Developments in Social Impact Assessment

Wherever possible, the articles in these volumes have been reproduced as originally published using facsimile reproduction, inclusive of footnotes and pagination to facilitate ease of reference.

For a list of all Edward Elgar published titles visit our website at
www.e-elgar.com

Developments in Social Impact Assessment

Edited by

Frank Vanclay

Professor of Cultural Geography
University of Groningen, The Netherlands

An Elgar Research Collection
Cheltenham, UK • Northampton, MA, USA

© Frank Vanclay 2014. For copyright of individual articles, please refer to the Acknowledgements.

All rights reserved. No part of this publication may be reproduced, stored in a retrieval system, or transmitted in any form or by any means, electronic, mechanical, photocopying, recording, or otherwise without the prior permission of the publisher.

Published by
Edward Elgar Publishing Limited
The Lypiatts
15 Lansdown Road
Cheltenham
Glos GL50 2JA
UK

Edward Elgar Publishing, Inc.
William Pratt House
9 Dewey Court
Northampton
Massachusetts 01060
USA

A catalogue record for this book is available from the British Library

Library of Congress Control Number: 2013954356

MIX
Paper from
responsible sources
FSC® C013056

ISBN 978 1 78254 719 8

Printed and bound in Great Britain by T.J. International Ltd, Padstow

Contents

Acknowledgements xi
Introduction Frank Vanclay xv

PART I   CURRENT OVERVIEW OF SIA

1. Ana Maria Esteves, Daniel Franks and Frank Vanclay (2012), 'Social Impact Assessment: The State of the Art', *Impact Assessment and Project Appraisal*, **30** (1), March, 34–42   3
2. Ciaran O'Faircheallaigh (2009), 'Effectiveness in Social Impact Assessment: Aboriginal Peoples and Resource Development in Australia', *Impact Assessment and Project Appraisal*, **27** (2), June, 95–110   12
3. Stewart Lockie (2001), 'SIA in Review: Setting the Agenda for Impact Assessment in the 21st Century', *Impact Assessment and Project Appraisal*, **19** (4), December, 277–87   28
4. Frank Vanclay (2004), 'The Triple Bottom Line and Impact Assessment: How do TBL, EIA, SIA, SEA and EMS Relate to Each Other?', *Journal of Environmental Assessment Policy and Management*, **6** (3), September, 265–88   39
5. Frank Vanclay (2012), 'The Potential Application of Social Impact Assessment in Integrated Coastal Zone Management', *Ocean and Coastal Management*, **68**, November, 149–56   63

PART II   GUIDELINES AND PRINCIPLES

6. Frank Vanclay (2003), 'International Principles for Social Impact Assessment: Their Evolution', *Impact Assessment and Project Appraisal*, **21** (1), March, 3–4   73
7. Frank Vanclay (2003), 'International Principles for Social Impact Assessment', *Impact Assessment and Project Appraisal*, **21** (1), March, 5–11   75
8. Interorganizational Committee on Principles and Guidelines for Social Impact Assessment (2003), 'Principles and Guidelines for Social Impact Assessment in the USA', *Impact Assessment and Project Appraisal*, **21** (3), September, 231–50   82
9. Frank Vanclay (2006), 'Principles for Social Impact Assessment: A Critical Comparison between the International and US Documents', *Environmental Impact Assessment Review*, **26** (1), January, 3–14   102

PART III ETHICS AND VALUES

10. Richard Howitt (2005), 'The Importance of Process in Social Impact Assessment: Ethics, Methods and Process for Cross-Cultural Engagement', *Ethics, Place and Environment*, **8** (2), June, 209–21   117
11. Robert Fisher (2008), 'Anthropologists and Social Impact Assessment: Negotiating the Ethical Minefield', *Asia Pacific Journal of Anthropology*, **9** (3), September, 231–42   130
12. Michael Gismondi (1997), 'Sociology and Environmental Impact Assessment', *Canadian Journal of Sociology*, **22** (4), Autumn, 457–79   142

PART IV UNDERSTANDING SOCIAL IMPACTS

13. Roel Slootweg, Frank Vanclay and Marlies van Schooten (2001), 'Function Evaluation as a Framework for the Integration of Social and Environmental Impact Assessment', *Impact Assessment and Project Appraisal*, **19** (1), March, 19–28   167
14. Frank Vanclay (2002), 'Conceptualising Social Impacts', *Environmental Impact Assessment Review*, **22** (3), May, 183–211   177
15. Stewart Lockie, Susan Rockloff, Danielle Helbers, Maharlina Gorospe-Lockie and Karen Lawrence (2009), 'Assessing the Social Impacts of Extensive Resource Use Activities', *Journal of Environmental Planning and Management*, **52** (4), June, 437–55   206

PART V THEORETICAL FRAMEWORKS

16. Thomas Dietz (1987), 'Theory and Method in Social Impact Assessment', *Sociological Inquiry*, **57** (1), Winter, 54–69   227
17. Helen Ross and Tara K. McGee (2006), 'Conceptual Frameworks for SIA Revisited: A Cumulative Effects Study on Lead Contamination and Economic Change', *Impact Assessment and Project Appraisal*, **24** (2), June, 139–49   243
18. Nigel Rossouw and Shakti Malan (2007), 'The Importance of Theory in Shaping Social Impact Monitoring: Lessons from the Berg River Dam, South Africa', *Impact Assessment and Project Appraisal*, **25** (4), December, 291–99   254
19. Stewart Lockie (2007), 'Deliberation and Actor-Networks: The "Practical" Implications of Social Theory for the Assessment of Large Dams and Other Interventions', *Society and Natural Resources*, **20** (9), 785–99   263

PART VI SIA IN PRACTICE

20. Ciaran O'Faircheallaigh (2010), 'Public Participation and Environmental Impact Assessment: Purposes, Implications, and Lessons for Public Policy Making', *Environmental Impact Assessment Review*, **30** (1), January, 19–27   281

21. Ana Maria Esteves and Frank Vanclay (2009), 'Social Development Needs Analysis as a Tool for SIA to Guide Corporate–Community Investment: Applications in the Minerals Industry', *Environmental Impact Assessment Review*, **29** (2), February, 137–45 — 290

22. Ana Maria Esteves and Mary-Anne Barclay (2011), 'Enhancing the Benefits of Local Content: Integrating Social and Economic Impact Assessment into Procurement Strategies', *Impact Assessment and Project Appraisal*, **29** (3), September, 205–15 — 299

23. Dianne Buchan (2003), 'Buy-in and Social Capital: By-Products of Social Impact Assessment', *Impact Assessment and Project Appraisal*, **21** (3), September, 168–72 — 310

24. Annelies Stolp, Wim Groen, Jacqueline van Vliet and Frank Vanclay (2002), 'Citizen Values Assessment: Incorporating Citizens' Value Judgements in Environmental Impact Assessment', *Impact Assessment and Project Appraisal*, **20** (1), March, 11–23 — 315

PART VII VARIOUS ISSUES OF INTEREST

25. Deanna Kemp and Frank Vanclay (2013), 'Human Rights and Impact Assessment: Clarifying the Connections in Practice', *Impact Assessment and Project Appraisal*, **31** (2), 86–96 — 331

26. Philippe Hanna and Frank Vanclay (2013), 'Human Rights, Indigenous Peoples and the Concept of Free, Prior and Informed Consent', *Impact Assessment and Project Appraisal*, **31** (2), 146–57 — 342

27. Ciaran O'Faircheallaigh (1999), 'Making Social Impact Assessment Count: A Negotiation-Based Approach for Indigenous Peoples', *Society and Natural Resources*, **12** (1), 63–80 — 354

28. Keith Storey (2010), 'Fly-In/Fly-Out: Implications for Community Sustainability', *Sustainability*, **2** (5), May, 1161–81 — 372

29. Stewart Lockie, Maree Franettovich, Vanessa Petkova-Timmer, John Rolfe and Galina Ivanova (2009), 'Coal Mining and the Resource Community Cycle: A Longitudinal Assessment of the Social Impacts of the Coppabella Coal Mine', *Environmental Impact Assessment Review*, **29** (5), September, 330–39 — 393

30. Daniel M. Franks, David Brereton and Chris J. Moran (2010), 'Managing the Cumulative Impacts of Coal Mining on Regional Communities and Environments in Australia', *Impact Assessment and Project Appraisal*, **28** (4), December, 299–312 — 403

31. Doreen Stabinksy (2000), 'Bringing Social Analysis into a Multilateral Environmental Agreement: Social Impact Assessment and the Biosafety Protocol', *Journal of Environmental Development*, **9** (3), September, 260–83 — 417

32. C.J. Barrow (2010), 'How is Environmental Conflict Addressed by SIA?', *Environmental Impact Assessment Review*, **30** (5), September, 293–301 — 441

PART VIII CASE STUDIES OF SIA AROUND THE WORLD

33. Bettina Gransow (2007), 'Social Transformation in China and the Development of Social Assessment', *International Review of Sociology*, **17** (3), November, 539–58   453

34. Mostafa Ahmadvand, Ezatollah Karami, Gholam Hossein Zamani and Frank Vanclay (2009), 'Evaluating the Use of Social Impact Assessment in the Context of Agricultural Development Projects in Iran', *Environmental Impact Assessment Review*, **29** (6), November, 399–407   473

35. Jacobus A. du Pisani and Luke A. Sandham (2006), 'Assessing the Performance of SIA in the EIA Context: A Case Study of South Africa', *Environmental Impact Assessment Review*, **26** (8), November, 707–24   482

36. Bryan Tilt, Yvonne Braun and Daming He (2009), 'Social Impacts of Large Dam Projects: A Comparison of International Case Studies and Implications for Best Practice', *Journal of Environmental Management*, **90** (3), July, S249–S257   500

PART IX HISTORICALLY SIGNIFICANT DOCUMENTS

37. Magoroh Maruyama (1973), 'Cultural, Social, and Psychological Considerations in the Planning of Public Works', *Technological Forecasting and Social Change*, **5** (2), 135–43   511

38. C.P. Wolf (1974), 'Social Impact Assessment: The State of the Art', *EDRA Proceedings*, **5** (2), 1–44   520

39. Sue Johnson and Rabel J. Burdge (1974), 'Social Impact Statements: A Tentative Methodology', *EDRA Proceedings*, **5** (2), 69–84   564

40. Lynn Llewellyn, Elaine Bunten, Clare Goodman, Gail Hare, Richard Mach and Ralph Swisher (1975), 'The Role of Social Impact Assessment in Highway Planning', *Environment and Behavior*, **7** (3), September, 285–306   580

41. Mark A. Shields (1975), 'Social Impact Studies: An Expository Analysis', *Environment and Behavior*, **7** (3), September, 265–84   602

42. James C. Cramer, Thomas Dietz and Robert A. Johnston (1980), 'Social Impact Assessment of Regional Plans: A Review of Methods and Issues and a Recommended Process', *Policy Sciences*, **12** (1), June, 61–82   622

43. C.P. Wolf (1980), 'Getting Social Impact Assessment into the Policy Arena', *Environmental Impact Assessment Review*, **1** (1), March, 27–36   644

44. Kurt Finsterbusch (1985), 'State of the Art in Social Impact Assessment', *Environment and Behavior*, **17** (2), March, 193–221   654

45. William R. Freudenburg (1986), 'Social Impact Assessment', *Annual Review of Sociology*, **12**, 451–78   683

46. Rabel J. Burdge (1991), 'A Brief History and Major Trends in the Field of Impact Assessment', *Impact Assessment*, **9** (4), 93–104 — 711
47. Robert Gramling and William R. Freudenburg (1992), 'Opportunity–Threat, Development, and Adaptation: Toward a Comprehensive Framework for Social Impact Assessment', *Rural Sociology*, **57** (2), June, 216–34 — 723
48. Christiane Gagnon, Philip Hirsch and Richard Howitt (1993), 'Can SIA Empower Communities?', *Environmental Impact Assessment Review*, **13** (4), July, 229–53 — 742
49. Kurt Finsterbusch (1995), 'In Praise of SIA – A Personal Review of the Field of Social Impact Assessment: Feasibility, Justification, History, Methods, Issues', *Impact Assessment*, **13** (3), September, 229–52 — 767
50. Rabel J. Burdge and Frank Vanclay (1996), 'Social Impact Assessment: A Contribution to the State of the Art Series', *Impact Assessment*, **14** (1), March, 59–86 — 791

Acknowledgements

The editor and publishers wish to thank the authors and the following publishers who have kindly given permission for the use of copyright material.

Annual Reviews, Inc. via the Copyright Clearance Center for article: William R. Freudenburg (1986), 'Social Impact Assessment', *Annual Review of Sociology*, **12**, 451–78.

Blackwell Publishing Ltd for articles: Thomas Dietz (1987), 'Theory and Method in Social Impact Assessment', *Sociological Inquiry*, **57** (1), Winter, 54–69; Robert Gramling and William R. Freudenburg (1992), 'Opportunity–Threat, Development, and Adaptation: Toward a Comprehensive Framework for Social Impact Assessment', *Rural Sociology*, **57** (2), June, 216–34.

Canadian Journal of Sociology for article: Michael Gismondi (1997), 'Sociology and Environmental Impact Assessment', *Canadian Journal of Sociology*, **22** (4), Autumn, 457–79.

Elsevier Ltd for articles: Magoroh Maruyama (1973), 'Cultural, Social, and Psychological Considerations in the Planning of Public Works', *Technological Forecasting and Social Change*, **5** (2), 135–43; C.P. Wolf (1980), 'Getting Social Impact Assessment into the Policy Arena', *Environmental Impact Assessment Review*, **1** (1), March, 27–36; Christiane Gagnon, Philip Hirsch and Richard Howitt (1993), 'Can SIA Empower Communities?', *Environmental Impact Assessment Review*, **13** (4), July, 229–53; Doreen Stabinksy (2000), 'Bringing Social Analysis into a Multilateral Environmental Agreement: Social Impact Assessment and the Biosafety Protocol', *Journal of Environmental Development*, **9** (3), September, 260–83; Frank Vanclay (2002), 'Conceptualising Social Impacts', *Environmental Impact Assessment Review*, **22** (3), May, 183–211; Frank Vanclay (2006), 'Principles for Social Impact Assessment: A Critical Comparison between the International and US Documents', *Environmental Impact Assessment Review*, **26** (1), January, 3–14; Jacobus A. du Pisani and Luke A. Sandham (2006), 'Assessing the Performance of SIA in the EIA Context: A Case Study of South Africa', *Environmental Impact Assessment Review*, **26** (8), November, 707–24; Ana Maria Esteves and Frank Vanclay (2009), 'Social Development Needs Analysis as a Tool for SIA to Guide Corporate–Community Investment: Applications in the Minerals Industry', *Environmental Impact Assessment Review*, **29** (2), February, 137–45; Bryan Tilt, Yvonne Braun and Daming He (2009), 'Social Impacts of Large Dam Projects: A Comparison of International Case Studies and Implications for Best Practice', *Journal of Environmental Management*, **90** (3), July, S249–S257; Stewart Lockie, Maree Franettovich, Vanessa Petkova-Timmer, John Rolfe and Galina Ivanova (2009), 'Coal Mining and the Resource Community Cycle: A Longitudinal Assessment of the Social Impacts of the Coppabella Coal Mine', *Environmental Impact Assessment Review*, **29** (5), September, 330–39; Mostafa Ahmadvand, Ezatollah Karami,

Gholam Hossein Zamani and Frank Vanclay (2009), 'Evaluating the Use of Social Impact Assessment in the Context of Agricultural Development Projects in Iran', *Environmental Impact Assessment Review*, **29** (6), November, 399–407; Ciaran O'Faircheallaigh (2010), 'Public Participation and Environmental Impact Assessment: Purposes, Implications, and Lessons for Public Policy Making', *Environmental Impact Assessment Review*, **30** (1), January, 19–27; C.J. Barrow (2010), 'How is Environmental Conflict Addressed by SIA?', *Environmental Impact Assessment Review*, **30** (5), September, 293–301; Frank Vanclay (2012), 'The Potential Application of Social Impact Assessment in Integrated Coastal Zone Management', *Ocean and Coastal Management*, **68**, November, 149–56.

Environmental Design Research Association for articles: C.P. Wolf (1974), 'Social Impact Assessment: The State of the Art', *EDRA Proceedings*, **5** (2), 1–44; Sue Johnson and Rabel J. Burdge (1974), 'Social Impact Statements: A Tentative Methodology', *EDRA Proceedings*, **5** (2), 69–84.

Multidisciplinary Digital Publishing Institute for article: Keith Storey (2010), 'Fly-In/Fly-Out: Implications for Community Sustainability', *Sustainability*, **2** (5), May, 1161–81.

Sage Publications via the Copyright Clearance Center's RightsLink service for articles: Mark A. Shields (1975), 'Social Impact Studies: An Expository Analysis', *Environment and Behavior*, **7** (3), September, 265–84; Lynn Llewellyn, Elaine Bunten, Clare Goodman, Gail Hare, Richard Mach and Ralph Swisher (1975), 'The Role of Social Impact Assessment in Highway Planning', *Environment and Behavior*, **7** (3), September, 285–306; Kurt Finsterbusch (1985), 'State of the Art in Social Impact Assessment', *Environment and Behavior*, **17** (2), March, 193–221.

Springer Science and Business Media B.V. for article: James C. Cramer, Thomas Dietz and Robert A. Johnston (1980), 'Social Impact Assessment of Regional Plans: A Review of Methods and Issues and a Recommended Process', *Policy Sciences*, **12** (1), June, 61–82.

Taylor and Francis Group, LLC (http://www.tandfonline.com) for articles: Ciaran O'Faircheallaigh (1999), 'Making Social Impact Assessment Count: A Negotiation-Based Approach for Indigenous Peoples', *Society and Natural Resources*, **12** (1), 63–80; Stewart Lockie (2007), 'Deliberation and Actor-Networks: The "Practical" Implications of Social Theory for the Assessment of Large Dams and Other Interventions', *Society and Natural Resources*, **20** (9), 785–99.

Taylor and Francis Ltd (http://www.tandfonline.com) for articles: Rabel J. Burdge (1991), 'A Brief History and Major Trends in the Field of Impact Assessment', *Impact Assessment*, **9** (4), 93–104; Kurt Finsterbusch (1995), 'In Praise of SIA – A Personal Review of the Field of Social Impact Assessment: Feasibility, Justification, History, Methods, Issues', *Impact Assessment*, **13** (3), September, 229–52; Rabel J. Burdge and Frank Vanclay (1996), 'Social Impact Assessment: A Contribution to the State of the Art Series', *Impact Assessment*, **14** (1), March, 59–86; Roel Slootweg, Frank Vanclay and Marlies van Schooten (2001), 'Function Evaluation as a Framework for the Integration of Social and Environmental Impact

Assessment', *Impact Assessment and Project Appraisal*, **19** (1), March, 19–28; Stewart Lockie (2001), 'SIA in Review: Setting the Agenda for Impact Assessment in the 21st Century', *Impact Assessment and Project Appraisal*, **19** (4), December, 277–87; Annelies Stolp, Wim Groen, Jacqueline van Vliet and Frank Vanclay (2002), 'Citizen Values Assessment: Incorporating Citizens' Value Judgements in Environmental Impact Assessment', *Impact Assessment and Project Appraisal*, **20** (1), March, 11–23; Frank Vanclay (2003), 'International Principles for Social Impact Assessment: Their Evolution', *Impact Assessment and Project Appraisal*, **21** (1), March, 3–4; Frank Vanclay (2003), 'International Principles for Social Impact Assessment', *Impact Assessment and Project Appraisal*, **21** (1), March, 5–11; Dianne Buchan (2003), 'Buy-in and Social Capital: By-Products of Social Impact Assessment', *Impact Assessment and Project Appraisal*, **21** (3), September, 168–72; Interorganizational Committee on Principles and Guidelines for Social Impact Assessment (2003), 'Principles and Guidelines for Social Impact Assessment in the USA', *Impact Assessment and Project Appraisal*, **21** (3), September, 231–50; Richard Howitt (2005), 'The Importance of Process in Social Impact Assessment: Ethics, Methods and Process for Cross-Cultural Engagement', *Ethics, Place and Environment*, **8** (2), June, 209–21; Helen Ross and Tara K. McGee (2006), 'Conceptual Frameworks for SIA Revisited: A Cumulative Effects Study on Lead Contamination and Economic Change', *Impact Assessment and Project Appraisal*, **24** (2), June, 139–49; Bettina Gransow (2007), 'Social Transformation in China and the Development of Social Assessment', *International Review of Sociology*, **17** (3), November, 539–58; Nigel Rossouw and Shakti Malan (2007), 'The Importance of Theory in Shaping Social Impact Monitoring: Lessons from the Berg River Dam, South Africa', *Impact Assessment and Project Appraisal*, **25** (4), December, 291–99; Robert Fisher (2008), 'Anthropologists and Social Impact Assessment: Negotiating the Ethical Minefield', *Asia Pacific Journal of Anthropology*, **9** (3), September, 231–42; Ciaran O'Faircheallaigh (2009), 'Effectiveness in Social Impact Assessment: Aboriginal Peoples and Resource Development in Australia', *Impact Assessment and Project Appraisal*, **27** (2), June, 95–110; Stewart Lockie, Susan Rockloff, Danielle Helbers, Maharlina Gorospe-Lockie and Karen Lawrence (2009), 'Assessing the Social Impacts of Extensive Resource Use Activities', *Journal of Environmental Planning and Management*, **52** (4), June, 437–55; Daniel M. Franks, David Brereton and Chris J. Moran (2010), 'Managing the Cumulative Impacts of Coal Mining on Regional Communities and Environments in Australia', *Impact Assessment and Project Appraisal*, **28** (4), December, 299–312; Ana Maria Esteves and Mary-Anne Barclay (2011), 'Enhancing the Benefits of Local Content: Integrating Social and Economic Impact Assessment into Procurement Strategies', *Impact Assessment and Project Appraisal*, **29** (3), September, 205–15; Ana Maria Esteves, Daniel Franks and Frank Vanclay (2012), 'Social Impact Assessment: The State of the Art', *Impact Assessment and Project Appraisal*, **30** (1), March, 34–42; Deanna Kemp and Frank Vanclay (2013), 'Human Rights and Impact Assessment: Clarifying the Connections in Practice', *Impact Assessment and Project Appraisal*, **31** (2), 86–96; Philippe Hanna and Frank Vanclay (2013), 'Human Rights, Indigenous Peoples and the Concept of Free, Prior and Informed Consent', *Impact Assessment and Project Appraisal*, **31** (2), 146–57.

World Scientific Publishing Company Pte Ltd for article: Frank Vanclay (2004), 'The Triple Bottom Line and Impact Assessment: How do TBL, EIA, SIA, SEA and EMS Relate to Each

Other?', *Journal of Environmental Assessment Policy and Management*, **6** (3), September, 265–88.

Every effort has been made to trace all the copyright holders but if any have been inadvertently overlooked the publishers will be pleased to make the necessary arrangement at the first opportunity.

In addition the publishers wish to thank the Library at the University of Warwick, UK, and the Library of Indiana University at Bloomington, USA, for their assistance in obtaining these articles.

Introduction
Developments in Social Impact Assessment: An introduction to a collection of seminal research papers
Frank Vanclay

This Edward Elgar research collection comprises 50 of the key journal articles in the field of social impact assessment (SIA) as it has developed over time. As discussed in more detail below and in the papers in this collection, the general understanding of SIA has changed over time and will likely continue to change into the future. SIA is now understood to be the process of managing the social issues associated with a planned intervention (in other words, project, policy, plan or programme). The approach used in SIA is also applied to assess the impacts of a disaster; however, SIA is primarily intended to be an *ex ante* (in advance) mechanism to anticipate likely social issues associated with planned interventions and to address them through management actions or by changing the planned intervention. *Ex post* assessment is also important to improve the knowledge base used to make *ex ante* judgements. SIA can be applied to policies, programmes, and plans, although the majority of attention has been at the project level.

The term 'social impact assessment' has multiple levels of meanings. At a very narrow understanding, it can refer to the discrete act of predicting the social impacts of a planned intervention as part of an environmental impact assessment (EIA) process or as a standalone SIA, whether in a regulatory context or not. SIA can also refer to all the activities associated with managing the social issues of a planned intervention, including: facilitating community engagement activities; designing and implementing mitigation and enhancement measures; developing local employment and local procurement procedures; influencing siting and operational decisions especially to mitigate impacts; managing resettlement programmes; assisting in re-establishing and improving livelihoods; considering and implementing appropriate compensation mechanisms; designing and implementing grievance procedures; facilitating appropriate activities to assist people in a community in coping with change; and ensuring compliance with local and international requirements relating to social issues and human rights – in short, everything that in the corporate world tends to be called 'social performance', or social relations and corporate social responsibility. A final level of understanding is that, just like many other applied fields of practice such as planning, architecture and social work, SIA is a paradigm or discourse, a body or group of practitioners and scholars, an applied field of research and practice. While SIA currently lacks the status of being a recognized profession and is taught in only a small number of universities around the world, thus lacking the distinction of being an academic discipline or subdiscipline in its own right, it is nonetheless an inter-disciplinary or trans-disciplinary (even post-disciplinary) field of enquiry. As a paradigm or field of practice, SIA comprises a knowledge base, a suite of methods and theories, a compendium of case-study examples, and a worldview or overarching philosophy encompassing values and attitudes. Much of the understanding of the current SIA paradigm is articulated in the first paper in this collection, the most recent state of the art paper (Esteves et al. 2012, Chapter 1, this volume), and in Chapter 7 of this volume (Vanclay 2003), the 'International principles for social impact assessment', a document developed under the auspices of the International Association for Impact Assessment (www.iaia.org).

Understanding SIA as being a paradigm or field of practice is important. Most significantly, such an understanding means that it does not really matter what the terms 'social', 'impact' and 'assessment' mean individually (on their own) or collectively (together). What is important is how the paradigm/discourse of SIA constructs itself, defines itself and determines what is included within SIA and what is not included. SIA is thus continuously defined and redefined by the people in the SIA section of the International Association for Impact Assessment and by the editors and reviewers of the two primary journals where SIA scholars and practitioners publish: *Impact Assessment and Project Appraisal* and *Environmental Impact Assessment Review*. The papers in this research collection, having been compiled by a key figure in the field, also articulate the paradigm of SIA and the way it has changed over time. Finally, a significant recent paper (the very first paper in this volume) is 'Social impact assessment: The state of the art' (Esteves et al. 2012). It and other 'state of the art' type papers in previous decades have also contributed to defining the field in their respective time periods.

It should be noted that some confusion exists around the term 'social impact assessment'. First, as with all paradigms, there has been some debate over appropriate terms and their meanings. Although the term 'social impact assessment' has prevailed, various other wordings have been used by certain authors and/or institutions. For example, in the World Bank, 'social analysis' and 'social assessment' have been used at different times, and now 'poverty and social impact analysis' is being applied. Within the US Agency for International Development (USAID), the term 'social soundness analysis' was used. 'Community impact assessment' was the preferred term of the US Department of Transport. The terms 'socio-economic impact assessment', 'societal impact assessment' and 'cultural impact assessment' have also been employed alongside a host of other terms – in fact, Vanclay (2004a, Chapter 4, this volume) identified over 100 terms. The various terms and their associated literatures are mostly included within the SIA paradigm, and some examples of them are included in this collection.

A second confusion exists with the rise in the past ten years of another field also confusingly called 'social impact assessment' or 'social impact analysis'. This field/discourse stems from the philanthropy sector and is concerned with measuring the 'social impact' of their investments – in other words, the benefits achieved beyond any immediate economic return. While the first field above considers social impact *on* society and culture, this second field considers the social impact *of* their programme. It is thus quite a different discourse to the field discussed in this collection and probably should have been called 'social return on investment' (SROI) or similar (noting, however, that SROI refers to a specific methodology). Although this second field overlaps with the discourse of SIA as in this collection in that we are also interested in ensuring that social investments achieve their full potential, there are substantial differences in assumptions, premises, understandings, experiences, case studies invoked, literature accessed, and so on, between the two fields. They are very different paradigms. For an access point to that field, please refer to the guides produced by the New Economics Foundation (2004, 2008) or the UK Cabinet Office (2009).

Choosing the 50 articles to include in this research collection was not easy and no doubt other compilers may have chosen a somewhat different collection of papers. It is important to appreciate that it includes only journal articles and not any of the many books, booklets or book chapters that are also significant (for example, Vanclay 1999, 2002a, 2004b). However, a listing of key books is provided later in this introduction. Articles for inclusion were chosen for their centrality to the SIA field as understood in this discourse. A range of other criteria were also applied to select papers to ensure that this collection: (a) was interesting to readers; (b) was indicative of the diverse range of SIA; (c) included the first papers in the field of SIA; and (d) included the current cutting-edge papers. In this research collection, the 50 papers are grouped into nine parts: (1) papers that provide a current overview of the field of social impact assessment; (2) the various guidelines and principles that govern the SIA field; (3) discussion of the ethics and values that underpin the SIA field and its practice; (4) papers that provide an understanding of the social impacts people and communities experience; (5) theoretical frameworks for SIA; (6) discussion of SIA in practice; (7) various issues of interest that currently influence the SIA field; (8) various case studies of SIA around the world; and (9) significant documents in the history of the field of SIA.

This introductory chapter provides some background information about SIA. It describes what SIA is and how it is done. It discusses what social impacts are and describes some of the key concepts. It discusses the philosophy of SIA and outlines the values expected of SIA practitioners. It sketches the history of SIA and the transition over time from being a regulatory tool to being a corporate tool. It advocates the business case for doing SIA. Finally, it outlines current issues and future directions. It draws on many of the papers included in this research collection, particularly those of Vanclay (2002b, Chapter 14; 2003, Chapter 6; 2012, Chapter 5) and Esteves et al. (2012, Chapter 1).

What Is Social Impact Assessment?

As described above, the field of SIA deals with the processes of managing the social impacts of planned interventions. The traditional (or original) understanding of SIA was that it was the *ex ante* prediction of the likely social consequences of a planned intervention (typically within a regulatory framework) in order to enable the decision maker (competent authority) to determine whether project approval should be given and, if so, with what conditions/ conditionalities. Over time, along with changing trends in society, SIA has also changed. The purpose of the SIA now varies according to the target audience or key stakeholder for the SIA. Where the intended audience is a regulatory authority, the purpose is likely to be about deciding whether approval should be given. Originally, SIA was something required by government agencies and resisted by companies. Over time – especially with the neoliberal withdrawal of government, the rise of corporate social responsibility and the emergence of a strong international non-governmental organization (NGO) watchdog sector (discussed later) – companies now see the business case for doing SIA for themselves and SIA has become part of good corporate management. In this new environment, SIA needs to align with corporate requirements, systems and processes. SIA can also be done for and/or by potentially impacted communities. Information from an SIA could assist a community in deciding whether it should give its 'free, prior and informed consent' (Hanna and Vanclay 2013, Chapter 26, this volume) to a project, and would assist a community in negotiating an 'Impacts and Benefits Agreement' with a company (Gibson and O'Faircheallaigh 2010; Nish and Bice 2011). SIA would also assist a community in visioning its future, and in implementing ways of coping with the change that a planned intervention could bring about. SIA also assists financial institutions, especially those that subscribe to the Equator Principles, in determining whether the appropriate social and human rights issues have been considered by a project developer and therefore whether project financing should be provided. Finally, an effective SIA also works closely with local government in considering community needs and aspirations, in discussing community infrastructure issues, especially as they might be affected by the project and the population influx it may bring, and in implementing mitigation measures and developing options for social investment.

In the early twenty-first century, around the world SIAs are routinely undertaken for large projects like new mines, dams, and oil and gas extraction projects, and for significant extensions of existing projects. In these sectors, there is an expectation that they be done irrespective of whether it is required by the host country. Depending on local regulatory requirements, SIAs may be undertaken for major highway construction projects and other infrastructure projects, new factories, windfarm developments, and so on. In some jurisdictions, SIAs are expected even for very small projects. Because of different histories in terms of the experience of SIA, there is considerable variation around the world in the extent to which they are required. In principle, SIA is good planning and, at an appropriate scale, should be done for every new development project regardless of size.

There are many activities involved in conducting an SIA. An SIA process is a composite of many steps depending on the particulars of the specific project. A wide range of social research methods are used. Therefore, it is not feasible to fully describe the practical details of how to do an SIA in this introductory chapter. However, to give a general impression of what is included, it can be stated that SIA addresses the following topics. It should be noted that a participatory approach is applied throughout the whole process.

Gaining an understanding of the communities affected by the project (policy, plan or programme)

- collation of existing baseline data and establishing what extra data needs to be collected
- developing local and regional community profiles
- stakeholder mapping and analysis
- community engagement.

Scoping the key elements of the social environment likely to be significantly impacted

- identifying key social issues
- providing feedback to project planners and stakeholders
- selecting social variables to measure.

Predicting the social changes that may result from the project

- comparisons with similar cases elsewhere
- trend projection and forecasting
- population multiplier methods
- scenario building using expert panels.

Estimating the significance of predicted changes, and determining how affected groups and communities will likely respond

- comparative analysis
- stakeholder input
- expert judgements
- field investigations.

Identifying ways of mitigating potential impacts and maximizing positive opportunities

- avoiding or minimizing potential impacts
- addressing irreversible impacts by providing offsets
- identifying opportunities for communities to benefit in the long term
- considering appropriate compensation arrangements.

Developing a monitoring plan and adaptive management response mechanism to track implementation, variations from mitigation actions and any unanticipated social changes/impacts

- outlining additional steps to be taken if scope or scale of impacts differs from predictions
- establishing ongoing community and government involvement in monitoring
- implementing a grievance procedure.

Reporting to key stakeholders

- communicating and validating findings with the affected community
- communicating findings to the proponent and negotiating mitigation and enhancement possibilities
- reporting findings to the competent authority.

Implementing findings

- working with the proponent to develop a Social Impact Management Plan
- working with the community and proponent to develop an Impacts and Benefits Agreement
- working with all parties to develop a review process.

What Are Social Impacts?

The key paper discussing social impacts is 'Conceptualising social impacts' (Vanclay 2002b), which is included in this collection (Chapter 14). That paper is a thorough analysis of all possible social impacts, identifying around 80 potential social impacts. Essentially, a social impact is something that is experienced or felt, whether in a perceptual (cognitive) or a corporeal (bodily, physical) sense at all levels, for example individual, economic unit (family/household), social group (circle of friends), workplace (a company or government agency), or by community/society generally. These different levels are affected in different ways by an impact or impact-causing action. Death, for example, is perhaps the most significant impact affecting an individual. But it also has a severe emotional and financial impact on the family or other people who may be economically dependent on the deceased person. The death of a person also affects all that person's friends. It can lead to reduced capacity in the organization where that person worked, and, in some circumstances, it can have a profound effect on society at large.

A social impact potentially could be anything, and therefore social impact assessment should address everything that is relevant to people and how they live. Environmental impacts, for example, can also be social impacts because people depend on the environment for their livelihoods and because people may have place attachment to the places where development is occurring.

Building on Armour (1992), Vanclay (2002b, Chapter 14, this volume, pp. 185–6, slightly edited) suggests that social impacts include changes to:

- people's way of life – that is, how they live, work, play and interact with one another on a day-to-day basis;
- their culture – that is, their shared beliefs, customs, values and language or dialect;
- their community – its cohesion, stability, character, services and facilities;
- their political systems – the extent to which people are able to participate in decisions that affect their lives, the level of democratization that is taking place and the resources provided for this purpose;
- their environment – the quality of the air and water that people use; the availability and quality of the food that they eat; the level of hazard or risk, dust and noise to which they are exposed; the adequacy of sanitation, their physical safety and their access to and control over resources;
- their health and well-being – where 'health' is understood in a manner similar to the World Health Organization definition: 'a state of complete physical, mental, and social well-being, not merely the absence of disease or infirmity';
- their personal and property rights – particularly whether people are economically affected, or experience personal disadvantage, which may include a violation of their civil liberties; and
- their fears and aspirations – their perceptions about their safety, their fears about the future of their community and their aspirations for their future and the future of their children.

For a given project, the social impacts on an individual will depend on the:

- characteristics of the project;
- characteristics of the operator, for example their prior reputation and the extent to which they demonstrate genuineness in community engagement;
- characteristics of any mitigation;
- characteristics of the community, specifically its vitality, viability, resilience and impact history; and
- characteristics of the individuals themselves, for example how they are positioned in society, their stage in the life cycle, their personal psychological resilience, their willingness to accept change and adapt to new circumstances and opportunities.

Another way of saying this is that people are differentially affected by impacts. However, it is important to realize that impacts are not stable; that is, how a person responds to an impact may change over time.

A significant conceptual contribution of the Vanclay (2002b, Chapter 14, this volume) paper relates to the differentiation between a social change process and a social impact. Not all change-inducing processes are impacts. A given change may or may not cause impacts (depending on the characteristics mentioned above). For example, the influx of population is not necessarily a negative social impact. In certain circumstances it may be a benefit. The issue for SIA is how to ensure that the process of in-migration is understood, prepared for and managed to minimize negative impacts and maximize the benefits.

While SIA is sometimes described as being a social form of environmental impact assessment, there are many differences. Primarily, (direct) environmental impacts only occur when the first sod of soil is turned, whereas social impacts can happen the moment there is a rumour that something might happen. Rumour leads to speculation and speculative behaviour. In some cases, for example a socially undesirable factory or other locally unwanted land use, rumour may create considerable fear and anxiety, whether or not the rumour has any foundation, and whether or not the project actually eventuates. As a result, people may move away from the site of the likely project. If they are homeowners, there may be a drop in the value of their property as a result of loss of perceived attractiveness of the location. In other cases, especially in developing countries, in a process known as the 'honey pot effect', people may move to the site either to attempt to become regarded as an affected person and therefore eligible for compensation, or in search of work.

Because of the existence of at least basic regulatory oversight in most countries, many major impacts are unlikely to occur. Therefore, the major concerns of many people often relate to the fear and anxiety created by the project. Fear and anxiety are real social impacts and should not be dismissed, but they need to be managed effectively. It is important to realize that the level and effectiveness of community engagement has a huge bearing on the amount of fear and anxiety generated. The extent of social impacts experienced is thus largely contingent on contextual factors such as the genuineness of the engagement mechanisms used and the extent to which the views of all stakeholders were considered and reflected in the various reports and mitigation actions.

Social impacts are also created by projects that raise false expectations in a community, either by inappropriately and knowingly promising things that will not eventuate, or inadvertently by allowing rumour to escalate expectations through not deliberately managing expectations. It is particularly important for project developers to be realistic about the number of jobs likely to be created by a project. Communities can feel 'ripped-off' when the benefits they anticipated receiving from a project do not eventuate.

A final social impact relates to lost opportunities. Sometimes with only very little additional effort or expense the benefits of a project to a local community can be substantially improved or enhanced. Infrastructure can be modified (expanded) and/or shared to ensure that there is a benefit to local communities. Effort can be expended to ensure the local procurement of as many goods and services as possible. Thought can be given as to what issues may arise and how these can be addressed so that jobs can be given to local people and goods and services can be sourced locally. The major impact causing events, such as resettlement, need to be minimized and carefully managed to reduce harm.

The Overarching Philosophy of the SIA Profession

As indicated earlier, SIA is a paradigm or field of research and practice. As a paradigm, a certain 'understanding' of the field can be presumed, encompassing theoretical and methodological knowledge, awareness of certain case studies, a knowledge of the history of the field and a comprehension of the ethical issues likely to be faced. These topics are all addressed in the papers included in this collection (especially the 'International Principles for Social Impact Assessment', Vanclay 2003, Chapter 7) as well as in some papers that could not be included (for example, Vanclay et al. 2013).

An SIA practitioner has multiple stakeholders to please/appease, including the client or proponent, regulatory agencies, community liaison committees, peer reviewers where used, affected communities and the multiple groups within them, other interested stakeholders, professional peers and society in general. While in the physical sciences there is a naïve assumption about scientists being 'objective' and value-free, in the social sciences these concepts are contested. Instead, the SIA profession professes the following values (adapted from Vanclay 2003, Chapter 7, this volume):

- commitment to sustainability
- openness and accountability
- fairness and equity
- preservation of human rights
- empowerment of local peoples, specifically women, minority groups and disadvantaged
- capacity building
- acceptance of multiple value systems.

The History of Social Impact Assessment

The concept of 'social impact assessment' (as implied by the discourse in this book) arguably emerged in the early 1970s alongside environmental impact assessment (EIA) with the passage of the National Environmental Policy Act (NEPA) of the USA in 1969 (42 USC 4321–4544).

However, it is very difficult to date exactly when the term 'social impact assessment' was first used. The very first conference on social impact assessment was held in 1974 in conjunction with the fifth conference of the Environmental Design Research Association in Milwaukee, Wisconsin, USA. A 'state of the art' summary of the emerging field was written by Charlie Wolf and presented at that conference (and is included in this collection, Chapter 38). The first published journal article I can find that clearly belongs to the SIA field (as constructed by a NEPA framing) was written by Magoroh Maruyama and published in 1973 (also included in this collection, Chapter 37), noting that it does not specifically mention 'social impact assessment'. However, from the discussions in the early papers on SIA and the references cited therein, it is clear that there was much activity and interest in the nascent field of SIA and many grey-literature reports about SIA (broadly speaking) were published, especially within the transport and water management sectors in the USA, most of which unfortunately are no longer readily accessible. In a 1974 report (a bibliography on SIA specifically) for the US Army Engineer Institute for Water Resources, Mark Shields states that he made use of the Office of Water Resources Research abstracts which indexed over 3,000 items on the 'social aspects of resource management' (Shields 1974). Wolf (1974, Chapter 38, this volume) and Shields (1975, Chapter 41, this volume) cite several references from 1971, 1970, 1969 and even earlier that mention 'social impacts' or 'socio-cultural impacts', making it evident that there had been much discussion about assessing social impacts (in other words, SIA) before the passage of NEPA. An example is a 1965 book of over 600 pages, *The Impact of Large Installations on Nearby Areas* (Breese 1965), which discussed the social impacts of military establishments. It is appropriate, however, to point out that the NEPA legislation was years in the making (for discussion on the history of NEPA see Dreyfus and Ingram 1976).

The passage of NEPA in the USA was a significant event in environmental history around the world. Particularly important and something of an innovation in policy was the concept of a triggering or action-forcing mechanism that compelled action in certain situations (Dreyfus and Ingram 1976). NEPA, however, only applied if US Federal land, laws or monies were involved and thus not to private actions (Burdge 1991, Chapter 46, this volume). In the decade after NEPA was introduced at the US federal level, many of the US states adopted similar legislation to apply to state actions (these were termed 'little NEPAs'). A fundamental limitation remained, however, that much development initiated by the private sector was not included in this regulatory framework. Despite this, the NEPA legislation was widely praised (Friesema and Culhane 1976), and many countries around the world began implementing EIA legislation loosely based on the NEPA concept, although typically being applicable to all development actions, private and public. Australia, New Zealand, Canada and the Philippines were among the first countries to adopt such legislation. In most cases, the 'environment' was broadly defined to include people and their connection to place, and not just the biophysical issues. Thus, the socio-economic component was an essential (if badly done) part of EIA (Vanclay 2004a, Chapter 4, this volume). The spread of NEPA and its widening focus around the world led to the rapid growth of SIA in the mid-to-late 1970s and 1980s (see Figure 1), and by 1985 some ten major texts on SIA had been produced (see Box 1). These textbooks give the impression of a mature discourse. The requirement for a social component in Environmental Impact Statements and rapid development in many countries led to a boom in the number of SIA consultants and larger environmental consulting firms who claimed SIA expertise.

Figure 1 charts the annual growth from 1970 of mentions of 'social impact assessment' (as currently available on the internet and to the Google Scholar search engine). There is no (correctly coded) record of any item accessible to the Google search engine before 1970. It should be appreciated that the graph is indicative rather than completely accurate because it only measures what is accessible on the internet at this point in time. Much grey literature that has not been digitized or recorded in a digital catalogue would not be currently accessed. As at 23 August 2013, Scopus had a total of 504 documents for 'social impact assessment' (search on title, abstract, keywords); Google Scholar had 13,300 items; and Google had 723,000 hits.

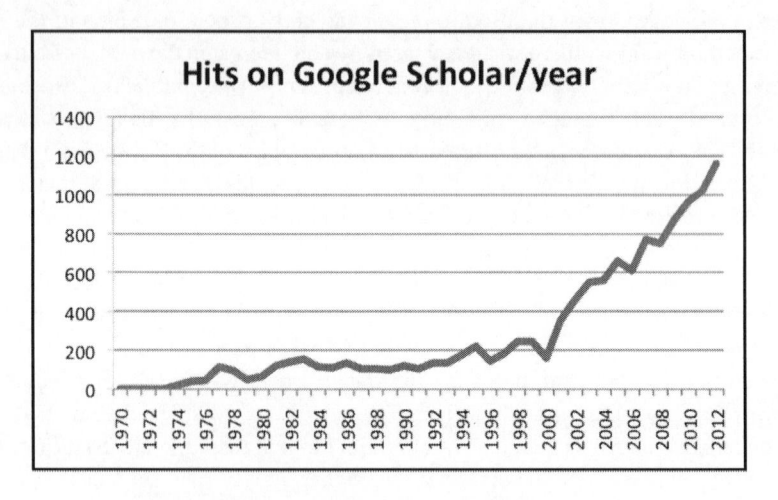

Note: The graph records the number of hits for the search term 'social impact assessment' using Google Scholar and a custom date range restricting the search to each calendar year. Obvious miscodings deleted. No valid document is identified before 1970. Search performed 7 August 2013.

Figure 1 Growth in interest in social impact assessment over time

Box 1 lists significant books in the field of SIA. In addition to the books listed in Box 1 are many documents (reports, guidelines, primers), booklets and leaflets published by various parties to promote awareness of SIA in certain specific regions or sectors. Many of them were highly significant in their own context at the time of their publication and circulation.

Box 1: Significant Books in the Field of Social Impact Assessment

1974 Wolf, C.P. (ed.) *Social Impact Assessment*. Part 2 of Carson, D. (ed.) EDRA 5: Man–Environment Interactions: Evaluations and Applications – The State of the Art in Environmental Design Research. Milwaukee: Environmental Design Research Association.

1977 Jacobs, S.-E. *Social Impact Assessment: Experiences in Evaluation Research, Applied Anthropology, and Human Ethic*. Starkville, MS: Mississippi State University.

1977 Finsterbusch, K. and Wolf, C.P. (eds) *Methodology of Social Impact Assessment*. Stroudsburg, PA: Dowden Hutchinson Ross (second edition published in 1981).

1977 Fitzsimmons, S., Stuart, L. and Wolf, P. *Social Assessment Manual: A Guide to the Preparation of the Social Well-Being Account for Planning Water Resources Projects.* Boulder, CO: Westview.

1977 McEvoy, J. and Dietz, T. (eds) *Handbook for Environmental Planning: The Social Consequences of Environmental Change.* New York: Wiley.

1978 Dixon, M. *What Happened to Fairbanks: The Effects of the Trans-Alaska Oil Pipeline on the Community of Fairbanks, Alaska.* Boulder, CO: Westview.

1980 Torgerson, D. *Industrialisation and Assessment: Social Impact Assessment as a Social Phenomenon.* Toronto: York University.

1980 Finsterbusch, K. *Understanding Social Impacts: Assessing the Effects of Public Projects.* Beverly Hills, CA: Sage.

1981 Tester, F.J. and Mykes, W. (eds) *Social Impact Assessment: Theory, Method and Practice.* Calgary: Detselig.

1981 Bowles, R.T. *Social Impact Assessment in Small Communities.* Toronto: Butterworth.

1981 Soderstrom, E.J. *Social Impact Assessment: Experimental Methods and Approaches.* New York: Praeger.

1981 Leistritz, F.L. and Murdock, S. *The Socioeconomic Impact of Resource Development: Methods of Assessment.* Boulder, CO: Westview.

1982 Geisler, C., Usner, D., Green, R. and West, P. (eds) *Indian SIA: The Social Impact Assessment of Rapid Resource Development on Native Peoples.* Ann Arbor, MI: University of Michigan Natural Resources Sociology Research Laboratory.

1983 Murdock, S., Leistritz, F.L. and Hamm, R. *Nuclear Waste: Socioeconomic Dimensions of Long-Term Storage.* Boulder, CO: Westview.

1983 Daneke, G., Garcia, M. and Delli Priscoli, J. (eds) *Public Involvement and Social Impact Assessment.* Boulder, CO: Westview.

1983 Finsterbusch, K., Llewellyn, L.G. and Wolf, C.P. (eds) *Social Impact Assessment Methods.* Beverly Hills, CA: Sage.

1984 Carley, M. and Bustelo, E. *Social Impact Assessment and Monitoring: A Guide to the Literature.* Boulder, CO: Westview.

1984 Branch, K., Hooper, D.A., Thompson, J. and Creighton, J. *Guide to Social Assessment: A Framework for Assessing Social Change.* Boulder, CO: Westview.

1984 Burch, W. and DeLuca, D. *Measuring the Social Impact of Natural Resource Policies.* Albuquerque: University of New Mexico Press.

1985 Derman, W. and Whiteford, S. (eds) *Social Impact Analysis and Development Planning in the Third World.* Boulder, CO: Westview.

1985 Cernea, M.M. (ed.) *Putting People First: Sociological Variables in Rural Development*, Washington, DC: The World Bank.

1985 Halstead, J., Chase, R., Murdock, S. and Leistritz, F.L. *Socioeconomic Impact Management: Design and Implementation*. Boulder, CO: Westview.

1985 Detomasi, D. and Gartrell, J. *Resource Communities: A Decade of Disruption*. Boulder, CO: Westview.

1985 Gold, R. *Ranching, Mining, and the Human Impact of Natural Resource Development*. New Brunswick, NJ: Transaction Books.

1986 Elkind-Savatsky, P.D. (ed.) *Differential Social Impacts of Rural Resource Development*. Boulder, CO: Westview.

1986 Leistritz, F.L. and Ekstrom, B. *Social Impact Assessment and Management: An Annotated Bibliography*. New York: Garland.

1988 Hyman, E. and Stiftel, B. *Combining Facts and Values in Environmental Impact Assessment: Theories and Techniques*. Boulder, CO: Westview.

1989 Brealey, T., Neil, C. and Newton, P. (eds) *Resource Communities: Settlement and Workforce Issues*. Melbourne: CSIRO Publications.

1990 Taylor, C.N., Bryan, H. and Goodrich, C.G. *Social Assessment: Theory, Process and Techniques*. Lincoln, NZ: Centre for Resource Management, Lincoln University (later editions published in 1995, 2004).

1990 Finsterbusch, K., Ingersoll, J. and Llewellyn, L. (eds) *Methods for Social Analysis in Developing Countries*. Boulder, CO: Westview Press.

1992 Neil, C., Tykkyläinen, M. and Bradbury, J. (eds) *Coping with Closure: An International Comparison of Mine Town Experiences*. London: Routledge.

1994 Burdge, R.J. *A Conceptual Approach to Social Impact Assessment*. Middleton, WI: Social Ecology Press (later edition published in 1998).

1994 Freudenburg, W. and Gramling, R. *Oil in Troubled Waters: Perceptions, Politics and the Battle over Offshore Drilling*. Albany, NY: SUNY Press.

1995 Burdge, R.J. *A Community Guide to Social Impact Assessment*. Middleton, WI: Social Ecology Press (later editions published 1998, 2004).

1995 Vanclay, F. and Bronstein, D. (eds) *Environmental and Social Impact Assessment*. Chichester, UK: Wiley.

1996 Lichfield, N. *Community Impact Evaluation: Principles and Practice*. London: UCL Press.

1997 Becker, H.A. *Social Impact Assessment: Method and Experience in Europe, North America, and Developing World*. London: UCL Press.

1997 Barrow, C.J. *Environmental and Social Impact Assessment: An Introduction*. London: Arnold.

1997 Cernea, M. and Kudat, A. (eds) *Social Assessment for Better Development*. Washington, DC: The World Bank.

1998 Rietbergen-McCracken, J. and Narayan, D. (eds) *Participation and Social Assessment: Tools and Techniques*. Washington, DC: The World Bank.

1999 Murdock, S., Krannich, R. and Leistritz, F.L. *Hazardous Wastes in Rural America: Impacts, Implications and Options for Rural Communities*. Lanham, MD: Rowman & Littlefield.

2000 Barrow, C.J. *Social Impact Assessment: An Introduction*. London: Arnold.

2000 Goldman, L.R. (ed.) *Social Impact Analysis: An Applied Anthropology Manual*. Oxford: Berg.

2001 Dale, A., Taylor, C.N. and Lane, M. (eds) *Social Assessment in Natural Resource Management Institutions*. Collingwood, Vic.: CSIRO Publishing.

2003 World Bank Social Development Department *Social Analysis Sourcebook: Incorporating Social Dimensions into Bank-Supported Projects*, Washington, DC: The World Bank.

2003 Becker, H.A. and Vanclay, F. (eds) *The International Handbook of Social Impact Assessment*. Cheltenham, UK and Northampton, MA, USA: Edward Elgar Publishing Ltd.

2004 Burdge, R.J. *The Concepts, Process and Methods of Social Impact Assessment*. Middleton, WI: Social Ecology Press.

2006 Coudouel, A., Dani, A. and Paternostro, S. (eds) *Poverty and Social Impact Analysis of Reforms: Lesson and Examples from Implementation*. Washington, DC: The World Bank.

2007 World Bank, *Tools for Institutional, Political, and Social Analysis of Policy Reform: A Sourcebook for Development Practitioners*. Washington, DC: The World Bank.

2011 Vanclay, F. and Esteves, A.M. (eds) *New Directions in Social Impact Assessment: Conceptual and Methodological Advances*. Cheltenham, UK and Northampton, MA, USA: Edward Elgar Publishing Ltd.

It is important to realize that while NEPA led to a flurry of interest by scholars in SIA and did lead over time to the formalization of a designated and widely accepted SIA procedure, there was already a long tradition of academic interest in the social consequences of change, especially within anthropology and sociology. Papers by Fred Cottrell (1951), 'Death by dieselization: A case study in the reaction to technological change' and Lauriston Sharp (1952) 'Steel axes for stone age Australians', are classic case-study examples. A 1936 paper by Robert Merton, 'The unanticipated consequences of purposive social action', is a classic theoretical example. A 1957 paper by Carl Kraenzel considered the social consequences of river-basin development, specifically in the Tennessee and Missouri basins. A 1969 paper by Eric Schwimmer was one of the earliest papers to consider the social impacts of a natural disaster. Although these papers may not be part of the current SIA paradigm, they are part of an earlier intellectual interest in this general topic.

There has been much debate over when the first SIA was done. While some scholars like Burdge (1991, Chapter 46, this volume) would only consider SIA to have been done in a post-NEPA context, other scholars – who consider that SIA is, in effect, the search for no-regret strategies – can find much earlier examples. Prendergast (1989) suggests that the Marquis de Condorcet did the first SIA in 1795 when he analysed the likely impacts on mortality rates of the Picardy canal in France. Becker (1997) posits that Johan de Witt, the Grand Pensionary of Holland, was the inaugurator of SIA in 1671 when he assessed the price of the annuities being sold to raise funds for a war with England and France. Whether these are examples of SIA or not is a moot point. The point is that there is a long tradition in thinking about the social consequences of change, and therefore linking SIA solely to NEPA is a very limited perspective.

A much repeated story about the origins of SIA (for example, Burdge 1991, Chapter 46, this volume) relates to the Berger Inquiry in Canada. While the Berger Inquiry might not be responsible for the birth of SIA, it certainly was significant in terms of developing a model for the operationalization of SIA/EIA and it is widely held up as an exemplar of best practice (for example, Howitt 1989, Craig 1990). It is one of the few EIA/SIAs discussed in *Science* (Gamble 1978). Nevertheless, it had its detractors at the time (for example, Lotz 1977), and subsequent assessment of it yields an ambivalent outcome (see Sabin 1995, Abele in press). Officially known as the Mackenzie Valley Pipeline Inquiry and chaired by Justice Thomas Berger, it ran from 1974 to 1977 producing two reports (Berger 1977) totalling over 500 pages and over 40,000 pages of other documentation. What was innovative about it was that, in addition to formal hearings with legal cross-examination of expert witnesses, Berger enabled participation by the various Indigenous peoples by having community hearings in their own villages, in their own languages and in their own culturally appropriate ways (Gamble 1978). In his letter to the Minister, which served as something of an executive summary to the report, Berger (1977 Vol. 1, p. vii) wrote:

> At the formal hearings of the Inquiry in Yellowknife, I heard the evidence of 300 experts on northern conditions, northern environment and northern peoples. But, sitting in a hearing room in Yellowknife, it is easy to forget the real extent of the North. The Mackenzie Valley and the Western Arctic is a vast land where people of four races live, speaking seven different languages. To hear what they had to say, I took the Inquiry to 35 communities – from Sachs Harbour to Fort Smith, from Old Crow to Fort Franklin – to every city and town, village and settlement in the Mackenzie Valley and the Western Arctic. I listened to the evidence of almost one thousand northerners. I discovered that people in the North have strong feelings about the pipeline and large-scale frontier development. I listened to a brief by northern businessmen in Yellowknife who favour a pipeline through the North. Later, in a native village far away, I heard virtually the whole community express vehement opposition to such a pipeline. Both were talking about the same pipeline; both were talking about the same region – but for one group it is a frontier, for the other a homeland.

Berger (1977 Vol. 1, p. xiii) made strong recommendations 'that no pipeline be built and no energy corridor be established across the Northern Yukon, along either route'. He indicated that a potential alternative had been suggested (along the Alaska highway) but added that 'I am in no position to endorse such a route: an assessment of social and economic impact [of that proposal] must still be made, and native claims have not been settled' (Berger 1977 Vol. 1, p. xiv). Whether Berger's recommendations were accepted or not is subject to conjecture given the changing energy scene at the time (Sabin 1995, Abele in press). Nevertheless, the Berger report was profoundly influential, with one commentator likening the Inquiry to a truth and reconciliation commission (Stanton 2012). Berger went on to become a champion of Indigenous peoples' rights, producing several more major works (Berger 1981, 1985, 1992).

From Regulatory Mechanism to Company Procedure

SIA has come a long way since the Berger Inquiry, and NEPA (or NEPA-like legislation) is no longer the sole basis of SIA. In fact, there have been several trends over the last decade or two that have profoundly affected the positioning of SIA, shifting it away from being a regulatory tool (determining what the impacts are and advising a competent authority whether to approve the project or not) to being an industry tool (the process of managing the social issues of development). Instead of the SIA consultant submitting a statement of social impacts akin to an Environmental Impact Statement, the consultant now tends to work with the proponent in developing and implementing a social impact management plan. In fact, best practice in environmental regulation would be to consider the social impact management plan, not the statement of impacts (Franks and Vanclay 2013). The trends or forces that have led to this shift are described separately below but in reality are intertwined. Every trend is not necessarily happening everywhere in the world, but in general these trends are taking place, depending on the local context.

First, there has been a growing realization that *the regulatory model did not work*. Governments lacked conviction to implementing thorough procedures, specifically in relation to setting conditions (conditionalities) and ensuring compliance with them. There was a lack of 'follow-up' (in other words, compliance monitoring). Proponents were not committed to the process and viewed it as a bureaucratic hurdle rather than something that was beneficial to their business. Consultants were often disingenuous, acting often as advocates for the project rather than as defenders of the community. The procedure was excessively costly and time-consuming. EIA/SIA was done far too late in the project implementation process to have any meaningful influence on project design, and since many of the social impacts are caused by fear and anxiety and the 'honey pot effect' which occur early on, the procedure was not effective in dealing with many of the social impacts created by projects. The regulatory model of impact assessment arguably suited the regulator's needs, but failed to address the management of the issues.

Second, around the world there has been a growing *change in the way governments see their responsibilities*, often referred to as *neoliberalism*. Neoliberalism refers to a free market ideology of small government and a belief in market-based rather than state-based solutions to social and environmental problems, a shift away from state paternalism and the nanny state. The influence of neoliberalism in certain specific countries and the world generally has resulted in the withdrawal of basic social services (especially in rural regions), the elimination of the welfare state, the rollback of regulatory oversight mechanisms, deregulation and/or an acceptance of industry self-regulation, privatization of state-owned enterprises, the dismantling of protectionist trade barriers, and the privatization of property rights over natural resources that had previously been vested in the state or community (through the creation of land titles and water rights etc.) (Tonts and Jones 1997; McCarthy and Prudham 2004; Liverman and Vilas 2006; Young and Matthews, 2007). Neoliberalism has meant that there is little government interest in EIA/SIA procedures in the way it developed in the period shortly after NEPA was passed and as manifested by the Berger Inquiry.

Third, *communities* have come to *want more than the 'do no harm' approach taken in EIA. Mitigating the harmful impacts is no longer enough.* Communities want projects to contribute positively to their development. They realize that all the harmful impacts will never be fully mitigated and positive benefits are needed to overcome residual harm. Positive benefits could be in the form of job opportunities or contributions to community development. More than just jobs, *communities want opportunities for enhancement of business opportunities.* Instead of importing all goods and services, projects can make a huge positive benefit to local economies through local procurement. Furthermore, although the NEPA model of EIA/SIA allowed for, if not required, community consultation, communities have come to expect more than to be merely consulted – they want greater involvement and to be fully engaged in the processes of determining community vision, what is good development, how impact assessment should be undertaken, and in determining what appropriate mitigation and compensation should be. Rather than insisting that all harm be mitigated even if at ludicrous cost, communities in trusting relationships with companies are willing to consider appropriate trade-offs. These arrangements between a project and a community are increasingly being written into Impacts and Benefits Agreements (or community development agreements) (Gibson and O'Faircheallaigh 2010; ICMM 2010; O'Faircheallaigh 2011; Nish and Bice 2011).

Fourth, along with increasing community expectations came increasing community activism and the *rise of the concept of social risk* or non-technical risk (Joyce and Thomson 2000). Communities have become empowered and better resourced, including by international environmental NGOs. The internet and associated globalization have expanded the reach and influence of individuals and groups. Communities, or disgruntled components within communities, are willing to protest and to blockade, thus causing disruption and delay as well as gaining national and international media attention. They might also take direct action in the form of sabotage. They might also engage in peaceful, but politically powerful, protest that results in loss of political support. Finally, they might also pursue legal action and, whether or not they are successful, the legal case can be costly, time-consuming, delay-inducing, and may lead to reputational risk. All of these issues are real risks a business faces. Thus in the same way that there is technical risk and financial risk, there are also non-technical risks such as social risk that need to be seriously considered by a business. The fact that most businesses have accepted this point means that they are now very appreciative of the need to be aware of and manage these risks. Rio Tinto, for example, makes its policy statement on social risk publicly available: http://www.riotinto.com/documents/Social_risk_analysis_guidance_2011_2014.pdf

Fifth, NEPA and related legislation in other countries were typically implemented in an era of corporate irresponsibility and the manifest need for government control, often in the wake of environmental disasters. Even though the concept of corporate social responsibility (CSR) arguably dates from the 1950s and thus before NEPA (Bowen 1953; van der Ploeg and Vanclay 2013), over the last two decades or so there has been a marked rise in the attention being given to CSR (Carroll 1999, Matten and Moon 2008). *Sustainable development and corporate social responsibility are now part of the corporate mentality and culture.* Many industry sectors have adopted a sustainable development ethos (for example, IIED 2002; ICMM 2003) and many industry bodies have developed codes of practice, sometimes specifically on SIA (see Box 2). Companies are willing to do more than the minimum required by governments, and many of them frame their business strategy to be 'the developer of choice', and are being encouraged to do so by leading management consultants (for example Accenture 2012).

Sixth, related to CSR and growing community empowerment is the concept of *social licence to operate* (SLO). This refers to the extent to which a company meets the 'demands on and expectations for a business enterprise that emerge from neighbourhoods, environmental groups, community members, and other elements of the surrounding civil society' (Gunningham et al. 2004, p. 308). Essentially, corporations realize that they need to meet more than regulatory requirements: they also need to meet the expectations of a wide range of stakeholders including international NGOs and local communities. If they do not, they risk not only reputational damage and the reduced opportunities that might bring, they also risk being subject to strikes, protests, blockades, sabotage, legal action and the financial consequences of those actions. Even though the concept is criticized (Owen and Kemp 2013), 'social licence' has become part of the language of business (Nelson 2006), actively influences if not drives the business strategy of many companies, and is part of the governance landscape (Prno and Slocombe 2012).

Seventh, there has been a rise in the standing of the *business and human rights agenda* and a widening of what are understood as human rights (Kemp and Vanclay 2013, Chapter 25, this volume). As a result of the appointment of a 'United Nations Special Representative of the Secretary-General on the issue of human rights and transnational corporations and other business enterprises', Prof. John Ruggie, from 2005 to 2011, and the subsequent United Nations adoption of the *United Nations Guiding Principles on Business and Human Rights* (UNGP 2011), the issue of human rights has gained substantially more standing. The business responsibility to respect human rights has been clarified in Ruggie's (2008) protect, respect, remedy framework. Alongside Ruggie, there has been much discussion about what the human rights are. Although the minimum standards for human rights observance were made explicit by Ruggie, the UNGP also requires businesses to consider additional standards as may be appropriate depending on host and home state circumstances. This has led to much discussion, leading to the notion of 'emerging rights'. Two previously considered emerging rights, the right to water and the right to sanitation, have now been confirmed as basic rights by the United Nations (UNGA 2010). Other emerging rights relate to the right to food, the right to a livelihood, the right to housing, the right to live in a healthy environment, the right to health and healthcare, the right to an adequate standard of living, the right to cultural integrity, the right to education, the right to adequate information and the right to participation (Kemp and Vanclay 2013, Chapter 25, this volume; Sanz-Caballero 2013). Whether confirmed as fundamental human rights or not, project developers will need to consider all these issues. An implication of the growth of the human rights agenda is that social impacts are now potentially infringements of human rights, and impacted stakeholders are now rights holders who may have legal redress. SIA will of necessity incorporate human rights, and will gain an increased mandate because of the human rights agenda. The legal standing of human rights and the increasing awareness that business has an obligation to respect human rights increases corporate interest in ensuring that they are meeting their responsibilities and in SIA as a mechanism to do this.

Finally, there is very little evidence of the regulatory model actually policing projects, especially in the current neoliberal environment. Instead, *the 'regulators' of today are international NGO watchdog organizations and local litigious community groups.* It is not only government regulators who hold companies accountable, it is civil society. This is partly connected to the concept of 'social licence to operate' mentioned earlier. The standards a company has to meet are not just those specified by government, it is those expected by local and distant civil society actors. With the rise of human rights, there is a growing legal basis for community and NGO action against companies. Irrespective of whether the legal case is strong or not, and whether successful or not, in many cases of civil society action the reputational damage to a company can be considerable.

These eight societal trends are the basis of the shift in SIA away from being a regulatory tool to being a company process of managing the social issues of project development. Intellectually, there were also some concerns with the regulatory approach. Primarily, the regulatory model with its point-in-time assessment presumed that SIA could be an all-knowing and all-powerful tool – that it could actually predict all the impacts and that whatever mitigation measures were recommended they would be effective and fully implemented. Those assumptions were dubious. Given the complexity of social interactions and human response, it is highly unlikely that an SIA could predict all the social impacts, especially the second and higher-order, indirect and cumulative impacts. What is clearly needed is an ongoing adaptive management process. Also, unless the SIA is closely aligned to a company and the business case for mitigation is very clear to the company, it is highly unlikely that mitigation measures will be fully implemented. It is important to realize that SIA is not constrained to being a business tool and that discussion about the shift in focus from being a regulatory tool to being a business tool does not negate the valuable role SIA can play as a tool for communities or governments.

Box 2: Indicative SIA Guidelines
(Please note that no endorsement should be inferred by being listed here)

PROFESSIONAL ASSOCIATION GUIDELINES
International Association for Impact Assessment: Vanclay, F. 2003 'International Principles for Social Impact Assessment', *Impact Assessment and Project Appraisal* 21(1), 5–11.
http://www.iaia.org/publicdocuments/sections/sia/IAIA-SIA-International-Principles.pdf

Planning Institute of Australia 2010 *Social Impact Assessment Position Statement*
http://www.planning.org.au/documents/item/250

INDUSTRY LEVEL GUIDELINES
Cement industry: World Business Council for Sustainable Development 2005 *Cement Sustainability Initiative Environmental and Social Impact Assessment Guidelines*
http://www.wbcsdcement.org/pdf/cement_esia_guidelines.pdf

Oil and Gas industry: IPIECA 2004 *A Guide to Social Impact Assessment in the Oil and Gas Industry*
http://www.ipieca.org/publication/ipieca-guide-social-impact-assessment-oil-and-gas-industry

CORPORATE LEVEL GUIDELINES
Anglo American 2012 Socio-Economic Assessment Toolbox
http://www.angloamerican.com/development/social/seat
Rio Tinto 2011 *Social Impact Assessment Guidance*
http://www.riotinto.com/documents/Social_impact_assessment_guidance_2011_2014.pdf

INSTITUTIONAL LEVEL GUIDELINES
African Development Bank 2003 *Integrated Environmental and Social Impact Assessment Guidelines*
http://www.afdb.org/fileadmin/uploads/afdb/Documents/Policy-Documents/Integrated%20Environmental%20and%20Social%20Impact%20Assesment%20Guidelines.pdf

United Nations Economic and Social Commission for Asia and the Pacific 2001 *Multistage Environmental and Social Impact Assessment of Road Projects: Guidelines for a Comprehensive Process*
http://www.unescap.org/ttdw/Publications/TIS_pubs/pub_2177/esiaguidelines01.pdf

GOVERNMENT LEVEL GUIDELINES
Greenland (national government): Bureau of Minerals and Petroleum 2009 *Guidelines for Social Impact Assessments for mining projects in Greenland*
http://www.bmp.gl/images/stories/minerals/sia_guideline/sia_guidelines.pdf

Suriname (national government): Office of Environmental and Social Assessment 2005 *Environmental Assessment Guidelines Volume IV: Social Impact Assessment* (NIMOS Nationaal Instituut voor Milieu en Ontwikkeling in Suriname)
http://www.nimos.org/smartcms/default.asp?contentID=611

Queensland Government (state government, Australia): Coordinator General 2013 *Social Impact Assessment Guideline*
http://www.dsdip.qld.gov.au/resources/guideline/social-impact-assessment-guideline.pdf

Lake Macquarie City Council (peri-urban local government, NSW Australia) 2012 *Social Impact Assessment Guideline*
http://www.lakemac.com.au/downloads/Att%2021%2012STRAT005%20Social%20Impact%20Assessment%20Guidelines.pdf

Randwick City Council (urban local government, NSW Australia) 2006 *Social Impact Assessment Guidelines for Assessing Development Applications*
http://www.randwick.nsw.gov.au/library/scripts/objectifyMedia.aspx?file=pdf/27/58.pdf&siteID

CO-MANAGEMENT AGENCY GUIDELINES
Mackenzie Valley Environmental Impact Review Board 2007 *Socio-Economic Impact Assessment Guidelines*
http://www.reviewboard.ca/process_information/guidance_documentation/guidelines.php

The Business Case for SIA

As discussed above, there has been a shift in SIA away from being a regulatory tool to being a business tool. This is beneficial for the objectives of SIA because it means that there is greater commitment by companies to undertaking the SIA seriously and in implementing the findings. It also means that the SIA process is able to influence the project at a much earlier stage in the project life cycle, and given that many of the social impacts happen early, this is substantially beneficial to the potentially affected communities.

The business case for why corporations should do SIA can also be presented. There are many reasons why it is in the best interests of companies to be committed to good SIA (Esteves and Vanclay 2009, Chapter 21, this volume; Esteves et al. 2012, Chapter 1, this volume; Vanclay 2012, Chapter 12, this volume). These essentially connect to all of a company's business drivers. Social impact assessment enables a company to:

- have more effective risk identification and management processes;
- achieve enhanced access to land and resources;
- gain increased access to local workforce and suppliers;
- have the ability to identify and act on issues much earlier;
- achieve cost reductions (for example, through earlier remediation);
- achieve full cost consideration of all likely costs;
- create greater certainty for investors, government and society;
- enhance a company's legal and social licence to operate and to grow;
- improve stakeholder relations and thereby achieve efficiencies;
- maintain and enhance company and product reputation;
- avoid delays, shutdowns and potentially the untimely closure of projects; and
- increase short-term and long-term success.

Emerging Issues

As some of the papers in this research collection discuss, there are several contemporary developments that are set to have a major influence on SIA in the near future. Already discussed above in the section on the shift in SIA from regulatory mechanism to company procedure is the rise of *the business and human rights agenda* (also see Kemp and Vanclay 2013, Chapter 25, this volume). This will have an increasing impact on SIA and will give renewed vigour to SIA by providing a legal mandate. However, it will also mean that SIA practitioners will need to become thoroughly versed in human rights law. While there is a lot of compatibility between human rights issues and social issues, a human rights approach is a different paradigm to the current SIA paradigm. Whether human rights impact assessment emerges as a completely independent new field in competition with SIA, or whether they exist amicably alongside each other and supporting each other remains to be seen and is perhaps something for SIA to consider and manage.

Alongside the rise of human rights generally has been the increasing attention given to the rights of Indigenous peoples, especially with the passing of the United Nations Declaration of the Rights of Indigenous Peoples (UN 2007) and Convention 169 of the International Labour

Organization (ILO 1989). Discussed further by Hanna and Vanclay (2013, Chapter 26, this volume), a specific element of these documents that is of great relevance to SIA is the concept of *free, prior and informed consent* (FPIC). Although the legal status and precise meaning of FPIC is contested, there is a growing sense of FPIC being a philosophy about the rights of any community (IIED 2002; Hill et al. 2010) to be consulted without duress or coercion (free), before any project work takes place (prior), on the basis of full information about the project and a full understanding of what it will mean for the community (informed), and with the ability to collectively say no or yes (consent) and have their view listened to and acted upon (Vanclay and Esteves 2011). FPIC increases the need for effective community engagement processes, for effective social impact assessments, and for project developers to seriously consider how impacted peoples can be converted from impactees to engaged beneficiaries.

The need to clarify the relationship with impacted communities and to treat them with respect has led to the development of *Impacts and Benefits Agreements* (IBAs) (O'Faircheallaigh 1999, Chapter 27, this volume). Typically, these are legally binding agreements between a developer and a community specifying what the project entails, what the likely impacts will be, what the developer promises to do in relation to the impacts and what compensation and/ or community development assistance will be provided. These agreements should emerge as an outcome of an SIA process, or at least be informed by an SIA process and be developed alongside SIA. Discussion of how the benefits from projects will be distributed should be based on a sound knowledge and understanding of what the likely social impacts will be, and on a basis of an understanding of the issues associated with visioning the future for a community. The agreements must also be made in a manner consistent with FPIC. While IBAs so far have tended to be developed only with Indigenous communities and in relation to large extractive projects, there is no reason why they should not be used as a normal part of a good SIA and project development, irrespective of the context.

The shift from regulatory tool to company procedure has been accompanied by *a shift from mitigation to enhancement* (João et al. 2011). Doing no harm is no longer good enough for communities; they want opportunities for positive development. SIA therefore needs to be much more concerned with assisting communities in ensuring they receive benefits from projects, and not just with mitigating harmful impacts. Thinking about opportunities for benefit enhancement and developing local procurement strategies will be necessary. Also necessary will be the ability of SIA practitioners to be able to demonstrate the business case why this extra investment in enhancement is appropriate to project developers. SIA practitioners will require a wider set of skills in the future. They need to be influential within the companies they are working with.

A final external factor that may influence SIA, and somewhat in contradiction to neoliberalism discussed earlier, is the rise of *resource nationalism*. Resource nationalism refers to national governments exerting control over their natural resources in order to advance policy goals (Stanislaw 2009; Bremmer and Johnston 2009). While this (in some circumstances at least) is a legitimate right of sovereign nations, the process does provoke concern in certain quarters. Resource nationalism may impact SIA in various ways. In some circumstances, especially in countries that have little need for foreign currency, it may lead to strategic bargaining by the state to increase the revenue gained from natural resources, including by seeking co-ownership in a joint-venture company. In situations where a country has a dire need for foreign currency, it may lead to state actions that ensure the rapid flow of financial benefits from project development, potentially without doing proper EIA, SIA or other forms of due diligence assessment. It may also lead to accepting a bid from a company that returns less longer-term benefit in exchange for a more rapid flow of carnings.

Conclusion

Social impact assessment (SIA) has changed much over time. Once conceived primarily as being a regulatory tool, SIA is now recognized as having multiple formats, and perhaps primarily being a corporate process of managing the social impacts of development. Once governed by a government regulatory agency, SIA is now 'regulated' primarily by impacted peoples and national and international watchdog NGOs in direct negotiation with a company and/or by legal action. Once seen as a bureaucratic hurdle to be overcome, SIA is now being seen as not only necessary but a potentially valuable tool for businesses to utilize to improve their social licence to operate, to meet their free, prior and informed consent procedures, and to add value to their business. While there will continue to be changes in SIA, driven from within the paradigm and by external factors, the discourse or paradigm of SIA is here to stay.

References

Abele, F. in press 'The immediate and lasting impact of the Inquiry into the construction of a pipeline in the Mackenzie Valley, 1974–77', in G. Inwood and C. Johns (eds), *Commissions of Inquiry and Policy Change: A Comparative Analysis*, University of Toronto Press [online]. Available at: http://s3.amazonaws.com/isuma.attachments/Abele_BergerInquiryArticle.pdf [accessed 28 August 2013].

Accenture (2012), *Achieving High Performance for Mining in 2020: Six Strategies for Safe, Sustainable and Superior Operations* [online]. Available at: http://www.accenture.com/SiteCollectionDocuments/PDF/Accenture-Achieving-High-Performance-Mining-2020.pdf [accessed 28 August 2013].

Armour, A. (1992), 'The challenge of assessing social impacts', *Social Impact: The Social Impact Management Bulletin*, **1** (4), 6–9.

Becker, H.A. (1997), *Social Impact Assessment: Method and Experience in Europe, North America, and Developing World*, London: UCL Press.

Berger, T.R. (1977), *Northern Frontier, Northern Homeland: The Report of the Mackenzie Valley Pipeline Inquiry*, 2 vols, Ottawa: Minister of Supply and Services [online]. Available at: http://yukondigitallibrary.ca/digitalbook/northernfrontiersocialimpactenvironmentalimpact/ [accessed 28 August 2013].

Berger, T.R. (1981), *Fragile Freedoms: Human Rights and Dissent in Canada*, Toronto: Clarke & Irwin.

Berger, T.R. (1985), *Village Journey: The Report of the Alaska Native Review Commission*, New York: Hill and Wang.

Berger, T.R. (1992), *A Long and Terrible Shadow: White Values, Native Rights in the Americas, 1492–1992*, Vancouver: Douglas & McIntyre.

Bowen, A.B. (1953), *Social Responsibilities of the Business Man*, New York: Harper & Row.

Breese, G. (1965), *The Impact of Large Installations on Nearby Areas*, Beverly Hills, CA: Sage.

Bremmer, I. and Johnston, R. (2009), 'The rise and fall of Resource Nationalism', *Survival: Global Politics and Strategy*, **51** (2), 149–58.

Burdge, R. (1991), 'A brief history and major trends in the field of impace assessment', *Impact Assessment*, **9** (4), 93–104.

Cabinet Office (2009), *A Guide to Social Return on Investment*, London: The Cabinet Office [online]. Available at: http://www.socialevaluator.eu/ip/uploads/tblDownload/SROI%20Guide.pdf [accessed 28 August 2013].

Carroll, A.B. (1999), 'Corporate social responsibility: Evolution of a definitional construct', *Business and Society*, **38**, 268–95.

Cottrell, W.F. (1951), 'Death by dieselization: A case study in the reaction to technological change', *American Sociological Review*, **16** (3), 358–65.

Craig, D. (1990), 'Social Impact Assessment: Politically oriented approaches and applications', *Environmental Impact Assessment Review*, **10** (1), 37–54.

Dreyfus, D. and Ingram, H. (1976), 'The National Environmental Policy Act: A view of intent and practice', *Natural Resources Journal*, **16** (2), 243–62.

Esteves, A.M., D. Franks and F. Vanclay (2012), 'Social impact assessment: The state of the art', *Impact Assessment & Project Appraisal*, **30** (1), 35–44.

Esteves, A.M. and F. Vanclay (2009), 'Social Development Needs Analysis as a tool for SIA to guide corporate-community investment: Applications in the minerals industry', *Environmental Impact Assessment Review*, **29** (2), 137–45.

Franks, D. and Vanclay, F. (2013), 'Social Impact Management Plans: Innovation in corporate and public policy', *Environmental Impact Assessment Review*, **43**, 40–48.

Friesema, H.P. and Culhane, P.J. (1976), 'Social impacts, politics, and the environmental impact statement process', *Natural Resources Journal*, **16** (2), 339–56.

Gamble, D.J. (1978), 'The Berger Inquiry: An impact assessment process', *Science*, **199** (4332), 946–52.

Gibson, G. and O'Faircheallaigh, C. (2010), *IBA Community Toolkit: Negotiation and Implementation of Impact and Benefit Agreements*, Ottawa: Walter & Duncan Gordon Foundation [online]. Available at: http://www.ibacommunitytoolkit.ca [accessed 28 August 2013].

Gunningham, N., Kagan, R. and Thornton, D. (2004), 'Social license and environmental protection: Why businesses go beyond compliance', *Law & Social Inquiry*, **29** (2), 307–41.

Hanna, P. and F. Vanclay (2013), 'Human rights, indigenous peoples and the concept of Free, Prior and Informed Consent', *Impact Assessment & Project Appraisal*, **31** (2), 146–57.

Hill, C., Lillywhite, S. and Simon, M. (2010), *Guide to Free Prior and Informed Consent*, Carlton, Vic.: Oxfam Australia.

Howitt, R. (1989), 'Social Impact Assessment and resource development: Issues from the Australian experience', *Australian Geographer*, **20** (2), 153–66.

ICMM (2003), *ICMM Sustainable Development Framework: ICMM Principles* (Document Ref: C 020/290503), London: International Council on Mining and Metals [online]. Available at: http://liveassets.iucn.getunik.net/downloads/minicmmstat.pdf [accessed 28 August 2013].

ICMM (2010), *Indigenous Peoples and Mining: Good Practice Guide*, London: International Council on Mining and Metals.

IIED (International Institute for Environment and Development) (2002), *Breaking New Ground: The Report of the Mining, Minerals and Sustainable Development Project*, London: Earthscan [online]. Available at: http://www.iied.org/mmsd-final-report [accessed 28 August 2013].

ILO (1989), *Convention Concerning Indigenous and Tribal Peoples in Independent Countries* (Convention 169), Geneva: International Labour Organization [online]. Available at: http://www.ilo.org/dyn/normlex/en/f?p=1000:12100:0::NO::P12100_ILO_CODE:C169 [accessed 28 August 2013].

João, E., Vanclay, F. and den Broeder, L. (2011), 'Emphasising enhancement in all forms of impact assessment', *Impact Assessment and Project Appraisal*, **29** (3), 170–80.

Joyce, S. and Thomson, I. (2000), 'Earning a social licence to operate: Social acceptability and resource development in Latin America', *Canadian Institute of Mining Bulletin*, **93** (1037), 49–53.

Kemp, D. and F. Vanclay (2013), 'Human rights and impact assessment: clarifying the connections in practice', *Impact Assessment & Project Appraisal*, **31** (2), 86–96.

Kraenzel, C. (1957), 'The social consequences of river basin development', *Law and Contemporary Problems*, **22** (2), 221–36.

Liverman, D. and Vilas, S. (2006), 'Neoliberalism and the environment', *Annual Review of Environment and Resources*, **31**, 327–63.

Lotz, J. (1977), 'Northern pipelines and southern assumptions', *Arctic*, **30** (4), 198–204.

Maruyama, M. (1973), 'Cultural, social, and psychological considerations in the planning of public works', *Technological Forecasting and Social Change*, **5** (2), 135–43.

Matten, D. and Moon, J. (2008), 'Implicit and explicit CSR: A conceptual framework for a comparative understanding of corporate social responsibility', *Academy of Management Review*, 33, 404–24.

McCarthy, J. and Prudham, S. (2004), 'Neoliberal nature and the nature of neoliberalism', *Geoforum*, 35 (3), 275–83.

Merton, R.K. (1936), 'The unanticipated consequences of purposive social action', *American Sociological Review*, 1 (6), 894–904.

Nelson J. (2006), 'Social license to operate', *International Journal of Mining, Reclamation and Environment*, 20 (3), 161–2.

New Economics Foundation (2004), *Measuring Social Impact: The Foundation of Social Return on Investment* (colloquially called the SROI Primer) [online]. Available at: http://sroi.london.edu/Measuring-Social-Impact.pdf [accessed 28 August 2013].

New Economics Foundation (2008), *Measuring Social Impact: A Guide to Social Return on Investment* [online]. Available at: http://commdev.org/userfiles/files/2196_file_SROI.nef2008.pdf [accessed 28 August 2013].

Nish, S. and Bice, S. (2011), 'Community-based agreement making with land-connected peoples', in F. Vanclay and A.M. Esteves (eds), *New Directions in Social Impact Assessment: Conceptual and Methodological Advances*, Cheltenham, UK and Northampton, MA, USA: Edward Elgar Publishing Ltd, pp. 59–77.

O'Faircheallaigh, C. (1999), 'Making Social Impact Assessment count: A negotiation-based approach for Indigenous peoples', *Society and Natural Resources*, 12 (1), 63–80.

O'Faircheallaigh, C. (2011), 'SIA and Indigenous social development', in F. Vanclay and A.M. Esteves (eds), *New Directions in Social Impact Assessment: Conceptual and Methodological Advances*, Cheltenham, UK and Northampton, MA, USA: Edward Elgar Publishing Ltd, pp. 138–53.

Owen, J. and Kemp, D. (2013), 'Social licence and mining: A critical perspective', *Resources Policy*, 38, 29–35.

Prendergast, C. (1989), 'Condorcet's canal study: The beginnings of social impact assessment', *Impact Assessment Bulletin*, 7 (4), 25–37.

Prno, J. and Slocombe, S.D. (2012), 'Exploring the origins of "social license to operate" in the mining sector: Perspectives from governance and sustainability theories', *Resources Policy*, 37, 346–57.

Ruggie, J. (2008), *Promotion and Protection of all Human Rights, Civil, Political, Economic, Social and Cultural Rights, including the Right to Development – Protect, Respect and Remedy: A Framework for Business and Human Rights*. Report of the Special Representative of the Secretary-General on the Issue of Human Rights and Transnational Corporations and Other Business Enterprises, John Ruggie. UN Doc. A/HRC/8/5.

Sabin, P. (1995), 'Voices from the hydrocarbon frontier: Canada's Mackenzie Valley Pipeline Inquiry (1974–1977)', *Environmental History Review*, 19 (1), 17–48.

Sanz-Caballero, S. (2013), 'Children's rights in a changing climate: A perspective from the United Nations Convention on the Rights of the Child', *Ethics in Science and Environmental Politics*, 13, 11–14.

Schwimmer, E.G. (1969), *Cultural Consequences of a Volcanic Eruption Experienced by the Mount Lamington Orokaiva*. Department of Anthropology, University of Oregon.

Sharp, L. (1952), 'Steel axes for stone age Australians', *Human Organization*, 11 (2), 17–22.

Shields, M.A. (1974), *Social Impact Assessment: An Analytic Bibliography* (A Report Submitted to the US Army Engineer Institute for Water Resources), Providence, RI: Brown University.

Stanislaw, J.A. (2009), *Power Play: Resource Nationalism, the Global Scramble for Energy, and the Need for Mutual Interdependence*, Houston, TX and Washington, DC: Deloitte Center for Energy Solutions [online]. Available at: http://www.deloitte.com/assets/Dcom-Canada/Local%20Assets/Documents/ca_en_Stanislaw_PowerPlay.pdf [accessed 13 January 2014].

Stanton, K. (2012), 'Looking forward, looking back: The Canadian Truth and Reconciliation Commission and the Mackenzie Valley Pipeline Inquiry', *Canadian Journal of Law and Society*, 27 (1), 91–9.

Tonts, M. and Jones, R. (1997), 'From state paternalism to neoliberalism in Australian rural policy: Perspectives from the Western Australian wheatbelt', *Space and Polity*, 1 (2), 171–90.

UN (2007), *United Nations Declaration on the Rights of Indigenous Peoples. A/RES/61/295*, New York: United Nations General.

UNGA (2010), *64/292. The Human Right to Water and Sanitation*, United Nations General Assembly, UN Doc. A/RES/64/292.

UNGP (2011), *Guiding Principles on Business and Human Rights: Implementing the United Nations 'Protect, Respect and Remedy' Framework*, United Nations Human Rights Council, UN Doc. HR/PUB/11/04.

van der Ploeg, L. and Vanclay, F. (2013), 'Credible claim or corporate spin: A checklist to evaluate corporate sustainability reports', *Journal of Environmental Assessment Policy and Management*, **15** (3), 1350012 (21 pages).

Vanclay, F. (1999), 'Social impact assessment', in J. Petts (ed.), *Handbook of Environmental Impact Assessment* (Volume 1), Oxford: Blackwell Science, pp. 301–26.

Vanclay, F. (2002a), 'Social impact assessment', in M. Tolba (ed.), *Responding to Global Environmental Change*, Chichester, UK: Wiley, pp. 387–93.

Vanclay, F. (2002b), 'Conceptualising social impacts', *Environmental Impact Assessment Review*, **22** (3), 183–211.

Vanclay, F. (2003), 'International Principles for Social Impact Assessment', *Impact Assessment & Project Appraisal*, **21** (1), 5–11.

Vanclay, F. (2004a), 'The Triple Bottom Line and Impact Assessment: How do TBL, EIA, SIA, SEA and EMS relate to each other?', *Journal of Environmental Assessment Policy & Management*, **6** (3), 265–88.

Vanclay, F. (2004b), 'Assessing the social consequences of planned interventions', in R. White (ed.), *Controversies in Environmental Sociology*, Melbourne: Cambridge University Press, pp. 257–75.

Vanclay, F. (2012), 'The potential application of Social Impact Assessment in integrated coastal zone management', *Ocean & Coastal Management*, **68**, 149–56.

Vanclay, F., Baines, J. and Taylor, C.N. (2013), 'Principles for ethical research involving humans: Ethical professional practice in impact assessment Part I', *Impact Assessment and Project Appraisal*, **31** (4), 243–53.

Vanclay, F. and Esteves, A.M. (2011), 'Current issues and trends in social impact assessment', in F. Vanclay and A.M. Esteves (eds), *New Directions in Social Impact Assessment: Conceptual and Methodological Advances*, Cheltenham, UK and Northampton, MA, USA: Edward Elgar Publishing Ltd, pp. 3–19.

Young, N. and Matthews, R. (2007), 'Resource economies and neoliberal experimentation: The reform of industry and community in rural British Columbia', *Area*, **39** (2), 176–85.

Wolf, C.P. (1974), 'Social Impact Assessment: The State of the Art', *EDRA Proceedings*, **5** (2), 1–44.

Part I
Current Overview of SIA

Social impact assessment: the state of the art

Ana Maria Esteves[a]*, Daniel Franks[b] and Frank Vanclay[c]

[a]Community Insights Pty Ltd, Groningen, The Netherlands; [b]Centre for Social Responsibility in Mining, Sustainable Minerals Institute, University of Queensland, Brisbane, Australia; [c]Department of Cultural Geography, Faculty of Spatial Sciences, University of Groningen, Groningen, The Netherlands

(Received 11 September 2011; final version received 29 December 2011)

Social impact assessment (SIA) is now conceived as being the process of managing the social issues of development. There is consensus on what 'good' SIA practice is – it is participatory; it supports affected peoples, proponents and regulatory agencies; it increases understanding of change and capacities to respond to change; it seeks to avoid and mitigate negative impacts and to enhance positive benefits across the life cycle of developments; and it emphasizes enhancing the lives of vulnerable and disadvantaged people. We analyse the strengths, weaknesses, opportunities and threats facing SIA. We assert that the SIA community needs to revisit core concepts, such as culture, community, power, human rights, gender, justice, place, resilience and sustainable livelihoods. It is incumbent on SIA practitioners to educate proponents, regulators and colleagues about these concepts, and to embed them into practice norms. Stronger engagement with the emerging trends of free, prior and informed consent (FPIC); human rights impact assessment; social performance standards; supply chain management; governance; local content and economic development will improve the relevance and demonstrable value of SIA to all stakeholders.

Keywords: social impact assessment; impact and benefit agreements; community development agreements; social impact management plan; social sustainability; FPIC

Introduction

Social impact assessment (SIA) is about the processes of managing the social issues associated with planned interventions (Vanclay 2003a, 2006). SIA is a field of research and practice, a discourse, paradigm, or subdiscipline in its own right. The corpus of practitioners and scholars who profess this field have an established body of knowledge about theory and methods, a stock of tools, accumulated practical experience, insight and a collected history of case studies. Their shared professional values and understandings have been codified in the 'International principles for social impact assessment' (Vanclay 2003a) and in the core literature on SIA (see IAIA 2009). Many individuals identify as being an SIA practitioner or include SIA as a key interest area. There is a community of scholars engaged in research on SIA. The International Association for Impact Assessment (http://www.iaia.org) provides SIA practitioners and researchers with a professional home, and there are journals where SIA professionals publish, notably *Impact Assessment and Project Appraisal*.

SIA is an interdisciplinary and/or transdisciplinary social science that incorporates many fields including sociology, anthropology, demography, development studies, gender studies, social and cultural geography, economics, political science and human rights, community and environmental psychology, social research methods and environmental law, among others.

Originally (but now only in its narrowest conceptualization) SIA was regarded as a technique for predicting social impacts as part of an environmental impact assessment (EIA) in the production of an environmental impact statement (EIS), or as a stand-alone process, usually in the context of national legislation. Now SIA researchers and practitioners are interested in the processes of analysing, monitoring and managing the social consequences of planned interventions, and by logical extension the social dimensions of development in general. In addition to being a field of research, SIA is conceived as being a methodological approach or framework. SIA practitioners use this approach to contribute to the development process. SIA practitioners work with communities to achieve better development outcomes for communities. They also work with development agencies and private sector companies to design better projects and policies, and they work with regulatory agencies to provide information for the development approval process and ongoing regulation of projects. The approach is elaborated in many textbooks (see IAIA 2009) and is adapted to suit local circumstances.

The origins of social impact assessment

Contemporary SIA arguably began along with EIA in the early 1970s in response to the formal requirements of the National Environmental Policy Act (NEPA) 1969 of the USA. However, various writers – notably Burdge and Vanclay (1995), Becker (1997) and Vanclay (1999) – have argued that the consideration of social impacts existed long before NEPA. Nevertheless, it is clear that SIA formalized in terms of legal requirements and/or as part of normal project planning is linked to the spread of NEPA-like legislation and thinking around the world. A scrutiny of listings in Google Scholar (on 11 August 2011)

*Corresponding author. Email: amesteves@communityinsights.com.au

Box 1. Current good practice SIA

The activities typically undertaken in an SIA process are well established and documented (see IAIA 2009). Whether proponent-led or community-led, SIA essentially involves:

- creating participatory processes and deliberative spaces to facilitate community discussions about desired futures, the acceptability of likely impacts and proposed benefits, and community input into the SIA process, so that there can be a negotiated agreement with a developer based on free, prior and informed consent;
- gaining a good understanding (i.e. profiling) of the communities likely to be affected by the policy, programme, plan or project including a thorough stakeholder analysis to understand the differing needs and interests of the various sections of those communities;
- identifying community needs and aspirations;
- scoping the key social issues (the significant negative impacts as well as the opportunities for creating benefits);
- collecting baseline data;
- forecasting the social changes that may result from the policy, programme, plan or project;
- establishing the significance of the predicted changes, and determining how the various affected groups and communities will likely respond;
- examining other options;
- identifying ways of mitigating potential impacts and maximizing positive opportunities;
- developing a monitoring plan to inform the management of change;
- facilitating an agreement-making process between the communities and the developer ensuring that principles of free, prior and informed consent (FPIC) are observed and that human rights are respected, leading to the drafting of an impact and benefit agreement (IBA);
- assisting the proponent in the drafting of a social impact management plan (SIMP) that puts into operation all benefits, mitigation measures, monitoring arrangements and governance arrangements that were agreed to in the IBA, as well as plans for dealing with any ongoing unanticipated issues as they arise;
- putting processes in place to enable proponents, government authorities and civil society stakeholders to implement arrangements implied in the SIMP and IBA and to develop their own respective management action plans and embed them in their own organizations, establish respective roles and responsibilities throughout the implementation of those action plans, and maintain an ongoing role in monitoring.

Adapted from Vanclay and Esteves (2011, pp. 11–12)

for 'social impact assessment' for different years of publication confirms this. Discounting a few mis-codings, 'social impact assessment' makes its first appearance with one citation in 1973, 14 in 1974, just over 30 in 1975 and 1976, 97 in 1977, a dip for the next three years, and from 1981 to 1992 a fairly constant rate of around 100 citations per year. Since then, it has been steadily increasing (linearly) from 120 in 1993 to 624 in 2010.

The first 'state of the art' papers on SIA (Wolf 1975, 1976, 1977) contributed to establishing the field. The mid 1980s and mid 1990s saw further state of the art papers: Finsterbusch (1985), Freudenburg (1986), Murdock et al. (1986a, 1986b) and Burdge and Vanclay (1995, 1996). Subsequent state of the art papers include Vanclay (1999, 2002a) and Lockie (2001). Many more papers contribute to the knowledge base of SIA.

There are significant documents in the history of SIA, each responding to unease about SIA. Essentially they were developed to codify the state of the art and prescribe best practice (see Box 1). The first was the publication of the *Guidelines and principles for social impact assessment* by the [US] Interorganizational Committee on Guidelines and Principles for Social Impact Assessment (1994). This committee represented various scholarly and professional organizations in the USA that had an interest in impact assessment. The publication was a milestone because it represented agreement as to the core procedures and understanding of SIA at that time. Although clearly based on the regulatory framework operating in the USA, it enabled general guidance in any jurisdiction.

Over time there was demand to develop international guidelines and principles and in 1997 a task force was established for this purpose. However, the task force became embroiled in a major analysis of SIA as a paradigm. It became evident that, in international contexts without the regulatory requirements of the USA, there is a wider purpose for SIA (Vanclay 2003b, 2006). SIA had to be a mechanism that could be effective in the absence of regulation, it had to be able to deal with multiple regulations (e.g. the World Bank and bilateral aid agencies and in some cases national legislation), and it had to enhance the outcomes of development projects.

Developments in the practice of SIA around the world

SIA is widely practised internationally as a predictive study that is part of the regulatory approval process for infrastructure and resource extraction projects. Here SIA is usually included as a component of an EIS. Despite the widespread and longstanding practice of SIA, the legislative context has historically favoured biophysical impacts in most jurisdictions.

While its use in project approvals is still the predominant form of SIA, the drivers and focus for SIA have shifted. Some organizations and companies have implemented ongoing processes – assessment, management and monitoring – to improve the identification of the social impacts that occur during project implementation and to respond proactively to change (Franks et al. 2009,

Franks 2011, Kemp 2011, Vanclay and Esteves 2011). This view of SIA as part of an ongoing management process to respond to impacts is linked to the field of community relations (Kemp 2009) and recognizes the importance of social issues as drivers of business risk. Stakeholder-related risks have been identified to be significant influencers on the success, timeliness and cost of projects (Ruggie 2010). The business benefits of improved processes for assessing and managing social impacts are now widely recognized, and include:

- greater certainty for project investments and increased chance of project success;
- avoidance and reduction of social and environmental risks and conflicts faced by industry and communities;
- improved ability to identify issues early on, and therefore to reduce costs and to incorporate unavoidable costs into feasibility assessments and project planning;
- improved planning for social and physical infrastructure;
- a process to inform and involve internal and external stakeholders and to assist in building trust and mutually beneficial futures;
- improved quality of life for employees and improved attraction and retention of skilled workers;
- a positive legacy beyond the life of the project;
- increased competitive advantage through enhanced social performance and corporate reputation.

International codes and standards, particularly when written into conditions of project financing, have provided an additional driver. The International Finance Corporation's Performance Standards, which have been adopted by some private lenders as the Equator Principles, are an example. The 2006 IFC Performance Standards (a revision of its safeguard policies in place since 1998) require the preparation of environmental and social action plans for all projects. These plans summarize the findings of the impact assessment; outline measures for mitigation and community development; provide estimates of the timing, frequency, duration and cost of management measures; and establish monitoring and reporting procedures.

In some jurisdictions, social management processes are required for project approval. In Queensland, Australia, resource projects must submit a social impact management plan (SIMP) as part of their EIS. SIMPs outline the strategies to be undertaken during all phases of a development (including closure) to assess, monitor, report, evaluate, review and proactively respond to change (QDITR 2008, Franks et al. 2009, QDIP 2010). South Africa introduced social and labour plans (SLP) in 2004 as a requirement of mining projects. SLPs are prepared by the proponent and submitted with an application for a mining right. They address human resources, career progression and local community development (SADME 2006, Franks et al. 2009). A similar system, the Social Development and Management Program, exists for mining projects in the Philippines (Minerals Development Council 2007).

SIA methods and tools are now frequently applied in natural resource management (Dale et al. 2001, Fenton et al. 2003, Cooper et al. 2006), in peace-building and conflict initiatives (International Alert 2005), in international development cooperation projects (Dani and Beddies 2011), in due diligence processes (Joyce and MacFarlane 2001) and in disaster preparation (Benson and Twigg 2007).

Current strengths and weaknesses

The strengthening of SIA practice is evidenced by greater recognition of the importance of social issues and a corresponding proliferation of social specialists in lending institutions, governments, project developers and engineering consultancies. The increased capacities of individuals and organizations, and the greater responsibilities placed on them, are matched by similar trends of increased and expanded corporate policy, standards and tools in SIA and related fields. Project developers engaged in leading practice in impact assessment implement ongoing social monitoring and management programmes, and community feedback mechanisms.

SIA methods are used to assist decision-making and prioritization of social investments by project proponents. Social investments often form part of the corporate social responsibility initiatives of companies and their community development commitments to affected communities. Proponents seek to improve the balance of costs and benefits of projects by enhancing positive outcomes and mitigating negative impacts (João et al. 2011). Esteves and Vanclay (2009) developed a social development needs analysis (SDNA) tool to assist managers to evaluate community development alternatives. SDNA can assist with the alignment of a project and its social investments with community needs and regional planning priorities, while simultaneously addressing the strategic risks faced by project developers. Applying SIA methods to social investments can help navigate the potentially contradictory trends of contributing to local communities while reducing dependency on short-term projects.

These encouraging transformations should not be overstated. Compared to the extent of analysis and resources devoted to biophysical issues, SIA usually has a minor role. Social practitioners have insufficient influence in shaping project/development alternatives, and, despite the increase in social roles within many organizations, the project managers who are responsible for commissioning and delivering impact assessments often have little social experience. The limited capacity of regulators and the limited resources devoted to quality control have a significant impact on the standard of SIAs, with a tendency for proponents to produce assessments that only just pass the minimum expectations of regulators.

In transition regions and where multiple projects overlap, data currency is a key issue. Secondary data sources quickly become outdated and it is often necessary to supplement desktop research with local data collected by skilled social researchers. Primary data helps strengthen baseline information and better identify what unmet needs exist. Methodological issues such as reliability and validity, robustness and significance levels are weaknesses in many SIA studies. Many reports lack adequate details about methods, sources and assumptions. The quality of analysis is another area of variability. Assessments are sometimes little more than a social and economic profile of the impacted communities compiled from secondary data sources. Analysis sometimes lacks identification of the spatial, temporal and stakeholder distribution of impacts and benefits. Integration with environmental, health and cultural heritage issues can be superficial. While there are legitimate constraints on the level of analysis that is possible, better use of scoping and issue prioritization can assist in allocating resources efficiently and in ensuring that in-depth analysis is undertaken for all key issues. Regulators can assist by better formulation of the terms of reference for SIA and EIA studies.

The adequacy of public participation continues to be an issue. SIAs often do not meet public expectations of being a deliberative process to determine the acceptability of a project. Rather they are seen at best as a process for incremental project improvement, and at worst as being little more than a feeble attempt at project legitimization. Public participation ranges from being the provision of periods for public comment and the supply of information, to being the active involvement of stakeholders in shaping the SIA process and the opening-up of governance processes to include local communities in decision-making about projects.

The demands of community consultation can lead to fatigue in communities and local governments, particularly in situations with multiple developments. These challenges are exacerbated where there is limited engagement, leading participants to question the value of their involvement. Some proponents have addressed these issues through joint engagement processes (Franks et al. 2010).

The public availability of SIA reports, SIMPs, baselines and agreements is an ongoing issue. Even publicly available SIAs can be difficult to locate after submission, especially in the absence of online repositories.

Finally, cumulative social impacts require greater attention in project-level and strategic assessments (Brereton et al. 2008, Lockie et al. 2008, Franks et al. 2010, 2011). Other SIAs undertaken in the local area are rarely cross-referenced, and co-ordination and collaboration between project developers is rare. SIAs are seldom used by local government to manage impacts at local or regional levels. Where regional and strategic assessments have been conducted, few give adequate attention to social issues (Vanclay 2004).

External influences on the practice of SIA

Here we explore the opportunities presented by several emerging trends: (1) the increasing acceptance of the concept of free, prior and informed consent; (2) heightened attention to human rights; (3) the evolution of social performance standards; (4) enhanced management of social performance in supply chains; (5) improved governance of resource extraction projects; and (6) the rise of local content requirements.

1. Free, prior and informed consent (FPIC)

Advocated in the International Labour Organization (ILO) Convention 169 on Indigenous and Tribal Peoples (1989) and the United Nations Declaration on the Rights of Indigenous Peoples (2007), FPIC recognizes various fundamental rights of Indigenous peoples. The FPIC concept has been adopted by the IFC and other international entities. There is evidence of the FPIC philosophy being applicable to all project-affected peoples (Hill et al. 2010, Nish and Bice 2011). The evolving requirements for FPIC potentially shift the statutory basis of SIA from being subordinate to EIAs, to being the process that enables FPIC to occur. The output of such a process could be an impact and benefit agreement (Gibson and O'Faircheallaigh 2010, ICMM 2010, Nish and Bice 2011, O'Faircheallaigh 2011). Agreements should be informed by an SIA process, with decisions on how the compensation for impacts and benefits from projects will be distributed based on a sound knowledge and understanding of the likely social impacts, and of the issues associated with visioning the community's future (Vanclay and Esteves 2011).

The practical challenges in putting FPIC principles into operation (Cariño 2005, Macintyre 2007) are similar to those that have plagued SIA over time (see Burdge and Vanclay 1995, Vanclay 1999), including:

- defining who has the right to give consent and who represents the affected communities and therefore has a right to be compensated and/or to benefit;
- ensuring informed consent in contexts where traditional understandings differ from Western scientific understandings;
- deciding who has legitimacy as an information provider;
- the issue of veto and the potential undermining of state sovereignty and eminent domain;
- the right and/or ability of communities to withdraw consent at a later stage;
- implications for project costs and delay;
- addressing the power imbalances between affected peoples and developers;
- mechanisms for redress in the absence of FPIC.

FPIC is not understood in the same way by all. For example, in the recent review of its Performance Standards, IFC did not define consent in terms of veto (the power to say 'no') but in terms of consensus by all parties on the outcomes of the negotiations (refer to IFC 2012, Performance Standard 7, point 12). This conflicts with the position generally understood by many others (Hill et al. 2010, Nish and Bice 2011) that Indigenous peoples have a fundamental right to self-determination, and that FPIC is the ultimate statement of respect for this right vesting in them the right to say 'no'.

Similar to SIA, FPIC faces the risk of being treated only as token consultation rather than being a powerful instrument to build respectful relationships among those who have a stake in the outcome. The growing rhetoric towards supporting FPIC by various organizations is not yet commensurate with formal legal and policy structures for protecting the right of communities to grant or withhold their consent. One exception is the Indigenous Peoples Rights Act (1997) of the Philippines. As with SIA, FPIC requires significant commitment and investment by the community, government and proponent. FPIC is a philosophy; SIA is a process to build knowledge and understanding and manage change; and agreements are the outputs of these processes (Vanclay and Esteves 2011).

2. Human rights

While many in the SIA community argue that rigorous SIA should consider human rights (Vanclay 2003a), as typically practised SIA does not adequately address human rights, and explicit attention should be given to due diligence when it comes to issues such as forced evictions, community access to cultural heritage and human trafficking (IFC 2012). The emergence of human rights impact assessment (HRIA) has been given impetus by the United Nations Special Representative on Human Rights and Business, John Ruggie. His 'Protect, Respect and Remedy' framework is based on three core principles: 'the state duty to protect against human rights abuses by third parties, including business; the corporate responsibility to respect human rights; and greater access by victims to effective remedy, both judicial and non-judicial' (Ruggie 2008, p. 1). Ruggie's final report, endorsed by the Human Rights Council of the United Nations, provided a set of 'Guiding Principles on Business and Human Rights' to assist in implementing the framework (United Nations 2011).

HRIA studies are being commissioned. One example was conducted on Goldcorp's Marlin mine in Guatemala (On Common Ground 2010). The IFC has sponsored an online guide for HRIA (IBLF 2007), and the responsibility of the private sector to respect human rights has been explicitly addressed in the revised IFC Performance Standards (IFC 2012). Early signs point to HRIA and SIA co-existing, with HRIA being conducted primarily to demonstrate due diligence. As with FPIC, a human rights perspective provides SIA practitioners with a legitimate mandate distinct from EIA.

3. Social performance standards

Numerous social responsibility and performance standards are emerging that are consistent with the values underpinning SIA. In 2011, approximately 12% of global assets were managed according to socially responsible investment principles, a share predicted to grow to 30% by 2015 (Just Economics 2011). Relevant standards include (modified from UNCTAD 2011):

(1) Intergovernmental organization standards such as the UN Global Compact (established 2000); numerous ILO conventions and declarations, OECD Guidelines on Multinational Enterprises (endorsed 2008); UN Principles for Responsible Investment (endorsed 2006).
(2) Multilateral financial institution standards (e.g. IFC) which have social performance standards including the need for SIA that they expect their clients to uphold.
(3) Multi-stakeholder initiative standards, mostly developed by civil society and business actors, such as the International Organization for Standardization's *ISO 26000 Guidance on Social Responsibility* (2010). Some private banks have adopted most of IFC's standards in an initiative known as the Equator Principles (first launched in 2003). The Equator Principles require borrowers for high risk projects to conduct a social and environmental assessment and propose mitigation and management measures.
(4) Industry association codes typically jointly developed by companies within an industry to define social performance elements for their industries, such as the International Council on Mining and Metals and the International Petroleum Industry Environmental Conservation Association.
(5) Individual company codes of practice.

The existence of social performance standards strengthens the argument that SIA processes should lead to the development of a social impact management plan which is effectively linked to the proponent's systems and processes (Vanclay and Esteves 2011). Unfortunately, much discussion on the assessment of social impacts is removed from the SIA discourse. For example, the ISEAL Alliance (http://www.isealalliance.org), the global association for social and environmental standards, requires standards systems to develop an assessment plan that includes all the steps required to assess their contributions to impact. While the term 'impact assessment' is used, it is based in the field of programme evaluation. Philanthropic and social investment fields also employ social impact terminology when describing the quantification of benefits associated with a programme, using financial proxy methods such as social return on investment (see Nicholls et al. 2009). The European Commission's *Impact Assessment Guidelines* (European Commission 2009) also promote assigning monetarized values to predicted social impacts, something which the SIA community has always resisted. While no group should claim a monopoly on a term, the underlying premises between the various applications need to be differentiated.

4. Social performance management in supply chains

Increasingly, complex supply chains are demonstrating a sense of shared responsibility by implementing systems and procedures to enforce social performance standards and provide incentives for good performance by all participants in the chain, and by recognizing differing cultural and contextual requirements. More proponents are collaborating with contractors in early-stage planning and assessments, agreeing on environmental and social obligations and standards, and investing in local capacity building. Proponents are encouraging adoption of social standards in pre-qualification and tender processes; designing contracts to provide incentives for good practice; assisting contractors in developing social management plans; supporting local community liaison officers; and building trust and accountability with external stakeholders through public reporting, engagement, resolution of grievances and oversight by third-party organizations (Wilson and Kuszewski 2011).

5. Improved governance of resource extraction projects

The link between governance and the performance of natural resource abundant economies is increasingly under scrutiny. Good governance is demonstrated by political stability and absence of violence, government effectiveness, the extent to which citizens have a voice in selecting their government, freedom of expression, freedom of association, free media, regulatory quality over private sector development, operation of the rule of law and control of corruption (World Bank 2006). Governance refers to the appropriate social and institutional arrangements (at all levels) to achieve these ends. Below are examples of initiatives where SIA is used to strengthen the dimensions of good governance of resources extraction projects.

The *Extractive Industries Review*, an independent review of the World Bank's involvement in the extractive industries sector, recommended that to contribute to poverty reduction the World Bank must ensure that countries meet three criteria: pro-poor public and corporate governance aimed at poverty alleviation through sustainable development; more effective social and environmental policies; and respect for human rights (Extractive Industries Review 2003). Integrated environmental and social impact assessments were also emphasized.

Multi-stakeholder initiatives to strengthen governance are being catalysed by private sector developers. In 2006, ALCOA partnered with the Getulio Vargas Foundation's Center for Sustainability Studies and the Brazilian Biodiversity Fund to develop a draft sustainable development agenda for the municipality of Juruti and the wider region in the state of Pará, Brazil, which was experiencing rapid change brought about by a bauxite mine (Centre for Sustainability Studies 2008). Another example is the rural community of Clermont, Australia. Here Rio Tinto Coal Australia (RTCA) worked with local government to address infrastructure-related impacts associated with the closure of one mine and the opening of another mine. A community strategic planning initiative begun in 2007 was coordinated by the Belyando Shire Council and facilitated by Central Queensland University. The resultant 20-year community plan guides development and provides a framework for ensuring investments align with community goals (Miles 2008, Franks et al. 2010).

Indigenous peoples are leading initiatives to strengthen governance of developments. For example, the Taku River Tlingit First Nation (2007) developed a mining policy to provide guidance to developers in British Columbia. Based on the EIA process, an accommodation agreement, and an impacts and benefits agreement, this First Nation gives consent and support if the proposal achieves the policy objectives.

A government-led example of a policy promoting collaborative regional planning is the Queensland State Government's Sustainable Resource Communities Policy. A number of measures were initiated to improve the assessment and management of social impacts, particularly cumulative impacts, to provide for greater co-ordination and collaboration between stakeholders, and to address resource governance issues (QDTRDI 2008), including the establishment of a dedicated SIA function in government. Proponents are also required to prepare a SIMP outlining the forecasted changes to communities, agreed strategies for mitigation of impacts, and responsibility of various parties for management (see Franks et al. 2009, 2010).

These are examples of initiatives that aim to strengthen the governance of projects by shifting oversight closer to project-affected peoples. The trend towards improving governance further establishes the need for instruments such as SIA to provide opportunities for affected peoples to be involved in project development and management.

6. Local content requirements

Local content refers to the participation of local peoples in the workforce and supply chain of a project. The requirement for a specified level of local content raises challenges for developers and governments. While the sourcing of local labour, goods and services has obvious benefits, it can not necessarily be assumed that local content is always a 'positive' to be maximized. The extent to which local communities will benefit from a local content requirement depends on their capacity to take up the opportunities, the extent to which these opportunities align with community values and aspirations, and their ability to adapt to the business cycle of the project and changing circumstances (Esteves and Barclay 2011, Esteves et al. 2011, Wilson and Kuszewski 2011).

In order to achieve sustainable regional development, an analysis of potential social impacts should be used as a guide against which to assess strategies for local economic development (Ivanova et al. 2007, Ivanova and Rolfe 2011a, 2011b). This will ensure the baseline conditions for human and economic capital are considered and potential negative consequences averted. Potential negative consequences include distorting markets, drawing local people from other businesses and much-needed services in the area, vulnerability to business cycles of large corporates, community dissatisfaction from seeing only menial works being given to local people, and reinforcing elite structures (Esteves and Barclay 2011). Strengthening the internal local economy and linkages with external markets requires understanding which strategies for local economic development are appropriate for different types of communities. The analysis should be a collaborative activity between the proponent and local government to identify which are the key sectors that contribute to the region's economic development, and to engage in local procurement with those key sectors.

Conclusion: where to next for SIA?

There is strong consensus on what 'good' SIA practice looks like – it is participatory; supports affected peoples, proponents, regulatory and support agencies; increases their understanding of how change comes about and increases their capacities to respond to change; and has a broad understanding of social impacts (Vanclay 2002b, 2003a, Howitt 2011, Vanclay and Esteves 2011). In comparison with other forms of impact assessment, the SIA community has always believed that there should be an emphasis on enhancing the lives of vulnerable and disadvantaged people, and in particular, that there should be a specific focus on improving the lives of the worst-off members of society (Vanclay 2003a).

One of the barriers to innovative, positive development outcomes is the limited understanding and skills of those who commission SIAs. The following quotation sums this up from a developer's perspective:

> These studies are usually not commissioned by social scientists. They are typically commissioned by environmental scientists or by permitting or project managers, most of whom have a scientific (or possibly legal) training with little understanding of the more progressive/innovative end of the impact assessment topic. This is a powerful barrier, particularly when the social analyses are often inherently messy, and with uncertain outcomes in terms of implications for the project (i.e. they stick with what they know). (Jon Samuel, Head of Social Performance, Anglo American plc, personal communication, 21 June 2011)

SIA requires an understanding of its core concepts such as culture, community, power, human rights, gender, justice, place, resilience, sustainable livelihoods and the capitals, as well as of the theoretical bases for participatory approaches. It is crucial to understand how these concepts influence the way social relationships are created, change and respond to change, and hence how such concepts should frame analysis in an SIA (Ross and McGee 2006, Howitt 2011). These understandings also require all those involved in SIA to reflect on potential biases. It is incumbent upon SIA practitioners to develop practical guidelines and to educate proponents, regulators and impact assessment colleagues from other professions on these core concepts so that they become embedded in the terms of reference for SIA.

A number of opportunities for SIA have been presented in this paper. The ability of the SIA community to take advantage of these opportunities will depend on its willingness to take an external stakeholder orientation, ironically an orientation that it itself promotes. Engagement with human rights, FPIC, social performance standards, supply chain management, governance, local content and economic development will maintain the relevance and demonstrable value of SIA to affected communities, regulators, civil society and developers. We hope that the maturing of the FPIC discourse and the involvement of the SIA community in that discourse will encourage a speedier shift towards participation as a valued end in itself, rather than merely being a means by which projects are legitimized. Such a shift requires transformational change in the way SIA is practised.

References

Becker, H., 1997. *Social impact assessment: method and experience in Europe, North America and the developing world*. London: UCL Press.

Benson, C., and Twigg, J., 2007. *Tools for mainstreaming disaster risk reduction: guidance notes for development organisations*. Geneva: ProVention Consortium.

Brereton, D., et al., 2008. *Assessing the cumulative impacts of mining on regional communities*. St Lucia: Centre for Social Responsibility in Mining, Centre for Water in the Minerals Industry, and the Australian Coal Association Research Program.

Burdge, R., and Vanclay, F., 1995. Social impact assessment. In: F. Vanclay and D. Bronstein, eds. *Environmental and social impact assessment*. Chichester: Wiley, 31–66.

Burdge, R., and Vanclay, F., 1996. Social impact assessment: a contribution to the state of the art series. *Impact Assessment*, 14 (1), 59–86.

Cariño, J., 2005. Indigenous peoples' right to free, prior, informed consent: reflections on concepts and practice. *Arizona Journal of International and Comparative Law*, 22 (1), 19–39.

Center for Sustainability Studies, 2008. *Sustainable Juruti: a proposed model for local development* [online]. Sao Paolo: Center for Sustainability Studies of the Getulio Vargas Foundation. Available from: http://www.alcoa.com/brazil/pt/juruti_info_page/Juruti_ingles.pdf [Accessed 10 September 2011].

Cooper, S., Maher, M., and Greiner, R., 2006. *The people impacts of NRM: a simple training package for building social and economic impact assessment in regional natural resource management*. Brisbane: Department of Natural Resources, Mines and Water.

Dale, A., Taylor, N. and Lane, M., eds., 2001. *Social assessment in natural resource management institutions*. Collingwood, Victoria: CSIRO Publishing.

Dani, A., and Beddies, S., 2011. The World Bank's poverty and social impact analysis. In: F. Vanclay and A.M. Esteves, eds. *New directions in social impact assessment: conceptual and methodological advances*. Cheltenham: Edward Elgar, 306–322.

Esteves, A.M., and Barclay, M.A., 2011. Enhancing the benefits of local content: integrating social and economic impact assessment into procurement strategies. *Impact Assessment and Project Appraisal*, 29 (3), 205–215.

Esteves, A.M., and Vanclay, F., 2009. Social development needs analysis as a tool for SIA to guide corporate–community investment: applications in the minerals industry. *Environmental Impact Assessment Review*, 29 (2), 137–145.

Esteves, A.M., et al., 2011. Enhancing the benefits of projects through local procurement. In: F. Vanclay and A.M. Esteves, eds. *New directions in social impact assessment: conceptual and methodological advances*. Cheltenham: Edward Elgar, 234–250.

European Commission, 2009. *European Commission Impact Assessment Guidelines*. Brussels: European Commission.

Extractive Industries Review, 2003. *Striking a better balance: the Extractive Industries Review*. Jakarta and Washington, DC: Extractive Industries Review.

Fenton, M., Coakes, S., and Marshall, N., 2003. Vulnerability and capacity measurement. In: H. Becker and F. Vanclay, eds.

The international handbook of social impact assessment: conceptual and methodological advances. Cheltenham: Edward Elgar, 211–230.

Finsterbusch, K., 1985. State of the art in social impact assessment. *Environment and Behavior*, 17 (2), 193–221.

Franks, D., 2011. Management of the social impacts of mining. In: P. Darling, ed. *SME mining engineering handbook*. 3rd ed. Littleton, CO, USA: Society for Mining, Metallurgy, and Exploration, 1817–1825.

Franks, D., et al., 2009. *Leading practice strategies for addressing the social impacts of resource developments*. St Lucia: Centre for Social Responsibility in Mining, Sustainable Minerals Institute, The University of Queensland, and Department of Employment, Economic Development and Innovation, Queensland Government.

Franks, D., Brereton, D., and Moran, C., 2010. Managing the cumulative impacts of coal mining on regional communities and environments in Australia. *Impact Assessment and Project Appraisal*, 28 (4), 299–312.

Franks, D., Brereton, D., and Moran, C., 2011. Cumulative social impacts. In: F. Vanclay and A.M. Esteves, eds. *New directions in social impact assessment: conceptual and methodological advances*. Cheltenham: Edward Elgar, 202–220.

Freudenburg, W., 1986. Social impact assessment. *Annual Review of Sociology*, 12, 451–478.

Gibson, G., and O'Faircheallaigh, C., 2010. *IBA community toolkit: negotiation and implementation of impact and benefit agreements* [online]. Ottawa: Walter & Duncan Gordon Foundation. Available from: http://www.ibacommunitytoolkit.ca [Accessed 10 September 2011].

Hill, C., Lillywhite, S., and Simon, M., 2010. *Guide to free, prior and informed consent*. Carlton, Victoria: Oxfam Australia.

Howitt, R., 2011. Theoretical foundations. In: F. Vanclay and A.M. Esteves, eds. *New directions in social impact assessment: conceptual and methodological advances*. Cheltenham: Edward Elgar, 78–95.

IAIA, 2009. *Social impact assessment key citations* [online]. Fargo, ND: International Association for Impact Assessment. Available from: http://www.iaia.org/resources-networking/key-citations.aspx [Accessed 10 September 2011].

IBLF, 2007. *Guide to human rights impact assessment and management* [online]. London: International Business Leaders Forum. Available from: https://www.guidetohriam.org/welcome [Accessed 10 September 2011].

ICMM, 2010. *Indigenous peoples and mining: good practice guide*. London: International Council on Mining and Metals.

IFC, 2012. *Performance Standards on environmental and social sustainability*. [online]. Available from: www1.ifc.org/wps/wcm/connect/topics_ext_content/ifc_external_corporate_site/ifc+sustainability+framework/2012+edition/2012-edition#PerformanceStandards [Accessed 10 September 2011] Washington, DC: International Finance Corporation

International Alert, 2005. *Conflict-sensitive business practice for extractive industries*. London: International Alert.

International Labour Organization, 1989. *C169 Indigenous and Tribal Peoples Convention, 1989* [online]. Available from: http://www.ilo.org/ilolex/cgi-lex/convde.pl?C169 [Accessed 10 September 2011]

International Organization for Standardization, 2010. *ISO 26000 Guidance on Social Responsibility*. Geneva: International Organization for Standardization.

[US] Interorganizational Committee on Guidelines and Principles for Social Impact Assessment, 1994. Guidelines and principles for social impact assessment. *Impact Assessment*, 12 (2), 107–152.

Ivanova, G., and Rolfe, J., 2011a. Using input–output analysis to estimate impact of coal industry on regional and local economies. *Impact Assessment and Project Appraisal*, 29 (4), 277–288.

Ivanova, G., and Rolfe, J., 2011b. Assessing development options in mining communities using stated preference techniques. *Resources Policy*, 36 (3), 255–264.

Ivanova, G., et al., 2007. Assessing social and economic impacts associated with changes in the coal mining industry in the Bowen Basin, Queensland, Australia. *Management of Environmental Quality: An International Journal*, 18 (2), 211–228.

João, E., Vanclay, F., and den Broeder, L., 2011. Emphasising enhancement in all forms of impact assessment: introduction to a special issue. *Impact Assessment and Project Appraisal*, 29 (3), 170–180.

Joyce, S., and MacFarlane, M., 2001. *Social impact assessment in the mining industry: current situation and future directions*. MMSD Paper no. 46. London: IIED and World Business Council for Sustainable Development.

Just Economics, 2011. *Investing for sustainable development? A review of investment principles: trends and impacts*. London: International Institute for Environment and Development.

Kemp, D., 2009. Community relations in the global mining industry: exploring the internal dimensions of externally orientated work. *Corporate Social Responsibility and Environmental Management*, 17, 1–14.

Kemp, D., 2011. Understanding the organizational context. In: F. Vanclay and A.M. Esteves, eds. *New directions in social impact assessment: conceptual and methodological advances*. Cheltenham: Edward Elgar, 20–37.

Lockie, S., 2001. SIA in review: setting the agenda for impact assessment in the 21st century. *Impact Assessment and Project Appraisal*, 19 (4), 277–288.

Lockie, S., et al., 2008. Democratisation versus engagement? Social and economic impact assessment and community participation in the coal mining industry of the Bowen Basin, Australia. *Impact Assessment and Project Appraisal*, 26 (3), 177–187.

Macintyre, M., 2007. Informed consent and mining projects: a view from Papua New Guinea. *Pacific Affairs*, 80 (1), 49–66.

Miles, R.L., ed., 2008. *Clermont Preferred Future: Clermont Community Development Strategy, final report prepared for Belyando Shire Council*. Australia: Central Queensland University.

Minerals Development Council, 2007. *Investor's prospectus on Philippine mining*. Quezon City: Minerals Development Council, The Republic of the Philippines.

Murdock, S., Leistritz, F., and Hamm, R., 1986a. The state of socioeconomic impact analysis in the United States: limitations and opportunities for alternative futures. *Journal of Environmental Management*, 23 (2), 99–117.

Murdock, S., Leistritz, F., and Hamm, R., 1986b. The state of socioeconomic impact analysis in the United States. *Impact Assessment Bulletin*, 4 (3/4), 101–132.

Nicholls, J., et al., 2009. *A guide to social return on investment*. London: Office of the Third Sector, Cabinet Office.

Nish, S., and Bice, S., 2011. Community-based agreement making with land-connected peoples. In: F. Vanclay and A.M. Esteves, eds. *New directions in social impact assessment: conceptual and methodological advances*. Cheltenham: Edward Elgar, 59–77.

O'Faircheallaigh, C., 2011. SIA and Indigenous social development. In: F. Vanclay and A.M. Esteves, eds. *New directions in social impact assessment: conceptual and methodological advances*. Cheltenham: Edward Elgar, 138–153.

On Common Ground Consultants Inc. 2010. *Human rights assessment of Goldcorp's Marlin Mine* [online]. Vancouver, BC: On Common Ground Consultants Inc. Available from: http://www.hria-guatemala.com/en/MarlinHumanRights.htm [Accessed 10 September 2011].

QDIP, 2010. *Social impact assessment. Guideline to preparing a social impact management plan*. Brisbane: Queensland Department of Infrastructure and Planning.

QDTRDI, 2008. *Sustainable Resource Communities Policy: social impact assessment in the mining and petroleum industries*. Brisbane: Queensland Department of Tourism, Regional Development and Industry.

Ross, H., and McGee, T., 2006. Conceptual frameworks for SIA revisited: a cumulative effects study on lead contamination and economic change. *Impact Assessment and Project Appraisal*, 24 (2), 139–149.

Ruggie, J., 2008. *Promotion and protection of all human rights, civil, political, economic, social and cultural rights, including the right to development – Protect, Respect and Remedy: a framework for business and human rights. Report of the Special Representative of the Secretary-General on the Issue of Human Rights and Transnational Corporations and Other Business Enterprises, John Ruggie*. UN Document A/HRC/8/5.

Ruggie, J., 2010. *Business and human rights: further steps towards the operationalisation of the 'Protect, Respect and Remedy' framework. Report of the Special Representative of the UN Secretary-General on the Issue of Human Rights, and Transnational Corporations and Other Business Enterprises*, 9 April.

SADME, 2006. *Social and labour plan guidelines for the mining and production industries*. Pretoria: South Africa Department of Minerals and Energy.

Taku River Tlingit First Nation, 2007. *Mining policy* [online]. Available from: http://fnbc.info/content/mining-policy-taku-river-tlingit-first-nation [Accessed 10 September 2011]

UNCTAD, 2011. *World Investment Report 2011: non-equity modes of international production and development*. Geneva: United Nations Conference on Trade and Development.

United Nations, 2007. *United Nations Declaration on the Rights of Indigenous Peoples 2007*. United Nations General Assembly Resolution 61/295 adopted 13 September 2007

United Nations, 2011. *Report of the Special Representative of the Secretary-General on the Issue of Human Rights and Transnational Corporations and Other Business Enterprises, John Ruggie. Guiding principles on business and human rights: implementing the United Nations 'Protect, Respect and Remedy' framework*. United Nations Human Rights Council, Seventeenth session, Agenda item 3. UN Document A/HRC/17/31.

Vanclay, F., 1999. Social impact assessment. In: J. Petts, ed. *Handbook of environmental impact assessment* (Vol. 1). Oxford: Blackwell Science, 301–326.

Vanclay, F., 2002a. Social impact assessment. In: M. Tolba, ed. *Responding to global environmental change*. Chichester: Wiley, 387–393.

Vanclay, F., 2002b. Conceptualising social impacts. *Environmental Impact Assessment Review*, 22 (3), 183–211.

Vanclay, F., 2003a. International principles for social impact assessment. *Impact Assessment and Project Appraisal*, 21 (1), 5–11.

Vanclay, F., 2003b. International principles for social impact assessment: their evolution. *Impact Assessment and Project Appraisal*, 21 (1), 3–4.

Vanclay, F., 2004. The triple bottom line and impact assessment: how do TBL, EIA, SIA, SEA and EMS relate to each other? *Journal of Environmental Assessment Policy and Management*, 6 (3), 265–288.

Vanclay, F., 2006. Principles for social impact assessment: a critical comparison between the international and US documents. *Environmental Impact Assessment Review*, 26 (1), 3–14.

Vanclay, F., and Esteves, A.M., 2011. Current issues and trends in social impact assessment. In: F. Vanclay and A.M. Esteves, eds. *New directions in social impact assessment: conceptual and methodological advances*. Cheltenham: Edward Elgar, 3–19.

Wilson, E., and Kuszewski, J., 2011. *Shared value, shared responsibility: a new approach to managing contracting chains in the oil and gas sector*. London: International Institute for Environment and Development.

Wolf, C.P., 1975. Social impact assessment: the state of the art. In: D. Carson, ed. *Man–environment interactions, Part 1*. Stroudburg, PA: Dowden, Hutchinson & Ross, 1–44.

Wolf, C.P., 1976. Social impact assessment: the state of the art restated. *Sociological Practice*, 1, 56–70.

Wolf, C.P., 1977. Social impact assessment: the state of the art updated. *Social Impact Assessment*, 20, 3–22.

World Bank, 2006. *A decade of measuring the quality of governance: governance matters 2006* [online]. Washington, DC: World Bank. Available from: http://info.worldbank.org/governance/wgi/resources.htm [Accessed 3 November 2011].

[2]

Effectiveness in social impact assessment: Aboriginal peoples and resource development in Australia

Ciaran O'Faircheallaigh

Definitions of and judgments regarding effectiveness in social impact assessment (SIA) depend on how the purposes of SIA are understood. They are defined differently by various interests that participate in, or are affected by, impact assessment processes, and the concept of 'effectiveness' and the issue of what is required to achieve it are both contested and contextual. This article reviews a number of different approaches to SIA and outlines what effectiveness might mean for each. It then considers, at two levels, what 'effective SIA' involves in the context of large-scale resource development on Aboriginal land in Australia. The first level involves control of SIA. For indigenous peoples who have historically been excluded from and ignored by SIAs undertaken as part of government approval processes, Aboriginal control is an essential prerequisite for 'effective SIA'. However, control only creates the potential for effectiveness. The second level of analysis involves the practical activities that must be undertaken, and issues that must be addressed, to realize this potential. The author develops a matrix designed to help identify and manage these activities and issues in a systematic way.

Keywords: social impact assessment, effectiveness, Aboriginal peoples, exclusion, indigenous control

DURING RECENT YEARS, major oil and gas companies, including Shell, BP, Chevron, Total and BHPBilliton, have identified large reserves of natural gas in the Browse Basin, off the coast of the Kimberley region in the northwest corner of Western Australia. The region's Aboriginal peoples maintain strong connections to their ancestral lands and a vibrant cultural and ceremonial life, reflected in the fact that, with the assistance of their regional land organization, the Kimberley Land Council (KLC), they have won recognition within Australia's legal system that they continue to hold native title[1] to some 50% of the region (KLC, 2008a). At the same time, like many indigenous populations in industrialized countries, they face threats to the social and economic sustainability of their communities. Less than 20% of working-age Aboriginal people are in formal employment, and there is a heavy reliance on welfare payments; life expectancy is some 20 years less than for non-Aboriginal Australians; access to education and housing is poor; and communities face serious social issues, including substance abuse, family violence and child abuse (Taylor, 2006, 2008).

To date there has been no large-scale industrial development on the Kimberley coast. Extraction of natural gas and its processing into liquefied natural gas (LNG) for export has the potential to severely damage the social and cultural fabric of local Aboriginal societies. For example, construction of pipelines, the building and operation of LNG plants, and shipping of LNG could threaten the integrity of coastal environments that support the wildlife and fish populations on which many Aboriginal people depend; some species (for example turtles) are also

---

Ciaran O'Faircheallaigh is at the Department of Politics and Public Policy, Griffith University, 170 Kessels Road, Nathan, Queensland 4111, Australia; Email: Ciaran.Ofaircheallaigh@griffith.edu.au

Paper submitted for special issue of Impact Assessment and Project Appraisal on Effectiveness in Impact Assessment

Effectiveness in social impact assessment

of great cultural significance. Immigration of non-indigenous workers and large infusions of cash could exacerbate problems with substance abuse and family violence. Equally, the development of LNG has the potential to help address the severe economic and social disadvantage currently experienced by Aboriginal people, for instance by generating training and employment initiatives and providing revenue streams for Aboriginal communities that could create further economic opportunities and support education, health, housing and other services (KLC, 2008a, 2008b).

In this context the application of 'effective' SIA could greatly enhance the prospects for positive outcomes by identifying and minimizing negative social and cultural effects and identifying potential positive effects and assisting Aboriginal people to take advantage of them. In contrast, 'ineffective' SIA can not only result in a failure to manage risks and grasp opportunities, but can itself represent a negative impact (Finsterbusch, 1995: 23). This is especially so in an indigenous context where SIA that fails to address local interests can reinforce the mistrust and alienation generated by the historical marginalization of indigenous peoples from 'mainstream' governance institutions (see below).

What exactly is 'effective SIA', and what is required to achieve it? There is little consensus in the literature about how 'effectiveness' in SIA might be defined, or about how best to pursue it. This reflects the essentially contested and political character of SIA and of impact assessment (IA) generally. This point is explored in the next section, which also indicates different ways in which 'effectiveness' might be defined and pursued, given different understandings of the purpose of SIA. Subsequent sections explore the question of how effectiveness might be defined and pursued in the context of large-scale resource development on Aboriginal lands. Critical in this regard is the link between Aboriginal control over SIA processes and the potential for achieving 'effective SIA'. This consideration is absent from 'mainstream' models for pursuing effective SIA, for example that developed by the Interorganizational Committee on Principles and Guidelines for SIA (IGPGSIA).[2] Also vital is the need to address numerous practical issues and challenges if the potential created by Aboriginal control is to be realized.

Effectiveness in social impact assessment

In exploring alternative approaches to effectiveness in SIA, three preliminary points should be noted. First, writing that focuses specifically on effectiveness in SIA is limited, and so it is necessary to also draw on the wider literature on environmental impact assessment (EIA). Second, IA researchers and practitioners are not always explicit or consistent in their definition of 'effectiveness'. Their understanding of it must often be gleaned from the priority they attach to various aspects of or approaches to IA, and/or what they say about 'problems' or 'limitations' affecting it, on the basis that if those problems or limitations were removed, then the resultant IA would be 'effective' or 'more effective' (see, for example, Becker, 2001; Hickie and Wade, 1998; Kapoor, 2001; Lockie, 2001; McKillop and Brown, 1999; Paci *et al.*, 2002; Tollefson and Wipond, 1998). Third, although authors often claim to be dealing with the effectiveness of 'impact assessment', in reality they often deal only with one aspect of it (see, for example, Baker and McLelland, 2003: 582–84, who slip between discussing the effectiveness of EIA and that of 'EA participation policy').

Two distinct issues arise in relation to effectiveness in SIA. The first relates to what SIA is or consists of, i.e. what must occur if a set of activities are to be regarded as constituting SIA. If any such activities are missing or incomplete, then by definition SIA cannot be 'effective'. The second issue, discussed below, involves the purpose of SIA, or what SIA is for. The two issues are related, because the way in which the purpose of SIA is defined will affect views regarding the activities that should constitute it.

SIA is generally seen as a subset of EIA that specifically seeks to predict the effects on people – as opposed to the biophysical environment – of planned activities, and in particular of large industrial or infrastructure projects (Becker, 2001: 311–12; ICGPSIA, 2003: 31).[3] It also involves finding ways of intervening to avoid or mitigate the negative impacts and maximize the positive impacts that projects are expected to create (Becker, 2001: 313; ICGPSIA, 2003: 247–48; Lockie, 2001: 279). Where projects proceed, SIA may also encompass ongoing monitoring of social impacts and of intervention strategies; identification of any unanticipated impacts created by projects; and the development of alternative or additional intervention strategies where those initially adopted proved insufficient or ineffective (Becker, 2001: 34; ICGPSIA, 2003: 31–32).

'Effectiveness' in SIA also refers 'to whether something works as intended and meets the purposes for which it is designed' (Sandham and Pretorius,

> **There is little consensus in the literature about how 'effectiveness' in SIA might be defined, or about how best to pursue it. This reflects the essentially contested and political character of SIA and of impact assessment (IA) generally**

2008: 229; see also Jay *et al.*, 2007: 290; Kauppinen *et al.*, 2006). From this perspective, how 'effective SIA' is defined and pursued depends on what assumptions are made regarding the purposes of SIA (Cashmore *et al.*, 2004: 296–99; Finsterbusch, 1995; Lawrence, 1997a: 4). Those purposes can be understood in a number of ways. One focuses on the proponents of the projects involved, and in this regard it must be remembered that in many jurisdictions SIA is undertaken by the private companies seeking to construct or expand major projects, or by consultants retained by them. It is usually conducted as a component of EIA, and as part of regulatory requirements that project proponents must meet in order to obtain approval from government authorities (Jay *et al.*, 2007: 288; Joyce and MacFarlane, 2001: 7,12, 18–19; Sandham and Pretorius, 2008: 238).

Given that, for proponents, the major purpose of SIA is to obtain project approval, then 'effective SIA' is SIA that facilitates timely and positive completion of regulatory processes, helps secure project approvals, and avoids the imposition of conditions by regulatory authorities that might undermine project economics. Thus, for instance, negative findings regarding the potential social effects of a project or activity are unlikely to be welcomed. Proponents attach a premium to an approval process that is speedy and avoids project delays; the main 'product' of the SIA is a report to the regulatory authority that supports the granting of project approvals; and the 'endpoint' of the SIA is the granting of such approvals. From this perspective, SIA processes should be tightly controlled by both proponent and regulator. Participation by the public (and especially by socially marginalized groups) should be minimized, as it is likely to extend timelines for approval and increase the chances that potentially negative impacts and demands for major project modifications, or project cancellation, will be raised (Buckley, 1997: 4; Doelle and Sinclair, 2006: 190; Lockie, 2001: 278–79; Joyce and MacFarlane, 2001; Rosenberg *et al.*, 1995: 146; Suagee, 2002: 234).

In principle, governments might be expected to pursue a broader set of interests than those of proponents, and so to define the purpose of SIA as providing inputs to a rigorous and balanced assessment of social impacts, allowing rejection of projects that threaten net social costs (an approach considered below). However, especially in jurisdictions where the level of economic activity relies substantially on large-scale resource development, governments often driven by an 'ideology of development', are strongly supportive of corporate interests, and are similarly reluctant to consider SIA processes or findings that might constrain or delay development (Kapoor, 2001: 270; Mulvihill and Baker, 2001: 377–82; Rosenberg *et al.*, 1995: 146; Suagee, 2002; Tollefson and Wipond, 1998).

More recently, the priorities of project proponents may have been modified to some extent as a result of the growing emphasis on corporate social responsibility and 'stakeholder engagement' policies. Corporations are increasingly convinced that they cannot continue to operate profitably unless they seek to meet the needs of specific stakeholders, for instance employees, customers, and communities adjacent to their operations and, more broadly, achieve the support of the societies in which they operate (Ali and O'Faircheallaigh, 2007; Jones, 1999). As a result, they may adopt policies that require more systematic engagement with stakeholders, especially when they are considering major new developments, and thus an additional purpose of SIA may be to facilitate this engagement (Jones, 1999). Yet the fundamental purpose remains to secure approval for proposed projects.

A different perspective assumes that the primary purpose of SIA is to provide regulators and politicians with the information to ensure that the net social impact of projects is positive in the longer term, in other words that development is socially sustainable. SIA allows informed public decisions regarding whether projects should be allowed to proceed and, if so, under what conditions (Becker, 2001; ICGPSIA, 2003; Jay *et al.*, 2007: 290–291; Sandham and Pretorius, 2008: 229). From this perspective, 'effective SIA' would produce comprehensive and rigorous information of the sort required by public decision makers, in a form easily accessible by them. Effectiveness would be gauged in terms of the capacity of SIA to influence decision making and the shape of projects, and hence ultimately their social outcomes (Becker, 2001: 315; Cashmore *et al.*, 2004: 296–98, 303–305; Nitz and Holland, 2000: 1–3).

Underlying an approach that contemplates the use of SIA to affect social outcomes is the assumption that social impacts are subject to modification though intervention by regulatory authorities, proponents and potentially affected populations. Such intervention can be designed to mitigate or avoid negative effects, or enhance positive effects, either by changing project configurations to alter predicted impacts, or by implementing initiatives in response to impacts that cannot be avoided. From this perspective the purpose of SIA is not just to predict impacts, but also to address them (Devlin and Yap, 2008: 17; Finsterbusch, 1995: 247–48; Lockie, 2001: 279–80).

This last point highlights the link between the purposes of SIA and the activities that constitute it. If its purpose is to shape impacts, the activities it encompasses must include the development of strategies to allow this to occur. In turn, strategies can only be effective if they are maintained over time and their effectiveness regularly evaluated. Recognition of this reality has lead to a growing focus on 'post-approval' elements of SIA. This focus has been sharpened by the realization that, historically, SIA findings and reports have often been ignored once project approval is secured. Among other factors, this reflects the absence of incentives for either

Effectiveness in social impact assessment

developers or governments to monitor or act on impacts once projects are under way; the lack of resources devoted to monitoring and managing social impacts; and the frequent absence of specific and binding commitments by proponents in EIA reports and in regulatory approvals (Brown and Jacobs, 1996: 4,10; Gagnon, 1995: 282–84; Joyce and MacFarlane, 2001: 16–17, 20; Lawe *et al.*, 2005; MVEIRB, 2006; O'Faircheallaigh, 1999, 2007; Sandham and Pretorius, 2008: 230). In addition, it is clear that in many cases impacts were not fully or accurately predicted when the initial SIA was conducted, and that many projects are altered significantly after regulatory approval has been granted. The result is that original assumptions regarding project impacts often proved incorrect (Cashmore *et al.*, 2004: 302; Gagnon, 1995) Growing awareness of these realities has led a number of scholars and organizations to posit models of SIA that explicitly require monitoring and evaluation of project impacts over time. It also involves reassessment of impact management strategies and project configuration in the light of information about *actual* impacts, as opposed to the impacts originally predicted (see, for example, Finsterbusch, 1995; ICGPSIA, 2003; MVEIRB, 2006).

From this perspective, effective SIA must include the development and ongoing implementation of strategies designed to minimize negative impacts and maximize positive ones; the allocation of sufficient resources to ensure post-approval impact monitoring and evaluation of mitigation strategies; and reappraisal of project impacts where project design has changed significantly post approval.

Other perspectives on the purpose of SIA are associated with the growing emphasis on using SIA to facilitate public participation in decision making. Indeed, the need to secure such participation and the conditions under which it can be secured represents one of the most dominant themes in recent literature on IA (for a sample see Del Furia and Wallace-Jones, 2000; Devlin and Jap, 2008; Doelle and Sinclair, 2006; Geurts and Joldersma, 2001; Hartley and Wood, 2005; Kapoor, 2001; Lockie, 2001; Morrison-Saunders and Early, 2008; Stewart and Sinclair, 2007; Wiles *et al.*, 1999). However, the reasons for seeking public participation vary, indicating further differences in how the purposes of SIA and hence the requirements for effective SIA are understood.

In some cases the desire to achieve or enhance public participation reflects a belief that it is required so that decision makers in corporations and regulatory agencies have access to full and robust information on affected populations, on the nature of social impacts, and on the likely efficacy of mitigating strategies. The fears and hopes that accompany people's own predictions of the likely effects of projects are themselves an important component of social impact, and those who actually experience impacts have unique insights into their nature and significance. As Ross (1990: 192) notes, 'Impact analyses are likely to be wide of the mark if they discount the impacted people's values, social dynamics, and beliefs about events. The people concerned are in the best position to say how they actually experienced events'. Affected populations can also offer valuable information on the likely efficacy of mitigating strategies, and knowledge of their aspirations is critical in making judgements about the significance of predicted impacts (Lane *et al.*, 2003; Lockie, 2001: 281; Mayoux and Chambers, 2005; Paci *et al.*, 2002: 115).

Another perspective on public participation is that its purpose is not just to help meet the information needs of proponents, regulators or politicians, but to help achieve ethical, political or philosophical goals. Given that it is 'the public' or sections of it that experience social impacts, it can be seen as unethical or undemocratic not to take account of their views and assessments in decision making, which cannot be done in any rigorous manner unless they participate in the SIA process (Geurts and Joldersma, 2001: 301; Hartley and Wood, 2005: 327–35; Lane *et al.*, 2003). In a similar vein, Howitt (1989) argues that public participation is essential if the public interest is to be protected against profit-maximizing companies, governments concerned with the pursuit of short-term political gain, or impact assessment professionals pursuing their personal ambitions. From this perspective, what is required is not just public consultation by decision makers, but active participation in decision making by affected people and groups (Doelle and Sinclair, 2006: 189; Lawrence, 1997b: 92; Lockie, 2001: 284; Stewart and Sinclair, 2007: 168).

Because the context and motivation for seeking participation vary greatly, so does the precise definition of 'effectiveness'. For instance, a concern with ensuring full access to information for decision makers will only seek public participation to the extent required to secure access to the relevant data (Lane *et al.*, 2003: 97). Thus 'effective SIA' secures precisely this degree of public participation and no more, so that the SIA process remains firmly under the control of the proponent and the regulatory authority. If the relevant information was available from other sources, for instance an earlier SIA of a similar project in the same area, 'effective SIA' would require no public participation. An approach based on the principle that citizens should be included in decisions that affect them would regard SIA as effective only if public participation is sufficient to sway the choices of decision makers.

Other perspectives stress that the purpose of SIA is not to inform value-free, 'rational' decision processes, but rather to contribute to political decisions and judgements. For instance, Cashmore *et al.* (2007: 528) have criticized the tendency in IA to 'neglect contextual factors' and to assume that IA operates 'within an institutional, sociocultural and political vacuum'. All decisions about proposed projects create benefits for some individuals and groups in society and costs for others, and thus are inherently political. A key purpose of SIA is, therefore, to provide information on the potential costs and benefits of projects, on who will be winners and losers, thereby facilitating transparent, fair and democratic political decision making (Finsterbusch, 1995: 234–36).

A more radical position is that SIA is not limited to calculating potential costs and benefits and so contributing to political choices. SIA can also be used by socially marginalized groups as a platform from which to negotiate change to the social order, and so help alter in basic ways the distribution of costs and benefits of development. Thus while Finsterbusch (1995: 234) argues that SIA is not 'an instrument for the revolution of social institutions to equalize power and results', Cowell *et al.* (2001: 273) see SIA as ensuring direct community participation in the processes that 'determine the distribution of costs and benefits of mining project(s)' (273). Gagnon (1995: 273, 286) sees SIA as one of the most important and useful tools in empowering 'local community members to exercise increased control over their own territory, social environment and future development' (see also Gagnon *et al.*, 1993: 229; Gondolf and Wells, 1986; Howitt, 1989). Such an approach, which sees SIA as a means of pursuing social justice, would define 'effective SIA' as facilitating the political mobilization of affected communities and allowing the renegotiation of power relationships between affected groups, corporations and governments.

In summary, the definition of 'effective SIA' depends very much on how the purposes of SIA are defined. For instance, effective SIA means something very different to a proponent concerned to achieve prompt project approval with minimal impact on the commercial viability of a proposed project, and a community activist seeking to bring about a fundamental change in the distribution of political power and hence the allocation of social and other costs and benefits from development.

Aboriginal exclusion from SIA

How might 'effective SIA' be understood by Aboriginal peoples experiencing the effects of large resource projects? A fundamental starting point in addressing this question is the recognition that historically in industrialized countries, including Australia, Aboriginal people have been almost entirely excluded from participation in IA processes, and their interests ignored by those conducting SIAs. In many cases, despite the fact that Aboriginal communities would be directly and obviously affected by development, their existence was ignored in the terms of reference provided by regulators to proponents conducting IAs, and IA reports often made no reference to Aboriginal people or dealt with them only cursorily. Even where their interest in development outcomes was recognized formally, Aboriginal groups faced many practical barriers to participation in IA processes. These included:

- The failure of governments and proponents to afford legitimacy or weight to indigenous ecological, cultural and social knowledge, or to consider indigenous challenges to dominant epistemologies;
- The culturally alien character of IA processes, including their adversarial nature, their insistence on use of written rather than oral submissions, and their failure to recognize the need to facilitate communication with indigenous participants, for instance through the provision of interpreters;
- Lack of financial resources required to attend regulatory hearings and gain access to the technical expertise needed to challenge proponents and regulators;
- The short periods of time allowed for submission to IA inquiries, which exacerbated the impact of resource constraints and were often inconsistent with the need for consultation with Aboriginal communities. (For an extensive discussion of these points and of other obstacles to Aboriginal participation in Australia, and also in North America, see Chase, 1990; Craig, 1990: 41–42; Geisler *et al.*, 1982; Howitt, 1989; Jobes, 1986; Lajoie and Bouchard, 2006; Lawe *et al.*, 2005; O'Reilly, 1996; Wismer, 1996).[4]

The exclusion of Aboriginal people from IA processes and the tendency to ignore their interests and concerns reflected their economic, social and political marginalization within dominant societies. In particular, it reflected the effects of dispossession from their ancestral lands; the fact that they were denied basic human rights, including political rights, until at least the mid-1960s; suffered from deep-seated racism in relation to every aspect of their lives; were forced into highly institutionalized settings (in particular government or mission reserves), leaving them little room for the exercise of individual freedoms and political expression; and suffered sustained (albeit ultimately unsuccessful) attempts by the dominant society to destroy indigenous culture and social forms (for a detailed analysis see O'Faircheallaigh, 2002).

Exceptions to this pattern of exclusion occurred both in Australia and in other industrialized countries, where projects or activities achieved a high political profile, created considerable political controversy, and had potential social consequences that were obvious and dramatic. In these cases governments might decide that a different approach was required to minimize the risk of negative political fallout. Examples from the mid-1970s include the Berger Inquiry into the proposed construction of the Mackenzie Valley gas pipeline in Canada's Northwest Territories, and the Ranger Inquiry into uranium mining in Australia's Northern Territory. Both

Effectiveness in social impact assessment

involved extensive participation by affected Aboriginal people and led, in large measure because of concerns regarding negative social impacts on indigenous groups, to government decisions not to allow a project to proceed (Mackenzie Valley pipeline), or to reduce the scale of development and attach numerous conditions to it (uranium in the Northern Territory) (Berger, 1988; Commonwealth of Australia, 1977). However, these *were* exceptions. For instance, when the proponent of the Century zinc mine, located in a region inhabited predominantly by Aboriginal people, submitted its three-volume Environmental Impact Statement in 1994, just half of one page addressed potential social and cultural impacts on the Aboriginal people (Dames and Moore, 1994).

Increased recognition of indigenous rights arising from recent legal and policy developments, some of which are discussed below, have removed some of the most blatant manifestations of exclusion. Yet obstacles to Aboriginal participation in mainstream SIA processes continue. These include the fact that a group treated so badly by state institutions is often reluctant to participate in government-run IA processes; the ongoing impact of racism, which means that if indigenous people do try to participate they are often met with suspicion or hostility by other participants in the political process; the continuing ambiguity of state actors regarding the desirability of Aboriginal participation, often fuelled by a conviction that Aboriginal groups are fundamentally 'anti-development'; and the continuing disjuncture between Aboriginal and mainstream cultural norms. Also significant is the fact that their formal exclusion from public life over a period of 200 years means that some (though by no means all) indigenous groups have limited experience in identifying strategies and establishing political structures designed to maximize their effective participation in regulatory and policy forums (O'Faircheallaigh, 2002).

Aboriginal control of SIA

Against this background, for Aboriginal people a key purpose of SIA is to help end their marginalization from decision making about development on their ancestral lands. It can only serve this purpose, however, if Aboriginal people have a strong degree of control over IA processes, because all of their experience suggests that they have little to gain from processes controlled by proponents and/or state institutions. Thus at a fundamental level, for them, 'effective SIA' is SIA controlled by Aboriginal people (Craig, 1989; Geisler *et al.*, 1982; Gondolf and Wells, 1986; Howitt, 1989, 1993; O'Faircheallaigh, 1999; Ross, 1990). One approach, pioneered by Aboriginal organizations in the Cape York region of Queensland in the 1990s, is for Aboriginal groups to undertake their own community-based SIAs (Holden and O'Faircheallaigh, 1995; O'Faircheallaigh,

2000). In some cases SIAs are conducted independently of government approval processes, and then used as a basis for negotiating legally binding agreements with developers and governments regarding the terms on which Aboriginal groups would support development on their traditional lands (O'Faircheallaigh, 1999). In other cases the Aboriginal groups involved negotiated an arrangement with regulators whereby the SIA Activity was 'extracted' from the formal EIA, conducted by the community, and the community's SIA Report was then 'inserted' into the regulatory process as a part of the proponent's environmental impact statement (EIS). This approach was adopted, for instance, in relation to the EIS for Alcan's proposed new bauxite mine and port in 1996–1997. In all cases SIAs focus overwhelmingly on the potential impacts, both positive and negative, of proposed developments on affected Aboriginal communities, and use approaches to communication and consultation carefully designed to maximize the potential for Aboriginal participation (see, for example, Holden and O'Faircheallaigh, 1995, O'Faircheallaigh, 2000).

A similar approach has been adopted by the KLC in relation to LNG development in the Kimberley region. In 2007, Inpex, a Japanese oil and gas company, commenced regulatory approval procedures for the construction of an LNG processing plant on the Maret Islands, off the Kimberley coast. Construction would have a major physical impact on the islands themselves, which are rich in Aboriginal cultural heritage. The project would generate far-reaching economic and social effects in a region with little existing industrial development, involving construction costs of more than US10 billion over three years; a construction workforce peaking at some 3,000 people; an operating workforce of about 800; and an operating life of at least 30 years. The company proposed a conventional EIA process, including an SIA, to be undertaken by consultants retained by Inpex (Inpex Browse Ltd, 2007). The KLC insisted on establishing an Aboriginal-controlled SIA process parallel to the government statutory approval process, and in July 2007 negotiated an agreement with Inpex for the company to fund an 'Aboriginal Social Impact Assessment' which would be undertaken with the maximum possible participation by Aboriginal traditional owners.

As mentioned earlier, Inpex is only one of a number of companies that have identified gas reserves off the Kimberley coast. Concerned at the prospect that a piecemeal, project-by-project site approval process would result in extensive development along the coast, and unacceptable environmental and social impacts, the government of Western Australia (WA) established a Northern Development Taskforce (NDT) to identify a single site or 'hub' for LNG processing, to which natural gas from the various fields could be piped. The WA government sought the involvement of the KLC and of Aboriginal traditional owners along the Kimberley coast in this process, and the arrangements it negotiated with the KLC included allocation of funds to support an Aboriginal SIA of the proposed 'hub' (Western Australia, 2008).

The ability of the KLC and Aboriginal traditional owners to negotiate these arrangements reflects a number of factors. The High Court's 1992 recognition of inherent rights is central, as both the Maret Islands and a number of potential sites for a processing hub were subject to native title claims. Australia's native title legislation (the *Native Title Act, 1993*) does not confer a veto on native title claimants or holders, and so traditional owners could not use the threat of halting development as part of their negotiations with Inpex and Western Australia. However, the procedural rights available to traditional owners could potentially be used to cause significant project delays which, given the scale of the proposed developments, could impose large costs on developers and governments. Thus Inpex's agreement to fund an Aboriginal Social Impact Assessment followed on from legal action by the KLC to delay granting of permits for vegetation clearance on the Maret Islands which, if successful, could have substantially delayed the project (KLC, 2007).

As research on the outcomes of negotiations between Aboriginal people and developers clearly shows (O'Faircheallaigh, 2006), the existence of a strong regional political organization, in the form of the KLC, is also of critical importance. The KLC is a grassroots community organization founded 30 years ago, during one of a number of major confrontations between Kimberley Aboriginal people and resource developers in the late 1970s and early 1980s, and it has been instrumental in helping Kimberley Aboriginal people maintain their culture and win recognition of their economic and political rights. Because of its capacity to mobilize Aboriginal people on a regional basis, and also to draw on substantial financial and human resources, it has been able to engage in political, legal and technical arenas relevant to gas development in a way that would be difficult or impossible for individual groups of Aboriginal traditional owners to do. Finally, broader international developments in relation to recognition of indigenous rights (United Nations Economic and Social Council, 2006; United Nations General Assembly, 2007) are also significant, as indicated by the WA government's acceptance of the principle that development should not take place on Aboriginal lands without the informed consent and substantial economic participation of traditional owners (Carpenter, 2006).

It cannot be assumed that other indigenous groups will be able to replicate the approaches adopted in the Kimberley and in Cape York, and indeed Aboriginal groups in regions of Australia where dispossession has been more long-lasting and extensive and political organization is less robust have found it difficult or impossible to win similar recognition of their right to be involved in development decisions (O'Faircheallaigh, 2006). The vulnerability of arrangements of the sort negotiated by the KLC to changes in corporate strategy and government policy must also be recognized, especially as, given the limited nature of their own resources, Aboriginal groups must rely on industry or government to fund SIA work. In September 2008 Inpex announced that for economic reasons it would seek to process its gas in the Northern Territory rather than Western Australia (Inpex Browse Ltd, 2008). Significant impacts have arisen from Inpex's pre-development activities, for instance its site investigation work on the Maret Islands and the social impact of the economic opportunities created by its preparatory work. However resources are no longer available to complete SIA work or implement relevant mitigative strategies. Also in September, 2008 Western Australia's Labour government lost the state election and has been replaced by a Liberal/National party government whose continued support for the NDT process and for high levels of Aboriginal participation is far from certain.

In addition, although Aboriginal control of SIA processes may be a prerequisite to achieve 'effective SIA' from an Aboriginal perspective, it is far from guaranteeing it. We explore this point in the next section.

Realizing the potential for effective SIA

As noted at the beginning of this paper, large-scale resource development creates significant risks as well as opportunities for Aboriginal people. The stakes are very high. Given the serious economic and social disadvantages they face, any benefits that can be generated by these projects are greatly valued. On the other hand, large-scale development has the potential to seriously damage the land and sea on which they rely for sustenance and for maintenance of their cultural vitality. Damage to, or destruction of, these resources could be disastrous for people with limited participation in the mainstream economy, and whose social circumstances are in many respects perilous. In this situation it is essential that SIA should accurately predict social impacts; identify effective intervention strategies to minimize negative social impacts and maximize positive ones; help ensure that these interventions are actually implemented; and support the ongoing review of both project operations and intervention strategies to ensure that net social benefits continue to be maximized. There are substantial obstacles to ensuring that SIA can perform these roles, including the economic and social disadvantages currently faced by Aboriginal communities, and the paucity of human and financial resources associated with this.

A rigorous approach to SIA is required to address the complex array of issues and challenges involved in this situation. The following discussion attempts to make a contribution in this regard, drawing on the earlier general discussion of effectiveness in SIA; the

Effectiveness in social impact assessment

> **It is essential that SIA should accurately predict social impacts; identify effective intervention strategies to minimize negative social impacts and maximize positive ones; help ensure that these interventions are actually implemented; and support the ongoing review of both project operations and intervention strategies to ensure that net social benefits continue to be maximized**

literature on indigenous SIA; and the author's practical experience in organizing SIAs in indigenous communities (Holden and O'Faircheallaigh, 1995; O'Faircheallaigh, 1999). The approach adopted is summarized in the matrix outlined in Table 1. This has parallels with other models for effective SIA – for instance that developed by the ICGPSIA – but also departs from and/or adds to them in important ways. It assumes that the potentially affected group of Aboriginal people plays a central and indeed controlling role in the SIA. It includes components absent from other models, for instance the 'revisiting' of impact factors and 'spheres of impact' (Activity 6) and the negotiation of binding strategies to maximize net benefits (Activity 10). It identifies practical considerations that may not arise in other contexts, such as the need to communicate complex technical information across cultural frames, and to develop baseline data whose existence could be taken for

Table 1. Activities of SIA that is effective for Aboriginal people

Activities of effective SIA	Key questions/ issues	Key participants	Key resources: time, information, money.	Sources of information	Key policy/ political issues
1. Understand nature and extent of impact factors associated with proposed project/activity (e.g. demand for land and water, labour demand, immigration)	What is the 'project'? What are its impacts?	SIA team; Project proponents (i.e. developers, Government); specialist independent advice to verify proponent information	Information on project; time for SIA team to collect, verify and absorb; funding for SIA team and independent experts	Proponent's regulatory submissions e.g. initial Expression of Interest, Environmental Impact Statement, industry sources on comparable projects, experience of independent experts	How narrowly/widely is project and its impacts conceptualised? (e.g. are 'indirect effects' such as increased tourism due to project infrastructure considered?) Is project considered on a 'standalone' basis or in a cumulative context?
2. Initial estimation of 'sphere of impact'.	Where (geographically) will impacts occur and what is the affected population?	SIA team	Time and funding for SIA team; information on impacts of comparable projects	Activity 1.; information on actual impacts of comparable projects elsewhere	Definition of sphere of impact: developers may want to minimize, government and community groups to maximize
3. What are the existing social, cultural, economic and political conditions (baseline) within the 'sphere of impact'?	What are peoples lives like at the moment?	SIA team; specialist informants (e.g. demographers); community and government service delivery organizations.	Time and funding for SIA team and specialists.	Census data; household surveys; data held by government and service delivery organizations.	Access to confidential data; sensitivity about documentation of 'problems' in community from government and community members.
4. What are the values and priorities of affected groups/ peoples? (Answer may be different for different components of population)	How do people define the 'good life'? What would make life worse or better for them?	Affected groups; SIA team	Time and funding for SIA team; community meetings; small group engagement; surveys (where appropriate)	Existing reports (e.g. community planning); SIAs for earlier projects; engagement with community members	Conflicting values and priorities may be expressed by different groups or community members
5. Communicate nature and extent of impact factors and key baseline data to affected groups in forms they can most readily comprehend	How can potentially affected groups be made fully aware of what is likely to happen?	SIA team; communication specialists (graphic artists, interpreters); project proponents	Funds for SIA team and specialists; for information materials (e.g videos, models); to conduct community engagement. Time to develop and communicate information materials	Activities 1–4.	Omission of groups that believe they will be affected; over-concentration on specific affected groups that can exercise political leverage

(continued)

Table 1. (continued)

Activities of effective SIA	Key questions/ issues	Key participants	Key resources: time, information, money.	Sources of information	Key policy/ political issues
6. Revisit issues of impact factors and of 'sphere of impact', e.g. some affected groups may indicate they will not feel impact; may draw attention to others who will feel effects; unanticipated impacts may be identified	Where (geographically) will impacts occur and what is the affected population?	SIA team	Funding for SIA team	Activities 1 – 5.	Definition of sphere of impact: developers may want to minimize, government and community groups to maximize
7. Understand nature and extent of social impacts if no intervention, and identify interventions (strategies) that minimize costs and maximize benefits, given values/priorities of affected groups	What will effect of project be if no specific measures taken to affect it? What can be done to minimize or maximize impacts?	SIA team; affected groups; community and government organizations whose involvement required to make strategies effective	Funding for SIA team and for engagement with affected groups; input from relevant organisations	Activities 1– 4; data on actual impacts of comparable projects; information on effectiveness of strategies attempted in other contexts; scenario building with affected groups; agencies responsible for service provision	Access to confidential data; sensitivity about documentation of 'problems' in community from government and community members.
8. Communicate proposed strategies to affected groups and so enable them to make informed decisions in relation to the project	How can potentially affected groups be made fully aware of available strategies and their likely efficacy?	SIA team; communication specialists	Funds for SIA team and specialists; for information materials; to conduct community engagement. Time to develop and communicate information materials	Activities 1– 4, 7	Conflicting values and priorities may be expressed by different groups or community members
9. Negotiate agreed strategies with decision makers; devise and sign off mechanisms to ensure strategies are implemented	What is it politically feasible to negotiate? How can implementation be achieved?	Community leaders and negotiators, with support from SIA team; proponent and government negotiators	Funds to support ongoing flow of information from SIA team; for negotiations; for engagement with community re proposed agreement provisions and implementation strategies	Negotiated outcomes achieved in relation to comparable projects; negotiation positions and implementation mechanisms developed in other contexts. Activity 3. (e.g. baseline information re organizational capacity).	Conflict between affected groups and developers and governments re strategies. Failure to reach agreement, projects being 'pushed' through against opposition of affected groups
10. Monitor impacts and effectiveness of strategies throughout project life (including closure), reconsider project parameters (to extent feasible), adjust strategies where required, e.g. in response to changing circumstances, unanticipated impacts	What mechanisms can be put in place to make sure that social impacts continue to receive the resources and attention they need? How to ensure that strategies are maintained, and adjusted over time as required?	Community and project operator monitoring teams; periodically, SIA specialists; where adjustment to conditions or strategies required, community leaders and negotiators	Funds to support monitoring efforts; development of new strategies; engagement between project operators and community leaders/negotiators	Information from monitoring activity on project impacts; on alternative or additional strategies attempted at other projects	Proponents or governments unwilling to fund continued monitoring and unwilling to consider changes to project to minimize impacts; government reluctant to expend political capital to insist on project changes

granted in other contexts (see, for example, ICGPSIA, 2003: 236). Finally and critically, it recognizes (in the final column) that many of the specific activities involved in SIA (and not just the wider issue of SIA effectiveness) are inherently political, and that failure to accept this and to manage the political ramifications of each activity may derail the whole enterprise.

Table 1 identifies 10 key Activities of 'effective SIA'; the second column notes key questions

Effectiveness in social impact assessment

identified with each Activity, to highlight the critical matters each must address. Although the Activities are discussed in sequence here, in reality they are likely to overlap. So, for instance, the collection of baseline data (Activity 3) may be taking place while the analysis of impact factors (Activity 1) is still under way. The next three columns represent the need to ensure that, if these Activities are to be completed, the key participants in each are identified and the resources required for implementation (time, information, money) made available. The references in these columns to an 'SIA Team' assume that the Aboriginal community appoints its own team to conduct the SIA. This would typically involve a mix of professional staff with extensive experience in SIA, and community members whose local knowledge and cultural expertise are critical to the efficient conduct of an SIA in a cross-cultural context and within limited time frames (Holden and O'Faircheallaigh, 1995; Craig, 1989; Ross, 1990). The final column raises key policy or political issues associated with each Activity.

Ten critical SIA Activities

Understanding impact factors

The first Activity involves the need to understand the 'impact factors' associated with the proposed project, and the key questions involve defining what the project is and quantifying aspects of the project that will generate social impacts (e.g. demand for land, for immigrant labour). Much of this information will be generated by the proponent, and its accuracy will need to be verified for the SIA team by independent experts. Resources required include the funding for the SIA team and independent advisers, and the time for the SIA team to collect, analyse and understand project information. Time is a critical resource at every stage of the process. Typically, project proponents are operating under tight time constraints and will be pushing to have IA completed, and regulatory approvals granted, as quickly as possible.[5] Key policy or political issues raised by this Activity include the definition of 'the project' – for instance, whether it is defined as a 'standalone' activity or as just one of a number of developments affecting the area of impact; and whether only core project activities (in this case the production and transport of LNG) are considered, or whether 'ancillary' activities and indirect impacts (such as the use of project infrastructure by tourists) are also included.

Initial estimate of sphere of impact

The second Activity involves an initial estimation of the project's 'sphere of impact', both spatially (i.e. *where* will impacts happen) and socially (*who* will be affected), based on project characteristics and on knowledge regarding the actual impacts of similar projects elsewhere, where this information is available. This estimation will be revisited as the SIA process unfolds (see below), especially where information on comparable situations is limited. Even a preliminary identification of the sphere of impact is essential at this stage, however, because it defines the basis on which the following Activity (for example the collection of baseline data, communication of information on impact factors) is undertaken. Defining the sphere of impact can also be highly political. Proponents and their supporters in government may wish to define it narrowly and so limit the scope of SIA work, and in particular the number and range of potentially affected people who need to be consulted. The SIA team and Aboriginal organizations may wish to take a more expansive approach, however, believing that it is unacceptable to risk omitting areas and people that may be affected as a result of defining the sphere of impact too narrowly.

Compiling baseline data

The third Activity focuses on compiling baseline data on people and communities within the 'sphere of impact', and focuses on the question: 'What are peoples' lives like at the moment'? Full and accurate baseline data regarding potentially affected people and communities are essential, for example to estimate the potential of community members to take up employment opportunities; to establish the adequacy or otherwise of physical and social infrastructure to deal with a population influx; and to assess the cultural and social resilience of communities and their capacity to absorb impacts and take advantage of opportunities. In the absence of such data it is impossible to assess likely impacts and opportunities, to devise effective strategies for dealing with them, and, later, to monitor and evaluate the actual impact of development.

The quality and coverage of existing baseline data for Aboriginal communities is often poor, creating a significant challenge for SIA work. This is certainly the case in the Kimberley region, where the Census data that provides much of the available baseline information on economic, social and cultural conditions is deficient in important respects (Taylor, 2006, 54, 67, 2008, 35–36, 40). First, some of it is seriously inaccurate or incomplete in relation to the demographic, social and economic variables it purports to describe. For example, Taylor (2008: 4) estimates that as many as one in four Aboriginal people may have been overlooked by the Census. This can result in a serious underestimate of the number of people requiring and using public services. Second, existing data may have been collected in such a way that it misrepresents social and economic reality. As Taylor notes, the process of Census data collection can be described as a 'collision of [cultural] systems' which can 'produce answers that can be nonsensical in terms of describing the reality of Indigenous social and economic life' (2006: 7). In his view, the existing data 'selectively describe the relative condition of Indigenous people, but contain no Indigenous voice' (2006: 7). A third problem is that there are important social, cultural and economic indicators in relation to which the existing baseline information is entirely silent. For instance, there are no systematic indicators of cultural and social vitality, of Aboriginal people's access to their traditional lands, and of their subjective sense of wellbeing, all of which are extremely important for an accurate assessment of their capacity to absorb impact and take advantage of development opportunities.

Extensive research must often be undertaken to address gaps in existing baseline data. This demands the allocation of substantial resources, and the work involved takes time which, as indicated earlier, may be a significant issue given tight project schedules. In addition, proponents may be reluctant to fund what they regard as 'general' research that lacks a specific bearing on their project. Other policy or political issues that require careful management are sensitivities concerning access to information held by Aboriginal health, education, cultural and other organisations; and the possible opposition of Aboriginal leaders and mainstream politicians to the exposure of social pathologies for which they may be held responsible.

Understanding Aboriginal aspirations and concerns

As indicated in the earlier discussion of participation and SIA, the collection of baseline data often requires engagement with Aboriginal people, who may be the only source of critical information. Such engagement will certainly be essential for Activity 4, which focuses on another key requirement: an understanding of the aspirations, concerns and values of Aboriginal people and communities. It is one thing to document the likely impacts of a project, but quite another to make judgements regarding the significance of those impacts. For example, a project's capacity to generate employment will be viewed quite differently depending on the relative values attached to the generation of cash incomes and the maintenance of traditional land use and associated cultural practices. Similarly, the sorts of strategies that will be appropriate in addressing potentially negative social impacts, and in taking advantage of positive opportunities, will depend on community goals and values. For instance, in a non-indigenous context it may be acceptable to allow market forces to determine the allocation of employment and business opportunities associated with large projects. In an Aboriginal community, there may be a strong belief that those whose traditional lands are most directly affected by a project should have first priority in relation to employment opportunities, and so education and training initiatives designed to prepare people for employment may need to be targeted to this group.

Productive engagement with Aboriginal people will require the application of appropriate field work and consultation methodologies by the SIA team. For instance, public meetings, often used as part of consultation processes in non-indigenous contexts, may not be appropriate because of people's reluctance to speak out in public, or the tendency of certain groups to defer to others (for instance younger people to elders). Small group meetings on people's traditional lands, informal engagement with family groups, story-telling and a range of other techniques may be employed (for a detailed discussion see Berger, 1988; Craig, 1989: 51–60; Gondorf and Wells, 1986; Holden and O'Faircheallaigh, 1995; Ross, 1990). These forms of engagement are resource intensive, both because of the considerable amounts of time they require, and because of the high cost of bringing together Aboriginal groups that can be widely scattered, often across very remote regions. At a political level, a key issue that must be addressed at this stage is the need to manage conflicting values and priorities that may emerge between individuals and groups within Aboriginal communities (Gondolf and Wells, 1986: 376–79). Indeed, this task must be undertaken on an ongoing basis as the SIA moves to form judgements regarding the net impacts of proposed projects and appropriate strategies for dealing with them (see below).

Communicating information on impacts and baseline

Activity 5 involves communication of information on key impact factors and on baseline data to potentially affected groups, to ensure they are aware of the consequences of proposed projects. This is not a simple task. For instance, information on proposed projects is usually contained in written documents that employ complex or 'high' technical language and are impossible for many Aboriginal people – for whom English is often a second or third language – to understand. This is certainly the case in relation to LNG development on the Kimberley coast, where much such information is contained in engineering studies prepared by company consultants, some of which are hundreds of pages long (see, for example, Gaffney Cline, 2008).

Converting this information to a form that can be communicated to Aboriginal traditional owners is a major challenge. The task is not simply one of preparing summaries of key documents in 'plain English' or in Aboriginal languages, or of ensuring that interpreters are present when company or government engineers give oral presentations: there is also the fact that what is being discussed is beyond the experience of many traditional owners and is difficult to translate into terms that are meaningful for them. For instance, engineers estimate that 1,000 hectares will be required for an LNG processing hub in the Kimberley, but how can traditional owners understand what this might mean if the hub was located on their country? Environmental scientists

Effectiveness in social impact assessment

stress that major impacts on wildlife such as turtles could result from 'light pollution' from a hub, but how can the concept of light pollution be explained in a context where people have no experience of major industrial facilities? In this case, the first issue was addressed by preparing computer-generated images that imposed an area of 1,000 hectares on top of places with which traditional owners were familiar, such as local townships and regional centres. The second was addressed by taking a small number of traditional owners from each potentially affected group to see an existing LNG plant in the Pilbara region, south of the Kimberley. The second exercise in particular was expensive, and leaves those who visited the LNG plant with the task of trying to explain what they saw to other community members.

Another issue is that there is often a mismatch between the value frames within which project information was prepared and those of Aboriginal groups. For instance, Aboriginal people see themselves as intimately connected to past and future generations, and as having close relationships with the animals and birds that share their traditional lands (KLC, 2008a: 4–6). Thus the fundamental assumptions made by company staff or consultants in gathering, interpreting and presenting information about likely project impacts on cultural heritage or on animal behaviour, for example, may not be shared by the Aboriginal people receiving that information. Information may have to be 'reinterpreted' by them with the assistance of specialists familiar with both Aboriginal and non-Aboriginal cultural norms and world views.

This discussion again raises the critical issue of resources. Preparation of appropriate communication tools is expensive. More broadly, the range of tasks required to complete the Activities outlined in Table 1 do not just need substantial funding: they also require access to people with the cultural, demographic, engineering, economic, environmental, communication and other skills required to collect and understand relevant information and communicate it in a form that is comprehensible to Aboriginal people both linguistically and in terms of their world views.

Revisiting the 'sphere of impact'

Once information on a project, its likely impacts and relevant baseline data is communicated to potentially affected people, the issue of that project's 'sphere of impact' needs to be revisited (Activity 6). Additional information on the project and on local populations may now be available, and Aboriginal traditional owners may identify impacts not initially anticipated by an SIA team, for instance because the latter have limited information on Aboriginal interests in land (which can be complex and multifaceted), on land use patterns, or on the behaviour of fish and game taken by Aboriginal hunters. This process does not inevitably involve a widening of the 'sphere of impact'. Groups that initially felt they would be affected may decide they will not be once the nature of the project and related activities becomes clearer.

Thus a clearer picture of potential impacts is developed through an iterative process involving the provision of information by project proponents and regulators; interpretation and communication of this information by the SIA team; and augmentation of it and responses to it by the potentially affected population.

As noted in relation to Activity 2, defining the scope of project impacts can be a highly political exercise, not only between proponents and potentially affected communities, but also within communities. For instance, where project benefits are expected to 'follow' project impacts, traditional owners close to projects may wish to define impacts narrowly, whereas traditional owners whose land is some distance away may wish to define them broadly.

Design intervention strategies

Once a clear picture of potential impacts is formed, it is necessary to consider what the consequences of a failure to intervene may be, and to design intervention strategies that can minimize potential project costs and maximize benefits (Activity 7). This process also requires input from Aboriginal people, who have a first-hand understanding of which intervention strategies are likely to be effective and which are not. Scenario building can be an important part of this interaction, with the insights of local people combining with the SIA team's experience of other projects and communities to identify and consider the likely efficacy of alternative strategies in allowing negative impacts to be addressed and opportunities grasped.

Communicate strategies assist informed decision making

Communication of information on predicted impacts, as modified through viable intervention strategies, is essential for Aboriginal communities to make informed decisions regarding proposed projects (Activity 8). If a community believes that the balance of impacts is likely to be negative even with the best available interventions, it may decide that it will oppose the project as currently configured. This may involve outright opposition where the community's view is that there are no circumstances in which the project could be acceptable, as occurred with the Mirrar people's opposition to development of the Jabiluka uranium project (Katona, 2002). In this case any additional SIA work would be redundant. Alternatively, the community may take the view that fundamental reconfiguration of the project is required before approval can be reconsidered. This occurred with the Voisey's Bay nickel project in Labrador, Canada, where Innu and Inuit traditional owners determined that a project on the scale proposed by the developer, Inco Ltd, was unacceptable, but that one on a much smaller scale and with a longer mine life might generate an acceptable balance of benefits and costs (Gibson, 2006). If a substantially revised configuration can be agreed (as was the case with Voisey's Bay, which eventually proceeded at less than half the scale initially proposed), further SIA work may be needed, focusing on the revised proposal. Given the key role of Activity 8 in determining community responses to a project, it is highly political. For instance, community leaders who favour development may wish to suppress or water down negative assessments, expecting them to mobilize community opposition to a project.

Negotiation of agreed, binding intervention strategies

If a project is 'in principle' regarded as capable of generating net social benefits, there remains the issue of ensuring that recommendations for intervention and mitigation arising from SIA reports are actually put into practice and reviewed on a regular basis. As noted above, there is a widespread failure to act on the recommendations and findings of SIA reports once project approval is secured. One approach (Activity 9) is to negotiate with project proponents and, where appropriate, governments, agreed intervention strategies whose implementation over time is secured through legally binding contracts. Such an approach is not part of the SIA, as indicated by the fact that the primary participants are community leaders, with the SIA team playing only a supporting role (see Table 1). However, it can be regarded as integral to effective SIA, as in its absence all the work involved in the previous Activity may have little practical effect on project outcomes.

In Cape York, for example, Aboriginal communities have used their community-controlled SIAs as a basis for negotiating legally binding agreements with developers and governments regarding the terms on which they would support development on their traditional lands. These agreements encompass strategies to maximize positive impacts (for instance, the creation of education and employment opportunities for traditional owners, establishment of community development funds) and minimize negative ones (for example cultural heritage protection provisions, participation of traditional owners in environmental management). This approach clearly involves a basic change from the historical function and use of SIA, which in Cape York has become a tool for an affected community to use in negotiating responses to expected project impacts so as to maximize the net benefits (for a discussion of this 'negotiation-based approach' to SIA and of specific agreement provisions, see O'Faircheallaigh, 1999).

A key political issue in relation to this Activity is the possibility that all three sides will fail to reach agreement, possibly with the result that attempts will be made to push projects through against Aboriginal opposition. If this occurs, Aboriginal groups may have to resort to wider political strategies, for instance designed to delay project development, and use the additional leverage gained in this way to support further attempts to secure agreement (Gibson, 2006). The SIA work undertaken earlier can be very useful in such situations. For instance, information on potential project impacts and on existing conditions in affected communities may play a key role in media campaigns and in garnering support from potential political allies.

Ongoing monitoring and adjustment of strategies

Finally, Activity 10 involves ongoing monitoring of impacts and the effectiveness of intervention strategies throughout the life of the project and, where necessary, the adjustment of existing strategies or the development of new ones to account for changing circumstances or new information. This is especially important given the tendency for projects to change after regulatory approval is granted; the potential for unanticipated impacts; and the likelihood that changes in the broader social environment within which projects operate will require changing responses if net social benefits are to be maximized. Specific attention must be focused on these matters, given that IA processes tend to be 'one off' in nature, focusing on the grant of project approvals, and to lack an approach based on adaptive management in the context of changes in project configurations, in knowledge regarding impact processes, and in the wider social environment (Brown and Jacobs, 1996; Joyce and McFarlane, 2001: 3–17; O'Faircheallaigh, 2007: 322). Negotiated agreements can also be helpful in this area. For example, they can require proponents to provide resources for ongoing monitoring of social impacts, and establish joint management structures with representation from affected communities and project operators that evaluate and adjust intervention strategies to take account of changing circumstances (O'Faircheallaigh, 1999, 2007).

Conclusion

There is no consensus on what SIA is or on what its purposes are, and so no single definition of 'effective SIA' is possible. SIA is understood differently, for instance, by those who see it as a tool to help make an initial decision about project approval and/or approval conditions, and those who see it as a tool for managing project impacts. Its purposes are defined differently by project proponents, for example, and by those who consider that SIAs are undertaken in political systems characterized by fundamental social and economic inequalities, and so should provide a platform for the pursuit of social justice.

The approach of Aboriginal people to SIA highlights this diversity and hence the definition of

Effectiveness in social impact assessment

effective SIA. Given their history of exclusion from SIA (and wider legal and political processes) and the fact that proponents and SIA consultants have in the past ignored their interests, a fundamental starting point for them is that a key purpose of SIA is to help end their marginalization regarding development on their traditional lands. Given this fact and their history of exclusion from mainstream SIA processes, to be 'effective' SIA must be controlled by Aboriginal people. However, this is only a starting point, one that creates a potential for effective SIA. To realize that potential a series of activities must be undertaken and challenges addressed. These include the need for accurate identification of project characteristics and impacts, and to communicate this information to potentially affected populations; to devise effective strategies to minimize negative impacts and maximize positive ones; to ensure that those strategies are put into effect by proponents, developers and affected communities; and to establish ongoing processes to monitor impacts, identify unanticipated effects, and revise intervention strategies to ensure their continued effectiveness. Each component of SIA creates demands for personnel, resources and information, and each has political ramifications that must be recognized and managed. The discussion in the final section above outlines an approach that can be used to identify the specific requirements for effective SIA in relation to resource development on the traditional lands of indigenous peoples.

Many of the issues and challenges addressed also arise in non-indigenous contexts, and so the approach adopted here, appropriately modified, should assist in pursuing effective SIA in other situations. Two specific examples highlight this point. The first is the fact that many of the activities involved in SIA are inherently and unavoidably political, and that SIA can only be 'effective' if this is recognized and appropriate strategies developed. The second is that SIA can only be effective if mechanisms are identified to translate its findings and recommendations into action, not just when a project is approved but on an ongoing basis. These mechanisms may not be developed or implemented as part of SIA, but they are as important to its effectiveness as anything that occurs within SIA itself.

Notes

1. In Australia, 'native title' refers to the recognition, for the first time, of inherent indigenous rights in land by the High Court of Australia in its 1992 *Mabo* decision, subsequently given legislative expression in the Commonwealth *Native Title Act 1993*. In other words, the High Court recognized that Australia was owned by its indigenous inhabitants when Britain colonized it in 1788. The High Court also determined that indigenous people in Australia may still hold rights in land, if those rights have not been extinguished by valid grants of title by Australian governments and if the indigenous groups involved have maintained their connection to their land.
2. Only one of the six principles that underlie the ICPGSIA 'Principles and guidelines for social impact assessment in the USA' (ICGPSIA 2003) might address this issue, that calling for 'environmental justice issues to be fully described and analyzed'. But this principle calls for SIA specialists to ensure that they consider 'underrepresented and vulnerable stakeholders' and 'consider the distribution [of] all impacts … to different social groups (including ethnic/racial and income groups)', not for control of SIA by indigenous or other vulnerable groups (ICGPSIA 2003, 233).
3. Some SIAs do focus on activities other than project development and on government policies (see, for example, Becker, 2001: 316–17; Kauppinen *et al.*, 2006), but most are concerned with large projects (Smith, 1993: 15), and that is the focus here.
4. Some of these experiences are shared with non-indigenous groups (Hartley and Wood, 2005; Doelle and Sinclair, 2006; Stewart and Sinclair, 2007), but their combined impact over extended periods has been especially onerous for indigenous people, who often disproportionately bear the ill effects of large-scale development in remote regions.
5. Inpex's decision to move to the Northern Territory was due to a perceived inability of the WA government to accommodate its need to deliver natural gas to Japan by a specific date. However, if insufficient time is available for SIA work, it may be fatally compromised, a point we return to below.

References

Ali, S and C O'Faircheallaigh 2007. Extractive Industries, Environmental Performance and Corporate Social Responsibility. *Greener Management International: The Journal of Corporate Environmental Strategy and Practice*, **52**, 5–16.

Baker, D C and J N McLelland 2003. Evaluating the effectiveness of British Columbia's environmental assessment process for first nations' participation in mining development. *Environmental Impact Assessment Review*, **23**, 581–603.

Becker, H A 2001. Social impact assessment. *European Journal of Operational Research*, **128**, 311–321.

Berger, T 1988. *Northern Frontier, Northern Homeland: The report of the Mackenzie Valley Pipeline Inquiry*. Vancouver: Douglas and McIntyre.

Brown, D and P Jacobs 1996. Adapting environmental impact assessment to sustain the community development process. *Habitat International*, **20**, 493–507.

Buckley, R 1997. Economic and technology issues in EIA. *Resources*, **59**, 1–5.

Carpenter, A 2006. West Kimberley onshore liquefied natural gas processing facilities: Statement by Premier. Perth: Legislative Assembly, Western Australia, 21 November. Available at http://www.parliament.wa.gov.au/hansard/hans35.nsf/16ab30a0303e54f448256bf7002049e8/c8dbf3c3ba5613a04825723000 20d180? OpenDocument, last accessed 19 January 2009.

Cashmore, M, A Bond and D Cobb 2007. The contribution of environmental assessment to sustainable development: towards a richer empirical understanding. *Environmental Management*, **40**, 516–530.

Cashmore, M, R Gwilliam, R Morgan, D Cobb and A Bond 2004. The interminable issue of effectiveness: substantive purposes, outcomes and research challenges in the advancement of environmental impact assessment theory. *Impact Assessment and Project Appraisal*, **22**(4), 295–310.

Chase, A 1990. Anthropology and impact assessment: development pressures and indigenous interests in Australia. *Environmental Impact Assessment Review*, **10**, 11–23.

Commonwealth of Australia 1977. *Uranium: Australia's Decision*. Canberra: Australian Government Publishing Service.

Cowell, S, M Lane, B Burke and R Crisp 2001. Social assessment and indigenous peoples: Aboriginal versus bureaucratic agency. In *Social Assessment in Natural Resource Management Institutions*, eds A Dale, N Taylor and M Lane, pp. 266–280. Collingwood: CSIRO.

Craig, D 1989. *The Development of Social Impact Assessment in Australia and Overseas and the Role of Indigenous Peoples*. Canberra: East Kimberley Impact Assessment Project, Working Paper No. 31.

Craig, D 1990. Social impact assessment: politically oriented approaches and applications. *Environmental Impact Assessment Review*, **10**, 37–54.

Dames and Moore 1994. *The Century Project: Draft Impact*

Assessment Study Report, Volume 1, Volume 2, Volume 3. Brisbane: Dames and Moore.
Del Furia, L and J Wallace-Jones 2000. The effectiveness of provisions and quality of practices concerning public participation in EIA in Italy. *Environmental Impact Assessment Review* **20**, 457–479.
Devlin, J F and N T Yap 2008. Contentious politics in environmental assessment: blocked projects and winning coalitions. *Impact Assessment and Project Appraisal*, **26**(1), 17–27.
Doelle, M and J A Sinclair 2006. Time for a new approach to public participation in EA: Promoting cooperation and consensus for sustainability. *Environmental Impact Assessment Review*, **26**, 185–205.
Finsterbusch, K 1995. In praise of SIA: a personal review of the field of social impact assessment: feasibility, justification, history, methods, issues. *Impact Assessment*, **13**, 229–252.
Gaffney Cline 2008. Browse Basin Gas Technical Report Development Options Study: Report 1 of 3: LNG Plant Site Selection Validation: Report for the Northern Development Taskforce. Sydney: Gaffney Cline. Available at http://www/dmp/wa/gov/au/documents/appendix_1_Gaffney_Cline_and_Associates_-_Addendum_to_Report_1.pdf , last accessed 19 January 2009.
Gagnon, C 1995. Social impact assessment in Quebec: issues and perspectives for sustainable community development. *Impact Assessment*, **13**, 273–288.
Gagnon, C, P Hirsch and R Howitt 1993. Can SIA empower communities? *Environmental Impact Assessment Review*, **13**, 229–253.
Geisler, C C, R Green, D Usner and P C West (eds) 1982. *Indian SIA: The social impact of rapid resource development on native peoples*. Ann Arbor: University of Michigan Press.
Geurts, J L A and C Joldersma 2001. Methodology for participatory policy analysis. *European Journal of Operational Research*, **128**, 300–310.
Gibson, R B 2006. 'Sustainability assessment and conflict resolution: Reaching agreement to proceed with the Voisey's Bay nickel mine'. *Journal of Cleaner Production*, **14**(3/4), 334–48.
Gondolf, E W and S R Wells 1986. Empowered Native Community, Modified SIA: the case of Hydaburg, Alaska. *Environmental Impact Assessment Review*, **6**, 373–383.
Hartley, N and C Wood 2005. Public participation in environmental impact assessment – implementing the Aarhus Convention. *Environmental Impact Assessment Review*, **25**, 319–340.
Hickie, D and M Wade 1998. Development of guidelines for improving the effectiveness of environmental assessment. *Environmental Impact Assessment Review*, **18**, 267–287.
Holden, A and C O'Faircheallaigh 1995. *Economic and Social Impact of Mining at Cape Flattery*. Brisbane: Centre for Australian Public Sector Management, Griffith University.
Howitt, R 1989. Social impact assessment and resource development: issues from the Australian experience. *Australian Geographer* **20**(2), 153–166.
Howitt, R 1993. Social impact assessment as 'applied peoples' geography. *Australian Geographical Studies*, **31**(2), 127–140.
Inpex Browse Ltd 2007. *Ichthys Gas Field Development Draft Environmental Scoping/Guidelines Document*. Perth: Inpex Browse Ltd. Available at http://www/inpex.co.jp/english/news/inpex/2007/0312/pfd, last accessed 19 January 2009.
Inpex Browse Ltd 2008. INPEX Announces Northern Territory for Ichthys LNG Facility. Perth: Inpex Media Release, 26 September. Available at http://www.inpex.com.au/news/2008/inpex_announces_northern_territory_location_for_ichthys_lng_facility.aspx, last accessed 19 January 2009.
ICGPSIA (Interorganizational Committee on Guidelines and Principles for Social Impact Assessment) 2003. Guidelines and principles for social impact assessment in the USA. *Impact Assessment and Project Appraisal*, **21**(3), 231–250.
Jay, S, C Jones, P Slinn and C Wood 2007. Environmental impact assessment: retrospect and prospect. *Environmental Impact Assessment Review*, **27**, 287–300.
Jobes, P C 1986. Assessing impacts on reservations: a failure of social impact research. *Environmental Impact Assessment Review*, **6**, 385–394.
Jones, M G 1999. Environmental and social impact management adds value to business. Paper delivered to IAIA Annual Conference, Glasgow, June.
Joyce, S A and M MacFarlane 2001. *Social Impact Assessment in the Mining Industry: Current Situation and Future Directions*. London: Mining, Minerals and Sustainable Development.
Kapoor, I 2001. Towards participatory environmental management?

Journal of Environmental Management, **63**, 269–279.
Katona J 2002. Mining uranium and indigenous Australians: The fight for Jabiluka. In *Moving Mountains: Communities Conflict Mining & Globalisation*, eds G Evans, J. Goodman and N Lansbury, pp. 195–206. London: Zed Books.
Kauppinen, T N, K Nelimarkka and K Perttila 2006. The effectiveness of human impact assessment in the Finnish Healthy Cities Network. *Public Health*, **120**, 1033–1041.
KLC (Kimberley Land Council) 2007. Kimberley Land Council moves to protect Maret Islands from disturbance. Broome: KLC Media Release, 26 April. Available at http://www/klc/org/au/media/070426_Media Release_Maret_DEC_Appeal1.pdf. Last accessed 19 January 2009.
KLC 2008a. *Prospectus for the Kimberley Land Council*. Broome: KLC. Available at http://www.klc.org.au/pdfs/KLC_Prospectus.pdf , last accessed 19 January 2009.
KLC 2008b. Informed consent of traditional owners key to sustainable gas development in the Kimberley. Broome: KLC Media Release 11 January. Available at http://www/klc/org/au/media/080111_GAS_DEVELOPMENTS_InformedConsent_TOs.pdf. Last accessed 19 January 2009.
Lajoie, G and M A Bouchard 2006. Native involvement in strategic assessment of natural resource development: the example of the Crees living in the Canadian taiga. *Impact Assessment and Project Appraisal*, **24**(3), 211–220.
Lane, M B, H Ross, A P Dale and R E Rickson 2003. Sacred land, mineral wealth, and biodiversity at Coronation Hill, Northern Australia: indigenous knowledge and SIA. *Impact Assessment and Project Appraisal*, **21**(2), 89–98.
Lawe, L B, J Wells and Mikisew Cree First Nations Industry Relations Corporation 2005. Cumulative effects assessment and EIA follow-up: a proposed community-based monitoring program in the Oil Sands Region, northeastern Alberta. *Impact Assessment and Project Appraisal*, **23**(3), 205–209.
Lawrence, D P 1997a. EIA – do we know where we are going? *Impact Assessment*, **15**, 3–13.
Lawrence, D P 1997b. The need for EIA theory-building. *Environmental Impact Assessment Review*, **17**, 79–107.
Lockie, S 2001. SIA in review: setting the agenda for impact assessment in the 21st century. *Impact Assessment and Project Appraisal*, **19**(4), 277–287.
Mayoux, L and R Chambers 2005. Reversing the paradigm: quantification, participatory methods and pro-poor impact assessment. *Journal of International Development*, **17**, 271–298.
McKillop, J and A L Brown 1999. Linking project appraisal and development: the performance of EIA in large-scale mining projects. *Journal of Environmental Assessment Policy and Management*, **1**(4), 407–428.
MVEIRB (Mackenzie Valley Environmental Impact Review Board) 2006. *Raising the Bar for Socio-economic Impact Assessment*. Yellowknife: MVEIRB. Available at http://www.mveirb.nt.ca/upload/ref_library/SEIA_Workshop_Report_May_29_2006.pdf. Last accessed 19 January 2009.
Morrison-Saunders, A and G Early 2008. What is necessary to ensure natural justice in environmental impact assessment decision-making. *Impact Assessment and Project Appraisal*, **26**(1), 29–42.
Mulvihill, P R and D C Baker 2001. Ambitious and restrictive scoping: Case studies from Northern Canada. *Environmental Impact Assessment Review*, **21**, 363–384.
Nitz, T and I Holland 2000. Does environmental impact assessment facilitate environmental management activities? *Journal of Environmental Assessment and Policy*, **2**(1), 1–17.
O'Faircheallaigh, C 1999. Making social impact assessment count: a negotiation-based approach for indigenous peoples. *Society and Natural Resources*, **12**, 63–80.
O'Faircheallaigh, C 2000. *Negotiating Major Project Agreements: The 'Cape York Model'*, Australian Institute for Aboriginal and Torres Strait Islander Studies, Research Discussion Paper No 11, Canberra 2000.
O'Faircheallaigh, C 2002. Overcoming severe obstacles to public participation: indigenous people and impact assessment procedures in Australia. In *Public Participation and Innovations in Community Governance*, ed. P McLaverty, pp.13–34. Aldershot: Ashgate Press.
O'Faircheallaigh, C 2006. Aborigines, mining companies and the state in contemporary Australia: a new political economy or 'business as usual'? *Australian Journal of Political Science*, **41**(1), 1–22.
O'Faircheallaigh, C 2007. Environmental agreements, EIA follow-up and Aboriginal participation in environmental management:

Effectiveness in social impact assessment

The Canadian experience. *Environmental Impact Assessment Review*, **27**(4), 319–342.
O'Reilly, K 1996. Diamond mining and the demise of environmental assessment in the north. *Northern Perspectives*, **24**, 1–5.
Paci, C, A Tobin and P Robb 2002. Reconsidering the Canadian Environmental Impact Assessment Act: A place for traditional environmental knowledge. *Environmental Impact Assessment Review*, **22**, 111–127.
Rosenberg, D M, R A Bodaly and P J Usher 1995. Environmental and social impacts of large scale hydro-electric development: who is listening? *Global Environmental Change*, **5**(2), 127–148.
Ross, H 1990. Community social impact assessment: a framework for indigenous peoples. *Environmental Impact Assessment Review*, **10**, 185–193.
Sandham, L A and H M Pretorius 2008. A review of EIA report quality in the North West province of South Africa. *Environmental Impact Assessment Review*, **28**, 229–240.
Smith, L G 1993. *Impact Assessment and Sustainable Resource Management*. Harlow, Essex: Longman.
Stewart, J M P and A J Sinclair 2007. Meaningful public participation in environmental assessment: perspectives from Canadian participants, proponents and government. *Journal of Environmental Assessment Policy and Management*, **9**(2), 161–183.
Suagee, D B 2002. NEPA in Indian country: compliance requirement to decision-making tool. In *Justice and Natural Resources: Concepts, Strategies and Applications*, eds K M Mutz, G C Bryner and D S Kenney, pp. 225–251. Washington: Island Press.
Taylor, J 2006. *Indigenous People in the West Kimberley Labour Market*. Canberra: Working Paper No. 35/2006, Centre for Aboriginal Economic Policy Research, Australian National University.
Taylor, J 2008. *Indigenous Labour Supply Constraints in the West Kimberley*. Canberra: Working Paper No. 39/2008, Centre for Aboriginal Economic Policy Research, Australian National University.
Tollefson, C and K Wipond 1998. Cumulative environmental impacts and Aboriginal rights. *Environmental Impact Assessment Review*, **18**, 371–390.
United Nations Economic and Social Council 2006. *Report on the Expert Seminar on Indigenous Peoples' permanent Sovereignty and their Relationship to Land*. Geneva: UNESC.
United Nations General Assembly 2007. *United Nations Declaration on the Rights of Indigenous People*. New York: United Nations.
Western Australia 2008. Northern Development Taskforce. Available at http://www.doir.wa.gov.au/5649.aspx. Last accessed 7 October 2008.
Wiles, A, J McEwan and M H Sadar 1999. Use of traditional ecological knowledge in environmental assessment of uranium mining in the Athabasca Saskatchewan. *Impact Assessment and Project Appraisal*, **18**(2), 107–114.
Wismer, S 1996. The nasty game: how environmental assessment is failing Aboriginal communities in Canada's north. *Alternatives Journal* **22**(4).

SIA in review

SIA in review: setting the agenda for impact assessment in the 21st century

Stewart Lockie

This article reviews the literature and practice of social impact assessment (SIA) to address some of the perennial questions faced by all fields of impact assessment. What scope is there to extend impact assessment beyond individual projects? How might the different branches fit together? What is the relationship between scientific assessments and public participation? It argues that the relative marginalization of SIA has limited the effectiveness and influence of all aspects of impact assessment. However, this marginalization cannot be blamed entirely on the technocratic world views and political agendas of project proponents, governments and scientific agencies. The strength of SIA is undermined also by a failure to resolve fundamental theoretical contradictions concerning the objects and methods of impact assessment, in particular, the contested role of prediction in SIA. While closure on these issues may not be possible, acknowledgement and clarification of them does suggest positive routes forward for impact assessment.

Keywords: social impact assessment; project appraisal

Dr Stewart Lockie is Director, Centre for Social Science Research, Central Queensland University, Rockhampton QLD 4702, Australia; Tel: +61 7 49306539; Fax: +61 7 49306402; Email: s.lockie@cqu.edu.au.

MY TITLE FOR THIS REVIEW is deliberately provocative. Even though the necessity of addressing social impacts has been acknowledged since the earliest institutionalization of impact assessment through the US *National Environmental Policy Act 1969* (Burdge *et al*, 1995), in practice it has remained something of the poorer cousin of environmental impact assessment (EIA) (Glasson, 1995).

By way of illustration, a review of general texts on impact assessment written over the last ten years shows that some give social impacts and social impact assessment (SIA) no more than passing reference (for instance, Biswas and Agarwala, 1992; Fortlage, 1990; Glasson *et al*, 1994; Wathern, 1990). Others attest to the importance of social impacts but accord them little discussion (for instance, Gilpin, 1995; Thomas, 1998; Wood, 1995). This implies, whether deliberately or not, that the assessment of social impacts is either straightforward or something that follows the assessment of environmental impacts.

Some authors collapse social and economic assessment into 'socio-economic impact assessment' which, despite the obvious relationships between the two, belies the very different methodological and theoretical expertise necessary to evaluate social and economic change. There are exceptions to this pattern, of course (for instance, Barrow, 1997; Erikson, 1994; Lee and George, 2000; Morris and Thérivel, 1995; Vanclay and Bronstein, 1995), but it is telling that the general literature on impact assessment devotes far more attention to public consultation and participation than to SIA.

While the practice of SIA itself remains marginal, it is increasingly recognized that all impact assessment professionals must come to terms with how

Social impact assessment in review

actively to engage with impacted communities and other stakeholders. With an ever-expanding literature on public participation that makes no reference to the role of independent social impact assessors (for instance, del Furia and Wallace-Jones, 2000; McNab, 1997; Palerm, 1999) it is not unreasonable to contemplate what relevance SIA retains.

This paper argues that SIA must take a significantly more prominent role in setting the agenda for all aspects of impact assessment if impact assessment is to maintain, if not increase, its relevance to the resource management decisions of the 21st century. Is this just another plea from another branch of impact assessment for a bigger slice of the action? No. While I do advocate a more substantial role for SIA, it is one that is oriented towards expanding impact assessment, not merely colonizing the space currently occupied by environmental, ecological, economic, or any other form of impact assessment.

The question of how meaningfully to expand the focus of impact assessment temporally and spatially beyond individual projects has troubled impact assessors for some time. So too have questions of how the different branches of impact assessment fit together and the relationship between scientific assessments and public participation. It is not surprising, then, that over the last decade or so the concept of strategic environmental assessment (SEA) — or undertaking more integrated assessment of the potential impacts of a wider range of policy and project options earlier in the planning and decision-making process (Partidário and Clark, 2000; Thérivel et al, 1992; Thérivel and Partidário, 1996) — has become quite popular among impact assessment researchers. By itself, however, SEA only goes part way to resolving these questions.

The review will begin by considering briefly what social impacts are and what aspects of their analysis social impact assessors largely agree with each other about. This will be used to argue that, beneath the surface-level consensus on a number of issues, there remain theoretical and methodological differences that relate to the question of whether SIA is principally about the prediction of impacts, their measurement and monitoring, or a process and tool to facilitate negotiation among stakeholders. This debate, it is argued, is of broad relevance as it demonstrates the potential contribution of SIA to more holistic, strategic and effective impact assessment. For more specific guidance on the techniques deployed by social impact assessors readers are referred to the literature cited.

What are social impacts?

The US Interorganizational Committee on Guidelines and Principles for Social Impact Assessment defines social impacts as (Burdge *et al*, 1995, page 11):

"the consequences to human populations of any public or private actions — that alter the ways in which people live, work, play, relate to one another, organize to meet their needs, and generally cope as members of society. The term also includes cultural impacts involving changes to the norms, values, and beliefs that guide and rationalize their cognition of themselves and their society."

This is an extremely broad definition that provides scope to focus on almost any aspect of social change associated with a development or policy innovation. Although the lack of specificity may seem surprising to some, its strength is that it encourages social impact assessors to focus on those changes that are important within a particular situation rather than on those that are easy to measure or with which the assessor may be familiar or comfortable (Burdge *et al*, 1995, page 35). This requires the social impact assessor to allocate some sort of priority to potential changes under circumstances where statistical measures of significance are by themselves unlikely to provide satisfactory answers.

It is at this point, perhaps more than at any other, that the SIA literature reveals the absolute dependence of effective SIA on equally effective public participation strategies. I will elaborate on the various roles attributed to public participation in greater detail below, but it is worth pointing out that SIA researchers and practitioners tend to view SIA and public participation as different, but inseparable (Burdge and Robertson, 1998; Coakes, 1999; Vanclay, 2000). Further, they consider it necessary to begin participation/social assessment as early in the life of a project as possible so as to be able to incorporate community concerns, local knowledge and mitigation strategies in project design (SIAU, 2000).

That public consultation and participation programs for major developments and policy changes are, in many instances, conducted by different consultants and with few links to the SIA component is extremely problematic. This separation often results in formal consultation activities being reduced to little more than public relations exercises and, to the extent that SIA activities provide scope for more meaningful participation, duplication in the demands made on community members and other stakeholders (Holden and Gibson, 2000; see also SIAU, 2000).

So what's the problem?

Technocratic rationality

One of the most frequently identified reasons for the marginalization of SIA is the technocratic rationality that dominates natural resource decision-making and assessment (Burdge and Vanclay, 1995). Technocratic rationality supports the "instrumental manipulation and engineering of people (and nature)" in the pursuit of unexamined goals such as economic development (Dryzek, 1990, page 55). It constructs impact assessment as a technique largely for "measuring, predicting and reporting" on the impacts of proposals in order to objectively investigate alternatives and select the course of action with "the greatest net benefits for society" (Formby, 1990, page 191; see also Howitt, 1989; Lane et al, 1997).

Despite the aura of objectivity, technocratic rationality is ill-equipped to deal either with the competing interests, beliefs, values and aspirations that characterize complex social situations, or with the active participation of multiple stakeholders in working through these situations. Technocratic rationality is often favoured by professionals who are trained in engineering or the natural sciences and are uncomfortable with, or sceptical about, the involvement of what they regard to be an ill-informed public (Dugdale and West, 1991, page 454).

However, this is not just about conflicting worldviews — it is about power (Rickson et al, 1998). It is about whose definition of an impact, an aspiration, a value and a fact is considered legitimate and whose is dismissed as subjective, emotional and irrelevant (Lockie et al, 1999). In privileging the quantifiable, technocratic rationality empowers governments and developers by highlighting apparently positive impacts, such as regional economic and employment growth, while ignoring: those that are not measurable; the variable impact of changes within affected communities; and the subjective and cultural meanings that these changes hold within communities (Howitt, 1989; Burdge and Vanclay, 1995; Lockie et al, 1999).

There is no shortage of examples from around the world of technocratic approaches to impact assessment being used to exclude consideration of social impacts, undermine public participation, avoid independent scrutiny of impact statements and minimize public accountability for decisions (Dale et al, 1997; Formby, 1990). Far from simply privileging a 'natural' scientific view over a more sociological one, technocratic rationality potentially undermines the scientific integrity of all branches of impact assessment (Formby, 1990). As Palerm's (1999) study of public participation in EIA in Hungary suggests, more adequate consideration of social impacts is a necessary prerequisite to the improvement of both public participation and environmental assessment.

Importantly, however, the most appropriate manner in which to undertake SIA remains contentious. The most obvious dimension of conflict is that which lies between development proponents and SIA practitioners (Lockie et al, 1999). As Howitt (1989, page 154) observes, "the impact assessment process itself is part of a process of social change with significant social and political consequences". It is not surprising then that many development proponents, afraid of political mobilization and opposition, resist anything other than the most technocratic approaches to social impact assessment.

Competing definitions of SIA

As important as this conflict continues to be in limiting the consideration of social impacts to those that lend themselves most readily to quantification (if they are considered at all), in this review I focus more attention on the less readily apparent differences in approach among SIA practitioners and researchers themselves. Some may argue that my assessment of these differences is overstated, that they are differences in emphasis rather than orientation, and that SIA professionals are largely united in their opposition to technocracy and advocacy of a more adequately 'socialized' impact assessment.

Writing a decade ago, Craig (1990) identified a sharp divide between SIA studies that were oriented towards the technical collection of primarily quantitative data with which to determine 'objectively' the nature of impacts, and those that were oriented towards providing a process through which the interests and aspirations of impacted communities could be represented in decision-making by facilitating community participation (see also Howitt, 1989). There has been no shortage of attempts since then to develop methodological approaches that transcend this dichotomy by applying technical measurement tools within more participatory frameworks (for instance, Lane et al, 1997) on the basis that attempts to specify and quantify social impacts can provide useful foci for community learning, discussion and empowerment (Burdge, 1999).

So are we left then with dimensions of difference among SIA practitioners that, with the exception of obviously bad practice,[1] are really only a matter of emphasis? It is worth considering in this regard a couple of definitions of social impact assessment, both of which come from attempts to specify guidelines and principles for SIA, the first in the USA and the second internationally:

> "we define *social impact assessment* in terms of efforts to assess or estimate, *in advance*, the social consequences that are likely to follow from specific policy actions (including programs, and the adoption of new policies), and specific government actions (including

Despite the aura of objectivity, technocratic rationality is ill-equipped to deal with the competing interests, beliefs, values and aspirations that characterize complex social situations, or with the active participation of multiple stakeholders

Social impact assessment in review

buildings, large projects, and leasing large tracts of land for resource extraction), particularly in the context of the US *National Environmental Policy Act of 1969* or 'NEPA' …" (Burdge *et al*, 1995, page 12, emphasis in original)

"Social Impact Assessment (SIA) is the process of analysing and managing the intended and unintended consequences of planned interventions on people so as to bring about a more sustainable biophysical and human environment." (Vanclay, forthcoming)

It would be misleading to imply that either of these definitions presupposes a technocratic approach, although neither entirely precludes it either. It is also important to note that, while the second definition represents an attempt to encapsulate what many social impact assessors think SIA should ideally be about, the first is constrained by the requirements of a particular piece of national legislation.

My use of these definitions here is designed to illustrate the very different emphasis that is placed on the act of *prediction* within SIA. In the US Guidelines and Principles, prediction is presented as the heart and soul of SIA, while in the proposed International Guidelines and Principles it is not even explicitly mentioned. While it is not explicitly precluded either, at least as much emphasis is placed on the ongoing monitoring and modification of projects, policies and mitigation programs before, during and following implementation.

This raises an interesting question for all impact assessors. If predicting the consequences that might follow an action is not necessarily the primary function of social impact assessment, is there any reason to assume that other branches of impact assessment should not be similarly subjected to critical scrutiny? Is SIA a special case? To what extent can the lessons learned from its practice be generalized?

The rest of this review will be organized around a consideration of the place of prediction in SIA and the theoretical assumptions that underlie both predictive and non-predictive approaches. It will argue that what will be referred to as negotiation-based approaches contain within them the potential to radically transform the entire field of impact assessment and to promote strategic, adaptive and democratic planning and decision-making.

Predicting social impacts

Can social impacts be predicted?

The SIA literature is somewhat divided on the question of how successful social impact assessors have been at predicting social impacts. To make a somewhat crude categorization, those authors who believe that SIA has developed adequate tools of prediction tend to be less committed to the notion of prediction for its own sake while those critical of SIA's predictive power tend to be rather more committed to a technocratic vision for impact assessment. I will deal with these latter authors first.

A rather extreme, but instructive example, is provided by Soderstrom (1981). Soderstrom believes that SIA has largely failed as a predictive tool because of the basic lack of an empirically grounded knowledge base and theoretical foundation from which to make sound predictions. This is a common criticism (see also Beckwith, 2000; Dietz, 1987; Dale *et al*, 1997; Rickson *et al*, 1990), but it is not one that is as straightforward as it might seem.

Soderstrom (1981) is concerned with the positivist conception of theory as sets of statements that can explain causal relationships between variables (that is, if x then y). Translated into impact assessment terms it means that under a known set of conditions it is possible to predict a given set of outcomes with a calculable degree of certainty. The theoretical approaches advocated by many other authors (Dietz, 1987; Dale *et al*, 1997; Rickson *et al*, 1990) focus on more abstract theoretical notions such as the nature of power, institutions and social interaction.

Given that writers from both perspectives believe the alternative to be atheoretical, a more accurate criticism may be that many SIA studies fail to clearly identify the theoretical assumptions that have guided them. This is not an indication that no theoretical assumptions have guided analysis, but evidence of a lack of theoretical transparency that takes its own 'scientific' basis for granted.

For Soderstrom (1981), the lack of empirically grounded causal theory for SIA is problematic in the first instance because it leaves open the possibility that important variables may be excluded from analysis. Further, even though SIA is based on prediction, it cannot account for whether parameters may change over time, and neither can it deal with the possibility that social phenomena may turn out to be inherently indeterminate or unpredictable.

Given this absence of theoretical and empirical knowledge, Soderstrom advocates an experimental approach through which proposed interventions and mitigation strategies are scientifically tested on a small scale in relation to measurable social indicators selected with input from both project proponents and opponents. The political, moral and practical problems with this proposed approach are obvious enough. A section of potentially impacted community cannot simply be fenced off for experimentation in the same way that we might conduct re-vegetation trials on disturbed land. Nevertheless, what if part of Soderstrom's analysis is correct and social phenomena do turn out to be essentially indeterminate or unpredictable?

There are very good reasons, in fact, to suspect that the particular sorts of social phenomena with which we are concerned here are largely unpredictable. Torgerson (1979, cited in Caley and Derow,

> Despite the preference of bureaucratic élites for technocratic approaches that reinforce their dominance, those approaches have largely failed in the exercise of social explanation and prediction

1980), for example, argues that the technocratic emphasis on measurement in early SIA reflected the functionalist assumption that communities had monolithic and discernable social goals, and simply ignored competing interest groups, imbalances of power and ambiguous and subjective social phenomena.

Taking this further, Dryzek (1990) argues that attempts to predict and control the outcomes of policy interventions not only impose often unstated goals and values, they pre-empt the outcomes of debates and decision-making processes through which the values, aspirations, perceived interests and political positions of stakeholders are likely to change. In other words, while predictive SIA may attempt to avoid functionalist assumptions by identifying different interest groups within impacted communities, defining the interests and values of each group and the likely effects of change on them, before policy interventions have even been set in place, the social milieus in which they are deployed have invariably been transformed — new groups have emerged, new alliances formed, values and aspirations redefined, new forms of political struggle identified and so on (Lockie et al, 1999). Despite the preference of bureaucratic élites for technocratic approaches that reinforce their dominance, those approaches have largely failed in the exercise of social explanation and prediction (Dryzek, 1990).

Comparative analysis, participation and democracy

In stark contrast to the argument that predicting social impacts is inherently technocratic and unfeasible stands the argument that attempts to "estimate, *in advance*, the social consequences that are likely to follow from specific policy actions" (Burdge et al, 1995, page 12) are essential to democratic debate (Dietz, 1987) and to the identification of potentially disadvantaged groups that may not otherwise have the political resources to participate in that debate (Bass, 1998). Comparative analysis is central to this approach, as is the involvement of potentially impacted communities.

Comparative analysis involves using *post hoc* studies of similar developments or policies elsewhere to identify possible impacts at the site of interest (Burdge et al, 1995; Burdge and Johnson, 1998). What is offered then is substantially less focus on precision — particularly in terms of mathematically reducing all impact variables to common denominators — and more on the identification of possible change scenarios (Becker, 1997).

According to Taylor *et al* (1990), compelling change scenarios may be developed following inductive reasoning (that is, by formulating and revizing predictions until all available data can be accommodated). From the positivist perspective, inductive reasoning is logically flawed because of the possibility that more than one explanation may be able to account for the same data, and hence that the incorrect explanation will be chosen (Beckwith, 2000). However, according to the US Interorganizational Committee on Guidelines and Principles for Social Impact Assessment, 'proof' of impacts cannot be established with absolute confidence in advance of the actions that cause them, and the purpose of impact assessment is to cautiously identify all those potential impacts that cannot, with confidence, be ruled out (Burdge et al, 1995, page 40).

Public involvement is particularly important in demarcating this approach from more technocratic ones. Social impact assessment that incorporates a public involvement dimension is seen as something that should occur early in the life of a proposal in order to ensure that:

- the entire impact assessment process may incorporate local knowledge about social conditions, processes and likely impacts;
- attitudes and perceptions towards proposed change can be identified;
- subjective and cultural impacts that relate to the ways in which people construct (that is, understand or conceptualize) their social and natural environment, and their own place within them, may be identified;
- appropriate mechanisms to involve different groups in the decision-making process may be identified;
- the outcomes of the SIA and the views of the public may be incorporated at the stage of project design and used to maximize benefits rather than simply to compensate the losers following implementation;
- potential alternatives may be identified and adequately assessed; and,
- conflict over projects may be minimized by ensuring that as many interests as possible are considered in decisions and appropriate mitigation strategies are put in place (see Burdge et al, 1995; Bisset, 2000; Burdge and Robertson, 1998; Dale et al, 1997).

Public involvement is not seen simply then as an additional source of data or as a means of educating impacted communities, but a mechanism to strengthen inductive reasoning through triangulation (that is, use of multiple data sources) and public debate about conclusions. Implicit in this approach to

Social impact assessment in review

SIA is a model of pluralistic interest group politics enacted within the framework of NEPA and a host of US institutions and laws (see also Becker, 1997; Burdge and Robertson, 1998). It reflects, in other words, a particular legislative and institutional framework and culture of decision-making that presumes individual rights to political representation, protection of property and compensation.

This does not mean that alternative approaches may not be relevant to the US context, but it does mean that the further one gets from the type of institutional, legal and cultural context that the US provides the more important it is to reassess the assumptions on which public involvement in SIA is based.[2] More importantly, when examining the logic of this approach it becomes possible to argue that, despite the definitional importance attributed to the process of predicting possible impacts, these are only likely to facilitate better decision-making to the extent that impacted communities and other stakeholders are involved in this process to a degree that extends beyond the contribution of data.

Unfortunately, this is not always the case. As we have seen, in practice SIA and public participation are increasingly treated as distinct processes, presumably because SIA is still interpreted in far too many cases as an exercise in counting demographic changes and the increased demand that will be placed on community services during and following development (for instance, Chadwick, 1995; Marriot, 1997). It can be all too easy for SIA reports to list possible impacts and claim to have engaged in appropriate consultation without ever taking the necessary steps to ensure that impacted communities do actually participate in decision-making — either directly or by having their interests represented fairly.

Improved decision-making may be understood in many different ways, but if it does include genuine public contribution to decision-making, reduced conflict and maximization of positive benefits (not just compensation for loss of property), as implied above, one must critically examine the dominant focus of SIA. Is it the improved estimation of possible impacts that improves the quality of decisions? Or is it the increased understanding and negotiation among stakeholders that has accompanied attempts to identify, analyse and manage those impacts? If the latter is the case, should not these be regarded as fundamentally more important than the task of prediction? If prediction is but one possible focus for analytic effort, what are the others?

I will turn now to a range of approaches often labelled as political or participatory SIA, all of which attempt, in some way, to answer these questions.

Should SIA be about something else?

Debates over whether social impact assessment should be a social–scientific exercise of prediction undertaken to enlighten decision-making, or a means of mobilizing public involvement in the decision process, have a history almost as long as SIA itself (Caley and Derow, 1980). While it is possible to attribute the continued predominance of predictive approaches to the more comfortable fit they achieve with technocratic decision-making processes, it remains important to consider very carefully the arguments for and against so-called political and participatory approaches (Craig, 1990).

This section elaborates on some of the arguments that have been made for more overtly political and participatory approaches to SIA before seeking to extend these in order to argue that there are important lessons to be learnt here for all branches of impact assessment and resource management.

Political and value-laden nature of decision-making

Craig (1990) puts the argument that many of the issues raised in resource management disputes are not technical in nature but, rather, questions of values. They are about what sort of social and natural environment people want to live or work in, their livelihood aspirations, lifestyle goals, sense of cultural identity and aesthetic judgments. They are as much, if not more, for example, about what sorts of development will provide opportunities to enhance local lifestyles and traditions as about which development options may objectively create more employment or economic growth.

Restricting SIA to technical and quantifiable questions misses the point and serves only to privilege some values over others. In such circumstances, Craig argues, open political processes are clearly the most appropriate basis for decision-making. Dale and Lane (1994) put a similar argument in relation to planning situations where multiple stakeholders with competing interests are involved and power is dispersed and fragmented. Centralized planning, even when supported by sound technical SIA, is poorly suited to these situations because of its inability to accommodate the perspectives and interests of the full range of stakeholders in planning outcomes.

SIAs that are either highly technical or too project-focused may fail to engage with the myriad stakeholders whose own goals and projects will eventually make or break the project under immediate consideration. It is of no use to successfully implement an infrastructure development plan only to find that intended beneficiaries are either not interested or do not have the resources to make use of that infrastructure.

Constructedness and fluidity of social impacts

No matter how many alternative development scenarios (including the no-development scenario) impact assessors consider, the predictions they make are likely to be outdated by the time decisions are taken, because the social terrain they describe will already have shifted. Negotiation-based approaches to SIA are not, therefore, based solely on the democratic value of participation but on a range of practical and theoretical arguments that suggest they are necessary simply to maintain the empirical integrity of impact assessments.

On a very practical level, it has already been noted that, despite the focus of impact assessment on 'big projects' and 'big decisions', these are themselves implemented in far more complex social and political environments. Even if these projects go ahead they may just as easily be undermined in the longer term by myriad alternative decisions and actions.

On a somewhat more conceptual level, it is also possible to argue that negotiation-based approaches may enhance the scientific validity of impact assessments. Public scrutiny of results is the more obvious dimension of this, but there are also good epistemological reasons to believe that the integration of SIA with full public involvement, negotiation and decision-making gets us closer to 'the truth of the matter'.

The argument that will immediately be levelled against this claim is that people are not always capable of predicting what will happen to them following a proposed change and are, therefore, only likely to benefit from objective assessment of those impacts (Beckwith, 2000). Local residents may, for example, expect to benefit from an increase in local economic activity following development, only to discover afterwards that most of the wealth created leaves the immediate region. They may also be aware of all sorts of other impacts left unexamined by 'expert' social impact assessors.

The point here is not whether impacted communities or specialist assessors are in better or worse positions to estimate impacts, but that many of the social impacts with which we are concerned are socially constructed through the processes of conflict and negotiation that emerge around proposed change — not waiting independently to be discovered and evaluated (Lockie et al, 1999). Again, we are not dealing with a straightforward causal process here (whereby a proposed change a, under conditions b, equals impact c). Rather, we are dealing with the fluid and contested *meanings* that are associated with spaces, activities, communities and proposed changes by those involved (Pollard et al, 1998). Both the composition of communities of interest and the things they value most highly are likely to change throughout the life of a proposal.[3]

Deliberative processes for enhanced validity

Acknowledgement that neither impacted communities nor SIA specialists are either wholly ignorant or completely knowledgeable about the impacts of change, and that impacts are potentially fluid social constructs, very strongly suggests a need for all stakeholders to work their way cooperatively through the impact assessment and planning process. Approaches to this process in the literature range from methods to bring members of impacted communities formally into the assessment process as co-researchers (Kruger and Shannon, 2000), to the development of normative criteria with which to assess participation (Webler et al, 1995), and the reconceptualization of impact assessment and planning as a collaborative learning exercise (Daniels and Walker, 1996; Daniels et al, 1996).

Although these authors draw on a range of theoretical perspectives to support their particular approaches, there is a broad consistency with the notion of communicative or discursive rationality (Dryzek, 1990; Habermas, 1984). This is based on the assumption that, while it is not possible in many circumstances for all claims to be satisfied (for instance, in use of a resource), it is possible for people's views "to be swayed by rational arguments and to lay aside particular interests and opinions in deference to overall fairness and the common interest of the collectivity" (Miller, 1992, page 56).

The role of communicatively rational deliberation is not to establish universal standards of 'right' and 'wrong', or to find the one 'correct' answer to a dispute or problem, but to arrive at decisions that participants believe fair and reasonable. This is not a recipe for political expediency over empirical reality. Utilizing the methods of the social sciences to support deliberation over the goals, impacts and management of proposed change offers more scope to come to terms with the shifting empirical reality of change than does the objectifying gaze of the 'expert' social scientist.

Importantly, it is not just social scientists whose work is likely to be improved by engaging in communicatively rational processes of deliberation and co-learning with proponents, impacted communities and other stakeholders. Indeed, I would suggest that undertaking such engagement is fundamental to the process of moving impact assessment away from its project orientation and towards more strategic processes of ongoing adaptive management. Resource management is inherently characterized by complexity, uncertainty and indeterminacy.

At the very least this suggests the need for multidisciplinarity, since no "single party, agency, organization, or discipline holds the key to understanding a particular natural resource management

The role of communicatively rational deliberation is not to establish universal standards of 'right' and 'wrong', or to find the one 'correct' answer to a dispute or problem, but to arrive at decisions that participants believe fair and reasonable

situation" (Daniels and Walker, 1996, page 75), and that more be done to integrate disciplinary perspectives. However, there is a temporal dimension as well associated with longer-term and cumulative impacts.

There is no simple answer to the challenges these raise for impact assessment. Although economic tools such as contingency valuation exist to translate otherwise incommensurate forms of data into the common denominator of money (Wattage *et al*, 2000) — and quite irrespective of how well or not they do this (see Vaughan *et al*, 2000) — we are still left with problems of constant change, redefinition of interests and values, unintended consequences and so on.

The recently popularized concept of adaptive management is a notable attempt to come to terms with these issues (Daniels and Walker, 1996), but its implementation is dependent on appropriate institutional arrangements that foster constant dialogue, deliberation and learning among stakeholders — including the scientific community. According to Dryzek (1987), such deliberation has real potential to promote more 'ecologically rational' decision-making by: encouraging decision-makers to consider options holistically and look beyond self-interest to collective and ecological well-being; decentralizing decision-making and making social choice processes more sensitive to ecological feedback signals; and involving more participants in what appear to be supra-local issues (Dryzek, 1987).

SIA, bargaining and negotiation

What might an approach to SIA based in deliberation look like and how will it differ from predictive approaches? One model advocated by Dale and Lane (1994) is the systematic and iterative application of standard social science research methods (such as interviews and surveys) to an articulation of the values, knowledge, attitudes and aspirations of all relevant interest groups throughout the impact assessment and planning process. The 'social maps' generated through this process are made available to stakeholders in order to provide a platform for negotiation based on thorough understandings of who is affected by decisions.

This has potential to: help avoid conflict based on misunderstanding and histories of prior conflict; ensure that the perspectives of those groups without the resources for active participation in decision-making are not ignored; and identify opportunities to capitalize on stakeholder capacity and aspirations. Most importantly, this is an iterative process that is repeated constantly as interest groups redefine themselves, their relationships with other interest groups and their collective aspirations. This approach acknowledges not only that multiple stakeholders with competing interests and values have legitimate interests in development and policy change, but also that there are usually many decision-makers, big and small, that have an ability to influence the long-term success or failure of those changes.

Another useful example is provided by O'Faircheallaigh (1999; see also Lane and Dale, 1995; Ross, 1992) that draws on the experience of indigenous communities in Australia. O'Faircheallaigh's argument is based on the observations that:

- indigenous communities have often been denied access to participate in SIAs despite their clear traditional associations with land under development;
- even where indigenous people have been admitted to participate in SIAs this has not necessarily been sufficient to influence decision-making because of a lack of resources and the incompatibility of formal impact assessment procedures with indigenous decision-making processes;
- the values and beliefs of indigenous people are often not recognized by the project-approval and conflict-resolution frameworks within which SIA is conducted; and
- the project-by-project and impact-mitigation orientation of impact assessment is poorly equipped to maximize the long-term benefits associated with successive initiatives.

Irrespective of the degree to which social impact assessors attempt to incorporate indigenous values and encourage participation in the process of predicting impacts, this cannot, in itself, guarantee participation in decisions over project approval or access to broader political and institutional structures:

"perhaps the most noticeable feature of the existing literature on indigenous people and SIA is its almost total failure to address the issue of how the findings and recommendations generated by impact assessment can be effectively fed into decision-making processes, and so help to generate a more favourable balance of benefits and costs for indigenous people." (O'Faircheallaigh, 1999, page 67)

The solution advocated by O'Faircheallaigh (1999) is the integration of SIA into processes of negotiation between developers and impacted indigenous communities that produce legally binding agreements. While this particular process may not be relevant to all impacted communities (although there is no reason to assume its applicability is limited to indigenous communities), the generalizable point here is that involvement in SIA must also provide a concrete avenue for participation in meaningful decision-making, not just provide data to decision-makers elsewhere.

Deliberation is meaningless unless linked directly to the outcomes of decisions. This does not mean that predictive and technical SIA methods such as comparative analysis are unimportant, but it does mean that they are decentred as the actual goals of SIA and deployed, as Dale and Lane (1994) suggest, where necessary to support bargaining and negotiation. "[T]he results of SIA do not flow automatically into the negotiation process. Arrangements must be put in place to ensure that they do so" (O'Faircheallaigh, 1999, page 77).

Conclusion

There is no doubt that estimating in advance the impacts of proposed change is a vital planning activity, but it is not the only vital planning activity and it must be decentred as the primary function of impact assessment if impact assessment is to move beyond the focus on 'big projects' and 'big decisions' and deal more adequately with strategic issues. Arguing this does not imply that impact assessment is solely about the facilitation of public participation.[4] Rather, it is an argument that the most basic criteria against which all impact assessment activities should be evaluated is their contribution to communicatively rational deliberation.

Such a contribution, and the co-learning that is implied, is dependent on scientific rigour and honesty, flexibility, and active engagement with the full range of stakeholders involved in, or affected by, proposed change so that they may use, challenge, reinterpret and add to the knowledge created. It is not about 'telling people how it is' so that they can go away and make a decision. Such arrogance serves only to perpetuate technocratic rationality and the narrow range of interests it serves.

Examination of existing practice in social impact assessment suggests that even when SIAs are conducted within a predictive framework, decision-making is vastly improved when the involvement of impacted communities extends beyond the contribution of data and to involvement in decision-making processes. Models that have been developed explicitly to facilitate such processes offer great potential in increasing the relevance and influence of SIA.

In the end, it is not radically new scientific procedures or types of impact assessment that are needed to move impact assessment beyond the project focus so much as radically new types of institutional arrangements that foster different kinds of decision-making. While this may appear, at face value, to be out of the hands of impact assessors, it should also be noted that the more technocratic the practice of impact assessment the more support is lent to existing arrangements and their frequent incapacity to deal with uncertainty in a strategic and participatory manner.

The more our own practice as impact assessors is democratized according to the principles of communicatively rational deliberation the more we do to foster the institutional arrangements that will allow such processes to be seen increasingly as good practice rather than as a threat. It is my view that this is what holds the key to more widespread implementation of the call of strategic environmental assessment for earlier and more frequent impact assessment of a wider range of proposed changes, and to the application of impact assessment tools to the many more scattered, diffuse and small decisions that on a cumulative basis have major socio-environmental impacts — that is, to extend the reach of all impact assessment.

Notes

1. Much bad practice in SIA can be explained by its continued marginalization and the all too common practices of either devoting insufficient resources to SIA studies or of assigning them to people who are poorly qualified (often junior staff within engineering consultancy firms that have been contracted to undertake EIAs) and who are most likely unsympathetic towards, if they are even aware of, these debates (Dale et al, 1997; Holden and Gibson, 2000).

2. It would be trite and unhelpful to try to address in this paper the unique issues that are raised for impact assessment in cultural and legal contexts that do not support the rights to political representation and compensation for loss of property — whether material or cultural — as found in the USA and elsewhere. While more communal notions of property rights, for example, may serve simply to redefine the parameters of appropriate participation and mitigation, they may also be used to justify the alienation of resources from the politically weak.

    While the theoretical argument of this paper is consistent with the issues of empowerment and participation that are obviously raised in such contexts, the paper will not attempt to resolve how these might, in practice, be addressed. One useful example, however, is provided by Richardson et al (1998), in their discussion of the potential for NGOs (non-governmental organizations) to sponsor public participation programs in parallel with formal impact assessment activities, in countries where the capacity or willingness of governmental institutions and development proponents to support public participation themselves is inadequate.

3. While the composition of some communities of interest may appear relatively straightforward — as is reflected in popular terminology such as 'the Aboriginal community' and 'the fishing community' — it is important that these are not taken for granted. Within Australia, for example, at the time of European colonization there were some 600 language groups, meaning that many developments and other proposed changes involve more than one group of traditional land owners who frequently express different aspirations and development preferences. Fishers are routinely divided into recreational and commercial fishers, each represented by distinct lobby groups and other industry organizations.

    There are many more communities of interest, however, that cannot be so readily identified. These may include residents of a town, district, or other spatial unit that until a change is proposed have limited sense of common identity or formal representative institutions, and are divided over the proposal in question. In all cases it must be recognized though that the legitimacy of organizations to define and speak for a community of interest is a contingent, and potentially contestable, achievement.

4. As Beckwith (2000) points out, the equation of pubic participation with SIA can be a convenient way for weak SIA practitioners to avoid analytical techniques in which they are not competent.

References

Barrow, C J (1997), *Environmental and Social Impact Assessment: an Introduction* (Arnold, London).

Social impact assessment in review

Bass, R (1998), "Evaluating environmental justice under the national environmental policy act", *Environmental Impact Assessment Review*, 18, pages 83–92.

Becker, H (1997), *Social Impact Assessment* (UCL Press, London).

Beckwith, J A (2000), "Social impact assessment: can it deliver?", paper presented to the Annual Meeting of the International Association for Impact Assessment, Hong Kong, June.

Bisset, R (2000), "Methods of consultation and public participation", in Lee and George (2000), pages 149–160.

Biswas, A, and S Agarwala (1992), *Environmental Impact Assessment for Developing Countries* (Butterworth–Heinemann, Oxford).

Burdge, R (editor) (1998), *A Conceptual Approach to Social Impact Assessment: Revised Edition* (Social Ecology Press, Middleton, WI).

Burdge, R (1999) *A Community Guide to Social Impact Assessment: Revised Edition* (Social Ecology Press, Middleton, WI).

Burdge, R, P Fricke, K Finsterbusch, W Freudenberg, R Gramling, A Holden, L Llewellyn, J Petterson, J Thompson and G Williams (1995), "Guidelines and principles for social impact assessment", *Environmental Impact Assessment Review*, 15, pages 11–43.

Burdge, R, and S Johnson (1998), "Social impact assessment: developing the basic model", in Burdge (1998), pages 13–29.

Burdge, R, and R Robertson (1998), "Social impact assessment and the public involvement process", in Burdge (1998), pages 183–192.

Burdge, R, and F Vanclay (1995), "Social impact assessment", in Vanclay and Bronstein (1995), pages 31–65.

Caley, M, and E Derow (1980), *Social Impact Assessment: a Cross-Disciplinary Guide to the Literature* (Policy Studies Institute, London).

Chadwick, A (1995), "Socio-economic impacts 2: social impacts", in Morris and Thérivel (1995), pages 29–49.

Coakes, S (1999), *Social Impact Assessment: a Policy Maker's Guide to Developing Social Impact Assessment Programs* (Bureau of Rural Sciences, Agriculture, Fisheries and Forestry Australia, Canberra).

Craig, D (1990), "Social impact assessment: politically oriented approaches and applications", *Environmental Impact Assessment Review*, 10(1/2), pages 37–55.

Dale, A, and M Lane (1994), "Strategic perspectives analysis: a procedure for participatory and political social impact assessment", *Society and Natural Resources*, 7(3), pages 253–267.

Dale, A, P Chapman and M McDonald (1997), "Social impact assessment in Queensland: why practice lags behind legislative opportunity", *Impact Assessment*, 15(2), pages 159–179.

Daniels, S, and G Walker (1996), "Collaborative learning: improving public deliberation in ecosystem-based management", *Environmental Impact Assessment Review*, 16, pages 71–102.

Daniels, S, R Lawrence and R Alig (1996), "Decision-making and ecosystem-based management: applying the Vroom-Yetton model to public participation strategy", *Environmental Impact Assessment Review*, 16, pages 13–30.

Del Furia, L, and J Wallace-Jones (2000), "The effectiveness of provisions and quality of practices concerning public participation in EIA in Italy", *Environmental Impact Assessment Review*, 20, pages 457–479.

Dietz, T (1987), "Theory and method in social impact assessment", *Sociological Inquiry*, 57(1), pages 54–69.

Dryzek, J (1987), *Rational Ecology: Environment and Political Economy* (Blackwell, Oxford).

Dryzek, J (1990), *Discursive Democracy: Politics, Policy and Political Science* (Cambridge University Press, Cambridge).

Dugdale, M, and S West (1991), "Public participation in natural resources planning and management", in Proceedings of the International Hydrology and Water Resources Symposium (Institute of Engineers, Perth) pages 454–459.

Erikson, P (1994), *A Practical Guide to Environmental Impact Assessment* (Academic Press, San Diego).

Formby, J (1990), "The politics of environmental impact assessment", *Impact Assessment Bulletin*, 8(1/2), pages 191–196.

Fortlage, C A (1990), *Environmental Assessment: a Practical Guide* (Gower, Brookfield, VM).

Gilpin, A (1995), *Environmental Impact Assessment: Cutting-Edge for the Twenty-First Century* (Cambridge, Cambridge).

Glasson, J, R Thérivel and A Chadwick (1994), *Introduction to Environmental Impact Assessment: Principles and Procedures, Process, Practice and Prospects* (UCL Press, London).

Habermas, J (1984), *The Theory of Communicative Action, Volume One: Reason and the Rationalisation of Society* (Polity Press, Cambridge).

Holden, A, and R Gibson (2000), "Opportunities for better practice social impact assessment in Queensland, Australia", paper presented to the Annual Meeting of the International Association for Impact Assessment, Hong Kong, June.

Howitt, R (1989), "Social impact assessment and resource development: issues from the Australian experience", *Australian Geographer*, 20(2), pages 153–166.

Kruger, L, and M Shannon (2000), "Getting to know ourselves and our places through civic social assessment", *Society and Natural Resources*, 13, pages 461–478.

Lane, M, and A Dale (1995), "Project assessment in Australian indigenous domains: the case for reform", *Australian Journal of Environmental Management*, 2, pages 30–39.

Lane, M, H Ross and A Dale (1997), "Social impact research: integrating the technical, political, and planning paradigms", *Human Organization*, 56(3), pages 302–310.

Lee, N, and C George (editors) (2000), *Environmental Assessment in Developing and Transitional Countries: Principles, Methods and Practice* (Wiley, Chichester).

Lockie, S, S Momtaz and B Taylor (1999), "Meaning and the construction of social impacts: water infrastructure development in Australia's Gladstone/Calliope region", *Rural Society*, 9(3), pages 529–542.

Marriot, B (1997), *Environmental Impact Assessment: A Practical Guide* (McGraw Hill, New York).

McNab, A (1997), "Scoping and public participation", in J Western (editor), *Planning and Environmental Impact Assessment in Practice* (Longman, Essex) pages 60–77.

Miller, D (1992), "Deliberative democracy and social choice", *Political Studies*, 40, pages 56–67.

Morris, P, and R Thérivel (editors)(1995), *Methods of Environmental Impact Assessment* (UCL Press, London).

O'Faircheallaigh, C (1999), "Making social impact assessment count: a negotiation-based approach for indigenous peoples", *Society and Natural Resources*, 12, pages 63–80.

Palerm, J (1999), "Public participation in EIA in Hungary: analysis through three case studies", *Environmental Impact Assessment Review*, 19, pages 201–220.

Partidário, M R, and R Clark (editors) (2000), *Perspectives on Strategic Environmental Assessment* (Lewis Publishers, Boca Raton).

Pollard, L, M Booth and L Stocker (1998), "Expressing community meanings through the hermeneutic process in social impact assessment", paper presented to the Annual Meeting of the International Association for Impact Assessment, Christchurch, April.

Richardson, T, J Dusik and P Jindrova (1998), "Parallel public participation: an answer to inertia in decision-making", *Environmental Impact Assessment Review*, 18, pages 201–216

Rickson, R, T Hundloe and J Western (1990), "Impact assessment in conflict situations: World Heritage listing of Queensland's northern tropical rainforests", *Impact Assessment Bulletin*, 8(1/2), pages 179–190.

Rickson, R, J Western and R Burdge (1998), "The use of social impact assessment knowledge in development decisions", in Burdge (1998), pages 79-91.

Ross, H (1992), "Opportunities for Aboriginal participation in Australian social impact assessment", *Impact Assessment Bulletin*, 10(1), pages 47–76.

SIAU, Social Impact Assessment Support Unit (2000), *Social Impact Assessment in Queensland* (Department of Families, Youth and Community Care, Brisbane).

Soderstrom, E (1981), *Social Impact Assessment: Experimental Methods and Approaches* (Praeger, New York).

Taylor, C N, C H Bryan and C Goodrich (1990), *Social Assessment: Theory, Process and Techniques* (Centre for Resource Management, Lincoln University, Lincoln, NZ).

Thérivel, R and M R Partidário (editors) (1996), *The Practice of Strategic Environmental Assessment*, (Earthscan, London).

Thérivel, R, E Wilson, S Thompson, D Heany and D Pritchard (1992), *Strategic Environmental Assessment* (Earthscan, London).

Thomas, I (1998), *Environmental Impact Assessment in Australia: Theory and Practice* (Federation Press, Sydney).

Vanclay, F (2000), "Social impact assessment", in Lee and George (2000), pages 125-135.

Vanclay, F (forthcoming), "Social impact assessment", in *Encyclopaedia of Global Environmental Change* (Wiley, Chichester, UK).

Vanclay, F and D Bronstein (editors)(1995), *Environmental and Social Impact Assessment* (Wiley, Chichester, UK).

Vaughan, W, C Russell, D Rodriguez and A Darling (2000), "Uncertainty in cost-benefit analysis based on referendum contingent valuation", *Impact Assessment and Project Appraisal*, 18(2), pages 125–137.

Wathern, P (editor)(1990), *Environmental Impact Assessment: Theory and Practice* (Routledge, London).

Wattage, P, A Smith, C Pitts, A McDonald and D Kay (2000), "Integrating environmental impact, contingent valuation and cost–benefit analysis: empirical evidence for an alternative perspective", *Impact Assessment and Project Appraisal*, 18(1), March, pages 5–14.

Webler, T, H Kastenholz O Renn (1995), "Public participation in impact assessment: a social learning perspective", *Environmental Impact Assessment Review*, 15, pages 443–463.

Wood, C (1995), *Environmental Impact Assessment: a Comparative Review* (Longman, Essex).

THE TRIPLE BOTTOM LINE AND IMPACT ASSESSMENT: HOW DO TBL, EIA, SIA, SEA AND EMS RELATE TO EACH OTHER?

FRANK VANCLAY

Tasmanian Institute of Agricultural Research
University of Tasmania, Australia
Frank.Vanclay@utas.edu.au

Received 5 January 2004
Revised 13 July 2004
Accepted 19 July 2004

Triple bottom line (TBL) reporting is a concept that is sweeping across the business sector, government and NGOs. However, many of the issues faced by consideration of the social in TBL are very similar to issues faced by social impact assessment (SIA) in its connections with biophysical environmental impact assessment (EIA) and the financial considerations associated with projects including economic and fiscal impact assessment, and cost-benefit analysis. It would appear that the advocates of TBL and the institutions that have adopted TBL are ignorant of SIA and other forms of impact assessment. The view presented here is that TBL is a fad that presents little that is new, and that TBL would learn a great deal by considering the experience of SIA.

Keywords: Triple bottom line; sustainability; social impact assessment; environmental management systems; strategic environmental assessment; TBL reporting; social indicators.

Introduction

The relatively new concept of the triple bottom line (TBL) of social, environmental and economic performance has increasing corporate, government and NGO support. Although initially intended as a philosophy or way of thinking about sustainability, akin to the concept of corporate social responsibility, it has become a framework for accounting and reporting. While the economic and environmental indicators are relatively easy to identify, select and measure, the social indicators are not. Consequently, there has been a flurry of panic about what the social TBL indicators might be.

This paper argues that the concept of TBL, and the role of the social within TBL, are not fundamentally different to the well-established field of impact assessment. Therefore, the relationship between social impact assessment (SIA) and environmental impact assessment (EIA) may assist thinking about the triple bottom line.

To some extent the paper is critical of TBL, not because the author is opposed to sustainability or the need to think about social and environmental, as well as economic, criteria, or the need for corporate social responsibility — far from it — but rather because the originators of TBL and its current advocates seem to be ignorant of the field of impact assessment. An underlying criticism is that although TBL was meant to be a way of thinking and a heuristic, the accounting requirements have meant that there is a preoccupation with identifying indicators, which often have not proved adequate. By contrast, in the author's primary research field of social impact assessment, there is an adage that one should focus on the things that count, not the things that can be counted!

What is the Triple Bottom Line?

The "triple bottom line" is variously described as:

- social, environmental and economic performance;
- sustainable development, sustainable environment, sustainable communities;
- impact on society, the environment, and economic sustainability;
- economic, environmental and social sustainability;
- economic prosperity, environmental quality, and social justice;
- economic growth, ecological balance and social progress;
- economic growth, social progress and environmental health;
- economy, environment, equity;
- profit, people, planet (or planet, people, profit); and
- landscapes, lifestyles and livelihoods.

The term "triple bottom line" was allegedly coined by John Elkington in 1995 (Sarre and Treuren, 2001) although it did not become popularised until the widespread take-up of his 1997 book, *Cannibals with Forks: The Triple Bottom Line of 21st Century Business*. The title of this book comes from a question posed by the Polish poet Stanislaw Lec, "Is it progress...if a cannibal uses a fork?" (Elkington, 1997, vii). Elkington applies the question to contemporary capitalism. While the wording of the question/title would suggest that Elkington was sceptical, in a confusing way he states that he believes that "it can be" (ibid.) in a logic that is not altogether apparent. Surely progress and genuine corporate social responsibility requires more than the adoption of some greenwashing to makeover big business and/or government.

Elkington's consultancy company, SustainAbility, which he founded in 1987, gives a big picture description of TBL, as well as an accounting concept.

> The triple bottom line (TBL) focuses corporations not just on the economic value they add, but also on the environmental and social value they add — and destroy. At its narrowest, the term "triple bottom line" is used as a framework for measuring and reporting corporate performance against economic, social and environmental parameters.
>
> At its broadest, the term is used to capture the whole set of values, issues and processes that companies must address in order to minimize any harm resulting from their activities and to create economic, social and environmental value. This involves being clear about the company's purpose and taking into consideration the needs of all the company's stakeholders — shareholders, customers, employees, business partners, governments, local communities and the public. (SustainAbility, 2003, website)

TBL is meant to be a way of thinking about corporate social responsibility, not a method of accounting. On this point, Elkington (1997, 70) is unambiguous, likening TBL to a Trojan Horse which is wheeled in by corporations. In the beginning they succumb to an accounting procedure, but ultimately they are meant to embrace a wider vision of sustainability. Unfortunately, too many agencies and companies have not appreciated the philosophy behind TBL, and are responding only to the reporting requirements. An Australian scoping study by TBL Victoria (Vandenberg, 2002) revealed that there was considerable confusion about the definition and philosophy behind TBL in the 32 organisations surveyed.

TBL has achieved considerable imprimatur because corporations such as Shell and BP have adopted it (see BP Australia's *Triple Bottom Line Report*). The World Business Council for Sustainable Development, a coalition of 160 international companies, has also given strong endorsement to the concept (see Holliday *et al.*, 2002). Various government agencies at all levels have been required to implement TBL, and have struggled because the social (and in some cases environmental) indicators have not been determined. But they have lost sight of the intention. TBL should be a philosophy, not a set of accounts.

TBL advocates could learn much from the field of impact assessment, as this paper will show. It could also be that TBL is redundant given the existence of SIA. Alternatively, maybe TBL will provide a new raison d'etre for SIA.

What is Impact Assessment?

Impact assessment

"Impact assessment can be broadly defined as the prediction or estimation of the consequences of a current or proposed action (project, policy, technology)" (Vanclay and Bronstein, 1995, xi). Or, as on the website of the International Association for Impact Assessment (IAIA, 2003), "Impact assessment, simply defined, is the process of identifying the future consequences of a current or proposed action". Impact assessment is a generic term that can mean either an integrated approach or the composite/totality of all forms of impact assessment such as environmental impact assessment (EIA), social impact assessment (SIA), health impact assessment (HIA), etc.

Environmental impact assessment

EIA "is a process of identifying and predicting the potential environmental impacts... of proposed actions, policies, programmes and projects, and communicating this information to decision makers before they make their decisions on the proposed actions" (Harvey, 1998, 2). EIA emerged as a discipline in the early 1970s with the introduction of the United States National Environment Policy Act of 1969 (NEPA) (Ortolano and Shepherd, 1995).

The major dilemma across the world is what does "the environment" in EIA mean? For most writers, and Harvey (1998, 2) is typical, environmental impacts means "bio-geophysical, socio-economic and cultural" — in other words, EIA is a triple bottom line phenomenon. This holistic notion of EIA is present in some regulatory contexts. In Australia, the Federal Government's Environment Protection and Biodiversity Conservation Act of 1999 (EPBC) (Section 528), defines the environment as including:

> (a) ecosystems and their constituent parts, including people and communities; and
> (b) natural and physical resources; and
> (c) the qualities and characteristics of locations, places and areas; and
> (d) the social, economic and cultural aspects of a thing mentioned in paragraph (a), (b) or (c).

Other Australian legislation, such as Local Government (Planning and Environment) Act 1990 of the State of Queensland, use a similar definition but with sub-sections (c) and (d) slightly reworded to emphasise the social.

(c) the qualities and characteristics of locations, places and areas, however large or small, that contribute to their biological diversity and integrity, intrinsic or attributed scientific value or interest, amenity, harmony, and sense of community; and
(d) the social, economic, aesthetic, and cultural conditions that effect, or are affected by, things mentioned in paragraphs (a) to (c).

In Australia, therefore, at least until recently, the "environment" was broadly understood. Unfortunately, in some subsequent legislation, for example the Gene Technology Act 2000 (Section 10) this definition has been watered down. The Explanatory Memorandum relating to the Gene Technology Act (page 48) states very bluntly, "It is intended that the definition of environment include all animals (including insects, fish and mammals), plants, soils and ecosystems (both aquatic and terrestrial)".

Around the world, definitions of "the environment" vary enormously with some countries having very limited definitions, while others reflect an holistic understanding (see Donnelly, Dalal-Clayton and Hughes, 1998).

Social impact assessment

"Social impact assessment is analysing, monitoring and managing the social consequences of development" (Vanclay, 2003a, 6). SIA emerged in the early 1970s along with EIA and as a consequence of NEPA (Burdge and Vanclay, 1995). To some extent, SIA is a component of EIA, especially when "the environment" is understood broadly. In that sense, social TBL is just another name for SIA within EIA.

However, SIA is more than a technique or step, and is more than a component of EIA, it is philosophy about development and democracy (Vanclay, 2002a). Ideally SIA considers:

- pathologies of development (i.e. harmful impacts);
- goals of development (clarifying what is appropriate development, improving quality of life); and
- processes of development (e.g. participation, building social capital).

SIA has become a significant field of research such that three levels of SIA can be conceived. This creates a confusion in developing a definition (Vanclay, 2002a). At the lowest level, SIA is a technique or method within (i.e., subordinate to) EIA (the prediction of social impacts in an environmental impact statement). More commonly, SIA is considered as a methodology in its own right (the process of managing the social issues of a planned intervention) and equal in standing, i.e., comparable, and compatible with EIA. Finally, SIA can be considered as a body corporate, a group of scholars and practitioners, field of research and practice, and/or a paradigm or sub-discipline of applied social science understanding.

With over 30 years of existence, the discipline of SIA has something to contribute, and has achieved profound learning. Unfortunately, many of the advocates of TBL are ignorant of SIA, and many are ignorant of the other forerunners of TBL in the history of the concept of sustainability. It is true that in its 30 year history, SIA has had various ups and downs. However, over time, considerable progress has been made. Two significant documents have assisted in codification of the discipline. The first was the 1994 report of the Interorganizational Committee for Guidelines and Principles, *Guidelines and Principles for Social Impact Assessment*, which was developed for the USA/NEPA context. The second was the 2003 *International Principles for Social Impact Assessment* (Vanclay, 2003a). The variables/issues to be considered have been documented although they need to be substantiated in each case through a local scoping process (Vanclay, 2002b). There are several textbooks on SIA (Barrow, 2000; Becker, 1997; Becker and Vanclay, 2003; Branch *et al.*, 1984; Burdge, 1998; 1999; Lane *et al.*, 2001; Taylor *et al.*, 1995). A comprehensive on-line bibliography (electronic database) is also available on the IAIA website (Vanclay and Nauta, 2003). Finally, SIA practitioners have a professional body as part of the International Association for Impact Assessment (www.iaia.org), an organisation which was founded in 1980 having several thousand members across over 100 countries.

TBL and the History of Sustainability

As indicated earlier, TBL is a concept that was ostensibly coined by John Elkington in 1995, and publicly articulated in 1997. But it is a concept that has connections to many earlier ideas, and that is totally consistent with ecologically sustainable development (ESD) thinking that was espoused in the Brundtland Report (WCED, 1987) and in the 1992 Rio Declaration and Agenda 21. In Chapter 4 of his book, Elkington (1997, 70) makes this clear saying that "none of this was new".

The essence of ESD thinking was popularised as a three-legged stool that has become so ubiquitous that establishing the originator of this concept is impossible. The three legged stool, now somewhat contested, was a powerful metaphor because with three legs, each was equally important, and all necessary for support. If a fourth leg is added (for example culture, see Hawkes, 2001), the allegory of support no longer works. The terms describing each leg were meant to be understood broadly. Sustainability represented the intersection of all three domains. The diagram was a useful heuristic and the legs were never intended to be quantified or operationalised.

One consequence of the 1992 Earth Summit, which was reinforced by the United Nations Environment Program and the organisation for Economic Cooperation and

Development, was that many countries agreed to undertake State of the Environment (SoE) reporting. With a broad holistic definition of the environment, and with the noble sentiments of the Rio Declaration and Agenda 21, it would be expected that some discussion of the social environment be included in the SoE reports. While some writers (Goodland and Daly, 1995) articulated social sustainability in general terms, the SoE reports required quantitative indicators to measure performance and change over time. Therefore, the difficult process of defining and operationalising social constructs began. As the social scientist engaged to consider the role of social science data in the National Land and Water Resources Audit, my report indicated how difficult this was (Vanclay, 1998).

Current Trends in Impact Assessment

In the field of impact assessment, there are five obvious trends happening at present:

- moving impact assessment upstream to the policy level through the development of strategic environmental assessment (SEA);
- ensuring that all possible considerations are included through the development of a myriad of additional forms of impact assessment to cater for each specific issue;
- an increasing focus on integration and integrative approaches;
- broadening the definitions; and
- mainstreaming impact assessment through environmental auditing and environmental management systems (EMS).

Thinking about these trends provides a warning about what will happen, or at least could happen, with TBL if there is a failure to consider these issues through the abandonment of past learnings. The naïve adoption of a TBL framework will be a regressive step.

Trend 1: Strategic environmental assessment

Although EIA and SIA were always intended to be applicable at the policy level as well as the project level (Becker, 1997; Taylor *et al.*, 1995; Vanclay, 1999), the practice and experience of EIA and SIA has been at the project level. EIA and SIA have also failed to consider the positive outcomes of development, have not considered the goals of development, and in the case of SIA, has tended to emphasize the impacts on individuals rather than on societies as a whole (Vanclay, 2002a). Cumulative effects have been ill-considered, as have the upstream and downstream impacts, and the second and higher-order impacts (Slootweg *et al.*, 2001; Vanclay, 2002b). Nevertheless, Boothroyd (1995, 90) identified several reasons why EIA and

SIA have been constrained at the project level:

- Projects are tangible, dramatic, highly organised, discrete geographically and temporally, and for all these reasons amenable to systematic IA.
- Localized negative impacts of individual projects are perceived to be able to be mitigated, or are regarded as insignificant in comparison to project benefits, thus EIA can be applied rigorously on a case-by-case basis without threatening the current unsustainable development path and those most benefiting from it.
- Policy-making is secretive, or at least guarded. Power-holders feel threatened by increasing explicit systematization and the public accountability it produces or seems to imply. Rejection of a well-defined policy proposal because of an EIS would be regarded as causing loss of public confidence in the proponent — the higher the proponent, the more serious this loss.
- The most important policies are unwritten, often unspoken, certainly not reviewed, and are therefore not assessable.

To counter the deficiencies in EIA, a new field called strategic environmental assessment (SEA) has emerged as "a form of impact assessment that can assist managers and leaders in policy, planning and programmatic decisions" (Partidário, 2000, 647). Although perhaps first introduced by Wood and Dejeddour (1992), the field only became popular in the later half of the 1990s (e.g., Partidário and Clark, 2000; Thérivel and Partidário, 1996). Since then, it has been a veritable growth industry. The definition of SEA is much discussed in the literature with many shying away from a precise definition preferring instead to opt for some general description (see Partidário, 1996; 1999; Verheem and Tonk, 2000).

While SEA is seen as an important advance in the field of impact assessment, some doubt remains about the extent to which it provides anything different than the project level thinking that characterizes much of impact assessment, and about the extent to which it involves social as well as biophysical impacts. There is also terminological and methodological confusion. Boothroyd (1995, 100) considers that SEA "is limited by its: (1) positivism; (2) binding but unempowering formality; and (3) narrow scope. These limitations result from SEA being an extension of reductionist, linear, environmental IA." He also accuses it of failing to integrate across sectors, of only being applied to specific proposals, and of having a short impact horizon. SEA was spawned from within the technical EIA paradigm in complete ignorance of an already established field of policy assessment (see Boothroyd, 1995).

There are many lessons here for TBL. First, it is clear that there is a need for thinking at the policy level. Secondly, policy level thinking is different to project level thinking. Third, the lesson for Social TBL is how to ensure that adequate attention is given to the social and that TBL does not continue the marginalisation of social considerations. Finally, it is important not to reinvent the wheel.

Trend 2: Every other form of impact assessment

EIA and SIA emerged more or less simultaneously in the early 1970s. In addition to these methods, cost benefit analysis (CBA) was also a common dimension to establishing the feasibility of a project (Leistritz, 1995). It has a lengthy history dating to the 19th century. These three methods together could be considered as the triple bottom line.

In the early period of impact assessment, however, these three methods were already augmented by several other methods. Technology assessment, which with the closure of the USA Congressional Office of Technology Assessment in 1995 is a largely by-passed or superseded concept, was developed in the 1960s (see Porter, 1995). It was specifically focussed on new technology, and tended not to be prominent outside of the USA. Policy assessment (see Boothroyd, 1995) was a field that predated EIA and that continues to exist outside the impact assessment fold. Risk assessment (or risk analysis) was another field that predates EIA and that continues to exist independently of EIA, but is also well integrated with EIA (Carpenter, 1995). These fields represented the main fields of impact assessment that existed in the early 1990s.

Although EIA was meant to be an all-inclusive framework for consideration of environmental and social issues, it failed to adequately address the social, and therefore SIA developed. Likewise, while SIA was meant to be an all-inclusive framework to include all social considerations, the practice of SIA has been inadequate. While there is a strong attempt in SIA to re-establish the all-encompassing nature of SIA (see Vanclay, 1999; 2002a; 2003a), there is also the development of separate strands of various types of impact assessment to cater for narrow specific interests (see Table 1).

In many cases, "social impacts" became "socio-economic impacts" and the socio-economic impact assessment (SEIA) and the socio-economic impact statement (SEIS) would then only consider the economic impacts or demographic impacts. Therefore, some people claimed that "culture" was not included in "social", and therefore there was pressure to have cultural impact assessment. Over time, specialist interests led to the development of well over 100 different types of impact assessment (see Table 1). The list in Table 1 is unlikely to be complete as new terms are being invented constantly. Some of the terms are slight variations on other terms, while some refer to the affected group, others refer to the domain/sector of interest, while others refer to the type of activity.

Most of the types listed in Table 1 are minor, and are not meant to be taken as major forms of impact assessment. Sometimes they refer to a sector (mining, dams,

Table 1. Types of impact assessment.

(The number refers to the number of search results using the Google Search Engine with the term in inverted commas. All searches performed on 19 May 2003.)

(1)	Aboriginal impact assessment	7	(51)	family impact assessment	71
(2)	aesthetic impact assessment	43	(52)	fauna impact assessment	70
(3)	agriculture impact assessment	74	(53)	fiscal impact assessment	408
(4)	air quality impact assessment	947	(54)	fisheries (+fishery) impact assessment	231
(5)	analytical strategic env assessment	177			
(6)	archaeological impact assessment	906	(55)	fisheries resource impact assessment	23
(7)	Arctic impact assessment	18	(56)	flora impact assessment	6
(8)	beneficiary assessment	1,660	(57)	food (chain) impact assessment	4
(9)	benefit cost assessment	1,060	(58)	forestry impact assessment	14
(10)	benefit incidence analysis	547	(59)	gender assessment	1,200
(11)	biodiversity impact assessment	327	(60)	gender impact assessment	1,980
(12)	business impact assessment	1,990	(61)	GIS impact assessment	19
(13)	climate impact assessment	2,720	(62)	GIS-based impact assessment	23
(14)	climate change impact assessment	1,140	(63)	Greenhouse impact assessment	1
(15)	coastal impact assessment	55	(64)	habitat impact assessment	196
(16)	community impact assessment	1,550	(65)	health impact assessment	10,400
(17)	comprehensive impact assessment	996	(66)	health technology assessment	24,800
(18)	conflict impact assessment	1,240	(67)	heritage impact assessment	570
(19)	conflict risk and impact assessment	3	(68)	historical impact assessment	39
(20)	consumer impact assessment	88	(69)	historical resources impact assessment	137
(21)	corporate impact assessment	19	(70)	HIV/AIDS impact assessment (& HIV IA)	190
(22)	corporate privacy impact assessment	2			
(23)	cost benefit analysis	322,000	(71)	human impact assessment	229
(24)	cumulative impact assessment	2,120	(72)	human rights impact assessment	411
(25)	cumulative effects assessment	2,620	(73)	impact assessment	377,000
(26)	cultural heritage assessment	568	(74)	indigenous impact assessment	1
(27)	cultural heritage impact assessment	241	(75)	infrastructure impact assessment	145
(28)	cultural impact assessment	505	(76)	institutional impact assessment	65
(29)	dam impact assessment	94	(77)	integrated impact assessment	1,280
(30)	demographic impact assessment	35	(78)	landscape impact assessment	375
(31)	development impact assessment	2,070	(79)	legal impact assessment	33
(32)	disability impact assessment	21	(80)	leisure impact assessment	19
(33)	disaster assessment	5,490	(81)	lifecycle impact assessment	15
(34)	disaster impact assessment	136	(82)	mental health impact assessment	31
(35)	drainage impact assessment	227	(83)	microfinance impact assessment	244
(36)	ecological assessment	15,000	(84)	mining impact assessment	33
(37)	ecological impact assessment	1,260	(85)	navigation impact assessment	4
(38)	ecology impact assessment	347	(86)	noise impact assessment	1,840
(39)	economic impact assessment	6,510	(87)	odour impact assessment	158
(40)	enterprise development impact assessment	835	(88)	overflight impact assessment	16
			(89)	park(s) impact assessment	125
(41)	environmental health assessment	3,360	(90)	participatory impact assessment	444
(42)	environmental health impact assessment	895	(91)	participatory poverty assessment	3,980
			(92)	peace impact assessment	4
(43)	environment impact assessment	6,060	(93)	pest impact assessment	64
(44)	environmental impact assessment	171,000	(94)	pesticide impact assessment	3,910
(45)	environmental risk assessment	24,100	(95)	policy assessment	13,800
(46)	epidemiological impact assessment	4	(96)	policy impact assessment	945
(47)	equality impact assessment	2	(97)	political impact assessment	15
(48)	equity impact assessment	47	(98)	political risk impact assessment	1
(49)	erosion impact assessment	39	(99)	poverty assessment	13,500
(50)	facility impact assessment	15	(100)	poverty impact assessment	404

Table 1. (*Continued*)

(101) poverty and social impact analysis	1,230
(102) poverty and social impact assessment	601
(103) privacy impact assessment	1,820
(104) psycho-social impact assessment	6
(105) rapid environmental (impact) assessment	727
(106) rapid impact assessment	315
(107) regional impact assessment	536
(108) regulatory impact assessment	14,300
(109) rural impact assessment	29
(110) risk assessment	1,290,000
(111) risk impact assessment	351
(112) site impact assessment	160
(113) social analysis	49,100
(114) social assessment	15,600
(115) social capital assessment	353
(116) social impact analysis	4,020
(117) social impact assessment	13,600
(118) social risk assessment	209
(119) social soundness analysis/assessment	170
(120) socio-economic impact assessment	1,820
(121) strategic environment assessment	556
(122) strategic environmental assessment	14,700
(123) strategic impact assessment	735
(124) strategic integrated assessment	43
(125) sustainability assessment	5,980
(126) sustainability impact assessment	2,290
(127) system impact assessment	444

(128) technology assessment	291,000
(129) technology impact assessment	484
(130) trade impact assessment	511
(131) tourism impact assessment	215
(132) transboundary impact assessment	88
(133) transport impact assessment	684
(134) uranium impact assessment	298
(135) urban impact assessment	46
(136) vegetation impact assessment	22
(137) vibration impact assessment	267
(138) visual impact assessment	2,760
(139) water impact assessment	141
(140) welfare impact assessment	22
(141) wildlife impact assessment	362
(142) workforce impact assessment	5
environmental audit	50,000
environmental management systems	118,000
environmental monitoring	283,000
project appraisal	36,000
project evaluation	145,000
public participation	472,000
public consultation	254,000
public involvement	298,000
stakeholder analysis/assessment/mapping	15,000
social monitoring	5,120
triple bottom line	33,600

coastal development) and therefore are intended to be similar to general EIA/SIA applied in that situation. Others, however, are narrow areas of specific interest and are therefore a component of a higher form of impact assessment. Thus, for example, in addition to health impact assessment there is mental health impact assessment (and psycho-social impact assessment), disability impact assessment, HIV impact assessment, and epidemiological impact assessment.

Health impact assessment (HIA) is a legitimate field lying at the intersection of EIA and SIA. HIA is also a field that is becoming very well established and becoming mandated in the same way that EIA has been, even surpassing SIA in regulatory standing. HIA has been given official imprimatur by the World Health organisation and many other agencies. While some argue for culture to be the fourth leg of sustainability (e.g., Hawkes, 2001) (and therefore the quadruple bottom line), health professionals argue that health should be.

The mandated use of a form of assessment does give it a degree of legitimacy, but it does bring a number of problems. One of the problems for HIA is the perennial problem of definitions and demarcations — what is health? While the World Health organisation (1946) defines "health is a state of complete physical, mental and social well-being and not merely the absence of disease or infirmity", not all share this broad definition. In fact such a definition, especially when understood in the full context of WHO philosophy, is very much a social phenomenon. The Ottawa Charter for Health Promotion (WHO, 1986) advocates that "an individual or group must be able to identify and to realise aspirations, to satisfy needs, and to change or cope with the environment.... Health is a positive concept emphasizing social and personal resources, as well as physical capacities". Since there are clear links between the spiritual and cultural integrity of indigenous cultures and their physical, mental and social wellbeing, it is obvious that health is a multi-faceted, multi-disciplinary phenomenon (Rattle and Kwiatkowski, 2003). Health therefore is unambiguously a social rather than medical phenomenon.

The problem is that general understandings of "health" tend to be limited to physical concepts of health, and the medical profession has appropriated the field of health through their political and professional power (known in sociological terms as medical dominance).

Birley (1995, 153) considers that HIA is "a multi-disciplinary activity that cuts across traditional boundaries between public health, medical services, environmental and social science ... and that it is a necessary component of project planning in all countries and part of Environmental Impact Assessment (EIA)". By "health impacts" he refers to the "positive and negative changes in community health that are attributable to a development project". He argues that there are five categories of health impact: communicable diseases, non-communicable diseases, malnutrition, injuries, and mental disorder. In Birley's view, although there is an overlap with social impact assessment, there is quite a clear delineation in focus. The overlap is greater in that the five categories of health impact (experience) have social and institutional precursors. Risk-taking behaviour (which lead to injuries), health related behaviours such as smoking, drug use and substance abuse, violence and suicide are also of concern. HIV/AIDS and other sexually transmitted diseases are forms of communicable disease that have special significance.

Herein is the dilemma. If HIA is to accept a fully social definition of health as promoted by the WHO, it would be no different to SIA. But SIA would require the technical expertise of HIA practitioners to consider the health impacts of projects and policies. But HIA practitioners do not see themselves as subordinate to SIA, and now with official imprimatur and regulatory support, the field of HIA is growing rapidly.

Because of the overlap between health and social considerations, it has been proposed that perhaps there should be a new field called "human impact assessment" (HuIA) (STAKES, 2000; 2002). Such a concept would overcome the limited understanding that exists of what is "social", and the limited understanding of what is "health". It would also eliminate the problems caused by the overlap and the gap in things that are not considered. Developing a new field would also potentially overcome the project-based thinking that has constrained SIA. Human impact assessment could emerge from the beginning as a contribution for policy-making and decision making, applicable to policies, programs, plans and projects. Arguments about what should rightfully be included would be eliminated, with the new procedure defined to be broad and all-encompassing. It would be a manifestation of a new planning culture (STAKES, 2000). But it might also be argued that SIA is supposed to do all this already, and that inventing a new term is just contributing to the plethora of new concepts that do not fundamentally change practice or address fundamental issues.

The message for TBL here is that there are not three bottom lines, there are multiple bottom lines, and a language of Multiple Bottom Line may be more appropriate. However, discussion about a quadruple (or quintuple or whatever) bottom line is not beneficial. At the same time, it is important that it be understood that the terms economic, environmental (or ecological) and social all be understood broadly.

Trend 3: Integration

Partly because of the splintering in impact assessment that is occurring, another major trend is integration. While integration can be variously defined, with Scrase and Sheate (2002) identifying 14 meanings, there are three primary reasons for integration. The first is because everything is inherently interconnected. Some social impacts are caused by biophysical changes, and some biophysical impacts are caused by the social processes that occur because of social impacts (Slootweg *et al.*, 2001). A complete understanding of all the impacts can only be achieved by a comprehensive and integrated assessment. The second reason for integration is logistics. Agencies can not manage the multiple processes that are required when there are too many different forms of assessment that are required. An integrated assessment might also be more efficient (cost and time). Finally, since EIA has legal mandate, which most other forms of impact assessment do not, by piggy-backing on EIA (if not being truly integrated), these other issues can achieve greater consideration.

A perennial concern in discussions of integration/separation is whether a topic (say social issues or gender considerations) would be better served by being separate and potentially ignored (subordinate), or by being integrated or mainstreamed and potentially subordinated in terms of all the other things that need to be considered. There is no easy answer to this question. However, it is perhaps safe to conclude that neither strategy (being integrated or being separate) will work if there is not a commitment to considering the issue in question. Perhaps it is the commitment rather than the process that is important. Scrase and Sheate (2002, 291) argue that integration might not encourage sustainable development, rather it "may be merely promoting the prevailing economically driven paradigm".

The lessons for TBL are probably that while there should be an awareness of Multiple Bottom Lines, there should not be a process of trying to define what they are. Secondly, the commitment to the issues is more important than the process.

Trend 4: Broadening the definitions

The fourth significant trend that is apparent in impact assessment is a broadening of the definitions applying to impact assessment. Instead of impact assessment pertaining strictly to the prediction of impacts within a regulatory process, impact assessment is seen broadly as a philosophy about development and democracy (Vanclay, 2002a). This is evident in the way the definition of SIA has been codified by official documents. The first official statement (undertaken for the USA context) is thoroughly regulatory context driven, and focussed only on the prediction of impacts.

> We define social impact assessment in terms of efforts to assess or estimate, in advance, the social consequences that are likely to follow from specific policy actions (including programs and the adoption of new policies), and specific government actions (including buildings, large projects and leasing large tracts of land for resource extraction), particularly in the context of the U.S. National Environmental Policy Act of 1969 or NEPA (PL 91-190, 42 USC. 4371 et seq.). (Interorganizational Committee on Guidelines and Principles, 1994, 108)

This definition can be contrasted with the definition adopted as part of the International Principles for Social Impact Assessment.

> Social Impact Assessment includes the processes of analysing, monitoring and managing the intended and unintended social consequences, both positive and negative, of planned interventions (policies, programs, plans, projects) and any social change processes invoked by those interventions. Its primary purpose is to bring about a more sustainable and equitable biophysical and human environment. (Vanclay, 2003a, 6)

Vanclay (2002a; 2003b) considers that the original understanding of SIA is inherently limiting in that it presumes an adversarial regulatory system. It denies that assessment might be carried out internally by a corporation or by government, or even by a community itself independent of a regulatory process. The assessment of impacts of past developments is excluded. There is no role for the management, mitigation and monitoring of impacts, or for contribution of SIA participants in the redesign of the project or in decision-making about what constitutes an appropriate project.

SIA practitioners consider that SIA as a discipline is more than the prediction of negative impacts, it is philosophy about development and democracy which considers the pathologies of development (i.e., harmful impacts), goals of development (such as poverty alleviation), and processes of development (e.g., participation, capacity building) (Vanclay, 2002a). SIA needs to be process oriented, and to ensure that social issues are included in project design, planning and implementation as well as ensuring that development is acceptable, equitable and sustainable (Branch and Ross, 1997). The improvement of social wellbeing (and quality of life), with a particular focus on poverty reduction and an emphasis on democratisation, should be explicitly recognised as an objective of development projects and plans, and as such should be a performance indicator considered in any form of impact assessment.

SIA is an umbrella or overarching framework that encompasses all matters that may impinge on humans. SIA is not limited to a narrow or restrictive understanding of the concept "social". Vanclay (2002b), for example, lists some 80-odd considerations, but strongly resists the identification of variables or indicators as this is antithetical to the way of thinking about social processes. A paradox will befall TBL — if it is to be true to its broadest conceptualisation as a way of thinking, it must not succumb to the development of indicators.

Trend 5: Environmental auditing and environmental management systems

The final significant trend is the mainstreaming of impact assessment considerations through environmental auditing and/or environmental management systems (EMS). EMS and environmental auditing are effectively the same thing (see Buckley, 1995). EMS "is a generic term used to describe any systematic approach used by an enterprise or organisation to manage its impacts on the environment" (EMS Working Group, 2001, 6). EMS, although a voluntary code of conduct or management framework, has official endorsement in many countries, and has a degree of recognition because of an International organisation for Standardisation standard ISO 14001 which can provide an external certification. Consumer and citizen demand for EMS accreditation is promulgating the adoption of EMS by business. EMS plans typically focus on environmental impacts and legal responsibilities. The exact content is not specified as this is to be determined by each individual business. They are not meant to be about the achievement of a static goal, rather they are meant to encourage a process of continuous improvement, with goals changing to adapt to differing circumstances and local issues. Thus, potentially, EMS frameworks could include social as well as biophysical environmental issues. The more that sustainability considerations are analysed, the more it becomes obvious that for EMS to be a true sustainability process, a very wide range of issues need to be included. "Best practice EMS, therefore, calls for companies to integrate public participation and strategic environmental thinking into the corporate culture" (van der Vorst *et al.*, 1999, 9). Some leading companies are even starting to include corporate social responsibility (CSR) concerns in their EMS plans, or moving from EMS to a CSR framework completely. In general, however, the practice of EMS has failed tending to remain at a limited range of biophysical concerns. In theory, EMS is rather similar to TBL, and it could be said that with EMS, TBL is unnecessary except as a concept to remind everyone, that the social issues also need to be considered and not just the biophysical environmental and economic ones.

Failings / Limitations / Barriers of Social Impact Assessment

While offering much as an ideal, SIA has failed in practice. SIA failed to obtain sufficient legal mandate so it is rarely done, and when it is done, it is rarely done well. Because of being done badly, too often it is seen as legitimating bad development rather than being a path to good development. The potential role of SIA is inadequately understood, and many groups including academics, government agencies and the general public are frequently completely ignorant of SIA. Even within EIA, the potential contribution of SIA has not been adequately considered. SIA has been marginalised and given the minuscule proportion of project funding. Social considerations have rarely been treated seriously. If this is the experience of SIA after 30 years, why will TBL be more successful?

Many limitations or problems with SIA can be articulated (Freudenburg and Keating, 1982; Burdge and Vanclay, 1995; Dale *et al.*, 1997; Vanclay, 1999). The essence of all these issues is that SIA is not, nor can be, nor should be, a decision algorithm. Nevertheless, too many technocrats expect SIA to provide definitive answers. Unlike economics, where cost-benefit analysis, contingent valuation and other methods return dollar values providing simple decisions, SIA can not do this. Social impacts cannot be precisely defined, and they can not be quantitatively valued. They are not consistent across the community. They impact on individuals differentially. All SIA can do is to indicate that some sections of the population will likely experience certain impacts, while other sections will likely experience certain other impacts. A decision to proceed, or not to proceed, cannot be based on the blind application of impact assessment techniques. The decision remains political because decision-makers have to weigh the impacts and interests of the various groups affected or involved in any proposal being considered. This will not be different for TBL. In fact, insisting on a literal social bottom line is a further extension of the technocratic mentality that has dogged SIA.

The great potential of SIA, therefore, is not in decision-making, but in process management. SIA should be seen as a process, not as a once-off report. For SIA to be truly effective in its role of minimising impacts and maximising benefits through the development of mitigation mechanisms, and in facilitating public participation, SIA has to be considered as a process of management of change. The benefits of SIA being seen as a process is that in construction of new development projects, public participation can contribute through local knowledge to development decisions, siting decisions and so on. Effective public participation is also one way of alleviating fear and feelings of unfairness. TBL is seen as a decision algorithm and therefore fails to deal with the process issues.

Thirty years of existence as a discipline reveals that there are five major barriers confronting SIA. These barriers will also affect TBL (adapted from Burdge and Vanclay, 1995).

(i) There are issues in the social sciences in that they do not have an applied tradition, are not practical, and they are not used to providing proactive recommendations. Worse, there is a theoretical snobbery and an ostracisation of those social scientists who dabble in this area. As a result, SIA is not widely taught nor practiced. People tend to enter the field from the technical sciences rather than from the social sciences.

(ii) There are difficulties in applying the social sciences to SIA, particularly because consideration of social issues is descriptive and discursive not predictive, qualitative not quantitative, and they tend to involve values, with different value-weightings being applied by different groups, and which may change over time.

(iii) There are difficulties with the SIA process itself, particularly in terms of the paucity of quality studies, the lack of effective techniques, tools and models, and the quality of available data. There may be a shortage of skilled SIA professionals and even social planners particularly in the employment of all levels of government.

(iv) There are problems with the procedures applying to SIA, particularly because the SIA discipline has not instigated a formal registration system, and regulatory agencies have not demanded that SIAs be done by appropriately qualified consultants. With no formal review process, no evaluation process, and with no generally agreed standards for SIA, many SIAs have been inadequate. Dale *et al.* (1997) complain that administrative structures have not facilitated the use of SIA.

(v) Finally, there exists an 'asocietal mentality' or disciplinary prejudice or bias amongst various groups of people that leads to a perception by developers, regulatory agencies, and sometimes by environmental professionals, that social issues are unimportant. This has led to a lack of commitment to SIA. Freudenburg and Keating (1982, 75) report that one community resident frustrated with the lack of consideration given to social impacts stated that "Sometimes I think they'd pay more attention to us if we grew antlers". Similar sentiments have been expressed by a Dutch resident who considered that they "would be better off if I was a rare reptile or a dead Roman in the old castle" (Stolp, 2003, 255).

In addition to the above barriers, Vanclay (1999) addresses at length a number of internal fundamental unresolvable issues in SIA.

(i) Who have legitimate interests in the community? How is the "affected community" to be defined and identified?
(ii) What should be the role of community participation in the SIA?
(iii) What is the role of compensation in SIA?
(iv) What impacts are to be considered?
(v) How should impacts be weighted?
(vi) Who judges?

After 30 years of experience, SIA has established that these are difficult political questions. TBL will also be plagued with these issues.

TBL Compared with Various Other Approaches

The main argument of this paper is that TBL is a fad, introduced and promoted by people ignorant of the field of impact assessment and which offers nothing in addition to other approaches that are already available. Table 2 provides a comparison of a range of leading approaches with TBL.

TBL is focused at the level of an organisation (company, government department or NGO). In that respect it differs from EIA, SIA and SEA, but not from EMS and environmental auditing. Because of the failure of the proponents of TBL to consider the field of impact assessment, the learning in the field of impact assessment about what impacts are, and how to identify, define and measure them, have not been considered. Consequently, what are offered as the social TBL indicators, and quite possibly the economic and environmental ones as well, are inadequate.

Table 2. Comparison of various approaches.

	TBL	EIA	SIA	SEA	EMS
When established	ca 2000	ca 1970	ca 1973	ca 1995	ca 1990
Intended scope	Social, environmental and economic considerations usually in relation to organisational achievements	Environmental impacts of projects (and arguably policy, plans and programmes)	Analysing, monitoring and managing the social consequences of planned interventions (projects, policies, plans and programmes)	Environmental impacts of policy, plans and programmes	Environmental and potentially social issues as decided by the organisation
Coverage of social in theory	Social is meant to be one of three equal dimensions	Varies in intention — some jurisdictions require full treatment of social; others include only biophysical	Should cover all social issues broadly defined (anything affecting a community or individual)	Varies in intention	Social can be included if this is established as a goal by the organisation
Coverage of social in actual practice	Inadequate	When required, it is inadequate in practice	Range of "social" usually too limited	Inadequate	Inadequate
Data expectations	Predefined, discrete, quantitative indicators	Primarily quantitative indicators relevant to the activity as determined by a scoping process	Qualitative and quantitative indicators relevant to the activity as determined by a scoping process	Qualitative and quantitative indicators relevant to the activity, usually determined by experts	Qualitative and quantitative indicators relevant to the activity as determined by the organisation
Technocratic or participatory	Technocratic	Should have a participatory dimension, but tends to be technocratic	Should be participatory	Should be participatory, but tends to be technocratic	Usually participatory
Established tradition	No	Yes	Yes	Developing	Developing
Theoretical basis	No	Yes	Yes	Arguably yes	No
Professional association	No	Yes	Yes	Yes	Not directly

284   F. Vanclay

Conclusion: What Can TBL Learn from IA?

A number of lessons and key points can be drawn from this analysis. The most important of these is that while TBL might be a new buzzword and a current fad, it is not a new concept and is substantially similar to the field of impact assessment. TBL proponents could learn a lot from the literature on impact assessment.

The second major point is that TBL is meant to be a heuristic. The concept of expanding the bottom line was meant to encourage corporations to think beyond pure profit motive and to consider the environmental and social implications of their activities. TBL was meant to be a philosophy about corporate social responsibility, not a decision algorithm. This way of thinking should not degenerate into a simple set of indicators. A push to a language of accounting or economics is likely to ignore many of the truly social issues. The experience in SIA has shown that there needs to be a focus on the things that count, not the things that can be counted. Andrew Campbell's (2004) concept of a triple helix, which interlocks and interconnects the interactions of landscapes, lifestyles and livelihoods may be a better metaphor than the triple bottom line.

The experience in impact assessment has shown that there will be a degree of contestation over what is included and what the three lines of TBL actually refer to. While TBL should resist becoming a quadruple or quintuple bottom line, a terminology of 'multiple bottom line' may be more appropriate.

Acknowledgments

Prof Vanclay's position is partly funded by the Grains Research and Development Corporation (www.grdc.com.au). This paper is a revised version of conference presentations to (1) The Social Dimensions of the Triple Bottom Line in Rural Australia workshop (26 February 2003) Canberra: Bureau of Rural Sciences; and (2) the 2003 International Association for Impact Assessment annual conference held in Marrakech, Morocco, June 2003.

References

Australia (1999). *Environmental Protection and Biodiversity Conservation Act 1999* (No 91, 1999).
Australia (2000). *Gene Technology Act 2000* (No 169, 2000).
Australia (2000). *Gene Technology Bill 2000 Explanatory Memorandum.*
Barrow, C (2000). *Social Impact Assessment.* London: Arnold.
Becker, H (1997). *Social Impact Assessment.* London: UCL Press.

Becker, H and F Vanclay (eds.) (2003). *The International Handbook of Social Impact Assessment: Conceptual and Methodological Advances*. Cheltenham: Edward Elgar.

Birley, M (1995). Health impact assessment. In *Environmental and Social Impact Assessment*, F Vanclay and D Bronstein (eds.), pp. 153–170. Chichester: Wiley.

Boothroyd, P (1995). Policy assessment. In *Environmental and Social Impact Assessment*, F Vanclay and D Bronstein (eds.), pp. 83–126. Chichester: Wiley.

BP Australia (2001). *Triple Bottom Line Report*. Melbourne: BP Australia.

Branch, K et al. (1984). *Guide to Social Assessment: A Framework for Assessing Social Change*. Boulder, Co: Westview Press.

Branch, K and H Ross (1997). The evolution of Social Impact Assessment: Conceptual models and scope. Paper presented to the annual meeting of the International Association for Impact Assessment, New Orleans.

Buckley, R (1995). Environmental auditing. In *Environmental and Social Impact Assessment*, F Vanclay and D Bronstein (eds.), pp. 283–301. Chichester: Wiley.

Burdge, R (1998). *A Conceptual Approach to Social Impact Assessment* (rev edn). Middleton: Social Ecology Press.

Burdge, R (1999). *A Community Guide to Social Impact Assessment* (rev edn). Middleton: Social Ecology Press.

Burdge, RJ and F Vanclay (1995). Social impact assessment. In *Environmental and Social Impact Assessment*, F Vanclay and D Bronstein (eds.), pp. 31–66. Chichester: Wiley.

Campbell, A (2004). Landscapes, lifestyles and livelihoods. Paper presented to the National Extension Policy Forum, Sydney, 21 July 2004.

Carpenter, R (1995). Risk assessment. In *Environmental and Social Impact Assessment*, F Vanclay and D Bronstein (eds.), pp. 193–219. Chichester: Wiley.

Dale, A, P Chapman and M McDonald (1997). Social impact assessment in Queensland: Why practice lags behind legislative opportunity. *Impact Assessment*, 15(2), 159–179.

Donnelly, A, B Dalal-Clayton and R Hughes (eds.) (1998). *A Directory of Impact Assessment Guidelines*, 2nd edn. London: International Institute for Environment and Development.

Elkington, J (1997). *Cannibals with Forks: The Triple Bottom Line of 21st Century Business*. Oxford: Capstone.

Environmental Management Systems Working Group (2001). *Towards a National Framework for the Development of Environmental Management Systems in Agriculture: A Public Discussion Paper Prepared by the Environmental Management Systems Working Group*. Canberra: Natural Resource Management Standing Committee Discussion Paper.

Freudenburg, W and K Keating (1982). Increasing the impact of sociology on social impact assessment. *The American Sociologist*, 17, 71–80.

Goodland, R and H Daly (1995). Environmental sustainability. In *Environmental and Social Impact Assessment*, F Vanclay and D Bronstein (eds.), pp. 303–322. Chichester: Wiley.

Google Search Engine (2003). (on-line resource) http://www.google.com. [accessed 19 May 2003].

Harvey, N (1998). *Environmental Impact Assessment: Procedures, Practice and Prospects in Australia*. Melbourne: Oxford University Press.

Hawkes, J (2001). *The Fourth Pillar of Sustainability: Culture's Essential Role in Public Planning*. Melbourne: Cultural Development Network.

Holliday, CO, S Schmidheiny and P Watts (2002). *Walking the Talk: The Business Case for Sustainable Development*. Sheffield: Greenleaf.

IAIA (2003). International Association for Impact Assessment home page 2003. http://www.iaia.org [accessed 3 April 2003].

[US] Interorganizational Committee on Guidelines and Principles for Social Impact Assessment (1994). Guidelines and principles for social impact assessment. *Impact Assessment*, 12(2), 107–152.

Lane, M, A Dale and N Taylor (eds.) (2001). *Social Assessment in Natural Resource Management Institutions*. Melbourne: CSIRO Publishing.

Leistritz, FL (1995). Economic and fiscal impact assessment. In *Environmental and Social Impact Assessment*, F Vanclay and D. Bronstein (eds.), pp. 129–139. Chichester: Wiley.

Ortolano, L and A Shepherd (1995). Environmental impact assessment. In *Environmental and Social Impact Assessment*, F Vanclay and D. Bronstein (eds.), pp. 3–30. Chichester: Wiley.

Partidário, M (1996). Strategic environmental assessment: Key issues emerging from recent practice. *Environmental Impact Assessment Review*, 16(1), 31-55.

Partidário, M (1999). Strategic environmental assessment: Principles and potential. In *Handbook of Environmental Impact Assessment*, J Petts (ed.), pp. 12–32. London: Blackwell Science.

Partidário, M (2000). Elements of an SEA framework: Improving the added-value of SEA. *Environmental Impact Assessment Review*, 20(6), 647–663.

Partidário, M and R Clark (eds.) (2000). *Perspectives on Strategic Environmental Assessment*. Boca Raton, Fl: CRC-Lewis.

Porter, A (1995). Technology assessment. In *Environmental and Social Impact Assessment*, F Vanclay and D Bronstein (eds.), pp. 67–81. Chichester: Wiley.

Rattle, R and R Kwiatkowski (2003). Integrating Health and Social Impact Assessment. In *International Handbook of Social Impact Assessment*, H Becker and F Vanclay (eds.), pp. 92–107. Cheltenham: Edward Elgar.

Sarre, R and G Treuren (2001). The triple bottom line: Balancing social, environmental and financial outcomes in business (paper prepared for the South Australian Business Vision 2010) (on-line resource) http://business.unisa.edu.au/cae/tbl/tbldownloadables/sabv2010fin.rtf [accessed 3 April 2003].

Scrase, JI and WR Sheate (2002). Integration and integrated approaches to assessment: What do they mean for the environment. *Journal of Environmental Policy and Planning*, 4, 275–294.

Slootweg, R, F Vanclay and M van Schooten (2001). Function evaluation as a framework for the integration of social and environmental impact assessment. *Impact Assessment and Project Appraisal*, 19(1), 19–28.

Stolp, A (2003). Citizen values assessment. In *International Handbook of Social Impact Assessment*, H Becker and F Vanclay (eds.), pp. 231–257. Cheltenham: Edward Elgar.

STAKES (2000). *Human Impact Assessment Ideacard 4/00*. Helsinki: National Research and Development Centre for Welfare and Health.

STAKES (2002). Human impact assessment (on-line resource) http://www.stakes.fi/sva/huia/ [accessed 3 April 2003].

SustainAbility (2003). The triple bottom line (on-line resource) http://www.sustainability.com/philosophy/triple-bottom/tbl-intro.asp [accessed 3 April 2003].

Taylor, CN, CH Bryan and CG Goodrich (1995). *Social Assessment: Theory, Process and Techniques*, 2nd edn. Christchurch: Taylor Baines and Associates.

Thérivel, R and M Partidário (eds.) (1996). *The Practice of Strategic Environmental Assessment*. London: Earthscan.

Vanclay, F (1998). Inclusion of social data in the National Land and Water Resources Audit. *Rural Society*, 8(1), 39–48.

Vanclay, F (1999). Social Impact Assessment, In *Handbook of Environmental Impact Assessment*, Vol 1, J Petts (ed.), pp. 301–326. Oxford: Blackwell Science.

Vanclay, F (2002a). Social impact assessment. In *Responding to Global Environmental Change*, M Tolba (ed.), pp. 387–393. Chichester: Wiley.

Vanclay, F (2002b). Conceptualising social impacts. *Environmental Impact Assessment Review*, 22(3), 183–211.

Vanclay, F (2003a). International principles for social impact assessment. *Impact Assessment and Project Appraisal*, 21(1), 5–11.

Vanclay, F (2003b). Conceptual and methodological advances in social impact assessment. In *International Handbook of Social Impact Assessment*, H Becker and F Vanclay (eds.), pp. 1–10. Cheltenham: Edward Elgar.

Vanclay, F and D Bronstein (1995). Editors' Preface: The state of the art of Impact Assessment. In *Environmental and Social Impact Assessment*, F Vanclay and D Bronstein (eds.), pp. xi–xiii. Chichester: Wiley.

Vanclay, F and M Nauta (2003). *Social Impact Assessment Bibliography* (on-line resource) http://www.iaia.org/Non_Members/SIA%20Database/SIA_interface.asp [accessed 13 July 2004].

Vandenberg, M (2002). TBL *Victoria Scoping Study: How Victorian Businesses, Governments and Non-government Organisations are Taking the Journey towards the Triple Bottom Line*. Report for the Victorian State Government, Department of Premier and Cabinet, Melbourne: Encompass. (on-line resource) http://www.ethyka.com/tbl/resources/TBL%20Scoping%20Study.pdf [accessed 3 April 2003].

van der Vorst, R, A Grafe-Buckens and WR Sheate (1999). A systemic framework for environmental decision making. *Journal of Environmental Assessment Policy and Management*, 1(1), 1–26.

Verheem, R and J Tonk (2000). Strategic environmental assessment: One concept, multiple forms. *Impact Assessment and Project Appraisal*, 18(3), 177–182.

Wood, C and M Dejeddour (1992). Strategic environmental assessment: EA of policies, plans and programmes. *Impact Assessment Bulletin*, 10(1), 3–23.

288   F. Vanclay

World Commission on Environment and Development (1987). *Our Common Future* (Australian edition). Melbourne: Oxford University Press.

World Health Organization (1946). Preamble to the Constitution of the World Health Organization as adopted by the International Health Conference, New York, 19–22 June, 1946; signed on 22 July 1946 by the representatives of 61 States (Official Records of the World Health Organization, no. 2, p. 100) and entered into force on 7 April 1948. http://www.who.int/about/definition/en/ [accessed 3 April 2003].

World Health Organization (1986). Ottawa Charter for Health Promotion (on-line resource) http://www.who.int/hpr/archive/docs/ottawa.html [accessed 3 April 2003].

[5]

The potential application of social impact assessment in integrated coastal zone management

Frank Vanclay*

Department of Cultural Geography, Faculty of Spatial Sciences, University of Groningen, PO Box 800, 9700AV Groningen, The Netherlands

ARTICLE INFO

Article history:
Available online 23 May 2012

ABSTRACT

Integrated coastal zone management (ICZM) would be significantly enhanced if there was greater connection to the field of social impact assessment (SIA). SIA is the process of managing the social issues of planned interventions (projects, policies, plans, and programs). SIA can also be used to consider the effects of gradual landscape change. Key concepts in SIA that are applicable to ICZM include: sense of place and place attachment, islandness, cumulative effects, social carrying capacity, not in my backyard (NIMBY) responses, resilience and vulnerability, corporate social responsibility, social legitimacy, social license to operate, seachange communities and second home ownership. SIA incorporates stakeholder analysis, public participation and community engagement not only to predict the impacts of planned interventions or policy changes, but also to develop effective adaptive management and enhancement strategies. The paper presents a general case outlining the potential use of SIA in ICZM, with reference to the Wadden Sea Region where applicable. Important lessons (aphorisms, frankisms) from SIA are highlighted.

© 2012 Elsevier Ltd. All rights reserved.

1. Introduction: place attachment in significant regions

Landscapes, including specific regions and places such as the Wadden Sea Region of northwest Europe, are important social constructions in the sense of being created, contrived and imagined in social ways (Greider and Garkovich, 1994; Vanclay, 2008). The people who live within them often have strong attachments to their region and it may well form part of their personal identity (either explicitly or implicitly). Their livelihoods may depend on the landscape and its associated habitats in various ways, for example, people who are dependent on fishing. It should be noted that significant landscapes (however they are defined) attract tourists (daytrippers and holidaymakers) and when this becomes repeat or return visitation, these people can also develop a strong attachment to those places. Significant places also attract second home owners ('weekenders', summer houses) who also can have strong place attachment, which is often stronger than that of permanent residents (Stedman, 2006; Halfacree, 2012). Islands can be particularly significant places to the people who identify with them (Baldacchino, 2004, 2007; Clark, 2004; Conkling, 2007; Hay, 2006; Stratford, 2008). Finally, when landscapes and/or regions are significant biodiversity reserves, world heritage sites or have significant cultural heritage values, or are highly socially valued for some other characteristic, many individuals may develop strong custodianship or stewardship notions over them, albeit vicarious, and feel they are a legitimate stakeholder in decision making about a specific location or landscape, even if they don't live there and sometimes even if they have never actually been there. These people will expect to be included in decision making, and will scrutinise any decisions and the implementation of plans for acceptability from their personal perspectives. Thus, there are potentially a very large number of stakeholders who need to be considered when decisions are being made about regions, landscapes and specific places (Cocklin et al., 1998; Conrad et al., 2011; Selman, 2004; van der Aa et al., 2004).

Coastal zone management has been much criticised for its failure to address a range of issues (Christie, 2005), specifically for its perceived 'democratic deficit', that is its failure to enable or facilitate community engagement sufficiently (Shipman and Stojanovic, 2007). Curiously, the counter argument has also been made, that integrated coastal zone management (ICZM) "has focused largely on socioeconomic aspects and has not always incorporated scientific information effectively" (Cheong, 2008: p.1090). However, the view that the lack of good governance is the most important issue in ICZM, rather than the lack of good science, is widely held (Olsen et al., 1997; Turner, 2000).

The argument of this paper is that the management of the Wadden Sea Region in particular, and of all coastal regions and any

* Tel.: +31 631179966.
E-mail address: frank.vanclay@rug.nl.

0964-5691/$ – see front matter © 2012 Elsevier Ltd. All rights reserved.
doi:10.1016/j.ocecoaman.2012.05.016

region or place in general, would be greatly improved by utilising the approach and understandings of the field of social impact assessment (SIA). SIA is the process of managing the social issues associated with development (Vanclay, 2003, 2004; Esteves and Vanclay, 2009). Although typically undertaken in the context of specific projects (Vanclay and Esteves, 2011; Esteves et al., 2012), SIA can also be utilised in a wider range of situations, including incremental landscape change (Schirmer, 2011). The understandings, experiences, philosophy and methods of SIA would greatly enhance democratic decision making and planning processes, and would do much to address the many criticisms of integrated coastal zone management (Voyer et al., 2012).

2. Current best practice in social impact assessment

Social impact assessment (SIA) is typically defined as including "the processes of analysing, monitoring and managing the intended and unintended social consequences, both positive and negative, of planned interventions ... and of any social change processes invoked by those interventions. Its primary purpose is to bring about a more sustainable and equitable biophysical and human environment" (Vanclay, 2003: p.6).

'Planned interventions' refers to:

- specific projects such as the construction, installation, implementation and operation of a new offshore gas platform or windfarm, the hosting of an event or mega-event such as a major festival, or the removal/dismantling of a specific feature from the landscape;
- policies such as the planned implementation of new biodiversity policy or habitat directive;
- plans such as to increase tourism in a region; and
- programs (i.e. collections of various change actions) which might be the implementation of a policy or plan, and would likely involve a series of projects. An example might be a series of management actions relating to Natura-2000 (the Birds and Habitats Directive) which could involve: changing the zoning of and access to a number of locations; the changing of fishing and shooting provisions; the closure of various walkways and roads and the corresponding opening-up or expansion of others; and the relocation of various facilities or installations.

Although typically undertaken in a prospective (ex-ante) setting so that it can contribute to decision making and planning, SIA is also retrospective (ex-post) studying past events to build a knowledge base from which to make predictions about current or future issues. SIA is similar to environmental impact assessment (EIA), except that SIA emphasises the impacts on humans and communities, and is more concerned with the management of the impacts rather than just their prediction. SIA has an important role in the project approval process, but is of greater use when it is involved in the planning and design stages considering issues such as how to mitigate, monitor and manage the impacts likely to be experienced. Recent developments have focussed on ensuring that local communities benefit from development activities (Esteves and Vanclay, 2009; João et al., 2011; Vanclay and Esteves, 2011; Esteves et al., 2012).

The four p's (projects, policies, plans and programs) are not mutually exclusive and have many similarities with each other. They also interact in that a policy or plan may lead to projects, and a program comprises a series of projects. They all start as a concept and progress through various iterations before becoming a formal proposal. If approved and if they proceed, they then progress through an implementation phase, become established and operational, and may eventually lapse or be decommissioned. Potentially there are social and environmental impacts at each stage, although the impacts will likely vary between the different stages. Formal impact assessment can and arguably should be undertaken at all stages, or preferably an integrated and holistic impact assessment process should be undertaken that considers the full life of the project, policy, plan or program.

Although SIA has primarily developed in the context of planned interventions and particularly the project context, the approach taken can also be used to consider the social impacts of events like disasters (storms, floods, major fires, drought, earthquakes, tsunamis, volcanic eruptions), both in terms of understanding the experience of the event, but more importantly in planning and organizing recovery programs and in pre-disaster preparation (Cottrell and King, 2011; ProVention Consortium, 2007). SIA can also be applied to the consideration of landuse and landscape change (Schirmer, 2011).

SIA is primarily the process of managing the social issues. It is a multi-faceted activity that deals with all stakeholders. It assists communities in visioning the future, in thinking about appropriate development, and in coping with change. It assists regulatory agencies in providing information to be used in the assessment of proposals, the determination of conditionalities and the appropriateness of compensatory arrangements. It also works with proponents (both private sector and government) in engaging with stakeholders, in considering the social issues in planning; in conceiving and designing mitigation measures to reduce harm, and in developing enhancement actions. It potentially can be used to coordinate the collection and utilisation of the local knowledge of nearby communities in project development.

The tasks of SIA essentially involve (adapted from Vanclay and Esteves (2011)):

- creating participatory processes and a deliberative space to facilitate community discussions about desired futures, the acceptability of likely negative impacts and proposed benefits, and community input into the SIA process, so that they can come to a negotiated agreement with a proponent — preferably on the basis of the emerging legal principle of 'free, prior and informed consent' (FPIC);
- gaining a good understanding of the communities and stakeholders likely to be affected by the policy, program, plan or project (i.e. profiling) including a thorough stakeholder analysis to understand the differing needs and interests of the various sections of those communities;
- identifying the needs and aspirations of the various communities;
- scoping the key social issues (the significant negative impacts as well as the opportunities for creating benefits);
- identifying key indicators and collecting baseline data;
- forecasting the social changes that may result from the policy, program, plan or project and the impacts these are likely to have on different groups of people;
- establishing the significance of the predicted changes, and determining how the various affected groups and communities will likely respond to them;
- identifying ways of mitigating potential negative impacts and maximising positive opportunities;
- developing a monitoring plan to track implementation, variations from mitigation actions, and unanticipated social changes, especially negative impacts;
- facilitating an agreement making process between the communities and the proponent ensuring that FPIC principles are observed and that human rights are respected and that leads to the drafting of an Impact and Benefit Agreement (IBA);
- assisting the proponent in the drafting of a Social Impact Management Plan (SIMP) that operationalizes all benefits,

mitigation measures, monitoring arrangements and governance arrangements that were agreed to in the IBA, as well as plans for dealing with any ongoing unanticipated issues as they arise;
- putting processes in place to enable proponents, regulatory authorities and civil society stakeholders to implement arrangements implied in the SIMP and IBA and to develop their own corresponding management action plans, establish respective roles and responsibilities throughout the implementation of action plans, and maintain an ongoing role in monitoring.

It is important to realize that SIA is more than a technique or a tool, it is a field of research and practice, a body of scholars and practitioners, a discourse, and a community of practice that has existed since the early 1970s (Vanclay, 2003). Like all such fields, it has established theoretical understandings and methodologies, case study experience, and shared norms and values. There is a professional association to which SIA practitioners belong, the International Association for Impact Assessment (www.iaia.org); journals in which to publish (particularly *Impact Assessment and Project Appraisal* and *Environmental Impact Assessment Review*); and various other networking resources, such as the SIAhub, www.socialimpactassessment.com. The core literature that defines the field of SIA has been identified by the International Association for Impact Assessment in its Key Citations series (IAIA, 2009). A landmark document that demarcates the field is the "International Principles for Social Impact Assessment" (Vanclay, 2003, 2006).

3. The potential application of social impact assessment to coastal zone management and the Wadden sea region

In many respects, especially from a social perspective, there is nothing fundamentally different about coastal zones to any other location when it comes to the processes of assessment and management of the social issues associated with projects, policies, plans and programs. SIA is equally relevant and valuable in coastal zones as elsewhere. Perhaps there are some unique social issues to consider in coastal zones, and especially on islands (Baldacchino, 2004, 2007), but the procedures and methodologies are fundamentally the same.

A project such as the development of a new hotel at an island location needs to be assessed in terms of the impacts of the physical structure itself, the way the facility will be operated (who its patrons will be and how they behave), as well as the manner in which it will be constructed. Typical planning questions such as whether the building is consistent with the identity of the local community should be considered. The question of whether the project is compatible with the social carrying capacity of the island community also needs to be considered. An important consideration therefore is the issue of cumulative impacts (Franks et al., 2011). Even if the one particular hotel being considered is acceptable (when considered on its own), what does this mean for the aggregate number of tourists and the incremental effect of many hotels? The impacts will be different if the new hotel is replacing an existing structure, or whether the construction of the hotel is intending to service an anticipated expansion in the number of tourists. If that is the case, many questions need to be considered such as the adequacy of a whole range of services to cope with the increased number of visitors. The key social question in this context is whether expansion of tourism is consistent with the identity of the local community and with their vision of the future (Conway et al., 2008).

The effects of new policies, plans and programs can also be considered by SIA. Effective ICZM is likely to lead to a range of decisions including the rezoning of areas of land to protect valuable habitats. This is likely to entail fencing those areas off, erecting signage, changing access routes (pedestrian, cycle and vehicle). It might involve remedial works such as the removal of paths and the removal of invasive weeds. Where there has been erosion, it could involve revegetation activities. The effect of these activities could lead to the exclusion of some people from their favourite places, or at least from places to which they had some sort of connection. If such decisions are imposed, in other words have no legitimacy with those who are affected, there is likely to be resistance, resentment and potentially noncompliance. Gaining social legitimacy — or in other discourses, a "social license to operate" (see Gunningham et al. (2004)) — is therefore important for the success of the goals of ICZM. This can be achieved through the use of effective community engagement methods (Agrawal and Gibson, 1999; Cliquet et al., 2010; Lane et al., 2007; Vanclay et al., 2004). In fact, the listing of the Wadden Sea Region on the World Heritage Register was amidst considerable opposition from local peoples — who would normally have been expected to support such a listing. The primary reasons for this resistance were "a perceived loss of autonomy and a lack of clarity about the possible impact of nomination" (van der Aa et al., 2004: 301). Other marine parks around the world have also been resisted by local communities (Cocklin et al., 1998).

Although SIA has primarily been applied in the project setting, it is increasingly being realised that the methods, approaches and understandings of SIA can be applied in a range of other areas including to incremental landscape change (Schirmer, 2011). Landscape change can often be a planned intervention, or at least can be a known (predicted) consequence that will follow from the implementation of regional plans and policies, or the implementation of a particular project. Although landscape change is often considered to be insidious, frequently it can also be reasonably predicted in situations where there is a planning vacuum, especially when there is an understanding of the basic geographical and social change processes that are taking place (Slootweg et al., 2001; Vanclay, 2002). Thus, SIA can be applied in both retrospective and prospective forms to consider the social experience of landscape change where there is a will that it be done. Where it is done, the findings from SIA can be used to make better planning decisions, to implement mitigation, to develop enhancement strategies, and to assist communities to cope with change.

Into the near future there are numerous foreseeable projects, policies, plans and incremental changes that are likely to occur and/or need to be considered in the Wadden Sea Region, including: deepening (dredging) the shipping lanes and an increasing amount of shipping traffic, the construction of new gas platforms, the establishment of offshore and onshore windfarms, industrial developments of various kinds, proposals for waste disposal facilities, modifications to dykes and other storm protection mechanisms, land drainage activities, agricultural and aquacultural developments, increasing numbers and types of tourism potentially above social carrying capacity, an increasing number and size of festivals and concerts, increasing numbers of amenity migration residents (newcomers, seachange communities), a changing demographic composition of settlements, changing dependency ratios, changing lifestyle and livelihood bases, expansion of protected areas for biodiversity reasons, and various contestations over landuse including between commercial/industrial use, residential use, recreation use, habitat protection, and the protection of new and old archaeological finds and heritage. All of these issues potentially create a degree of immediate nuisance and many have associated dangers and risk of accidents which also need to be considered. All will benefit from the application of SIA thinking, experience, understandings and methodologies.

4. Some important lessons from the SIA field

A number of important lessons that have relevance to ICZM can be drawn from the SIA field are described below. These aphorisms have been developed over many years of personal reflection on the theory and practice of SIA, and can be colloquially regarded as 'frankisms' (i.e. adages, epigrams, maxims, or simply 'frank sayings').

Lesson 1: *The 'community' is never homogeneous — always say 'communities' or 'publics' in the plural.* Although it is very tempting and common practice to singularise and reify 'the community', it is a bad habit because it fails to acknowledge the diversity that always exists. Every locality will always have multiple social subgroups, each of which will be affected in different ways and have different interests, and will need to be separately considered. Some common examples are males/females, old/young, those in employment/those who are unemployed or on fixed incomes, home owners/renters, newcomers/oldtimers. But even these dualisms do not adequately reflect the diversity in any community. A planned intervention is never uniformly good or bad for a community, it will affect different stakeholders in different ways. Therefore, always be wary of saying or referring to 'the community', instead always consider phrases such as 'multiple stakeholders' or 'diverse publics'.

Lesson 2: *The impacts of any planned intervention are always differentially distributed.* Because of the diversity in any local community, and especially because different groups within an affected region are positioned differently, there is always a differential distribution of the benefits and costs associated with any planned intervention. This reinforces the previous point (**Lesson 1**), that rather than a singular statement of the impacts, it is necessary to consider and report how the different groups are differentially affected.

Lesson 3: *The needs of the worst-off members of society must always be considered.* The worst-off members of society are typically never involved and therefore there is a special responsibility to ensure that their interests are considered. The worst-off members of society don't advocate for their rights in the way some other groups in society can and they lack the social capital and resources to defend their own interests. They are usually excluded from participatory processes, sometime deliberately, and sometimes inadvertently. While in any case it may be difficult to engage them in participatory processes, at the very least all planned interventions should actively seek to consider how the worst-off members in society will be affected, and there should be an attempt to improve their wellbeing. Related to this is our responsibility to all future generations, and the Indigenous peoples' concept of appointing someone in all meetings to speak on behalf of the seventh generation so that their interests are considered.

Lesson 4: The environmental (biophysical) impacts only occur when the first sod of soil is turned; social impacts occur the moment there is speculation or rumour that something will change. The direct biophysical impacts of a project can only be caused when the project commences construction, when the first sod of soil is turned. Social impacts, however, start the moment there is a rumour or speculation. Immediately many people will respond. In some cases, for example a socially-undesirable factory, there may be considerable fear and anxiety created (whether or not the rumour has any foundation, and whether or not the project actually eventuates). As a result, people may move away from the site of the likely project. If they are home owners, there may be a drop in the value of their property as a result of loss of perceived attractiveness of the location. In other cases, especially in developing countries, in a process known as the 'honey pot effect', people may move to the site either to attempt to become regarded as an affected person and therefore eligible for compensation, or in search of work. In richer countries, amenity landscapes (potentially including the Wadden Sea islands) can be subject to sudden upturns in reputation that increase their perceived attractiveness and real estate values. In both cases, this mass movement of people to a place can cause considerable environmental and social harm.

Lesson 5: *Even the act of doing a social or environmental impact assessment can create social impacts.* Because many organisations try to keep their plans secret till regulatory approval is required, often the first time many people in the community hear of a proposed project is when the social and/or environmental impact assessment is being done. The irony is that the social research being done in support of the interests of the impacted communities may be the trigger to their fear and anxiety. Even if they had been aware of an intended project, it may not be until the actual SIA that they actually think about what it may mean for them. Perhaps they may have thought about the project and decided that it was not harmful, but the fact that an EIA or SIA was being done can engender concern. Awareness of this possibility and appropriate remedies need to be considered by SIA practitioners.

Lesson 6: *Often the biggest social impact is the fear and anxiety caused by the project or policy.* Because of the existence of at least basic regulatory oversight in many countries, the most significant social impact is often the fear and anxiety created by the project. Fear and anxiety are real social impacts and should not be dismissed, instead they need to be managed effectively.

Lesson 7: *Process is everything.* It is important to realise that the level and effectiveness of community engagement has a huge bearing on the amount of fear and anxiety experienced. The extent of social impacts felt is largely contingent on contextual factors such as the genuineness of any community engagement mechanisms and the extent to which the views of all stakeholders were considered and reflected in the outcome. Good social process reduces social impact, poor process creates concern and fear and anxiety.

Lesson 8: *Perception is reality.* Perceived impacts are real social impacts. Although some scientists and engineers might discount people's perceptions because they are not real and may be based on incorrect information, the important social understanding is that, right or wrong, the way individuals perceive things affects their feelings. Fear and anxiety (which is often the biggest social impact, refer to **Lesson 6**), in other words stress, may well be caused by (mis)perception, but they are real and harmful to people just the same as (and in many cases more than) any 'real' impact. It is not helpful to denigrate people's concerns by dismissing them as perceptions or by emphasising their 'perceived' basis. People act on their perceptions and people feel as a result of their perceptions. Perceived impacts are real social impacts.

Lesson 9: *A key concept is trust — if the past experience of a community with projects* (i.e. their impact history) is bad, new projects will be regarded very sceptically, even if they are in fact beneficial and best practice. The fear and anxiety stakeholders experience is related to their perception of the trustworthiness of the proponent and of the various regulatory bodies and relevant government agencies. Where trust in these institutions is low, fear and anxiety will be much higher. The experiences that stakeholders have of past projects affects the way they relate to new projects. Thus a new proponent will be afflicted by the reputation created by previous proponents. And, although it is only a cliché, there is truth in the saying, 'once bitten, twice shy'.

Lesson 10: *Second and higher order impacts tend to cause more harm than first order impacts.* Analysis of the case history of projects reveals that first order impacts (the ones caused directly by the project) tend not to be as significant as second and higher order impacts. This makes prediction of social impacts difficult, and something that should not be done by inexperienced or unqualified personnel. It also means that the use of checklists of impacts is inappropriate because their use may stifle thinking about what the likely impact pathways will be. This means that more important than impact prediction is having an ongoing monitoring and adaptive management process.

Lesson 11: *A good way of thinking about the possible impacts of a project is to conceive of 'upstream' and 'downstream' as metaphors for all inflows and outflows of a project.* A thorough assessment of any project should not only be of the site itself, but of all the inputs into the site and project, as well as of anything that leaves the site. This is true for social issues as well as for biophysical concepts. The concepts of upstream and downstream apply both in their literal (or geographical) sense and in their metaphorical sense. Labour, for example, is an input and the labour demands of a big project can have consequences for where the workers come from, as well as at the site and surrounding areas where they are located. The outflows from a site include not only the products but also the waste products and pollution including a range of disturbances (noise, light, odour, vibration etc), all of which have social as well as environmental consequences. Often the products can often have downstream social impacts.

Lesson 12: *Almost all projects almost always cause almost all impacts – and thus more important than predicting impacts and having checklists is having an ongoing process of monitoring and adaptive management.* Because of the difficulties of predicting impacts and of knowing how people will respond, and because their response may change over time, and given that second and higher order consequences tend to be more harmful (see **Lesson 10**), even small (and relatively environmentally harmless) projects have the potential to cause significant social impacts and social upset, especially because many projects do not have social acceptance or legitimacy and are often poorly implemented with respect to engaging with the various publics. All of this means that almost all projects almost always cause almost all (social) impacts. Given this, much more important than attempting to predict all impacts in advance (and relying solely on these predictions for management and decision making) is having an ongoing monitoring process and a process of adaptive management to respond to any issues that emerge. Monitoring in a social sense includes tracking pre-established and fit-for-purpose social indicators from various data sources, but also refers to having an ongoing process of community engagement where community observations about unexpected consequences can be raised. The corporate social responsibility obligations of proponents require that they allow for this as a project related expense.

Lesson 13: *A major impact of many projects is the foregone benefits that could have been obtained. Another impact is the failure to deliver on promised benefits.* Many projects over-promise on the likely benefits either deliberately in order to gain approval or inadvertently. This can happen, for example, because the proponents fail to take account of likely new technological developments which can reduce labour requirements and therefore promised jobs to the local community. When this happens, communities can feel cheated and deceived, lowering their trust in the proponent and in the regulatory bodies. Another negative impact, although it is not usually experienced as such, is the failure to achieve the potential benefits that exist in every project – that could be achieved if a little more care and attention was given and if a 'social' way of thinking was present on the Board and in management.

Lesson 14: *Focus on what counts, not on what can be counted.* Too often, especially in the selection of indicators for monitoring, there is a tendency to select indicators for which data are readily available, whether or not they are relevant to the real issues facing affected people. This variation of a quote normally attributed (albeit dubiously) to Einstein is good advice. Excessive concern about tracking indicators, especially those that are inadequate, can lead to perverse outcomes. Effort needs to be expended on developing indicators that have validity (measure what they purport to measure) as well as having reliability (measure accurately). Because of the complexity of social issues, finding easily measurable indicators is very difficult. Having a range of qualitative approaches to monitoring, evaluation and assessment might be more valid than an obsession with quantification.

Lesson 15: *Labelling the opposition of local peoples as 'NIMBY' is not helpful.* While it is common for proponents to be dismissive of the opposition of local peoples by using the pejorative label, NIMBY (not in my backyard), this is not helpful and may well exacerbate conflict. There are some important points to appreciate. Because there are different stakeholders with different motivations, values and interests, there will always be a degree of conflict over planned interventions. However, strong opposition will tend to occur because of the failure of the proponent to establish the social legitimacy of the project or policy, to gain a social license to operate. The concerns of local peoples should be accepted as being legitimate responses which need to be addressed respectfully, not by denigration. It is highly recommended that use of the NIMBY term cease altogether.

Lesson 16: *One size does not fit all.* While there is much learning in the field of SIA that means that experienced SIA people can have a reasonably good idea of what is likely to happen in particular situations, and while people often react in similar ways the world over, there is always a local specificity that must be considered. Care must be taken to ensure that standard solutions are not rolled out uniformly. And even where there may be common solutions, people want to be involved in the decision making processes that affect their lives. People in deliberative settings may well come to the same decisions as experts, but they needed to have that process of engagement in order to accept the outcome.

Lesson 17: *You may not be responsible, but you will be held accountable.* Organisations often deny that certain things are their responsibility and quite often they may not have legal responsibility for particular events. But if it is the view of some groups (not necessarily in the local community but potentially anywhere in the world) that an organisation is responsible, a corporation can suffer reputational harm, may lose its social license to operate, either locally or in other places, and may experience a stock market reaction. Thus the question of legal responsibility is a moot point, what is of concern is whether people are likely to believe that a company should have acted in a certain way whether they were required to or not. There is a strong business case for corporate social responsibility.

5. Future challenges for the Wadden sea region from an SIA perspective

Applying an SIA perspective to thinking about the future challenges for the protection, restoration and sustainable use of the Wadden Sea Region results in the identification of numerous topics deserving of consideration. These topics arguably apply to all regions of the world rather than just the Wadden. To a large extent, these topics are perennial and intractable, but nevertheless there is much experience in SIA and related fields that can be of use in addressing them.

Challenge 1: Developing and implementing effective community engagement processes in order to gain social legitimacy (and a social license to operate), and the need to accept the time, resources and professional skills that this takes – There is an enormous volume of literature on community engagement and public participation. Approximately half of this literature sings the praises of community engagement, the other half is full of stories how participation processes did not work (at least when not done properly). Dare et al. (2011a, 2011b) are useful starting points. Hartz-Karp and Pope (2011) outline some contemporary methods of engagement. It is important to realise that good community engagement takes time and resources, and needs to be undertaken by people with appropriate professional skills and experience — effective process is more than "just talking with people".

Challenge 2: *Accepting, appreciating and respecting (if not celebrating) the differences between various stakeholders* — As **Lessons 1 and 2** above argued, not only is there considerable diversity in all communities which needs to be appreciated, understanding how they are differentially affected by the impacts and benefits of a project is important. But it is not only the people who are affected by a project who are stakeholders. Especially when dealing with natural resource management issues, there can be a very large number of people who have an interest in decision making. A proper definition of stakeholder therefore includes not just those with a vested interest and those who are affected by a project, but also those who have the power to influence a project. Put another way, the stakeholders can be considered to be those who are impacted, those who are interested, and those who are influential (Dare et al., 2011a). Some commentators suggest that because of the potentially large number of stakeholders and the inability of organisations to deal with them all, that they be classified by notions such as power, legitimacy and urgency (Mitchell et al., 1997). Buanes et al. (2004), for example, have applied this concept in the context of coastal planning in Norway.

Challenge 3: *Realising that conflict is inevitable and needs to be managed appropriately* — Again, because of the diversity of stakeholders, each with different interests and each being impacted differently, solutions or outcomes that are win—win for everyone are unlikely. Participatory processes fail not because there is anything wrong with participation and community engagement as concepts, but because the varying interests of different parties make it difficult. This is in fact normal and to be expected. The varying impact experiences of different groups also means that there might be very low levels of initial trust between the impacted peoples and the proponent, but also between the various groups. Good process needs to provide opportunities for healing and sharing, for past experiences and current feelings to be aired, for anger to be vented, and for trust-building and empathy to occur. Conflict is inevitable, but can be accommodated and managed. Some useful resources are Dare et al. (2011a,b), Sairinen (2011) and Peltonen and Sairinen (2010).

Challenge 4: *Finding creative solutions that address differences by using participatory and deliberative methods* — There is a wide range of new methods of participation and engagement based on concepts of deliberative democracy that increase the extent of deliberativeness in the planning process and that have considerable potential to be used in impact assessment and planning (see Gastil and Levine (2005), Hartz-Karp and Pope (2011)). "Deliberation involves people with manifestly divergent viewpoints reasoning together in an environment of mutual understanding and trust, endeavouring to understand the reasons behind others' viewpoints as well as their own, devising potential options, then weighing those options according to what is valued, and finally working through their differences to arrive at decisions that have the broad and legitimate agreement of the deliberators" (Hartz-Karp and Pope, 2011: 255—256). There is considerable potential to use deliberative methods to enable greater public involvement in planning, and in so doing to come to better decisions; decisions which will be more sound, more sustainable, and have greater legitimacy — and therefore invoke greater commitment and compliance.

Challenge 5: *Creating shared community visions and developing and utilising commitment to ensure that such visions are attained* — There has been a shift in impact assessment to focussing on enhancement rather than just mitigation (João et al., 2011). Now, every project presents opportunities for each community to progress towards a better future. But planning, especially at the local level, has tended to be a reactive rather than a proactive process. Ideally, every place (geographical community) should consider what it wants to be like in the future. Then, plans and proposals could be assessed against their contribution to that vision, and enhancement actions could be designed to assist in the achievement of that vision. Such visions need to be developed in a participatory and preferably deliberative way to ensure broad support and legitimacy. To ensure the realization of a vision, a process of 'backcasting' is also necessary — the development of strategies to get from the present situation to the desired future situation (Robinson, 2003; Robinson et al., 2011). Scenario planning is all very well, but a bit pointless unless there is a real strategy to ensure that the preferred scenario is achieved.

Challenge 6: *Developing socially-legitimate methods to determine the intrinsic value (social and ecological worth) of landscapes, nature, biodiversity, habitats and heritage, etc, in a way that has broad agreement and can be used in decision making* — Although the field of environmental and/or ecological economics has come a long way in developing methods to give economic value to landscapes, nature, wildlife and even 'peace and quiet', such values seldom have legitimacy amongst members of the public. This is partly because the field of economics is disconnected from people and its language is exclusionary and alienating. For existence value, intrinsic value, non-use value and amenity value and related concepts (see Attfield (1998)) to be valid in decision making as numbers (rather than as generic concepts), these concepts and the methods they use will need to earn greater acceptance and legitimacy in the community. Stolp et al. (2002) present one method of developing socially-constructed assessments of value.

Challenge 7: *Protecting cultural heritage, especially intangible cultural heritage* — Determining what is heritage is always contentious. Protecting tangible cultural heritage (objects, buildings, ruins etc) is difficult enough, and when the alleged heritage impinges on development opportunities of other groups, there will likely be local opposition in the same way as there can be opposition to other planned interventions. Protecting intangible cultural heritage is even harder, especially as it is difficult to define or explain. "It is the culture that people practise as part of their daily lives. It is beliefs and perspectives, ephemeral performances and events that are not tangible objects of culture like monuments, or paintings, books or artefacts. It is often described as the underlying 'spirit' of a cultural group" (Kurin, 2004: p.67). The problem with culture is that it can not be locked up in a museum, it must be free to be expressed, to be lived, but it also needs to adapt. Here comes the difficult question, the preservation of culture (intangible cultural heritage) requires that there be a degree of change. The ecological concept of 'sustainable use' is useful in relation to cultural heritage. Rather than a 'fence and forget' or 'lock it up in a museum' approach, the protection of culture and heritage requires its ongoing sustainable use, to keep it alive, to recognize its social value, to gain legitimacy, to create enjoyment and commitment. Such principles are recognized in the Council of Europe Framework Convention on the Value of Cultural Heritage for Society. Many other ecological principles are applicable to cultural landscapes, albeit with some modification (see Moreira et al. (2006)).

Challenge 8: *Establishing legitimate ways to trade-off new opportunities against social impacts* — Old models of impact assessment were primarily about preventing harm (almost at any cost). New thinking in impact assessment focuses as much on maximising the benefits and opportunities that can arise from planned interventions. New developments potentially can provide many benefits and resources to communities, provided that care is taken to ensure that they are achieved and that whatever deals and trade-offs are made are done on the basis of free, prior and informed consent (FPIC) (Vanclay and Esteves, 2011). Impact and Benefit Agreements are one way of developing and recording arrangements pertaining to a planned intervention (see Gibson and O'Faircheallaigh (2010)). Agreements should be informed by and developed through an SIA process and on the basis of a thorough understanding of how the benefits will be distributed, an understanding of what the likely social impacts will be, and on an understanding of the issues associated with visioning the future for a community.

Challenge 9: *Implementing non-patronising measures to safeguard vulnerable communities from exploitation* – The shift to a focus on benefits in impact assessment potentially means that there is less of a critical voice and it raises the possibility that companies will buy their way to gain approval for projects – the philosophy of FPIC has already been tarnished by the colloquial expression, "first pay in cash", in certain industry sectors. Vulnerable communities – those with few options and high unemployment – become easy prey for less responsible operators. While Impact and Benefit Agreements are in general beneficial, there does need to be a non-patronising safety-check to ensure that vulnerable communities are not exploited. One way that this will be done into the future is by notions of corporate social responsibility. Companies (and governments) will be judged and held accountable for their past deeds, and there may well be future legal liability if there has been a failure to disclose pertinent information or act in particular ways (to exercise a duty of care). Establishing mechanisms or rather processes for allowing grievances to be aired and addressed, as advocated by United Nations Special Representative for Business and Human Rights, John Ruggie, is another dimension to safeguarding communities and groups against exploitation (see Sherman (2009)).

6. Conclusion

The critical role of community engagement has been well recognized in Integrated Coastal Zone Management. Social Impact Assessment, however, does much more than facilitate public participation. SIA applies an analytical framework in conjunction with participatory and deliberative processes to manage effectively the social issues that arise from planned interventions – projects, policies, plans and programs. Its experiences and understandings can also be applied to consider gradual landscape change and to assess the social consequences of unplanned events like disasters. The effectiveness of ICZM would be significantly increased by a greater incorporation of SIA within the ICZM field and practice.

SIA improves the quality of decision making, it improves the legitimacy of decisions, it reduces harm experienced by communities, and potentially it increases the likely benefits that flow from the project or policy. Thus, doing SIA properly is not a cost, but an investment in risk management that will reduce likely future expenditures in the early identification and remedy of potential issues that would otherwise lead to litigation, delays to approval, costs in the form of managing protest actions, and business lost through reputational harm. Reducing risk also leads to reduced costs of capital, and for publicly-listed corporations to increases in shareholder value. SIA has the potential to identify local knowledge that could be used to guide siting decisions and reduce costs that come from poor siting. While much information can be gained from technical surveys and model predictions, they are no substitute for the lived experiences of local peoples. Thus there are many reasons why doing SIA properly makes good sense for the private sector and government, whether the project is for commercial purpose or a planned change in landuse. Social impact assessment should become part of the repertoire and skill set of coastal managers.

References

van der Aa, B., Groote, P., Huigen, P., 2004. World heritage as NIMBY? The case of the Dutch part of the Wadden Sea. Current Issues in Tourism 7 (4–5), 291–302.
Agrawal, A., Gibson, C., 1999. Enchantment and disenchantment: the role of community in natural resource conservation. World Development 27 (4), 629–649.
Attfield, R., 1998. Existence value and intrinsic value. Ecological Economics 24 (2–3), 163–168.
Baldacchino, G., 2004. The coming of age of island studies. Tijdschrift voor Economische en Sociale Geografie 95 (3), 272–283.
Baldacchino, G., 2007. Islands as novelty sites. Geographical Review 97 (2), 165–174.
Buanes, A., Jentoft, S., Karlsen, G., Maurstad, A., Søreng, S., 2004. In whose interest? An exploratory analysis of stakeholders in Norwegian coastal zone planning. Ocean & Coastal Management 47 (5–6), 207–223.
Cheong, S., 2008. A new direction in coastal management. Marine Policy 32 (6), 1090–1093.
Christie, P., 2005. Is integrated coastal management sustainable? Ocean & Coastal Management 48 (3–6), 208–232.
Clark, E., 2004. The ballad dance of the Faeroese: biocultural geography in an age of globalisation. Tijdschrift voor Economische en Sociale Geografie 95 (3), 284–297.
Cliquet, A., Kervarec, F., Bogaert, D., Maes, F., Queffelec, B., 2010. Legitimacy issues in public participation in coastal decision making processes: case studies from Belgium and France. Ocean & Coastal Management 53 (12), 760–768.
Cocklin, C., Craw, M., McAuley, L, 1998. Marine reserves in New Zealand: use rights, public attitudes, and social impacts. Coastal Management 26 (3), 213–231.
Conkling, P., 2007. On islanders and islandness. The Geographical Review 97 (2), 191–201.
Conrad, E., Christie, M., Fazey, I., 2011. Is research keeping up with changes in landscape policy?: a review of the literature. Journal of Environmental Management 92 (9), 2097–2108.
Conway, S., Cameron, R., Navis, I., 2008. Methods, tools and techniques for measuring sustainability in tourism based communities. WIT Transactions on Ecology and the Environment 115, 97–102.
Cottrell, A., King, D., 2011. Disasters and climate change. In: Vanclay, F., Esteves, A.M. (Eds.), New Directions in Social Impact Assessment: Conceptual and Methodological Advances. Edward Elgar, Cheltenham, pp. 154–170.
Dare, M., Schirmer, J., Vanclay, F., 2011a. Handbook for Operational Community Engagement within Australian Plantation Forest Management. Cooperative Research Centre for Forestry, Hobart. Available online: http://www.crcforestry.com.au/publications/downloads/CRCForestry-CE-FINAL.pdf.
Dare, M., Vanclay, F., Schirmer, J., 2011b. Understanding community engagement in plantation forest management: Insights from practitioner and community narratives. Journal of Environmental Planning and Management 54 (9), 1149–1168.
Esteves, A.M., Vanclay, F., 2009. Social development needs analysis: adapting SIA methods to guide corporate-community investment in the minerals industry. Environmental Impact Assessment Review 29 (2), 137–145.
Esteves, A.M., Franks, D., Vanclay, F., 2012. Social impact assessment: the state of the art. Impact Assessment and Project Appraisal 30 (1), 35–44.
Franks, D., Brereton, B., Moran, C., 2011. Cumulative social impacts. In: Vanclay, F., Esteves, A.M. (Eds.), New Directions in Social Impact Assessment: Conceptual and Methodological Advances. Edward Elgar, Cheltenham, pp. 202–220.
Gastil, J., Levine, P. (Eds.), 2005. The Deliberative Democracy Handbook: Strategies for Effective Civic Engagement in the 21st Century'. Jossey-Bass, San Francisco, pp. 80–110.
Gibson, G., O'Faircheallaigh, C., 2010. IBA Community Toolkit: Negotiation and Implementation of Impact and Benefit Agreements. Walter & Duncan Gordon Foundation, Ottawa. Available online: www.ibacommunitytoolkit.ca.
Greider, T., Garkovich, L., 1994. Landscapes: the social construction of nature and the environment. Rural Sociology 59 (1), 1–24.
Gunningham, N., Kagan, R., Thornton, D., 2004. Social license and environmental protection: why businesses go beyond compliance. Law & Social Inquiry 29 (2), 307–341.
Halfacree, K., 2012. Heterolocal identities? Counter-urbanisation, second homes, and rural consumption in the era of mobilities. Population, Space and Place 18 (2), 209–224.
Hartz-Karp, J., Pope, J., 2011. Enhancing the effectiveness of SIA through deliberative democracy. In: Vanclay, F., Esteves, A.M. (Eds.), New Directions in Social Impact Assessment: Conceptual and Methodological Advances. Edward Elgar, Cheltenham, pp. 253–272.
Hay, P., 2006. A phenomenology of islands. Island Studies Journal 1 (1), 19–42.
IAIA, 2009. Social Impact Assessment Key Citations. International Association for Impact Assessment, Fargo. Available online. www.iaia.org/resources-networking/key-citations.aspx.

João, E., Vanclay, F., den Broeder, L., 2011. Accentuating the positive: emphasising enhancement in all forms of impact assessment. Impact Assessment and Project Appraisal 29 (3), 170–180.

Kurin, R., 2004. Safeguarding intangible cultural heritage in the 2003 UNESCO Convention: a critical appraisal. Museum International 56 (1–2), 66–77.

Lane, R., Vanclay, F., Wills, J., Lucas, D., 2007. Museum outreach programs to promote community engagement in local environmental issues. The Australian Journal of Public Administration 66 (2), 159–174.

Mitchell, R., Agle, B., Wood, D., 1997. Toward a theory of stakeholder identification and salience: defining the principle of who and what really counts. Academy of Management Review 22 (4), 853–886.

Moreira, F., Queiroz, A., Aronson, J., 2006. Restoration principles applied to cultural landscapes. Journal for Nature Conservation 14 (3–4), 217–224.

Olsen, S., Tobey, J., Kerr, M., 1997. A common framework for learning from ICM experience. Ocean & Coastal Management 37 (2), 155–174.

Peltonen, L., Sairinen, R., 2010. Integrating impact assessment and conflict management in urban planning: experiences from Finland. Environmental Impact Assessment Review 30 (5), 328–337.

ProVention Consortium, 2007. Social Impact Assessment: Tools for Mainstreaming Disaster Risk Reduction Guidance Note 11. ProVention Consortium, Geneva.

Robinson, J., 2003. Future subjunctive: backcasting as social learning. Futures 35 (8), 839–856.

Robinson, J., Burch, S., Talwar, S., O'Shea, M., Walsh, M., 2011. Envisioning sustainability: recent progress in the use of participatory backcasting approaches for sustainability research. Technological Forecasting & Social Change 78 (5), 756–768.

Sairinen, R., 2011. Environmental conflict mediation. In: Vanclay, F., Esteves, A.M. (Eds.), New Directions in Social Impact Assessment: Conceptual and Methodological Advances. Edward Elgar, Cheltenham, pp. 273–287.

Schirmer, J., 2011. Landuse change. In: Vanclay, F., Esteves, A.M. (Eds.), New Directions in Social Impact Assessment: Conceptual and Methodological Advances. Edward Elgar, Cheltenham, pp. 171–185.

Selman, P., 2004. Community participation in the planning and management of cultural landscapes. Journal of Environmental Planning and Management 47 (3), 365–392.

Sherman, J., 2009. Embedding a Rights Compatible Grievance Processes for External Stakeholders with Business Culture. Corporate Social Responsibility Initiative Report No. 36. John F. Kennedy School of Government, Harvard University, Cambridge, MA.

Shipman, B., Stojanovic, T., 2007. Facts, fictions, and failures of integrated coastal zone management in Europe. Coastal Management 35 (2), 375–398.

Slootweg, R., Vanclay, F., van Schooten, M., 2001. Function evaluation as a framework for the integration of social and environmental impact assessment. Impact Assessment and Project Appraisal 19 (1), 19–28.

Stedman, R.C., 2006. Understanding place attachment amongst second home owners. American Behavioral Scientist 50 (2), 187–205.

Stolp, A., Groen, W., van Vliet, J., Vanclay, F., 2002. Citizen values assessment: incorporating citizens' value judgements in environmental impact assessment. Impact Assessment and Project Appraisal 20 (1), 11–23.

Stratford, E., 2008. Islandness and struggles over development: a Tasmanian case study. Political Geography 27 (2), 160–175.

Turner, R., 2000. Integrating natural and socio-economic science in coastal management. Journal of Marine Systems 25 (3–4), 447–460.

Vanclay, F., 2002. Conceptualising social impacts. Environmental Impact Assessment Review 22 (3), 183–211.

Vanclay, F., 2003. International principles for social impact assessment. Impact Assessment and Project Appraisal 21 (1), 5–11.

Vanclay, F., 2004. The triple bottom line and impact assessment: how do TBL, EIA, SIA, SEA and EMS relate to each other? Journal of Environmental Assessment Policy and Management 6 (3), 265–288.

Vanclay, F., 2006. Principles for social impact assessment: a critical comparison between the International and US documents. Environmental Impact Assessment Review 26 (1), 3–14.

Vanclay, F., 2008. Place matters. In: Vanclay, F., Higgins, M., Blackshaw, A. (Eds.), Making Sense of Place. National Museum of Australia Press, Canberra, pp. 2–11.

Vanclay, F., Esteves, A.M., 2011. Current issues and trends in social impact assessment. In: Vanclay, F., Esteves, A.M. (Eds.), New Directions in Social Impact Assessment: Conceptual and Methodological Advances. Edward Elgar, Cheltenham, pp. 3–19.

Vanclay, F., Lane, R., Wills, J., Coates, I., Lucas, D., 2004. 'Committing to Place' and evaluating the higher purpose: Increasing engagement in natural resource management through museum outreach and educational activities. Journal of Environmental Assessment Policy and Management 6 (4), 539–564.

Voyer, M., Gladstone, W., Goodall, H., 2012. Methods of social assessment in marine protected area planning: Is public participation enough? Marine Policy 36 (2), 432–439.

Part II
Guidelines and Principles

Guest editorial

International Principles for Social Impact Assessment: their evolution

Frank Vanclay

THIS ISSUE OF *Impact Assessment and Project Appraisal* (IAPA) is special because it contains the long-awaited International Principles for Social Impact Assessment (SIA). They are the output of a formal International Association for Impact Assessment (IAIA) project, initially approved as a project by the IAIA Board in 1998, with the final document being endorsed in early 2003.

To some extent, the Principles were inspired by the US Interorganizational Committee's Guidelines and Principles for Social Impact Assessment which were published in IAPA's predecessor journal, *Impact Assessment*, in 1994. Their Guidelines and Principles (G&P) were well received by the SIA community at large. However, consistent with their purpose, they were strictly only appropriate to the US National Environmental Policy Act jurisdictional setting. Even in that context, they had a number of problems; primarily that it was not always clear whom they were addressing.

At IAIA's New Orleans conference in 1997, two committees were established to review the G&P. One was to consider them for application within the American context, while the second was charged with the responsibility of developing a set of International Guidelines and Principles. Rabel Burdge, an original member of the Interorganizational Committee, became Convenor of the US-based Committee, while Frank Vanclay was appointed Convenor of the International Committee.

Establishing the membership of the International Committee was a fraught process. There were many willing volunteers, but mostly from the developed world. Even so, without funding, how could the International Committee actually meet to do its business? Furthermore, there was an awareness that developing truly international guidelines and principles would be difficult. Once the regulatory context is removed, different cultures are considered, and different development priorities are comprehended, it becomes a rather unsettling process. Therefore it was decided to have a small Project Team that would oversee the process of development, provide comment to the Convenor at strategic points, and maximise input through a series of participatory workshops at a number of venues around the world.

Initially, this proved to be a good strategy. Over time, however, problems emerged. It became apparent that the concept of an impact-predicting SIA as part of a regulatory system was not a suitable model for SIA in a development context. What this meant was that no consensus emerged in the workshops that were held. Various meetings did make major leaps of understanding, but when these were revisited at subsequent workshops, which often contained different people, the discussion would start from square one again.

Therefore, it took several years before sufficient discussion had occurred for the Project Team to have the faith to agree that the concept (and later the document) was finalised. Even so, because the change in the concept of SIA is considerable, people who are locked into old ways of thinking may find it hard to accept the new understanding of SIA.

Prof Frank Vanclay is at the Tasmanian Institute of Agricultural Research, University of Tasmania, Private Bag 98, Hobart, Tasmania 7001, Australia; Tel: +61 3 6226 2618; Fax: +61 3 6226 7450; E-mail: Frank.Vanclay@utas.edu.au. He is Convenor of the Project Team.

Guest editorial

Ultimately, part-day workshops were held at IAIA conferences in Christchurch (1998), Hong Kong (2000) and The Hague (2002), with full-day workshops being held in Glasgow (1999) and Cartagena (2001). In addition to IAIA conferences, additional input was gained from workshops or presentations at: (1) the IAIA South Africa Affiliate's conference at Cathedral Peak (1998); (2) Community Development conferences in Bangkok (1998) and Ho Chi Minh City (2000); (3) a Capacity Building workshop in Hoi An (2001); (4) the World Congress of Rural Sociology in Rio de Janeiro (2000); (5) the International Conference on Impact Assessment in the Development Process at the University of Manchester (1998); (6) the World Bank (2001); and (7) at several presentations in Australia.

All in all, several hundred people participated in the process and over 50 made a substantial contribution. The final text was drafted by the Convenor and was subject to the editorial scrutiny of the Project Team.

Membership of the Project Team changed over time, but the following people participated at some time: James Baines (SIA Section Convenor); Hobson Bryan; Di Buchan; Rabel Burdge; Gary Cox; Allan Dale; Amber Frugte; Stewart Lockie; Abdoulaye Sene; Pierre Senecal; Roel Slootweg; Nick Taylor; and Frank Vanclay (Convenor).

At the beginning of the process, the discussion mostly centred on what international G&P ought to represent: a statement of minimum standards or an ideal model. It also considered whether it was desirable for there to be a single specified model for SIA. Central to that debate was the question "what exactly is SIA; a practice, a process, or a philosophy?" Ultimately, it was decided that SIA is a multi-level concept and that it should be more mindful of its proactive community development role.

The process therefore led to the development of a new definition of SIA, the precise wording of which has been discussed at great length. Like all definitions developed by a committee, it represents something of a compromise. Irrespective of the precise wording, however, there was strong agreement on the concept being conveyed. Nevertheless, the International Principles are intended to be reviewed periodically and to change over time. They are also intended to be the basis of several sets of guidelines to be developed with relevant industry groups and in national contexts.

Several lessons were learned in the process. The most important for a general audience is that there is widespread uncertainty about what 'principles' and 'guidelines' are. It became necessary to define these terms and to constantly remind ourselves of these definitions. In defining them, and thinking about the meaning of them, it became clear that guidelines derive from principles, and principles derive from values. Guidelines should not be developed in advance of principles, which in turn should not be developed before a discussion about values.

It also became clear that it was a pointless exercise for an organisation such as IAIA to develop guidelines to foist on to industry. Guidelines so developed would have no legitimacy and would not be adopted. Guidelines become relevant not by being written on paper, but through their legitimacy and the commitment industry would have to abide by them. The gaining of this commitment and legitimacy requires a participatory process. It requires 'ownership' by industry. The benefit of guidelines, therefore, is not the having of them, but the process of their development.

It was also clear that in a rush to develop guidelines, there would be a lack of reflection about the discipline. It is only through discussion of core values, fundamental principles, key objectives and so on, that true reflection and learning occurs. We believe that this has occurred in the SIA community and that this new learning and understanding of SIA is documented in the International Principles for Social Impact Assessment (pages 5–11 in this issue). I commend them to you.

[7]

SIA principles

International Principles For Social Impact Assessment

Frank Vanclay

The "International Principles for Social Impact Assessment" is a statement of the core values of the SIA community together with a set of principles to guide SIA practice and the consideration of 'the social' in environmental impact assessment generally. It is a discussion document for the impact assessment community to be used as the basis for developing sector and national guidelines. In the process of being developed explicitly for an international context, increasing pressure was placed on the conventional understanding of SIA and a new definition, with official imprimatur of an international professional body, has been formalised. "Social Impact Assessment includes the processes of analysing, monitoring and managing the intended and unintended social consequences, both positive and negative, of planned interventions (policies, programs, plans, projects) and any social change processes invoked by those interventions. Its primary purpose is to bring about a more sustainable and equitable biophysical and human environment."

Keywords: social impact assessment; human rights; core values; principles; guidelines; international conventions; development; environmental impact assessment

This document was prepared over a five-year period for the IAIA by Frank Vanclay to whom feedback should be provided. Workshops were held at several IAIA and other conferences across six continents. Several hundred people were consulted and some 50 made substantial contributions. Rabel Burdge initiated the project, and James Baines and Richard Morgan supported it along the way. The International Principles is a living document that will continue to be modified. Revised versions will be available on the IAIA website (www.iaia.org).

Prof Frank Vanclay is at the Tasmanian Institute of Agricultural Research, University of Tasmania, Private Bag 98, Hobart, Tasmania 7001, Australia; Tel: +61 3 6226 2618; Fax: +61 3 6226 7450; E-mail: Frank.Vanclay@utas.edu.au.

Why have Principles for SIA?

There has been considerable interest in producing "International Guidelines and Principles for Social Impact Assessment". An international document produced under the auspices of a major organisation such as the International Association for Impact Assessment (IAIA) could:

- Assist in the development of legislation and policy at the national level;
- Provide standards for SIA practice in international contexts (transboundary projects, development cooperation, foreign investments, international banking);
- Increase the appeal of SIA to a wider range of audiences, through increasing its legitimacy/standing;
- Establish minimum standards for SIA practice;
- Provide an articulation of best practice in SIA as a model to aspire to;
- Remove confusion over terminology by establishing a definitive glossary;
- Establish the appropriate scope of the social component of impact assessments;
- Promote the integration of SIA in all impact assessments (especially environmental impact assessment and strategic environmental assessment).

The process of developing international guidelines and principles however has been difficult. In a truly international context, there are many issues to consider and little can be taken for granted. The regulatory context varies, the cultural/religious context varies, and social and economic priorities for development vary. As the process of developing international guidelines and principles progressed, increasing pressure was placed on the conventional understanding of SIA, and a new concept of what SIA was about emerged. This resulted in a revised definition of SIA.

It also became apparent that a definitive document containing the "International Guidelines and Principles" was a flawed concept. Firstly, because most such documents tend to emphasise guidelines rather than principles. They fail to realise that guidelines need to be deduced from principles, and principles need to be derived from core values. Only by first establishing the core values of the community of practice, then deriving the principles, and only then developing guidelines, can truly appropriate guidelines emerge. The second flaw is that guidelines and principles are often developed in non-participatory processes. Even where participatory processes are involved, too often they do not include the people to whom the guidelines are directed. These are the people who ultimately need to develop 'ownership' of the guidelines if they are to be adopted and be utilised.

This document serves as a discussion document for the impact assessment community. It promulgates a new understanding of SIA. It is intended that this be available to practitioners around the world. It can provide them with the basis for developing national guidelines in consultation with a range of stakeholders and users in their own countries.

Defining and describing SIA

In general terms, SIA is analysing, monitoring and managing the social consequences of development. However, there are different levels by which to understand the term 'SIA'. SIA is a field of research and practice, or a paradigm consisting of a body of knowledge, techniques, and values. Various individuals identify themselves as SIA professionals, or list SIA as one of their disciplines or specialty areas. There is a community of individuals engaged in research and practice of SIA. These people practice the methodology of SIA and undertake associated social and environmental research to inform the practice of SIA. As a methodology or instrument, SIA is the process that SIA professionals follow in order to assess the social impacts of planned interventions or events, and to develop strategies for the ongoing monitoring and management of those impacts. SIA should not be understood only as the task of predicting social impacts in an impact assessment process.

Social Impact Assessment includes the processes of analysing, monitoring and managing the intended and unintended social consequences, both positive and negative, of planned interventions (policies, programs, plans, projects) and any social change processes invoked by those interventions. Its primary purpose is to bring about a more sustainable and equitable biophysical and human environment.

The important features of this understanding of SIA are that:

1. The goal of impact assessment is to bring about a more ecologically, socio-culturally and economically sustainable and equitable environment. Impact assessment, therefore, promotes community development and empowerment, builds capacity, and develops social capital (social networks and trust).
2. The focus of concern of SIA is a proactive stance to development and better development outcomes, not just the identification or amelioration of negative or unintended outcomes. Assisting communities and other stakeholders to identify development goals, and ensuring that positive outcomes are maximised, can be more important than minimising harm from negative impacts.
3. The methodology of SIA can be applied to a wide range of planned interventions, and can be undertaken on behalf of a wide range of actors, and not just within a regulatory framework.
4. SIA contributes to the process of adaptive management of policies, programs, plans and projects, and therefore needs to inform the design and operation of the planned intervention.
5. SIA builds on local knowledge and utilises participatory processes to analyse the concerns of interested and affected parties. It involves stakeholders in the assessment of social impacts, the analysis of alternatives, and monitoring of the planned intervention.
6. The good practice of SIA accepts that social, economic and biophysical impacts are inherently and inextricably interconnected. Change in any of these domains will lead to changes in the other domains. SIA must, therefore, develop an understanding of the impact pathways that are created when change in one domain triggers impacts across other domains, as well as the iterative or flow-on consequences within each domain. In other words, there must be consideration of the second and higher order impacts and of cumulative impacts.
7. In order for the discipline of SIA to learn and grow, there must be analysis of the impacts that occurred as a result of past activities. SIA must be reflexive and evaluative of its theoretical bases and of its practice.
8. While SIA is typically applied to planned interventions, the techniques of SIA can also be used

Social Impact Assessment is analysing, monitoring and managing the social consequences of development

to consider the social impacts that derive from other types of events, such as disasters, demographic change and epidemics.

SIA is best understood as an umbrella or overarching framework that embodies the evaluation of all impacts on humans and on all the ways in which people and communities interact with their socio-cultural, economic and biophysical surroundings. SIA thus has strong links with a wide range of specialist sub-fields involved in the assessment of areas such as: aesthetic impacts (landscape analysis); archaeological and cultural heritage impacts (both tangible and non-tangible); community impacts; cultural impacts; demographic impacts; development impacts; economic and fiscal impacts; gender impacts; health and mental health impacts; impacts on indigenous rights; infrastructural impacts, institutional impacts; leisure and tourism impacts; political impacts (human rights, governance, democratisation etc); poverty; psychological impacts; resource issues (access and ownership of resources); impacts on social and human capital; and other impacts on societies. As such, comprehensive SIA cannot normally be undertaken by a single person, but requires a team approach.

The nature of SIA in an international context

The objective of SIA is to ensure that development maximises its benefits and minimises its costs, especially those costs borne by people (including those in other places and in the future). Costs and benefits may not be measurable or quantifiable and are often not adequately taken into account by decision-makers, regulatory authorities and developers. By identifying impacts in advance: (1) better decisions can be made about which interventions should proceed and how they should proceed; and (2) mitigation measures can be implemented to minimise the harm and maximise the benefits from a specific planned intervention or related activity.

An important feature of SIA is the professional value system held by its practitioners. In addition to a commitment to sustainability and to scientific integrity, such a value system includes an ethic that advocates openness and accountability, fairness and equity, and defends human rights. The role of SIA goes far beyond the ex-ante (in advance) prediction of adverse impacts and the determination of who wins and who loses. SIA also encompasses: empowerment of local people; enhancement of the position of women, minority groups and other disadvantaged or marginalised members of society; development of capacity building; alleviation of all forms of dependency; increase in equity; and a focus on poverty reduction. SIA complements the economic and technical models that characterise the thinking of many development professionals and agencies.

SIA can be undertaken in different contexts and for different purposes. This creates difficulties in

Awareness of the differential distribution of impacts among different groups in society, and particularly the impact burden experienced by vulnerable groups in the community should always be of prime concern

defining or evaluating it. The nature of an SIA done on behalf of a multinational corporation as part of that company's internal procedures may be very different to an SIA undertaken by a consultant in compliance with regulatory or funding agency requirements, or an SIA undertaken by a development agency interested in ensuring best value for their country's development assistance. These, in turn, may be very different to an SIA undertaken by staff or students at a local university on behalf of the local community, or an SIA undertaken by the local community itself. Each of these applications of SIA is worthwhile, and none should pretend to be the definitive statement. Evaluation of an SIA needs to consider its intended purpose.

Some conceptualisations of SIA are related to protecting individual property rights, with clear statements of adverse impacts required to ensure that individual rights are not transgressed. Where these rights are violated, SIA could be seen as contributing to mitigation and compensation mechanisms. In these situations, SIA tends to concentrate on the negative impacts. In other contexts, however, particularly in developing countries, there should be less emphasis on the negative impacts on small groups of individuals or on individual property rights. Rather, there should be greater concern with maximising social utility and development potential, while ensuring that such development is generally acceptable to the community, equitable and sustainable. SIA should also focus on reconstruction of livelihoods. The improvement of social wellbeing of the wider community should be explicitly recognised as an objective of planned interventions, and as such should be an indicator considered by any form of assessment. However, awareness of the differential distribution of impacts among different groups in society, and particularly the impact burden experienced by vulnerable groups in the community should always be of prime concern.

What are social impacts?

SIA is much more than the prediction step within an environmental assessment framework. Social impacts are much broader than the limited issues often

International Principles for Social Impact Assessment

considered in EIAs (such as demographic changes, job issues, financial security, and impacts on family life). A limited view of SIA creates demarcation problems about what are the social impacts to be identified by SIA, versus what is considered by related fields such as health impact assessment, cultural impact assessment, heritage impact assessment, aesthetic impact assessment, or gender impact assessment. The SIA community of practitioners considers that all issues that affect people, directly or indirectly, are pertinent to social impact assessment.

A convenient way of conceptualising social impacts is as changes to one or more of the following:

- people's way of life – that is, how they live, work, play and interact with one another on a day-to-day basis;
- their culture – that is, their shared beliefs, customs, values and language or dialect;
- their community – its cohesion, stability, character, services and facilities;
- their political systems – the extent to which people are able to participate in decisions that affect their lives, the level of democratisation that is taking place, and the resources provided for this purpose;
- their environment – the quality of the air and water people use; the availability and quality of the food they eat; the level of hazard or risk, dust and noise they are exposed to; the adequacy of sanitation, their physical safety, and their access to and control over resources;
- their health and wellbeing – health is a state of complete physical, mental, social and spiritual wellbeing and not merely the absence of disease or infirmity;
- their personal and property rights – particularly whether people are economically affected, or experience personal disadvantage which may include a violation of their civil liberties;
- their fears and aspirations – their perceptions about their safety, their fears about the future of their community, and their aspirations for their future and the future of their children.

Activities comprising SIA

SIA comprises most of the following activities. It:

- participates in the environmental design of the planned intervention;
- identifies interested and affected peoples;
- facilitates and coordinates the participation of stakeholders;
- documents and analyses the local historical setting of the planned intervention so as to be able to interpret responses to the intervention, and to assess cumulative impacts;
- collects baseline data (social profiling) to allow evaluation and audit of the impact assessment process and the planned intervention itself;

All issues that affect people, directly or indirectly, are pertinent to SIA

- gives a rich picture of the local cultural context, and develops an understanding of local community values, particularly how they relate to the planned intervention;
- identifies and describes the activities which are likely to cause impacts (scoping);
- predicts (or analyses) likely impacts and how different stakeholders are likely to respond;
- assists evaluating and selecting alternatives (including a no development option);
- assists in site selection;
- recommends mitigation measures;
- assists in the valuation process and provides suggestions about compensation (non-financial as well as financial);
- describes potential conflicts between stakeholders and advises on resolution processes;
- develops coping strategies for dealing with residual or non-mitigatable impacts;
- contributes to skill development and capacity building in the community;
- advises on appropriate institutional and coordination arrangements for all parties;
- assists in devising and implementing monitoring and management programs.

Guidelines, Principles and Core Values

Core Values are fundamental, ideal-typical, enduring, statements of belief that are strongly held and accepted as premises (is-statements).

Principles are general statements of either a common understanding or an indication as to a course of action about what ought to be done (ought-statements).

Guidelines are statements by which to plan a specific course of action and which clarify how it should done (action-statements).

Guidelines can be described as statements which provide advice or direction by which to plan a specific course of action. They are written as specific statements of instruction about what to do and/or how to do it. Typically they are "action-statements". A principle is a macro statement that provides a general guide to a course of action about what ought to be done. They are written as "ought-statements". Core values are statements about fundamental beliefs that are deeply held. They are typically "is-statements". Values determine principles, from which guidelines can be written.

Core Values

The core values of SIA are:

The SIA community of practice believes that:

1. There are fundamental human rights that are shared equally across cultures, and by males and females alike.
2. There is a right to have those fundamental human rights protected by the rule of law, with justice applied equally and fairly to all, and available to all.
3. People have a right to live and work in an environment which is conducive to good health and to a good quality of life and which enables the development of human and social potential.
4. Social dimensions of the environment – specifically but not exclusively peace, the quality of social relationships, freedom from fear, and belongingness – are important aspects of people's health and quality of life.
5. People have a right to be involved in the decision making about the planned interventions that will affect their lives.
6. Local knowledge and experience are valuable and can be used to enhance planned interventions.

Fundamental principles for development:

The SIA community of practice considers that:

1. Respect for human rights should underpin all actions.
2. Promoting equity and democratisation should be the major driver of development planning, and impacts on the worst-off members of society should be a major consideration in all assessment.
3. The existence of diversity between cultures, within cultures, and the diversity of stakeholder interests need to be recognised and valued.
4. Decision making should be just, fair and transparent, and decision makers should be accountable for their decisions.
5. Development projects should be broadly acceptable to the members of those communities likely to benefit from, or be affected by, the planned intervention.
6. The opinions and views of experts should not be the sole consideration in decisions about planned interventions.
7. The primary focus of all development should be positive outcomes, such as capacity building, empowerment, and the realisation of human and social potential.
8. The term, 'the environment', should be defined broadly to include social and human dimensions, and in such inclusion, care must be taken to ensure that adequate attention is given to the realm of the social.

International Principles for Social Impact Assessment

Principles specific to SIA practice

1. Equity considerations should be a fundamental element of impact assessment and of development planning.
2. Many of the social impacts of planned interventions can be predicted.
3. Planned interventions can be modified to reduce their negative social impacts and enhance their positive impacts.
4. SIA should be an integral part of the development process, involved in all stages from inception to follow-up audit.
5. There should be a focus on socially sustainable development, with SIA contributing to the determination of best development alternative(s) – SIA (and EIA) have more to offer than just being an arbiter between economic benefit and social cost.
6. In all planned interventions and their assessments, avenues should be developed to build the social and human capital of local communities and to strengthen democratic processes.
7. In all planned interventions, but especially where there are unavoidable impacts, ways to turn impacted peoples into beneficiaries should be investigated.
8. The SIA must give due consideration to the alternatives of any planned intervention, but especially in cases when there are likely to be unavoidable impacts.
9. Full consideration should be given to the potential mitigation measures of social and environmental impacts, even where impacted communities may approve the planned intervention and where they may be regarded as beneficiaries.
10. Local knowledge and experience and acknowledgment of different local cultural values should be incorporated in any assessment.
11. There should be no use of violence, harassment, intimidation or undue force in connection with the assessment or implementation of a planned intervention.
12. Developmental processes that infringe the human rights of any section of society should not be accepted.

Other guiding principles

There are many International Agreements and Declarations that contain notable statements. Principle 1 of the 1992 Rio Declaration on Environment and Development, for example, states that "Human beings are at the centre of concerns for sustainable development. They are entitled to a healthy and productive life in harmony with nature." Principle 17 calls for impact assessment to be undertaken. Article 1 of the 1986 Declaration on the Right to Development states that "The right to development is an inalienable human right by virtue of which every human person and all peoples are entitled to participate in, contribute to, and enjoy economic,

International Principles for Social Impact Assessment

Human beings are at the centre of concerns for sustainable development (Principle 1 of the Rio Declaration)

social, cultural and political development, in which all human rights and fundamental freedoms can be fully realised. The human right to development also implies the full realization of the right of peoples to self-determination, which includes, subject to the relevant provisions of both International Covenants on Human Rights, the exercise of their inalienable right to full sovereignty over all their natural wealth and resources."

In international agreements and declarations, social issues are often implied but rarely given adequate emphasis. Nevertheless, the statements that are given in those declarations can be rewritten to refer to social issues more specifically. The following is a list of international principles in common usage rewritten to apply more directly to social issues.

Precautionary Principle: In order to protect the environment, a concept which includes peoples' ways of life and the integrity of their communities, the precautionary approach shall be applied. Where there are threats or potential threats of serious social impact, lack of full certainty about those threats should not be used as a reason for approving the planned intervention or not requiring the implementation of mitigation measures and stringent monitoring.

Uncertainty Principle: It must be recognised that our knowledge of the social world and of social processes is incomplete and that social knowledge can never be fully complete because the social environment and the processes affecting it are changing constantly, and vary from place to place and over time.

Intragenerational Equity: The benefits from the range of planned interventions should address the needs of all, and the social impacts should not fall disproportionately on certain groups of the population, in particular children and women, the disabled and the socially excluded, certain generations or certain regions.

Intergenerational Equity: Development activities or planned interventions should be managed so that the needs of the present generation are met without compromising the ability of future generations to meet their own needs.

Recognition and Preservation of Diversity: Communities and societies are not homogenous. They are demographically structured (age and gender), and they comprise different groups with various value systems and different skills. Special attention is needed to appreciate the existence of the social diversity that exists within communities and to understand what the unique requirements of special groups may be. Care must be taken to ensure that planned interventions do not lead to a loss of social diversity in a community or a diminishing of social cohesion.

Internalisation of Costs. The full social and ecological costs of a planned intervention should be internalised through the use of economic and other instruments, that is, these costs should be considered as part of the costs of the intervention, and no intervention should be approved or regarded as cost-effective if it achieves this by the creation of hidden costs to current or future generations or the environment.

The Polluter Pays Principle. The full costs of avoiding or compensating for social impacts should be borne by the proponent of the planned intervention.

The Prevention Principle. It is generally preferable and cheaper in the long run to prevent negative social impacts and ecological damage from happening than having to restore or rectify damage after the event.

The Protection and Promotion of Health and Safety. Health and safety are paramount. All planned interventions should be assessed for their health impacts and their accident risks, especially in terms of assessing and managing the risks from hazardous substances, technologies or processes, so that their harmful effects are minimised, including not bringing them into use or phasing them out as soon as possible. Health impacts cover the physical, mental and social wellbeing and safety of all people, paying particular attention to those groups of the population who are more vulnerable and more likely to be harmed, such as the economically deprived, indigenous groups, children and women, the elderly, the disabled, as well as to the population most exposed to risks arising from the planned intervention.

The Principle of Multisectoral Integration. Social development requirements and the need to consider social issues should be properly integrated into all projects, policies, infrastructure programs and other planning activities.

The Principle of Subsidiarity. Decision making power should be decentralised, with accountable decisions being made as close to an individual citizen as possible. In the context of SIA, this means decisions about the approval of planned interventions, or conditions under which they might operate, should be taken as close to the affected people as possible, with local people having an input into the approval and management processes.

International Principles for Social Impact Assessment

Developing Guidelines

Because guidelines are specific recommendations for action, they need to be developed in the context in which they are to be applied and they need to be addressed to a specific audience. Therefore, they need to be developed in conjunction with the relevant parties. They need to become accepted as the guidelines of that group rather than being imposed.

There are many different groups who are potentially interested in guidelines for SIA. They include:

- SIA practitioners – require guidelines to improve their practice;
- Regulatory agencies – require guidelines in order to specify or audit the scope of SIA activities they commission as well as the quality of SIA reports they receive;
- Policy and program developers – require guidelines to ensure that policy and program development considers social impacts;
- Affected peoples and NGOs – require guidelines to be able to participate effectively in SIA processes. Local action groups (resident action groups) and NGOs often act like a regulatory agency in checking the appropriateness of SIA processes.
- Developers (proponents) and Financiers – require guidelines to be committed to good practice in environmental and social impact assessment, to adequately resource such practice, to liaise effectively with practitioners and interested and affected parties, and with regulatory agencies.

IAIA seeks to liaise with sector groups to develop SIA Guidelines applicable to their practice

- Development agencies (multilateral and bilateral aid organisations) – require guidelines to ensure that the most benefit is obtained from their aid projects, that SIA components are adequately resourced, and that the aid projects themselves do not have unintended environmental or social consequences.

In addition, various sectors of the community may have special interests, and it may be appropriate for guidelines to be developed to address those special interests, such as Indigenous Peoples.

IAIA seeks to liaise with the groups listed above to develop SIA Guidelines applicable to their practice.

Project Team

The Project Team has at various times included the following: Frank Vanclay (chair), James Baines, Hobson Bryan, Di Buchan, Rabel Burdge, Gary Cox, Allan Dale, Amber Frugte, Stewart Lockie, Abdoulaye Sene, Pierre Senecal, Roel Slootweg and Nick Taylor. Many other people participated in workshops and gave comments.

[8]

US principles and guidelines

Principles and guidelines for social impact assessment in the USA

The Interorganizational Committee on Principles and Guidelines for Social Impact Assessment

The 2003 version of Principles and Guidelines for Social Impact Assessment (SIA) in the USA provides guidance for the conduct of SIA within the context of the US National Environmental Policy Act of 1970. Guidelines are integrated within six principles focusing on: understanding of local and regional settings; dealing with the key elements of the human environment; using appropriate methods and assumptions; providing quality information for decision making; ensuring that environmental justice issues are addressed; and establishing mechanisms for evaluation/monitoring and mitigation. A social impact assessment model is outlined followed by suggested social impact assessment variables. The document concludes with the detailed steps in the SIA process.

Keywords: social impact assessment; principles; guidelines; steps; SIA variables; SIA model

The Committee was:[1] *Rabel J Burdge, Professor of Sociology and Environmental Studies, Western Washington University, Bellingham; Susan Charnley, Social Scientist, Forest Experiment Station, USDA Forest Service, Portland, Oregon; Michael Downs, Social Scientist, EDAW, San Diego, CA; *Kurt Finsterbusch, Professor of Sociology, University of Maryland, College Park; *Bill Freudenburg, Professor of Environmental Studies, University of California at Santa Barbara; *Peter Fricke, Social Anthropologist, National Marine Fisheries Service, Silver Springs, Maryland; *Bob Gramling, Professor of Sociology, University of Southwestern Louisiana, Lafayette; Michael Smith, Natural Resources Planning, Department of Environmental and Natural Resource Sciences, Humboldt State University, Arcata, California; Brenda C Kragh, Social Science Analyst, FHWA, Office of Planning, Washington, DC; *Richard Stoffle, Professor of Anthropology, Bureau Applied Research, University of Arizona, Tucson; *James G Thompson, Professor of Rural Sociology, Department of Agricultural and Applied Economics, University of Wyoming, Laramie; *Gary Williams, St Marys College, St Marys City, Maryland and the Clark Group, Washington, DC.

SINCE PASSAGE OF the US National Environmental Policy Act (NEPA) of 1970, environmental impact assessment has become the key component of environmental planning and decision making in the United States. Agency planners and decision makers have recognized a need for better understanding of the social consequences of policies, plans, programs and projects (PPPPs).

In response to this need, a group of social scientists formed the Interorganizational Committee on Guidelines and Principles for Social Impact Assessment[1] (SIA) in 1992, with the purpose of outlining a set of guidelines and principles that would assist public- and private-sector agencies and organizations to fulfill their obligations under the NEPA, related authorities and agency mandates (IOCGP, 1993). This monograph is the decade update of the original.

In the 2003 version, we continue to define social impact assessment in terms of efforts to assess, appraise or estimate, in advance, the social consequences that are likely to follow from proposed actions. These include: specific government or private projects, such as construction of buildings, siting power generation facilities, large transportation projects, managing natural resources, fish and wildlife; and preserving or leasing large tracts of land and the adoption of new policies and resulting plans

---

Box 1. Social impacts

By social impacts we mean the consequences to human populations of any public or private actions-that alter the ways in which people live, work, play, relate to one another, organize to meet their needs and generally cope as members of society. The term also includes cultural impacts involving changes to the norms, values, and beliefs that guide and rationalize their cognition of themselves and their society.

US principles and guidelines for SIA

and programs. The actions and their consequences are considered particularly in the context of the NEPA (P.L. 91-190, 42 U.S.C. 4371 *et seq*) and state laws and regulations that reflect NEPA.

The central requirement of NEPA is that before any agency of the federal government may take major actions potentially significantly affecting the quality of the human environment, that agency must first prepare an environmental assessment (EA) or environmental impact statement (EIS) requiring the integrated use of the social sciences. Similar requirements for state agencies are found in US States that have laws and/or regulations that reflect NEPA.

The social science components of EISs are given various labels, including social analyses, socio-economic assessments, community impact assessments, social impact assessments, or simply SIAs. The term social impact assessment first appeared when the Department of the Interior was preparing the EIS for the Trans-Alaska pipeline in the early 1970s.

Within federal agencies that have developed SIA guidelines there is variation on how the social component of NEPA is to be implemented. Prior to publishing the 1993 *Guidelines and Principles for SIA* there had not been a systematic, inter-disciplinary statement from the social science community as to what should be the content of an SIA. This version provides discretionary guidance on how to work through the SIA process in the context of the NEPA Statute and the Council on Environmental Quality (1986) NEPA implementing regulations.

The organizations and individuals in the Interorganizational Committee represent the relevant social science disciplines and design arts as well as social scientists who have done SIA in federal agencies, for the private sector, and for international donor agencies. In addition, most of the individuals do social impact assessment research and teach workshops and courses on the topic.

This document provides systematic and interdisciplinary principles and guidelines to assist government agencies and private-sector interests in using SIA to make better decisions under NEPA, related mandates and administrative requirements. The guidelines and standards provided are also designed for communities and individuals likely to be affected by proposed actions, in order that they might conduct independent assessments or evaluate the adequacy of an agency SIA.

Within these pages we cannot cover over three decades of research on social effects, much less every contingency that may occur in the course of implementing an approved action. However, we do provide a broad overview, focusing less on methodological details and more on the principles and guidelines for the preparation of technically and substantively adequate SIA within reasonable time and resource constraints.

How does SIA help in the decision process?

An SIA is focused on human environment problems and their resolution. Government policies, plans, programs, and projects are developed in response to identified or anticipated opportunities or problems. An impact assessment, whether social, economic or environmental, is a tool to help make decisions. Properly done, SIAs help the affected community or communities and the agencies plan for social change resulting from a proposed action or bring forward information leading to reasons not to carry out the proposal.

The SIA process also brings local knowledge to the decision process. Those who live in the affected area are knowledgeable about their human environment. With the use of local knowledge, SIA saves both time and money as affected populations are identified and involved in the process. It also ensures that key stakeholders are identified and consulted during decision making. Thus, SIA can help improve both the scoping and public involvement processes, which are key requirements under NEPA.

In summary, as a decision tool, SIA provides information to agencies and communities about social and cultural factors that need to be considered in any decision; provides a mechanism for incorporating local knowledge and values into the decision; and can help a decision-maker identify the most socially beneficial course of action for local, regional, and national interests.

What is new in the 2003 version?

We have benefited from almost ten years of comments and wide use of the *Guidelines and Principles (G&P) for Social Impact Assessment*. Over 3,000 copies of the 1993 version have been distributed worldwide and been reprinted in professional journals and SIA books. In addition, most federal agencies have used the *G&P for SIA* as rationale to include social impact assessment during their planning and assessment process.

The new version expands the focus away from projects to include policies, plans, and programs. These we refer to as the four Ps (PPPPs). By policies we mean general approach to such issues as immigration, hazard and contaminated waste disposal, the relocation of households, global warming and the maintenance of food stocks. By plans we mean such issues as land-use designations, growth management or the general plan used to implement a policy. Programs are the outcomes of plans; examples might be striped bass management or a program to return wild salmon to Pacific Northwest Rivers. A project would be the building of irrigation facilities to enhance agricultural development or the expansion of an airport. We use examples at all four levels throughout this document.

The next section outlines the principles that guide the assessment as well as any good social science analysis. This is followed by guidelines for doing social impact assessments. Next there is a basic model for SIA, followed by an outline of the steps in doing an SIA. We conclude with a list of applicable publications and websites. Details regarding federal mandates, a glossary of terms and a list of acronyms may be found at <www.nmfs.noaa.gov/sfa/reports.htm> and <www.socialimpactassessment.net>.

Principles for social impact assessment

The following principles guide the concepts, process, and methods for doing social impact assessment. These principles are based on expert judgment of professional sociologists, anthropologists, social psychologists, geographers, land-use planners, economists, natural resource social scientists and landscape architects. These principles are meant to ensure sound scientific inquiry and the best practices established in the field over the last three decades. Figure 1 summarizes the principles and related guidelines.

US principles and guidelines for SIA

Achieve extensive understanding of local and regional settings to be affected by the action or policy
- Identify and describe interested and affected stakeholders and other parties
- Develop baseline information (profiles) of local and regional communities

Focus on key elements of the human environment
- Identify the key social and cultural issues related to the action or policy from the community and stakeholder profiles
- Select social and cultural variables which measure and explain the issues identified

Identify research methods, assumptions and significance
- Research methods should be holistic in scope, i.e. they should describe all aspects of social impacts related to the action or policy
- Research methods must describe cumulative social effects related to the action or policy
- Ensure that methods and assumptions are transparent and replicable
- Select forms and levels of data collection analysis which are appropriate to the significance of the action or policy

Provide quality information for use in decision-making
- Collect qualitative and quantitative social, economic and cultural data sufficient to usefully describe and analyze all reasonable alternatives to the action
- Ensure that the data collection methods and forms of analysis are scientifically robust
- Ensure the integrity of collected data

Ensure that any environmental justice issues are fully described and analyzed
- Ensure that research methods, data, and analysis consider underrepresented and vulnerable stakeholders and populations
- Consider the distribution all impacts (whether social, economic, air quality, noise, or potential health effects) to different social groups (including ethnic/racial and income groups)

Undertake evaluation/monitoring and mitigation
- Establish mechanisms for evaluation and monitoring of the action, policy or program
- Where mitigation of impacts may be required, provide a mechanism and plan for assuring effective mitigation takes place
- Identify data gaps and plan for filling these data needs

Figure 1. Principles and guidelines for social impact assessment

Principle 1: Achieve extensive understanding of local and regional populations and settings to be affected by the proposed action, program or policy. The use of SIA provides the best source of scientific knowledge necessary to understand the social and cultural consequences of planned and unplanned actions.

Principle 2: Focus on the key elements of the human environment related to the proposed action, program or policy. Application of the SIA process will ensure that the social and cultural concerns, values, consequences (costs) and benefits for human communities and populations will be included in the decision-making process.

Principle 3: The SIA is based upon sound and replicable scientific research concepts and methods. The SIA process subscribes to the ethic that good science (scholarship) will lead to informed and better decisions. To ensure the best and most appropriate methods are used, SIA practitioners should use trained and qualified social scientists. Protecting the confidentiality of study participants is a guiding tenet.

Principle 4: Provide quality information for use in decision-making. The 'good science' ethic requires the collection of quality data representative of all issues and perspectives, and holistic and transparent analyses of information and alternatives, clearly presented. To ensure the quality and completeness of information and analysis, an SIA should be peer-reviewed after scoping and prior to release.

Principle 5: Ensure that any environmental justice issues are fully described and analyzed. SIA practitioners must identify disadvantaged, at risk and minority populations (for instance, race, national origin, gender, handicap/disability and religion) affected by the proposed action, program, or policy and incorporate information about these populations in the SIA descriptions and analyses.

Principle 6: Undertake project, program or policy monitoring and evaluation and propose mitigation measures if needed. Use of the research design and databases established for the assessment of impacts should be the basis for monitoring and evaluating the actual impacts of the chosen alternative.

Guidelines for social impact assessment

In general, there is consensus, in federal and state mandates and among social impact practitioners, on: the types of impact that need to be considered; and on the need for

> **There is general consensus on: the types of impact to be considered; the need to include discussion of the proposed action; the components of the human environment where the impacts may be felt; likely social impacts; and the possible steps to enhance positive impacts and mitigate negative ones**

US principles and guidelines for SIA

the SIA to include a discussion of the proposed action. There is also general consensus on: the components of the human environment where the impacts are likely to be felt; likely social impacts; and the steps that could be taken to enhance positive impacts and to mitigate any negative ones.

Briefly, the consensus on types of impact to be considered would include social, cultural, demographic, economic, social–psychological, and sometimes political impacts. The discussion of the proposed action would describe, for example, any policy, plan, program, project or proposed facility. The consensus on the components of the human environment is that they would include descriptions and analyses of affected neighborhoods, communities and regions. The likely impacts are generally defined as the difference between the likely futures of the affected human environment with versus without the proposed action. There is also a general consensus that preferred alternatives should, when possible, avoid negative impacts and costs by appropriate modifications, efforts to minimize negative impacts and the provision of compensation for any that cannot be avoided or ameliorated.

As SIA textbooks point out (Burdge, 1999; Branch, *et al*, 1984; Taylor *et al*, 1995) and as suggested by the Council on Environmental Quality (CEQ) *Regulations for Implementing the Procedural Provisions of NEPA* (CEQ, 1986), the SIA practitioner should focus on the more significant impacts, should use appropriate measures and information, should provide qualitative and quantitative indicators where feasible and appropriate, and should present the social impacts in a manner that can be understood by decision-makers and affected communities alike.

The following guidelines are derived from the principles in the previous section. They are benchmarks for conducting an SIA. The principles are restated for clarity and flow of the discussion.

Principle 1.   Achieve extensive understanding of local and regional settings to be affected by the action or program or policy

Guideline 1a. Identify and describe interested and affected stakeholders and other parties. Because different social groups have a 'stake' in the outcomes associated with public- and private-sector actions, the assessor must be proactive in identifying these social groups (stakeholders) and understand their interests and values. Through public involvement, the SIA practitioner begins to understand the local context and identify and involve all potentially interested and affected groups at the very early stages of the assessment process.

Public involvement can facilitate the SIA process by identifying potentially affected groups, and by providing an opportunity to hear the 'meaning' of social and biophysical impacts. Public involvement is crucial in recruiting participants for the planning process who are truly representative of affected groups. However, involvement must be truly interactive with communication flowing both ways between the proponent agency and affected parties.

Guideline 1b. Develop baseline information (profiles) of local and regional communities. The community profile is a 'map' of the existing conditions and past trends associated with the human environment in which the proposed action is to take place. The terms community profiles and the baseline study are here used interchangeably. Baseline simply means a time line and associated social, cultural and community information from which to start the assessment.

For example, with construction projects, a geographical area is identified along with the distribution of special populations at risk. For policies, plans, programs, or other special assessments (for instance, technology, health, natural resources management), the relevant human environment may be a dispersed collection of interested and affected parties, pressure groups, organizations, and institutions. Typically, community and regional profiles include population and other demographic information, economic and employment data, descriptions of social and cultural institutions and their relationships to community and regional life, and an accounting of both social and economic capital and their distribution in the community and region.

Principle 2.   Focus on key elements of the human environment

Guideline 2a. Identify the key social and cultural issues related to the action or policy from the community and stakeholder profiles. NEPA regulations require public involvement in order to identify key issues for focusing the assessment of impacts (and eliminating or minimizing less important issues). SIA practitioners must contend with stringent time and resource constraints that affect the scope of the assessment and what can be achieved in the time available. Given such constraints, a central question emerges: "If you cannot cover the social universe, on what should you focus?" The answer is, first, the most significant impacts in order of priority, and secondly, all significant impacts for all interested and affected parties must be identified early using a variety of rapid appraisal or public involvement techniques.

Impacts identified by the public: Clearly, impacts identified as important by the public must be given high priority. Many of these will surface during the NEPA scoping process; however, as noted earlier, some groups low in power that may be adversely affected are rarely early participants in the planning process. It is essential that broadly based public involvement occur throughout the SIA process, but additional means (for instance, key informants, participant observation and, if funds and time are plentiful, surveys of the general population) often must be used to ensure that the most significant public concerns are addressed.

Impacts identified by SIA practitioners: SIA practitioners have the expertise to help prioritize impact issues using a review of the SIA literature, analysis of similar settings, and professional experience. These professionals will suggest issues unrecognized or unarticulated by either the general public or the agencies.

Provide feedback on social impacts: Identify issues that could be solved with changes to the proposed action or alternatives early in the process. Findings from the early SIA stages should feed back to the project planners and thus into the design of the proposed action to minimize adverse impacts and enhance positive impacts. The assessment process, therefore, should be designed as a dynamic one involving cycles of design, assessment, redesign, and reassessment.

This process should be conducted before the agency becomes strongly committed to some form of action. Therefore, it may need to be carried out informally with agency planners prior to publication of the assessment for public comment. Public input early in the process appears to be very influential.

Guideline 2b. Select social and cultural variables that measure and explain the issues identified. SIA variables point to measurable change in human populations, communities, and social relationships resulting from a proposed action. Social impact assessment variables can be grouped under the general headings of: population change; community and institutional structures; political and social resources; community and family changes; and community resources.

While the social profiles of communities and regions will contain as much information as possible on a wide variety of social variables, the SIA must focus on the action proposed and the human environment involved. Not all SIA variables (issues) identified by the public and SIA practitioners will have sufficient information to satisfactorily measure and explain potential changes and issues identified. Often it will be necessary to triangulate impacts using a variety of variables assessed with different measures. Social and cultural assessment variables are outlined in the next section under "A basic model for social impact assessment".

Principle 3.   Identify methods and assumptions and define significance

Guideline 3a. Research methods should be holistic in scope, that is, they should describe all aspects of social impacts related to the proposed action. The methods and assumptions used in the SIA should be summarized in the draft environmental impact statement or environmental assessment to allow decision makers and affected publics to evaluate the assessment process (as required by NEPA).

Practitioners will need to consult the CEQ Regulations. Definitions and examples of effects (primary, secondary and cumulative) are provided in 40 CFR 1508.7 and 1508.8 (CEQ, 1986). In these regulations "effects" and "impacts" are used synonymously. The CEQ Regulations are clear that an EIS has to focus on impacts found to be "significant" and Section 1508.27 defines significance in terms of "context" and "intensity" considerations. Context includes such considerations as society-as-a-whole, affected regions, affected interests and locality (for instance, when considering site-specific projects, local impacts assume greater importance than those of a regional nature).

The probable social impacts will be formulated in terms of predicted conditions without the actions (baseline condition), the predicted conditions with the actions and the predicted impacts that can be interpreted as the difference between the future with and without the proposed action. The empirical procedure is based on the social impact assessment model outlined below (Figure 2 in the next section).

Investigation of the probable impacts involves five major sources of information: detailed data from the sponsoring agency on the proposed action; the record of previous experience with similar actions as represented in the literature including other EIAs/SIAs; census and vital

SIA should use easily understood methods and assumptions that can be duplicated in similar settings: information must be collected using accepted social science methods and assumptions, and must be subjected to independent, formal peer-review

statistics; documents and secondary sources; and field research, including informant interviews, public hearings, group meetings and, if funds are available, surveys of the potentially impacted population. The investigation of the social impacts identified during scoping is the most important component.

Guideline 3b. Research methods must describe secondary and cumulative social effects related to the action or policy. Cumulative impacts are those that result from the incremental impacts of an action added to other past, present, and reasonably foreseeable future actions regardless of which agency or person undertakes them (see CEQ, 1986, 40 CFR 1508.7). A community's residential and retail growth and pressures on government services following the locating of a highway interchange are examples of secondary impacts. Cumulative impacts would add historical events in the vicinity of the interchange to the mix.

While they are more difficult to estimate precisely than primary impacts, it is very important that secondary and cumulative impacts be clearly identified in the SIA. CEQ (1997b) has prepared a *Cumulative Effects Handbook* which provides guidance on the subject and is available on-line on NEPA net (<http://ceq.eh.doe.gov/nepa/nepanet.htm>).

Guideline 3c. Ensure that methods and assumptions are transparent and replicable. Good scientific and research practice requires that any SIA should use methods and assumptions that are easily understood and can be duplicated in other similar settings. The Data Quality Act (2001) [P.L. 106-554, §515] reinforces this practice for any influential information and data, such as that used in environmental assessments or SIAs for federal actions, and guidance has been issued by the Office of Management and Budget [*Federal Register* 67(36), pages 8451–8460].

Information must be collected using accepted social science methods and assumptions, and must be subjected to an independent, formal peer-review before it can be used. Where data are to be kept confidential, the researcher must document the research design, methods and means of analysis and these must also be peer-reviewed to ensure that the methods and assumptions are transparent and replicable.

Guideline 3d. Select forms and levels of data collection and analysis that is appropriate to the significance of the

US principles and guidelines for SIA

action or policy. Published scientific literature and primary and secondary data from the affected area are the three sources of data for all SIAs. Balance among the three may vary according to the type of the proposed action, as well as specific considerations noted below, but all three will be relevant. The SIA practitioner must be sure, for federal projects, that any information and data used meet the requirements for the Data Quality Act (2001).

Published scientific literature The SIA should draw on existing, previously reviewed and screened social science literature that summarizes existing knowledge of impacts based on accepted scientific standards. Examples include journals, books and documents available from similar projects. A list of easy to obtain and recommended sources is provided in the bibliography. Existing documentation is needed in identifying which social impacts are likely to accompany the proposed action. When it is possible to draw potentially competing interpretations from the existing literature, the SIA should provide a careful discussion of relative methodological merits of available studies.

As pointed out under "A basic model for social impact assessment" in the next section, the best guidance for future expectations is past experience. Therefore, consideration of existing literature should err on the side of inclusiveness, not on exclusion of potentially relevant cases. Caution is needed when the SIA presents a conclusion that is contradicted by the published literature; in such cases, the reasons for the differences should be explicitly addressed. For example, anthropological data on rural, and ethnically and racially diverse communities is best for understanding the cultural context of the impacted community.

Secondary data sources The best sources are the Bureau of Census, and vital statistics, geographical data, and routine data collected by state and other federal agencies. Examples of other secondary data sources include: agency caseload statistics (for instance, from mental health centers, social service agencies and other human service providers, law enforcement agencies, and insurance and financial regulatory agencies); published and unpublished historical materials (often available in local libraries, historical societies, and school district files); compilations produced by service organizations (such as chambers of commerce, the better business bureaus, tourist offices, social organizations, and church groups); and the files of local newspapers.

These secondary sources can be used in conjunction with key-informant interviews, to allow for verification of informant memories and of potential sources of bias in the available documentary record.

Primary data from the affected area Survey research, oral histories and informant interviews are examples of primary data that may be collected to verify other findings. If a social assessor concludes that community impacts will differ from those documented elsewhere, this decision must be based on the collection and analysis of primary data that specifically show why such alternative conclusions are more credible. Local residents are an important source of expertise, both about local social and economic conditions and the broader range of likely impacts from a proposed action. If a community has a particularly unique history and structure, it may react to a development event or policy change differently than other communities. Following a basic tenet of social science research the practitioner must protect the confidentiality of study participants.

Principle 4.   Provide quality information for use in decision-making

Guideline 4a. Collect qualitative and quantitative social, economic and cultural data sufficient to usefully describe and analyze all reasonable alternatives to the action. Within the boundaries of good scientific and research practice, it is more important to identify likely social impacts than to precisely quantify the more obvious social impacts. All assessors strive to identify and quantify significant impacts, thereby providing decision makers and the affected public with information that is both as complete and as accurate as possible.

In cases where this desirable goal cannot be met, it is better to be roughly correct on important issues than to be precisely correct on unimportant ones. Within the context of the social impact statement, there are two important differences between impact identification (what are the general categories or types of impact that are likely to occur) and impact evaluation (precisely how 'significant' are those impacts likely to be?).

Research has identified social impacts resulting from many types of action, and the experienced SIA practitioner can identify plausible and potentially significant impacts relatively quickly and efficiently. On the other hand, an accurate evaluation is a resource-intensive process and deals with the question of significance. Research on the decision-making process has found that experts and policy makers were particularly prone toward premature closure.

Given a partial listing of potential impacts, experts tended to assume they have been given a complete list and, in most cases, fail to recognize the potential impacts that have been omitted from consideration. While empirical estimates can appear to be quite precise, demographic and economic projections have been shown by empirical analysis to have an average absolute error in the range of 50–100%.

We support the use of qualitative and quantitative measures of social impact assessment variables, but realize that the evaluation of significance has an important judgment component. The OMB (2001) Guidance for the Data Quality Act [*Federal Register* 67(36), pages 8451–8460] and the subsequent guidance issued by the federal agency sponsoring the action will assist the SIA practitioner in setting appropriate levels of significance for data analysis.

It is important to be on the 'conservative' side in reporting likely social impacts. The purpose of the EIS is to provide an even-handed treatment of the potential for impacts, offering a scientifically reasonable assessment of this potential in advance of the proposed action. It is a very different matter from providing solid proof of impacts after all the evidence is in!

All EISs and SIAs are by their nature anticipatory. Therefore, questions about the 'proof' of impacts cannot be answered with true confidence in advance of the actions in question. Accordingly, if the evidence for a potential social and economic impact is not definitive in either direction, the 'conservative' conclusion is that the impact cannot be ruled out with confidence, and not that the impact 'is not proven.' In cases of doubt, in terms of statistical terminology, the proper interpretation is the

Type II test for power/sensitivity, and not the Type I test for the strength of consistency of an association.

Guideline 4b. Ensure that the data collection methods and forms of analysis are scientifically robust. The fewer reliable data there are on the human environment effects of projects or policy change, the more important it is to have the SIA work performed by competent social scientists. There are two possible exceptions to the rule-of-thumb that SIA practitioners be trained social scientists.

In some cases, proposed actions are considered by reasonable persons (specifically those within the agency with demonstrated social science and SIA expertise and those in the potentially effected community) to be likely to create only negligible or nonexistent impacts on the human environment. In these situations, a finding of no significant impact (FONSI) would be issued by the agency and an environmental assessment (EA) would be conducted instead of an EIS.

In other cases a significant body of empirical findings is available from the social science literature that can be applied relatively directly to the proposed action in question, and should be referenced, summarized, and cited by the person(s) preparing the SIA section of the EIS.

Thus, the rigor of SIA data collection and analysis requires the use of professional social science expertise and inclusion of the relevant literature. Any other course would be imprudent for both the agency and affected groups and communities.

Guideline 4c. Ensure the integrity of collected data. Both good scientific and research practice and the provisions of the 2000 Data Quality Act ensure the integrity of collected data. Trained social scientists employing social science methods will provide the best results and the most legally defensible. The courts have demonstrated deference to agency scientists in exercising their expert judgment.

To ensure integrity of the SIA process, the need for professionally qualified, competent people with a social science background cannot be overemphasized. Protection of the confidentiality of collected data is also key to integrity. However, the assessor must remember his/her responsibilities under the Freedom of Information Act (FOIA) in planning the assessment design.

An experienced SIA practitioner will 'know the data,' and be familiar and conversant with existing social science evidence pertaining to impacts that have occurred elsewhere and therefore are relevant to the impact area in question. This breadth of knowledge and experience can prove invaluable in identifying important impacts that may not surface as public concerns or as mandatory considerations found in agency NEPA compliance procedures. A social scientist will be able to identify the full range of important impacts and select the appropriate measurement procedures.

Having a social scientist as part of the EIA/SIA team will also reduce the probability that an important social impact could go unrecognized. In assessing social impacts, if the evidence for a potential type of impact is not definitive in either direction, then the appropriate conservative conclusion is that it cannot be ruled out with confidence. In addition, it is important that the SIA practitioner be conversant with the technical and biological perspectives brought to bear on the project, and the cultural context of the agency in which he/she works.

The SIA practitioner should identify disadvantaged, at risk and minority populations, describe and measure their social and cultural characteristics, and incorporate this information into the SIA and the baseline data sets

Guideline 4d. Gaps in data or information. SIA practitioners may be required to produce an assessment in the absence of relevant or even necessary data. The three elements of this guideline are intended to supplement the guidance already provided by CEQ (1986) 40 CFR 1502.22, as amended by the removal of the requirement for a "worse-case analysis" (*Federal Register* 51, No. 80, Friday, April 25, 1986, pages 15818-626):

"When an agency is evaluating reasonably foreseeable significant adverse effects on the human environment in an environmental impact statement and there is incomplete or unavailable information, the agency shall always make clear that such information is lacking. (a) If the incomplete information … is essential to a reasoned choice among alternatives and (b) the overall costs of obtaining it are not exorbitant, the agency shall include the information in the environmental impact statement."

Only if the relevant information "cannot be obtained because the overall costs of obtaining it are exorbitant or the means to obtain it are not known," is the EIS permitted a gap in relevant information. In such cases, moreover, the EIS needs to include:

"(1) a statement of relevance of the incomplete or unavailable information … (2) a summary of existing credible scientific evidence [that] is relevant …, and (3) the agency's evaluation of such impacts based upon theoretical approaches or research methods generally accepted in the scientific community." (CEQ, 1986, 40 CFR 1502.22)

Principle 5. Ensure that any environmental justice issues are fully described and analyzed

Guideline 5a. Ensure that research methods, data, and analysis consider underrepresented and vulnerable stakeholders and populations. The Executive Order 12898 on Environmental Justice (Executive Office of the President of the United States, 1994) requires federal agencies to consider the impacts of any action on disadvantaged, at risk and minority populations. In the course of the SIA, the practitioner should take care to identify these special populations, describe and measure their social and cultural characteristics, and incorporate this information into the SIA and the baseline data sets. The assessor should be

US principles and guidelines for SIA

alert for different social meanings of environmental impacts as interpreted through the values of these different groups.

Examples abound in the literature of special populations that could be considered poor, sensitive, vulnerable and/or low-powered. The elderly have been identified as a category of persons sensitive to involuntary displacement and relocation. Children have suffered learning problems resulting from long-term exposure to various forms of transportation noise (for instance, vehicular traffic, rapid rail). Minority and low-income persons in the 1960s were disproportionately targeted as optimal sites for road construction, waste disposal sites and similar undesirable land uses.

Persons with some form of disability or impairment constitute another sensitive category with important needs. Farmers often are affected by transmission lines, water projects, or housing and commercial developments that take large amounts of land. Commercial fishers are often impacted by coastal and harbor development that restricts fishing opportunities or reduces available dock space.

Women have different financial, health and social concerns and may be vulnerable to changes in community focus. For example, a change from a textile manufacturing base (employing women) to a power plant (employing men) could lead to significant unemployment. The reverse could happen if the local economy changes from logging to tourism. The special impacts on these populations should be highlighted in an SIA, not lost in undifferentiated summary statistics.

Guideline 5b. Clearly identify who will win and who will lose, and emphasize vulnerability of under-represented and disadvantaged populations. Impacts should be specified for differentially affected populations and not just measured in the aggregate. Identification of all groups likely to be affected by a proposed action is central to the concept of impact equity. There will always be 'winners' and 'losers' (benefits and burdens) as the result of a decision to construct a dam, build a highway or close an area to timber harvesting. However, no category of persons, particularly those that might be considered more sensitive or vulnerable as a result of age, gender, ethnicity, race, occupation or other factors, should have to bear the brunt of adverse social and biophysical impacts.

While most proposals are not zero-sum situations and there may be varying benefits for almost all involved, the SIA practitioner has a special duty to identify those whose adverse impacts might be lost in the aggregate of benefits. The assessor must be attentive to those groups that lack political efficacy; such 'low-powered' groups often are not heard and therefore do not have their interests properly represented.

Principle 6. Undertake evaluation/monitoring and mitigation

Guideline 6a. Establish mechanisms for evaluation/monitoring of the proposed action that involve agency and stakeholders and/or communities. Crucial to the SIA process is the monitoring of significant social impact variables and the mitigation programs that have been put in place. As indicated earlier, the identification of impacts might depend on the specification of contingencies. For example, if the in-migration of workers during the construction phase is a work force of 1,000, special and additional housing will be needed, but if it is only 50 and the community is large, present accommodation may be sufficient.

Identifying and monitoring infrastructure needs is a key element of the local planning process. Two important points are: monitoring and mitigation should be a joint agency (proponent)–community responsibility; and both activities should occur on an iterative basis throughout the project life cycle (Figure 3).

Depending on the nature of the proposal and time horizons for completion/implementation, the focus of long-term responsibility for monitoring and mitigation is not easily defined. Research shows that trust and expertise are key factors in choosing the balance between proponent and community monitoring activities. Few federal agencies have the resources to continue monitoring for an extended period and therefore local communities should be provided resources to assume a portion of the monitoring and mitigation responsibilities.

Guideline 6b. Where mitigation of impacts is required, provide analyses and assessments of alternatives. A social impact assessment not only forecasts impacts, it should identify means to mitigate adverse impacts. Mitigation includes: avoiding the impact by not taking or modifying an action; minimizing, rectifying, or reducing the impacts through redesign or operation of the project or policy; or compensating for irreversible impacts by providing substitute facilities, resources, or opportunities (see CEQ, 1986, 40 CFR 1508.20; and under "Steps in the social impact assessment process").

Ideally, mitigation measures are built into the selected alternative, but it is appropriate to identify them even if they are not immediately adopted or if they would be the responsibility of another organization or government unit. Also, if an agency prepares an EA and identifies potentially significant social impacts, then that agency will be required to identify and implement mitigation measures to reduce the impact(s) below the threshold of significance if they wish to implement the action based on a FONSI rather than go on to prepare an EIS.

Guideline 6c. Identify data gaps and assess data needs. As the SIA progresses, data gaps and related methodological problems will emerge. These should be fully documented and incorporated with the findings of the SIA. For example, in natural resource management agencies, federal actions and programs will be changed and modified over time necessitating development of a new SIA. Knowledge of data gaps and data needs permit agencies to collect new information and to build baseline data sets.

A basic model for social impact assessment

Link between EIA and SIA

Impacts on human environment both resemble and differ from biophysical impacts.

- Social impacts can vary in desirability, ranging from the positive to the adverse.
- They also vary in scale — the question of whether a facility will create 50 or 1,000 jobs, for example, or

whether it will have the potential to spill 50 or 1,000 gallons of toxic waste.
- Another consideration involves the extent or duration of impacts in time and space. Like biophysical impacts, some social impacts can be of short duration, while others can last a lifetime; and some communities 're-turn to normal' quite quickly once a source of disruption is removed, while others do not.
- Social impacts can also vary in intensity or severity, a dimension that may be defined differently in a different context, just as the same 'objective' biophysical impact (for instance, a predicted loss of 75 sea otters) might have an almost imperceptible effect on populations in one location (for example, off the coast of Alaska) while amounting to a significant fraction of the remaining population in another location (off the coast of California).
- Similarly, there are differences in the degree to which social impacts are likely to be cumulative, at one extreme, or mutually counterbalancing, at the other.

In addition, it is important to consider the social equity or distributions of impacts on different populations. Just as the biological sections of EISs devote particular attention to species having special vulnerabilities, the social and economic sections of EISs must devote particular attention to the impacts on vulnerable and disadvantaged segments of the human population. Examples include: the poor, the elderly, adolescents, or unemployed women; members of minority and/or other groups that are racially, ethnically, and/or culturally distinctive; or occupational, cultural, political or value-based groups for whom a given community, region, or use of some component of the biophysical environment is particularly important.

In addition to the types of disturbance that can affect other species, humans are affected by changes in the distinctly human environment, including those associated with the phenomenon referred to as the 'social construction of reality'. Social constructions are not mere perceptions or emotions, to be distinguished from reality; rather, how we view a social situation determines how we behave. Furthermore, social constructions of reality are characteristic of all social groups, including the agencies that are attempting to implement change as well as the communities that are affected.

In the case of proposed actions that involve controversy (attitudes and perceptions toward a proposed policy change are one of the variables that must be considered in determining the significance of impacts (CEQ, 1986, 40 CFR 1508.27(4)), participants are often tempted to dismiss the concerns of others as being merely imagined or perceived. There are two important reasons not to omit

We use a comparative SIA method to study the course of events in a location where planned environmental change has occurred and to extrapolate from that analysis what is likely to happen in another location where a similar action is proposed

such concerns from SIAs and EISs. First, the positions taken by all sides in a given controversy are likely to be shaped by (differing) perceptions of the proposed action. The decision to accept one set of perceptions while excluding another may not be scientifically defensible. Second, if a proponent asserts that their critics are emotional or misinformed, for example, they are guaranteed to raise the level of hostility between themselves and community members and will stand in the way of a successful resolution of the problem.

In summary, some of the most important aspects of social impacts involve not, for example, the physical relocation of human populations, but the meanings or significance attached to these changes.

Social impact assessment model

To predict the probable impact of development, we seek to understand the behavior of individuals and communities affected by agency developments or policy changes. We use a comparative SIA method to study the course of events in a location where planned environmental change has occurred and to extrapolate from that analysis what is likely to happen in another location where a similar action is proposed. As shown in Figure 2, if we wish to know the probable effects of a proposed power plant in location (b), one of the best places to start is to assess the effects of a power plant that is operational in location (a). Example SIA variables to access impacts are shown later in this section.

It is almost impossible to catalogue all dimensions of social impacts because change has a way of creating other changes. A freeway extension that facilitates residential growth can lead to increased traffic and air pollution, creation of new schools, retail centers and other services, and the decline of downtown commercial centers.

```
                                    Power plant
Comparative study (a)         T₁ₐ--------x-------->T₂ₐ
(development)

                                    Proposed power plant
Impact study (b)              T₂ᵦ--------x-------->T₃ᵦ


Control study (c)    T₁c------------>T₂c------------>T₃c------------>T₄c
                     (past)       (present)    (future without)  (far future)
```

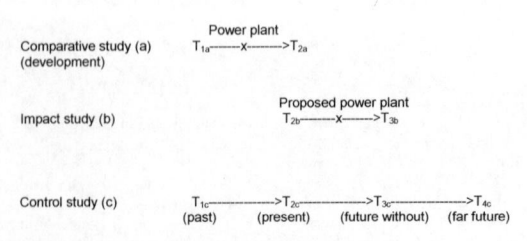

Figure 2. Basic social impact assessment model

US principles and guidelines for SIA

In Table 1 (later in this section) we have identified some basic social dimensions that can be measured; they reflect fundamental and important characteristics of a community. Studied over time, these characteristics give us insight as to how social structure will be altered when change occurs. Faced with a proposal to implement a new ski area, for example, the community and the agency proposing the change can profit from the experience of other communities that have developed ski areas and thereby gain a reasonably accurate expectation of how the project will affect their community.

Forecasted impacts are the difference in the human environment between a future with the proposed action and a future without (see Figure 2). Since we cannot see the future, we look at other communities that have experienced similar policies or projects in the past. Thus, the social impact assessment model is comparative — the social impacts in one community may be projected to a location where a similar action is proposed. The model in Figure 2 also permits a follow-up SIA of the impacted community to assess what the actual impact has been, so that the fit between forecasts and outcome can be matched (the difference between T_{1a} and T_{2a}).

One way to capture the dynamic quality of something as far-reaching and complex as social impacts is to metaphorically take a series of snapshots over time as implementation of the agreed action unfolds and fill in what happened in between. Ideally, information about the community or geographic area of study is available both before and after the event to help in measurement. Social impacts then become the changes taking place between the two measurement points (T_{2b} and T_{3b}). The social assessor then attempts to forecast the change associated with the proposed action based on the research and information accumulated from comparative studies of similar impact settings (T_{1a} and T_{2a}).

Based on the directives outlined in NEPA and the CEQ regulations, we also need to identify irreversible and undesirable social effects of development before they occur to make recommendations for mitigation. As we point out in a later section, the appropriate federal agency in co-operation with state and local governments and the local community bears responsibility for coordinating mitigation efforts. The SIA model also allows us to address the issue of alternative plans and alternative impacts of a proposed action. Moreover, because social impacts can be measured and understood, recommendations for mitigating actions on the part of the agencies can be made. In the next section we outline a procedure for mitigating potentially adverse impacts.

Another strength of the comparative SIA model is that, with appropriate data sources (those that can be collected frequently, such as, land transfer records, population and employment numbers), it allows for a dynamic interpretation of events and can provide monitoring of short-term impacts. Moreover, this kind of frequent monitoring provides a continual source of evaluation or check on the direction of forecasts made about social impacts.

Stages in policy/project development

All projects go through a series of steps or stages, starting with initial and detailed planning (to include impact assessment), followed by implementation and/or construction carrying through to operation and maintenance (Figure 3). At some point the implemented action might be abandoned or decommissioned, or official policy could change. Social impacts will be different for each stage.

Scoping of issues prior to analysis may lead the assessor to focus only on one stage. For example, one community might be concerned about public reaction resulting from a proposal to site a hazardous waste disposal facility, another with the construction aspects of reservoirs, while a third might be faced with a change in the designation of adjacent public land from timber production to wilderness use. The specific stage is an important factor in determining impacts; and not all social (or biophysical) impacts will occur at each stage. Figure 3 illustrates the stages in federal agency planning and implementation.

Stage 1. General planning/policy development and preliminary impact assessment Social impacts actually begin the day the proposed action is announced and can be measured from that point. We often assume that no impacts will take place until stage 3 (construction/implementation begins) through dirt-moving operations or, for example, restrictions on water use. However, real, measurable, and often significant impacts on the human environment begin to take place as soon as there are changes in social or economic conditions following announcement. From the time of the earliest announcement of a pending policy change or rumor about a project, both hopes and hostilities can begin to mount; speculators can lock up potentially important properties, politicians can maneuver for position, and interest groups can form or redirect their energies. These changes occur by merely introducing new information into a community or region.

Depending upon the proposed action, activities in this stage include: creation of a public involvement program; system planning; preliminary project concept; attentive action design; notification of both public officials and the general public and gathering their input; relevant 'outside' agency contacts and gathering their input; preliminary 'fatal flaw' impact assessment; preliminary work toward acquisition of property or right-of-way permits; licensing;

| Stage 1. General planning/policy development and preliminary impact assessment |
| Stage 2. Detailed planning, funding and impact assessment |
| Stage 3. Construction/implementation |
| Stage 4. Operation/maintenance |
| Stage 5. Decommissioning/abandonment |

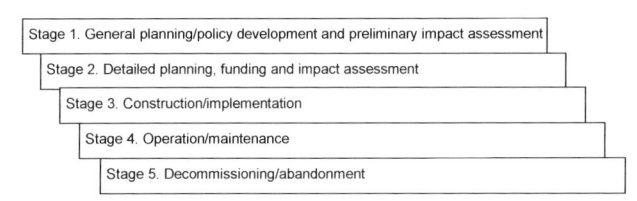

Figure 3. Stages in project/policy development

and groundwork for any necessary changes in laws, regulations, or procedures. Basic policy decisions, such as the mix of problem solutions and prioritizations of implementation, are determined. These policy decisions determine the benefits and burdens of, and to, individuals and communities that are immediately and ultimately impacted.

Stage 2. Detailed planning, funding and impact assessment Once the local land-use plan is in place, reality and fiscal aspects come into play. Prioritized implementation activities with designated funding sources guide these more detailed activities. As funds and funding sources are recognized, more detailed project planning takes place, including the assessment of social impacts. Examples include detailed project design, revision, continuing public input, licensing, evaluation of alternatives and their varied impacts, and, ultimately, the decision to proceed with the proposed action or an alternative.

Stage 3. Construction/implementation The construction/implementation stage, begins when a decision is made to proceed, a permit is issued or a law or regulation takes effect. For typical construction projects, this involves clearing land, building access roads, developing utilities, and so on. Acquisition of needed right of way, displacement and relocation of people, if necessary, occur during this phase.

Depending on the scale of the project, the buildup of a migrant construction work force also may occur. If significant in-migration occurs, the new residents may create a strain on community infrastructure, and social stresses as a result of changing patterns of social interaction. Communities may have difficulties in responding to the increased demands on school, health facilities, housing and other social services. Further stresses may be created by resentments between newcomers and long-term residents, by sudden increases in the prices for housing and local services, and even by increased uncertainty about the future.

Stage 4. Operation/maintenance The operation/maintenance stage occurs after the construction is complete and/or the policy is fully operational. In many cases, this stage will require fewer workers than the construction/implementation phase, and, particularly if operations continue at a relatively stable level for an extended period of time, the effects during this stage can often be the most beneficial of any stage. Communities seeking industrial development will often focus on this stage, for example, because of the long-term financial benefits that may follow. It is also during this stage that the communities can adapt to new social and economic conditions, accommodation can take place and the expectations of positive benefits, such as stable population, quality infrastructure and employment opportunities, can be realized.

In natural resource management, the operational stage will see shifts in activities by stakeholders. Where resource allocation is insufficient to support previous operations, consolidation will occur or stakeholders will switch to alternative activities. In farming, grazing or forestry, land may be sold or leased, thus reducing the number of operators. Alternatively, small stakeholders may stay in business but supplement their income with second jobs, or, in the case of commercial fishing, switch to other fisheries.

The projects and policy decisions that require, and benefit from, SIA range from prison and plant sitings to highway, reservoir, power plant construction, and managing old growth forests to maintain a biologically diverse region

Stage 5. Abandonment/decommissioning Abandonment/decommissioning begins when the proposal is made that the project or policy and associated activity will cease at some time in the future. As in the planning stage, the social effects of decommissioning begin when the intent to close down is announced and the community or region must again adapt, but this time to the loss of the project or an adjustment to a policy change.

Sometimes this means the loss of the economic base as a business closes its doors. At other times, the disruption to the local community may be lessened or at least altered if one type of worker is replaced by another. Such a case was the 1994 closing of the Hanford Facility in Washington State, where nuclear production facilities closed down, but employment actually increased as environmental cleanup specialists were hired to help deal with the contamination at the facility.

In other cases, disruption may be exacerbated if the community is not only losing its present economic base, but has lost the capacity to return to a former economic base. Morgan City, Louisiana which had been the self-proclaimed "shrimp capital of the world" in the 1950s is a good example of this. During the 1960s and 1970s, employment in this community shifted to offshore oil development. When oil prices collapsed in the 1980s, the community found it could not return to the shrimp industry because shrimp-processing facilities had closed down, and most of the shrimp boats had been allowed to decay or their crews had left the area.

Policy and project decision settings

The projects and policy decisions that require, and benefit from, social impact assessment range from prison and plant sitings to highway, reservoir, power plant construction, and managing old growth forests to maintain a biologically diverse region. Accordingly, the location of proposed actions may range from isolated wilderness areas to urban neighborhoods, each with special characteristics that can affect social impacts.

Social impacts (and economic and biophysical changes) will vary depending on the type of activity and existing social structure. The following examples of policies, plans, programs and projects (PPPPs) were taken from the *Digest of Environmental Impact Statements*, which is a cumulative listing of all the environmental impact statements done by federal agencies in the USA.

- mineral extraction, including surface and underground mining, and new oil and gas drilling;

US principles and guidelines for SIA

- federal health-care policies to include social security, Medicare and Medicade;
- hazardous and sanitary waste sites, including the construction and operation of disposal sites for a variety of hazardous and sanitary wastes (also included are facilities that burn or otherwise destroy chemical and toxic wastes);
- power plants including both nuclear and fossil-fuel electrical generating facilities and associated developments;
- reservoirs, including all water impoundments for flood control, hydro power, conservation, recreation, and cooling lakes and diversion structures;
- industrial plants (manufacturing facilities built and operated by the private sector, for instance, refineries, steel mills and assembly lines);
- land-use designations, such as, zoning activity, comprehensive growth-management plans, and the reclassification of land use (timber production to wilderness);
- living natural resource management plans, including fisheries, endangered species, bird and wildlife, and range and forest;
- military and governmental installations, including base closures and openings;
- schools; both public and private, primary, secondary and university;
- transportation facilities, including airports, streets, terminals;
- linear developments, including subways, railroads, highways, power lines, aqueducts, bike paths, bridges, pipelines, sewers, fences, walls and barrier channels, green belts, waterways;
- trade facilities, including businesses, shopping centers;
- designation of sacred sites;
- parks, preserves, refuges, cemeteries, recreation areas;
- housing facilities, including apartments, office buildings, hospitals.

Identifying social impact assessment variables

SIA variables point to measurable change in human population, communities, and social relationships resulting from a proposed action. Based on a half century of research on local community change, rural industrialization, reservoir and highway development, natural resource development, and social change in general, we outline a list of social variables under the general headings of: population change; community and institutional structures; political and social resources; community and family changes; and community resources (Table 1).

- Population change refers to present population and expected change; ethnic and racial diversity, influxes and outflows of temporary residents, and the arrival of seasonal or leisure residents.
- Community and institutional structures mean the size, structure, breadth and level of organization of local government, and linkages to the larger political systems. Also included are historical and present patterns of employment and industrial diversification, the size and level of activity of voluntary associations and interest groups, religious organizations and, importantly, how these institutions relate to each other.
- Political and social resources refer to the distribution of power authority, the identification of interested and affected parties, and the leadership capability and capacity within the community or region.
- Community and family changes refer to factors that influence the daily life of individuals and families, including family living and work arrangements, attitudes, perceptions, family characteristics and friendship networks. These changes range from attitudes toward the policy to an alteration in family and friendship networks and perceptions of risk, health, and safety.
- Community resources include patterns of natural resource and land use, and the availability of housing and community services to include health, police and fire protection and sanitation facilities. A key to the continuity and survival of human communities is their historical, archaeological and cultural resources. Under this collection of variables we examine possible changes for indigenous populations and religious sub-cultures.

At this point in the discussion of an SIA model we have demonstrated a conceptual procedure for both examining and accumulating information about social impacts. We have also outlined a matrix that demonstrates that social impacts will be different depending on the project/policy type and the stage of development. The next step in the development of the model is to suggest the social impact variables for stages in project development given different project/policy types and settings.

SIA variables, project/policy stage and setting

The five stages of project/policy development affect the social processes that produce changes in characteristics of the community or region. The SIA specialists must construct a matrix to direct their investigation of potentially significant social impacts. Sample matrices are shown in Tables 1 and 2. For each project/policy stage, the assessor should identify potential impacts on each SIA variable identified in the matrix. This approach ensures that no critical areas are overlooked.

We emphasize that Table 1 does not represent all social impact assessment variables that may be of interest for any project. It is presented to illustrate the issues that represent the beginning of such a task. The task for the assessor is to spell out the magnitude and significance of impacts for each cell like those identified in the illustrations.

Table 2 provides an abbreviated illustration of how the SIA variables (as suggested in Table 1) might be applied within the context of both the setting type and the stage of the SIA process. The first example is the siting of a hazardous waste facility. Perceptions about problems of public health and safety, and concerns as to how different agencies work together could emerge during the planning stages. If a decision is made to go ahead, construction would be accompanied by an influx of temporary workers. In the case of the new highway, displacement and relocation concerns will surface during planning and safety concerns during the operational stage. These analytic procedures would be repeated for each of the SIA variables for each stage in the assessment process. The procedures for accomplishing this task are outlined the next section on steps in the SIA process

Steps in the social impact assessment process

The social impact assessment itself may contain the ten steps outlined in Figure 4. These steps are logically

US principles and guidelines for SIA

Table 1. Matrix relating project stage to social impact assessment variables

Social impact assessment variables[a]	General planning, policy development preliminary assessment	Detailed planning, funding & impact assessment	Construction implement	Operation/ maintenance	Decommission/ abandonment
Population change					
Population size density & change					
Ethnic & racial comp. & distribution					
Relocating people					
Influx & outflows of temporaries					
Presence of seasonal residents					
Community & institutional structures					
Voluntary associations					
Interest group activity					
Size & structure of local government					
Historical experience with change					
Employment/income characteristics					
Employment equity of disadvantaged groups					
Local/regional/national linkages					
Industrial/commercial diversity					
Presence of planning & zoning					
Political & social resources					
Distribution of power & authority					
Conflict newcomers & old-timers					
Identification of stakeholders					
Interested and affected parties					
Leadership capability & characteristics					
Interorganizational cooperation					
Community and family changes					
Perceptions of risk, health & safety					
Displacement/relocation concerns					
Trust in political & social institutions					
Residential stability					
Density of acquaintanceships					
Attitudes toward proposed action					
Family & friendship networks					
Concerns about social well-being					
Community resources					
Change in community infrastructure					
Indigenous populations					
Changing land use patterns					
Effects on cultural, historical, sacred & archaeological resources					

Note: [a] These variables are suggestive and illustrative and are intended to provide a beginning point for the social assessor. Taylor *et al* (1995) (and the US Forest Service Manual and Handbook (1982)) use the categories of: population change; life style; attitudes, beliefs and values; and social organization. Burdge (1999) uses population impacts; community and institutional arrangements; communities in transition; individual and family-level impacts; and community infrastructure needs. Branch et al (1984) use the categories of social impact assessment variables in their social organization model: direct project inputs; community resources; community social organization; and indicators of individual and family well-being. The US Bureau of Reclamation (BOR) (2002) uses the seven categories of population; community composition; community infrastructure needs; community attitudes and institutional structure; community identity and attitudes toward water; individuals and families; and social justice and Native American responsibilities.

sequential, but often overlap in practice. This sequence is patterned after the EIA steps as listed in the 1986 *CEQ Guidelines*. The corresponding NEPA steps are included within Figure 4.

Public involvement

This means developing an effective public involvement plan to involve all potentially affected public groups. It requires identifying and working with all potentially affected individuals and groups starting at the very beginning of planning for the proposed action and alternatives. Groups affected by proposed actions include: those who live nearby; those who will hear, smell or see a development; those who are forced to relocate because of a project; and those who have an interest in the proposal but may not live in proximity.

Others affected include those who might normally use the land on which the project is located (such as farmers who have to plow around a transmission line). Also there are those affected by the influx of seasonal residents because they may have to pay higher prices for food or rent,

US principles and guidelines for SIA

Table 2. Social impact assessment variables, by policy/project setting (type) and stage in SIA process

Policy/ project settings	Stage in SIA process				
	General planning, policy develop preliminary assessment	Detailed planning funding & impact assessment	Construct/ implement	Operation/ maintenance	Decommission/ abandonment
Hazardous waste site	Inter-organization cooperation	Perceptions of risk, health & safety	Influx of temporary workers	Trust in political/social institutions	Alteration in size of local government
Highway project	Formation of attitudes toward the project	Displacement & relocation concerns	Residential stability	Perceptions of risk, health & safety	Community infrastructure
Forest Service to Park Service Management	Attitude toward proposed action	Interested & affected parties	Trust in political & social institutions	Influx of recreation users	Re-distribution of power authority

or pay higher taxes to cover the cost of expanded community services.

The practitioner must be aware of literacy levels, language barriers, and cultural differences in preparing the public involvement program. Potentially affected public groups also may be identified through spatially oriented census data, literature review, networking with agency contact lists or referrals from field staff. Once identified, representatives from each interested and affected party should be systematically consulted to determine potential areas of concern/impact and ways each representative might be involved during initial planning and the final decision. A full range of public involvement techniques should be used to collect information about public response to a proposed action. In this first step, the pieces are put in place for a public involvement program which will last through implementation and become the foundation for monitoring. Most agencies will have a public involvement unit for support.

Describe proposed action

This involves describing the proposed action or policy and, if appropriate, reasonable alternatives. During this step, the proposed action is described in enough detail to begin to identify the data requirements needed from the

Steps	Category
1. Develop public involvement program	Public involvement
2. Describe proposed action and alternatives	Identification
3. Describe relevant human environment and zones of influence	Community profile
4. Identify probable impacts	Scoping
5. Investigate probable impacts	Projection of estimated effects
6. Determine probable response of affected parties	
7. Estimate secondary & cumulative impacts	
8. Recommend changes in proposed action or alternatives	Formulation of alternatives
9. Mitigation, remediation, and enhancement plan	Mitigation
10. Develop and implement monitoring program	Monitoring

← Include interested and affected parties in all steps of the SIA process ..→

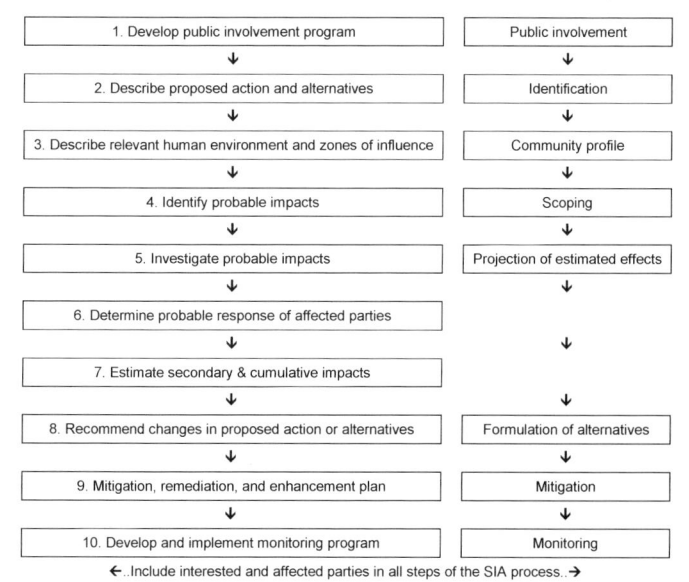

Figure 4. Steps in the social impact assessment process

proponent to do a preliminary assessment. For example, in new road construction, the assessor would need to know location; land requirements; need for ancillary facilities (transmission lines, sewer and water lines); construction schedule; size of the work force (construction and operation, by year or month); facility size/shape; need for local work force; and institutional resources.

The list of social impact assessment variables shown in Table 1 is used as a guide for obtaining data from project proponents. Sometimes the description of the proposed alternatives may not include all the information needed for an SIA. Another problem is the provision of summary numbers when disaggregated numbers are needed. For example, the social assessor may be given numbers for the total peak work force of a construction project, when information is needed on local and non-local commuting workers as well as those hired from outside the area.

Community profiles (baseline study)

This stage involves describing the relevant human environment/zones of influence and baseline conditions. The community profile is the existing conditions and past trends associated with the human environment in which the proposed action is to take place. The terms community profiles and the baseline study are here used interchangeably. Baseline simply means a geographical and time line to start the assessment. For example, with construction projects, a geographical area is identified along with the distribution of special populations at risk; but for policies, plans, programs, or other special assessments (such as, technology, health), the relevant human environment may be a more dispersed collection of interested and affected parties, pressure groups, organizations, and institutions.

The example dimensions for investigation of the human environment listed below apply for construction projects and geographically located programs and policies (the social impact assessment variables listed in Table 1 provide additional guidance for the community profile):

- Relationships with the biophysical environment, including: ecological setting; aspects of the environment seen as resources/problems; areas having economic, recreational, esthetic and/or symbolic significance to indigenous populations; residential arrangements and living patterns, including relationships among communities/social organizations; and if available, attitudes toward environmental and patterns of natural resource use.
- Historical background, including: initial settlement and subsequent shifts in population; key developmental events and eras, including experience with boom–bust effects and a discussion of broader employment trends; past or ongoing community controversies, particularly those involving technology and/or the environment; and other experiences likely to affect the level or distribution of the impacts of, and/or local receptivity to, the proposed action.
- Political and social resources, includes: who has the authority and resources to address issues and problems; the capacities of relevant systems or institutions (for instance, the school system); friendship networks and patterns of cleavage or cooperation among potentially affected groups; levels of residential stability; distributions of socio-demographic characteristics such as age and ethnicity; presence of distinctive or potentially vulnerable groups (for instance, low income); and linkages among geopolitical units (federal, state, county, local and inter-local).
- Culture, attitudes and social-psychological conditions, including: attitudes toward the proposed action; trust in political and social institutions; perceptions of risks; relevant psychological coping and adjustment capacity; cultural cognition of society and environment; assessed quality of life; and important values that may be relevant to, or affected by, the proposed action.
- Economic and financial background (to the extent not listed in other parts of the community profile) include: historical numbers of persons employed by financial sectors and type of firm; payroll size and the amounts of business and sales receipts and taxes by sector and type of firm.
- Population characteristics including: the demographics of relevant groups (including all significant stakeholders and underrepresented and disadvantaged populations and groups); major industrial and agricultural activities; the labor markets to include available labor by occupational category by race and nation origin; unemployment and underemployment numbers; present population and expected changes; availability of housing, infrastructure and services; size, gender and age structure of households; and seasonal migration patterns to include both leisure and labor migrants.

The level of effort devoted to the description of the human environment should be commensurate with the size, cost and degree of expected impacts of the proposed action. At a minimum, the existing literature on comparable or analogous impact events, key local informants and readily available documents such as government reports should be consulted. On-site investigations are a must. If available, always use the findings from previous field studies, general surveys, rapid appraisals and mini-surveys.

Scoping

After obtaining a technical understanding of the proposed action, identify the full range of probable social impacts that will be addressed based on discussion/interviews with sponsoring agency and potentially affected populations. During initial scoping, the SIA practitioner selects the SIA variables for further assessment situations. Consideration needs to be devoted to both the impacts perceived by the sponsoring agency and those perceived by

After obtaining a technical understanding of the proposed action, identify the full range of probable social impacts that will be addressed based on discussion/interviews with sponsoring agency and potentially affected populations

US principles and guidelines for SIA

interested and affected publics and key stakeholders. At this point in the process, available methods are reviews of the existing social science literature and public scoping based on appropriate public participation techniques. Ideally, all affected publics contribute to the selection of SIA variables for assessment, either through a participatory process or by review and comment on the decisions made by responsible officials and the interdisciplinary SIA–EIA team.

Relevant criteria for selecting 'significant' social impacts comparable to those spelled out in the CEQ (1986) Regulations (40 CFR 1508.27), include the:

- probability of the event occurring;
- number of people and/or indigenous populations that will be affected;
- duration of impact (long term vs short term);
- value of benefits and/or costs (benefits and burdens) to impacted groups (intensity of impacts);
- extent to which identified social impacts are reversible or can be mitigated;
- likelihood that an identified impact will lead to secondary or cumulative impacts;
- relevance for present and future policy decisions;
- uncertainty over possible effects;
- presence or absence of controversy over the issue.

Investigate probable impacts

This involves investigating the probable social impacts, which will be formulated in terms of predicted conditions without the actions (baseline condition), the predicted conditions with the actions and the predicted impacts, which can be interpreted as the differences between the future with and without the proposed action. The empirical procedure is based on the social impact assessment model outlined (see Figure 2).

Investigation of the probable impacts involves five major sources of information: detailed data from the sponsoring agency on the proposed action; record of previous experience with similar actions as represented in reference literature to include other EIAs–SIAs; census and vital statistics; documents and secondary sources; and field research, including informant interviews, hearings, group meetings and, if funds are available, surveys of the general population. Population 'pockets' within the area need to be over-sampled if there is reason to believe there will be disproportionate impacts. The investigation of the social impacts identified during scoping is the most important component.

Methods of projecting the future lie at the heart of the SIA process and much of the process of analysis is tied up in this endeavor. Care must be taken to ensure the quality and transparency of methods and data and to provide for critical review (compare with Data Quality Act, 2001). Most of the methods to analyze social impacts fall into the following categories:

- Comparative method: The SIA model (Figure 2) uses the comparative research approach. The present is compared to the future with the proposed action. Based on past research and experiences in similar cases, determination of significance is made based on the comparative data presented.
- Straight-line trend projections means taking an existing trend and simply projecting the same rate of change into the future; we assume that what happened in the past is likely to happen in the future. For example, recreation visitations increase each year at about the same rate they did in the past.
- Population multiplier methods means each specified increase in population implies designated multiples of other variables, such as jobs, housing units and other infrastructure needs.
- Statistical significance means calculations to determine probabilistic differences between with and without the proposed action. A social assessor could employ comparative statistical methods to determine statistical significance for appropriate SIA variables.
- Scenarios refers to logical-imaginations based on construction of hypothetical futures through a process of mentally modeling the assumptions about the SIA variables in question.
- Expert judgment: persons familiar with the study area could be asked to present scenarios and assess the significant implications for the proposed action.
- Calculation of 'futures forgone': a number of methods have been formulated to determine what options would be given up irrevocably as a result of a plan or project, for instance, river recreation and agricultural land use after the building of a dam. The wetlands mitigation strategy is such an example.

The record of previous experience is very important to the estimation of future impacts. It is largely contained in case reports and studies and the experience of other assessors. Variations in the patterns of impacts and responses in these cases also should be registered. Expert knowledge is used to enlarge this knowledge base and to judge how the proposed action is likely to deviate from typical patterns. The documents and secondary sources provide information on existing conditions, plans, reported attitudes and opinions, and contribute to the present assessment. The field research involves interviews with persons who have different interests at stake, different perspectives, and different kinds of expertise.

Wherever feasible, it should also involve a search through a wide range of documentation that is often available in forms ranging from official statistics to the minutes of organizations, the meetings and letters to the editor. The opinions of the various publics toward the proposed action should also be part of the record. If time and funding permits, surveys of the general population are valuable to assess public opinion, because spokespersons do not always represent the views of the rank and file. Public meetings should be used to identify possible impacts but not to collect data for projections.

Determine responses to impacts

This step involves determining the significance of the identified social impacts. Projecting is both a very important and a very difficult assessment task, but the responses of affected parties frequently will have significant higher-order impacts. After the direct impacts have been estimated, the assessor must next estimate how the affected publics will respond in attitude and actions. Their attitudes before implementation predict their attitudes afterwards, though there is increasing data that show fears are often overblown and that expected (often promised) benefits fail to meet expectations.

The actions of affected publics are to be estimated

using comparable cases and interviews with those affected about what they expect to do. So much depends on whether local leadership arises and the objectives and strategies of these leaders, that this assessment step often is highly uncertain, but at least policy makers will be notified of potential problems and unexpected results.

This step is also important because adoption and responses of affected publics can have consequences of their own, whether for an agency that proposes an action (as when political protest stalls a proposal) or for the affected communities, whether in the short term or in the longer term (as in the previously noted example of Morgan City, Louisiana).

Patterns in previous assessments guide this analysis, and expert judgment and field investigations are used to determine whether the study case is following the typical patterns or how it is developing uniquely. Being able to show both the proponent and potentially affected publics that significant impacts are being incorporated into the assessment is critical to the success of this step.

Secondary and cumulative impacts

This involves estimating subsequent impacts and cumulative impacts. Secondary or indirect impacts are those caused by the primary or direct impacts; they often occur later both in time and geographic distance than primary impacts. Cumulative impacts are those resulting from the incremental impacts of an action added to other past, present, and reasonably foreseeable future actions regardless of which agency or person undertakes them (see CEQ, 1986, 40 CFR 1508.7)

A community's residential and retail growth and pressures on government services following the siting of a highway interchange are examples of secondary impacts. Cumulative impacts would be the sum of the proposed action plus past and present activity in the same area. While they are more difficult to estimate precisely than primary impacts, it is very important that secondary and cumulative impacts be clearly identified in the SIA.

Alternatives to the proposed action

This involves recommending new or changed alternatives and estimate or project their consequences. Each alternative or recommended change in the proposed action should be assessed separately. The methods used in step five (estimation) apply here but usually on a more modest scale. More innovative alternatives and changes probably should be presented on an experimental basis. Expert judgment and scenarios are helpful in developing alternatives or variations. The number of iterations here will depend upon time, funding and the magnitude of the proposed action.

Mitigation

A social impact assessment not only forecasts impacts, it should identify means to mitigate adverse impacts. Mitigation includes avoiding the impact by not taking or modifying an action; minimizing, rectifying, or reducing the impacts through redesign or operation of the project or policy; or compensating for irreversible impacts by providing substitute policies, facilities, resources, or opportunities (see CEQ, 1986, 40 CFR 1508.20).

Ideally, mitigation measures are built into the selected alternative, but it is appropriate to identify mitigation measures even if they are not immediately adopted or if they would be the responsibility of another organization or government unit. (Federal legislation that mandates mitigation measures may be found at <www.nmfs.noaa.gov/sfa/reports.htm>.)

We suggest a sequencing strategy to manage social impacts modeled after one used with wetland protection and other natural resource issues. During the first sequence, the wetlands managers strive to avoid all adverse impacts if possible. In the second sequence, managers strive to minimize any adverse impacts that cannot be avoided. During the third sequence, managers compensate for adverse impacts. Compensation for the loss of a wetland, for example, could be to acquire a different wetland, enhance a degraded site, or create a new wetland. The amount of compensation can be based on the type of wetland or resources damaged/lost, the severity of the impact and location of the wetland mitigation site.

The first two steps of sequencing — avoiding and minimizing — can apply to the project itself or to the host community or the impacted region. For example, the project may be revised to avoid or minimize adverse social impacts (for instance, by extending the construction period to minimize in-migration), or the community may be able to take steps to attenuate, if not avoid, any adverse effects. Application of the sequencing concept for the mitigation of adverse social impacts requires that the assessor first rank the level of importance of each significant SIA variable determined during the estimated effects SIA step.

The first step in evaluating potential mitigation for each social impact variable is to determine whether the proponent or sponsoring agency could modify the proposed action to avoid adverse social impacts. For example, a road that displaces families could be re-routed.

Next is to identify ways to minimize adverse social impacts. For example, most citizens are uncomfortable with the idea of locating a waste facility or prison near their community. Attitudes (particularly negative ones) formed about an undesirable land use, cannot be eliminated, but might be moderated if the public has complete information about the proposal and is included in the decision-making process or is provided with sufficient legal and structural arrangements that assure safe operation.

There are at least three benefits of identifying irresolvable social impacts that may result from a proposed action. The first is identifying methods of compensating individuals and the community for unavoidable impacts. The second occurs when the community may identify

> **By articulating the impacts that will occur and making efforts to avoid or minimize the adverse consequences, or compensating the residents or the community for the losses, benefits may be enhanced and avoidable conflicts can be managed or minimized**

US principles and guidelines for SIA

ways of enhancing other quality of life variables as compensation for adverse effects. The third happens when the identification of the irresolvable social impacts makes community leaders and project proponents more sensitive to the feelings of community residents. By articulating the impacts that will occur and making efforts to avoid or minimize the adverse consequences, or compensating the residents or the community for the losses, benefits may be enhanced and avoidable conflicts can be managed or minimized.

Monitoring

A monitoring program must be developed that is capable of identifying both deviations from the proposed action and unanticipated social impacts (Magnuson-Stevens Act [compare with §302(g) and §302 (h)]). Furthermore, the monitoring plan should track project/program development and compare real impacts with projected impacts, and should spell out the nature and extent of additional steps to be taken when unanticipated impacts or impacts larger than the projections occur.

Monitoring programs are necessary for projects and programs that lack detailed information or have high variability or uncertainty. It is important to recognize, in advance, the potential for 'surprises' that may lie completely outside the range of options considered during the assessment process. If monitoring procedures cannot be adequately implemented then mitigation agreements should work to the benefit of all parties involved in a decision-making process and should allow an approved action to move forward.

It is generally only at this stage that the community or affected groups have the influence to 'get it in writing.' For example, a monitoring program, with subsequent provision for mitigation, was negotiated between the US Department of Energy and the State of Texas to build the Super Conducting Super Collator Laboratory. The process allowed for the payment of approximately US$800,000 to local jurisdictions to monitor the impacts of the construction activity.

Conclusion

Social impact assessment is predicated on the notion that decision makers should understand the consequences of their actions before they act and that the people affected will not only be apprised of the effects, but have the opportunity to participate in designing their future. The social environment is different than the biophysical environment because it reacts in anticipation of change, but can adapt in reasoned ways to changing circumstances if it is a participant in the planning process. In addition, persons in different social settings interpret social change in different ways and react in different ways.

Perhaps because of this complexity, or the political consequences of making explicit the social consequences of policies, plans, programs and projects, social impact assessment has not been well integrated into US federal agency decision making. The principles and guidelines presented herein are designed to assist agencies and other institutions in implementing SIA within the context of the NEPA process. If a well-prepared SIA is integrated into the decision-making process, better decisions will result.

Notes

1. *Members of the original team. For more administrative details contact Rabel J Burdge at burdge@cc.wwu.edu or go to <www.nmfs.gov/sfa/reports.htm>.

Social impact assessment bibliography

The following bibliography is limited to English language serialized scholarly and professional journals, retrievable government documents and bulletins, and books and monographs with an ISBN number. 'Gray literature', such as papers, meeting presentations and proceedings and documents with limited distribution are not included. Articles and chapters in special issues of journals and books are not cited separately if the entire issue or volume is devoted to social impact assessment. If available, we include an ISBN number and a website for ordering books and monographs.

Textbooks and guides to SIA

Branch, Kristi, Douglas A Hooper, James Thompson and James C Creighton (1984), *Guide to Social Impact Assessment* (Westview Press, Boulder CO) ISBN 0-86531-717-8.
Burdge, Rabel J (1999), *A Community Guide to Social Impact Assessment: Revised Edition* (Social Ecology Press, Middleton WI) ISBN 0-941042-17-0.
IOCGP, Interorganizational Committee on Principles and Guidelines for Social Impact Assessment (1993), *Guidelines and Principles for Social Impact Assessment*, US Department of Commerce NOAA Tech Memo NMFS-F/SPO-16, reprinted in *Impact Assessment*, 12(2), 1994, pages 107–152.
Taylor, Nicholas C, Hobson Bryan and Colin Goodrich (1995), *Social Assessment: Theory, Process and Techniques* (Taylor Baines and Associates, PO Box 8620, Riccarton, Christchurch, New Zealand) ISBN 0-473-03245-7.

Regulations, content and administrative procedures

Berger, Thomas R (1983), "Resources, development, and human values", *Impact Assessment Bulletin*, 2(2), pages 129–147.
CEQ, Council on Environmental Quality (1986), *Regulations for Implementing the Procedural Provisions of the National Environmental Policy Act* (40 CFR 1500-1508) (Government Printing Office, Washington DC).
CEQ, Council on Environmental Quality (1997a), *Environmental Justice: Guidance Under the National Environmental Policy Act* (Office of the President, Washington DC).
CEQ, Council on Environmental Quality (1997b), *Cumulative Effects Handbook* available at <http://ceq.eh.doe.gov/nepa/nepanet.htm>.
Executive Office of the President of the United States (1994), "Executive Order 12898: federal actions to address environmental justice in minority populations and low-income populations", *Federal Register*, 59, pages 7629 et seq.
Llewellyn, Lynn G, and William R Freudenburg (1990), "Legal requirements for social impact assessments: assessing the social science fallout from Three Mile Island", *Society and Natural Resources*, 2(3), pages 193–208.
NEPA, National Environmental Policy Act (1970), Public Law 91-190:852-859.42, U.S.C and as amended Public Law 94-52 and 94-83 42 U.S.C., pages 4321-4347.

United States federal agencies social assessment procedures (selected)

McCold, L N, and J W Saulsbury (1998), "Defining the no-action alternative for National Environmental Policy Act analysis of continuing actions", *Environmental Impact Assessment Review*, 18, pages 353–370.
US Bureau of Reclamation (USDI) (2002), *Social Analysis Manuel Volume I: Manager's Guide to Using Social Analysis*; *Volume II Social Analyst's Guide to Doing Social Analysis* (Resource Management and Planning Group. Technical Service Center, Denver Federal Center D-8580, Bldg. 67. Denver, CO 80225-0007).

US Forest Service (1982), "Guidelines for economic and social analysis of programs, resource plans, and projects: final policy", *Federal Register*, 47(80), 26 April, pages 17940–17954.

US Department of Transportation (1996), "FHWA-PD-96-036 HEP-30/8-96 (10M)P: Community impact assessment — a quick reference for transportation", September, available at <http://www.fhwa.dot.gov/environment/nepa/cia.htm>.

US Environmental Protection Agency (2002), *Community Culture and the Environment: A Guide to Understanding a Sense of Place*, Publication No EPA 842-B-01-003, November (for copies call +1-800-490-9198 or +1-513-489-8190).

State-of-the-art and literature reviews

Burdge, Rabel J (2002), "Why is social impact assessment the orphan of the assessment process?", *Impact Assessment and Project Appraisal*, 20(1), March, pages 3–9.

Carley, Michael J (1984), *Social Impact Assessment: A Cross-Disciplinary Guide to the Literature* (Westview Press, Boulder CO) ISBN 0-86531-529-9.

Finsterbusch, K (1995), "In praise of SIA: a personal review of the field of social impact assessment", *Impact Assessment*, 13 (3), pages 229–252.

Lockie, Stuart F (2001), "SIA in review: setting the agenda for impact assessment in the 21st century", *Impact Assessment and Project Appraisal*, 19(4), pages 277–287.

Conceptual guidelines for social impact assessment

Burdge, Rabel J (1998), *A Conceptual Approach to Social Impact Assessment: Revised Edition Collection of Writings by Rabel J Burdge and Colleagues* (Social Ecology Press, Middleton WI) ISBN 0-941042-16-2.

Freudenburg, William R, and Robert Gramling (1992), "Community impacts of technological change: toward a longitudinal perspective", *Social Forces*, 70(4), pages 937–955.

Freudenburg, William R, and Susan K Pastor (1992), "Public responses to technological risks: toward a sociological perspective", *Sociological Quarterly*, 33(3), pages 389–412.

Freudenburg, William R, and Kenneth M Keating (1985), "Applying sociology to policy: social science and the environmental impact statement", *Rural Sociology*, 50(4), pages 578–605.

Gramling, Robert, and William R Freudenburg (1992), "Opportunity-threat, development, and adaptation: toward a comprehensive framework for social impact assessment", *Rural Sociology*, 57(2), pages 216-234.

Rickson, Roy E, Rabel J Burdge and Audrey Armour (editors) (1990), "Integrating impact assessment into the planning process: international perspectives and experience", special issue of *Impact Assessment Bulletin*, 8(1/2), 357 pages.

Slootweg, R, F Vanclay and M van Schooten (20010, "Function evaluation as a framework for the integration of social and environmental impact assessment", *Impact Assessment and Project Appraisal*, 19(1), pages 19–28.

SIA methodology

Conyers, Diane (1993), *Guidelines on Social Analysis for Rural Area Development Planning* (FAO, Rome, Training Manuel No 73) ISBN 92-5-103439-7.

Chambers, R (1994), "The origins and practice of participatory rural appraisal", *World Development*, 22(7), July, pages 953–969.

Dale, Allan, C Nicholas Taylor and Marcus Lane (editors) (2001), *Social Assessment in Natural Resource Management Institutions* (CSIRO Publishing, Victoria, Australia) ISBN 0-643-06558X or go to <www.publish.csiro.au/books/>.

Denq, Furjen, and June Altenhofel (1997), "Social impact assessments conducted by federal agencies: an evaluation", *Impact Assessment*, 15, pages 209–231.

Finsterbusch, Kurt, J Ingersol and Lynn Llewellyn (editors) (1990), *Methods for Social Analysis in Developing Countries* (Westview Press, Boulder CO) ISBN 0-8337-829-X.

Finsterbusch, Kurt, Lynn G Llewellyn and C P Wolf (editors) (19830, *Social Impact Assessment Methods* (Sage, Beverly Hills CA) ISBN 0-8039-2142.

Goodrich, Colin, and C Nicholas Taylor (editors) (1995), "Special issue on social assessment", *Project Appraisal*, 10(3), pages 141–196, ISSN 0268-8867.

King, Thomas F (1998), "How the anthropologists stole culture: a gap in American environmental impact assessment practice and how to fill it", *Environmental Impact Assessment Review*, 18, pages 117–134.

Mulvihill, Peter R, and Peter Jacobs (1998), "Using scoping as a design process", *Environmental Impact Assessment Review*, 18(1), pages 350–370.

O'Faircheallaigh, C (1999), "Making social impact assessment count: a negotiation-based approach for indigenous peoples", *Society and Natural Resources*, 12(1), pages 63–80.

Rickson, Roy E, Tor Hundloe, Geoffrey T McDonald and Rabel J Burdge (editors) (19900, "Social impact of development: putting theory and methods into practice", special issue of *Environmental Impact Assessment Review*, 10(1/2).

Stolp, A, W Groen *et al* (2002), "Citizen values assessment: incorporating citizen's value judgments in environmental impact assessment", *Impact Assessment and Project Appraisal*, 20(1), pages 11–23.

Research findings

Burnigham, K (1995), "Attitudes, accounts and impact assessment", *The Sociological Review*, 43(1), pages 100–122.

Burdge, Rabel J (Guest Editor) (2003), "The practice of social impact assessment", *Impact Assessment and Project Appraisal*, 21(2&3), June and September, pages 84–250 (two issues).

Cernea, Michael M (editor) (1995), *Putting People First: Sociological Variables in Rural Development* (Published for the World Bank by Oxford University Press, New York, 2nd edition).

Dixon, Mim (19780, *What Happened to Fairbanks: the Effects of the Trans-Alaska Oil Pipeline on the Community of Fairbanks, Alaska* (Westview Press, Boulder CO) ISBN 0-89158-961-9.

Freudenburg, William R, and Robert Gramling (1992), "Community impacts of technological change: toward a longitudinal perspective", *Social Forces*, 70(4), pages 937–955.

Freudenburg, William R, and Robert Gramling (1994), *Oil in Troubled Waters: Perceptions, Politics and the Battle Over Offshore Drilling* (State University Press of New York, Albany) ISBN 0-7914-1882-0.

Freudenburg, William R, and Robert E Jones (1992), "Criminal behavior and rapid community growth: examining the evidence", *Rural Sociology*, 56 (4), pages 619–645.

Gramling, Robert, and William R Freudenburg (1990), "A closer look at 'local control: communities, commodities, and the collapse of the coast", *Rural Sociology*, 55(4), pages 541–558.

Greider, Thomas, and Lorraine Garkovich (1994), "Symbolic landscapes: the social construction of nature and the environment", *Rural Sociology*, 59(1), pages 1–24.

Goldman, Laurence R (editor) (2000), *Social Impact Analysis: An Applied Anthropology Manuel* (Berg, Oxford).

Murdock, Steven H, Richard S Krannich and F Larry Leistritz (1999), *Hazardous Wastes in Rural America: Impacts Implications and Options for Rural Communities* (Rowman and Littlefield, Lanham Maryland) ISBN 0-8476-9100-4.

Smith, Michael D, Richard S Krannich and Lori M Hunter (2001), "Growth, decline, stability, and disruption: a longitudinal analysis of social well-being in four western rural communities", *Rural Sociology*, 66(3), pages 425–450.

Stoffle, Richard W, *et al* (1991), "Risk perception mapping: using ethnography to define the locally affected population for a low-level radioactive waste storage facility in Michigan", *American Anthropologist*, 93(3), pages 611-635.

Stoffle, Richard W, and Richard Arnold (2003), "Confronting the Angry Rock: American Indians' situated risks from radioactivity", *Ethnos*, 68(2), pages 230–248.

Public involvement and social impact assessment

Howell, R E, M E Olsen and D Olsen (1987), *Designing a Citizen Involvement Program* (Western Rural Development Center, Corvallis OR, WREP 105).

O'Connor Center for the Rocky Mountain West (2000), *Reclaiming NEPAs Potential: Can Collaborative Processes Improve Environmental Decision Making?* (O'Connor Center for the Rocky Mountain West, University of Montana, Missoula, MT) available from <http://www.crmw.org/Our%20Products.asp?p=NEPA/>.

Roberts, Richard (1995), "Public involvement: from consultation to

US principles and guidelines for SIA

participation", in F Vanclay and D Bronstein (editors), *Environmental and Social Impact Assessment* (Wiley and Sons, Chichester) pages 221–246.

World Bank (1996), "Guidelines for using social assessment to support public involvement in World Bank–GEF projects", World Bank, Environmental Department, Global Environment Division, Washington DC.

Peer reviewed journals

American Anthropologist, <www.ameranthassn.org>.

Australian Geographical Studies, <www.ssn.flinders.edu.au/geog/iag/iagags.htm>.

Environmental Impact Assessment Review, go to Editor <ejohnson@ecosite.co.uk> or <www.elsevier.co.jp/homepage/>.

Environmental Monitoring and Assessment: An International Journal.

Human Organization, <www.epa.gov/enap/index_txt.html>.

Impact Assessment and Project Appraisal (formerly *Impact Assessment Bulletin*, shortened to *Impact Assessment* and combined with *Project Appraisal* in 1998) go to Editor at <editor.iapa@man.ac.uk> or the IAIA website <www.iaia.org>.

Project Appraisal (now combined with *Impact Assessment*).

Rural Sociology, <www.ruralsociology.org>

Society and Natural Resources, <www.tandf.co.uk/>; <samplesnr@tandfpa.com>.

Journal of Environmental Assessment and Management, <www.et.ac.uk/jeapm/>.

Journal of Environmental Assessment Policy and Management, <www.et.ic.uk/jeapm/>.

Social impact assessment related websites

International Association for Impact Assessment was organized in 1980 to bring together researchers, government employees, practitioners, and users of all types of impact assessment, <www.iaia.org>.

International Association for Public Participation (IAP2) was established in 1990 to serve as a focal point for networking about public involvement activity and techniques. The journal is Interact: the Journal of Public Participation, published semi-annually, <www.pin.org/iap2.htm>.

National Association of Environmental Professionals was founded in 1975 for persons who work on a variety of environmental planning issues. They publish The Environmental Professional, <www.naep.org>.

US Council on Environmental Quality has NEPA guidance, regulations, scoping procedures, and links to other US Federal agencies environmental programs, <http://ceq.eh.doe.gov/nepa/nepanet.htm>.

US Department of Transportation web site on Community Impact Assessment is <www.ciatrans.net>. The Florida DOT/FHWA CIA website is <www.ciatrans.net>.

Canadian Environmental Assessment Agency has excellent links to sites in other organizations and countries, or write to CD_ROM Library, 200 Sacre Couer Blvd. Hull, QC K1A 0H3, <http://www.ceaa.gc.ca/index_e.htm> also <http://founder.library.ualberta.ca/FTP/EN/Laws/Chap/C/>.

Australian EIA Network has information on environmental impact assessment (EIA) and its process within Australia, <http://www.environment.gov.au>.

New Zealand Ministry of the Environment has a range of information on recent publications, <http://www.mfe.govt.nz>.

<www.socialimpactassessment.net>, web site on social impact assessment maintained by Rabel Burdge. Includes updated SIA bibliographies, recent publications, workshops, training guides, job opportunities, conferences, ordering SIA publications, course outlines, consultation opportunities and links to other sites.

Homepage of the EIA Centre at the University of Manchester, United Kingdom. See the Leaflet Series, Index of Leaflets <http://www.art.man.ac.uk/eia/EIAc.htm>.

[9]

Environmental Impact Assessment Review

Environmental Impact Assessment Review 26 (2006) 3–14

Principles for social impact assessment: A critical comparison between the international and US documents

Frank Vanclay[*]

Tasmanian Institute of Agricultural Research, University of Tasmania, Private Bag 98, Hobart, Tasmania 7001, Australia

Received 1 April 2005; accepted 1 May 2005
Available online 11 July 2005

Abstract

The "International Principles for Social Impact Assessment" and the "Principles and Guidelines for Social Impact Assessment in the USA", both developed under the auspices of the International Association for Impact Assessment and published in 2003, are compared. Major differences in the definition and approach to social impact assessment (SIA) are identified. The US Principles and Guidelines is shown to be positivist/technocratic while the International Principles is identified as being democratic, participatory and constructivist. Deficiencies in both documents are identified. The field of SIA is changing to go beyond the prevention of negative impacts, to include issues of building social capital, capacity building, good governance, community engagement and social inclusion.
© 2005 Elsevier Inc. All rights reserved.

Keywords: Social impact assessment; SIA; Guidelines and Principles; International Principles; NEPA

1. Introduction

Two significant documents were published in 2003: the International Principles for Social Impact Assessment ('International Principles' for short) and the Principles and

---

[*] Fax: +61 3 6226 7450.
 E-mail address: Frank.Vanclay@utas.edu.au.

0195-9255/$ - see front matter © 2005 Elsevier Inc. All rights reserved.
doi:10.1016/j.eiar.2005.05.002

Guidelines for Social Impact Assessment in the USA ('US Principles and Guidelines' for short). Each document is important in its own right, with each being a landmark document representing a codification of the field of social impact assessment (SIA). The two documents make an interesting comparison because together they embody several of the tensions in the discipline, particularly relating to the contextual setting in which SIA occurs.

The US Principles and Guidelines is attributed to a collective authorship of 12 people, the 'Interorganizational Committee', which was convened by Rabel Burdge who is, in effect, primary author of that document. By contrast, the International Principles is largely developed by Frank Vanclay (the author of this commentary) and published as a sole authored paper (Vanclay, 2003a) but with acknowledged input in the form of ideas and comments from a wide range of people numbering several hundreds in total, with some 50 or so making a substantial contribution. As discussed in an editorial (Vanclay, 2003b), the International Principles was subject to the editorial scrutiny of a somewhat dynamic 'Task Force' of around 5 people at any time, but which over time included a total of 12 people, including Rabel Burdge. Thus, while the two documents were developed independently, they were not in ignorance of each other. They are both direct descendents of a 1993/1994 document, Guidelines and Principles for Social Impact Assessment ('G&P' for short). This commentary is written by the primary author of the International Principles (Vanclay), so it is perhaps a somewhat one-sided account. Nevertheless, the comparison is interesting because it highlights varying understandings of SIA.

2. A little history

With the passage of the National Environmental Policy Act (NEPA) in the USA on the 1st of January 1970, environmental impact assessment (EIA) was formally established. NEPA required that social issues be considered as part of the definition of the environment (unlike legislation in some other countries). However, there was little comprehension about what considering social issues really meant, and how this would or could actually be done. It was not until the 1973 environmental impact study for the Alaskan Pipeline from Prudoe Bay on the Arctic Sea to Valdez on Prince William Sound, that social issues really came to the fore: "Now that we have dealt with the problem of the permafrost and the caribou and what to do with hot oil, what about changes in the customs and ways of my people?" (cited by Dixon, 1978:4; Burdge and Vanclay, 1995). This concern then led to the establishment of strong interest in social impact assessment as an issue, and a specific methodology and theoretical basis to the field gradually developed.

Throughout the late 1970s and early 1980s, SIA flourished in the USA. It was an era of a boom economy, with many large-scale energy projects requiring SIA studies. Gradually, people in the SIA business realized that there was not sufficient control over the quality of the SIA projects being undertaken. Agencies were unable to properly assess the quality of SIA reports, and many consultants were not properly trained. A further problem was that there was confusion over what social impacts were legitimate to consider. One of the members of the original Interorganizational Committee, Charlie Wolf (personal communication) attributes the initiative for the development of the G&P to Gary Williams who could not convince his employer at the time (a US government agency) that quality of life issues were valid issues to consider in an SIA of the proposed superconducting supercollider. It was thought that by creating a formal statement that had the endorsement of many professional associations, regulatory agencies and other bodies could be encouraged to consider social issues more thoroughly. The statement would certainly give more power to individual SIA practitioners who were arguing that a broader range of issues should be considered in SIA.

Consequently, a committee was formed in 1989 containing one or two representatives from a range of social science organizations which had a membership base in the USA. The committee was called the Interorganizational Committee on Guidelines and Principles for Social Impact Assessment (usually abbreviated Interorganizational Committee). The organizations represented included the International Association for Impact Assessment, the Rural Sociological Society, the American Psychological Association, the American Sociological Association, the American Anthropological Association (together with the Society for Applied Anthropology), the Agricultural Economics Association, and four members at large who were recognized as having specific experience that would be useful in the development of the guidelines and principles.[1] As most members of this Committee were members of the International Association for Impact Assessment (IAIA), even if they were not formally representing IAIA, it was agreed that IAIA would be the lead association, and when the Committee finalized their report, copyright in the report was assigned to IAIA.

The first version of the report was completed in 1993 with the formal copyright date being given as December 14, 1993, but most public versions of the report were released in 1994. The report was subsequently published in May 1994 by a consortium of US agencies, and as a Technical Memorandum of the National Oceanic and Atmospheric Administration (NOAA).[2] It was also published in IAIA's journal, Impact Assessment (1994a,b) and in the Environmental Impact Assessment Review (1995).

Intellectually, at least, the initial G&P document was well received by the SIA community at large, judging by discussions at IAIA conferences. However, the actual cited use of the G&P was disappointing (Burdge, 2002). Even though they were developed for the USA context, the document had an international standing. However, consistent with their purpose, they were strictly only appropriate to the US NEPA jurisdictional setting. Even in that context, they had a number of problems; primarily that it was not always clear whom they were addressing (see below). Because of their desired use outside of the original USA-NEPA context, some criticism of the G&P developed and it became evident that the document needed updating.

---

[1] The names of the members of the Interorganizational Committee and the associations represented changes between the various versions of the document. The information here is from the original 1993 IAIA version of the document — the same information is contained in the version published as a NOAA Technical Memorandum.

[2] The Consortium included the US Department of Commerce, the National Oceanic and Atmospheric Administration, and the National Marine Fisheries Service. NOAA Technical Memorandum NMFS-F/SPO-16. Available on line (access date 22 September 2004) in both HTML http://www.st.nmfs.gov/tm/spo/spo16.pdf and PDF versions http://www.st.nmfs.gov/tm/spo/spo16.pdf.

At IAIA's New Orleans conference in 1997, two committees were established to revise the G&P. One committee was to modify the G&P for application within the American context, while a second committee was charged with the responsibility of developing a set of International Guidelines and Principles. Rabel Burdge, an original member of the Interorganizational Committee, became Convenor of the US-based Committee, while Frank Vanclay was appointed Convenor of the International Committee. Vanclay (2003b) provides more information about the process of development of the International Principles. The International Principles and the US Principles and Guidelines published in 2003 are the products of those committees.

3. Brief outline of the original Guidelines and Principles

The original document comprised seven sections, commencing with a brief introduction that contained a specific (narrow) definition of SIA and of social impacts (see discussion below). The second section outlined the relevant sections of NEPA and the Council on Environmental Quality's (CEQ) Regulations for Implementing the Procedural Provisions of the National Environmental Policy Act. Section 3 outlined a basic model for SIA including a checklist (or matrix) of SIA variables. The fourth section outlined the Steps in the SIA process, entrenching a particular model of SIA. The fifth section identified nine 'Principles' for SIA. Sections 4 and 5 presented lengthy explanations of the steps in the model, and a full discussion of the nine principles. A final two sections presented a very short conclusion, and a list of SIA literature.

4. Critiquing the original Guidelines and Principles

There were a number of problems with the original G&P which were identified through workshops held in the process of developing the International Principles and the 2003 US Principles and Guidelines. There have also been various mentions in the literature about problems with them (e.g. Seebohm, 1997; Lockie, 2001). Burdge and Vanclay (1995) and Vanclay (1999) have provided improved wording for the principles mentioned in the G&P.

From an international perspective, the primary criticism was that they were developed for the US NEPA-CEQ regulatory framework. This is hardly a fair criticism, since it was the document's stated purpose. However, this criticism was an indication of the need for an international version of the document, which is now provided by the International Principles.

Because the G&P were based on the US regulatory context, the document reflected a proponent-adversary approach to SIA, where SIA was seen as a discrete activity that occurred at the beginning of a project cycle, rather than as a process of participation, or as a process of ensuring optimal development from the community's perspective. The model and philosophy of SIA that were articulated in the G&P were focussed on the protection of individual property rights–impact prediction, mitigation and compensation mechanisms (the negative impacts on affected parties)–and not on the betterment in wellbeing and improved sustainable livelihoods of the whole community. This might be an unimportant distinction in industrialized countries where most projects are activities where benefits largely accrue to the private sector and costs are borne by the public sector and the community, but in development (where the intention is the betterment of the whole community) the balance of macro-public good versus (minor) harm on a small group of people may be assessed differently.

Although the word 'policy' was mentioned in many places in the G&P, consistent with the proponent-adversary approach of SIA/EIA embedded in NEPA, the G&P tends to reflect project-based thinking. Despite the mention of policy, there was no addressing of policy issues.

There were some practical problems with the G&P. The document failed to identify its target audience. Potentially, guidelines and principles can be directed to many different groups, each of whom have different interests. For SIA, the potential list of audiences could include: policy makers (who need to consider environmental management policy); regulatory agency managers (who need to consider what should be specified in tender documents, and whether a particular SIA study adequate); advocates for SIA within agencies (who need to convince the agency what must be done); SIA practitioners (consultants) (who need standards for practice so as to justify the cost indicated in a tender, or to prove to a client/agency that investigation of a wide range of issues is necessary); developers (who need to be convinced why SIA is necessary); and the community and academics with an interest in SIA. The G&P document seemed to be addressing different audiences in different places and therefore it was not clear which audience was being addressed at any one location. The document also suffered from internal inconsistency and from a confusion about its purpose. The principles and guidelines that are discussed seem to be at different levels, and were not necessarily, strictly speaking, principles or guidelines.

5. What was new in 2003

As indicated above, one of the major initiatives in the development of the second round of the G&P was the creation of a separate document for international purposes, as well as an explicit statement in the title that the American document was for use in the USA. However, despite that purpose, it is curious to note that the US document has been generalised, rather than being made more specific. In addition to cosmetic and formatting changes and a slight re-ordering of content, one section that was present in the original version has been deleted—the section on the legal and regulatory basis of SIA in the USA. In other respects, however, whereas the International Principles presents quite a different view of SIA, the underlying philosophy and approach to SIA in the US Principles and Guidelines is rather similar to that in the original G&P.

Some changes that are noteworthy include the expansion of the number of stages of a project or policy from four to five, with the planning stage being split into preliminary planning and detailed planning stages. The principles have changed considerably in both scope and tone becoming more technocratic. The short conclusion remains the same, and the Bibliography has been updated but remains US-centric and patchy.

The 2003 version of the US Principles and Guidelines (p. 232) claims that they "have benefited from almost ten years of comments" but it is not clear that the Interorganizational Committee has fully responded to all the concerns raised above. In the section headed *'What is new in the 2003 version?'*, about the only major statement of change is that "the new version expands the focus away from projects to include policies, plans, and programs" (p. 232). But the original G&P version was always meant to include policies—the definition of SIA being: "In this monograph, however, we define social impact assessment in terms of efforts to assess or estimate, in advance, the social consequences that are likely to follow from specific policy actions (including programs, and the adoption of new policies), and specific government actions" (p. 1). It is true that it was a major criticism of the original G&P, that even though policies were mentioned, there was very little attention given to anything other than the project level. Despite the comment in the 2003 version, there has been very little change to give increased recognition to the policy level, and it is true to say that the same criticism applies—there is inadequate attention of the policy, plan and program levels.

6. Principles, guidelines and values

In the process of developing the International Principles, it became apparent that there were varying understandings of what 'guidelines' and 'principles' were, and few people had any understanding of a formal definition of these terms. It became necessary to define these terms and to constantly remind the Task Force and other participants of the definitions adopted. In defining them, and thinking about the meaning of them, it became clear that guidelines derive from principles, and principles derive from values. Guidelines, therefore, should not be developed in advance of clarification of principles, which in turn should not be developed before a discussion about values. This is the reason why both the International and US documents have put principles first.

It also became obvious to the International Task Force that it would be a pointless exercise for a non-government organization like IAIA to independently develop a set of guidelines to foist on to industry without their engagement in that process. Guidelines so developed would have no legitimacy, no 'ownership' by industry, and would not be adopted by industry. Guidelines become relevant and effective, not by being written on paper, but through a process of development which engages with the people they are intended to influence. The benefit of guidelines, therefore, is not the having of them, but the process of their development. It is through this participatory process that the guidelines gain legitimacy and commitment by industry.

The International Principles Task Force therefore resolved that it would not develop guidelines, but it would articulate the values of the SIA community, and the principles that SIA should address. The US Interorganizational Committee agreed with the International Principles Task Force in prioritising principles over guidelines, a change between 1993 and 2003.

The International Principles Task Force (Vanclay, 2003a: 8) defined the key terms as follows.

Core Values:	Fundamental, ideal-typical, enduring, statements of belief that are strongly held and accepted as premises (is-statements).
Principles:	General statements of either a common understanding or an indication as to a course of action about what ought to be done (ought-statements).
Guidelines:	Statements by which to plan a specific course of action and which clarify how it should done (action-statements).

Guidelines can be described as statements which provide advice or direction by which to plan a specific course of action. They are written as specific statements of instruction about what to do and/or how to do it. Typically they are 'action-statements'. A principle is a macro-statement that provides a general guide to a course of action about what ought to be done. They are written as 'ought-statements'. Core values are statements about fundamental beliefs that are deeply held. They are typically 'is-statements'. Values determine principles, from which guidelines can be written.

It will be observed that the majority (if not all) of the nine original principles in the 1993 G&P, and the six principles in the 2003 US Principles and Guidelines, do not conform to the above definition of principles.

7. Comparing the International and US documents

7.1. Definition of SIA

SIA was defined by the US Interorganizational Committee in 1993 (p. 1) as follows:

> In this monograph, however, we define social impact assessment in terms of efforts to assess or estimate, in advance, the social consequences that are likely to follow from specific policy actions (including programs, and the adoption of new policies), and specific government actions (including buildings, large projects and leasing large tracts of land for resource extraction), particularly in the context of the U.S. National Environmental Policy Act of 1969 or "NEPA" (P.L. 91-190, 42 U.S.C. 4371 *et seq.*).

Their 2003 definition is substantially similar, although broadening the scope to include private projects and state regulations as well as the federal setting (NEPA) (pp. 231–232).

> In the 2003 version, we continue to define social impact assessment in terms of efforts to assess, appraise or estimate, in advance, the social consequences that are likely to follow from proposed actions. These include: specific government or private projects, such as construction of buildings, siting power generation facilities, large transportation projects, managing natural resources, fish and wildlife; and preserving or leasing large tracts of land and the adoption of new policies and resulting plans and programs. The actions and their consequences are considered

particularly in the context of the NEPA (P.L. 91-190, 42 U.S.C. 4371 *et seq.*) and state laws and regulations that reflect NEPA.

In contrast, the International Principles (Vanclay, 2003a: 6) presents a very different concept of SIA.

> Social Impact Assessment includes the processes of analysing, monitoring and managing the intended and unintended social consequences, both positive and negative, of planned interventions (policies, programs, plans, projects) and any social change processes invoked by those interventions. Its primary purpose is to bring about a more sustainable and equitable biophysical and human environment.

About the only point of agreement in these definitions is the focus on planned actions (interventions). The International Principles recognizes that the methodology can be applied to events other than planned interventions, such as disasters, demographic changes and epidemics, but the primary intention is the consideration of planned interventions. The significant differences in the definitions, from the perspective of the International Principles Task Force, are the following:

- SIA should not necessarily be tied to a regulatory context. SIA can and should be undertaken in many situations and not just when a specific jurisdiction requires it. Private sector companies ought to routinely and systematically do SIA as part of their corporate social responsibility, good neighbour, or triple bottom line processes. Communities ought to do SIA in planning development. SIA is beneficial in any context and should not just be seen as part of a regulatory process, initiated because of environmental regulation.
- SIA should not just be ex-ante or 'in advance'. The emphasis on 'in advance' highlights a view that SIA is a project-driven, responsive or reactive (rather than proactive) once-off event, and not a community-driven process leading to appropriate sustainable development.
- SIA needs to consider how to ensure the achievement of the intended positive consequences or goals of development as well as preventing unintended negative outcomes. Therefore, SIA needs to be goal-oriented and proactive and not just reactive.

The International Principles also indicates that there are three different levels in the meaning of 'SIA': (1) a paradigm or field of research and practice; (2) a social research process or methodology, and (3) a discrete step (or specific task) of predicting social impacts in some impact assessment process. The concept of SIA embodied in the US Principles and Guidelines hovers between level (2) and level (3). The concept of SIA in the International Principles rejects level (3) and straddles levels (1) and (2).

7.2. SIA variables

There is minimal change between the 1993 G&P and 2003 US Principles and Guidelines in the description of social impact variables that should be considered. Table 1 in the 2003 version lists 32 variables categorised under five headings. Although a note to the table (p. 243) states that "These variables are suggestive and illustrative and are intended to provide a beginning point for the social assessor", there are many reasons to avoid using a checklist, one of which is to avoid the development of a checklist mentality (Vanclay, 2002). The presentation of the variables in a matrix format emulates a Leopold Matrix, one of the original methodologies of EIA (Leopold et al., 1971). This creates an impression of the US Principles and Guidelines as being technocratic, something that was undoubtedly intended.

The International Principles does not contain a list of impact variables, this being a deliberate decision by the author and the Task Force. Instead, the International Principles suggests that SIA is an umbrella or overarching framework that embodies the evaluation of all impacts on humans, and it then goes on to include a long list of areas that should be considered. It also describes social impacts in very general terms.

Analysing the 32 variables of the US Principles and Guidelines reveals many deficiencies. It is disappointing that there is no engagement with Vanclay's (2002) analysis of SIA variables which reveal some 80-odd concepts and which was a solid critique of the variable listing of the 1993 G&P. Given the minimal change between 1993 and 2003, the listing of variables in the US Principles and Guidelines would be subject to the same criticisms made by Vanclay (2002).

7.3. The basic framework for SIA

Both the 1993 G&P and the 2003 US Principles and Guidelines articulate a basic model for SIA. While the 2003 version has updated the model, the essential elements are the same. "We use a comparative SIA method to study the course of events in a location where planned environmental change has occurred and to extrapolate from that analysis what is likely to happen in another location where a similar action is proposed" (p. 239). An experimental method showing an experimental group (the impact study), a control, and a prior comparative study is provided in Fig. 2, giving the appearance of scientific rigor. Ten steps are outlined in a linear flow chart of action (Fig. 4).

In contrast, the International Principles provides a list of 17 dotpoints of things that SIA comprises, not prescribing a specific order. The International Principles Task Force considered that it was not necessary to endorse a specific model as there were sufficient textbooks to provide this type of information.

7.4. The principles themselves

The US Principles and Guidelines (p. 233) outlines six principles which inform a total of 16 guidelines.

1. Achieve extensive understanding of local and regional populations and settings to be affected by the proposed action, program or policy.
2. Focus on the key elements of the human environment related to the proposed action, program or policy.

3. The SIA is based upon sound and replicable scientific research concepts and methods.
4. Provide quality information for use in decision-making.
5. Ensure that any environmental justice issues are fully described and analyzed.
6. Undertake project, program or policy monitoring and evaluation and propose mitigation measures if needed.

The International Principles contains eight fundamental principles that relate to development in general and seek to influence the shape of policies and projects. It then specifies a further 12 principles that relate specifically to SIA practice. As a bonus, it then outlines how 12 leading international environmental principles from International Agreements such as the Rio Declaration can be interpreted to have a social dimension. The principles that relate specifically to SIA practice are (Vanclay, 2003a, 9):

1. Equity considerations should be a fundamental element of impact assessment and of development planning.
2. Many of the social impacts of planned interventions can be predicted.
3. Planned interventions can be modified to reduce their negative social impacts and enhance their positive impacts.
4. SIA should be an integral part of the development process, involved in all stages from inception to follow-up audit.
5. There should be a focus on socially sustainable development, with SIA contributing to the determination of best development alternative(s)—SIA (and EIA) have more to offer than just being an arbiter between economic benefit and social cost.
6. In all planned interventions and their assessments, avenues should be developed to build the social and human capital of local communities and to strengthen democratic processes.
7. In all planned interventions, but especially where there are unavoidable impacts, ways to turn impacted peoples into beneficiaries should be investigated.
8. The SIA must give due consideration to the alternatives of any planned intervention, but especially in cases when there are likely to be unavoidable impacts.
9. Full consideration should be given to the potential mitigation measures of social and environmental impacts, even where impacted communities may approve the planned intervention and where they may be regarded as beneficiaries.
10. Local knowledge and experience and acknowledgment of different local cultural values should be incorporated in any assessment.
11. There should be no use of violence, harassment, intimidation or undue force in connection with the assessment or implementation of a planned intervention.
12. Developmental processes that infringe the human rights of any section of society should not be accepted.

Comparing the 6 principles from the US Principles and Guidelines with the 12 principles from the International Principles reveals the different approaches of the two documents. The positivist/technocratic character of the US Principles and Guidelines is obvious in contrast to the more democratic, participatory, constructivist International Principles.

8. Conclusion

If the US Principles and Guidelines, instead of being published because it is an official statement, was a paper submitted to a journal for refereeing, and I was the referee, I would have to reject it. It failed to engage with the literature, and it has not considered a range of developments in the field of SIA. While I was a strong advocate of the original 1993 Guidelines and Principles, I am disappointed in the lack of updating of the 2003 version of the now US Principles and Guidelines. The Interorganizational Committee failed to do the hard work that was necessary to update their document. They have instead made minimal changes, many of which have failed to address the critiques of the original version. Given that the Interorganizational Committee was constantly kept informed of the development of the International Principles, saw draft versions of the International Principles especially in the last 2 years or so of their development, and that the International Principles was published first, the complete lack of acknowledgement or reference to the International Principles is surprising. Whereas the expectation was that the US Principles and Guidelines would become more attuned to the US NEPA-CEQ regulatory context, leaving the International Principles to become the general statement of SIA, the US Principles and Guidelines has also become generalised. Instead of more connection with US legislation, there is less—the only major change from 1993 to 2003 being the removal of the section on legal mandates and administrative procedures.

In contrast, while the International Principles is some ways incomplete, it presents a very different picture of SIA to that presented in the US Principles and Guidelines. While the document, too, is inadequate and is unlikely to fulfil all of the objectives listed at the beginning of the document, it at least does address the criticisms made of the original G&P, and the various critiques of SIA in general. It genuinely does attempt to consider a broad range of social issues, and to extend from the project level to the policy level.

The need for SIA is as great now as it ever was, and internationally at least (if not in the USA), there is increased demand for SIA, or at least for social analysis of some description. Unfortunately, whereas a technocratic appearance to SIA might be necessary to gain legitimacy in the USA (given the asocietal nature of American society, politics and culture), the technocratic appearance of the American model of SIA makes it unattractive to an international audience. Internationally, new concepts, approaches and methodologies are emerging, which SIA is having to compete with, and integrate. These approaches include social risk assessment, sustainability assessment, triple bottom line accounting, and corporate social responsibility (Becker and Vanclay, 2003; Vanclay, 2004). There is a concern, not with the prevention of negative impacts, but on building social capital, on capacity building, good governance, community engagement and social inclusion. None of these terms are mentioned in the US Principles and Guidelines. To survive into the future, SIA will need to include the new language and to adapt to new expectations of a wide range of regulatory and de-regulated contexts. Becoming established as a quality assurance process, like a social version of an environmental management system (ISO 14000) may be desirable.

References

Becker H, Vanclay F, editors. The international handbook of social impact assessment: conceptual and methodological advances. Cheltenham, UK: Edward Elgar; 2003.

Burdge RJ. Why is social impact assessment the orphan of the assessment process? Impact Assess Proj Apprais 2002;20(1):3–9.

Burdge RJ, Vanclay F. Social impact assessment. In: Vanclay F, Bronstein DA, editors. Environmental and social impact assessment. Chichester: Wiley; 1995. p. 31–65.

Dixon M. What happened to Fairbanks: the effects of the trans-Alaska oil pipeline on the community of Fairbanks. Alaska: Westview Press; 1978.

Interorganizational Committee on Guidelines and Principles. Guidelines and Principles for Social Impact Assessment, c/- IAIA, Box 70, Belhaven, NC 27810, 1993 [this is no longer the address for IAIA].

Interorganizational Committee on Guidelines and Principles for Social Impact Assessment. Guidelines and principles for Social Impact Assessment. NOAA Technical Memorandum NMFS-F/SPO-16 1994 [on-line resource accessed 23 Sept 2004], http://www.st.nmfs.gov/tm/spo/spo16.pdf.

Interorganizational Committee on Guidelines and Principles for Social Impact Assessment. Guidelines and principles for social impact assessment. Impact Assess 1994;12(2):107–52 [Reprinted in Environmental Impact Assessment Review 1995; 15(1):11–43].

Interorganizational Committee on Principles and Guidelines for Social Impact Assessment. Principles and Guidelines for Social Impact Assessment in the USA. Impact Assess Proj Apprais 2003;21(3):231–50.

Leopold LB, Clarke FE, Hanshaw BB, Balsley JR. A procedure for evaluating environmental impact. Geological Survey Circular, vol. 645. Washington, DC: Government Printing Office; 1971.

Lockie S. SIA in review: setting the agenda for impact assessment in the 21st century. Impact Assess Proj Apprais 2001;19(4):277–88.

Seebohm K. Guiding principles for the practice of social assessment in the Australian water industry. Impact Assess 1997;15(3):233–51.

Vanclay F. Social impact assessment. In: Petts J, editor. Handbook of Environmental Impact Assessment, vol. 1. Oxford: Blackwell Science; 1999. p. 301–26.

Vanclay F. Conceptualising social impacts. Environ Impact Asses Rev 2002;22(3):183–211.

Vanclay F. International principles for social impact assessment. Impact Assess Proj Apprais 2003a;21(1):5–11.

Vanclay F. International principles for social impact assessment: their evolution. Impact Assess Proj Apprais 2003b;21(1):3–4.

Vanclay F. The triple bottom line and impact assessment: how do TBL, EIA, SIA, SEA and EMS relate to each other? J Environ Assess Policy Manag 2004;6(3):265–88.

Frank Vanclay is professor of rural sociology in the Tasmanian Institute of Agricultural Research at the University of Tasmania. He was convenor of the International Association for Impact Assessment's task force to develop International Principles for social impact assessment. He has published numerous articles on social impact assessment and is co-editor of The International Handbook of Social Impact Assessment (Edward Elgar, 2003).

Part III
Ethics and Values

[10]

The Importance of Process in Social Impact Assessment: Ethics, Methods and Process for Cross-cultural Engagement

RICHARD HOWITT
Department of Human Geography, Macquarie University, NSW, 2109, Australia

ABSTRACT *Social impact assessment (SIA) presents an important opportunity to draw cross-cultural encounters arising from project-based development efforts into wider procedures of engagement and negotiation that might address the imbalance in relationships between local communities, project proponents and states. In the SIA literature, however, ethical considerations have received relatively little explicit attention, with greater attention given to outcomes in the form of negotiated agreements and financial and employment results. This paper considers the question of SIA methods from the standpoint of recent Australian national guidelines on ethical engagement with Australian Indigenous people, and argues for much greater attention being given to process and its implications for just and sustainable outcomes in SIA research.*

In thinking about the practices of cross-cultural engagement, whether it is in the form of personal encounters with cultural difference, formal processes of intercultural consultation in professional fields such as planning and service provision or structured settings such as cross-cultural negotiation and social assessment, we are often confronted with circumstances that are somewhat distant from social theory's complex abstractions of relationships between abstract selves and abstract others. Concern with difference and alterity has really driven much of Western philosophy for more than 50 years, producing some of the most exciting and frustrating debates in social science. Yet it is the performance rather than theorising of cross-cultural engagements that constitutes and reconstitutes societies and the social and environmental relationships within and between them. It is also the performance of these engagements that challenges societal assumptions of how things are, can be and should be.

The field of social impact assessment (SIA) is one in which cross-cultural relationships, or at least the interface between co-existing cultural groups in the context of a development project, is subject to some degree of critical scrutiny

210   R. Howitt

from social researchers. In the case of SIA involving Indigenous Australians, participatory methods have become relatively standard practice, and a negotiations-based approach (for example O'Faircheallaigh, 1999) is widely seen as appropriate.

Much of the SIA research carried out by academics, however—along with a lot of other research involving Aboriginal or Torres Strait Islander peoples—is undertaken as 'consultancies', outside the normal scrutiny of formal ethical oversight by peers in institutional ethics committees or similar arrangements. A lot of the research is not widely published, being circulated in limited numbers within the 'grey' literature of reports that are available for limited time periods and to restricted audiences. Work is often covered by 'confidentiality' agreements which restrict wider publication or circulation. From the outside, it might be assumed that such work is already ethically 'engaged' if it is commissioned by Aboriginal or Torres Strait Islander organisations such as land councils or native title representative bodies. In my own experience, however, these bodies are sometimes poorly equipped to deal with questions about research ethics and research methods. They are also themselves subject to significant political, financial and institutional limitations that have implications for SIA and negotiations-related research. Restrictions on publication are difficult to remove, and accountability to the most directly affected people whose concerns are ostensibly at the heart of the SIA or negotiation-oriented research is difficult to scrutinise externally. While, in some cases, robust and effective controls are in place, in others, the procedures seem, at best, to be indirect and far from transparent. In some cases, there is incorporation of some formal peer review prior to acceptance of a report, but this approach is not generally used in studies commissioned by development proponents as part of the environmental impact assessment (EIA) component of their project approval process.

The limited circulation and scrutiny of SIA reports that are not formally published also limit the capacity of local groups not directly involved in a study to learn from the achievements and shortcomings of a particular study. It is in the nature of many of the community-based organisations involved that staff turnover and poor internal communications reduce the awareness of even effective SIA work within the organisations beyond the project team itself. This risks imposing a situation where each new SIA starts again from an earlier level of understanding (or ignorance) rather than building on an accumulation of methodological and conceptual understanding.

Further, it is in the nature of much SIA research that the researchers are in a close relationship with a project proponent, relying on them for funding, information and implementation. While independence is typically secured through arm's-length contracts, often involving procedural oversight by a third party—typically an Aboriginal organisation—protection of independence in such research has long plagued impact assessment research. Yet, the proximity to the proponent and to other stakeholders and decision makers also facilitates iterative and contextually sensitive work that can insert crucial information into decision making, approval and evaluative procedures. This paradoxical situation, which juxtaposes dependence and scrutiny in complex ways, is at the heart of the ethical challenge addressed in this paper. In the field of SIA, my concern is with the need for independent evaluation of research in which ethical standards, transparency and accountability might better address the needs, concerns and aspirations of marginalised local groups who are so often left to carry the burden of development projects in which the benefits at the local scale are illusory or conditional.

In particular, the lack of transparency in decision making between research findings and recommendations in SIA reports and the implementation phase—the absence of independent evaluation, monitoring and follow-up of SIA research that has been commented on critically over many decades (for example Boothroyd et al., 1995; Gagnon, 2003)—raises the difficult issue of distinguishing the 'research' phase, which is really the core concern of ethical oversight in formal ethics committees, and the 'action' phase, which may well be of more significance for community-based research participants, but inaccessible to university-based ethical oversight.

The 2003 National Health and Medical Research Council Guidelines:
Values and Ethics

The recent adoption of new formal guidelines regarding ethical conduct in Aboriginal and Torres Strait Islander health research by Australia's National Health and Medical Research Council (NHMRC) (2003) offers a benchmark against which such research activities and accountability procedures might be compared. The NHMRC first adopted guidelines in this field in 1991 (NHMRC, 1991) in response to an increasingly articulate Aboriginal critique of research practices, particularly in relation to health research (Humphrey, 2001). Many of the concerns arising in health research, however, were also relevant to wider social science research (for example Howitt et al., 1990). The fact that all grant-funded social research in Australia is legally required to comply with a range of ethical guidelines, including those regarding the interests of Aboriginal and Torres Strait Islander peoples, has not guaranteed compliance from university-sector researchers. Indeed, I was recently interviewed by a Ph.D. student from a major university who was working on an Australian Research Council (ARC)-funded project who clearly neither had specific ethical approval for her work, nor understood the principles of ethical research conduct. In my own institution, where I am a member of the Human Ethics Review Committee, we consistently seek out ways to increase researcher awareness of the ethical issues that arise in applied social research and cross-cultural 'consultancy' research activities.

In 2003 an academic anthropologist published a populist piece titled 'Why I don't want to be an "ethical" researcher', which sought to dismiss ethical oversight of research involving Aboriginal and Torres Strait Islander Australians as 'political correctness', 'simplistically and crudely bandied about by research police, including those bodies who euphemistically...call themselves ethics committees' (Rolls, 2003, p. 1). Rolls's controversial paper received prominent attention in the *Australian Higher Education Supplement* (Lane, 2003). In the context of the NHMRC issuing new guidelines (NHMRC, 2003) which shift the focus of ethical oversight of work involving Aboriginal and Torres Strait Islander people away from a 'protectionist' framework towards a much more collaborative and creative one, this paper considers just why process matters—ethically, methodologically and politically—in SIA and related cross-cultural research, and what implications arise for the practices of SIA, and related researchers. Rolls's suggestion that public scrutiny of the ethical implications of public research is reducible to a problem of political correctness raises serious issues about the way in which public intellectuals contribute to society. In the case of the shift to a more collaborative approach as advocated by the new guidelines, Rolls's position reverts to a deeply disempowering paternalism, in which the researcher is seen as best placed to decide what is appropriate. This is ethically indefensible, but Rolls's advocacy of this position frames a wider challenge to participatory and action-oriented research, including SIA, outside the domain of publicly funded projects.

At one level the new NHMRC guidelines are quite straightforward. They identify six principles and 'draw out the implications of each value for research, and how researchers and research proposals might demonstrate engagement and consistency with each value' (NHMRC, 2003, p. 8). In each case researchers, ethics committees and 'participating communities' are exhorted to consider how proposed research demonstrates consideration of and responsiveness to these values. In each case, researchers and ethics committees are also directed to the relevant sections of the *NHMRC Statement on Human Experimentation and Supplementary Notes 1992* (NHMRC, 1992), which is binding on all Australian researchers. The six values identified are:

- *reciprocity*—inclusion and mutual recognition lay the foundation for reciprocity in research relationships that ensure that 'research outcomes include equitable benefits of value to Aboriginal and Torres Strait Islander communities or individuals...[which should be defined] according to their own values and priorities' (p. 10);
- *respect*—research relationships which 'acknowledge and affirm the right of people to have different values, norms and aspirations' (p. 11) and in which 'the trust, openness and engagement of participating communities and individuals is as important as the scientific rigour of the investigation' (pp. 11–12);
- *equality*—a commitment to 'distributive fairness and justice' and to 'advance the elimination of inequalities', because to 'treat people less favourably is not only unethical, but discriminatory' (p. 14);
- *responsibility*—'researchers carry responsibilities in addition to the science of their inquiry', including responsibilities 'for which they or those of the community with whom they work may be held accountable' (p. 16);
- *survival and protection*—where researchers or institutions have ignored, denied or undermined Aboriginal and Torres Strait Islander values and distinctiveness, it is common for research to be perceived as an 'exploitative exercise', and to overcome such legacies, researchers and institutions 'will need to demonstrate through ethical negotiation, conduct and dissemination of research that they are trustworthy and will not repeat the mistakes of the past' (p. 18);
- *spirit and integrity*—a 'continuity of values and bonds that has sustained and been sustained by the overarching value of spirit and integrity' which underpins community decision making about research (p. 19).

Constructing a transparent and accountable demonstration of how research has considered and engaged with these issues is a challenging, but quite reasonable expectation in a cross-cultural setting. Far from constructing ethics committees as the 'research police' (Rolls, 2003, p. 1), the NHMRC guidelines exhort researchers, participating communities and institutional ethics committees towards engaged partnerships in which each challenges the others to consider ways in which the challenges of ethical engagement might best be met, without seeking to endorse only those preferred projects of a politically correct view of the world. Indeed, in the case to which Rolls refers to defend his advocacy of a rejection of the demands of ethical oversight—the case of the disputed construction of a bridge and marina at Hindmarsh Island in South Australia—the processes advocated by the NHMRC guidelines could have accommodated rigorous and divergent research collaborations with both sides of the Aboriginal dispute without having to resort to decisive claims about truth. In contrast to Rolls's individualistic solution, however, there would have been both transparency and accountability constructed into research relationships negotiated consistently with the guidelines—regardless of the political preferences of the various community factions involved.[1]

Negotiations-based SIA: Paradoxes and Challenges

This brings me back to SIA research and the grey areas of consultancy research, commercial research for (or about) Aboriginal and Torres Strait Islander groups and research that is embedded in negotiated relationships, such as the research component of negotiations-based SIA research.

In the context of negotiations between development proponents, such as mining companies or infrastructure companies in the resource and tourism sectors, and Aboriginal people with interests in land and waters affected by a project, SIA research can provide an important framework for affected Indigenous peoples to reflect on the issues that have affected, or will affect, their communities, their way of life and their culture, and to develop considered and well-supported negotiation positions. But one of the key principles of negotiation processes involving Indigenous peoples must be the principle of self-determination (Agius et al., 2004), and it is crucial that negotiation positions reflect internal processes and politics rather than developing as an artefact of research or negotiation methodologies. In other words, the development of structures that hold SIA research accountable to affected Aboriginal groups should itself be negotiated in ways that do not insist on a standardised outcome, but in which the groups themselves govern the outcome. Transparency and accountability against appropriate local values and governance structures, and within appropriate geographical and temporal scales, are crucial, but hard to achieve.

In some cases, SIA research is conducted in accordance with published guidelines, using explicit peer review and community-based oversight, and with full publication of final reports. For example, the Resource Assessment Commission's benchmark study of the Kakadu Conservation Zone and Coronation Hill mining proposal in the early 1990s (Lane et al., 1990) has been discussed in terms of its terms of reference, research methods and conclusions (see for example Howitt, 2001). Similarly, the Kakadu Region Social Impact Study (KRSIS) of the mid-1990s was undertaken against excellent terms of reference, under the oversight of a stakeholder committee and an Aboriginal Project Committee, with published reports (Levitus & Aboriginal Project Committee, 1997; Project Advisory Committee, 1997)—yet there has been no explicit discussion of the ethical engagement, oversight and accountability of either of these projects. Indeed, in the KRSIS example, the Project Advisory Committee report ignored or filtered much of what the Aboriginal Project Committee emphasised, and several years after the publication of these reports, and an implementation report (Collins, 2000), there is little evidence to suggest that the SIA facilitated any major change in relationships between the parties on the ground. While there was no specific scrutiny of the process by a formal ethics committee, the work was much more publicly accountable than many of the SIAs undertaken as contract research. And yet the KRSIS demonstrably failed to meet some of the aspirations enshrined in its terms of reference.

The apparent process failures in the KRSIS case raise significant concerns about the efficacy of scrutiny. In much contract research, the drivers for accountability can be, and often are, quite robust, even if there is an absence of external scrutiny in a formal structure. To what extent, then, does this lack of transparency to the 'external' world restrict the effectiveness of internal accountability? In the case of projects which remain within the 'grey' literature, with limited publication of terms of reference, final reports and so on, reviewing and assessing the ethical engagement and practical accountability of the work undertaken is even harder than is the case in even flawed public proceedings. Indeed, in many cases, reports are withheld from any public scrutiny, there are no publicly available terms of reference and there are exceptionally restricted grounds for consideration of ethical accountability.

This presents a somewhat paradoxical situation, in which neither approach to SIA research offers an externally transparent means of reviewing the ethical standards of the research against guidelines such as those adopted by the NHMRC. The values specified in the *Values and Ethics* document certainly establish a framework within which to construct appropriate standards of research practice and mutual accountability between researchers, affected community groups, project proponents, state agencies and other stakeholders. But there are significant challenges.

Let me illustrate with two cases in which I have been directly involved. In the Western Cape York Economic and Social Impact Assessment I was part of a research team led by Ciaran O'Faircheallaigh (Griffith University), along with Annie Holden (ImpaxSIA Consulting). I was recruited into the team because of my previous experience with the Aboriginal community at Napranum, and also because of my previous SIA research experience. When recruited, the terms of funding for the project had largely been finalised between the Cape York Land Council and Comalco Ltd, and I signed a contract, through Macquarie University's research consultancy arm, to provide my research services for a study which would review the impacts of more than 30 years of bauxite mining on the community most directly affected. That work was carried out under the close supervision of a local Aboriginal steering committee, with oversight from the Cape York Land Council. The time frames, the commercial confidentiality, my role in the research team and the lack of any ethical oversight within Macquarie Research Ltd at that time all meant that this work was not submitted to any institutional ethics committee for review nor was it subject to any other formal or independent ethical oversight. It was ethically engaged, and in many ways it actually exemplified many of the values referred to in the NHMRC guidelines. While O'Faircheallaigh (1999) has reflected on the process in a published paper, and the subsequent negotiations built on our SIA work culminated in the finalisation of the Western Cape Communities Coexistence Agreement in March 2001 (Cape York Partnerships, 2003; Comalco Ltd, 2003), the details of the research methods, findings and recommendations in the reports remain generally inaccessible. It was only in early 2005 that Comalco staff accepted that it might, in fact, be valuable to have wider public scrutiny of that material as an illustration of good SIA practice (O'Faircheallaigh, pers. comm.). In the absence of any such publication, judging the 'benefit' of the research is restricted to consideration of one of its quite direct outcomes—the Western Cape Communities Coexistence Agreement—and the limited discussion in the public domain of a largely confidential process.

In the second case, the SIA research on the Alice Springs to Darwin railway project, I led a small team which investigated the social impacts of the railway on affected Aboriginal people in the Northern and Central Land Council regions. The terms of reference were negotiated between the land councils and the Northern Territory government before there was any practical discussion of the research. The land councils discussed the proposed research and possible terms of reference for a research contract, and were willing to comply with the government's thinking, which required the scope of the research to be restricted to the 'tangible physical impacts' of the new railway—until it became quite clear that to do so would be unethical because it would limit the capacity of the research to consider a range of direct detrimental impacts and potential beneficial opportunities. While my co-researcher Sue Jackson and I have published on our research methodology (Howitt & Jackson, 2000), the two land councils have refused to release the full text of our report for public scrutiny. In late 2004 I approached the project operators to discuss cooperation with a formal *post facto* review of the project's impacts and the adequacy and efficacy of the SIA report, but received a brief response indicating that the operator could see 'no value' in such a study. In this case, I am less confident that the work undertaken for the SIA exemplifies the values at the heart of the NHMRC guidelines because the scope of the work was so vast, and our capacity to secure meaningful local benefits extraordinarily circumscribed. Nevertheless, I would welcome public scrutiny of the work—if it could be released. Indeed, given that this public infrastructure has proceeded with a range of public costs and benefits, it would be appropriate for such monitoring and scrutiny to be explicitly mandated. If critical documentation such as the SIA report are not publicly accessible, it becomes impossible for the public (either the general public or the affected Aboriginal publics) to audit the project's performance, or to monitor against predicted consequences. For us as researchers, there is no mechanism to maintain our accountable presence during the construction and operational phases of this project—as these both occurred after the research and reporting phases of the SIA.

The railway project had a number of controversies during construction which revealed divergence from detail of the proposal that was assessed in the EIA and SIA processes. One incident, the bulldozing of Gouldian finch habitat, resulted in the appointment of an officer within the Department of Environment and Heritage to monitor construction. Despite an explicit recommendation for a parallel structure to monitor and report publicly on social impacts, there was no capacity in the public arena for anybody to know what the social impacts actually were. One of the problems is that privately contracted studies facilitate governments relinquishing their mandated duty of care to evaluate costs and benefits of development projects in the interests of the entire society—and to minimise harm to any particular groups within society. Such shortcomings inevitably entrench less than satisfactory practices as an effective standard in SIA research—at significant cost to Aboriginal and general public interests in jurisdictions such as the Northern Territory.

Ethical Oversight: Do Researchers Have a 'Right to Research'?

In my view, it could be said that my colleagues and I failed to construct procedures that were adequately transparent and accountable to external scrutiny, even though a significant public interest might be said to exist in doing so. I should hasten to say that not all my colleagues agree that this is a significant failure, or that we failed to reach an appropriate standard. We occupied different positions in these projects and experienced the local accountability structures differently, and the significance of a lack of external transparency is no simple matter. Indeed, in the context of our shared acceptance that Aboriginal people have a right to self-determination, protecting Aboriginal processes from intrusive external scrutiny is enormously important in empowering people to pursue their own view of their own interests. In these two cases, we operated within constraints that affected funding, timing, terms of reference, methodologies, relationships with research participants, relationships with development proponents, relationships with Aboriginal organisations and local Indigenous governance processes. In both cases we did some of the best research that I have ever been involved in, and in my judgement this was highly ethical research which engaged with and reflected precisely the values identified in the NHMRC guidelines—but to some extent, the public is forced to accept this claim at face value, because the relevant reports cannot be read. The outcomes cannot even be monitored against our recommendations because there is no published version of our recommendations against which either public or Aboriginal authorities might be asked to report. In the case of the Northern Territory study, there have since been other linear projects evaluated, but affected groups have not had easy access to our report, even where they are working for the same organisations that commissioned our work (Sue Jackson, pers. comm.).

Clearly I am uncomfortable with this situation and this paper invites debate on how such work might better proceed. This work has drawn me to a reflection on much of the work that we undertake as applied social researchers, our work as activist researchers, our work in spaces of cross-cultural engagement and the work of my students and graduates in this field, where there is no formal accreditation of SIA professionals and no professional body from which one can be disqualified if one fails to meet appropriate ethical standards. There is no body to which we can appeal when those who contract our services seek to secure inappropriate influence, or themselves act in ways that are inconsistent with standards such as those put forward in the *Values and Ethics* guidelines (NHMRC, 2003).

As a member of an institutional ethics committee, I have observed that many publicly funded researchers operate as if our positions as university employees give us something like a right to research. Ethics oversight for these researchers is dehistoricised and reconfigured as a restraint on or interference with university staff members' 'right to research' on any topic they like. In the context of work in indigenous studies, we neglect the historical context of unethical research at our peril. I accept Rolls's (2003) important observation that many Aboriginal claims rely on research that was undertaken in ways that would now not be approved by any institutional ethics committee—but that is not the point. One of the lessons of the history of research ethics is that research is always undertaken in a social context, and that research cannot be divorced from its social and cultural settings. None of us has a 'right' to research. Our opportunities (and obligations) to undertake research are circumscribed by our circumstances, and privileging the research traditions of, for example, colonial anthropology or geography in the context of Australian research, because it produces some historically significant information, and then setting that as an appropriate standard for contemporary research practice is simply wrong (see Howitt & Jackson (1998) for discussion relevant to geography). Changing social values, legal requirements, technological capacities and theoretical frameworks all insist on calibrating contemporary practices to contemporary standards—including ethical standards. It is, perhaps, easier to see the point of ethical oversight in the treatment of animals, of genetic material, of reproductive technologies, and even of psychological research and health research involving risk, than for observational social research, or contracted SIA research.

But just what sort of value might external ethical review add to SIA research undertaken in a negotiations-based approach such as the Western Cape York and Northern Territory railway studies? Clearly, this is not a simple question, but it is relevant to university-based researchers accepting research contracts in a range of cross-cultural settings. In the case of my own university, social science and humanities researchers have worked hard to avoid ethical oversight being reduced to a censorious methodological review. Indeed geographers at Macquarie have been central for nearly a decade to challenging the idea research ethics could, or should, only be applied in a narrowly biomedical mode, contributing significantly to the development of supportive and facilitative ethical oversight of participatory and action-oriented methodologies, qualitative research approaches and cross-cultural research. In particular, the development of iterative approval procedures, which allow researchers to construct increasingly sophisticated collaborative research with indigenous participants without requiring them to pre-empt the outcomes of consultative and negotiation-based exploration of what will be researched and how it will be researched, has encouraged much more open-ended and robust engagements with the NHMRC principles at Macquarie than were previously possible for many researchers. The value of this ethical oversight is that we collectively support the exploration of how the ethical engagement anticipated in the NHMRC guidelines might work in practice.

So, in stark contrast to Rolls's (2003) assertion that ethical accountability in research institutions is restricted to some sort of enforcement of political correctness,

218   R. Howitt

we do not assume that either a researcher's personal 'good intentions' or their research rigour will produce adequate research. For my own part, this means that I am always ready to face demanding questioning from my research peers, my students, my research collaborators—both community- and industry-based and professional colleagues—and groups affected by or involved in my research. I recognise that university research resources—however pitiful they may seem to us from time to time, and however much we may decry research funding policies and priorities—are an important part of the structures of power, privilege and disadvantage in contemporary Australia and that Aboriginal and Torres Strait Islander peoples will continue to see research activities as ambiguous and potentially negative while researchers' ethical engagement is less than transparent, accountable and open to challenge. Of course, being open to challenge from an institutional ethics committee and being available to challenges from the people who are affected by or interested in our research are quite different matters. I want to assert that the ethical engagement envisaged by the NHMRC guidelines is central to the research enterprise generally, and is absolutely central to any concept of research that involves cross-cultural engagement such as SIA research (see Howitt & Stevens, 2005). Given that ethics committees can be considered a key point at which accountability and ethical engagement of research is overseen and facilitated, the failure to bring social impact research to that arena is significant, yet simply bringing contracted SIA research under the scrutiny of institutional ethics committees will not achieve the sort of outcomes that I am hoping to catalyse here. Again, the paradoxical challenges of improving external scrutiny and responding to indigenous rights to self-determination are more apparent than a solution.

In cases where corporate or government sponsorship of the research is involved, as they were in the case of both the Western Cape York and Northern Territory railway studies, there is a substantial argument to support the need for external ethical review and mandating both publication and formal follow-up, including public participation in monitoring and implementation of recommendations. Yet in relation to practices of self-determination, external scrutiny by yet another non-indigenous authority that claims a right to oversee (and overrule) indigenous decision making and authority is not the answer.

Universities increasingly value externally funded research projects such as contract-funded SIA projects, and the corporatist university will support research dollars coming in from almost any source and rationalise almost any research that can stand some peer review scrutiny. Yet researchers working in indigenous studies must recognise that state and private sector interests are not, and historically have never been, committed to any form of Aboriginal or Torres Strait Islander self-determination or self-government. Universities do not sponsor research with Aboriginal and Torres Strait Islander peoples as part of a strategy for increased Indigenous participation in university affairs or for recognition of Indigenous rights. As critical social scientists, we really do need to recognise the contexts in which we research; to recognise that Aboriginal and Torres Strait Islander organisations that are authorised by legislation are not always the vehicle for Aboriginal and Torres Strait Islander self-determination. And we must see that well-intentioned research, well-intentioned negotiations may well contribute to and even initiate processes that usurp peoples' rights to self-determination, self-government and self-representation (see also Agius *et al.*, 2004; Macduff, 2003).

Process Really Does Matter: Questions for Research Practice

The NHMRC guidelines offer a very strong foundation for challenging ourselves about how ethically engaged we are in cross-cultural work with Aboriginal and Torres Strait Islander peoples. They are not prescriptive, nor are they censorious. They provide a set of reference points and challenges that it is appropriate for us to meet every time we occupy the privileged position of 'researcher'. External review, for example by an institutional ethics committee, may well be difficult and inconvenient at times. And it may not produce easy responses to difficult questions and challenges—but it is better than no ethical review, and it is a basis for increasingly equitable, awkward and challenging partnerships to develop between researchers, research institutions and Aboriginal and Torres Strait Islander peoples and their own institutions and customary procedures that will open new possibilities for challenging the role of research in cross-cultural relations in Australia.

Clearly, process does matter—and ethical engagement is about process. It is a means for focusing researchers on precisely those elements that the input and output obsession of university funding models and career assessment models in the corporatist and managerialist universities we work in so effectively ignore. It focuses precisely on those issues of the social construction of knowledge and its socialised application that critical applied social research should prioritise and acknowledge.

The NHMRC guidelines are a useful opening to a long and complex discussion about appropriate ethical standards and procedures in SIA research, and a reference point in terms of key principles that will need to be considered. The guidelines offer discussion of examples of different models of research, collaboration and management. There is no assertion of a politically correct approach in the guidelines, and there is the prospect for a great diversity of outcomes and approaches to be generated from the guidelines. But there is some common ground in insisting that research is not a detached procedure that can be abstracted from the social, political, historical and geographical context of its participants, subjects and audiences. The models suggested all share:

> ... explicit recognition and commitment to respect for Aboriginal and Torres Strait Islander cultural values and principles. The models also promote local relationships to ensure that the nuances of judgement and practice necessary to promote trustworthiness and trust are created and maintained. They also illustrate important aspects of accountability and transparency in standards, and process and structures. (NHMRC, 2003, p. 5)

As a starting point for debating how Aboriginal and Torres Strait Islander peoples' rights may be best protected and advanced in just, equitable and sustainable ways through contract and applied research such as SIA research, the challenges raised in the NHMRC guidelines are both constructive and challenging. In reflecting on the challenges experienced in work I have been involved in over the past decade,

220   R. Howitt

I think I have provided a starting point for a fruitful debate about the multiple audiences and axes of accountability that such research constructs. I hope that we might also see some new sorts of procedures emerge which challenge the privileges accorded to 'research' in contexts where Aboriginal and Torres Strait Islander peoples and their representative bodies may well see things differently from researchers, universities and research funding agencies.

Note

[1] It is beyond the scope of this paper to provide an overview of the Hindmarsh Island affair, and there is a substantial literature available that presents various facets of this complex matter. See, for example, Brunton (1996), Langton (1996), Fergie (1996), Gelder & Jacobs (1997), Weiner (1997), Bell (1998) and Simons (2003). Transcripts of the South Australian Royal Commission are available online at http://www.library.adelaide.edu.au/gen/H_Islnd/ and papers from a conference on the legal case, which found in favour of the Aboriginal women who refused to testify to the Royal Commission, can be obtained online at http://www.aas.asn.au/hindmarsh.htm

References

Agius, P., Davies, J., Howitt, R., Jarvis, S. & Williams, R. (2004) Comprehensive native title negotiations in South Australia, in: M. Langton, M. Tehan & L. Palmer (Eds) *Negotiating Settlements: Indigenous Peoples, Settler States and the Significance of Treaties and Agreements*, pp. 203–219 (Melbourne: Melbourne University Press).
Bell, D. (1998) *Ngarrindjeri Wurruwarrin: A World that Is, Was, and Will Be*, (Melbourne: Spinifex Press).
Boothroyd, P., Knight, N., Eberle, M., Kawaguchi, J. & Gagnon, C. (1995) The need for retrospective impact assessment: the megaprojects example, *Impact Assessment*, 13(3), pp. 253–271.
Brunton, R. (1996) The Hindmarsh Island bridge and the credibilty of Australian anthropology, *Anthropology Today*, 12(4), pp. 2–7.
Cape York Partnerships (2003) Traditional owners, Comalco and government sign historic agreement. Available at: http://www.capeyorkpartnerships.com/media/releases/his-agree-com-14-3-01.htm
Collins, B. (2000) *Kakadu Region Social Impact Study Community Report: Report on Initiatives: November 1998–November 2000*, Darwin, Parks Australia.
Comalco Ltd (2003) Western Cape Communities Coexistence Agreement. Available at: http://www.comalco.com/freedom.aspx?pid=502
Fergie, D. (1996) Secret envelopes and inferential tautologies, *Journal of Australian Studies*, 48, pp. 13–24.
Gagnon, C. (2003) Methodology of social impact follow-up modeling, in: R. O. Rasmussen & N. E. Koroleva (Eds) *Social and Environmental Impacts in the North: Methods in Evaluation of Socio-economic and Environmental Consequences of Mining and Energy Production in the Arctic and Sub-Arctic*, pp. 479–489 (Dordrecht: Kluwer Academic).
Gelder, K. & Jacobs, J. (1997) Promiscuous sacred sites: reflections on secrecy and scepticism in the Hindmarsh Island affair, *Australian Humanities Review*, June. Available at: http://www.lib.latrobe.edu.au/AHR/archive/Issue-June-1997/gelder.htm
Howitt, R. (2001) *Rethinking Resource Management: Justice, Sustainability and Indigenous Peoples* (London: Routledge).
Howitt, R. & Jackson, S. (1998) Some things do change: indigenous rights, geographers and geography in Australia, *Australian Geographer*, 29(2), pp. 155–173.
Howitt, R. & Jackson, S. (2000) Social impact assessment and linear projects, in: L. R. Goldman (Ed.) *Social Impact Analysis: An Applied Anthropology Manual*, pp. 257–294 (Oxford: Berg).
Howitt, R. & Stevens, S. (2005) Cross-cultural research: ethics, methods and relationships, in: I. Hay (Ed.) *Qualitative Research Methods in Human Geography*, 2nd edn (Melbourne: Oxford University Press) pp. 30–50.
Howitt, R., Crough, G. & Pritchard (1990) Participation, power and social research in central Australia, *Australian Aboriginal Studies*, 1, pp. 2–10.

Humphrey, K. (2001) Dirty questions: Indigenous health and "Western research", *Australian and New Zealand Journal of Public Health*, 25(3), pp. 197–202.

Lane, B. (2003) Why I'm not an ethical researcher, *Australian Higher Education Supplement*, 5 March, p. 23.

Lane, M. B., Dale, A., Ross, H., Hill, A. & Rickson, R. (1990) *Social Impact of Development: An Analysis of the Social Impact of Development on Aboriginal Communities in the Region* (Canberra: Australian Government Publishing Service).

Langton, M. (1996) How Aboriginal religion has become an administrable subject, *Australian Humanities Review*, July. Available at: http://www.lib.latrobe.edu.au/AHR/archive/Issue-July-1996/langton.html

Levitus, R. & Aboriginal Project Committee (1997) *Kakadu Region Social Impact Study: Report of the Aboriginal Project Committee* (Canberra: Supervising Scientist).

Macduff, I. (2003) What would you do—with a *taniwha* at the table? *Negotiation Journal*, 19(3), pp. 195–198.

NHMRC (1991) *Guidelines on Ethical Matters in Aboriginal and Torres Strait Islander Health Research* (Canberra: NHMRC).

NHMRC (1992) *NHMRC Statement on Human Experimentation and Supplementary Notes 1992* (Canberra: NHMRC).

NHMRC (2003) *Values and Ethics: Guidelines for Ethical Conduct in Aboriginal and Torres Strait Islander Health Research* (Canberra: NHMRC).

O'Faircheallaigh, C. (1999) Making social impact assessment count: a negotiation-based approach for Indigenous peoples, *Society and Natural Resources*, 12, pp. 63–80.

Project Advisory Committee (1997) *Kakadu Region Social Impact Study Community Action Plan: Report of the Study Advisory Group* (Canberra: Office of the Supervising Scientist).

Rolls, M. (2003) Why I don't want to be an "ethical" researcher, *Australian Humanities Review*, January. Available at: www.lib.latrobe.edu.au/AHR/archive/Issue-Jan-2003/rolls1.html

Simons, M. (2003) *The Meeting of the Waters: The Hindmarsh Island Affair* (Sydney: Hodder Headline).

Weiner, J. F. (1997) "Bad Aboriginal" anthropology: a reply to Ron Brunton, *Anthropology Today*, 13(4), pp. 5–8.

[11]

Anthropologists and Social Impact Assessment: Negotiating the Ethical Minefield[1]

Robert Fisher

The approval of major infrastructure and industrial developments is often dependent on the results of environmental and social impact assessments (EIA and SIA, respectively). Depending on the recommendations of 'experts' undertaking the assessments, projects are approved, rejected or modified to take account of unintended negative consequences. In practice, there are pressures on consultants to come up with favourable results, and unfavourable results are often ignored. These pressures may be subtle. For example, because consultants are usually employed by somebody with an interest in seeing projects go ahead, any consultant with a reputation for being too negative is unlikely to get work. The present paper explores issues faced by anthropologists in SIA, as well as the structure of interests within which SIA is carried out, and ways in which ethical dilemmas can be negotiated. It asks whether simply opting out of the process altogether is an ethical option preferable to critical engagement.

Keywords: Social impact assessment; Environmental impact assessment; Consultancy; Professional practice; Professional ethics

Introduction

The old system of hiring consultants to evaluate a proposed project was efficient, cost-effective and mutually beneficial for all the players involved. Typically the World Bank would hire Northern engineering firms that had often worked with the proposed contractors—that is, the firms who were expected to build the infrastructure ... to collect and analyze data to assess a project. More often than not, the engineering firms would find that indeed the project was feasible (or would be, with certain modifications) and that its negative impacts could be mitigated through some additional investment—for example a drainage system might be

Correspondence to: Dr Robert Fisher, Australian Mekong Resource Centre, School of Geosciences, Madsen Building (FO9), University of Sydney, NSW 2006, Australia. Email: rjfisher@ozemail.com.au

ISSN 1444-2213 (print)/ISSN 1740-9314 (online)/08/030231-12
© 2008 The Australian National University
DOI: 10.1080/14442210802251670

> added to resolve a potentially leaky irrigation system. As long as the project was not shown to be *in*feasible (a highly unusual occurrence), these impact assessments could lead to an increase in the size of a loan and the work for engineering firms and builders. (Goldman 2001, p. 196, emphasis in original)

Approval of major development projects is commonly dependent on the results of an environmental impact assessment (EIA) and a social impact assessment (SIA). In theory, at least, projects are approved, rejected or modified depending on the recommendations of 'expert' consultants.

Given that large developments usually involve actors with vested interests, consultants are often under pressure—sometimes fairly obvious, sometimes (perhaps more often) subtle—to reach favourable findings. Such favourable findings often disadvantage some people. The subtle pressures include the reality that consultants cannot always be negative—or too negative—if they want future consultancy work in EIA/SIA. It would, in principle, seem to be easier for an academic anthropologist, or someone otherwise employed, to take strong negative stands than it is for someone whose income largely depends on consultancy.

If we take the view that major infrastructure developments will occur (and many of them are genuinely desirable), and that it is a good idea in principle that interventions with possible human consequences should be subject to a process of impact assessment, then the dilemma is how to be critically and ethically, and therefore selectively, involved—how to navigate through the complexities. I think it is not enough to throw up our hands in despair at the difficult choices.

The aim of the present paper is to explore some of the ethical dilemmas involved for anthropologists doing impact assessments as consultants and to try to suggest ways of dealing with them. The paper is informed by discourse about the relationships between power and 'professional knowledge' and is a critical reflection on experiences in conducting EIA/SIA. In this sense, the paper can be seen very much as an example of participant observation of a consultancy process leading to an ethnography of the 'developers' rather than the usual ethnography of the 'developees'.

Although the paper is primarily about anthropologists and SIA, it draws on the experience of people who are not necessarily anthropologists but who, nevertheless, are expected to make anthropologically informed judgements. The consultant industry does not, after all, necessarily respect disciplinary boundaries. Much of what is being discussed here applies to non-anthropologists doing similar work and, for that matter, a lot of it is relevant to more than SIA. It should be noted that SIA is frequently subsumed into EIA and is not always identified separately. For this reason, I draw on literature concerned with EIA and sometimes use the terms more or less interchangeably.

I will now look at two case studies. The first is the Theun Hinbon Dam and Power Station in Laos. I was not personally involved in any of the SIAs involved in this case, although I have visited the site and discussed the process with many of the actors (usually referred to as 'stakeholders' in SIA).[2] Much of the history of this case is available in the public domain. It highlights some of the real dilemmas involved in impact assessment, as well as some of the pressures placed on practitioners. The second case, in which I was involved directly as a consultant, concerned minerals processing in India.

Theun Hinboun Hydropower Project (Lao PDR)

The Theun Hinboun Hydropower Project is managed by a private company, the Theun Hinboun Power Company (THPC).[3] The company is owned jointly by Electicité du Laos, a state-owned utility (60 per cent share), a Thai company (MDX Lao) and Nordic Hydropower (a Swedish company). MDX Lao and Nordic Hydropower each own 20 per cent shares. The total cost of the project was US$240 million, of which US$60 million (most of the Lao government's investment) was financed by a loan from the Asian Development Bank (ADB). The project will be handed over to the Lao government after thirty years. Almost all the electricity produced is sold to Thailand.

The project diverts water from the Theun-Kading river, through a tunnel that feeds the power station and then into the Hai and Hinboun rivers. The holding dam is on the Theun river above the tunnel entrance. Thus, the water flow in the Theun river is reduced and the flow in the Hai–Hinboun rivers is increased whenever there are surges in water flow during periods of peak power demand. Sometimes the rate of increase is very fast. People were killed by sudden increases in water level early in the period of dam operation and complaints were made when banks and fields were washed away. The changes in the flow of the river would seem to suggest, *a priori*, that the project would lead to environmental changes.

The project was completed in 1998. The ADB claimed it was a model project that was essentially environmentally benign and had no effect on livelihoods. Both before and after the completion of the project, non-government organisations (NGOs) published critiques of the EIA (which supposedly incorporated SIA) and argued that livelihoods were threatened. Even before the dam was completed, a report by FIVAS, a Norwegian NGO, criticised Norwegian involvement in the project for not taking into account environmental and social costs (FIVAS 1996). In particular, the report criticised the lack of consultation prior to the commencement of the project with people affected and the lack of a formal policy for compensating them. FIVAS criticised an EIA undertaken by the Norwegian partner (Norpower 1993) that claimed positive environmental effects and denied that there would be major social impacts. The FIVAS report argued that many villages would be affected.

Subsequently, following a visit just prior to the official opening of the dam, Shoemaker (1998), a consultant for the international NGO the International Rivers Network, reported that 'ALL [villages] reported experiencing various harmful effects from the project' (emphasis in original). Further, 'villagers reported substantial declines in fishing catches' (ranging from 30 per cent to 90 per cent). Shoemaker continues:

> Villagers also reported being impacted by the loss of riverbank vegetable gardens, the loss of dry season drinking water sources, and transportation difficulties. In

some areas, villagers must relocate their homes and do not feel they are receiving adequate assistance with this process.

All this occurred before the power station was formally opened. Following these critiques, and others, the ADB held a review mission and the Bank and the company commissioned a study of the impact on fish populations and fisheries (Warren 1999). The study aimed to identify impacts and to recommend mitigation measures. It was very much a technical study that raised issues of concern, but was only mildly critical. Nevertheless, the ADB and the THPC refused to release the report. Warren, the consultant who authored the report, subsequently gave a public presentation on impacts at a conference held in June 2000 (Warren 2000). The original report—which was never accepted by the THPC—was placed on the International Rivers Network website (Warren 1999). The public release of findings demonstrated considerable professional courage on Warren's part.

In 2001 the company commenced a Mitigation and Compensation Program. The program established village development committees and provided funds for a variety of livelihood activities and programs, such as credit funds. In 2003, the THPC and the International Rivers Network made an agreement to appoint mutually acceptable consultants to carry out a joint review, the Environmental Management Division, which managed the Mitigation and Compensation Program. The consultants were contracted by the THPC. The company, which had originally agreed to release the draft of the consultants' report for public review, refused to do so when the draft was completed. The reason given to the consultants was that the company regarded it as an internal matter and did not want outsiders to intervene.

The International Rivers Network withdrew from the agreement. Unfortunately, the original agreement was not a formal contract and the contract was not available until after the work had begun. Subsequently, the THPC published an amended version of the review report (Blake, Carson, & Tubtim 2005). Among other changes, this version omitted discussion of the effects of a proposed extension of the project on the grounds that it was not in the original contract, which the company claimed was restricted to the Mitigation and Compensation Program. At least two of the consultants reluctantly agreed to the amendments, believing that the amended report was better than nothing. Subsequently, one of them published an article (Blake 2005) arguing that, although having some achievements, the program did not adequately compensate people for the negative impacts of the project upon them.[4]

This case illustrates some of the difficulties faced by consultants who attempt to undertake EIA/SIA on behalf of parties with financial interests in a project. In both the fisheries review by Warren and the review of the Mitigation and Compensation Program, the company and/or the ADB were clearly unhappy with the findings and rejected or revised the reports.

The EIAs and SIAs undertaken on behalf of NGOs were instrumental in drawing attention to significant issues and, through the advocacy of the NGOs, forced the ADB and the company to undertake further reviews and, subsequently, to develop a program of mitigation. However, the contracting agencies were not prepared to accept the findings of their independent consultants or to honour a verbal agreement about the consultancy process.

One strategy used by the company has been the use of science (and claims of objectivity) to criticise the quality of unfavourable reports. The Theun Hinboun case is characterised by a series of studies, some commissioned on behalf of advocacy groups and others commissioned by partners in the joint venture. All were subjected to competing claims of bias and lack of scientific rigour. In this context, it is hard to see how it can be maintained that EIA/SIA is an objective technical process. Who could be an honest broker in the process, especially given that both the government of Laos and the ADB strongly supported the project?[5]

The pressures to come up with favourable findings, and where unfavourable findings are revised before release, are obvious here. Clearly not all EIA/SIA activities are so obviously distorted by the interests of the employer, but it is not easy to navigate the complex structures of interests as a critical professional.

A Copper Smelter in North Eastern India

The second case study relates to a combined environmental and social impact assessment undertaken as part of a project design mission for a potential bilaterally funded project carried out in a largely tribal state. Owing to potential concerns about a 'commercial-in confidence' contractual clause, I cannot be too specific. The potential project involved the application of new technology to the processing of copper ore at an existing smelter. In terms of the scale of the existing smelter, the proposed development was a small add-on, which aimed to reprocess ore to capture valuable trace elements. Therefore, it contributed only incrementally to existing positive and negative effects.

The engineering company that had developed the technology was funded by the donor to carry out a mission to implement a detailed design for the new technology. This was part of an aid program intended to subsidise or 'kick start' business connections between the donor country and India. The design mission included EIA and SIA. An international consulting firm was contracted to undertake the impact assessments. The team leader for this activity was an environmental engineer employed by the consultancy company. His job was to assess the environment within the plant. Two other individual consultants were subcontracted, one to undertake an assessment of the impacts of the proposed new technology on local environment and agriculture, and the other (me) to assess the social impacts. The three-person impact assessment team worked closely with the technical design team, but prepared its report for the donor.

Given the relatively small scale of the project and the already large impacts of the existing smelter, the impact assessment exercise was relatively minor and only about two weeks were set aside for the fieldwork. The methods adopted for the environmental and social impacts were essentially rapid appraisal methods, rather than comprehensive surveys and studies. The SIA aspect could be thought of as rapid ethnography.

A methodological challenge was how to assess the potential impacts of the new add-on technology, given the scale of the changes. The strategic decision was to identify, but not quantify, the impacts of the existing operation and to assume that the new technology would add incrementally, but not quantifiably, to the existing impacts, both positive and negative.

The smelter was situated on the banks of a river in an area largely populated by tribal people (in the Indian sense of 'scheduled tribes'). A town across the river had grown mainly as a result of the smelter operations. A significant aspect of the smelter operations was the provision of considerable employment, both for migrant labour and local tribal people. There was also a great deal of economic activity arising from services, shops, restaurants and the like. In many ways, the area was an island of economic development in a very economically depressed area. Many tribal people were employed in the plant and this was an important positive impact.

The two major sources of environmental change arising directly from the smelter were chemical pollution flowing into the river and pollution from the smoke plume flowing from the smelter's chimneys. A survey of the river condition downstream showed some effects of pollution, although the river was surprisingly healthy. The ecologist's view was that much of the damage was due to pollution from the town—including from sewerage fed into the river—rather than being a direct impact of the smelter operations. Nevertheless, good EIA and SIA take a systemic perspective and consider indirect impacts (good and bad) as well as direct impacts.

Downstream, it was clear that local fishers were collecting much reduced catches of fish and crustaceans. They reported collecting only three or four kilograms a day, compared with much larger quantities in the past. It is not clear whether the decrease was a result of pollution or declined stock resulting from overfishing to feed the urban population. Either way, the decreased income for the fishers was a direct or indirect result of the smelter's activity.

Just as the impact assessment team looked downstream to examine the environmental and social impacts of river pollution, examination of the impacts of the smoke plume was explored by assessing sites 'downstream' of the chimneys, in terms of prevailing wind direction. There were some signs of declining soil fertility, and interviews with farmers reported reduced productivity. It was not clear, without chemical analysis, how much of the decline was a result of pollution and how much was a result of inadequate inputs and reduced fallow periods resulting from increasing pressure on the land. The point is that there were changes that could be plausibly linked with the smelter and associated population.

What was emerging from this is the picture of a migrant and local population that was relatively prosperous as a result of the economic activity generated by the smelter. At the same time, much of the population did not participate in the mainstream activity associated with the smelter, but rather occupied very specific economic niches, some resulting from the presence of the smelter and associated activities. This sort of economy characterised by small groups occupying narrow niches is common in India. Artisanal fishing was one such niche occupation. Another was fuel wood collection, which was an important source of income for tribal women. The advantage was that the urban population created a demand for fuel wood, but deforestation made it more time-consuming due to increased distances. One other specialist niche related to women who sifted through the piles of processed ore, finding pieces with enough copper for reprocessing and selling them to the smelter. In terms of income, it was a marginal activity, but nevertheless a source of income. One downside of the small but important incomes of economically marginal groups is that the overall cost of living was apparently higher in the area than in other parts of the state.

Identifying various occupational niches was an important step in identifying groups likely to be affected differently by the smelter and associated economy. Various groups were affected differently by changes in economic opportunity, pollution-related damage to resources and so on. The detail is not necessary here. The important thing is that we were able to identify both positive and negative impacts of the smelter operation and associated urbanisation and economic change.

Ultimately, the conclusions of the EIA/SIA were that the proposed new technology would lead to an incremental addition to the existing positive and negative impacts of the existing smelter—strong local economy and negative effects on some segments of society, such as reduced income and increased labour. The report recommended some mitigating measures, such as an increased contribution to the existing 'social' programs run by the smelter—including income-generating activities for women—and funding for aquaculture for the affected artisanal fishers. Overall, it identified no reasons why the project should not proceed, except to sound a warning that conflict within the state between tribal movements and the government may lead to the donor being caught up in local politics. (Ultimately, the project did not go ahead, apparently because of these political risks.)

So, what were the ethical issues involving SIA in this case? I should start by stressing that the various parties involved behaved with integrity and honesty and that the findings of the impact team were, in my opinion, appropriate given the scale of the existing activities, the fact that they provided substantial economic benefits to the local population and the very limited—so limited to be unquantifiable—positive and negative impacts of the new activities. I had worried that the fact that the impact team was, to some extent, answerable to an engineering company with an interest in seeing the project going ahead may lead to pressure to make favourable findings. In fact, this did not happen—except at one point when the impact team was considering whether it should consider the impacts on another state of India, which was the source of some of the ore used in the smelter. According to the Terms of Reference (TOR) for the impact assessment, remote impacts were also to be explored, so there was some discussion of where the boundaries should realistically be set. The leader of the engineering team expressed the view that this was beyond the TOR. The leader of the impact team said that this was the responsibility of the impact assessment team to decide. This resolved the issue immediately and no further pressure was applied. Ultimately, the EIA and SIA specialists decided that extending the boundaries to such an extent was impractical and would not affect the overall findings. I do not believe that the decision resulted from the intervention by the engineering team leader.

This incident demonstrates that the sort of pressures for favourable findings—or, more correctly, the willingness to ignore, override or not release unfavourable findings—evident in the Theun Hinboun case are not always present. In fact, they are not very common. The position taken by the leader of the impact team illustrates the importance of professional reputation—including the reputation of a major international consulting company—and integrity.

The underlying issue is whether, even in relatively straightforward impact assessment tasks, implied pressure can affect the outcomes of a study. Does the very structure of the consultancy industry imply pressure to avoid highly critical findings? The fact that many consultants are dependent on getting future jobs clearly puts them in a situation where a reputation for being very critical may reduce their chances for future work. It is, of course, hard to test how much this implicit threat actually affects the results that consultants give, although it seems plausible that it may. In the India case, this was not really an issue, because the proposed new technology had very small impacts compared with the existing operation. However, if there were serious issues, this sort of implied pressure may have come into play.

Discussion

Before discussing individual strategies that may assist anthropologists (and others) to deal with the ethics of engagement, it is useful to consider whether there are ways to make the impact assessment process more objective and more equitable through institutional or structural reform.

Given that impact assessments are generally prepared on behalf of project proponents who have a vested interest in seeing their projects approved, it would be an obvious advantage to have a neutral agency—an 'honest broker'—involved in commissioning or assessing impact assessments. However, this is not as easy as it may seem. Agencies, such as governments, and donors, such as the international development banks, often have their own preferences for projects to go ahead. Both the government of Laos and the Asian Development Bank were anxious to see the Nam Theun-Hinboun project go ahead. Neither of these could be regarded as independent assessors in that project. Who would appoint the 'honest broker'? And who would recognise the 'honest broker'?

An associated suggestion is that a professional association of consultants could provide an independent body to ensure that guidelines for professional practice are followed. Although this has potential, it is doubtful whether—at least in broader international development—membership of such an association would assist in the appointment of consultants. Contractors could simply choose consultants who did not belong to the association. It is only if the major development agencies and national governments made membership of professional associations a condition of employment as an impact assessment consultant that the professional associations could act as honest brokers. But it is not clear that national governments and large donors would support such a system given that the current system works well *for them*.

If we accept that this sort of structural or institutional reform to the impact assessment process will be difficult to achieve, at least in the near future, I suggest another alternative is for consultants to have strategies or guidelines to assist them to assess potential contracts.

At the beginning of this essay I made the point that non-engagement in SIA can also have ethical consequences. It is clear that advocacy for dissenting interests is one form of engagement that is often an option that anthropologists feel comfortable with. Nevertheless, this is often a reactive position—reacting to development decisions that seem to be flawed. (I will return to this option later.) The question is whether there are ways to engage more critically in the process as it is generally practised in development. Short of asserting that the entire consultancy process for SIA is intrinsically and inevitably unethical, the question is how can professional anthropologists become critically engaged in impact assessment as it is generally practised?

I believe that the concept of 'structures of interest' can help to guide potential consultants through the minefield. There are a number of questions that can help a consultant decide whether to become involved in advance:

- Who is the employer—direct and indirect?
- Do employers have expectations of a specific outcome—or may they have such expectations? Do they have vested interests?
- What do the TOR allow in terms of the scope of the enquiry, the boundaries, the scope for findings and recommendations?
- Who would gain or lose from decisions based on findings?
- How could the findings be used?
- How much control of—or even access to—the findings would the consultant have? In other words, does the consultant have the right to publish or distribute findings independently of the organisation that commissions the study?
- How is the assessment process structured? Are there opportunities for dissenting voices—such as local people—to be heard?[6]

Some consultancies can be fairly easily ruled out by such an analysis. For example, I was once asked to undertake a consultancy that involved making recommendations about whether resident people should be resettled out of a protected area. The task included recommending mitigation and compensation measures and it seemed clear at the time that resettlement was an assumed outcome. I rejected the consultancy because, in my experience, such resettlement schemes never provided acceptable outcomes. I concluded that I could not honestly accept a consultancy in which I could not, in good faith, consider options envisioned in the TOR. In any case, it would have been very likely that there would be pressure to make such recommendations had I accepted the job.

Underlying the need to assess the structure of interests in terms of the opportunities for independent findings, two key themes are the importance of transparency and public scrutiny and the space for negotiation of outcomes with stakeholders, especially locally affected people. These are potential filters by which potential consultancies can be assessed.

If understanding the structure of interests is essential to assessing the ethical opportunities and threats involved in potential SIA contracts, then the question of potential transparency and public scrutiny is of fundamental importance. Chambers (1987) argues that 'the major ethical issues that have a direct bearing on applied research have to do with client relationships and "secret" or proprietary research' (p. 328). Howitt (2005) strongly urges the need for public scrutiny of SIA reports. Ensuring that contracts deal satisfactorily with this issue is a challenge and a point on which many ethical issues may revolve.

The second key theme is the potential for negotiation of outcomes. Howitt (2005) stresses the importance of process in SIA and this is perhaps one way around the issues of power. Participatory approaches to SIA have been advocated and tried in various contexts, and are sometimes explicitly built into the SIA process. Howitt (2005) and O'Faircheallaigh (1999) both argue for negotiations-based approaches. The implication is that potential consultants should consider ensuring that opportunities for negotiation are built into impact-assessment processes before contracts are signed.

If a negotiations-based approach is not built into an impact-assessment process, another professional option is to specifically recognise the political nature of the process and to support civil society in commissioning and implementing alternative and competing SIAs, as in the Theun Hinboun case. This option—SIA as politics—provides opportunities to correct the excesses of SIAs driven by parties with vested interests. The idea of competing SIAs explicitly recognises the political and non-objective reality of the impact assessment process.[7]

The questions listed above are useful pointers to issues that can potentially undermine an honest SIA process. Sometimes the answers to the questions are obvious in advance, especially from an analysis of the contractual arrangements. In practice, the answers are not always obvious. The case of the arrangements for independent consultants being asked to review the Mitigation and Compensation Program of the THPC suggests that negotiated arrangements for transparency can be ignored, undermined or reversed by parties with vested interests who are not happy with the conclusions. Contractual provisions can be ignored. Nevertheless, it is not reasonable always to assume bad faith.

I have used the two case studies discussed in the present paper to help explore some of the dilemmas and to help me to identify some working questions. There are no absolute right answers to some ethical issues. As the Australian social critic Hugh Mackay (2004) says, trying to recognise and think about ethical issues and trying to weigh up the consequences of actions is the key to ethics. The challenge is to maintain that awareness in a pressured industry.

Notes

[1] This is a revised version of paper originally presented at the Australian Anthropological Society Conference held in Cairns, 26–29 September 2006, as part of a session held in honour of Doug Miles by former students. I participated as Doug had been my honours supervisor. Doug's role in the controversy over the Tribal Research Centre at Chiang Mai during the Vietnam War reflected his insistence that anthropologists have ethical responsibilities and cannot hide behind the claim that they are carrying out objective research without human consequences. His concerns remain an inspiration and are very relevant to the practice of modern anthropology. I am grateful to Ronlyn Duncan, Michael Allen and two anonymous referees for very useful comments on an earlier draft.
[2] This occurred in the context of a workshop and field exercise involving academics from a number of universities in the Mekong region as part of a program called the Mekong Learning Initiative, which involves academics from these universities and the Australian Mekong Resource Centre at the University of Sydney.
[3] An overview of ownership arrangements and financing is available from Australian Mekong Resource Centre 2006. For a detailed discussion of the history of NGO involvement in the controversy, see Soutar (2007).
[4] Disputes about impact assessment continue in a current expansion phase for the Theun-Hinboun. According to a statement circulated by email from the IRN and FIVAS on 20 December 2007: 'The environmental scientist originally hired to conduct the environmental impact assessment (EIA) for the Theun-Hinboun Expansion Project in Laos has disassociated his group from the official report. Instead of accepting Dr. Murray Watson's original – and highly critical – report, the Company ceased communicating with him and hired a Norwegian company, Norplan, to complete the EIA.'
[5] The development banks often present themselves as honest brokers. For a discussion of this point see Witoon (2000).
[6] I am indebted to Ronlyn Duncan for highlighting this point.
[7] Spry (1976) argues that, instead of relying on the idea that Environmental Impact Statements should be partial and subjective, there might be advantages in having EISs that are 'explicitly partisan', because 'the assessor [or decision-maker] would be aware that he must investigate the problem himself and challenge every fact and opinion before accepting it' (p. 255).

References

Australian Mekong Resource Centre (2006) *The Theun Hinboun Hydropower Project*, Mekong brief no. 3, Australian Mekong Resource Centre, University of Sydney.

Blake, D. (2005) 'A future in doubt: reviewing dam builder's efforts to restore river-based livelihoods in Laos', *World Rivers Review*, vol. 20, no. 1, pp. 6–7, 15.

Blake, D., Carson, B. & Tubtim, N. (2005) *Review of the Environmental Management Division, Theun-Hinboun Power Company Limited*, report submitted to Theun Hinboun Power Company. (Unpublished)

Chambers, E. (1987) 'Applied anthropology in the post-Vietnam era: anticipations and ironies', *Annual Review of Anthropology*, vol. 16, pp. 309–37.

FIVAS (1996) *More Water, More Fish? A Report on Norwegian Involvement in the Theun Hinboun Hydropower Project in Lao PDR, Based on FIVAS's Study Tour to Lao PDR and Thailand*

December 1995–January 1996, Foreningen for Internasionale Vannstudier, retrieved 1 May, 2008, from http://www.fivas.org/sider/tekst.asp?side=107

Goldman, M. (2001) 'The birth of a discipline: producing authoritative green knowledge, World Bank-style', *Ethnography*, vol. 2, no. 2, pp. 191–217.

Howitt, R. (2005) 'The importance of process in social impact assessment: ethics, methods and process for cross-cultural engagement', *Ethics, Place and Environment*, vol. 8, no. 2, pp. 209–21.

Mackay, H. (2004) *Right & Wrong: How to Decide for Yourself*, Hodder, Sydney.

Norpower (1993) *Nam Theun/2 Hydropower Project. Feasibility Study, Vol. 3*, Environmental Impact Assessment Report. (Unpublished)

O'Faircheallaigh, C. (1999) 'Making social impact assessment count: a negotiation-based approach for indigenous peoples', *Society and Natural Resources*, vol. 12, no. 1, pp. 63–80.

Shoemaker, B. (1998) *Trouble on the Theun-Hinboun: A Field Report on the Socio-economic and Environmental Effects of the Nam Theun-Hinboun Hydropower Project in Laos*. International Rivers Network, retrieved 1 May, 2008, from http://internationalrivers.org/files/Trouble%20on%20the%20Theun-Hinboun.pdf

Soutar, L. (2007) 'Asian Development Bank: NGO encounters and the Theun-Hinboun dam, Laos', in *NGOS as Advocates for Development in a Globalising World*, ed. B. Rugendyke, Routledge, London, pp. 200–221.

Spry, A. (1976) 'A consultant's views on Environmental Impact Statements in Australia', *Search*, vol. 7, no. 6, pp. 252–255.

Warren, T. (1999) *A Monitoring Study to assess the Localized Impacts Created by the Nam Theun-Hinboun Hydro-scheme on Fisheries and Fish Populations: Final Report*, Prepared for the Theun-Hinboun Power Company (THPC), Vientiane, Lao P.D.R., June 1999, retrieved 1 May, 2008, from http://www.irn.org/programs/mekong/twstudy.pdf

Warren, T. (2000) 'Impacts on fish populations and fisheries created by the Nam Theun-Hinboun Hydropower Project, Lao P.D.R.', paper presented at conference *Accounting for Development*, University of Sydney, retrieved 1 May, 2008, from http://www.mekong.es.usyd.edu.au/events/past/Conference2000/Papers/Warren.pdf

Witoon Permpongsacharoen (2000) 'ADB: "Honest broker" for whom?', Summary of presentation at conference *Accounting for Development*, University of Sydney, retrieved 1 May 2008, from http://www.mekong.es.usyd.edu.au/events/past/Conference2000/Papers/WitoonADB.pdf

[12]
Sociology and Environmental Impact Assessment[1]

Michael Gismondi

Abstract: The paper indicates how a critical sociology could contribute to environmental impact assessment (EIA), and argues sociologists must become involved in evaluating the EIA process itself. Topics examined include: how EIA excludes and frames social issues; why social science should precede natural science; the social construction of impact science; bias and the circulation of EIA consultants; and fairness when talking in public hearings. The author proposes an activist role for sociologists.

Résumé: Cette étude démontre comment une sociologie critique pourrait contribuer au processus d'étude d'impact environnemental (EIE). Elle soutient que les sociologues doivent s'engager dans l'évaluation de l'EIE elle-même. Les thèmes abordés sont: comment l'EIE exclut et conçoit des questions sociales; pourquoi les sciences sociales devraient précéder les sciences naturelles; la construction sociale des sciences d'impact; le parti-pris et la circulation des experts-conseils de l'EIE; l'équité des orateurs dans les audiences publiques. L'auteur propose une fonction activiste de la part des sociologues.

Introduction

[If] there had been proper EARP [environmental assessment review process] scoping sessions, we might have seen 20 professional social scientists here from the federal government, as we saw natural scientists this morning. It would have been, I think, a recognition that socio-economic impact issues are just as important a study, and that communities need as much assistance in coming to understand what this [pulp mill] project's impacts might be as the assistance they need in understanding the impacts on the water, air, and wildlife. Michael Gismondi (Public Hearing Proceedings, 1989: 2959)

---

1. Preparation for this paper was funded in part by the SSHRC Grant # 806–92–0040. Thanks to Joan Sherman, who helped with research and writing in all aspects of the paper.

Speaking before the Alberta-Pacific Environmental Impact Assessment review panel in 1989, at federal-provincial public hearings on the world's largest single-line bleached kraft pulp mill proposed near Athabasca — my home town — I was one frustrated sociologist. Two dozen federal natural scientists had just concluded days of scientific and technical testimony on whether the Peace and the Athabasca rivers could assimilate more pulp-mill pollution. Representing research centres across Canada, and joined by Alberta government scientists, these fisheries specialists, water quality experts, pulp-mill pollution control technicians, biologists, chemists, engineers, computer simulation programmers, and science bureaucrats tore into Alberta-Pacific (Alpac) studies predicting environmental impacts. They questioned completeness, accuracy, narrowness or breadth of research, reliability, applicability, proposed mitigation and more. Alpac fought back with science consultants (private and academic), experts from PAPRICAN (the Canadian pulp and paper research institute), and technical specialists from the United States and Scandinavia.

Extensive questioning by government specialists of the social sections of Alpac's environmental impact assessment (EIA) did not occur. Science was the primary concern of the official EIA process. Sociological analysis of the natural science conventions used in EIA appeared to be the last thing on the minds of review panel members. But should EIA review be so one-dimensional?

In Canada, if a large-scale project such as the Alpac pulp mill or the Arctic Diamond Mine (Gibson, 1993; Richardson, et al., 1993; Wismer, 1996) is likely to cause significant adverse environmental effects, an independent EIA assessment is ordered. This also applies to international projects with substantial federal funding (Appiah-Opoku, 1994; Lawrence, 1994; United Nations, 1987). The environment minister appoints an EIA review panel, calls for public hearings and sets out terms of reference to consider environmental and socio-economic effects. The panel hears from public servants, scientists, and the impacted communities before establishing the scope of impacts that the proponent must follow when preparing its EIA. The EIA statement is made public and hearings are held to "integrate public values with scientific/technical information about potential environmental effects of a project, in order to permit informed decision-making by Ministers" (Regulatory Advisory Committee, 1996). It may take up to two years before the minister has a report upon which to make a decision on project approval (Gilpin, 1995).

Environmental policies, review procedures, and impact science in EIA are permeated by political, social, and ethical issues that require broad debate. As a sociologist who joined Friends of the Athabasca Environmental Association (FOTA) to fight the Alpac pulp mill, my experience during the Alpac EIA gave me an appreciation for the applicability, and silence, of the social sciences in the applied context of the review. Nine years later, from my point of view as a FOTA activist and sociologist concerned about the place of the public and the social sciences in EIA, not much has changed (Regulatory Advisory Committee, 1996). This paper outlines where critical sociological scrutiny of EIA process, research, and underlying assumptions could assist the public with strategies for effective public intervention. Five themes stand out: excluding social issues from EIA; putting critical social science first; social construction of impact science; circulation of consultants and epistemic communities; and fairness when talking in public hearings.

Excluding Social Issues from EIA

What we should be deciding is whether we want projects of this kind in the first place before we have environmental hearings. Merilyn Peruniak[2]

Development

In the late 1980s the Alberta government commissioned five pulp mills, setting the context for a series of industrial project proposals that would undergo individual EIAs (Pratt and Urquhart, 1994; Marchak, 1996). Yet the terms of reference of public review did not extend to the political and economic policies that drove these development proposals. This is not uncommon. Tester's study of 36 federal EIAs subjected to panel review in Canada revealed that "consideration of the underlying development issues was consistently discouraged and most deliberations were focused on the mitigation of negative effects" (1992: 39). Freudenberg and Keating discovered in their review of EIA in the United States that even "widely respected researchers rarely will question the developments themselves" (1982: 75). Instead of providing the public an opportunity to criticize development assumptions, the EIA procedure "has 'subverted' the agenda of dealing with conflicts over development policy" (Levidow, 1992: 120).

What is excluded during an EIA reveals premises and assumptions embedded in the practice. Alpac's EIA statement excluded issues the public wanted to discuss, such as foreign ownership and the implications of a project that would produce pulp for export but would not commit to value-added local job opportunities. Citizen demands to see studies of previous mega-projects against which to test Alpac's development claims were common. Many argued that opportunity costs of futures foregone should be included in any cost-benefit analysis (there was not one), and suggested the millions of dollars in government loans and grants promised to the Alpac project be used for several small-scale developments, forestry research projects, or eco-tourism (Richardson, et al.,

---

2. Author interview with Merilyn Peruniak. Athabasca, 1994.

1993: Chapter 2). Some people asked the panel to go beyond mitigating project impacts and to place long-term ecological goals before short-term economic goals. Each request went unpursued.

Values

The public sought to extend conventional impact assessment in other ways. For example, one woman criticized the adequacy of EIA to engage the value of "community" held by the people in the farming district proposed for the megamill:

The main shortcoming [of EIA] was not being able to put a value on community, and to do anything about the effects of uprooting people ... Why do people have to make that kind of sacrifice? ... if we start breaking up community, then that is to the detriment of the larger society. Merilyn Peruniak[3]

The company did commission surveys to measure people's values and perceptions about changes that would occur in the community from a hypothetical pulp mill — a practice Freudenberg and Keating characterize as "roughly akin to asking someone about a blind date s/he has never met" (1982: 73). No social theory to explain the purpose for the studies was provided, and the expert survey completely ignored one key social value — the freedom to choose — as expressed by this farmer:

[The Alpac] development was announced and dropped in our lap. ... Is it going to be development designed by the community, or is it going to be development that's foisted on a community? Emil Zachkewich[4]

Households within a six-mile radius of the proposed mill were surveyed, with an 85 per cent return. Communities outside the six-mile radius, either downwind or along the transportation corridor, were also surveyed, and their response rate was 40 per cent. Bold, clear questions such as Merilyn Peruniak's — whether some farm families near the mill site should be sacrificed for the betterment of others in the larger region — were not asked. Fifty-four per cent of those surveyed in the extended region indicated they would like to see economic development and employment in the area. Within a six-mile radius of the mill, however, 61 per cent feared the community would break down, and 43 per cent said they wished the community to remain as is. The company's consultants concluded the findings were mixed. Disgusted, area farmers referred to Alpac's surveys as "demobilization studies ... commissioned in order to build information to assist in overcoming resistance to the proposed development"

---

3. Author interview with Merilyn Peruniak. Athabasca, 1994.
4. Author interview with Emil Zachkewich. Athabasca, 1994.

(Friends of the Athabasca Environmental Association, 1991: 157; Equus Consulting, 1989).

Pointing to other value judgements in development planning and EIA information gathering, a woman from Athabasca asked how forestry expansion and five pulp mills might benefit women — 43.28 per cent of the workforce:

> goods-producing industries, such as the proposed pulp mill, employ only 14.11 per cent [women], while service industries employ 85.89 per cent. Perhaps we should be concentrating on a different area of job creation, so that we are not almost excluding nearly half of the our work force. Ann Stiles (Public Hearing Proceedings, 1989: 3300–3301)

Studying job creation in the resource hinterlands of northern Ontario, Heald (1991) found many gender-blind assumptions, while MacGregor (1995) alerts us to patriarchal assumptions and techniques in urban planning. Likewise, Priya Kurian observes the need "to identify to what extent EIA as practiced in the Third World is a gendered practice" (1995: 168). Ann Stiles shows that EIA in Canada also needs a sociology of gender.

The absence of social scientists on the Alpac EIA review panel may explain why community, gender and development were poorly addressed, or ignored. The problems appear deeper. Freudenberg and Keating find "sociological expertise is severely underrepresented in the impact statement process — not only in final decisions, but in the impact statements themselves'" (1982: 71). They found broad community profiles in some EIAs, which described social life — as did Alpac's 1989 community study — without referencing sociological reasons for selecting or ignoring certain issues (1982: 72). Alberta's two mega-pulp mills, Daishowa near Peace River and Alpac, will operate for 25–50 years. Yet, sociologists examining the mills' EIAs will find no substantial research into long-term socio-economic issues, the boom-and-bust cycles in a resource economy, or studies of a northern pulp industry dependent on southern and international sources for capital, labour, spare parts, and technology (Dunk, 1991). Likewise, while some community values are reported or described in these Canadian EIAs, they are not analysed or integrated into EIA deliberations in any clear manner — despite the existence of approaches to testimonial evidence and values analysis in applied ethics and the social sciences (Attfield and Dell, 1989; Dunk, 1994; Pendelton Banks, 1990; McDonald, Stevenson, Cragg, 1992; Feit, 1995). Recently, Burningham confirmed a preference in EIA for quantitative work which "has led to a situation where the more intangible impacts of projects, and data that cannot easily be quantified, are often excluded from assessments" (1995: 103).

During the Alpac EIA review, it was as if, *prima facie*, a $1.3 billion pulp mill meant sustainable socio-economic development. Repeatedly, the politics of exclusion prior to, and inside, EIA blunts, frames, and blocks out issues and inquiries. In such politics, calls for using more knowledge from social science in development projects (Cornea, 1991) appear naive, almost make-believe.

Putting Critical Social Science First

[a] careful examination of the socio-economic aspects of the proposal should be top priority ... because if the jobs are not there, we do not have to concern ourselves with these natural science effects. Barry Johnstone (Public Hearing Proceedings, 1989: 3870)

Orthodoxy in Social Impact Assessment (SIA)

A recent review of 75 mega-projects confirms that in the Canadian experience local gains are usually disappointing: "existing residents and communities receive limited benefits ... most of the economic benefits ... appear to 'leak out of the regional economy' " (Knight, et al., 1993: 17).[5] Poor social science during and following EIA is one explanation. Alpac's identification of socio-economic impacts was orthodox. Its EIA sketched local and mill-site community profiles, and made employment and purchasing predictions. It calculated spin-off jobs based on multiplier estimates, and outlined business opportunities. Lifestyle disruptions, population increase during construction or during operations, and whether existing housing, classrooms, police, and hospitals would be adequate were discussed. Freudenberg and Keating note that SIA typically stresses "economics and logistics ... the impact of people on service agencies ... [and has] less to say about social systems than they do about sewer and water systems" (1982: 73). The EIA panel accepted Alpac's framing of socio-economic impacts, and its basic measurement techniques.[6] The framing appears objective, therefore a reader could easily fail to detect that certain social questions were screened out.

Community members were more perceptive. They doubted Alpac's claims about the number of local business opportunities and local jobs, and disputed the definition of a "local person" (i.e., living within 50 km or 150 km of the site; long-time resident or just arrived with rumours of the mill). Critics questioned the estimates of taxes and royalties to be paid by Alpac, and its choice of multipliers to predict economic spin-offs. (There were no probabilities or ranges in Alpac's calculations.) Many debated the fit between skills required of mill employees and those held by people in the regional labour market, and doubted claims of minimal economic leakage to Edmonton, the urban centre 120 kilometres south.

---

5. For example, Alpac's coverall cleaning contract went to an Edmonton firm. A local drycleaner, equipped for the task, commented: "the minute they won the coverall contract, they sent a salesman through town and he promptly stole three or four of my accounts. So, the net result was, not only did I not get an opportunity to bid ... it actually cost me money. The economics of bringing a truck up [from Edmonton] supported coming in and undercutting my prices." Interview with local businessman. Athabasca, 1995.
6. Examining the sociology of technique, Power shows "how certain cultural entitlements to claim expertise are exhibited, sustained and reproduced" (1995: 318).

Generally the public asked for an EIA process that addressed basic sociological research starting points: more primary data about impacted communities; critical review of the secondary literature cited in the proponent's EIA; and comparative evidence from similar mega-projects. Illustratively, the Athabasca Health Unit asked for animal and human health baseline studies prior to mill approval. Citizens identified impacts on the elderly and people on fixed incomes, or wondered about job commitments for native people. Unclear of what government and industry meant by sustainable development, and concerned about changes in traditional lifestyle, forest destruction and wildlife decline, native people and environmentalists asked the panel to consider equity for future generations. Such research requests — some quantitative, some qualitative — were not carried out. Once again, value judgements revealed themselves in impact research that was not conducted. Moreover, Beder (1993b) counsels us to assess critically recent attempts by economists at cost-benefit analysis or economic valuation of nature.

Site Selection

The provincial cabinet chose the southern boreal forest along the Athabasca River as the location for the pulp mill because the region had an unemployment rate said to be 8-10 percentage points above the average. Alpac compared nine sites to "ensure selection of the environmentally, socially and economically optimal mill location" (Alberta-Pacific Forest Industries Inc, 1989: 2.4). The farming community of Prosperity in Athabasca County (site #2) was chosen for the mill, yet many locals found Alpac's differential cost comparison of sites biased.

There is considerable evidence that the choice of the [mill] site in the community of Prosperity was politically motivated ... the company admitted their first choice from an environmental point of view was Site #1 (Friends of the Athabasca Environmental Association, 1991: 103).

The main social criteria identified in the EIA was that the mill be located no further than a 45-minute drive from a local community to avoid creation of a new town or "operations residential camp." Locating the mill at site #1 (the environmentally preferred site north of the County of Athabasca and closer to logging activities and native communities) was rejected because it would have added driving time from nearby towns. Socio-economically homogenous depictions of the region, combined with heavy lobbying by the primarily non-native County of Athabasca, shifted $4 million in annual tax revenue out of mostly native communities, to save between 10 to 15 minutes driving time from the equi-distant local towns Boyle, Athabasca and Lac La Biche. Ironically, many mill employees decided to live in the countryside on acreages, farms, or in hamlets closer to the workplace, and not in local towns. Serious public discussion and critical sociological analysis of the high rates of poverty and unemployment in nearby native communities — as social justice issues in sustainable development — might have checked the systemic racism hidden in the assumptions underlying siting decisions, and driving time.[7]

Distributional Effects and Restrictive Scoping

Following Habermas, Thomas Dietz presents an alternative strategy whereby "SIA can be an effective tool for informing the public, encouraging participation in policy debates ... translating policy consequences into social consequences that are comprehensible and salient to the public." Deitz suggests disaggregating impact assessment by location, income, occupation, and ethnicity as a method of identifying groups with the most to gain or lose from a policy or project, and to motivate them "to actively participate in discussion" (1987: 60–63). Similarly, Carter and Willard suggest an evolving scoping process, which identifies issues as the EIA progresses "where an adversarial model of multiple parallel studies, responsive to different interested 'publics,' is employed." These strategies seem consistent with studies sought by the public in the Alpac hearings, and reflect a Canadian philosophy of providing the public with some intervenor funding for EIA counter-studies. Like the public in the Alpac hearings, however, Carter and Willard found generic impact studies "curtail impact areas, limit impact variables, and restrict 'publics' to be considered." Limitations on scoping begin even before the EIA process starts, or become "fixed relatively early" (1993: 266).

Limits can be resisted. A persistent public forced the Alpac panel to commission a review of Alpac's Price Waterhouse economic and social impact feasibility study, which was withheld for most of the public review. It was found to be an "optimistic (rather than realistic) portrayal of how the project will affect the region and the province." Just as the public had doubted Alpac's local job claims, the panel's consultant strongly criticized Price Waterhouse's multiplier assumptions for direct and spin-off jobs, concluding that "employment opportunities for local residents would be quite limited." He also calculated logging royalties would be modest, and discovered millions of dollars in concealed subsidies:

it would be just as economically feasible for the Government of Alberta to take the subsidies that would be paid to support Alberta Pacific and use an equivalent amount of money to directly create

---

7. The Town of Athabasca unemployment rate in 1986 was 8.1 per cent. Income Data for Postal Code Areas in 1985 showed the Town of Athabasca at 83 per cent of the Canadian Index; whereas the native community of Calling Lake north of the river was at 21 per cent of the Canadian index. Urban FSA and Postal Code Summary Data, Statistics Canada, 1984 and 1985.

new [and more] jobs for existing residents of northern Alberta ... and the vast amounts of timber required for the mill would remain standing, none of the possible environmental problems associated with the mill need occur (Praxis, 1989: 11–13).[8]

It was too late. Two and one-half years of Alpac open-house sessions, information meetings, glossy brochures, and positive economic forecasts presumably swayed much public opinion about environmental trade-offs. Thus, the rational debate Dietz and Habermas hope for can be stifled by industrial and political manoeuvring, that controls information and captures the imagination of the public.

EIA, as practised, offers few mechanisms for answering questions about job creation and economic sustainability, despite long-standing advice that no single change "could make as much difference in the quality of SIA as the ability to do a greater proportion of impact research that is empirical rather than anticipatory" (Freudenberg and Keating, 1985: 584). Unfortunately, longitudinal studies of economic and community impacts, once a project goes ahead, seldom occur and the public is left with no follow-up on EIA commitments and predictions (Gismondi, 1992). Because local business contracts and jobs, native and women's employment, provincial economic spin-offs and royalty income, corporate taxes, and other socio-economic topics are considered private information, a mega-project's economic impacts are left open to manipulation by public relations experts (Sherman and Gismondi, 1997). To prevent closure on gathering social and economic information for public deliberation, the politics of what gets researched, and when, has to be open to public debate early in EIA scoping. To prevent manipulation of public values about environmental trade-offs, the development and job creation claims of a proponent should be examined early, loudly, comprehensively, and first.

This will be controversial. Even less likely to be received by EIA practitioners, bureaucrats, and industry are the suggestions of Brian Wynne, who advocates social science involvement "upstream in the ... processes of constructing scientific knowledge or technological artifacts," thus moving sociology out of its role "subordinate to the precommitments and agenda of the natural sciences" (1994: 170). Putting social theory and research on the same footing with natural science, or before the construction of scientific studies, would contradict what appears to be an implicit assumption in EIA: social science knowledge is secondary.

---

8. Alpac received $250,000 to finance its feasibility study, $75 million for road and rail infrastructure, and $400 million in government debentures.

Social Construction of Impact Science

[E]xperts or scientists.... it's funny how they don't agree and that's not helpful because it seems to me [that] presented with the same data, the same information, you should have the same conclusions, but they don't. Ron Epp[9]

Web of Conventions

The study of the biophysical in EIA is considered a technical exercise, carried out by experts and scientists, based on scientific principles of fact collection that are assumed to be neutral and unaffected by political or commercial bias, or ethical and moral values. As in the conflict between experts in the law courts (Smith and Wynne, 1989), however, confrontations in EIA hearings between industry, government and citizen scientists debating pollution impacts on water, air, soil, animals and humans reveal "scientific knowledge in the making, [where] adversarial pressure forces the premises and conventions of each side out into the open" (Wynne, 1989: 33).

One disarming EIA practitioner declares "EIAs are not science ... EIAs always contain unexamined and unexplained value assumptions ... EIAs will always be political" (Beattie, 1995: 109). While Beattie feels his admissions do not reduce the importance of EIA, others disagree and question the privileged role of EIA experts and impact science. For sociologists, EIA proceedings leave a rich trail. Alpac's experts made claims about pollution impacts supported by models, theories, industrial trials, arguments, and footnoted references in the EIA statement. Their claims and the written counterpoints from government scientists, the review panel, and citizen scientists are public documents, as are transcripts of EIA hearing presentations by Alpac's science team reciting credentials, responding to panel questions, and deflecting criticisms. Debate is captured on transcripts, and body language and vocal inflections on videotape. Thus, science in context is open for deconstruction:

[F]ar from providing a fixed, objectively verifiable body of knowledge of nature's workings — through privileged access to the essential physical reality — science itself exists as a social construct, in which doctrines of 'objective' practice rest on a web of conventions, practices, understandings and negotiated indeterminancies (Wynne in Grove White, 1993: 22).

The next sections examine key conventions.

Peer Review and Adequacy in Science

The science sections of EIAs are large and complex, and imposing when presented in public by heavily credentialed experts. Yet, Alpac's EIA came

---

9. Author interview with Alpac EIA panel member Ron Epp. Athabasca, 1994.

under fire from scientists and members of the public for using confidential or unidentified sources, consultants' reports, industry and manufacturers' tests, or evidence from studies that were not peer reviewed, or reviewed in refereed journals. Defending the credibility of such sources, Alpac's consultants felt "it was currently impractical to analyze a proposal on state-of-the-art technology purely on the basis of publications," and equally impractical to wait for peer review before going through the EIA process, thus losing a company's competitive edge in the marketplace (Richardson, et al., 1993: 158).

In a report by the Aquatic Science Committee of the Royal Society of Canada, the authors note that only 16 per cent of all research on the Mackenzie River basin, which includes the Peace and the Athabasca rivers, has appeared in refereed journals. They conclude "the great majority of reports have not passed through this widely accepted test of adequacy and internal value. On balance it is not possible to draw a firm conclusion about the adequacy of aquatic science in the Mackenzie Basin" (1995: 52). Their report is cautious about identifying as unacceptable unpublished industrial studies, and consultancy work, but they did state such research presented a problem for public review:

the lack of an information base obtained through research widely accepted as adequate can hinder constructive discussion of policy alternatives. While university, collaborative and some federal laboratory research usually involves independent evaluation of adequacy, most consultant, industry and departmental research does not ... such research is most susceptible to criticism (1995: 71).

One role for sociology in EIA would be to quantify the number of peer reviewed and non-peer reviewed research findings supporting a proposal, and assess whether references are partial, taken out of context, or represent the most favourable reading of a spectrum of probable outcomes. Such analysis would assist a community's appreciation of the adequacy of science — revealing that one of the main pillars of certainty associated with scientific methodology is weak, if not missing.

Bias and Credibility

Concerns about science in EIA extend far beyond Canada.[10] In the case of the Sydney, Australia, deepwater outfalls for sewage disposal into the ocean, Sharon Beder discovered that scientists working on EIA make value judgements about the definition of the problem, scope of impacts covered, data sampling time periods, areas covered, the scale of study, data interpretation, and even presentation of findings.

---

10. Science conventions in the Alpac case are well covered in *Winning Back the Words*. Here, I introduce similar findings from other EIAs, to demonstrate the general nature of the issues.

> The goal of a completely objective [EIA] document is illusory because science itself is socially constructed ... biases are ... subtle and arise from the many value judgements made at every stage of the preparation of an EIS (Beder, 1993a: 28).

Beattie, the EIA practitioner, acknowledges that most EIAs "are made under strict deadlines — [and] data gaps and simplifying assumptions are the norm under these conditions" (1995: 110).

Beder's work concludes that "engineers played an active role in shaping public perceptions and moulding impressions. Their studies set out to justify, legitimate, and sell the technological solutions which they preferred, ones that used the ocean for sewage treatment"(1996: 39). Freudenberg and Keating, when writing with "technically oriented" people concluded that

> social scientists can improve the scientific basis for decision-making ... by identifying the extent to which engineers and various scientists are contributing value-based input, if only by selecting certain variables and options while overlooking others (1985: 590).

In *Toxic Fish and Sewer Surfing* (Beder, 1989), choices, assumptions, and conventions operating in EIA are shown to be misleading and rooted in the power and authority of a profession's way of doing or explaining things. Typically, environmental scientists select valued ecosystem components — key species of wildlife, plants, water systems — for a region under study, raising the questions: "What components are to be valued? And who will decide what is of value?" (Salleneve, 1994). Beder analyses pollution statistics to show how quantification or mathematics — techniques of EIA that seem less affected by values — may hide inadequacies behind professional claims to precision.[11] Beder also reconstructs how the release of information from bioaccumulation studies of fish contaminated with organochlorines were the focus of "a struggle to control the flow and interpretation of information to the public" (1990: 136).

Opening up apparently solid facts, practices, and conventions these authors reveal choices, values, and uncertainty in EIA science. Beder holds that "an EIS should incorporate discussion of assumptions, choice of methods and different interpretations that can be made of the studies" (1989; 1993), and Beattie (1995: 113) believes that admitting "in advance that these assumptions reflect certain values can help focus debates about EIAs."[12]

---

11. Discussing the social nature of precision, Wise notes "how intensely local are the cultural meanings attached to any given project for attaining numerical precision and setting standards...values may be located by method, discipline, and ideology, as well as economic interest and geographical region" (1995: 9).
12. Brian Campbell's study (1985) of the Mackenzie Valley pipeline inquiry maintained "the political effectiveness of expertise is not diminished by the use of uncertainty arguments. Concretely, Judge Berger used scientists as expert sources in justifying his extremely firm uncertainty position"(Cited in Rip, 1992, Note 3).

Sometimes the EIA process offers opportunities, often unintentionally, for citizens to introduce contending systems of knowledge and representations of nature. In the Alpac hearings, the knowledge of local ecosystems held by native people or farmers and fishers worked as a feedback or evaluative check on official or expert knowledge, allowing the public to identify incompetent or dishonest uses of expert knowledge in Alpac's EIA. It provided serious, reliable knowledge about the community — qualitative and quantitative, spatial and temporal — that drew from practical experience and collective memory to correct, verify, complement, and clarify the official accounts in the EIA. At some hearing sites the meeting of expert knowledge and local knowledge revealed ethnocentric or normative assumptions in western science techniques such as classification, aggregation of data, or the setting of standards that disclose social disadvantage and institutional racism (Gismondi and Sherman, 1996; Wynne, 1994).

A sociology of science that helps communities recognize the social, cultural, and moral shaping of techniques and conventions in EIA would lessen the political power and legitimacy of experts, especially when confronting local knowledge.

Ecology, River Uses and the Sociological Survey

Sociology has its own web of conventions. Between 1991 and 1996, the governments of Canada, Alberta, and the Northwest Territories carried out a survey of the consumptive and non-consumptive uses of the Athabasca, Peace, and Slave rivers, as part of the Northern River Basins Study (NRBS). Natural-science focused, the NRBS committed to the use of an ecosystem-based perspective and native traditional ecological knowledge in all its research. It conducted one major social science study — "Other River Uses" (NRBS, 1996).

Key to "Other River Uses" was a householder survey using a stratified random sample of residents in the river basins. A draft circulated in the summer of 1994 hypothesized that water uses and values related to use of northern rivers would differ between rural and urban populations, and between natives and non-natives. The survey designers also assumed a community's economic base would influence the way water was used, and valued.

To test these hypotheses, the researchers proposed a telephone survey instrument of city dwellers (centres over 4000) and town, hamlet and village dwellers. Three basic assumptions (settlement size, economic base, and ethnicity) provided the framework for developing the population stratification groups to be used in the stratified random sample. The authors then identified eleven population subsets, linking them to telephone number prefixes in order to implement the survey.

Because the NRBS championed an ecosystem perspective, FOTA proposed that ecological criteria (such as sub-regions of the river ecosystem, sub-watersheds, and reaches of the river systems) be used for identifying the population subsets instead of socio-economic criteria. As well, questions seeking public values about water use were poorly designed. They sought information mostly about current and past use, few asked what might be needed for the future of the ecosystem. Not many questions tested people's willingness to participate in shaping that future by altering their river uses, and lifestyles. FOTA proposed several values questions: "Would you accept diminishment of environmental quality in exchange for job creation and economic development?" "How much and why?" and "Would you accept less economic development in exchange for better conservation and preservation of the river system?"

FOTA's intervention altered the householder survey to an ecosystem-based sociological survey model, which should be of interest to EIA practitioners, community groups, and sociologists working towards a sociology of nature and ecology (Macnaghten and Urry, 1995; Murphy, 1995). Ironically, the Other River Uses study does not credit the intervention by the public.[13]

Circulation of Consultants and Epistemic Communities

We had $37,000 of intervenor funding given to us. Right?
The first thing our individual did, he said:
"How much intervenor funding did you say?"
"$37,000."
"Well, let's see now, we'll do this, this, and this."
" That's $5,000, $6,000, $10,000, $3,000... $37,299."
"Think you can manage the $299?" Emil and Elaine Zachkewich[14]

Situated Actions and Vocabularies of Motive

The assumption that science is objective (who carries out the research for whom does not influence the experimental design or interpretation of findings) has facilitated the growth of epistemic communities of consultants who move across and between countries to design, defend, or review projects undergoing EIA. In Canada, consulting scientists, social scientists, engineers, risk analysts, and others circulate from industry, government, and universities to private practice and back again, sometimes in quick succession, or with a foot in more than one camp. For example, the EIA consultant hired by the Prosperity farmers to

---

13. Correspondence between author and Dr. Peter Larkin, Chair of the NRBS Science Advisory Committee. August, 1994.
14. Author interview with local farm family. Athabasca, 1994.

challenge Alpac's site selection had earlier co-authored a report on environmental regulatory framework (Review Panel on Environmental Law Enforcement, 1987) for the provincial Minister of Environment, helped Weyerhaeuser — Alpac's competitor — prepare its bid for the Athabasca mill and forest concession, and was later appointed to the federal-provincial-territorial Northern River Basins Study to consider the impacts of industrialization, especially the mills, upon the river basin. Similarly, Alpac's lead EIA consultant had quarterbacked the public review of the Alberta Newsprint mill EIA in 1988 before leading the Alpac team into its EIA hearings. He disappeared at the time the Alpac EIA was severely criticized by civil servants and the public, but reappeared as advisor to the science curriculum for the Alberta Science in the Schools program, and was later appointed to the Alberta Energy and Utilities Board, a provincial agency that reviews energy projects. As Brian Martin explains,

> the dominant group of experts in any field is usually closely linked to other power structures, typically government, industry, or professional bodies. The links are cemented through jobs, consultancies, access to power and status, training, and other methods (1996: 5).

Recognizing consultants in such different contexts, it is not unreasonable to assume pressure on their objectivity. One anthropologist who has worked on all sides in EIA explained: "at a certain point you develop a sympathy with the person/group you are working with, you adapt to them, their worldview, and your own work may be tempered by that." Likewise, he felt government specialists can be under pressure in EIA "often the ability of the civil servant to speak candidly is circumscribed by the various agencies for whom they work or the individuals for whom they work in government."[15]

Fearnside maintains the problem is not one of individual ethics, rather structural pressures such as oaths of secrecy in professions or anonymity in EIA documents, and how these "together with the realization of all consultants that their future prospects for contracts depend on discretion, ensure that inconsistencies between detailed findings and the conclusions remain interred" (1994: 51). In writing EIAs, for example, the standard in Canada is that authors of various sections remain anonymous. Anonymity makes it difficult to recognize when a consultant may be in conflict of interest, or taking one position while working for industry and another in academic, government or public life.[16] Putting a face on environmental consultants and firms, their linkages and

---

15. Author interview with George Kupfer. Calgary, 1994.
16. Recently, consultants for a municipal waste engineering firm were found to be promoting a toxic waste disposal proposal in China, and at the same time were contracted by the Lesser Slave Lake Indian Regional Council to intervene against the same disposal process at the Swan Hills hazardous waste and incineration site in Alberta.

ownership patterns, their circulation within epistemic communities, and unearthing consistency or inconsistency in project evaluation and conclusions is a long overdue sociological task.

Fairness When Talking in Public

[D]iscussion became so emotional ... It made me realize that there was so much more at stake here than a specific proposal, ... there are people's lives, people's values, and a sense of powerlessness that I think was driving the emotion. Esmeralda Cabral[17]

The EIA as a Context of Unequal Power

Public hearings are held near the end of the EIA process. They are designed as forums in which "expert opinions on technical subjects as well as value judgements or choices of society intersect and merge"(Study Group on Environmental Assessment Hearing Process, 1988). Yet, the shortcomings of EIA identified by the public — excluding development issues, scoping restrictions, failing to disaggregate impacts, poor economic analysis, values, bias and uncertainty in science, social pressure on the objectivity of consultants — question the value-free status of expert opinions in EIA hearings. It is too large a burden on the democratic process to suggest that such problems will come out in the wash at the public hearing stage.

As it stands, studies of environmental hearings show that the interactions between experts, panel members, and lay people are not always fair (Forester, 1985; Richardson, et al., 1993; Waddell, 1996; Wynne, 1982). For many who study how citizen values and expert opinions on technical subjects merge and intersect in environmental public hearings, rhetoric, discourse, and expert language reveal themselves as tools used to legitimate the authority of scientists, experts, bureaucrats, lawyers and business people, and to silence the testimony of non-experts (Sherman, et al., 1996).

Critical sociology provides an understanding of the social interaction of talking in contexts of unequal power: conversation analysis and discourse analysis. They need not be mutually exclusive.

Conversation Analysis and Talking Structures

Sociological studies of the negotiation of meaning and status in public speaking, and analysis of effectiveness in making oral presentations before panels, show

---

17. Author interview with Esmeralda Cabral, former Alberta Environment Community Affairs Branch employee assigned to Alpac EIA. Vancouver, 1995.

obstacles that lay people, women, and minorities must overcome when talking in public forums. Some examples are differential control over conversational division of labour; interruption; holding the floor; asking questions; and controlling topics (Fisher and Groce, 1990; Caesar-Wolf, 1984; Kathlene, 1994).

In *Who Need Not Be Heard: Deciding Who Is Not An Expert*, Rifkin uses conversation analysis to study expert status in Water Board hearings on toxic waste issues:

Expert status represents a high participation status in a conversation ... connotes the authority to talk and set the topic of conversation. It is the expert who tells people what factors are relevant to their concerns (1994: 61).

Water Board members decide expert status or decide who is not an expert by applying the criterion of relevance based on "information offered, a testifier's identity, and norms and rituals of the hearing process." Rifkin identifies the ethnomethods of establishing acceptance before a panel through linguistic triggers, mimicry of those with status, and jousting as a means for testing expertise. He notes gender differences in presentation style and self-assurance that also influence acceptance. His conclusion that "who gets to talk is more important than what is said,' is helpful, but says little about forms of public resistance that reject such presentation of self as expert.

For example, focused rudeness — or intentionally disrupting highly ritualized hearing procedures — was a prime tool used by farmers to attract the Alpac EIA review panel's attention and to pierce the "performances" of experts. In native communities, traditional prayer, pipe ceremonies, and a round dance with community, company and panel members were used to counter secular rituals of public hearings and western science.

Discourse Analysis

Not all power at play in public hearings is captured in the sociological net of conversation analysis. Many find power in the discourses spoken in public hearings (Downey, 1988; Litfin, 1994; Waddell, 1996; Waller, 1995).

Kurian's study of gender, development, and traditional knowledge of women in EIA in a Third World context focuses less on talking structures, and more on the discourses and worldviews of EIA decision makers and activists. Examining how well these decision makers listen when women speak, she discovers a predominately masculine worldview deaf to the feminine. Kurian shows how males view issues through the lens of economic progress, while women discuss social justice issues. Where men talk technology, she finds women talk social-cultural issues. Mostly, women's concerns and their gender-specific relationship to nature is not addressed or valued in EIA. For Kurian, the sexist assumptions in Indian culture about women's relationship to nature are replicated in environmental and development discourses that see women as natural appendages of men: "there has been a reinforcement of social, economic, and political processes that simultaneously silence women's voices while marginalizing them" (1995: 175).

Power is also intertwined with scientific and technical knowledge. In *Ozone Discourses*, Litfin explains that

> the power of scientists to interpret reality has itself become a productive source of political power.... Scientists' power derives from their socially acceptable competence as interpreters of reality. Yet they are not simply powerful agents wielding an arsenal of knowledge; rather, discourse itself is a source of power, facilitating the production of identities and interests (1994: 29).

Many EIA conventions described in this paper are examples of knowledge as a discursive source of power. Applied to EIA hearings, conversation analysis and discourse analysis could pry open conventions and suggest tactics for lay people, minorities, and women to overcome obstacles, and make the hearing process more fair. Another strategy would be to use sociological findings about talking in public to problematize the EIA hearing itself, to force debate about power imbalances between lay people and experts when talking in a democracy, and to make fairness in hearings part of the scoping, and terms of reference.

Taking Sides

The role for critical sociology in EIA that I have outlined is not neutral, or cloaked in claims to objectivity. It begins from the premise that knowledge is socially constructed. Biologist Mary O'Brien, whose research on pulp-mill pollution helped FOTA members raise questions before the Alpac panel, argues that being a scientist means taking sides. She maintains that sometimes "you must publicly interpret your research and the research of others; testify at a public hearing; prepare an affidavit for an environmental lawsuit; respond to citizen activists who ask questions when you would rather be doing your research" (1993: 707). Because not taking sides means supporting the status quo, O'Brien recommends acting as scientifically knowledgeable citizens in the public interest, and "participating in those processes that promote environmental integrity, biological diversity, public health, and democracy" (1993: 707). For Brian Martin, the critic of establishment experts, effective participation means that good arguments of critics have to avoid becoming academic and "need to be linked to interest groups, in the same manner that establishment experts are linked to vested interests" (1996: 179).

Over a decade ago Freudenberg and Keating, frustrated by the paucity of sociology in impact assessment, invoked C. Wright Mills who argued what social scientists "ought to do for society ... is to help build and strengthen self-cultivating publics"(1985: 594–595). Joining public groups in environmental confrontations was their advice for making the discipline relevant to EIA. It remains sound counsel.

References

Alberta-Pacific Environmental Impact Assessment Review Board
    1989   *The Proposed Alberta-Pacific Pulp Mill: Report of the EIA Review Board, March 1990.* Edmonton, Alberta: Alberta Environment.

Alberta-Pacific Forest Industries Inc.
    1989   *Alberta-Pacific Forest Industries Inc. Environmental Impact Assessment Bleached Kraft Pulp Mill Main Report.* Edmonton, Alberta: Alberta-Pacific Forest Industries Inc.

Appiah-Opoku, Seth
    1994   "Theoretical orientations of environmental assessment in Canada: Application to the Third World." *Environments* 22 (3): 103–110.

Aquatic Science Committee of the Royal Society of Canada
    1995   *Aquatic Science in Canada: A Case Study of Research in the Mackenzie Basin.* Vancouver: Royal Society of Canada.

Attfield, Robin and Katherine Dell (eds.)
    1989   *Values, Conflict, and the Environment.* Oxford: Ian Ramsey Centre.

Beattie, Robert B.
    1995   "Everything you already know about EIA (but don't often admit)'" *Environmental Impact Assessment Review* 15: 109–114.

Beder, Sharon
    1989   *Toxic Fish and Sewer Surfing.* North Sydney, Australia: Allen and Unwin Australia Pty Ltd.
    1990   "Science and control of information: An Australian case study." *The Ecologist* 20 (July / August): 136–140.
    1991   "The many meanings of means." *Search* 22 (3): 88–90.
    1993a   "Bias and credibility in environmental impact assessment." *Chain Reaction* (68) (February): 28–30.
    1993b   *The Nature of Sustainable Development.* Newham, Australia: Scribe Publications.
    1996   "Sewerage treatment and the engineering establishment." In Brian Martin (ed.), *Confronting the Experts.* Albany, New York: State University of New York Press.

Breyman, Steve
    1993   "Knowledge as power: Ecology movements and global environmental problems." In Ronnie D. Lipschutz and Ken Conca (eds.), *The State and Social Power in Global Environmental Politics.* New York: Columbia University Press.

Burningham, Kate
    1995   "Attitudes, accounts and impact." *The Sociological Review* 43 (1): 100–122.

Caesar-Wolf, Beatrice
    1984   "The construction of 'adjudiciable' evidence in a West German civil hearing." *Text* 4 (1–3): 193–223.

Campbell, Brian L.
    1985   "Uncertainty as symbolic action in disputes among experts." *Social Studies of Science* 15 (3): 429–453.

Carter, Lewis F. and William Willard
    1993   "Issues of restricted scope in social impact assessment: Case study of assumptions about impacts of the proposed Hanford high-level nuclear waste repository." *Research in Social Problems and Public Policy* 5: 243–268.

Cornea, Michael M.
    1991   *Using Knowledge from Social Science in Development Projects.* World Bank Discussion Papers: 114.

476   Canadian Journal of Sociology

Deitz, Thomas
1987   "Theory and method in social impact analysis." *Sociological Inquiry* 57: 54–69.

Downey, Gary L.
1988   "Structure and practice in the cultural identities of scientists: Negotiating nuclear wastes in New Mexico." *Anthropological Quarterly* 61 (1): 26–38.

Dunk, Thomas (ed.)
1991   *Social Relations in Resource Hinterlands*. Thunder Bay, Ontario: Centre for Northern Studies, Lakehead University.
1994   "Talking about trees: Environment and society in forest workers' culture." *Canadian Review of Sociology and Anthropology* 31 (1): 14–34.

Equus Consulting Group
1989   *Values and Perceptions Baseline Study in the Grassland / Prosperity Area of Alberta. Draft: Prepared for Prosperity and Area Community Members and Alberta Pacific Forest Industries Inc.* Edmonton: Author.

Fearnside, Philip M.
1994   "The Canadian feasibility study of the Three Gorges Dam proposed for China's Yangzi River: A grave embarrassment to the impact assessment profession." *Impact Assessment* (Spring): 21–57.

Feit, Harvey
1995   "Hunting and the quest for power: The James Bay Cree and whitemen in the twentieth century." In R. Bruce Morrison and C. Roderick Wilson (eds.), *Native Peoples: The Canadian Experience,* 2d ed. Toronto: McClelland and Stewart Inc.

Fisher, Sue and Stephen B. Groce
1990   "Accounting practices in medical interviews." *Language in Society* 19: 225–250.

Forester, John (ed.)
1985   *Critical Theory and Public Life*. Cambridge: Massachusetts Institute of Technology Press.

Freudenberg, William R. and Kenneth M. Keating
1982   "Increasing the impact of sociology on social impact assessment: Toward ending the inattention." *The American Sociologist* 17: 71–80.
1985   "Applying sociology to policy: Social science and the environmental impact statement." *Rural Sociology* 50 (4): 578–605.

Friends of the Athabasca Environmental Association
1991   *The FOTA Files: Pulp Mill Pollution and Politics 1988–1991*. Athabasca, Alberta.

Gibson, Robert B.
1993   "Environmental assessment design: Lessons from the Canadian experience." *The Environmental Professional* 15: 12–24.

Gilpin, Alan
1995   *Environmental Impact Assessment*. Cambridge: Cambridge University Press.

Gismondi, Michael
1992   "Mega project slow to deliver on promises." *First Reading* 10 (5) 6–7.

Gismondi, Michael and Joan Sherman
1996   "Pulp mills, fish contamination, and fish eaters: A participatory workshop on the politics of expert knowledge." *Capitalism Nature Socialism* 7 (4): 127–137.

Goldman, Michael
1997   " 'Customs in common': The epistemic world of the commons scholars." *Theory and Society* 26(1): 1–37.

Grove White, Robin
　1993　"Environmentalism: A new moral discourse for technological society?" In Kay Milton (ed.), *Environmentalism: The View From Anthropology*. London: Routledge.

Haas, Peter
　1989　"Do regimes matter? Epistemic communities and Mediterranean pollution control." *International Organization* 43.

Heald, Susan
　1991　"Projects and subjects: Women, the North, and job creation." In Thomas Dunk (ed.), *Social Relations in Resource Hinterlands*. Thunder Bay, Ontario: Centre for Northern Studies, Lakehead University.

Kathlene, Lyn
　1994　"Power and influence in state legislative policymaking: The interactions of gender and position in committee hearing debates." *American Political Science Review* 88 (3): 560–576.

Knight, Nancy, Peter Boothroyd, Margaret Eberle, June Kawaguchi and Christiane Gagnon
　1993　*What We Know About the Socio-Economic Impacts of Canadian Megaprojects: An Annotated Bibliography of Post-Project Studies*. Vancouver: University of British Columbia, Centre for Human Settlements.

Kurian, Priya A.
　1995　"Environmental impact assessment in practice: A gender critique." *The Environmental Professional* 17: 167–178.

Lawrence, David P.
　1994　"The characteristics and aims of environmental impact assessment." *Plan Canada* (March): 6–10.

Levidow, Lev
　1992　"Impact assessment: Whose rationality?" *Capitalism Nature Socialism* 3 (1): 117–124.

Litfin, Karen T.
　1994　*Ozone Discourses: Science and Politics in Global Environmental Cooperation*. New York: Columbia University Press.

MacGregor, Sherilyn
　1995　"Deconstructing the man made city: Feminist critiques of planning thought and action." In Margrit Eichler (ed.), *Change of Plans: Towards a Non-Sexist Sustainable City*. Toronto: Garamond Press.

Macnaghten, Phil and John Urry
　1995　"Towards a sociology of nature." *Sociology* 29 (2): 203–220.

Marchak, M. Patricia
　1996　*Logging the Globe*. Montreal and Kingston: McGill-Queen's University Press.

Martin, Brian
　1979　*The Bias of Science*. Canberra: Society for Social Responsibility in Science, A.C.T.
　1996　*Confronting the Experts*. (ed.) Albany, NY: State University of New York Press.

McDonald, Michael, J. T. Stevenson and Wesley Cragg
　1992　"Finding a balance of values: An ethical assessment of Ontario hydro's demand / supply plan." *Report to the Aboriginal Research Coalition of Ontario*.

Murphy, Raymond
　1995　"Sociology as if nature did not matter: An ecological critique." *British Journal of Sociology* 46 (4): 667–707.

Northern River Basins Study
   1996   *Characterization of Aquatic Uses Within the Peace, Athabasca and Slave River Basins.* Synthesis Report 7. Edmonton, Alberta: Northern River Basins Study.

O'Brien, Mary H.
   1993   "Being a scientist means taking sides." *BioScience* 43 (10): 706–708.

Pendelton Banks, E.
   1990   "Ethnography: An essential tool for impact prediction." *Impact Assessment Bulletin* 8 (4): 19–30.

Power, Michael
   1995   "Auditing, expertise and the sociology of technique." *Critical Perspectives on Accounting* 6: 317–339.

Pratt, Larry and Ian Urquhart
   1994   *The Last Great Forest: Japanese Multinationals in Alberta's Northern Forests.* Edmonton: NeWest Press.

Praxis, A Social Planning Company
   1990   *Alberta-Pacific Forest Industries Inc. Bleached Kraft Pulp Mill: A Review of the Economic and Social Implications.* Calgary.

Price Waterhouse
   1988   *Crestbrook Forest Industries Ltd.: Economic Impact Study Proposed Pulp Mill.*

Public Hearing Proceedings
   1989   *The Alberta-Pacific Environmental Impact Assessment Review Board Public Hearing Proceedings Vol 1–55.* Edmonton: J. G. Moore & Associates.

Regulatory Advisory Committee Subcommittee
   1996   "Procedures for an assessment by a review panel." Working draft. Hull, Quebec: Canadian Environmental Assessment Agency.

Review Panel on Environmental Law Enforcement
   1987   *An Action Plan for Environmental Law Enforcement in Alberta.* Edmonton: Queen's Printer.

Richardson, Mary, Joan Sherman and Michael Gismondi
   1993   *Winning Back the Words: Confronting Experts in an Environmental Public Hearing.* Toronto, Ontario: Garamond Press.

Rifkin, William D.
   1994   "Who need not be heard: Deciding who is not an expert." *Technology Studies* 1 (1): 60–96.

Rip, Arie
   1992   "Expert advice and pragmatic rationality." In Nico Stehr and Richard V. Ericson (eds.), *The Culture and Power of Knowledge: Inquiries into Contemporary Cultures.* New York: Walter de Gruyter.

Sallenave, John
   1994   "Giving traditional ecological knowledge its rightful place in environmental impact assessment." *Northern Perspectives* 22 (1): 16–19.

Shapcott, Catherine
   1989   "Environmental impact assessment and resource management, a Haida case study: Implications for native people of the North." *The Canadian Journal of Native Studies* 9 (1): 55–83.

Sherman, Joan, Michael Gismondi and Mary Richardson
1996 "Not directly affected: Using the law to close the door on environmentalists." *Journal of Canadian Studies* 31 (1): 102–118.

Sherman, Joan and Michael Gismondi
1997 "Jock talk, goldfish, horse logging and Star Wars: How a pulp company communicates a green image." *Alternatives Journal* 23 (1): 14–20.

Smith, Roger and Bryan Wynne (eds.)
1989 *Expert Evidence: Interpreting Science in the Law.* London: Routledge.

Stehr, Nico and Richard V. Ericson (eds.)
1992 *The Culture and Power of Knowledge: Inquiries Into Contemporary Societies.* New York: Walter de Gruyter.

Study Group on Environmental Assessment Hearing Procedures
1988 *Public Review: Neither Judicial, Nor Political, But An Essential Forum For the Future of the Environment.* A Report Concerning the Reform of Public Hearing Procedures for Federal Environmental Assessment Reviews. Ottawa: Supply and Services Canada.

Tester, Frank
1992 "Reflections on Tin Wis: Environmentalism and the evolution of citizen participation in Canada." *Alternatives: Perspectives on Society, Technology and Environment* 19 (1): 34–41.

United Nations
1987 "Goals and principles of environmental impact assessment." Decision 14/25 of the Governing Council of UNEP, of 17 June 1987.

Waddell, Craig
1996 "Saving the Great Lakes: Public participation in environmental policy." In Carl G. Herndl and Stuart Brown (eds.), *Green Culture: Rhetorical Analyses of Environmental Discourses.* Madison, Wisconsin: University of Wisconsin Press.

Waller, Tom
1994 "Expertise, elites, and resource management reform: Resisting agricultural water conservation in California's Imperial Valley." *Journal of Political Ecology* 1: 12–42.
1995 "Knowledge, power, and environmental policy: Expertise, the lay public, and water management in the Western United States." *The Environmental Professional* 17: 153–166.

Wise, M. Norton
1995 *The Values of Precision.* Princeton: Princeton University Press.

Wismer, Susan
1996 "The nasty game: How environmental assessment is failing aboriginal communities in Canada's North." *Alternatives Journal* 22 (4): 10–17.

Wynne, Brian
1982 *Rationality and Ritual: The Windscale Inquiry and Nuclear Decisions in Britain.* Chalfont St. Giles, England: The British Society for the History of Science.
1989 "Establishing the rules of laws: Constructing expert authority." In R. Smith and B. Wynne (eds.), *Expert Evidence Interpreting Science in the Law.* London: Routledge.
1994 "Scientific knowledge and the global environment." In Michael Redclift and Ted Benton (eds.), *Social Theory and the Global Environment.* London: Routledge.

Part IV
Understanding Social Impacts

Function evaluation

Function evaluation as a framework for the integration of social and environmental impact assessment

Roel Slootweg, Frank Vanclay and Marlies van Schooten

Social impact assessment and environmental impact assessment have developed as separate entities, but a full appreciation of all impacts requires a thorough understanding of all the biophysical and social changes invoked by a planned intervention. Biophysical impacts also have social impacts, and social changes can cause changes in the biophysical environment, which create biophysical impacts. To date, there has not been an adequate framework for integrating biophysical and social impact assessment. This paper presents a method for such integration using function evaluation as a conceptual framework. This has led to a better understanding of the full extent of human impacts, and the impact pathways that lead from interventions to the experience of impacts.

Keywords: function evaluation; social impact assessment; environmental impact assessment

Roel Slootweg, PhD, is with Geoplan International, The Netherlands; E-mail: general@geoplan-international.nl. Frank Vanclay, PhD (contact author) is at the Centre for Rural Social Research, Charles Sturt University, Locked Bag 678, Wagga Wagga NSW 2678, Australia; E-mail: fvanclay@csu.edu.au. Marlies van Schooten, MSc, is a private consultant in The Netherlands; Email: mvsrs@xs4all.nl.

The theoretical framework presented is partly based on unpublished work of Rob Koudstaal and Roel Slootweg commissioned by the Wetland Group Foundation. The Netherlands Ministry of Foreign Affairs made further elaboration possible by commissioning a decision support system to assist donor organisations to determine the potential impacts of proposed projects. The authors would like to thank Anneke Wevers for her support in this innovative and challenging endeavour.

THERE IS A GROWING CONCERN about the environmental and social consequences of development efforts. The developed world potentially faces enormous costs because of the need to restore and to protect the environment to safeguard natural resources for future generations. Developing countries must consider how their social and economic development can be combined with protection of the environment and preservation of their natural resources, not as a luxury, but as a necessity for sustainable development.

When applied in the earliest stages of the decision-making process, environmental impact assessment (EIA) and social impact assessment (SIA) can become important project planning instruments. They provide information on the consequences of specific development activities in a way that allows these consequences to be taken into account and used in the process leading to a final decision and in designing mitigation measures. Proper application of EIA and SIA can significantly improve the quality of project proposals and will eventually lead to important savings on project implementation because of reduced negative impacts and better acceptance of the project objectives.

Since the publication of the *Brundtland Report* (WCED, 1987) and the UNCED (UN Conference on Environment and Development), or Earth Summit, in Rio de Janeiro in 1992, the concept of sustainable development has gained wide acceptance and the idea that environment and development are strongly interrelated is recognised by many. Further, poverty and gender assessments are likely to become widely used instruments of planning in development cooperation.

Since EIA is the most developed instrument, backed by a legal framework in many countries, it is increasingly used to assess as well the social and economic impacts of planned interventions. The obvious consequence of the desire to integrate environmental, social and economic aspects of project assessment is the apparent need for an integrating framework. So far, the worlds of environmental impact assessment, in the strict sense, social impact assessment, and economic cost–benefit analysis have operated in their separate realms.

In this paper, an attempt is made to construct a conceptual framework that provides a harmonised and integrated way of thinking and will assist in the identification of potential environmental, social and economic impacts of a planned intervention. The framework is designed to have broad application, and it provides insight in, and understanding of, the complex cause–effect chains that may lead to desired or undesired effects. It is partially based on an approach that translates nature and natural resources into functions for human society, often referred to as 'function evaluation' (R S de Groot, 1992). This concept bears some similarity to the discussion of environmental goods and services that exists in some countries.

We realise that the terminology used in this discussion can easily lead to misunderstandings, since some terms may have a different meaning in other contexts. To assist, we provide a glossary of the terms we use in a specific way in Appendix 1.

Settings

The conceptual framework presented here aims to provide insight into the relations between human society and the biophysical environment. The focus of this conceptualisation is the characterisation and classification of the functions provided by the biophysical environment and the assessment of their value for supporting human activities. The framework is based on the so-called 'function evaluation' of nature. Leading authors in this field are, among others, R S de Groot (1992) and W T de Groot (1992).

The starting point in this approach is that society utilises products and services that are provided by the biophysical environment. In economic terms, society constitutes the demand side, and the environment constitutes the supply side (see Figure 1). Simply stated, sustainability deals with the equilibrium in supply and demand, now and in the future! Perceived imbalances in this equilibrium trigger institutions to act by managing either the supply from nature or the demand from society.

Institutions can, in this sense, be national, regional or local authorities with their formal instruments and regulations, or they can be traditional chieftains or village elders with their traditional techniques and customary laws. In a globalised world, international agencies that exert effective control over human activities could also be included, for example, potentially the Framework Convention on Climate Change, the Biodiversity Convention, or the Montreal Protocol on Substances that Deplete the Ozone Layer.

Three main settings can be identified (see Figure 1):

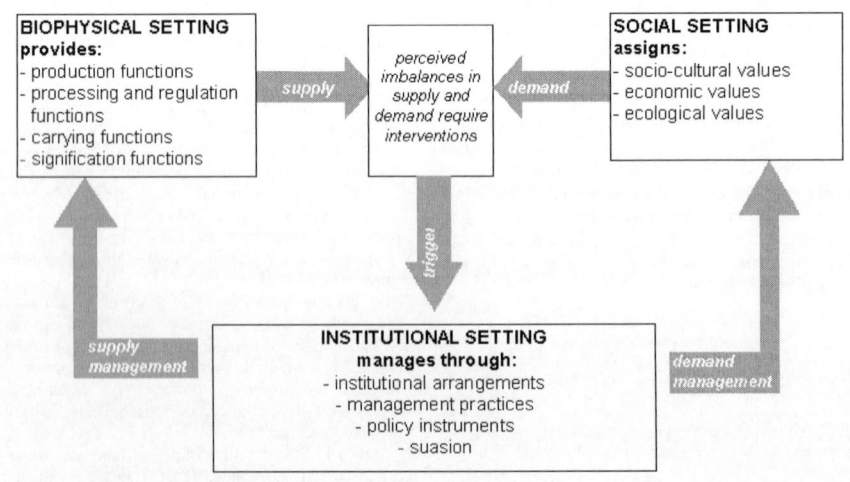

Figure 1. Main settings in function evaluation

Source: Concept developed further from an original idea conceived in conjunction with Rob Koudstaal in a study for the Wetland Group Foundation: "Wise use of wetlands: a methodology for the assessment of functions and values of wetlands" (unpublished document)

- The natural environment (or biophysical setting) comprises a combination of living and non-living resources and their interactions. Resources perform functions in providing goods and services which are used by each society.
- Human society (or the social setting) encompasses all human activities, knowledge, beliefs and values. As a result of human activities and social values (which are influenced by societal knowledge and beliefs, that is, culture), environmental goods and services (that is, the functions of the biophysical environment) are valued in a social context. These environmental values can be expressed in economic, socio-cultural (including spiritual) or ecological terms. To a large extent, these values depend on the societal context, differing between cultures, and also for different groups within a society.
- The institutional setting consists of the institutional arrangements (authorities, legal framework, traditional laws and regulations), management practices (such as physical structures — dykes, roads, and so on), policy instruments (permits, subsidies, quota, and so on), and the use of suasion by governments or agencies in an attempt to change people's beliefs or behaviour.

Figure 1 depicts how the need for action is triggered by a perceived disequilibrium in the relation between supply and demand. The demand for goods and services from nature may surpass the available supply, which leads to a present or expected future problem (for instance, over-exploitation or insufficient supply). The opposite may also occur; some of the functions of the natural environment are not exploited and, to the extent that they are recognised, this represents a development opportunity.

Both problems and opportunities may trigger an initiative from the policy- or decision-makers, who through their institutional arrangements, policy instruments, management practices and suasion will try to solve the problem or benefit from the development opportunity. This intervention either works via the side of the biophysical setting by managing the supply of environmental goods and services (provision of agriculture, forestry, hydraulic engineering, and so on), or via the side of the social setting by managing the demand for goods and services (through tax incentives, setting of quota, trade negotiations, and so on).

> The natural system comprises many environmental functions that provide goods and services that can be utilised by humanity: whether all these functions are actually utilised is dependent on the social, economic and cultural 'behaviour' of the society

Biophysical setting

The natural system comprises many environmental functions that provide goods and services that can be utilised by human society. Whether all these functions are actually utilised is dependent on the social, economic and cultural 'behaviour' of the society concerned, its state of development, technical knowledge, and so on. Of course, it is not necessary that all the identified functions of an ecosystem are used, and furthermore, ecosystems may possess functions that are not as yet identified — one of the primary arguments in support of biodiversity protection. Combining the clear but somewhat simplified classification of R S de Groot (1992) and the theoretically more appropriate classification of W T de Groot (1992), four categories of environmental functions can be distinguished: production; processing and regulation; carrying; and signification functions.

Production functions refer to the ability of the natural environment to generate useful products for humanity. A distinction is made between natural production functions and nature-based human production functions.

Natural production functions include products that the natural environment largely produces on its own, that is, without human input other than humans being harvesters (hunting and gathering). Products can be produced over a short term (for instance, firewood, fruit, streamwater, ocean fisheries) or over a long time period (for instance, oil, minerals, fossil groundwater). The former are often referred to as renewable resources, while the latter are considered non-renewable. The logging of old-growth forests for lumber or pulp would be renewable if undertaken on a sustainable yield basis, or would arguably be non-renewable if done by clear-felling operations with little or no regeneration of native forests.

Nature-based human production functions refer to the production of biological (animal or plant) products by the biophysical environment in ways that involve active management and inputs by people. Examples include most agricultural and horticultural activities, forestry plantations and managed forests, and fish ponds (aquaculture and mariculture).

Processing and regulation functions (or maintenance functions) relate to the maintenance of ecosystem support systems. The interactions between biotic and abiotic components result in complex processes that influence the conditions for maintenance of life support systems. These functions are often not recognised until they are disturbed. They refer to the ability of ecosystems to maintain or restore dynamic equilibria within the system, or in other linked ecosystems through physical, biological and chemical processes and interactions.

Processing functions often undo the harm caused by human activities or reduce the risk to humans. They include the sequestration of carbon dioxide, the dilution of pollutants, and the active chemical transformation of harmful substances such as organic waste. Examples of regulation functions include: maintenance of groundwater levels, maintenance of biological diversity, protection against natural forces (coastal protection by mangroves) and protection against harmful cosmic radiation (ozone shield). Water storage in wetlands is an example of a regulation function for river flow regulation.

Carrying functions are related to space or a substrate that is suitable for certain activities and for which there may be a demand. The availability of space together with a particular set of environmental conditions associated with that space make an area more or less suitable to perform certain functions for humans. Examples include suitability of an area for human habitation and settlement, nature conservation areas, areas for nature-based recreation (such as mountain climbing, bushwalking, skiing, beach tourism), waterways for navigation, and sites for energy conversion (for instance, hydropower reservoirs).

Signification functions refer to the social values that are ascribed to nature itself (natural heritage values) and to other features of the landscape including the human constructed landscape (cultural heritage values). Nature provides opportunities for spiritual enrichment, aesthetic enjoyment, cognitive development (contemplation, meditation) and recreation. Different from the provision of physical space as in carrying functions, these functions refer to the meaning (significance) associated with the biophysical environment.

The world's largest economic sector, tourism, is largely based on this function — that is, human appreciation of nature and landscape. Examples include aesthetic information (scenery, landscape), spiritual and religious information (religious and sacred sites), psychological information (emotional attachment, nostalgic attachment to place), historic information (historic and archaeological elements), cultural and artistic information (inspiration for folklore, music, dance, art), and educational and scientific information (natural science classes, research, environmental indicators).

The difference between the 'classical' approach to describe nature in terms of natural resources (water, soil, forest, and so on) and function evaluation is that the latter provides much more insight into the multifunctionality of resources. For example, instead of just describing the resource, 'water', function evaluation provides insight into the multiple functions of water, such as production function for agriculture, carrying function for shipping and recreation, regulation function to counterbalance seawater intrusion, and signification function for science or religious groups or nature-based tourism. By identifying the functions, the relevant units of measurement can be identified and decision-making can be based on a more profound understanding of the role the biophysical environment plays for human society.

It is important to realise that many functions can occur simultaneously (see example for water above), but that with human intervention these functions may become mutually exclusive. The creation of a dam to enhance water storage in a river basin will block the pathway for migratory fish as well as for long-river water transport. Intensive exploitation of freshwater for agricultural productivity will reduce or exclude other functions such as shipping, balancing the intrusion of seawater, and maintenance of downstream wetlands.

Social setting

The social setting creates the demand for environmental goods and services. The existence of goods and services that derive from environmental functions is what determines the perceived value of those functions for humanity. This perceived value is also related to what is socially valued in that society, which in turn, is related to the culture of that society, the level of technology and so on. Three broad categories of values can be distinguished: social; economic; and ecological.

Social values refer to the quality of life in general and can be expressed in many different units, depending on the social context and cultural background of the situation/society. Some examples are: health and safety (expressed as prevalence of diseases or number of people protected from forces of nature); housing and living conditions; space for settlement; the value of the environment as a source of food (or in-kind income) in subsistence economies; and religious and cultural values.

The economic value of an environmental function refers to the monetary value of the goods and services that are provided. It can be assigned to individual economic activities (agriculture, industries, fisheries, construction), to household income (as an overall indicator of the financial conditions of the population), or to *per capita* gross regional or domestic product, as an indicator of the income of the society as a whole.

Ecological values refer to the value that society places/derives from the maintenance of the earth's life support systems (particularly the processing and regulation functions). They come in two forms. Temporal ecological values refer to the potential future benefits that can be derived from biological diversity (genetic, species and ecosystem diversity) and key ecological processes that maintain the world's life support systems for future generations. The appropriate way(s) to express these values is hotly debated. A simple, regularly used measure is the proportion of endemic species (that is, only locally occurring species) as a measure of uniqueness of the area. Other measures try

Function evaluation in integrating SIA & EIA

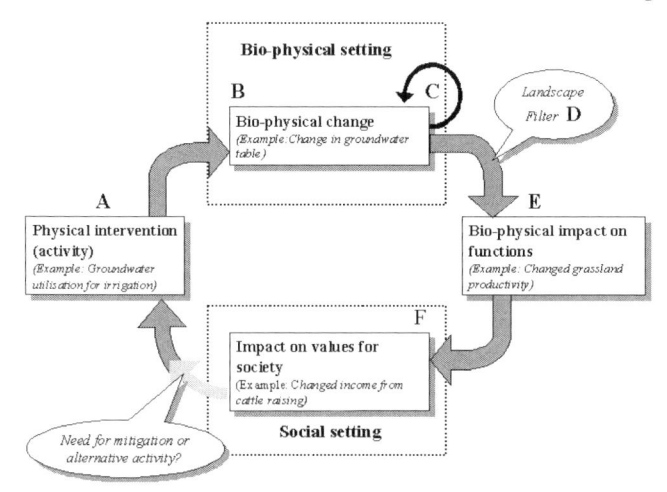

Figure 2. Steps in determining impacts resulting from physical interventions

to indicate the 'naturalness' of an area, that is, the level at which natural processes can still structure and maintain the environment and its functions.

Spatial ecological values refer to the interactions ecosystems have with other systems, and thus perform functions for the maintenance of other systems. Coastal lagoons and mangroves that serve as breeding grounds for marine fish provide a good example. The ecological value of the mangroves is the support they provide for economic activity elsewhere — without mangroves there would be less fish. Other examples are wintering areas for migratory birds or flood plains that recharge groundwater aquifers for neighbouring dry lands or act as a silt trap that prevent downstream rivers and reservoirs from silting up.

These values are not mutually exclusive, since functions cannot always be unequivocally assigned an economic or a social value. For example, the suitability of a certain area for a traditional crop (production function) can be valued in economic (for instance, income, employment, subsistence) as well as social terms (for instance, cultural preservation), or even in ecological terms (for instance, the use of a traditional and unique variety of salt-resistant rice that merits being maintained in a seed bank for future uses). It is important to realise that values differ for different (groups of) individuals in a society. Therefore, the identification of values should include the views and opinions of many people.

Interventions, changes and impacts

As shown in Figure 1, imbalances between the supply of goods and services provided by the biophysical environment and the demand for these goods and services from society may lead to the identification of an actual or a perceived current or future problem or opportunity. The problem or opportunity, in its turn, will trigger a reaction from the institutional setting to undertake interventions (or activities, projects, and so on) to address the issue. Interventions may be designed to have direct influence on the biophysical setting, or on the social setting.

In impact assessment, we are interested in predicting the environmental (biophysical and social) impacts of such planned interventions. There are several key questions for impact assessment:

- How can social and biophysical impacts be integrated in one process, and more importantly, how are social and biophysical impacts interlinked?
- What are the chains of events that lead from a proposed intervention to expected impacts?
- Can second- and higher-order effects be identified?
- Can off-site impacts (away from the site of the intervention) be identified?

We use the function evaluation framework as a way of understanding how impacts develop from physical interventions. Separating the concepts of a change in the biophysical setting from the impact to the environmental functions, and the impact experienced by people as a result of those biophysical impacts, is useful (see Figure 2).

Figure 2 shows that physical interventions (A) create changes to the characteristics of the natural resources in the biophysical setting (B). These biophysical changes can be measured and quantified. A change in the characteristics of a natural resource will occur under all circumstances, irrespective of the type of ecosystem or land-use type in which the intervention is carried out. For example, a project

Function evaluation in integrating SIA & EIA

Biophysical impacts are expressed in terms of changes in the products and services provided by the environment and will consequently have impacts on the values of these functions for human society

(intervention) which will divert water from one watercourse into another will change the downstream hydrology (the biophysical change), whether it be in the Amazon River, a mountain stream (natural ecosystems), or an irrigation feeder canal (an artificial land-use type). Magnitude and direction of change are determined by the combined characteristics of the intervention and the natural resource involved. This conceptual framework, however, only allows for the identification of likely biophysical changes. Field Hobservations and detailed information on the proposed interventions are needed to determine the actual magnitude and the direction of the change.

The biophysical change that directly results from an intervention is a first-order change. This change may in turn cause second- and higher-order biophysical changes (C). As in the example above, a river diversion is likely to result in a change in river hydrology (first-order change); this may lead to a change in flooding regime in downstream floodplains, or change the salt and other pollutant concentration along the river (second-order changes).

The example in Figure 2 shows that changes in the physical and biological properties of natural resources will change the functions of the natural environment (E), that is, the goods and services provided by nature. These changes are called the biophysical impacts. The type and quality of the biophysical environment determine the functions affected.

For example, a change in groundwater level in forested upland areas will affect functions such as wood production, and the provision of water for lowland areas. In coastal lowlands, however, the same biophysical change in groundwater level will affect functions such as the prevention of underground seawater intrusion, and productivity of meadowlands.

From this framework, then, a long list of potential impacts can be derived for all imaginable environmental conditions. However, field observations are needed to confirm or reject the potential impacts.

With some knowledge of the specific location, it would be possible to improve the identification of potential impacts by using the concepts of ecosystem and land-use type. By knowing the ecosystem or land-use type in which a biophysical change occurs, it would be possible to indicate the functions that potentially will be affected. The long list of potential impacts can thus be narrowed down considerably by introducing a 'landscape filter' (D). For practical reasons, the combined term landscape is used, being defined as a biologically and/or geographically recognisable unit representing either a natural ecosystem (for example, a lowland rainforest), a semi-natural ecosystem (such as managed forest) or a human land-use type (irrigated cropland). This landscape filter 'filters' the relevant impacts from the long list of potential impacts.

When the first- and higher-order biophysical changes that result from an intervention are known, the area of impact can be determined. Many changes will only occur in the area where the intervention is carried out and will result in on-site impacts that can be determined when the landscape type in which the intervention is carried out is identified.

However, some biophysical changes will have a broader geographical range of impact. For example, air pollution drifts to other areas by wind; interventions in river hydrology may have impacts on the entire river basin (upstream and downstream); an airport or road produces noise that travels along noise contour lines. For each physical change, the geographical range where changes can be expected can be defined. By defining this range, the so-called off-site impacts of any intervention can be determined.

An example is the geographical range of a change in peak discharge of a river downstream from an intervention site. By determining the landscape types that lie downstream of the intervention site and that depend on river water, the off-site impacts can be determined. If, for example, the peak discharge will be significantly diminished, the identified downstream floodplains will suffer from reduced or total absence of flooding, and the estuary where the river empties will experience a change in the fresh–salt water balance. The impacts in each landscape type will be very different, but they result from the same intervention and the same biophysical change.

Biophysical impacts are expressed in terms of changes in the products and services provided by the environment and will consequently have impacts on the values of these functions for human society (F). Changes in the functions of nature will lead to changes in the values assigned to nature. For example, when, due to the construction of a dam, the surface area of floodplains downstream changes (physical change), downstream fish productivity will change (biophysical impact) which in turn influences society, that is, a change in the economic livelihoods of downstream fisherfolk.

These impacts on society are considered to be indirect human impacts. The word 'indirect' in this case refers to the fact that the impact on humans takes place through biophysical changes and impacts, in contrast to the direct impacts where the proposed intervention directly leads to changes and impacts in society.

The word 'human' instead of 'social' is introduced to avoid semantic discussions on what should be considered 'social' impacts. Human impacts are the real and perceived impacts experienced by humans (at individual and higher aggregation levels) as a result of biophysical and/or social change processes caused by planned interventions. We assume that human impacts encompass all final impact variables that are studied in environmental impact assessments, social impact assessments, health impact assessments, and even biodiversity impacts assessments given that the maintenance of biological diversity (a function of nature) is currently valued by society (as an ecological value) to guarantee the livelihoods of future generations.

Decision-making in relation to a proposed project is (or should be) based on the assessment of all these values, and on possibilities of defining alternatives or mitigation measures in the case of undesirable impacts. Changes to the proposed intervention, or the implementation of mitigation measures is a new intervention, making the process circular. Over time, too, the type of new projects that are proposed (A) is dependent on the experience of past interventions (F).

Social change processes and human impacts

We have presented a framework to derive human impacts that result from physical interventions (changes to the biophysical setting). We now elaborate further the framework to address also the human impacts that result from social interventions (changes in the social setting). Among SIA practitioners, there is general agreement that social impacts relate to

"all social and cultural consequences to human populations of any public or private actions that alter the ways in which people live, work, play relate to one another, organise to meet their needs, and generally cope as members of society." (Interorganisational Committee, 1994, page 107)

In contrast to biophysical impacts, human impacts can occur as soon as there are changes in social conditions, even from the time when a project is anticipated. People do not simply experience social changes, they react to them and are able to anticipate them. This makes prediction of social changes and human impacts difficult and situation specific. As a consequence, and for many other reasons elaborated by Burdge and Vanclay (1995), too many social impact assessment studies have been inadequate, often presenting little more than demographic or economic predictions.

In the context of our approach, human impacts should be seen in the broadest sense. This means that they refer to quantifiable variables such as economic or demographic issues, as well as to changes in people's norms, values, beliefs and perceptions about the society in which they live, the gendered differentiation of impacts and all other facets of life. See Vanclay (1999) or Vanclay et al (2001) for a full discussion of the nature of human impacts.

Analogous to the distinction between biophysical changes and biophysical impacts in the biophysical setting, we argue that a distinction between social change processes and human impacts should be identified in the social setting. Policies or project interventions cause social change processes. These can be intended (for instance, conversion of economic activities) or unintended (for instance, job loss). In our opinion, social change processes take place regardless of the social context of society (groups, nations, religions or whatever). The resettlement or relocation of local people due to the building of a dam, or the influx of new residents whether permanent, seasonal or weekenders, are social change processes, and are not in themselves social impacts.

Under certain conditions, depending on the characteristics of the existing community and the nature of mitigation measures, these social processes may cause impacts. There is, therefore, a distinction to be made between social change process and human impacts that is rather akin to the difference between biophysical changes and biophysical impacts. Conceptually too, it is obvious that an 'impact' has to be experienced or felt in a corporeal (physical) or cognitive (perceptual) sense, whether at the level of individual, household, or society/community. An increase in population, or the presence of strangers, is not the experienced impact, the experienced impact is likely to be changed perception about the nature of the community ('communityness', community cohesion), changed perception about personal attachment to the community, and possibly annoyance and upset as a result of the project.

The ways in which the social change processes are perceived, given meaning, or valued, depends on the social context in which various societal groups act. Some sectors of society, or groups in society, are able to adapt themselves quickly and make use of the opportunities of a new situation. Others are less able to adapt themselves (for instance, various vulnerable groups) and will bear most of the negative consequences of change.

Integrating biophysical and social settings

Figure 3 presents a revised version of the framework combining all elements, the biophysical setting, the social setting, and interlinkages. In particular it shows that the social setting can be influenced by interventions through two pathways: indirect and direct. Indirect human impacts result from changes in the natural resource base and the derived functions, that is, from biophysical impacts. Direct human impacts originate directly from (social) interventions (via the social change processes), and are either especially designed to influence the social setting (objectives) or are an unintended consequence of the intervention.

Change has a way of creating other changes. This notion of circularity or iteration has been incorporated in the framework in several ways. Social change

Function evaluation in integrating SIA & EIA

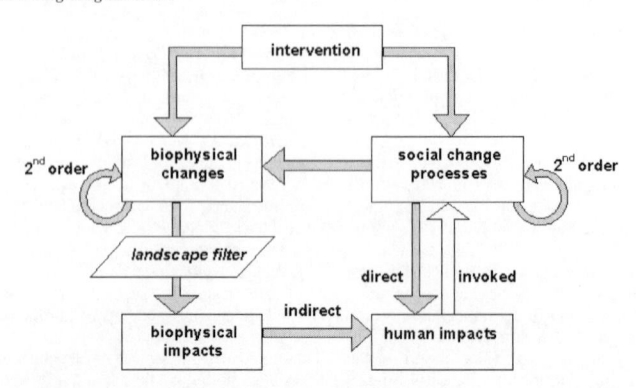

Figure 3. Pathways to derive biophysical and human impacts

processes that result directly from the intervention, the so-called first-order changes, can lead to (several) other social change processes, the second- and higher-order changes. For example, resettlement can lead to processes of rural to urban migration and changes in food production. In addition, the social experience of change (that is, the human impacts) can provoke people to undertake other behaviour or further social change processes. For example, the negative human impacts (experiences) associated with unemployment can activate the social change process of rural to urban migration in search of work.

Social change processes can also provoke biophysical changes. Economic developments which increase the number of tourists in a particular area can have serious influence on land use and water quality, which in their turn, can have indirect human impacts through a reduction in agricultural production and subsequently on income level for smallholder farmers.

A social filter?

So far, there has been a close comparison between the biophysical setting and the social setting. Somewhat analogous to the landscape filter in the biophysical setting, we can conceive of a social group filter. The aim of such a filter would be that, by using information about the types of social groups present, it might be possible to narrow down the long list of potential human impacts and identify the relevant impacts for that group. The filter would be placed between the social change processes and the human impacts and between the biophysical impacts and the human impacts (see Figure 3).

Conceptually, this is straightforward, especially once the logic of the framework is accepted. However, the construction of such a social filter in any practical application of this framework appears to be very complicated, and there is resistance amongst SIA professionals to consider the possibility. In the biophysical setting, biophysical impacts are related to ecosystems and landscape types. The classification of ecosystems or landscapes into meaningful units is reasonably established and accepted amongst EIA professionals and the ecology discipline. In contrast, there is not a generally accepted classification of social groupings for which sufficient knowledge exists to make predictions about the likely experience of human impacts. Further, landscape or ecosystem units have common elements around the world, but cultural groupings tend to be unique in many respects.

It is clear that the concept of a social filter still needs further thinking. The fact that most (all?) social scientists who have worked for some time in a community can identify vulnerable groups, or can predict (to a certain extent) the likely effects of a specified intervention, proves that intrinsic social filter mechanisms exist. The challenge is to articulate and operationalise the criteria that underlie this intrinsic knowledge.

What's new with our approach?

The framework presented in this paper is an attempt to provide a means to structure social and biophysical knowledge in impact assessment. It should be stressed that it is not a procedural framework for impact assessment and that it is not a predictive model, but rather it is a way of thinking. Impact assessment has always dealt with the identification of the cause–effect chains that may result from a planned intervention. By providing an integrating framework that

It is our strong conviction that all impacts are human impacts, but the pathways through which these impacts arise can be complex and include both the social and the biophysical settings

combines the biophysical and the social aspects of impacts, we hope that the separate worlds of EIA and SIA can join forces for better impact assessment, better project design, and hopefully to bring about better livelihoods for present-day and future people.

We have deliberately introduced the term 'human impact', so as to avoid the sometimes difficult and unfruitful discussion about whether SIA encompasses EIA, or whether EIA should encompass both the social and the biophysical dimensions. It is our strong conviction that all impacts are human impacts, but the pathways through which these impacts arise can be complex and include both the social and the biophysical settings. It makes no sense to separate the biophysical from the social environment.

The framework forms the basis of a computerised instrument that assists in identifying (qualitatively) the potential impacts of proposed projects. For that purpose, the authors have been forced to create a rigid and unequivocal framework of thinking. In doing so, it was realised that the analytical side of EIA and SIA practice could be strongly enhanced. Very often, implicit knowledge is used in both EIA and SIA without this being realised. For example, in many terms of reference for EIA studies, impacts on water quality are considered negative impacts, without any statement of the reasons why this should be the case. Implicitly, water is assumed to have functions for public water supply, irrigation or for fisheries. Would water quality be an issue if the water drained into an uninhabited area without any living organisms?

The rigid division between change processes (being tangible, objectively verifiable and measurable processes) and impacts (as subjective, context-dependent final variables of impact studies) provides considerable analytical assistance in the early identification of potential impacts. It adds something new to both EIA and SIA. EIA studies usually stop at the level of biophysical changes, such as changes in the quality or quantity of air, water, or soils. The notion of functions provides a mechanism to translate these changes into explicitly identified issues that are of relevance to human society. Water quality *per se* does not provide insight; the functions of this water and its values for society provide the relevant information.

For SIA studies, the separation of social change processes from the experience of (social or human) impacts is new. Many social scientists state that each situation is unique and that SIA studies are by definition context specific. However, nobody will doubt that inundation of populated areas will cause migration if not relocation, or that the creation of new factories will increase employment opportunities. These change processes do not give any clue as to the nature and severity of impacts that may be expected. This depends on the context of different groups in society and should be subject to SIA studies.

We believe that the framework presented in this paper provides a useful tool in the identification of issues that should be subject to impact studies. It also provides the means to focus on relevant issues thus avoiding lengthy scoping processes, and it reduces the risk of overlooking important issues. Furthermore, by providing simple and clearly defined links between the biophysical and social environments, the division of tasks and the communication between members of multidisciplinary study teams can be greatly enhanced.

Appendix 1. Glossary of working definitions for terminology used in the framework

The terminology in this paper is only used to distinguish steps in the presented framework. The authors make no pretensions as to the wider meaning of the terms. To avoid semantic discussions on terminology, we use the following working definitions:

- *Physical intervention*: planned human activity that physically intervenes in, and possibly alters, the biophysical environment.
- *Social intervention* planned human activity that intervenes in, and possibly alters, the social environment.
- *Biophysical change*: change in the characteristics of a natural resource, including soil, water, air, flora and fauna, resulting from a physical intervention.
- *Biophysical impact*: change in the quality (or quantity) of the goods and services that are provided by the biophysical environment, that is, a change affecting the functions of the biophysical environment.
- *First-order change*: change that results directly from the intervention.
- *Second- and higher-order changes*: changes that may result from the first order change through a causal chain of events or processes.
- *Landscape type*: a recognisable area with a consistent set of natural, semi-natural or managed resources — water, land, climate, and flora and fauna.
- *On-site impacts*: impacts resulting from a physical (or social) intervention that occur in the area where the intervention is conducted.
- *Off-site impacts*: impacts caused by a physical (or social) intervention, but that occur away from the location where the intervention is conducted, as a result of biophysical or social changes that influence distant areas. Off-site impacts are usually, but not necessarily always, second- or higher-order impacts.
- *Social change process*: a discrete, observable and describable process which changes the characteristics of (parts of) a society, taking place regardless of the societal context (that is, independent of specific groups, nations, religions and so on). These change processes may, in certain circumstances and depending on the context, lead to the experience of human impacts.
- *Human impact*: the effect resulting from social change processes or biophysical impacts, as experienced (felt) by an individual, family or household, community or society, whether in corporeal (physical) or perceptual (psychological) terms.
- *Direct human impacts*: human impacts that result directly from an intervention through social change processes. They may be the intention of specially designed interventions to influence the social setting (intended impacts, project goals, objectives), or may unintentionally result from the interventions (unintended consequences).
- *Indirect human impacts* human impacts that result from changes to the biophysical environment, affecting the functions that the environment provides to people.
- *Invoked social change processes*: because of the ability of people to act in response to perceived or real impacts, human impacts may in their turn cause other social change processes to occur.

Function evaluation in integrating SIA & EIA

References

R J Burdge and F Vanclay (1995), "Social impact assessment", in F Vanclay and D A Bronstein (editors), *Environmental and Social Impact Assessment* (Wiley, Chichester) pages 31–65.

Interorganisational Committee on Guidelines and Principles for Social Impact Assessment (1994), "Guidelines and principles for social impact assessment", *Impact Assessment*, 12(2), pages 107–152.

R S de Groot (1992), *Functions of Nature: evaluation of nature in environmental planning, management and decision making* (Wolters-Noordhoff, Groningen).

W T de Groot (1992), *Environmental Science Theory: concepts and methods in a one-world, problem-oriented paradigm* (Elsevier, Amsterdam).

F Vanclay (1999), "Social impact assessment", in J Petts (editor), *Handbook of Environmental Impact Assessment* (vol 1) (Blackwell Science, Oxford), pages 301–326.

F Vanclay, M van Schooten and R Slootweg (2001), "Social impact assessment", in C Briffett and J Obbard (editors), *Environmental Assessment in East Asia* (Institute of Southeast Asian Studies, Singapore, in press).

WCED, World Commission on Environment and Development (1987), *Our Common Future* (Oxford University Press, Oxford).

Conceptualising social impacts

Frank Vanclay*

Tasmanian Institute of Agricultural Research, University of Tasmania, GPO Box 252-54, Hobart, Tasmania 7001, Australia

Received 1 April 2001; received in revised form 1 November 2001; accepted 1 November 2001

Abstract

The conceptual framework based on environmental function evaluation of Slootweg et al. [Impact Assess. Proj. Appraisal 19 (2001) 19–28.] is used as the basis for conceptualising social impacts. Existing lists of social impact variables, such as those of the Interorganizational Committee for Guidelines and Principles for Social Impact Assessment, are examined and found to be inadequate and contradictory. A new listing of some 80-odd indicative social impacts is developed reflecting a change from project-based thinking to inclusion of the impacts of policies and programs, from thinking only about negative impacts to including positive benefits, and from thinking about unintended consequences to including intended consequences. The importance of differentiating between social impacts and social change processes is highlighted. Many of the variables typically measured in social impact assessment (SIA) studies are not in themselves impacts, but rather represent the measurable outcomes of social change processes, which may or may not cause impacts depending on the situation. Caution is expressed in the use of the list of impacts as a checklist. © 2002 Elsevier Science Inc. All rights reserved.

Keywords: Social impact assessment, SIA; Scoping; Social impact variables; Social indicators

1. Introduction

Ideally, the issues to be considered in a social impact assessment (SIA) study should derive from the scoping exercise conducted as part of the study. The

---

* Tel.: +61-3-62261804; fax: +61-3-62267450.
  E-mail address: Frank.Vanclay@Utas.edu.au (F. Vanclay).

social impacts likely to be significant will vary from place to place, from project to project, and the weighting assigned to each social impact will vary from community to community and between different groups within a given community. Since the factors to be considered in a SIA study should be determined in conjunction with input from the community, it might at first be regarded that there is little utility in having a well-developed list of social impacts to consider.

There are many arguments against the development of a checklist. At worst, a checklist would mean that charlatan consultants — those with little training in the social sciences (see Burdge and Vanclay, 1995) — may use the checklist instead of undertaking a proper scoping process. They may just use so-called 'expert judgements' to specify likely impacts rather than undertaking field work or involving the public in determining locally important issues. In the process of specifying impacts, consultants using a checklist approach may not properly think through the complex causal mechanisms that produce social impacts, especially the higher-order impacts or flow-on effects (Slootweg et al., 2001). Expert opinions often vary markedly from local community opinion about likely social impacts and the desirability of alternatives. Many SIA studies have substantially underestimated the social impacts that have been experienced by affected communities.

On the other hand, a comprehensive list of impacts may increase awareness of the full range of social impacts, and may lead to improved assessments as a result. There is also considerable demand for a generic list of social impacts. Cursory analysis of existing lists of social impacts indicates a high degree of inconsistency between such lists and internal inconsistency within many of the lists.

This paper reviews the literature on social impact variables and concepts, analyses consistencies and contradictions in the various lists of variables, and presents a new listing of social impacts, which was partly developed using the function evaluation framework for integrating social and environmental impact assessment as elaborated by Slootweg et al. (2001). While there has been an attempt at completeness, the social impacts listed are quite likely to exhibit various prejudices and biases. Other people — particularly those from other cultures and/or economic settings, economists and/or institutional development specialists — may well classify impacts differently.

2. Existing social impact variable lists

Many publications provide a generic classification of types of social issues that should be considered in SIA. Few publications include lists of specific social impacts. In these publications, social impacts can refer to quantifiable variables such as numbers of immigrants (newcomers), but can also refer to qualitative indicators such as cultural impacts involving changes to people's norms, values, beliefs, and perceptions about the society in which they live. Most social impact specialists stress that it is impossible to detail all dimensions of social impact—social change has a way of creating other changes. Further, most of the changes are seen as situation specific and are therefore dependent on the social, cultural, political, economic, and historic context of the community in question, as well as the characteristics of the proposed project and of any mitigation measures implemented.

The ambiguity associated with impacts, the lack of operational definitions for many constructs, as well as an asocietal mentality (Burdge and Vanclay, 1995), has led to a focus on investigation on measurable impacts (e.g. economic and demographic) and/or politically convenient indicators such as population change, job creation, or use of services (Gramling and Freudenburg, 1992). At the other extreme, Cernea (1994) complains that there have been some in-depth social analyses that have a tendency to become lengthy social overviews without any focus on the likely future social impacts. Mining companies have tended to favour these 'social monitoring' projects (see, for example, Banks, 1999a,b, 2000).

Attempts have been made by various social scientists to develop classifications of types of social impacts, but few have developed lists of specific social impacts, and fewer still have provided operational definitions of their variables. Amongst the classifications are the following.

Audrey Armour (1990):

- people's way of life—how they live, work, play, and interact with one another on a day-to-day basis;
- their culture—shared beliefs, customs, and values;
- their community—its cohesion, stability, character, services, and facilities.

Vanclay (1999), expanding Audrey Armour's list, has identified the following as important:

- people's way of life—that is, how they live, work, play, and interact with one another on a day-to-day basis;
- their culture—that is, their shared beliefs, customs, values, and language or dialect;
- their community—its cohesion, stability, character, services, and facilities;
- their political systems—the extent to which people are able to participate in decisions that affect their lives, the level of democratisation that is taking place, and the resources provided for this purpose;
- their environment—the quality of the air and water that people use; the availability and quality of the food that they eat; the level of hazard or risk, dust, and noise in which they are exposed to; the adequacy of sanitation, their physical safety, and their access to and control over resources;

- their health and well-being — where 'health' is understood in a manner similar to the World Health Organisation definition: "a state of complete physical, mental, and social well-being, not merely the absence of disease or infirmity";
- their personal and property rights — particularly whether people are economically affected, or experience personal disadvantage, which may include a violation of their civil liberties; and
- their fears and aspirations — their perceptions about their safety, their fears about the future of their community, and their aspirations for their future and the future of their children.

Juslén (1995) considered that a universal list of social impacts that would suit every case was not possible but argued that a checklist would be useful, especially in scoping. He identified several general impact categories:

1. 'standard' social impacts concerning noise level, pollution, and so on;
2. psychosocial impacts (such as community cohesion, disruption of social networks);
3. anticipatory fear;
4. impacts of carrying out the assessment;
5. impacts on state and private services; and
6. impacts on mobility (such as transportation, safety, obstacles).

In more general typologies, Taylor et al. (1995) identified lifestyles, attitudes, beliefs and values, and social organisation. Branch et al. (1984) highlighted community resources, community social organisation, and indicators of individual and community well-being.

Gramling and Freudenburg (1992) distinguish between six systems of the human environment:

1. Biophysical and health systems;
2. Cultural systems;
3. Social systems;
4. Political/legal systems;
5. Economic systems; and
6. Psychological systems.

The Interorganizational Committee on Guidelines and Principles for Social Impact Assessment (1994) included a list of social impact variables. These variables point to measurable change in human population, communities, and social relationships resulting from a development project or policy change. Rabel Burdge, a member of the Interorganizational Committee, produced a similar list (see Box 1), which has been subsequently modified in the 1999 revised version of his manual.

Box 1: Comparison of social impact variable lists of the Interorganizational Committee on Guidelines and Principles for Social Impact Assessment (1994) and Burdge (1994)

Interorganizational Committee	Burdge's List of 26
Population characteristics 1. Present population and expected change 2. Ethnic and racial diversity/distribution 3. Relocated populations 4. Influx or outflow of temporary workers 5. Seasonal residents	Population characteristics (demographic effects) 1. Population change 2. Dissimilarity in age, gender, racial or ethnic composition (ethnic and racial distribution) 3. Relocated populations 4. Influx or outflow of temporary workers 5. seasonal (leisure) residents
Community and institutional structures 6. Voluntary associations 7. Interest group activity 8. Size and structure of local government 9. Historical experience with change 10. Employment/income characteristics 11. Employment equity of minority groups 12. Local/regional/national linkages 13. Industrial/commercial diversity 14. Presence of planning and zoning activity	Community and institutional structures (public involvement) 6. Formation of attitudes towards the project (voluntary associations) 7. Interest group activity 8. Alteration in size and structure of local Government 9. Presence of planning and zoning activity 10. Industrial/commercial diversity 11. Enhanced economic inequities 12. Employment equity of minority groups 13. Changing occupational opportunities
Political and social resources 15. Distribution of power and authority 16. Identification of stakeholders 17. Interested and affected parties 18. Leadership capability and characteristics	Conflicts between local residents and newcomers 14. Presence of an outside agency 15. Introduction of new social classes 16. Change in the commercial/industrial focus of the community 17. Presence of weekend residents (recreational)
Individual and family changes 19. Perceptions of risk, health, and safety 20. Displacement/relocation concerns (perceptions) 21. Trust in political and social institutions 22. Residential stability 23. Density of acquaintanceship 24. Attitude toward policy/project 25. Family and friendship networks 26. Concerns about social well-being	Individual and family changes (cultural effects) 18. Disruption in daily living and movement patterns 19. Dissimilarities in religious practices 20. Alteration in family structure 21. Disruption of social networks 22. Perceptions about public health and safety 23. Change in leisure opportunities
Community resources 27. Change in community infrastructure 28. Native American tribes 29. Land use patterns 30. Effects on cultural, historical, and archaeological resources	Community resources (infrastructure needs) 24. Change in community infrastructure 25. land acquisition and disposal 26. Effects on known cultural, historical and archaeological resources

3. Analysis of the impact lists

The first observation in the analysis of lists of social impacts is that there is a strong reluctance by SIA researchers to provide variable lists, often because of a view that everything is always context dependent and therefore unique. The second observation is that where lists are provided, there are substantial differences both in terms of the range of impacts that are included and in the way that impacts are categorised or grouped. Many potential social impacts are entirely missing from the lists, there is a focus only on negative impacts, and impacts are described in ethnocentric terms. It is clear that there are wide discrepancies about what constitutes social impacts.

Although the Interorganizational Committee on Guidelines and Principles for Social Impact Assessment (1994) had a policy that impact assessments should focus on the things that count and not the things that can be counted, there does appear to be an emphasis in the Interorganizational Committee's list on empirical measures. A particular issue is that many of the variables in the Interorganizational Committee's list (and in Burdge's list) are not in themselves necessarily social impacts. Taking the first grouping of variables "population characteristics" from the Interorganizational Committee's list (see Box 1), for example, none of the five 'variables' listed constitute an 'impact' where an impact is an actual experience of an individual or community. Traditionally measured social impact variables like increase in population, increase in ethnic or racial diversity, relocation, presence of temporary workers, and/or seasonal residents are not in themselves impacts. Under certain circumstances, they will result in social impacts such as loss of community cohesion, fear and uncertainty amongst residents, fluctuating real estate (property) values, shortage of housing, etc., but if properly managed, these demographic changes might not create impacts. Whether impacts are caused will depend on the characteristics and history of the host community and the extent of mitigation measures that are implemented.

In the second grouping of impact variables in the Interorganizational Committee's list, i.e. Community and Institutional Structures, many of the listed indicators also are not in themselves social impacts. Rather, they refer to intervening variables that provide an indication of the characteristics of a community and whether the community is likely to experience impacts. The presence of voluntary associations, the size and structure of local government, and historical experience with change are obvious examples of this point. Local government and other formal organisations, as well as informal organisations such as community groups may experience impacts, but the actual presence of these organisations is not the impact.

It is obvious therefore that the list provided by the Interorganizational Committee is *not* a list of social impacts, but, rather, it is a list of indicators that should be considered in a study to provide information that could be used to determine social impacts that might exist in a particular community.

More distressing is the realisation that many social impacts are entirely missing from the lists. First and foremost are occupational health and safety issues. Many construction activities create danger to the community, as well as to workers (who may belong to the local community). Many projects alter patterns of daily life that expose people to risk. Death and injury are social impacts that can be the direct result of a project, for example, especially if a project increases the volume of traffic in a neighborhood. Many projects increase exposure of residents and/or workers to diseases, especially vectored diseases (e.g. malaria, bilharzias) because of changed ecological conditions. Social changes, especially relating to work practices (e.g. men away from home for work) may result in increased sexually transmitted diseases (such as HIV/AIDS). Tourism and its associated prostitution can also lead to increased spread of communicable diseases (Truong, 1990).

There is no mention of human rights. Violation of human rights is a social impact. Violation of human rights can occur when governments use force to allow a project to occur, or when public comment in opposition of the project is suppressed. Violation of the right of free speech occurs in developing countries, as well as developed countries. For example, in the USA, project proponents have threatened community activists with legal action over public statements they may make about a project. The use of so-called SLAPPS (strategic lawsuits against public participation) has the effect of silencing opposition (Beder, 1997; Canon and Pring, 1988).

While the Interorganizational Committee does include perceptions of risk, health, and safety as impacts, it fails to appreciate that actual risks are impacts, too. In restricting themselves to a small number of impacts, the Interorganizational Committee has not adequately represented the full range of social impacts, and they have trivialised some impacts. Clearly, existing lists of social impacts are inadequate, and there is need for a more comprehensive list. It is also clear that there is a strong Western orientation to the lists that have been developed. They demonstrate concern about individual property rights. Broader social objectives and goals of development are entirely missing from such lists. Despite the rhetoric of many SIA writers, it is clear that the lists of social impacts produced and the variables considered in most SIA studies relate only to the negative social impacts of projects. Positive impacts, the impacts of policies and programs, and the benefits, goals, or objectives of planned interventions are not seriously considered, despite rhetorical statements that they should be.

4. Definitions of SIA and associated conceptions of social impact

The inadequacy of many SIA studies derives in part from the lack of a regulatory agency definition of SIA and the lack of appropriate peer review of studies to ensure professional best practice. As a result, many studies have not been of a satisfactory standard and many have failed to consider the full range of social impacts that might be experienced. Consensus about a definition of SIA and an agreement about the variables that at a minimum need to be considered would enhance the quality of studies. It was this thinking that led to the establishment of the Interorganizational Committee on Guidelines and Principles for Social Impact Assessment in the USA and the production of its report in 1994. Anchored in the context of the National Environmental Policy Act (NEPA) of 1969, the Interorganizational Committee's report was not written in a general format suitable for adoption internationally. Burdge and Vanclay (1995, p. 32) modified the Interorganizational Committee's definition to be more generally applicable.

> Social impact assessment can be defined as the process of assessing or estimating, in advance, the social consequences that are likely to follow from specific policy actions or project development, particularly in the context of appropriate national, state or provincial environmental policy legislation. Social impacts includes all social and cultural consequences to human populations of any public or private actions that alter the ways in which people live, work, play, relate to one another, organise to meet their needs, and generally cope as members of society. Cultural impacts involves changes to the norms, values, and beliefs of individuals that guide and rationalise their cognition of themselves and their society.

However, this is not useful when considering projects in developing countries, when SIA needs to be considered more as "a framework for incorporating participation and social analysis into the design and delivery of development projects" (World Bank, 1995) and/or as "a process for research, planning and management of change arising from policies and projects" (Taylor et al., 1995, p. 1). Thus, SIA needs to be process oriented to ensure that social issues are included in project design, planning, and implementation, as well as ensuring that development is acceptable, equitable, and sustainable (Branch and Ross, 1997). The improvement of social well-being, with a particular focus on poverty reduction and an emphasis on democratisation, should be explicitly recognised as an objective of development projects and plans, and as such, should be a performance indicator considered in any form of impact assessment. Vanclay (2002, p. 388) expanding from Goodland (2000, p. 12) writes:

> SIA is more than a technique or step, rather, it is a philosophy about development and democracy. As such, ideally it considers pathologies of development (i.e. harmful impacts), goals of development (such as poverty alleviation), and processes of development (e.g. participation, capacity building).

With input from participants at conferences of the International Association for Impact Assessment, Vanclay (2002, p. 388), defines SIA in the following manner:

> Social impact assessment is the process of analysing (predicting, evaluating and reflecting) and managing the intended and unintended consequences on the human environment of planned interventions (policies, programs, plans, projects) and any social change processes invoked by those interventions so as to bring about a more sustainable and equitable biophysical and human environment.

SIA, therefore, is an umbrella or overarching framework that encompasses all human impacts including aesthetic (landscape analysis), archaeological and heritage, community, cultural, demographic, development, economic and fiscal, gender, health, indigenous rights, infrastructure, institutional, political (human rights, governance, democratisation etc.), poverty-related, psychological, resource issues (access and ownership of resources), the impacts of tourism and other impacts on societies. SIA is not limited to a narrow or restrictive understanding of the concept 'social.'

5. A framework for conceptualising social impacts

With a broad definition of social impact, it is difficult to delineate the specific social impacts that may occur in any situation. The integrated framework of Slootweg et al. (2001) identifies the pathways by which environmental and social impacts derive from specific projects (see Fig. 1) and assists in thinking about social impacts. Derived from the environmental functions analysis of R.S. de Groot (1992a) and W.T. de Groot (1992b) (see Slootweg et al., 2001), the framework separates a physical change to the environment from a physical impact, that is, a change in the functions provided by the environment (i.e. the environmental products and services). For example, a fluctuating watertable (a physical change) may or may not cause an environmental impact (change to the environmental services). The distinction between a change process and impact in physical environment encouraged a thinking about social impacts in much the same way. Many social changes are not in themselves 'impacts.' If 'social impact' refers to the impacts actually experienced by humans (at individual and higher aggregation levels) in either a corporeal (physical) or cognitive (perceptual) sense, then many impact variables commonly measured in SIA studies — for example, population growth, presence of construction workers, etc. — are not impacts, but change processes that lead to impacts.

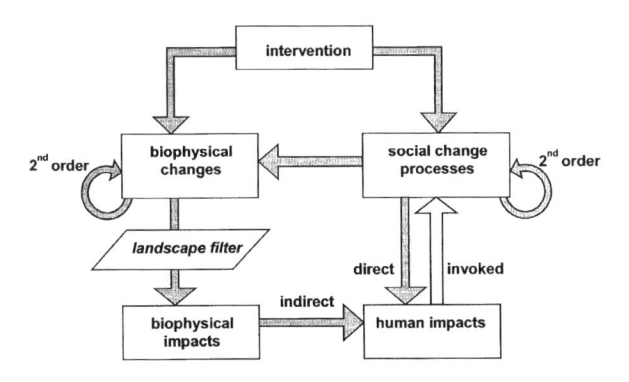

SOURCE: Slootweg, Vanclay and van Schooten (2001)

Fig. 1. Integrated framework for environmental and social impact assessment.

An increase in population, or the presence of strangers, are not the 'felt' impacts. Instead, the impacts that will likely result from these change processes are changed perceptions about the nature of the community (communityness, community cohesion), changed perceptions about personal attachment to the community, and possibly annoyance and upsetness as a result of the project. The ways in which the social change processes are perceived, given meaning, or valued depends on the social context in which various social groups act. Some sectors or groups in society are able to adapt quickly and make use of the opportunities that arise from the new situation. Others are less able to adapt (e.g. various vulnerable groups) and will bear most of the negative consequences of change.

To complete the interpretation of the figure, some explanation of the iterations and feedback mechanisms is required. Social change processes that result directly from the intervention, the so-called first-order changes, can lead to (several) other social change processes, the second- and higher-order change processes. For example, resettlement can lead to processes of rural-to-urban migration and changes in food production. In addition, the social experience of change (that is, the human impacts) can also provoke people to undertake other behaviour that leads to further social change processes. For example, the negative human impacts (experiences) associated with unemployment can activate the social change process of rural-to-urban migration in search of work. Social change processes can also provoke biophysical changes. Economic developments that increase the number of tourists in a particular area can have serious influence on land use and water quality, which, in their turn, can have indirect human impacts through a reduction in agricultural production and subsequently on income level for small holder farmers (Slootweg et al., 2001).

In the SIA literature, no distinction is made between the social change processes and the social impacts that are experienced. Social change processes are set in motion by project activities or policies. They take place independent of the local social context. Resettlement, for example, is a social change process, set in motion by, for example, the activity of land clearance (for a road or an agricultural project), or by inundation of an area by dam construction. Social change processes can lead to several other, second-order, social change processes. Resettlement can lead to processes such as rural-to-urban migration and changes in food production. Depending on the characteristics of the local social setting and mitigation processes that are put in place, social change processes can lead to social impacts.

Direct social impacts result from social change processes that result from a planned intervention. They may be the intention of specially designed activities to influence the social setting (intended impacts), or may unintentionally result from these activities. Indirect social impacts are a result of changes in the biophysical environment. Biophysical changes can affect the functions the environment provides for people. For example, if an activity causes land degradation, one of the biophysical impacts can be that the productive capacity of the land will decrease. The resulting reduction of income from farming activities is an indirect social impact. Biophysical changes can also have effects on disease organisms or disease vectors that lead to health impacts: An example is the introduction of irrigated agriculture. This leads to social change processes such as the creation of jobs and an increase in food supply. A direct social impact resulting from these social change processes is the raising of social well-being. However, the same activity leads to biophysical changes such as the creation of breeding sites for mosquitoes and snails, resulting in biophysical impacts such as increased transmission of malaria and schistosomiasis and, consequently, in the reduction of health (indirect social impact).

The framework presented by Slootweg et al. (2001) presents a useful way of thinking about the integration of social and environmental impacts and for conceptualising the full range of social impacts that are likely to occur from a given intervention. By following impact pathways, or causal chains, and, specifically, by thinking about the iterations that are likely to be caused, the full range of impacts can be identified. This makes the model a useful scoping mechanism and an heuristic aid.

6. Social change processes

It is impossible to identify all social change processes that could occur in any given project or amongst a range of projects and to particularly identify all the background social change processes that are taking place in society. While there are many social change processes, part of the problem of identification is also a lack of clarity about what exactly constitutes a social change process, and the level of detail at which these processes should be specified. Below are some examples of the social change processes that are important in SIA. This list is not complete, it is simply an indicative list of examples of social change processes. It is likely, however, that the categorisation of social change processes into a number of groupings of social change processes is appropriate and likely to be robust across a range of situations. The social change processes are likely to comprise the following groupings:

(A) Demographic processes (changes in the number and composition of people);
(B) Economic processes (relating to the way in which people make a living and economic activity in the society);
(C) Geographical processes (changes in land use patterns);
(D) Institutional and legal processes (relating to the efficiency and effectiveness of institutional structures including government and nongovernment organisations);
(E) Emancipatory and empowerment processes (increasing influence in decision making processes);
(F) Sociocultural processes (affecting the culture of a society); and
(G) Other processes.

6.1. Demographic processes

Demographic processes are those that relate to the movement and/or composition of people in the region(s) affected by the project. They include the following.

• *In-migration.* Rapid population growth can place strain on a local area in relation to a wide range of economic, social, and environmental issues. 'Boomtowns' — towns established because of, or which become affected by, rapid development — have many unique issues that need to be addressed. In-migration is not an impact in itself, but potentially leads to impacts such as inadequacy of services.

• *Out-migration.* Projects can also lead to a decline in population size where people move out because the area affected by a project becomes less desirable as a place to live, or because a project some distance always lures people in search of work. Decline in population (especially if associated with a changing demographic composition) can have profound effects on the viability and vitality of a place.

• *Presence of newcomers.* The social impacts of in-migration are exacerbated when the newcomers (new settlers) are different from, or perceived as being different from, 'old timers.' The physical presence of newcomers is not an impact because actual impacts depend on the impact history of the community and the nature of any mitigation mechanisms, as well as characteristics of the community and the newcomers themselves.

• *Presence of (temporary) construction workers.* Impacts are often different when the newcomers are construction workers or other project personnel who are resident in the project area on a short-term (or commuting/fly in, fly out) basis. The types and severity of impacts caused depends on the number, composition, and (dis)similarity of these 'project people,' as well as logistical arrangements and mitigation processes. As with newcomers, their presence will have impacts on infrastructure needs such as housing and health facilities, roads and shops — however, because of the temporary nature of their presence, many construction workers do not develop an attachment to place or affiliation with the local community, and construction camps may demand a range of services such as prostitution and alcohol outlets (and sometimes other drugs) that cause concerns for existing residents. The nature of construction and life away from home often leads to a 'work hard, play hard' mentality and can lead to lower levels of social control (and self control) than those usually expected in an adequately functioning community. There are also problems associated with the boomtown nature of construction camps — often, when they leave, the local community is left with an overcapacity.

• *Presence of seasonal residents.* Some projects, especially tourism-related projects, may lead to the presence of seasonal residents, that is, people who live for only some part of the year (perhaps summer or winter) in a particular region. In one sense, they may have legal rights as citizens to participate in decisions about the community, but they may also be profoundly different from permanent (year-round) residents. In some cases, especially in areas of southern France, Spain, rural areas of Italy, and beautiful places anywhere, the seasonal residents may be much wealthier than permanent residents and may come from different cultural backgrounds (e.g. from England, Germany, or The Netherlands). In other cases, they may be itinerant workers going from harvest to harvest in search of work and may be much poorer than local residents. In either case, their presence can lead to seasonal demands on infrastructure and can lead to changes in cultural and social values when the seasonal residents are socially and/or culturally dissimilar to the local population.

• *Presence of weekenders.* Similar to seasonal residents is the phenomenon of weekenders. This refers to the influx of people who do not live permanently in the community, but who regularly visit, say on weekends, and who may own property in the community. They may be different from permanent residents, and conflicts about issues affecting the community may develop. Because the primary affiliation of weekenders is to some other place, and because expenditure patterns and regional multipliers for weekenders do not augur well for economic activity in the community, projects that lead to large increases in the number of weekenders may cause social impacts.

• *Presence of tourists and day-trippers.* The presence of tourists may be seen as a source of revenue for local populations, but it can also lead to a wide range of social impacts, especially when the tourists are substantially different from local people. The range of services demanded by tourists means that the local community changes. Tourism can also cause local inflation or price escalation.

• *Resettlement* refers to coopted or coerced process by which local people surrender land for a project (such as dam) and are relocated elsewhere as part of a compensation package.

• *Displacement and dispossession* refer to the processes by which development projects and policies cause people to lose land and other assets, or lose access to resources, but for which they are not (adequately) compensated. The land lost may be their homes or agricultural lands, or other areas on which they are dependent for resources. Displacement may result in physical dislocation, loss of income, and other related processes and impacts such as impoverishment, social disintegration, etc.

• *Rural-to-urban migration.* Many projects accelerate the rate of rural-to-urban migration as jobs or social services become increasingly only available in the cities, or because of a growing perception of the attractiveness (lure) of life in the city (cultural hegemony). This form of migration has consequences both for rural areas (declining viability and vitality, changed demographic structure) but also for urban areas in that it creates areas of rapid housing growth, especially in the rural/urban fringe (periurban development), and may lead to large slum areas. Urban infrastructure becomes stretched because it cannot meet the increasing demand.

• *Urban-to-rural migration.* In many European countries with improved transportation and communication networks, many previously urban people are now choosing to live in rural environments, significantly altering the demographic and cultural characteristics of those areas.

6.2. Economic processes

Economic processes are those that affect the economic activity in a region including the way people make a living, as well as macroeconomic factors that affect society as a whole. They include the following.

• *Conversion and diversification of economic activities.* Planned interventions (projects and policies) may stimulate a process of change in the nature of economic activity from one type of production to other types of production. At the macrolevel, this might be from agricultural to industrial forms of production. At lower levels, it might be from subsistence farming to cash cropping. In the commercial sector, it might be from small family-owned-and-operated small holder businesses to larger companies with a workforce or employees.

• *Impoverishment* is the process by which certain groups in society experience a downward spiral of poverty, usually involving displacement (loss of land or access to resources and markets) and disempowerment (loss of power in decision making).

• *Inflation* is a process of escalating prices. It can occur at the national level as a result of macroeconomic factors, or it can occur at local levels caused by the spending power of increasing numbers of high-income people, which may arise through expansion of tourism, presence of imported workers, etc.

• *Currency exchange fluctuation (devaluation).* Changes in the exchange rates of local currency can have major effects on a community. Fluctuation itself creates uncertainty and a degree of hedging that can have profound effects on the economy and society including hoarding and shortages. Devaluation increases the costs of both imported and local goods (at least those that are potentially exportable). Commodities like oil become increasingly expensive, and this contributes to inflation generally.

• *Concentration of economic activity.* At the sectoral level, concentration of economic activity refers to the lack of diversification in the country as a whole — it refers to concentration of activity in a single industry. This makes the society and nation vulnerable to the fortunes of that commodity. At geographical scale, it refers to concentration of economic activity in a small number of places. This potentially leads to uneven economic development across the country. Sometimes, both sectoral and geographical concentration occur together, both at national levels (such as in Papua New Guinea with reliance on a very small number of mines, giving the mining companies a very large influence in the nation's affairs), and at very local levels when the phenomenon of boomtown or company town can occur. Boomtowns and company towns can have major influences on people's lives depending how they are organised.

• *Economic globalisation (conversion to global market-oriented production).* Globalisation — i.e. the incorporation of the local into the global — of the local economy is a multifaceted process. It means that economies change from being locally oriented to being globally oriented. This means that locally produced goods have to compete with imported goods (which may be cheaper). It also means that the focus of local production changes towards international markets instead of local or regional markets. This can have profound influence on the environment and on other activities. For example, the transition from traditional mixed agriculture to monocropping of cash crops, and the shift from payment in kind to payment in cash, may have serious impacts on households primarily dependent on agriculture.

6.3. Geographical processes

Geographical processes are those that affect the land use patterns of a society, including the following.

- *Conversion and diversification of land use.* Planned interventions may also lead to a change in the way land is utilised, both in terms of the area of land appropriated for a particular activity (extensification), the intensity of utilisation of the land (intensification) through the use of artificial inputs and whether there are areas of land not utilised for production, and in the type of land use activities and the pattern or mix of those activities.

- *Urban sprawl* is the expansion of urban areas into previously rural or peri-urban areas with associated land use changes and pressure on urban infrastructure.

- *Urbanisation* is both the process that promotes rural-to-urban migration, as well as the process of transforming smaller centres (towns) into more densely populated cities, resulting in a change in social relations of those who live there.

- *Gentrification* is the process whereby usually inner city suburbs become converted from lower class areas to middle or upper class suburbs. It has significant impacts on the existing residents, particularly the lower-income renters who may no longer be able to afford to live in what once might have been their community.

- *Enhanced transportation and rural accessibility.* Improvements in transport facilities result in increased accessibility, which results in various demographic changes. At a macrolevel (such as through improved air travel), it can mean increased tourism and the cultural consequences that flow from exposing new regions to tourism. At local levels (such as through improved ground transportation, e.g. better roads), it can result in the presence of newcomers, weekenders, or the development of rural areas as dormitory suburbs for the city. It can also result in telework where urban professionals conduct business from their country homes. In all cases, it means substantial change for the previously less accessible areas.

- *Physical splintering.* Infrastructure projects like highways, railways, transmission corridors, irrigation canals, and the impoundment of water can lead to the physical division or splintering of communities, which can lead to social impacts such as loss of social networks, loss of access to resources, and, in the worst cases, to displacement and dispossession.

6.4. Institutional and legal processes

Institutional and legal processes are those processes that affect the efficiency and effectiveness of various organisations that are responsible for the supply (and security of supply) of the goods and services on which people depend. These organisations include government agencies, nongovernment organisations, and the commercial sector. Important processes include the following:

- *Institutional globalisation and centralisation.* The incorporation of the local into the global in terms of institutions related to the loss of autonomy of decision making at the local level. Local organisations are increasingly required to do what central management dictates, whether or not what is being stipulated is locally relevant.
- *Decentralisation.* Somewhat as a counter force to institutional globalisation is the process of decentralisation, that is, of change from a centralised to a decentralised public administration system. This can lead to impacts on the workload at local community levels and to the adequacy of services.
- *Privatisation* refers to the process of transfer of responsibilities from the public to the private sector. It is often associated with the sale of state-owned enterprises.

6.5. Emancipatory and empowerment processes

Emancipatory and empowerment processes are ones that lead to an increase in the ability of local people to affect (contribute to) the decision making that affects their life.

- *Democratisation* is the process by which people are granted increased influence in political decision making.
- *Marginalisation and exclusion* refer to the processes by which various groups in society are denied access to services or to participation.
- *Capacity building* refers to increasing knowledge, networking capacity, and increasing skill base amongst local people.

6.6. Sociocultural processes

Sociocultural processes are those that affect the culture of a society, that is, all aspects of the way that people live together, including the following:

- *Social globalisation.* The incorporation of the local into the global at the sociocultural level refers to the change in the nature of the local culture, particularly as a result of the cultural hegemony of American cultural expression, often described as McDonaldization or 'Coca-Cola development.' American fast food competes with local food, American popular culture (music, cinema, dress) competes with local costume and custom. Many 'normal' Western products (including medicine and contraceptives) become locally available creating a challenge for the preservation of local culture and local values.

• *Segregation* refers to the process of creation of social difference within a community.

• *Social disintegration* refers to the dissolving or loss of social capital, the falling apart of social, cultural, and kinship networks, and the abandonment and lack of relevance of cultural practices. Cultures have well-developed systems that allow them to cope with a degree of change, provide survival mechanisms, and provide for the effective functioning of those societies. When change is too rapid, or when there are exogenous shocks with which the system cannot cope, there may be disregard for traditional cultural practices by members of society, which means that the culture does not provide the benefits it once did. This is a double bind, because there is an expectation by some members of the society that these systems should work, and because they were in place in the past, there are not alternative mechanisms to provide for those services in the present when those cultural practices are not adhered to.

• *Cultural differentiation* refers to the increase in the differences, or perceived differences, between various groups in a community based on cultural values, traditions, rituals, language, traditional skills, etc. This process of 'othering' creates division within a community.

In addition to the above-mentioned sociocultural processes is the issue of deviant social behaviour. Sociologically, deviant behaviour is a feature of a society and is therefore a part of the culture. It is well accepted that various planned interventions (projects) lead to an increase in various types of social behaviours that might be considered deviant or antisocial by some. It is rather more difficult to argue that an increase in these behaviours necessarily leads to cultural change. Nevertheless, these issues are important, because they cause division in the community. For example, many projects lead to an increase in prostitution. The presence of construction workers and tourists—in both cases, groups eager to utilise the services of prostitutes and with the economic means to pay for them—will lead to the movement to the area of prostitutes, or the supply of prostitution services by local women (and men). Prostitution, in itself, is not a social impact. However, prostitution can cause social impacts such as health impacts (through the spread of HIV and other sexually transmitted diseases). Prostitution may cause moral outrage, a range of gender impacts, and other concerns. It also provides economic opportunities and employment—which, in fact, can lead to further social impacts. Prostitution itself is not an (experienced) impact, but in this schema, it is considered to be a social activity (process) that leads to impacts.

Various other social behaviours are treated in a similar way, for example, alcohol consumption, legal and illegal drug use, other types of substance abuse (such as petrol, glue, and solvent sniffing), various types of risk taking behaviours, gambling, and vandalism. They can have serious impacts on the social and economic well-being of the community, as well for the individuals/ households involved. While these social behaviours can be caused directly by planned interventions and the impacts of these social behaviours might be avoided by good mitigation, these kinds of behaviour can also be a sign of social tension in the community as well as create social tension.

6.7. Other processes

The list of social change process given above is not intended to be complete and, in fact, it is argued that no list could ever be complete. New technologies and new social phenomenon continuously occur, and it is impossible to predict them and their likely social influence. For example, 20 years ago (and maybe even 10 years ago), who could have predicted the social impact of the Internet? It is always important to be aware that new processes are always potentially arising and that SIA theory and practice must never become stagnant. It is also clear that processes are not uniquely definable, conceptually clear, or mutually exclusive phenomena. They are theoretical constructions that provide explanation for what the observer is seeking to describe or explain. Thus, the types of processes identified by a particular theorist is linked to the purposes, objectives, and interests of the observer.

There are different levels at which social processes can be described. Some social processes are macroprocesses that entail many other processes. For example, in the SIA literature, there is often discussion of normalisation (see inter alia Brealey et al., 1988)—the process by which boomtowns become normalised communities. This is, in fact, a complex process that involves many subordinate changes, including demographic changes, economic changes, geographical changes, institutional and legal changes, sociocultural changes, and quite possibly emancipatory changes as well.

7. Social impact variables and concepts

In this paper, the need for a reconceptualisation of the nature of social impacts has been emphasised. Social change processes need to be differentiated from social impacts that are experienced or felt in corporeal or perceptual terms. The SIA literature has confused impacts and social change processes. While an overview of the social change processes that occur is given above, an outline of the indicative social impacts (concepts) is given below. It should be noted very strongly that this is not a checklist of possible impacts of any particular project, nor is it a list of variables or indicators. As repeatedly indicated, checklist thinking does not encourage the analytical thinking about the impact causing mechanisms that lead to impacts, especially the second- and higher-order impacts, and the indirect impacts. The variables that are important must be locally defined, and there may be local considerations that a generic listing does not adequately represent. In addition, any listing is a product of its author's conceptualisation about what impacts to include and how they should be described. A key factor is the level of detail that describe compound impacts. Given the interests, disciplinary backgrounds and allegiances of the author of this listing, it is quite likely to exhibit a Western bias and may not adequately represent economic and institutional impacts. The list was developed progressively by reviewing the SIA literature, SIA/EIA reports, and socioenvironmental impact statements, and by tapping into the practical experiences of SIA and EIA consultants including personal experiences.

The concepts that are presented are dimensions of the individual, family, community, and societal experience of social impacts and vary in their specificity. Some are macroconcepts that may be difficult to measure, while others may lend themselves to operational definition, variable creation, and measurement easily. For the purposes of this paper, however, the intention was only to expand or broaden the understanding of social impacts.

Social impacts must be experienced or felt. To be true to the broad definition of SIA used (i.e. Vanclay's, 2002 definition), the list of impacts must potentially be capable of addressing positive benefits, as well as negative ones. In addition, because social impacts (that is, *all* impacts on humans) cover a wide variety of issues, the list must be broad. Some impacts are experienced at the level of an individual, other impacts are experienced at the level of a family or household unit, and other impacts are experienced by social organisations, institutions, or a community or society as a whole. Some impacts are corporeal—that is, felt by the body as physical reality—other impacts are perceptual or emotional. Some macrolevel impacts are quite removed from individuals but nonetheless are important social impacts.

The conceptualisation of social impacts has been divided into seven categories. The categorisation is intended to provide a general grouping to assist in thinking about the range of impacts. It is accepted that others may well group impacts in different ways.

Box A: Indicative Health and Social Well-being Impacts

- Death of self or a family member – personal loss.
- Death in the community – loss of human & social capital.
- Nutrition – adequacy, security and quality of individual and household food supply.
- Actual health and fertility (ability to conceive) of family members.
- Perceived health and fertility.
- Mental health and subjective well-being – feelings of stress, anxiety, apathy, depression, nostalgic melancholy, changed self image, general self esteem (psycho-social factors).
- Changed aspirations for the future for self and children.
- Autonomy – changes in an individual's independence or self-reliance.
- Experience of stigmatisation or deviance labelling – the feeling of being 'different' or of being excluded or socially marginalised.
- Uncertainty – being unsure about the effects or meaning of a planned intervention.
- Feelings (positive or negative) in relation to the planned intervention – which may result in formation of interest groups.
- Annoyance – a feeling/experience such as due to disruption to life, but which is not necessarily directed at the intervention itself.
- Dissatisfaction (betrayal) due to failure of a planned intervention to deliver promised benefits.
- Experience of moral outrage – such as when a planned intervention leads to violation of deeply held moral or religious beliefs.

Health issues are social issues. Health impact assessment (HIA) (see Birley, 1995; Birley and Peralta, 1995) is needed as a process to identify the health impacts. While HIA professionals have a wide range of health indicators they consider, the dimensions listed are the ones likely to be important from a social perspective. Death is perhaps the most severe impact that can be experienced by an individual, and also has major consequences for other members of the family or household (both in terms of grieving and economic impacts if the deceased is a major contributor to the household economy). Death also has a community level impact in terms of the loss of human and social capital. It is often said that one of the greatest impacts of many projects is the uncertainty or fear associated with a project, and that the impacts that are perceived in anticipation of the planned intervention can be many times greater than the impacts that ultimately result from a planned intervention (Burdge and Vanclay, 1995). Somewhat related to this, although in an opposite direction, is that some interventions raise expectations about what will come, more jobs, more economic growth, etc. Quite a few interventions are accepted by many communities on the basis of a cargo-cult mentality. In these cases, usually the promised flow-on development does not occur. Proponents too often exaggerate the benefits of projects in order to secure approval. In one example, in a logging community in Australia, some 600 forestry jobs were promised by the company. Only 1 year later, only 34 jobs had eventuated with the company claiming that there had been technological improvements with new logging and wood processing technologies requiring less workers. According to a member of the local government (personal communication), the local community felt that they had been cheated. When there are heightened expectations caused by projects, disappointment, resentment, or dissatisfaction can result.

Other emotional concepts include the feelings created by being marginalised in society, such as through a process of the creation of social divisions within a community. People with strong views or moral codes may experience moral outrage as a result of certain projects or policies. For example, the legalisation of prostitution in Australia, and the creation of brothels in many local government areas, has caused a great deal of moral outrage amongst certain sections of the community. The placement of needle exchange services, used syringe containers, and discussion about the distribution of syringes and condoms in prisons has also evoked strong moral outrage. While planned interventions (projects or policies) are more likely to invoke feelings of upsetness or resentment, some projects or policies may create positive feelings. These feelings (positive or negative) may result in formation of interest groups, sometimes used as an indicator of the degree of feeling in the community about an issue.

Yet, another emotional feeling, especially for older citizens, is nostalgic melancholy. The experience of change and other changes in the community can lead to a situation where they dream constantly of the past, the "good old days." An issue in the mitigation of social impacts is whether there should be reminders of the past. This is particularly the case in resettlement. Reminders of the previous village can invoke feelings of nostalgia. On the other hand, like grief experiences, reminders of the past allow people to process their feelings and adjust better. In resettlement, especially where there is to be inundation or destruction of buildings, decisions need to be made about whether buildings need to be relocated. In some cases, for example, in the case of some towns that were inundated in the Snowy Mountains Hydro Electricity Scheme in Australia, whole villages (buildings and all) have been relocated. In other cases, villages have been submerged with perhaps only one or two significant buildings being relocated. A special consideration in the case of inundation is whether there will be protruding reminders of the village, such as church spires. It needs to be recalled that such protrusions can be irregular, such as at times of exceptional low water levels. The community needs to be consulted in relation to these matters. Some communities chose actively to keep such protrusions as a gentle reminder (and as a way of coping), others may choose to have buildings relocated or destroyed so that the reminders of the past are removed.

Box B: Indicative Quality of the Living Environment (Liveability) Impacts
- Perceived quality of the living environment (i.e. work and home environment or neighbourhood) – in terms of exposure to dust, noise, risk, odour, vibration, blasting, artificial light, safety, crowding, presence of strangers, commuting time etc.
- Actual quality of the living environment.
- Disruption to daily living practices (which may or may not cause annoyance).
- Leisure and recreation opportunities and facilities.
- Aesthetic quality – visual impacts, outlook, vistas, shadowing etc.
- Environmental amenity value – the non-market, non-consumptive aesthetic and moral value ascribed to a location or experience.
- Perception of the physical quality of housing.
- Actual physical quality of housing.
- Perception of the social quality of housing (homeliness) – the degree to which inhabitants feel that their house is their 'home'.
- Availability of housing facilities.
- Adequacy of physical infrastructure – impact on the existing infrastructure of the community (water supply, sewage, land, roads, etc.).
- Adequacy of social infrastructure – change in the demands for and supply of basic social services and facilities, such as education, police, libraries, welfare services, etc.
- Perception of personal safety and fear of crime.
- Actual personal safety and hazard exposure.
- Actual crime and violence.

A second major category of social impact relates to the quality of the living environment, or in other words, the liveability of the neighborhood and workplace. This category contains many of the variables traditionally considered in SIA and EIA studies. Some of these variables relate directly to the physical environment and in the Slootweg et al. (2001) model (see Fig. 1) come through the pathway from the biophysical impacts. Exposure to dust, exposure to noise, exposure to artificial light, exposure to odors, and similar issues could all be given as individual impacts but have been grouped under this single heading, "quality of the living environment." This macroconcept has both a perceptual dimension and an actual dimension. Because of the significance of one's own house as a place to live, concepts related to housing are also included, separate from quality of the living environment (which might be regarded as outside of the home). Housing indicators include adequacy of housing in the community, as well as perceived and actual physical quality of housing. In addition, a perceived social quality of housing indicator is included. One finding from rehousing projects is that even though the physical quality of houses may improve, many resettled people find that their new house is not 'home' anymore. This view is also one of the reasons why people are reluctant to move, even when compensation packages are generous.

At the community level, the adequacy of infrastructure, both physical and social, is a major area for potential impacts. Population growth, especially rapid growth, in a community can mean that the physical limits of existing infrastructure are reached. Town water supplies and the local sewerage system may not be able to cope with the increased demand. Social services and social facilities, too, may not be able to cope.

Also included in the liveability grouping is how people feel about their surroundings. Recreational opportunities near where they live or holiday, and the aesthetic quality of the places with which they are familiar are also listed under this heading. A final concept is of environmental amenity value, sometimes referred to as existence value (McNeely et al., 1990). This refers to the nonmarket, nonconsumptive value of a place or experience — in other words, the vicarious satisfaction experienced by people in relation to their knowledge about a place or object. Potentially, it also includes the moral or intrinsic values that may be ascribed to a place or species (as in the case of biodiversity protection) (Norton, 1988). These values can be affected by desecration of the place or by changed knowledge or meaning about the place. A forest that has been logged is no longer 'pristine.' A natural area that has a road put through is no longer 'wilderness.' A river that has been dammed or otherwise modified is no longer 'wild.'

Box C: Indicative Economic Impacts and Material Well-being Impacts
- Workload – amount of work necessary in order to survive and/or live reasonably.
- Standard of living, level of affluence – a composite measure of material well-being referring to how well off a household or individual is in terms of their ability to obtain goods and services. It is also related to the cost of living, and is affected by changes in local prices etc.
- Access to public goods and services.
- Access to government and/or other social services.
- Economic prosperity and resilience – the level of economic affluence of a community and the extent of diversity of economic opportunities.
- Income – both cash and inkind income.
- Property values.
- Occupational status/prestige and type of employment.
- Level of unemployment in the community – underutilisation of human capital.
- Loss of employment options.
- Replacement costs of environmental functions – the cost of replacing a product or service that was formerly provided by the environment, such as clean water, firewood, flood protection, etc.
- Economic dependency or vulnerability – the extent to which an individual or household (or higher entity) has control over economic activities, the degree of incorporation into larger production systems.
- Disruption of local economy – the disappearance of local economic systems and structures.
- Burden of national debt – such as the intergenerational transfer of debt.

Economic impacts and material well-being relate to the wealth and prosperity of individuals and the community as a whole. While employment opportunities, income, and property (real estate) prices might be obvious impact variables in industrialised countries, issues like workload — that is, the amount of work that is required in order to live reasonably — is more important in a development context. Some concepts can be quite complex. Income in some African villages, for example, might not be shared in the household, so a conversion to cash cropping that brings cash income to men, might not result in reduced workload for women. The gendered differentiation of income is considered separately in the group of variables dealing with gender relations. Property prices (real estate values) is also a complex measure. Rising property prices is not necessarily a social good. Rising property prices is only a personal individual good if this commercial value is to be realised through sale or through mortgage. In general terms, high property prices excludes locals (or the children of local people) from access to property. Certain rural areas, such as southern France, Spain, and Wales, are subject to land purchases by foreigners, thereby creating a local inflation of property prices. To restrict this trend, in the Peak District of England near Manchester, for example, regulations have been implemented to restrict settlement to genuine local people.

Another important impact, rarely considered in SIA, is the burden of national debt. When governments borrow money to build dams or for the construction of other major infrastructure, or to finance structural adjustment, it is easy to consider the immediate social impacts of the development project or loan itself. However, the money borrowed is a burden for future generations that must be repaid. That, too, is a social impact. When current pension schemes provide generous benefits for current older age persons but that are funded not from the contribution of those older age persons during their own lifetimes but from the contributions of currently working people, there is a potential financial burden on future generations, especially given the changing demographic structure of Western societies (Kotlikoff, 1992).

Box D: Indicative Cultural Impacts
- Change in cultural values – such as moral rules, beliefs, ritual systems, language, and dress.
- Cultural affrontage – violation of sacred sites, breaking taboos and other cultural mores.
- Cultural integrity – the degree to which local culture such as traditions, rites, etc. are respected and likely to persist.
- Experience of being culturally marginalised – the structural exclusion of certain groups because of their cultural characteristics, thus creating a feeling of being a second class citizen.
- Profanisation of culture – the commercial exploitation or commodification of cultural heritage (such as traditional handicrafts, artefacts) and the associated loss of meaning.
- Loss of local language or dialect.
- Loss of natural and cultural heritage – damage to or destruction of cultural, historical, archaeological or natural resources, including burial grounds, historic sites, and places of religious, cultural and aesthetic value.

Cultural impacts include all impacts (changes) on the culture or cultures in an affected region, including loss of language, loss of cultural heritage, or a change in the integrity of a culture (ability of the culture to persist). Cultural affrontage implies the violation or desecration of sacred sites, or the violation of cultural taboos. A commonly reported cultural impact, especially in relation to tourist areas, is profanisation of culture through the commodification of cultural (sometimes sacred) artefacts for sale to tourists, and the loss of meaning to those objects as a result.

Box E: Indicative Family and Community Impacts
- Alterations in family structure – such as family stability, divorce, number of children at home, presence of extended families.
- Changes to sexual relations.
- Obligations to living elders.
- Obligations to ancestors.
- Family violence – physical or verbal abuse.
- Disruption of social networks – impacts on the social interaction of household members with other people in the community.
- Changed demographic structure of the community.
- Community identification and connection – sense of belonging, attachment to place.
- Perceived and actual community cohesion.
- Social differentiation and inequity – creation of perceived or actual differences between various groups in a community or differentiation in level of access to certain resources.
- Social tension and violence – conflict or serious divisions within the community.

Family and community impacts includes impacts related to the family, social networks, and the community generally. A change to family structure is a major family impact that can be caused by the enticement away from home of young people, or by the periodic or long-term absence of adults for work. Various changes to life can cause disruption to sexual relations and to social networks. Changes in the community can affect perceived and actual community cohesion and the extent to which residents like where they live and/or feel that they belong there (community identification, attachment to place). The creation of social division within the community is a social impact, as is the creation of tension or hostility. Obligations to living elders or to deceased ancestors can also be problematic, especially where resettlement or physical splintering occurs. In some Asian cultures, the need to fulfil obligations to ancestors is a strongly held belief protecting one's own good fortune in the after-life, and this means that current or future material well-being (such as through compensation for resettlement) cannot be traded off against this obligation.

Box F: Indicative Institutional, Legal, Political and Equity Impacts
- Workload and viability of government or formal agencies – capacity of the formal institutions to handle additional workload generated by a planned intervention.
- Workload and viability of non-government agencies and informal agencies including community organisations.
- Integrity of government and government agencies – absence of corruption, competence in which they perform their tasks.
- Loss of tenure, or legal rights.
- Loss of subsidiarity – a violation of the principle that decisions should be taken as close to the people as possible.
- Violation of human rights – any abuse of the human rights, arrest, imprisonment, torture, intimidation, harassment etc., actual or fear or censorship and loss of free speech.
- Participation in decision making.
- Access to legal procedures and to legal advice.
- Impact equity – notions about fairness in the distribution of impacts across the community.

There is a range of impacts on institutions, such as regulatory agencies, those that lead to exceeding the capacity to cope with the extra workload that is generated by development activities. Many development projects are promoted by large corporations who have strong commercial interests in seeing their project approved with a minimum of delay and minimal conditions of approval. This creates a potential for the offering of bribes (graft) and other favours in return for favourable treatment. Individuals can have their legal and human rights violated, or be subject to intimidation or harassment. Governments may quell publication of opposing views or dissent in relation to a particular project. Protecting the freedom of speech is an important aspect of (social) impact assessment. Other times, higher level governments (or authorities) may overrule a local or state (provincial) government (or authority) and members of that lower government or authority and their constituents may feel that the principle of subsidiarity is violated. This principle, from the European Union, refers to the notion that decisions should be taken as close to the people that are affected by a decision as possible.

Box G: Indicative Gender Relations Impacts

❖ Women's physical integrity – refers to the right of women to be able to make informed decisions about their own body, health and sexual activity, having control over fertility and childbearing and child-rearing practices, and having the resources to implement those decisions safely and effectively, and to be free from coercion, violence and discrimination in the exercise of those decisions.
❖ Personal autonomy of women – the level of independence, self-reliance and self-respect in physical, economic, political and socio-cultural aspects.
❖ Gendered division of production-oriented labour – refers to the unequal distribution of workload between men and women in relation to production, in terms of cash cropping, subsistence food production, wage-labour and other household (cash) income strategies.
❖ Gendered division of household labour – refers to the gendered and uneven distribution of workload in relation to the maintenance of the household, that is fetching water and fuel, preparing food, washing, cleaning and decorating the house.
❖ Gendered division of reproductive labour – refers to the gendered and uneven distribution of workload in relation to the care and maintenance of household members, that is the personal burden of childbearing and childrearing.
❖ Gender-based control over, and access to, resources and services – including land, water, capital, equipment, knowledge, skills, employment opportunities and income, and services such as health facilities, education and agricultural extension services.
❖ Equity of educational achievement between girls and boys.
❖ Political emancipation of women – women's influence on decision making at household, community and society levels.

A recent World Bank (2001, p. 1) report on the role of gender in development began with the words "Gender discrimination remains pervasive in many dimensions of life—worldwide. ... In no region of the developing world are women equal to men in legal, social, and economic rights. Gender gaps are widespread in access to and control of resources, in economic opportunities, in power and political voice." Women tend to bear the largest and most direct social impacts. For these reasons, gender is a core social impact issue, and a development objective in its own right, requiring explicit consideration in the form of gender assessments (DGIS, 1994; Feldstein and Jiggins, 1994; Gianotten et al., 1994; Guijt and Shah, 1998; NEDA, 1997; Peiris, 1997). While all social impacts should be gender disaggregated — which means that there needs to be a separate consideration of the social impacts on women as well as on men — there also needs to be a consideration of the impacts on gender relations. To this end, eight dimensions of gender relations impact can be conceived, which cover the major areas in which gender differentiation takes effect, and each can be the focus of improvement. In undertaking gender analysis, it is important not to homogenise women. The social position and likely impact experience of women are different from men, but there is also diversity amongst women that also needs to be appreciated.

8. Conclusion

Despite rhetoric in SIA about considering the benefits of planned interventions, as well as the negative impacts, and about considering the impacts of policies and programs, as well as projects, it is clear given the variables typically considered in SIA studies and that comprise the variable lists of the Interorganizational Committee on Guidelines and Principles for Social Impact Assessment (1994) and others, that there is no consideration given to the indicators that would be necessary to describe the positive benefits of projects, or the different impacts that are invoked when the consequences of policies and programs are considered, as well as those of projects. In the list of social impacts presented, although still potentially inadequate and perhaps still affected by a Western cultural bias, there has been specific consideration given to expanding consideration from negative to include positive, from unintended consequences to include intended consequences, and from the impacts of projects to include the impacts of policies and programs.

The listing of indicative social impacts does capture most of the potential social impacts that are likely to occur across a range of planned interventions. However, while awareness of the list is useful for expanding awareness of the full range of social impacts, the list should not be used as a checklist. Because of the existence of second- and higher-order impacts, the complex iterative processes by which impacts are caused, and the complex impact pathways and causal chains, a thorough analysis using the conceptual framework of Slootweg et al. (2001) is advocated. Awareness of the local meaning associated with impacts is also important.

An important dimension of the conceptual framework is the separation of the concept of social change process from the concept of social impact. This is an important conceptual distinction not previously made in the SIA literature. It is clear that many previously measured SIA variables are not in themselves social impacts, but rather social change processes or intervening variables that might lead to social impacts under certain conditions, depending on the characteristics of the impacted community and of any mitigation measures.

Through a greater awareness of the processes by which impacts are caused, acceptance of the potential for a greater range of impacts such as presented here, and by utilisation of the Slootweg et al. (2001) conceptual framework, better scoping of SIA studies will occur, leading to better impact predictions. This will improve SIA and EIA studies, and potentially to better planned interventions and improved quality of life in affected communities.

Acknowledgments

This paper is a further development of collaborative work with consultants Marlies van Schooten and Roel Slootweg, which was funded by the Netherlands Ministry of Foreign Affairs and to be published as van Schooten, Vanclay, and Slootweg, "Conceptualising social change processes and social impacts," which will appear in *The International Handbook of Social Impact Assessment*, being edited by Henk Becker and Frank Vanclay and published by Edward Elgar. Anneke Wevers of the Ministry of Foreign Affairs is acknowledged for her role in initiating and supervising the initial project that led to our collaboration. I am very grateful to Marlies and Roel for involving me in the project and for challenging my ideas. In addition, I thank Annelies Stolp (of the Netherlands Ministry of Transport, Public Works, and Water Management) for the encouragement, perspective, and balance, and for being a sounding board. Many colleagues in the World Bank Social Development Department also provided input, but in particular, I thank Lyn Bennett for her specific comments on this paper. The usual caveats apply.

References

Armour A. Integrating impact assessment into the planning process. Impact Assess Bull 1990; 8(1/2):3–14.

Banks G. Keeping an eye on the beasts: social monitoring of large-scale mines in New Guinea. Resource Management in Asia Pacific (RMAP) Working Papers No. 21. Canberra: Research School of Pacific and Asian Studies, Australian National University, 1999a.

Banks G. Business as unusual. In: Filer C, editor. The dilemmas of development: the social and economic impact of the Porgera gold mine 1989–1994. Canberra: Asia-Pacific Press, 1999b. pp. 222–59.

Banks G. Social impact assessment monitoring and household surveys. In: Goldman LR, editor. Social impact analysis: an applied anthropology manual. Oxford: Berg, 2000. pp. 297–343.

Beder S. Global spin: the corporate assault on environmentalism. Melbourne: Scribe, 1997.

Birley MH. The health impact assessment of development projects. Norwich: Her Majesty's Stationary Office, 1995.

Birley MH, Peralta G. Health impact assessment. In: Vanclay F, Bronstein DA, editors. Environmental and social impact assessment. Chichester: Wiley, 1995. pp. 153–70.

Branch K, Ross H. The evolution of social impact assessment: conceptual models and scope. Paper presented to the annual meeting of the International Association for Impact Assessment, New Orleans, 1997.

Branch K, Hooper DA, Thompson J, Creighton JC. Guide to social assessment. Boulder, CO: Westview Press, 1984.

Brealey TB, Neil CC, Newton PW, editors. Resource communities: settlement and workforce issues. Melbourne: CSIRO, 1988.

Burdge R. A community guide to social impact assessment. Middleton: Social Ecology Press, 1994.

Burdge R. A community guide to social impact assessment (rev. edn.). Middleton, Wisconsin: Social Ecology Press, 1999.

Burdge R, Vanclay F. Social impact assessment. In: Vanclay F, Bronstein DA, editors. Environmental and social impact assessment. Chichester: Wiley, 1995. pp. 31–65.

Canon P, Pring G. Strategic lawsuits against public participation. Social Problems 1988;35(5):506–19.

Cernea MM. Using knowledge from social sciences in development projects. Proj Appraisal 1994;9(2):83–94.

de Groot RS. Functions of nature: evaluation of nature in environmental planning, management and decision making. Groningen: Wolters-Noordhoff, 1992a.

de Groot WT. Environmental science theory: concepts and methods in a one-world problem-oriented paradigm. Amsterdam: Elsevier, 1992b.

DGIS. Gender Assessment Study; a guide for policy staff. The Hague: Special Programme on Women and Development, Directorate General for International Co-Operation, Netherlands Ministry of Foreign Affairs, 1994.

Feldstein H, Jiggins J, editors. Tools for the field: gender analysis in farming systems research and extension West Hartford: Kumarian Press, 1994.

Gianotten V, Gorverman V, van Walsum E, Zuidberg L. Assessing the gender impact of development projects: case studies from Bolivia, Burkino Faso and India. London: Intermediate Technology Publications, 1994.

Goodland R. Social and environmental assessment to promote sustainability: an informal view from the World Bank. Environment Department Papers No 74. Washington, DC: The World Bank, 2000.

Gramling R, Freudenburg WR. Opportunity-threat, development, and adaption: toward a comprehensive framework for social impact assessment. Rural Sociol 1992;57(2):216–34.

Guijt I, Shah M, editors. The myth of community: gender issues in participatory development. London: Intermediate Technology Publications, 1998.

Interorganizational Committee on Guidelines and Principles for Social Impact Assessment. Guidelines and principles for social impact assessment. Impact Assess 1994;12(2):107–52.

Juslén J. Social impact assessment: a look at Finnish experiences. Proj Appraisal 1995;10(3):163–70.

Kotlikoff L. Generational accounting: knowing who pays, and when, for what we spend. New York: Free Press, 1992.

McNeely J, et al. Conserving the world's biological diversity. Gland: IUCN—The World Conservation Union, 1990.

NEDA. Gender and environment; a delicate balance between profit and loss. Working paper 1. Women and Environment. The Hague: NEDA, 1997.

Norton B. Commodity, amenity, and morality: the limits of quantification in valuing biodiversity. In: Wilson EO, editor. Biodiversity. Washington, DC: National Academy Press, 1988. pp. 200–205.

Peiris K. Weaving a future together: women and participatory development. Utrecht: International Books, 1997.

Slootweg R, Vanclay F, van Schooten M. Function evaluation as a framework for the integration of social and environmental impact assessment. Impact Assess Proj Appraisal 2001;19(1):19–28.

Taylor CN, Bryan CH, Goodrich CG. Social assessment: theory, process and techniques 2nd ed. Christchurch: Taylor Baines and Associates, 1995.

Truong T. Sex, money and morality: prostitution and tourism in South-East Asia. London: Zed Books, 1990.

Vanclay F. Social impact assessment. In: Petts J, editor. Handbook of environmental impact assessment, vol. 1. Oxford: Blackwell, 1999. pp. 301–26.

Vanclay F. Social impact assessment. In: Munn T, editor. Encyclopedia of global environmental change, vol. 4. Chichester: Wiley, 2002. pp. 387–93.

World Bank. Social assessment. Environment Department Dissemination Notes Number 36. Washington, DC: World Bank, 1995.

World Bank. Engendering development: through gender equality in rights, resources, and voice. New York: Oxford Univ. Press, 2001 (A World Bank Policy Research Report).

Frank Vanclay is currently a Principal Research fellow with the Tasmanian Institute of Agricultural Research at the University of Tasmania in Australia. Previously he was with the Centre for Rural Social Research at Charles Stuart University. A specialist on social impact assessment, he has also worked for the World Bank and was a consultant to the World Commission on Dams.

Assessing the social impacts of extensive resource use activities

Stewart Lockie[a]*, Susan Rockloff[b], Danielle Helbers[a], Maharlina Gorospe-Lockie[a] and Karen Lawrence[a]

[a]Research School of Social Sciences, The Australian National University, Canberra, ACT 0200, Australia; [b]Institute for Health and Social Science Research, Faculty of Sciences, Engineering and Health, Central Queensland University, Bundaberg, QLD 4670, Australia

(Received January 2007; final version received July 2008)

Extensive forms of resource use are rarely subject to detailed environmental and social assessment. This paper outlines a potential methodology for assessment of the social impacts of extensive resource use activities based on the Pressure-State-Impact-Response (PSIR) model of integrated indicator development. It then tests this methodology through a case study of changed water flow regimes in Central Queensland's Fitzroy River catchment. While resource degradation associated with interruptions to flow was expected to force all resource users to face higher costs and greater uncertainty, negative social impacts were particularly concentrated among vulnerable groups and downstream industries. Extension of the PSIR framework and methodology proved useful in linking social and biophysical research and would thus appear to offer some potential as a model for incorporating social concerns within natural resource decision making.

Keywords: integrated resource management; social impact assessment; social indicators

1. Introduction

Extensive forms of resource use, such as agriculture, fisheries and forestry are, as Duffy (2004, p. 175) states, responsible for enormous environmental impacts. This is recognised in "soil conservation measures, environmental farm plans, forestry practice codes, and fish harvesting limits and habitat management". However, in contrast with physical infrastructure projects such as mines, dams, industrial plants, etc, that produce point-source pollutants and other impacts, extensive forms of resource use are seldom subjected to systematic environmental analysis – they are the 'orphans' of environmental impact assessment (EIA) (Duffy 2004). Of course, if systematic evaluation of extensive resource use is the 'orphan' of EIA, social impact assessment (SIA) might be considered its 'poor cousin'. Despite some notable exceptions (see Powell and Jiggins 2003; Fenton et al. 2003), the application of SIA to activities such as agriculture, fisheries and forestry is rare.

The most obvious reason for this is the history of environmental and social impact assessment as natural resource management (NRM) tools applied to 'planned interventions' which propose to alter significantly the natural and social

---

*Corresponding author. Email: stewart.lockie@anu.edu.au

environment. This casts impact assessment as an anticipatory activity applied most frequently to the legislative approval of large development projects (Burdge 2004). No clear trigger exists in the majority of jurisdictions to initiate EIA or SIA in relation either to unplanned changes in resource use and condition or in relation to the cumulative activities and impacts of multiple resource users. One response to this limitation is the concept of strategic environmental assessment (SEA), which advocates more integrated assessment of the potential impacts of a wider range of policy and project options earlier in the planning and decision-making process (see Partidário and Clark 2000). SEA has gained a certain amount of traction among policy makers and has been adopted in some form by a number of international organisations and national legislatures including, notably, EU sectoral plans for agriculture (Chaker et al. 2006).

This paper seeks to contribute to efforts to conceptualise a broader role for impact assessment, in general, and social impact assessment, in particular, in two ways. First, the paper seeks to outline a conceptual framework and methodology for the assessment of social impacts relevant to the management of extensive resource use activities. These are based on an adaptation of the Pressure-State-Impact-Response (PSIR) model of environmental and social indicator development and reporting. Second, the paper seeks to evaluate this framework and methodology in terms of its ability to contribute to our understanding of the social consequences of changing natural resource condition in a predominantly agricultural catchment. The context for this lies in an exploratory case study of altered water flow regimes in a large agricultural catchment in Central Queensland, Australia.

2. Conceptualising SIA in relation to extensive resource use activities

The most influential definition of SIA is that put forward by the US Interorganisational Committee on Social Impact Assessment, which states that SIA is designed "to assess or estimate, *in advance*, the social consequences that are likely to follow from specific ... actions" including programmes, new policies, large projects, etc. (Burdge et al. 1995, p. 12, emphasis in original). Impacts themselves may be understood as any alteration to "the ways in which people live, work, play, relate to one another, organise to meet their needs, and generally cope as members of society", as well as "cultural impacts involving changes to the norms, values and beliefs that guide and rationalise [peoples'] cognition of themselves and their society" (Burdge et al. 1995, p. 11). The method that is proposed for identifying and measuring these impacts is a comparative one based on the use of *post hoc* studies of similar developments or policies instituted elsewhere to identify possible impacts at the site of interest (Burdge et al. 1995). International Principles for SIA developed more recently through a collaborative process involving SIA practitioners (see Vanclay 2003) reinforce the need to apply SIA in response to planned interventions, but seek also to reduce the emphasis on a specific method of impact identification, to stress the applicability of SIA to unplanned events and processes of social change, to engage more proactively with the entire process of development planning, and to consider the relevance of SIA to concepts such as sustainability assessment, triple-bottom line accounting and corporate social responsibility (Vanclay 2006), together with larger spatial scale management interventions.

This broadening of scope for SIA has stimulated a variety of conceptual and methodological innovations (see Becker and Vanclay 2003), some of which have been directed to extensive resource management contexts such as forestry industry restructuring (Fenton et al. 2003) and agricultural land management (Powell and

Jiggins 2003). The focus of the current study on alterations in a water flow regime suggested a need to articulate with integrated catchment management initiatives underway within the Fitzroy River Basin and with the natural resource monitoring and reporting programmes required of those initiatives (see Australian Government 2003). The research process used here was, therefore, based on an adaptation of the Pressure-State-Response (PSR) model already used widely for State of the Environment Reporting in Australia and elsewhere (Rapport and Singh 2006). This framework links pressures on the environment as a result of human activities with changes in the state, or condition, of the environment and with subsequent management or policy interventions. The model has been adapted in a variety of ways (e.g. the 'Condition-Pressure-Response' and 'Condition-Implications-Pressures/Response-Implications' frameworks) although the most important adaptation, for the purposes here, has been the expansion of the PSR model to include consideration of the impacts of changes in environmental condition on human welfare (Turner 2000, Turner et al. 1998, 2003).

The resultant Pressure-State-Impact-Response (PSIR) model has been adopted by a number of OECD (Organisation for Economic Co-operation and Development) countries and by the World Bank. By including the impacts of changes in environmental state indicators on social welfare it is possible to begin understanding and managing bio-regions as one co-evolving eco-social system while focusing the attention of natural resource managers and SIA practitioners on those social and economic issues of most direct relevance to NRM and avoiding those issues with little connection to natural resource management practice or outcomes. Put more simply, the PSIR model asks: What are the key features of this ecosystem? What causes change in those features? What does this mean for human communities? What should we do about it?

3. Methodology

Figure 1 illustrates the relationships between the methodological steps described below and the conceptual framework provided by the PSIR model. Identification of key resource use pressures and subsequent dimensions of environmental change, as described in Figure 1, were undertaken through:

- A desktop review of scientific reports, environmental impact statements and historical documents;
- Focus group interviews with representatives (6–8 per sector group) of a variety of sectors including heavy industry, agriculture, government agencies, conservation and natural resource management groups, tourism and economic development, Indigenous groups, and community services and education; and,
- Semi-structured interviews with scientists and stakeholders representative of the same sectors, but whom had not participated in focus group interviews.

Focus group and individual interviews focused on participants' perceptions regarding the most likely types and levels of resource use pressure facing the catchment over the next 20 years, threats to these scenarios, threats to the ecological and social health of the catchment and waterways, strategies to manage pressures and resulting threats, the distribution of costs and benefits among stakeholders, and any other relevant issues they wished to raise. Outcomes from this stage of the research led to a focus for the SIA component of the study on impacts associated

Pressure:
Definition: human activities causing environmental impacts.
Task: clarify type, magnitude & timeframe for resource use pressures on Fitzroy system.

State:
Definition: condition of key environmental indicators.
Task: identification of current & potential environmental changes associated with water flow regimes and likely magnitude of changes

Response:
Definition: legislative, government administration, economic instruments, community action, etc.
Task: communicate findings to relevant natural resource management groups and agencies.

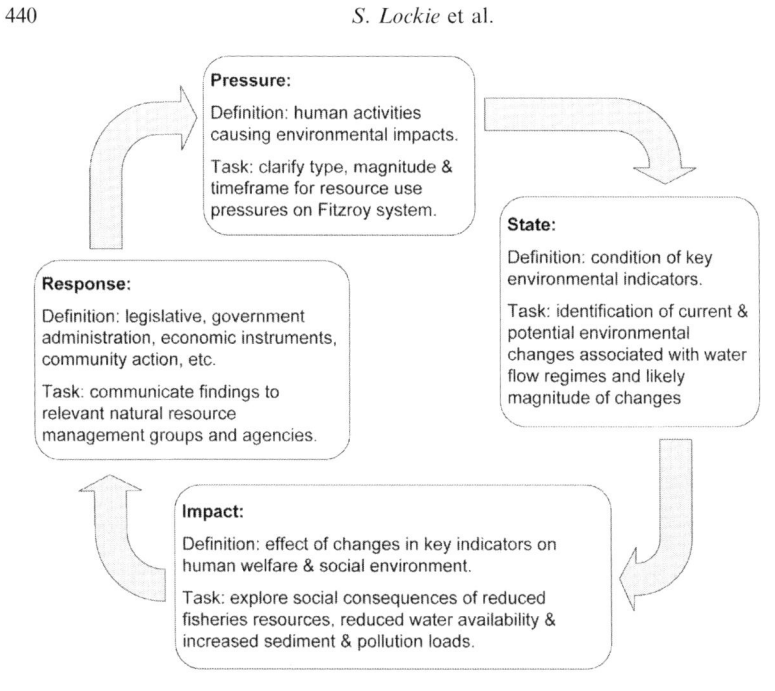

Impact:
Definition: effect of changes in key indicators on human welfare & social environment.
Task: explore social consequences of reduced fisheries resources, reduced water availability & increased sediment & pollution loads.

Figure 1. Conceptual and methodological framework.

with a reduction in the fishery resource, a reduction in the volume of water available for consumptive uses, and increased sediment and pollution loads due to altered river dynamics.

Identification of social impacts was based mostly on a series of over 30 semi-structured interviews with representatives of the various stakeholders affected as well as with scientists, natural resource planners, social service providers and sectoral groups. In these interviews, participants were asked to focus more specifically on the issues identified in the previous phase of research, to articulate what they saw as the distribution of costs and benefits among stakeholders, and to identify potential data sources with which to provide additional verification of the scale and distribution of impacts and to potentially underpin the development of indicators with which to monitor impacts over time. The reliance of the impact assessment phase of the research on stakeholder interview data highlights a limitation of the current study in that issues were identified during this consultative process that beg more detailed quantitative analysis and/or verification through use of other data sources. Nevertheless, the value of an exploratory study of the type conducted here lay in the ability to begin consideration of a wide and complex array of issues and to provide a forum for relevant stakeholders to share their own knowledge and perspectives.

4. Case study context

Covering a total area of 143,000 square kilometres, the Fitzroy River drains the largest water catchment in Queensland and flows into the World Heritage listed

Great Barrier Reef lagoon. The region's population is approximately 184,000, of which people of Aboriginal and Torres Strait Island descent comprise 4.2% (CQRPAC no date).

Located on the Tropic of Capricorn, the catchment incorporates sub-tropical, sub-humid and semi-arid climatic zones (Coastal CRC 2003). This leads to climatic conditions that are highly variable on both a spatial and a temporal basis. In the central catchment, annual rainfall ranges from 250 to 1400 millimetres, but usually falls in the range 500 to 800 millimetres (Coastal CRC 2003). Along the coastal fringe, average annual rainfall tends to exceed 800 millimetres, with years in which rainfall exceeds 1800 millimetres. Therefore, the entire catchment is characterised by a large number of years with significantly below average rainfall punctuated by sporadic and intense rainfall events. With hot daytime temperatures prevailing over the entire catchment, average evaporation exceeds average rainfall through the entire year, meaning that it is these sporadic and intense rainfall events that are responsible both for a significant proportion of overland and in-stream water flow and for the downstream ecological processes that are stimulated by these flows (e.g. fish breeding). While temperatures are generally not high enough to be destructive to plant growth (Coastal CRC 2003), evidence is emerging that mean temperatures are increasing and that this is associated with both decreasing mean rainfall and water availability (Miles *et al.* 2005).

Spatially, the dominant land use (approximately 90% of land area) within the Fitzroy is agriculture (Fitzroy Basin Association 2004). While most of the land area devoted to agriculture accommodates beef grazing, dryland and irrigated cropping, and irrigated horticulture are also significant land uses. Other major uses of land and water include forestry (6% of land area), conservation (6%), urban and industrial use including power generation and minerals processing (0.5–1%), and mining (0.4%) (FBA 2004). The coastal zone and estuary support a scallop, prawn and fish industry as well as tourism and recreation industries. This combination of resource uses affects the volume and quality of water flows in a number of ways including: point source and diffuse water pollution; groundwater accessions and withdrawals; the interruption of overland and in-stream flows; and extraction from the river system.

According to the Fitzroy Basin Association (2004), the highest risks to water quality within the catchment are posed by low levels of vegetative ground cover, rising water tables and soil salinity, intense episodic rainfall, seasonal variability, invasive plant and animal species, riparian and floodplain modification, wetland modification, coastal development, dams and weirs, water contaminants, and lack of understanding of Indigenous values. Medium to high risks include water extraction, cattle access to riverbanks, overfishing, land clearing, urban and industrial pollution and water flow management. Steps to address these risks have included state government-driven processes of water allocation planning, the introduction of market principles to water allocation pricing and transfers, restrictions on activities that impede the overland flow of water, use of fish ladders on major water impoundments, riparian revegetation, and detailed research on the level and source of sediments and other pollutants in the estuarine reaches of the river. Despite these steps, the FBA (2004) also identifies insensitive government policy and legislation, capacity to pay for improved natural resource management, lack of co-ordination and integration in resource management, lack of monitoring, and lack of producer and community involvement in research as additional risks to water quality.

In addition, while some individual policies and resource management activities have been subjected to social and/or economic impact assessment (especially in relation to the distribution of compliance costs among resource users), little consideration has been given to the social impacts of changing resource condition at a catchment level and outside the community of direct resource users.

5. Results

As stated above, the SIA component of the study was focused on social impacts associated with a reduction in the fishery resource, a reduction in the volume of water available for consumptive uses, and increased sediment and pollution loads due to altered river dynamics. It sought to strengthen the integrated approach taken by resource managers by making explicit the connection between the changed state of the ecosystem and human well-being. The social issues participants believed associated with these changes illustrate the importance of water flows for ecosystem and social health. The main social issues identified by participants included:

- Increased costs to agriculture, industry and domestic water consumers to access water, along with increased irregularity of supply (including restrictions on new developments and expansion of existing rural towns);
- Health and availability of fish and seafood resources for traditional hunting and fishing by Indigenous people, together with the continuation of cultural and spiritual practices;
- Development of higher rates of social pathologies from deterioration of community identity, bonds and social cohesion within Indigenous communities;
- Health and availability of fish and seafood resources to sustain commercial fishing activity;
- Recreational opportunities along foreshore, waterways and in-shore coastal areas;
- Attractiveness of the area and resources for tourism activities;
- Public health burden and human health decline from exposure to contaminated recreational waters and fish and seafood;
- Breakdown in social cohesion with conflict over access and the future viability of resources;
- Participation in the fishery resource changed through regulation and the resultant structure of the resource sector favouring larger operators and export markets; and
- Negative perceptions of the resource creating human health risk, environmental health and resource supply security concerns within the Indigenous community and broader community.

These issues are summarised in Table 1. Table 1 illustrates the relationships between secondary environmental impacts that arise as an outcome of changed water flow regimes, the social issues that are associated with those environmental impacts, the social impacts that comprise those issues, and the stakeholders who are most affected. For the purposes of Table 1, the only substantive difference between a social issue and a social impact is the level of abstraction. In contrast with the assertion made by van Schooten et al. (2003) (see also Slootweg et al. 2003) that there is a real

Table 1. Summary of social impacts associated with changes in water flows and quality.

Secondary environmental impacts	Social issues	Stakeholders affected	Social impacts
Reduced fish and seafood stocks	Reduced opportunity for recreational and commercial fishing of estuarine fish species → Shift in fishing activity to coast and offshore	Local community Fishers Indigenous community	• Altered system favours less desirable fish species above the barrage • Reduced fishing opportunities for communities above the barrage • Declining recreational fish catches • Significant change to amount of commercial fishing in Great Barrier Reef Marine Park • Changed river structure – no separate waterholes now for recreational use • Infrastructure affects traditional use of the river by Indigenous people (e.g. social gatherings, swimming and fishing)
	Conflict between commercial and recreational fishers over access to limited fishery resource and the sustainability of the resource	Fishers	• Negative public perceptions of commercial fishers (even though not all commercial fishers are large-scale operators).
	Changed access to fisheries resource in Great Barrier Reef Marine Park due to reduced fishery stock	All fishers but commercial fishers more affected Small commercial fishers and family owned businesses Local community Local fish/seafood retailers	• Controlled access to fishing areas and gear used • Bag and size limits reduce the recreational fish catch • Fishermans' Cooperative retail and wholesale stores sold to private businessperson and local buyers affected • Larger commercial fishery operators at an advantage as they export to overseas markets

(continued)

Table 1. (Continued).

Secondary environmental impacts			
	Social issues	Stakeholders affected	Social impacts
	Indigenous peoples' dependency on the river changes due to food and food sources being affected by sedimentation	Traditional Owners Other stakeholder groups due to established access and lack of understanding of traditional hunting and fishing rights	• Fishing closures of 2.5 months affect prawn fishers • Commercial fishers required to look for off-season employment • Fish effort indicates fisheries are in decline • Cultural connection and identity to food source • Social and economic reliance on fishery resource - estuary fish, turtle, dugong • Good health relies on fish and seafood as staple diet • Perceived health risk to consuming fish • Fish caught above the barrage are perceived to have poor taste • Community affected through health, breakdown in social structures, relationships with other stakeholders and Traditional Owner groups • Displacement of fisheries influences population shift to access the resource

(continued)

Table 1. (Continued).

Secondary environmental impacts	Social issues	Stakeholders affected	Social impacts
	Resource accessibility and use affected by crocodiles above the barrage	Recreational river users Indigenous community	• Shift of fishery activities puts increased pressure on other areas • Prevents use of the river for social and competitive sporting events • Presence of crocodiles deters use of river for recreation and social gatherings
Lack of accessible water	Competing interests for a limited water resource → need for equitable allocation of water use amongst current and future users	Local community Farmers Industry Mining Fishers Indigenous community	• Environment (flora and fauna) above Fitzroy barrage changed due to water extraction • Agriculture benefits with regular water supply • Licenses have low flow conditions on them reducing water available for extraction • Development increases demand for resources, population increases, traditional laws and culture of Indigenous people affected • Water supply for agriculture sector and urban areas affected
Sediment and pollutants	Increased pollutants, sediment and nutrients impacts on: (1) visual appearance of the river,	Local community Fishers Recreational users of the river and causeway	• Change in frequency of use of recreation areas • Effect on marine flora and fauna, with negative impact on diving

(continued)

Table 1. (Continued).

Secondary environmental impacts			
Social issues	Stakeholders affected	Social impacts
(2) blue green algae affecting recreational use, (3) marine habitat and fish and seafood stock and (4) water pollutants affecting human use and consumption	Irrigators Indigenous community Tourists Tourism operators/small businesses	• Decline in aesthetics of coastal beaches and river result in loss of tourist appeal and community use • Accessibility to river for boats and use of ramps • Blue green algae impacts on treatment process, cost of treatment and ability to treat available water • Fish kills from algae reduce fish stock • Water high in nutrients and sediment effected estuary and river resource (2–3 month shift in prawn inshore fishery) • Impact on fish habitat and spawning from runoff into estuary - low water flows, stagnant water and pollutants cause poor fish catch and low fish meat quality • Concern water quality impact on tourism – expectation of tourists and deter visitors • Impacts on water supply, affect tourism and local community, including farms supplying local markets

(*continued*)

Table 1. (*Continued*).

Secondary environmental impacts	Social issues	Stakeholders affected	Social impacts
			• Pollution from yachts, tankers etc in creeks and beach affecting use and consumption of fish • Indigenous people have limited recreational access/use of creek and lagoon and loss of meeting places • Indigenous public health issue – children get sore eyes and ears from swimming in creek and water not good for human consumption or use • Sediment is washed into river affecting the health and management of riparian zone • Shallow water levels prevent boating activities
	Access and use of recreational areas due to sediment deposit	Community Recreational fishers	

and fundamental difference between social impacts and other processes of social change, it is suggested that these differences are primarily rhetorical and make no claim that the categorisation of processes as issues or as impacts in Table 1 is anything other than a matter of convenience.

Figure 2 provides a pictorial representation – using the PSIR model – of how these social issues and impacts interrelate with the resource use pressures and key environmental changes identified in the first phase of research, as well as with some of the existing management responses. The remainder of this section discusses in more detail two of the social impacts illustrated in Figure 1 (namely, the effects of reduced fish and seafood availability and consumption and the effects of a decline in water quality on Indigenous hunting and fishing activities).

5.1. Effects of reduced resource condition and availability

Although there was some uncertainty among stakeholders regarding current levels of water quality and a view that, on a catchment-wide level, water extraction was not yet exceeding supply, the potential for negative impacts given both existing levels of development and projected climate change impacts was widely accepted. Reduced river flows and water quality due to water storage infrastructure, drought events and water extraction could be expected to affect the freshwater and marine environments as well as fisheries and other natural resources. In turn, these environmental changes could be expected to impact on the social environment by limiting resource access and quality, by reducing opportunities for cultural and recreational activities, and by creating human health risks.

It was generally accepted that the cost of access to water is increasing for agriculture, industrial users and domestic water consumers alike. It was also generally accepted that all water consumers faced increased irregularity of supply. Population pressures, irregular rainfall and more demand for water by industry (in particular from mining and irrigated agriculture), were placing increasing pressures on supply, thereby resulting in local governments having to restrict new development in rural towns. Some localities were experiencing almost constant water restrictions and had been forced to place moratoriums on particular developments until water pressures subsided. Nevertheless, some stakeholders believed that planning was geared primarily toward economic development without the infrastructure to protect availability of water supply in place to support that development in the long term.

For commercial fishers, it was secondary impacts associated with the effect of water resources on other ecological processes that determine, ultimately, the size and health of fisheries that were more at issue. Research has shown that a relationship exists between the frequency of periods of high freshwater flow in the river and the recruitment and growth of tropical estuarine fish including key commercial species such as barramundi (Staunton-Smith et al. 2004, Robins et al. 2006). Fishers believed that with heavy extraction from water sources and capturing of water before it reaches water courses, high flow periods were occurring less often and fish were triggered to move upstream to spawn less often, reducing the number of fish available. Furthermore, flushing events were occurring less frequently and so waters were more likely to become stagnant and experience problems with algae. Fishers believed that polluted water impacts upon the health of fish and seafood, especially among bottom dwelling species that tend to feed where the polluted matter is in highest concentration. When algae is prolific, it tends to reduce water oxygen levels

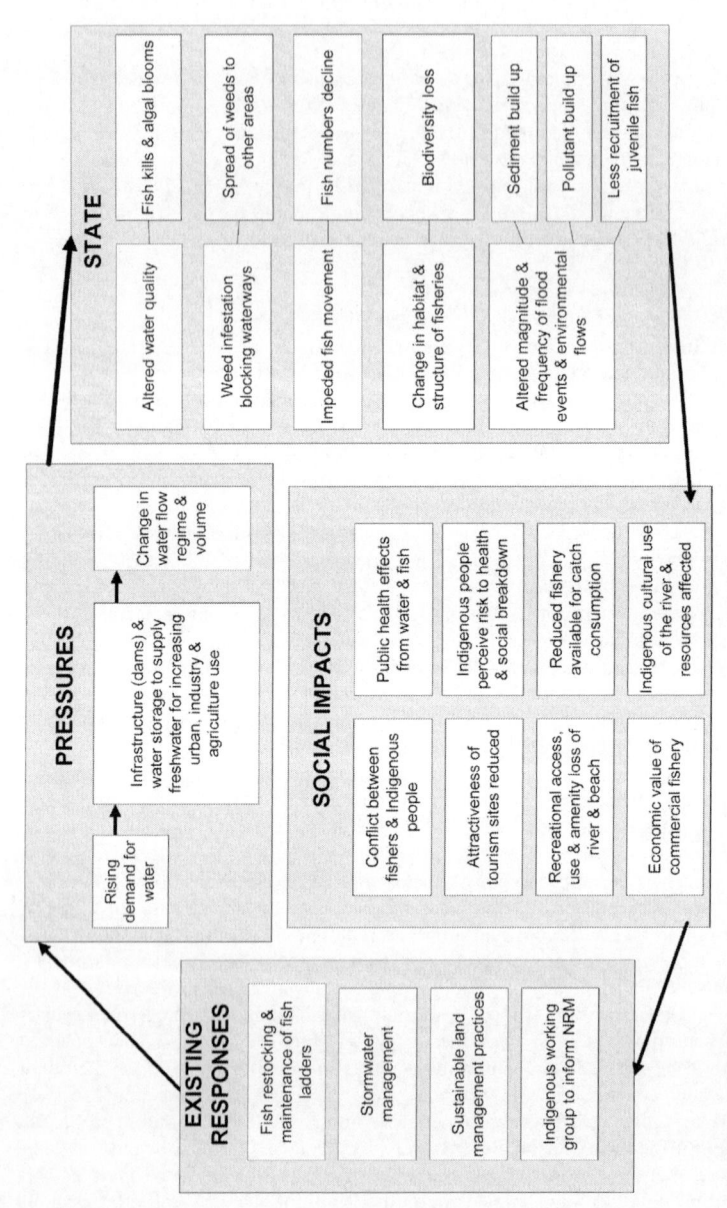

Figure 2. Relationships between changed water flow regimes, social impacts and management responses.

and fish will also die in these conditions. Therefore, fisheries resources were very much under threat, as were commercial operators, especially small operators. Small operators tended not to have more expensive equipment and had smaller boats that were not able to travel vast distances to access remote locations where fish were in more plentiful supply. This also puts upward pressure on seafood processors and the availability and cost of seafood to consumers.

For some stakeholders, the value of water resources lay not only in their economic use value (for irrigating crops or underpinning industrial processes), but also in their aesthetic and cultural values. For tourism and recreation businesses, for example, the impact of water resources on the physical attractiveness of the area was important. These stakeholders believed that high sediment loads entering the estuary and coastal zone were discolouring sandy beaches and coastal waters. Visibility was an important concern for tourist operators as the tropical fish are difficult to see in murky water, and tourists may be less satisfied with their experience. Furthermore, sediment coats the seagrass beds, mangrove areas and coral where fish and seafood feed. It can kill plant life and alter the accessibility, productivity and/or carrying capacity of nursery habitats, which will reduce the availability of food for fish and seafood and impact upon their numbers. Hence, it is in the interest of tourist operators that seabeds and coral remain healthy in order to ensure the sustainability of tourism in the local area.

For recreational users, additional problems were identified with the build-up of sediment on boat ramps (creating safety hazards) and in popular fishing locations. Further compounding these issues were changes to fishery zoning policy that were affecting access and use of areas. With reduced fish supplies, recreational anglers were tending to travel to more remote spots and purchasing more expensive equipment in order to successfully catch fish. Obviously, this places extra pressure on remaining fish stocks. However, it also creates additional safety issues with people travelling to sites where there is both a greater chance of experiencing dangerous conditions such as large waves and where emergency services are less accessible. Those without the equipment to travel to less isolated locations may simply engage less frequently in this particular recreational pursuit. Furthermore, in order to protect sites from further degradation, there were increasing regulations and restrictions attached to accessing places that may have been, in the past, favourite locations for fishing, picnicking or other activities. It was believed that sites that remained accessible were experiencing higher levels of traffic and use and were at higher risk of degradation.

With some resource users identifying the activities of other resource users as responsible for their own increasing costs of access – not to mention the uncertainties surrounding the future impact of climate change – many were concerned about conflict over resource access and viability and a resulting breakdown in social cohesion. These conflicts went beyond upper and lower catchment resource users. Recreational and commercial fishers were in conflict both over who was responsible for greatest fishing effort and how to manage ongoing access to the resource. Developers and residents were also in conflict. Coastal residents were concerned about population growth and development, which they believed changed the character of small towns, placed pressure on water supplies, promoted building that was insensitive either to other residents (e.g. by blocking views) or the environment (e.g. on low lying and flood-prone land) and rising costs of living. A number of management challenges had arisen in resolving these conflicts, not the least of which was arriving at fair and equitable outcomes in situations characterised by high degrees of uncertainty.

5.2. Effects on Indigenous communities

Aboriginal Australians have occupied the Central Queensland region for at least 20,000 years and today there are a number of Aboriginal nations and tribes in the region (Rockloff and Lockie 2006). In the coastal zone, these groups include the Woppaburra (part of the Darumbal nation) who traditionally inhabit the Fitzroy estuary and nearby coast and islands, and the Bailai and Goorang Goorang people of the Port Curtis area. Aspects of Indigenous cultural heritage relevant to waterway management include: protection of sites of cultural and spiritual significance such as eating places and art sites; access to resources such as waterways, land and fisheries for cultural and economic purposes; and rights as Traditional Owners to participate in decision making and management of natural resources. Importantly, it is both difficult and potentially misleading to draw firm distinctions between Indigenous peoples' cultural and spiritual activities and the seemingly more tangible aspects of economic and physical well-being. Seeing themselves as part of the land, Aboriginal people involved in this research saw processes such as sedimentation, pollution and eutrophication in the river and estuarine environments as significant threats to the health of their communities both directly (by degrading an environment they see as part of themselves) and indirectly (through reduced economic opportunities and consumption of contaminated seafood).

Access to ecologically healthy waterways for traditional purposes was seen by Indigenous people as vital to community well-being. Indeed, the simple opportunity for physical access was, even by itself, extremely important. Reduced flows caused by damming, changed water courses and over-extraction had both reduced access and led to the buildup of toxicants in various spots and fewer instances of natural flushing events as there were fewer occasions of higher flow. Indigenous people in the Fitzroy area have traditionally enjoyed a diet based heavily on fish and seafood; however, they feared their health might be affected if they eat these fish. Furthermore, they noted that the fish did not look as healthy. Various spots no longer had water and/or were unsafe for swimming and fishing.

Indigenous people believed that these issues of access, safety and health were associated with the deterioration of community identity, bonds and social cohesion within Indigenous communities. Indigenous people rely heavily on the health of the land, its waterways and the environment to sustain cultural practices such as stories, traditional fishing and hunting, traditional knowledge and the social structure of the various traditional groups. When water resources are degraded and changed then traditional knowledge and practices that are embedded in the health and vitality of these systems are lost and traditional relationships that are important to Indigenous culture are also eroded.

Elders in the Indigenous community have traditionally held powerful roles in their clans associated with their knowledge of medicines, hunting, care of the land, weather patterns, other foodstuffs, weaving and tools. The loss of an elder was always considered a tragedy to his/her clan as survival traditionally depended on that person's wisdom during times of crisis. Another important role of the elder was to teach the younger generations his/her area of expertise so that traditional knowledge was preserved; for example, where to hunt and fish, at what times, and which fish to catch and which ones to throw back. Often, such knowledge is embedded in traditional stories, myths and/or experiences that have been passed on from generation to generation, and which may also be based upon land formations and features in the area. When water resources and land formations are changed by human intervention, which had been the case in recent times, the knowledge of the elders becomes less relevant and their importance is undermined and devalued. Hence, elders' role in raising Indigenous youth and passing on knowledge, not only on traditional practices such as fishing and hunting, but also on traditional Indigenous values such as respect for self, family, elders and country are also impacted. With a changed social structure, is a loss of identity and changed family relationships that also fracture bonds between clans and lower self-esteem.

Stakeholder interviews conducted during the course of this research suggested that there exist a number of institutional barriers to more thorough consideration of impacts on Indigenous communities. Most natural resource managers and planners were unaware of impacts on Indigenous communities and tended not to recognise how their organisation could involve Indigenous people, or whether it was even appropriate to do so. This was slowly changing with regional NRM groups having designated regional Indigenous facilitators. However, some stakeholders felt that it was the role of organisations that provide services to Indigenous communities themselves to take responsibility for Indigenous interests. Often arrangements involving Indigenous communities and NRM exist separate from mainstream NRM activities, and the setting of regional targets for monitoring purposes neglects to encompass socio-economic indicators to cover Indigenous issues.

Without an understanding of social impacts arising from resource change, there is the potential to further marginalise and disadvantage these communities. For example, sites of historical and/or cultural significance that may be negatively impacted by NRM activities are common. Impeding the natural flow of the water has affected various waterholes along the Fitzroy that were traditionally used as popular gathering and recreational sites. Rarely are these sites known unless Indigenous people are consulted directly. Further, the significance of these sites to the public (and not just to Indigenous people themselves) is not often explored. Frequently, sites are lost or destroyed with little consideration to their significance at a regional or state scale because of the lack of information in this area. The cumulative effect of numerous small-scale changes to the environment across a region has the potential to have a major impact on the preservation of Indigenous sites and culture. Even when mitigation strategies are implemented in response to identified impacts there is no follow-up on the amelioration or management of these impacts on Indigenous people and communities.

6. Discussion and conclusion

Extensive forms of resource use such as agriculture and forestry tend to lack the clear decision points, approval processes and licensing conditions that typically trigger detailed environmental and/or social impact assessment. This does not mean that extensive forms of resource use are not subjected to any form of assessment or planning, but it does mean that even where management is organised at what appears to be a logical scale, such as the watershed or bioregion, significant challenges remain in dealing with the cumulative impacts of multiple decisions and actions (small and large) by large groups of stakeholders over an extended period of time. Connected to this problem is the inadequate involvement and consideration of those less visible or 'at risk' communities and groups already marginalised socially and economically. Within this context, the research reported here tested the proposition that SIA research and methods are most likely to be useful in extensive resource use contexts when applied in concert with other conceptual frameworks such as the Pressure-State-Impact-Response model of integrated indicator development and monitoring.

The exploratory study conducted here thus highlights some of the key social impacts associated with resource use pressures and changes in ecosystem health within a large agricultural catchment. In relation, more specifically, to alternations in water flow regimes, the case study suggests that:

- Even where the negative social impacts of natural resource management appear relatively minor, there is potential for those impacts to be concentrated among small and vulnerable groups. Indigenous groups, for example, in the Fitzroy Basin benefited little from the economic activities responsible for reduced water flows and quality, but bore substantial negative social impacts from declining access to waterways and the cultural and economic opportunities they offer.
- The viability of downstream industries, such as fishing and coastal tourism, is reliant on management activities undertaken upstream. While the economic impacts within the Fitzroy system of discrete land management activities on downstream fisheries have not been quantified, there was a perception among fishers and tourism operators that they were the 'victims' of larger and more powerful industries. Although there is debate over the extent to which this is actually the case, the absence both of detailed monitoring, and of planning forums in which all resource users have equal representation, has fostered conditions in which conflict between resource users appeared likely to escalate.
- Increasing costs of access to water resources, combined with increasing irregularity of supply, is likely to be the trend for some time. As the cost of resource access increases, some users will implement resource conserving measures in order to reduce costs (e.g. improved irrigation infrastructure). For others, however, less money will be available to implement improved management, and practices that do not save costs or improve productivity (e.g. fencing riverbanks) will not be undertaken without assistance. The issue of capacity to pay for NRM measures will, therefore, increase in prominence.

Translating these findings into meaningful natural resource management actions requires an extension of the work reported here in at least two ways. First, while the exploratory study reported here identified a range of issues that warrant ongoing consideration, the level of detail in which these issues were explored may be considered more appropriate to the setting of priorities for detailed investigation than to the finalisation of management interventions. This was particularly the case in relation to the social impacts of changes in ecosystem health. Despite the inherent uncertainty in predicting future resource use pressures and their implications for ecosystem health, stakeholders participating in the research were able to draw on a far more extensive body of knowledge on biophysical ecosystem processes when estimating environmental outcomes than they were when speculating on the social consequences of these outcomes. At the same time, it was evident that while some areas of social impact would have been amenable to greater levels of quantification than those achieved here (e.g. toxicant levels and health implications), others require a more collaborative and consultative approach between resource managers and impacted stakeholders (e.g. resource use conflicts and amenity values).

Second, translation of these findings requires closing the loop of the PSIR model through more detailed consideration and planning of management responses. Although this was outside the scope of the current study, the PSIR model of integrated indicator development offered a useful framework for the identification of social impacts that were demonstrably linked to changes in resource use and condition and, by implication, to changes in resource management practice. Using the PSIR model to link such assessment exercises with indicator development programmes appears to have some potential as a model for incorporating social concerns within natural resource decision making in a manner that avoids *ad hoc*, overly costly, and potentially inefficient, indicator selection and monitoring.

Acknowledgements

This research was supported by the Cooperative Research Centre for Coastal Zone, Estuary and Waterway Management.

References

Australian Government, 2003. *National natural resource management monitoring and evaluation framework*. Canberra: Commonwealth Government of Australia.

Becker, H. and Vanclay, F., eds., 2003. *The international handbook of social impact assessment: conceptual and methodological advances*. Cheltenham: Edward Elgar.

Burdge, R., 2004. Social impact assessment: definition and historical trends. *In*: R. Burdge, ed. *The concepts, process and methods of social impact assessment*. Middleton, WI: Social Ecology Press, 3–11.

Burdge, R., *et al.*, 1995. Guidelines and principles for social impact assessment. *Environmental impact assessment review*, 15, 11–43.

Central Queensland Regional Planning Advisory Committee, no date. *Central Queensland regional growth management framework*. Rockhampton: CQ A New Millennium.

Chaker, A., *et al.*, 2006. A review of strategic environmental assessment in twelve selected countries. *Environmental impact assessment review*, 26, 15–56.

Coastal CRC, 2003. *Central Queensland information paper*. Brisbane: Cooperative Research Centre for Coastal Zone, Estuary and Waterway Management.

Duffy, P., 2004. Agriculture, forestry and fisheries: the orphans of environmental impact assessment. *Impact assessment and project appraisal*, 22 (3), 175–176.

Fenton, M., Coakes, S., and Marshall, N., 2003. Vulnerability and capacity assessment. *In*: H.A. Becker and F. Vanclay, eds. *The international handbook of social impact assessment: conceptual and methodological advances*. Cheltenham: Edward Elgar, 211–230.

Fitzroy Basin Association, 2004. *Central Queensland strategy for sustainability*. Rockhampton: Fitzroy Basin Association.

Miles, R., *et al.*, 2005. *Climate change impacts and adaptations in the Fitzroy Basin area: report to the Australian greenhouse office*. Rockhampton: Institute for Sustainable Regional Development, Central Queensland University.

Partidário, M. and Clark, R., eds., 2000. *Perspectives on strategic environmental assessment*. Boca Raton: Lewis Publishers.

Powell, N. and Jiggins, J., 2003. Learning from participatory land management. *In*: H.A. Becker and F. Vanclay, eds. *The international handbook of social impact assessment: conceptual and methodological advances*. Cheltenham: Edward Elgar, 42–55.

Rapport, D.J. and Singh, A., 2006. An ecohealth-based framework for state of environment reporting. *Ecological indicators*, 6 (2), 409–428.

Robins, J., et al., 2006. Variable growth rates of the tropical estuarine fish barramundi *Lates calcarifer* (Bloch) under different freshwater flow conditions. *Journal of fish biology*, 69 (2), 379–391.

Rockloff, S. and Lockie, S., 2006. Democratisation of coastal zone decision-making for Indigenous Australians: insights from stakeholder analysis. *Coastal management*, 34 (3), 251–266.

Slootweg, R., Vanclay, F., and van Schooten, M., 2003. Integrating environmental and social impact assessment. *In*: H.A. Becker and F. Vanclay, eds. *The international handbook of social impact assessment: conceptual and methodological advances*. Cheltenham: Edward Elgar, 56–73.

Staunton-Smith, J., et al., 2004. Does the quantity and timing of fresh water flowing into a dry tropical estuary affect year-class strength of barramundi (*Lates calcarifer*)? *Marine and freshwater research*, 55 (8), 787–797.

Turner, R., 2000. Integrating natural and socio-economic science in coastal management. *Journal of marine systems*, 25, 447–460.

Turner, R., et al., 1998. Coastal management for sustainable development: analysing environmental and socio-economic changes on the UK coast. *The geographical journal*, 164, 269–281.

Turner, R., et al., 2003. Towards an integrated environmental assessment for wetland and catchment management. *The geographical journal*, 169, 99–116.

Vanclay, F., 2003. International principles for social impact assessment. *Impact assessment and project appraisal*, 21 (1), 5–11.

Vanclay, F., 2006. Principles for social impact assessment: a critical comparison between the international and US documents. *Environmental impact assessment review*, 26, 3–14.

van Schooten, M., Vanclay, F., and Slootweg, R., 2003. Conceptualising social change processes and social impacts. *In*: H.A. Becker and F. Vanclay, eds. *The international handbook of social impact assessment: conceptual and methodological advances*. Cheltenham: Edward Elgar, 74–107.

Part V
Theoretical Frameworks

[16]

Theory and Method in Social Impact Assessment*

Thomas Dietz, *George Mason University*

> Social Impact Assessment (SIA) is a method of policy analysis that offers great potential for integrating scientific policy analysis into a democratic political process. This potential has not been realized in large part because there has been no theoretical framework to guide SIA. In this paper I propose such a framework, using Habermas' (1970) pragmatistic approach to policy. The framework suggests heavy emphasis on use of SIA early in the policy process and on methods that emphasize impact identification and portrayal.

Over the last twenty-five years, scientific analysis has become a key element in debate about social and environmental problems. Research in the social and environmental sciences has helped identify and clarify many problems. But in addition to this research on problems per se, techniques of scientific policy analysis, including benefit-cost analysis, systems analysis, and risk analysis have become very influential in policy debates. These techniques are meant to rationalize the policy process, and thus, presumably, to improve the quality of the policies adopted to address social and environmental problems. Benefit-cost analysis was justified as a method of guarding against "pork-barrel" politics and enhancing the economic efficiency of public projects. Systems analysis was intended to eliminate unintended consequences and bottlenecks in public programs. Risk analysis was meant to target those hazards that may cause the most harm. But as critics of these techniques have noted, they may be invoked for political purposes (Hoos, 1983). Habermas, in particular, has argued that there are inherent tensions between the use of science in the policy process and democracy (Habermas, 1970).

In contrast, impact assessment, including technology assessment, environmental impact assessment and especially social impact assessment, while generally viewed as scientific methods of policy analysis, also have great potential for enhancing democratic participation in the policy process. Unfortunately, that potential has seldom been realized, and impact assessments have usually remained technical documents subject to the same criticisms as benefit-cost, systems and risk analyses (Schnaiberg, 1980; Meidinger and Schnaiberg, 1980).

In large part, I believe that the weakness of many impact assessments and in particular of SIAs, has resulted from a lack of a theoretical or conceptual basis for conducting impact assessment. The U.S. National Environmental Policy Act (NEPA) and a number of similiar international, national, state, and local laws have mandated impact assessments but have not provided clear conceptual guidance about how to do such assessments. Thus, while benefit-cost and risk analyses are guided by efficiency notions derived from welfare economics, and systems analysis rests on systems theory, impact assessment is done on an ad-hoc basis. Several volumes of SIA methods (McEvoy and Dietz, 1977; Finsterbusch and Wolf, 1981; Finsterbusch, Llewellyn and Wolf, 1984) have appeared in the last decade, but they apply traditional social analysis tools, including ethnography, survey research, social indicators and demographic analysis, without providing a framework to guide SIA. The best critique of SIA, offered by Meidinger and Schnaiberg (1980) argues for SIA as a means of enhancing participation but does not detail methods appropriate to that task.

In this paper, I shall attempt to provide a theoretical framework for SIA that emphasizes the potential of SIA as a mechanism of reducing the conflict between scientific policy analysis and democracy. Such a framework is critical for improving impact assessment practice. Only clear thinking about *why* an SIA is being conducted can lead to an appropriate choice of methods. And in turn high quality SIAs may help to reconcile the science-democracy conflict. I will begin by defining SIA and discussing current practice. Then I will discuss the practical utility of SIA, and, drawing on Habermas, discuss the potential of SIA for integrating scientific analysis with democratic process. These views on the purpose of SIA suggest the kinds of impacts likely to be important. After discussing these, I turn to practical constraints of conducting SIAs. Comparisons of practical constraints with potential leads to specific suggestions on the use of SIA and on ways of improving practice in the intermediate and long term.

What is Social Impact Assessment?

No definition is sufficient to completely delineate a mode of research. But a good definition can serve as a base for excursions into the underbrush of an approach to analysis. Those unfamiliar with the terrain will find that a good definition provides a clear map, while those with more experience will be able to see where a map is fuzzy and how the map provided by a particular definition differs from others, and therefore can use the definition to initiate discussion.

After offering a definition, I will briefly discuss several issues raised by it, including the nature of the impact assessment process, the importance of subjective and objective impacts, the definition of the event generating impacts, assessment of net rather than gross effects and boundaries on the impact assessment. In the context of discussing those issues, I will provide some suggestions regarding the scope of an SIA.

My favorite definition of social impact assessment is one which first defines social impact assessment, then defines social impacts. It was developed by Duncan and Jones (1976) and is discussed in Cramer, Dietz and Johnston (1980). A social impact assessment is defined to be the identification, analysis, and evaluation of the social impacts resulting from a particular event. A social impact is a significant improvement or deterioration in people's well-being or a significant change in an aspect of community concern.

By my definition, SIA is a process composed of three steps: identification, analysis, and evaluation. Methods will differ from one step to another. Identification of impacts requires imagination, creative thinking, and an understanding of the people being impacted and the social systems in which they live and work. Analysis assigns probabilities to possibilities uncovered in the identification stage and attempts to elaborate sketchy ideas, providing quantitative and qualitative data as appropriate. Evaluation integrates the information from the identification and the analysis into an overall image of the impacts resulting from the proposed action. Evaluation does not require the reduction of all impacts to a single dimension but does require a clear, informative display of data. The impact assessor may wish to provide an overall rating for a proposed plan, but the information on which such a rating is based should be as accessible to the reader as the summary judgment.

The definition includes two criteria for an impact: a subjective one and an objective one. Subjective impacts are those perceived by, or of concern to, those affected, whether or not an outsider finds those concerns realistic. Objective impacts are those considered important by an outside expert whether or not those impacts are of concern to those affected. Many SIAs consider only objective impacts. This is inappropriate. Outside experts will often minimize the importance of those social changes which are of greatest importance to those affected by a project. The result can be an assessment which ignores the factors which are most important to the development of political opposition to or support for a policy (Cramer, Dietz and Johnston, 1980).

The definition refers to an event. In many cases the event is the implementation of a policy and thus stretches over several years. Different stages of the policy may have different impacts, so the SIA must examine changes over time. In assessing the impacts of a policy, the analyst can assume that the policy will be implemented as proposed, or can construct what seems to be a realistic implementation scenario. Most analysts act as if policies are followed carefully, so analysts tend to examine only policies-as-proposed. This is necessary for an adequate SIA but not sufficient. Because practice can deviate substantially from policy, the impacts of practice may be very different from the impacts of a hypothetical, perfectly implemented policy. So the analyst should construct a realistic implementation scenario and indicate how deviations from the written policy will change impacts. If the analyst wishes to limit the assessment to the policy as proposed, he or she should provide convincing evidence that previous policies have been implemented as proposed.

All assessments are implicitly of net impacts, that is, of the impacts caused by the policy rather than of all social change. To ascertain net impacts, the future with the policy must be compared to the future without the policy. This may seem cumbersome, but impact assessment practice under the U.S. National Environmental Policy Act (NEPA) requires consideration of a "no project" or "continuation of current practice" alternative, so the assessment of net impacts does not add to the complexity of most impact assessment work.

The definition does not specify boundaries for the analysis. Boundary, or externality, issues are a problem for all modes of policy analysis. For example, in benefit-cost analysis, the discount rate reduces the importance of future events and thus delineates a time boundary. The economic effects of many policies are local, so the spatial horizon in economic analysis is sharply limited. SIA should not have comparable limits on the horizons of analysis. Regional, national, and global effects, and intermediate (10–25 years), long term (25–50 years) and very long term (50 + years) effects should be identified then analyzed and evaluated as carefully as possible.

Legal Status of Social Impact Assessment

While the definition and subsequent discussion deals with SIA in a generic, common sense way, current practice in SIA has been driven by the specific requirements of laws and regulations. In addition to the mandates of NEPA at the U.S. federal level, there are a number of state and local laws calling for SIA as part of general environmental impact assessment process or in response to certain kinds of proposed developments, particularly those with a "boomtown" potential (Atherton, 1977). In the last decade a number of international agencies including the World Bank and the Inter-American Development Bank have begun exploring the use of SIA as a tool in development planning. So far these efforts have produced some interesting experimental efforts but no large scale systematic use of SIA methods.

In contrast, SIA has been conducted on an ad-hoc basis in response to the requirements of various laws and regulations. In the U.S., the National Environmental Policy Act (NEPA) in Section 102(2) (A and B) requires federal agencies to "(a) utilize a systematic, interdisciplinary approach which will insure the integrated use of the natural and social sciences and the environmental design arts in planning and decision-making which may have an impact on man's environment" and "(b) identify methods and procedures . . . which will insure that presently unquantified environmental amenities and values may be given appropriate consideration in decision-making along with economic and technical consideration" (Atherton, 1977:9-10). This act and parallel laws at other levels of government mandate SIA without specifying its content. The court interpretations of NEPA make it clear that social impacts must be considered in the environmental impact assessment process, but they provide little guidance to the contents of social impact assessment or the methods appropriate to carrying out the assessment (Atherton, 1977; Freudenburg, 1986; Meidinger and Freudenburg, 1983). Most federal agencies have prepared in-house guidelines for preparation of SIAs as part of the environmental impact assessment process. But there is great variation in the methods used and in the utility of the information produced.

A Conceptual Framework

As noted above, the most important contribution of SIA to policy analysis comes from the ability of impact assessment to display the implications of a policy option in a form which generates focused, rational debate on the policy and diffuses rigid, single issue attacks. In evaluating a policy, a large body of research and conjecture on the current situation, the absolute and relative effectiveness and efficiency of alternate policies, and many other factors must be considered. Making a decision for one policy option on purely technical grounds would be a formidable task, but many important issues cannot be addressed with a technical analysis. Individuals within our society vary considerably in the value they assign to the consequences of alternative policies. These value differences, translated into the positions of various interest groups, lead to strong political pressures. Integrating the diverse values of the public with the information derived from scientific analysis is the key problem of policy analysis in a democracy.

Some ideas derived from the work of Jurgen Habermas provide a useful framework for understanding the problems of technical policy analysis in a democracy. For Habermas (1979:178-188) unconstrained communication is a requisite of democracy. A society is democratic if and only if all members of the society can participate equally in unconstrained discussions of political and policy issues. It is through this discussion that values come to bear on political and policy issues. This condition is difficult to meet when technical analysis plays an important role in the policy process (Habermas, 1970, 1971). Members of the general public lack the background to fully understand the details of benefit-cost analysis, risk analysis and other techniques. Indeed, specialists with technical training in one scientific discipline often cannot assess work done by analysts using the tools of a different discipline. Two problems for democracy result. First, parts of the discussion become unintelligible to non-specialists, so all members of a society cannot participate freely in debate. Second, because technical analysis is viewed as scientific, it carries great legitimacy in industrial societies. This legitimacy is a source of power for those whose position on a policy is supported by the technical analysis. Both of these problems are departures from the ideal discussion process used to integrate values into the policy process.

Under these circumstances, there are three modes that can be used to integrate values and technical analysis into politics. The first mode is a *decisionistic* approach which subordinates science to politics. Decisions are made in response to the pressures of interest groups and so reflect the product of the value positions of those groups and the relative power they possess. Scientific analysis has two functions in this mode. First, it can clarify the implications of a policy to the interest groups concerned and lead to some "fine-tuning" within the general policy selected on political grounds. Second, technical analysis may be used to justify decisions which are made on a political basis. But the critical decisions are not based on a scientific analysis. This mode of decision-making is problematic because it concentrates on a political balancing act, trying to reconcile a general mandate to promote the public interest with the positions of uncompromising special interest groups. The public interest is ill-served, because a rational overview of the impacts of a policy is not used in allocating resources.

In Habermas' *technocratic* mode of integrating scientific information and value questions, politics is subordinated to technical analysis. Decisions are made on the basis of the costs and benefits of policy options. Value questions and the political process are used only to legitimate decisions to the public. The current emphasis on using benefit-cost analysis to justify regulation is an attempt to promote technocratic analysis. Indeed, some advocates of scientific policy analysis explicitly question the viability of democratic approaches to decision-making. To quote John Kemeny, chair of the presidential commission which investigated the Three Mile Island accident:

> I've heard many times that although democracy is an imperfect system, we somehow always muddle through. The message I want to give you, after long and hard reflection, is that I'm very much afraid it is no longer possible to muddle through. The issues we deal with do not lend themselves to that kind of treatment. (Quoted in Dickson 1981:63-64)

There is a perception that the political process, dominated by special interest groups, has produced irrational and counter-productive policies and that the only resolution to this problem is to remove many key decisions from the political arena, leaving them to be made on wholly technical grounds.

For Habermas, the ideal mode of decision-making is one that integrates values and scientific analysis. He advocates a *pragmatistic* mode, where discussion by an informed public integrates values and scientific information. In this mode, all debate about policy is unconstrained, with no individual or group able to wield any power beyond the validity of their arguments. Policies are selected by the merits of arguments pro and con. Values are brought to bear through the debate itself, since arguments for and against a policy must reference the value structure of the debaters. And over time, community value structures will evolve in response to these debates so that there is a dynamic relationship between values and science.

Unfortunately, Habermas provides no guidance as to how societies may move from the current mix of technocratic and decisionistic modes of integrating science and policy towards a pragmatistic mode. A major problem with the pragmatistic approach lies in developing an informed public motivated to discuss a policy in a constructive way. The public has little information about most policies. The information that is available is presented in a form which is difficult to understand and which does not link the impacts of the policy to the everyday interests and experience of the public. The exception to this general condition occurs when interest groups publicize policy impacts. But this usually does not lead to informed discourse, because the groups will emphasize only those aspects of a policy related to their value positions. The result is a polarized public debate, where compromise and rationality are more difficult to achieve.

I believe that SIA can be an effective tool for informing the public, encouraging their participation in policy debate, and reducing disproportionate influence of special interest groups in the decision-making process. That is, SIA can be designed to make the mode by which science and values are integrated into policy closer to Habermas' pragmatistic ideal. SIA can translate all policy consequences into social consequences which are comprehensible and salient to the public. A rancher might not understand nor care much about the cost-effectiveness of a particular public lands policy. But he or she will understand and be concerned with the impact of a policy on his or her ranch, neighbors, and town. An Ohio steelworker won't care about or understand a loss of plant diversity in a section of range, but he or she may be concerned about a reduction in sightseeing or hunting opportunities. Broadening and deepening public interest and understanding can also depolarize debate. If a rancher's only source of information about a policy is the Cattlemen's Association, he or she will think only about the economics of the plan. If an SIA points out the consequences of alternative policies for ranch economics, hunting opportunities, and local service costs, the rancher will have a better view of the tradeoffs inherent in any decision and will be less inclined to support all or nothing positions.

SIA can also clarify the relationship between scientific information and values. When science subordinates politics or politics subordinates science, it is difficult to understand the line between fact and values. An SIA can clearly display all known impacts, the facts derived from scientific analysis. Then the values assigned to each impact in the process of making a decision are also clear. A policy may preserve a Native American burial ground but hurt the income of the timber industry. Another policy may destroy the burial ground but improve timber production. If each set of impacts is clearly portrayed, when a particular policy is chosen, it is obvious that the resource manager has valued the cultural resources over the economic productivity or vice versa. The SIA does not indicate which decision is best, but it does differentiate scientific or factual information from values or political judgments.

An outstanding example of the approach I am advocating is the Berger Inquiry into the proposed Mackenzie Valley Pipeline (Gamble, 1978). The inquiry provided a forum for public debate on the pipeline, sponsored well-publicized hearings, and provided funds to organizations interested in participating. The process was very successful at opening up debate on a large complex project. As Gamble (1978:951) concludes, the inquiry " . . . demonstrates that the obligation of the expert in industry and government is to expose, at a very early stage, the whole range of issues to the 'expert' scrutiny of all citizens. The citizens' input has now been shown to be essential to an assessment process." This general approach to facilitating public scrutiny and debate has also been used successfully in the evaluations of Community Development Block Grants (Kotz, 1981) and in the evaluation of proposed urban developments (Francis, 1975).

Implications for Practice

Benefit-cost analysis is justified as a means of increasing the efficiency of public resource allocations. This justification legitimates the use of benefit-cost analysis and guides its practice. SIA can be justified as a means of moving the policy process closer to a pragmatistic mode, a means of democratically integrating science and values. This justification will legitimate SIA to those concerned with the quality of public participation in policy and with mechanisms of conflict management. More important for the purposes of this paper, a pragmatistic view of SIA provides a conceptual framework for conducting SIAs. In this section of the paper I will examine some of these implications for SIA practice.

Integrating Impacts

Many analysis techniques translate all identified impacts into a single dimension. For cost-benefit and cost-effectiveness analysis, this translation is done by assigning market values. Multiattribute utility analysis uses an empirically derived utility function (Keeney, 1972, 1973), and some varieties of social impact assessment use measures based on the social well-being or quality of life (Freeman, Frey, and Quint, 1982; Olsen, Melber, and Merwin, 1981). All these techniques assign weights based on values to the various types of impacts, multiply these weights by a quantitative estimate of the magnitude of the impact, and sum over impacts to produce an overall assessment. There are two problems with these approaches. First, the assignment of weights is a value question which should be the subject of public discussion. But in most cases, the weighting procedure as practiced is highly technical, and its assumptions are not easily identified and debated. Second, the magnitudes of impacts are difficult to estimate and may be substantially in error. For example, economic and demographic models that are central to many impact assessments are very sensitive to the quality of input data and to assumptions they incorporate. Assumptions of structural stability over time in social systems are dubious, and baseline data are of poor quality. As a result, impact analysis based on economic-demographic modeling is very imprecise and may obscure more than it clarifies (Dietz, 1981; Meidinger, 1977). When quantitative models of this sort are used to estimate the magnitude of impacts the results may be little more than noise. But since the results appear scientific, the public may give undo weight to these analyses.

Some aggregation of values must be done before policy choices can be made. Quantitative techniques can aid the public and decision-makers in coming to a better understanding of a complex problem. My concern is that the imprecision and judgments inherent in these techniques can be masked by their technical complexity. SIA allows the use of a different approach to the problem of assigning and aggregating values. Emphasis is placed on multidimensional display rather than on developing a single evaluative criterion. For each policy option, all known impacts are exhibited. Detailed analysis of particular impacts, including estimates of magnitude, distributional characteristics, and importance to various subpopulations should be included in the display. But no attempt is made to aggregate across categories of project effects to form an overall, or net, assessment of a proposal. Each person reading the SIA is free to assign values to each category of impact, to debate those values with others, and aggregate them into an overall evaluation of the policy. By following debate the resource manager can learn about the weights interest groups assign to impact categories and the value positions taken by the group. This approach does not always lead to an unambiguous selection of one option over another, but it does clarify the issues and avoids the obfuscation which is inherent in many aggregation techniques.

Of course, it is not sufficient to provide an unstructured list of impacts, as is often done in SIAs. While such a list is preferable to hiding value judgments in an evaluative procedure, a simple list makes it difficult for concerned members of the public to understand how a proposed policy will change their lives. Care should be taken to discuss impacts in a fashion that educates and informs the public and sparks informed discussion. Unfortunately, there has been little research of impact display, in part because the goal of and audience for that display has been poorly defined (Johnston, 1975).

Impact Categories

The kinds of impacts that should be considered in an SIA depend on the policy being assessed. As a result, it is not useful to develop a general checklist of impacts. Indeed as I have argued elsewhere (Cramer, Dietz and Johnston, 1980), such checklists may be counterproductive because they limit imagination. But it is useful to consider briefly some categories of impacts that are important in almost all circumstances and that are often neglected.

Few, if any, policies produce costs and benefits that are identical for all citizens. Individuals vary in their ability to adapt to changes in resource allocation. A policy change which has minimal average impact may have an overwhelming effect on part of the population. Meidinger and Schnaiberg (1980; Schnaiberg, 1980) have noted the importance of focusing on distributional impacts, but their arguments have not yet had much effect on SIA practice. Disaggregating the impact assessment by location, income, occupation, and ethnicity will identify any groups who are disproportionately affected by a policy. This disaggregation, properly publicized, can motivate those groups with the most to gain or lose to actively participate in discussion of proposed policy, thus broadening the planners' understanding of the impacts on those groups.

Many public policies have moderate impact on the nation as a whole but have massive impact on local communities. Certainly any policy that involves construction of facilities or that changes allocation of resources to particular types of communities, such as those with military bases, colleges, etc., will have very substantial local impacts. Small communities and neighborhoods lack mechanisms for monitoring and influencing policy changes that affect them. SIAs should pay particular attention to such local impacts as a way to engage the community or neighborhood in discussion of policy. There is a body of research on "boomtowns" in rural areas that can guide the analyst in considering such local impacts (for a review, see Freudenburg, 1986), but more work on local impacts in urban areas is badly needed.

At the opposite end of the scale from community level impacts are impacts on the nation as a whole, the planet, and future generations. I have lumped these broad effects together under the term macro impacts. It is difficult to assess the impacts of a specific policy on the overall condition of the nation, the world, or future generations. Indeed, a single policy may have little impact in itself. But it may be representative of a set or type of policy whose cumulative effects are substantial. To insure adequate consideration of these macro effects, the cumulative impacts of policies of the same kind should be considered. It has been argued that this approach may place an unfair burden on a specific policy proposal, which is judged not on its own merit but on the basis of real and hypothetical policies of a similiar character (Gamble, 1978). If SIAs produced a single metric that aggregated all impacts, then the use of the proposed policy as a surrogate for all similar policies would be inappropriate. But a disaggregated SIA simply includes a cumulative "if we all did this" analysis as one of several views of project impacts. It is not, in itself, damning but may indicate unpleasant and otherwise unanticipated consequences for the nation, the globe, or future generations.

Practical Constraints

SIA methods must be frugal in their use of time, money, and technical expertise. Agencies have limited funds for planning and few social scientists with expertise in impact assessment, yet must prepare a large number of impact assessments in a short time. Techniques that work well when used by a team of specialists with long lead times may perform poorly in a realistic agency environment. To be useful, an SIA method must perform well when used with typical resource limitations.

Most agencies develop a diversity of types of policies. Some call for very little change from current practice. Others bring about massive, permanent change with significant regional and national impacts. SIA methods must be capable of examining many different kinds of plans and the multitude of impacts associated with them. If analytic resources were abundant, special methods might be developed for each sort of policy and type of impact, but since that is not practical, general purpose methods are required.

Since both subjective and objective impacts must be considered, an effective SIA technique must identify, analyze, and evaluate both sorts of impacts. Most techniques used today emphasize either subjective or objective impacts, so the analyst must compensate at the evaluation stage and attempt to integrate the results of various methods into a balanced image of the project which does justice to both subjective and objective inputs. It is better to use a set of methods which can integrate subjective and objective impacts from the start of the process.

An impact assessment tool should be frugal of time, money, and expertise yet be flexible enough to integrate a wide range of impacts. These demands can be met by using techniques which emphasize impact identification over analysis and evaluation. Analysis and evaluation of a list of impacts which does not include all important consequences of a plan will not yield an adequate assessment. But a list of impacts from a careful identification process can often serve as a full impact assessment. If all salient impacts are identified and are sufficiently disaggregated that individuals can understand how they will be affected, the resulting debate about the policy can generate much of the information which would result from staff analysis and evaluation. This is not to suggest that the analysis and evaluation processes are unimportant. But an impact assessment process should concentrate resources on careful identification.

Timing

SIA is usually conducted at the end of the planning process. By the time social consequences are examined in a systematic way, only a few alternatives are being considered. This has the advantage of simplifying the analytical task to be accomplished, but it also minimizes the usefulness of SIA. Most environmental impact studies give the impression that decisions have been made long before the impact analysis was finished and that public debate is intended to make marginal changes in policy rather than develop policy. Because impact assessments are irrelevant to decisions, they are a low priority activity. Because there are few resources expended on impact assessment, the resulting impact statements are dull *pro forma* documents that provide little significant new information about the project. This in turn reinforces the position that impact assessments are more or less useless and that scarce agency resources should be devoted to other parts of the planning process.

For SIA to realize its potential, it must be integrated into the planning process at a point at which the impact assessment and the public discussion it generates can actually influence decisions. First, SIA should be used to identify issues at the beginning of the process. SIA can be used to generate general information to identify key impacts that would result from a continuation of current practice. The impacts identified are the social issues that should be considered in developing policy. Then SIA should be used in formulating alternative plans. Since early plans are vague and include rather crude analyses, planners are defensive about them and reluctant to share them with a wide audience. I suggest that an in-house abbreviated SIA be conducted on sketch plans. Informal but systematic procedures can produce information that is very useful in improving plans. This approach to SIA can be viewed as one step in the preparation of a draft plan rather than a formal evaluation of the draft.

After several iterations, a tentative set of policy plans emerge and must be scrutinized by other organizations and the public. An SIA on each proposed alternative should be completed before public release of the plan and presented with it. This is, in essence, the environmental impact assessment process. Again, it is critical that assessment be done early enough to have an impact on decision-making. The SIA should emphasize open options and should clearly indicate what actions have already been dropped from consideration.

Specific Tools

As I noted in the beginning of the paper, each step in the impact assessment process requires its own methods. One weakness of current practice is that it emphasizes tools for analyzing impacts without giving sufficient attention to impact identification. Instead, impact identification tools that are frugal, flexible, and able to deal with both objective and subjective impacts should be used. Previous work with planning and development agencies have shown that a structured group process, using panels of experts, can meet all these requirements (Cramer, Dietz and Johnston, 1980; Dietz, 1984; Dietz and Pfund, 1983). The panels are inexpensive to run, requiring only a small amount of staff time. The panels are flexible because their composition can be changed to reflect the local, regional, and national concerns most important in considering a given policy and because the members can think through general statements in a plan or even the rough ideas in a sketch plan. By structuring the panels to include both technical experts and individuals familiar with the local setting, both subjective and objective impacts can be identified. The panels can also develop priorities for focusing limited staff resources on analysis of the most important, least understood impacts. The panels can develop a summary evaluation of impacts. A technique for using expert panels in SIA is described in Dietz (1984). It should be noted that the use of expert panels for SIA requires careful training of the staff who will be leading the panels. Effective training will make the difference between a useful, creative SIA process and a pointless and frustrating procedure.

An emphasis on impact identification does not reduce the importance of analysis and evaluation. Most agencies do not have the resources to conduct an extensive analysis for all social impact statements. In most situations, the analysis phase must be restricted to a few site visits, an examination of secondary statistics, and a review of the published literature on the sort of impact identified. This work can provide new insights, particularly if it is focused on a few salient impacts.

Goals for the evaluation phase should also keep practical constraints in mind. A clear and graphic display of impacts, broken down by areas and groups impacted and accompanied by importance ratings from the panels, can facilitate public discussion. More elaborate approaches to analysis and evaluation should be deferred until there is a significant increase in research on socal impacts and social impact methods.

Long Range Considerations

There are four information needs that must be met to improve SIA practice. First, agencies should begin a program to monitor the social consequences of policies already in effect. This sort of basic evaluation study provides the data critical to all other SIA work. Second, methodological studies should be conducted to determine how well SIA methods perform in practice and what kinds of SIA techniques have been most effective in improving policy. Third, careful *ex post facto* impact assessments should be carried out to improve basic knowledge about the most important and common consequences of policies. Fourth, experience in public participation and mediation should be used to develop better methods for impact display. SIA is a new field. Its potential contribution to rational policy-making is great, but that potential can be realized only if an investment is made in improving the data base and techniques available for SIA.

Conclusion

Jefferson once wrote that "whenever people are well informed they can be trusted with their own government." I view SIA as a tool for making citizens better informed about complex policies. Working from that perspective, this paper sketches some thoughts on how the Social Impact Assessment can be used in the policy process. I hope that it is of practical value and that it also contributes to fruitful discussions of the tensions between science and values in a democratic society.

ENDNOTES

*The ideas presented here were developed in part while preparing a paper on social impact assessment in rangelands management for the U.S. National Research Council (Dietz, 1984). I thank C. Orsburn, R. Frey, S. Groth, R. Johnston, A. Kasper, P. Stern, S. Schwartz, W. Freudenburg, Sociological Inquiry's anonymous reviewers, and especially J. Cramer for comments and the Graduate School of George Mason University for research support.

REFERENCES

Atherton, C. C.
    1977   "Legal requirements for environmental impact reporting." Pp. 9–64 in J. McEvoy and T. Dietz (eds.), Handbook for Environmental Planning. New York: Wiley-Interscience.

Cramer, J. C., T. Dietz, and R. A. Johnston
    1980   "Social impact assessment of regional plans: A review of methods and issues and a recommended process." Policy Science 12:61-82.

Dickson, D.
    1981   "Limiting democracy: Technocrats and the liberal state." Democracy 1:61-79.

Dietz, T.
    1981   "The Use of Demographic Information in Social Impact Assessment." Pp. 196-206 in K. Finsterbusch and C. P. Wolf (ed.), Methodology of Social Impact Assessment. Second edition. Stroudsburg, Penn.: Hutchinson and Ross.

Dietz, T.
    1984   "Social Impact Assessment as a Tool for Rangelands Management." Pp. 1613-1634 in National Research Council (eds.), Developing Strategies for Rangelands Management. Boulder, Colo.: Westview.

Dietz, T., and A. Pfund
    1983   Issues related to the Trinidad and Tobago Health Project. Washington, D.C.: Inter-American Development Bank.

Duncan and Jones
    1976   Methodology and Guidelines for Assessing the Social Impacts of Development. Berkeley, Calif.: Duncan and Jones, Inc.

Finsterbusch, K., L. Llewellyn, and C. P. Wolf
    1984   Social Impact Assessment Methods. Beverly Hills, Calif.: Sage.

Finsterbusch, K., and C. P. Wolf
    1981   Methodology of Social Impact Assessment. Second edition. Stroudsburg, Penn.: Hutchinson and Ross.

Francis, M.
    1975   "Urban impact assessment and community development." Environment and Behavior 7:373-404.

Freeman, D. H., R. S. Frey, and J. M. Quint
    1982   "Assessing resource management alternatives. A social well-being framework with a national level application." Environmental Impact Assessment Review 3:59-73.

Freudenburg, W.
    1986   "Social impact assessment." Annual Review of Sociology. 12:451-478.

Gamble, D.
    1978   "The Berger inquiry: An impact assessment process." Science 199:946-952.

Habermas, J.
    1970   Toward a Rational Society. Boston, Mass.: Beacon.
    1971   Knowledge and Human Interests. Boston, Mass.: Beacon.
    1979   Communication and the Evolution of Society. Boston, Mass.: Beacon.

Hoos, I.
    1983   Systems Analysis and Public Policy: A Critique. Second edition. Berkley, Calif.: University of California Press.

Johnston, R.
    1975   "Assessing Social and Economic Impacts." Pp. 113-157 in R. Corwin and P. Hetternan (eds.), Environmental Impact Assessment. San Francisco, Calif.: Freeman, Cooper and Company.

Keeney, R. I.
    1972   "Utility functions for multiattributed consequences." Management Science 18:276-287.

1973 "A decision analysis with multiple objectives: The Mexico City airport." Bell Journal of Economics 4:101-117.
Kotz, N.
1981 "Citizens as experts." Working Papers for a New Society 8 (2):42-48.
McEvoy, J., and T. Dietz
1977 Handbook for Environmental Planning. New York: Wiley-Interscience.
Meidinger, E.
1977 "Projecting secondary jobs: An empirical examination and epistemological critique." Paper presented to the Annual Meeting of the American Sociological Association, Chicago, Illinois, September.
Meidinger, E., and W. Freudenburg
1983 "The legal status of social impact assessment: Recent developments." Environmental Sociology 34:30-33.
Meidinger, E., and A. Schnaiberg
1980 "Social impact assessment as evaluation research: Claimants and claims." Evaluation Review 4:507-536.
Olsen, M. E., B. D. Melber, and D. J. Merwin
1981 "Methodology for Conducting Social Impact Assessments Using Quality of Social Life Indicators." Pp. 48-78 in K. Finsterbusch and C. P. Wolf (ed.), Methodology of Social Impact Assessment. Second edition. Stroudsburg, Penn.: Hutchinson and Ross.
Schnaiberg, A.
1980 The Environment: From Surplus to Scarcity. New York: Oxford University Press.

SIA conceptual frameworks

Conceptual frameworks for SIA revisited: a cumulative effects study on lead contamination and economic change

Helen Ross and Tara K McGee

This article trials three conceptual frameworks on an Australian case study of a small remote city suffering lead contamination, with cumulative effects from concurrent economic change due to downsizing in the mining industry. It interprets the usefulness of these frameworks, and explores two questions: can they apply to circumstances other than project assessment, and what are their relative merits as guides to SIA? All the frameworks reviewed can be used in non-project and cumulative SIA, although, if they had been used to predict the impacts in our case study, we may easily have been misled as to the resilience of the community. Choosing among these frameworks becomes a matter personal preference: each has different merits.

Keywords: social impact assessment, theory, cumulative impact assessment, lead contamination, economic change

Professor Helen Ross (contact author) is at the School of Natural and Rural Systems Management, The University of Queensland, Gatton, Queensland 4343, Australia; Email: hross@uqg.uq.edu.au; Tel: +61 7 5460 1648; Fax: +61 7 5460 1324. Dr Tara K McGee is Associate Professor, Department of Earth and Atmospheric Sciences, University of Alberta, T6G 2G8, Canada; Email: tmegee@ualberta.ca.

The authors thank the residents of Broken Hill, Australia, who participated in the research for this article, and the Australian Department of Human Services and Health for R&D Grant funding. They thank Professor Valerie Brown for her role in the originating project, and anonymous reviewers for suggestions for improvement.

IN OVER 30 YEARS of publication in the field of social impact assessment (SIA), there have been many case studies, some reviews and publications on methods, but comparatively few attempts to develop theory specifically for SIA. Becker (2003) attributes this to the majority of SIA practitioners having been trained in the applied and technical, rather than social, sciences. It could also reflect the dominance of sociology in the early development of SIA, allowing a majority of SIA practitioners to draw on theory from a shared parent discipline.

Like Becker (2003) we argue that there is a need for SIA to have explicit conceptual frameworks, or conceptual models,[1] to enhance its practice. Burdge and Vanclay (1995: 44) point out that social science traditions, especially sociology, tend to be "critical and discursive rather than predictive and explanatory". This may have limited theoretical contributions to the highly practical field of SIA. We need to be able to focus on the question: what happens to societies and individuals in the case of a particular type of intervention (project, policy or plan)?

Further, as SIA has attracted a broad range of practitioners, including psychologists, anthropologists, human geographers and planners, it cannot rely solely on theory from parent disciplines that are not fully shared. Rather, it needs to integrate theory from a range of disciplines. Theory in SIA could be enriched by the other disciplines and applied fields contributing to SIA, for instance, by combining psychological, cultural and place-based dimensions

Conceptual frameworks for SIA revisited

with the sociological, to offer clarity with respect to different social scales and relationships with environments.

Meanwhile, much of the SIA content published continues to be attempted without an explicit theoretical basis concerning the affected societies, or social change processes (Burdge and Vanclay, 1995; Becker, 2003). This is particularly disturbing where SIA is part of project-based environmental impact assessment (EIA) studies. In this case, it may also suffer from being peripheral to the EIA content, possibly conducted by non-social scientists, and data is frequently chosen for its availability more than for its relevance to the types of social change one might expect in the particular society, and from the particular type of project (Ross and Lane, 2001; Lane *et al*, 2003).

While EIA technical reports do not require theoretical frameworks to be made explicit — indeed doing so may run counter to the desire to keep reports brief and accessible to the general public — the work should be well-informed. As the social sciences are rich in theory on social change, and on the dynamics of most societies, the lack of apparent theoretical basis for much of the research is disappointing. It is possible, and necessary, to share learning from our existing disciplinary understanding of societies and social change, and combine these with perspectives particular to social impact assessment, to develop the theory needed to provide a more rigorous basis for SIA.

Taylor *et al* (1995: 42) argue that we are far from having a single integrated theory underlying the practice of SIA. They suggest that what is more important is to appreciate the guiding and informing role of theory, to know what to ask (what data to collect) and how to interpret it (what the data means). In their view, and ours, a single underlying theory may be undesirable, and perhaps unattainable. In attempting to be sufficiently general, it could also fail to provide enough guidance for particular SIAs in different contexts.

Theory means different things to different people (Robson, 2002). It comes in different forms, with deductive or inductive directions of reasoning, and may explain different levels of social reality. It may be a formal, large-scale and general theory, or 'substantive', applying to a particular area of social concern. It may seek to predict, or to explain. Theoretical frameworks provide collections of assumptions, concepts and forms of explanation (Neumann, 2000). Theory about what is happening and why, especially when expressed in diagrammatic form, is sometimes referred to as a conceptual framework (Robson, 2002). The theory currently provided within SIA encompasses:

- Conceptual frameworks (or conceptual models) designed to guide and inform the collection and interpretation of data (Blishen *et al*, 1979; Bowles, 1981; Branch *et al*, 1984; Little and Krannich, 1988). Becker (2003: 130) describes these as meta-theories, as they provide "informed guesses" as to people's future behaviour without referring to any specific forms of behaviour.
- Key concepts that have emerged as central to SIA, such as that communities respond actively and differently to new developments (or policies, programs), and are far from being 'passive victims' of change (for instance, Edelstein, 1988; Ross, 1990). Thus communities help to shape the impacts they experience. Another is the concept of cumulative impacts, that impacts can have synergistic effects in space and time that are more than the sum of their parts.
- Summaries of knowledge, generalisations made from review of many examples (Becker, 2003: 129; Finsterbusch, 1980).
- Procedural models, principally focused on the ability to identify change trajectories from a baseline situation with and without a proposed intervention, or to monitor change from a baseline study (Burdge and Vanclay, 1995; Burdge, 1998; Fenton *et al*, 2003). There are similar models of project cycles (Becker, 2003: 131).

Conceptual frameworks

In this article we consider conceptual frameworks, a category of theory designed to provide a basis for collecting and interpreting data. While conceptual frameworks are intended to guide researchers, it is a moot point whether their developers intend to rest here — at pointing out social dimensions for consideration — or to go further to help explain or forecast impacts. The frameworks we have chosen also incorporate aspects of the second type of theory above, key concepts. We review three conceptual frameworks: Blishen *et al* (1979) and Bowles (1981); Branch *et al* (1984); and Little and Krannich (1988). We compare their relevance to a case study of the cumulative impacts of lead contamination and mining industry downsizing in a remote Australian city, Broken Hill, in the early 1990s (McGee, 1996).

The frameworks chosen represent all those known to the authors and colleagues as having been developed explicitly for SIA, at a scale suited to informing the selection of dimensions for an SIA study. Higher-order (and more recent) conceptual frameworks are available, but are insufficiently specific to inform the design of an SIA study in any detail. For example, Slootweg *et al* (2001, repeated in Vanclay, 2002 and elaborated in Slootweg *et al*, 2003) focus on the interactions between environmental and social impacts, recognising social change processes as a contributing factor.

Becker (1997: 12–17), also working at a high level of abstraction, provides a conceptual framework tracing interactions between an action system and a target system, its societal context, and the system of science that influences the actors' understandings of social problems and also receives contributions to its body of knowledge. Meanwhile, at finer scales, much work has been done on lists and typologies of social impact variables (see van Schooten *et al*, 2003; Interorganizational Committee, 1994). While informative, these tend not to be articulated in theoretical terms to explicate the dynamics of social change possible.

The conceptual frameworks we have chosen were originally derived from the North American SIA research experience of their authors, and were designed for small, relatively remote communities. All have been inspired by similar sociological and community development literature, and they cite one another. They all focus on social, economic and, to some extent, political dimensions of communities, but differ with respect to relative emphasis on social structures and processes, and the extent to which culture and values are apparent.

Our purpose is to offer some validation and interpretation of the usefulness of these frameworks, none of which appears to have been tested widely (or reported as having been) beyond the studies from which they were generated.[2] All are now at least 15 years old, ample time for testing, had practitioners been so inclined.

We encourage other researchers to use and report on their experiences with the conceptual frameworks we review, and others, in the interests of advancing theory and informing practice in SIA. We need to know how well the frameworks apply in different project and national contexts, and whether they can be generalised (perhaps with adaptation) beyond their original purpose as guides for the analysis of impacts of large, externally imposed developments on small, geographically remote communities.

After reviewing the same three frameworks that are analysed here, Kelly (2000) concludes that they have limitations in fully capturing the complex nature of communities, and they suffer from ignoring the physical environment, and from minimal reference to the time dimension. She proposes an alternative framework based on data from a study of change in country towns associated with the forest industry in south-west Western Australia.

Ramsey and Smit (2002) have published a framework, which also recognises the physical environment, as well as health outcomes. Theirs is also a valuable contrast to previous frameworks in that it deals with social and economic trends: their choice of similar key concepts to those reviewed here suggests that the frameworks are valid beyond the specific project scenarios for which they were developed. This paper extends the analysis completed to date, by examining the relevance of the three frameworks to a case study of lead contamination and mining industry downsizing.

We know that our case study broadly follows the patterns of community response to contamination identified by Edelstein (1988) in *Contaminated Communities*. However, it is also a remote, socially cohesive small city, affected not by a commercial development (as anticipated in the conceptual frameworks we analyse) but by a severe health threat discovered during a period of economic change for the community. It thus provides an opportunity to explore how far three conceptual frameworks designed for project impacts can in fact extend to other impact situations, including cumulative impacts.

The frameworks reviewed here are essentially guides for analysis. They supplement researchers' knowledge of social science theory by helping them to identify what they need to study and to look for connections between factors. Although the works in which they are published sketch out some of the theory underlying them (most comprehensively in the case of Bowles (1981)), they are not sufficient on their own. A researcher also needs a familiarity with the culture, history and local dynamics of the society being studied, and sound social research skills, in order to conduct a useful study.

For convenience, we have drawn on descriptions given by the original authors to label each framework reviewed. These descriptions were not necessarily intended as names for these frameworks by their authors.

Community response model

A very simple conceptual framework, in that sets of variables are grouped into three memorable cluster variables, has been published by two teams (possibly originating from the same Canadian research work): Blishen *et al* (1979), and Bowles (1981). It is designed to analyse how different communities respond to potential impact situations, and to predict their abilities to cope with the impacts of projects imposed by external agents. It consists of three dimensions, described slightly differently in the two publications (the following comes from Blishen *et al*):

- social vitality — patterns of social behaviour (interactive or private), representing community 'health';
- economic viability — the degree to which communities are economically dependent on, or

> **Our purpose is to offer some validation and interpretation of the usefulness of three frameworks, none of which appears to have been tested widely (or reported as having been) beyond the studies from which they were generated**

Conceptual frameworks for SIA revisited

independent of, the regional, provincial or national economy; and

- political efficacy — the extent to which social vitality and economic viability are associated with the mobilisation of political power or processes (including the extent of local political debate and participation).

These key dimensions summarise theory about the social and economic dynamics of communities, and their relationships with other communities and institutions. Blishen *et al* list the indicators they used in working with eight communities in British Columbia, and explain their interpretation. For instance, under 'social vitality' they consider mutual assistance norms, labour transaction norms, norms for resolving social problems, conflict resolution, status recognition, norms for achieving social and economic mobility, private ownership of property, and induction, socialisation and rejection norms.

The communities in which the Blishen *et al* version of this model was developed were native American, or included indigenous members. The model was therefore created for societies in which strongly collective social dynamics are typical.

This model was used by Lane *et al* (1990; Lane *et al*, 1997; Ross, 2001; Lane *et al*, 2003) in their predictive study of the social impacts of the proposed Coronation Hill mine in northern Australia on Aboriginal people of the region. They found that the Jawoyn Aboriginal people had strong social vitality and political efficacy, yet low economic viability, although there were emerging prospects for a diversified economy. The first two characteristics were dominant in shaping resilience to deal with the proposal. Economic viability affected value differences among the Jawoyn people, and hence their divided views as to whether the project should go ahead. All three characteristics appear to have helped the Jawoyn people's recovery from the social and individual stresses of contesting the proposal (it was eventually rejected), and then reconstruction of relationships amongst themselves and with other stakeholders.

The model has also been used by Coakes and Fenton (2001: 262; Fenton and Marshall, 2001; Fenton *et al*, 2003) in studies of social impacts or changes in resource access for forestry and fishing communities. The dimension of economic viability conceptually underpins a quantitative methodology for assessing economic and social impacts that may occur at a distance from the intervention location, for instance, in the towns where purchasing (of different types) occurs or children are sent to school (Fenton and Marshall, 2001; Fenton *et al*, 2003).

Social organisation model

The social organisation model (Branch *et al*, 1984) was published as the centrepiece of one of the first guides to SIA. It recognises that different people and different communities react differently to similar

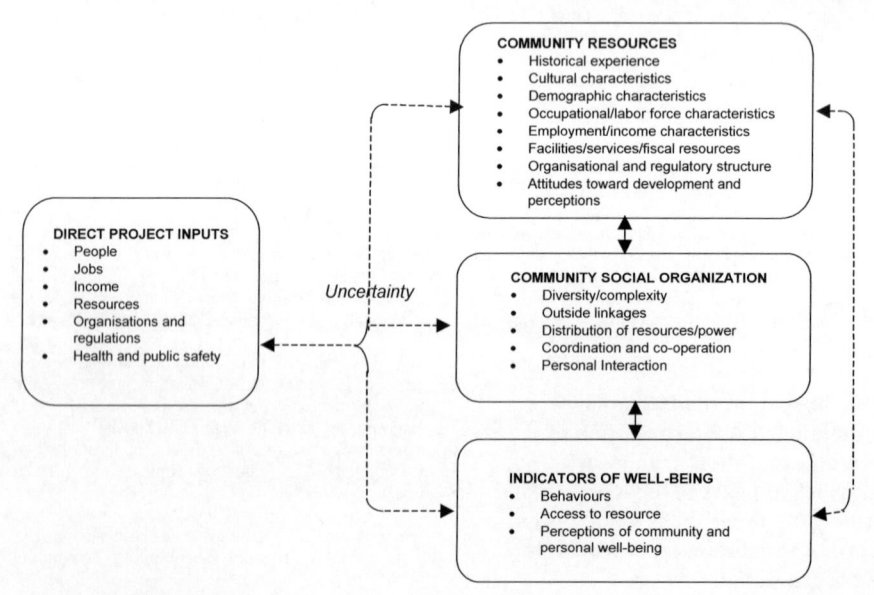

Figure 1. Social organisation model
Source: Branch *et al* (1984: 27)

events, so that the impact of any project is as much due to the way the community is organised and the way it responds, as to the particular characteristics of the project.

The model (see Figure 1) considers links among four components:

- the nature of direct project inputs (such as the number of people employed in the different stages of the project), and their effects on
- community resources (such as historical experience, cultural and demographic characteristics),
- community social organisation (including diversity and complexity, outside linkages, distribution of resources and power, coordination and cooperation, and personal interaction[3]), and
- well-being (behaviours, access to resources, and perceptions of community and personal well-being).

The Branch et al (1984) book elaborates the meaning of these components and their indicators, and explains why the indicators were chosen and how to obtain information on them and interpret them.

Community organisation model

A community organisation model was proposed by Little and Krannich (1988) (see Figure 2). It presents linkages between:

- shared values, which "orient and shape the actions, attitudes, beliefs and perceptions of persons residing in the area" (1988: 27);
- community structures: economic (production and distribution), political (public institutions), formal social (non-public institutions and organisations) and informal social (non-public groups and networks);

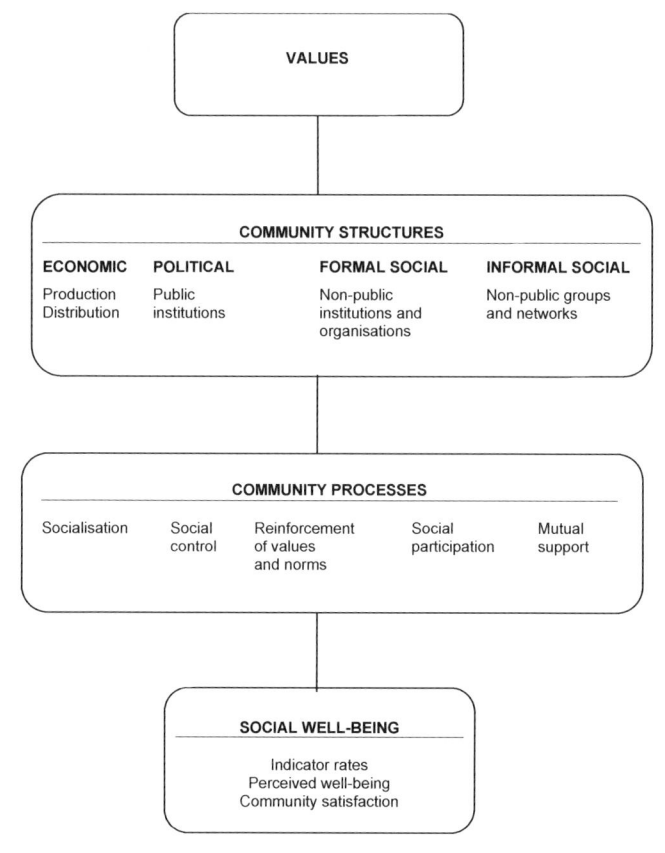

Figure 2. Community organisation model
Source: Little and Krannich (1988: 30)

Conceptual frameworks for SIA revisited

- community activities and processes, including socialisation, social control mechanisms, behaviours that reinforce local norms and values, opportunities for social participation, and mutual support patterns; and
- social well-being, which is related to behavioural dimensions of social integration and psychological distress (assessed partly through indicator variables representing social problems), and to community satisfaction and perceived well-being.

The minor differences between this and the previous model (Branch *et al*, 1984) are in its emphasis on values, and the substitution of processes for resources. The authors of this model, like the Blishen–Lockhart team, have used their experience with communities of indigenous people to inform their thinking. While Little and Krannich do not make cultural differences explicit in their model, the categories within their model, especially social organisation and values, are key dimensions of culture.

Broken Hill case study

Broken Hill is located in semi-arid far western New South Wales, Australia, and has a population of 22,600. The city grew up alongside the area's first mining operations, which commenced in 1883. Subsequent mining operations of lead–silver–zinc have included underground and open cut mining, and retreatment of mining waste and tailings. The numerous mines in the Broken Hill field have played a central part in shaping the nature of the community and providing the major source of employment for most of Broken Hill's history.

The city is also well known for its labour unions, and has been characterised as a 'union town', rather than a 'company town'. The Barrier Industrial Council, a peak body of unions formed in 1923 (under previous names) has influenced the social, economic, health and political nature of the community through its unconventional involvement in issues of law, pricing of commodities, regulation of access to the local labour market, commercial, industrial and domestic disputes (Howard, 1990).

Throughout much of the city's history, most Broken Hill residents enjoyed the prosperity of the mines, which provided a secure source of well-paid employment for local men. Until the early 1980s, married women worked in the home, leaving unionised jobs to single women and men. Mine workers and their families also received a range of benefits including the sickness fund, dental clinic, co-operative housing finance, credit assistance for purchasing household appliances, holiday camps, local parks and amenities, scholarships and other educational assistance. Residents also enjoyed strong social ties with friends and family. The historical prosperity and security began to change in the 1980s, with alterations in mining technology and industrial practices, and reductions in the mining workforce.

> **Blood lead levels as low as 10 μg/dL can result in decreased intelligence and impaired neuro-behavioural development, decreased stature or growth, and other serious problems: levels higher than 25 μg/dL were reported in children in Broken Hill**

In early 1992, the community of Broken Hill became engaged in the process of dealing with chronic environmental lead contamination, which was brought to public attention with the release and associated media coverage of the results of a Regional Public Health Unit blood lead survey. The survey of 899 local children aged 0–4 reported that 20.3% of children tested had blood lead levels higher than 25 micrograms per decilitre (μg/dL), the National Health and Medical Research Council level of concern at that time.

The potential biophysical health effects of young children's exposure to relatively low levels of lead are widely recognised. Lead affects virtually every system in the body and, once absorbed, it enters the blood, soft tissues and mineralising systems such as bones and teeth. Lead is particularly harmful to the developing brain and nervous system of foetuses and young children (see for example Smith *et al*, 1989; Needleman, 1992). Blood lead levels as low as 10 μg/dL have been found to result in decreased intelligence and impaired neuro-behavioural development, decreased stature or growth, decreased hearing acuity and decreased ability to maintain a steady posture (Centers for Disease Control, 1991).

During the study period (1992–96), the Regional Public Health Unit responded to the results of the blood lead-level survey with a program that included providing information about potential biophysical health effects of lead exposure, blood lead testing, environmental sampling and suggested lead risk reduction measures to be implemented by parents, such as lowering dust levels in houses and gardens. Residents responded to the information about the lead contamination in a variety of ways. Some appeared to be very concerned, while others questioned the existence of a hazard (McGee, 1999).

One year after the release of the blood lead-level survey results, Broken Hill experienced a significant change in the local mining industry, when one of the major mines closed and the other restructured, reducing the mining workforce by 37% to 846. Thus the community was involved in dealing with cumulative impacts of the discovery of lead contamination and the retrenchments. These were not merely contemporaneous events. Mining was central to both the health and the economic impacts, since it was the main employer, and the sources of the lead contamination include dust from open-cut mining and exposed tailings dumps, as well as natural erosion of the ore body.

In a detailed qualitative study, McGee (1996; 1999) examined how residents and other local stakeholders responded to the chronic environmental lead contamination and mining industry retrenchments in Broken Hill, and the resulting effects on the health and well-being of individuals, organisations and the community.

Application of the frameworks

We shall first discuss the results of the Broken Hill study in terms of the Blishen team (1979) and Bowles (1981) community response model.

Social vitality

The Broken Hill community was found to have strong social networks of family, friends and mine co-workers, which underpin its social vitality. Many residents were third and fourth generation locals, with extended family living in the city. Many mine co-workers developed close bonds with workmates who shared work, coping with work hazards, work breaks, and sports and other leisure activities.

Throughout its history, local residents have come together for collective events, from sports meetings, craft fairs and other informal social gatherings, to the more formal St Patrick's Day races and the annual agricultural fair. Broken Hill's social networks serve several functions, including socialising, passing along information, and providing assistance in times of need. Thus, in terms of social vitality (Blishen *et al*, 1979; Bowles, 1981), Broken Hill should be well placed to deal with threats.

However, in contrast to the response that might be expected in such a socially vital community, the lead contamination in Broken Hill was dealt with at an individual, rather than collective, level (McGee, 1999). Parents usually dealt with it by themselves, by seeking information and participating in the blood lead-testing program, rather than turning to their social networks for support. Many parents felt that they should have been able to prevent, and subsequently eliminate, their children's exposure to lead.

This response reflected a range of factors including the nature of the Public Health Unit's intervention program, which focused on parents' actions that could reduce exposure, and cultural beliefs about self-sufficiency and parenting roles. A sense of stigma was attached to the issue, parents feeling their families to be stigmatised and the population at large fearing adverse consequences for the city's emerging tourism industry.

When residents did turn to their social networks for assistance, in some cases they received social and financial support to help them implement lead risk reduction measures, while in others they received little support, or social undermining in the form of the disapprobation of others. This lack of support in part reflected the diversity of beliefs held about the nature of the lead contamination risk, and about appropriate responses. Those who were concerned about the threat were socially undermined, or not supported, by those who were not concerned.

In addition to their beliefs about what was a 'normal' amount of concern, residents identified what they deemed to be 'normal' actions for a parent with young children. Parents whose behaviour deviated from the presumed norm by doing more to reduce children's lead exposure, or not doing enough, were also not supported.

This largely individual response contrasts with many other communities, where active community groups facilitated a collective response to environmental contamination (see, for example, Edelstein, 1988; Levine, 1982; Brown and Mikkelsen, 1990). In Broken Hill, several individuals became activists, but there was not a group of concerned residents working together (see discussion of political efficacy).

Economic viability

Broken Hill's economy has historically been heavily dependent on the local mining industry. Most local men, particularly tradespeople, were employed in the mines and, until the 1980s, mine workers essentially had a job for life. Single women worked in the local shops and hospital, and as office workers at the mines. In accordance with local union policy, married women worked at home. Those employed in the mines received high wages, which provided a multiplier effect supporting other parts of the local economy. The mining companies also contributed to the city's economy through the payment of rates to the city council for water and electricity, and financial contributions to community services and facilities.

The dominance of the mining industry in the local economic base has declined over recent years, with the expansion of tourism and other activities, and an increase in mechanisation and productivity in the mining industry. Mining was the leading source of employment until 1991 (16%, down from 21% in 1986) but, by 1996, the main industries were retail trade, health and community service, with mining offering 11% of the city's employment (Australian Bureau of Statistics Census data of 1986, 1991 and 1996). The city's historical dependence on the mining industry placed it in a position of low economic viability, with little resilience to downturns in the industry.

The 'control capacity' of industry in industry-dependent communities involves control over jobs, the threat of job loss to individual employees, and the threat of economic decline for the host

Conceptual frameworks for SIA revisited

community resulting from closure of a key industry (Gould, 1991). The threat of job loss, and a decline in the community's economic viability — a normal uncertainty associated with the mining industry — was particularly potent in Broken Hill because of the continued decline in mine employment since 1986, and the large number of retrenchments that occurred in the city in February 1993. The fears of retrenchment reduced public discussion and activism in response to the lead contamination (McGee, 1996). Consistent with community response theory, then, the Broken Hill community's low economic viability restricted its ability to deal with the lead contamination threat.

Political efficacy

Levels of local participation in determining, mediating and negotiating social and economic initiatives affect a community's resilience to impacts. Historically, the Barrier Industrial Council (union) looked after many aspects of the daily living of local workers and their families. The strong leadership and support provided by union, local government and other community leaders has also played a significant role in protecting the community from threats. For example, in the early to mid-1980s, the unions played a significant role in the campaign against a proposal for a toxic waste incinerator near the city. Other threats throughout Broken Hill's history have included water shortage, and loss of government services including health care. In late September 1991, a rally of approximately 8,000 to 10,000 people protested against state government cutbacks that resulted in a decline in local services in the city. The strong combination of union, local government and other community leaders dealt effectively with threats.

Although they had organised politically in many other cases, the unions, local government and many of the other community leaders did not encourage community participation in response to the lead contamination. Indeed, in some cases, they actively discouraged it, for a range of reasons including fears that active resident concern about lead contamination would threaten the city's growing tourism industry, or would cause further reduction in local mining employment. Instead, a small number of residents, including parents with young children, doctors, and mine employees, were publicly active.

Several of those who were publicly active, particularly early on in the community response process, received considerable social undermining, including threatening phone calls. Attempts to discredit these activists were also made. A similar lack of community support of activists has been noted elsewhere (see, for example, Couch and Kroll-Smith, 1985; Brown and Mikkelsen, 1990). Thus, in addition to community leaders' lack of support of collective resident action, individual activists received little social support. Meanwhile, the city's reliance on

Using the community response model, the community has a high level of social vitality, but is not uniformly supportive; it has apparent political efficacy, but this is the preserve of established organisations; it is low in economic viability

established formal leadership for its political efficacy, with low participation by individual residents, restricted its ability to respond to the lead contamination threat.

The three key variables of the community response model are easily described and, at a broad level, seem pertinent to the response. The community has a high level of social vitality, but it turns out that this is not uniformly supportive in all circumstances. It has apparent political efficacy, but this is the preserve of established organisations, on which the city community has been dependent for its political responses. It is low in economic viability, a factor that influenced social and political response when the community was faced with the cumulative impacts of lead contamination and mine closure.

The model does not assist us in seeing how the variables combine, nor what happens when some characteristics are strong, others weak. The case study suggests the interactions between social vitality, economic viability and political efficacy can be complex, and not necessarily reliable for predictive purposes (compare with Kelly, 2000). Broken Hill's social vitality and political efficacy failed to produce the support the community was clearly capable of, because other factors, such as cultural factors, the nature of the health intervention program and the reliance on mining jobs (hence reluctance to be seen as criticising the employer) became dominant.

Culture and values

The Branch *et al* (1984) social organisation and Little and Krannich (1988) community organisation models both identify cultural characteristics as central to a community's resilience to impacts. The Branch model includes cultural characteristics as a component of community resources, whereas Little and Krannich (1988) focus on values as a key dimension of the socio-cultural context in which impacts occur, since they shape the actions, attitudes, beliefs and perceptions residing in the community. (Values are a key cultural characteristic, but far from the only one.)

Cultural factors significantly affected the nature of the Broken Hill community's response to lead contamination. One of our fundamental cultural assumptions is that we live in "a benevolent, safe world" (Janoff-Bulman, 1992; Lerner, 1980). Many local residents had positive feelings and beliefs about the city that has provided them with prosperity and security throughout much of its history. These encouraged residents to minimise the perceived lead contamination threat, and to accept it, rather than moving away from the city. As one local parent said:

> We love Broken Hill — it's a great place ... Broken Hill has got a lot of advantages. Lead is minor when you compare all of the advantages of Broken Hill.

A cultural value of independence, which characterises residents in many rural communities (Larson and Dearmont, 2002), was fostered by the city's isolation. Highly valued by many residents, this independence discouraged public expression of concern and collective action, and encouraged residents' use of private rather than public coping methods.

As our outline of Broken Hill's social vitality showed, values and social norms were important in shaping the community's response to lead contamination. While our retrospective analysis shows how a set of values interacted, it would have been very difficult to identify the combined roles of these values in any predictive analysis.

Mediating factors

Other factors besides characteristics of the community affected the unfolding of events and shaping of the social impacts. The nature of lead as a contaminant was one such factor. Scientific information was in short supply at first, and never able to offer precision about the sources of the contamination (natural and industrial), its distribution or duration. The invisibility of the contamination, shown up only by scientific testing, allowed some to minimise the threat cognitively, while others suffered stress associated with the uncertainties.

The diversity of beliefs about the contamination reduced the likelihood of a collective response, or even social support, developing around a shared understanding (McGee, 1999). Further, the fact that one of the main health threats in lead contamination is reduced cognitive development undoubtedly encouraged parents to keep quiet about their children being affected. Some adults drew the conclusion that they also had probably been exposed to lead throughout their own lives, and might well have suffered impaired development.

The Regional Public Health Unit's well-intended response focused on improved housework and children's play places as a pragmatic way of reducing children's exposure to the lead-laden dust that pervaded the city. There were also recommendations for grass cover in gardens to reduce dust loads. Practical difficulties of maintaining tight domestic control over dust in a hot and dry climate (average 32°C in summer, average annual rainfall 248mm) where water is scarce and expensive, and windows need to be kept open for breeze relief, were overlooked.

All three frameworks we consider in this article are vague about such influences. In the Branch *et al* model, the nature of the contaminant and organisational responses could be considered part of the 'project inputs', although the public health interventions could be considered a third cumulative impact factor alongside the lead contamination and loss of employment.

Role of the physical environment

All the frameworks reviewed here virtually ignore the physical environment,[4] yet it was highly relevant as the source of both the economic benefits (mining) and the health threat (lead in the local environment). More subtly, it is a dry area, with little vegetation to prevent dust flying around and, because this is a semi-arid area, water to grow vegetation is very expensive. The design of much of the old, inexpensive housing made it difficult to exclude dust, even if one were prepared to shut windows in such a hot climate. Thus, individual responses to the lead threat were influenced by the physical environment. This provides a reminder that future SIA theoretical frameworks should provide for interactions between the physical environment and social and economic processes (compare with Slootweg *et al*, 2003).

Conclusion

If we had tried to use any of these frameworks to predict the impacts of what happened in Broken Hill, from soon after the discovery of lead contamination in 1992, how well would they have helped us? Would we have forecast the dramatic industry downsizing and been able to assess its interacting effects with the lead contamination? Would we have been misled by the community's strong social vitality and apparent political efficacy into assuming that the community would provide strong social support through the crisis? Would we have realised that economic dependence on a particular industry would have such an effect on people's willingness to confront a health threat related to that industry? The community response model highlights economic viability as a factor in community resilience to impacts, but it is hard to grasp the potential subtleties of interaction between the economic, social and political factors from the generalised statement of theory.

Moving to the social organisation (Branch *et al*, 1984) and community organisation (Little and Krannich, 1988) models, would we have been assisted to identify which among several values held strongly in Broken Hill would prove pivotal? In such a socially cohesive community, why did values of individualism prevail over those of social support,

Conceptual frameworks for SIA revisited

even among kin? While the social and economic structure is easily documented under the headings outlined by Little and Krannich, the social processes related to these are subtle. We might not have picked the disempowerment of private individuals, which proved to be the counterpart of having strong formal organisations. As we said in relation to the community response model, we would have placed undue faith in the social cohesion of the community to adapt to its problems.

We set out to validate and examine the usefulness of these conceptual frameworks. While we have ascertained that these frameworks, on their own, would have had limitations in enabling us to forecast the eventual impacts effectively, we do not believe this undermines their usefulness as a guide to project design and analysis. The frameworks do provide a useful theoretical basis, highlighting key social dimensions for study and showing how these typically interact.

We believe the problem lies not in the frameworks, but in the complexity of social dynamics in any given situation (Becker, 2003). Any SIA forecast remains a 'best guess': as our case study shows, events can take different turns from those expected. One possible solution to this is to recognise that frameworks at this level are useful, though blunt, instruments, that need some supplementation. This could come through combining the framework with summaries of knowledge, where available, in the domain of study, or in the form of more detailed, context-specific frameworks (Ross, 1999).

The frameworks appear more different than they actually are, because of the ways in which the variables are clustered. For instance, social organisation (Branch *et al*; Little and Krannich) provides structural underpinnings for social vitality and political efficacy (Blishen *et al*; Bowles). Which framework one uses comes down to preference, and perhaps a scoping of characteristics that seem important in each new study.

The community response framework has an active orientation, in which there is a clear role for each key variable in confronting, or adapting to, whatever new situation has prompted study. These social dynamics are more obscure in the other frameworks. The social organisation models provide a stronger focus on culture, and Little and Krannich correctly emphasise the important role of values in shaping evaluations and responses.

A similarity among the frameworks is an underlying assumption about communities' capacities to manage social impacts themselves, using their own resources, perhaps with some guidance.[5] This may apply better to developed countries than to less developed countries, where power relations between project proponents, governments and communities can be far more pronounced, and traditions of activism and self-sufficiency not necessarily present.

Despite the complexities of their interpretation in particular settings, it is clear that each of the three theoretical frameworks is adaptable to impact situations beyond the project development context for which they were devised. This is a useful finding, since the dominant concerns of SIA have moved beyond the large project developments of the 1970s and early 1980s, to include corridor projects, such as roads and pipelines, and hazardous materials.

Emerging concerns are the global reach of technologies and policies (such as telecommunications and biotechnology), and region-wide natural resource management strategies (Branch and Ross, 1998). New or adapted theory also needs to cater for different types of society, such as urban and densely settled areas, which may have social dynamics and ways of organising politically that are different from those understood in the existing theoretical frameworks.

Notes

1. In this article we use these terms interchangeably, following Robson (2002: 63) and Becker (2003), partly because the originating authors of the conceptual frameworks we have chosen use the term 'model' to describe their work. We recognise that some authors (for instance, Fenton *et al*, 2003: 211) distinguish conceptual frameworks subtly from conceptual models according to the degree of causal explanation offered.
2. Some have been used, for instance, by Lane *et al* (2003) and Ross (2001). We are unaware of the reasons for lack of testing, as opposed to use, but surmise this could represent the relative lack of interest in theoretical development in SIA.
3. Note the similarities here with the three characteristics outlined in the Blishen *et al*/Bowles model.
4. This point is also made by Kelly (2000).
5. We acknowledge an anonymous reviewer for this insight.

References

Becker, H 1997. *Social Impact Assessment*. London: UCL Press.
Becker, H 2003. Theory formation and application in social impact assessment. In *Conceptual and Methodological Advances in Social Impact Assessment* eds. H Becker and F Vanclay, pp. 129–142. Cheltenham UK: Edward Elgar.
Blishen, B R, A Lockhart, P Craib and E Lockhart 1979. *Socio-Economic Impact Model for Northern Development*. Hull: Department of Indian and Northern Affairs.
Bowles, R T 1981. *Social Impact Assessment in Small Communities: An Integrative Review of Selected Literature*. Toronto: Butterworths.
Branch, K, D A Hooper, J Thompson, and J Creighton 1984. *Guide to Social Assessment*. Boulder CA: Westview Press.
Branch, K and H Ross 1998. SIA in the age of complexity, tight budgets and participation. *Papers from IAIA Conferences 1997 and 1998* on CD ROM. North Dakota State University, Fargo: International Association for Impact Assessment.
Brown, P and E J Mikkelsen 1990. *No Safe Place: Toxic Waste, Leukemia, and Community Action*. Berkeley CA: University of California Press.
Burdge, R 1998. *A Conceptual Approach to Social Impact Assessment*. Middleton WI: Social Ecology Press.
Burdge, R and F Vanclay 1995. Social impact assessment. In *Environmental and Social Impact Assessment*, eds. F Vanclay and D A Bronstein, pp. 31–65. Chichester, UK: Wiley.
Centers for Disease Control 1991. *Preventing Lead Poisoning in Young Children*. Atlanta GA: US Department of Health and Human Services/Public Health Service.
Coakes, S and M Fenton 2001. Social assessment in the Australian forest sector. In *Social Assessment in Natural Resource Management Institutions*, eds. A Dale, N Taylor and M Lane, pp. 255–265. Victoria: CSIRO Publishing.

Couch, S R and J S Kroll-Smith 1985. The chronic technical disaster: toward a social scientific perspective. *Social Science Quarterly*, **66**(3), 564–575.

Edelstein, M R 1988. *Contaminated Communities: the Social and Psychological Impacts of Residential Toxic Exposure*. Boulder CA: Westview Press.

Fenton, D M and N Marshall 2001. *A Guide to the Fishers of Queensland, Part A: TRC — Analysis and Social Profiles of Queensland's Commercial Fishing Industry*, CRC Reef Research Centre Technical Report no 36. Townsville, Queensland: CRC Reef Research Centre.

Fenton, M, S Coakes and N Marshall 2003. Vulnerability and capacity measurement. In *Conceptual and Methodological Advances in Social Impact Assessment*, eds. H Becker and F Vanclay, pp. 211–230. Cheltenham UK: Edward Elgar.

Finsterbusch, K 1980. *Understanding Social Impacts: Assessing the Effects of Public Projects*. Beverly Hills CA: Sage Publications.

Gould, K A 1991. The sweet smell of money: economic dependency and local environmental political mobilization. *Society and Natural Resources*, **4**, 133–150.

Howard, W A 1990. *Barrier Bulwark: The Life and Times of Shorty O'Neil*. Melbourne Victoria, Willry Pty Ltd.

Interorganizational Committee on Guidelines and Principles for Social Impact Assessment 1994. *Impact Assessment*, **12**(2), 107–152.

Janoff-Bulman, R 1992. *Shattered Assumptions: Towards a New Psychology of Trauma*. New York: The Free Press.

Kelly, G 2000. *Rural Communities Adapting to Change: Case Studies from South Western Australia*. Unpublished PhD thesis. Perth, Western Australia: Curtin University of Technology.

Lane, M, A Dale, H Ross, A Hill and R Rickson 1990. *The Social Impact of Development: an Analysis of the Social Impact of Development on Aboriginal Communities of the Region*. Resource Assessment Commission Kakadu Conservation Zone Inquiry. Canberra, NSW).

Lane, M B, H Ross and A P Dale 1997. Social impact research: integrating the technical, political and planning paradigms. *Human Organization*, **56**, 302–310.

Lane, M B, H Ross, A P Dale and R Rickson 2003. Sacred land, mineral wealth, and biodiversity at Coronation Hill, Northern Australia: indigenous knowledge and SIA. *Impact Assessment and Project Appraisal*, **21**(2), June, 89–98.

Larson, N and M Dearmont 2002. Strengths of rural farming communities in fostering resilience of children. *Child Welfare*, **81**(5), 821–835.

Lerner, M J 1980. *The Belief in a Just World: a Fundamental Delusion*. New York: Plenum Press.

Levine, A G 1982. *Love Canal: Science, Politics and People*. Toronto, Canada: D.C. Heath and Company.

Little, R L and R S Krannich 1998. A model for assessing the social impacts of natural resource utilization on resource-dependent communities. *Impact Assessment Bulletin*, **6**(2), 21–35.

McGee, T K 1996. *Shades of Grey: Community Responses to Chronic Environmental Lead Contamination in Broken Hill, New South Wales*. Unpublished PhD thesis. Canberra, NSW: The Australian National University.

McGee, T K 1999. Private responses and individual action: community responses to chronic environmental lead contamination. *Environment and Behaviour*, **31**, 66–83.

Needleman, H L 1992. *Human Lead Exposure*. Florida: CRC Press.

Neumann, W L 2000. *Social Research Methods: Qualitative and Quantitative Approaches*. Boston MA: Allyn and Bacon.

Ramsey, D and B Smit 2002. Rural community well-being: models and application to changes in the tobacco-belt in Ontario, Canada. *Geoforum*, **33**, 367–384.

Robson, C 2002. *Real World Research*. Oxford, UK: Blackwell.

Ross, H 1990. Community social impact assessment: a framework for indigenous peoples. *Environmental Impact Assessment Review*, **10**(1–2), 185–193.

Ross, H 1999. A social impact and negotiation model for the mining industry and Aboriginal Australians. Paper presented at International Symposium on Society and Natural Resource Management, Brisbane, Queensland, 7–10 July.

Ross, H 2001. Social impact assessment: Coronation Hill. In *Working on Country: Contemporary Indigenous Management of Australia's Lands and Coastal Regions*, eds. R Baker, J Davies, and E Young, pp. 320–336. Melbourne, Victoria: Oxford University Press.

Ross, H and M Lane 2001. Social assessment and resources management at the Australian Federal level: trapped in an epistemological corner?. In *Social Assessment in Natural Resource Management Institutions*, eds. A Dale, N Taylor and M Lane, pp. 93–104. Collingwood, Victoria: CSIRO Press.

Slootweg, R, F Vanclay and M can Schooten 2001. Function evaluation as a framework for the integration of social and environmental impact assessment. *Impact Assessment and Project Appraisal*, **19**(1), 19–28.

Slootweg, R, F Vanclay and M van Schooten 2003. Integrating environmental and social impact assessment. In *Conceptual and Methodological Advances in Social Impact Assessment*, H Becker and F Vanclay, pp. 56–73. Cheltenham, UK: Edward Elgar.

Smith, M A, L D Grant and A I Sors eds. 1989. *Lead Exposure and Child Development: An International Assessment*. Dordrecht: Kluwer.

Taylor, C N, C H Bryan and C G Goodrich 1995. *Social Assessment: Theory, Process and Techniques*, 2nd edn. Christchurch, NZ: Taylor Baines and Associates.

van Schooten, M, F Vanclay and R Slootweg 2003. Conceptualizing social change processes and social impacts. In *Conceptual and Methodological Advances in Social Impact Assessment*, eds. H Becker and F Vanclay, pp. 74–91. Cheltenham UK: Edward Elgar.

Vanclay, F 2002. Conceptualising social impacts. *Environmental Impact Assessment Review*, **22**, 183–211.

The importance of theory in shaping social impact monitoring: lessons from the Berg River Dam, South Africa

Nigel Rossouw and Shakti Malan

The outputs and outcome of a social-monitoring programme is a direct result of the theoretical framework used by the practitioner. One approach is to adopt social impact monitoring frameworks that identify impacts through a deductive process of objective rationality. This often results in checklist reporting and a myopic focus on predetermined themes (such as employment, housing, education, health). This approach blinds the practitioner to issues that fall outside their frame of analysis. This paper is a narrative reflection by the authors on the changing theoretical frameworks evident at the different stages of social monitoring on the Berg River Dam. Lessons learnt are that: the purpose of social monitoring is to promote social sustainability; explicit theoretical models at each stage of the environmental assessment and management process (that is, at the social impact assessment, environmental management plan (EMP) design and EMP implementation stage) are imperative to guide the monitoring programme; and for social monitoring to become dynamic it needs to develop in a reflexive and inductive manner.

Keywords: social impact monitoring, social sustainability model, social science theory, environmental management plans, Berg River Dam, South Africa

THIS PAPER POSITS that social-monitoring programmes implemented as part of environmental management plans (EMPs) should be:

- executed using a clear and robust theoretical framework;
- periodically reviewed and revised in response to the different project phases; and
- context-specific to the project's dynamic social environment.

The Berg River Dam in South Africa, which is presented as a case study, illustrates that an EMP, while being a valuable method for environmental management, should not be used in a static and uncritical manner. If the social-monitoring programme contained in the EMP is used as a deductive framework, then predetermined responses (that is, the proposed mitigation actions) to listed predicted impacts are merely executed without inductive verification of their appropriateness for the social environment at that stage in the project cycle. In addition, if the social-monitoring programme is executed without an explicitly articulated theoretical framework or model, then its implementation can be flawed or be guided in a direction not originally intended by the designers of the EMP.

When the Berg River Dam social-monitoring programme was initiated it replicated the categories and

Nigel Rossouw and Shakti Malan are with TCTA (Trans-Caledon Tunnel Authority), 3 Reservoir Street-East, Franschhoek, 7690, South Africa; Tel: +27 21 876 8700; Fax: +27 21 876 8701; Email: nrossouw@tcta.co.za.

Nigel Rossouw is TCTA's Environmental Manager for the construction of the Berg River Dam and Shakti Malan is a Social Anthropologist contracted as project leader for the social-monitoring programme. Liza van der Merwe, a Sociologist consulting to TCTA participated in the initial conceptualisation of this paper. Support and approval from TCTA for the authors to compile this paper is gratefully acknowledged. Opinions expressed and conclusions drawn are those of the authors.

The importance of theory in shaping social impact monitoring

lists contained in the EMP. The theoretical framework within which social monitoring was understood remained implicit and unstated. In the absence of an explicit theoretical framework, the checklists became like the walking stick of the blind, with the social-monitoring programme following the EMP in the land of theoretical 'blindness'. Attachment to the listed categories and predicted impacts identified in the initial EMP created a myopic lens through which the social environment was viewed. It resulted in certain key issues being ignored because these existed outside the field of view or framework of analysis.

A review of some social-monitoring programmes of large-scale construction projects indicates that social monitoring often focuses on: a) site-specific issues to be addressed (for instance, housing and basic services for workers); b) managing public relationships; and c) managing land claims (see Banks, 1999; Inter-American Development Bank and Corporacion Andina de Fomento, 2002). Thus, the focus areas for social monitoring are stipulated before operations begin and monitoring is focused on achieving these predetermined goals. This leaves little room for inductive analysis and observation of social changes related to the project that have not been predicted.

Where social monitoring focuses on identifying social changes, this is often done in a 'hands-off' way, much like a surveillance approach. Banks (1999) criticises the "surveillance" approach to social monitoring, where it is done through sporadic surveys, thus eliminating the need for any direct engagement with local communities. Foucault (1977) argues that social surveillance is a major mode of control and the means by which power is expressed in modern society. Social monitoring, if done without reflexive awareness, can perpetuate existing systems of power.

The goals or focus areas of social monitoring are often a result of the (often implicit or unknowingly chosen) understanding of communities' social needs. Table 1 provides a list of the key theoretical positions on social needs and their corresponding focus areas. Issues that fall outside the frame provided by the theory constitute the 'blindness', especially where these positions are unknowingly followed.

The conventional ('objective') approach to poverty measures social sustainability in terms of people's income or consumption (Ravallion, 1992). This understanding appears to be shared quite widely by decision-makers (that is, developers, politicians and authorities) in South Africa, who measure the social sustainability of development mainly by the number of jobs created and the income stream to local communities.

A second and related understanding (typically held by welfare institutions and local authorities) is that social sustainability is promoted when basic needs (water, sanitation, electricity, housing and so on) are met. The post-1994 South African Government introduced a plethora of policies in which it articulated an explicit understanding that social sustainability and well-being requires people not only to have income and basic services, but also to have institutional access to resources, power and decision-making. Thus, for instance, South Africa's National Environmental Management Act (NEMA) emphasises equity, justice, access and participation as key aspects of social sustainability. The human development approach used by some international aid organisations includes an appreciation for human resources, but neglects the impact of people's access to power and decision-making structures.

In an attempt to broaden the understanding of social sustainability, Caroline Moser (1998) developed a model that analyses and identifies the constraints on sustainable livelihoods. Moser (1998) called this model the Asset Vulnerability Framework, within which livelihoods are understood as the capacities, assets (material and social) and activities required for a means of living (Moser, 2005). This model includes all the focus areas of the theoretical positions identified in Table 1. The model developed by Moser (1998) within the context of poverty-reduction strategies can also be usefully applied as a model for understanding how project implementation impacts on the

Table 1. List of some of the key theoretical positions and their corresponding specific areas of focus.

Theoretical position/framework	Focus areas
Lack of income	Focus on level of income
Inadequate resources to satisfy basic needs (social welfare approach)	Access to basic services eg water, housing, sanitation, etc
Societal structures that lead to social exclusion	Impact of biased institutional structures on social needs; community preferences for service delivery
Barriers to human development	Human development index: longevity (life expectancy at birth), education attainment (adult literacy, educational enrolment ratios), standard of living (GDP and purchasing power parity)
Constraints on sustainable livelihoods	Local perspectives on factors that enable or constrain sustainable livelihoods

Source: Parnell et al (1999)

different kinds of capital that are essential for social sustainability.

The evolution of the Berg River Dam social impact monitoring programme was influenced by specific turning points. These occurred because of a conscious process of reflexivity and inquiry by the authors, who were the key architects and implementers of the Berg River Dam social impact monitoring programme. Reflexivity refers to the process of having constantly to think about, or reflect upon, the circumstances in which we live our lives (Giddens, 2001). Giddens (2001) believes that the knowledge we gain about society can affect the way in which we act in it. In other words, reflection and knowledge determines the interventions we use in society.

Reflexivity occurs when we become aware of how our observations or actions affect the very situations they are observing. It also occurs when the theory being formulated is disseminated to, and affects the behaviour of, the individuals or systems. In *Seeing like a State*, James Scott (1998) argues that bureaucracies have a tendency to perceive only those aspects of social realities that fit within their existing frameworks. This paper argues that, without conscious reflexivity, monitoring on large construction projects such as the Berg River Dam can have a tendency to be limited by myopic social realities.

We argue that, in the absence of an explicit theoretical framework, social impact monitoring can revert to an implicit and simplistic model of social sustainability (such as the social welfare model). This paper documents the implementation of the Berg River Dam's social-monitoring programme as it changed from the initial deductive 'checklist' approach (with a hidden theoretical model and a rigid attachment to the original form of the EMP) to a dynamic and inductive process using an explicit model of social sustainability. This paper is intended as a contribution (by illustrating a specific case study and social environment in South Africa) to the existing body of knowledge in the social impact monitoring field.

Background and social environment

The Berg River Dam is situated in the upper reaches of the Berg River system and is located less than 6km west of the town of Franschhoek in the Western Cape Province of South Africa (Figure 1). The rationale for the construction of the dam is to increase the yield of the Western Cape water supply system by 18%. The Berg River Dam comprises a concrete-face rock-fill dam (the embankment is 60m high and more than 900m wide) and a supplementary scheme 10km downstream whereby water will be diverted and pumped back into the dam.

The population of Franschhoek, which is located close to the dam, was estimated at 16,443 in 2001 in the South African census data. It is likely that the combination of the annual growth rate and in-migration has increased the total population to about 40,000. The communities residing in the project area range widely in terms of their socio-economic profile. According to Bloom (2003), 4.47% of the population in the project area have no income, while 65.8% have an income of less than US$6,500 per annum.

According to a household survey conducted as part of the Berg River Dam social-monitoring programme, 34% of workers in formal employ are reliant on seasonal labour on farms. The scenic beauty of Franschhoek with its surrounding winelands makes it a popular tourist destination. Work skills in the previously disadvantaged population are therefore aligned to the tourism and agricultural sectors. Franschhoek is also home to a significant percentage of highly skilled professionals and business people with considerable resources.

Planning phase of social impact monitoring

The planning phase of the Berg River Dam social-monitoring programme consisted of the social impact assessment (completed in 1996) conducted during the environmental impact assessment (EIA)

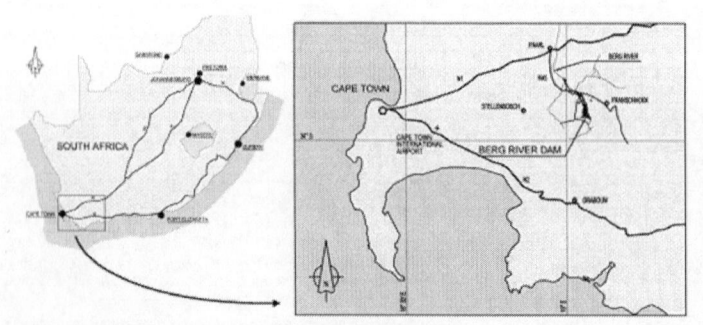

Figure 1. The Berg River Dam is located in the south west of South Africa, near the town of Franschhoek

The importance of theory in shaping social impact monitoring

> **The socio-economic strategy of the EMP aimed to develop strategies to compensate/mitigate social concerns and maximise social benefits: the strategies were developed by listing identified social impacts, grouping them into related issues, and mapping linked compensation strategies**

and the development of the socio-economic strategy (completed in 2003) prepared as part of the EMP. The framework for the social-monitoring programme is contained within the social impact assessment conducted as part of the EIA. The EIA for the Berg River Dam identified a range of potential social impacts (Table 2).

The social impact assessment report lacked a methodological description and therefore a theoretical link could not be made between the EIA and EMP stages. Because there was a seven-year gap between the completion of the EIA and the EMP, the process of developing the socio-economic strategy consisted of capturing issues and concerns identified by interested and affected parties. The focus of the socio-economic strategy was thus provided by key issues raised by stakeholders during the EMP stage.

The goal of the socio-economic strategy of the EMP was to develop effective strategies to compensate and mitigate any social concerns and maximise social benefits. The strategies were developed, first, by listing all identified social impacts. Secondly, impacts were grouped into categories of related issues. Thirdly, compensation and mitigation strategies were then mapped and linked to the impacts. The structure of the EMP socio-economic strategy included the following broad categories (ARUP, 2003):

- Community institutional and economic enhancement strategy
- Employment strategy
- Procurement policy
- Housing and infrastructure policy
- Education strategy
- Health strategy
- Traffic safety strategy
- Safety and security strategy
- Social monitoring and evaluation strategy

Berg River Dam social monitoring

Social monitoring on the Berg River Dam was initiated at the onset of the project as a response to the requirements of the EMP. It evolved through three distinct phases that are described below.

First phase (October 2004–January 2006)

The social-monitoring function was contracted to independent consultants. Monitoring initially focused on surveying the social impacts in the twelve geographic areas that had been identified as part of the project social environment. Social monitoring was undertaken strictly according to the requirements of the EMP.

Populating checklists The socio-economic strategy section of the EMP was taken as a direct and literal guideline. Social-monitoring data interpretation and reports were therefore structured according to the main categories that constituted the EMP socio-economic strategy (see list above). This use of the socio-economic strategy headings as a structure for social-monitoring reporting was a somewhat

Table 2. Summary of the key socio-economic impacts predicted in the EIA report

Negative impacts	Positive impacts
- economic losses for the forestry company associated with the inundation of forestry land;	- the provision of 70 million cubic meters of water for urban use and agriculture;
- the loss of approximately 20 forestry jobs;	- the creation of approximately 150 temporary jobs for the local community during the construction phase;
- the loss of approximately 25 jobs due to inundation of the trout farm;	- post construction benefits to the local community in terms of training and skills;
- the loss of employment of the approximately 150 local workers after the end of the construction period;	- the transfer of construction housing and infrastructure after the construction period;
- the possible immigration of unemployed people to the Franschhoek area in search of employment; and	- a boost to the local and regional economy during the construction phase; and
- the possible negative impact on the character and ambience of Franschhoek as a result of the increase in population, traffic congestion, noise, safety, crime and pollution during the construction phase.	- the potential to develop recreation and tourism associated with the dam.

Source: DWAF (1996)

forced reinterpretation of the original intention of the socio-economic strategy. The sections listed each contained potential impacts that the project had to consider and address as part of the EMP. The socio-economic strategy headings effectively became the 'checklist' for social monitoring and there was a focus on populating the checklists, albeit in narrative rather than quantitative format. As a result the following happened:

1. Headings assumed their own meaning. The headings of the socio-economic strategy were printed out and used as visual guidelines for monitoring. The original EMP was based on a prediction of potential impacts and response mechanisms needed. These predicted impacts did not necessarily match what respondents reported on. For this reason the reports produced for each section often pursued a different direction from what the original EMP expressed. So, for instance, the Housing and Infrastructure section of the EMP focused specifically on a housing and infrastructure development that was part of the Berg River Dam project. The report for this section focused on a variety of housing needs and concerns that interviewees spoke about but that had little to do with the Berg River Dam.
2. Social welfare theory by default. Because social monitoring was directed by the EMP checklist, there was no explicit statement on how the social environment was understood, or what the theoretical foundation or the research paradigm of the work was. As a consequence, the interpretation of data receded into one of the dominant societal discourses in South Africa, namely the social welfare understanding of community needs. This model works on the understanding that social vulnerability results from basic needs not being fulfilled. The classical response of social welfare institutions is to identify what 'things' to provide people with in response to the 'things' they lack. The provision of welfare grants, housing and basic services by the state is often an expression of this discourse.

The social welfare discourse typically uses institutionally expressed categories of social need. The EMP socio-economic strategy listed institutional categories of need (that is, housing and infrastructure, safety and security, education and so on). The result was that the reporting focused on a detailed listing of social needs in the project area that could be identified under each EMP heading. So, for instance, the following social needs were listed under the heading Welfare:

- Teenage pregnancies
- Drug abuse
- Promiscuity
- Lack of recreational facilities
- Alcoholism

Such a listing provides a particular lens through which local communities are viewed. One of the unintended consequences of this (implicit) theoretical model is that it identifies people through what they lack. The 'deficit' model of social development has been criticised in contemporary practice as disempowering and objectifying people (Escobar, 1996: 138). Another consequence is that the social-monitoring function drifted away from the issues related to the Berg River Dam processes and issues identified got a life of their own.

3. 'Things' get a life of their own. Some social needs identified under each heading in the monitoring reports then became compelling and started to get a life of their own (that is, separate and unrelated from the direct and cumulative impacts that could be identified with the Berg River Dam). Since interviewees spoke, for instance, with much concern about the increase of drug use amongst the youth, social-monitoring reports elaborated on the nature of this social concern and expressed the need for a response from the developers. This was the case even though there is no identifiable relationship between drug use by teenagers in the project area and the Berg River Dam, for which social monitoring was being done.

Data interpretation During the first phase of social monitoring, the lack of a social theory also resulted in a superficial interpretation and analysis of data. As a result, initial reports expressed conclusions such as:

People coming from outside are responsible for the substance abuse and subsequent teenage pregnancies in the area.

Upon review of the interview transcripts, it is clear that this statement in the report is an uncritical reiteration of an opinion held by an interviewee. Because social monitoring was conducted from a position that excludes an understanding of how power, agency and positionality affect discourse, the statement of the interviewee was taken to be factual evidence. The statement holds a number of assumptions, such as a relationship between:

- people from outside and substance abuse;
- substance abuse and teenage pregnancies; and
- teenage pregnancies and people coming in from outside the project area.

The list of assumptions reflects an unexpressed, unknowing and uncritical social welfare paradigm. The implications of the statement for the project could be huge. For example, large construction projects are often associated with in-migration or work seekers and therefore it could be read that 'people coming from outside' are people who

The importance of theory in shaping social impact monitoring

have come to work on the Berg River Dam. While this relationship was not expressed in the reports, the fact that the statement is made in a Berg River Dam social-monitoring report implies that the project stimulated the in-migration of people who are responsible for substance abuse and that the project has thus resulted in an increase in teenage pregnancies.

Mitigation and response A significant consequence of the checklist approach is that its focus on analysing *things* does not encourage a strategic understanding of *systems* and *processes*. Even if impacts are identified, their definition is often so devoid of context that it is difficult to determine response mechanisms and factors that would catalyse positive change. This was clearly evident during the first phase of social monitoring, which lacked any clear expression of impacts and even less indication of responses required. In effect, social monitoring remained a listing of distinct social phenomena that did not appear to have much to say to the Berg River Dam.

In summary, the approach used during the first phase of social monitoring on the Berg River Dam narrowly adhered to the requirements set out by the EMP categories. This dilemma is not unique to the Berg River Dam. For example, the Australian National Land and Water Resources Audit established that the indicators used to gather social and economic information for this substantial national audit are often not linked to clear questions that these indicators are meant to answer (Webb *et al*, 2004; ABARE, 2005). Similarly, during the phase 1 social monitoring, it was not always clear how the data gathered related to questions of impact and processes of the Berg River Dam. After a brief period of in-depth reflection and analysis, it was decided that social monitoring should be undertaken directly by TCTA as the developer.

Second phase (February 2006–May 2006)

In February 2006, the need for an explicit theoretical framework for social monitoring was recognised and a decision was made to simplify Moser's (1998) Asset Vulnerability Framework and adapt it for use as a model for social sustainability. For the Berg River Dam, Moser's model has been simplified to a focus on three kinds of capital: social, productive and human (Box 1).

The second phase of social monitoring continued with a focus on the various areas that had been identified as constituting the project social environment. The project interpretation of Moser's (1998) livelihoods model (see Box 1) replaced the EMP headings as the structuring elements of social-monitoring reports. Reporting became focused on analysing social, productive and human resources and structures that are likely to be impacted by the project's activities

---

Box 1. Forms of capital/resources required for social sustainability

Social capital is the value that people get from their social structure. It consists of two aspects: informal/horizontal social networks, such as family structures, and community/ neighbourhood relationships; and institutional or hierarchical relationships, such as with government institutions, development organisations and employers. An understanding of people's access to social capital requires an understanding of power dynamics, access and equity in their vertical and horizontal social relationships.

Productive capital concerns the resources people need to maximise their ability to produce livelihood resources. This includes access to employment opportunities and to resources (anything from finances to environmental resources) that are used to sustain livelihoods.

Human capital concerns the resources people need in order to sustain their health and well-being. This includes education and skills, health, safety, housing and basic services.

Source: Adapted from Moser (1998)

---

and processes. It thus became easier to identify and follow direct and cumulative social impacts.

Monitoring findings The theoretical framework within which social monitoring was now done, provided a new set of lenses through which the project social environment could be viewed. Monitoring methods and interpretation strategies were expanded to include:

- discourse analysis of transcribed in-depth individual and focus group interviews;
- a conscientious taking of field notes on what researchers observe and how they experience research encounters;
- the use of rapid rural appraisal methods (such as drawings by children depicting how they see their community having changed in response to the dam construction project); and
- visual (photo and video) research recording and analysis.

As a result of the widened lens used for research, hitherto unaddressed project social consequences came into view (Box 2 outlines one such field).

Monitoring methods and interpretation strategies were expanded to include: discourse analysis of in-depth interviews; a conscientious taking field notes on what researchers observe; rapid rural appraisal methods; and photo and video research recording and analysis

> **Box 2. Narrative of the Berg River Dam core workers and their associated impact on the social system**
>
> A significant social intervention brought about by the Berg River Dam (as with all large construction projects) was the introduction of a new social population, namely the skilled workers who were brought in by the contractors from elsewhere in the country to build the Berg River Dam (the core workers brought in by contractors are in fact not a homogenous social population but a diverse collective of people from all over the country who were brought together in the project area with one shared, and very defined, purpose). Social monitoring indicated that the social relationships between local residents and the imported skilled labour could be resulting in significant social changes and/or impacts. One example is sexual relationships between core workers and local women. These relationships have the potential to, for instance, alter the existing social support systems of local women, to diversify the social web to which local women are connected (by indirectly or directly linking them to the homesteads elsewhere in the country of workers, as well as the future working environments of the workers), to change the social and economic expectations of women (who perceive core workers to have financial stability), to change existing sexual and household relationships (where relationships involve women with existing partners), to change social behaviour patterns and to alter existing social contracts within local communities. During phase 1, social monitoring did not focus on the core staff that had been brought in, because the EMP focused on the monitoring of local communities. Within the new theoretical paradigm, however, it became clear that direct interviewing of core workers was essential for understanding the impact of the project on the social capital of local communities.

The change in research field in this case study (from only interviewing people from local communities to also interviewing core workers) came about because of more rigorous reflexivity on our part. We noticed that local people were reluctant to make any comments about the core workers; possibly because they were concerned about the consequences of their comments. Initially, core workers refused to be interviewed by TCTA researchers because they suspected that the research would be used to incriminate them with their employers (who in turn are contracted by TCTA). As we started to engage the core workers with clarity about the power dynamics involved, they became willing and co-operative in sharing their experiences. This enabled us to gain social perspectives on the lives of construction workers that would otherwise have remained hidden to us as the project developer.

Response mechanisms The method of inquiry in social monitoring shifted from an identification of needs (checklists of things to be monitored) to understanding the patterns and processes that impact on the flow of social, human and productive resources. The identification of appropriate social responses to project impacts and social concerns could therefore be contextualised and analysed within a robust model of social sustainability.

To improve the impact of reporting on decision-making, the social-monitoring reporting framework was changed to an executive summary style in which identified social impacts or concerns are linked to potential response mechanisms. Because TCTA, as the developer, was directly undertaking the monitoring and authoring the reports, mitigatory responses were internalised in the project's processes. To prevent inadvertent bias in social monitoring and reporting, a high level panel of experts was appointed to periodically review and critique the monitoring programme and its mitigation measures.

Third phase (June 2006–January 2008)

As indicated above, the theoretical framework used during the second phase of social monitoring started to make visible some potentially significant social implications of the project. By the end of the second phase, social monitoring and fieldwork had been undertaken in all the geographic areas that were identified as the Berg River Dam social environment and zones of influence.

The next step was to explore further the areas of social change that research during the second phase (and a reinterpretation of the first phase) suggested. Rather than continuing to focus on area-based monitoring, the social-monitoring team now focused on an in-depth investigation of specific issues that had been highlighted in previous social monitoring. These issues were developed into full specialist study areas relating to the forms of capital that impact on people's livelihood security. Here are some examples.

Social capital

Core staff studies Phase 2 monitoring indicated that the social networks and support systems of local communities may have been altered by the presence of core workers from elsewhere in the country. Specialist studies were conducted in the main core staff communities and results were communicated to contractors. TCTA realised that the impact of core workers on local communities is an industry-wide phenomenon and thus embarked on a plan to influence operating frameworks for the use of core workers in the industry. In addition, findings are being used to reformulate tender agreements for future TCTA projects.

In-migration In-migration into local communities by work seekers (other than the core workers who were brought in by their employers) can also result in social changes in local communities. A substantial migration survey was conducted to explore the view held by many phase 1 interviewees that the Berg River Dam has resulted in people moving into Franschhoek to work on the project. The study tracked people's movement patterns and the reasons for their movement.

The importance of theory in shaping social impact monitoring

Human capital

Impact of training Training done on the Berg River Dam has the potential to be a human capital resource for local communities. Many interviewees expressed scepticism about the actual benefit that training for local workers on the project will have for these workers. This study is an in-depth investigation of the nature of training on the project. It involves a discursive study of skills acquisition and a tracking of the socio-economic benefits that have come with training.

Productive capital

Livelihood studies TCTA recognises that the form of productive capital that the project has offered (that is, employment during the construction phase) has a limited life span. In-depth research is being done in local communities to develop an understanding of the various livelihood strategies that households employ. These include formal and informal income streams, multiple earners in one household, pension-based earning and social exchange. The results of these studies will be used as an input to the Berg River Dam Exit Strategy, which aims to support the existing livelihood strategies of local residents, supporting new opportunities and reducing the negative socio-economic impact associated with the cessation of construction.

Specialist studies are in many cases a further exploration of broad hypotheses that have come from the first and second stages of social monitoring. Because the project now applies a critical theoretical framework for social monitoring, statements made by interviewees are no longer taken as a report on the state of things but as situated positions that are to be understood within a discursive context. In essence, they direct the attention of the research team to those contexts and patterns that require further exploration.

The EMP becomes a responsive tool

During the third phase of social monitoring, the socio-economic strategy was revised. The aim was to change the EMP from a static tool defined by pre-construction period predictions of impacts to a dynamic process that responds to the changing project cycle and the realities of the social environment. The proposed changes are a result of:

- the need to update the EMP as a living document in keeping with best practice;
- the changes observed in the local social environment;
- the need to reflect the stage in the project cycle and its associated processes;
- the findings of the social-monitoring programme, which has revealed that the social impacts predicted in the EMP have largely not been realised because predicted activities have been taken into account in contract documentation and have been mitigated before construction commenced: the mitigation measures specified in the EMP thus required reformulation; and
- the shift in methodological approach from deductive monitoring where the EMP was previously taken as a prescriptive checklist, to the current inductive approach where qualitative monitoring is being undertaken in a strategic, critical and discursive manner.

Conclusions

What the social-monitoring practitioner observes and identifies as social changes related to the project, depends on the theoretical choices made. We have argued that the identification, monitoring, evaluation and mitigation of social impacts as part of project implementation requires a deep understanding of the dynamics operating in the social environment. Environmental and social practitioners at times take it for granted that social impacts can be identified through a deductive process of objective rationality based on a checklist approach. A checklist approach to social monitoring and evaluation leads the practitioner to a myopic focus on pre-determined checklist themes (for instance, employment, housing, education, health).

At the onset of social monitoring on the Berg River Dam the socio-economic strategy themes contained in the EMP were taken as direct and literal guidelines. Social monitoring therefore developed in a deductive manner, with a blind focus on data collection for monitoring the EMP themes. This approach blinded the practitioners to the impacts that the Berg River Dam was having on social networks, social processes, social structures and resources. Monitoring changed and adopted a model that distinguished among social, productive and human capital required for social sustainability.

The authors believe that having a clearly articulated theoretical foundation to social monitoring achieved the following objectives:

- it helped make explicit how the Berg River Dam is intervening in the social environment and how it is connected to the way social, productive and human capital are accessed by the local population;
- it made it possible to identify clear, effective and appropriate response mechanisms;
- it provided a robust research and inquiry orientation to social monitoring;
- it reflected the stance the practitioners adopted in the monitoring process;
- it framed the study and therefore provided a clear boundary for inquiry; and
- it enabled the data collection methods and reporting to have a clearly identifiable epistemological perspective and theoretical framework.

References

ARUP, engineers and consultants 2003. *Berg Water Project: Environmental Management Plan*. Cape Town: report prepared for TCTA.

ABARE, Australian Bureau of Agricultural and Resources Economics 2005. *Signposts for Australian Agriculture: a Framework for Developing Economic and Social Indicators*. Canberra: report prepared for the Australian National Heritage Trust.

Banks, G 1999. *Keeping an EYE on the Beasts: Social Monitoring of Large-scale Mines in New Guinea*. Working Paper no 21, Resource Management in Asia Pacific Project, Research School of Pacific and Asian Studies.

Bloom, J 2003. *An Economic Assessment of the Berg Water Project, Franschhoek*. Cape Town: report prepared for TCTA.

DWAF, Department of Water Affairs and Forestry 1996. *Skuifraam Dam Feasibility Study: Environmental Impact Assessment*. Cape Town: Ninham Shand.

Escobar, A 1996. Planning. In *The Development Dictionary: a Guide to Knowledge as Power*, ed. W Sachs, pp. 132–145. Johannesburg: Witwatersrand University Press.

Foucault, M 1977. *Discipline and Punish: the Birth of the Prison*. New York: Pantheon.

Giddens, A 2001. *Sociology*, 4th edn. Cambridge: Polity Press.

Inter-American Development Bank and Corporacion Andina de Fomento 2002. *Environmental and Social Monitoring Report, Camisea Natural Gas and Natural Gas Liquids Project*. Washington DC: Inter-American Development Bank.

Moser, C 1998. The asset vulnerability framework: reassessing urban poverty reduction strategies. *World Development*, 26(1), 1–19.

Moser, C 2005. Assets, livelihoods and social policy. Unpublished conference paper, Arusha conference on New Frontiers of Social Policy: Development in a Globalizing World, Arusha, Tanzania, 12–15 December. Washington DC: World Bank.

Parnell, S, O Crankshaw, D Crosoar, E Pieterse, M Poyser and J Wilson 1999. *Key Performance Indicators: Poverty Indicators and the Seven Strategic Priorities of the City of Cape Town*. Cape Town: Isandla Institute.

Ravallion, M 1992. *Poverty Comparison: a Guide to Concepts and Methods. Living Standards Measures*. Working Paper no 8. Washington DC: World Bank.

Scott, J 1998. *Seeing Like a State: How Certain Schemes to Improve the Human Condition Have Failed*. New Haven: Yale University Press.

Webb, T, K Cody, B Harrison, A Sincock and C Mues 2004. *Social and Economic Information for Natural Resource Management*. Canberra: report prepared for the Australian National Heritage Trust.

Deliberation and Actor-Networks: The "Practical" Implications of Social Theory for the Assessment of Large Dams and Other Interventions

STEWART LOCKIE

Faculty of Sciences, Engineering and Health, Central Queensland University, Rockhampton, Queensland, Australia

> This article reviews the potential contribution of deliberative theory and actor-network theory to the practice of social impact assessment (SIA). With reference to a case study of the World Commission on Dams, it argues for an approach to SIA that goes beyond documenting social change and that (1) targets consensus building among those impacted by planned interventions as a basic starting point for social scientific investigation; (2) places greater emphasis on the ways in which peoples' values, aspirations, perceived interests, and political coalitions change throughout the life of a proposal and shape their experience of project outcomes; (3) seeks to unravel the often unstated assumptions about who and what is important that are built into social data and stakeholder representative structures; and (4) challenges the separation of the "social" and the "natural" by fostering a more productive engagement between scientific and lay knowledges about the processes and impacts of change.
>
> **Keywords** actor-network theory, deliberative theory, social impact assessment, World Commission on Dams

The motivation for this article lies in four challenges that, in the author's experience, characterize the contemporary practice of environmental social science. The first of these is to contribute knowledge that makes a "practical" contribution to the management of natural resources. With concepts like sustainable development and triple-bottom-line reporting now commonplace, social scientists are increasingly called on to add the missing "social dimension" to environmental monitoring and decision making. The second challenge is to ensure that the application of the social sciences to environmental matters is theoretically informed. According to Rickson et al. (1998), without an understanding of basic sociological concepts such as power, would-be environmental social scientists risk failing to identify the underlying social causes of environmental degradation and conflict. But there is more to environmental social theory than the application of existing concepts to natural resource management. The third challenge, therefore, is to contribute to the development of theory that is uniquely placed to help understand and transform the relationships between humans and their environment. Unfortunately, this leads to a fourth

---

Received 26 January 2005; accepted 12 February 2007.
Address correspondence to Associate Professor Stewart Lockie, Faculty of Sciences, Engineering and Health, Central Queensland University, Rockhampton, QLD 4702, Australia. E-mail: s.lockie@cqu.edu.au

challenge, the large gap that exists between some of the more interesting innovations in environmental social theory and our capacity to apply these in any practical sense to inform environmental decision-making.

This article is concerned, therefore, with examining two theoretical perspectives on the relationships between humans and their environments in terms of the implications of these perspectives for the practical application of environmental social science. These theoretical approaches are (1) deliberative theory and (2) actor-network theory (ANT). ANT is also known as the sociology of scientific knowledge, the sociology of science and technology, the sociology of translations and the sociology of associations. This article by no means undertakes an exhaustive survey of environmental social theory. Nevertheless, it is suggested that deliberative theory and ANT are of particular relevance to this review due to the very different perspectives they bring to bear on the relationships between humans and the environments with which they interact. To illustrate this, the article examines the implications of each theoretical perspective for social impact assessment (SIA) and its application to large-scale environmental intervention through the well-known World Commission on Dams (WCD). The article does not offer a comprehensive assessment and critique of the WCD, but uses the WCD as an illustrative case study. The article begins with a brief description of the major theoretical debates that have characterized at least one of the environmental social sciences—environmental sociology—and the manner in which deliberative and actor-network theories seek to step outside these debates. It then turns to SIA and the questions raised for the practical application of environmental social sciences by these perspectives.

Bringing Nature into Social Theory

One of the defining characteristics of environmental sociology since it emerged as a distinct subdiscipline in the 1960s and 1970s has been vigorous debate over how best to bring nature into social theory. In what is generally represented as a debate between "realists" and "constructivists" (Dickens 1996), one of the main points of agreement between protagonists has been the need to move beyond the application of existing sociological concepts to environmental matters to an approach that more fundamentally rethinks the implications for the social sciences of humans' biological interdependence with the rest of nature. The former approach results in accounts of environmental movements, for example, that are rich in political and sociodemographic detail but make no mention of ecosystems processes or degradation. For constructivists, the implication is a minor one. The material reality of nonhuman nature is not contested. Pragmatically, however, a methodological stance is taken that restricts the focus for environmental social science to the "claims-making" activities that underpin environmental conflict and action while remaining agnostic toward the actual existence or severity of environmental conditions (Burningham 1998). This is justified on the grounds that opportunities are thus created to reduce environmental conflict. But it is also criticized for offering no explicit analysis of the moral and political implications of its subject matter (Hamlett 2003) and for ruling out of consideration the role of nature "in the social practices of everyday life" (Van Koppen 2000, 308).

Realists, by contrast, argue that nature-society relationships need to be understood historically and dialectically. According to Dickens (1996), the lives of humans are conducted in relation to a nature that is both subject to and resistant to transformation through human labor. Both ecological Marxists and ecofeminists discuss the alienation of humanity from nature and the manner in which a dualistic distinction between "nature" and "society" has historically been used in Western philosophy to legitimate the subordination of groups (such as women and slaves) that were defined as somehow "closer to nature" and thereby as less human (Dickens 1996; Merchant 1987). Norgaard's (1994) coevolutionary sociology takes a similarly dialectical approach in its examination of the ways in which environments, knowledge, technology, values, and forms of organization adapt to each other in unpredictable and potentially destructive ways. Despite substantial differences between these dialectical approaches, they have in common a view that nature should be attributed a sense of agency, a capacity to act, independently of human intervention.

Dialectical conceptions of "society" and "nature" are attractive in the sense that they allow for the possibility of sociological analyses that are at once socially and environmentally sensitive. It can also be argued, however, that dialectical approaches rely, in the end, on the same dualistic separation of nature and society that defines mainstream social theory (FitzSimmons and Goodman 1998) and that tends to favor distinctively social explanations for environmental "problems." Hence the interest of this article in deliberative theory and actor-network theory. Both of these perspectives attempt (although in very different ways) to subvert far more thoroughly the nature-society dualism. The question is whether this is an issue of purely theoretical interest or whether it can add utility to those conceptual and methodological tools used by environmental social scientists.

Social Impact Assessment and the World Commission on Dams

The practice of social impact assessment is used as a case study in this article due to its overt focus on the practical application of social scientific knowledge, as opposed to sociological analysis undertaken either solely for its own sake or in the hope that results might indirectly influence policy makers or other political actors. SIA developed initially in response to the U.S. *National Environmental Policy Act of 1969* and was defined by leading exponents as the practice of assessing or estimating, in advance, the social consequences likely to arise from specific policy actions and projects such as resource development, construction works, and so on (Burdge et al. 1995, 12). These consequences, Burdge et al. stated, could be considered in relation to any aspect of the ways "in which people live, work, play, relate to one another, organize to meet their needs, and generally cope as members of society" as well as "changes to the norms, values, and beliefs that guide and rationalize their cognition of themselves and their society" (Burdge et al. 1995, 11). More recently, an international group of leading SIA exponents extended this definition of SIA to link analysis of the intended and unintended consequences of planned interventions on people to the management of those consequences (Vanclay 2003).

One of the most enduring debates among SIA scholars concerns whether SIA should primarily be about predicting and/or measuring the impacts of intervention with certainty and precision (the technical paradigm), or whether it should primarily be about providing a mechanism to facilitate public involvement and empowerment in decision making (the participatory paradigm) (Lockie 2001). Many, however, regard the technical and participatory aspects of SIA as inseparable. Predictive techniques allow assessors to inform democratic debate by cautiously identifying a range of potential impacts (Burdge et al. 1995) and by identifying more clearly those interest groups who may not otherwise have the political resources to ensure their interests are represented (Bass 1998). Participatory techniques add to this in two broad ways (see Lockie 2001). First, they extend the scope of information that is made available to inform democratic debate. This information includes local knowledge about social conditions, processes, and potential impacts; subjective and cultural impacts relating to the ways in which people understand their social and natural environment; and the attitudes and perceptions that are likely to shape stakeholders' responses to proposed change. Second, participatory techniques provide specific mechanisms through which to involve different groups in decision-making processes. This is seen to encourage mutual understanding between stakeholders and a focus on maximizing the positive impacts of change for all stakeholders rather than simply compensating losers following project implementation. Together, these content and process aspects of participatory techniques may help to minimize conflict over projects by ensuring that as many interests as possible are considered in decisions and that appropriate mitigation strategies are put in place to manage adverse impacts (Lockie 2001).

It is worth noting here that despite what would appear to be very good reasons to integrate technical and participatory approaches to SIA, there is a growing trend in impact assessment practice to treat SIA and public consultation and participation as separate components of the planning and assessment process, with a correspondingly greater emphasis on the latter at the expense of technical SIA (Lockie 2001).

At face value, the World Commission on Dams incorporates something of both the technical and participatory paradigms. Bringing together representatives of governments, civil society, the private sector, international financial institutions, and affected peoples, in a process initiated by the World Bank and the World Conservation Union, the WCD was charged with undertaking an independent evaluation of the development effectiveness of large dams. The rationale for this lay in more than two decades of escalating conflict over the costs and benefits of large dams: conflicts that were seen to stem, at least in part, from a generalized failure in planning and decision-making processes to give adequate consideration to the negative social and environmental impacts of large dams (WCD 2000a). The WCD began its deliberations in 1998 and delivered its final report in 2000.

The WCD based its findings on analysis of 8 detailed case studies of large dams, a survey of 125 additional dams, 2 country reviews, and 17 thematic reviews on issues associated with dam development (WCD 2000a). Large dams, it was argued, are possibly unique in the spatial and temporal scales of their impact. Lengthy decision-making processes, extensive inundation areas, changes to downstream water flows and ecologies, substantial construction workforces, and the potential creation of new water and energy resources all contribute to a complex balance sheet of winners and losers. Despite the many social and economic benefits of large dams, the WCD (2000b) found that some 40–80 million people worldwide have been forced to relocate due to the construction of large dams. Many of these people have not adequately been recognized or documented, contributing to a failure to provide them with compensation, resettlement options, or alternative livelihoods. Millions more living downstream of large dams have had their livelihoods disrupted through changes to resource quality and access. Often, those living near reservoirs have also experienced adverse livelihood and health outcomes. Further, the WCD found, indigenous and tribal peoples, as well as ethnic minorities, have suffered a disproportionate rate of displacement and disruption to their livelihoods, culture, and spiritual

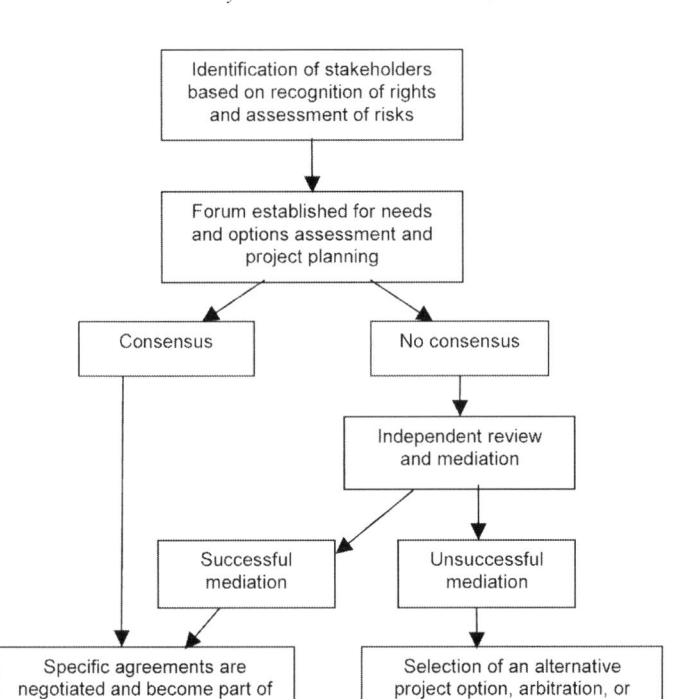

[Figure: flowchart showing WCD framework from "Identification of stakeholders based on recognition of rights and assessment of risks" → "Forum established for needs and options assessment and project planning" → branching to "Consensus" or "No consensus"; "No consensus" → "Independent review and mediation" → "Successful mediation" or "Unsuccessful mediation"; "Consensus" and "Successful mediation" → "Specific agreements are negotiated and become part of project compliance framework"; "Unsuccessful mediation" → "Selection of an alternative project option, arbitration, or judicial review".]

Figure 1. From rights and risks to negotiated agreements: the WCD framework for options assessment and project planning (adapted from WCD 2000b, 23).

existence, and the gender gap has widened in many affected communities. On the economic side, the WCD found that construction delays, cost overruns, and failure to meet physical targets for water supply or power generation have led, in the majority of cases, to lower than expected levels of cost recovery and profitability.

For the WCD, management of these impacts and the complex decision-making environment in which they are embedded is best undertaken through what is described as a "rights-and-risks" -based approach to the identification of legitimate stakeholders, the issues they need to consider, and thence to the negotiation of development plans in an open and transparent manner (see Figure 1). Further, they argue, this approach assists in the reduction of conflict and in the integration of social, economic, and environmental considerations in a holistic assessment of the costs and benefits of possible development paths. Deliberative theory, to which the article now turns, offers some conceptual insight as to why negotiation may be so important to the identification of social impacts.

Deliberation as a Model of Integration

Deliberative theory is particularly concerned with collective choice mechanisms, the rationalities—or ways of thinking—that they reflect, and possibilities for their reform. Of particular relevance here is Dryzek's (1996) notion of ecologically rational deliberation. To highlight what is meant by this concept, Dryzek (1996) contrasts this with instrumental rationality—a model for thinking and acting based on identifying the most efficient means with which to attain predetermined ends. Instrumental rationality, Dryzek (1996) argues, encourages the exploitation of resources for short-term gain, the discounting of future benefits and of intrinsic value in nature, and a reductionist outlook that ignores complexity and interdependence. Although many authors have pointed to the destructiveness of instrumental reason, Dryzek departs from other analyses in two important ways. To begin, he argues that instrumental rationality is not innate to particular social and bureaucratic institutions. However, he also argues that education about alternatives is not sufficient to challenge instrumental reason because education does not, by itself, address the forms of social organization, such as liberal capitalism, that make discounting the future and other forms of instrumental action appear rational and inevitable. Addressing these requires the promotion of collective choice mechanisms that support what he refers to as ecological *intersubjectivity*: that is, collective choice mechanisms that both acknowledge the inseparability of the social and the natural and seek to embed recognition of that inseparability in the attempts of participants in natural resource decision making to achieve mutual understanding. To illustrate this, Dryzek (1996) argues that what distinguishes situations where natural resources have been managed sustainably over long periods of time from those that have not is that the agencies and stakeholders involved have developed ways to communicate and interact with each other. These groups have also developed the ability to learn whom to trust and about the effects that their actions have on each other and on the resource, and they have developed norms, patterns of reciprocity, and institutions to solve problems and conflicts.

According to deliberative theorists, there is no universally applicable institutional structure or process with which to ensure that participants achieve ecological intersubjectivity or what might be described, in contrast with instrumental rationality, as ecological rationality. At issue is the coordination of action in a manner that is based on consensus reached through free and unconstrained debate among communicatively competent equals, and thus founded solely on the merits of arguments rather than on the defence of particular interests or points of view (Habermas 1984; Dryzek 1990). According to Miller (1992), the role of deliberation is not to establish universal standards of "right" and "wrong," or to embark on a process of discovery to find the one "correct" answer to a dispute or problem, but to arrive at decisions that participants believe fair and reasonable. Decisions may be based as much on participants' assessments of appropriate procedures or norms as on their assessment of empirical "facts." Communicatively rational deliberation is based on the assumption that while it is not possible in many circumstances for all claims to be satisfied (e.g., in use of a resource), it is possible for people's views "to be swayed by rational arguments and to lay aside particular interests and opinions in deference to overall fairness and the common interest of the collectivity" (Miller 1992, 56). Deliberative theory is not, therefore, concerned with developing a precise science of ecological rationality (Little 2000) but with encouraging the decentralisation of decision making to local communities, sensitivity to ecological feedback signals, and deliberation that looks beyond self-interest to consider collective and ecological well-being (Dryzek 1987).

What is the significance of this for the environmental social sciences? Dryzek (1996, 33) argues that the environmental social sciences must highlight the ways in which particular ways of thinking come to be taken for granted in the material practice of natural resource management and thence contribute to sustained debate over alternatives. In doing so, the emphasis is shifted away from attempts to predict and control the outcomes of policy and project interventions and toward the facilitation, in various ways, of flexible, open and participatory processes of deliberation (Dryzek 1990). Too often, attempts to predict and control the outcomes of policy and project interventions impose unstated goals and values that may not be shared among those affected by those interventions. At the very least, this is likely to result in questionable conclusions and dissatisfaction with outcomes (Dryzek 1990). However, it may also preempt the outcomes of debates and decision-making processes through which the values, aspirations, perceived interests, and political positions of stakeholders are likely to change. Social impacts are not, in this sense, waiting to be discovered by independent and objective researchers, but constructed actively through the processes of conflict, negotiation, and reflection emerging around proposed change. Before policy interventions even have been put in place, the social milieu that was subjected to the impact assessment will have been transformed—new interest groups will have emerged, new alliances formed, values and aspirations redefined, and new forms of political struggle identified (Lockie et al. 1999; Lockie 2001). The question is, if the environmental social sciences are to disentangle the rationalities that shape natural resource decision making in order to reflect these to potential participants in collective choice, what conceptual and methodological tools are they to apply in doing so? On this, deliberative theory has less to say. It is a theory more of what the environmental social sciences *should* be doing to contribute to political debate than it is a theory of *how* they should be doing it. In this respect, actor-network theory could hardly be more different.

Actor-Network Theory and Rationality

Actor-network theory (ANT) is notoriously agnostic (and much criticized) on the politics and appropriate focus of the social sciences. Making no stronger political statement than that social scientists should attempt to *represent* the social to itself in all its consequences and uncertainties (Latour 2000), ANT puts forward three basic theoretical propositions (see Latour 2005). First, it must be accepted that nonhuman species, ecosystem processes, and technologies make a material difference to social affairs. Second, the sorts of categorizations that are traditionally used to describe the social (categorizations such as gender, occupation, place, ethnicity, etc.) have no intrinsic explanatory power. Instead, the formation, stabilization, and transformation of groups are phenomena that themselves need to be explained. Third, the task of social science is not to deconstruct or debunk the so-called "grand narratives" of modernity and thus to explain away scientific knowledge, for example, as a mere set of "social constructions" no different to any other knowledge claim. Rather, it is to explore how new procedures, techniques, concepts, and institutions are used to pull the social together in whatever (unstable) form the social scientist might find it.

It is for the first of these propositions that ANT is most (in) famous. ANT makes no theoretical or methodological distinction between the social and the natural. Social networks, it claims, are "hybrid assemblages" of humans and nonhumans, beings and things (Latour 1993). From this perspective, understanding the role of the nonhuman is fundamental not only to what we recognize as explicitly environmental issues, but to any kind of sociological knowledge or theory. Not surprisingly, this argument attracts criticism for falsely attributing distinctly human traits (such as the capacity for language, consciousness, reflection, and intentional resistance) to the actions of nonhumans (see Hacking 1999). However, ANT does not dispute that there are real and substantial differences between humans and nonhumans. The point is that concepts such as agency and power should not be seen as the properties of individuals but as the outcomes of interactions within a network. The resources that help an actor to exert considerable influence in one social setting may have little or no value in another. Thus, as Hindess (1996; see also Foucault 1986) argues, power can take many forms, at times concentrated and hierarchical and at times dispersed. As a consequence, actor-network theorists argue that rather than attempting to define or attribute power and agency in theoretical terms, they should be treated simply as empirical research questions (Callon and Law 1995; Latour 1999).

The key concept here is that of "translation." Translation refers to the processes through which actors are enrolled and mobilized within networks. As the term "translation" implies, actors are not brought into association with each other unchanged. They are displaced, redefined, and transformed (Callon 1986), often in ways that are not readily apparent (Law 1994). Translation takes actors from one world and—by aligning their properties, actions, interests, or concerns—places them in another (Leigh Star 1991). Translation can be both violent and forceful, or mutually consensual, but it can also be more subtle and complicated. ANT research on science and technology has pointed to the use of "various kinds of devices, inscriptions, forms and formulae" that attempt to "sum up" (that is, record, calculate, and represent) and coordinate the interactions of multiple actors across a variety of sites (Latour 1999, 17). Statistics, law, science, accounting, media, auditing, and mapping are common examples of such techniques, and telephones, ships, compasses, and computers are common examples of the devices on which they rely. The concept of "action at a distance" is used by Latour (1987, 219) to study the apparently global extension of networks through the deployment of technologies of knowledge that allow for the consistent collection and transmittal of information across space and time. Localized scientific practice is used to render the world outside the laboratory knowable and manipulable "at a distance." Other technologies of knowledge—such as the collection of statistics—are similarly deployed to render those aspects of the social world beyond the immediate sphere of state control knowable and calculable (Murdoch and Ward 1997). None of these techniques, of course, offers any guarantee of success, and networks are often characterized by fluidity and instability as actors resist translation and/or attempt to mobilize competing networks (Callon 1986).

The theoretical and empirical arguments of ANT are drawn from what is presented as a highly open-ended ethnographic approach to social research based on "following the actors"—whoever and whatever they may be—as they engage in processes of translation and enrolment (Latour 1987). The only injunction here is that established by the principle of analytical symmetry; that is, the idea that the contributions of humans and nonhumans to the phenomena in which we are interested need to be given equal analytical priority (Callon 1986). No-body, and no-thing, should be assumed a priori to be more important than another. As Latour (2005) argues, the point of this analytical and political agnosticism is not to deconstruct the notion of the social, the importance of science, or the reality of inequity and disadvantage. The point, rather, is to focus analytical attention on *how* particular social arrangements come to be: drawing out those elements of network construction that are not necessarily apparent at first glance (Leigh Star 1991); exploring the character of distributive strategies and the resources on which they are based (Law 1991); highlighting the costs imposed on actors because of their membership or nonmembership of networks (Leigh Starr 1991); assuming that no matter how entrenched and naturalized relations appear, things "*could be otherwise*" (Law 1991, 6, italics in original); and representing the social to itself in all its consequences and uncertainties (Latour 2000). Thus, we are asked not to abandon analysis of the social relations that surround resource degradation and change, but to develop accounts that tie together processes of ecosystem change and social interaction, rather than treating one as the cause of the other.

Deliberative Theory, ANT and SIA

At face value, deliberative theory would appear to offer additional support both to the WCD process and outcomes and to participatory forms of SIA in general. However, it would also suggest that participation, for its own sake, is not sufficient to guarantee reform in decision making. In fact, consultation and participation may be used by assessors, development proponents, and other agencies simply to secure public support for proposed change, marginalize political dissent from minority groups, capture local knowledge, and divert attention from other projects. In guarding against this, deliberative theory provides a number of criteria based on ideal-typical models of communicative rationality and ecological intersubjectivity against which to evaluate natural resource planning and decision-making processes. As we have seen, these criteria relate to the coordination of action through decision-making processes that are open to all stakeholders; that promote free and unconstrained debate; that take practical steps to ensure all contributors are able to participate as communicatively competent equals; that focus on the merits of arguments and the interests of the collectivity rather than on the defence of particular interests; and that aim, ultimately, to reach decisions that all participants believe fair and reasonable. To what extent was this achieved by the WCD? According to at least one insider:

> The overriding lesson [from the WCD] is that a way forward can be found when the space is created for people to meet in a civilized and constructive atmosphere, listen to each other with mutual respect and together decompose the problems into their component parts and construct appropriate solutions. Participation has become a byword in development circles. The question is how to ensure it is effective and move from a culture of talking past each other to meaningful participation where the discussions are more open and inclusive, are conducted in good faith and have a demonstrable influence on the outcome. (Bird 2002, 113)

Thus the WCD case presents itself as evidence that interest groups can put aside their differences in deference to the common good. Certainly, the WCD report was eagerly awaited by many and has had some influence on the practices of a number of governmental and multilateral institutions (Bird 2002). Although they are not linked to any binding legal framework, the report and its recommendations have attained a moral authority that is difficult for such institutions to ignore without justification (Dingwerth 2005). Nevertheless, implementing the WCD process did require sustained work on the perceptions of fairness surrounding its activities and explicit attention to processes of mediation between stakeholders (Brinkerhoff 2002). Conflict and scepticism surrounded the entire WCD process and its proposed rights-and-risk approach to dam assessment and planning received significant criticism (see Brinkerhoff 2002; Fujikura et al. 2003; Fujikura and Nakayama 2003). This is not to deny the very real achievements of the WCD (see Bird 2002). After all, the consensus model of decision making promoted by the WCD is something that the WCD itself achieved to only a limited extent. The consensus view put forward by the WCD was the consensus view of the 12 commissioners who led the process. It was not the consensus view of the 70 member stakeholder forum or the hundreds of other people consulted during preparation of the report (Brinkerhoff 2002). While it can be argued that data gathering within the WCD was participatory, to a point, it certainly cannot be argued that decision making was anything other than the preserve of a small elite. Nor can it be argued that these elite were representative of broader constituencies for—apart from the absence of any legitimate electoral process to select such representatives—the very notion of sectoral representativeness understates the tremendous diversity of interests to be found within the so-called state, civil society, and private sectors from which commissioners were drawn (see Dingwerth 2005). Further, no guidance was provided in the WCD's proposed model of decision making on the relative importance that the interests of different stakeholders should receive (Dingwerth 2005) or on the management of situations in which one or more stakeholders refuse to consider compromise in light of the interests and views of others (see Fujikura and Nakayama 2003). The WCD model suggests that, in the absence of consensus between legitimate stakeholders, independent arbitration should be used to arrive at decisions. However, no criteria are provided to guide such arbitration, particularly where it does not, by itself, facilitate movement toward consensus.

Of course, at the same time that deliberative theory may be used to evaluate the participatory claims of the WCD, the experience of the WCD may be used, conversely, to reflect on the utility of deliberative theory as a tool to inform impact assessment and other applications of environmental social science. Deliberative theory certainly has been criticized as a utopian and ultimately impractical set of normative principles that are unlikely to be realized in practice on any sort of widespread scale (Little 2000). Justice research has established empirically that while a sense of procedural fairness can help people to accept the legitimacy of decision-making processes from which they are likely to emerge as "losers," it does not always guarantee compliance with the decisions that emerge from those processes (Nancarrow and Syme 2001). Securing compliance in situations of compromise requires that participants recognize themselves as members of some sort of collectivity to which they are responsible and accountable (Syme et al. 2006). Broadly speaking, this may seem less likely to be the case in transboundary and other spatially extensive disputes over resource access and management than in relatively localized disputes. This should not, however, be assumed. As the current fashion for triple-bottom-line and corporate social responsibility reporting shows, even the largest and most transnational of resource users can face significant risks and costs associated with disputes over resource use.

On this basis, it might be argued that the greatest potential contribution of deliberative theory to SIA and similar tools is not the broad support it offers for participatory approaches but its contextualization of collective choice within different models of decision-making rationality linked to wider political projects. Missing, however, is a comprehensive set of conceptual tools with which to examine the concrete processes through which any given rationality is actually incorporated within SIA and other practices. ANT, by contrast, moves us beyond broad critiques of technocratic manipulation by examining *how* particular rationalities of governance and technologies of knowledge are deployed in specific spatial and temporal settings. ANT raises questions regarding how actors are enrolled in specific networks, what they gain and/or give up in order to participate, how they are (re)defined by others and themselves in this process, the projects they intend to pursue, and how they are constrained by the rationalities and knowledge claims of others. Neither membership in particular communities of interest, nor the identities inscribed on actors by virtue of their membership in those communities, are taken for granted. Instead, the concept of translation encourages SIA practitioners to examine in more detail the strategies that are used to mobilize, stabilize, and transform networks around planned intervention; the destruction or exclusion of other networks, identities and projects inconsistent with such interventions; and the changing identities and relationships experienced by actors as both positive and negative impacts of network mobilisation, marginalisation, and/or dissolution around intervention. Would greater consideration of these questions have led to a fundamentally different approach to the WCD? Or to potentially different outcomes?

The efforts made by the WCD to increase the relative visibility of women and ethnic minorities (e.g., indigenous peoples) and the differential impacts of dam construction they experience (Adams 2000; WCD 2000a) certainly show awareness of issues of exclusion. However, by conceptualizing power as a network effect, ANT suggests that, in addition to examining more obvious cases of marginalisation and exclusion, SIA researchers should pay more attention to the subtle and often indirect ways in which actors are influenced "at a distance." In practical terms, this means questioning where knowledge comes from and the assumptions on which it is based—for example, questioning the use of fixed and predefined categories within statistical data that may tell us little about the local relevance of such categories or how they articulate with the social networks to which actors belong, and the identities they would prefer to adopt. The point here is not that social assessors should be dismissive of statistical and secondary data, but that they should strive to be aware of who and what is excluded from statistical definitions and how the abstracted realities of data can be reimposed on the worlds they portend to reflect (see also Murdoch and Ward 1997). The same is true of the categories used to select and organize participants in decision-making processes. The WCD stakeholder forum, for example, was seen as broadly representative, including delegates from "multilateral agencies, bilateral agencies, export credit guarantee agencies, government agencies, utilities, research institutes and individual researchers, private sector firms, river basin authorities, engineers, NGOs, environmentalists, and indigenous and affected peoples groups" (Brinkerhoff 2002, 1292). In addition to participating in consultation, delegates were charged with disseminating and building support for the WCD's findings among their constituencies. There is an obvious resonance here with the challenge identified earlier of fostering among stakeholders in decision making a sense that they belong to, and are accountable to, a distinct collectivity: a challenge that was made all the more difficult in this case by two factors. First, the constituencies represented by stakeholder forum members were vaguely defined and offered limited avenues for direct involvement in the WCD. Second, as the spatial and temporal scale of planned intervention increases, it is reasonable to expect that finding ways to describe network membership is likely to become more difficult. As Adams (2000) advocates in one of the WCD thematic review papers, fostering a genuine sense of belonging is best achieved through widespread participation in the design and interpretation of data gathering exercises *throughout the life of an intervention*. The composition of target groups and proposed decision-making strategies must, therefore, be revisited regularly as projects progress if they are to keep pace with the processes of social change surrounding major interventions. There is little evidence that such a degree of negotiated flexibility was applied to the WCD itself.

The final issue addressed here concerns the ANT principle of analytical symmetry and its suggestion that SIA practitioners should avoid excluding claims about the biophysical aspects of planned interventions from their analysis. This can represent something of a challenge in circumstances where social assessors must take projected ecological and economic changes associated with planned intervention—as determined by expert assessors in these fields—as starting points in the identification of social impacts. Thus we find in WCD reports on social issues a starting assumption that social impacts are derived from environmental and economic impacts, and thence a predominant concern with the distribution of costs and benefits as opposed to the facilitation and documentation of debate over the technical, environmental and/or other aspects of dams (Adams 2000). While it is true that these reports do advocate participatory processes and sensitivity to local knowledge in the planning, design, and construction of dams (Adams 2000), they do not clearly address the roles of participation and local knowledge in environmental impact assessment or the potential for SIA more generally to inform understanding of environmental and economic impacts. The issue here is not one of highlighting the constructedness of the scientific knowledge claims on which environmental impact assessments are based but of acknowledging the interdependencies among people, technologies, and ecologies within planned interventions and the ensuing roles of local knowledge and actions in coconstructing the biophysical outcomes of that intervention. In practical terms, this suggests using SIA as a conduit to facilitate genuine involvement among impacted stakeholders in the full cycle of project planning, assessment, implementation and monitoring; taking seriously the "local" knowledge of those stakeholders; and fostering the collaborative evolution of new knowledge and understanding (Adams 2000). SIA conceivably may play a very constructive role here in providing a process through which to mediate competing knowledge claims and link these more closely with proposed interventions.

Conclusion

As stated earlier, this article has not sought to offer a detailed review either of environmental social theory or of the World Commission on Dams. Rather, it has sought to examine two quite divergent, and at times obtuse, theoretical perspectives to see what they may offer in the practical application of the environmental social sciences. With the value of public participation in natural resource management widely recognized, the question is what the two theoretical perspectives reviewed here might have to offer, in a practical sense, that any other reflexive and sensitive approach to the environmental social sciences might not. In light of recent trends to separate SIA and public consultation for large projects, this question takes on a special significance. Together, deliberative and actor-network theories suggest a number of conclusions of particular relevance to SIA.

First, Dryzek (1996) argues that collective choice mechanisms based on intersubjectivity (not public participation for its own sake) have been shown empirically to offer the most opportunities for sustainable resource use. Without wishing to prescribe this as a universally applicable goal, the pursuit of genuine consensus provides a useful starting point in any consideration of the ends to which the social sciences may be applied. Second, deliberative theory also suggests that participation in decision making is not only a matter of peoples' right to self-determination or of the pragmatic need to secure their compliance with decisions based on those processes. As important as these are, fostering participation in decision making is also critical to the basic empirical validity of social assessments. Although any planned intervention is likely to generate unexpected outcomes, it is crucial to remember that the subjective factors that shape peoples' experience and evaluation of outcomes (i.e., their values, aspirations, perceived interests, and political coalitions) are all likely to change throughout the life of an intervention and through interaction with other stakeholders.

Third, the environmental social sciences play a key role in the facilitation of free democratic discourse by drawing out the rationalities (the ways of thinking and other unstated assumptions) that underlie the data on which decisions are based. Key issues here include the categorizations that are used to define, monitor, and enroll stakeholders in processes of planning, assessment, and decision making; the exclusions and redefinitions that are inherent in any system of categorization; the goals and outcomes that are accorded legitimacy; and the stakeholder representative structures that are set up in response to these categorizations and goals. Fourth, ANT suggests that social impact assessors might constructively challenge an exclusively human model of intersubjectivity by exploring who seeks to speak on behalf of the animals, plants, microbes, and ecosystems that are, ultimately, just as critical to sustainable natural resource management as the people with whom they interact. The task here is not to pretend expertise across an ever-expanding range of disciplines, but to facilitate discourse that encourages all stakeholders to engage both seriously and critically with the knowledge claims of others. Such a process seeks neither to romanticize local knowledge nor to deconstruct scientific knowledge. Rather, it seeks to open both to new perspectives and hypotheses and to extend the notion of peer review to a wider community. As mentioned earlier in relation to specifically sociological knowledge, intersubjective processes of deliberation may be expected to improve the robustness of scientific knowledge, not to undermine it.

References

Adams, W. 2000. *The social impact of large dams: Equity and distributional issues.* Cape Town, South Africa: World Commission on Dams.

Bass, R. 1998. Evaluating environmental justice under the national environmental policy act. *Environ. Impact Assess. Rev.* 18:83–92.

Bird, J. 2002. Nine months after the launch of the World Commission on Dams report. *Water Resources Dev.* 18:111–126.

Brinkerhoff, J. 2002. Partnership as a social network mediator for resolving global conflict: The case of the World Commission on Dams. *Int. J. Public Admin.* 25:1281–1310.

Burdge, R., P. Fricke, K. Finsterbusch, W. Freudenberg, R. Gramling, A. Holden, L. Llewellyn, J. Petterson, J. Thompson, and G. Williams. 1995. Guidelines and principles for social impact assessment. *Environ. Impact Assess. Rev.* 15:11–43.

Burningham, K. 1998. A noisy road or a noisy resident?: A demonstration of the utility of social constructionism for analysing environmental problems. *Sociol. Rev.* 46:536–563.

Callon, M. 1986. Some elements of a sociology of translation: Domestication of the scallops and the fishermen of St. Brieuc Bay. In *Power, action and belief: A new sociology of knowledge?*, ed. J. Law, 196–229. London: Routledge and Kegan Paul.

Callon, M. and J. Law. 1995. Agency and the hybrid collectif. *S. Atlantic Q.* 94(2):481–507.

Dickens, P. 1996. *Reconstructing nature: Alienation, emancipation and the division of labour.* London: Routledge.

Dingwerth, K. 2005. The democratic legitimacy of public-private rule making: What can we learn from the World Commission on Dams. *Global Governance* 11:65–83.

Dryzek, J. 1987. *Rational ecology: Environment and political economy.* Oxford, UK: Basil Blackwell.

Dryzek, J. 1990. *Discursive democracy: Politics, policy and political science.* Cambridge, UK: Cambridge University Press.

Dryzek, J. 1996. Foundations of environmental political economy: The search for homo ecologicus? *N. Polit. Econ.* 1(1):27–40.

FitzSimmons, M. and D. Goodman. 1998. Incorporating nature: Environmental narratives and the reproduction of food. In *Remaking reality: Nature at the millennium*, ed. B. Braun and N. Castree, 194–220. London: Routledge.

Foucault, M. 1986. Disciplinary power and subjection. In *Power*, ed. S. Lukes, 229–242. Oxford, UK: Blackwell.

Fujikura, R. and M. Nakayama. 2003. Perception gaps among stakeholders regarding the WCD guidelines. *Int. Environ. Agreements Polit Law Econ.* 3:43–57.

Fujikura, R., M. Nakayama, and K. Mori. 2003. Applicability of the World Commission on Dams' recommendations for public financial assistance: A case for Japanese yen loan assistance. *Hydrol. Processes* 17:2737–2751.

Habermas, J. 1984. *The theory of communicative action, volume one: Reason and the rationalisation of society.* Cambridge, UK: Polity Press.

Hacking, I. 1999. *The social construction of what?* London: Harvard University Press.

Hamlett, P. 2003. Technology theory and deliberative democracy. *Sci. Technol. Hum. Values* 28:112–140.

Hindess, B. 1996. *Discourses of power: From hobbes to foucault.* Oxford, UK: Blackwell.

Latour, B. 1987. *Science in action: How to follow scientists and engineers through society.* Cambridge, MA: Harvard University Press.

Latour, B. 1993. *We have never been modern.* Cambridge, MA: Harvard University Press.

Latour, B. 1999. On recalling actor-network theory. In *Actor network theory and after*, ed. J. Law, 15–25. Oxford, UK: Blackwell.

Latour, B. 2000. When things strike back: A possible contribution of "science studies" to the social sciences. *B. J. Sociol.* 51(1):107–123.

Latour, B. 2005. *Reassembling the social: An introduction to actor-network theory.* Oxford, UK: Oxford University Press.

Law, J. 1991. Introduction: Monsters, machines and sociotechnical relations. In *A sociology of monsters: Essays on power, technology and domination*, ed. J. Law, 1–23. London: Routledge.

Law, J. 1994. *Organizing modernity.* Oxford, UK: Blackwell.

Leigh Star, S. 1991. Power, technology and the phenomenology of conventions: On being allergic to onions. In *A sociology of monsters: Essays on power, technology and domination*, ed. J. Law, 26–56. London: Routledge.

Little, A. 2000. Environmental and eco-social rationality: Challenges for political economy in late modernity. *N. Polit. Econ.* 5(1):121–134.
Lockie, S. 2001. Social impact assessment in review: Setting the agenda for impact assessment in the Twenty-First Century. *Impact Assess. Project Appraisal* 19(4):277–287.
Lockie, S., S. Momtaz, and B. Taylor. 1999. Meaning and the construction of social impacts: Water infrastructure development in Australia's Gladstone/Calliope region. *Rural Society* 9:529–542.
Merchant, C. 1987. *The death of nature: Women, ecology and the scientific revolution.* San Francisco: Harper and Row.
Miller, D. 1992. Deliberative democracy and social choice. *Polit. Stud.* 40:56–67.
Murdoch, J. and N. Ward. 1997. Governmentality and territoriality: The statistical manufacture of Britain's "national farm." *Polit. Geogr.* 16(4):307–324.
Nancarrow, B. and G. Syme. 2001. Challenges in implementing justice research in the allocation of natural resources. *Social Just. Res.* 14:441–452.
Norgaard, R. 1994. *Development betrayed: The end of progress and a coevolutionary revisioning of the future.* London: Routledge.
Rickson, R., J. Western, and R. Burdge. 1998. The use of social impact assessment knowledge in development decisions. In *A conceptual approach to social impact assessment: Revised edition*, ed. R. Burdge, 79–91. Middleton, WI: Social Ecology Press.
Syme, G., E. Kals, B. Nancarrow, and L. Montada. 2006. Ecological risks and community perceptions of fairness and justice: A cross-cultural model. *Hum. Ecol. Risk Assess.* 12:102–119.
Vanclay, F. 2003. *Social impact assessment: International principles.* Fargo, ND: International Association for Impact Assessment, Special Publication Series No. 2.
Van Koppen, C. 2000. Resource, arcadia, lifeworld. Nature concepts in environmental sociology. *Sociol. Rural.* 40:300–318.
World Commission on Dams. 2000a. *Dams and development: A new framework for decisionmaking. The report of the World Commission on Dams.* London: Earthscan.
World Commission on Dams. 2000b. *Dams and development: A new framework for decisionmaking. The report of the World Commission on Dams: An overview.* Cape Town, South Africa: World Commission on Dams.

Part VI
SIA in Practice

Environmental Impact Assessment Review

Public participation and environmental impact assessment: Purposes, implications, and lessons for public policy making

Ciaran O'Faircheallaigh *

Department of Politics and Public Policy, Griffith Business School, Griffith University, Queensland 4111, Australia

ARTICLE INFO

Article history:
Received 13 February 2009
Received in revised form 24 April 2009
Accepted 3 May 2009
Available online 26 May 2009

Keywords:
Public participation
Environmental impact assessment
Social impact assessment
Public policy

ABSTRACT

In recent years the need to enhance public participation in Environmental Impact Assessment (EIA), and the efficacy of alternative mechanisms in achieving this goal, have been central themes in the EIA literature. The benefits of public participation are often taken for granted, and partly for this reason the underlying rationale for greater public participation is sometimes poorly articulated, making it more difficult to determine how to pursue it effectively. The reasons for seeking public participation are also highly diverse and not always mutually consistent. There has been limited analysis of the implications of different forms and degrees of public participation for public decision making based on EIA, and little discussion of how experience with public participation in EIA relates to debates about participation in policy making generally. This paper distinguishes various purposes for public participation in EIA, and discusses their implications for decision making. It then draws on some general models of public participation in policy making to consider how approaches to participation in EIA can be interpreted and valued, and asks what EIA experience reveals about the utility of these models. It argues that the models pay insufficient attention to the interaction that can occur between different forms of public participation; and to the fact that public participation raises issues regarding control over decision making that are not subject to resolution, but must be managed through ongoing processes of negotiation.

© 2009 Elsevier Inc. All rights reserved.

1. Introduction

Even a cursory glance at recent writing on EIA and related decision making processes shows that the issue of public participation in EIA is a major focus for scholars and practitioners (Chavez and Bernal, 2008; Cooper and Elliott, 2000; Del Furia and Wallace-Jones, 2000; Devlin and Yap, 2008; Diduck and Mitchell, 2003; Doelle and Sinclair, 2006; Hartley and Wood, 2005; Kapoor, 2001; Lockie, 2001; Lockie et al., 2008; Mayoux and Chambers, 2005; Morrison-Saunders and Early, 2008; Stewart and Sinclair, 2007). While some scholars do indicate that public participation can in certain circumstances have negative consequences (Cooper and Elliott, 2000, p. 342; Lawrence, 2003, p. 270–71), the overwhelming view is that it is highly desirable and that the key issue for scholars and practitioners is to find ways of making it more effective. For instance Stewart and Sinclair (2007, p.161) state that 'The benefits of public participation have been clearly described in both theoretical and practical terms ... [but] the design and implementation of specific public participation programs remain contentious'. Similarly, Hartley and Wood (2005, p. 333) state that while public participation 'is widely documented as being a valuable component of the EIA process', debate continues about how to undertake it (see also Chavez and Bernal, 2008, p.167; Cooper and Elliott, 2000, p. 342; Daneke et al., 1983; Doelle and Sinclair, 2006, p. 186; Lemon et al., 2004, p. 191–92; Lockie et al., 2008, p. 178–80; Vanclay, 2003).

Perhaps because its benefits are assumed to be obvious and substantial, the specific rationale for seeking greater public participation is not always clearly articulated. In many cases multiple purposes are listed without differentiation between them or without discussion of how they relate to each other, or of whether certain potential benefits are omitted because they are not considered significant. For instance Momtaz and Gladstone (2008, p. 223) include in the objectives of public participation 'sharing information, involving the community at an early stage of decision making, taking community aspirations into considerations and giving the community the ability to influence the outcome of decision making'. Stewart and Sinclair (2007, p. 162) envisage an even wider range of benefits, including access to local knowledge; broadening the range of solutions considered; avoiding costly litigation; strengthening the democratic fabric of society; acting as a vehicle for individual and community empowerment; and promoting broadly-based individual and social learning, so enabling the transition to sustainability (see also Andre et al., 2006; Chavez and Bernal, 2008, p. 168–69; Del Furia and Wallace-Jones, 2000, p. 460–61; Lockie et al., 2008, p. 178–80; Peterlin et al., 2006, p. 184–86; Sinclair et al., 2007, 400–01; Yang, 2008, p. 93–98).

A number of problems are associated with the identification of multiple objectives and the assumption that the key issue involved is

---

* Tel.: +61 11 61 7 3735 7736; fax: +61 11 61 7 3735 7737.
E-mail address: Ciaran.Ofaircheallaigh@griffith.edu.au.

0195-9255/$ – see front matter © 2009 Elsevier Inc. All rights reserved.
doi:10.1016/j.eiar.2009.05.001

how to pursue effective participation. First, many of the objectives involve quite different concepts, activities and consequences. For instance sharing information with the public is a very different matter to allowing a community to influence government decisions or 'empowering' individuals and communities. Given this fact, it is difficult to see how one can pursue the issue of 'effective participation' without first differentiating clearly between different goals and considering what each involves and implies. Second, reflecting the fact that the term can encompass many different things, the consensus implied in the literature regarding the benefits of participation is in fact more apparent than real (Lawrence, 2003, p. 272). In the real world of public policy decisions, the issue of public participation is contested and highly political. To cite a specific case, Chinese authorities may well be keen to promote public participation if it improves the quality of information available to government decision makers, but may not respond at all well to Yang's call (2008, p. 97) for the public to be 'given power to contribute to and influence decision-making by participating in the formulation of a proposal, the whole EIA process, the implementation and the evaluation of a proposal' (Tang et al., 2008).

A third issue is that even some of the individual objectives identified in the literature are complex and require careful definition and analysis. For instance a frequently-cited goal is to allow community aspirations or priorities to be taken into account in decision making. Yet such a requirement could encompass many different approaches, from treating community views as one of numerous variables considered in decision making, to immediately excluding options that fail to win community support (Becker et al., 2004; Devlin and Yap, 2008; Lockie, 2001).

Another difficulty is that the possibility that different facets of public participation would interact is rarely acknowledged. It seems to be assumed that use of public participation to enhance the quality of empirical information for decision makers, for instance, can occur independently of its use as a tool of community empowerment. In the rare cases where the potential interaction between different forms of participation is recognised, its treatment tends to be perfunctory and to assume that these aspects are likely to reinforce each other in a positive manner. For example Sinclair et al. (2008, p. 422) comment that more 'passive' forms of participation may provide 'on-ramps to more deliberative mechanisms'. Del Furia and Wallace-Jones (2000, p. 459), while acknowledging that there may be an interrelationship between the various goals they list for public participation, assume that the satisfaction of one goal can contribute to the achievement of another, and limit further discussion of the matter to a footnote. In fact there is no logical reason to exclude the possibility that pursuit of one objective might not undermine pursuit of another (OECD, 2001, p. 36). The relationship between them certainly warrants more careful investigation.

The failure to consider the interaction between different forms of public participation is in fact also a feature of general models of public participation in policy making. This raises a further issue. The broader implications of experience with public participation in EIA for public policy making are rarely considered. Given that EIA is, overwhelmingly, undertaken as a component of public policy decisions regarding (mainly) large-scale project development and (less commonly) public programs and policies, it seems important to consider how issues regarding public participation in EIA relate to wider debates about public participation in policy making. For example, one proposed purpose for enhancing public participation in EIA is to 'empower' individual communities. What are the broader implications of such 'empowerment' for public policy making, and how are public policy actors likely to respond to demands for greater power at the community level?

This article seeks to contribute to the debate regarding public participation in EIA in three ways. The first involves the modest but important goal of clearly distinguishing between a range of distinct purposes for public participation. The second is to consider how such purposes can be interpreted and valued, drawing on the wider literature on public participation in policy making. The third is to consider how experience with public participation in EIA can assist in assessing the utility of various models of public participation in policy making generally. In pursuing the second and third goals the primary objective is not to offer definitive responses to the issues raised, but to highlight their importance and the fact that they deserve greater attention from researchers.

One definitional matter should be clarified before proceeding, involving the term 'public participation'. The concept has long been contested and subject to a range of definitions (Bishop and Davis, 2002). Some analysts insist that use of the term is only justified where the public is *actively* involved and where decision makers are substantially influenced by that involvement (Bishop and Davis, 2002, p. 15–17). However given that a key goal of the article is to identify and explore the full range of ways in which members of the public relate to EIA processes, a restrictive definition is not appropriate. Thus 'public participation' is defined here as any form of interaction between government and corporate actors and the public that occurs as part of EIA processes.

As EIA occurs as part of public decision making processes, it is logical to consider the purposes of public participation as falling in three broad areas, depending on their relationship to those processes: as an aid to decision making which remains separate from the participating public; as a mechanism for achieving a role for the public as joint decision makers; and as a mechanism for reconstituting decision making structures. In making this distinction, no assumption is made that these areas are discrete either in the sense that the boundaries between them can be precisely delineated, or that chains of causality may not run between them, with actions in one having consequences in others. Yet at a conceptual level they do involve distinctions that are useful in identifying different approaches and exploring their implications. Table 1 summarises some more specific purposes included under each broad approach; these are discussed in the following sections.

2. Participation as input for decision makers

2.1. Provision of information

The public may be involved in EIA as recipients of information, with decision makers providing them with details of proposed projects or activities, of their timing, and of their expected impact on particular groups and localities. While not requiring the public's active participation and regarded in some cases as of little value to it (see Section 5), such information provision can be important in allowing affected groups to prepare for project impacts. It may be an essential prerequisite for the following two purposes, which involve transmission of information *to* decision makers by the public; and may assist in securing the smooth implementation of projects or programs (Del Furia and Wallace-Jones, 2000, p. 472; Tang et al., 2008).

2.2. Filling information gaps

In many cases the desire to achieve or enhance public participation in EIA reflects a belief that it is required so that decision makers in

Table 1
Defining purposes for public participation in EIA.

Broad purpose	Specific purposes and activities
Obtain public input into decisions taken elsewhere	1. Provide information to public
	2. Fill information gaps
	3. Information contestability
	4. Problem solving and social learning
Share decision making with public	1. Reflect democratic principles
	2. Democracy in practice
	3. Pluralist representation
Alter distribution of power and structures of decision making	1. Involve marginalised groups
	2. Shift the locus of decision making
	3. Entrench marginalisation

government and corporations have access to full and robust information on impacted ecologies and populations, on the nature of impacts, and on the likely efficacy of mitigative strategies (Andre et al., 2006; Hartley and Wood, 2005, 320). In this approach public participation 'is designed essentially to ensure that all relevant information, including input from those affected, is available so that the decision-maker can make the most informed and well-considered decision. The public participation is not an end in itself. Nor does it actually provide a role for the public in the actual decision making' (Morrison-Saunders and Early, 2008, p. 39; see also Momtaz and Gladstone, 2008). The information involved may relate to existing ecological or social conditions, as where Chinese authorities utilised public participation to gain accurate demographic data on a population that would be affected by resumption of agricultural land for industrial development (Tang et al., 2008, p. 64–65). In addition, it may only be through public participation that all of the issues potentially associated with proposed actions can be identified and that information can be obtained on the fears and hopes that accompany people's own predictions of the likely effects of projects, which are themselves an important component of social impact (Becker et al., 2004; Chavez and Bernal, 2008; Lemon et al., 2004; Robinson and Bond, 2003).

Decision makers also make judgments regarding the *significance* of predicted impacts and the risks associated with development alternatives. In this regard knowledge regarding the aspirations and values of affected populations is critical, and public participation may be required to obtain this information (Lane et al., 2003; Lockie, 2001, p. 281; Lockie et al., 2008, p. 180; Paci et al., 2002, p. 115; Tauxe, 1995). It may also be essential to provide decision makers with information about the distribution of costs and benefits from proposed projects, allowing them to undertake what many analysts regard as a critical component of EIA, calculation of the *political* consequences of alternative decisions they might take (Finsterbusch, 1995, p. 234–36; Usher, 1993, p. 99).

Where the underlying rationale for seeking public participation is gaining access to information, decision makers are likely to seek only the degree of participation needed to elicit the required information and no more (Lane et al., 2003, p. 97). This participation may be 'active' as, for example, where indigenous elders travel with officials to their traditional lands and expose them to environmental and cultural knowledge by demonstrating traditional life styles and practices. However participation in this case represents a technique designed to elicit information, not any sharing of control over decision making, and the implications of public participation for the nature of policy processes are unlikely to be substantial. If the relevant information is available from other sources, for instance an earlier EIA of a similar project in the same area, there will be no requirement for public participation.

2.3. Information contestability

Decision makers may wish not simply to extract specific types of information from potentially affected people, but may also wish to create contestability in relation to a wide range of information on projects and expected impacts. This is especially so given that the Environmental Impact Statements (EISs) or EIA reports that represent a critical input into public decision making are generally prepared by proponents or their consultants, who are far from disinterested in their selection, interpretation and presentation of information. Proponents wish their projects to be approved, and as a result are likely to ignore or downplay negative impacts or risks, and to exaggerate potential project benefits, and in particular may be prone to exaggerate the economic benefits that usually constitute the major justification for large industrial projects (Doelle and Sinclair, 2006, p.190; Lockie, 2001, p. 278–79; Lockie et al., 2008; Momtaz and Gladstone, 2008; Rosenberg et al., 1995, p. 146). Public participation can be indispensable if proponent information is to be contested and if alternatives to those favoured by the proponent are to be properly scrutinised (Lockie, 2001; Tilleman, 1995).

It is not only that proponents may engage in obfuscation or in deliberate exaggeration, though this certainly occurs (see Weitzner, 2008 for extensive documentation of a contemporary case in relation to EIA of a bauxite project in Suriname). Also important are the world views, epistemologies and values that specific professionals engaged by proponents and their consultants bring to bear in identifying and assessing potential impacts (Tauxe, 1995). For instance, engineers or economists are likely to emphasise the concrete and the quantifiable, and so are likely to focus on and privilege certain types of impacts and ignore others (Chase, 1990; Kapoor, 2001). In contrast committed environmentalists or indigenous elders, given that they see the world and their own place in it quite differently, are likely to pursue alternative sources and types of information and to understand the same information differently. In relation to the latter point, it may be agreed, for example, that a proposed project will result in the death annually of a specific number of turtles. But this impact will be assessed very differently by an economist who sees it in terms of the market value of an equivalent quantity of meat, and an indigenous elder who believes that people and turtles are spiritually linked and live in a relationship of mutual dependency and obligation. Decision makers may also wish to ensure that no one professional perspective world view is allowed to dominate.

2.4. Problem solving and social learning

Public participation may be sought by decision makers not just as a way of obtaining information or testing its robustness, but also to assist with problem solving by suggesting ideas, concepts, solutions and resources that can be mobilised to address complex environmental and social issues (Diduck and Mitchell, 2003; OECD, 2001). Public participation can be a source of creativity and innovation (Joldersma, 1997), allowing decision makers to draw on alternatives that are not present in their existing array of responses. A related approach increasingly discussed in the literature involves the concept of social and organizational learning, in which stakeholders work together, sharing information to identify effective, socially acceptable strategies to mitigate impacts and identify opportunities (Chavez and Bernal, 2008; Diduck and Mitchell, 2003; Fitzpatrick, 2006; Van den Howe, 2006; Webler et al., 1995). Van den Howe argues that stakeholder involvement is essential given 'the irreducible plurality of stand-points that stems from the complex nature of [environmental] issues …' (2006, p. 12). According to Sinclair et al. collective learning and the social mobilisation that can accompany it are required to achieve 'the perspective transformation necessary for changing unsustainable resource use patterns' (2008, p. 425) and to address 'the need for institutional innovation and generative change in response to the sustainability imperative' (2008, p. 416).

Social learning by definition involves a flow of ideas that is not unidirectional. However when it is undertaken as in input into decision making located elsewhere, the public's contribution of ideas and potential solutions, while possibly offering opportunities for acquiring scientific, technical and social knowledge, does not allow it to determine *which* solution will be adopted (for illustrations see Diduck and Mitchell, 2003; Momtaz and Gladstone, 2008). As noted in Section 3.2, social learning can also take other forms where public participation does involve a degree of control over decision making (Fitzpatrick, 2006; Sinclair et al., 2008).

3. Public participation in decision making

What distinguishes this broad perspective is that participation involves an element of control over decisions by the public, through existing decision making structures and processes. Both the extent of this control and the mechanisms through which it is exercised can vary substantially.

3.1. Democratic principles and 'influencing' decisions

One approach involves the argument that it is 'the public' or sections of it which experience relevant environmental and social impacts, and that it is unethical or undemocratic for them not to be involved in decisions (Hartley and Wood, 2005, 327–35; Lawrence, 2003, p. 277; Morrison-Saunders and Early, 2008, p. 33; Vanclay, 2003, p. 9). A key issue, of course, is the nature of that involvement. Lockie (2001, 284) for example stresses the need for participation to be 'meaningful' and 'not just [provision of] data to decision makers elsewhere', while the public's capacity to 'influence' decisions is often seen as critical (Hartley and Wood, 2005, p. 328, 331; Yang, 2008, p. 97). But how are concepts such as 'meaningful decision making' and 'influence over decision making' translated into operational terms? How much influence should the public have? Some argue that in fact EIA should be used to obtain the *consent* of those affected by proposed projects, on the basis that the legitimacy of government derives from the consent of the governed (Creighton, 1983; Barton, 2002: p. 87–88). This latter approach, if taken to its logical conclusion, has profound implications for the conduct of public policy as it would require that EIA encompass a mechanism such as the referendum that allowed city residents in Italy to have the final say on a proposed gas terminal (Del Furia and Wallace-Jones, 2000). In 'wicked' policy areas such as the siting of waste disposal facilities, the outcome may be policy paralysis (see Section 3.3).

3.2. Democratic practice and capacity

A second strand involves the argument that participation is of value in its own right, that people cannot develop their full potential as citizens except by participating in the work of governance. Participation thus fulfils an educative function, allowing citizens to develop a fuller understanding of their system of government, giving them insights into the interests of their fellow citizens and of society as a whole, and in the process allowing them to contribute to government decision making and so fulfil the obligations which, along with rights, are associated with citizenship. Participation is essential for the full development of individual capabilities (Barton, 2002: p. 102–103; Hindess, 2002, p. 36–37). Social and organizational learning is also highly relevant in this case, as joint learning and problem solving creates opportunities for citizens to enhance their understanding of each other and to engage in the collective decision making at the heart of democracy (Fitzpatrick 2006; Renn, 2006; Sinclair et al., 2008, p. 416). From this perspective EIA represents one of many spheres of political life in which people can participate and both be educated in the exercise of their citizenship and at the same time fulfil their duties as citizens. The capacity for EIA to serve as an arena for personal development and a focus for exercise of citizenship is truncated if EIA procedures allocate decision making power solely to senior bureaucrats and/or government ministers. Again, a critical issue involves the extent to which and the way in which decision making power is shared between public officials, appointed and elected, and citizens. We return to this issue in Section 5.

3.3. EIA as a political arena: pluralism and representation

Another basis for public participation, and one which renders moot the issue of degrees of public influence over decision making, rests on the starting point that decision making in modern democracies involves a contest between representatives of various interests in society, usually in the form of interest groups. From this viewpoint, the purpose of public participation in EIA is to provide avenues for these contending interests to pursue their desired outcomes and to resolve conflicts between them (Barton, 2002, 90–94; Chavez and Bernal, 2008, 166; Lockie, 2001, p. 281–82). A 'representative pluralist' approach takes the view that the role of EIA is not just to generate information on the distribution of costs and benefits for decision makers, including the public, to consider. Rather, EIA processes represent fora in which conflicts are resolved and winners and losers *are decided* through the contest of competing interests. The proponent represents one such interest and will push for rapid development of the project at least possible cost, while other interests (for instance environmental or indigenous groups, other economic producers using resource the proponent will monopolise or affect) will be pushing for different outcomes.

The various interests will lobby for their preferred outcomes both by participating in the EIA process, and subsequently seeking to influence government decision makers, for instance the minister ultimately responsible for rejecting or approving a project or setting conditions for its approval, or cabinet where it has the final say on project approval. Individual components of the state (for instance a mines department or an environmental protection agency) may also be perceived as constituting distinct interests pushing for their preferred outcomes. The agency that is responsible for overseeing the EIA process may be seen in a similar light, or alternatively may be viewed as a referee who oversees the contest and ensures that the 'rules of the game', as set out in relevant legislation and administrative procedures, are observed (Devlin and Yap, 2008, p. 19).

From this perspective there is no necessity for members of the public to participate directly in EIA processes or to lobby governments, only for the groups that represent them to participate.

An important issue that arises in relations to group participation in EIA involves its implications for pursuit of a general public interest, defined as the general good or the aggregate interest of the political community as a whole (Hindess, 2002, p. 31–32). Where participation revolves around promotion of specific group interests, it can be seen as promoting specific and even narrow interests at the expense of the wider social good (Hindess, 2002, p. 34). This is especially the case where EIA is being conducted in relation to siting of projects or activities that are widely reviewed as undesirable, for instance waste disposal facilities, power stations and prisons. Indeed in such cases public participation may simply constitute public resistance, with the result that policy making is paralysed, facilities for which an urgent need exists are not constructed, and society incurs significant costs (Barton, 2002, p. 119; Holland, 2002).

On the other hand it can be argued that claims of incompatibility between group participation and pursuit of broad societal interests are based on the assumption that government decision makers would, in the absence of such participation, pursue the public good. This assumption may not in fact be valid in relation to EIA, which can be dominated by project proponents, consultants on their payroll, government agencies that are subject to 'capture' by proponents, and politicians intent on promoting short-term economic growth to boost their electoral prospects (Curran and Hollander, 2008; Weitzner, 2008). Broadly-based group participation may be required to avoid such an outcome (Barton, 2002, p. 88; Doelle and Sinclair, 2006, p. 187, 189–90; Kapoor, 2001, p. 270; Lockie, 2001, p. 279).

4. Reframing decision making: shifting the balance of power

4.1. Empowering marginalised groups

The broad approaches outlined in Sections 2 and 3 assume that existing decision making structures and the distribution of power they reflect are acceptable and will remain unchanged. In the first case, public or corporate officials will make decisions, in part by utilising information and ideas provided by the public. The second approach assumes that the existing distribution of power allows citizens to participate in decision making in 'meaningful' ways or, from a pluralist perspective, that it reflects a democratic political contest between groups that represent citizens' interests. A third broad approach takes the view that the existing distribution of power is in fact uneven and inequitable, that in this context marginalised groups will exist that cannot exercise any significant impact on decision making, and that this situation is unacceptable. Thus a fundamental goal of public participation in EIA is to achieve a more equitable distribution of political power and change existing decision structures. EIA can be used by socially marginalised groups as a platform from which to change the social order, and in so doing alter in basic ways the distribution of costs and benefits from development.

Thus while Finsterbusch (1995, p. 234) argues that impact assessment is not 'an instrument for the revolution of social institutions to equalize power and results', Gagnon (1995, p. 273, 286) sees SIA as one of the most important and useful tools in empowering 'local community members to exercise increased control over their own territory, social environment and future development'. Similarly, Vanclay (2003, 7) argues that the role of impact assessment 'encompasses empowerment of local people; [and] enhancement of the position of ... disadvantaged or marginalised members of society' (see also Barton, 2002; Gagnon et al., 1993; Howitt, 1989; Lawrence, 2003, Chapter 7).

This approach has major implications for policy making, implying the need for a realignment of political roles and structures that place previously marginalised groups in a position to influence decision making in EIA. An important consideration in this regard is how marginalised groups, given their disadvantaged status, can in practice achieve such a position. The powerless in society are in fact the least likely to participate in EIA, both because they lack the resources to do so and often find the processes involved alien and intimidating (Esteves and Vanclay, 2009, p. 141). While long recognised in the literature (Freudenberg, 1983, p. 231), this dilemma is frequently not addressed by analysts calling for a redistribution of political power. Thus for example Dale and Lane (1994, p. 264) state that 'local Aboriginal people have little influence and control over environmental decision making' and note the need 'for more effective participation', but do not indicate how, at a political level, such an outcome can be achieved.

Another important consideration involves the response of decision makers and existing developer and other interests to marginalised groups that do mobilise and push for change. It appears unlikely that those who hold power will yield gracefully to groups pushing for a share of it. In this context the latter may first need to work outside impact assessment processes in order to enhance their negotiating position, and then insert or re-insert themselves from this stronger position. For instance, Lawrence (2003) reports a case involving an impact assessment of a planned oil shale project on fruit farmers in Queensland, Australia. While an SIA conducted by the proponent identified a range of likely impacts, it offered no solutions acceptable to the fruit farmers. The fruit growers carried out their own strategic planning process outside the SIA to investigate a full range of possible responses, some of which had been foreclosed by the proponent. One of these, involving a complete buy-out of the growers, was eventually accepted by the government. As Lawrence notes, 'the growers found a way to broaden and redefine the SIA process. However to have the necessary control over their own fate, they had to go outside the SIA process, employ a parallel planning process, and then reshape the SIA process ...' (2003, p. 268).

4.2. Shifting the locus of decision making

Groups that are subject to systemic marginalisation may find it impossible to reshape existing structures, and may respond by establishing impact assessment processes separate to the statutory ones, bypassing government and using their impact assessment as a basis for negotiating terms of development directly with project proponents. For instance during the 1990s a number of Aboriginal groups in Cape York, Queensland, having been effectively excluded from EIA decision making for many years (Chase, 1990), opted out of the public project assessment process and undertook their own impact studies. They used these studies as a basis for negotiating legally-binding agreements with project developers. These agreements deal with matters (including environmental management and cultural heritage protection) that are also addressed in legislation and public regulation, and in at least some cases they contain provisions that appear to appropriate for Aboriginal people decision making powers usually monopolised by governments. For instance one agreement allocates to a joint Aboriginal–company management structure control over environmental and cultural issues arising from mining operations (O'Faircheallaigh, 1999, 70). While the government does possess the ultimate authority to impose its legislation, in effect it is unlikely to intervene if project development is proceeding smoothly, and to date the Queensland government has not done so. The outcome is that Aboriginal communities gain a significant degree of influence over impact assessment and the conditions under which development occurs. Similar outcomes have been achieved by some indigenous groups in Canada using what are referred to there as 'Impact and Benefit Agreements' (Gibson, 2006).

4.3. Reinforcing powerlessness

While the literature dealing with marginalised social groups generally focuses on the use of EIA to enhance their political position, impact assessment can also be utilised to reinforce marginalisation or marginalise social groups even further. For example Tang et al. (2008, p. 66–70) note that Chinese officials responsible for an environmental assessment of a major industrial development regarded villagers who would lose their land as 'policy recipients', that the purpose of the EIA was to 'justify already-made project decisions', and that officials prevailed on a lawyer hired by villagers opposing the development not to take their case. Hildyard et al. (1998) report that Indonesian officials undertook impact assessment processes solely because these were required by international aid agencies, and continued to ignore the interests of villagers whose land was being lost to agribusiness projects. Tauxe (1995, p. 9–10) describes how public consultation procedures which supposedly incorporated ranchers affected by oil development in Montana further marginalised them by invoking 'dominant organizational, ideological, and discursive forms' which devalued the ranchers' values and rhetorical styles.

5. A wider perspective: public participation in policy making

How should these different approaches to public participation be interpreted and how should they be valued? The general literature on public participation in policy making may provide insights in this regard. In turn, the experience with public participation in EIA may offer useful insights into the utility and validity of models of pubic participation included in that literature.

The approaches outlined above could be interpreted within frameworks that establish a hierarchy of forms of participation, such as Arnstein's 'ladder of participation', cited regularly in the literature on public participation in EIA and on public participation generally (for example Chavez and Bernal, 2008; Cooper and Elliott, 2000; Diduck and Mitchell, 2003; Tritter and McCallum, 2006). Arnstein (1969) constructs a hierarchy of participation in terms of the degree of control over policy decisions enjoyed by public participants. Use of EIA to provide information to the public or to generate information for decision makers would be defined as 'tokenism' in Arnstein's framework, because it fails to deliver citizen's control over policy. Use of public participation in EIA to help to shift the balance of power in society would be highly regarded, given that the ultimate goal of public participation is 'the redistribution of power that enables have-not citizens, presently excluded from the political and economic processes, to be deliberately included in the future' (Arnstein, 1969, p. 216; see also Hildyard et al., 1998).

One difficulty with such approaches is that they dismiss forms of public participation that, as the EIA experience reveals, can substantially enhance the quality of public decision making by expanding the available information base. This is especially so when public participation is utilised to create contestability in relation to information available to decision makers (Barton, 2002, p. 100–101; Tilleman, 1995, p. 428–29; Weitzner, 2008). They also treat each form of participation as separate and distinct, denying the possibility that they may in fact interact in dynamic ways. Thus for example Arnstein argues that citizens only achieve access to the 'upper rungs' of the ladder by refusing to participate in forms of participation that equate to the lower rungs (1969, p. 122). But in reality provision of information to decision makers can provide a basis for achieving a share of decision making power. For instance Tauxe (1995, p. 8) discusses how a developer's association in Montana was able to provide authoritative figures on the projected impacts of energy development, which were then utilised by state planning agencies and consultants, earning the developers 'a strong lobbying voice' with decision makers. In another context, Keck and Sikkink (1998) show that the capacity to generate and control information has been crucial to the ability of non-government organizations to influence international policy regimes.

An alternative framework is proposed by Thomas (1990). He argues that a range of different approaches to public participation may be appropriate depending on the nature of the policy problem or issue involved. Participation may serve quite different ends in different policy areas, and so no particular approach to participation is inherently desirable or undesirable. The degree of public involvement 'depends on the attribute of the core problem; some problems demand more involvement, others less' (1990, p. 435). Thomas models five different approaches to decision making, ranging from a situation in which a public manager makes an 'autonomous managerial decision' without public involvement, to one in which 'the manager and the public attempt to reach agreement on a solution'. The key task for decision makers is to classify policy problems and 'choose among [the] five decision-making approaches, varying in the extent of group involvement and potential approaches' (1990, p. 436; for another similar approach see Shand and Arnberg, 1996).

While this approach has the advantage of drawing attention to the potential benefits of various types of public participation, it has two major drawbacks. First, it assumes that fundamental choices regarding the nature of policy issues or problems and regarding the appropriate approach to public participation should be made by public officials; such participation may be extensive in certain cases, but only where public officials determine that this should be so. This position itself embodies a very specific approach to public participation. Second, it assumes acceptance by the public of the degree of participation that officials determine is appropriate, denying agency to people or groups that are offered specific forms of participation. As we shall see, the EIA experience suggests that this assumption is seriously flawed.

Bishop and Davis (2002, p. 21–26) adopt a somewhat different and less normative approach based on 'aggregating contemporary practice'. They identify six different forms of public participation, ranging from 'Participation as Consultation' to 'Participation as Control'. Their classification has the virtue that it does recognise the possibility of agency on the part of the public, arising for instance from its ability to use administrative law to *insist* on a role in decision making and in some cases to have government decisions reversed or modified ('Participation as Standing'). However in common with the approaches discussed above, this classification tends to treat different forms of participation as separate and mutually exclusive categories; to ignore the dynamic relationship that can exist between various forms of participation; and to downplay the capacity of the public to devise strategies to redefine the basis on which their participation occurs.

The importance of addressing these matters is well illustrated by public participation in EIA. For example, officials and proponents may determine that public participation should serve purely as a means of generating information they can use to take decisions. However seeking information from a potentially affected public is likely to raise public awareness of a project and this in turn may result in demands for more substantial public participation (Devlin and Yap, 2008, p. 19). Indeed the willingness to allow this may become a precondition for providing the information originally sought by the proponent or government officials. Official requests for information on indigenous cultural heritage that may be affected by a proposed project provide a good illustration of such responses. Typically, indigenous people are reluctant to release such information unless they are fully informed about the proposed project and are given the opportunity to enter into negotiations with government and the proponent on management of cultural heritage (O'Faircheallaigh, 2008). If such demands for greater involvement are met, then the character of public participation and its implications for policy making change significantly, illustrating the fact that control over information can in itself represent a significant source of power. Alternatively, if such requests for greater involvement are denied by decision makers, members of the public may feel that they are facing attempts to coopt them into a process over which they will have no control, and may simply withdraw, undermining the objectives of public officials (Hildyard et al., 1998; Tauxe, 1995, p. 7).

Critically, EIA experience shows that withdrawal may only be from the specific participative processes the public finds overly restrictive, rather than from relevant decision making arenas. Groups can utilise a range of strategies to 'break open' decision making processes through what Devlin and Yap (2008, p. 19) term 'transgressive contention' that rejects the 'rules of the game' initially laid down by public officials. They note that 'Even quite closed and technocratic processes can be broken open if the public becomes aware of the project and begins to mobilize against it' (2008, 19; see also Feit, 2005, p. 269). Thus Holland (2002), for instance, describes how groups dissatisfied with the assessment process being applied to the selection of a nuclear waste disposal facility in Australia used court action, and political strategy focused on minority parties in the Australian Senate, to undermine and eventually derail the entire site selection process (for other examples of 'transgressive action' by the public, see Hildyard et al., 1998; Lawrence, 2003; Lucas, 2002, 313–314). Similarly, Non-Government Organizations (NGOs) in Canada are mounting court challenges to Federal Government attempts to constrain public participation in EIA processes for the proposed Red Chris mine in northern British Columbia (Mining Watch Canada, 2009). Indeed it may even be the case that EIA processes that allow little opportunity for public control of decisions themselves provide opportunity for acquisition of skills, such as communication strategies and methods of social mobilisation (Diduck and Mitchell, 2003), that can later be turned against decision makers.

This discussion of models of public participation highlights the fact that static frameworks that place different forms or levels of public participation into separate categories characterised by rigid boundaries are unhelpful, especially where it is also suggested that policy makers have the freedom to choose between them. In reality the three broad forms of public participation outlined in previous sections are not insulated from each other, but rather interact in the context of a political dynamic that inevitably surrounds public decisions regarding major project developments and other activities subject to EIA. This can be illustrated in relation to a key issue around public participation, the question of control over decision making.

Public officials, appointed or elected, generally prefer to keep public participation 'within tightly circumscribed limits' and display a 'propensity towards centralized control' (Lawrence, 2003, p. 273), a tendency that seems nearly universal across political systems (Chavez and Bernal, 2008, p. 167; Doelle and Sinclair, 2006, p. 187; OECD, 2001; Tang et al., 2008). Indeed in politically sensitive areas government may prefer to avoid public participation, because of the risk of policy paralysis (Holland 2002, 81). The argument that public officials must ultimately control decision making gets substantial support in the EIA literature and in writing on public participation generally. As Daneke argued over two decades ago, 'Most researchers agree that it is not the purpose of public involvement to make the decision, but rather to merely improve decision making' (Daneke, 1983, p. 24). Kane and Bishop (2002, p. 87) are critical of the 'tendency to view consultation as an exercise in policy determination by the public rather than as public input … whose ultimate use is to be defined by the elected decision makers' (see also Lucas, 2002, p. 345–46; Lemon et al., 2004, p. 193).

But the political reality is that if officials refuse to share decision making power, public participation may be seen as tokenistic, and the public quickly becomes cynical and withdraws. Thus Stewart and Sinclair (2007, 168) cite informants in a study of public participation as stressing the need for 'genuine opportunity to influence the decision … People sense very quickly when something's a done deal; then they stop participating' (see also Curran and Hollander, 2008; Hartley and Wood, 2005, p. 328; OECD, 2001, p. 21–24, 41–43; Webler et al., 1995, p. 459).

Government needs public participation, for instance because of its valuable role in filling information gaps and rendering information contestable; in ensuring that government is aware of the full range of policy options; and in removing potential obstacles to project or policy implementation. But unless it is convinced that participation will involve some real influence over decision making, the public will be reluctant to participate. This reluctance may not be limited to a specific project or policy area, but may result in a general cynicism that makes it very difficult to involve citizens when officials wish to do so, and ultimately threatens the legitimacy of government (Curran and Hollander 2008, p. 22; OECD, 2001; Webler et al., 1995, p. 459).

In addition, as mentioned above public actors may well react by finding ways to undermine or circumvent existing policy structures. Thus what faces officials is not a menu of 'participation options' from which they can chose what they consider appropriate for the circumstances. Rather what faces them is an ongoing negotiation regarding the terms on which the public will participate, and the need to constantly manage the tension between their 'propensity towards centralized control' and the 'decentralizing tendencies of public involvement' (Lawrence, 2003, p. 273). This does not deny the need for policy makers to be clear about the distinction between various forms of public participation, and transparent about their willingness to allow public participants to influence decision making. To do otherwise is to invite public cynicism, and withdrawal from participation. But attempts to establish hard-and-fast rules regarding the relationship between public participation and decision making are likely to be counterproductive. Maintaining flexibility in relation to the nature and extent of public participation is essential to its successful incorporation into public policy making.

While the public is not powerless in dealing with government, EIA experience highlights the fact that public participation occurs in dynamic political environments and that, as a result, the trend will not inevitably be towards greater public control. Decision makers, driven by wider policy and political imperatives and reacting to what they see as threats to their ability to respond to these, may act to roll back public participation. Indeed the very success of groups in achieving greater control over decision making can lead to political responses which push public participation back to a 'lower' level, again emphasising the relationship between different dimensions of public participation.

Site identification and impact assessment procedures utilised in 2007–2008 in relation to a liquefied natural gas (LNG) processing facility in the Kimberley region of Western Australia offer a good illustration of this point. Historically, Kimberley Aboriginal people have been excluded from decisions about resource development on their traditional lands. From the late 1970s they began to actively oppose such developments, using litigation and direct action to delay and in some cases halt major projects (Hawke and Gallagher, 1985). After 2000, the regional Aboriginal land organization, the Kimberley Land Council, was able to use this record of opposition to major projects, the Australian High Court's legal recognition of inherent Aboriginal rights in land (arising from the 1992 *Mabo* case), and the growing international recognition of indigenous rights to push for a much stronger role for Aboriginal landowners in impact assessment and project approval processes (Kimberley Land Council, 2008a,b). It achieved considerable success in this regard, to such an extent that when the (Labor) Government of Western Australia contemplated establishing an LNG facility on the Kimberley coast in 2006, it stated that development would only occur with the informed consent of the Aboriginal traditional owners of proposed sites (Carpenter, 2006). In other words, the government was not only sharing its decision making powers, but allowing traditional owners the final say. A site identification and impact assessment process was established on this basis during 2007 and 2008.

In October 2008 a newly-elected Liberal/National Party Government reversed this position, believing that it was unacceptable for any section of the public to have what it termed a veto over government decisions. The government indicated that while it would consult with traditional owners regarding measures for impact mitigation and community benefits, the existing site selection process would be discontinued. It has since announced its preferred site for the LNG facility, and indicated that it will use compulsory acquisition powers to enforce its decision if traditional owners oppose it (Government of Western Australia, 2008; O'Brien, 2008).

6. Conclusion

This article has proposed a classification of purposes for public participation in EIA based around three fundamental relationships between the public and decision making structures and processes. These involve public input to decisions taken separately from the public; public involvement in decision making; and attempts to change the distribution of power in society so as to reconfigure decision making. Ten different purposes are identified, each of which differs significantly in the degree and form of participation and in its implications for public decision making. The point of this exercise is not to argue that this is the only basis on which alternative purposes for public participation in EIA can be classified and their implications explored. Rather it is to highlight the need to be clear and specific regarding what these purposes are, how they may be distinguished from one another, what each implies in terms of the role of public participation in decision making process, and the implications of each for decision making.

It is one matter to distinguish between different purposes for public participation in EIA, another to form judgments regarding their desirability. There is also the important issue, little addressed in the literature, of what experience with public participation in EIA implies for participation in policy making generally. The general literature on public participation in policy making offers some arguments and insights regarding the value of various types of participation, but tends to adopt rigid positions in favour either of specific forms of public participation, or to privilege the authority of public officials in determining which form should be adopted. Both approaches ignore two important and inter-connected realities, highlighted by the experience with public participation in EIA. The first is the dynamic and political nature of public participation as an issue. This involves inherent tensions between the desire of public officials to keep control over decisions; their need for public involvement; and the agency of the public in responding to opportunities for participation, in some cases by circumventing decision making processes created by public officials and legislators. The second is that alternative purposes for public participation are in fact not bounded and discrete but relate to each other, in ways that require further exploration. Thus for instance use of public participation to obtain information for corporate and government officials can lead to pressures for public control over decision making; the success of groups in gaining control over decision making can in turn generate reactions from public officials, resulting in a redefinition of the purposes and limits of public participation.

More research is needed on the way in which the dynamic political processes within which EIA is embedded work out in specific contexts and influence the shape and extent of public participation in EIA, and on the way in which various forms of public participation relate to each other. These matters receive less attention than they deserve not only in research on public participation in EIA, but also in the wider literature on public policy making. Thus such a focus would not only enhance understanding of EIA, but also represent an important contribution to knowledge regarding public participation in policy making generally.

References

Andre P, Enserink D, Connor D, Croal P. Public participation international best practice principles. Special publication series no. 4. Fargo, USA: International Association for Impact Assessment; 2006.
Arnstein S. A ladder of citizen participation. J Am Instit Plann 1969;35(4):216–24.
Barton B. Underlying concepts and theoretical issues in public participation in resources development. In: Zillman D, Lucas A, Pring G, editors. Human rights in natural resources development: public participation in the sustainable development of mining and energy resources. Oxford: Oxford University Press; 2002. p. 77–119.
Becker D, Harris C, Nielsen E, McLaughlin W. A comparison of a technical and a participatory application of social impact assessment. Impact Assess Proj Apprais 2004;22(3):177–89.
Bishop P, Davis G. Mapping public participation in policy choices. Aust J Publ Admin, 2002;61(1):14–29.
Carpenter A. West Kimberley onshore liquefied natural gas processing facilities: statement by Premier. Perth: Legislative Assembly, Western Australia; 2006. Online resource: http://www.parliament.wa.gov.au/hansard/hans35.nsf/16ab30a0303e54f448256bf7002049e8/c8dbf3c3ba5613a0482572300020d180?OpenDocument [last accessed 19 January 2009].
Chase A. Anthropology and impact assessment: development pressures and indigenous interests in Australia. Environ Impact Assess Rev 1990;10:11–23.
Chavez B, Bernal A. Planning hydroelectric power plants with the public: a case of organizational and social learning in Mexico. Impact Assess Proj Apprais 2008;26(3):163–76.
Cooper L, Elliott J. Public participation and social acceptability in the Philippine EIA process. J Environ Assess Pol Manag 2000;2(3):339–67.
Creighton J. An overview to the research conference on public involvement and social impact assessment. In: Daneke G, Garcia M, Priscolin J, editors. Public involvement and social impact assessment. Boulder: Westview Press; 1983. p. 1-10.
Curran G, Hollander R. A tale of two pulp mills: realising ecologically sustainable development in Australia. Aust J Publ Admin 2008;67(4):483–97.
Dale A, Lane M. Strategic perspectives analysis: a procedure for participatory and political social impact assessment. Soc Nat Resour 1994;7:253–67.
Daneke G. Public involvement: what, why, how. In: Daneke G, Garcia M, Priscolin J, editors. Public involvement and social impact assessment. Boulder: Westview Press; 1983. p. 11–34.
Daneke G, Garcia M, Priscolin J, editors. Public involvement and social impact assessment. Boulder: Westview Press; 1983.
Del Furia L, Wallace-Jones J. The effectiveness of provisions and quality of practices concerning public participation in EIA in Italy. Environ Impact Assess Rev 2000;20:457–79.
Devlin JF, Yap N. Contentious politics in environmental assessment: blocked projects and winning coalitions. Impact Assess Proj Apprais 2008;26(1):17–27.
Diduck A, Mitchell B. Learning, public involvement and environmental assessment: a Canadian case study. J Environ Assess Pol Manag 2003;5(3):339–64.
Doelle M, Sinclair J. Time for a new approach to public participation in EA: promoting cooperation and consensus for sustainability. Environ Impact Assess Rev, 2006;26:185–205.
Esteves A, Vanclay F. Social Development Needs Analysis as a tool for SIA to guide corporate-community investment: applications in the minerals industry. Environ Impact Assess Rev, 2009;29:137–45.
Feit H. Re-cognizing co-management as co-governance: visions and histories of conservation at James Bay. Anthropologica 2005;47:267–88.
Finsterbusch K. In praise of SIA: a personal review of the field of social impact assessment: feasibility, justification, history, methods, issues. Impact Assess 1995;13:229–52.
Fitzpatrick P. In it together: organizational learning through participation in impact assessment. J Environ Assess Pol Man 2006;8(2):157–82.

Freudenberg W. The promise and peril of public participation in social impact assessment. In: Daneke G, Garcia M, Priscolin J, editors. Public involvement and social impact assessment. Boulder: Westview Press; 1983. p. 227–34.
Gagnon C. Social impact assessment in Quebec: issues and perspectives for sustainable community development. Impact Assess 1995;13:273–88.
Gagnon C, Hirsch P, Howitt R. Can SIA empower communities? Environ Impact Assess Rev 1993;13:229–53.
Gibson RB. Sustainability assessment and conflict resolution: reaching agreement to proceed with the Voisey's Bay nickel mine. J Clean Prod 2006;14(3/4):334–48.
Government of Western Australia. Liberal-National Government makes decision on LNG precinct. Perth: Department of the Premier and Cabinet; 2008. Online resource: http://www.mediastatements.wa.gov.au/Lists/Statements/DispForm.aspx?ID=131095 [last accessed 6 February 2009].
Hartley N, Wood C. Public participation in environmental impact assessment — implementing the Aarhus Convention. Environ Impact Assess Rev 2005;25:319–40.
Hawke S, Gallagher M. Noonkanbah, whose land, whose law. Fremantle: Fremantle Arts Centre; 1985.
Hildyard N, Hedge P, Wolvekamp P, Reddy S. Same platform, different train: the politics of participation. Unasylva: An international journal of forestry and forest industries 1998;49(3) Online resource: http://www.fao.org/docrep/w8827W/w8827e00.HTM [last accessed 4 November 2008].
Hindess B. Deficit by design. Aust J Publ Admin 2002;61(1):30–8.
Holland I. Consultation and contest: the danger of mixing modes. Aust J Publ Admin 2002;61(1):76–86.
Howitt R. Social impact assessment and resource development: issues from the Australian experience. Aust Geogr 1989;20(2):153–66.
Joldersma C. Participatory policy making: balancing between divergence and convergence. Eur J Work Organ Psychol 1997;6(2):207–18.
Kane J, Bishop P. Consultation and contest: the danger of mixing. Aust J Publ Admin 2002;61(1):87–94.
Kapoor I. Towards participatory environmental management? J Environ Manag 2001;63:269–79.
Keck M, Sikkink K. Activists beyond borders: advocacy networks in international politics. Ithica: Cornell University Press; 1998.
Kimberley Land Council. Prospectus for the Kimberley Land Council. Broome: KLC; 2008a. 2008 Online resource: http://www.klc.org.au/pdfs/KLC_Prospectus.pdf [last accessed 19 January 2009].
Kimberley Land Council. Completed agreements. Broome: KLC; 2008b. 2008 Online resource: http://www.klc.org.au/agrees_complete.htm [last accessed 18 March 2008].
Lane M, Ross H, Dale A, Rickson R. Sacred land, mineral wealth, and biodiversity at Coronation Hill, Northern Australia: indigenous knowledge and SIA. Impact Assess Proj Apprais 2003;21(2):89–98.
Lawrence D. Environmental impact assessment: practical solutions to recurrent problems. New Jersey: John Wiley and Sons; 2003.
Lemon M, Jeffrey P, McIntosh B, Oxley T. Understanding perceptions of change: a pathways contribution to community consultation and environmental decision making. J Environ Assess Pol Manag 2004;6(2):189–211.
Lockie S. SIA in review: setting the agenda for impact assessment in the 21st century. Impact Assess Proj Apprais 2001;19(4):277–87.
Lockie S, Franetovich M, Sharma S, Rolfe J. Democratisation versus engagement? Social and economic impact assessment and community participation in the coal mining industry of the Bowen Basin, Australia. Impact Assess Proj Apprais 2008;26(3):177–88.
Lucas A. Canadian participatory rights in mining and energy resource development: the bridges to empowerment? In: Zillman D, Lucas A, Pring G, editors. Human rights in natural resources development: public participation in the sustainable development of mining and energy resources. Oxford: Oxford University Press; 2002. p. 307-53.
Mayoux L, Chambers R. Reversing the paradigm: quantification, participatory methods and pro-poor impact assessment. J Int Dev 2005;17:271-98.
Mining Watch Canada. Supreme court to hear Red Chris case; January 2 2009. Online resource: http://www.miningwatch.ca/index.php?/Imperial_Metals/Red_Chris_SCC_for_newsletter [last accessed 21 April 2009].
Momtaz S, Gladstone W. Ban on commercial fishing in the estuarine waters of New South Wales, Australia: community consultation and social impacts. Environ Impact Assess Rev 2008;28:319–42.
Morrison-Saunders A, Early G. What is necessary to ensure natural justice in environmental impact assessment decision-making. Impact Assess Proj Apprais 2008;26(1):29–42.
O'Brien A. I'll take native title land: Barnett. Australian; December 11 2008. Online resource: http://www.theaustralian.news.com.au/story/0,25197,24782899-5013945,00.html [last accessed 6 February 2009].
OECD. Citizens as partners: information, consultation and public participation in policy-making. Paris: OECD; 2001.
O'Faircheallaigh C. Making social impact assessment count: a negotiation-based approach for indigenous peoples. Soc Nat Resour 1999;12:63–80.
O'Faircheallaigh C. Negotiating protection of the sacred? Aboriginal-mining company agreements in Australia. Dev Change 2008;39(1):25–51.
Paci C, Tobin A, Robb P. Reconsidering the Canadian Environmental Impact Assessment Act: a place for traditional environmental knowledge. Environ Impact Assess Rev 2002;22:111–27.
Peterlin M, Kross B, Kontic B. Information in an EIA process and the influence thereof on public opinion. J Environ Assess Pol Manag 2006;8(2):183–204.
Renn O. Participatory processes for designing environmental policies. Land Use Pol 2006;23:34–43.

Robinson M, Bond A. Investigation of different stakeholder views of local resident involvement in environmental impact assessments in the UK. J Environ Assess Pol Manag 2003;5(1):45-82.

Rosenberg D, Bodaly R, Usher P. Environmental and social impacts of large scale hydro-electric development: who is listening? Global Environ Change 1995;5(2):127-48.

Shand D, Arnberg M. Background paper. In: OECD, editor. Responsive government: service quality initiatives. Paris: OECD; 1996.

Sinclair P, Cowell S, Lofstedt R, Clift R. A case study in participatory environmental systems assessment with the use of multimedia materials and quantitative LCA. J Environ Assess Pol Manag 2007;9(4):399-421.

Sinclair A, Diduck A, Fitzpatrick P. Conceptualizing learning for sustainability through environmental assessment: critical reflections on 15 years of research. Environ Impact Assess Rev 2008;28:415-26.

Stewart J, Sinclair A. Meaningful public participation in environmental assessment: perspectives from Canadian participants, proponents and government. J Environ Assess Pol Manag 2007;9(2):161-83.

Tang B, Wong S, Chi-hong Lau M. Social impact assessment and public participation in china: a case study of land acquisition in Guangzhou. Environ Impact Assess Rev 2008;28:57-72.

Tauxe C. Marginalizing public participation in local planning. J Am Plann Assoc 1995;61(4):471-81.

Thomas J. Public involvement in public management: adapting and testing a borrowed theory. Pub Admin Rev 1990;50(4):435-45.

Tilleman W. Public participation in the environmental impact assessment process: a comparative study of impact assessment in Canada, the United States and the European community. Columbia J Transnat Law 1995;33:337-435.

Tritter J, McCallum A. The snakes and ladders of user involvement: moving beyond Arnstein. Health Pol 2006;76:156-68.

Usher P. Northern development, impact assessment, and social change. In: Dyck N, Waldram J, editors. Anthropology, public policy, and native peoples in Canada. Montreal: McGill-Queen's University Press; 1993. p. 98-130.

Van den Hove S. Between consensus and compromise: acknowledging the negotiation dimension in participatory approaches. Land Use Pol 2006;23:10-7.

Vanclay F. International principles for social impact assessment. Impact Assess Proj Apprais 2003;21(1):5-11.

Webler T, Kastenholz H, Renn O. Public participation in impact assessment: a social learning perspective. Environ Impact Assess Rev 1995;15:443-63.

Weitzner V. Missing pieces: an analysis of the draft environmental and social impacts reports for the Bakhuis Bauxite Project. West Suriname. Ottawa: North-South Institute; 2008.

Yang S. Public participation in the Chinese Environmental Impact Assessment (EIA) system. J Environ Assess Pol Manag 2008;10(1):91-113.

Ciaran O'Faircheallaigh is Professor of Politics and Public Policy at Griffith University, Brisbane. His research focuses on the interrelationship between large-scale resource development and indigenous people, and he has published numerous articles and books in the fields of impact assessment, negotiation, public policy, and indigenous studies. He is the author of *A New Approach to Policy Evaluation: Indigenous People and Mining* (Ashgate, 2002) and editor (with Saleem Ali) of *Earth Matters: Indigenous Peoples, the Extractive Industries and Corporate Social Responsibility* (Greenleaf, 2008). For over a decade Professor O'Faircheallaigh has worked with indigenous organizations in Australia and Canada on negotiation of agreements with mining companies.

[21]

Social Development Needs Analysis as a tool for SIA to guide corporate-community investment: Applications in the minerals industry

Ana Maria Esteves [a,*], Frank Vanclay [b]

[a] *Community Insights Pty Ltd, Australia*
[b] *Tasmanian Institute of Agricultural Research, University of Tasmania, Australia*

ARTICLE INFO

Article history:
Received 12 February 2008
Received in revised form 19 August 2008
Accepted 20 August 2008
Available online 11 October 2008

Keywords:
Social Impact Assessment
SIA
Sustainable development
Mining
Social development
Needs analysis
Needs assessment
Capacity-building
Social investment

ABSTRACT

Mining companies are faced with growing societal demands that a sufficient portion of the benefits from mining should flow to local communities to ensure they are adequately compensated for the negative social impacts they experience. This paper considers how a more equitable benefit distribution system can be achieved through voluntary initiatives, recognising companies as potential agents for social development through the provision of improved services and infrastructure, capacity-building, employment and local economic development initiatives. Social Development Needs Analysis is introduced as an enhancement to participatory Social Impact Assessment methods to give practical guidance to site managers in evaluating community investment alternatives. Social Development Needs Analysis aims to identify the priority social issues that need to be addressed in order for a company to contribute to a net positive impact in the community while building assets for the business.

© 2008 Elsevier Inc. All rights reserved.

1. Introduction

If corporate interventions to address issues in the social environments in which companies operate are to have significant outcomes, they must also contribute to the long-term profitability of the corporation itself. This requires that community investment objectives clearly demonstrate how programs add value to both the business and the communities in which they operate. Obvious though this is, it represents a deviation from current practice dominating the mining industry. This paper supports Labonne's (1999) prescription for success in dealing with affected communities—the mining company should view the local community as a source of valuable human, natural and physical assets that can be utilised when developing the mine, and that the community must be able to articulate its own development aspirations. While Social Impact Assessment (SIA) is a means of integrating development and sustainability into core business strategies and can assist in building collaboration between the company and communities and government, in practice its application is typically limited to being a project-planning tool (Esteves, 2008a,b).

* Corresponding author. Community Insights Pty Ltd, 13/47-51 Domain Street, South Yarra, Vic 3141, Australia. Tel.: +61 408 506607.
E-mail addresses: amesteves@communityinsights.com.au (A.M. Esteves), Frank.Vanclay@utas.edu.au (F. Vanclay).

0195-9255/$ – see front matter © 2008 Elsevier Inc. All rights reserved.
doi:10.1016/j.eiar.2008.08.004

Changing the orientation of SIA from predicting and mitigating the negative social consequences of projects towards facilitating positive social development outcomes within a sustainable development framework is consistent with the philosophy expressed in the International Principles for SIA (Vanclay, 2003) and the Sustainable Livelihoods Approach (DfID, 1999). This paper attempts to connect SIA practice in the minerals industry with these broader international approaches and introduces a practical method to assist managers to undertake a needs analysis from both business and community perspectives. The 'Social Development Needs Analysis' (SDNA) outlined in this paper attempts to address on behalf of a company the following question: *What are the priority social issues that should be addressed in order for us to contribute to sustainable development of the community and create value for our business?* While this paper focuses on the minerals industry, the approach has general applicability to any private-sector industry and their local community.

Social Development Needs Analysis seeks to address the higher-level challenge of how to reconcile, within a sustainable development paradigm, business needs with community needs, and at a practical level to assist managers in allocating limited resources to community investments. The goal is to embed concepts of sustainability and social development into core business strategies by linking the future of the company with the future of the local community. This approach differs from most practical applications of SIA which tend to be oriented only towards mitigating negative impacts associated with point-in-time assessments—as demonstrated by an empirical analysis of the large-scale mining sector conducted by Esteves (2008a,b). The premise underlying the SDNA approach is that communities and companies would both obtain greater benefit by closer alignment of interests.

Social Development Needs Analysis as presented in this paper is an advancement in SIA as currently practiced. While needs assessments have been part of SIA all along (see Burdge, 2004a), in this paper SDNA is positioned theoretically in a way not previously done and the benefits to the proponent as well as to the community are advocated. The main focus of this paper, therefore, is to provide rationale for a Social Development Needs Analysis with an outline of the approach, and how it should be incorporated with other SIA methods. The paper does this by discussing the application of the analytical approach in a mining context. It is therefore desirable to discuss some of the social issues in mining to provide some background.

2. Social development in a mining context

There is a wide range of issues that mine site managers face when making decisions about social investment that an effective SIA should address (Uglow, 1998). Mining is a two-edged sword. It is portrayed as presenting opportunities for the production of substantial wealth for companies, governments and potentially communities, while at the same time contributing to the destruction of the environment and social life. Connell and Howitt (1991), for example, found that while mining presents challenges to local Indigenous societies, paradoxically, it can also reinforce traditional knowledge and relationships, by these being valorised as a basis for negotiation and compensation payments. Gibson (2000) suggests that mining could be considered acceptable when any negative effects are promptly remediated and when socioeconomic benefits contribute to the sustainability and wellbeing of the local community.

2.1. Economic arguments of the benefits of mining for communities

A common argument in favour of mining is that its economic benefits enhance the wellbeing of local communities. A mining company contributes in a number of ways:

- Taxes and royalties to local governments;
- Royalty and compensation payments to landowners;
- Employment (wages);
- Local procurement (the purchase of goods and services as inputs for the mine);
- Investment in services and infrastructure which may have spin-off benefits to the wider community and to unrelated businesses;
- Investment in community programs, to achieve outcomes in areas such as capacity-building, environment, arts and recreation, health and wellbeing;
- Support for volunteering efforts by employees in the community sector;
- Provision of inputs for downstream business activities, such as processing, refining and fabrication; and
- Indirect benefits through the multiplier effects of the above activities.

In many locations around the world, but especially in areas that are remote, mining may be the only likely development option. It is often the only means some people have to secure a capital base for involvement in the wider economy. By injecting cash into the economy and through associated multiplier effects, the welfare of some individuals and groups can be improved. Investment in health care services and community health programs, for example, are other ways by which many large mining corporations contribute to local economies. Mining, therefore, is potentially a means of helping to achieve locally-defined economic and social goals.

2.2. Taking a broader view of development

There has been only limited evaluation of the effectiveness of mining investment into the development of communities. Most of the focus of both ex-ante impact assessments and follow-up assessments or audits in mining has been on the adverse environmental effects associated with its extractive nature, the disturbance of land and the finite nature of mining, and their associated social impacts. For example, there has been discussion of adverse health impacts resulting from chronic and transient environmental exposure to air, water, soil and noise pollution, as well as to incidents such as tailings dam failures. Increased heavy vehicle traffic, water scarcity, ecosystem disruption, loss of biodiversity, increased exposure to vector-borne diseases due to changed environmental conditions, decreased crop yields, and loss of pastureland are amongst the impacts identified with large-scale mining development (Noronha, 1999; Ripley et al., 1996). However, there are many more social impacts, both positive and negative, that have not been considered by the mining industry (discussed below).

The International Principles for SIA (Vanclay, 2003, p. 6) argues that "the goal of impact assessment is to bring about a more ecologically, socio-culturally and economically sustainable and equitable environment". It argues that the focus of concern of SIA should be "a proactive stance to development and better development outcomes" and that "assisting communities and other stakeholders to identify development goals and ensuring that positive outcomes are maximised, can be more important than minimising harm from negative impacts".

It is necessary to consider what social development might be in any particular local context. Developing this idea further from Uglow (1998), who cites the 1990 United Nations Development Program's Human Development Report, human development can be conceived as having three fundamental components. The first is the ability to live a long and healthy life. This means not only access to health care services but to live in a peaceful and healthy community—a society in which good health is achievable. Health, according to the International Principles for SIA (Vanclay, 2003, p. 8), modifying the World Health Organisation's definition slightly, is "a state of complete physical, mental, social and spiritual wellbeing". The second dimension of human development is to be able to acquire knowledge. This means to have access to educational facilities and libraries, and to have time in the week to be able to devote to this. The third fundamental component is to have sufficient access to resources to ensure a basic standard of living. There are additional dimensions that are also important, including economic, political and social freedom; opportunities to be creative and productive; the ability to enjoy self respect; and guaranteed human rights.

Development has also been expressed as 'freedom', and contrasted with 'growth' by Nobel Prize winning economist Amartya Sen (1999). Development requires the removal of the major sources of 'unfreedom': poverty, tyranny, poor economic opportunities, systemic social deprivation, neglect of public facilities, and the passive tolerance of repressive states. The United Nations Millennium Declaration (2000) underlined the importance of social development, basing the Millennium Development Goals (MDGs) on fundamental values that are essential to international relations in the 21st century. These include freedom, equality, solidarity, tolerance, respect for nature, and shared responsibility. In addressing the MDGs, Sachs (2005) emphasised the need to end the poverty trap and identified low-cost interventions that can make a difference in living standards and economic growth. Sachs argued that each of his six identified types of capital is needed for an effective, well-functioning economy: human capital, business capital, infrastructure, natural capital, public institutional capital, and knowledge capital. Further, success in any single area depends on investments across all forms of capital.

The concept of 'the capitals' (or assets) is used by many writers, albeit in various formulations. For example, it is the basis of the challenge Porritt (2005) puts to the corporate sector to change the way they do business in order to contribute to a sustainable future. It also forms the essence of Moser's (1998) Asset Vulnerability Framework for social sustainability, and is the core of the Sustainable Livelihoods Approach (DfID, 1999).

2.3. Defining social development

To address the broader view described above, social development can be defined as being "the processes of fulfilling the basic needs of people, achieving a fair distribution of wealth gained as a result of economic growth, building human and social capital, expanding the scope of opportunities of individuals and communities, promoting social justice and equal opportunities, and eradicating poverty and illiteracy" (Esteves, 2008c, p. 43). In this view, a company's contribution to development should be more than improving the local and/or national economy. We concur with Uglow (1998, p. 2), "Good economic growth promotes human development in all its dimensions: it generates full employment and security of livelihoods; it fosters people's freedom and empowerment; it distributes benefits equally; it promotes social cohesion and co-operation, and it safeguards future human development."

Unfortunately, this good economic growth, or social development, is not always an outcome from mineral exploitation. There has been much debate about the broader social benefits of mining-led development, which has been primarily focused at the macro level (Auty, 1994; Friends of the Earth, 2000; Pegg, 2006; Ross, 2001; Sachs and Warner, 1995). An example of a regional-level analysis is Cademartori (2002) who discusses the social performance of the Escondida Mine in Chile's Antofagasta region since its start in 1990 in terms of human development and quality of life indices. In that example, most human development indicators showed very low values, at odds with the economic growth in the region. Davis and Tilton (2005) argue that mining can promote economic development and address poverty, and has done so in some countries. We support their view that the debate should not be generalised about whether mining should or should not be encouraged within all countries, as this presumes that the correct policy choice will be the same under all conditions and for all countries. Instead, we believe that mining may contribute to social development when companies are committed to this and when they do the analyses that are necessary to determine what is needed. We believe that the tool, Social Development Needs Analysis, as described below, will be useful.

At the local level, what is primarily at issue is whether local communities will receive an appropriate balance of benefits to compensate for the costs associated with the negative impacts on their livelihoods and whatever socio-cultural and political problems may be created. It tends to be the case that while the local community bears most of the environmental and social costs of mining, most of the profits (rents) flow elsewhere. This has led to growing demands that a sufficient portion of the benefits/rents should flow to local communities to ensure they are adequately compensated. Labonne (2002) argues for an equitable rent distribution system as a means of ensuring that mining becomes an agent for sustainable livelihoods. She suggests that this system should take the form of: (1) improved services and infrastructure as well as direct contributions, considering the temporary nature of mining; (2) participatory capacity-building activities to enable the community to make informed choices and to learn to take control of their development needs; and (3) balancing short-term job opportunities and dependency on mining activity with long-term objectives of protecting the natural resource base and sustaining post-mining development.

2.4. Identifying the social impacts of mining

The social impacts of an operation are difficult to establish, not least because the social meanings of actions vary according to each stakeholder's perspective (Burdge and Vanclay, 1995; Taylor et al., 2004; Uglow, 1998; Vanclay, 1999). The impacts of mining may be beneficial to one group of stakeholders, but may be detrimental other groups. Thus, trade-offs between the benefits and costs of the social impacts are inevitable. The impacts are also typically difficult to quantify. The matter is further complicated by the varying nature of the social impacts of a mining operation. Mines vary in size, lifespan, location, mineral deposit and regulatory framework. Each of these potentially affects the likely social impacts from the mining operation. The social impacts are in themselves complex and a function of the nature and strength of the pre-existing social system. Social impacts also change over the lifespan of a mining operation, from exploration through operation, to closure.

Mining companies have attempted to increase their capacity to predict social impacts, with a view to increasing their attempts to mitigate these impacts. A constructive and effective approach to mitigation, although rare in its application, requires the structuring of mining projects from the outset and throughout the lifecycle of mines in ways that maximise benefits to the local community and minimise the disruptive impacts. SIA is a tool with the potential to fulfill these objectives. In addition to the question of 'which impacts?', SIA is also concerned with 'who gains and who loses?', that is, the differential distribution of benefits and costs. SIA also considers both direct and indirect impacts (the 'second-order' and 'higher-order' effects of direct impacts).

2.5. Governance and social development interventions

This paper supports the view of Newbold (2003) that because tax revenues from mining activities do not always adequately serve the infrastructure needs of local communities, mines should participate in voluntary programs that provide immediate and direct benefits to communities, with a view to developing the region so that it can attract a diverse range of other industries. This is particularly important where all aspects of life in the mining town have historically been organised by the company, and the resultant dependency of workers and their families on the company can be a major barrier to sustainability.

The likely success of these programs is influenced by levels of community capacity and governance. In developing countries especially, the situation for a mining company is rarely one of going about its business and addressing its environmental and social obligations as prescribed by a regulatory body. Operations are often located in regions characterised by: weak local government; a lack of strategic social and economic planning at national, regional and local levels; and growing dissatisfaction in local communities because of the perceived weak alignment between the economic returns from mining and their own livelihood priorities.

Realistically, taking a 'strategic' approach to social investments will necessarily involve entering into what is typically regarded as the domain of government (Esteves, 2008a). In some developing countries, a focus on sustainable development also raises an expectation to consider a much wider range of social commitments than would typically be the case in developed countries, for example: education and health, programs for promoting local economic activity, support for Indigenous peoples, and institution building (Humphreys, 2001). They all come at a cost to companies, a cost which in developed countries can be shared with a wide range of other contributors. In most developing countries, however, companies have to bear these costs on their own. This issue has practical implications in that companies are uncertain as to how far they should intrude into those responsibilities traditionally seen as belonging to government. Companies accept that a fundamental principle of long-term success is the ability to align the interests of communities in the locations where they wish to operate with their own interests, and to develop business operations within those communities on the basis of mature and respectful partnerships. Facilitating local development needs to be undertaken in such a way that is not overly paternalistic nor usurps the functions of national and local governments. Companies do not want to be responsible for social costs that might not be sustainable in the event of an economic downturn or mine closure.

It is generally accepted that companies are ill-equipped to address social problems (Burke and Logsdon, 1996). A company is more likely to be committed to social projects that directly support 'core business', such as utilising local employment, building a local supply base, ensuring that the infrastructure and service needs of employees and their families are met, and facilitating skills transfer between employees and community groups. Gaining support from senior management of mine sites to long-term social projects is easier when focus areas are shown to benefit the site's strategic goals.

It may be necessary to reconceptualise transnational mining companies as being key players in a country's governance (Ferguson, 2006). While this blurs the lines between business and government, it does not necessarily mean a withdrawal by the State. Instead, the logic is that if business takes on a larger responsibility than previously, government can target its development programs more effectively. However, in order to avoid a 'Santa Clause' scenario, care needs to be taken not to enter into long-term, unilateral commitments to community development programs since these can generate false expectations and community dependency, as well as undermine the proper role of the State, especially given the commercial volatility of mining (Petkoski and Twose, 2003). Greater sustainability and reduced liability will occur where companies partner with local government on community projects, aligning their social investment programs with the strategic social and economic priorities of a legitimate democratic local planning process. Petkoski and Twose (2003, p. 26) suggest that "where such political and planning processes are either absent, fledgling or corrupted … the company should seek to 'lead from behind'—[to] avoid undermining the proper role of government and yet play a transparent and graduated part in building the capacity of local authorities to plan and implement social and economic development". This type of social investment is particularly appropriate for those in developing countries where good governance is lacking.

2.6. Considerations in countries with conflict

Social investment can also play a role in peace-building where companies operate in countries with conflict. Unless well-managed, this can be fraught. While companies seldom intend to start conflict, their actions can directly or indirectly contribute to it. Social investments also have the potential to be a source of conflict within the community and to create dependency. They can also reinforce negative behaviour, for example, by using social investment as a tool for managing disturbances, companies often inadvertently reward violent behaviour. International Alert (2005) has provided guidance on how to avoid the potentially harmful impacts of social investment and how to maximise the potential of social investment to be a conduit for contributing to peaceful societies. Some recommendations include looking at social investment through an operations lens, rather than as an add-on; conducting a context analysis and impact assessment prior to designing a social investment policy; ensuring that social investment projects address root causes, and are not just reactions to episodic symptoms; involving the government; collaborating with others; focusing on impact rather than input; and being clear about the objectives of social investment projects.

3. Social Impact Assessment and social development

While SIA is widely accepted as a project-planning tool amongst the largest mining companies, in practice it has not typically advocated the inclusion of social development and sustainability into core business strategies and the building of collaborations with government and communities (Esteves, 2008a). There is some suggestion that SIA has not achieved its full potential in its applications in the mining industry (O'Faircheallaigh, 1999). Nevertheless, some companies are seeking to redress this, for example Anglo American plc, whose Socio-Economic Assessment Toolbox (SEAT) is linked to improving the implementation and contribution of activities such as: increasing local procurement and outsourcing to support local business development; establishing new community investment initiatives; developing human capital; setting up partnerships; and post-closure planning.

The International Principles for SIA (Vanclay, 2003, p. 6) considers that SIA "includes the processes of analysing, monitoring and managing the intended and unintended social consequences, both positive and negative, of planned interventions (policies, programs, plans, projects) and any social change processes invoked by those interventions. Its primary purpose is to bring about a more sustainable and equitable biophysical and human environment". SIA can be of particular value in understanding broader sustainability issues (both pre-existing and those triggered by a mine development) and in addressing these through the company's community contributions program. Rather than being limited to a narrow understanding of the concept 'social', "SIA is best understood as an umbrella or overarching framework that embodies the evaluation of all impacts on humans and on all the ways in which people and communities interact with their socio-cultural, economic and biophysical surroundings. SIA thus [encompasses] … aesthetic impacts (landscape analysis); archaeological and cultural heritage impacts (both tangible and nontangible); community impacts; cultural impacts; demographic impacts; development impacts; economic and fiscal impacts; gender impacts; health and mental health impacts; impacts on indigenous rights; infrastructural impacts, institutional impacts; leisure and tourism impacts; political impacts (human rights, governance, democratisation etc); poverty; psychological impacts; resource issues (access and ownership of resources); impacts on social and human capital; and [all] other impacts on societies" (Vanclay 2003, p. 7).

A conceptual distinction is made between a social change process (such as population growth) and an impact (caused by social change processes) (Slootweg et al., 2001). Impacts are experienced at various levels: as an individual; as a family, household or economic unit; and at the community level. Impacts can be experienced in a perceptual or corporeal (physical) sense (Vanclay, 2002).

The multi-disciplinary nature of the field of SIA has led to a void of well-developed SIA-specific theoretical underpinnings (Burdge and Vanclay, 1995; Vanclay, 1999). However, SIA falls within the overarching field of Impact Assessment, defined simply as "the process of identifying the future consequences of a current or proposed action" (Becker, 1997, p. 2). In spite of differences in the attitudes and backgrounds of their respective practitioners, SIA has much in common with EIA, SEA and other forms of impact assessment and ex-ante evaluation (Vanclay, 2004). Primary questions addressed by SIA include whether the proposed project is consistent with the needs identified by the affected population, and what the likely differences will be in the community's quality of life as a result of the proposed action.

The SIA process broadly follows four phases (adapted from Burdge and Vanclay, 1995):

(i) Identifying and understanding the issues associated with the project/intervention/mine;
(i) Projection and prediction of likely impacts from change strategies or development projects that are to be implemented;
(i) Development of mitigation strategies in order to minimise potential or unforeseen social impacts; and
(i) Development of monitoring programs to identify unanticipated social impacts that may develop as a result of social change.

SIA, as a well-developed field, has shown itself to be an effective means of understanding how communities function and how to involve affected communities in problem solving and developing community goals. Esteves (2008a), however, argues for a shift in thinking from using SIA as a short-term project-planning tool that is used mainly to mitigate impacts, to:

- being a source of data integrated within company decision-making systems;
- providing structured, regular information to the company about its social environment in a way that guides business planning processes;
- providing information to the community about the company's operations and their impacts; and
- involving the community in decisions around the most appropriate social investments.

SIA that is participatory, proactive and oriented towards social development also needs the support of a government policy framework which is visibly aligned to sustainable development (Taylor et al., 2004). Such a policy framework requires addressing issues such as dependency/autonomy, local and regional resource planning, regional development, employment and livelihoods, small business development, housing and residential infrastructure and community vitality, viability and health. Decision criteria typically applied by government assessors, or standards used to make judgments about whether environmental and social effects are positive or negative, are often not explicitly specified, and may be difficult to specify as they reflect a range of human values (Taylor et al., 2004). This is a further justification for grounding SIA in a sustainable development policy framework.

In the field of SIA, there is a something of a schism between technocratic (product oriented) and participatory (process oriented) approaches (Becker et al., 2004; Taylor et al., 2004). Technocratic approaches, which emphasise objectivity and tend towards the use of empirical data, have been criticised by many writers including Chambers (1997), Geisler (1993), Lane et al. (1997) and Lockie (2001). Participatory approaches, by contrast, use the knowledge and experiences of those most affected by the proposed development as the basis for determining impacts and the management of change (Becker et al., 2004). They emphasise early consultation and resolution of potential conflicts in planning and decision-making. The process helps to mobilise communities and interest groups to participate in change. Participatory SIA is much more than public consultation and includes the community in all stages of the SIA including problem identification, project design and implementation, and monitoring. It involves the interested and affected parties in deciding on the indicators of environmental and social impacts, and on the evaluation of effects and monitoring (Becker et al., 2004; Buchan, 2003).

An underlying premise of this paper is that impacts should be assessed first from the perspective of those directly affected and then from the perspective of the wider society. Public involvement, therefore, is a vital component of the SIA, which cannot be done without input from the potentially impacted community. Further, since the meaning of sustainable development is partly determined through societal consensus-building processes, it too relies heavily on participation (Rao, 2000; Reid, 1995; Smith, 1996). Participation is regarded as the key issue of sustainable development in political documents such as the 1992 Rio Declaration on Environment and Development and Agenda 21. An OECD report (Gramberger, 2001, p. 19) also emphasised the importance of participation, stating that: "Broad participation helps to open up debate to new ideas and sources of information ... and develop a consensus on the need for action that leads to better implementation [of sustainable development]. Central government must be involved ... but multi-stakeholder processes are also required involving decentralised authorities, the private sector and civil society, as well as marginalised groups." The participatory characteristic of sustainable development is one of the reasons why the concept is so elusive (Sillanpää and Wheeler, 1997).

The emphasis in a participatory approach to SIA is in helping the potentially impacted population cope with change, and of raising the awareness of assessors to the complexity of social change. Being sensitive to the existence of social impacts may be even more important than actually being able to identify them (Buchan, 2003; Vanclay, 2002). An important outcome for all participants in the SIA process is an awareness and understanding of how their community works. To understand the likely impacts of the proposed action and alternatives, communities and decision-makers need to know how the community is organised, how the community views and adapts to change, and how the community makes decisions. These variables are captured and monitored as part of the SIA, alongside variables measuring change in service and infrastructure demand, quality of life, community resilience, community aspirations and strengths.

An SIA oriented to social development also holds its challenges. While social development could encourage local communities to influence and share control over decisions and resources that affect them, in practice, this may be difficult for mining companies given their conventional orientation towards project management, where control is essential for running an efficient and profitable operation, including working to tight timeframes. Social development also challenges the view that professionals and experts know best. While it makes inherent sense that affected people should have a say in their own development, genuinely valuing local knowledge runs counter to the conventional approach in the mining industry where expert opinions are sought, consultants are brought in to advise on specific issues, and employees are expected to work in a managerial way.

Another significant challenge is reaching people who are most vulnerable; that is, those who are typically the most marginalised and the least vocal members of a community. Standard community engagement processes tend to gravitate to the more visible and influential players in a community; that is, those people or groups who have the greatest capacity to threaten an operation's social licence to operate.

Despite their many benefits, all SIAs, whether technical or participatory, are inevitably "a value-laden and a fundamentally political process in which peoples' biases cannot be entirely divorced from the projection of impacts" (Becker et al., 2004, p. 178). Public involvement, too, has its limitations. It does not necessarily systematically represent the community (Burdge and Vanclay, 1995; Vanclay, 1999). Individuals involved in public participation processes are often higher educated, better informed, have relatively more time, and a higher level of interest in the project than the average citizen (Stolp et al., 2002). A holistic view is required whereby the strengths of each approach are used to address the deficiencies of other approaches (Becker, 1997; Becker et al., 2004). A multi-methods approach: (a) allows for local residents' perspectives of social impacts to be gathered through a range of qualitative and quantitative techniques; (b) incorporates an analysis of quantitative indicators; (c) combines primary and secondary data sources; and (d) allows for the inclusion of the expert judgement of experienced SIA practitioners. The combination of methods (often called triangulation) provides multiple sources of data, a converging approach to indicator selection and impact projection, and ultimately serves to increase community trust in predicted impacts. Trust in the process (how the impacts have been assessed), and community acceptance of how impacts will be managed, is vital to the effectiveness of social development initiatives in which companies invest.

4. Social Development Needs Analysis as a methodological enhancement to SIA

Social Development Needs Analysis is a process that seeks to identify the significant social issues that need to be addressed in order for a company to contribute to the sustainable development of the local community over time, while creating value for the business. It is an additional set of methods that should be applied within the context of a broader SIA process in order to fully capitalize on the opportunities presented by the corporate activities. It links to a broader, ongoing, social monitoring program over the life of a company's operations, and should be mainstreamed into business planning and decision-making processes. This ensures that the company's engagement with governments and communities remains focused, relevant and appropriate to achieving sustainable development at the local level.

Fig. 1 depicts the normal SIA process with the four phases of SIA indicated. The activities within each phase have been slightly modified to include SDNA activities so as to give the overall SIA a social development orientation. The four phases and activities overlap in a temporal sense and may be iterative. The way SDNA is implemented in SIA is described below. This description of the four phases does not detail a standard SIA process since this is available in many places elsewhere (see for example Barrow, 2000; Becker, 1997; Branch et al., 1984; Burdge, 2004b; Goldman, 2000; Taylor et al., 2004; Vanclay, 1999), but describes how SDNA is incorporated into the SIA process.

4.1. Phase 1: Understanding the issues and opportunities

One of the main differences between the common practice of SIA in industry, and an SIA that incorporates SDNA, is the latter's emphasis on understanding the capitals/assets accessed by communities. The SDNA approach asserts that SIA practice and the resultant mitigation and social investment programs should be underpinned by theoretically robust social sustainability frameworks. These frameworks guide the selection of impact variables, seeking to avoid the risks associated with a checklist approach. Listings tend to be developed using deductive reasoning based on literal interpretations of discourse, ignoring how discourse is affected by power, agency and positionality (Rossouw and Malan, 2007). An uncritical approach to needs assessment also reinforces social welfare thinking that "identifies people through what they lack" (p. 295). An inductive, soft-systems approach to identifying impacts, for example, using a capitals framework demonstrates how the business is potentially connected to and affects a community's sustainability by influencing its capitals/ assets. It also facilitates the identification and monitoring of indirect and cumulative impacts.

The initial phase typically involves the following activities:

- Developing a community profile to understand the various dynamics constituting the social environment of the project or business and to understand the full range of capitals/assets accessed by the community;
- Collecting baseline data;
- Consulting stakeholders to identify potential impacts associated with the mining activity on social sustainability elements, and social development risks and opportunities;
- Selecting the salient impact variables to consider in further assessment; and
- Collecting business activity data, such as training, employment and procurement needs.

The community profile is a key element describing the existing conditions and past trends associated with the human environment in which the proposed action is to take place. 'Baseline' refers to a point in time and a geographical location to start the assessment. An important feature is in giving participants awareness and understanding of how their community works (Buchan, 2003). To understand the likely impacts of the proposed action and alternatives, companies, communities and decision-makers need to know how the community is organised; how the community views and adapts to change; and how the community makes decisions.

Recognition of community vulnerability and resilience as part of the profiling stage is important to enable positive change through all phases of the mine lifecycle. Community resilience refers to the ability of a community to adapt when faced with change. It is important because a lack of resilience increases the likelihood of harm from unforeseen risks and indicates that the community is more vulnerable to the impacts of change. Assessing resilience (and/or vulnerability) involves understanding the community's risk factors in order to develop a strategy that benefits their wellbeing and livelihood, while respecting their culture, customs, beliefs and values.

Conducting a baseline assessment usually requires primary data collection and analysis of secondary data, such as census surveys, government regional development plans and other strategic planning documents. Taylor et al. (2004) provide guidance on typical data sources for a community profile which collectively provide a comprehensive picture of a community and its capacity to cope with change associated with the effects of mining activity.

The baseline assessment process also assists in the identification of the mine's stakeholders. The International Finance Corporation (2007, p. 10), part of the World Bank Group, defines the stakeholders of a project to be: "persons or groups who are directly or indirectly affected by a project, as well as those who may have interests in a

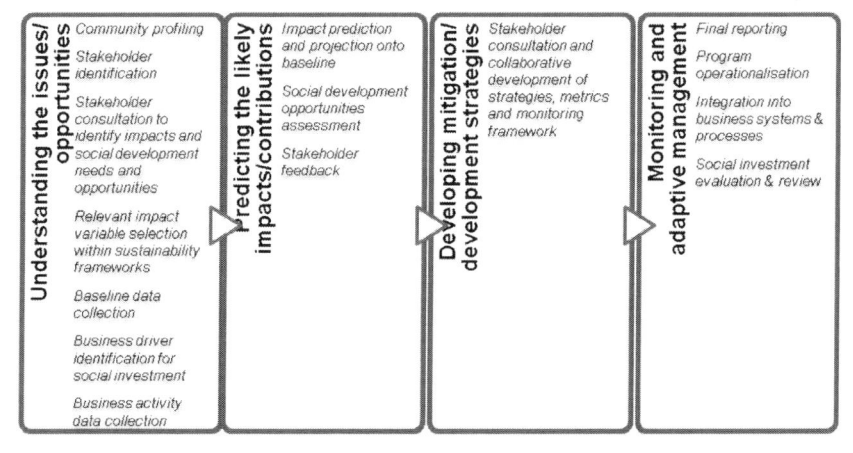

Fig. 1. Participatory SIA process with a social development orientation.

project and/or the ability to influence its outcome, either positively or negatively. Stakeholders may include locally affected communities or individuals and their formal and informal representatives, national or local government authorities, politicians, religious leaders, civil society organizations and groups with special interests, the academic community, or other businesses". Affected or 'local' communities may not necessarily be located in the immediate vicinity of the mine. The terms 'upstream' and 'downstream' should be used figuratively as well as literally to assist in defining the boundaries of an affected community. Upstream refers not only to a geographical location, but to anywhere that contributes inputs to the project (including for example where workers previously resided), while downstream also refers to the pathway of outputs (products and discharges). It is important to note that impacts can be direct or indirect, and that often the second or higher order impacts can be of greater significance. Consideration also needs to be given to the cumulative effects of projects over time as well as to the catalytic effects of different impacts occurring simultaneously.

As an input into the baseline assessment, a program of stakeholder consultation is undertaken using qualitative and quantitative methods. In a Social Development Needs Analysis, the purpose of this program goes beyond the traditional SIA focus of identifying perceived impacts associated with the mining activity. Perceptions relating to issues affecting the future sustainability of the region are sought as well as preliminary suggestions for strategies that would benefit from community, government and industry collaboration. Interested stakeholders are invited to participate in providing ongoing input into a social development strategy. Baseline assessment and consultation findings are shared with stakeholders for validation and further insights into complex issues, and to promote transparency, openness and a willingness to work collaboratively.

Concurrent with the community process, a needs analysis should be undertaken from a company perspective. A pivotal assumption of this paper is that the company should seek to undertake 'strategic social investments'. This involves identifying how the range of business success factors can be leveraged beyond the traditional emphasis on reputation and seeking stakeholder approval, to address business drivers such as human capital, risk management, cost savings and productivity, and access to land (Esteves, 2008a). Specific objectives linked to these higher-level drivers are developed using an 'ends and means', or value-tree, approach. This requires preliminary analysis of workforce data, procurement data and mine development plans to understand how business activities will be influenced by changes in the social environment, such as a transitory population and a competitive employment environment.

4.2. Phase 2: Predicting the likely impacts and contributions

The consultation phase is followed by an assessment of the community's social development needs which considers the nature, scale and significance of the identified issues. Sometimes this will be undertaken in conjunction with an assessment of predicted social impacts potentially created by a new mining development. In other situations, it may be done during normal operations of a mine as part of the ongoing monitoring program.

Applying a capitals framework to the assessment can assist in maximising the opportunities brought about by the development. This includes ensuring a sustainable future for the community when the mine eventually closes. An assessment and monitoring framework designed around all capitals is useful in guiding community and government stakeholders through this planning and transition. Brereton and Pattenden (2007) argue that the benefits of applying a capitals framework include ensuring that equal attention is given to: the full range of potential project impacts (rather than the common practice of focusing on economic and environmental impacts); the interconnectedness of the system in which impacts are experienced;

and to the potential contribution companies can make to the development of a community and/or region. The model also facilitates a structured deliberative process regarding potential substitutions and trade-offs. The selection of indicators that measure the flow of capital through the relevant domains is critical, as they need to provide useful data on change and early identification of emerging areas of concern.

The reliability of data is checked through triangulation. The assessment phase may involve methods such as expert panels, Delphi panels, citizen juries, the building of scenarios as well as the use of multipliers and other projection methods. Ivanova et al. (2007), for example, applied choice modelling techniques and experimental workshops amongst community representatives to make choices about alternative community development scenarios in the Bowen Basin, a region in Australia experiencing a coal mining boom.

4.3. Phase 3: Developing mitigation/development strategies

In the typical approach adopted in mining industry SIAs, the next step is the development of strategies to mitigate predicted negative impacts. In the SDNA-enhanced SIA, in addition to this, a major emphasis in this phase is the alignment of the social investment decisions of the company with the social development goals of the community. Partnerships are widely promoted as vehicles for corporate social investment to address sustainability issues, as they bring together diverse types of organisations with different skills and resources. In addition to consideration of the issues being addressed, companies also need to take into account the organisational aspects of strategy implementation. Emerging relationships between governments, businesses, and civil society organisations blur the boundaries between sectors (Selsky and Parker, 2005). The literature points to a growing acceptance that traditional sector solutions cannot address certain challenges and therefore must be enhanced by learning and borrowing from organisations in other sectors.

Business Partners for Development (2001) have tackled the common myth that successful partnerships are primarily shaped around a common or shared long-term vision or aim. They argue that evidence suggests that successful partnerships are those shaped around common or shared activities that first and foremost deliver against the individual aims of each partner, particularly where these have been legitimised within the partnership.

Multi-criteria decision analysis (MCDA) techniques are useful to incorporate partner aims into evaluating potential areas for investment focus (refer to Esteves, 2008a), so that both community and business can benefit. The result of the MCDA is a shortlist of priorities for further examination with community, government and expert input. After this, there follows an iterative and participatory process in which community projects are defined, 'lead' and 'lag' performance measures are developed for ongoing monitoring and review, and appropriate governance arrangements are put in place.

4.4. Phase 4: Monitoring and adaptive management

The monitoring and evaluation framework for mitigation and development programs is developed by stakeholders during the previous phase and formalised through partnering agreements. Implementation occurs during this final phase. At the end of the project life, the framework forms the basis for a post-project review. Performance of corporate-community partnerships can be measured at three levels: the direct impact on the issue and its stakeholders; the impact on building capacity, knowledge, and reputational capital that can attract new resources; and any influence on social policy or system change. Selsky and Parker (2005) suggest that learning (or capacity-building) is also an important outcome, for example, interpersonal and administrative skills, technical skills in the issue area, reflective skills that can change mind-sets and habits, and social learning that can lead to innovation. A simple input–output systems model or logframe approach ignores these benefits, yet unfortunately appears to be commonly used in evaluating partnerships. The following checklist for the monitoring and evaluation of partnership programs has been offered by Business Partners for Development (2002, p. 26):

- Actual benefits delivered through the partnership and their sustainability
- Extent to which the partnership's intended outcomes have been achieved
- Any unintended/unexpected/spin-off sustainable development outcomes or business benefits
- Any negative consequences of the partnership for communities, government, or business
- Overall, whether there is evidence that the partnership has 'added value' in terms of its impact
- Indication of the financial and nonfinancial costs and benefits of the partnership
- Evidence of institutional change brought about in the business, government agencies, or civil society organisations
- How the key lessons from the partnership are being recorded, reflected upon, and disseminated within the partnership (and with the respective constituents and other parties).

Another useful established evaluation model is Bennett's hierarchy, which is an outcomes-focussed approach. Bennett (1975) suggested seven categories of criteria for evaluating programs, which are based on a seven-link 'chain of events'. Evidence of program impact becomes stronger as the hierarchy is ascended. First in the chain are inputs, the resources expended by the project. These inputs produce activities that involve people who have reactions (positive and negative). People involved may change their knowledge, attitudes, skills and aspirations (KASA). Practice change occurs when people apply their KASA change to their working and personal lives. What follows from these practice changes are end results, which include accomplishing the social outcomes of the program.

Irrespective of the evaluation tool selected, it is critical that the monitoring framework considers how strategies and indicators are mainstreamed into the operation's core business planning, budgeting, review, performance management, reporting, and reward and recognition systems.

5. Conclusion

Corporations are facing increasing societal expectations that they will not only provide benefits to host communities and leave a positive legacy post-closure, but that they will also take an active role in addressing poverty at local, national and international levels. This paper calls for more effective corporate social investments. The premise is that a more rigorous approach to decision-making and a clear logic in the links between investment decisions, business value and community needs, will increase the chances of success. The advocated approach requires setting investment priorities that represent the development aspirations of the community and identifying how core business activities can contribute to sustainable development.

Social Development Needs Analysis is a conceptual and practical enhancement to the typical Social Impact Assessment process and is a useful device to guide corporate-community investment. While this paper has focused on mining communities, the approach has broader application. We have advocated a business case approach to social investments, which facilitates a shift in thinking from impact mitigation to value creation for both businesses and local communities.

Using SDNA within SIA to strengthen the rigour with which community investment decisions are made will result in more effective initiatives, ultimately leading to credibility being built amongst the community and other stakeholders, the company being rewarded by financial markets, corporate commitment to social investment being reinforced, and social and environmental outcomes being achieved.

References

Auty R. Patterns of development: resources, policy, and economic growth. London: Edward Arnold; 1994.
Barrow C. Social Impact Assessment: an introduction. London: Arnold; 2000.
Becker H. Social Impact Assessment: method and experience in Europe, North America and the developing world. London: UCL Press; 1997.
Becker D, Harris C, Nielsen E, McLaughlin W. A comparison of a technical and participatory application of social impact assessment. Impact Assess Proj Appraisa 2004;22(3):177–89.
Bennett C. Up the hierarchy. J Ext 1975;13(2):7–12.
Branch K, Hooper D, Thompson J, Creighton J. Guide to social assessment: a framework for assessing social change. Boulder: Westview; 1984.
Brereton D, Pattenden C. Measuring what matters: monitoring the contribution of a new mining project to community sustainability. Conference proceedings from 3rd International Conference on Sustainable Development Indicators in the Minerals Industry, June 2007, Milos, Greece; 2007. p. 327–32.
Buchan D. Buy-in and social capital: by-products of social impact assessment. Impact Assess Proj Apprais 2003;21(3):168–72.
Burdge R. Community needs assessment and public involvement techniques. In: Burdge R, editor. The concepts, process and methods of Social Impact Assessment. Middleton: Social Ecology Press; 2004a. p. 223–33.
Burdge R. A Community Guide to Social Impact Assessment. (third edition). Middleton: Social Ecology Press; 2004b.
Burdge R, Vanclay F. Social impact assessment. In: Vanclay F, Bronstein D, editors. Environmental and Social Impact Assessment. Chichester: Wiley; 1995. p. 31–65.
Burke L, Logsdon J. How corporate social responsibility pays off. Long Range Plan 1996;29(4):495–502.
Business Partners for Development. Endearing myths, enduring truths: enabling partnerships between business, civil society and the public sector; 2001. Online resource: http://www.bpdweb.com/endearing_myths.pdf [last accessed 24 June 2008].
Business Partners for Development. Putting partnering to work; 2002. Online resource: http://www.bpdweb.com/docs/main1or5.pdf [last accessed 24 June 2008].
Cademartori J. Impacts of foreign investment on sustainable development in a Chilean mining region. Nat Resour Forum 2002;26(1):27–44.
Chambers R. Whose reality counts: putting the first last. London: Intermediate Technology Publications; 1997.
Connell J, Howitt R, editors. Mining and indigenous peoples in Australasia. Sydney: Sydney University Press; 1991.
Davis G, Tilton J. The resource curse. Nat Resour Forum 2005;29(3):233–42.
DfID. Sustainable livelihoods guidance sheets London. Department for International Development; 1999. Online resource: http://www.livelihoods.org/info/info_guidancesheets.html [last accessed 24 June 2008].
Esteves AM. Evaluating community investments in the mining sector using multi-criteria decision analysis to integrate SIA with business planning. Environ Impact asses Rev 2008a;28(4-5):338–48.
Esteves AM. Evaluating social investments in the mining industry using Multi-Criteria Decision Analysis. Unpublished PhD thesis; 2008b.
Esteves AM. Mining and social development: refocusing community investment using multi-criteria decision analysis. Resour Policy 2008c;33(1):39–47.
Ferguson J. Global shadows: Africa in the neoliberal world order. Durham: Duke University Press; 2006.
Friends of the Earth. Treasure or Trash? The World Bank's flawed defense (sic) of mining as a tool for economic development; 2000. Online resource: http://www.foe.org/camps/intl/worldbank/teasureortrouble.pdf (sic) [last accessed 24 June 2008].
Geisler C. Rethinking SIA: why ex ante research isn't enough. Soc Nat Resour 1993;6(4):327–38.
Gibson R. Favouring the higher test: contribution to sustainability as the central criterion for reviews and decisions under the Canadian Environmental Assessment Act. J Environ Law Pract 2000;10(1):39–54.
Goldman L, editor. Social impact analysis: an applied anthropology manual. Oxford: Berg; 2000.
Gramberger M. Citizens as partners: OECD handbook on information, consultation and public participation in policy-making. Paris: OECD Publishing; 2001.
Humphreys D. Sustainable development: can the mining industry afford it? Resour Policy 2001;27(1):1–7.
International Finance Corporation. Stakeholder engagement: a good practice handbook for companies doing business in emerging markets. Washington: IFC; 2007. Online resource: http://www.ifc.org/ifcext/enviro.nsf/AttachmentsByTitle/p_StakeholderEngagement_Full/$FILE/IFC_StakeholderEngagement.pdf [last accessed 24 June 2008].
International Alert. Conflict-sensitive business practice: guidance for extractive industries. London: International Alert; 2005. Online resource: http://www.iisd.org/pdf/2005/security_conflict_sensitive_business.pdf [last accessed 24 June 2008].
Ivanova G, Rolfe J, Lockie S, Timmer V. Assessing social and economic impacts associated with changes in the coal mining industry in the Bowen Basin, Queensland, Australia. Man Environ Qual: An Intern J 2007;18(2):211–28.
Labonne B. The mining industry and the community: joining forces for sustainable social development. Nat Resour Forum 1999;23(4):315–22.
Labonne B. Commentary: harnessing mining for poverty reduction, especially in Africa. Nat Resour Forum 2002;26(1):69–73.
Lane M, Ross H, Dale A. Social impact research: integrating the technical, political, and planning paradigms. Human Organ 1997;56(3):302–10.

Lockie S. SIA in review. Impact Assess Proj Apprais 2001;19(4):277–88.
Moser C. The asset vulnerability framework: reassessing urban poverty reduction strategies. World Dev 1998;26(1):1–19.
Newbold J. Social consequences of mining and present day solutions: Region II in Chile highlighted. Sust Dev 2003;11(2):84–9.
Noronha L. Mining in Goa: the need to integrate local regional and national interests. In: Mayer J, Chambers B, Farooq A, editors. Development policies in natural resource economies. Cheltenham: Edward Elgar; 1999. p. 155–71.
O'Faircheallaigh C. Making social impact assessment count: a negotiation-based approach for indigenous peoples. Soc Nat Resour 1999;12(1):63–80.
Pegg S. Mining and poverty reduction: transforming rhetoric into reality. J Clean Prod 2006;14(3–4):376–87.
Petkoski D, Twose N, editors. Public policy for corporate social responsibility. WBI Series on Corporate responsibility, accountability, and sustainable competitiveness. Washington: World Bank Institute; 2003.
Porritt J. Capitalism as if the world matters. London: Earthscan; 2005.
Rao P. Sustainable development: economics and policy. Oxford: Malden; 2000.
Reid D. Sustainable development: an introductory guide. London: Earthscan; 1995.
Ripley E, Redmann R, Crowder A. Environmental effects of mining. Delray Beach: St. Lucie Press; 1996.
Ross ML. Extractive sectors and the poor: An Oxfam report. Boston: Oxfam America; 2001.
Rossouw N, Malan S. The importance of shaping social impact monitoring: lessons from the Berg River Dam, South Africa. Impact Assess Proj Apprais 2007;24(4):291–9.
Sachs J. The end of poverty: how we can make it happen in our lifetime. London: Penguin; 2005.
Sachs J, Warner A. Natural resource abundance and economic growth. NBER working paper series, vol. 5398. Working Paper; 1995. Online resource: http://www.cid.harvard.edu/ciddata/warner_files/natresf5.pdf [last accessed 24 June 2008].
Selsky J, Parker B. Cross-sector partnerships to address social issues: challenges to theory and practice. J Manag 2005;31(6):849–73.
Sen AK. Development as freedom. Oxford: Oxford University Press; 1999.
Sillanpää M, Wheeler D. Integrated ethical auditing: The Body Shop International, UK. In: Zadek S, Pruzan P, Evans R, editors. Building corporate accountability. London: Earthscan; 1997. p. 102–28.
Slootweg R, Vanclay F, van Schooten M. Function evaluation as a framework for the integration of social and environmental impact assessment. Impact Assess Proj Apprais 2001;19(1):19–28.
Smith RJ. Sustainability and the rationalisation of the environment. Environ Polit 1996;5(1):25–47.
Stolp A, Groen W, van Vliet J, Vanclay F. Citizen values assessment: incorporating citizens' value judgements in environmental impact assessment. Impact Assess Proj Apprais 2002;20(1):11–23.
Taylor CN, Bryan CH, Goodrich CG. Social assessment: theory, process and techniques. Third ed. Middleton: Social Ecology Press; 2004.
Uglow D. Social performance indicators. Coventry: mining and energy research network, Corporate Citizenship Unit, Warwick Business School, University of Warwick; 1998.
United Nations. The millennium declaration. New York: United Nations; 2000. Online resource: http://www.un.org/millennium/declaration/ares552e.pdf [last accessed 24 June 2008].
Vanclay F. Social impact assessment. In: Petts J, editor. Handbook of environmental impact assessment (Volume 1). Oxford: Blackwell Science; 1999. p. 301–26.
Vanclay F. Conceptualising social impacts. Environ Imp Assess Rev 2002;22(3):183–211.
Vanclay F. International principles for social impact assessment. Impact Assess Proj Apprais 2003;21(1):5–11.
Vanclay F. The triple bottom line and impact assessment: how do TBL, EIA, SIA, SEA and EMS relate to each other? J Environ Assess Policy Manag 2004;6(3):265–88.

Ana Maria Esteves is a consultant in the resources sector specialising in corporate-community investment, community engagement and social research. This paper is partly based on the work comprising a PhD recently completed through the University of Melbourne.

Frank Vanclay is professor of rural and environmental sociology with the Tasmanian Institute of Agricultural Research at the University of Tasmania. He is a specialist in the field of Social Impact Assessment and the social aspects of natural resource management.

Enhancing the benefits of local content: integrating social and economic impact assessment into procurement strategies

Ana Maria Esteves and Mary-Anne Barclay

One of the most encouraging recent developments in supply chain management has been the concerted effort to incorporate local small-to-medium enterprises (SMEs) into the supply chains of multi-national corporations. However, local SME procurement can lead to adverse social impacts. This paper demonstrates how the integration of social and economic impact assessment (SEIA) into sourcing strategy can be an effective tool to enhance the benefits associated with projects to local communities. Drawing on research into the mining, oil and gas sectors, the contribution of this paper is the application of impact assessment methodologies to local procurement. The paper recommends the development of a local procurement strategy and offers a step-by-step process for applying a Local Procurement Social Risks and Opportunities Assessment to local procurement planning.

Keywords: supply chain management, local content, development, mining, oil and gas, social impact assessment, economic impact assessment, procurement, enhancement

THERE IS GROWING INTEREST globally in enhancing the opportunities for locally based businesses to participate in the supply chains of major resource projects. Several companies, especially in the mining, oil and gas sectors, have adopted policies and standards aimed explicitly at increasing 'local procurement' or 'community content',[1] recognising that local economic participation has benefits for companies and communities alike. From a corporate perspective, local economic participation is seen as one means of maintaining a social licence to operate, by giving communities a stake in the project, as well as of ensuring reliability of supply by having a supplier located nearby. From a community perspective, the participation of local businesses in the resource project is a means by which the benefits of resource development can flow into their communities. The benefits of supply chain participation have become particularly apparent in Indigenous communities where there are now a number of agreements between companies and Indigenous groups that are aimed at enabling greater Indigenous economic participation and which include commitments to support the development of Indigenous-owned enterprises.

This paper draws on the research undertaken by the authors in developing a good practice local procurement guide for the Australian mining, oil and

---

Ana Maria Esteves is Director of social development consultancy Community Insights Pty Ltd (Akerkhof 28, 9711JC Groningen, The Netherlands), which has a speciality in the mining, oil and gas sector; Email: amesteves@communityinsights.com.au. Mary-Anne Barclay is a Research Fellow at the Centre for Social Responsibility in Mining, Sustainable Minerals Institute, The University of Queensland, Brisbane St Lucia, Queensland 4072, Australia; Email: m.barclay@smi.uq.edu.au. Ana Maria and Mary-Anne share a common research interest in identifying how the benefits of mining operations can be shared with local communities. They have collaborated on a number of research projects for the mining industry on topics such as corporate community investment, the evaluation of community funds and foundations and Indigenous employment initiatives, as well as their work on local procurement.

For acknowledgements see page 214.

gas sectors (Esteves et al, 2010, 2012). The project included a comprehensive research methodology. First, an extensive review of procurement practices around the world was undertaken. Next, 49 interviews were conducted in 2009 with key stakeholders operating in the mining, oil and gas sectors throughout Australia. The purpose of these interviews was to identify the key challenges in incorporating local small-to-medium enterprises (SMEs) into the supply chains of major mining, oil and gas companies and to identify successful strategies for their incorporation. Finally, the researchers looked at 23 companies in the mining, oil and gas sectors to consider how their supply chain practices can contribute to the social and economic development of local communities. This research strategy resulted in the development of a number of 'mini case studies', drawn from both Australian and international contexts, that identified the corporate practices involved in successful local SME participation.

This paper focuses in particular on the mining, oil and gas sectors. Because of the huge global demand for oil, gas and metals to fuel economic development, and the desire of developing nations to exploit their natural resources to lift themselves out of poverty, the resources sector is enormously powerful. The sector's impacts, both positive and negative, affect us all. Therefore, the lessons that can be learned from its good practices and efforts to mitigate its negative impacts are important to everyone, in particular, those marginalised communities who would benefit most from more corporate practices that contribute to employment and business development opportunities. These lessons are also relevant to other sectors that have the potential to draw on community assets, such as manufacturing, forestry and agribusiness supply chains.

General stories about the success of local procurement strategies have led many in the impact assessment community to embrace local procurement initiatives as a means of enabling local economic development. A cursory review of the social impact statements submitted as part of the approvals process for new resource developments reveals that there is a common assumption among assessors that local sourcing is a 'positive' to be maximised and an effective instrument for gaining community and government support for resource development. Economic impact assessment reports submitted to permitting authorities also reveal a range of persuasive arguments in favour of the multiplier effects of project spend.

However, the extent to which the local community will actually benefit from local procurement initiatives is dependent on the capacity of the community to supply goods and services to the project, on the extent to which there is a local multiplier effect and, even more importantly, on the ability of communities to adapt to the inevitable changes that accompany large-scale resource development (Esteves et al, 2010). The central argument of this paper is that planning for local procurement can be enhanced by

The central argument of this paper is that planning for local procurement can be enhanced by the adoption of an integrated social and economic impact assessment (SEIA) approach, where SEIA is the process of managing the social and economic issues associated with local procurement

the adoption of an integrated social and economic impact assessment (SEIA) approach, where SEIA is the process of managing the social and economic issues associated with local procurement.

Therefore the intent of this paper is to provide guidance to supply chain managers and impact assessment practitioners, with a view to maximising the long-term socio-economic development benefits for communities and regions, while considering commercial interests. The paper begins by outlining the current trends in corporate procurement from local SMEs. Then the paper reviews current frameworks and methods applied to develop procurement strategy, including an analysis of weaknesses in relation to planning for local procurement. Next, consideration is given to the potential contribution of SEIA to local procurement strategies. Herein is the main contribution of this paper. A step-by-step process is recommended to enhance the positive impacts of local procurement and mitigate the negative consequences by adapting contract strategy planning and applying a Local Procurement Social Risks and Opportunities Assessment. The paper concludes with some observations on applying the SEIA process to local procurement management planning, to provide lasting socio-economic benefits to local communities and reduce social risk to businesses.

Current trends in local procurement

There is a growing awareness among practitioners that procurement from local SMEs can bring significant social and economic benefits to communities. In addition to creating business for suppliers, local procurement can stimulate economic activity and attract further investment, both through suppliers engaging other suppliers for inputs and through the multiplier effects of employees of local businesses spending some of their wages in their communities. Other benefits include improving the quality of life for employees and business owners and operators, dissemination of new technologies and innovation to other market participants, and attraction of investment in social infrastructure (SEAF, 2007).

Another important development in the area of local procurement has been the emergence of partnerships between governments, support institutions and development agencies to establish supplier linkage programs. SME linkage programs have been especially successful in enabling SMEs to access financing and skills development programs, particularly those that provide technical mentoring and support for the development of business management skills (Deloitte, 2004; Jenkins et al, 2007; Nelson, 2007; Ruffing, 2006; UNCTAD, 2001). Linkage programs also focus heavily on institutional strengthening activities to encourage an enabling environment for SME development. One particular area of success has been in assisting women to establish their own small businesses by providing them with access to legal, business and financial systems, thereby reducing the gender gap that prevents many women from participating in economic life (ODI, 2005; Wise and Shtylla, 2007).

There has, however, been very little written in either the academic or the practitioner literature on the other social and economic consequences (positive or negative) that may flow from an increase in local procurement. These consequences potentially include:

- Demographic change associated with in-migration;
- The concentration of economic activity around the project area;
- Changes in the level of economic diversification;
- Changes in patterns of land use; and
- Institutional change.

Before promoting the benefits of local procurement, it is important to consider these changes if an accurate picture of social and economic impacts of a new project development is to be obtained.

Typically, the social considerations associated with the design and implementation of procurement arrangements have not received the same attention as technical considerations, such as those associated with constructing a pipeline, a transport route, an accommodation camp or water supply. However, there is now clear evidence that the resources sector, at least, is learning that social issues are important and is starting to change its practices in response. Previous research (Esteves et al, 2010; Esteves and Vanclay, 2009) indicated that corporate attitudes towards local procurement are continually evolving. For example, for companies with leading practices, the corporate drivers for local procurement have shifted over time. In many instances, the initial motivation was a need to comply with formalised commitments, to a host government, an investment partner, or an Indigenous community. Compliance was deemed necessary in order to secure access to resources. Over time, however, these companies had become increasingly motivated by the desire to establish and maintain enduring partnerships with local suppliers for mutual benefit.

Resource companies are now engaging in a range of local procurement interventions that are designed to increase local business access to contract opportunities. These strategies include assigning higher preference weightings to local businesses in competitive bidding processes; sole sourcing arrangements with local suppliers; price matching, that is allowing local suppliers to match the price of other suppliers; breaking large contracts into smaller ones (unbundling) to create opportunities for smaller local suppliers; requiring non-local suppliers to sub-contract locally or to enter joint ventures with local suppliers; providing technical and management training and mentoring; and linking local businesses to other service providers and agencies that promote technological innovation and provide access to finance.

While the success of these strategies indicates that SMEs can be an effective vehicle for economic growth and poverty reduction, local SME procurement strategies can also lead to adverse social impacts. Setting inappropriate key performance indicators (KPIs) and targets for local spend can encourage perverse behaviour. One example of this is 'fronting', where companies are established with the prescribed local ownership or address, but the decision-making and benefits are held by other individuals, who are not targeted beneficiaries of the local procurement policy.

Another common scenario in mining communities is that because of the high wages paid by the large resources companies, local people are often drawn away from other businesses in town. As a result of these losses, local communities can find their already limited services sector shrinking even further. The loss to communities is compounded because they may also suffer a major loss in human capital, as experienced retailers, administrators, nurses and teachers leave their professions to work in the resources sector.

A third example of unanticipated negative impacts of local procurement strategies is community dissatisfaction that can result from seeing only menial works being given to local people. Community perceptions that particular groups have been favoured in the allocation of business opportunities can negatively affect social cohesion, as can disputes within groups over the distribution of profits and employment opportunities.

Even for those SMEs that are part of the resource sector supply chain there can be negative impacts, especially if the resource company is their sole, or major, client. These companies can be left vulnerable to the business cycles of the larger company and there may be little in the way of opportunities for diversification. Given the range of factors that can limit the effectiveness of local procurement strategies, this paper advocates the adoption of a SEIA approach to local procurement planning as a means of identifying, mitigating and managing these potential negative impacts and enhancing the positive impacts.

Theoretical frameworks for local procurement strategies

Local procurement during the development of procurement strategies involves (Warner, 2011): (1) understanding the business case and the level of priority the business should give to local procurement when compared to price, time, quality and schedule; (2) identifying the future demand for goods and services, and the capacity of local suppliers to meet this demand (while also considering the demand of other companies competing in the same supplier markets); and (3) selecting appropriate procurement strategies, including the packaging of work, selection process, extent of client control and contract terms. These activities are guided by management theories, which are briefly reviewed in this section.

Supply chain management

Supply chain management (SCM) has emerged over the last three decades as an increasingly important area to both business practitioners and academics. The concept is defined by the Council of Supply Chain Management Professionals (CSCMP, 2011: 1) as follows:

> Supply Chain Management encompasses the planning and management of all activities involved in sourcing and procurement, conversion, and all logistics management activities. Importantly, it also includes coordination and collaboration with channel partners, which can be suppliers, intermediaries, third-party service providers, and customers. In essence, supply chain management integrates supply and demand management within and across companies.

A dominant model applied in SCM practice is the Kraljic Purchasing Portfolio Management Model, which seeks to minimise the company's supply risk and make the most of its buying power (Kraljic, 1983). The model includes the construction of a portfolio matrix that classifies products according to two dimensions: profit impact and supply risk ('low' versus 'high'). The result is a classification of procurement demand in four categories: bottleneck, non-critical, leverage and strategic items (see Figure 1).

Each of the four categories calls for a specific strategy towards suppliers. Non-critical items (low profit impact, low risk) require efficient processing, standardisation, order volume and inventory optimisation. Leverage items (high profit impact, low risk) allow the buying company to exploit its full purchasing power, such as through competitive tendering. Bottleneck items (low profit impact, high risk) cause significant problems and risks, which should be handled by insurances, controls, security of inventories and backup plans. Strategic items (high profit impact, high risk) require development of long-term supply relationships, careful analysis and management of risks, and contingency planning.

Kraljic (1983) also recommends a further market analysis of the strategic items. The firm's buying strengths are plotted against the strengths of the supply market, to identify three basic power positions and associated supplier strategies: balance, exploit and diversify. According to Kraljic (1983), supply managers should develop long-term relationships with their suppliers based on mutual trust and openness under the strategic quadrant, and conversely, in the non-critical quadrant, they should take a short-term transactional exchange focus and spread purchase volume among multiple suppliers. Macbeth (2002) refers to the two quadrants respectively as the 'important few' and the 'trivial many' (see Figure 1).

While the simple two-dimensional nature of the model has been criticised, on the whole, practitioners find the portfolio approach useful in positioning commodities in the different segments and in developing differentiated purchasing strategies

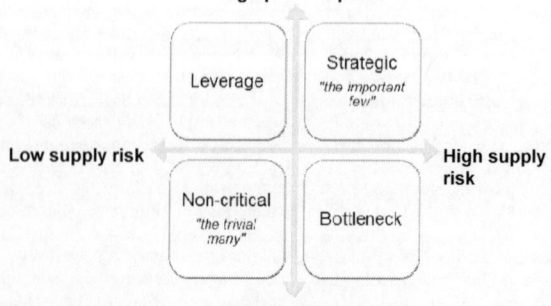

High profit impact

Leverage	Strategic *"the important few"*
Non-critical *"the trivial many"*	Bottleneck

Low supply risk ← → **High supply risk**

Low profit impact

Figure 1. Purchasing Portfolio Management Model (adapted from Kraljic, 1983; Macbeth, 2002)

(Gelderman and Van Weel 2003). For example, the model was adapted to forecast and segment future demand in order to develop local suppliers for the Chad–Cameroon Oil Development and Pipeline Project (IFC and Esso Exploration & Production Chad, Inc, 2008). Positioning business opportunities on the matrix led to identifying three clusters of business opportunities, and classifying these using a three tier system (see Box 1).

A further illustration is found in Peru, where a detailed market analysis of strategic commodities was undertaken to support mining cluster development in Cajamarca. Here, Vargas (2010) drew on Michael Porter's frameworks (1980, 1985) and identified the determinants of industrial competitiveness with regard to factors of production; factors of demand; support and related industries; and the strategies, structures and rivalry among mining firms to identify the relative power of market participants.

However, recent trends in risk management and stakeholder research raise questions around the appropriateness of the Kraljic model in identifying how supply chain performance can be aligned with social and environmental considerations and be responsive to stakeholder and societal expectations of performance (Frankel et al, 2008). For instance, Macbeth's (2002) classification of low complexity/low contribution to profit suppliers as the 'trivial many' may be brought into question in areas where there are weak markets and project-affected local communities have high expectations of participation and the ability to prevent continuity of operations. These trends call for a change in how firms think about their supply chain performance.

This paper proposes that for every local procurement strategy there needs to be an assessment of the impacts on markets and affected communities. For example, small suppliers can be disadvantaged by long-term partnering strategies (relational exchange). Applying resource dependency theory and transaction cost economics, Barringer (1997) developed a conceptual framework on relational exchange in the small supplier/large buyer context. The framework focuses on advantages and disadvantages for small suppliers. Advantages of relational exchange include reduced transaction costs, more certain access to critical resources, reliable customer base, and quality and cost. However, small suppliers can be negatively impacted through loss of autonomy and flexibility, dependence on the buyer, weaker negotiating position, and having to share confidential cost and other information. These disadvantages have led Larson et al (2005) to hypothesise that relational exchange may be more suitable for large suppliers than smaller ones.

Supply chain risk management

Supply chain risk management (SCRM) is a field within SCM that is also commonly used within the mining, oil and gas sectors and is applicable to all large-scale extractive and manufacturing industries with significant infrastructure costs and lengthy supply chains. SCRM is typically a formal process that involves identifying potential losses, understanding the likelihood of potential losses, and assigning significance to these losses (Giunipero and Eltantawy, 2004). The results lead to management responses that include avoidance, transfer, mitigation, monitoring or even acceptance of risk (Khemani, 2007). For example, the results can also be used to guide decisions on supplier development programs (Trkman and McCormack, 2009).

A key argument of this paper is that SCRM processes give little attention to the prediction of social impacts (negative and positive). SCRM would be enhanced by considering the impacts of the procurement intervention on the entrepreneurs, their employees, households, communities and regions. This crucial information would identify those exogenous material considerations that impact the business through value creation or protection.

Using SEIA and social risk and opportunities assessment to enhance local procurement strategies

The field of impact assessment offers a number of methods to assess systematically each alternative available to project developers intent on making opportunities accessible to local businesses, building local business capacity to meet contract requirements, and improving their competitiveness. Integrating SEIA into contracting strategy involves the following steps:

1. Categorise future demand opportunities using the four Kraljic (1983) categories (see Figure 1), each of which calls for a specific strategy towards suppliers.
2. Determine and assign relative weightings to criteria for assessing (1) opportunities according to local suppliers' ability and interest to take them up, and (2) potential for community benefit.
3. Within each of the four Kraljic categories, rate each opportunity according to criteria, and rank and prioritise opportunities. This will require a basic understanding of local suppliers and of their capability.

Box 1.	Three clusters of business opportunities (IFC and Esso Exploration & Production Chad, Inc, 2008)
Level I	— basic services and labour requirements.
Level II	— intermediate services and contractor requirements.
Level III	— highly critical, complex, specialised services and construction activities.

Enhancing the benefits of local content: integrating SEIA into procurement strategies

4. Determine what will be the potential 'community content' component of each priority opportunity, based on a more rigorous supply side analysis. Design a plan to realise the targeted community content by selecting appropriate procurement methods and supplier development strategies. This, in essence, is the local procurement strategy.
5. Identify the potential social and economic impacts associated with the local procurement strategy. The objective is to understand the likely responses of affected businesses, their communities and the regional economies to which they belong.
6. Assess the potential impacts using a social risk and opportunities assessment.

Demand side analysis and identifying potential opportunities for local procurement

Steps 2 and 3 (the 'demand side' analysis) can be assisted by applying multicriteria methodologies to rank and prioritise opportunities. As an example, in early 2011, the authors assisted an oil and gas company operating in Australia in seeking to identify potential opportunities for Indigenous businesses to participate in a facilities management contract. The contract comprised approximately 70 activities, or 'scopes of work'. A set of criteria and relative weightings were reached through consensus among procurement decision-makers and Indigenous liaison personnel. The criteria were expanded to take into account aspects such as the existing capability and capacity of Indigenous suppliers to deliver the scopes of work, the extent of potential employment benefits, a very rough estimation of the extent of 'cultural fit', as well as the sustainability of the opportunity. The seven criteria proposed to be used for prioritising opportunities were:

- Cultural fit with Indigenous community, and perceived levels of community interest;
- Potential for direct job creation;
- Supply risk;
- Capital outlay;
- Consistency of demand/sustainability;
- Existing local business capability gap; and
- Technical and managerial complexity.

Each scope of work was then rated, for each criteria, by systematic application of a scoring scale unique to each criteria. Table 1 shows the scoring scale and weighting for each criteria.

The simple 'rate and weight' exercise, followed by ranking the weighted averages for each scope of work, generated a number of opportunities for Indigenous sourcing for further investigation. For example, the following scopes of work were given a higher weighted average:

- Artwork;
- Biodiesel;
- Canteen serving, clean-up and cooking;
- Food scraps removal/recycling;
- Indoor plant supply and maintenance;
- Lawn maintenance;
- Maintenance of personnel uniforms;
- Plant supply;
- Recycled soaps; and
- Watering, weeding, pruning.

In this example, the decision-makers proceeded to agree on a process to engage the Indigenous community to explore their interest in taking up the opportunities, to inform of the contract requirements and procurement process, and to determine the nature and scale of supplier development that would be required to ensure Indigenous businesses are able to deliver to company standards and have access to the required capital. In essence, the output of these steps would be a local Indigenous procurement strategy for the facilities management contract. The company's intent was to learn from the process and replicate across other contract areas.

Table 1. Criteria used to score, rank and prioritise opportunities for Indigenous-owned businesses in a facilities management contract of an Australian oil and gas company

Criteria	Scoring scale	Weighting
Cultural fit with Indigenous community	3 = activity undertaken outdoors, 2 = indoors, in a workshop environment with a group of Indigenous workers, 1 = indoors	20%
Potential for direct job creation	1 = one full time equivalent employee, 2 = more than one, 3 = at least five employees	20%
Supply risk	0 = 'show-stopper', 1 = high supply risk, 2 = moderate, 3 = low	20%
Capital outlay	1 = heavy machinery required, 2 = vehicle, 3 = no/minor capital requirements	10%
Consistency of demand/sustainability	3 = daily, 2 = at least monthly, 1 = less frequent	10%
Existing local business capability gap	1 = weak capability, 2 = moderate, 3 = strong	10%
Technical and managerial complexity	1 = specialised training required, 2 = basic training plus health, safety and environment training, 3 = routine task, basic training	10%
Total		100%

The following two examples demonstrate the kinds of alternative procurement strategies that are considered during impact assessment:

- *Sole sourcing versus competitive bidding:* A sole sourcing strategy in an environment where social capital within the community is low and distrust is high may be more harmful than a competitive bidding process (all else being equal). Further, giving a preference weighting to a local contractor who will need to import expertise may create less local employment benefits in the short term than bringing in a large, non-local contractor and requiring them to sub-contract locally.
- *Investing in supplier development programs with or without collaboration:* Evaluation of procurement strategies from a social impact perspective would assist in determining whether collaborating with other industry players to invest in supplier development would lead to greater benefit than would be obtained with a supplier development program aimed at meeting the demand of only a single operator. One example here is the case of the partnership between Anglo Ferrous Brazil (Minas Gerais, Brazil), local government, a local trade association and other major industries operating in the area. These partners worked together to design a supplier development program for building the capacity of local SMEs. The program addresses management training, business development and growth, improvements to unprofitable businesses, and creation of new enterprises.

Supply side analysis and identifying the potential impacts

In addition to a segmentation of prospective demand using Kraljic (1983), a local supply side analysis should be conducted to assess the level of community interest and capacity in accessing business opportunities, and to identify potential constraints. A comprehensive mapping of local SMEs is helpful in identifying their capabilities and in determining which businesses could benefit most from the opportunity to participate in local supply chains.

The Chad–Cameroon Pipeline example described earlier (IFC and Esso Exploration & Production Chad, Inc, 2008) classified suppliers using a star system. Supplier development strategies are developed according to their level of competency (see Box 1 for descriptions of these three types of levels). One star suppliers are established SMEs capable of performing basic (Level I) services, have proper administration and paperwork, but lack basic management tools and practices. Two star suppliers are aspiring world-class suppliers, with the attributes to perform Level II services. These suppliers are fairly well managed, use modern supply practices and specialise in specific sectors. They also have the capacity for growth. Three star companies are world-class suppliers, with the attributes to perform Level III services. Tenders are advertised specifying the rating required for bid applicants. Contracts are awarded on the basis of the capacity of the SME to perform the contract. This rating system has the extra advantage of adding transparency to the procurement process.

In addition to a supplier mapping and issues identification, an industry analysis is also required, which includes identification of the factors influencing an effective, well-functioning economic environment and, at the micro level, those factors critical to the success of local SMEs.

The issues scoping should be aimed at empowering stakeholders such as chambers of commerce, local government authorities and business associations. This is best achieved by involving them in early stages of local procurement strategy development, and in the evaluation and monitoring of social and economic impacts associated with local procurement. The scoping phase is also the right time to alert developers and stakeholders to the significant barriers faced by SMEs that can be disincentives to participation, and which tend to place SMEs in a weaker bargaining position.

The major disincentives to SME participation in the supply chains of large companies include communication breakdowns and the often rigid contracting requirements of the major resource companies. Local business owners are often unaware of tendering opportunities, or information is provided too late to allow for clustering, joint ventures or investing in the necessary equipment. The complex procedures and costs associated with prequalification and the tendency of major contractors to sub-contract to suppliers already known to them present further barriers to participation. However, these barriers can be overcome with persistence, genuine engagement between interested business owners and the company, and the right local knowledge. By involving stakeholders in the scoping process, solutions to some of these common problems can be found.

The scoping phase reveals that successful local procurement depends on investments across a number of areas. In establishing a baseline of local SME capacity, it is important that companies incorporate local knowledge, engage a broad range of stakeholders, and seek opportunities for collaboration with governments, local organisations and development agencies with the required expertise and responsibility.

Assessment of risks and opportunities

Having scoped the issues and opportunities, the next phase of the impact assessment involves narrowing the potential impacts for further analysis, and assessing the significance of risks and opportunities likely to result from each local procurement strategy under consideration.

The selection and analysis of impact variables requires drawing on a range of disciplines, the use of quantitative and qualitative methodologies, and a combination of expert and participatory processes. Figure 2 proposes a comprehensive framework for social risk and opportunities assessment of procurement strategies. The criteria reflect local procurement impact variables compiled from Esteves *et al* (2010, 2012), SEAF (2007), World Business Council for Sustainable Development (WBSCD) (2009), and WBSCD and IFC (2008). It is clear when scrutinising the variables that each requires its own techniques for measurement, and each technique brings its own problems. For this reason, it is important to select methods to support the derivation of proxies, rather than pursuing an indisputable, objective measure. Also, if a predicted impact is significant in the assessment, then it is essential to find a way to measure it, even if this requires developing new methods or data collection procedures. Measurability is never exact and a mixed methods approach in SEIA (as in most social and economic research) is useful to compensate for each method's weaknesses.

Three predictive methods often used in impact assessment are impact pathway analysis, scenario anal-

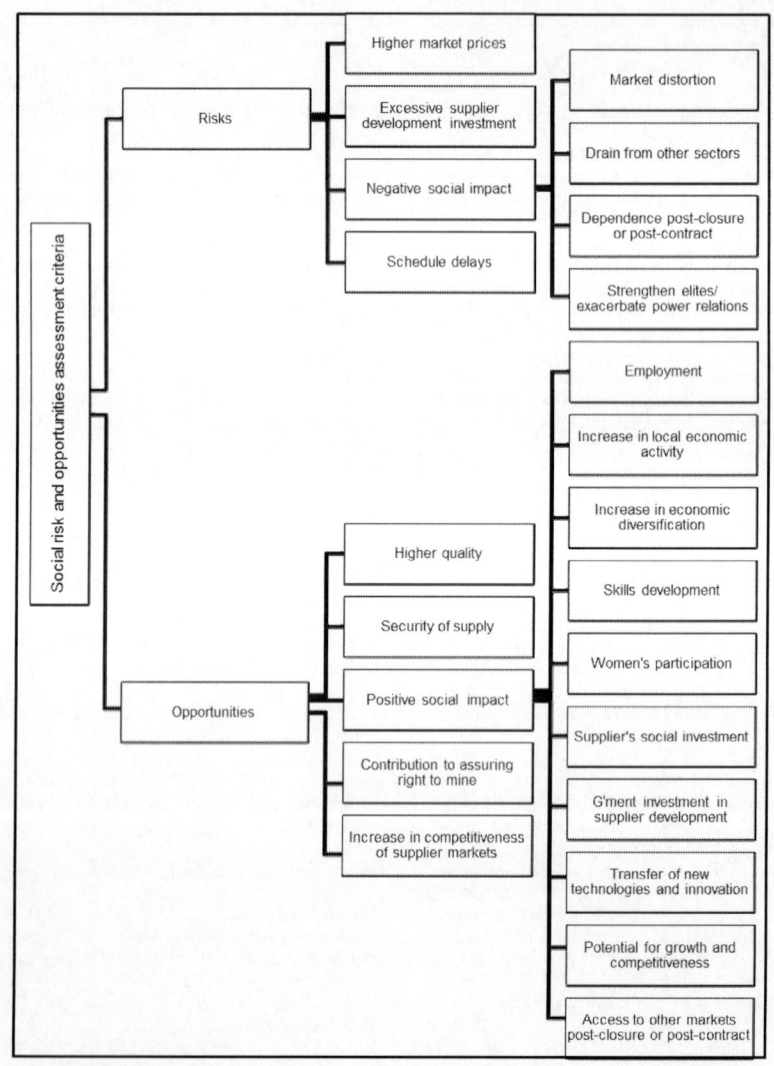

Figure 2. Social risk and opportunities assessment criteria (compiled from Esteves et al, 2010, 2012; SEAF, 2007; WBSCD, 2009; WBSCD and IFC, 2008)

ysis and modelling. One weakness to date has been the economic modelling conducted within SEIA, which has been largely irrelevant in informing local procurement strategies and identifying measures to enhance the employment and supplier development impacts of major projects. There is, however, an increasing awareness of the need to strengthen this area. In a recent development, Warner (2011) has applied economic impact optimisation (EIO) modelling to assess the commercial and public policy implications of different regulations and strategies for local content and supplier development. The model uses dialogue processes to quantify the impacts of different local content scenarios on dimensions such as costs, schedule, net present value and internal rate of return, payback period, national revenues and taxes, jobs created (direct, indirect and induced), and investments in local supplier competitiveness.

The model is applied when comparing different contracting strategies. Once a thorough knowledge of the negative impacts has been achieved, a rating is assigned, based on an assessment of likelihood (ranging from rare to almost certain) and consequence (insignificant to catastrophic). Common risk ratings that are assigned are as follows:

- *Low:* it will not have an influence on the decision.
- *Moderate:* it should have an influence on the decision unless mitigated.
- *Extreme or high:* it should influence the decision regardless of any possible mitigation.

The risk ratings are used to guide the adaptation of contracting strategies determined by the Kraljic (1983) approach to mitigate significant risks. Strategies to enhance identified opportunities can be assessed using approaches such as cost–benefit analysis. Considering the residual risks and feasible enhancements, the supply chain manager then goes about selecting strategies to make opportunities accessible to local businesses, building their capacity to meet contract requirements, and improving their competitiveness.

Monitoring of contracting strategies

It is important to note that, as it is impossible to predict all direct and indirect impacts, having a monitoring and adaptive management process in place is necessary to deal with any unintended consequences of the chosen procurement strategy plus check that proposed improvements are indeed working. The monitoring process should not be limited to selected social impact indicators and trends; the business value to the company from investing in local procurement and supplier development also requires attention. Investing in supplier development programs should not be approached as a philanthropic act, but rather as a form of business investment.

Taking the perspective that local procurement provides mutual gains to project developers and their communities, measures of business value also need to be incorporated in monitoring. Indicators should be linked to the business drivers for procuring from the local communities, which will vary across project stage and country context. Examples of business activity/output indicators include value of goods and services procured locally by the company; number of local suppliers; number of local employees hired by local suppliers; local procurement as a percentage of total corporate procurement; and company procurement spend as a proportion of overall procurement of goods and services in the area. Examples of business outcome indicators include faster timeframes for project approvals due to community and government support; reduced costs associated with delays in delivery; reduced costs of closure or decommissioning; and increased quality of supply to the company and reduced risk of protest action.[2]

Conclusions and recommendations

This paper has examined the increasingly common assertion in the mining, oil and gas industry that there are mutual benefits to be gained if affected communities believe that they will gain in the long term from living near a major resource development, and if local businesses believe they have equitable access to all opportunities within the company's supply chain. With local procurement practice on the rise, the commonly stated intent is to contribute to diverse, thriving local economies that are not dependent on a single operation. This intent is not only demonstrated by industry; local procurement also has the support of governments and development institutions who promote private sector-led development and poverty reduction by strengthening the SME sector.

These trends have meant that local procurement interventions require company staff to assume a greater responsibility for engagement with government, suppliers and civil society to create a supportive and sustainable business environment. The core argument of this paper is that this shift in the role of industry requires companies and governments to build their own capacity in terms of understanding the social and economic change processes in local communities, and how procurement and supplier development interventions affect these. While the focus of the paper has been on one sector (mining, oil and gas), the concepts can also be applied to public procurement, development assistance and other private industry sectors. The main contributions of the paper can also be generalised to these other sectors: (1) in proposing that SEIA has the potential to provide supply chain managers with the required knowledge and legitimacy within affected communities, and (2) in providing guidance on how contract strategy should be adapted in practice.

Enhancing the benefits of local content: integrating SEIA into procurement strategies

When integrated into contract strategy, SEIA can be an effective tool to promote collaboration and to enable communities to be active agents in their social and economic futures

When integrated into contract strategy, SEIA can be an effective tool to promote collaboration and to enable communities to be active agents in their social and economic futures. Local procurement can play a vital role in community's self-determination and well-being. However, scholarship is lagging behind practice, and local procurement practice faces the risk of becoming another 'siloed' managerial activity undertaken solely by staff in supply chain management roles and experts from economic disciplines. Potential research questions include: How can governments and industry design local content policies in a way that market-development outweighs market-distortion? How can women in developing countries benefit from supply chain participation? How can social and economic impact assessment methodologies be enhanced to guide local procurement planning? How can supply chain value be created through local SME participation? The interface between procurement practice and the community environment requires interdisciplinary understanding, and the emerging area of local procurement practice, both within the extractive industries and in other industry sectors, will benefit from further scholarship.

Acknowledgements

The authors are grateful to David Brereton, the editors of this special issue and the anonymous reviewers for enhancements to this paper.

Notes

1. Local content is the proportion of inputs to a product or service (e.g. materials, parts, services) that have been made in that country rather than imported. A foreign company might be required to use a certain amount of local content to gain the right to produce or manufacture in a particular place.
2. An outcome is defined as changes in the behaviour of the organisations and individuals impacted by a program or policy intervention. Outcomes tend to be related to a program's end goals. Outputs, or program activities, can lead to program outcomes, although they do not necessarily cause the outcomes.

References

Barringer, B R 1997. The effects of relational channel exchange on the small firm: a conceptual framework. *Journal of Small Business Management*, **35**(2), 65–79.

CSCMP, Council of Supply Chain Management Professionals 2011. *CSCMP Supply Chain Management Definitions*. Lombard Illinois: CSCMP. Available at <http://cscmp.org/aboutcscmp/definitions.asp>, last accessed 27 February 2011.

Deloitte, Deloitte Touche Tohmatsu Emerging Markets Ltd 2004. *Partnerships for Small Enterprise Development*. New York: UNDP; and Vienna: UNIDO.

Esteves, A M and F Vanclay 2009. Social development needs analysis: adapting SIA methods to guide corporate–community investment in the minerals industry. *Environmental Impact Assessment Review*, **29**(2), 137–145.

Esteves, A M, D Brereton, D Samson and M A Barclay 2010. *Procuring from SMEs in Local Communities: A Good Practice Guide for the Australian Mining, Oil and Gas Sectors*. Brisbane: Centre for Social Responsibility in Mining, Sustainable Minerals Institute, University of Queensland.

Esteves, A M, D Brereton, D Samson and M A Barclay 2012. Enhancing the benefits of projects through local procurement. In *New Directions in Social Impact Assessment: Conceptual and Methodological Advances*, eds F Vanclay and A M Esteves. Cheltenham: Edward Elgar (in press).

Frankel, R, Y A Bolumole, R A Eltantawy, A Paulraj and G T Gundlach 2008. The domain and scope of SCM's foundational disciplines: insights and issues to advance research. *Journal of Business Logistics*, **29**(1), 1–30.

Gelderman, C J and A J Van Weel 2003. Handling measurement issues and strategic directions in Kraljic's purchasing portfolio model. *Journal of Purchasing & Supply Management*, **9**, 207–216.

Giunipero, L and R Eltantawy 2004. Securing the upstream supply chain: a risk management approach. *International Journal of Physical Distribution and Logistics Management*, **34**(9), 698–713.

IFC, International Finance Corporation, and Esso Exploration & Production Chad, Inc 2008. *A Manual for Practitioners Based on the Procurement Experience in Chad*. Washington: IFC.

Jenkins, B, A Ahalkatsi, B Roberts and A Gardiner 2007. *Business Linkages: Lessons, Opportunities, and Challenges*. Cambridge: IFC, International Business Leaders Forum, and the Kennedy School of Government, Harvard University. Available at <http://www.hks.harvard.edu/m-rcbg/CSRI/publications/report_16_BUSINESS%20LINKAGESFINAL.pdf>, last accessed 13 May 2011.

Khemani, K 2007. Bringing rigor to risk management. *Supply Chain Management Review*, **11**(2), 67–68.

Kraljic, P 1983. Purchasing must become supply management. *Harvard Business Review*, **61**(5), 109–117.

Larson, P D, P Carr and K S Dhariwal 2005. SCM involving small versus large suppliers: relational exchange and electronic communication media. *The Journal of Supply Chain Management*, Winter, 18–29.

Macbeth, D K 2002. Managing a portfolio of supplier relationships. In *Gower Handbook of Purchasing Management*, ed. M Day, pp. 51–62. Gower Publishing: Burlington, VT.

Nelson, J 2007. *Building Linkages for Competitive and Responsible Entrepreneurship*. Cambridge: UNIDO, Harvard University. Available at <http://www.unido.org/fileadmin/user_media/Services/PSD/CSR/Building_Linkages_for_Competitive_and_Responsible_Entrepreneurship.pdf>, last accessed 27 February 2011.

ODI, Overseas Development Institute 2005. *Levers & Pulleys: Extractive Industries and Local Economic Development: Incentivising Innovation by Lead Contractors through Contract Tendering*. Briefing Note 3, London: ODI. Available at <http://www.odi.org.uk/resources/specialist/business-development-perfomance-briefings/3-extractive-industries-local-economic-development.pdf>, last accessed 27 February 2011.

Porter, M 1980. *Competitive Strategy: Techniques for Analyzing Industries and Competitors*. New York: The Free Press.

Porter, M 1985. *Competitive Advantage: Creating and Sustaining Superior Performance*. New York: The Free Press.

Ruffing, L 2006. *Deepening Development through Business Linkage*. New York and Geneva: United Nations.

SEAF, Small Enterprise Assistance Funds 2007. *From Poverty to Prosperity: Understanding the Impact of Investing in Small and Medium Enterprises*. Washington, DC: SEAF.

Trkman, P and K McCormack 2009. Supply chain risk in turbulent environments — A conceptual model for managing supply chain network risk. *International Journal of Production Economics*, **119**, 247–258.

UNCTAD, United Nations Conference on Trade and Development

2001. *World Investment Report 2001: Promoting Linkages*. New York and Geneva: United Nations.

Vargas, O 2010. *Cajamarca: A Mining Cluster?* Master's thesis, University of Cesar Vallejo, Trujillo, Peru.

Warner, M 2011. *Local Content Solutions: Participation of Domestic Industry in Procurement for Oil, Gas and Mining Projects*. Sheffield: Greenleaf Publishing.

Wise, H and S Shtylla 2007. *The Role of the Extractive Sector in Expanding Business Opportunity*. Corporate Social Responsibility Initiative No. 18. Cambridge, MA: Kennedy School of Government, Harvard University. Available at <http://www.hks.harvard.edu/m-rcbg/CSRI/publications/report_18_EO%20Extractives%20Final.pdf>, last accessed 27 February 2011.

WBCSD, World Business Council for Sustainable Development 2009. *Measuring Impact Framework Case Study Newmont: Supporting Local Economic Growth in Ghana*. Available at <http://www.wbcsd.org/DocRoot/awRR7UodI8FqWpF7itUm/NewmontIFC%20casestudyFINAL.pdf>, last accessed 27 February 2011.

WBCSD, World Business Council for Sustainable Development, and IFC, International Finance Corporation 2008. *Measuring IMPACT Framework Methodology*. April version 1.0. Available at <http://www.wbcsd.org/DocRoot/gB1QYq9Fx9A5R2hCnD8R/MIMethodology.pdf>, last accessed 27 February 2011.

Involving communities

Buy-in and social capital: by-products of social impact assessment

Dianne Buchan

Participatory impact assessment is a term frequently used and often abused. It refers to an approach that includes interested and affected parties in deciding indicators and measures of environmental and social impacts, in evaluation of effects and monitoring. Involving communities in a participatory manner facilitates skill transfer, fosters buy-in and creates local social capital. This paper describes a participatory exercise initiated by a local authority (Council) in New Zealand. Based on the reported assessment and that of two others, five essential ingredients are identified for a genuine participatory exercise. Time and flexibility are key components.

Keywords: participatory social assessment; social capital; community consultation; SIA practitioner

Dianne Buchan is an SIA practitioner with Corydon Consultants Ltd, Wellington, New Zealand. She may be reached at PO Box 27-145, Marion Square, Wellington, New Zealand; E-mail: db@corydon.co.nz.

SOCIAL IMPACT ASSESSMENT (SIA) has changed so that the emphasis is now on involving those who are affected by a proposal in the analysis of impacts and identification of appropriate mitigation strategies. In the early days, the SIA was more technocratic in the sense that there was a strong, almost total, focus on the use of quantitative data, written information sources and 'expert' observations. Process design, identification of relevant information and data analysis were largely seen as the domain of the expert social impact assessor.

Since the 1980s, there has been increasing recognition of the importance of the views, values and priorities of stakeholders and communities affected by proposals. This change grew out of community development theory, which says that communities are best placed to define their needs and identify appropriate solutions (Shirley, 1982, page 21). Community consultation became a principal tool in the SIA methodology, and an important objective of the exercise was the development of an informed community, able not only to articulate its interests but also to make personal and collective decisions in response to the proposal (Carter, 1981).

However, still this new community-based approach tends to be largely designed and managed, and the information collected is still interpreted, solely by the social impact expert. Consultation is largely undertaken with organised stakeholders at the expense of the non-organised — those who may be affected by decisions but remain uninvolved.

Participatory impact assessment is a term which is frequently used and, I would argue, often abused. For 'participation' often comprises nothing more than giving people the opportunity to express their opinions. In my view, participatory IA refers to an approach that includes affected parties in deciding on the indicators and measures of effects, evaluating their relative importance, and even in monitoring the effectiveness of mitigation measures during project implementation.

The best social impact assessments are based on a combination of three approaches: technical; consultative; and participatory.

- Rigorous, measurable data is needed.
- Input from those affected by the proposal is needed in order to understand accurately their experiences, values and priorities.
- The community needs to be involved in defining impact measures and indicators, and in identifying appropriate responses to anticipated effects. By involving affected parties and communities in this way, not only is community buy-in to the proposed development fostered, but it is possible also to create social capital — the social 'glue' (community norms, values and networks) that helps people understand, and take ownership of, social issues and to work collaboratively for common purposes (Putnam, 1993).

Without this glue, co-operation and social cohesion break down, resulting in human alienation and environmental degradation. If local people are involved throughout the process, SIA can become an instrument for increasing awareness of issues that affect them, generating common understandings, empowering communities through increased knowledge of, and access to, decision-making processes, thus promoting greater accountability among decision-makers.

In a recent paper, Lockie (2001) described the benefits of community participation in impact assessment as follows (Lockie, 2001, page 285):

"… the most basic criteria against which all impact assessment activities should be evaluated is their contribution to communicatively rational deliberation. … Such a contribution, and the co-learning that is implied, is dependent on scientific rigour and honesty, flexibility and active engagement with the full range of stakeholders involved in, or affected by, proposed change so that they may use, challenge, reinterpret, and add to the knowledge created."

Over the past ten years I have been involved in three large-scale SIAs where, to varying degrees, I have tried to apply this community participatory approach: they were in New Zealand (Buchan, 1991), the Cook Islands (assessing the effects of the economic reforms in that county (Buchan, 1997)) and one in Tuvalu (monitoring the impacts of a national trust fund on social well-being (Buchan, 2001)).

Space constraints preclude a discussion on all but the New Zealand example. From my experience in implementing these three projects, I have concluded that there are five ingredients (which tend to overlap) that are essential to a successful community participatory approach:

- Adequate funding: since the process tends to be more time-consuming and less efficient than one where the 'experts' set about their task with controlled input from the affected community, this approach tends to take longer and require extra resources and therefore can be more expensive.
- Sufficient time: because of the need to train community participants in the process of SIA, data gathering and data analysis, and for participants to be highly informed about the details of the proposal, the process takes longer. Under the participatory approach, the technological transfer, which occurs through the training of local participants, can be as important as the impact assessment itself.
- Flexibility: it is important to be responsive to the needs of participants in the process. These are usually difficult to predict at the outset, especially when operating in developing countries.
- A willingness by those in power to involve the community in decision-making (as opposed to simply consulting them). This includes a willingness by the proponent of the project being assessed (be it a government or a developer) to disclose all relevant information.
- A skilled SIA practitioner who is able to:
  - teach local people SIA theory and techniques, and convey information about the proposal in an accessible way;
  - process data in a way and at a level that the community participants can understand;
  - be sensitive to cultural differences when working in communities foreign to their own: this may require some professional restraint (such as accepting less effective indicators of change as a first step in the learning process, if the community insists that those are what should be measured).

Five ingredients, which tend to overlap, are essential to a successful community participatory approach: adequate funding; sufficient time; flexibility; a willingness to involve the community; and a skilled SIA practitioner

Buy-in and social capital

Example of a participatory approach

The project in Hutt City, New Zealand involved the construction of a four-lane road bridge into Hutt City, the widening of the river adjacent to the central city, the demolition of a section of the shopping centre, the construction and landscaping of new stop-banks, minor relocation of local roads, and the construction of walkways, cycle-paths and so on.

The main points of the process were:

- As a social impact consultant, I was contracted by the Lower Hutt City Council to develop a brief for an impact assessment and community consultation process for the proposed project. This brief was developed in consultation with over 100 potentially affected people, including residents, business people and representatives of community organisations and institutions adjoining the proposed development site. The brief, which identified the matters to be assessed, the extent of the area to be included in the assessment, the structures and mechanisms to be established for community involvement and for information distribution, was, over the following planning and construction period, implemented in its entirety by the City Council.
- Three community resource (focus) groups were established to work with the impact assessor in reviewing the plans as they were developed and to identify potential impacts. One group was made up of representatives of the affected residents from each side of the river and included men and women with a mix of ages and life-styles (working age, retired and students). The other two groups represented affected businesses, and local institutions and agencies. A separate consultation process for the tangata whenua (the Maori tribe with primacy over the area affected) was run by the City Council in accordance with an established governance protocol. However, the social impact assessors maintained contact with the Maori tribal council and included their concerns and requirements in the impact assessment report.
- The community resource groups agreed a terms of reference (TOR) with the social impact assessor and the Council. The TOR set out what was expected of the members and what they could expect from the Council staff and contractors. This in essence became a contract. On at least one occasion this document was used to address a situation in which a Council consultant proved reluctant to attend resource group meetings and to provide information that the resource groups considered important.
- The social impact assessment team undertook a demographic and land-use analysis of the area affected, shopper surveys, area-use surveys and interviews with key informants as part of the data-gathering exercise. In addition to providing ideas about the information to be collected, the resource groups gave input into the identification and analysis of impacts.
- Once the draft SIA was compiled and agreed on by the members of the three resource groups, the groups joined together to review the detailed plans as they were developed. At this stage, about half the participants considered they had provided sufficient input to ensure their interests were adequately represented and, with other pressures on their daily lives, chose to withdraw from the process. The remaining members still comprised a representative sample of the affected population with a cross-section of residents as well as affected business operators.
- The plan analysis phase involved joint meetings with the Council's engineers, planners and landscape architects. Plans were drafted and discussed, site visits were held when necessary, and examples of materials to be used for certain aspects of the construction were brought to meetings to get the views of participants as to their suitability.
- Through this iterative process, agreement was reached on the need for the project to be at the scale proposed and for specific changes to be made to such aspects as the provision and design of public spaces along the river, the width and location of walking and cycle paths, the location of vehicle parking areas and other, more minor details.
- The final project was approved by an independent planning commission of engineering and environmental professionals established by the Council to hear, and decide on, the case. Approval was subject to a number of conditions, many of which (including specific measures to protect the economic viability of the affected business area, repair the river ecology, alleviate construction impacts, and to establish procedures for managing any accidental discovery of Maori burial sites) had been recommended in the SIA.
- At the request of the Mayor, the resource group continued meeting as necessary during the construction phase to monitor contractors' compliance with the conditions. They were provided with contact details for reporting any breaches to a designated Council officer.

The entire process, including impact assessment, project design, approval and construction took three years. The community representatives continued meeting at regular intervals on a voluntary basis throughout this period. At the end of each year, the City Council invited the participants to lunch with the council staff and consultants involved in the project. At these events, participants were formally thanked for their efforts.

Over the three years, the participant's knowledge of Council functions and responsibilities, types of flood mitigation measures and of each other greatly increased. Over that period some of the student representatives passed their senior school exams and went on to university. One participant had a baby, several changed careers and one of the elderly members died. As well as coming to understand each others' values and needs, the members shared the sadness and joy of these life experiences with each other.

The participants were committed to the ongoing process because they could see that they were influencing the project design in ways that reduced the negative effects and enhanced the social benefits of the project. The value of this influence was confirmed by the respect, support and credibility accorded to the process by the council's politicians, staff and consultants. The timeframe was not driven by a project deadline but by the need for the community participants to be confident that the negative effects of the project would be minimised, all potential benefits would be realised and long-term security against flooding in the city's central business district would be assured.

The process was empowering for the participants because they were given an active role both in analysing the significance of potential impacts and in developing mitigation measures that would address their concerns. Giving participants copies of the conditions of consent, a contact number to call in the case of breaches, and the Mayor's support for their role as monitors, meant they were empowered to protect their community's interests during the construction phase.

Assessing the processes

Much can be gained from a truly participatory approach (based on community development principles) to social impact assessment — much more than just identifying impacts. Such a process will become a vehicle for sharing local knowledge and building awareness about the components of a local community. It can help build consensus among those with disparate views and experiences as to what is important and what should be done. By increasing community awareness and knowledge, the process becomes a vehicle for making decision-makers more accountable to the people they serve.

The three participatory impact assessments mentioned earlier all included a much greater degree of stakeholder involvement than would have been the case using the traditional approach to community consultation as an input to impact assessment. However, of the three, the most successful was the New Zealand example, which was able to deliver all five of the essential ingredients: adequate time to enable community decision-making capacity to develop through shared knowledge and understanding; adequate funding; flexible process; commitment to the process by the decision-makers and staff; and skilled SIA and consultation facilitation.

The other two projects only partially fulfilled their potential. While both were successful in raising awareness and knowledge of the development concerned and of their own communities and decision-making structures, in both cases they failed in the area of technological transfer. This was largely because those who commissioned the work provided insufficient time and funding to enable the participants to be involved in the data processing and impact analysis processes. Lack of capacity in the communities concerned meant that, in order to achieve a fully participatory process, extra resources and supervision was required. The inflexibility of the consultancy contracts and administrative procedures meant that the SIA processes could not be adapted in time to meet these and other needs as they emerged.

Discussion

With the current emphasis on pre-determined budgets and timetables, flexibility of approach and adequate timeframes are perhaps the most difficult ingredients to achieve for social impact assessment practitioners. If we are to pay more than lip-service to the term 'participatory assessment', those who commission and fund this work must recognise the importance of these two ingredients and adjust their own budget-setting and administrative processes accordingly.

We must stop using the term 'participatory assessment' for processes that do not acknowledge, and provide for, all the ingredients necessary to give substance to that term. This includes allowing sufficient time for proponents and affected communities to exchange and consider information and ideas and to identify appropriate responses to potential impacts. Enhancing the capacity of communities to contribute to decision-making in this way can generate buy-in and social capital, which, in the long-run, will reduce costs.

References

Buchan, D, Rivers Buchan Associates (1991), *Social Impact Assessment: Ewen Floodway Project: Parts I and II* (2 volumes) (available from Corydon Consultants Ltd, Wellington, New Zealand).

Buchan, D (1997), *Cook Islands Economic Reforms to April 1997: Social Impact Assessment*, (NZODA, Ministry of Foreign Affairs and Trade, Wellington, New Zealand).

Buchan, D (2001), *Social and Economic Wellbeing Survey prepared for the Asian Development Bank*, TA No 3221/TUV: Island Development Program Implementation, Tuvalu, Asian Development Bank, Manila (Nimmo Bell and Company, Wellington, New Zealand).

Carter, Novia (1981), "SIA: new wine in old bottles" in Frank Tester and William Mykes (editors), *Social Impact Assessment — Theory, Method and Practice* (Detselig Enterprises Ltd, Calgary, Canada).

Lockie, Stewart (2001), "SIA in review: setting the agenda for impact assessment in the 21st century", *Impact Assessment and Project Appraisal*, 19(4), December, pages 277–287.

Buy-in and social capital

Putnam, Robert (1993), *Making Democracy Work — Civil Tradition in Modern Italy* (Princeton University Press, Princeton, USA).

Roberts, Richard (1995), "Public involvement: from consultation to participation", in F Vanclay and D Bronstein (editors), *Environmental and Social Impact Assessment* (Wiley and Sons, Chichester, UK).

Shirley, Ian (editor) (1982), *Development Tracks: The Theory and Practice of Community Development* (Dunmore Press, Wellington, New Zealand).

Citizen values assessment

Citizen values assessment: incorporating citizens' value judgements in environmental impact assessment

Annelies Stolp, Wim Groen, Jacqueline van Vliet and Frank Vanclay

Citizen values assessment (CVA), developed in the Netherlands Ministry of Transport, Public Works and Water Management, is a research method that assesses citizens' judgements about the qualities of their living environment. CVA considers how planned developments may affect environmental qualities from the perspective of people who live in, or otherwise use, the area affected by the project. A case study relating to the proposed redesign of an inner city highway is presented. CVA provides valuable additional information that can be used in environmental impact assessment (EIA) procedures, and a specific technique for incorporating social considerations, thereby assisting in the integration of social impact assessment within EIA.

Keywords: social impact assessment; SIA methodology; citizen values; scoping; living environment; EIA; environmental values; community profile

Annelies Stolp (contact author) is Leader of the CVA Team, Ministry of Transport, Public Works and Water Management, Civil Engineering Division, PO Box 20000, 3502 LA Utrecht, The Netherlands; Tel: +31 30 2857833; Fax: +31 30 2858195; E-mail: a.stolp@bwd.rws.minvenw.nl. Wim Groen and Jacqueline van Vliet were Project Manager of CVA studies (1997–2001 and 1995–1998 respectively). Professor Frank Vanclay from the Tasmanian Institute of Agricultural Research, University of Tasmania, Hobart, Tasmania 7001, Australia is an international adviser to the CVA method development project; E-mail: Frank.Vanclay@utas.edu.au.

EXPERT OPINIONS OF ENVIRONMENTAL values and impacts, including those of social impact assessment (SIA) practitioners, can be different from the way citizens feel about the state of their living environment (where they live, work and play) and how intended activities may impact on the various attributes of that environment. Therefore, in environmental impact assessment (EIA), SIA and other planning procedures, it is necessary to investigate the way people judge their living environment, and how they think a planned project may affect its qualities. This may provide additional relevant information to decision-makers.

Unfortunately, consideration of citizens' value judgements is not routinely undertaken in EIA or SIA. Both tend to remain technocratic in orientation avoiding any detailed consideration of the ways people are affected (Burningham, 1995; Dale and Lane, 1994; 1995; Gagnon *et al*, 1993; Ortolano and Shepherd, 1995).

Despite awareness within SIA of differences in perceptions among social groups, and between experts and the affected communities, the SIA literature has very little specification of the actual methods used to determine citizen values. In fact, SIA does not have many specified techniques, despite endorsement of a general procedure in the Interorganizational Committee's "Guidelines and principles for social impact assessment" (ICGP, 1994) and despite the outlines provided by Freudenburg (1986), Taylor *et al* (1995), Burdge (1998) and Vanclay (1999).

Incorporating citizens' value judgements in EIA

Although SIA is said to be a fully recognised component of EIA (Burdge and Vanclay, 1995), social impacts are rarely included in EIA studies.

The need to consider differences between citizens and experts in the perceived qualities of the environment, together with the lack of specified techniques, led to the development of citizen values assessment (CVA). The CVA research method was conceived and developed within the Directorate-General for Public Works and Water Management (Rijkswaterstaat) of the Netherlands Ministry for Transport, Public Works and Water Management.

The method has been utilised in over 20 applications at a total cost of more than two million euros. CVA studies have been conducted for: infrastructure projects (highways, railways); the siting of depots for highly contaminated sediment; dike reinforcement; harbour development; river embankment design; coastal protection structures; and risk analyses related to flood protection and river dredging. Development of CVA began in 1995 with one part-time person. Now, it has grown into a CVA Unit employing eight professionals, contracting out much work to consultants.

Characterisation of CVA

Central to CVA is the difference that an intended activity will make to the living environment of people potentially affected by a project, and that in any EIA this must be described from the perspective of those people. So, CVA is primarily an instrument to incorporate within an EIA the importance people attach to particular environmental attributes.

The term 'citizen values' is interpreted here to mean the value judgements of individuals about the quality of their living environment and its various attributes. The living environment comprises the area in which people live, work and play. By citizens, we mean all residents and other users of an area potentially affected by an intended activity. The word 'citizen' was chosen because it reinforces the notion that the level of analysis is the individual, and it does not refer to citizenship or nationality.

CVA provides an inventory of the values people in affected communities assign to their living environment through in-depth interviews with individual citizens. This is later validated by a quantitative survey of a representative sample of the population. Selected key values are presented in a citizen values profile (CVP) which forms the basis of assessment by which project alternatives are evaluated. The CVP is translated into evaluation criteria, which are subsequently operationalised by qualitative and quantitative variables.

CVA thus combines a 'normative approach', using subjective value judgements of individual citizens and the meanings they attach to the qualities of the living environment, with a 'technocratic approach' using scientifically rigorous and technically sound data. By identifying the key values of the living environment rather than opinions about alternatives, CVA is not influenced by fears, public resistance or the positions of interest groups. By providing systematic and 'neutral' information, CVA provides a rational basis for decision-making. This information is complementary to expert judgements and can be added to the analysis of impacts in environmental impact statements (EISs) and other policy evaluation reports.

CVA does not measure attitudes, nor is it an instrument to investigate citizens' preferences or opinions about alternative plans or projects. The method does not measure community views about the future impacts of projects, nor does it evaluate the extent of acceptance of, or resistance to, intended activities. Instead, it is an EIA instrument that measures citizens' judgements about the qualities of the living environment, and provides a framework for analysis by which the possible impacts of project alternatives on those environmental attributes can be evaluated.

CVA does not provide an overview of the full range of possible social impacts of a given project. It only applies to those social impacts associated with perceived environmental values, and not to other dimensions of social impact such as health and social well-being, economic impacts and material well-being, cultural impacts, family and community impacts, gender impacts, and so on. Furthermore, CVA is not designed to understand why people behave as they do in relation to their living environment. Nor does it predict how they will respond to possible changes in the living environment as a result of a proposed development.

A crucial difference between CVA and public involvement is that CVA is a structured research process providing an overview of citizen values and how a project may affect those values, whereas public involvement is intended to obtain input and gain support by discussing alternatives directly with representatives of affected communities and other interest groups. Public involvement does not necessarily systematically represent the community (Burdge and Vanclay, 1995; Vanclay, 1999). Those individuals involved in public participation processes are often higher educated, better informed, have relatively more time, and a higher level of interest in the project than the average citizen.

Public involvement does not guarantee a representative overview of what the environment means to all potentially affected citizens. An adequate and representative consideration of citizen's judgements of environmental attributes, and how project alternatives may affect these qualities, requires a structured research process, which CVA provides.

Premises of CVA

CVA was founded on three basic premises. First, decisions about what matters in the environment and

An adequate and representative consideration of citizen's judgements of environmental attributes, and how project alternatives may affect these qualities, requires a structured research process, which citizen values assessment provides

what is studied as part of an EIA should be based on value orientations that are explicit and these should not come exclusively from technical experts. The people who are actually living in an area have important knowledge to share, based on their use and experience of the local environment and their observations of the operations of facilities and infrastructure. Their lived rationality should not only be incorporated by means of public involvement during the project planning and EIA process, but should also be incorporated in the final document that describes, evaluates and compares alternatives.

Second, the inclusion of citizen values explicitly in the EIA process increases the quality of the EIS, because it provides a broader overview of positive and negative aspects of alternatives. Adding CVA to EIA improves the rational basis for decision-making because it provides additional information on environmental values, project and mitigation design, impacts, and comparison of alternatives. Moreover, including citizen values in an EIS puts them on an equal footing with scientific and technical information. This increases the legitimacy of the document from the perspective of the public (van Vliet, 1996).

Third, citizen values are best reflected if the research approach used furnishes a detailed understanding of the meaning of the living environment to citizens themselves. This requires a research approach that respects citizens' perceptions of reality in the process of collecting and analysing data.

Detailed outline of CVA

CVA consists of four phases and a follow-up step related to integration of the outcomes of CVA in the EIS or other policy evaluation document. Phase 1 consists of problem definition, delineation and identification of interest groups, and the collection of background information.

Phase 2 is a preliminary qualitative study to provide in-depth understanding of local peoples' connections to the area affected by the project. Semi-structured interviews are conducted with people from all relevant interested and affected parties, including residents, commuters, workers, day-trippers and tourists. The outcome is a listing of the selected key values of the affected community (a preliminary profile).

In Phase 3, a quantitative survey is conducted to validate the key values identified in Phase 2, to determine the relative importance of those key values, and how respondents feel about their present living environment in respect of these key values. The outcome is an assessment matrix or citizen values profile.

In Phase 4, the CVP is translated into evaluation criteria. Qualitative or quantitative variables are identified for each of the assessment criteria. Impacts are determined and alternatives are compared.

After the CVA study is completed, the results should be integrated in the EIA or other policy evaluation document. A possible way to integrate CVA outcomes in an EIS is the development of a citizen values scenario complementary to other scenarios like an economic scenario or a nature scenario.

Phase 1: basic groundwork

Phase 1 is a brief investigation to identify the likely area of impact, the geographical area in which impacts may occur (that is, the study area), and the groups of citizens that are potentially affected. It provides insight into landuse patterns, relevant groups of landusers and the organisations representing them. Relationships among interests, and between interests and the proposed development, are analysed.

The study area may differ from that considered by the various experts, depending on how alternatives are defined, and how the zone of impact is determined. In CVA, the study area is usually defined as the area where impacts can be experienced by the sensory perception of those who live in, and/or use, it.

A preparatory study starts with an analysis of relevant documents, such as maps, photographs, municipal guides, reports, newspapers, and other information, to identify landuse patterns and relevant interest groups. An interest group is considered relevant when the interest(s) it represents are likely to be affected by the proposed development. This includes small local-interest groups representing specific activities or neighbourhoods, as well as large, professional, national (and potentially international) organisations, such as nature conservation associations.

These organisations provide information for understanding the study area through interviews with key informants, often the representatives of the interest groups. Note that these representatives are not specifically involved as respondents in Phase 2, as they represent specific interest groups. Telephone interviews are conducted with key informants, liaison contacts for relevant groups, and other knowledgeable local individuals.

The preparatory study results in a research plan,

Incorporating citizens' value judgements in EIA

defines categories of respondents, and identifies a process for selecting representatives of the various groups. Respondent groupings are typically based on factors such as geographic distribution, landuse patterns and specific activities.

Phase 2: identifying key values

The primary objectives of Phase 2 are to: investigate the baseline conditions of the study area; collect data illustrating the location-specific relationships of citizens with their living environment; and identify the environmental values that are considered relevant by citizens. This information becomes the basis for the development of a preliminary profile.

The identification of the key values is the core of a CVA study. Data are collected by face-to-face interviews with citizens. These provide detailed understanding about what the environment means to citizens. The interviews are semi-structured, with the course of the conversation led by the interviewer following strategically arranged discussion themes (see Box 1). Respondents are invited to discuss these themes in their own way, using their own words, and from their own perspective. Interviews last approximately one hour.

Interviews are conducted with representatives of relevant groups, such as residents, commuters, workers, day-trippers and tourists. For accuracy, CVA requires skilled professional interviewers committed to its premises. They should be able to approach respondents in an unbiased way and respect differing perceptions of reality. Interviews are tape-recorded and transcribed for qualitative data analysis.

The large quantity of information collected is organised into a coherent picture by a process of 'open coding' and 'analytical memo writing' (Neuman, 1996). Each transcript is examined for mention of elements of the living environment, and for specific meanings associated with those elements. This results in a listing of 'element-meaning pairs' — elements of the environment together with the meanings ascribed to those elements by interviewees.

Then follows a process of sorting (interview themes), categorising (types of values), and synthesising a listing of key values underlying the perceived attributes of the living environment. This phase requires social researchers adequately skilled in qualitative analysis.

The results are presented in a separate report structured along the interview themes. One intention of CVA is to allow citizens to recognise themselves in the outcomes, showing them that they have been heard and listened to, and reinforcing the legitimacy of citizens' values and rationality in the EIA process. To achieve this, many quotations are used to illustrate and justify the descriptions of what the living environment means to citizens. The outcome of Phase 2 is a listing of the key values.

The report, or at least a summary, from this phase should be sent to all respondents. This is an important step to check whether the analysis is perceived to be adequate. Ideally, the outcomes of this phase are discussed with community representatives. The report, and preliminary drafts of it, should be distributed to the proponent's project team, so that the information can be used as an input for project mitigation and design and as feedback on the impact of the communication strategies of the proponent.

If CVA is initiated early enough, the (preliminary) outcomes can be used to profile the content of the EIA study. The use of these preliminary results is a substantial part of the total contribution of CVA to the EIA process. An example is discussed in Box 2.

Phase 3: constructing a citizen values profile

In Phase 3, the preliminary profile is transformed into a final assessment matrix, or citizen values profile (CVP). The CVP represents the importance of the environmental values from the perspective of citizens. Data are collected by a quantitative survey, normally a mail survey, of a random sample of the potentially affected population. This is done to:

- validate the preliminary profile. Data are collected to confirm whether the set of key values is comprehensive and that each is actually relevant.

Box 1. Discussion themes in a CVA interview with residents (Phase 2)

- **Perceptions of environmental qualities** Why did the resident choose to live here? What is the specific connection with this living environment? What makes the person feel 'rooted' in the area? What is special about this living environment? What factors cause nuisance? How does the resident make use of the area?
- **Observed and expected changes in environmental qualities** What changes has the resident recently observed? Are these changes positive or negative? Why? What changes does the resident anticipate will occur in the near future? Are these changes positive or negative, and why?
- **Problem underlying the proposed project** Does the resident know about the underlying issue? Does the resident acknowledge the problem? Does the resident agree that the problem should be tackled in the way intended by the proponent? What is the resident's opinion of the proposed project?
- **Opinion towards proposed project** [Note: this information is used to increase understanding of residents' value judgements about environmental qualities and impacts on environmental qualities; this information is not meant to investigate the extent of public acceptance or resistance.] What is the opinion of the resident about the project and the alternatives that are relevant to them? (maps, drawings and/or artist impressions of alternatives are shown to the resident to provide background).
- **Perceptions of possible impacts** Interviewee is asked which environmental qualities may be affected by the proposed alternatives (as before, maps, drawings and/or artist impressions may be shown).
- **Issues relevant for design** What measures should be taken to minimise those possible impacts that are relevant to the resident? What other measures could the resident think of to compensate for those impacts that cannot be avoided?

> **Box 2. Example of the use of preliminary results of CVA during Phase 2**
>
> An EIA study was conducted on the upgrading of the highway bypass (ring road) round the city of Eindhoven in the south of The Netherlands. The upgrading was intended to solve traffic jams on major connecting highways. The identification of key values in the CVA study conducted as part of that EIA provided useful location-specific information on recreational use of the areas surrounding the highways as well as on traffic nuisance. This included: information about horses crossing the highways being blinded by car lights (the area is known for equestrian activities); the importance of openness of the landscape (even a green sound barrier would cause serious harm to the aesthetics of the landscape); the increase of noise nuisance even after noise-reduction measures in other locations; the nature of traffic nuisance (local traffic versus highway traffic); and nuisance caused by through traffic in local streets (specifying particular locations).
>
> The CVA interviews provided insight about how the public judged the alternatives. It also revealed that the residents had very different perceptions to the experts about how effective the various alternatives would be at addressing the various issues in the ring road upgrading, specifically in relation to one of the alternatives. As a result of this information, the project team was able to reconsider the information being provided about that alternative, and made changes to it to correct the potential miscommunication.

> **Box 3. Outline of a CVA questionnaire (Phase 3)**
>
> - **Introduction** Description of the objective of the study and a brief description of the proposed project and the underlying problem.
> - **Part 1. Evaluation of the present living environment** For each selected key value in Phase 2, respondents are asked to consider: (1) whether or not they consider the key value relevant in terms of their living environment; and (2) how they judge the quality of their current living environment in relation to this key value. Space exists for respondents to nominate new key values under an 'other' heading. Any additional value must be scored in the same way.
> - **Part 2. Relative importance of the key values** Respondents are asked to judge the key values (which may include the values added by the respondent), by scoring each key value on a scale from 1 to 10 (or 100), or to rate them on a Likert Scale.
> - **Part 3. Mitigation and compensation measures** Different questions are formulated depending on the type of project and the project environment. Questions may relate to impacts such as noise nuisance or loss of visual amenity, or to design and siting issues such as road layout, location of facilities or land reclamation.
> - **Part 4. General demographic and socio-economic characteristics of the respondents**

- determine the importance of each of the key values by asking respondents to prioritise them. Potentially, this can be done in three ways: scoring each of the key values on a scale (say from 1 to 10, or 1 to 100); rating each value on a Likert Scale; or ranking them. Ranking is not usually practical since the large number of values makes it too taxing on respondents. Statistically, it is preferable for Likert scales to contain more categories (that is, 5 or 7) to provide greater differentiation, but respondents generally prefer less categories. The aggregated scores across all respondents provide the basis for determining the weighting to be assigned to each key value.
- score the present living environment in respect of the key values.
- collect information to assist in developing mitigation measures and/or for the consideration of compensation.

The questionnaire consists of four sections (Box 3). To avoid large non-response bias, it is very important that the questionnaire and accompanying letter are citizen-friendly (no jargon; no official language). They must clearly describe the status of CVA within the EIA process to prevent inflated expectations of what will be done with the outcomes of the CVA.

When the proposed project has alternative locations, separate samples are required. In this situation, the key values may differ among locations requiring different questionnaires. To ensure validity and reliability of the results, the sampling procedures need to be justified explicitly, and the way in which key values are translated into questions needs to be transparent.

The results of this phase are presented in a separate report in which the final CVP is presented. The CVP may consist of a number of different sub-profiles for different locations and/or different alternatives. Each sub-profile lists the key values in order of importance.

Phase 4: determining impacts of project alternatives

In Phase 4, the CVA researcher translates the key values into evaluation criteria. The outcome is an overview, from the perspective of citizens, of the potential impacts of alternatives on the attributes of the living environment. This phase starts after the design of alternatives has been finalised. It consists of the following steps:

- translation of key values into evaluation criteria;
- operationalisation of evaluation criteria by identification of quantitative or qualitative variables, and identification of data sources;
- determining importance of impacts for each criterion;
- recommendations for mitigation and/or compensation.

The crucial step in this phase is how the CVP is transformed into evaluation criteria. This involves selection and judgement of the available information by the CVA researcher. Transparency and justification are essential. There should be no doubt about how the criteria were operationalised.

The first step is the selection of those key values that discriminate between alternatives. For example, concern about safety in a residential area may be relevant for assessing impacts of an infrastructure project when the factors that make people feel unsafe are related to traffic (for instance, shortcuts through residential areas). However, safety concerns may not be relevant to the CVA when such concern is caused by anti-social behaviour unrelated to the proposed project. In the second step, each discriminating key value is translated into an evaluation criterion. For each criterion, the underlying meanings, how they are operationalised, whether by means of qualitative or quantitative variables, and what data sources exist, need to be explained on the basis of the outcomes of Phase 2.

The primary and most appropriate data sources are the various impact studies (expert studies) carried out by the EIA team. For example, a criterion 'quiet, green living environment' may be operationalised by utilising expert studies on noise nuisance, traffic patterns and visual amenity. The importance of probable impacts can be determined, either directly from the empirical results of the expert studies, or it can be derived from interpretations of these studies made by the CVA researcher.

However, the information needed for the determination of impacts considered relevant by citizens will not always be available in the expert studies. When a criterion cannot, or can only partly, be linked with the expert judgements, additional variables have to be conceived.

For example, in the case of a proposed highway, the evaluation criterion 'preservation of outlook or vista' (referring to the scenic or aesthetic values of a residential area) might be connected with the variable 'road surface height' in terms of height above (or below) ground level. If so, this may provide an indication of the extent to which the road embankments will block the view of citizens.

In some cases, situations may arise in which the majority of required data is not available in the expert studies. To overcome this, workshops to derive impact measures could be held with a selection of experts, representatives of interest groups and knowledgeable citizens. A Delphi technique could be applied with participants to come to consensus on the weightings (Taylor *et al*, 1995).

Ultimately, each alternative requires a score for each evaluation criteria. This can be done with a five-point scale (such as ++, +, 0, −, − −). Another option is to rank the alternatives for each criterion. An overall assessment is conducted by considering all scores of each alternative, together with the weighting for each criterion.

Qualitative analysis can be used, resulting in an overview of positive and negative aspects of each alternative. Such an analysis can be summarised in a final score based on an average appreciation of an average user of a local area. The weights can be used in an analysis of the essential differences between alternatives. The analysis should focus on those criteria that have relatively high weights, and/or those criteria for which the impacts score relatively high.

Alternatively, multi criteria analysis (MCA) can be used, using various weighting techniques (such as using a five-point scale ++, +, 0, −, − −; rankings; or quantitative techniques) (see de Vries, 1999). When alternatives are located in different sub-areas, CVA may result in different criteria and/or varying weights. In these cases, criteria need to be clustered into coherent themes at a higher abstraction level, before MCA is applied. In any case, simple forms of CVA are preferable. A complicated MCA procedure implies a degree of quantitative precision and does not reflect the character of CVA, which is primarily a qualitative instrument.

The outcome of Phase 4 is the final (and full) CVA report in which the whole process is described, the outcomes of each phase are summarised, the impacts of alternatives are presented and alternatives are compared.

There are several problems that can be encountered in Phase 4. The CVA researcher plays an important role in interpreting data and drawing conclusions, which means that it is very important that this input be validated. Transparency and justification of interpretations are an important basis for quality control, but they cannot prevent all bias.

Ideally, verification is achieved through short workshops, in which representatives of project planners, experts involved in impact assessment, and community and other interest groups, discuss the operationalisations proposed by the researcher. This, however, is labour intensive. Preferably, verification is integrated in the ongoing communication process, for instance, through discussion in existing advisory groups in which community groups and other interested parties are represented.

To be able to make optimal use of the impact studies conducted in the EIA process, specific periods of information exchange between the CVA study and the expert studies should be planned. Thus, CVA should start in the very early stages of project design (and the EIA process) so that its preliminary results can be used as input for scoping.

Working with the outcomes of the various studies used as part of the EIA has revealed that there is considerable variation in the scales used to score impacts. This makes results hard to compare.

> The information needed for the determination of impacts considered relevant by citizens will not always be available in the expert studies: when a criterion cannot be linked with the expert judgements, additional variables must be conceived

Further, it is clear that in many EIA sub-reports, interpretations are often implicit. When justification is lacking, a secondary analysis of these data is difficult for the CVA researcher. Some harmonisation between CVA, SIA and EIA is required, and greater recognition of the role of CVA (and SIA) in EIA is desirable.

Follow-up phase: integrating CVA in the EIS

The results of a CVA need to be integrated into the final EIS. This is crucial for the potential role of CVA in decision-making. The more explicit and elaborate the CVA outcomes that are presented in the EIS, the greater the chance that they will influence decision-making. Furthermore, the more explicitly they are presented, the more recognizable citizens' value orientations will be to the citizens who read the EIS. This will potentially increase the legitimacy of the EIS in their eyes.

There are four ways in which CVA outcomes can be incorporated in the EIS. Presenting the outcomes of a full CVA independently gives the strongest statement of commitment that citizens' values will be respected. This option emphasises the different nature of the information CVA presents, being based on citizens' perspectives rather than that of experts. It allows for the development of a 'most citizen-friendly' alternative as a counterpart to the 'most environment-friendly' alternative often defined in EIA studies.

A second way of presenting CVA outcomes is as one of the sub-components of the topic 'living environment'. This places them alongside the expert impact studies on other sub-components such as noise nuisance and emissions. However, this option not only reduces the prominence of the CVA outcomes within the overall EIA, it neglects the distinct character of data provided by CVA. This option can also lead to confusion because some aspects, such as landscape or recreation, may be presented twice in the final table (under technical sections as well as in the CVA).

Third, a citizen values scenario can be developed. Here, the outcomes of the CVA study are used as input for a MCA applied to the main themes in the overall assessment matrix. The citizen values scenario can be compared with other scenarios, such as a nature or an economic one. The CVP is used to assign weights to these aspects or themes in the overall assessment matrix.

Two approaches are possible in developing the scenario. In one, the CVA assessment matrix is matched with the expert assessment matrix. All variables in the expert assessment matrix that are not mentioned by citizens are deleted. The weights for the remaining variables are calculated by translating weights from the CVA into ones in the expert evaluation matrix.

Alternatively, weights can be assigned only to the main categories (aggregates of variables) in the assessment matrix. In both procedures, a ranking of alternatives is constructed by means of MCA. The development of a citizen scenario may be used as the sole outcome of a CVA study, in which case Phase 4 of the CVA method can be omitted. However, this reduces the potential value of the data collected earlier.

The final option, and weakest form of applying CVA, is to use the information from the CVP to comment on any list of impacts provided by other sources. For example, a CVA/SIA practitioner may be asked by an EIA team to comment on the impacts of alternatives. Here, information about the community could be used by the CVA practitioner to assign weights on behalf of the community. This option is relatively cheap and can be undertaken in a relatively short timeframe (because Phase 4 is not required), but it seriously reduces the potential of the method.

Case study of Rotterdam highway options

Introduction

Highway A20 (see Figure 1) is a major part of the transport network in The Netherlands specifically linking Rotterdam City and its harbour (arguably the world's largest port) with Amsterdam airport Schiphol (a major airfreight centre) and other major Dutch cities, Amsterdam, The Hague, Utrecht, and ultimately Germany, Belgium, France and England. A bottleneck occurs with north–south traffic travelling along the A16 and A13 being forced to traverse a seven kilometre section of the A20 between the highway junctions Terbregseplein and Kleinpolderplein in inner Rotterdam (a city of some 600,000 inhabitants).

Here, the congestion chance (that is, the probability of being in a traffic jam on a specific highway section over a 24-hour period) was above 20% in 1995, much higher than the accepted national standards of 2% for international access highways (A20 and A16) and 5% for other national highways (A13). It was considered that, if no action were taken, the congestion chance would increase to over 35% by 2010.

The consequences of this increasing congestion include declining accessibility and longer journey times, as well as severe negative effects on residential areas particularly declining quality of the living environment and safety. With only small distances between the roadway and buildings, noise nuisance and air pollution are considerable. There was concern about the extent of 'barrier effect' caused by the highway going through a neighbourhood. Traffic jams also occur on the feeder roads. Nuisance is caused by cars traversing residential areas, often at high speed, in an attempt to avoid traffic jams. An English translation of the Dutch word, *sluipverkeer*, for this phenomenon is 'sneaky traffic'.

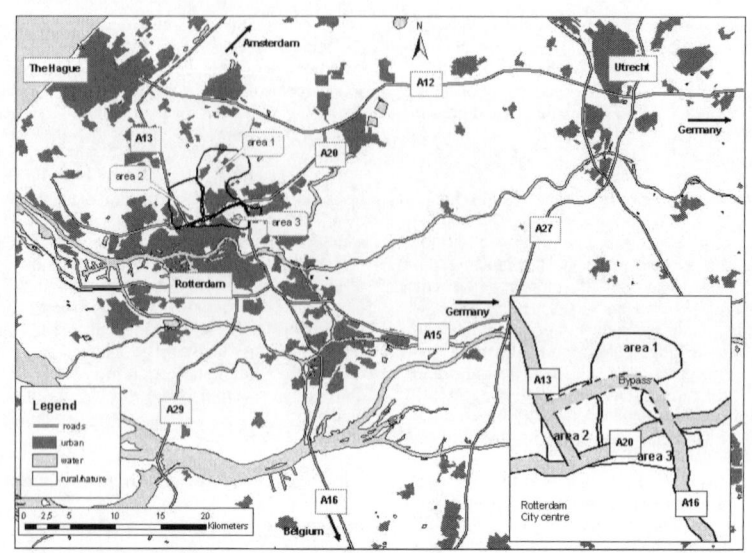

Incorporating citizens' value judgements in EIA

Figure 1. Highway network around Rotterdam and study areas
(prepared by M van der Zel, Rijkswaterstaat, 2002)

Rijkswaterstaat, together with a steering committee comprising representatives of the Rotterdam City Council, the Greater Rotterdam Regional Council, and the Province of South Holland, identified two main alternatives for addressing the problems, one involving the reconstruction and upgrading of the existing highway (itself having two alternatives relating to the construction, or not, of an additional local road), the other being the construction of an alternative route or deviation between the A16 and A13 bypassing the inner city area. An EIA procedure started in 1996 in which CVA was an integral part. The EIS was completed in February 2000.

For each of the three major alternatives there were a number of possible technical options related to the number and length of tunnels, the number of traffic lanes, precise siting, layout and integration with existing (local or feeder) road networks. To simplify the analysis, the EIA was based on a consideration of two 'packages of options' for each of the three major alternatives. Thus there were six variants in total to be considered. The packages of options represented contrasts, or minimal and maximal options, for the problem-solving capacity of each of the alternatives in relation to traffic flow and environmental considerations.

Basic groundwork

A conclusion of the groundwork phase was that the study area should be conceived as three sub-areas, related to alternatives and the functions of these areas for citizens. The construction of the bypass would have major impacts on the northern residential area of Rotterdam and the rural area outside Rotterdam (Area 1). Special characteristics of this area are wealthy neighbourhoods in a semi-rural setting, recreational areas (forest, golf course, artificial ski hill, cycling, sailing, horse riding and so on), and rural areas.

The reconstruction of the existing highway would have impacts on Areas 2 (to the north-west of the A20) and 3 (to the south-east). Area 2 is the area traversed by the A13. Further away is Rotterdam airport and nearby is an industrial estate. Area 3 is a densely populated residential area situated directly alongside the A20. Away from the A20, the area is less densely populated with important recreational areas. Four different user groups were identified: citizens; holiday-makers and day-trippers; farmers; and nature lovers.

Key values

Fifty in-depth interviews were conducted with representatives across the four user groups. A wide range of issues was mentioned as being important, and which could be grouped into three headings: living environment; traffic; and recreation and nature. There were few differences between the three areas of the study. Frequently mentioned comments related to the peacefulness and tranquillity of their neighbourhood, a green environment, recreation facilities, and accessibility to the facilities of Rotterdam. For example, one respondent from Area 1 said "it's great recreation here, just because of that I don't want to leave".

Traffic nuisance was also an issue. However, despite the fact that all interviewees lived near the highway, in all three sub-areas most emphasised the issues above and not issues such as noise. Traffic was an issue because of traffic jams, exhaust gases and sneaky traffic, but not because of noise. One respondent said: "in the morning I wake up with exhaust gases up my nose". In Area 1, respondents frequently mentioned sneaky traffic, while in Area 2, traffic jams on highway A13 were identified: "when you want to leave at 6.00 pm, you can't get through".

An unexpected outcome was that, in contradiction to the expectations of the EIA team, there was no suggestion that the highways were regarded as barriers dividing communities. Instead, the opposite was emphasised with citizens highlighting the accessibility of the facilities of Rotterdam. The CVA team concluded that was because of the long length of time the highways had existed, and that therefore the residential areas had developed independently over the years and people had became used to the limited number of crossing-points.

Citizen values profile

Because the preliminary profile revealed that the key values were largely similar across the three areas, it was decided to construct one questionnaire. Key values that could not possibly discriminate between alternatives and were not relevant to this project (including comments about aircraft noise, train noise at night, neighbourly relations, and crime) were deleted. The remaining 18 key values were included in the questionnaire.

A mail survey was sent to a random sample of 3,800 households. This number was determined by statistical estimations of projected response rates and the need for statistical significance. Address lists were provided by the local governments. The mail survey contained a reply-paid envelope and instructions for completion of the survey, including which individual in the household should respond (to control for age and gender effects).

An unexpected outcome of the interviews was that there was no suggestion that the highways were regarded as barriers dividing communities: instead, citizens highlighted the accessibility of the facilities of Rotterdam

The response rate was about 30%, resulting in 1,100 usable responses. Additionally, 139 holidaymakers and day-trippers were interviewed at different recreation areas. The results of the survey confirmed the preliminary profile. The key values were comprehensive and each was considered relevant. Only a few respondents mentioned other values, including having good neighbours and dog droppings (neither relevant to the project).

Although the key values were largely similar across the three sub-areas, the specific environmental qualities differed. For the determination of impacts, two assessment frameworks were constructed, one for the areas surrounding the A20 (Areas 2 & 3), and one for the area surrounding the proposed bypass (Area 1). Table 1 presents the two sub-profiles. The results showed that the most important key values of Area 1 were a quiet living environment, the high quality and level of facilities, the accessibility of the city centre, and recreation facilities. The most important values for Areas 2 and 3 were mostly similar to Area 1, although traffic exhaust was also ranked highly.

In Area 1, the 'quality of the living environment of the neighbourhood' and 'recreation' were the key values that the largest percentage of respondents scored highly. 'Traffic annoyance' had the largest negative score. In Areas 2 and 3, 'facilities in the

Table 1. Citizen values profile

Area 1: Bypass construction (ranking)	Key Value	Areas 2 & 3: A20 reconstruction (ranking)
1	quiet living environment	1
2	facilities in the neighbourhood	2
3	accessibility to centre of Rotterdam	4
4	recreational facilities	5
5	different species of plants and animals	7
6	large nature area	9
7	cycling possibilities	8
8	noise nuisance of highway	6
9	accessibility of recreational areas	17
10	traffic exhaust	3
11	heavy traffic on local roads	11
12	diversity of recreational facilities	15
13	rural character of the living environment	10
14	traffic jams on highways	12
15	noise nuisance of local roads	14
16	sneaky traffic	13
17	view of/over highway	16
18	accessibility of aquatic areas	18

Incorporating citizens' value judgements in EIA

neighbourhood' and 'short distance to the city centre' were the most frequently reported highly scored attributes. Respondents were negative about traffic issues, specifically exhaust, traffic jams and sneaky traffic.

Impacts of project alternatives

The first step was to translate the key values into evaluation criteria. Each key value had to be operationalised and the appropriate data source identified. The key value 'quiet living environment', for example, was operationalised by considering the concept in detail. Respondents associated it with peacefulness, but also with images of children playing on streets, slow-moving traffic, and so on. Given this, it seemed reasonable to select traffic volume in residential areas as the indicator. The underlying assumption was that the less traffic, the more people would judge their neighbourhood as being quiet. Data about the traffic volumes in residential streets was obtainable from the traffic impact study.

After translating all key values into assessable evaluation criteria, scores for each criterion for each of the six alternatives were determined using a five-point scale (– –, –, 0, +, + +) (see Table 2). Where possible, scores were based on data from the expert studies. Some key values were easier to operationalise than others because they linked directly with expert studies. For example, 'noise nuisance', 'traffic jams on highways' and 'traffic exhaust' all had direct parallels in data collected in various studies for the EIA.

In several cases, expert studies could not be used, largely because of inadequate description in the EIA reports. In those cases, experts were interviewed to provide a score. Another problem was the use of different scales in the EIA impact studies — sometimes only indicating presence or absence of the issue. Here, interpretation by the CVA researchers was necessary. Only for the criterion 'sneaky traffic' was it impossible to determine impacts for the alternatives. On this matter, data sources were unreliable and traffic experts found it impossible to predict how the alternatives would affect this issue.

Project alternatives compared

MCA was undertaken to compare the variants of each of the alternatives (see Table 2). Two forms of the MCA were considered. One considered each key value as being equally weighted. The other was an experimental procedure that used the ranking as a proxy weighting. In both cases, there were only 17 items because sneaky traffic could not be assessed. In the experimental process, the project alternatives were compared by multiplying the scores (– – to ++) with the ranking (reversed) and summed. This procedure, although user-friendly, has ultimately not been accepted as standard practice because using the reverse ranking as a proxy weighting potentially

Table 2: Assessment matrix

Key values	A20 without local road		A20 with local road		Bypass	
	min	max	min	max	min	max
quiet living environment	0	0	0	0	0	0
facilities in the neighbourhood	0	0	0	0	0	0
accessibility of city centre	0	0	0	0	0	0
recreational facilities	0	0	–	– –	–	0
different plants and animals	+	+	–	– –	–	0
large nature area	0	+	0	– –	– –	–
cycling possibilities	0	0	0	0	0	0
noise nuisance of highway (reduction)	+	+ +	+	+ +	+	+
accessibility of recreational areas	0	0	+	+	+	+
traffic exhaust (reduction)	–	–	–	–	0	–
heavy traffic on local roads (reduction)	–	0	–	+	+	–
diversity of recreational facilities	0	0	0	0	0	0
rural character of living environment	0	0	0	0	–	–
traffic jams on highways	+	+	+	+	+	+
noise nuisance from local roads (reduction)	0	0	+	+	+	+
view of/over highway	+	+	+	0	– –	–
accessibility of aquatic areas	0	0	0	0	0	0
Total score	+10	+41	–23	–52	–40	–21
Total without ranking	+2	+5	0	–2	–3	–2

excessively accentuates the differences between the key values. A more valid way of determining weightings is required.

Table 2 presents a comparison of the six variants assessed according to the key values nominated by citizens (not including sneaky traffic). The first conclusion in comparing alternatives was that, from the perspective of citizens, the reconstruction of the A20 without a local road is the preferred alternative (the minimal and maximal variants had the highest scores). The reason for this preference is that no new road will be built, while other alternatives expose people who have not previously been exposed to highway impacts. Also, within this preferred alternative, the 'maximal variant' is preferred to the 'minimal variant', mainly because the additional tunnels of this variant further reduce noise nuisance.

Curiously, in the alternative A20 with local road, the 'maximal variant' scores much lower than the 'minimal variant' mainly because of its impacts on recreational facilities, variety in plant and animal species, and the destruction of a large nature area. This variant is a 2×2-lane road at surface level which passes through forest and recreational areas. The 'minimal variant' is a smaller road (2×1 lanes) which is 'minimal' in solving traffic problems, but has a tunnel under the forest and recreational areas. Citizens (that is local residents as opposed to highway users) had a marked preference for greater use of tunnels because of the advantages for noise reduction, improved views, reduction in traffic exhaust, and the ability to develop/maintain green areas on top of tunnels.

Integration of CVA with the EIA study

In the final EIS, the alternatives were compared from different perspectives: the human perspective (using the definition of 'liveability' based on government policy); the citizen perspective (based on CVA); the nature and landscape perspective (based on ecological and landscape values); and the traffic/economic perspective. Each perspective was assigned a set of weights for the four major themes (and sub-themes) investigated in the EIA study (traffic, spatial development, economy, and environment) (see Table 3). The sum of the weightings in each case is 1.00. It should be emphasised that the processing of the CVA results was beyond the responsibility of the CVA team. They were assigned by the EIA project team based on their interpretations of the outcomes of various studies and of the logic of the each of the perspectives.

Application of the weights in Table 3 to a multiple criteria analysis of the six variants (Table 4) revealed that, in the human perspective, improving the A20 with an additional local road scored negative and constructing the bypass scored neutral. Improving the existing highway without constructing an additional local road scored slightly positive.

In comparison, from the citizens' perspective, constructing the bypass scored negative and improving the A20 with an additional local road scored negative for the 'minimum variant' but slightly positive for the 'maximum variant' (which actually contradicts the outcomes of the CVA study; see Table 2). Improving the existing highway without constructing an additional local road scored the highest from the citizens' perspective. While the differences between the citizen and human perspectives were not great, they differed considerably from the traffic and economic perspective.

Conclusions of case study

The case study demonstrates that including citizen values in an EIS is feasible and that the CVA research method was easily applied in the EIA context. The CVA study provided information on differences between alternative plans and information relevant for developing compensation and/or mitigation measures. Combining the citizens' perspective with the experts' perspective caused no difficulties, and in fact added a dimension to the analysis that would not otherwise have been present. The added value of the CVA study was that the study provided new insights and put some assumptions of experts in a new perspective.

Noise nuisance appeared to be less important than was expected, and, despite the noise nuisance in several areas, some of these areas were very positively judged for other attributes. The conviction of the experts that the existing highways were serious barriers in the living environment was not confirmed at all. Instead the traffic jams were considered a serious problem. The outcomes of the CVA study showed clear differences with the expert assessment of 'liveability', highlighting the different emphases between citizens and experts. Thus, the CVA study did provide a broader overview of positive and negative impacts of alternatives.

One problem in this application of CVA was that it was not adequately integrated in the timeframe of project design, and, as a result, information from Phases 2 and 3 could not be fully used in the process of detailing designs of project alternatives. Another problem was that, because the CVA used data from

Table 3. Distribution of weights for four perspectives

Theme	Sub-theme	Human perspective	CVA perspective	Nature and landscape perspective	Traffic and economic perspective
Traffic	Traffic flow	0.05	0.15	0.05	0.25
	Traffic safety	0.15	0.01	0.05	0.15
Spatial development	Local and regional impacts	0.15	0.11	0.15	0.14
Economy	Direct and indirect impacts	0.10	0.15	0.10	0.40
Environment	Air quality	0.13	0.10	0.10	0.01
	Water and soil	0.05	0.01	0.15	0.01
	Ecology	0.05	0.22	0.15	0.01
	External safety	0.13	0.01	0.05	0.01
	Landscape aesthetics	0.05	0.01	0.15	0.01
	Noise and vibration	0.14	0.23	0.05	0.01
Total		1.00	1.00	1.00	1.00

Incorporating citizens' value judgements in EIA

Table 4. Results of multi-criteria analysis

Variant	Human perspective	CVA perspective	Nature and landscape perspective	Traffic and economic perspective
A20 without local road min	+0.03	+0.14	+0.03	+0.29
A20 without local road max	+0.08 (best)	+0.19 (best)	+0.05 (best)	+0.24
A20 with local road min	−0.11 (worst)	−0.09 (worst)	−0.26	+0.23 (worst, but still beneficial)
A20 with local road max	−0.04	+0.05	−0.19	+0.38
Bypass min	−0.01	−0.02	−0.35 (worst)	+0.49 (best)
Bypass max	+0.01	−0.08	−0.27	+0.48

other impact studies, the CVA report was one of the last to be completed. This required a certain degree of flexibility and creativity to integrate the results in the final EIS and in project design. For the optimal use of a CVA, it is of great importance that this is taken into account in planning the EIA process.

Postscript

The EIS for the Rotterdam Highway situation was completed in February 2000. However, changing government policy about major infrastructure development resulted in a reassessment of priorities, which led to a redesignation of the status of this project. As a result, at this time (early 2002), no government funding will be made available for the project before 2010. Public release of the EIS was deemed to be inappropriate since no action was likely to be taken. The exact role of CVA in decision-making in this particular case, therefore, is not clear, but we remain convinced of its potential role.

Conclusion

CVA is a useful addition to the EIA process because it adds information that has been systematically collected, which represents the way citizens assess the qualities of the environment, and which provides a systematic comparison of alternatives from the citizens' perspective. By incorporating citizen values

> **The case study demonstrates that including citizen values in an environmental impact statement is feasible and that the citizen values assessment research method was easily applied in the environmental impact assessment context**

in the EIS — the document that describes, judges and compares alternatives and that is the basis of project approval — citizens are recognised as being relevant experts to define the quality and attributes of their own living environment. CVA broadens the scope of an EIS, thus providing an improved overview of positive and negative aspects of alternatives.

CVA does have limitations. What citizens observe and expect does not necessarily include all aspects relevant to them, neither will citizens' judgements be based on a clear picture of the situation at the time the project is intended to be implemented (which may involve long time spans). For a complete overview of social impacts, a full SIA study is required.

The value of including citizen values explicitly in the EIA process, however, is that they become a serious (rational) component of what is considered the rational basis for decision-making: the EIS. An EIS that puts citizen values on an equal footing with scientific and technical information provides a broader overview of positive and negative aspects of alternatives than conventional EISs. Moreover, combining public rationalities and scientific rationalities in an EIS may make the document legitimate from a public point of view.

Successful application of CVA requires commitment of the project team. Many scientists and engineers still need to be convinced that social considerations should be part of EIA procedures. When members of a project team are sceptical about the added value of a CVA study, the added value will be limited. Another factor determining the successful integration of CVA in EIA is quality control. Social impact practitioners with relevant expertise need to be involved to guarantee high quality results. Ideally, feedback with representatives of the community should take place at each research phase.

The development of CVA in The Netherlands contributes to the integration of social considerations in Dutch EIA. Furthermore, its development stimulated the discussion on the role of a social component in Dutch EIA. The development of CVA also contributes to the development of SIA expertise in The Netherlands, tuned to the specific requirements of EIA.

CVA is an instrument that has the potential to be

applied much more widely than just within EIA. 'Liveability' or 'quality of the living environment' is becoming a major factor in many decision-making arenas. It has a potential to contribute to decision-making on spatial development, public safety (risk perception), and environmental and nature management.

What is even more important than the application of the CVA instrument itself, is the explicit recognition by politicians of the relevance of systematic information on citizen values as a data source for decision-making. This requires a change in attitude towards experts' judgements: they should be considered an appropriate but not exclusive information source.

Acknowledgements

The authors wish to thank Annemarie Rodenhuis, Jacqueline Snoek, Anne Sorber, Dimitri Terlien, Anouk Tompot, Wilko de Vlieger, Danielle Vollering, Elly van Welie and Inez Ytsma for their valuable contributions as team members of the CVA development project. They are also grateful to Angelique Bergers, Hans Brouwer, Otto Cox, Henk Laagland, Heleen Sarink, Michiel de Vries, and Jan Wuisman for their valuable input in specific phases of the project.

References

Burdge, R J (1998), *A Conceptual Approach to Social Impact Assessment* (Social Ecology Press, Middleton, Wisconsin USA, revised edition).

Burdge, R J, and F Vanclay (1995), "Social impact assessment" in F Vanclay and D A Bronstein (editors), *Environmental and Social Impact Assessment* (Wiley, Chichester) pages 31–65.

Burningham, K (1995), "Attitudes, accounts and impact assessment", *The Sociological Review*, 43(1), pages 100–122.

Dale, A, and M Lane (1994), "Strategic perspectives analysis: a procedure for participatory and political social impact assessment", *Society and Natural Resources*, 7(3). pages 253–268.

Dale, A, and M Lane (1995), "Queensland's social impact assessment unit: its origins and prospects", *Queensland Planner*, 35(3), pages 5–10.

Freudenburg, W R (1986), "Social impact assessment", *Annual Review of Sociology*, 12(4), pages 51–78.

Gagnon, C, P Hirsch and R Howitt (1993), "Can SIA empower communities?", *Environmental Impact Assessment Review*, 13(4), pages 229–253.

ICGP, Interorganizational Committee on Guidelines and Principles for Social Impact Assessment (1994), "Guidelines and principles for social impact assessment", *Impact Assessment*, 12(2), pages 107–152.

Neuman, W L (1996), *Social Research Methods: Qualitative and quantitative approaches* (Allan and Bacon, Boston).

Ortolano, L and A Shepherd (1995), "Environmental impact assessment: challenges and opportunities". *Impact Assessment*, 13(1), pages 3–30.

Taylor, C N, C H Bryan and C G Goodrich (1995), *Social Assessment; Theory, Process and Techniques* (Taylor Baines and Associates, Ricarton New Zealand, second edition).

Vanclay, F (1999), "Social impact assessment", in J Petts (editor), *Handbook of Environmental Impact Assessment* (volume 1) (Blackwell Science, Oxford) pages 301–326.

van Vliet, J (1996), *M.e.(e)r. waarde belevingsonderzoek* (*The Added Value of Citizen Values Profiling in EIA*) (Directorate General of Public Works and Water Management, Civil Engineering Division, Utrecht, The Netherlands).

de Vries, M S (1999) *Calculated Choices in Policy-Making: Theory and Practice of Impact Assessment* (Palgrave, Houndmills/London).

Part VII
Various Issues of Interest

Human rights and impact assessment: clarifying the connections in practice

Deanna Kemp[a]* and Frank Vanclay[b]

[a]Centre for Social Responsibility in Mining, Sustainable Minerals Institute, The University of Queensland, Brisbane, Australia;
[b]Department of Cultural Geography, Faculty of Spatial Sciences, University of Groningen, Groningen, The Netherlands

> Historically, impact assessment practice has not explicitly considered human rights. That human rights are relevant to business has been confirmed through the United Nations Human Rights Council's endorsement of the 'Guiding Principles on Business and Human Rights'. Special Representative to the Secretary-General on business and human rights, Professor John Ruggie, advocated awareness of 'rights-holders' and 'duty-bearers' and a shift from third parties "naming and shaming" companies as a way of addressing human rights harms to companies also "knowing and showing" how they are taking responsibility for their human rights impacts and managing their human rights risks. Consideration of human rights should therefore be central to impact assessment for private sector projects, especially those affecting livelihoods, environment, health, safety and security, land and property, culture and gender dynamics. We provide an introduction to the business and human rights debate, discuss the relevance of human rights to the field of impact assessment, and examine a range of challenges associated with integrating the fields of human rights and social impact assessment.

> **Keywords:** Human rights impact assessment; social impact assessment; due diligence; corporate social responsibility; social licence to operate

Introduction

Extraordinary expansion in the reach and power of the private sector in last half-century has been accompanied by a corresponding increase in the nature and intensity of its impacts – both positive and negative – on the social and bio-physical environment. Many of these impacts have wide-ranging implications for the enjoyment of human rights, which are considered to be the inherent dignities and freedoms to which all human beings are entitled (UNGA 1948). Multinational companies and heavy-footprint industries in particular – including agriculture, mining, manufacturing, tourism, telecommunications and infrastructure – all have considerable potential to impact on human rights. Impact assessment is an established domain of practice in these and other industries; however, its methodologies and scope have tended not to cover the human rights impacts of projects, plans, programmes and policies in any substantive sense, beyond suggesting that human rights are integral to the core values of the social impact assessment (SIA) community (MacNaughton & Hunt 2011; Vanclay 2003, 2006). Forging stronger connections between human rights and impact assessment can bridge this gap and help ensure that businesses uphold their human rights responsibilities.

Internationally agreed human rights were enshrined in the *Universal Declaration of Human Rights* (UDHR), which was adopted by the United Nations (UN) in 1948. It is now well established that human rights are inalienable, universal, indivisible, interdependent and interrelated, and apply equally to all human beings (UNGA 1993). The UDHR, together with the *International Covenant on Civil and Political Rights* (UNGA 1966a) and the *International Covenant on Economic, Social and Cultural Rights* (UNGA 1966b), form the *International Bill of Human Rights*. In broad terms, 'civil and political rights' are associated with physical security such as freedom from torture and arbitrary detention, the right to a fair trial, and freedom of religion and free speech (UNGA 1966a). The 'economic, social and cultural rights' include considerations such as the right to a livelihood; the right to participate in the cultural life of a community; the right to a fair wage, health care and other social services; the right to family life; and freedom from gender and other types of discrimination (UNGA 1966b). As will be elaborated below, while the Bill of Human Rights and a range of other international human rights legal instruments apply to signatory states, the UN has confirmed that international human rights law holds particular relevance to business (UNHRC 2011).

In this article, we outline the development of the 'business and human rights' agenda, and explain the key elements of contemporary human rights thinking, especially with respect to the responsibilities of business. An introduction to the business and human rights debate is provided, before discussing the relevance of human rights to the field of impact assessment and examining a range of conceptual and operational challenges associated with integrating the fields of human rights and SIA.

Business and human rights: An introduction to the debate

Human rights has become a prominent political discourse on a global scale. Evidence of its emergence as a 'field of practice' lies in the inexorable growth of human rights organisations (Ergas 2009) as well as its emergence as a specialist field of academic research and teaching (Morrison & Vermijs 2011; Risse 2009). The arena of 'business and human rights' has also expanded amid clashes between a rights-based approach to development and market-based notions of access and entitlement to

---

*Corresponding author. Email: d.kemp@smi.uq.edu.au

© 2013 IAIA

resources (De Feyter 2005; Newell & Wheeler 2006). The business and human rights debate has been shaped by a series of egregious cases of alleged human rights abuses by business entities (Wright 2008).

A long-standing and emblematic case involves Shell and the Ogoni people in Nigeria (Frynas 2001; Obi 1997; Welch 1995; Boele et al. 2001). Shell had been operating in Ogoniland since 1958. As a result of severe environmental degradation, a lack of benefits to local people, and no 'social licence to operate' (amongst other things), the Movement for the Survival of the Ogoni People (MOSOP) was founded in 1990 to seek self-determination for the Ogoni People. MOSOP prepared and presented an Ogoni Bill of Rights to advance their cause (MOSOP 1991). It also began a vigorous, non-violent campaign of opposition against the Nigerian government and the oil companies. A repressive response by the Nigerian government ensued. A Human Rights Watch (1995, online) report, which documented the human rights abuses, stated that:

> In the wake of the murders [of four Ogoni chiefs in May 1994], which occurred under disputed circumstances, the Rivers State Internal Security Task Force embarked on a series of punitive raids on Ogoni villages. These raids were characterised by flagrant human rights abuses, including extrajudicial executions, indiscriminate shooting, arbitrary arrests and detention, floggings, rapes, looting, and extortion.

The murders provided a pretext for the military government to arrest MOSOP leader, Ken Saro-Wiwa, and eight colleagues, accusing them of inciting the murders. Following a sham trial, which violated international norms for judicial procedure, the Ogoni Nine were executed on 10 November 1995 amidst widespread international pleas for clemency and condemnation of Shell and the Nigerian government. The British government, for example, called it "judicial murder" (Wettstein 2012, p. 50). Shell was accused of complicity in various human rights abuses including killings and torture, and of "a vicarious role in the executions" (Wheeler et al. 2002, p. 301; Frynas 2001; Wettstein 2012). As a consequence, Shell suffered a significant reputational loss, was the subject of organised boycotts and sabotage attacks on their retail outlets around the world, and considerable disinvestment and an associated fall in share price (Wheeler et al. 2002). Civil cases using the Alien Tort Claims Act (which allows US courts to hear cases brought by non-US citizens in relation to activities that occurred outside the USA) are still underway.

Another notable case of human rights concern relates to Anvil Mining's alleged complicity and logistical support of a 2004 massacre by the Congolese military in a village near its Katanga copper mine (McBeth 2008). This event led to separate legal trials in the Democratic Republic of Congo, Australia and Canada and an investigation by the International Finance Corporation (IFC) Compliance Advisor/Ombudsman (CAO) at the request of the President of the World Bank (CAO 2005a). Although no court action against the company has been successful, the costs to the company and to its reputation have been considerable.

Another example is Barrick Mining. Barrick was accused of the systematic rape of local women by security staff at the Porgera Joint Venture in Papua New Guinea (Human Rights Watch 2011). For years Barrick denied all charges, until finally initiating a series of investigations, which confirmed many of the original claims. The company has since developed a framework of remediation initiatives to help confront violence against women in the Porgera Valley (Barrick Mining 2012).

A final example, also now emblematic, is that of the Marlin Mine in the San Marcos Department of south-western Guatemala. In 2002, the Guatemalan government gave endorsement to Montana Exploradora, a subsidiary of Glamis Gold to develop the mine. In 2004, the IFC approved a US$45 million loan to the mine and it commenced operation in 2005. In 2006, Glamis Gold merged with Goldcorp, a Canada-based company. From the beginning, the mine was vigorously opposed by the local Indigenous (Mayan) people and in January 2005 they blockaded the access road, delaying a delivery convoy by over a month. Police action to enable the convoy to pass resulted in the killing of one protester and several injuries (Fulmer et al. 2008). The Guatemalan President, Oscar Berger, defended the police action by saying that, "We have to protect the investors" (Nolin & Stephens 2010, p. 53). Since then, there has been a range of concerns about damage to the environment relating in particular to the cyanide leaching process used, water use, royalty payments to the central government, and the benefits that flow to local people. A major concern relates to the notion that large-scale land disturbance is incompatible with the Mayan 'cosmovision' and that development has nothing to offer them: "We don't want gold; what we want is to defend our way of life and our water" (Fulmer et al. 2008, p. 93). In 2005, a complaint was lodged with the IFC's CAO, raising issues of reduced community access to water and contamination of waterways, and that the project proceeded without adequate consultation with the local Indigenous people and in violation of their rights. The subsequent report (CAO 2005b) rejected concerns about reduced water quality and access. On the matter of consultation, the report said:

> The CAO found a genuine difference in understanding amongst the parties about the purpose of consultation with and disclosures to local people. Without endorsing either perspective, CAO found that the project sponsor and IFC believe it was sufficient to inform parties of the impending project, some of its potential impacts and solicit input for associated development projects. Many of the local leaders in Sipacapa believe that they should have the right to determine whether or not the project should be allowed to operate in their territory. (CAO 2005b, p. ii)

Although the mine has contributed to the local community in various ways, it is clear that there was significant opposition to the mine, with the protestors managing to gain considerable international interest in their cause. In early 2008, a group of institutional investors in Goldcorp who were committed to ethical investment – specifically

Ethical Funds, First Swedish National Pension Fund, Fourth Swedish National Pension Fund, Public Service Alliance of Canada Staff Pension Fund, and SHARE – sent a delegation to Guatemala to inspect the site. Subsequently they called upon Goldcorp to undertake an independent human rights assessment, which was completed by a Canadian consulting firm (On Common Ground 2010).

In the face of mounting international pressure from these and other cases, the issue of business and human rights was taken up by the UN in 2005 and given particular prominence through the appointment of Professor John Ruggie as the "United Nations Special Representative of the Secretary-General on the issue of human rights and transnational corporations and other business enterprises". Ruggie is the Berthold Beitz Professor in Human Rights and International Affairs at Harvard University's Kennedy School of Government. Ruggie, who has an extensive background in UN work, including the development of the Global Compact and the Millennium Development Goals, was appointed to identify and clarify standards of corporate responsibility and accountability with regard to human rights. Often referred to as the 'Ruggie mandate', indicating a long-term international mission authorised by the UN, Ruggie sought to address the uncertainty created by the *Draft Norms on Transnational Corporations and Other Business Enterprises* (2003), which sought to impose on companies the same range of human rights duties under international law as states (refer to Ruggie 2007 for details). The Draft Norms created confusion, division and tension amongst a range of stakeholders in relation to the responsibilities of business and other actors on the issue of human rights (Kinley & Chambers 2006), and were never adopted by the UN (United Nations 2010).

After three years and a process of broad-based global consultation, in 2008 Ruggie proposed the *Protect, Respect and Remedy* framework to clarify the responsibilities of business and government in relation to business-related human rights harm.

> The framework rests on differentiated but complementary responsibilities. It comprises three core principles: the State duty to protect against human rights abuses by third parties, including business; the corporate responsibility to respect human rights; and the need for more effective access to remedies. Each principle is an essential component of the framework: the State duty to protect because it lies at the very core of the international human rights regime; the corporate responsibility to respect because it is the basic expectation society has of business; and access to remedy, because even the most concerted efforts cannot prevent all abuse, while access to judicial redress is often problematic, and non-judicial means are limited in number, scope and effectiveness. The three principles form a complementary whole in that each supports the others in achieving sustainable progress (Ruggie 2008, pp. 4–5).

The mandate was subsequently extended in order to focus on operationalising the framework, recognising the significant challenge of implementation. This led to the UN *Guiding Principles on Business and Human Rights* (hereinafter 'UNGP'), which the UN Human Rights Council unanimously endorsed in 2011. In addition to the official, internal UN version (Ruggie 2011), a public version has also been produced (United Nations 2011). This was the first time that the UN had ever endorsed standards to govern the adverse impacts of business activities on the human rights of individuals and groups. A range of companies and industry organisations officially recognised the UN framework on its release and have subsequently endorsed the UNGP.

Establishing standards for human rights observance by business

Because the contemporary concept of human rights is codified in the 1948 UDHR and other international human rights treaties, the responsibilities of states are well established. However, before the Ruggie mandate, the international legal framework for human rights did not adequately address the responsibilities of companies, and indeed there was a question as to what extent companies were subject to international human rights law. It is now clear that companies are subject to international human rights law (UNHRC 2008, 2011) and that various watchdog organisations will pursue companies that abuse human rights. However, the precise requirements that businesses need to follow to fulfil their human rights obligations in practice are still emerging.

The respect principle in the *Protect, Respect and Remedy* framework provided one way of establishing the minimum standard of business conduct: to avoid infringing the human rights of others, which Ruggie refers to as the "do no harm" principle (Ruggie 2010). However, in the UNGP, Ruggie is more specific about what constitutes the minimum standards for human rights observance. Principle 12 reads:

> The responsibility of business enterprises to respect human rights refers to internationally recognised human rights – understood, at a minimum, as those expressed in the International Bill of Human Rights and the principles concerning fundamental rights set out in the International Labour Organization's Declaration on Fundamental Principles and Rights at Work.

The four principles in the International Labour Organization's (ILO) Declaration of Fundamental Principles and Rights at Work (ILO 1998, online) are:

(a) freedom of association and the effective recognition of the right to collective bargaining;

(b) the elimination of all forms of forced or compulsory labour;

(c) the effective abolition of child labour; and

(d) the elimination of discrimination in respect of employment and occupation.

The UNGP states that businesses may need to consider additional standards, depending on host and home state circumstances. In many industries, particularly those that require land acquisition and/or cause disruption to culture and heritage, instruments such as the ILO Convention 169, which concerns Indigenous and tribal peoples, and the UN

Declaration on the Rights of Indigenous Peoples (UNDRIP) may be relevant. These instruments bring into frame the issue of 'free prior and informed consent' (FPIC) as a primary tool for securing and protecting Indigenous peoples' rights. While some companies and industry organisations have indicated 'in principle' support for these instruments (e.g. Rio Tinto 2012; ICMM 2011), FPIC remains highly contested in terms of how it is interpreted and applied in the business arena (Esteves et al. 2012; Hanna & Vanclay 2013). FPIC does not form part of the UNGP's 'minimum standard', but it is now embedded in other human rights-related regulatory regimes, such as the pervasive IFC's Performance Standards (2012), which apply to IFC-funded projects, and, by extension, the Equator Principles, which apply to an increasing number of financing institutions. There are many facets to the debate about FPIC and business, including the issues of representation, the power of veto and the applicability of FPIC beyond Indigenous peoples (Hanna & Vanclay 2013).

Debates about additional human rights standards also relate to some human rights not being explicitly enshrined in international law, such as the right to water. The right to water was not recognised as a distinct right in the UDHR, but observers have argued that the right to air and water were so obvious that the original drafters of the UDHR saw no reason to list them (IHRB 2009; Gleick 1999). In 2008, the UN Human Rights Council appointed an Independent Expert, Professor Catarina de Albuquerque, to consider the contentious issue of water as a human right. Ultimately, access to potable water was recognised by the UN General Assembly as a distinct human right, in conjunction with the human right to sanitation (UNGA 2010). For water-intensive industries such as mining, manufacturing and/or water infrastructure facilities (whether state or privately owned), these 'emerging rights' have considerable relevance to the business and human rights debate (Kemp et al. 2010a). Beyond water and sanitation, other emerging rights include, for example, the right to food (Narula 2006).

There are a wide range of other significant international developments and global initiatives that reinforce, consolidate, challenge and shift the boundaries of the business and human rights debate. In addition to those mentioned above, one of the most significant developments has been the 2011 revision of the OECD Guidelines for Multinational Enterprises. The Guidelines, which were originally adopted in 1976, apply to the current now 34 OECD member states, and outline what these governments expect of business. The 2011 revision aligns with the UNGP and includes a new chapter on human rights with reference to 'due diligence' – a concept embedded within the UNGP, which we elaborate below. The European Union has also endorsed the UNGP, and invited Member States to develop national plans for implementing the UNGP by the end of 2012. For individual states, new legislation such as the 'Dodd-Frank Wall Street Report and Consumer Protection Act' passed by the US Congress in 2010 has ushered in new corporate reporting requirements specifically in the context of conflict minerals (Earthworks 2010), although it is expected that the concept will be applied more generally.

A number of voluntary schemes have also aligned with the UNGP. The ISO 26000 Guidance on Social Responsibility (ISO 2010), for example, was revised to be consistent with the intent and substance of the UNGP (Atler 2011). The UN's flagship business and human rights scheme, the UN Global Compact (which was established and overseen by Ruggie a decade earlier) has released a guidance tool about the UNGP to support and enhance their implementation by businesses (UNGC 2011). The Office of the UN Office for the High Commissioner on Human Rights (2011) has also released an Interpretive Guide, providing guidance on the business responsibility to respect human rights.

Some stakeholders are concerned about the absence of enforcement provisions in the UNGP and the lack of ability to hold companies to account for human rights abuse (e.g. Amnesty International 2011, SOMO 2012). Certainly, not all countries have been willing to embrace the legal aspects relating to the 'protect' pillar of Ruggie's *Protect, Respect and Remedy* framework. Despite ongoing contention on the issue of 'enforceability', the intensity of the business and human rights debate has bolstered the strength of non-government organisation (NGO) campaign platforms by raising the profile and currency of the important issue of human rights abuses by companies (e.g. Human Rights Watch 2011). The UNGP are undoubtedly the most authoritative instrument in this realm. Their endorsement by the UN Human Rights Council has given weight to the notion that businesses have human rights responsibilities. This level of support has not previously been seen in the history of the debate about non state actors, or indeed the UN. Although the weaknesses inherent in the UNGP continue to be debated, there is no doubt that they provide an unprecedented global reference point for businesses to demonstrate their respect for human rights.

The UNGP, due diligence and impact assessment

Principle 17 of UNGP proposes the concept of 'human rights due diligence' as a mechanism for improved practice and a method for demonstrating respect for human rights. In the domain of business, the notion of human rights due diligence is as much routine as it is revolutionary. It is routine in the sense that businesses customarily conduct due diligence to satisfy themselves that a proposed business action, transaction or acquisition has no hidden risks to the business. It is revolutionary in the sense that instead of only considering risks to the business, human rights due diligence requires the business to consider risks to people. While the two approaches are not mutually exclusive, human rights due diligence requires a 180 degree shift from an approach that focuses solely on the business entity to one that has an equivalent focus on the human rights of individuals and groups affected by a business's activities or relationships. Ruggie (2010, p. 3) described human rights due diligence as a "game changer" in the sense that it moves the debate from only "naming and shaming" to also "knowing and showing". 'Naming and shaming' is a third-party response to the failure of companies to respect human rights, whereas 'knowing and showing' represents the internalisation of that respect by companies themselves through comprehensive human rights due diligence and reporting processes.

While the concept of due diligence lies at the heart of the corporate responsibility to respect human rights, impact assessment and the concept of human rights impacts are integral to any human rights due diligence process. The UNGP describes due diligence as a process that companies should undertake "to identify, prevent, mitigate and account for how they address their impacts on human rights" (Principle 15). The process should include: "assessing actual and potential human rights impacts, integrating and acting upon the findings, tracking responses, and communicating how impacts are addressed" (Principle 17). The UNGP explains the importance of undertaking a comprehensive due diligence process that considers whether a business causes, contributes to or is linked to adverse human rights impacts through its business relationships. Thus, undertaking ex ante impact assessment and regular ex post audits is essential for a company to respect human rights.

While human rights was always a consideration in SIA (Vanclay 2002, 2003, 2006), the reality is that they were seldom systematically considered in SIA practice (Maassarani et al. 2007). Following the Ruggie mandate and with increasing corporate interest in the business and human rights agenda, as well as with a change in SIA practice from the production of point-in-time reports of predicted impacts to a regulatory agency to being "the process of managing the social issues" (Vanclay 2004, p. 269; Vanclay 2012, p. 150; Esteves et al. 2012), SIA should now fully incorporate the assessment and management of human rights issues. The UNGP provides a stronger legal mandate than has existed in the past in terms of considering of social issues, now under the guise of human rights. Under the UNGP, project-affected peoples are no longer simply stakeholders or impacted communities; they are rights-holders with legitimate interests that need to be respected.

The burgeoning interest in business and human rights has given rise to a blossoming human rights impact assessment fraternity. While some in the fraternity connect with SIA, most come from a legal or para-legal background and do not necessarily connect with impact assessment. Human rights impact assessment (HRIA) differs from SIA in the sense that it proceeds from a clear starting point of the internationally recognised rights, whereas SIA proceeds following a scoping process whereby all stakeholders (including the affected communities) nominate key issues in conjunction with the expert opinion of the assessor in terms of what the key issues might be based on experience in similar cases elsewhere and a conceptual understanding.

While advances in SIA have been important in terms of managing impacts (Esteves et al. 2012; Vanclay & Esteves 2011), without specific consideration of all established human rights norms, it is possible that they might not all be considered. Therefore, impact assessment that provides comprehensive coverage of human rights would need to consider how a policy or project interacts with the full range of human rights by using agreed international human rights standards as the primary reference point and considering additional legal instruments that may have relevance. The systematic inclusion of human rights in this way will represent a significant shift in SIA practice in the coming years.

Challenges of integrating human rights into impact assessment practice

In many ways, the *Protect, Respect and Remedy* framework and the UNGP could be interpreted as clarifying and perhaps streamlining the myriad expectations that fall under the ever-broadening rubric of corporate social responsibility (CSR). From an impact assessment perspective, however, the issue of human rights brings with it a number of conceptual and operational challenges (discussed below) that are not immediately apparent when engaging in global debates about the human rights responsibilities of businesses.

Communicating human rights concepts

Business and human rights is a complex and specialised field characterised by legalistic language. A key challenge for the impact assessment community is to communicate human rights impacts in a language that businesses and other stakeholders can understand and respond to. The international human rights discourse introduces a new lexicon of responsible business, which requires a certain level of expertise or familiarity with international human rights law to engage with accuracy and precision. Principles 16 and 18 of the UNGP explicitly require that appropriate 'expertise' be utilised. As such, this area has increasingly become an arena for specialists with particular knowledge, rather than the domain of generalists. The high level of expertise required to assess human rights may be problematic, at least from an organisational change perspective. To successfully mainstream human rights into business, experts must ensure that the language, discourse and knowledge of human rights is somehow accessible to non-experts, including those within the business sector who may not have previously engaged with human rights language.

The challenge of connecting the discourses of human rights and conventional business was an issue canvassed by Ruggie (2010), who emphasised the need to engage business in order to influence conventional practice. HRIA may need to present findings and recommendations through mainstream business language (e.g. risk, cost, benefit) when communicating a human rights message, but overuse of conventional business concepts may inhibit the take-up of those ideas. Instead of gaining influence, the new language runs the risk of being subsumed within dominant industry constructs, or being positioned as an 'alternative' language that exists at the fringes of corporate practice. It is important that, as part of the assessment process, HRIA raises awareness of human rights so that it acquires meaning in corporate policy and practice. Careful and considered use of language can help to facilitate changes when the right balance is struck between organisational receptivity and resistance (Hardy et al. 2000, Kemp et al. 2010b). Embedding human rights requires sensitivity to existing systems within the organisation in order to achieve buy-in, particularly with managers and decision-makers who are unfamiliar with human rights concepts, processes and practices. Harrison (2011) has called for more research into the ways in which the HRIA process can be made accessible to a wider range of users while not losing its underlying robustness.

The challenge of change for business and the impact assessment family is significant given the nature of the discursive and conceptual shifts that accompany a human rights perspective. A case in point is the changing nature of what constitutes a 'key stakeholder', a core construct of CSR theory (Carroll 1991; Campbell 2007; Banerjee 2008; Brammer et al. 2011; EC 2011). No longer are 'stakeholders' the dominant theoretical construct, but rather 'rights-holders', 'duty-bearers' and 'responsible parties' are now central to the expanded notion of CSR. All individuals and some groups (such as Indigenous groups) hold human rights and are considered to be 'rights-holders'. In the context of business and human rights, the language of 'rights-holder' is used to refer to people whose rights have been (or may be) impacted by a decision or activity. While all stakeholders are in some way rights-holders, not all human rights of all stakeholders are put at risk in every circumstance. When using a human rights lens, impact assessors and businesses must focus on rights-holders who are affected by policies or projects, including the issue of direct and indirect responsibility for impacts. These and other shifts in language have the potential to complicate the human rights message and the generation of shared meaning between HRIA experts, impact assessors and the business community.

Approach to human rights and impact assessment: dedicated, integrated and issue-specific

Another challenge in connecting human rights and impact assessment is determining the appropriate approach for assessing human rights impacts; specifically, whether the assessment should be undertaken through a dedicated, integrated or issue-specific approach. Decisions about the approach to human rights and impact assessment have implications for scope, resourcing, expertise and methodology. In any case, the common feature in each of these approaches is that human rights is deliberately and explicitly considered, providing an evidence base for alignment with international human rights standards, and highlighting the need to change and transform established ways of conducting business.

A dedicated approach is captured by the term 'human rights impact assessment'. Various notions of HRIA have been utilised since the late 1990s by specialist human rights organisations, such as human rights institutes, commissions, NGOs, government and intergovernmental organisations (Harrison 2011). Some business and human rights practitioners use the terminology of HRIA on the assumption that dedicated assessments were implied by the UNGP; however, Ruggie was not specific on the form that impact assessment should take. Nonetheless, there are several companies that now undertake or require a dedicated HRIA as a part of doing business (*e.g.* BHP Billiton 2012). Some practitioners describe dedicated HRIAs as 'drawing on' SIA (Hunt & MacNaughton 2011), whereas others position HRIA as 'distinct from' SIA (Graetz & Franks 2013). Clearly, there are different interpretations on the point of whether HRIA is related to, or indeed an extension of, SIA or other forms of impact assessment (Kemp et al. 2010a).

Some organisations advocate integrated assessments as the default approach, where human rights are embedded within the scope of environment, social and health impact assessments (IPIECA in press). This approach would require the integration of human rights specialists into an assessment team and/or for generalist assessors to update their knowledge to the extent that they could cover this domain. Issues of expertise aside, an integrated assessment raises other issues in a multi-disciplinary impact assessment frame. SIA has traditionally been the weaker impact assessment discipline (Burdge 2002; Maassarani et al. 2007), largely because of the challenge of defining, predicting and measuring social change and impact, in addition to legal and regulatory frameworks for assessment that are persistently weak or ineffectual in terms of social impact (Esteves et al. 2012). In integrated mode, human rights may find itself 'competing for space' in an already weak area of impact assessment practice. This issue tends not to be discussed in documents providing guidance on integrating human rights into impact assessment.

Whether a dedicated or integrated approach is preferred, it may be necessary to tailor an assessment to a specific need, circumstance, situation or issue. An integrated assessment may, for example, highlight a need to understand a particular issue in more depth, in which case specialised human rights assessments may be commissioned. Similarly, a specific HRIA process may be warranted in the case of resettlement, when there is conflict, or where a group of people have suffered egregious harm. Alternatively, an issue-specific assessment may be triggered by a concern lodged through a project-level grievance mechanism. There are a range of possible approaches to assessing human rights impacts, including a desktop assessment of already completed environmental impact assessments or SIAs to determine the degree to which human rights considerations were covered in prior assessments. Whether a retrospective study would meet the intent of the UNGP in some circumstances, or would only ever be a preparatory step, is not entirely clear, but at a minimum, such a review would hopefully serve to draw attention to human rights considerations.

Operational challenges

Despite the recent focus on business and human rights, frameworks for assessing human rights impacts are still relatively immature. Nonetheless, there are important issues to consider, not least of which are how methods used to engage individuals and groups can impact on human rights such as freedom of expression, self-determination and non-discrimination. One important challenge emerges in jurisdictions where discussing human rights is forbidden or inhibited, governance frameworks are weak, corruption is high, human rights awareness is low, and/or where civil society activism is constrained by the state. In these jurisdictions, stakeholders may be unaware of their rights under law, and may not frame issues in a rights language, even where issues may relate directly to human rights. In traditional societies, rights to land and water are typically negotiated and based on customary tenure, social exchange and group interaction, rather than internationally conceived notions of 'universal' rights and duties. An impact assessment must be aware not only of international and national legal frameworks, but also the micro-context, including how issues are framed and negotiated in the local culture. While SIA practitioners face these challenges irrespective of whether human rights impacts are being explicitly addressed, this 'global to local' knowledge base is central to human rights impact assessment. Misinterpretations can result in misreading particular situations.

In some jurisdictions, stakeholders may not claim their rights or seek to hold the state or companies to account for violations or abuse, largely owing to the political context. Some individuals and/or groups would face persecution for even suggesting that impacts may constitute a corporate human rights abuse. This does not render human rights irrelevant, but rather calls attention to the challenges for an assessment team seeking to understand business-related human rights risks and impacts. The process for assessing rights in these contexts will require alternative methodologies. For situations where direct consultation may put groups at risk, it may be necessary to engage third parties, such as NGOs or other agencies or individuals who have worked closely with particular groups. Assessment teams must be vigilant about ensuring that individuals and groups are not put at risk by virtue of the human rights assessment itself. These situations raise the question of how (or indeed whether) an inclusive or participatory assessment can be undertaken if there is a risk of backlash.

It can be particularly difficult to engage with the issue of human rights where social and cultural protocols prevent or inhibit engagement with some groups or individuals. For example, in some cultures women are discouraged from participating in public meetings, or are prevented from meeting with outsiders where men are not present (Srinivasan & Mehta 2003; Lahiri-Dutt & Ahmad 2011). However, it cannot be assumed that, because women or other groups do not participate in an open meeting that they do not influence the process, as O'Faircheallaigh (in press) has highlighted in the context of gender and agreement-making in mining. At other times, lack of participation in the assessment process can relate to more practical aspects of assessment, such as the timing of meetings, the availability of translators and so forth. Nonetheless, it is important that the complex issue of local culture vs universal norms is addressed so that the human rights assessment process itself does not inadvertently privilege particular people or practices, and upholds human rights in the process. This challenge is amplified in impact assessments that seek to connect universal human rights and context-specific impact assessment processes.

Internalising the responsibility to respect

The prominence of the human rights discourse globally and the proliferation of human rights organisations in the face of continued violation and abuse raises important questions about putting principles into practice (Ergas 2009; Harrison 2011). Certainly there have been long-standing debates about the effectiveness of international human rights law and whether it makes a difference in terms of a country's human rights performance. Hathaway (2002), for example, completed an extensive study into the relationship between human rights treaties and human rights practice and found that, although countries that had ratified treaties had generally better practices than those that had not, non-compliance with treaty obligations was common. Hathaway concluded that not only was treaty ratification not infrequently associated with the *worst* human rights practices, but also that treaty ratification accrues reputation points and results in a reduced pressure to comply in practice. In the business and human rights arena, the risk that companies 'sign on' to international human rights standards with limited enforcements mechanisms and subsequently benefit in terms of reputation credits is significant. For the SIA community, the challenge is in ensuring that human rights and impact assessment processes provide mechanisms through which businesses can internalise or integrate human rights thinking in practice.

Following endorsement of the UNGP by the UN Human Rights Council on 16 June 2011, many companies incorporated human rights commitments into their policies, management systems and procedures (IHRB 2012). To be effective, management systems must provide useful information so that a business can avoid infringing upon human rights in its business activities and relationships (Boele et al. 2001). The challenge, however, is ensuring that HRIAs are a meaningful rather than superficial response to the emerging agenda. Companies can create policies, mechanisms and processes, but ultimately, alignment will be measured by a company's ability to link impact assessment to decisions and actions. In fact, implementation of normative guidance is considered to be one of the most significant challenges in the business and human rights arena (IHRB 2012), and impact assessment could play an essential role in this process.

Kemp et al. (2010) described a range of barriers relating to the implementation of a 'water and human rights' perspective in mining, including: disciplinary barriers between the dominant engineering and natural science professions and the minority social science professions; and lack of team integration both intra (i.e. within departments) and inter (i.e. between departments). There were also hierarchical considerations. Human rights policies are usually driven by corporate head-offices, whose representatives have engaged at the global level, whereas operational personnel – who are required to implement corporately mandated policies – are rarely involved in any substantive sense. Clearly there are both disciplinary and organisational factors to consider in policy development and implementation, as well as the methodological challenges outlined above.

The challenges associated with embedding knowledge from impact assessment into organisational realities are well recognised (Esteves & Vanclay 2009; Kemp 2011). However, the emphasis of impact assessment – even leading practice impact assessment – continues to focus on the impact that a policy or practice has on the external stakeholders or the bio-physical environment, rather than also considering organisational aspects. Rarely does the scope of an impact assessment include the project proponent's ability to understand or respond to assessment findings or recommendations (Kemp 2011). This lack of focus on internal or organisational dynamics continues to limit policy implementation, planning and integration of social considerations into organisational processes. An assessment of internal capacity and organisational capability may serve to open up space for capacity building as a prelude to, or in conjunction with, a human rights impact assessment so that non-expert managers and decision-makers can engage with the assessment process and potentially co-create forward strategies. Internal assessment may also serve to identify organisational barriers and enablers to human rights take-up so that constraints can be addressed from the outset. In the context of business and human rights concerns, organisational process considerations are more relevant than ever. Organisational diagnostic work would also enable adjustments to organisational structures and processes that support a business and human rights perspective, rather than relying only on an agency-based model where external assessors and other internal champions continually push for change from the periphery.

What role should advocacy play in impact assessment practice?

In the arena of business and human rights, campaigners and advocates have played and will continue to play a prominent role in driving an agenda for change. Alternative voices have long sought to open up space for public debate about business and human rights, including capacity building for civil society (SOMO 2012). With human rights entering mainstream business discourse, the issue becomes one of whether, and if so how, advocacy and assessment can constructively co-exist within a common frame. Human rights stems from an advocacy tradition that applies external pressure to raise awareness of particular issues in order to trigger a response. Impact assessment, on the other hand, stems from a permitting tradition that utilises project plans and processes as the basis for engagement. This is particularly so for environmental impact assessment, to which SIA remains connected in many cases.

Contemporary SIA encourages broad-based consultation, meaningful participation and transparency of assessment findings (Esteves et al. 2012; Vanclay 2003). However, the limited availability of corporate-commissioned HRIAs seems to suggest that confidentiality, rather than transparency, is standard practice. This tends not to be the case for NGO/civil society-driven SIAs, as demonstrated by Watson et al. (2013), where the HRIA was explicitly used as a campaign tool and a strategic lever to prompt industry change. Corporate-commissioned HRIAs may represent a shift from "naming and shaming" to "knowing and showing", but the lack of publicly available assessments raises questions about alignment with contemporary approaches to SIA, other than in exceptional cases, such as the Marlin Mine HRIA (On Common Ground 2010).

Whatever the approach to change, rarely will impact assessors hold formal authority in the organisational realm. Assessors are typically external to the project proponent organisation and hold only *informal* authority by virtue of their specialisation. They must therefore be adept at identifying and using effective levers for change. The point has been made above that this will require familiarity with context, including organisational dynamics. Assessors need to be well informed about the internal domain in order to calculate the tactical concessions that they may need to make in order to effectively raise human rights issues of significant concern. Assessors cannot afford to isolate themselves from project proponents as they will, in effect, lose influence. In the language of adaptive leadership, systems distress must be kept within the productive range (Heifetz 1994; Heifetz et al. 2009).

This, in turn, raises important ethical issues. If, for example, assessors find that a company has directly or indirectly caused or contributed to an abuse of human rights, assessors must be clear about what they do with this information, including how such abuse is to be reported within – or outside – the impact assessment frame. This is where the delineation between assessment and advocacy becomes less clear. These and other challenges must be discussed and debated within the assessment community to ensure that its own core values are upheld in each and every impact assessment.

Conclusion

Human rights are firmly established on the global agenda. Expectations of business in relation to human rights have increased markedly, as has industry's willingness to engage in the debate. Much progress has been made in terms of clarifying the roles and responsibilities of different actors, and the necessary processes to ensure that companies achieve at least minimum performance. While some clarity has been provided through the Ruggie mandate, the business and human rights agenda is far from static and continues to evolve. It is impossible to predict which points of contention will be resolved and which will continue to generate conflict into the future. Some questions are likely to fade from prominence, such as whether integrated or stand-alone HRIAs should apply – clearly, it will be a case of 'fit for purpose'. The greater issue is how to make rapid gains in the methodological realm, especially because a philosophy or culture of 'shared practice' is perhaps underdeveloped in this sector as companies try to obtain a competitive advantage in social performance.

As some issues are resolved, others will come to the fore. Issues likely to gain momentum include questions relating to how FPIC should be implemented, and about appropriate accountability mechanisms in cases of human rights abuse. One issue that has not been as prominent in debates about business and human rights is the role of business in improving the enjoyment of human rights. The focus of the current debate has been on harm minimisation, rather than realising rights and enhancing enjoyment, which was considered outside the scope of the Ruggie mandate. In effect, the current business and human rights discourse is largely framed in the negative, emphasising 'harm' and 'avoidance' and therefore does not tend to speak to broader debates, where 'development benefit' and 'shared value' sit at the forefront (Esteves & Vanclay 2009; João et al. 2011). While the point was clearly made in the *Protect, Respect and Remedy* framework that companies cannot offset human rights harm by doing good deeds elsewhere, substantive discussion about the link between human rights and human development has not been as prominent, despite the fact that a human rights-based approach has gained currency in the development sector and that companies often make substantial contributions to human rights enjoyment. Rarely are these contributions framed from a human rights perspective. It will be interesting to see whether human development and rights discourses forge closer connections over time, particularly in the context of the urgent need to accelerate progress in the achievement of other human rights-related frameworks, such as the UN's Millennium Development Goals, towards which several companies have indicated their support.

The role that impact assessment can play in contributing to these debates is considerable. The impact assessment community can play an important support role in helping companies determine their level of compliance with voluntary commitments and international human rights standards. Alternatively, it can take a more active role by advocating for improved human rights performance. Impact assessors also have an opportunity to build on the current momentum and identify other points of connection, not taken up in this paper. For example, impact assessment provides a key opportunity to strengthen the focus on access to remedy. The remedy landscape is important in any given development context, and impact assessment has an important role to play in understanding the effectiveness of existing mechanisms, in addition to highlighting the need for additional grievance mechanisms to fill an identified remedy gap. The UNGP states that the value of grievance mechanisms is to identify impacts and facilitate early remediation. The connection between impact assessment and the remedy pillar deserves careful thought and attention.

In this article we have provided an introduction to the business and human rights debate and considered many complexities associated with establishing a stronger connection between human rights and impact assessment. We have also highlighted several opportunities for impact assessment to meaningfully contribute to the emerging business and human rights agenda – in fact we suggested that impact assessment provides one of the cornerstones of the business responsibility to respect human rights. The UNGP provides impact assessment with a global authority that has never before underpinned impact assessment practice. Human rights offers a powerful pathway to renew and rejuvenate the very meaning of impact assessment and, with a commitment to shared learning and innovation, the impact assessment community could, in turn, support a global agenda for change.

References

Amnesty International [Internet]. 2011. The UN Human Rights Norms For Business: Towards Legal Accountability; [cited 2013 Jan 3]. Available from: http://www.amnesty.org/en/library/asset/IOR42/002/2004/en/c17311f2-d629-11dd-ab95-a13b602c0642/ior420022004en.pdf

Atler S. 2011. The Impact of the United Nations Secretary-General's Special Representative & The UN Framework on the Development of the Human Rights Components of ISO 26000. Corporate Social Responsibility Initiative Working Paper No. 64. Cambridge, MA: John F. Kennedy School of Government, Harvard University.

Banerjee SB. 2008. Corporate social responsibility: The good, the bad and the ugly. Cr Sociol. 34(1):51–79.

Barrick Mining [Internet]. 2012. A framework of remediation initiatives in response to violence against women in the Porgera Valley [cited 2012 Dec 23]. Available from: http://www.barrick.com/files/porgera/Porgera-Backgrounder-Framework-of-remediation-initiatives.pdf

BHP Billiton [Internet]. 2012. Community; [cited 2012 Dec 23]. Available from: http://www.bhpbilliton.com/home/aboutus/ourcompany/Documents/2012/Community.pdf

Boele R, Fabig H, Wheeler D. 2001. Shell, Nigeria and the Ogoni. A study in unsustainable development: I. The story of Shell, Nigeria and the Ogoni people – environment, economy, relationships: conflict and prospects for resolution. Sust. Dev. 9(2):74–86.

Brammer S, Jackson G, Matten D. 2011. Corporate social responsibility and institutional theory: New perspectives on private governance. Soc Econ Rev. 10(1):3–28.

Burdge RJ. 2002. Why is social impact assessment the orphan of the assessment process? Impact Assess Proj Appraisal. 20(1):3–9.

Campbell JL. 2007. Why would corporations behave in socially responsible ways? An institutional theory of corporate social responsibility. Acad Manage Rev. 32(3):946–967.

Carroll AB. 1991. The pyramid of corporate social responsibility: Toward the moral management of organizational stakeholders. Bus Horizons. 34(4):39–48.

Compliance Advisor/Ombudsman [Internet]. 2005a. CAO Audit of MIGA's Due Diligence of the Dikulushi Copper-Silver Mining Project in The Democratic Republic of the Congo. Washington: Office of the Compliance Advisor/Ombudsman, International Finance Corporation, Multilateral Investment Guarantee Agency, [cited 2013 Jan 3]. Available from: http://www.cao-ombudsman.org/cases/case_detail.aspx?id=94

Compliance Advisor/Ombudsman [Internet]. 2005b. Assessment of a Complaint submitted to CAO in relation to the Marlin

Mining Project in Guatemala. Washington: Office of the Compliance Advisor/Ombudsman, International Finance Corporation, Multilateral Investment Guarantee Agency, [cited 2013 Jan 3]. Available from: http://www.cao-ombudsman.org/cases/case_detail.aspx?id=95

De Feyter K. 2005. Human Rights: Social Justice in the Age of the Market. London: Zed Books.

Earthworks. 2010 Jul 16. Senate passes a landmark bill to rein in dirty deals in mining and drilling. Earthworks [Internet]. [cited 2013 Jan 3]. Available from: http://www.earthworksaction.org/media/detail/new_legislation_to_bring_greater_-accountability_for_extractive_industries#.UUqNQxfX89U

Ergas Y. 2009. Human rights impact: Developing an agenda for interdisciplinary, international research. J Hum Rts Prac. 1(3):459–468.

Esteves AM, Franks D, Vanclay F. 2012. Social impact assessment: The state of the art. Impact Assess Proj Appraisal. 30(1):34–42.

Esteves AM, Vanclay F. 2009. Social development needs analysis as a tool for SIA to guide corporate-community investment: Applications in the minerals industry. Env Impact Assess Rev. 29(2):137–145.

European Commission (EC) [Internet]. 2011. A renewed EU strategy for 2011-14 for corporate social responsibility. Communication from the Commission to the European Parliament, the Council, the European Economic and Social Committee and the Committee of the Regions; [cited 2012 Dec 20]. Available from: http://eur-lex.europa.eu/LexUriServ/LexUriServ.do?uri=COM:2011:0681:FIN:EN:PDF

Frynas JG. 2001. Corporate and state responses to anti-oil protests in the Niger Delta. African Aff. 100(398):27–54.

Fulmer ASM, Snodgrass Godoy A, Neff P. 2008. Indigenous rights, resistance, and the law: Lessons from a Guatemalan mine. Lat Am Polit Soc. 50(4):91–121.

Gleick P. 1999. The human right to water. Water Policy. 1(5):487–503.

Graetz G, Franks DM. 2013. Incorporating human rights into the corporate domain: Due diligence, impact assessment and integrated risk management. Impact Assess Proj Appraisal. 31(2):97–106.

Hanna P, Vanclay F. 2013. Human rights, Indigenous peoples and the concept of Free, Prior and Informed Consent in the extractive industries in Brazil. Impact Assess Proj Appraisal. 31(2):146–157.

Hardy C, Palmer I, Phillips N. 2000. Discourse as a Strategic Resource. Human Relat. 53(9):1227–1248.

Harrison J. 2011. Human rights measurement: Reflections on the current practice and future potential of human rights impact assessment. J Hum Rights Prac. 3(2):162–187.

Hathaway OA. 2002. Do human rights treaties make a difference? The Yale Law J. 111(8):1935–2042.

Heifetz RA. 1994. Leadership Without Easy Answers. Cambridge, MA: Harvard University Press.

Heifetz RA, Grashow A, Linsky M. 2009. The Practice of Adaptive Leadership: Tools and Tactics for Changing Your Organization and the World. Boston: Harvard Business Press.

Human Rights Watch [Internet]. 1995. The ogoni crisis: A casestudy of military repression in Southeastern Nigeria; [cited 2013 Jan 3]. Available at: http://www.unhcr.org/refworld/docid/3ae6a7d8c.html

Human Rights Watch [Internet]. 2011. Gold's costly dividend; [cited 2013 Jan 3]. Available from: http://www.hrw.org/en/reports/2011/02/01/gold-s-costly-dividend

ICMM [International Council of Mining and Metals] [Internet]. 2011. Good Practice Guide Indigenous Peoples and Mining. London, UK: ICMM, [cited 2013 Jan 3]. Available from: http://www.sdsg.org/wp-content/uploads/2011/06/ICMM_Indigenous_Peoples_and_Mining_GPG1.pdf

IHRB [Institute for Human Rights and Business] [Internet]. 2009. Business, human rights and the right to water: Challenges, dilemmas and opportunities: Roundtable consultative report (Draft); [cited 2012 Dec 23]. Available from: http://www.institutehrb.org/pdf/Draft_Report-Business_Human_Rights_and_Water.pdf

IHRB [Internet]. 2012. The "State of Play" of human rights due diligence: Anticipating the next five years; [cited 2012 Dec 23]. Available from: http://www.ihrb.org/pdf/The_State_of_Play_of_Human_Rights_Due_Diligence.pdf

International Finance Corporation [Internet]. 2012. IFC Performance Standards on Environmental and Social Sustainability. Washington, DC: International Finance Corporation, [cited 2013 Jan 3]. Available from: http://www1.ifc.org/wps/wcm/connect/c8f524004a73daeca09afdf998895a12/IFC_Performance_Standards.pdf?MOD=AJPERES

International Labour Organization [Internet]. 1998. ILO Declaration on Fundamental Principles and Rights at Work and its Follow-up [Adopted by the International Labour Conference at its Eighty-sixth Session, Geneva, 18 June 1998 (Annex revised 15 June 2010)]; [cited 2013 Jan 3]. Available from: http://www.ilo.org/declaration/thedeclaration/textdeclaration/lang–en/index.htm

International Organization for Standardization. 2010. ISO 26000 Guidance on Social Responsibility. Geneva: International Organization for Standardization.

IPIECA. in press. Preliminary guidance on integrating human rights into impact assessment in the oil and gas industry. London Joint IPIECA-DIHR Project

João E, Vanclay F, den Broeder L. 2011. Emphasising enhancement in all forms of impact assessment: introduction to a special issue. Impact Assess Proj Appraisal. 29(3):170–180.

Kemp D. 2011. Understanding the organizational context. In: Vanclay F, Esteves AM, editors. New Directions in Social Impact Assessment: Conceptual and Methodological Advances. Cheltenham: Edward Elgar. p. 20–37.

Kemp D, Bond CJ, Franks DM, Cote C. 2010a. Mining, water and human rights: making the connection. J Clean Prod. 18(15):1553–1562.

Kemp D, Keenan J, Gronow J. 2010b. Strategic resource or ideal source? discourse, organizational change and CSR. J Organ Change Manage. 23(5):578–594.

Kinley D, Chambers R. 2006. The UN human rights norms for corporations: The private implications of public international law. Hum Rights Law Rev. 6(3):447–497.

Lahiri-Dutt K, Ahmad N. 2011. Considering gender in social impact assessment. In: Vanclay F, Esteves AM, editors. New Directions in Social Impact Assessment: Conceptual and Methodological Advances. Cheltenham: Edward Elgar. p. 117–137.

Maassarani TF, Drakos MT, Pajkowska J. 2007. Extracting corporate responsibility: Towards a human rights impact assessment. Cornell Int Law J. 40:135–169.

MacNaughton G, Hunt P. 2011. A human rights-based approach to social impact assessment. In: Vanclay F, Esteves AM, editors. New Directions in Social Impact Assessment: Conceptual and Methodological Advances. Cheltenham: Edward Elgar. p. 355–368.

McBeth A. 2008. Crushed by an Anvil: A case study on responsibility for human rights in the extractive sector. Yale Hum Rights Dev Law J. 11:127–166.

Morrison J, Vermijs D. 2011. The "State of Play" of Human Rights Due Diligence: Anticipating the next five years. Volume One: General Overview. London: Institute for Human Rights and Business.

MOSOP (Movement for the Survival of the Ogoni People) [Internet]. 1991. Ogoni Bill of Rights, [cited 2013 Jan 3]. Available from: http://www.mosop.org/ogoni_bill_of_rights.html

Narula S. 2006. The right to food: Holding global actors accountable under international law. Colum J Transnat Law. 44:691.

Newell P, Wheeler J, editors. 2006. Rights, Resources and the Politics of Accountability. London: Zed Books.

Nolin C, Stephens J. 2010. "We have to protect the investors": Development & Canadian mining companies in Guatemala. J Rural Community Dev. 5(3):37–70.

Obi CI. 1997. Globalisation and local resistance: The case of the Ogoni versus Shell. New Polit Econ. 2(1):137–148.

O'Faircheallaigh C. in press. Women's absence, women's power: Indigenous women and negotiations with mining companies in Australia and Canada. Ethnic Racial Stud. DOI:10.1080/01419870.2012.655752

On Common Ground Consultants Inc [Internet]. 2010. Human Rights Assessment of Goldcorp's Marlin Mine. Vancouver, BC, Canada: On Common Ground Consultants Inc [cited 2013 Jan 3]. Available from: http://www.hria-guatemala.com/en/MarlinHumanRights.htm.

Risse M. 2009. Securing human rights intellectually: Philosophical inquiries about the universal declaration. HKS Faculty Research Working Paper Series RWP09-024, John F. Kennedy School of Government, Harvard University

Rio Tinto [Internet]. 2012. Community agreements guidance; [cited 2013 Jan 3]. Available from: http://www.riotinto.com/documents/Community_agreements_guidance_2012_2014.pdf

Ruggie J. 2007. Business and human rights: The evolving international agenda. Am J Int Law. 101(4):819–840.

Ruggie J. 2008. Promotion and protection of all human rights, civil, political, economic, social and cultural rights, including the right to development – protect, respect and remedy: A framework for business and human rights report of the special representative of the secretary-general on the issue of human rights and transnational corporations and other business enterprises, John Ruggie. UN Doc. A/HRC/8/5

Ruggie J. 2010. Report of the special representative of the UN secretary-general on the issue of human rights, and transnational corporations and other business enterprises. Business and human rights: Further steps towards the operationalization of the "protect, respect and remedy" framework. 9 April. UN Doc. A/HRC/14/27

Ruggie J. 2011. Report of the special representative of the secretary-general on the issue of human rights and transnational corporations and other business enterprises, John Ruggie. Guiding Principles on Business and Human Rights: Implementing the United Nations "Protect, Respect and Remedy" Framework. United Nations Human Rights Council, Seventeenth session, Agenda item 3. 21 March. UN Doc. A/HRC/17/31

SOMO [Internet]. 2012. How to use the UN Guiding Principles on Business and Human Rights in company research and advocacy. Amsterdam: SOMO (Centre for Research on Multinational Corporations), [cited 2013 Jan 3]. Available from: http://somo.nl/publications-en/Publication_3899/

Srinivasan B, Mehta L. 2003. Assessing gender impacts. In: Becker H, Vanclay F, editors. The International Handbook of Social Impact Assessment: Conceptual and Methodological Advances. Cheltenham: Edward Elgar. p. 161–178.

United Nations [Internet]. 2010. The UN "Protect, Respect and Remedy" framework for business and human rights; [cited 2013 Jan 3]. Available from: http://198.170.85.29/Ruggie-protect-respect-remedy-framework.pdf

United Nations. 2011. Guiding principles on business and human rights: Implementing the United Nations "Protect, Respect and Remedy" framework. United Nations Human Rights Council, UN Doc. HR/PUB/11/04

United Nations General Assembly [Internet]. 1948. Universal declaration of human rights; [cited 2013 Jan 3]. Available from: http://www.un.org/en/documents/udhr/

United Nations General Assembly [Internet]. 1966a. International covenant on civil and political rights; [cited 2013 Jan 3]. Available from: http://www2.ohchr.org/english/law/ccpr.htm

United Nations General Assembly [Internet]. 1966b. International covenant on economic, social and cultural rights; [cited 2013 Jan 3]. Available from: http://www2.ohchr.org/english/law/cescr.htm

United Nations General Assembly [Internet]. 1993. Vienna declaration and programme of action, as adopted by the world conference on human rights on 25 June 1993 UN doc. A/CONF/157/23; [cited 2013 Jan 3]. Available from: http://www.unhchr.ch/huridocda/huridoca.nsf/(symbol)/a.conf.157.23.en

United Nations General Assembly. 2010. 64/292. The human right to water and sanitation. UN Doc. A/RES/64/292

United Nations Global Compact [Internet]. 2011. United Nations. Guiding Principles on Business and Human Rights: Implementing the United Nations "Protect, Respect and Remedy" Framework; [cited 2013 Feb 26]. Available from: http://www.ohchr.org/Documents/Publications/GuidingPrinciplesBusinessHR_EN.pdf

United Nations Human Rights Council [Internet]. 2011. Special representative of the secretary-general on human rights and transnational corporation and other business enterprises; [cited 2013 Dec 23]. Available from: http://www.ohchr.org/EN/Issues/Business/Pages/SRSGTransCorpIndex.aspx

United Nations Office for the High Commissioner on Human Rights [Internet]. 2011. The corporate responsibility to respect human rights: An interpretive guide; [cited 2013 Feb 26]. Available from: http://www.unglobalcompact.org/docs/issues_doc/human_rights/Resources/CR_Respect_HR_Interpretive_Guide.pdf

Vanclay F. 2002. Conceptualising social impacts. Environ Impact Assess Rev. 22(3):183–211.

Vanclay F. 2003. International principles for social impact assessment. Impact Assess Proj Appraisal. 21(1):5–12.

Vanclay F. 2004. The triple bottom line and impact assessment: How do TBL, EIA, SIA, SEA and EMS relate to each other? J Env Assmt Pol Mgmt. 6(3):265–288.

Vanclay F. 2006. Principles for social impact assessment: A critical comparison between the international and US documents. Environ Impact Assess Rev. 26(1):3–14.

Vanclay F. 2012. The potential application of social impact assessment in integrated coastal zone management. Ocean & Coast Manage. 68:149–156.

Vanclay F, Esteves AM. 2011. Current issues and trends in social impact assessment. In: Vanclay F, Esteves AM, editors. New Directions in Social Impact Assessment: Conceptual and Methodological Advances. Cheltenham: Edward Elgar. p. 3–19.

Watson G, Tamir I, Kemp B. 2013. Human rights impact assessment in practice: Oxfam's application of a community-based approach. Impact Assess Proj Appraisal. 31(2):118–127.

Welch CE. 1995. The Ogoni and Self-Determination: Increasing Violence in Nigeria. J Mod Afr Stud. 33(4):635–650.

Wettstein F. 2012. Silence as complicity: Elements of a corporate duty to speak out against the violation of human rights.. Bus Ethic Quart. 22(1):37–61.

Wheeler D, Fabig H, Boele R. 2002. Paradoxes and dilemmas for stakeholder responsive firms in the extractive sector: lessons from the case of Shell and the Ogoni. J Bus Ethics. 39(3):297–318.

Wright M [Internet]. 2008. Corporations and human rights: A survey of the scope and patterns of alleged corporate-related human rights abuse. Working Paper No. 44, Corporate Social Responsibility Initiative, Havard Kennedy School; [cited 2013 Jan 3]. Available from: http://www.hks.harvard.edu/m-rcbg/CSRI/publications/workingpaper_44_Wright.pdf

Human rights, Indigenous peoples and the concept of Free, Prior and Informed Consent

Philippe Hanna and Frank Vanclay*

Department of Cultural Geography, Faculty of Spatial Sciences, University of Groningen, PO Box 800, 9700AV, Groningen, The Netherlands

> The human right to self-determination is enacted in various international treaties and conventions. In order to facilitate self-determination, it is necessary to provide Indigenous peoples with opportunities to participate in decision-making and project development. The obligation for governments and companies to engage impacted communities is recognized in international law, especially with the principle of 'Free, Prior and Informed Consent', which is outlined in the United Nations Declaration on the Rights of Indigenous Peoples and in the International Labour Organization Convention 169. The encounter between human rights, Indigenous peoples and mining and other extractive industries is discussed, especially as it is has played out in Brazil. We recommend that companies should fully endorse and respect these internationally recognized human rights, including self-determination, even where not required by national or local legislation. We also discuss the relationship between Free, Prior and Informed Consent and Impacts and Benefits Agreements.
>
> **Keywords:** social impact assessment; right to have rights; social licence to operate; corporate social responsibility; human rights impact assessment

Introduction

This paper discusses various contemporary issues surrounding human rights, Indigenous peoples and their relationship with the extractive industries, focusing on the Brazilian context. In particular, the concept of 'Free, Prior and Informed Consent' (FPIC) is detailed. A major demand of Indigenous peoples facing development projects likely to impact their livelihoods (e.g. mines, dams) is to be able to have a say about whether and how the project should proceed. In effect, this demand has been provided for with the provision of FPIC. However, the practical implementation of FPIC is often very far short of the ideal.

FPIC "recognizes indigenous peoples' inherent and prior rights to their lands and resources and respects their legitimate authority to require that third parties enter into an equal and respectful relationship with them based on the principle of informed consent. Procedurally, free, prior and informed consent requires processes that allow and support meaningful choices by indigenous peoples about their development path" (UN Sub-Commission on the Promotion and Protection of Human Rights 2004, p. 5). FPIC is intrinsically connected to the idea of self-determination, which basically argues that 'human beings, individually and as groups, are equally entitled to be in control of their own destinies, and to live within governing institutional orders that are devised accordingly' (Anaya 2009, p. 187). As stated in the Charter of the United Nations (United Nations 1945) and in Article 1 of the International Covenant on Economic, Social and Cultural Rights (UN General Assembly 1966), self-determination is to be provided to 'all peoples'.

The history of the relationship between the human rights discourse and Indigenous peoples is described, including a discussion of the anthropological contribution to this topic, particularly in the context of how it has played out in Brazil. In the first section of this paper, the process of recognizing human rights for Indigenous peoples as collective rights is described. The activities of companies and development agencies in relation to this issue are presented in the second section. In the third section, the concept of FPIC and its origins are described. Recommendations for companies wishing to respect human rights, particularly towards Indigenous peoples, are provided in the conclusion.

The Indigenous peoples' struggle for the 'right to have rights'

'Human rights are commonly understood as inalienable fundamental rights to which a person is inherently entitled simply because she or he is a human being' (Sepúlveda et al. 2004, p. 3). These rights, which are considered to be indivisible (apply equally to everyone) and inalienable (always apply and cannot be voided or extinguished), include the right to life, property, health, education, free association, among others (Sepúlveda et al. 2004). Human rights are intended to be universal, 'without distinction of any kind, such as race, colour, sex, language, religion, political or other opinion, national or social origin, property, birth or other status' (UN General Assembly 1948a, Article 2). However, Indigenous peoples still experience unequal access to human rights and systematic ethnic discrimination (Cobo 1986; Stavenhagen 2009; ILO 2012). They face higher levels of infant mortality and fare worse on most health indicators when compared with non-Indigenous groups (Stavenhagen 2003; Montenegro & Stephens 2006; Gracey & King 2009), a situation often described as the 'fourth world' (Dyck 1985; Wright 1988; Watkins 2005). Anaya (2004) classifies it as a dual discrimination – there is denial of access to land, basic resources and services, leading to difficulties in sustaining

---

*Corresponding author. Email: frank.vanclay@rug.nl

© 2013 IAIA

Box 1. Selection of the key international agreements that address Indigenous rights

Charter of the United Nations (1945) – Article 1, Clause 2 articulates 'the principle of equal rights and self-determination of peoples', which is still one of the major demands of Indigenous peoples (United Nations 1945).

Universal Declaration on Human Rights (1948) – This declaration addresses several universal rights, which also apply to Indigenous peoples, such as the right to life, property, health, education and free association, among others (UN General Assembly 1948a).

Convention on the Prevention and Punishment of the Crime of Genocide (1948) – Article 2 defines genocide as 'acts committed with intent to destroy, in whole or in part, a national, ethnical, racial or religious group'. Indigenous peoples historically were and still are targets of genocide, perpetrated in different ways by various national governments and racist groups (UN General Assembly 1948b).

UN Convention on the Elimination of All Forms of Racial Discrimination (1965) – This convention promotes the elimination of racial discrimination against ethnic groups, including Indigenous peoples (UN General Assembly 1965).

International Covenant on Economic, Social and Cultural Rights (1966, entered into force in 1976) – Article 1 of this UN covenant states that 'all peoples have the right to self-determination', and thus to 'freely determine their political status and freely pursue their economic, social and cultural development' (UN General Assembly 1966).

Indigenous and Tribal Peoples Convention (International Labour Organization C169 (1989) – This convention is a revision of the 1957 Indigenous and Tribal Populations Convention (ILO C107). Although C169 has been ratified by only 20 countries to date, it is the most important, legally binding international document about Indigenous rights. It promotes rights in different areas (e.g. education, health and land). It requires governments to consult Indigenous peoples regarding any administrative or legislative measures that affect them directly, and to guarantee that Indigenous peoples can participate in the process of decision-making (ILO 1989, Article 6).

World Bank Operational Directive 4.20 (1991) – This Operational Directive regulates how borrowers from the World Bank should proceed when their projects affect Indigenous peoples (World Bank 1991).

Declaration on the Rights of Persons Belonging to National or Ethnic Religious and Linguistic Minorities (1992) – The main provision of this UN Declaration is stated in Article 4, which require states to take measures to ensure that 'minorities may exercise fully and effectively their human rights and fundamental freedoms without any discrimination and in full equality before the law' (UN General Assembly 1992a).

Rio Declaration on Environment and Development (1992) – This Declaration is a product of the United Nations Conference on Environment and Development (or Earth Summit) held in Rio de Janeiro in 1992. Principle 22 establishes the crucial role of Indigenous peoples in environmental management because of their traditional knowledge (UN General Assembly 1992b).

Convention on Biological Diversity (1992) – Like the Rio Declaration, this Convention was signed at the Earth Summit. It recognizes the role of Indigenous peoples in promoting biodiversity through their traditional knowledge (UNEP 1992).

Vienna Declaration and Programme of Action (1993) – Article 1.20 outlined some basic principles, while Article 1.28 called for the establishment of a Working Group to prepare a Declaration on the Rights of Indigenous Peoples (which was not finalized until 2007). Article 1.2 states that 'The World Conference on Human Rights considers the denial of the right of self-determination as a violation of human rights and underlines the importance of the effective realization of this right' (UN General Assembly 1993).

UNESCO Universal Declaration on Cultural Diversity (2001) – 'The defence of cultural diversity is an ethical imperative, inseparable from respect for human dignity. It implies a commitment to human rights and fundamental freedoms, in particular the rights of persons belonging to minorities and those of indigenous peoples' (UNESCO 2001, Article 4).

Equator Principles (2003) – A voluntary set of standards developed by several major banks for assessing and managing risks related to development projects. Indigenous peoples are considered to be a stakeholder needing to be fully considered (Equator Principles Association 2003).

World Bank Operational Policy (OP) and Bank Procedure (BP) 4.10 (2005) – The OP/BP 4.10 replaces OD 4.20 for investment projects financed by the World Bank that affect Indigenous peoples (World Bank 2005).

International Finance Corporation (IFC) Performance Standard 7 (2006, updated in 2012) – IFC Performance Standards (PS) are similar to World Bank safeguard policies, but are adapted to be applicable to IFC borrowers. PS7 is related to Indigenous peoples and articulates specific procedures for projects that affect them (IFC 2006, 2012).

UN Declaration on the Rights of Indigenous Peoples (UNDRIP) (2007) – This Declaration addresses a large range of rights of Indigenous peoples. It affirms that governments should obtain 'free, prior and informed consent' from Indigenous peoples about any project that may affect their livelihoods (UN General Assembly 2007a, Articles 10, 19, 29 and 32).

traditional ways of life; in addition, there is systematic discrimination that arises especially when Indigenous peoples attempt to participate in the dominant society.

The Indigenous peoples' struggle to ensure respect for their human rights started with the demand for the 'right to have rights' (Stavenhagen 2003, linking to Arendt 1951), and has culminated in the drafting and endorsement of several international conventions and agreements that were conceived to guarantee the access of Indigenous peoples to human rights. A list of the various international documents that directly or indirectly address the rights of Indigenous peoples is provided in Box 1.

It is important to clarify that these documents do not provide Indigenous peoples with any 'extra' human rights that are not also accorded to non-Indigenous persons; nevertheless these documents are intended to guarantee that Indigenous peoples have equal access to human rights (Anaya 2009). However, as presently understood in a legal sense, FPIC is currently provided exclusively for Indigenous and other 'traditional peoples', such as the descendants of escaped slaves (*quilombolas* in Brazil) and tribal peoples in Africa, although there is a push to widen the application of FPIC (Goodland 2004; Hill et al. 2010; Vanclay & Esteves 2011). FPIC is not a 'right' per se, but a mechanism to ensure progress towards the right of self-determination for Indigenous Peoples (Anaya 2009). Even though FPIC itself may not be a right, Indigenous peoples do have the right to be consulted on issues that affect their lives, which we will refer to as the right to FPIC.

The process of establishing this international body of law (Box 1) has been controversial from the beginning. Anthropologists in general – as reflected in an American Anthropological Association (AAA) statement of 1947 (AAA, The Executive Board 1947) – were critical of the concept of universal human rights, which they considered to be a Western ethnocentric concept (Messer 1993; Preis 1996; Riles 2006). The major arguments of the AAA statement were that rights are culturally relative and that Western notions of progress should not be imposed on other cultures. Another reason that led to anthropologists boycotting the international human rights agenda was the predominantly legal approach that prevailed, allied to an exclusive focus on individuals rather than collective groups. However, with the Indigenous struggle for rights in the 1980s, anthropologists were addressing human rights through a sociocultural and political rather than legal framework (Messer 1993). They advocated for collective rights. This led to a change in the perspective of both sides, as the international discourse on human rights has now accepted the idea of collective rights and has even accepted 'some form of weak cultural relativism; that is, on a fundamental universality of basic human rights, tempered by a recognition of the possible need for limited cultural variations. Basic human rights are, to use an appropriately paradoxical phrase, relatively universal' (Donelly 1984, p. 419).

The anthropological perspective has also broadened, particularly around the formulations of social transformation and the anthropology of development (Messer 1993). In its 1999 Statement about Human Rights, the AAA embraced the human rights discourse; however, it pointed to the need for advocating for collective and cultural rights and for tolerance across different cultures (Messer 1993; AAA 1999; Engle 2001; Riles 2006). Wright (1988) discussed the dilemmas anthropology found itself in during those decades, as the native peoples it studied were facing a range of problems, as described above, and often their very survival was in question. Although Indigenous peoples played a major role themselves (Miranda 2010), Wright identified ways in which anthropologists were engaged in advocacy for Indigenous peoples. One way was through influencing international organizations and international law; and some positive results have occurred, such as the approval of the UNDRIP by a large number of countries, something that can be considered to be a major victory for Indigenous peoples, even if it was a long time coming.

The debate around collective and cultural rights was very important in the lead-up to and the drafting of the UNDRIP, as these rights clashed with the Western concept of individual rights (Clinton 1990; Anaya 2004). As explained by Wiessner (2011, p. 124):

> one of the major objections to the novel rights of indigenous peoples has been that they are largely rights of collectivities, not individuals. Thus, they appear to sit uneasily with the traditional human rights regime, which in the eyes of many is constructed around the interests and concerns of individual human beings.

The human right to self-determination is provided for in several international instruments. Many countries were reluctant to recognize the collective right of Indigenous peoples to self-determination because they feared it could threaten state sovereignty and lead to an escalation in claims for independence by Indigenous peoples (Engle 2011). A complicating factor is that there is a difference between internal and external self-determination. External self-determination refers to the aspiration of an ethnic group to claim statehood, sovereignty or secession, while internal self-determination provides some level of autonomy to operate within the existing state (Sterio 2009). The UNDRIP provides only for internal self-determination, which is comprehended by Engle (2011, p. 148) as a 'collective human rights demand rather than a claim for statehood'.

Another important argument towards collective human rights is that an individual cannot exercise their culture alone (Anaya 2004). This leads us to the question of cultural rights, which also became an important claim and one of the major strategies of Indigenous rights advocates since the 1990s (Engle 2011). Cultural rights, that is, the right of a particular ethnic group to maintain its own culture, are broad. For example, for Indigenous peoples, access to land and natural resources are fundamental to exercise and reproduce their culture. Thus, the human right to culture necessarily includes rights to land and its resources (Wiessner 2011).

The UNDRIP does not establish any new rights for Indigenous peoples that are not already provided by other international human rights instruments; however, it synthesizes how these rights need to be applied as a map of action for human rights policies towards Indigenous peoples (Stavenhagen 2009). Several authors (e.g. Royo 2009; Stavenhagen 2009; Wiessner 2011), as well most of the states voting in favour of the UNDRIP, clearly comprehend the Declaration as a non-binding legal instrument, or 'soft-law', which does not require ratification, and for which non-compliance by its signatories would not result in any sanctions. Burger (2009) argued that the Declaration brought no substantial change to what already existed, unless states would make changes to their own legislation and, above all, have the political will to do so. However, various authors (e.g. Anaya & Williams 2001; Royo 2009; Stavenhagen 2009) expect that, with time, full compliance with the UNDRIP and related instruments is likely as it will become part of customary international law (cf. Bradley & Goldsmith 1997), and thus be fully applied.

The role of corporations

Most transnational corporations in the extractives sector have adopted Corporate Social Responsibility standards for regulating their activities, sometimes including specific policies relating to human rights and/or Indigenous peoples. Despite the UNDRIP and Corporate Social Responsibility standards, human rights violations towards Indigenous peoples keep occurring, and the direct and indirect consequences of resources extraction by companies in or nearby Indigenous lands remain one of the major problems that Indigenous peoples continue to face (Stavenhagen 2003; ILO 2012; Verdum 2012).

Professor John Ruggie, the Special Representative of the UN Secretary-General on Human Rights and Transnational Corporations and Other Business Enterprises between 2005 and 2011, determined that companies should respect internationally recognized human rights, even if it was not required by host governments. In the Guiding Principles, Ruggie (2011) specified the minimum standards that companies should follow, specifically those expressed in the International Bill of Human Rights and the principles concerning fundamental rights set out in the International Labour Organization's Declaration on Fundamental Principles and Rights at Work. The right to self determination is thus included in the minimum standards. The lack of regulation or enforcement in national legislation to ensure that transnational companies comply with these standards is what Ruggie called a 'governance gap' (B&HRI 2010), which provides opportunities for companies to perform 'wrongful acts' without any legal consequences. A similar phenomenon is described by Stavenhagen (2009, p. 367) as the 'implementation gap between laws and practical reality'. This situation can be worsened in hybrid state–corporate enterprises where confluences of interest lead to conflicts of interest and role confusion, as highlighted by Miranda (2007, p. 139):

> Arguably, the most significant violations of indigenous peoples' land rights occur in the context of a hybrid state–corporate enterprise, where through a collaborative legal arrangement, a state effectively delegates many of its human rights responsibilities toward indigenous peoples to a joint corporate actor.

The governance gap is that, in these circumstances, the state fails in its duty to protect, partly because there frequently is no mechanism to verify compliance with human rights responsibilities. Also, there is no entity or legal instrument at the international level to enforce companies to comply. As mentioned earlier, the UNDRIP is not legally binding. Many authors have exposed a vast number of cases where Indigenous rights are threatened by industry activities (e.g. Colchester 2010; Haalboom 2012; Coumans 2012). Miranda (2007) warns of the need to create accountability mechanisms to ensure that companies respect the internationally recognized rights of Indigenous peoples.

A solution that has been proposed to address and prevent human rights violations in the development of large projects is to conduct a human rights impact assessment (HRIA) prior to project implementation. MacNaughton and Hunt (2011, p. 362) define HRIA as 'a process of predicting the potential consequences of a proposed policy, program or project on the enjoyment of human rights'. Maassarani et al. (2007) see the potential of HRIA to contribute to the progressive realization of human rights, if it is integrated into the early stages of company decision-making processes. The UN Global Compact (2011) created a Guidance Tool for companies, based on Ruggie's Guiding Principles (Ruggie 2011). The first step of their approach is to identify potential violations of human rights throughout the company production chain, including taking into account indirect violations, such as from suppliers or contractors. This can be achieved using the techniques typically used in HRIA and social impact assessment (SIA) (Esteves & Vanclay 2009; Esteves et al. 2012. After assessing the impacts, the Global Compact Guidance Tool emphasizes the need to involve the top management of the company in order to have a real commitment to respecting human rights. In addition to management support, training is needed for employees and contractors. Grievance mechanisms for affected communities and performance indicators are necessary to monitor if human rights are being respected, and to check whether improvements are being made (B&HRI 2010). This approach is well aligned with Messer's (1993) proposal, where anthropologists were seen as having a role in preventing, rather than simply reporting, human rights abuses in contexts of inter-ethnic conflict.

Human rights violations towards Indigenous peoples in Brazil often occur in the development of large projects, particularly mines and dams sponsored by Brazilian state–corporate enterprises. These situations can be characterized as contexts of inter-ethnic conflict, or a form of 'internal colonialism' (Cardoso de Oliveira 1978). This arises partly because of the perception of many Latin American elites that Indigenous cultures are 'backwards', and the lack of respect they have for Indigenous peoples, often believing that greater attention to Indigenous peoples' rights would slow down the development of the nation. This context of class struggle or 'inter-ethnic friction' (Cardoso de Oliveira 1978) has led to several conflicts, including deaths, violence and protracted legal battles (Coelho dos Santos 1981; Miranda 2007; Jampolsky 2012). The 'national interest' is often advocated as a reason to 'legitimately' violate Indigenous rights, especially in large development projects. This reason was even stated in a recent and controversial government act, Ordinance 303 (*Portaria 303 da AGU*), which was enacted on 16 July 2012 and states: 'the enjoyment of the riches of the soil, rivers and lakes existing in indigenous lands (art. 231, §2 of the Constitution) can be relativized whenever, as in art. 231, 6°, of the Constitution, there is relevant public interest of the Union, in the form of a supplementary law' (Brasil 2012, Article 1.1). Following protests, this Ordinance has been suspended, but not revoked (Mongabay 2012).

Another example, which has also been the subject of much controversy, is the planned Belo Monte dam in the State of Pará, Brazil. If built, Belo Monte would be the third largest dam in the world, would displace between 20,000 and 40,000 people, and would impact, directly or indirectly, on some 10 different Indigenous groups (Jampolsky 2012). The major argument against the construction of the Belo Monte dam (and other large projects) is the lack of genuine commitment to the principle of FPIC by the developers, and consequently a denial of the right to self-determination, arguably the most violated Indigenous right in the Brazilian development context (ILO 2012).

Free, prior and informed consent

It is hard to determine when the term 'Free, Prior and Informed Consent' first appeared, but the literature suggests that the FPIC idea arose in the mid 1980s as part of the Indigenous peoples' struggle for self-determination (Colchester & Ferrari 2007). Goodland (2004) concurs that FPIC appeared in the 1980s, particularly related to cases of involuntary displacement of Indigenous peoples. The term 'Free and Informed Consent', a precursor to the current concept of FPIC, first appeared in the International Labour Organization (ILO) *Convention Concerning Indigenous and Tribal Peoples in Independent Countries*, C169/1989. The concept has developed over time, with Vanclay and Esteves (2011, pp. 6–7) describing it as follows:

In both the formal and more general utilization of FPIC, each word contributes meaning to the concept. **Free**, meaning that there must be no coercion, intimidation or manipulation by companies or governments, and that should a community say 'no' there must be no retaliation. **Prior**, meaning that consent should be sought and received before any activity on community land is commenced and that sufficient time is provided for adequate consideration by any affected communities. **Informed**, meaning that there is full disclosure by project developers of their plans in the language acceptable to the affected communities, and that each community has enough information to have a reasonable understanding of what those plans will likely mean for them, including of the social impacts they will experience. **Consent**, meaning that communities have a real choice, that they can say yes if there is a good flow of benefits and development opportunities to them, or they can say no if they are not satisfied with the deal, and that there is a workable mechanism for determining whether there is widespread consent in the community as a whole and not just a small elite group within the community.

The right to FPIC is intrinsically linked to the right to self-determination, which is articulated in the 1945 Charter of the United Nations: 'To develop friendly relations among nations based on respect for the principle of equal rights and self-determination of peoples, and to take other appropriate measures to strengthen universal peace' (United Nations 1945, Article 1). Later, the UNDRIP would refer specifically to the rights of Indigenous peoples to self-determination (UN General Assembly 2007a). This right is about having the ability to choose to live accordingly to a group's institutions and traditional organization, and above all, by its own will. The right to self-determination may be seen as the basis or inspiration by which the right to FPIC was elaborated and claimed by Indigenous peoples, scholars and activists (Page 2004).

FPIC is also related to the concept of ethnodevelopment, which was elaborated by Stavenhagen (1985) around the same time as FPIC emerged, and was adopted into Brazilian law in 2004 (Resolução CONDRAF no. 44, Brasil 2004). Ethnodevelopment proposes that development should be defined according to each cultural context, giving the right to communities to decide over their own future and the use of their resources, as guided by their own cultural frameworks, which may differ from the Western notion of economic development (Stavenhagen 1985). Of course, inside the same community there may be political and inter-generational conflicts, with different perspectives for development. Even despite these possible divergences, ethnodevelopment is defined by the community itself, by its own cultural framework.

The terms self-determination, ethnodevelopment and FPIC are now embedded into international and national laws and have been incorporated into the discourse of Indigenous peoples when claiming their rights (e.g. Brasil 2004; Tauli-Corpuz et al. 2010; Hill et al. 2010). As previously mentioned, the ILO addresses it in its Convention 169, which states in Article 6(1):

governments shall: (a) consult the peoples concerned, through appropriate procedures and in particular through their representative institutions, whenever consideration is being given to legislative or administrative measures which may affect them directly; (b) establish means by which these peoples can freely participate, to at least the same extent as other sectors of the population, at all levels of decision-making in elective institutions and administrative and other bodies responsible for policies and programmes which concern them. (ILO 1989, p. 4)

According to MacKay (2004), the ILO Convention 169 does not require 'consent', although Article 6 obliges governments to 'consult' Indigenous peoples. Article 7(1) states that: 'The peoples concerned shall have the right to decide their own priorities for the process of development as it affects their lives, beliefs, institutions and spiritual well-being and the lands they occupy or otherwise use, and to exercise control, to the extent possible, over their own economic, social and cultural development'. This could be regarded as being a right to FPIC.

Tugendhat et al. (2009) consider that the ILO 169 is the only legally binding document regarding the rights of Indigenous peoples. Besides this Convention, the UNDRIP is the most referred to international document regarding the Indigenous right to FPIC, despite the fact that a UN Declaration does not have the same legal status as an ILO Convention. The Declaration is not legally binding, while the Convention provisions can be enforced in court. This may be one of the reasons why there are only 20 signatories to ILO Convention 169, but the UNDRIP was endorsed in 2007 by a vote of 143 countries in favour, 11 abstaining (Azerbaijan, Bangladesh, Bhutan, Burundi, Colombia, Georgia, Kenya, Nigeria, Russian Federation, Samoa and Ukraine), and four against (Australia, Canada, New Zealand and the United States). The four countries that voted against the declaration argued that 'they could not support it because of concerns over provisions on self-determination, land and resources rights and, among others, language giving indigenous peoples a right of veto over national legislation and State management of resources' (UN General Assembly 2007b, p. 1). Between 2009 and 2010, the four opposing countries changed their position and are now signatories to the Declaration, along with two of the abstaining countries, Colombia and Samoa. Nevertheless, at their respective announcements of endorsement, Australia, Canada, the United States and New Zealand all emphasized that they did not consider UNDRIP to be a legally binding document, but rather an aspirational goal (Engle 2011; Wiessner 2011).

FPIC is addressed in several places in the UNDRIP. According to the Declaration, governments need to consult Indigenous peoples in order to obtain their consent about the following topics: relocation (Article 10), administrative measures that affect them (Article 19), the storage of hazardous materials inside Indigenous land (Article 29) and utilization of their resources, as stated in Article 32:

> States shall consult and cooperate in good faith with the indigenous peoples concerned through their own representative institutions in order to obtain their free and informed consent prior to the approval of any project affecting their lands or territories and other resources, particularly in connection with the development, utilization or exploitation of mineral, water or other resources. (UN General Assembly 2007a, p.12)

Some international entities that recognize the right to FPIC are the Inter-American Commission on Human Rights and the Inter-American Court of Human Rights (Linde 2009). The World Bank's position on FPIC, however, is very controversial. Despite recommendations from the World Commission on Dams and the World Bank's own Extractive Industry Review, after a very long debate and an arguably inadequate consultation with Indigenous organizations (Linde 2009; Cariño & Colchester 2010), the World Bank adopted a lower standard – that of 'free, prior, and informed *consultation* resulting in broad community support' – in their Operational Policy on Indigenous Peoples, OP 4.10 (World Bank 2005). OP 4.10 is criticized by Indigenous organizations, nongovernmental organizations, academics and activists because it does not clearly recognize FPIC, but instead proposes this dubious concept of 'FPICon' (free, prior and informed consultation) (Caruso et al. 2003; MacKay 2005; Griffiths 2005). Goodland (2004), however, argues that 'meaningful participation', as required by the World Bank, can lead to FPIC if applied in good faith.

The World Bank's adoption of FPICon gave a mandate to other agencies to adopt similar requirements, including the International Finance Corporation (IFC) in its Performance Standard 7 (PS7), which provides guidelines for engagement between Indigenous peoples and the companies/projects it finances (IFC 2006). However, the 2012 revision of PS7 recognized the right to FPIC in special circumstances, such as 'Impacts on Lands and Natural Resources Subject to Traditional Ownership or Under Customary Use', 'Relocation of Indigenous Peoples from Lands and Natural Resources Subject to Traditional Ownership or Under Customary Use' and for projects that impact 'Critical Cultural Heritage' (IFC 2012).

Another institution that has adopted a concept similar to FPICon is the International Council on Mining and Metals (ICMM), with its 'Community Development Toolkit' containing guidelines for mining companies to engage with communities. Regarding Indigenous peoples, it proposed that 'all development programs should be based on engaging and consulting with Indigenous Peoples in a fair, timely and culturally appropriate way throughout the project cycle' (ICMM 2012, p. 22). In an earlier document focused exclusively on Indigenous peoples and mining, the ICMM stated that it agreed with the 'free, prior and informed' elements of FPIC, but not with the 'consent' component. ICMM members are expected to engage in FPIC only where it is required by national legislation. Their argument is that the right of FPIC is not feasible at present owing to the difficulties in implementation and definition (ICMM 2010). The position ICMM is taking could lead to breaches of international human rights standards, as companies might only do the minimum necessary to meet the requirements of local legislation (Haalboom 2012), potentially failing to recognize the right to FPIC, and thus infringing the Indigenous right to self-determination.

Arguably, the Philippines and Australia (somewhat ironically given that Australia was one of four objectors to UNDRIP) were the first countries to require FPIC or consent in local legislation (MacKay 2004). In the Philippines, the right to FPIC is provided by the Indigenous Peoples' Rights Act of 1997 and is effected through the mediation of a government agency responsible for Indigenous peoples in the country (National Commission on Indigenous Peoples, NCIP). The Act defines FPIC as:

> Free and Prior Informed Consent – as used in this Act shall mean the consensus of all members of the ICCs/IPs [Indigenous Cultural Communities/Indigenous Peoples] to be determined in accordance with their respective customary laws and practices, free from any external

manipulation, interference and coercion, and obtained after fully disclosing the intent and scope of the activity, in a language and process understandable to the community. (Indigenous Peoples' Rights Act of 1997, section 3)

MacKay (2004) suggests that FPIC has been required (albeit implicitly) in the Northern Territory of Australia for more than 30 years through the Aboriginal Land Rights (Northern Territory) Act 1976. Since then, New South Wales, Queensland and some other states have adopted similar regulations. However, while FPIC may be inferred to apply (and consent is specifically mentioned), none of this legislation specifically mentions FPIC per se, but requires a mining entrepreneur to formalize 'consent' in an agreement with the Aboriginal 'traditional owners', usually mediated by a Land Council or similar body.

Cariño and Colchester (2010) note that Bolivia, Venezuela, Colombia and Guyana adopted national laws recognizing the Indigenous right to FPIC and that New Zealand requires it for mining activities. In Venezuela, FPIC is implied in a law on biological diversity that also protects cultural diversity (Gupta 2002). In 2012 the Inter-American Court of Human Rights decided on a decade-long judicial battle, *Sarayaku v. Ecuador*, which was about rights over oil exploration in the Kichwa Sarayaku territory. With the Ecuadorian Government losing, this case can be considered an important legal precedent as it establishes a legal meaning on how and when FPIC should be applied (Amnesty International 2012).

Despite the fact that local law in many places requires FPIC, experience in the Philippines demonstrates that a regulatory process on its own is not enough to ensure that it is applied properly, as community consent has been manipulated through bribery or other coercion methods, as Cariño (2005, p. 39) informs:

> The experience of indigenous communities in the Philippines stands as a vehement reminder that surface level [i.e. superficial] change is not sufficient; despite progressive law that promises to involve indigenous communities in the future of their ancestral lands, the indigenous voice continues to be manipulated and ignored in the face of foreign owned mining firms. When industry interests clash with local interests, the former continues to prevail.

There is also the risk of FPIC becoming a box-ticking procedure made just to comply with local legislation, but with no real commitment to get a clear statement of consent from the impacted party. Cariño and Colchester (2010) call this kind of process the 'engineering of consent'. As shown in case of the Philippines, achieving FPIC might be done just to comply with government requirements, sometimes including the bribery of community leaders and government employees, in order to 'tick the box' of FPIC in the list of project requirements (Colchester & MacKay 2004; Cariño & Colchester 2010). According to Colchester and MacKay (2004, p. 26), 'extractive industries have consciously manipulated communities, introducing factionalism, dividing communities and promoting individuals, who may have no traditional authority as leaders, to represent the communities. The illusion of free, prior and informed consent is thus achieved by the exclusion of the majority of community members from effective participation in decision-making'.

Despite being a signatory to the ILO Convention 169 and the UNDRIP, the only legislation in Brazil that implies FPIC to any degree is the Brazilian Constitution of 1988, specifically Article 231 §3 (Brasil 1988). Even though not specifically referring to 'consent', it states that the use of water resources, potential for hydropower or mineral riches in Indigenous lands may only be exploited 'after hearing the communities involved'. However, there are no guidelines regarding how and when any consultation process must be applied. For that reason, in January 2012 a working group was formed by the government to develop and present a proposal for regulation (Verdum 2012), which at the time of finalizing our paper in early 2013 was yet to report.

In Brazil, mining can take place near Indigenous lands, but not inside their lands owing to regulatory restrictions. Because of this, various questions arise. For example, despite Indigenous peoples being directly affected by operations, where they are not the landowners of the actual mining lease, should their consent be required? Should the community have a veto power over the project? What defines consent, especially if the project is opposed by only a few community members?

In order to answer these questions, and notwithstanding our view that FPIC is not in itself a right but is in effect 'the right to be consulted', we believe, consistent with many others (e.g. Vanclay & Esteves 2011), that FPIC should be comprehended as a philosophy rather than a legal procedure. If operations affect Indigenous peoples' lives, they should have the right for their views to be considered and respected, regardless of the national legislation requirements. Cariño and Colchester (2010, p. 434) propose that "the spirit of FPIC is that development should become accountable to peoples' distinctive cultures, priorities, and unique paths to self-determination, not endanger their very survival". However, speaking about the practical operationalization of FPIC, Goodland (2004) suggests that consent should be regarded as the support from 51% or more of community members. However, this majority vote is a Western conception of democratic decision-making, and is not likely to be endorsed by many Indigenous political organizations, who, for example, depending on the ethnic group, may prefer that decisions be based on the elders' opinions or by reaching consensus between members (Bauman & Williams 2004; van Dam 2008).

Despite being recognized by international treaties, as at the time of writing in late 2012, only a small number of companies have made public statements of commitment to FPIC, including: Inmet, Newmont, Rio Tinto, Talisman and Xstrata (Voss & Greenspan 2012). Despite the expressed support of Talisman Oil for FPIC, Amazon Watch is criticizing them for their operations close to the Achuar Indigenous group on the border between Peru and Ecuador. Talisman alleges that they have community consent, although according to the nongovernmental organization, the Achuar oppose the project (Amazon Watch 2012).

This low level of corporate commitment to FPIC to date may be because companies might consider that their interests are threatened by recognition of an Indigenous community's right to FPIC. The argument provided is the same espoused by ICMM (2010), as mentioned earlier, for whom the consent part of FPIC was unclear and/or not feasible to be implemented in practice. Besides this argument, giving the power of veto to communities is seen as a menace that could tip the power balance in favour of communities and restrain possibilities for new ventures. Relations between companies and Indigenous communities are usually difficult, but that should not become a barrier to companies in adopting best practices and respecting internationally recognized human rights such as FPIC. In any case, we argue that when undertaken, FPIC can provide benefits to both sides. Companies that apply FPIC are likely to benefit from an improved social licence to operate and are likely to have a better public image than those who do not recognize the right to FPIC. Communities that enjoy their right of being informed, consulted and heard by the project proponents are able to provide positive feedback on project design, for example, that could contribute to cost savings. The enjoyment of this right also raises a community's confidence, as it becomes an important stakeholder during the whole project development process and puts it into a position that enables it to have a real opinion about the project's impacts and possible measures to avoid or mitigate these impacts. This could lead to simpler and cheaper solutions, as social impacts are identified at an earlier stage. Applying FPIC can also avoid conflicts with communities (De Echave 2010) and reduce costs and risks for companies (Davis & Franks 2011; Vanclay 2012).

Various authors suggest that the concept of FPIC should not be limited to Indigenous peoples, recommending its adoption to projects affecting all local communities (Goodland 2004; Hill et al. 2010; Vanclay & Esteves 2011; Langbroek & Vanclay 2012). According to Goodland (2004), we cannot advocate democracy only for some, leaving autocracy to the others. Thus, every affected community should have the right to be informed and to have its opinion on the developments that affect their lives fully considered. Useful tools for making the FPIC process more effective are SIA and HRIA, which can be perceived as the 'informed' component of FPIC, allowing both companies and communities to comprehend what the expected impacts are and, if they are acceptable to the community, the possible ways of avoiding or mitigating them. Vanclay and Esteves (2011) perceive that the FPIC and SIA processes are similar and that the basic steps for accomplishing them are fundamentally the same. Additionally, where there are unavoidable impacts, SIA can help ascertain what would be fair compensation to the community, and to formalize this in an Impacts and Benefits Agreement.

The relationship between FPIC and Impacts and Benefits Agreements

Impacts and Benefits Agreements (IBAs) are a form of community development agreement that communities negotiate with developers, usually without the mediation of government. They emerged in Canada and Australia as a way of formalizing the negotiations between extractives companies and Indigenous peoples. Earlier forms of arrangements failed to guarantee respect for Indigenous rights and/or their adequate participation in the process (O'Faircheallaigh 1999; O'Faircheallaigh & Corbett 2005). Before the IBA model, the social and environmental impacts of development projects on communities used to be addressed only through environmental impact assessment procedures, regulated by the government (Galbraith et al. 2007). Prno et al. (2010) consider that IBAs emerged as a community response to the 'business as usual' modus operandi that existed in Canada during the environmental impact assessment regime. IBAs have now become the standard model of negotiation between extractive companies and Indigenous peoples in Canada and Australia, and are being implemented in many other countries and contexts (O'Faircheallaigh 2010). In Brazil, although current laws forbid mineral extraction within Indigenous lands, a concept similar to IBA exists for where Indigenous peoples may be affected by developments close to their lands. Because of the context specificity and changing nature of IBAs, we endorse Caine and Krogman's (2010, p. 80) definition that IBAs are 'agreements that establish formal relationships between signatories, mitigate negative development impacts, and enhance positive development outcomes for Aboriginal communities'.

In the literature on the topic, IBAs are generally seen as positive tools for mitigating impacts, but some studies demonstrate that important issues, such as governance and implementation of the provisions, are often left out (Siebenmorgen 2009; O'Faircheallaigh 2010). Hitch (2006) also considers IBAs to be an innovative tool for promoting more equitable and sustainable development for all stakeholders, but suggests that, for IBAs to be successful in achieving their goals, it is crucial that companies have high levels of cultural sensitivity, apply participative and transparent approaches to decision making and work in collaboration with the communities. Similarly, O'Faircheallaigh (2010, p. 70) suggests that agreements can provide substantial benefits, but many issues need to be addressed, 'including confidentiality, Aboriginal support for projects, and Aboriginal access to judicial and regulatory systems. Also vital is the need to break down the barriers that often exist between processes for negotiating project agreements and broader processes for community planning and decision making'.

The existence of a signed IBA between a company and a community does not necessarily confirm that the conditions of FPIC were applied. For example, a signed agreement could be the result of coercion of various kinds (i.e. not free). Companies may not have acted in good faith by not revealing all relevant information and/or communities might not have understood the implications of what was going to happen (i.e. not informed). And quite often, agreements may have been finalized, and in some cases not even started, until after project activities had commenced (i.e. not prior). Thus the development of an IBA needs to be consistent with the philosophy of FPIC.

Because of potential future litigation (refer to the examples of human rights abuse in Kemp & Vanclay 2013), an issue for companies will be to ensure that they can establish into the future that FPIC was observed and fully applied. Although the mere existence of an IBA is not proof of FPIC (as discussed above), where IBAs are carefully written and document all the relevant details, it is likely that an IBA can establish that FPIC was observed. An IBA is an appropriate conclusion to an FPIC process.

conflict. However, companies need to be ready to listen and to accept 'no' as an answer sometimes, as not every community will be agreeable to accept all development projects affecting them, despite the potential benefits they might receive. Organizations (corporate and government) should not try to coerce communities into accepting a project. SIA and HRIA can be useful tools for ensuring that human rights are being respected in a company's projects and operations, if performed at an early stage and in a participatory manner. Companies that adopt the FPIC philosophy and fully implement it in practice, in addition to respecting the right of communities to participate in decisions that affect their lives, will probably benefit from reduced conflict, reduced likelihood of reputational damage, as well reduced risks and costs.

Conclusion

The concept of 'Free, Prior and Informed Consent' is a fundamental component of the Indigenous right to self-determination. Unfortunately, neither FPIC nor the right to self-determination are being respected in Brazil and many other countries. Violations of these rights are overlooked by governments, especially in the case of 'projects of national interest', and particularly in relation to Brazil's hybrid state–corporate enterprises. Violations can also happen when companies, as a box-ticking procedure, only do the absolute minimum required by environmental licensing processes and ignore international human rights standards.

FPIC should be taken seriously by companies that interface with Indigenous peoples. In order to achieve a legitimate social licence to operate and to refrain from violating human rights, companies need to respect FPIC, arguably with non-Indigenous as well as Indigenous communities. The right to self-determination is conceived as being applicable to all peoples (United Nations 1945), thus respecting FPIC in relation to all local communities would be complying with international human rights standards. Complying with FPIC should not be seen as being a voluntary measure that companies can choose to follow or not – it is necessary to ensure the self-determination of Indigenous peoples.

If companies are committed to fully respecting human rights, recognizing the right to FPIC, and actually implementing it, are important steps. The alleged difficulties in applying FPIC result from a lack of experience, with few initiatives so far. With good faith and qualified professionals, any company that chooses to adhere to FPIC, or is forced to by legislation, should be able to implement it. Also, there are now many handbooks available on how to implement FPIC, describing the successes and difficulties in different situations (e.g. Colchester and Ferrari 2007; Colchester 2008; Hill et al. 2010; Lehr and Smith 2010; Weitzner 2011; Persoon and Minter 2011). Therefore, although it can be considered as being difficult, as company–community relations usually are, it is not infeasible. In fact, relationships between companies and communities may become easier if FPIC is applied, as they will probably be based on trust instead of

References

AAA [Internet]. 1999. Declaration on anthropology and human rights. Arlington, VA: AAA; [cited 2012 Nov 8]. Available from: http://www.aaanet.org/about/Policies/statements/Declaration-on-Anthropology-and-Human-Rights.cfm

AAA, The Executive Board. 1947. Statement on human rights. Am Anthropol. 49(4):539–543.

Amazon Watch [Internet]. 2012. The Achuar and Talisman Energy. San Francisco, CA: Amazon Watch; [cited 2012 Nov 8]. Available from: http://amazonwatch.org/work/talisman

Amnesty International [Internet]. 2012. Ecuador: Inter-American Court ruling marks key victory for Indigenous Peoples. London: Amnesty International; [cited 2012 Nov 8]. Available from: http://www.amnesty.org/en/news/ecuador-inter-american-court-ruling-marks-key-victory-indigenous-peoples-2012-07-26

Anaya J. 2004. International human rights and Indigenous peoples: the move toward the multicultural state. Ariz J Int Comp L. 21:13–61.

Anaya J. 2009. The right of Indigenous peoples to self-determination in the post-declaration era. In: Chartres C, Stavenhagen R, editors. Making the declaration work: The United Nations Declaration on the Rights of Indigenous peoples. Copenhagen: International Work Group for Indigenous Affairs. p. 184–199.

Anaya J, Williams R. 2001. The protection of Indigenous peoples' rights over lands and natural resources under the Inter-American human rights system. Harv Hum Rts J. 14:33–86.

Arendt H. 1951. The Origins of Totalitarianism. New York, NY: Harcourt, Brace.

B&HRI. 2010. How to do business with respect for human rights: a guidance tool for companies. The Hague: Global Compact Network Netherlands.

Bauman T, Williams R. 2004. The business of process: research issues in managing indigenous decision making and disputes in land. Canberra: Native Title Research Unit, Australian Institute of Aboriginal and Torres Strait Islander Studies.

Bradley C, Goldsmith J. 1997. Customary international law as federal common law: a critique of the modern position. Harv L Rev. 111(4):815–876.

Brasil. 1988. Constituição da República Federativa do Brasil [Federative Republic of Brazil Constitution]. Brasília: Senado, In Portuguese.

Brasil. 2004. Resolução CONDRAF n. 44, de 13 de julho [CONDRAF resolution no. 44, 13 July]. Brasília: Diário Oficial da União, Ministério do Desenvolvimento Agrário, In Portuguese.

Brasil. 2012. Portaria n. 303, de 16 de julho [Attorney General of the Union, Ordinance no. 303, 16 July]. Brasília: Diário Oficial da União, Advocacia Geral da União (AGU), In Portuguese.

Burger J. 2009. Making the Declaration work for human rights in the UN system. In: Chartres C, Stavenhagen R, editors. Making the declaration work: The United Nations Declaration on the Rights of Indigenous peoples. Copenhagen: International Work Group for Indigenous Affairs. p. 304–313.

Caine J, Krogman N. 2010. Powerful or just plain power-full? A power analysis of impact and benefit agreements in Canada's north. Organ Environ. 23(1):76–98.

Cardoso de Oliveira R. 1978. A sociologia do Brasil Indígena [The Sociology of Indigenous Brazil]. Rio de Janeiro: Tempo Brasileiro, In Portuguese.

Cariño J. 2005. Indigenous peoples' rights to free, prior, informed consent: reflections on concepts and practice. Ariz J Int Comp L. 22(1):19–39.

Cariño J, Colchester M. 2010. From dams to development justice: progress with 'free, prior and informed consent' since the World Commission on Dams. Water Altern. 3(2):423–437.

Caruso E, Colchester M, MacKay F, Hildyard N, Nettleton G. 2003. Extracting promises: Indigenous peoples, extractive industries and the World Bank. Baguio City: Tebtebba Foundation.

Clinton R. 1990. The rights of Indigenous peoples as collective rights. Arizona L Rev. 32:739–747.

Cobo JM. 1986. Study of the problem of discrimination against Indigenous populations. International Covenant on Civil and Political Rights. Geneva: United Nations.

Coelho dos Santos S. 1981. Indigenismo e expansão capitalista: faces da agonia Kaingang [Indigenism and capitalist expansion: faces of the Kaingang Agony]. Cadernos de Ciências Sociais. Florianópolis: UFSC, In Portuguese.

Colchester M. 2008. Free, prior and informed consent and the Roundtable on Sustainable Palm Oil: a guide for companies. Moreton-in-Marsh: Forest Peoples Programme.

Colchester M. 2010. Palm oil and Indigenous peoples of South East Asia: land acquisition, human rights violations and indigenous peoples on the palm oil frontier. Moreton-in-Marsh: Forest Peoples Programme and the International Land Coalition.

Colchester M, Ferrari M. 2007. Making FPIC work: challenges and prospects for Indigenous peoples. Moreton-in-Marsh: Forest Peoples Programme.

Colchester M, MacKay F. 2004. In search of middle ground: Indigenous peoples, collective representation and the right to free, prior and informed consent. Moreton-in-Marsh: Forest Peoples Programme.

Coumans C. 2012. Mining, human rights and the socially responsible investment industry: considering community opposition to shareholder resolutions and implications of collaboration. JSFI [Internet].; [cited 2012 Nov 8]; 2(1):44–63. Available from: http://www.tandfonline.com/doi/pdf/10.1080/20430795.2012.702499

Davis R, Franks DM. 2011. The costs of conflict with local communities in the extractive industry. In: Brereton D, Pesce D, Abogabir X, editors. Proceedings of the First International Seminar on Social Responsiblity in Mining, 2011 Oct 19–21. Santiago: SRMinning; p. 1–13.

De Echave J. 2010. Guests at the big table? Growth of the extractive sector, Indigenous/peasant participation in multi-partite processes, and the Canadian presence in Peru. Ottawa: The North–South Institute and CooperAcción.

Donnelly J. 1984. Cultural relativism and universal human rights. Hum Rts Q. 6(4):400–419.

Dyck N. 1985. Aboriginal peoples and nation-states: an introduction to the analytical issues. In: Dyck N, editor. Indigenous peoples and the nation-state: 4th world politics in Canada, Australia and Norway. St John's: Institute of Social and Economic Research, Memorial University of Newfoundland; p. 1–26.

Engle K. 2001. From skepticism to embrace: human rights and the American Anthropological Association from 1947–1999. Hum Rts Q. 23(3):536–559.

Engle K. 2011. On fragile architecture: The UN Declaration on the Rights of Indigenous Peoples in the context of human rights. Eur J Int L. 22(1):141–163.

Equator Principles Association [Internet]. 2003. Equator Principles. Washington, DC: Equator Principles Association; [cited 2012 Nov 8]. Available from: http://www.equator-principles.com/resources/EPIII_PR.pdf

Esteves AM, Vanclay F. 2009. Social development needs analysis as a tool for SIA to guide corporate–community investment: applications in the minerals industry. Environ Impact Assess Rev. 29(2):137–145.

Esteves AM, Franks D, Vanclay F. 2012. Social impact assessment: the state of the art. Impact Assess Proj Appraisal. 30(1):35–44.

Galbraith L, Bradshaw B, Rutherford MB. 2007. Towards a new supraregulatory approach to environmental assessment in Northern Canada. Impact Assess Proj Appraisal. 25(1):27–41.

Goodland R. 2004. Free, prior and informed consent and the World Bank Group. SDLP. 4(2):66–74.

Gracey M, King M. 2009. Indigenous health part 1: determinants and disease patterns. Lancet. 374:65–75.

Griffiths T. 2005. Indigenous peoples and the World Bank: experiences with participation. Moreton-in-Marsh: Forest Peoples Programme.

Gupta AK. 2002. WIPO-UNEP Study on the role of intellectual property rights in the sharing of benefits arising from the use of biological resources and associated traditional knowledge. Ahmedabad: United Nations Environment Programme; [cited 2013 Feb 11]. Available from: http://www.wipo.int/tk/en/publications/769e_unep_tk.pdf

Haalboom B. 2012. The intersection of corporate social responsibility guidelines and Indigenous rights: examining neoliberal governance of a proposed mining project in Suriname. Geoforum. 43(5):969–979.

Hill C, Lillywhite S, Simon M. 2010. Guide to free prior and informed consent. Carlton: Oxfam Australia.

Hitch M. 2006. Impact and Benefit Agreements and the political ecology of mineral development in Nunavut [dissertation]. Waterloo: University of Waterloo.

ICMM. 2010. Indigenous peoples and mining: good practice guide. London: International Council on Mining and Metals.

ICMM. 2012. Community development toolkit. London: International Council on Mining and Metals.

IFC. 2006. Performance Standard 7 – Indigenous peoples. International Finance Corporation's Performance Standards on Social and Environmental Sustainability. Washington, DC: International Finance Corporation.

IFC. 2012. Performance Standard 7 – Indigenous peoples. International Finance Corporation's Performance Standards on Social and Environmental Sustainability. Washington, DC: International Finance Corporation.

ILO. 1989. Indigenous and Tribal Peoples Convention: C169. Geneva: International Labour Organization.

ILO. 2012. Report of the committee of experts on the application of conventions and recommendations (report III – Part 1A). Geneva: International Labour Organization.

Indigenous Peoples Rights Act of 1997 [Internet]. 1997. Republic Act no. 8371. Metro Manila: Congress of the Philippines; [cited 2012 Nov 8]. Available from: http://www.congress.gov.ph/download/ra_10/RA08371.pdf.

Jampolsky JA. 2012. Activism is the new black! Demonstrating the benefits of international celebrity activism through James Cameron's campaign against the Belo Monte Dam. Colo J Int Eviron L Policy. 23:227–256.

Kemp D, Vanclay F. 2013. Human rights and impact assessment: clarifying the connections in practice. Impact Assess Proj Appraisal. 31(2):86–96. http://dx.doi.org/10.1080/14615517.2013.782978

Langbroek M, Vanclay F. 2012. Learning from the social impacts associated with initiating a windfarm near the former island of Urk, The Netherlands. Impact Assess Proj Appraisal. 30(3):167–178.

Lehr A, Smith G. 2010. Implementing a corporate free, prior and informed consent policy. Boston, MA: Foley Hoag.

Linde E. 2009. Consultation or consent? Indigenous peoples' participatory rights with regard to the exploration of natural resources according the UN Declaration on Rights of Indigenous Peoples [dissertation]. Toronto: University of Toronto; [cited 2012 Nov 8]. Available from: https://tspace.library.utoronto.ca/bitstream/1807/18816/1/Linde_Eva_200911_Master_Thesis.pdf

Maassarani TF, Drakos MT, Pajkowska J. 2007. Extracting corporate responsibility: towards a human rights impact assessment. Cornell Int L J. 40:135–165.

MacKay F. 2004. Indigenous people's right to free, prior and informed consent and the World Bank's Extractive Industries Review. SDLP. 4:43–65.

MacKay F. 2005. The draft World Bank Operational Policy 4.10 on Indigenous peoples: progress or more of the same? Ariz J Int Comp L. 22:65–98.

MacNaughton G, Hunt P. 2011. A human rights-based approach to social impact assessment. In: Vanclay F, Esteves AM, editors. New directions in social impact assessment: conceptual and methodological advances. Cheltenham: Edward Elgar; p. 355–368.

Messer E. 1993. Anthropology and human rights. Annu Rev Anthropol. 22:221–249.

Miranda L. 2007. The hybrid state–corporate enterprise and violations of Indigenous land rights: theorizing corporate responsibility and accountability under international law. Lewis Clark L Rev. 11:135–183.

Miranda L. 2010. Indigenous peoples as international lawmakers. U. Pa. J. Int L. 32(1):203–263.

Mongabay [Internet]. 2012. Brazil decree opens tribal lands to mining, dams in 'national interest'. San Francisco, CA: Mongabay; [cited 2012 Nov 8]. Available from: http://news.mongabay.com/2012/0726-brazil-indigenous-directive.html

Montenegro R, Stephens C. 2006. Indigenous health in Latin America and the Caribbean. Lancet. 367:1859–1869.

O'Faircheallaigh C. 2009. Corporate–Aboriginal agreements on mineral development: the wider implications of contractual agreements. Proceedings of the rethinking extractive industries conference, 2009 Nov 5–7. Toronto: York University.

O'Faircheallaigh C. 2010. Aboriginal–mining company contractual agreements in Australia and Canada: implications for political autonomy and community development. Can J Dev Stud. 30(1–2):69–86.

O'Faircheallaigh C, Corbett T. 2005. Indigenous participation in environmental management of mining projects: the role of negotiated agreements. Eviron Policy. 14(5):629–647.

Page A. 2004. Indigenous peoples' free prior and informed consent in the Inter-American human rights system. SDLP. 4:16–20.

Persoon G, Minter T. 2011. Code of conduct for working with indigenous and local communities. Wageningen: Tropenbos International.

Preis A. 1996. Human rights as cultural practice: an anthropological critique. Hum Rts Q. 18:286–315.

Prno J, Bradshaw B, Lapierre D. 2010. Impact Benefit Agreements: are they working? Proceedings of the Canadian Institute of Mining, Metallurgy, and Petroleum conference, 2010 May 11. Vancouver: CIM.

Riles A. 2006. Anthropology, human rights, and legal knowledge: culture in the iron cage. Am Anthropol. 108(1):52–65.

Royo LRP. 2009. 'Where appropriate': monitoring/implementing of Indigenous peoples' rights under the declaration. In: Chartres C, Stavenhagen R, editors. Making the declaration work: The United Nations Declaration on the Rights of Indigenous Peoples. Copenhagen: International Work Group for Indigenous Affairs; p. 314–343.

Ruggie JG. 2011. Guiding principles on business and human rights: implementing the United Nations 'protect, respect and remedy' framework. Geneva: Human Rights Council, (A/HRC/17/31).

Sepúlveda M, van Banning T, Gudmundsdóttir G, Chamoun C, van Genugten WJM. 2004. Human rights reference handbook. Ciudad Colon: University for Peace.

Siebenmorgen P. 2009. Developing an ideal mining agenda: Impact and Benefit Agreements as instruments of community development in Northern Ontario [thesis]. Guelph: University of Guelph.

Stavenhagen R. 1985. Etnodesenvolvimento: uma dimensão ignorada no pensamento desenvolvimentista [Ethnodevelopment: an ignored dimension on developmentalist thinking]. Anu Antropol. 84:13–56, In Portuguese.

Stavenhagen R [Internet]. 2003. Indigenous peoples and their access to human rights. International Council on Human Rights Policy. Guadalajara: International Council on Human Rights Policy; [cited 2012 Nov 8]. Available from: http://www.ichrp.org/files/papers/102/123_Indigenous_Peoples_and_their_Access_to_Human_Rights_Stavenhagen__Rodolfo__2003.pdf

Stavenhagen R. 2009. Making the Declaration work. In: Chartres C, Stavenhagen R, editors. Making the Declaration work: The United Nations Declaration on the rights of Indigenous Peoples. Copenhagen: International Work Group for Indigenous Affairs; p. 352–371.

Sterio M. 2009. On the right to external self-determination: 'selfistans', secession and the Great Powers' rule. Minn J Int L. 19:1–28.

Tauli-Corpuz V, Enkiwe-Abayao L, De Chaves R, editors. 2010. Towards an alternative development paradigm: Indigenous peoples' self-determined development. Baguio City: Tebtebba Foundation.

Tugendhat H, Couillard V, Gilbert J, Doyle C. 2009. Business, human rights and Indigenous peoples: the right to free, prior and informed consent. Moreton-in-Marsh: Forest Peoples Programme.

UNEP [Internet]. 1992. UN Convention on biological diversity. Rio de Janeiro: United Nations Environment Programme; [cited 2012 Nov 8]. Available from: http://www.cbd.int/doc/legal/cbd-en.pdf

UNESCO [Internet]. 2001. Universal Declaration on cultural diversity. Paris: United Nations Educational, Scientific and Cultural Organization; [cited 2012 Nov 8]. Available from: http://www.unhcr.org/refworld/docid/435cbcd64.html

UN General Assembly [Internet]. 1948a. Universal Declaration of Human Rights. 217A (III). Paris: UN General Assembly; [cited 2012 Nov 8]. Available from: http://www.unhcr.org/refworld/docid/3ae6b3712c.html

UN General Assembly [Internet]. 1948b. Prevention and punishment of the crime of genocide. A/RES/260. Paris: UN General Assembly; [cited 2012 Nov 8]. Available from: http://www.unhcr.org/refworld/docid/3b00f0873.html

UN General Assembly [Internet]. 1965. International Convention on the Elimination of all Forms of Racial Discrimination. UN Treaty Series, 660:195. New York, NY: UN General Assembly; [cited 2012 Nov 8]. Available from: http://www.unhcr.org/refworld/docid/3ae6b3940.html

UN General Assembly [Internet]. 1966. International Covenant on Economic, Social and Cultural Rights. UN Treaty Series, 993:3. New York, NY: UN General Assembly; [cited 2012 Nov 8]. Available from: http://www2.ohchr.org/english/law/cescr.htm

UN General Assembly [Internet]. 1992a. Declaration on the Rights of Persons Belonging to National or Ethnic, Religious and Linguistic Minorities. A/RES/47/135. New York, NY: UN General Assembly; [cited 2012 Nov 8]. Available from: http://www.unhcr.org/refworld/docid/3ae6b38d0.html

UN General Assembly [Internet]. 1992b. Rio Declaration on Environment and Development. A/CONF.151/26 (Vol. I). Rio de Janeiro: UN General Assembly; [cited 2012 Nov 8]. Available from: http://www.un.org/documents/ga/conf151/aconf15126-1annex1.htm

UN General Assembly [Internet]. 1993. Vienna Declaration and Program of Action. A/CONF.157/23. Vienna: UN General Assembly; [cited 2012 Nov 8]. Available from: http://www.unhchr.ch/huridocda/huridoca.nsf/(symbol)/a.conf.157.23.en

UN General Assembly [Internet]. 2007a. United Nations Declaration on the Rights of Indigenous Peoples. A/RES/61/295. New York, NY: UN General Assembly; [cited 2012 Nov 8]. Available from: http://www.unhcr.org/refworld/docid/471355a82.html

UN General Assembly [Internet]. 2007b. Press release on the Declaration. GA/10612. New York, NY: UN General Assembly; [cited 2012 Nov 8]. Available from: http://www.un.org/News/Press/docs/2007/ga10612.doc.htm

UN Global Compact. 2011. UN Global Compact brochure. New York, NY: UN Global Compact Office.

United Nations [Internet]. 1945. Charter of the United Nations. 1 UNTS XVI. San Francisco, CA: United Nations, United Nations; [cited 2012 Nov 8]. Available from: http://www.unhcr.org/refworld/docid/3ae6b3930.html

UN Sub-Commission on the Promotion and Protection of Human Rights [Internet]. 2004. Report of the Working Group on Indigenous populations on its twenty-second session. E/CN.4/Sub.2/2004/28. Geneva: UN Sub-Commission on the Promotion and Protection of Human Rights; [cited 2012 Nov 8]. Available from: http://www.unhcr.org/refworld/docid/42d7b72f4.html

van Dam K. 2008. A Place called Nunavut: multiple identities for a new region. Circumpolar Studies no. 5. Groningen: University of Groningen.

Vanclay F. 2012. The potential application of social impact assessment in integrated coastal zone management. Ocean Coast Mgmt. 68:149–156.

Vanclay F, Esteves AM. 2011. Current issues and trends in social impact assessment. In: Vanclay F, Esteves AM, editors. New directions in social impact assessment: conceptual and methodological advances. Cheltenham: Edward Elgar; p. 3–19.

Verdum R. 2012. Povos Indígenas e comunidades tradicionais: Riscos e desafios no crescimento econômico [Indigenous peoples and traditional communities: risks and challenges in economic growth]. Orçam Polít Amb. 28:2–15, In Portuguese.

Voss M, Greenspan E [Internet]. 2012. Community consent index: oil, gas and mining company public positions on Free, Prior, and Informed Consent (FPIC). Oxfam America Research Backgrounder series; [cited 2012 Nov 8]. Available from: www.oxfamamerica.org/publications/community-consent-index

Watkins J. 2005. Through wary eyes: Indigenous perspectives on archaeology, Annu. Rev. Anthropol. 34:429–449.

Weitzner V. 2011. Tipping the power balance – making free, prior and informed consent work: lessons and policy directions from 10 years of action research on extractives with Indigenous and Afro-descendent peoples in the Americas. Ottawa: The North–South Institute.

Wiessner S. 2011. The cultural rights of Indigenous peoples: achievements and continuing challenges. Eur J Int L. 22(1):121–140.

World Bank [Internet]. 1991. Operational Directive 4.20: Indigenous peoples. Washington, DC: World Bank; [cited 2012 Nov 8]. Available from: http://www.ifc.org/ifcext/enviro.nsf/AttachmentsByTitle/pol_IndigPeoples/$FILE/OD420_IndigenousPeoples.pdf

World Bank [Internet]. 2005. Operational Policy 4.10 on Indigenous peoples. Washington, DC: World Bank; [cited 2012 Nov 8]. Available from: http://go.worldbank.org/TE769PDWN0

Wright R. 1988. Anthropological presuppositions of Indigenous advocacy. Annu Rev Anthropol. 17:365–390.

[27]

Making Social Impact Assessment Count: A Negotiation-Based Approach for Indigenous Peoples

CIARAN O'FAIRCHEALLAIGH

Griffith University
Nathan, Brisbane, Australia

In the past, indigenous people have often been entirely excluded from social impact assessments (SIAs) of projects or activities that affect them, or have faced major financial and cultural barriers in participating effectively and in having their perspectives accepted as legitimate. More recently, indigenous groups have achieved greater success in influencing SIA, but a fundamental problem remains. Their enhanced input into SIA has generally not increased the capacity of indigenous people to shape the outcomes of development projects in ways that favor their interests. This problem reflects a wider failure, extensively documented in the literature, to integrate SIA into decision-making. Drawing on case studies from Australia's Cape York Peninsula, this article shows how SIA can be integrated into the negotiation of legally binding agreements between developers and indigenous groups, offering a practical and effective way of ensuring that SIA findings influence the development and operation of resource projects. While the case studies relate to specific regional, political, and cultural contexts, the general approach outlined in the article should be of interest to indigenous communities and SIA practitioners.

Keywords Cape York Peninsula, indigenous peoples, negotiation, resource development, social impact assessment

SIA and Indigenous People

Indigenous people have experienced extensive problems with social impact assessment (SIA), which since the early 1970s has constituted part of the project approval process in many developed countries. In some cases indigenous people have been completely excluded from impact assessments of projects that affect them, particularly where SIA is conducted as part of assessment processes initiated by developers and controlled by state agencies that have an interest in promoting "development." Chase has shown how developers, state government officials, and consultants denied the right of Aboriginal people to participate in impact studies of a proposed silica sand mine at Shelburne Bay in Queensland, despite their traditional associations with the area involved (Chase 1990, 16–17). Similar situations are discussed by Jobes (1986), Justus and Simonetta (1982), Michalenko and Suffling (1982), Waldram (1984), and Ross (1989a).

In other cases, indigenous people have been admitted at a formal level, but have been unable to participate effectively in SIA and so have been powerless to influence its outcomes. This may be because the time allowed for SIA and for project

---

Received 14 May 1996; accepted 27 May 1997.

The author acted as negotiator and economic adviser to the Hope Vale community in relation to the Cape Flattery project, and to the Marpuna Corporation and the Cape York Land Council in relation to the Skardon River project. He was also the senior consultant for the Economic and Social Impact Assessments conducted for both projects. He expresses his appreciation to the Hope Vale and Mapoon communities for their permission to utilize information from these assessments, and his thanks to the many community members who participated in them.

Address correspondence to Ciaran O'Faircheallaigh, Faculty of Commerce and Administration, Griffith University, Nathan, Australia 4111. E-mail: Ciaran.Ofaircheallaigh@cad.gu.edu.au

approval more generally is excessively short, particularly given that indigenous decision-making processes may be protracted. Indigenous groups often lack the financial resources and the access to "technical" information and expertise required to ensure effective participation. The use of culturally alien forms of inquiry (such as highly formalized and legalistic public hearings) can also create problems.

More fundamentally, SIA and project approval procedures may fail to acknowledge the values and perspectives of indigenous people where these conflict with the dominant social ethos of the country concerned. Edelstein and Kleese (1995), for example, showed how native Hawaiian perspectives regarding the spiritual and religious significance of volcanos and the land surrounding them were rejected in the assessment of proposals for harnessing geothermal energy. The result was that native peoples affected by these proposals were marginalized from the project approval process. Edelstein and Kleese argued that the stress on supposedly "rational" and "scientific" approaches to impact assessment, which usually characterizes project approval processes, is in fact far from value neutral, because these approaches promote developmental agendas and deny the validity of perspectives and evidence put forward by indigenous peoples (Eldelstein and Kleese 1995, 20–22; see also Craig 1989, 2, 5–6; Howell 1983, 346–47).

Against this background, indigenous people have expressed cynicism and even hostility towards SIA, questioning whether it confers any benefits on themselves, as opposed to the consultants and university staff who undertake impact assessment studies (Nottingham 1990).

More general problems that are frequently associated with SIA have also created difficulties for indigenous people. One such problem is the tendency to focus on the impact of individual developments in isolation and over the short to medium term, which means that SIA may ignore the cumulative and longer term impacts that a succession of projects can have on indigenous communities (Ross 1989b; Nottingham 1990, 180).

A second problem is the tendency to assume that SIA should be *ex ante*, occurring prior to a decision on whether or not to proceed with a project or action, and designed to predict the impact of a negative or positive decision. According to Wolf (1981), for instance, SIA is concerned to "predict and evaluate the social effects of a policy, program or project while still in the planning stage—before those effects have occurred ... the task of SIA is anticipatory research" (1981, 27; see also Armour 1989, 29; Finsterbusch 1985, 195–6). But a purely *ex ante* approach may be inadequate. A project or development will often have consequences that cannot be predicted at the time of the SIA. In addition, a series of relevant factors—for example, people's values (including their attachment to traditional ways of life), government policies, and the nature of the development in question—will change over time, undermining the validity of assumptions that underlay the original study (Geisler 1993; Mulvihill and Keith 1989). Also relevant is the fact that SIA of projects initiated some decades ago, when the political position of indigenous people was weaker, may have been inadequate or nonexistent. People affected by these projects may now wish to have their impacts assessed so they can develop strategies designed to maximize the benefits they receive and minimize the costs they bear during the remainder of project life.[1]

Geisler called for SIAs that are "iterative and extend over the life of the development projects" (1993, 334; see also Blishen et al. 1979, 9). But he did not consider how indigenous people can fund such studies, who should carry them out, or what sorts of structures might facilitate their conduct, issues taken up later in this article.

A third general problem is that SIA is often regarded primarily as providing a basis for mitigating negative social impacts, which arise from projects that are expected to generate substantial economic benefits on a regional or national level (see, e.g., Craig and Tester 1982, 19; Geisler 1982a, 1; Finsterbusch 1985, 213; Interorganizational Committee 1995, 30–31; Schoepfle et al. 1984, 265, 268). However, indigenous communities do not want to be regarded solely as the object of "mitigation," but rather wish to share in the positive economic and social effects that can be associated with large development projects (Holden and O'Faircheallaigh 1995a, 1995b).

The problems just outlined have led to a number of responses, which can be grouped into two broad categories. The first involves attempts by indigenous people, and public officials sympathetic to them, to insist on more substantial indigenous input into formal, government-mandated SIA processes.

For example, the first impact assessment of the proposed Century zinc project in Queensland's Gulf region, carried out in 1994 by project developer Century Zinc Ltd (CZL), attracted sustained criticism from Aboriginal groups (and from concerned state government officials) because of its almost total failure to address indigenous interests. As a result CZL published a supplementary impact assessment that specifically dealt with Aboriginal issues. This also attracted criticism on the basis that its treatment was partial and lacking in depth, and in 1995 CZL published a second, and subsequently a third and much more extensive, supplementary impact statement (Carpentaria Land Council 1995). Similarly, pressure from tribes affected by the Glen Canyon dam and from officials in the Bureau of Indian Affairs led to eight tribes being incorporated into an impact assessment process initiated by the U.S. Department of Interior in 1990 (Austin and Bullets 1996). At a broader level, Nottingham (1990) described how consistent pressure by Maori people over an extended period of time resulted in their perspectives increasingly being taken into account in planning processes in New Zealand.

Gagnon et al. stressed the need for indigenous communities to take control of the "technical inputs" into SIA, to determine issues such as who directs research, what data are used, and which scenarios are considered. They saw this as substantially altering "the conventional balance of power in impact studies," and they indicated how one community successfully adopted such an approach (1993, 240–43). However, they acknowledged that indigenous people lack secure standing in most formal SIA procedures, with the result that their capacity to exert an element of control is contingent on prevailing corporate and government policies, which may of course be subject to change (1993, 245). More fundamentally, Ross (1989a, 8) argued that input by indigenous people into formal impact assessment procedures is unlikely to bring recognition of their interests when these procedures are part of a larger project assessment process over which they have limited control.

SIA occurs not only as part of a larger project assessment process, but also within broader political and institutional structures. A number of authors have argued that these structures distribute power in ways that make it difficult for indigenous people to influence the policy process, a fact that will be reflected in the outcomes of SIA (Craig 1989; Gagnon et al. 1993; Howitt 1989). But while these outcomes will certainly tend to reflect the political status quo, SIA can also play a role in attempts to bring about a realignment of political structures and of the "rules of the game" within which project assessment and government decision making occur, since it can provide indigenous people with access to information, which is of course an important source of political influence.

Another significant development has involved attempts by judges and government officials conducting SIA and similar processes to develop forms of inquiry that facilitate effective participation by indigenous people. Thomas Berger is widely credited with making important innovations in these areas, in conducting inquiries into resource projects and related developments in northern Canada and Alaska (Berger 1985, 1988). He held hearings in towns and villages throughout the regions in question, bringing inquiries to indigenous people rather than expecting them to travel to distant urban centers; established inquiry protocols that stressed informality and facilitated indigenous input; ensured funding for indigenous participants; and made extensive use of indigenous histories and of the direct evidence of indigenous people in his reports. The Seaman Inquiry into Aboriginal land rights in Western Australia adopted similar approaches, and in addition allowed all Aboriginal hearings to be chaired by Aborigines and to be conducted in a way chosen by Aboriginal people (Craig 1989; 46; see also Lane et al. 1993).

Efforts have also been made to develop research methods and protocols that are both more culturally appropriate and place more control in the hands of indigenous people. For example, the East Kimberley Impact Assessment Project (EKIAP) utilized innovative approaches in analyzing the impact of mining, tourism, and other developments on the East Kimberley region of Western Australia. In particular, it relied heavily on storytelling by Aboriginal participants (defined as "oral modes ranging from narrative story telling, to life and event-based histories, interviews and discussions") (Ross 1989b, 16). It thus sought to ensure that the issues highlighted and the perspectives provided were those of indigenous people themselves (Coombs et al. 1989; Ross, 1989b).[2]

The second broad category of responses has involved the conduct of SIA outside the formal project approval process. In some cases SIAs have been conducted by indigenous organizations themselves, which have set terms of reference, appointed professional staff, determined or approved methodologies, monitored research work, and received study findings. For example, Justus and Simonetta (1982) discussed the experience of the Cold Lake Indian Band. Dissatisfied with impact studies conducted by the proponent of a major oil sands project planned for construction near its reserve, the band commissioned its own SIA. This examined the experience of other Indian bands that had already felt the impact of oil sands projects, and sought advice from those bands regarding what measures they would have initiated, with hindsight, in order to minimize adverse impacts and maximize gains. On this basis, detailed recommendations were developed in relation to key impact areas.[3] In other cases SIA has been undertaken by the staff of university departments or independent research institutes, but the individuals and organizations involved have sought to ensure (with varying degrees of success) that the research agenda is driven by indigenous people and serves their interests (Ross 1989b, 10; Australian Institute of Aboriginal Studies 1984).

SIA and Development Outcomes

These responses in combination have enhanced the capacity of indigenous people to influence the conduct and content of impact assessment studies. However, it is not at all clear that this enhanced capacity has been translated into a greater ability to shape the nature and impact of the resource projects and other developments that are the subject of SIA. Indeed perhaps the most noticeable feature of the existing literature on indigenous people and SIA is its almost total failure to address the issue of how the findings and recommendations generated by impact assessment can be effectively fed into decision-making processes, and so help bring about outcomes that generate a more favorable balance of benefits and costs for indigenous people.

For example, Justus and Simonetta, in the study referred to earlier, developed a detailed list of measures relating to key impact areas such as environment, health, employment, and business development, which were intended to secure the interests of the Cold Lake Band. However they said little about how the band could secure implementation of this wide range of measures (1982, 250–56). Geisler (1982b) described how an Indian-controlled SIA generated recommended strategies aimed at enhancing the capacity of the tribe involved to deal with a major mining development adjacent to its land, but again, no clear indication was given as to how those recommendations might be put into effect. The EKIAP identified broad policy recommendations on the basis of its research; sought to provide research results to Aboriginal communities that would "enable them to develop their own strategies for dealing with social impact issues"; and called for Aboriginal participation "in planning and decision making on an equal footing" (Ross 1989b; Coombs et al. 1989, 135–36, 140). But in this case also little indication was provided of how policy goals are to be pursued, of what sorts of strategies are available to indigenous people in attempting to "deal with social impact issues," or of how their participation in planning and decision making is to be achieved. Similar comments could be made in relation to studies reported by Gondolf and Wells (1986), Stoffle et al. (1982), Lane et al. (1993), and Shera and Matsuoka (1992).

It may of course be the case that the indigenous groups involved did find ways of implementing the recommendations and strategies that emerged from SIA, and that their actions in this regard have simply not been reported in the literature. However, findings from the general literature on SIA would certainly not warrant such an assumption. A failure to ensure that its findings are integrated into decision making is widely regarded as a key weakness of SIA. In a 1991 status report on impact assessment and the planning process, Audrey Armour, a former president of the International Association for Impact Assessment, argued that impact assessment in general had not been integrated into decision-making processes, was increasingly carried out by "consultants and report writers" operating outside those processes, and tended to focus on compliance with procedural requirements rather than to address substantive issues (Armour 1991; see also Armour 1989; Craig 1989, 51; Howell 1983, 347).

Thus there is a very obvious need to devise strategies to ensure not only that indigenous people influence impact assessments of developments that affect them, but that the results of SIA help to shape the outcomes of these developments.

One such strategy is outlined in the remainder of this article. It involves the integration of SIA into negotiation processes designed to produce legally binding agreements with developers that address the aspirations and concerns of indigenous people. While the potential to utilize SIA findings within a negotiation framework has been acknowledged in the literature (Coombs et al. 1989, 132–33; Corbett 1990; Craig 1989, 8–9; Justus and Simonetta 1982, 253–54; Ross 1989a, 9), little detailed analysis or case study material exists that indicates how that potential can be realized.

The application of a negotiation-based approach to SIA is illustrated through two case studies, one detailed and the other more brief, from the Cape York region of Queensland, in Australia's north.

Cape York Peninsula

Cape York Peninsula occupies the most northern part of the state of Queensland (see locality map, Figure 1). During recent decades the indigenous population, decimated after European settlement by disease, dispossession, and the violent attacks of settlers, has grown rapidly, and today indigenous people account for just over half of the total population of 25,000, which is tiny in comparison to Cape York's land area. Most Aboriginal people now reside in some 10 Aboriginal settlements, none of which has more than about 1000 residents, and in small family-based "homeland centers" or "outstations," established since the 1970s as people have sought to reoccupy their traditional lands.

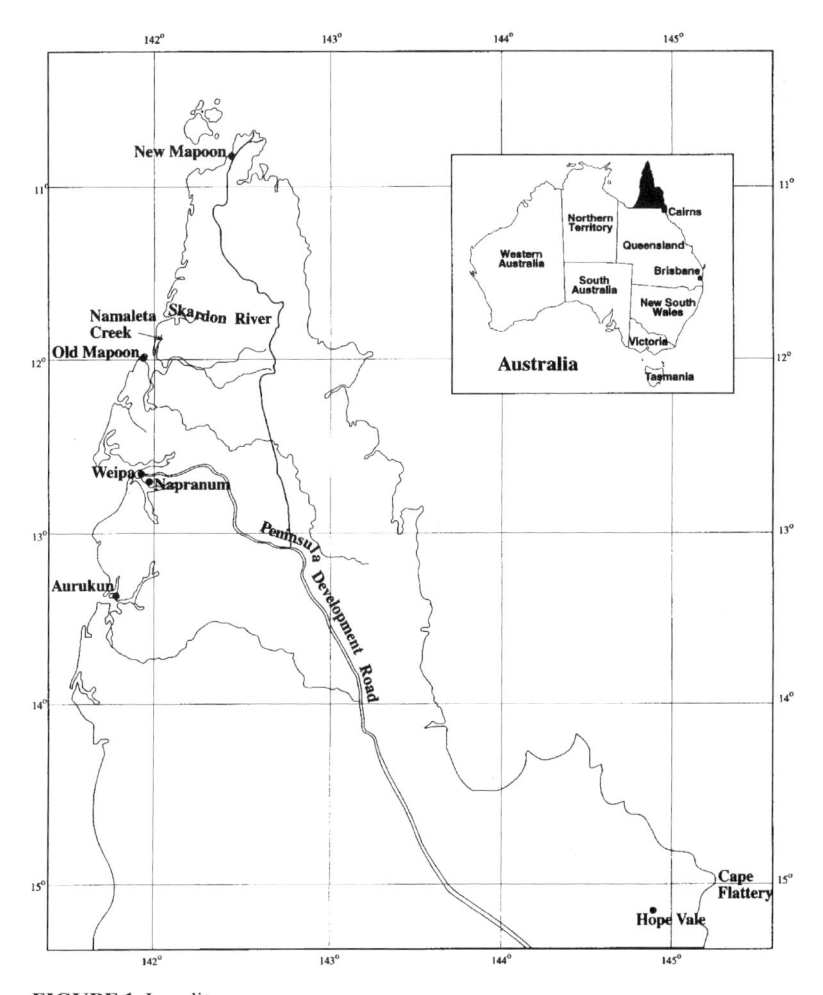

FIGURE 1 Locality map.

Despite the impact of settlers, governments, and missionaries, Aboriginal people retain important aspects of their traditional culture, spirituality, and social structures. It is estimated that two out of every three Aboriginal residents speaks at least one Aboriginal language; hunting and fishing are still very important sources of food, and especially of protein, for many people (particularly on outstations); and family or clan-based systems of kinship and reciprocity still constitute the core of social structures and the basis for much of economic and political life.

In the past, the mineral resources of Cape York have been developed with scant regard for the interests of its indigenous inhabitants. For example, on Western Cape York, reserves covering huge areas of land allocated for the use of Aboriginal people were revoked in the 1950s, and missions closed down or relocated and their residents expelled from their homes, to make way for exploration and mining. As late as the mid-1970s, exploration and mining leases were being granted over Aboriginal reserve land against the express wishes of traditional landowners. During the 1990s this situation has changed significantly, and as the following case studies reveal, SIA played a significant part in facilitating this change.

Silica Mining at Cape Flattery

Cape Flattery Silica Mines (CFSM), a fully owned subsidiary of Mitsubishi Corporation, has operated a silica mine at Cape Flattery since the late 1960s. The mine was established on Aboriginal reserve land, then under the control of Queensland's Department of Aboriginal and Islander Affairs (DAIA). It was located some 50 km from the Aboriginal community of Hope Vale, which at the time was run by a Lutheran mission (see Figure 1). Despite the mine's proximity to Hope Vale, travel between the two is difficult because of the absence of a surfaced road, and Hope Vale people working at Cape Flattery have always resided there, in single accommodation, for extended periods of time.

No SIA was conducted prior to the granting of mining leases, and Aboriginal people were not consulted regarding the establishment of the mine. By 1990 CFSM needed an additional mining lease to support its operations, and a number of its existing leases were due for renewal. Hope Vale had by then been granted title to the reserve (referred to as Deed of Grant in Trust or DOGIT) under Queensland legislation, and the community (numbering about 900) was administered by an elected Aboriginal Council. Under Queensland's Mineral Resources Act 1989, mining leases cannot be granted over DOGIT land unless the developer has first sought the consent of the Aboriginal trustees of the land, in this case the Hope Vale Council. This provided an opportunity for the community to enter into negotiations with CFSM regarding the terms of any new lease; since such a lease would be closely integrated with the company's existing operations, CFSM quickly agreed that the latter should also be addressed.

During 1990–1991 the Hope Vale Council prepared for the negotiations, in particular by commissioning the author and one of his graduate students to conduct an economic and social impact assessment (ESIA) of the mine. Though federal and state agencies responsible for indigenous affairs helped fund the ESIA, it was undertaken entirely under the control of the Hope Vale community, which set its terms of reference, appointed the consultants, nominated local people to work with them, and considered and approved draft and final reports.

A range of appropriate methodologies was employed to ensure maximum community participation in the ESIA process. The core of that process involved the dissemination of information regarding the Cape Flattery project; documentation of people's experience of the impact of CFSM's operations; identification of people's aspirations and concerns in relation to mining at Cape Flattery; and development of concrete strategies to deal with concerns and allow aspirations to be pursued, not only in the short term but well into the future (for a full description of methodology and findings, see Holden and O'Faircheallaigh 1995a).

When the ESIA process was complete, the council requested the author to join its negotiating team and to compile a draft negotiating position based on the ESIA report. This position was then ratified by the council, and formed the basis for negotiations with CFSM/Mitsubishi. Thus information on the impact of mining as experienced by Hope Vale people, and on their concerns and aspirations, was fed directly into the negotiation process. Negotiations with CFSM/Mitsubishi commenced in August 1991, and a final agreement was signed in April 1992.

The way in which the impact assessment process flowed through to the negotiation of legally binding arrangements between the community and the mining company is illustrated by Table 1. This summarizes, in the left-hand column, some of the demands and concerns expressed by Hope Vale people through the ESIA. The right-hand column indicates the provisions of the Hope Vale/Cape Flattery Agreement that sought to address these demands and concerns.

Much of the information presented in Table 1 is self-explanatory. However, an important point to stress is that the agreement created an institutional base that allows impact issues to be addressed on an ongoing basis.[4] In particular, it provided for the establishment of a Coordinating Committee, made up of equal numbers of representatives nominated by the Hope Vale Council and by CFSM. This body has "*control* over environmental, historical and Aboriginal issues which arise from mining operations" (my emphasis). In other words, its role is not advisory; it is authorized, under the Agreement, to take decisions in relation to these key (from an Aboriginal perspective) aspects of CFSM's operations. It also has a general responsibility to monitor implementation of the agreement. In addition, a Good Order Committee, with Aboriginal, trade union, and management representation, was established to deal with matters relating to workplace discipline and township administration.

The Coordinating and Good Order Committees are of crucial importance, as they provide forums through which implementation problems and new issues and circumstances can be addressed. However, the Hope Vale Council has had to devote significant resources and energy to ensuring that its representatives play an effective role on these committees, a fact that was not fully appreciated when the agreement was negotiated.

The Mapoon/Skardon River Agreement

Venture Exploration N.L., a Perth-based company, wished to develop an integrated kaolin mining and processing project on Aboriginal land that forms part of the Mapoon DOGIT. The mine site is approximately 15 km northeast of the community of Old Mapoon. Venture planned to mine kaolin in the headwaters of

TABLE 1 People's Concerns and Aspirations and Related Provisions of the Hope Vale/CFSM Agreement

Hope Vale people's concerns and aspirations	Provisions of the Hope Vale/CFSM Agreement
Royalty payments People saw a number of problems regarding the 3% profit royalty paid by CFSM • The payments were very low. • They were based on profits, and if the company made no profit, Hope Vale received no money at all. • The payments were made to the DAIA in Brisbane, and there were often long delays before the money reached Hope Vale.	The agreement provides for: • A much higher level of payments. • Payment is based on the value of minerals, not on profits. • Most royalty payments are made directly to Hope Vale.
Employment and training Hope Vale residents and workers at the mine expressed a number of concerns about employment and training: • Employment preference at Cape Flattery was for Aboriginal and Islander people in general, not Hope Vale people in particular. • Employment was limited to jobs in the mining and milling sections, whereas better paid and more highly skilled jobs went to non-Aborigines. • Hope Vale people did not have access to the training and educational opportunities that were necessary to get access to better jobs. • There were no established procedures for allowing Hope Vale workers to seek promotion within CFSM. • It was said that when Cape Flattery hired Hope Vale people they did not choose those who had been waiting for a job the longest, but people who were approved of by the management or supervisors. • There were no employment opportunities for Hope Vale women at Cape Flattery.	Under the agreement the company is to: • Give employment preference to Hope Vale people. • Establish training programs designed to ensure that Hope Vale employees have the opportunity to attain all positions at Cape Flattery, including senior management positions. • Provide a specified number of apprenticeships each year and a college or university scholarship. • Introduce a formal promotion process for all areas of the company's operations. • Hire workers from an "employment list" maintained by the Hope Vale Community Council. • Appoint a Liaison Officer from Hope Vale who, among other things, would implement the agreed recruitment procedures. • Introduce an affirmative action policy to facilitate employment of Hope Vale women at Cape Flattery, and provide specific employment opportunities for women.

TABLE 1 *Continued*

Hope Vale people's concerns and aspirations	Provisions of the Hope Vale/CFSM Agreement
Access to mining leases Numerous people complained that they were unhappy about restrictions on their access to CFSM's mining leases areas, in particular when they wanted to go fishing. (A number of important fishing areas could only be reached by traveling through the mining leases.) Signs at the lease boundaries stated that the permission of CFSM management was required prior to entry, which made people very angry, as they didn't feel they should have to ask permission to go on their own land.	Under the agreement: • Cape Flattery consents to Hope Vale Community members having access to all parts of the leases other than mining and other operational facilities. • It is stressed that Hope Vale residents do not require permission to enter the mining lease area. • Cape Flattery surrendered a number of its existing leases, and agreed to limit the extent of the new lease area to facilitate use of traditional hunting and fishing areas. It also undertook to construct and help to maintain a road to help Hope Vale people gain access to these areas.
The environment and sites of significance Many people complained that the company was not looking after the environment properly. A lot of people were also worried that important sites had already been disturbed or destroyed by mining and that more damage would occur in the future.	The agreement provides for: • An Aboriginal relations policy that requires protection of sites of significance from mining and vandalism. • The creation of a Coordinating Committee made up of equal numbers of representatives from Hope Vale and Cape Flattery. This Committee is given "control over environmental, historical, and Aboriginal issues that arise from mining operations," including the protection of sites of significance. There is a provision for appointment of a mediator where the Coordinating Committee cannot reach agreement on any issue. The Coordinating Committee also has a general responsibility to monitor the implementation of the Agreement.

(continued overleaf)

TABLE 1 *Continued*

Hope Vale people's concerns and aspirations	Provisions of the Hope Vale/CFSM Agreement
Accommodations for supervisors and arrangements for visitors	
• Some Hope Vale workers in supervisory positions complained that, unlike non-Aboriginal supervisors, they did not have their own houses. • Wives and families complained that it was difficult for them to visit the workers at Cape Flattery (who remain at the mine for several weeks at a time). They said that it was much easier for families of non-Aboriginal workers to visit them.	The agreement: • Ensures that Hope Vale workers in supervisory positions will, in line with general company policy, be provided with houses. • Explicitly agrees to visiting rights for families of employees. • Provides that the company will make available one of the empty barracks in the town for use by visiting families.
Working conditions and township administration	
• Workers complained that rules (about matters such as fighting and getting meals after hours) were not enforced fairly and that non-Aboriginal workers received more favorable treatment. • People complained that the management interfered too much in matters that were the business of township residents.	The agreement provides for the establishment of a "Good Order Committee" made up of representatives from Hope Vale workers, the trade union, and management. This committee's job is to develop and implement camp rules and a code of social behavior for the community at Cape Flattery, and to develop a consistent response to breaches of the rules that have been established.
Worker health	
A number of workers and/or their families expressed concern about possible adverse effects on their health as a result of working with silica sand at Cape Flattery.	The agreement provides for a system of x-ray checks once people had worked for Cape Flattery for 5 years, and also 5 years after such people stop working for Cape Flattery.

Note. From Holden and O'Faircheallaigh (1995a) and Hope Vale/CFSM (1992).

Namaletta Creek, then transfer it, in slurry form, through a pipeline to a processing plant near the Skardon River (see Figure 1).

The Aboriginal owners of the Mapoon DOGIT were dispersed in the early 1960s when the Queensland government closed, and then destroyed, the mission at Old Mapoon. Most now live at New Mapoon, near the tip of Cape York, at Napranum (near Weipa) and at Old Mapoon, where a community is being reestablished under the administration of the Marpuna Corporation. As in CFSM's case, Venture was required to undertake compensation negotiations with the Trustees of the DOGIT.

By mid-1994 the community was preparing for negotiations, with the help of the Cape York Land Council. It established a seven-person Steering Committee to oversee the negotiations, made up of representatives of the trustees, the Marpuna Corporation, and traditional landowners for the area concerned. The Steering Committee was determined that the environment should be protected and that the community should obtain an appropriate share of the benefits generated by Venture's project, but it was also keen to see the project proceed, particularly because of the employment it was expected to create.

In July 1994 Venture made an offer of compensation that was much more modest than that eventually agreed on. Anxious to quickly develop the project to take advantage of expected market opportunities, the company also sought agreement to a timetable that would have seen compensation negotiations completed by August 1994. The Steering Committee rejected the offer of compensation as fundamentally inadequate, and also rejected the proposed timetable, on the grounds that it wished to have relevant information (particularly an ESIA report) available before negotiating an agreement. However, it did all it could to expedite the process of preparation and negotiation, and an agreement was concluded in December 1994.

The ESIA process used in this case was similar to that employed at Hope Vale, though since the project was yet to be established the primary focus was on expected future impacts and on people's concerns and aspirations regarding these impacts. In addition, the pressure of time created by the project development schedule meant that research and reporting techniques had to be modified to some extent (Holden and O'Faircheallaigh 1995b).

The Mapoon/Skardon River Agreement is like that between CFSM and Hope Vale in a number of respects, for example, in relation to employment and training provisions and to protection of significant sites and the environment. It also creates an institutional framework for ongoing monitoring of, and response to, project impacts. However in this case and following from Hope Vale's experience, the company undertook to bear part of the Mapoon community's costs in participating in this framework.

There are also some significant differences between the two agreements, reflecting both the nature of Venture's planned project and the specific concerns articulated by the Mapoon community through the ESIA process. However, the link between that process and the eventual outcome is again very clear, a point that can be illustrated through a discussion of the arrangements for financial compensation.

A number of factors shaped the community's approach to financial compensation. Most people were supportive of the project and they recognized the need to design a compensation regime that would facilitate its establishment by not placing too heavy a financial burden on the project during its early years. However, there was also a strong feeling among community members that older people, who had borne the brunt of the earlier dispossession, should have a chance to share in income from the project before they passed away. Also relevant was the fact that mineral processing, as well as extraction, would take place on Aboriginal land. People forcefully expressed the view that the return they received should reflect the value of the processed product that left their land—a royalty should be charged not on the value of raw material extracted from the ground, as normally occurs, but on the value of products leaving the processing plant. Finally, the Mapoon community was attempting, with very limited resources, to reestablish itself on its traditional lands. From this perspective it was important to achieve a predictable flow of royalty revenues that could form the basis for longer term community planning and development (Holden and O'Faircheallaigh 1995b).

The financial regime contained in the Venture/Mapoon agreement consists of the following components:

- An "up-front" sum payable on issue of the mining leases, which is meant to ensure that older people in the community obtain some immediate benefit.
- A relatively low royalty that applies during years 1 to 5 of commercial production, based on a fixed amount per tonne of processed output, and linked to the Consumer Price Index (CPI) to protect against inflation.
- A higher royalty from year 6 onward, linked to weighted average prices for processed products, but with a "floor" royalty per tonne and a minimum total annual payment (the latter linked to CPI).
- A free issue of equity in the project.

This regime is designed to facilitate development of the project by easing royalty payments during its early years. However, it also seeks to ensure that the community will obtain substantial returns in later years. In addition, and very importantly, it guarantees the community a specific minimum level of income as long as mining continues, providing it with some protection against depressed prices and facilitating the use of mining income in community planning and development.

Both case studies discussed here involve situations where developers were obliged, by law, to negotiate with indigenous people. However, opportunities to negotiate can arise in the absence of such legal requirements. Thus Comalco Ltd, which has operated one of the largest bauxite mines in the world at Weipa (see Figure 1) since the early 1960s, is currently involved in negotiations with the Cape York Land Council and Aboriginal communities as a result of a policy decision by Comalco's parent company, CRA Ltd, to develop more satisfactory relationships with indigenous communities affected by its operations (Davis 1995). ESIAs similar to those carried out for Cape Flattery and Skardon River have provided the basis for negotiations in this case also.

Conclusion

These case studies demonstrate that it is indeed possible for indigenous people to take control of SIA and ensure that it reflects their experiences and their goals. Very importantly, they also show that a negotiation-based approach can allow SIA to help shape the outcomes of development projects in ways favorable to indigenous communities.

In addition, the case studies indicate that some of the more general problems associated with SIA and identified earlier in the article can be minimized. There is no need for SIA to be solely *ex ante*, as the Hope Vale case study shows. SIA can pay as much attention to the possibilities for achieving positive economic and social gains as to the mitigation of social costs. The creation of structures such as the Hope Vale/CFSM Coordinating Committee can help ensure that impact assessment is "iterative and ongoing" and continues long after the "consultants and report writers" have departed, and, as in the Skardon River case, developers can be required to share in the cost of supporting those structures.

The approach to SIA described here is project-based, but this does not imply that it cannot incorporate broader regional and indeed global or that cumulative impacts cannot be considered. The Hope Vale study, for instance, included an analysis of Mitsubishi's international corporate structures and of regional economic impacts, providing a way of addressing these wider contexts (Holden and O'Faircheallaigh 1995a, Chapters 10 and 11). The Mapoon ESIA had a strong "cumulative" focus in that its starting point in examining the likely effects of the Skardon River project was an analysis of the earlier impact of the mission closure and the dispersal of Mapoon people (Holden and O'Faircheallaigh 1995b, 23–32).

I do not wish to argue that a negotiation-based approach is unproblematic. One fundamental critique of such an approach emerges from the literature dealing with attempts to resolve environmental and land use conflicts through negotiation or mediation. Critics argue that such attempts may be misplaced because conflict in these areas often reflects basic value differences that are not subject to compromise. They also argue that, where an imbalance in power exists between the parties involved, negotiation may simply institutionalize existing inequalities, damaging the interests of the weaker party. In addition, negotiation can serve as a mechanism for cooption, with groups opposed to developer interests being persuaded to engage in negotiation processes that allow them to achieve only marginal gains, while at the same time they abstain from using legal or political avenues that might have yielded more positive outcomes. Drawing these points together, there is a perceived danger that those who lack power can be coopted into negotiations that are essentially tokenistic and as a result give way on matters that involve fundamental issues of principle (Amy 1983; Austin and Bullets 1996; Campbell and Floyd 1996; RuBino and Jacobs 1990).

These arguments could obviously be relevant in an indigenous context. Large-scale resource development can raise fundamental value conflicts for indigenous people; they do often suffer from an imbalance of power relative to developers and governments; and cooption into negotiation processes could, in this situation, result in (unnecessary) sacrifices in relation to fundamental values.

However, three opposing points can also be made. First, assuming that SIA processes are under community control and include appropriate participative methodologies, they should serve to highlight cases where conflict exists over fundamental values. In such cases it may indeed be inappropriate to proceed to negotiations, but there is no reason why such a decision should not in fact be the outcome of the (community-controlled) SIA process.

Second, SIA and negotiation processes of the sort outlined here can help shift the balance of power toward those who are relatively weak. The institutional arrangements negotiated as part of the Cape Flattery agreement, for example, enhance the power of the Hope Vale community relative to CFSM/Mitsubishi. More generally, a great deal of those processes involves providing communities with information and a capacity to apply that information, and this also can significantly enhance their relative power.

Third, there seems to be an assumption in the literature that any cooption that does occur affects only environmentalists, community groups, or (in the current case) indigenous people, and not developers. But is it not possible that developers can also be coopted through the negotiation process, and drawn away from using more traditional methods of dealing with indigenous people, which often involved ignoring them or mobilizing the state to protect developer interests?

Four more specific issues or potential problems should also be acknowledged. First, the mounting of an effective negotiation effort, and so the capacity to utilize SIA findings in the way outlined here, requires access to significant funding, which is often difficult for indigenous communities to secure, while substantial time and human resources must be invested in establishing structures and processes for consultation, negotiation, and implementation (see O'Faircheallaigh 1995 for a detailed discussion). On the other hand, the rewards for what is admittedly a substantial commitment of resources can be very great. Hope Vale, for example, recovered the entire costs of its negotiation effort with CFSM from the first year's additional royalty received under its revised compensation agreement.

Second, the broader legal and political framework may reduce the bargaining position of indigenous people, no matter how well they are organized for the negotiation effort. Of particular importance in this regard is the absence of any legislative framework that requires corporations or governments to achieve negotiated outcomes, leaving indigenous people at the mercy of shifts in corporate or public policies. This indicates the importance of more broadly based political campaigns by indigenous people to establish legal and constitutional recognition of their rights. But it also emphasizes the fact that where the bargaining power of indigenous people is currently limited, it is absolutely essential that they exercise it to maximum effect. SIA, by ensuring systematic identification of impacts, aspirations, and concerns and by helping people to establish priorities, can make a substantial contribution in this regard.

Third, the results of SIA do not flow automatically into the negotiation process. Arrangements must be put in place to ensure that they do so. It is enormously helpful if the indigenous people who will have ultimate responsibility for the negotiations, and any nonindigenous advisers, have been actively involved in the SIA process; the experience of hearing people speak directly about the impact of "development" on their lives is not only valuable in its own right, but also aids in understanding subsequent SIA reports. In the cases reviewed here, the inclusion of the senior SIA consultant in the negotiating team allowed a very direct flow of information. Where this is not considered possible or desirable, SIA consultants should be available to provide briefings both before and during negotiations, and provision for such briefing work should be included in SIA budgets.

Fourth, there is a risk that the negotiation process may take precedence over impact assessment, with the result that a thorough SIA is not conducted (Ross 1989a, 6, 10). This is a particular danger where project schedules place pressure on time frames, as occurred with Skardon River. But that case study also indicates that indigenous people can insist on time frames that allow them to undertake the key components of impact assessment while also acknowledging the developer's time constraints.

Thus there are potential problems that need to be addressed in adopting a negotiation-based approach to SIA. However, these problems are far from insurmountable, as the experience of Cape York communities demonstrates, and a negotiation-based approach can help ensure that indigenous people, in Green's words (1982, 14), "can be the engineers, rather than the recipients, of social change."

Notes

1. Such a situation is discussed in detail in a case study presented later; see also Gondolf and Wells (1986) and Austin and Bullets (1996).

2. Discussions of relevant methodological developments are provided by Blishen et al. (1979), Cowell (1987), Gondorf and Wells (1986), Holden and O'Faircheallaigh (1995a), Lane et al. (1993), Shera and Matsuoka (1992), and Stoffle et al. (1982).

3. For other similar examples see Gondolf and Wells (1986), Geisler (1982b), Fernando (1982), and the case studies presented later.

4. See Craig and Tester (1982) for a discussion of the importance of having an institutional dimension to SIA.

References

Amy, D. J. 1983. The politics of environmental mediation. *Ecol. Law Q.* 11(1):1–18.
Armour, A. 1989. Integrating impact assessment in the planning process: From rhetoric to reality. *Impact Assess. Bull.* 8(1–2):3–15.
Armour, A. 1991. Impact assessment and the planning process: A status report. *Impact Assess. Bull.* 9(4):27–33.
Austin, D. E., and A. Bullets. 1996. Placing dam management on a solid foundation: Southern Paiutes and the Bureau of Reclamation. In *Practical environmental directions*, 21st Annual Conference Proceedings of the National Association of Environmental Professionals, NAEP, 668–75.
Australian Institute of Aboriginal Studies. 1984. Aborigines and uranium: Consolidated report on the social impact of uranium mining on the Aborigines of the Northern Territory. Canberra: Australian Institute of Aboriginal Studies.
Berger, T. R. 1985. *Village journey: The report of the Alaska Review Commission*. New York: Hill and Wang.
Berger, T. R. 1988. *Northern frontier, northern homeland: The report of the Mackenzie Pipeline Inquiry*. Vancouver: Douglas and McIntyre.
Blishen, B. R., A. Lockhart, P. Craib, and E. Lockhart. 1979. Socio-economic impact model for northern development. Ottawa: Department of Indian and Northern Affairs Canada.
Campbell, M. C., and D. W. Floyd. 1996. Thinking critically about environmental mediation. *J. Plan. Literature* 10:235–47.
Carpentaria Land Council. 1995. Supplementary report on Aboriginal issues, Century Project Draft EIS: A submission from the Carpentaria Land Council. Burketown, Australia.
Chase, A. 1990. Anthropology and impact assessment: Development pressures and indigenous interests in Australia. *Environ. Impact Assess. Rev.* 10:11–23.
Coombs, H. C., H. McCann, H. Ross, and N. Williams (eds.). 1989. *Land of promises: Aborigines and development in the East Kimberleys*. Canberra: Centre for Resource and Environmental Studies. Australian National University, and Aboriginal Studies Press.
Corbett, R. 1990. From NIMBY to PIMBY: An alternative approach to social impact assessment. Paper presented at the International Symposium on Hazardous Materials, Toronto, October.
Cowell, N. M. 1987. The impact of bauxite mining on peasant and community relations in Jamaica. *Social Econ. Stud.* 36(1):171–216.
Craig, D. 1989. The development of social impact assessment in Australia and overseas and the role of indigenous peoples. East Kimberley Impact Assessment Project Working Paper No 31. Canberra: Centre for Resources and Environmental Studies. Australian National University.
Craig, F. E., and F. J. Tester. 1982. Indigenous peoples: Reassessing directions for SIA. In *Indian SIA. The social impact of rapid resource development on native peoples*, ed. C. C. Geisler, D. Usner, R. Green, and P. West, 16–40. Ann Arbor: University of Michigan Press.
Davis, L. 1995. New directions for CRA. Speech to the Securities Institute of Australia, Melbourne, March.
Edelstein, M. R., and D. A. Kleese. 1995. Cultural relativity and impact assessment: Hawaiian opposition to geothermal energy development. *Society and Natural Resources* 8:9–31.
Fernando, A. 1982. Upper Skagit: SIA development in Northwest Washington. In *Indian SIA: The social impact of rapid resource development on native peoples*, ed. C. C. Geisler, D. Usner, R. Green, and P. West. 97–106. Ann Arbor: University of Michigan Press.

Finsterbusch, K. 1985. State of the art in social impact assessment. *Environ. Behav.* 17(2):193–221.

Gagnon, C., P. Hirsch, and R. Howitt. 1993. Can SIA empower communities? *Environ. Impact Assess. Rev.* 13:229–53.

Geisler, C. C. 1982a. An Indian–SLA overview. In *Indian SIA: The social impact of rapid resource development on native peoples*, ed. C. C. Geisler, D. Usner, R. Green, and P. West, 1–12. Ann Arbor: University of Michigan Press.

Geisler, C. C. 1982b. Land ownership, control and use as sources of social impacts: The Sokaogan case. In *Indian SIA: The social impact of rapid resource development on native peoples*, ed. C. C. Geisler, D. Usner, R. Green, and P. West, 200–35. Ann Arbor: University of Michigan Press.

Geisler, C. C. 1993. Rethinking SIA: Why ex ante research isn't enough. *Society and Natural Resources* 6:327–38.

Gondolf, E. W., and S. R. Wells. 1986. Empowered native community, modified SIA: The case of Hydaburg, Alaska. *Environ. Impact Assess. Rev.* 6:373–83.

Green, R. 1982. Adapting SIA to unique Indian circumstances. In *Indian SIA: The social impact of rapid resource development on native peoples*, ed. C. C. Geisler, D. Usner, R. Green, and P. West, 13–15. Ann Arbor: University of Michigan Press.

Holden, A., and C. O'Faircheallaigh. 1995a. *The economic and social impact of silica mining on Hope Vale*. Aboriginal Politics and Public Sector Management Monograph No. 1. Brisbane: Centre for Australian Public Sector Management, Griffith University.

Holden, A., and C. O'Faircheallaigh. 1995b. Mapoon people and the Skardon kaolin project. An economic and social impact assessment. Centre for Australian Public Sector Management, Griffith University, Brisbane, January.

Hope Vale/CFSM. 1992. Hope Vale Aboriginal Council and Cape Flattery Silica Mines Pty Ltd, Deed of Compensation. Hope Vale, Australia: Hope Vale Community Council, unpublished.

Howell, B. J. 1983. Implications of the cultural conservation report for social impact assessment. *Hum. Organiz.* 42(4):346–50.

Howitt, R. 1989. Social impact assessment and resource development: Issues from the Australian experience. *Austr. Geog.* 20(2):153–66.

Interorganizational Committee on Guidelines and Principles for Social Impact Assessment. 1995. Guidelines and principles for social impact assessment. *Environ. Impact Assess. Rev.* 15(1):11–43.

Jobes, P. C. 1986. Assessing impacts on reservations: A failure of social impact research. *Environ. Impact Assess. Rev.* 6:385–94.

Justus, R., and J. Simonetta. 1982. Oil sands, Indians and SIA in Northern Alberta. In *Indian SIA: The social impact of rapid resource development on native peoples*, ed. C. C. Geisler, D. Usner, R. Green, and P. West, 238–57. Ann Arbor: University of Michigan Press.

Lane, M., H. Ross, and A. P. Dale. 1993. Social impact research: Integrating the technical, political and planning paradigms. Brisbane: School of Australian Environmental Studies, Griffith University, Mimeo.

Michalenko, G., and R. Suffling. 1982. Social impact assessment in Northern Ontario: The Reed Paper controversy. In *Indian SIA: The social impact of rapid resource development on native peoples*, ed. C. C. Geisler, D. Usner, R. Green, and P. West, 274–89. Ann Arbor: University of Michigan Press.

Mulvihill, P. R., and R. F. Keith. 1989. Institutional requirements for adaptive EIA: The Kativik Environmental Quality Commission. *Environ. Impact Assess. Rev.* 9:399–412.

Nottingham, I. 1990. Social impact monitoring: A Maori perspective—The Tahore case. *Environ. Impact Assess. Rev.* 10:175–83.

O'Faircheallaigh, C. 1995. Negotiations between mining companies and Aboriginal communities: Process and structure. Discussion Paper No. 86. Canberra: Centre for Aboriginal Economic Policy Research. Australian National University.

Ross, H. 1989a. Aboriginal control and participation in SIA. Paper presented to the International Association for Impact Assessment Conference, Montreal, June.

Ross, H. 1989b. Community social impact assessment: A cumulative study in the Turkey Creek area, Western Australia. East Kimberley Impact Assessment Project Working Paper No 27. Canberra: Centre for Resources and Environmental Studies, Australian National University.

RuBino, R. G., and H. M. Jacobs. 1990. *Mediation and negotiation for planning land use management, and environmental protection: An annotated bibliography of materials for the period 1980–1989*. Chicago: Council of Planning Librarians.

Schoepfle, M., M. Burton, and F. Morgan. 1984. Navajos and energy development: Economic decision making under political uncertainty. *Hum. Organiz.* 43(3):265–76.

Shera, W., and J. Matsuoka. 1992. Evaluating the impact of resort development on an Hawaiian island: Implications for social impact assessment policy and procedures. *Environ. Impact Assess. Rev.* 12:349–62.

Stoffle, R. W., M. Jake, M. Evans, and P. Bunte. 1982. Southern Paiute peoples' SIA responses to energy proposals. In *Indian SIA: The social impact of rapid resource development on native peoples*, ed. C. C. Geisler, D. Usner, R. Green, and P. West, 107–34. Ann Arbor: University of Michigan Press.

Waldram, J. B. 1984. Native people and social impact assessment in Canada. *Impact Assess. Bull.* Spring:56–62.

Wolf, C. P. 1981. Getting social impact assessment into the policy arena. *Environ. Impact Assess. Rev.* 1(1):27–36.

Sustainability **2010**, *2*, 1161-1181; doi:10.3390/su2051161

ISSN 2071-1050
www.mdpi.com/journal/sustainability

Article

Fly-in/Fly-out: Implications for Community Sustainability

Keith Storey

Department of Geography, Memorial University of Newfoundland, St. John's, Newfoundland, A1B 3X9, Canada; E-Mail: kstorey@mun.ca; Tel.: +1-709-737-8999; Fax: +1-709-737-3119.

Received: 22 March 2010; in revised form: 7 April 2010 / Accepted: 27 April 2010 / Published: 29 April 2010

Abstract: "Fly-in/fly-out" is a form of work organization that has become the standard model for new mining, petroleum and other types of resource development in remote areas. In many places this "no town" model has replaced that of the "new town." The work system has both beneficial and adverse implications for the sustainability of both existing communities near new resource developments and for the more distant communities from which workers are drawn. This paper explores these outcomes drawing upon examples from North America and Australia.

Keywords: fly-in/fly-out; community sustainability; commute work

1. Introduction

"Fly-in/fly-out" is one of a several terms used to refer to a set of work arrangements for resource operations that are typically located at a distance from other existing communities. The work involves a roster system in which employees spend a certain number of days working on site, after which they return to their home communities for a specified rest period. Typically the employer organizes and pays for transportation to and from the worksite and for worker accommodations and other services at or near the worksite. While most remote operations fly their workforces to and from their worksites, other modes of transport may be used. Fly-in/fly-out is used here as a generic term for these types of commute work arrangements.

This form of work organization is now the standard model for new mining, petroleum and many other types of resource development in remote areas. Over the past twenty-five years, and in Canada and Australia in particular, the "no town" model has replaced that of the "new town." In some recent developments this "temporary community" model is now being used in or adjacent to established communities to accommodate project labour, suggesting that it is not "remoteness" that is necessarily the principal driver in decisions regarding the use of this approach.

Fly-in/fly-out can have both beneficial and adverse implications for community sustainability both in the communities in the regions where it is used, referred to here as the "host" regions, and in those more distant communities from which much of the workforce is typically drawn, the "source" regions. Both beneficial and adverse outcomes can often be seen in the same communities at the same time. There is no simple answer as to whether these work arrangements are "good" or "bad" in community sustainability terms. What does seem certain is that use of fly-in/fly-out will continue to grow in the foreseeable future. This paper explores this complexity, drawing upon examples mainly from Canada, but also Alaska and Australia, in the hope that by identifying potential effects it will help key stakeholder groups—communities, governments and the resource companies—in negotiating strategies that will optimize outcomes for those affected.

2. Fly-in/Fly-out

Fly-in/Fly-out and the establishment of temporary accommodations at the worksite has its origins in the 1950s in the offshore oil industry in the Gulf of Mexico, where increasing distance of the work from the shore made daily commuting impractical [1].

Onshore use of fly-in/fly-out gathered momentum in the 1970s in both Canada and Australia, encouraged by the expansion of mining activity into increasingly remote areas at a time when corporate interests were focusing on "lean" and "flexible" modes of production and when governments were unwilling to support the development of new single-industry communities in remote areas [2]. While these same driving forces remain important today, labour shortages and strong and rapid growth in demand for labour in the construction, mining and petroleum production sectors have further encouraged fly-in/fly-out as a solution to delivering labour to remote locations.

3. Community Sustainability

Both "community" and "sustainability" are contested ideas and "community sustainability" is a term that compounds a number of vague and ambiguous concepts. In summarizing views on the concept Scanlon [3] notes that while the sustainability notion generally has been most extensively developed in relation to environmental concerns, community sustainability is a more recent derivation that has become increasingly broad in scope. The concept has become increasingly specific in that it looks at the practices and actions that are needed at the micro-level that contribute to or hinder sustainability, and more expansive in that it has moved beyond solely the economic dimensions of development, to encompass the social and cultural aspects of how communities cohere through time [4].

However, Scanlon also suggests that outside of an ecological or economic framework, little research work exists on the potential of cultural practices in strengthening communities and even within these frameworks there seems to be little agreement on what community sustainability entails beyond a very general level. Despite a growing literature on community sustainability, and while noting many of its positives including the emphasis on communities as agents of change and sites of participatory decision-making, Voth and Moon [5], conclude that "the idea of community sustainability *per se* hardly exists … Vague abstractions like "social capital" are discussed, but few details are provided about what really makes a community sustainable in terms of infrastructure, economics, culture, decision-making processes, and so on".

It is not the purpose of his paper to try to remedy this perceived deficiency, rather the purpose is to discuss the ways in which fly-in/fly-out work arrangements add to or reduce the challenges that people face in living in remote areas. For the purposes of this paper and acknowledging the limited scope of the definition, "community" here is used in the sense of "people living within a specific area, sharing common ties and interacting with one another" [6], while "sustainability" is taken to imply endurance and the long-term maintenance of wellbeing; "[i]n this sense it is a goal for the future, a prediction" [7].

Community sustainability implies that there is some sense of common goals and values with respect to wellbeing, progress toward achieving which can be measured. Herein lies one of the problems in that those common goals and values, where they exist, are more often implicit rather than explicit. The implications of fly-in/fly-out for community sustainability are not simply the net of the perceived pluses and minuses of the system. The effects are complex and whether over time the net result will mean improved or reduced prospects for community sustainability is not possible to say without a better understanding of what it is that makes a community sustainable. However, the conclusions drawn here may help point to actions that could be taken that can preserve or reinforce those characteristics that are valued by at least some community members, which in turn may contribute to the capacity for their communities to endure.

4. Fly-in/Fly-out and Host Regions

4.1. Fly-over Effects

Regional strategy documents, media reports and other materials repeatedly emphasize the view that resource development companies which operate in rural regions benefit from the resources in those regions but, by accessing their workforces and buying supplies and services from the larger metropolitan centres, they give little back to the regions [8]. These "fly-over" effects [9] are perceived to harm rural regions by failing to provide employment or training opportunities for people in those regions. As such it effectively encourages young people to leave their communities to find work elsewhere which, ironically, could mean back flying back to their own region, and by so doing, inhibits population growth or leads to population decline in rural communities.

Population decline in turn is reflected in business and government decisions that affect the regions negatively. Furthermore, the system is seen to decrease the share of the benefits to local communities from resource developments and effectively helps to undermine government policy with respect to decentralization and regional economic stability or growth. In Australia these perceived effects have led fly-in/fly-out operations to be referred to as the "cancer of the bush" [10].

Fly-over effects mean that many of the benefits of resource developments in remote areas accrue to the larger, distant, metropolitan urban centres. This is particularly evident in Western Australia where most commute workers live in the Perth region. Furthermore, the smaller regional centres not only fail to capture many of the benefits of development within their own regions [11], but often experience additional cost burdens resulting from the need to provide services for transient workers and operators with little return for their investment. This issue is discussed further in Section 4.2.

Government policy can go a long way to address these concerns by ensuring that development approvals are closely tied to industrial benefits planning strategies and impact benefits agreements that seek to maximize local area benefits from resource projects [12]. Fly-over effects can be mitigated by the inclusion of adjacency principles in impact agreements signed between the resource developer and local groups or governments in which hiring and purchasing preferences are given to local workers and businesses, providing that they meet certain capability and cost requirements. Such agreements are standard practice in Canada, but appear somewhat less well developed in Australia. At the same time communities need to clearly understand both industry requirements and their own capacities to ensure that the benefits they would like to see for their communities are realistic and achievable [11]. Benefits Agreements are discussed in greater detail in Section 4.4.

In the absence of a benefits planning process local community impacts may be significantly influenced by company decisions. For example, the Eskay Creek gold and silver mine in northwest British Columbia (1995–2007) operated a fly-in/fly-out operation with pick-up points in Vancouver, Pentiction, Kelowna, Kamloops, Prince George and Smithers. Barrick Gold, the operator chose to establish a regional pick-up point at Smithers rather than Stewart (see Figure 1), which effectively eliminated the latter from capturing some local benefits from the mine [13].

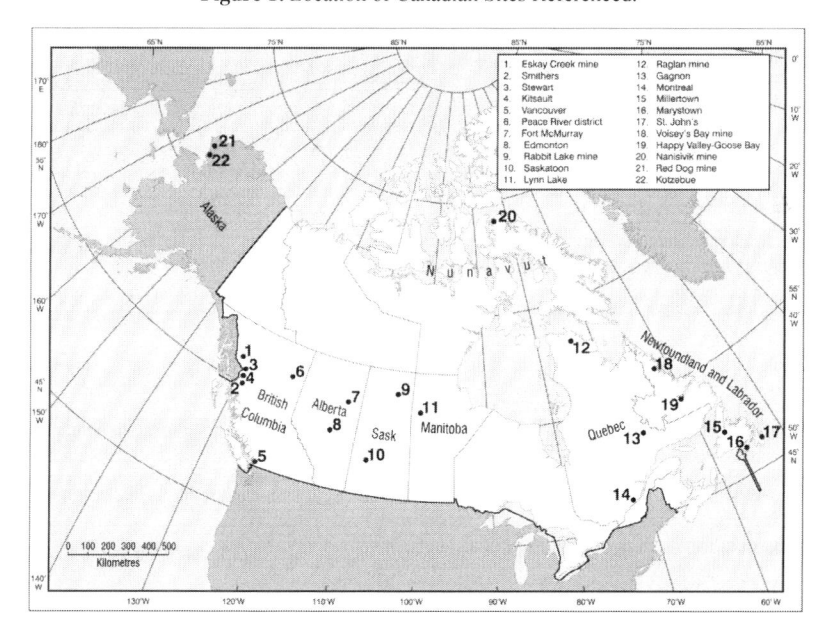

Figure 1. Location of Canadian Sites Referenced.

That said, even with the best of intentions companies may not be able to deliver local benefits as communities might wish. For example, in 2006 Aur Resources, when developing a copper-zinc deposit in central Newfoundland, proposed to base its workforce in the nearby community of Millertown (see Figure 1). However, workers were unwilling to relocate there and instead, over the protests of the local community, a commute operation with a camp near the mine site was established [14].

A similar issue was experienced by the Voisey's Bay mine/mill operation in Labrador. In an attempt maximize project benefits to Labrador, the company (now Vale Inco) tried to encourage workers from outside of Labrador to move into the region by initially agreeing only to pay for travel to the mine site from Happy Valley-Goose Bay in central Labrador (Figure 1). However, insufficient workers were willing to agree to these terms and given the short supply of labour the company had to back down from its original position and agree to payment of full transport costs for those living outside of the region. Once again the local community vigorously opposed the revised arrangements, but was unable to stop them [15].

4.2. Over-development

If lack of project-community interaction is a concern for some, too much interaction is a problem for others. For example, the pace and scale of oil and gas exploration and operations in northern British Columbia and oil sands development and operations activity in northern Alberta in Canada has increased significantly in the last decade, much of which has involved fly-in/fly-out or other types of commute work. Accompanying these developments have come community concerns about environmental disturbance, including ground water use, noise, dust, flaring and gas emissions, and other types of pollution. Aboriginal groups in particular have been concerned about the disturbance of spaces and places with spiritual value or the potential for hunting, fishing and other traditional activities to be adversely affected.

Concerns have also been expressed about the costs of development associated with a large transient population which makes little contribution to the community, but which may have high social costs as a result of increases in crime, drug use, prostitution, gambling and similar activities. These activities also have economic consequences as increased demands are placed upon infrastructure and services, the cost burden of which tends to fall on the community rather than the resource developer.

The growth of oil and gas activity in the Peace River District of northeastern British Columbia (see Figure 1) illustrates this type of problem and an approach to its resolution. The local economy has undergone a significant restructuring over the past two decades. Traditionally based on forestry and agriculture, a 40% growth in the oil and gas sector between 2001 and 2006 means that this sector now represents 30% of the regional economy [13]. This shift has placed significant demands on local physical and social infrastructure and services, demands on which local authorities have been unable to keep pace, largely because of their inability to raise revenue beyond property taxes. While forestry and mining activities often fell within municipal boundaries and were subject to local taxation, oil and gas activities generally take place either on private land or on crown lands beyond municipal control. Though not subject to local taxation, resource developers still benefit from the use of local infrastructure and services.

In 1993 the Province of British Columbia recognized the fiscal imbalances that development could cause and began negotiations for what would become the Fair Share Agreement (FSA). A memorandum of understanding was developed between the Province and local municipalities acknowledging that local governments should be compensated for services and infrastructure costs associated with resource developments taking place within their regions. The Agreement was renegotiated in 1998 and again in 2005. The current agreement is for a 15-year period and indexed against the 2004 rural industrial assessment base.

The FSA approach is one that has not been replicated elsewhere in British Columbia. It helps to address some of the direct costs incurred by local municipalities, but tensions remain about the effects of development on the environment, health and safety and lifestyles. The commute work approach to development is not seen as conducive to community stability, growth or long-term development. For many local residents there is considerable frustration with the responses of the industry to local concerns and with the apparent lack of planning for resource development generally. These frustrations have been manifested in the most extreme sense by a series of bomb attacks on gas pipelines in the region since October 2008 [13].

The problems of rapid growth and fly-in/fly-out are even more pronounced in the Regional Municipality of Wood Buffalo and Fort McMurray its main urban centre (see Figure 1), though to date responses have not been as extreme. Commercial development of the oil sands in the region began in the early 20th century, but activity levels have fluctuated over time. The "modern" oil sands era began in 1978 with the official opening of the Syncrude Project, but further stagnation in investment is reflected in the limited (1.1%) population growth in the area between 1986 (36,810) and 1996 (37,222). A revitalized interest in oil sands projects in the next decade saw the area population more than double (103%) by 2006 (75,717) and increase by another 36% to an estimated 103,334 by 2008. At the same time the number of fly-in/fly-out and other "mobile" workers in the area, those working in the municipality but with permanent residences elsewhere, increased from 3,568 in 1996 to 10,442 in 2006 and to 26,284 in 2008 [16].

The Municipality has struggled to keep pace with the growth in population and the associated growth in demand for all types of infrastructure and services. While fly-in/fly-out workers who live in camps place fewer demands on infrastructure and services than those who have migrated to the area and live in the community, their impacts and those of the projects where they work is not insignificant.

For example, the 435 km of Highway 63 between Fort McMurray and Edmonton to the southwest is the main route between the two centres. Project traffic and workers commuting to and from their work sites and their homes use it. It has some of the highest tonnage per kilometer of highway in Canada, among the largest and heaviest loads, and is among the most dangerous. Locally dubbed, the "Highway of Death" [17], there were 1,011 collisions between 2001 and 2005 in which 25 people died and 257 were injured. Increased activity in the area and greater highway use saw 22 people killed on the highway in 2007 alone. Provincial funding saw twinning of the highway begin in 2007 but the province has been criticized for not expediting the work while at the same time approving new projects in the area [18].

New project applications frequently use the argument that fly-in/fly-out will minimize demand on local infrastructure and services [19,20], however, the cumulative effects of multiple developments and growth of the community of Fort McMurray have meant that demands on medical and other services used by the local and transient populations have exceeded local capacities. With decisions regarding development of oil sands projects being made at the provincial level, but responses to those decisions expected to be addressed at the municipal level, the absence of an overall planning and funding process has meant that growth has outpaced the ability of the municipality to adequately respond. The economic downturn experienced in 2008 was, in the view of the Mayor of Fort McMurray, a welcome respite from the pace of growth that had been experienced and an opportunity to perhaps regroup and catch up with some of the demand on municipal infrastructure and service before the next growth phase [21].

Notwithstanding some evidence of forward planning efforts [22-25], similar problems of overdevelopment seem to be in store for the Surat Basin in southeast Queensland (see Figure 2). The Queensland government has identified mining and energy production as priority sectors, and the Surat Basin will play an increasingly important role in this development because of its large coal and gas resources. Nearly 50 mine and energy projects were expected to be up and running in the Basin by 2011, with a number of companies planning or developing coal seam gas, underground coal gasification and liquefied natural gas projects [26].

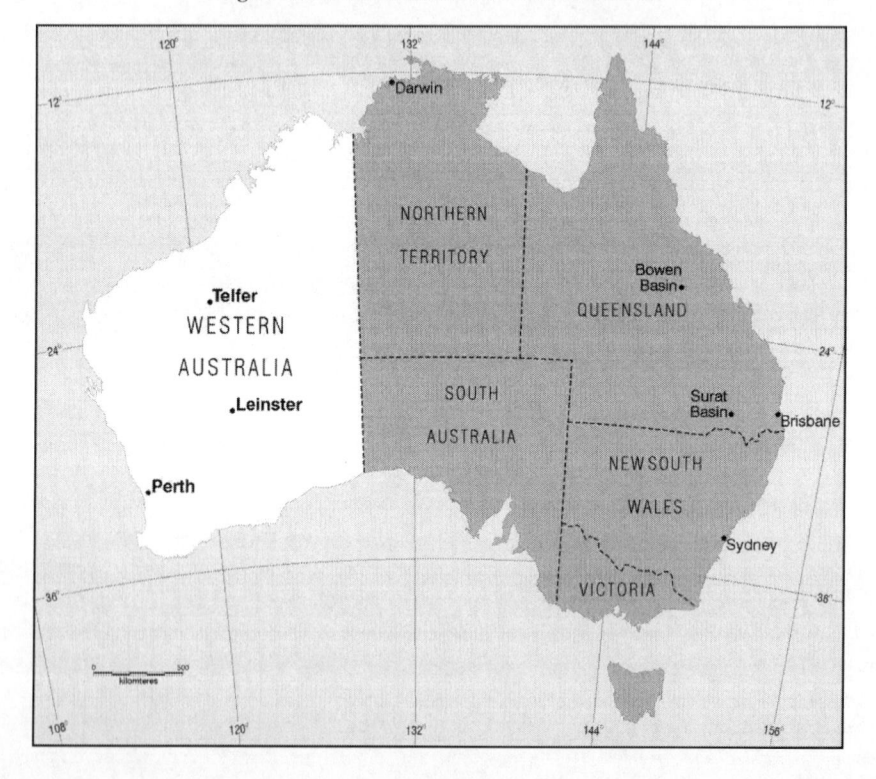

Figure 2. Location of Australian Sites Referenced.

Within the Surat Basin there are a number of relatively remote communities based on agriculture. Towns in the area are generally small and serve as community hubs for their rural catchment areas as well as centres for administration and commerce, and most have established infrastructure and service delivery networks that reflect their past roles and population distributions.

Prolonged periods of drought over the past two decades and rising fuel and labour costs have adversely affected the profitability of agriculture. Many younger people have left the area for larger urban centres or for better paid employment elsewhere, including the mining industry of central Queensland. In addition, a growing number of older people have moved to coastal areas and larger regional centres on retirement. As a result, the size of the populations of most of the smaller communities in the region fell between 1981 and 2007 [27].

The recent large scale and rapid resource development-led change has, not surprisingly, resulted in the emergence of numerous new social issues including employment and skills shortages, a shortage of affordable housing, social inequities and lack of appropriate infrastructure and services [27]. The adjacent Bowen Basin (see Figure 2) has faced similar transformations due to the exploitation of coal reserves in the recent past. The resulting socio-economic transformations included significant benefits, but also unintentional and socially undesirable effects that communities in the Surat region would like to avoid. Given the willingness of the State government to fast-track developments, this may be difficult. While there is local concern about the use of fly-in/fly-out [28], it appears that skills shortages and lack of local infrastructure to accommodate the required workforce means that there may be little choice but to use fly-in or drive-in roster arrangements if the proposed development schedule is to be maintained.

Some resource developers in the region, such as Arrow Energy, plan to draw on local or locally resident labour, arguing that living in the area and having a more settled career with the opportunity for good family life will prove more attractive to prospective employees than commuting [29]. Others are less convinced that this will be possible. The Curtis Island LNG project is expected to create some 5,000 direct jobs, however, a spokesperson for Australia Pacific LNG, the project developers, indicated that: "We are planning ... to have up to 80 per cent of our workforce fly in and out because we think we will only be able to attract 20 per cent of a local workforce" [29].

Even Government is anticipating infrastructure needs to facilitate fly-in/fly-out. As a spokesperson for Energy Skills Queensland noted: "The geographic spread of potential CSG/LNG sites means that jobs will be available from locations west of Toowoomba as far north as Townsville, with opportunities to either live in rural... locations or to fly in, fly out from coastal centres" [25].

Notwithstanding an apparent realization of the need for impact management planning to maximize the benefits and minimize the costs of resource development in the Surat Basin, it is difficult to imagine that, given the scale and rate of development proposed, investment in community and regional infrastructure and services will be able to keep pace with development, or that fly-in/fly-out will be the solution to minimizing local infrastructure and service demands. If so, little will have been learned from the Bowen Basin experience or from elsewhere.

4.3. Aboriginal Communities

Where the scale and pace of fly-in/fly-out activity has been more modest, host regions can benefit in ways that may be different from those associated with traditional town site development. Fly-in/fly-out was, for example, originally seen as a potentially valuable component of government affirmative action programs designed to encourage participation of Aboriginal peoples in resource development. The commute system allowed Aboriginal people to participate in the resource-based activity while at the same time minimizing potential adverse social interactions through the separation of home and workplace and allowing them to maintain elements of their traditional lifestyle [30].

In Canada the first fly-in/fly-out program specifically designed to incorporate Aboriginal labour was the Panarctic Oil Project, which included a commute for Aboriginal workers from (the former) Pond Inlet and Arctic Bay, Baffin Island, to exploration sites in the Arctic Islands. In 1974 Gulf Minerals Canada Ltd. established a fly-in/fly-out system between Aboriginal communities in the Athabasca/Fond du Lac River region in Northern Saskatchewan and its Rabbit Lake uranium mine (see Figure 1). Commuting from communities in this region to various uranium operations in northern Saskatchewan continues to this day [13].

In Canada in particular, the fly-in/fly-out model has been seen as a means of incorporating Aboriginal workers into the industrial work world. Experience in Saskatchewan serves to illustrate this [13]. In the 1970s mining companies in northern Saskatchewan saw the opportunity to tap into an undeveloped "local" labour source when they found themselves competing for labour in the north with the petroleum industry and an expanding potash sector and while employment levels were high in southern Saskatchewan [31]. From a government perspective, integration of northern Aboriginal peoples into the economic mainstream was consistent with policy, while at the same time there was little appetite for supporting the cost of development of new resource towns [32]. Furthermore, from an Aboriginal resource worker perspective, work that required relocation to towns was not an attractive proposition, while fly-in/fly-out work allowed participation without permanent relocation [33].

Both levels of government have supported and facilitated Aboriginal involvement in northern resource development projects. In Saskatchewan, the provincial government funded improved transportation infrastructure in the north, and both the federal and provincial governments have invested heavily in Aboriginal education and training programs.

4.4. Benefits Agreements

The past twenty-five years has seen significant changes in the political power of Aboriginal groups. In Canada, as a result of Aboriginal title decisions, land claims agreements, statutory requirements or government policy, Impact Benefits Agreements (IBAs) of various types have become a recognized part of the package of regulatory requirements associated with major resource projects [34]. Similarly, in Australia, Indigenous Land Use Agreements (ILUA), agreements on State land where native title has not been extinguished, may be signed between the proponent and the affected indigenous group as one of the conditions for development [35]. These are intended to address the concerns of Aboriginal people and other local residents regarding the potential adverse effects that large-scale development could have on their communities, while at the same time ensuring that local people and communities have the opportunity to benefit from the developments occurring in their region.

IBAs and ILUAs are legally enforceable, usually confidential, contracts in which the local group promises to support a proposed project in return for the developer's commitment to local benefits, environmental and cultural protection and other terms. Increased political power on the part of landowners and residents, and a greater awareness on the part of resource development companies of the need to demonstrate social responsibility have encouraged the negotiation of benefit agreements with (primarily indigenous) groups adjacent to new developments. The benefit of investing in "a social license" to conduct business can facilitate and help maintain local support for the project that might otherwise be affected through, for example, delays due to local resistance.

The nature of these agreements has changed over time [13]. In Canada, for example, in the 1970s and early 1980s they were mainly between industry and government, e.g., Surface Lease Agreements in Northern Saskatchewan, in which government was acting on behalf of the residents, particularly Aboriginal residents, in the region affected by the project. Today most agreements now take the form of IBAs and are made directly between industry and Aboriginal groups. Non-Aboriginal people, businesses and communities adjacent to the project may benefit from commitments made by the resource developer through preferential hiring of local workers or contract awards to local companies, but these commitments are usually to government and are made on behalf of rather than by those directly affected.

In Saskatchewan the first Surface Lease Agreement with Amok in 1979, included a requirement to employ 50 per cent "northerners." In order to facilitate this, a free 7/7 fly-in/fly-out schedule was to be established between the minesite and at least five points in northern Saskatchewan. Once established the schedule could only be altered if necessary and if approved by the employees.

Since then fly-in/fly-out systems have since become the standard model for delivering Aboriginal workers to Saskatchewan uranium and other northern resource operations, and there are now a variety of agreement mechanisms from Impact Benefits Agreements to Joint Venture Agreements designed to encourage northern Aboriginal employment, business development and other socio-economic effects of potential benefit [36]. While the involvement of Aboriginal people in northern resource development may not have grown as much or as quickly as was perhaps originally hoped, there has nonetheless been a significant increase in the number of Aboriginals working in the sector. In Saskatchewan, for example, overall employment of "northern residents" in northern mining operations increased from 18.5%, in 1989 to 34.2% in 1991 [37], and to 51% in 2006. In the latter case, 85% of northern resident employees were of Aboriginal ancestry [38].

In the early days expectations for Aboriginal involvement in mining and other resource developments were often unrealistic. The formal education and training requirements required for many positions could not be met by most Aboriginals given their low levels of education and training, and limited experience in working in a cash income economy. For example, at the start of production in 1976, the Nanisivik zinc mine (see Figure 1) had hoped for a 60% Aboriginal workforce, but by 1992 had settled for 25% or less, though it was still at the time seen as "one of the best hiring records in the Canadian North" [39].

Similarly, at the Cominco Red Dog mine north of Kotzebue, Alaska (see Figure 1), under the agreement negotiated in 1982, first preference in hiring was given to Northwest Alaska Native Association (NANA) Regional Corporation shareholders with the objective being to have 100% shareholder employment by 2002. In spite of on-site and off-site education and training programs, by this date only 50–60% of Red Dog employees were NANA shareholders and the 100% goal continues to remain elusive [39].

These earlier experiences have, however, benefited recent operations. Employment quotas are now less likely to be specified, but demonstration of "best efforts" to hire Aboriginal workers is required. Expectations for local hiring may now better reflect different regional conditions. For example, the

Agreement between the Makkivik Corporation and Falconbridge for the Raglan nickel operation in northern Quebec (see Figure 1) relies on best efforts with respect to Aboriginal hiring and here Inuit hires represent about 16% of the 300-person workforce [40]. By contrast, at the Vale Inco Voisey's Bay Mine/Mill in Labrador (see Figure 1), and even though Aboriginal hiring quotas are non-enforceable, the minimum expectation was for 25% Aboriginal hires, with 50% as the objective. In 2008 Innu and Inuit hires in fact represented 54% of the workforce [36].

While impact benefit agreements may give priority to hiring individuals from within the project region, there is no guarantee that income and other benefits will continue to flow to the communities from which they were hired. Most commute arrangements see workers travelling from designated pick-up points or their travel costs paid for from a variety of locations. This gives workers a greater choice over where they choose to live at no cost to themselves in terms of journey-to-work transportation costs.

In Saskatchewan, McBain [37] found that 36% of "northern hires" working in the north were living in the south. The definition of a "northerner" had changed over time and so not all of these may have been relocations, nevertheless, this out-migration represents a loss of key working members of northern Aboriginal communities and a reduction in potential multiplier effects of income expenditures in those communities [13]. A variety of reasons have been offered for the moves. For example, some had moved to larger southern centres to provide better opportunities for their families, while others had moved to avoid pressures from family and other community members to share the income that they had earned [31].

While over the last 40 years Aboriginal involvement in fly-in/fly-out work has increased significantly, industrial careers may not necessarily be what many are seeking. Aboriginal workers at Red Dog describe jobs at the mine as welcome opportunities, but mining may less often be considered as a career. Punctuality, consistency and hierarchical control structures, all common feature of industrial work, may not match traditional life characteristics [39]. Education achievement levels among Aboriginal people are still low compared with the rest of the Canadian and Australian workforces and many of those leaving school often lack the academic proficiencies to qualify for training programs or jobs in the professions or trades [41].

For some Aboriginal workers commute work is important in helping to support traditional lifestyle activities. Where work schedules are permissive or organized to allow absence from the workplace during important hunting or harvesting times, or during important ceremonial and spiritual events, conflict between the industrial work culture and Aboriginal culture can be minimized. At the same time cash income can facilitate ongoing engagement in traditional activities through the increased ability to purchase equipment and pay travel costs to access hunting, fishing and gathering areas more efficiently [31].

4.5. Community Re-designation

Single industry communities, particularly those based on non-renewable resources, often do not survive the depletion or decline in viability of their resource base. The mining "ghost towns" of the early 20th century bear are testimony to this. In Canada, closures followed by abandonment (e.g., Lynn Lake Manitoba), demolition (e.g., Gagnon, Quebec), or sell-off (e.g., Kitsault, BC) (see Figure 1), have been among the ways of dealing with traditional resource communities that are no longer viable. While fly-in/fly-out has been seen as a way of avoiding establishing "permanent" settlements with potentially short life-expectancies it has also been used as a transitional phase in the life-cycle of a number of permanent settlements.

There are few remaining "company towns" in Canada, but in Australia companies have been able influence community sustainability by choosing whether or not remain as "closed" towns with restricted residential access and whether or not to use fly-in/fly-out arrangements. The town of Telfer, WA, for example, was built in 1976 by Newmont Mining to accommodate workers at the Telfer gold mine (see Figure 2). By the early 1990s the population had grown to almost 1,000 and community services included a supermarket, police station, bank, community hall, library and sporting facilities. At this time the community had all of the characteristics of a remote mining town with a male/female ratio of 2.4/1, 50 per cent of the population under the age of 35 and an annual turnover in population of 20 per cent [42].

In 1996 the mine owners (now Newcrest Mining) made the decision to switch to fly-in/fly-out. The rationale was to give the mine access to a larger supply of skilled workers and to those who would otherwise have been unwilling to relocate to Telfer. The change in work arrangements resulted in all commercial services being withdrawn, only the recreational facilities were kept, and existing housing was used to accommodate fly-in/fly-out workers. In 2000 operations were suspended because of high operating costs, but in 2002 Newcrest announced a redevelopment plan and the mine reopened in 2004, once again as a fly-in/fly-out operation.

Leinster, also in WA (see Figure 2), has experienced a less dramatic, but for those permanent residents there, perhaps a crueler fate. Established as a "closed" or company town in 1976 to provide accommodation facilities for workers at the nearby Agnew nickel mine, it struggled for financial viability in the early 1980s and was eventually closed and both the mine and the town were placed under "care and maintenance". In 1989 the new owner WMC Resources (now part of BHP Billiton) recommenced mining and repopulated the town, providing accommodations for workers at its Leinster Nickel and Agnew Gold operations.

The town's status as a closed, company town added to its attractiveness as a residential option. Pattenden [43] reports that the metaphor of "an oasis in the desert" was a recurring theme in residents' description of the town. However, the situation changed in the 1990s when WMC offered workers the opportunity to either be resident in the town or work fly-in/fly-out rosters. By 2000 the population consisted of approximately 1,400, of whom 587 were residents (workers, children and non-working spouses) and the remaining two-thirds fly-in/fly-out workers. What had been a planned 210 residential unit community in 1977 had become a 1,100-person, predominantly fly-in/fly-out accommodation village.

The effects of this shift in the workforce balance are not surprising. Material infrastructure in the residential part of the town was less utilized and deteriorated. Town shops lost a large part of their client base and service to residents declined. There was a significant reduction in the number of people who had any involvement in the organization of and participation in community activities such as sport or social functions. The number of school children declined bringing into question the viability of schooling in the community and further reduced the opportunities for interaction activity and stimulation that parents regarded as necessary for healthy child development. Furthermore, the decline in the number of social contacts added to the "burn-out" factor associated with the intensity of living, working and socializing in close proximity with the same group of people and turnover in the residential workforce increased [43].

In 2000–2001 WMC conducted a review of the town's future. This created further tension and uncertainty with many residents believing that the outcome of the review would be the dismantling of the town's residential infrastructure and a conversion to fly-in/fly-out only. As yet that has not happened and workers still have the choice of being resident in Leinster or fly-in/fly-out commuters. How the current owners, BHP Billiton, see the future of the community is unknown. While the town is dependent on the life of the mine, the same cannot be said of the reverse. The mine could easily be sustained with an entirely fly-in/fly-out workforce and so the future of the town and that of its residents is far from clear. While there was never any indication that Leinster would ever have been "normalized" or that if it had it would have been sustainable, by switching to the fly-in/fly-out model either of those possibilities seems likely to have gone for ever.

5. Fly-in/Fly-out and Source Regions

5.1. Income and Lifestyle Support

Fly-in/fly-out can also have important consequences for source regions from which workers are drawn. In Saskatchewan, for example, the face of rural agriculture has been changing for many years and the family farm has been in decline. For some farmers wishing to retain their farms and stay in agriculture, the opportunity to work on a 7/7 roster at a uranium mine in northern Saskatchewan can fit well with wheat or other grain farming activities. Annual leave time can be combined with the leave period of the roster during planting and harvesting periods, the net effect being that commute work for some can effectively act as a *de facto* agricultural support program [44], while for others the farm can be a tax right-off against their mine income.

In Newfoundland and Labrador and other parts of the Atlantic Provinces of Canada, commute work has become an opportunity for many to be able to earn an income, or a higher income than would normally be possible locally, while at the same time maintaining their residence and family life in their home communities.

Until recently Newfoundland and Labrador has traditionally been the poorest of the Canadian provinces and unemployment rates at 15.3 per cent (September 2009) are still twice that for Canada as a whole [45]. Workers from the province have had a long history of going away to work, whether to the Labrador for the summer fishery, the north-east USA in the 19th and early 20th centuries to help build the skyscrapers of New York and Boston, since the 1950s to the Great Lakes to crew bulk carriers, or, most recently, to help construct oil sands processing facilities in Alberta. Data are poor and estimates vary, but in the order of 6–7% of the workforce are currently thought to be "mobile workers", workers who live in Newfoundland or Labrador but who work outside the province.

This migratory workforce exhibits a wide variety of work arrangements. Some are involved in seasonal work and may be absent from their home communities for several months at a time on no fixed roster, others work in the offshore petroleum sector either locally or internationally on regular 21/21, 28/28, or similar rosters. The majority however, travels to Alberta for construction work.

The Marystown area, on the Burin Peninsula in the southern part of Newfoundland (see Figure 1), exemplifies the current practice. Local industrial employment opportunities have traditionally been in the offshore fishery and fish processing, and more recently at the Marystown Shipyard and the Cowhead Marine Facility. The collapse of the fishery in 1992 saw the end of the offshore fleet and significant reductions in fish processing employment, while employment at the shipyard and at Cowhead over the years has at best been sporadic. When there is work, as was the case from April 2004 to August 2005 with the outfitting of the FPSO for Husky Oil's White Rose offshore oil project, local workers were able to stay at home and find employment. During times when there is no local work, they commute either regularly or periodically to places like Fort McMurray in Alberta and find work on the oil sands projects.

With local economic well being intimately connected to activity in the fishery and at the shipyards, employment and income levels can be highly volatile. Incomes flows from outside the province associated with commute work are therefore essential in helping to sustain the local economy on an ongoing basis. How long this will continue remains to be seen. Younger people may be more likely to weigh the trade-off between the perceived benefits of "home" and living a more settled existence elsewhere in favour of the latter, and indeed there has been a steady loss of population (19.4 per cent) from the area since 1996 [46,47]. Whether commute work in the absence of stable local employment can continue to sustain communities like Marystown over the long term is a question that as yet to be fully answered.

The boom in oil sands construction in Alberta between 2003 and the economic downturn in 2008 provided many workers with significant income earning opportunities. To date there have been no formal studies of commute work effects on source communities, but there is considerable anecdotal and visual evidence of local spin-off benefits in terms of new house construction and sales of trucks and recreational equipment such as snowmobiles and all-terrain vehicles.

5.2. Community Costs

While employment and income opportunities represent the upside for source communities, loss of local trades people, local volunteers and community leaders is part of the downside. Members of these groups are in increasingly short supply in rural Newfoundland in any event as a result of out-migration and an aging population. Temporary migration associated with commute work only serves to exacerbate the problem. Work away can mean on-the-job training for some and added experience for all. It can also mean that younger workers leave training programs before they complete them, lured away by the immediate income opportunities, with little thought for the future when formal qualifications might be a necessity.

Higher incomes can also bring with them imported issues associated with poor lifestyle choices such as increased drug and alcohol usage, gambling and increased incidences of sexually transmitted diseases. Likewise for some separation of work and home may place pressure on family relationships and contribute to family break-ups and family violence.

Much is made of these potential negative outcomes in the media, but there is only limited empirical to support these contentions. Newfoundland has a large number of mobile and commute workers, but overall divorce and separation rates continue to be the lowest in the country [48]. Similarly, research in Australia that examined the impact of commute work on children found nothing to substantiate that the work had any significantly different negative effects from "normal" work arrangements [49]. What is often ignored is that while commute workers may be away from the home and family for extended periods and while they may miss important family events, they also have extended periods at home and the opportunity to spend blocks of quality time with their families, something that may not be available to others who work a regular work week [44]. Other work arrangements, such as shift work, may have more negative consequences for workers and their families, and by extension their communities, but there is little comparative work to demonstrate this.

6. Conclusions

Fly-in/Fly-out can have both positive and negative effects on community sustainability and both may occur at the same place and at the time. While fly-in/fly-out use for land-based resource projects were established somewhat earlier in Canada than Australia, there are now significantly more such operations in Australia [50]. These differences notwithstanding, the evidence suggests that there are a number of significant common experiences with respect to fly-in/fly-out effects on community sustainability.

Scale of activity and proximity to existing communities are perhaps the most important factors influencing the effects of fly-in/fly-out on host region communities. The examples from Northern British Columbia, Northern Alberta and the Surat Basin Queensland illustrate how the cumulative effects of multiple projects without adequate planning and investment in infrastructure and services can adversely affect local communities.

In project host regions the nature of the economic effects of fly-in/fly-out resource development is largely a function of the degree of control that can be exercised by the local community or group over the resources in question. Where there is full land and resource ownership, as in the case of the NANA Regional Corporation in Alaska, control over the pace and scale of development can be exercised locally and the allocation of costs and benefits negotiated and more equitably distributed. IBAs in Canada and ILUAs in Australia may allow local Aboriginal groups to exercise similar control. However, as discussed earlier, even in these circumstances community sustainability may not be guaranteed if, for example, workers choose to relocate to other communities.

Where resource control is not the case, communities and groups may be dependent on government, acting on their behalf, to broker arrangements with the resource companies; Surface Lease Agreements in Saskatchewan are one such example. In other cases communities may have to depend on government to help them meet the incremental costs of development as in the case of the FSA in British Columbia. Where government objectives appear to be directed more to resource revenue generation than community impact management, as in the case of the Regional Municipality of Wood Buffalo and Fort McMurray in Alberta, and the Surat Basin in Queensland, then the community or regional authority may be largely on its own when trying to deal with demands for additional infrastructure and services to cope with development-related demands.

Fly-in/fly-out offers workers the opportunity for well-paid jobs without the need to permanently leave their home communities. For Aboriginal workers in both Canada and Australia it may be one of the few opportunities to be involved in the industrial wage economy without having to leave their particular social and cultural environments. Earned incomes mean taxes for government, and where incomes are spent locally there will be spin-off employment and income benefits for other community members and local businesses. For non-Aboriginal communities that have suffered employment losses in other sectors, as in rural Newfoundland and Labrador and Canada's Maritime provinces, these income opportunities may be, at least temporarily, what help to sustain those communities.

The downside of this may be the question of what happens to workers when the mine or other resource development closes. For Australian workers, particularly those from Western Australia, who may have access to a number of mine sites within range of Perth or other regional centres, switching workplace destinations may be relatively easy. In the Canadian North where there are fewer fly-in operations, distance and cost may make it impractical to draw on workers who had formerly worked at other fly-in/fly-out sites. In addition, jobs will likely first go to workers closer to the new operation under local hiring agreements. This was illustrated when the Nanisivik and Polaris zinc operations in Nunavut closed. The local economic effects were significant as local Inuit workers in the area lost their jobs, but did not have the opportunity to fly-in to work at other mining operations or to use their acquired skills (often not formally accredited) elsewhere in Nunavut or the Northwest Territories [51].

For many individuals fly-in/fly-out work offers opportunities for on-the-job training and career advancement at a faster rate than might be the case in more traditional workplaces. Particularly in Canada, where fly-in/fly-out employment is often associated with lack of opportunities in the home region, the skills and experience acquired may be repatriated to those home regions when opportunities arise. Depending on the particular roster arrangements, fly-in-fly-out can also provide the opportunity for all participants to spend extended quality time with family members during non-work periods and allow continued involvement by Aboriginal employees in traditional pursuits such as hunting and fishing, and participation in special community events.

At the same time, fly-in/fly-out work can be disruptive for communities where workers choose to relocate and live elsewhere while continuing to work fly-in/fly-out rosters. This is common to both Canada and Australia, but there are few data to illustrate that this is as important for Aboriginal workers and communities in Australia as it is in Canada or Alaska. Regardless of country, it can also be disruptive where well-paid fly-in/fly-out jobs create "have/have not" income divisions within the community. Similarly, for families everywhere, separations may mean added stress because one member is away for extended periods, while for communities those absences may mean less participation in volunteer, sports or other political, cultural and social activities. Those left at home may also find that their ability to participate in community affairs is reduced either because of lack of support resources (e.g., child-care) or social *mores* that may discourage participation of the temporarily single and usually female spouse or partner.

For workers, fly-in/fly-out requires a trade-off. Most would presumably prefer to work in well-paid, stable jobs close to home, obviating the need for long travel times and absence from their families, friends and communities. However, work in resource exploration, development and production typically requires a high degree of job mobility and time spent in remote locations. For some there will continue to be the opportunity to exercise their preference to live in (usually) small, remote communities. However, most workers appear not wish to do so and would rather live in larger, often metropolitan, centres with better access to services and infrastructure, employment and other perceived benefits. Australian art critic Robert Hughes is attributed with describing Australians as "a people obsessed with the outback but with little desire to live there" [52], a view corroborated by the distribution of the population in that country, and one which might well be equally applied to many Canadians with respect to their desire to live in the North.

Fly-in/fly-out might thus be seen as a benefit to larger or metropolitan centres as it adds further diversity to their economic bases. In Canada in particular, it has helped to maintain smaller rural communities that have lost their previous economic *raison d'être*, but in both countries it provides communities with opportunities for employment diversification. Likewise, in both Canada and Australia, it may contribute to the development of a new economic base for aboriginal communities previously outside of the industrial economy. At the same time fly-in/fly-out can be destructive to local communities where it results in infrastructure and service demands that the communities cannot meet, or erosive where a shift from "permanent" to fly-in/fly-out communities reduces the economic viability of local infrastructure and services, though the latter appears unique to Australia. Fly-in/fly-out, where it occurs near established communities, may also threaten those towns by reducing the number of workers who, through their relocation, might otherwise have been potential direct contributors to the social and financial well-being of those centres.

As noted in the introduction, there is no simple answer as to whether these work arrangements are "good" or "bad" in community sustainability terms. While the larger resource companies in particular work towards reducing labour requirements and addressing recruitment issues through hi-tech remote controlled mining and other measures, fly-in/fly-out is likely to remain the preferred option for delivering labour to remote places and, increasingly, for not so remote places, because it is cost-effective and maximizes access to a diminishing supply of skilled labour. While this remains the case some communities will find ways to use it to their advantage while others will struggle to deal with its consequences.

Acknowledgements

Thanks to Charlie Conway, Cartographer, Department of Geography, Memorial University for creating the maps used in the text and to two anonymous reviewers who provided comments on the paper.

References and Notes

1. Gramling, R. *Oil in the Gulf: Past Development, Future Prospects*; US Department of the Interior Minerals Management Service, Gulf of Mexico OCS Region: New Orleans, LA, USA, 1995.
2. Storey, K. Commute Work, Regional Development and Settlement Strategies. In *Proceedings of the Conference on the Role of the State in Population Movements: The Circumpolar North and Other Periphery Regions*, Rovaniemi, Finland, 26–28 October 2009.
3. Scanlon, C. *Community Sustainability*; Royal Melbourne Institute of Technology: Melbourne, Australia, 2005; Available online: http://www.communitysustainability.info/debate/frequently_asked_questions.html (accessed on 20 January 2010).
4. Lubbers, R.; Koorevaar, J. Primary Globalisation, Secondary Globalisation, and the Sustainable Development Paradigm—Opposing Forces in the 21st Century. In *Proceedings of EXPO 2000 OECD Forum for the Future Conference on 21st Century Social Dynamics: Towards the Creative Society*, Berlin, Germany, 6–7 December 1999.

5. Voth, D.E.; Moon, Z.K. Defining Sustainable Communities. Rural Infrastructure as a Cause and Consequence of Rural Economic Development and Quality of Life. In *Proceedings of a Regional Workshop*, Birmingham, AL, USA, 1997; Available online: http://www.uark.edu/depts/hesweb/hdfsrs/sustcom.pdf (accessed on 20 January 2010).
6. Lyon, L. *The Community in Urban Society*; Temple University Press: Philadelphia, PA, USA, 1987.
7. Costanza, R.; Patten, B.C. Defining and Predicting Sustainability. *Ecol. Econ.* **1995**, *15*, 193–196.
8. McHugh, B. *Fly-in-Fly-out in the Noughties*; ABC Rural: Perth, Australia, 2009; Available online: http://www.abc.net.au/rural/content/2009/s2764167.htm (accessed on 2 April 2010).
9. Storey, K.; Shrimpton, M. The Social and Economic Impacts of Long Distance Commuting on Employment in the Resource Sector. In *Proceedings of the Annual Meeting of the Canadian Association of Geographers*, McMaster University, Hamilton, Ontario, Canada, 26–30 May 1987.
10. Attributed to John Bowler then Minister for Industry and Resources, State Government of Western Australia, 2006.
11. Storey, K. Fly-in/fly-out and Fly-over: Mining and Regional Development in Western Australia. *Aust. Geogr.* **2001**, *32*, 133–148.
12. Storey, K.; Shrimpton, M. Industrial Benefits Planning in North America: Current Practice and Case Studies. In *Proceedings of the Regional Planning in Greenland Conference*, Nuuk, Greenland, Danmark, 23–24 January 2008.
13. Markey, S.; Storey, K.; Heisler, K. Fly-in/Fly-out Resource Development: Implications for Community and Regional Development. In *Demography at the Edge*: Remote Human Populations in Developed Nations; Carson D., Rasmussen, R.O., Ensign, P.C., Taylor, A., Huskey, L., Eds.; Ashgate Publishing: Farnham, UK, 2010, (in press).
14. *Registration*: *Duck Pond Camp. Environmental Assessment Registration*; Aur Resources: Millertown, NL, Canada, 2006; Available online: http://www.env.gov.nl.ca/env/env/EA%202001/pdf%20files%201221-1309/1297%20-%20DuckPondCamp/1297%20-Reg.pdf (accessed on 28 January 2010).
15. Baker, J. Voisey's Travel Subsidy Kosher. *The Telegram*, 18 August 2005. Available online: http://archives.cedrom-sni.com/WebPages/SearchResult.aspx (Accessed 28 January 2010.)
16. *Municipal Census 2008*; Regional Municipality of Wood Buffalo (RMWB): Alberta, Canada, 2008; Available online: http://www.woodbuffalo.ab.ca/business/demographics/pdf/2008_municipal_census.pdf (accessed on 28 January 2010).
17. Farrell, J. Road to Fort McMurray Dubbed "Death Highway". *Edmonton Journal*, 23 December 2007; Available online: http://www.canada.com/edmontonjournal/news/story.html?id=1ade6e44-1f45-4769-b554c2ccc80c769e&k=96617 (accessed on 28 January 2010).
18. Oil Sands Ministerial Strategy Committee. *Investing in Our Future*: Responding to the Rapid Growth of Oil Sands Development—Final Report; Government of Alberta: Edmonton, AB, Canada, 2007; Available online: http://alberta.ca/home/395.cfm (accessed on 3 February 2010).
19. *Socio-economic Assessment Joslyn North Mine Project—Phase I & II*; Report prepared by IPS Consulting Inc.; Deer Creek Energy: Edmonton, AB, Canada, 2006.

20. *Environmental Assessment of the Northern Lights Project: Volume 8 Land and People*; Report submitted by Synenco Energy Inc., Managing Partner, Northern Lights Partnership; Synenco Energy Inc.: Calgary, AB, Canada, 2006.
21. Pitts, G. The Waning of the Boom. *The Globe and Mail*, 28 December 2008; Available online: http://www.theglobeandmail.com/report-on-business/article729925.ece (accessed on 3 February 2010).
22. Schandl, H.; Darbas, T. *Surat Basin Scoping Study: Enhancing Regional and Community Capacity for Mining and Energy Driven Regional Economic Development*; Report to the Southern Inland Queensland Area Consultative Committee and Australian Government Department of Infrastructure, Transport, Regional Development and Local Government; CSIRO Sustainable Ecosystems: Canberra, Australia, June 2008; Available online: http://www.csiro.au/resources/SuratBasinScopingStudy.html (accessed on 2 April 2010).
23. *Surat Basin Future Directions Statement*; Queensland Government, Department of Employment, Economic Development and Innovation: Brisbane, QLD, Australia, 2010; Available online: http://203.210.126.185/dsdweb/v4/apps/web/secure/docs/4187.pdf (accessed on 2 April 2010).
24. Surat Basin Gets Funding To Handle CSG Boom. *Coal Seam Gas*, 19 March 2010; Available online: http://coal-seam-gas.blogspot.com/ (accessed on 2 April 2010).
25. $10 Million Program to Skill Workers for CSG-LNG Industry. *Licensing Line News*, 7 March 2010; Available online: http://www.licensinglinenews.com.au/Newsletter/Edition-76-March-2010/$10-million-program-to-skill-workers-for-CSG-LNG-industry.aspx (accessed on 2 April 2010).
26. Surat Basin Coal "Booming" Despite Queensland Job Cuts. *Coal Mining*, 15 January 2009; Available online: http://www.miningcoal.com.au/news/surat-basin-coal-booming-despite-queensland-job-cu (accessed on 2 April 2010).
27. *Surat Basin Population Report 2008—Full-Time Equivalent (FTE) Population Estimates at 30 June 2008*; Queensland Govternment: Brisbane, QLD, Australia, 2008; Available online: http://www.oesr.qld.gov.au/queenslandbytheme/demography/population/singlepublications/sura-basin-pop-report-2008/surat-basin-pop-report-2008.pdf (accessed on 2 April 2010).
28. Surat Mining Boom Offers Job Prospects. *9News*, 5 March 2007; Available online: http://news.ninemsn.com.au/article.aspx?id=230692 (accessed on 2 April 2010).
29. Problems on Horizon for LNG Plan. *Coal Seam Gas*, 19 March 2010; Available online: http://coal-seam-gas.blogspot.com/ (accessed on 2 April 2010).
30. Hobart, C. Company Towns or Commuting: Implications for Native People. In *Fly-in and the Future of Canadian Northern Development*; Northern Studies Series No. 1; Robson, R., Ed.; Institute of Urban Studies, University of Winnipeg: Winnipeg, MB, Canada, 1989; pp. 25–38.
31. Gagnon, J. Native Labour Commuting to Uranium Mines in Northern Saskatchewan: Its Economic Significance for Indigenous Communities. In *Coping with Closure: An International Comparison of Mine Town Experiences*; Neil, C., Tykkylainen, M., Bradbury, J., Eds.; Routledge: London, UK, 1992; pp. 291–309.
32. Robson, R. *Canadian Single Industry Communities: A Literature Review and Annotated Bibliography*; Rural and Small Town Research and Studies Programme; Department of Geography, Mount Allison University: Sackville, NB, Canada, 1986.

33. Nogas, F.R. Fly-in Program at Rabbit Lake. *CIM Bull.* **1976**, *69*, 125–128.
34. Kennett, S.A. *A Guide to Impact Benefits Agreements*; Canadian Institute of Resources Law, University of Calgary: Calgary, Alberta, Canada, 1999.
35. *Indigenous Land Use Agreements*; National Native Title Tribunal: Perth, WA, Australia, 2008–2010; Available online: http://www.nntt.gov.au/Indigenous-Land-Use-Agreements/Pages/default.aspx (accessed on 2 April 2010).
36. *Agreements between Mining Companies and Aboriginal Communities or Governments*; Natural Resources Canada (NRCAN): Ottawa Canada, 2008; Available online: http://www.nrcan-rncan.gc.ca/mms-smm/abor-auto/pdf/agr-ent-08-eng.pdf (Accessed 28 January 2010.)
37. McBain, L.A. *An Analysis of the Spatial Distribution of the Northern Labour Force Employed in Uranium Mining in Northern Saskatchewan*; Unpublished M.A. Thesis; Department of Geography, University of Saskatchewan: Saskatoon, SK, Canada, 1995.
38. *Aboriginal Engagement in the Mining and Energy Sectors*; Natural Resources Canada (NRCAN): Ottawa, Canada, 2009; Available online: http://www.nrcan.gc.ca/smm-mms/abor-auto/eng-eng/umi-min-eng.htm (accessed on 28 January 2010).
39. Storey, K.; Hamilton, L.C. Planning for the Impacts of Mega-Projects: Two North American Examples. In *Social and Environmental Impacts in the North*; Rasmussen R.O., Koroleva, N.E., Eds.; Kluwer Academic Publisher: Dordrecht, The Netherlands, 2003; pp.281–302.
40. *Aboriginal Engagement in the Mining and Energy Sectors: Case Studies and Lessons Learned*; Report to Energy and Mines Ministers; Natural Resources Canada (NRCAN): Ottawa, Canada, 2008; Available online: http://www.nrcan-rncan.gc.ca/mms-smm/abor-auto/eng-eng/stu-etu-eng.htm (accessed on 28 January 2010).
41. The Northern Labour Market Committee, Ministry of Advanced Education, Employment and Labour, Northern Region Office. *Northern Saskatchewan Regional Training Needs Assessment Report 2009–2010*; Northlands College: La Ronge, SK, Canada, 2009; Available online: http://career.kcdc.ca/fore/pdf/2009/2009RegionReportfinalwithcover.pdf (accessed on 28 January 2010).
42. Moore, G.G. *Mining Towns in Western Australia*; Chamber of Minerals and Energy of Western Australia: Perth, Australia, 1997.
43. Pattenden, C. *Shifting Sands: Transience, Mobility and the Politics of Community in a Remote Mining Town*; Unpublished Ph.D. Thesis; University of Western Australia: Perth, Australia, 2005.
44. Storey, K.; Shrimpton, M. *Impacts on Labour of Long Distance Commuting in the Canadian Mining Industry*; Report No. 3; Institute of Social and Economic Research, Memorial University: St. John's, NL, Canada, 1989.
45. *Labour Force Characteristics by Province, Seasonally Adjusted*; Statistics Canada: Ottawa, ON, Canada, 2009; Available online: http://www.statcan.gc.ca/pub/71-001-x/2009009/t003-eng.pdf (accessed on 1 February 2010).
46. *Census Analysis Series, A Profile of the Canadian Population: Where We Live*; Statistics Canada: Ottawa, ON, Canada, 2001; Available online: http://geodepot.statcan.ca/Diss/Highlights/Tables_e.pdf (accessed on 1 February 2010).

47. Marystown, Newfoundland and Labrador (Table). *2006 Community Profiles*; Statistics Canada: Ottawa, ON, Canada, 2007; Available online: http://www12.statcan.ca/census-recensement/2006/dp-pd/prof/92-591/index.cfm?Lang=E (accessed on 1 February 2010).
48. *Divorces and Crude Divorce Rates, Canada, Provinces and Territories, Annual, Table 101-6501-CANSIM (Database)*; Statistics Canada: Ottawa, ON, Canada, 2006; Available online: http://cansim2.statcan.gc.ca/cgi-win/cnsmcgi.exe?Lang=E&CNSM-Fi=CII/CII_1-eng.htm (accessed on 1 February 2010).
49. Kaczmarek, E.A.; Sibbel, A.M. The Psychosocial Well-being of Children from Australian Military and Fly-in/Fly-out (FIFO) Mining Families. *Community, Work Family* **2008**, *11*, 297–312.
50. Storey, K. The Evolution of Commute Work in Canada and Australia. Biography, Shift-labour and Socialisation in a Northern Industrial City—The Far North: Particularities of Labour and Human Socialisation. In *Proceedings of the International Conference in Novy Urengoy*, Novy Urengoy, Russia, 4–6 December 2008; Dzida, G.A., Stammler, F., Eilmsteiner-Saxinger, E., Pavlova, M.A., Vakhrusheva, T.A., Borlakova, Z.E., Nourieva, M.Kh., Eds.; Arktinen keskus Arctic Center: Rovaniemi, Finland, 2009; pp. 23–32; Available online: http://arcticcentre.ulapland.fi/docs/NURbook_2ed_100421_final.pdf (accessed on 28 April 2010).
51. Bowes-Lyon, L.M.; Richards, J.P.; McGee, T.M. Socio-Economic Impacts of the Nanisivik and Polaris Mines, Nunavut, Canada. In *Mining, Society, and a Sustainable World*; Richards, J., Ed.; Springer: Berlin, Germany, 2009; pp. 371–396.
52. Priestley, H. Fall of the Mining Town. Eastern Goldfields in Focus 2000; *Australia's Mining Monthly*, March 2000, pp. 38–41.

© 2010 by the author; licensee MDPI, Basel, Switzerland. This article is an open-access article distributed under the terms and conditions of the Creative Commons Attribution license (http://creativecommons.org/licenses/by/3.0/).

# Environmental Impact Assessment Review

Coal mining and the resource community cycle: A longitudinal assessment of the social impacts of the Coppabella coal mine

Stewart Lockie [a,*], Maree Franettovich [b], Vanessa Petkova-Timmer [b], John Rolfe [c], Galina Ivanova [d]

[a] *Institute for Health and Social Science Research, CQUniversity Australia, Rockhampton QLD 4702, Australia*
[b] *Institute for Health and Social Science Research, CQUniversity Australia, Mackay QLD 4741, Australia*
[c] *Centre for Environmental Management, CQUniversity Australia, Rockhampton QLD 4702, Australia*
[d] *Faculty of Business and Informatics, CQUniversity Australia, Rockhampton QLD 4702, Australia*

ARTICLE INFO

Article history:
Received 12 March 2008
Received in revised form 29 January 2009
Accepted 29 January 2009
Available online 9 March 2009

Keywords:
Coal mining
Central Queensland
Resource community cycle
Social impact assessment
SIA

ABSTRACT

Two social impact assessment (SIA) studies of Central Queensland's Coppabella coal mine were undertaken in 2002–2003 and 2006–2007. As ex post studies of actual change, these provide a reference point for predictive assessments of proposed resource extraction projects at other sites, while the longitudinal element added by the second study illustrates how impacts associated with one mine may vary over time due to changing economic and social conditions. It was found that the traditional coupling of local economic vitality and community development to the life cycle of resource projects—the resource community cycle—was mediated by labour recruitment and social infrastructure policies that reduced the emphasis on localised employment and investment strategies, and by the cumulative impacts of multiple mining projects within relative proximity to each other. The resource community cycle was accelerated and local communities forced to consider ways of attracting secondary investment and/or alternative industries *early* in the operational life of the Coppabella mine in order to secure significant economic benefits and to guard against the erosion of social capital and the ability to cope with future downturns in the mining sector.

© 2009 Elsevier Inc. All rights reserved.

1. Introduction

This paper reports the results of two social impact assessment (SIA) studies of Central Queensland's Coppabella coal mine. These studies were conducted both prior, and subsequent to, a major boom in coal prices and production. Additionally, both studies were undertaken outside Queensland's legislative framework for environmental impact assessment and project approval. This framework has been criticised for limiting impact assessment to major new projects, requiring assessment only at the beginning of those projects, and ignoring the influence of exogenous factors that may interact with the proposed project to affect economic and social outcomes (Rolfe et al., 2005; see also Vanclay, 2003). As a consequence, smaller projects, changes to or expansions of existing projects, cumulative impacts from multiple projects across a region, and impacts associated with project closure, are generally exempt from mandatory impact assessment, and few impact assessment studies are followed up post-development to test their accuracy, adjust mitigation strategies, or inform the assessment of other proposals. In light of the project delays, reputational damage, and other costs that may arise from unmitigated social impacts, it is becoming increasingly common for mining companies to undertake a variety of voluntary SIA and/or community consultation activities (Esteves, 2008; Esteves and Vanclay, 2009; Lockie et al., 2008).

In the case of Coppabella, the first SIA was conducted in 2002–2003, some 5 years after the commencement of mining operations, and the follow-up study was performed in 2006–2007. The longitudinal element that has been added to the Coppabella study provides additional insight into how impacts associated with one mine may vary over time due to changing economic and social conditions. Before proceeding to an analysis of Coppabella this paper will contextualise this analysis in a review of other ex-post SIA studies and the role they play in SIA methodology and theory building.

2. Social impact assessment, extractive industry and the resource community cycle

Ex-post studies of actual processes of change following the implementation of projects and policies were identified in the US *Guidelines and Principles for Social Impact Assessment* as the foundation on which social impact assessors should base predictions regarding the likely consequences of proposed change in other communities

* Corresponding author. Tel.: +61 7 49306539; fax: +61 7 49306402.
E-mail addresses: s.lockie@cqu.edu.au (S. Lockie), m.franettovich@cqu.edu.au (M. Franettovich), v.petkova@cqu.edu.au (V. Petkova-Timmer), j.rolfe@cqu.edu.au (J. Rolfe), g.ivanova@cqu.edu.au (G. Ivanova).

0195-9255/$ – see front matter © 2009 Elsevier Inc. All rights reserved.
doi:10.1016/j.eiar.2009.01.008

(Burdge et al., 1995). Despite continuing debate over whether the primary purpose of SIA ought to be predicting future impacts or, by contrast, facilitating public involvement in planning and decision-making (see Lockie, 2001), the comparative methodology outlined in the *US Guidelines and Principles* can be used, in principle, to inform either model by helping to identify the potential range and magnitude of impacts both of initial project proposals and of suggested alternatives. At the same time that public involvement may help to ensure that the predictions of assessors are sensitive to local values, perceptions, aspirations and knowledge, the insights provided through comparative analysis may help to support democratic debate among impacted publics through the systematic identification of potentially disadvantaged groups and of possible impacts which stakeholders may not otherwise have considered (Bass, 1998). Ideally, the body of knowledge on which comparative analysis is based should be sensitive to secondary and cumulative impacts, consider the entire life-cycle of development projects (including closure and decommissioning), and be accessible through peer reviewed publications (Burdge and Vanclay, 2004; Taylor et al., 2003). However, the predominant application of SIA through legislative processes of project approval has limited the development of such a body of knowledge and contributed to what Taylor et al. (2003) refer to as a 'treadmill' of case studies.

According to Taylor et al. (2003), one way to move beyond this treadmill is to treat SIA as an inductive process of theory-building regarding the chains of effects (that is, the ongoing processes of social transformation) that are likely to follow planned intervention. To illustrate this, they examine processes of community formation and change as stimulated by developments in the forestry, mining, agriculture, fishing, energy and tourism sectors. Based on a synthesis of SIA studies (including ex-post studies), they argue that assessing the impacts of any given proposal requires a parallel understanding of how communities are affected by a range of external linkages and processes. For small towns in rural New Zealand, they found that economic growth and decline was affected not only by the changing fortunes of the resource industries themselves, but by a range of inter-related factors including: technological changes that increased demand for skilled labour while reducing overall labour demand; multiple job holding by individuals and increased mobility promoting a regionalisation of labour pools; reduced opportunities for low skilled workers attracted to rural areas by relatively inexpensive accommodation; and an erosion of the human and social capital necessary to promote flexibility and entrepreneurialism. By mapping these factors against a conceptual model of the 'resource community cycle' (see Fig. 1), Taylor et al. (2003) are able to demonstrate their temporal relationships and to highlight a number of issues that typically receive limited attention in pre-approval SIA studies.

The resource community cycle draws explicit attention to the interplay between economic growth and decline, workforce and infra-structure decision-making, population dynamics and social capital. In doing so, it shows how decisions made prior to the implementation of a project have ongoing ramifications that, in the New Zealand case, have been shown to impact on a community's ability to cope with and move on from periods of economic stagnation in particular resource industries. While other types of social impact (e.g. criminality) will be more important in particular contexts, the dependence of rural communities on a limited number of resource industries means that conceptual models of change such as the resource community cycle are likely to remain useful in explicating the relationship of these impacts to planned interventions.

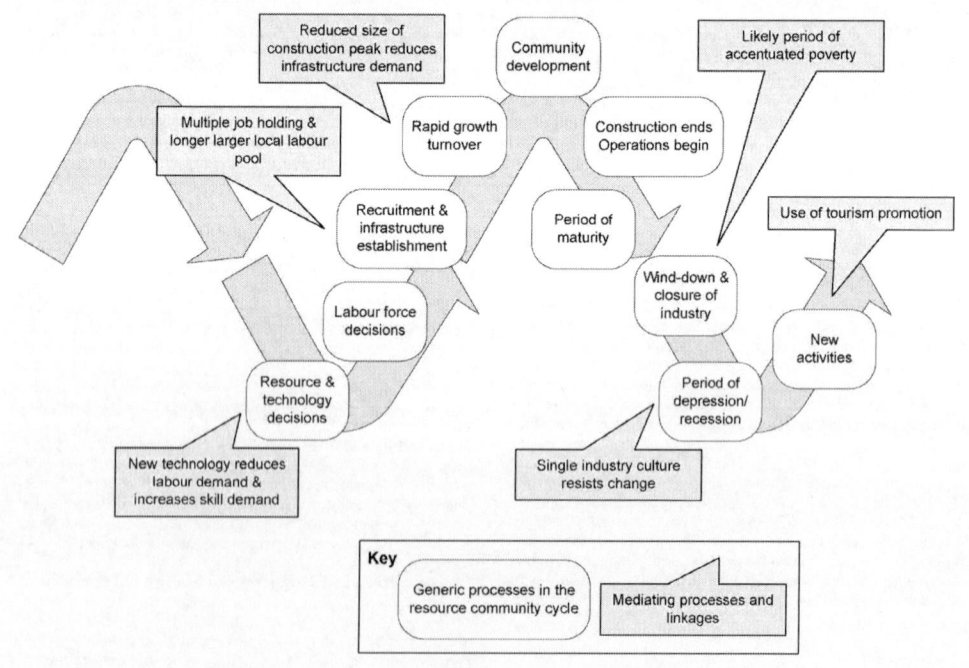

Fig. 1. The resource community cycle: recent findings from rural New Zealand (adapted from Taylor et al., 2003).

In applying this model to the Coppabella mine it is important to consider the outcomes of ex post SIA studies more specifically related to major resource extraction projects. Such studies have taken three broad foci: (1) the impacts of mines and their changing labour demands on resource dependent communities; (2) the social dynamics of purpose built mining towns; and (3) the impact of fly-in/fly-out or commuter workforce arrangements on workers and families. US research into social disruption and personal well-being in the resource development 'boomtowns' of the 1970s and 80s found that while these towns did not conform to the 'wild west' image of the popular imagination with rates, for example, of criminal victimisation that were no different to stable towns of similar size (Krannich et al., 1985), some towns and population sectors were vulnerable to rapid change. Freudenberg (1986) found that the declining density of acquaintanceship in smaller boomtowns led to a loss of informal surveillance and caring among community members that was associated with increases in criminal victimisation—albeit to levels that may still have been considered low. Krannich and Greider (1984), meanwhile, found that lack of integration within the community was highest among those living in temporary accommodation, such as mobile homes, while Freudenberg (1984) suggests that boomtown youth found the process of change more stressful than did adults.

Australian research over the same period concentrated on purpose built mining towns which many companies believed necessary to attract workers and minimise industrial disputes (Parker, 1988).[1] However, the majority of purpose built towns lacked the critical mass of population necessary to provide comprehensive human services, attract secondary investment, or achieve a balanced socio-demographic structure, providing residents with diminished quality of life and a sense of impermanence (Robinson and Newton, 1988; see also O'Faircheallaigh, 1988; Pilgrim, 1988; Sharma, 1983). Women especially were found to suffer more psychological stress and experience less social integration than did women in other rural towns (Cotterell, 1984; see also Williams, 1981). By the mid-1980s, these problems, together with declining terms of trade and regulatory changes that increased the cost of providing subsidised accommodation, saw movement away from the provision of social infrastructure and towards 'fly-in/fly-out' workforce arrangements (Newton and Robinson, 1987; Parker, 1988) which required both the periodic absence of workers from their permanent residences and the structuring of operations around compressed work schedules (generally involving 12 hour shifts worked in blocks of several days/nights on followed by a similar number of days off). Shiftwork of this nature is often associated with sleep disorders, fatigue and irritability (Knutsson, 2003); conditions that pose obvious risks to safety (at work and while commuting) and to participation in interpersonal relationships (Grosswald, 2003). While some families and individuals prefer long-distance commuting and compressed work schedules for the opportunities they present to earn relatively high incomes, to be flexible in where they choose to live, and to use the significant amount of time they have off work to pursue other interests or income, many complain of the difficulties workers face reintegrating into family life and the social and economic isolation they experience from the communities in which they ostensibly live (Shrimpton and Storey, 2001).

Fig. 2 summarises these findings in relation to the resource community cycle. It suggests that many of the social impacts on resource communities affected by major resource extraction projects from the mid-1980s on—as the profitability of mining declined and companies reduced investment in social infrastructure—related to a partial social and economic de-coupling of resource communities from the mines in their proximity. Lack of social integration became as much a function of compressed work schedules and long-distance commuting as it was of local population flows, while the ensuing need to attract secondary investment and/or alternative industries in response to economic malaise earlier in the operational life of mines accelerated the resource community cycle. However, at least two aspects of the resource community cycle warrant further attention. First, the regionalisation of labour pools and economic flows suggests a need to investigate whether alternative units of social organisation—such as the region as a network of resource communities—might offer additional insights into the distribution and management of impacts (see Fenton et al., 2003). Second, the boom in resource prices since 2004 has created a new set of conditions under which resource communities have been simultaneously exposed both to rapid localised population growth and to large non-resident workforces housed in mostly temporary accommodation while on shift. It is with the second of these issues that we are concerned in the assessment of Coppabella.

3. Case study

Coppabella coal mine is located in the Bowen Basin region of Central Queensland; Australia's premier coal producing region. A relatively small mine by Bowen Basin standards (shipping some 1.5 million tonnes of coal per annum and providing employment for about 340 people on-site when first opened), Coppabella began operations in 1998 at a time when falling real prices saw the focus of the industry shift from development to cost reduction. Common strategies included job shedding, the replacement of permanent with contract labour, the introduction of compressed shiftwork patterns, and moves away from the provision of accommodation and other social infrastructure. In 2004, however, a major boom in coal prices stimulated substantial increases in production, investment and employment. By mid-2006, there were 37 mines operating in the Basin (NRM, 2006), producing over AUS$12 billion worth of coal (OESR, 2006a), with a further 21 mines under development or active consideration (NRM, 2006).

The Coppabella mine exemplifies both recent and historical trends in resource sector development. The mine is located approximately 160 km southwest of the coastal City of Mackay (population 84 890 in 2006) in the rural Shire of Nebo (population 2521 in 2006). Nebo Shire is 10 009 km^2 with land use dominated by low-intensity beef grazing. It contains three small towns: Nebo (the administrative hub); Coppabella (established in 1971 to house Queensland Rail employees) and Glenden (purpose built in 1983 as the residential base for the nearby Newlands Mine). Glenden was the last dedicated mining town constructed in the region. Since then, the expectation has been either that existing towns would expand to accommodate workforces for new mines or that employees would stay in temporary workcamps while on-shift and commute to permanent residences in centres like Mackay when off-shift. At the time of these studies, the operator of Coppabella, Macarthur Coal, employed directly less than 10 people on-site (the remainder working for contractors) and operated no accommodation infrastructure. The mine itself was a conventional open cut producing a range of Pulverised Coal Injection and Thermal Coal for export. Based on initial estimates of resources, mine life was expected to be 25–30 years. Following the commencement of operations, mining was expanded both on-site with the opening of the Coppabella East extension and through the development of an additional mine (sharing processing infrastructure with Coppabella) which came on-line in 2004 at Moorvale. Coppabella was the first, therefore, of several mines which have, in the last several years, driven a change within Nebo Shire from the partitioning of mine workforces within stand-alone company towns to the transformation of existing

---

[1] Preference for single company towns resulted in some townships being constructed within 70 km of each other and foregoing the economies of scale that were achieved in those mixed company towns that were also established to service several mines. While in the 1970s some 80% of capital expenditure associated with mining projects was concentrated on the mine itself, a decade later this had declined to only 50%, the balance being spent on social and transport infrastructure. Between 1979-80 and 1984-85 the value of company-provided social infrastructure assets jumped from 12% to 35% of annual labour costs (Parker 1988).

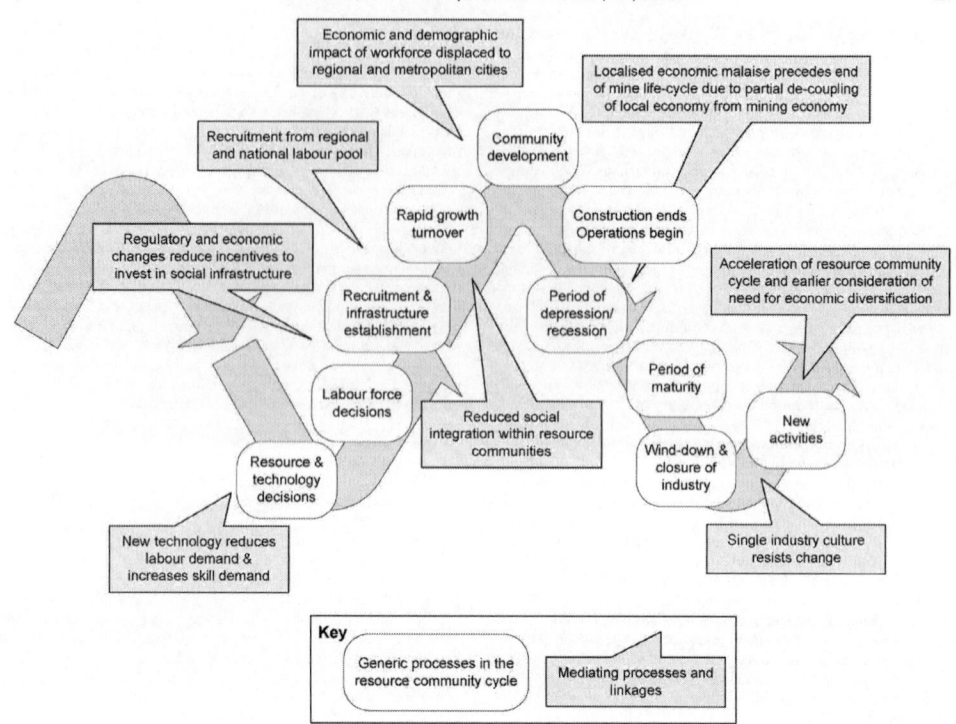

Fig. 2. The resource community cycle and recent trends in the management of major resource extraction projects.

agricultural and administrative service communities into mining boomtowns.

The methodology used for the first SIA study was based on a combination of comparative analysis and consultation with potentially affected stakeholders. A two phase methodology was adopted as detailed below.

3.1. Phase 1: scoping

The scoping phase aimed to identify all plausible impacts so that detailed plans could be developed for the rest of the study. Scoping involved two main activities. First, semi-structured interviews were conducted with stakeholder groups involved in, or affected by, the Coppabella Coal Mine to identify perceived social, economic and environmental impacts (positive and negative) and important elements of community structure. Second, a desktop study was undertaken of similar studies conducted elsewhere (see above) to identify potential impacts of which stakeholders may not have been aware.

3.2. Phase 2: baseline assessment of impacts and mitigation strategies

The assessment phase aimed to investigate further all plausible impacts identified through the scoping phase. Activities included:

- Estimation of social impacts. Based on more extensive community interviews and analysis of statistical data provided by a range of agencies, including the Australian Bureau of Statistics, an assessment was made of the actual magnitude of potential impacts identified during Phase 1.
- Stakeholder analysis. Given that the significance of many social and economic impacts depends on the value that is placed on them by relevant stakeholders, interviews with community representatives were utilised to:
  - Evaluate the significance of social and economic impacts to the community.
  - Identify mitigation and other strategies to enhance local capture of positive impacts and ensure equitable distribution of impacts.
- Workforce, business and resident surveys. Short quantitative surveys were conducted with mine workers, Nebo-based businesses and residents of Nebo and Mackay to compare perceptions of the social and environmental impacts of coal mining and to collect data regarding residential location preferences.

The second SIA study utilised much the same methodology with the exception that no additional scoping was undertaken in light of the data that were already available from the first study.

4. Results

The outcomes of both studies are summarised in Table 1. This paper will not present detailed data on all dimensions of either expected or actual impact but will concentrate on those that were greatest in

Table 1
Summary of social impact trends 2003–2006.

Preliminary social impacts/issues	Summary of 2003 findings	Summary of trends 2003–2006
Demographic change	Demographic picture had changed so as to increase vulnerability to downturns in mining industry. Dimensions included long-term population decline, low education levels, highly polarised income levels, dependence on mining for employment, and dominance of unskilled and semi-skilled positions.	No major changes in the nature of demographic change were evident at the time of this study. It is most likely, therefore, that the population of Nebo Shire was continuing its trend towards larger numbers, in absolute and relative terms, of men working in unskilled and semi-skilled occupations and with corresponding net loss of women, children and lower income earners.
Demand for human services	Little change to historically low level of human services availability. Establishment of full-time ambulance service. No permanent or visiting doctors. Expected increases in school enrolments not eventuating.	Human service availability remained low.
Demand for and cost of access to housing and accommodation	Considerable unmet demand for housing. Ability of market to meet housing demand constrained.	Some constraints on housing development removed (i.e. banks' reluctance to lend for housing in Nebo), but development of new accommodation still lagging behind demand contributing to dramatic inflation in purchase and rental markets. Considerable expansion of temporary accommodation facilities.
Demand for community infrastructure (e.g. recreation facilities)	Unresolved debate over who should pay for community infrastructure. Sport and recreation facilities inequitably distributed while shiftwork patterns limited participation in sport and leisure activities by mine employees.	Considerable expansion of temporary accommodation facilities. Debates over who should pay for community infrastructure in Nebo and Coppabella remained unresolved.
Crime	Perception of increased crime risk. Some increase in crime rates evident but overall rates remained extremely low. Anecdotal evidence that social problems simply exported to locations of permanent residence for mine employees.	Residents believed that criminal and anti-social behaviour had increased. While police reported that any increase was proportional to population growth (temporary and permanent), this still represented increased exposure to anti-social and criminal activity in absolute terms.
Community participation and integration	Participation in community activities and groups limited among mine employees. Extra burden placed on voluntary emergency service organisations. Increased volumes of commuter and commercial traffic.	Little change was evident with community and volunteer organisations still under considerable pressure.
Traffic and fatigue	Extra burden on voluntary and professional emergency services. Shiftwork practices encourage fatigue through long hours and disturbance of sleep patterns, although fatigue management programs may help reduce accident rates.	This trend appears to have intensified as more mines have come on-line.
Community identity	Nebo residents resistant to identity of 'mining town' as they believed this will limit economic diversification by discouraging new residents and investment in non-mining industries.	This was still evident in Nebo, but had also become an issue in Coppabella with the development of temporary accommodation in vicinity. No change.
Employment opportunities and labour availability	Extremely low unemployment levels in Nebo Shire reflected both employment opportunities in mining sector and low availability of affordable housing. Reduction in labour availability for non-mining businesses.	Nebo had experienced some industrial development although the continuation of this may be limited by increases in the price of land. Most development oriented towards servicing mines. Little diversification evident.
Business opportunities and constraints	Limited flow-on expansion of other businesses in response to mining. Question over whether non-mining business expansion will be sustainable beyond the life of coal mining.	No change.
Strength of local and regional institutions for planning and governance	Local government's capacity to participate in planning and governance limited by state-based approval processes and revenue flows. Perception that mines only do enough by way of communication, impact assessment and community contribution to progress mining development. Little engagement by the mining sector in regional planning processes that are more accessible to local institutions and people.	
Opportunities for Aboriginal people	The disturbance of country through mining is by itself a substantial negative impact. Macarthur's operations enhanced access to land for two Traditional Owner groups despite competing claims to Native Title over these lands. Cultural Heritage Management Plan negotiated with both groups that provided useful opportunities for capacity building and economic development. Consideration given in the rehabilitation plans for the mine sites for access and use by Traditional Owners post-mining for cultural and economic purposes. Training and employment programs largely successful, but challenges remained in recruiting Aboriginal people into senior positions within the mining industry and ensuring economic sustainability of Aboriginal enterprises post-mining. Support secured through Native Title compensation for a range of other community initiatives.	Some concern that training has not always translated into employment. Lack of input into non-mine related development.
Environmental impacts	Temporary accommodation facilities significant impact on visual amenity. Concern over long-term impacts of coal dust, land disturbance, tree clearing and water extraction on environment despite lack of evidence of immediate problem.	Expansion of temporary accommodation around both Nebo and Coppabella has increased the magnitude of this impact. Concern over water has intensified

magnitude and which illustrate most clearly the chains of effects that are likely to flow from and modify the resource community cycle as it pertains to communities impacted by extractive industries in the Bowen Basin.

4.1. Demographic change

The opening of the Coppabella mine had little immediate impact on the population of Nebo Shire. Despite an on-site workforce of 340, the permanent resident population of Nebo Shire decreased 5% from 2202 in 1996 to 2086 in 2001 (ABS, 2002). This proved a short-term trend, however, with the permanent resident population then growing 21% to 2521 in 2006 (ABS, 2007). In all likelihood, the early demographic impacts of the Coppabella workforce were offset by residential vacancies in mining towns that lay outside the Shire and which had suffered population declines during the 1990s. As those vacancies diminished and mines continued to expand post-2001, marked change was evident in both the permanent and temporary populations of Nebo Shire.

Of perhaps more importance than the absolute level of change in the permanent resident population was the type of population change. As Table 2 shows, the number of permanent residents fell in all age groups below 55 between 1996 and 2001 while those age groups 55 and above recorded substantial increases. With the largest fall in this period being in the 0–14 age group, it appeared that those leaving the community were families with children. This conclusion is borne out by Table 3, which shows that not only did the number of women in the community fall in the same age groups, but that the rate of population loss was greater among women than among men. Even as population loss was reversed post-2001, the lowest levels of population growth were in the 0–14 and 25–34 year age categories reflecting, again, the declining importance of families with children as a share of total population. In fact, the number of 'two parent with children' households in Nebo Shire declined from 353 (or 55% of all households) in 1996 to 267 (43%) in 2001 and 273 (42%) in 2006. Over the same 10 year period, the number of 'sole parent with children' households increased from a low 17 (<3%) in 1996 to 39 (6%) in 2006 (ABS, 2007) while the number of 'couple with no children' households grew from 155 (24%) to 182 (28%) in 2006 and the number of 'lone occupant' households increased from 108 (17%) to 137 (21%).

By 2003, mining had become the largest employer in Nebo Shire. An unemployment rate of only 0.6% in 2006 (OESR, 2007) suggests that locals either were recruited into the mines or forced to leave due to escalating housing costs (see below). Although this resulted in higher than average income levels, most mining jobs were in unskilled and semi-skilled categories and education levels were correspondingly low. Ethnic diversity was also low. Of particular note, few Aboriginal people lived in the area due to earlier periods of forced outmigration and limited employment opportunities.

Changes in the permanent resident population were, however, dwarfed by changes in the itinerant population of non-resident workers, with estimates that non-resident workers accommodated in various forms of single persons' quarters increased the population of Nebo Shire by around 20% on any given night in 2001 (QDLGP, 2001) and by over 150% in 2006 (PIFU, 2006). On census night 2006, 2082 non-resident visitors (of whom only 37 were above or below working age) were counted while 2263 Nebo Shire residents were counted at home.

One of the questions this raises is whether more mine employees and contractors would shift permanent residence to Nebo Shire if more suitable accommodation was available (see below). When mine employees were asked in 2003 whether they would like to move to a main town of residence closer to the mine site, 26% indicated that they would, 70% indicated that they would not, and 4% were undecided. For those indicating that they did not wish to move closer to the mine, the most important reasons related to their families' preferences not to move, together with the better employment, educational and recreational opportunities available to family members elsewhere. When temporary workcamp residents were interviewed 4 years later in 2007, 58% stated that they would prefer to continue living outside the area.

4.2. Housing

As indicated above, in 2003 approximately a quarter of the Coppabella mine workforce indicated that they would prefer permanent accommodation closer to the mine site while, in 2007, approximately one third of the residents of one of the major workcamps near Coppabella stated the same preference. Nevertheless, the ability of the market in 2003 to meet housing demand was severely constrained by a range of factors including reluctance among private entrepreneurs and banks to invest in residential development outside regional centres. Despite an increase in residential building approvals from zero in 2000 to around ten per year from 2003 to 2006, little change was evident in the total number of dwellings available for occupation. In fact, the number of occupied dwellings in Nebo Shire dropped from 645 to 622 between 1996 and 2001, before recovering to 647 in 2006 (ABS, 2007). No recovery, however, was evident in the availability of fully detached houses—the main and preferred dwelling type. While 579 fully detached houses were occupied in 1996, only 558 were occupied in 2001 and 2006. The increase in dwelling availability between 2001 and 2006 was almost entirely accounted for by temporary dwellings such as caravans (mobile homes), which grew in number from 15 to 77.

Shortages of both permanent and temporary accommodation led to dramatic inflation in the cost of buying and renting residential real estate. Residents of Nebo claimed that residential building blocks had increased in price from $20 000 to $160 000 and that workers were grouping together to share house rents of $600–750/week. According to census data, ten households in Nebo were paying over $550/week rent in 2006 (ABS, 2007). This was similar to the median weekly rent at the nearby mining town of Moranbah (Rolfe and O'Dea, 2007) and double the median rent of $300/week for a three bedroom house located in Queensland's state capital, Brisbane, in December 2006

Table 2
Permanent resident population by age, 1996–2006.

Age (years)	1996	2001	% change	2006	% change
0–14	628	528	−15.9	566	7.2
15–24	257	236	−8.2	321	36.0
25–34	431	404	−6.3	462	14.4
35–44	418	394	−5.7	479	21.6
45–54	281	265	−5.7	376	41.9
55–64	111	140	26.1	220	57.1
65–74	48	67	39.6	72	7.5
74 and over	28	52	85.7	27	−48.1
Total	2 202	2 086	−5.3	2 521	20.9

Table 3
Change in resident female population by age, 1996–2006.

	1996		2001		2006	
Age (years)	No. females	Females as % of total pop.	No. females	Females as % of total pop.	No. females	Females as % of total pop.
0–14	318	50.6	259	49.1	270	47.7
15–24	114	44.4	93	39.4	123	38.3
25–34	197	45.7	176	43.6	199	43.1
35–44	177	42.3	150	38.1	179	37.4
45–54	111	39.5	95	35.8	148	39.4
55–64	43	38.7	51	36.4	80	36.4
65–74	16	33.3	29	43.3	32	44.4
74 and over	18	64.3	10	19.2	13	48.1
Total	994	45.1	863	41.4	1 044	41.4

(RTA, 2007; see also OESR, 2006b). As a consequence, it was reported that low income earners were being forced out of town, that non-mine employers were finding it impossible to attract people to the town, and that a number of workers across all industries were resorting to sleeping in cars, caravans and tents.

4.3. Social integration

Participation in community activities and groups was extremely limited among mine employees in both 2002–2003 and 2006–2007 due to shiftwork patterns and the temporary nature of their residence in Nebo Shire. This created an extra burden for voluntary emergency service organisations such as the State Emergency Service due to the increase in road traffic in Nebo Shire associated with the movements of a workforce that provided no additional members to share the burden. Lack of integration and participation among mine employees suggested that when there is a downturn in the Shire's mining industry few will remain in the area or contribute to the development of new economic futures.

Lack of integration also promoted among residents of Nebo Shire a perception that they were at significantly greater risk of crime than prior to the development of the Coppabella mine due to the large number of unknown and temporary residents staying in camp-style accommodation around the town. While there was some evidence that that crime rates had increased since commencement of the Coppabella Coal Mine project, this may be entirely coincidental due to the diverse residence patterns of mining personnel and the location of staff from a number of other mining operations and industries in nearby towns. That said, offences against the person—especially sexual assault—increased in Nebo and the adjoining Belyando Shire rose from around 300 incidents per 100 000 people in 1998–1999 to 600 in 2000–2001 and 2483 in 2002–2003 (OESR, 2002, 2004). However, overall crime rates remained extremely low and a number of participants in the SIA study, including local police, believed that mine employees were subjected to surveillance and sanctions against anti-social behaviour while on-site and while in the general proximity of the mine. Formal surveillance included routine testing of mine employees for alcohol and other drugs, while informal surveillance operated through the communication networks operating between accommodation and other service providers.

By 2006, Nebo residents believed that crimes against property and general anti-social behaviour (public drunkenness, speeding etc) were accelerating. Conversely, Nebo police reported that any increases in criminal activity from 2003 to 2006 were proportional to the population increase over the same time. While in relative terms this would mean that there had been no increase in criminal activity, it would still signal an absolute increase in potential exposure to criminal activity. It would also suggest that as the itinerant population of the Shire grew, the application and effectiveness of informal sanctions fell.

4.4. Traffic and fatigue

Residents believed that traffic volumes—including volumes of large trailers and mining equipment—and accidents had increased both prior to and following the 2003 study. Road use statistics indicate that traffic volumes did increase with the bulk of additional traffic associated with miners travelling between their places of employment and residence area at the beginning and end of rostered blocks of 'days on.' Of the 204 accidents reported on the main road between Nebo and Mackay from January 1998 to September 2002, at least 28 were determined to have been related to fatigue. No data were available on accidents subsequent to 2002. Nevertheless, it is not unreasonable to speculate that the cumulative effects of fatigue may be an exacerbating factor in traffic safety for mining commuters and other road users. Di Milia's (2006) survey of over 1500 drivers, for example, on two major arterial routes from the Bowen Basin coalfields to the coast found that shift workers who had completed night shift accounted for approximately 11% of all road users. On average, these shift workers intended driving 211 km and the majority (76%) did not intend taking a driving break. Some 19% of these shift workers displayed symptoms of severe sleepiness compared with 1% of non-shift workers.

In 2003, both Macarthur Coal and the wider community demonstrated their awareness of this with a range of policies and programs in place to educate employees about fatigue management. However, what employees do once they are off shift lies outside company control and many respondents believed that workers regularly drove to the coast as soon as their block of 12 hour shifts was over and returned, similarly, just in time to start their next block.

4.5. Business opportunities and constraints

During the 1990s, mining took over from agriculture as the dominant industry and driver of economic activity in Nebo Shire. By 2003, there was some evidence that secondary industry (i.e. the provision of services to mining) was also beginning to expand. However, the flow-on effects to other sectors were limited and the ability of Nebo Shire to capture economic benefit from mining constrained by the relative lack of secondary industry compared with regional centres such as Mackay. While Nebo Shire Council had acted to attract investment by establishing a serviced industrial estate, initial take-up was slow due to the proximity to Mackay and difficulties faced by non-mining businesses in attracting labour. Virtually all employers, including mines, expressed difficulty in attracting suitably qualified staff, particularly in more specialised fields. Location, lack of facilities (e.g. education for families) and infrastructure (e.g. housing) all impacted on capacity to attract and retain staff. Non-mining businesses faced the additional issue of substantial disparities between what they could afford to pay workers and what those same workers might be paid by the mines with mine worker salaries up to three times those of similarly skilled workers in agriculture or local government.

It is perhaps a reflection of the magnitude of the mining boom that by 2006 the establishment of secondary industries in Nebo had increased dramatically despite even greater skills shortages. However, it is important to stress that non-mining business expansion was concentrated in the mine-service sector with little evidence, therefore, of economic diversification. In responding to this situation, stakeholders emphasised the need they perceived to build community infrastructure so as provide a more attractive environment for investment and to build transferable and entrepreneurial skills among residents.

4.6. Cultural heritage, native title and opportunities for indigenous people

Economic development of Nebo Shire has historically generated considerable negative impacts for Aboriginal people. Early European settlement of the area through the 1860s and 70s was characterised by extensive conflict between Aborigines and white settlers and it is likely that a substantial proportion of the Aboriginal population were killed either by diseases like smallpox or through fighting with the Native Mounted Police and vigilante groups (L'Oste-Brown et al., 2002). Those Aborigines who survived were either absorbed into the pastoral economy as stationhands and domestic workers, became fringe dwellers, and/or left. This, in part, explains the very small Aboriginal population of the Shire and the importance placed by the two Aboriginal groups claiming Native Title rights in Nebo Shire on access to traditional lands for group members wishing to return. Thus, it was found that despite the profound negative impact that open cut mining could be expected to impose on Aboriginal peoples' spiritual and cultural connections with traditional lands, those people still regarded the opportunities afforded by mining to access sites from which they had been excluded by pastoralism, and to participate in cultural heritage surveys on those sites, as a net gain.

While the Native Title and cultural heritage implications of resource development give Aboriginal people rights of participation in planning and management that extend beyond those of other stakeholders, the reality is that legislative uncertainty over the precise nature of these rights, combined with limited resources among Indigenous communities, means that Aboriginal people are frequently marginalised. By way of contrast, the Coppabella mine was seen in 2003 as notable for the positive relationships that had been developed with the two Aboriginal groups claiming Native Title rights over the mine site (groups that easily could have been played off against each other), and opportunities were identified and acted on to pursue cultural, economic and social development. Training and employment programs were put in place for Indigenous people and Aboriginal enterprises established to service the mine by providing for cultural heritage advice and management. In 2006, however, it was evident that the marginal position of Aboriginal groups within the wider community and economy had been reinforced by the dramatic expansion of mining in the region. Although there was no suggestion that Macarthur itself had sought to undermine its positive relationship with Native Title claimants, expansion of Coppabella and other mines saw the influx of a range of other business operators and the development of land for purposes other than mining. Concerns were raised that contractors were less committed to Indigenous community development and that non-mining land uses were not necessarily subject to the same detailed examination and management of cultural heritage as were mining lands.

5. The resource community cycle and the Coppabella mine

The concept of the resource community cycle is clearly applicable only to settlements in which the main determinant of economic vitality is the life-cycle of major natural resource use industries and projects. At the same time, proponents of this concept, such as Taylor et al. (2003), demonstrate that the chains of effects associated with development do not necessarily follow a straightforward pattern of positive benefits stimulated by economic growth followed by negative benefits associated with decline. Instead, the specific ways in which these chains of effects play out within the broad pattern of resource industry growth and decline are mediated by a host of technological, social and political processes such as the combined influence of labour saving technologies and multiple job holding on migration patterns. The two SIA studies of Coppabella coal mine illustrate a number of additional ways in which the impacts of the resource community cycle may be mediated; in particular, by labour recruitment and social infrastructure policies that reduce the emphasis on localised employment and investment strategies; and by the cumulative impacts of multiple projects within relative proximity to each other (see Fig. 3).

Most of the negative social impacts identified in the first ex post SIA study of Coppabella did not relate to social dislocation per se but to a failure to capture positive benefits that residents and local government had expected to flow from the establishment of major infrastructure. This was particularly evident in relation to the limited development of complementary and new enterprises and of more permanent housing. As a new mine, Coppabella could not de-couple from the local economy by compressing work schedules and reducing their provision of social infrastructure in favour of drive-in/drive-out workforce arrangements, as was the case with existing mines elsewhere in the Bowen Basin (see Fig. 2). However, the adoption of these same strategies to cope with tight terms of trade slowed the development of economic dependency on the mine among existing residents and businesses within Nebo Shire, and made many aware of the need to accelerate the resource community cycle by attracting secondary investment and/or alternative industries *early* in the operational life of the Coppabella mine if major economic benefits

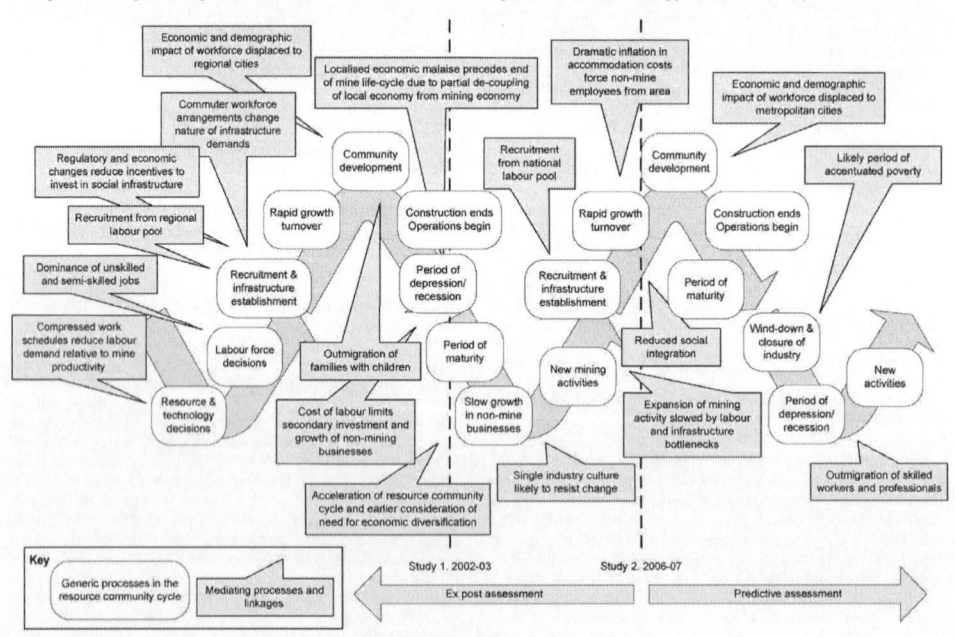

Fig. 3. The resource community cycle and Coppabella coal mine.

were to flow. In other words, the attraction of new activities was necessary not simply to replace mining as a source of employment and investment toward the end of the resource community cycle stimulated by the Coppabella mine, but to create the conditions under which employment and investment in the mining sector might contribute to higher levels of localised economic and community development throughout the cycle.

The most obvious cumulative social impact stemming from the increase in coal mining projects in the vicinity of Nebo Shire post-2004 was the acceleration of demographic changes associated with a more mining-dependent employment market and the dramatic rise in the number of non-resident workers housed in workcamps and other temporary accommodation. While these created a number of direct impacts (such as the perceived increase in criminal activity, traffic accidents etc), the impact that was of most direct relevance to the resource community cycle was the secondary impact on the community's likely capacity to cope with future downturns in the mining sector—whether as a consequence of falling profitability, technological innovations that reduce labour demands and/or the end of project life-cycles.

This can be illustrated with reference to indicators for the identification of vulnerable resource communities which were developed through the social impact assessment process used to inform Regional Forest Agreements (RFAs) in Queensland (QDNR et al., 1999). These indicators were grouped around three main concepts: (1) sensitivity to change in the local economy; (2) social values about resource use; and (3) the service capacity of the locale/region. Indicators relating to sensitivity to change in the local economy included: economic diversity, rates of unemployment, rates of employment in resource-use industries subject to change, levels of education and qualifications, income, housing ownership, purchasing and rental, and age. These indicators clearly point to areas of concern for Nebo. The Shire's economy was dependent on mining and agriculture with little evidence of diversification. Low unemployment was more a reflection of accommodation affordability than of employment opportunities and all businesses struggled to find sufficient labour—placing further constraints on diversification. Employment was thus concentrated in one industry—mining. Education levels were low and jobs were concentrated in the semi-skilled and unskilled categories. Housing availability was low. There was an increase in the population aged over 65. Social values on resource use in Nebo were conducive to mining, but recognised that the presence of mining in its current form was necessarily finite. The general community had no desire to become entirely dependent on mining and believed it necessary to use mining as a platform to support other development paths. However, the service capacity also placed constraints on the quality of life of residents and the ability of the Shire to attract investment and residents.

On the whole, the RFA indicators suggest that the capacity of the Nebo community to deal with any downturn in the mining industry will be limited. Further, with mining encouraging the masculinisation of the Nebo population without increasing participation in social activities and networks, it may be seen as having detrimental effects on those aspects of social capital that might support economic, social and cultural development; namely, constructive relationships between groups and individuals that support diversity, a climate of trust, acceptance of difference, and ability to resolve conflict (Flora et al., 1997; Gray and Lawrence, 2001). This is of concern due to the potential, in the event of a downturn in the mining industry, for Nebo to experience significant outmigration and income loss without sufficient capacity to generate alternative development paths and avoid the creation of a poverty trap for those left behind with unsaleable homes, limited capital and untransferable skills. Such a future is not inevitable and Macarthur Coal had engaged with some stakeholders in a manner that was likely to enhance capacity and social capital. The most obvious example of this was the capacity building approach that Macarthur took to dealing with Traditional Owners. However, as mining operations expand, other mines continue to come online, and the sector in general continues to rely on contractors for a major share of their operations, the capacity building activities of any one mine operator are likely to be insignificant in the absence of integrated sector-wide programs.

6. Conclusion

These social impact assessments confirm the conclusion of several earlier boomtown studies that the pathological effects of rapid growth on small communities are easily overstated. However, they also support the conclusion that closer attention to the effect of change on particular sub-sectors of the population may still identify significant social impacts, and speak to debates about the role of SIA in managing as well as in predicting change.

In 2003, many of the social impacts evident at that stage of the resource community cycle related to a failure by the community to capture positive benefits (in particular, economic development) despite increasing dependence on mining for employment and income. At the same time, while mining was responsible for only a small increase in population, demographic and social changes undermined the likely ability of the community to generate alternative economic and cultural futures. This was not inevitable, and Macarthur had engaged with some stakeholders—Aboriginal groups in particular—in a manner that enhanced capacity and social capital. However, the cumulative impact of multiple mine expansions and developments from 2003 to 2006 saw the magnification of these issues and the emergence of several acute social impacts. These included severe shortages of skilled labour in other industries; reduced accommodation access and affordability; increases in traffic and fatigue-related road accidents; increased pressure on emergency services (particularly those provided by volunteers); and increases in criminal and other anti-social behaviour.

The increase in anti-social behaviour between the two studies appeared to be linked to the declining density of acquaintanceship and informal surveillance associated with population growth. Maintaining our focus on the entire resource community cycle, this particular issue highlights the manner in which acute social impacts—while important in their own right—potentially mask or divert attention from underlying processes of social transformation that also warrant attention if longer-term impacts are to be anticipated and managed. In this case, increases (real and perceived) in anti-social behaviour reflected two major demographic changes. Most obvious was exponential growth in the temporary resident population between 2003 and 2006. Less obvious was the progressive masculinisation of the permanent resident population. While this latter trend can partly be attributed to competition for housing, it was also due to the negative impact of a large and demographically unbalanced itinerant population on the attractiveness of Nebo as a residential location for women and families. As the resource community cycle continues to turn, demand for labour in the mining sector can be expected to decline (Fig. 3). While it cannot be assumed that the permanent resident population will reflect, at that point, its current composition, questions do need to be asked about the human capital likely to be left behind in the event of a contraction in mining employment.

Concepts such as the resource community cycle that are inductively derived from multiple SIA studies play a useful role in building a body of theory and knowledge from which to anticipate the long-term, cumulative, and perhaps less obvious, impacts of resource development. Applying this concept to the studies at Coppabella has highlighted, for example, the importance of impact mitigation strategies that focus not only on immediate, or acute, concerns but on the development of human and social capital necessary for communities to cope with a wind-down of mining activity that is likely to see significant outmigration of skilled workers and professionals. However, identifying potential impacts such as these through the life-cycle of the project in question is only the first step in developing appropriate mitigation strategies. The long-term perspective encouraged by Taylor et al. (2003) serves to highlight the importance of integrating concepts such as the resource community cycle with SIA models designed specifically to facilitate the participation of impacted communities in planning and decision-making in ways that meet proponent needs (Esteves, 2008), build human and social capital (Esteves and Vanclay, 2009), and take account of the active roles that communities play in generating *unanticipated* outcomes as they interpret and respond to planned intervention (Lockie, 2007).

Acknowledgements

The authors would like to thank Macarthur Coal for their financial support of this research. They would also like to thank the residents, mine employees, local government officials and others who provided information for the studies. This research was approved by CQUniversity Australia's Human Research Ethics Committee (project number H06/09-158).

References

Australian Bureau of Statistics (ABS). 2001 Census Tables: Nebo (S)(Local Government Area. Canberra: Commonwealth of Australia; 2002.
Australian Bureau of Statistics (ABS). 2006 Census Tables: Nebo (S)(Local Government Area. Canberra: Commonwealth of Australia; 2007.
Bass R. Evaluating environmental justice under the national environmental policy act. Environ Impact Assess Rev 1998;18:83–92.
Burdge R, Fricke P, Finsterbusch K, Freudenberg W, Gramling R, Holden A, et al. Guidelines and principles for social impact assessment. Environ Impact Assess Rev 1995;15:11–43.
Burdge R, Vanclay F. The future practice of social impact assessment. In: Burdge R, editor. The concepts, process and methods of social impact assessment. Middleton, WI: Social Ecology Press; 2004. p. 283–92.
Cotterell J. Social networks of mining town women. Aust J Social Issues 1984;19:101–12.
Di Milia L. Shift work, sleepiness and long distance driving. Transportation Res 2006:278–85.
Esteves AM. Evaluating community investments in the mining sector using multi-criteria decision analysis to integrate SIA with business planning. Environ Impact Asses Rev 2008;28(4–5):338–48.
Esteves AM, Vanclay F. Social development needs Analysis as a tool for SIA to guide corporate–community investment: applications in the minerals industry. Environ Impact Asses Rev 2009;29(2):137–45.
Fenton M, Coakes S, Marshall N. Vulnerability and capacity measurement. In: Becker H, Vanclay F, editors. The International Handbook of Social Impact Assessment: conceptual and methodological advances. Cheltenham, UK: Edward Elgar; 2003. p. 211–30.
Flora J, Sharp J, Flora C. Entrepreneurial social infrastructure and locally initiated development in non metropolitan United States. Social Quart 1997;38:623–45.
Freudenberg W. Boomtown's youth: the differential impact of community growth on adolescents and adults. Am Sociol Rev 1984;49:697–705.
Freudenberg W. The density of acquaintanceship: an overlooked variable in community research. Am J Sociol 1986;92:27–63.
Gray I, Lawrence G. A future for rural Australia: escaping global misfortune. Cambridge: Cambridge University Press; 2001.
Grosswald B. Shift work and negative work—to family spillover. J Sociol Soc Welf 2003;30(4):31–56.
Knutsson A. Health disorders of shift workers. Occup Med 2003;53:103–8.
Krannich R, Greider T. Personal well-being in rapid growth and stable communities: multiple indicators and contrasting results. Rural Sociol 1984;49:541–52.
Krannich R, Greider T, Little R. Rapid growth and fear of crime: a four-community comparison. Rural Sociol 1985;50:193–209.
Lockie S. Social impact assessment in review: setting the agenda for impact assessment in the twenty-first century. Impact Assess Proj Apprais 2001;19:277–87.
Lockie S. Deliberation and actor-networks: the 'practical' implications of social theory for the assessment of large dams and other interventions. Soc Nat Res 2007;20: 785–99.
Lockie S, Franetovich M, Sharma S, Rolfe J. Democratisation versus engagement? Social and economic impact assessment and community participation in the coal mining industry of the Bowen Basin, Australia. Impact Assess Proj Apprais 2008.
L'Oste-Brown S, Godwin L, Porter C, in association with the Bowen Basin Aboriginal Steering Committee. Towards an indigenous social and cultural landscape of the Bowen Basin. Brisbane: Queensland Department of the Environment; 2002.
Natural Resources and Mines (NRM). Queensland mining and petroleum 2005: exploration, operations and developments. Brisbane: Queensland Government; 2006.
Newton P, Robinson I. Settlement options: avoiding local government with fly-in fly-out. In: Parker P, editor. Resource development and local government: policies for growth, decline and diversity. Canberra: AGPS Press; 1987. p. 72–81.
O'Faircheallaigh C. Economic base and employment structure in Northern Territory mining towns. In: Brealey T, Neil C, Newton P, editors. Resource communities: settlement and workforce issues. Melbourne: CSIRO; 1988. p. 41–63.
Office of Economic and Social Research (OESR). Small area crime profiles: 2000–01, Belyando (S), Nebo (S) Local Government Areas (LGAs). Brisbane: Queensland Government; 2002.
Office of Economic and Social Research (OESR). Small area crime profiles: 2002–03, Belyando (S), Nebo (S) Local Government Areas (LGAs). Brisbane: Queensland Government; 2004.
Office of Economic and Social Research (OESR). Queensland economic review. Brisbane: Office of the Government Statistician; 2006a.
Office of Economic and Social Research (OESR). Index of retail prices in Queensland Regional Centres. Brisbane: Office of the Government Statistician; 2006b.
Office of Economic and Social Research (OESR). Queensland regional profiles: Mackay Statistical Division. Brisbane: Office of the Government Statistician; 2007.
Parker P. The cost of remote locations: Queensland coal towns. In: Brealey T, Neil C, Newton P, editors. Resource communities: settlement and workforce issues. Melbourne: CSIRO Press; 1988. p. 79–95.
Pilgrim R. Normalisation of the Pilbara townships in Western Australia. In: Brealey T, Neil C, Newton P, editors. Resource communities: settlement and workforce issues. Melbourne: CSIRO Press; 1988. p. 245–60.
Planning Information and Forecasting Unit (PIFU). Full-time equivalent population estimates for nine local government areas in the Bowen Basin, June 2006. Brisbane: Queensland Government Department of Local Government, Planning, Sport and Recreation; 2006.
Queensland Department of Local Government and Planning (QDLGP). Whitsunday Hinterland and Mackay (WHAM) 2015 regional plan (draft). Brisbane: Queensland Government; 2001.
Queensland Department of Natural Resources (QDNR) CRA unit, agriculture, forestry and fisheries Australia: social impact assessment unit, Queensland CRA/RFA Steering Committee. South East Queensland Social Assessment Report. Brisbane and Canberra: Queensland Government and Commonwealth of Australia; 1999.
Residential Tenancies Authority (RTA). Median weekly rents for three bedroom houses for new bonds lodged each quarter December 2006. Residential Tenancies Authority, Brisbane; 2007. accessed online at www.rta.qld.gov.au/zone_files/ Stats_December_Quarter_2006/sa_3brm_houses.htm.
Robinson I, Newton P. Settlement options for non-renewable resource development in Canada and Australia: a comparative evaluation and decision framework. In: Brealey T, Neil C, Newton P, editors. Resource communities: settlement and workforce issues. Melbourne: CSIRO; 1988. p. 313–52.
Rolfe J, Lockie S, Ivanova G. Overview of social and economic issues associated with the Bowen Basin coal industry. Research report 1. Socio-economic impact assessment and community engagement to reduce conflict over mine operations. Rockhampton: Centre for Social Science Research. Central Queensland University; 2005.
Rolfe J, O'Dea G. Identifying the potential and constraints for the growth of Moranbah. Research report 1. Economic and social impacts of the Moranbah Mines Research Reports. Rockhampton: Centre for Environmental Management. Central Queensland University; 2007.
Sharma P. The new mining towns—'outback suburbias'? In: Richmond W, Sharma P, editors. Mining and Australia. St Lucia: University of Queensland Press; 1983. p. 150–79.
Shrimpton M, Storey K. The effects of offshore employment in the petroleum industry: a cross-national perspective. OCS Study MMS 2001-041. Herndon, VA: US Department of the Interior, Minerals Management Service, Environmental Studies Program; 2001.
Taylor N, Goodrich C, Fitzgerald G, McClintock W. Undertaking longitudinal research. In: Becker H, Vanclay F, editors. The International Handbook of Social Impact Assessment: conceptual and methodological advances. Cheltenham, UK: Edward Elgar; 2003. p. 13–25.
Vanclay F. International principles for social impact assessment. Impact Assess Proj Apprais 2003;21:5-11.
Williams C. Open cut: the working class in an Australian mining town. Sydney: Allen and Unwin; 1981.

Professor Stewart Lockie is a rural and environmental sociologist and Director of the Institute for Health and Social Science Research at CQUniversity Australia.

Ms Maree Franettovich is a researcher with the Institute for Health and Social Science Research and a member of the Faculty of Business and Informatics at CQUniversity Australia's Mackay campus.

Ms Vanessa Petkova-Timmer is a Research Officer with the Institute for Health and Social Science Research and Centre for Environmental Management at CQUniversity Australia.

Professor John Rolfe is a resource economist and Director of the Centre for Environmental Management at CQUniversity Australia.

Dr. Galina Ivanova is a lecturer in economics at CQUniversity Australia. Her research interests include economics of environmental protection, renewable energy and emissions reduction policy.

Managing the cumulative impacts of coal mining on regional communities and environments in Australia

Daniel M Franks, David Brereton and Chris J Moran

The expansion and contraction of the coal mining industry in Australia has placed pressure on regional communities and environments and multiplied the extent, magnitude and profile of cumulative impacts. While some mining communities have benefited from the expansion of the coal industry through the creation of jobs and the investment in economies, the compounding impacts of multiple mining operations have stretched environmental, social, human and economic systems and rendered conventional mine-by-mine governance approaches ineffective. In this paper we draw from examples in the Bowen Basin, Hunter Valley and Gunnedah Basin to traverse the range of cumulative impacts resulting from mining activities, and detail working examples of management and assessment practices that aim to enhance positive, and avoid and mitigate negative, cumulative impacts.

Keywords: cumulative effects, impact assessment, sustainable development, social licence to operate, regional development, strategic assessment, community development, mining

EFFECTIVE MANAGEMENT AND assessment of cumulative impacts requires holistic understandings, coordination, integration and cooperation across the industry, government and community sectors. The overwhelming number of components and the complexity of interactions challenge existing institutions and methodologies and demand a multitude of tailored approaches to reflect the diversity of situations in which cumulative impacts manifest (Canter and Kamath, 1995; Damman et al, 1995; Burris and Canter, 1997; Kennett, 1999;

Dr Daniel M Franks is a Research Fellow in, and Professor David Brereton is the Director of, the Centre for Social Responsibility in Mining, Sustainable Minerals Institute, The University of Queensland, Brisbane, Queensland 4072, Australia; Emails: D.Franks@smi.uq.edu.au and D.Brereton@smi.uq.edu.au; Tel: +61 7 3346 3164; Fax: +61 7 3346 4045. Professor Chris Moran is the Director of the Sustainable Minerals Institute, The University of Queensland; Email: C.Moran@smi.uq.edu.au.

This is part of a special issue on 'Cumulative effects assessment and management'.

For acknowledgements see page 310.

Duinker and Greig, 2006; Brereton et al, 2008; Franks et al, 2009a).

Resource provinces in Australia have experienced major transitions associated with an extended period of growth and are coming to terms with the compounding effects of multiple mining operations in a landscape already under environmental, economic and social strain (Brereton et al, 2008; Lockie et al, 2008; QDTRDI, 2008; QDIP, 2009). Resource development generates economic and employment benefits to towns and regions; however, the distribution of positive and negative impacts is uneven in scale and dimension as well as in space and time. These same regions also periodically contend with industry contraction.

In this paper we detail working examples of cumulative impact management and assessment with the aim to guide and encourage future practice. First, we discuss cumulative impacts in a mining context. Second, we introduce three major Australian coal resource provinces and the challenges confronting each region: the Hunter Valley in New South Wales, a mature high density mining region;

the Bowen Basin in Queensland, a relatively dispersed mining region; and the Gunnedah Basin in New South Wales, a prospective region. Finally, we outline assessment and management practices adopted to respond to the diversity of cumulative impacts in these regions.

Cumulative impacts and mining

In the broadest sense, cumulative impacts are the successive, incremental and combined impacts of one, or more, activities on society, the economy and the environment. Cumulative impacts result from the aggregation and interaction of impacts on a receptor and may be the product of past, present or future activities (Figure 1). Cumulative impacts can be both positive and negative and can vary in intensity as well as spatial and temporal extent. Cumulative impacts may interact such that they trigger or are associated with other impacts. They may aggregate linearly, exponentially or reach 'tipping points' after which major changes in environmental, social and economic systems may follow (Contant and Wiggins, 1991; Damman et al, 1995; Canter and Kamath, 1995; Moran et al, 2007; Brereton et al, 2008; Franks et al, 2009a).

Impacts can result directly from an action (or non-action) or from a pathway or chain of indirect impacts. Cumulative impacts may result from the aggregation and interaction of direct or indirect impacts. Depending on the context and the location in time and space, different receiving environments (such as a social group, river or geographic region) may experience the same impacts differently. A mining-related activity may generate multiple direct and indirect impacts and/or contribute towards existing stresses within social and environmental systems generated from other (non-mining) activities.

Cumulative impacts are not necessarily generated as part of a simple causal pathway; that is, a cumulative impact may result from the aggregation or interaction of impacts from multiple unrelated sources. An example of this may be the cumulative social impact experienced from the aggregation of different amenity impacts of mining (such as noise, dust, vibration, scenic amenity). The presence of one impact may also change how another may be experienced, independent of how that impact was generated.

An additional distinction that is evident in cumulative as well as direct and indirect impacts is that between source and sink impacts. A *sink impact* results from the addition of material to a receiving environment (the outputs of an activity; e.g. coal dust, greenhouse gas, or social investments). A *source impact* results from the extraction of natural, social, human or economic resources (the inputs of an activity; e.g. the water drawn from a river or additional pressures placed on health services).

Arguably the interactions between sink impacts and their environment are better understood in the mining context than source impacts. This is probably because the attention paid to discharges, such as air and water, has led to research to define thresholds above which impacts are considered significant. With the exception of impacts on air quality (most notably greenhouse gases) the spatial extents of most sink impacts arising from mining are local (vibration, noise, dust, and amenity) and more clearly bounded (e.g. watersheds and airsheds). Source impacts, such as changes to surface and groundwater, biodiversity, human resources and social services can be difficult to understand in both baseline and impacted states and may extend across ill-defined spatial extents.

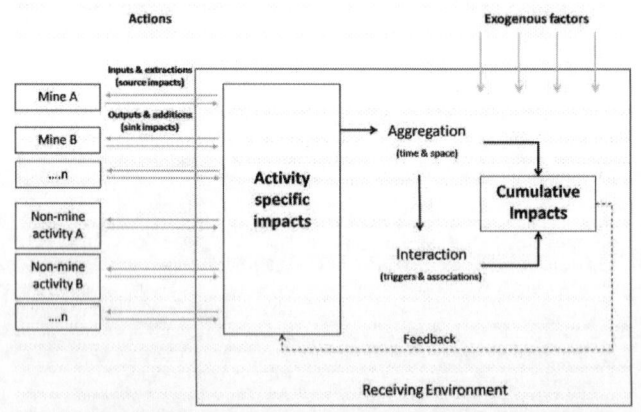

Figure 1. A conceptual framework of the cumulative impacts of mining. The definition of the receiving environment will vary for different impacts. Receiving environments may be influenced by external forces that are not activity generated impacts. These 'exogenous factors' may include variations in climate, global economic conditions or social and cultural trends
Source: Franks et al (2010)

The Australian coal industry

Australia is the world's largest exporter of black coal and the fourth largest producer. Black coal is mined for both metallurgical and energy production purposes. The industry generates AUD54.6 billion in exports and directly employs around 28,000 people (ABARE, 2009; MCA, 2010). Australian black coal production has experienced a period of expansion increasing from 345 Mt (raw) and 273 Mt (saleable) in 2001/02 to 421 Mt (raw) and 327 Mt (saleable) in 2007/08 (though production decreased slightly in 2008/09; ABARE, 2009).

Queensland is the largest producer of black coal in Australia with 54 active mines (15 underground, 39 open-cut; 2007 figures; ACA, 2009). In 2008/09 Queensland produced 222 Mt, up from 135 Mt a decade earlier (1997/98; figures are for raw coal; ABARE, 2009). The large majority of operations are in the Bowen Basin followed by the Surat, Galilee, Clarence-Moreton and Tarong Basins.

New South Wales is the second largest producer of black coal in Australia with 60 active mines (29 underground, 31 open-cut; 2007 figures; ACA, 2009). In 2008/09 the state produced 181 Mt, up from 134 Mt a decade earlier (1997/98; figures are for raw coal; ABARE, 2008). The Sydney Basin (that includes the Hunter coalfields) hosts the large majority of mines, with Gunnedah emerging as a prospective region.

The following sections profile three Australian coal provinces to highlight their varied operational contexts: the Bowen Basin, a dispersed mining region; the Hunter Valley, a 'mature', high density, coal mining region; and the Gunnedah Basin, a prospective region.

Bowen Basin (Queensland): a dispersed resource province

The Bowen Basin is a relatively dispersed mining region due to the size of the Basin and the relatively even distribution of the mining operations, though there are a number of locations where operations are closely spaced. The Bowen Basin covers an area of approximately 60,000 km^2 in Central Queensland stretching from Collinsville in the north to Theodore in the south (see Figure 2). The Basin hosts 47 operational coal mines and produces over 100 Mt of black coal annually (QDIP, 2008b; QDEEDI, 2009). A further 31 projects were under development or in an advanced stage of approvals, as of August 2009 (QDEEDI, 2009). Increasingly the Basin is also attracting development and exploration for coal seam gas extraction.

The Bowen Basin is serviced by communities including Collinsville, Nebo, Glenden, Moranbah, Clermont, Dysart, Middlemount, Tieri, Emerald, Blackwater and Moura. The Basin has a total population of around 70,000, with an additional 10,000 non-resident workers in company accommodations (e.g. single person quarters) while on roster that drive-in, drive-out (DIDO) and/or fly-in, fly-out (FIFO) to the coastal centres of Bowen, Mackay, Rockhampton and Gladstone (QDLGPSR, 2006). Coal from the Basin is mostly exported through ports near Mackay, Gladstone and Bowen. Glenden, Dysart, Tieri, Middlemount, Blackwater and Moranbah are purpose-built mining communities, while other communities were established to service rural industries, particularly grazing.

Expansion of coal mining in the Bowen Basin has contributed to the generation of a number of cumulative impacts, particularly pressure on social and economic infrastructure. The region has reported shortages in affordable accommodation and housing (e.g. rents in Emerald and Moranbah have been up to 95% more expensive than the state capital city of Brisbane; Rolfe et al, 2007; McKenzie et al, 2009), skills shortages in trades, difficulties in retaining staff in the non-mining sectors, and pressure on community services such as child care, employment and skills training, local medical and dental services (QDIP, 2009).

Increased mining activity has also brought positive economic cumulative impacts to the Basin with greater employment, and a larger population base to support services and facilities. In addition, the Bowen Basin has experienced positive cumulative impacts as a result of community development activities and funds, local business development from mine procurement, the development of human capital (skills, employment and training), and the provision (and subsidy) of water and transport infrastructure.

Due to the dispersed nature of mining in the region, impacts have most often arisen in the areas of regional infrastructure and services, rather than amenity issues associated with densely located operations. Where multiple mining operations are located close to towns, such as around Moranbah, the cumulative impacts of dust, noise, visual amenity and vibration are becoming increasingly evident (QDIP, 2009). Saline water discharge into the Fitzroy catchment, especially from mining operations subject to major flooding, has recently arisen as an issue of concern due to the cumulative impact on downstream ecosystems. Similarly, biodiversity impacts from vegetation clearing, on the maintenance of roads, the disruption to agricultural enterprises from exploration activities, fugitive greenhouse gas

---

Expansion of coal mining in the Bowen Basin has contributed to the generation of a number of cumulative impacts, particularly pressure on social and economic infrastructure

Managing the cumulative impacts of coal mining in Australia

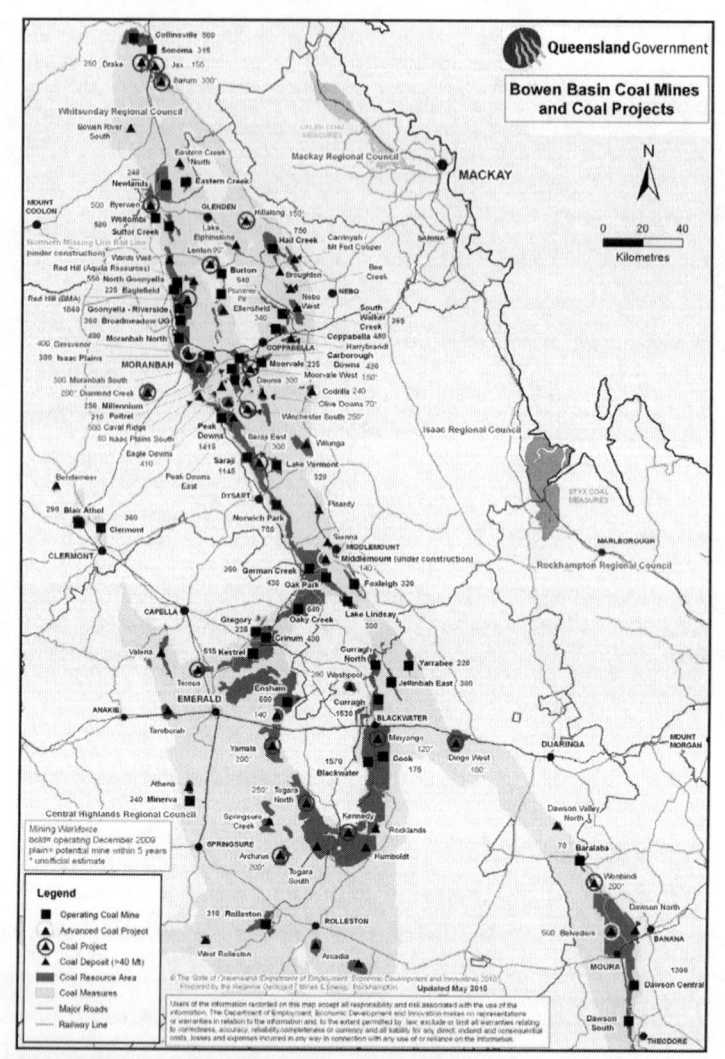

Figure 2. Coal mines and coal projects of the Bowen Basin, Queensland
Source: Queensland Department of Employment, Economic Development and Innovation

emissions, and mining subsidence also demonstrate a cumulative component.[1]

Hunter Valley (New South Wales): a high density resource province

Located in New South Wales to the northwest of Sydney, the Hunter Valley is a mature high density mining region. The Hunter coalfield hosts 18 mines with 12 expansions and new developments under way. The Hunter is one of a number of coalfields within the Sydney Basin (Figures 3 and 4). Coalfields in the vicinity of the Hunter include the Western coalfield (10 mines, 4 developments, 25.7 Mt), the Newcastle and Gloucester coalfields (14 mines, 4 developments, 18.9 Mt), the Central coalfield (no active mines), and the Southern coalfield (8 mines, 4 developments, 13 Mt; NSW DPI, 2009).

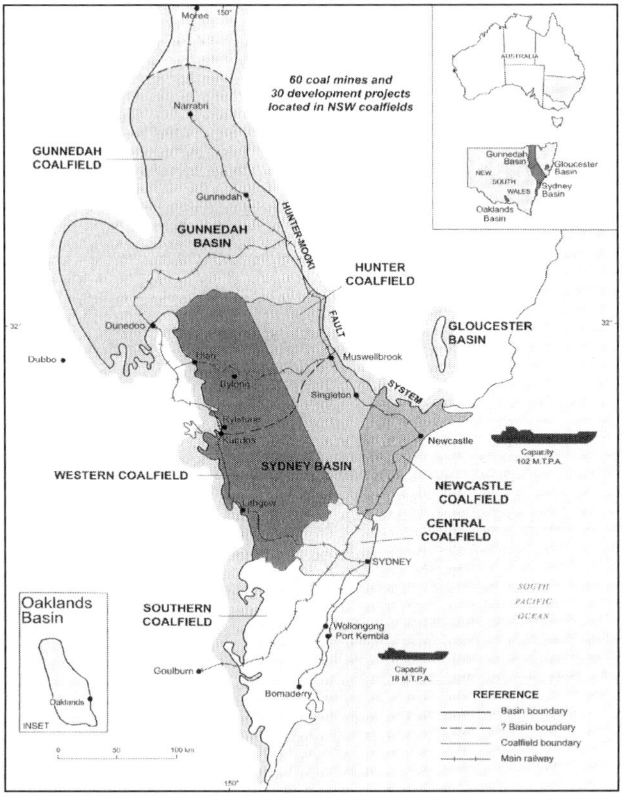

Figure 3. Coal mining regions of New South Wales
Source: NSW DPI (2009)

The Hunter Valley is approximately 50 km in width and 100 km in length, and has a population of around 50,000. The region is located in the headwaters and upper reaches of the Hunter River. The main towns of the region are Singleton, Muswellbrook, Denman, Aberdeen and Scone. Traditionally a rural-based economy, the region is now known for equine and wine industries, coal mining and energy production. Reference to cumulative impacts in the Hunter is most commonly in the context of environmental and amenity impacts (dust, water quality, noise, vibration, greenhouse gases, biodiversity, health and scenic amenity) though social impacts are also important.

In towns like Muswellbrook there was a distinct shift during the early 1990s from a community focus on direct impacts to one of cumulative impacts of multiple mining operations (URS, 2000). Muswellbrook, once a rural town in a dairy and farming district, is now surrounded by five mining operations (Figure 4). Cumulative issues of concern to the community in Muswellbrook include feelings of 'social dislocation' and changing sense of place, biodiversity, dust, noise, vibration, visual amenity, water quality and community infrastructure (URS, 2000; Brereton *et al*, 2008). Biodiversity and salinity discharge into the Hunter River are also cumulative impacts of community concern. Positive cumulative impacts include employment, local business and human capital development. For example, in Muswellbrook the mining industry directly employed 13–16% of the total Shire workforce between 1996 and 2006. Almost 30% of local businesses reported relying primarily on the mining and energy production industries for their business (Brereton *et al*, 2008).

*Gunnedah Basin (New South Wales):
a prospective resource province*

The Gunnedah Basin is a prospective coal province in New South Wales (see Figure 3). There are four current and four proposed coal mining projects in the Basin. In 2007/08 the Gunnedah Basin produced

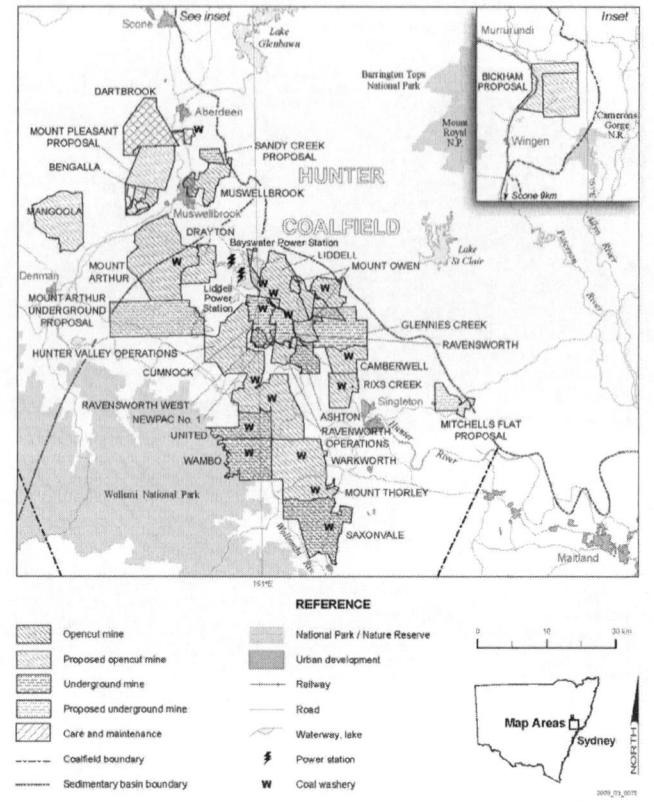

Figure 4. Coal mining operations of the Hunter coalfield
Source: NSW DPI (2009)

4.3 Mt of coal; however, the New South Wales Government projects the development of a number of small to medium sized mines with prospects for larger operations in the coming decade (NSW DPI, 2009). In 2006 the New South Wales Government issued an exploration licence for the Caroona area to BHP Billiton, and in 2008 an exploration licence was issued for the adjacent Watermark area to the China Shenhua Energy Company. As with the Surat and Bowen Basins there has also been significant interest and activity in the coal seam gas sector.

The Basin is approximately 150 km wide and 200 km in length, stretching from Dunedoo in the south to Narribri in the north (Figure 3). Towns in the Basin include Gunnedah, Tamworth, Quirindi, Narrabri, Caroona, Curlewis and Coonabarabran.

The Liverpool plains, one of Australia's most productive farming regions, is located in the Basin. These black soil alluvial plains lie between Gunnedah in the north and Murrurundi in the south and produce around one third of Australia's durum wheat and one fifth of its sorghum. Further coal development in the Basin would require that mining coexist with broad-scale agriculture and protect the features of the flood plain that make it attractive to farming. The farming community have raised concerns that coal mining may not be able to meet this requirement and may contribute to the generation of adverse cumulative impacts through interaction and aggregation with already existing impacts from non-mining activities, particularly in the form of impacts on the regional groundwater regime (CCAG, 2008). A regional groundwater study is currently under way to assess the potential impacts of mining development in the region.

Assessment of cumulative impacts

In Australia cumulative impacts are required to be assessed as part of the project approval process, which is primarily the responsibility of state governments.[2] Project-level impact assessments in both New South Wales and Queensland (the two states that account for the location of the vast majority of black coal mines) follow the same essential process:

1. The preparation of an initial advice statement (Queensland) or application for approval (New South Wales) by the proponent, which broadly outlines the scope of the proposal.
2. The development, by the relevant agency, of terms of reference (Queensland) or a report that details the environmental assessment requirements (New South Wales) to be covered in the assessment (in Queensland the terms of reference include provision for public comment, while in New South Wales the requirements must take into account the views of other government agencies).
3. The preparation of a draft Environmental Impact Statement (EIS) by the proponent (which includes social impacts).
4. A period of public review and comment and, if required by the relevant authority, a supplementary EIS to address issues raised by public submissions.
5. A decision whether to approve the proposal and an environmental assessment report by the relevant government agency that provides an overview of the process and indicates whether the EIS has complied with the Act.

In both New South Wales and Queensland the environmental impact assessment procedures require developments to address cumulative impacts. Table 1 lists the requirements to address cumulative impacts under relevant Australian, Queensland and New South Wales legislation and policy. In practice these requirements are specified in the terms of reference or assessment requirements of the impact assessment rather than in legislation.

In Queensland, cumulative impacts are not specifically mentioned in either the Environmental Protection Act 1994 or the State Development and Public Works Organisation Act 1971. These acts both specify that an EIS must be written in the form requested by the agency and, as such, guidance on the type of impacts that need to be assessed is given in the terms of reference developed by the agencies.

Under the Queensland Environmental Protection Act 1994 the development of a draft terms of reference is the responsibility of the proponent, with a period of public comment and then finalisation by the Department of Environment and Resource Management (DERM). While no definition of cumulative impacts is provided, the generic terms of reference does provide some guidance by stating that cumulative impacts 'must be considered over time or in combination with other (all) impacts in the dimensions of scale, intensity, duration or frequency of the impacts' (QDERM, 2010). Evidence of collaborative management is also required.

Cumulative impacts also play a role in the consideration of the level of impact assessment required. The Queensland Government considers the potential influence cumulative impacts may have on the overall impacts of a proposal when deciding whether, under the Environmental Protection Act 1994, the proposal is a standard application that does not require an EIS, a non-standard application that does not require an EIS, or a non-standard application that does require an EIS (QEPA, 2000).

In New South Wales, impact assessment is regulated under the Environmental Planning and Assessment Act 1979. The Act is supported by the State Environmental Policy (Major Projects) that was introduced in 2005 and defines the classification criteria for different levels of assessment. Mining projects generally fall into the 'Designated' and 'State Significant Development' categories (for more information see NSW DUAP, 2000).

The New South Wales Department of Urban Affairs and Planning has published a guideline for the preparation of EIS for coal mines and associated infrastructure (2000). The guidelines describe cumulative impacts as the result of 'a number of activities with similar impacts interacting with the environment in a region ... they may also be caused by the synergistic and antagonistic effects of different individual impacts ... [and] due to the temporal or spatial characteristics of the activities and impacts' (NSW DUAP, 2000: 37).

Cumulative impacts are required to be considered when prioritising issues, in site selection, the assessment of potential impacts, and management. Proponents must consider the resilience and capacity of the receiving environment to cope with impacts, the relationship to other mines and infrastructure, and must refer to existing regional, cumulative and strategic studies (such as the Upper Hunter Valley Cumulative Impacts Study), catchment or cumulative water quality management strategies and compliance arrangements (NSW DUAP, 2000).

For analysis of air quality the guidelines describe a suggested methodology of cumulative assessment and compel the proponent to take into account the cumulative effects of other developments that have been approved but are yet to commence. Measures to avoid and mitigate river impacts through discharge schemes, trading or supply to and from adjacent mines and industries, and reuse opportunities are also to be considered (NSW DUAP, 2000).

At a federal level the Commonwealth Environment Protection and Biodiversity Conservation Act 1999 (EPBC Act) includes an impact assessment function that is triggered in cases where the Minister believes there to be likely impacts on matters of national environmental significance from a proposal. Both Queensland and New South Wales have bilateral agreements with the Commonwealth to manage the assessments as a part of the state assessment process. While the EPBC Act does not specifically mention cumulative impacts, a number of Federal

Table 1. Requirements to address cumulative impacts in relevant Australian, Queensland and New South Wales legislation and policy

Legislation/terms of reference	Indicative extract
Commonwealth	
Commonwealth Environment Protection and Biodiversity Conservation Act 1999	No specific mention of cumulative impacts. Impact is defined to include direct, indirect and reasonably foreseeable consequences of actions. Federal Court rulings have interpreted the Act to include cumulative impacts. The 'Hawke' review of the EPBC Act has signalled that cumulative impacts will be a focus of reform.
Queensland	
Queensland Environmental Protection Act 1994	The Act makes no distinction between cumulative or other impacts, but expects an EIS to assess all such impacts. The draft terms of reference (ToR) must be 'in the approved form'. In practice this means that the project ToR must be based on the generic ToR developed by the Department of Environment and Natural Resource Management.
Queensland Department of Environment and Resource Management Generic ToR (2010) — Environmental Protection Act 1994	The generic ToR does not require a separate section for cumulative impacts, but rather requires them to be assessed in issue-related sections, such as those for ecology, social impacts, or noise. Indicative extracts from the generic ToR are: 'Describe any cumulative impacts on environmental values caused by the project, either in isolation or by combination with other known existing or planned development or sources of contamination.' 'The cumulative impacts of the project must be considered over time or in combination with other (all) impacts in the dimensions of scale, intensity, duration or frequency of the impacts.' 'Where impacts from the project will not be felt in isolation to other sources of impact, it is recommended that the proponent develop consultative arrangements with other industries in the proposal's area to undertake cooperative monitoring and/or management of environmental parameters. Describe such arrangements in the EIS.'
Queensland State Development and Public Works Organisation Act 1971	The Act makes no distinction between cumulative and other impacts. The Act requires compliance to the ToR finalised by the Coordinator General.
Queensland Coordinator General. Example Terms of Reference (2010) – Queensland State Development and Public Works Organisation Act 1971	'The EIS should summarise and describe cumulative impacts 'in combination with those of existing or proposed project(s) publicly known or advised by [the Department of Infrastructure and Planning] to be in the region, to the greatest extent practicable. Cumulative impacts should be assessed with respect to both geographic location and environmental values. The methodology used to determine the cumulative impacts of the project should be presented, detailing the range of variables considered, including where applicable, relevant baseline or other criteria upon which the cumulative aspects of the project have been assessed.' 'The EIS should provide a comparative analysis of how the project conforms to the objectives for 'sustainable development" ... 'This analysis should consider the cumulative impacts (both beneficial and adverse) of the project from a life-of-project perspective, taking into consideration the scale, intensity, duration and frequency of the impacts to demonstrate a balance between environmental integrity, social development and economic development.' 'The SIA will include an evaluation of the potential cumulative social impacts resulting from the project including an estimation of the overall size, significance and likelihood of those impacts. Cumulative impacts in this context is defined as the additional impacts on population, workforce, accommodation, housing, and use of community infrastructure and services, from the project, and other proposals for development projects in the area which are publicly known or communicated by [the Department of Infrastructure and Planning], if they overlap with the proposed project in the same time frame as its construction period.'
New South Wales	
New South Wales Environmental Planning and Assessment Act 1979	The Act makes no distinction between cumulative and other impacts (except in environmental assessment of fishing activities).
New South Wales Department of Urban Affairs and Planning. Coal Mines and Associated Infrastructure. EIS Guideline	'(a) identify other existing or proposed activities in the area with similar environmental impacts or which are likely to impact on the same elements of the environment (e.g. clearance of the same type of habitat)' '(b) assess the extent to which the environment affected by the proposal is already stressed' '(c) identify any likely long-term and short-term cumulative impacts, such as air quality, noise or traffic disturbance, visual impacts, surface water and groundwater issues, public health; or loss of heritage items, vegetation or fauna habitat' '(d) consider the receiving environment's ability to achieve and maintain environmental objectives', and '(e) consider options for integrating operations with adjoining mines to obtain operational synergies, reduce costs, prevent environmental impacts or lessen land degradation (e.g. spoil transfer, wastewater exchange for reuse, integrated rehabilitated landforms, joint rail or road haulage works, joint coal handling or treatment facilities, integrated and shared monitoring networks and programs).'

Court rulings have interpreted the Act in such a way that the Minister must consider cumulative impacts when considering the significance of an action.[3] The recently released independent review of the EPBC Act (the 'Hawke' review) has signalled that cumulative impacts are a focus of reform.

Despite these requirements the treatment of cumulative impacts in such assessments is mixed.[4] Recent examples exist in Queensland where the only mention of cumulative impacts in the EIS is in the terms of reference attached as an appendix (in one such case the mine was situated close to several other coal mines). Lockie et al (2008: 182) have also identified limitations in the analysis of cumulative assessment in project-level EIS in Australia finding that while a number of assessments acknowledged the potential for cumulative impacts on communities situated near multiple mines, not a single case proposed management or mitigation activities to address the identified issues.

There are legitimate difficulties that proponents face when undertaking cumulative impact analysis. Information on the plans and activities of other current and future operations are difficult to ascertain, impacts may have temporal and spatial extents beyond those which can be studied in a project-level assessment, limits and thresholds may be poorly understood, particularly in regions of transition or where little research exists, and when information is available there are often issues with the compatibility

> **Despite these difficulties, there are assessment methodologies relevant to project-level impact assessments that have the potential to address cumulative impacts, including forecasting, scenario analysis, impact pathway analysis and modelling**

of methodologies and data sets. Despite these difficulties, there are assessment methodologies relevant to project-level impact assessments that have the potential to address cumulative impacts, including forecasting, scenario analysis, impact pathway analysis and modelling (see Hegmann et al, 1999; Brereton et al, 2008; Duinker and Greig, 2006, 2007; Franks et al, 2009b, 2010).[5]

Strategic assessments

Strategic assessments are often promoted as a method to more effectively account for cumulative impacts as they are broader in spatial and sometimes temporal extent; they may make explicit regional standards, thresholds, and links to land use planning; and they often establish regional databases, protocols, management systems and tools for implementation (Dalal-Clayton and Sadler, 1998; Cooper and Sheate, 2004). Strategic assessments may also offer advantages for business by avoiding the duplication of project-level assessments, informing developers about the environmental and social context in which they operate, and giving the potential for more certainty in the approvals process. Strategic assessments may sometimes also remove the requirement for project-level assessments if the proposal is consistent with the scope of the strategic assessment. Such an approach has obvious benefits for business as it can provide certainty for development proposals, reduce the potential for consultation fatigue, reduce the regulatory burden, and shorten the approvals process.

The New South Wales Government, in particular, has utilised strategic assessments to specifically assess the cumulative impacts of coal mining in the Hunter Valley. In the mid-1990s the New South Wales Commission of Inquiry for the Bayswater No. 3 and Bengalla coal mines recommended that the Department of Urban Affairs and Planning undertake a study of the cumulative impacts of coal mining on the Upper Hunter Valley Region. This recommendation was prompted by pressure from community and local government. The study, the 'Upper Hunter Cumulative Impact Study and Action Strategy', developed triggers, indicators and an action strategy. The study provided guidance for project-level assessment and called for more focussed examination of cumulative impacts in assessments, improved regional and sub-regional planning, and strengthened monitoring and data sets (NSW DUAP, 1997).

A strategic assessment has also been developed to analyse the coal mining potential of the Upper Hunter Valley (New South Wales Department of Planning, 2005). The assessment takes into consideration coal resources, mine development potential, surface and groundwater, social and amenity issues, natural and cultural heritage, land and agriculture. In late 2006 the New South Wales Government initiated a strategic review of the impacts of underground mining in the Southern Coalfield, specifically subsidence. The findings of the independent review stressed the need for better assessment of cumulative and regional impacts and improved attention to cumulative impacts within project-level environmental impact assessments. Furthermore, the study recommended that regulatory agencies and industry consider collaborative efforts with other 'knowledge holders' to develop improved regional and cumulative environmental data sets for the Southern Coalfield (New South Wales Department of Planning, 2008).

Management of cumulative impacts

This section traverses a range of cumulative impact management approaches (strategic and regional planning; information exchange, networking and forums; pooling of resources to support initiatives and programs; and multi-stakeholder and regional monitoring). Working examples of collaboration and coordination are emphasised, including multi-stakeholder, cross-government, single company, multiple company and cross-industry approaches.

Strategic and regional planning

In response to social and economic infrastructure constraints in the Bowen Basin and Hunter Valley, the Queensland and New South Wales State Governments have led a series of initiatives to improve coordination and planning. In October 2004, the Coal Infrastructure Coordination Group was formed by the Queensland Government, later changing its name to the Queensland Government Coal Infrastructure Taskforce. The mandate of the Taskforce is to coordinate whole-of-government planning for the provision of coal infrastructure (transport, water, energy, housing and social infrastructure) in Queensland. The body, which is part of the Queensland Department of Infrastructure and Planning, reports to the Cabinet Budget Review Committee, thus providing the Taskforce with a direct line to state government decision-making and resources. The Taskforce is an attempt to expedite the infrastructure investments to cope with the sharp expansion of the coal industry since 2003 and to proactively address the cumulative impacts on physical and social infrastructure, especially in Bowen Basin mining communities. In 2005 the Queensland Government, with the support of the Queensland Resources Council (QRC), prepared the Coal Infrastructure Program of Actions (QDIP, 2008a). The program of actions is heavily focused on transport infrastructure, but areas such as water and power supply, workforce skills and social and housing infrastructure are also included. The Taskforce commissioned a Queensland Coal Industry Strategic Plan to determine future infrastructure needs of the state.

In September 2008, the Queensland Government introduced the Sustainable Resource Communities Policy to improve the assessment and ongoing management of social impacts, provide for greater coordination and collaboration between stakeholders, and address resource governance issues at multiple scales. Cumulative impacts were a key rationale for the development of the policy (QDTRDI, 2008).[6] The Sustainable Resource Communities Policy is designed to both maximise the opportunities presented by developments in Queensland resource regions and mitigate and avoid adverse impacts in areas such as social infrastructure, employment, housing, community services, amenity, quality of life, health and education. The policy is initially focused on three resource communities, the Bowen Basin, the Surat Basin and the North West Minerals Province, where resource development has significantly affected (or in the case of the Surat, has the potential to significantly affect) community infrastructure and services, and the social structure of communities.[7] The policy introduces a dedicated social impact assessment (SIA) function within government, and introduces social impact management plans (SIMPs) to outline the forecast changes to communities, the agreed strategies for mitigation of impacts, and the responsibility of various parties in relation to management (see Franks et al, 2009b). Regional planning also commands greater attention under the policy. Draft statutory regional plans have been recently developed for Central West, South West and Maranoa Districts, and further plans will be prioritised to provide guidance towards resource and community development.

The Sustainable Resource Communities Policy is complemented by a multi-stakeholder partnership between the state government, the Local Government Association of Queensland (LGAQ) and the Queensland Resources Council (QRC). In practical terms the partnership involves the formation of a partnership group and local leadership groups.[8] The partnership group aims to improve state-wide and regional coordination and includes representatives of the state government, the regional councils, the LGAQ and the QRC. The partnership group's role is to share strategic information, develop and coordinate solutions, undertake research into best practice and assessment methodologies, and facilitate cross-sector communication. At a resource province level, local leadership groups focus on regional planning, and developing projects that address the cumulative effects of resource developments (QDTRDI, 2008; QDIP, 2009; Franks et al, 2009b).[9]

New South Wales has also undertaken reforms of its planning instruments. Prior to the introduction of major legislative and procedural reforms in 2005, there were some significant structural impediments to consistent planning. A notable limitation was that the Department of Planning was responsible for granting planning approvals for new mines, but control of rehabilitation and post-mining land use was the responsibility of another area of government, the Department of Primary Industries. Similarly, approval and regulation of biodiversity offsets was the responsibility of the Department of Conservation and Environment. Not surprisingly, this division of responsibility presented some significant coordination challenges. The 2005 reforms have removed these impediments by clearly defining the Department of Planning as the pre-eminent planning body for New South Wales. In the case of mining, the powers of the Department now include the right to determine what offsets and rehabilitation will be required for new mining developments and the shape of final mining voids. The reforms were also designed to simplify planning controls and improve development assessment processes.

Industry too has led collaborative planning initiatives, though examples are less common. One such initiative is the Clermont Preferred Futures. In the small rural community of Clermont, also in the Bowen Basin, Rio Tinto has responded to local government requests for infrastructure development by facilitating a community strategic planning initiative. The requests for infrastructure followed the decision by Rio Tinto to open a second mine (Clermont coal mine) near the existing Blair Athol mine, which is due to close in 2015, and the potential additional impacts that would arise from these transitions. Clermont has become dependent on the economic activity of the mine, and the community visioning process provided an opportunity to target future investments to enable a positive post-mining legacy. The initiative was coordinated by the Belyando Shire Council (now part of the Isaac Regional Council) and facilitated by the Institute for Sustainable Regional Development at Central Queensland University. The community plan is a strategic framework to guide development in the community over the coming two decades and ensure investments meet community goals. The initiative was established in February 2007. The exercise was informed by a socio-economic baseline of the town. This consisted of stakeholder mapping, analysing the socio-economic characteristics of the region and the coverage of existing data, identifying previous work and existing plans and strategies, and developing partnerships. A vision was developed from targeted community consultation and input from a diverse steering committee. An action plan was formulated and an officer appointed to coordinate implementation. The position is jointly funded between the local government and Rio Tinto (ISRD, 2008).

Information exchange, networking and forums

Informal and formal networks can provide important opportunities to exchange experiences. Informal networks between environment and community relations practitioners are relatively common both within and between companies. Rio Tinto, for example, has internal professional networking for exchange of ideas and advice. The Muswellbrook Mine Managers Forum, in the Hunter Valley, is a more formal network to discuss common issues across multiple operations. Environmental officers in Muswellbrook also meet regularly. In the Bowen Basin the Central Queensland Mining Rehabilitation Group (CQMRG) is a collaborative forum through which members can share their experiences and information about environmental management of mine sites. CQMRG was formed in 1991. Most members are industry affiliated and major sponsors include URS, Sinclair Knight Mertz, Xstrata Coal, Rio Tinto Coal Australia, Anglo Coal and Central Queensland University. The group hosts tri-annual workshops and prepares regular newsletters (CQMRG, 2009).

Pooling of resources to support initiatives and programs

Where there are multiple mining projects operating in the same general area, there may be opportunities for these operations to focus and coordinate investments to target community and environment needs and generate the best value for each spend through pooling resources (Franks et al, 2009a). There may also be opportunities to involve government, other industries or organisations in such arrangements.

An initiative in the Hunter Valley that has taken this approach is the Upper Hunter River Rehabilitation Initiative. The Upper Hunter River Rehabilitation Initiative was a 5-year program, completed in 2007, which trialled river rehabilitation methods in the 10 km reach of the Hunter River south of Muswellbrook. The research was funded by the Australian Research Council, the New South Wales Department of Natural Resources, New South Wales Department of Primary Industries, the Hunter-Central Rivers Catchment Management Authority, New South Wales Department of Lands, Newcastle Ports Corporation, Mt Arthur Coal, Bengalla Mining Company (Coal and Allied) and Macquarie Generation (CMA, 2008).

In the Bowen Basin, BHP Billiton Mitsubishi Alliance (BMA) and Anglo Coal jointly funded a consultancy to conduct a voluntary impact assessment on the cumulative impacts of longwall coal mining on a 100 km stretch of the Isaac River in Central Queensland. The Queensland Department of Environment and Resource Management (DERM) was also a major stakeholder in the process. The assessment sought to identify the precise impacts of mining developments, primarily concerning river diversions and stream-bed subsidence, and to provide recommendations for mine planning and operations (Lucas et al, 2009).

In the Gunnedah Basin, advocacy by landholders concerned about the potential for cumulative impacts on groundwater systems has resulted in the Namoi Water Catchment Study. The aim of the study is to better understand the relationship between groundwater and surface water systems and the potential impacts of coal mining development. Participants in the Water Study Working Group include the Caroona Coal Action Group, New South Wales Farmers Association, Namoi Water, New South Wales Minerals Council, New South Wales Department of Primary Industries, the Commonwealth Department of the Environment, Water, Heritage and the Arts, and BHP Billiton.

Multi-stakeholder and regional monitoring

Cumulative impacts often extend well beyond the geographic location of an operation and may contribute to systems already impacted by other operations, industries and activities. Monitoring the activities of a single operation can therefore prove insufficient. Due to sampling and methodology limitations, the aggregation of data from individual operations also often fails to present a full picture. Regional and multi-stakeholder monitoring can help to address the cumulative impacts of multiple actions for important issues of high stakeholder concern.

The Hunter River Salinity Trading Scheme (HRSTS) is an example of a regional approach to monitor, mitigate and report on cumulative impacts in New South Wales. The geological composition of the Upper Hunter Valley is naturally high in salt, and the potential for mining to increase the salinity of the Hunter catchment has been a cause for concern in the local community. The disturbance of lands containing salt increases the potential for that salt to become dissolved in groundwater, and later enter the catchment system. Due to the pressures on the Hunter catchment from mining, agriculture and

---

Cumulative impacts often extend well beyond the geographic location of an operation and may contribute to systems already impacted by other operations, industries and activities

electricity generation, a comprehensive monitoring and regulation framework, the Salinity Trading Scheme, was trialled in 1994, and implemented in 2003. Market-based instruments, particularly trading schemes and offsets, have become a popular method to manage impacts, as they can be an efficient way of allocating entitlements or offsetting consumed capital.

Under the trading scheme, salty water can only be discharged when the salt concentration in the river is low. Under low river flow conditions, no discharges are permitted; under high flow conditions limited discharges are allowed as determined by a system of tradable salt credits. Under flood conditions, unlimited discharge is permitted (up to a threshold salt level; NSW EPA, 2003). Stakeholders hold a licence for a certain number of credits which permits them to discharge salt into a river block in proportion to the number of credits they hold (one credit allows the holder to contribute 0.1% of the total allowable discharge). There are a total of 1,000 credits in the trading scheme; these may be traded among stakeholders in the marketplace (NSW EPA, 2003). The ownership of credits, their price, and the volume and concentration of discharges are publicly reported to the community. The New South Wales Department of Environment, Climate Change and Water has reported that since the introduction of the scheme the target salinity level has not been exceeded as a result of discharges.

The Upper Hunter Air Quality Monitoring Network is a more recent initiative, announced in October of 2009. The New South Wales Government led initiative will develop an independent air quality monitoring network for the Upper Hunter Valley. The network will be developed in response to health and amenity concerns of dust pollution from coal mining and emissions from coal-fired electricity generation. The network is the result of a government–industry initiative, led by the New South Wales Department of Environment, Climate Change and Water (DECCW) and New South Wales Department of Planning, and consisting of New South Wales Health, Singleton Council, Muswellbrook Council, Upper Hunter Council, New South Wales Minerals Council, and the coal mining and electricity generation companies (Coal and Allied, Xstrata Coal, Ashton Coal, Integra Coal, Anglo Coal, Muswellbrook Coal, Hunter Valley Energy Coal, Rix's Creek, Wambo Coal, Macquarie Generation and Redbank Project). The network will expand an existing state government air quality monitoring network with an additional 14 particulate matter air quality monitoring stations in the Upper Hunter Valley, including in the towns of Singleton and Muswellbrook. Funding for the network will be provided through industry contributions with ongoing management and administration the responsibility of the New South Wales Government. Data will be accessible online through the DECCW's Regional Air Quality Index website. The partnership has been formalised through a memorandum of understanding (New South Wales Government, 2009).

Conclusion

The expansion and contraction of the coal mining industry has multiplied the extent, magnitude and profile of cumulative impacts in a number of Australian resource provinces. Mining can generate impacts that may aggregate and interact and/or contribute towards existing stresses within social and environmental systems generated from other (non-mining) activities. In this paper we have presented management and assessment approaches that seek to address the cumulative impacts of coal mining on regional communities and environments.

Due to the scale of cumulative impacts experienced in these resource provinces, focused attention is still required. In the area of assessment, government regulators are demanding greater emphasis on cumulative impact identification. There is scope to improve impact assessments through careful analysis of the different ways by which impacts aggregate and interact, collation and forecasting of information on announced and future projects, and collaborative research. Governments can also play a greater role in this area through the provision of strategic assessments, and explicit links between regional and land use planning and EIS.

The cumulative impact management approaches detailed here represent a range of institutional forms from single company initiatives and programs, to cross-industry and multi-stakeholder partnerships and networking. The approaches vary in complexity with each demanding a different degree of maturity of the collaborative relationship. Approaches such as information exchange, networking and forums are relatively straightforward and commonly practiced, while more advanced approaches, such as coordination and planning and multi-stakeholder monitoring, can be far more challenging to implement, but at the same time offering greater opportunities.

Acknowledgements

The authors would like to acknowledge the Queensland Department of Employment, Economic Development and Innovation, the Australian Coal Association Research Program, the Isaac Regional Council and the Sustainable Minerals Institute, University of Queensland, who funded aspects of the research presented here. Earlier versions of this work were presented at the International Association for Impact Assessment, Assessing and Managing Cumulative Environmental Effects Special Topic Meeting, and the International Conference on Sustainable Development Indicators in the Minerals Industry (Franks et al, 2009a). The authors acknowledge the Queensland Department of Employment, Economic Development and Innovation and the New South Wales Department of Primary Industries for permission to republish figures. The research forms part of a recently released good practice guide on cumulative impacts.

Notes

1. This paper focuses on the management of cumulative impacts at a regional scale. While the coal mining industry is a significant generator of greenhouse gas emissions this paper does not explicitly deal with their management. While some of the approaches detailed within may be relevant to the management of impacts that are global in scale there are a range of specific coordination issues at this scale that are beyond the scope of this paper.
2. Voluntary project-level impact assessments are also undertaken by resource developers independently of what is required by government. Such assessments are usually undertaken in response to a major change in the project or community, for example in preparation for closure or for a major expansion, or may be focused on the particular issues faced during exploration, resettlement, temporary scale down of operations, or for a community development program. A small, but increasing number of companies are now requiring all of their sites to undertake baseline studies and/or social impact assessments at periodic intervals.
3. See, for example, Brown v Forestry Tasmania, Wielangta Forest decision [2006] FCA F1729, and Queensland Conservation Council Inc v Minister for the Environment and Heritage, Nathan Dam case [2003] FCA 1463).
4. The standard does appear to be higher in New South Wales, perhaps a function of the higher density of mines and the longer period of time in which cumulative impacts have been an issue of public concern.
5. Brereton et al (2008) report on a 3-year Australian Coal Association Research Program funded research project to develop and test a framework for assessing, monitoring and reporting on the cumulative impacts of coal mining where multiple mines operate and refined methodological approaches. The study used the town of Muswellbrook in the Hunter Valley as a case study. Muswellbrook is surrounded by five coal mines (Mt Arthur Coal, Drayton, Bengalla, Muswellbrook Coal and Dartbrook), established vineyards, horse studs, irrigation and tourism industries. Impacts were prioritised through community consultation, and the research quantified and analysed visual amenity impacts, economic impacts, social impacts and water quality.
6. The policy builds upon the *Sustainable Futures Framework for Queensland Mining Towns*, published in July 2006 (QDLGPSR, 2006).The framework aimed to 'guide communities toward orderly and proper planning of towns impacted by mining projects'. The framework reviewed measures adopted in response to mining expansion and potential planning models; summarised population projections and the status of planning schemes; undertook consultation to determine the range of mining impacts on towns; scanned growth management issues for each of the resource towns of the Bowen and Surat Basins and planning considerations, responsibilities, and current actions for each issue identified.
7. Am AUD100 million 3-year program was announced to support the policy by providing physical and social infrastructure, such as upgraded roads, health facilities and schools in resource communities. As a demonstration of the difficulty of planning in regions of transition, in December 2008, 2 months after the announcement of the program, aud25 million of the aud100 million committed was brought forward and re-allocated toward capital projects in locations where mining jobs were lost in response to an anticipated downturn in the industry. The funds had originally been intended to be invested in infrastructure to manage growth.
8. Brereton et al (2008) recommended a similar high level consultative forum and a regional multi-stakeholder organisation be established in the Hunter Valley. The recommendations come out of a 3-year Australian Coal Association Research Program study of the cumulative impacts of mining in the town of Muswellbrook.
9. The local leadership groups build on the experience of the Moranbah Growth Management Group (MG2) an earlier commitment to assist the Belyando Shire Council (now part of the Isaac Regional Council), located in the Bowen Basin, to resolve issues related to the rapid growth in the purpose-built mining town of Moranbah. The MG2 reported directly to the Coal Industry Taskforce and consisted of representatives of the Department of Local Government Planning, Sport and Recreation, the office of the Coordinator General (Department of Infrastructure and Planning), Department of Mines and Energy, Isaac Regional Council, unions, BMA (BHP Billiton Mitsubishi Alliance) and Anglo Coal, and was chaired by the state government member for the region. The group led the preparation of the Moranbah preferred growth management strategy and commissioned the development of the Moranbah Strategic Plan.

References

ABARE, Australian Bureau of Agricultural and Resource Economics 2008. *Australian Commodity Statistics*. December. Canberra. 351p.

ABARE, Australian Bureau of Agricultural and Resource Economics 2009. *Australian Mineral Statistics 2009*. June Quarter. 36p.

ACA, Australian Coal Association 2009. *Black Coal Australia Statistical Summary*. 2p. Available at <http://www.australiancoal.com.au/resources.ashx/Publications/38/Publication/A3C9769373D6A8A7C7BF03F36284117C/BLACK_COAL_AUSTRALIA_160909.pdf>, last accessed 24 December 2009.

Brereton, D, C Moran, G McIlwain, J McIntosh and K Parkinson 2008. *Assessing the Cumulative Impacts of Mining on Regional Communities: An Exploratory Study of Coal Mining in the Muswellbrook Area of New South Wales*. Centre for Social Responsibility in Mining, Centre for Water in the Minerals Industry, and the Australian Coal Association Research Program. ACARP Project C14047.

Burris, R K and L W Canter 1997. Cumulative impacts are not properly addressed in environmental assessments. *Environmental Impact Assessment Review*, 17, 5–18.

Canter, L and J Kamath 1995. Questionnaire checklist for cumulative impacts. *Environmental Impact Assessment Review*, 15, 311–339.

CCAG, Caroona Coal Action Group 2008. *Proposal to Mine Liverpool Plains*. Fact Sheet. September. Available at <http://www.ccag.org.au/index.php?option=com_content&task=view&id=97&Itemid=74>, last accessed 16 December, 2008.

CMA, Hunter-Central Rivers Catchment Management Authority 2008. *The Upper Hunter River Rehabilitation Initiative*. Available at <http://www.hcr.cma.nsw.gov.au/uhrri/index.php3>, last accessed 23 December, 2008.

Commonwealth of Australia 2007. *Environmental Protection and Biodiversity Conservation Act 1999. Act No. 91 of 1999 as amended.* 1 July. Canberra: Office of Legislative Drafting and Publishing.

Contant, C and L Wiggins 1991. Defining and analyzing cumulative environmental impacts. *Environmental Impact Assessment Review*, 11, 297–309.

Cooper, L M and W R Sheate 2004. Integrating cumulative effects assessment into UK strategic planning: implications of the European Union SEA Directive. *Impact Assessment and Project Appraisal*, 22(5), 5–16.

CQMRG, Central Queensland Mining Rehabilitation Group 2009. Available at <http://www.cqmrg.org.au/index.html>, last accessed 10 March, 2009.

Dalal-Clayton, B and B Sadler 1998. Strategic environmental assessment: a rapidly evolving approach. In *A Directory of Impact Assessment Guidelines*, ed. A Donnelly, B Dalal-Clayton and R Hughes. London: International Institute for Environment and Development.

Damman, D, D Cressman and M Sadar 1995. Cumulative effects assessment: the development of practical frameworks. *Impact Assessment*, 13, 433–454.

Duinker, P and L Greig 2006. The impotence of cumulative effects assessment in Canada: ailments and ideas for redeployment. *Environmental Management*, 37(2), 153–161.

Duinker, P and L Greig 2007. Scenario analysis in environmental impact assessment: improving explorations of the future. *Environmental Impact Assessment Review*, 27(3), 206–219.

Franks, D M, D Brereton and C J Moran 2009a. Surrounded by change — collective strategies for managing the cumulative impacts of multiple mines. *Proceedings of the International Conference on Sustainable Development Indicators in the Minerals Industry*, 6–8 July, Gold Coast, Queensland, Australia. Australasian Institute of Mining and Metallurgy, Sustainable Minerals Institute and the Centre for Sustainable Resources Processing.

Managing the cumulative impacts of coal mining in Australia

Franks, D M, C Fidler, D Brereton, F Vanclay and P Clark 2009b. *Leading Practice Strategies for Addressing the Social Impacts of Resource Developments*. Centre for Social Responsibility in Mining, Sustainable Minerals Institute, The University of Queensland. Briefing paper for the Department of Employment, Economic Development and Innovation, Queensland Government. November. Brisbane.

Franks, D M, D Brereton, C J Moran, T Sarker and T Cohen 2010. *Cumulative Impacts: A Good Practice Guide for the Australian Coal Mining Industry*. Centre for Social Responsibility in Mining and Centre for Water in the Minerals Industry, Sustainable Minerals Institute, The University of Queensland. Australian Coal Association Research Program. Brisbane.

Hegmann, G, C Cocklin, R Creasey, S Dupuis, A Kennedy, L Kingsley, W Ross, H Spaling and D Stalker 1999. *Cumulative Effects Assessment Practitioners Guide*. Prepared for the Canadian Environmental Assessment Agency. Axys Consulting. February.

ISRD, Institute for Sustainable Regional Development 2008. *Clermont Preferred Future*. Clermont Community Development Strategy. Rockhampton. April. 76p.

Kennett, S 1999. *Towards a New Paradigm for Cumulative Effects Management*. Canadian Institute of Resources Law Occasional Paper No. 8. December. 57p.

Lockie, S, F Franetovich, S Sharma and J Rolfe 2008. Democratisation versus engagement? Social and economic impact assessment and community participation in the coal mining industry of the Bowen Basin, Australia. *Impact Assessment and Project Appraisal*, 26(3), 177–187.

Lucas, R, J Crerar, R Hardie, J Merritt and B Kirsch 2009. Isaac River cumulative impact assessment of mining developments. *Water in Mining 2009: From Contractor to Community — Protecting our License to Operate*, Conference Proceedings, September 2009, Perth. AusIMM, pp. 155–164.

MCA, Minerals Council of Australia 2010 *The Australian Minerals Industry and the Australian Economy*. Fact sheet. July.

McKenzie, F H, R Phillips, S Rowley, D Brereton and D Birdsall-Jones 2009. *Housing Market Dynamics in Resource Boom Towns*. Prepared for the Australian Housing and Urban Research Institute. AHURI Final Report No. 135, July. 107p.

Moran, C J, D Brereton, G McIlwian and J McIntosh 2007. Cumulative impacts of coal mining on a regional community. *3rd International Conference on Sustainable Development Indicators in the Minerals Industry*, June 2007, Milos island, Greece. 7p.

New South Wales Department of Planning 2005. *Coal Mining Potential in the Upper Hunter Valley — Strategic Assessment*. Sydney: New South Wales Government. December. 148p.

New South Wales Department of Planning 2008. *Impacts of Underground Coal Mining on Natural Features in the Southern Coalfield. Strategic Review*. Sydney: New South Wales Government. July. 158p.

New South Wales Government 2009. *Independent Air Monitoring Network Secured for the Upper Hunter*. Media Release, Minister for the Hunter, Jodi McKay. 21 October 2009.

NSW DPI, New South Wales Department of Primary Industries 2009. *New South Wales Coal Industry Profile*. Sydney: New South Wales Government. 302p.

NSW DUAP, New South Wales Department of Urban Affairs and Planning 1997. *Upper Hunter Cumulative Impact Study and Action Strategy*. Sydney: New South Wales Government.

NSW DUAP, New South Wales Department of Urban Affairs and Planning 2000. *Coal Mines and Associated Infrastructure. EIS Guideline*. Sydney: New South Wales Government. 55p.

NSW EPA, New South Wales Environment Protection Authority 2003. *Hunter River Salinity Trading Scheme: Working Together to Protect River Quality and Sustain Economic Development*. Sydney: New South Wales Government.

QDEEDI, Queensland Department of Employment, Economic Development and Innovation 2009. *Queensland's Coal — Mines and Advanced Projects*. Queensland Mines and Energy. August. 6p.

QDERM, Queensland Department of Environment and Resource Management 2010. *Generic Terms of Reference for an Environmental Impact Statement*. Brisbane.

QDIP, Queensland Department of Infrastructure and Planning 2008a. *Coal Infrastructure Program of Actions 2008*. Brisbane: Coal Infrastructure Taskforce. The State of Queensland. 16p.

QDIP, Queensland Department of Infrastructure and Planning 2008b. *Dysart Resource Summit. Record of Summit Discussions and Discussion Paper*. Brisbane: The State of Queensland. 47p.

QDIP, Queensland Department of Infrastructure and Planning 2009. *Resource Community Summits Final Reports — Dysart, Dalby and Mt Isa*. Brisbane: The State of Queensland.

QDLGPSR, Queensland Department of Local Government, Planning, Sport and Recreation 2006. *A Sustainable Futures Framework for Queensland Mining Towns. Discussion Paper*. Brisbane: Queensland Government. July. 39p.

QDME, Queensland Department of Mines and Energy 2007a. *Queensland's World Class Coal. Mine Production and Developments*. Brisbane: Queensland Government. November. 46p.

QDME, Queensland Department of Mines and Energy 2007b. *Queensland Mining Industries. A Report on the Economic Significance of Mining and Mineral Processing to the Central Region*. Brisbane: Queensland Government. 19p.

QDTRDI, Queensland Department of Tourism Regional Development and Industry 2008. *Sustainable Resource Communities Policy. Social Impact Assessment in the Mining and Petroleum Industries*. Brisbane: The State of Queensland. September. 7p.

QEPA, Queensland Environmental Protection Agency 2000. *Deciding the Level of Impact Assessment for the Mining Industry*. Guideline 4, Environmental Management in Mining Series. 26p.

Rolfe, J, B Miles, S Lockie and G Ivanova 2007. Lessons from the social and economic impacts of the mining boom in the Bowen Basin 2004–2006. *Australasian Journal of Regional Studies*, 13(2), 134–153.

State of New South Wales 2008. *Environmental Planning and Assessment Act 1979, No. 203, 10 December 2008*. Sydney: Parliamentary Counsel's Office. 365p.

State of Queensland 2007. *State Development and Public Works Organisation Act 1971. Reprint No. 5B, 16 November 2007*. Brisbane: Office of the Queensland Parliamentary Counsel. 188p.

State of Queensland 2008. *Environmental Protection Act 1994. Reprint No. 8C, 10 November 2008*. Brisbane: Office of the Queensland Parliamentary Counsel. 631p.

URS 2000. *The Mount Arthur North Coal Project Environmental Impact Statement*. Prepared for Coal Operations Australia Limited. Volume 2.

[31]

Bringing Social Analysis Into a Multilateral Environmental Agreement: Social Impact Assessment and the Biosafety Protocol

DOREEN STABINSKY

Negotiations under the UN Convention on Biological Diversity have recently concluded on a protocol governing the safe handling, transport, and use of living modified organisms (LMOs)—the Cartagena Protocol on Biosafety. One of the most contentious issues in these negotiations was the inclusion of socioeconomic considerations in the evaluation for import of an LMO. Many countries wanted the protocol to include provisions that enable an import ban or other trade-related measure to be taken if negative socioeconomic impacts are predicted that would have downstream consequences for the conservation and/or sustainable use of biological diversity. Other countries, principally the United States, believed such measures would run counter to national obligations under the World Trade Organization (WTO) agreements. The author considers the rationale for inclusion of socioeconomic considerations in evaluation of LMOs for import and evaluates the arguments that such provisions would not be WTO legal.

Graham Smith (1993) argued that social, economic, physical, environmental are so interconnected that impact assessment should not treat them separately but should link them. (Barrow, 1997, p. 226)

International environmental agreements have among their goals and purposes the management of the impact of humans on their environment. The implicit assumption made, of course, is that we can both assess and manage such impact through a process that includes environmental impact assessment (EIA). EIAs are not generally an explicit part of a multilateral environmental agreement (MEA) but implicit to the process of predicting and managing risks. Often included as part of the environmental assessment process in most national and international impact assessment practice is social impact assessment (SIA) of projects or developments.

In situations where an environmental impact assessment is proscribed in a multilateral environmental agreement, is there a need for also incorporating social impact assessment as part of the proscribed procedures? What about the situation in which the social impact of an enterprise—for example, displacement of a population for dam building into a previously uninhabited wilderness area—could have downstream effects (governed by the MEA) on the environment?

The UN Convention on Biological Diversity (CBD) has as its goals the conservation and sustainable use of biological diversity and the equitable sharing of benefits deriving from the use of biodiversity. To the extent that the social and economic impact may affect a community's ability to conserve biological diversity, we argue here that these impacts should be considered by states in the implementation of the convention.

Parties to the CBD have recently concluded negotiations on a protocol to the convention, pursuant to Article 19(3), which calls on parties to

> consider the need for, and modalities of, a protocol setting out appropriate procedures, including, in particular, advance informed agreement, in the field of the safe transfer, handling and use of any living modified organism resulting from biotechnology that may have adverse effect on the conservation and sustainable use of biological diversity. (UN Environment Programme, 1994, p. 16)

Central to the protocol is a procedure for advance informed agreement, whereby countries importing a living modified organism (LMO) would provide explicit consent to import that LMO based primarily on a risk assessment. Many developing countries, nongovernmental organizations (NGOs), and a small number of developed countries have argued that the risk assessment procedure should include consideration of social and economic impacts and their effects on a community's ability to conserve biological diversity.

This article reviews arguments for including SIA along with environmental risk assessment in the procedures of protocol. After a brief introduction to the protocol negotiations, we begin by addressing potential socioeconomic effects of the handling, transfer, and use of LMOs, particularly from the developing country perspective. We then outline how socioeconomic effects are dealt with in various national laws. We look at how the socioeconomic impact of LMO introduction has been addressed in international law in the Biosafety (Cartagena) Protocol. We conclude by considering the relevance of arguments that inclusion of such considerations for decisions on import of LMOs would be a violation of a country's obligations under the World Trade Organization (WTO).

A Brief History of Protocol Negotiations

An open-ended ad hoc group of experts, established by the first Conference of the Parties (COP) to the CBD, met in Madrid in July of 1995, to consider whether a protocol was in fact necessary, as requested by Article 19(3). Though consensus was not reached, the vast majority of country representatives present did, in fact, consider a biosafety protocol necessary. The second COP, in its decision II/5, established a working group, the Open-Ended Ad Hoc Working Group on Biosafety, to negotiate a protocol. Negotiations commenced in July 1996 in Aarhus, Denmark, and concluded in Montréal, Canada, in the early hours of January 29, 2000, a year after the unexpected collapse of the talks at what was to be the final negotiating session in February 1999 in Cartagena, Colombia.

At the deliberations in Madrid, countries outlined a broad array of components to be included in the protocol. These included a procedure for advance informed agreement (AIA) and 12 additional items. Of the 12, 3 were nonconsensus items, desired primarily by developing countries: consideration of socioeconomic impact of LMOs, liability and compensation for damage caused by LMOs, and a financial mechanism. After six negotiating sessions, all of the nonconsensus items were still on the table and unresolved, although only socioeconomic considerations were the subject of an article in the final text.

Socioeconomic Concerns Related to Biotechnology

> [Negative] social and economic impacts often greatly overshadow hoped-for development benefits.... Social and poverty issues are as often as not at the core of environmental impacts in developing countries. (Barrow, 1997, pp. 230, 241)

Many of the concerns about genetically engineered organisms, or LMOs as they are referred to in the CBD and protocol, involve those organisms destined for large-scale release into the environment, that is, genetically engineered crop plants that will be planted on a commercial scale. Crops are currently being engineered for three general purposes: alteration of production characteristics (e.g., herbicide, insect, or disease tolerance), alteration of downstream processing characteristics (e.g., to increase starch content in potatoes so they absorb less oil when being fried), and production of specialty, often nonfood, chemicals for use as industrial feedstocks (e.g., canola that produces lauric acid for use in shampoos and as a food additive).

Environmental concerns are many and include the following: escape of an engineered plant that eventually becomes a weed; escape of the transgene (the gene that was engineered into the plant) through pollen transfer to related varieties, with resulting impacts on the accidentally pollinated population, or impacts on populations of other plants that are outcompeted by the new hybrids; poisoning of nontarget insects by pollen or leaf material from genetically engineered plants; generation of new types of plant viruses through recombination with viral material engineered into the crops. All these concerns clearly fit under the mandate of the CBD, to conserve biological diversity.

No less important to many developing countries are concerns about socioeconomic impacts that might then have downstream effects on the conservation and sustainable use of biodiversity. Negative impacts to biodiversity can be the result of a chain of consequences, direct and indirect, intentional or accidental. Impacts that must be considered in the context of biosafety, therefore, include indirect harm (e.g., harm through economic or social consequences that lead to changes in forestry or agriculture, etc., and thus have an impact on local biota) or harm whereby an effect of an LMO release crosses a boundary (say by altering climatic conditions, or affecting migratory species, or by causing social or economic impacts on human populations that lead to refugees' crossing borders and harming—perhaps by numbers alone—new ecosystems).[1]

There are many ways that social and economic impacts could influence a community's ability to conserve and sustainably use their biological diversity. For example, genetic engineering of traditional crops may allow them to be grown, or allow products to be produced from their growing their cells outside of the agroclimatic zones where they are normally cultivated. This would have an impact on producers who normally grow that crop—and affect their ability to conserve or sustainably use it. A number of firms in the biotechnology industry are engineering plants or tissue culture cells that can produce, in Northern climates, many products that are now imported from developing countries. Tissue culture cells are being engineered to produce vanilla, which can be sold as real, not artificial, vanilla. Plants also can be engineered to produce compounds not naturally found in them. A canola plant has been engineered to produce lauric acid, a compound presently derived from coconut and palm kernel oils. Small-scale producers in both Madagascar and the Philippines will feel the effects of these crop substitutions.

The Rural Advancement Foundation International (RAFI) has been warning of these types of socioeconomic impacts of the new biotechnologies for more than 10 years. Some other impacts they note regard the following: coffee,

> Coffee is now a smallholder crop in most areas of the world. Biotechnologies will facilitate shift to large-scale production which will become concentrated in fewer countries (Rural Advancement Foundation International [RAFI], 1989, p. 1);

---

1. I am indebted to Professor Philip Bereano for elaboration of this point.

cacao,

> Development of high-yielding cacao varieties could lead to overproduction and jeopardize price and stability of cacao-producing countries while shifting production from small-scale producers to large-scale plantations; the use of biotechnology to convert low-priced oils into cacao butter could drastically reduce the demand and price for cacao beans. (RAFI, 1987, p. 1);

and pyrethrins,

> U.S. is the world's largest importer of natural pyrethrins. Development of "bio-pyrethrin" substitute could displace over 200,000 small farmers who grow pyrethrum flowers in Kenya, Tanzania, Rwanda, and Ecuador. (RAFI, 1992, p. 1)

Certainly one key concern of NGOs and others regarding the potential impacts of new genetically engineered crops is the impact that structural change in agriculture brought about by their introduction may have on food security. As RAFI notes, their introduction may facilitate a transition to large-scale monoculture or encourage a switch from planting food crops to cash crops, or to planting genetically engineered food crops that peasants cannot afford to grow.

Changes in the structure of agriculture are certainly significant for both food security and biodiversity conservation. It is important to emphasize here, though, that of these impacts, the CBD only covers those specific to the conservation and sustainable use of biodiversity; for socioeconomic considerations to be part of a legal instrument under the convention, harm to biodiversity must be demonstrated or shown to be possible. Therefore, it is necessary to be able to link socioeconomic impacts with their downstream effects on biodiversity. We detail below three general ways in which socioeconomic impacts may have such downstream effects.

The Green Revolution and the New Biotechnologies

One well-studied example of the social impact of a particular set of technologies is the impact of the introduction of Green Revolution high-yielding varieties in traditional agricultural systems. Researchers have documented socioeconomic impacts from the introduction of these varieties. In a social impact assessment of the Green Revolution, Bowonder (1979) found an uneven distribution of benefits and consequences—poor farmers were made poorer and rich farmers richer. Numerous researchers before and since then have come to the same conclusions regarding the impacts of the introduction of high-yielding varieties on different socioeconomic classes of agriculturists (see, for example, Bray, 1994; Cleaver, 1972; Griffin, 1974; Hewitt de Alcántara, 1976; Shiva, 1991; Wright, 1990). These impacts on small farmers include employment changes, debt, loss of land, marginalization, social changes, regional economic disparity, dependency for inputs and credits, unrest, and migration (Barrow, 1997).

In terms of the potential for socioeconomic impacts on traditional agricultural systems, there appears to be little difference between impacts seen from the introduction of the high-yielding products of the Green Revolution and the products that will be offered by the plant biotechnology industry. New technologies tend to reflect and reinforce existing social structures, and there is no indication that the products of genetic engineering will be any different.

Much of the planet's biological diversity is stewarded by small farmers, local communities, and indigenous peoples. A small farm is a reservoir for agricultural biological diversity; it is also a socioeconomic entity. To the extent that the introduction of any new technology or product is detrimental to the socioeconomic status of agriculturists, these technologies will also alter their ability to conserve biological diversity. In the eyes of most developing nations party to the protocol negotiations, changes in the socioeconomic conditions of their small farmers and other custodians of biological diversity may have significant impacts on their ability to conserve that diversity.

Cultural Impact

The CBD itself defines harm to biodiversity very broadly and includes in its mandate for protection, in addition to ecosystems and habitats, sociocultural aspects of biodiversity:[2] For example, Article 8(j) calls on parties to "respect, preserve and maintain knowledge, innovations and practices of indigenous and local communities embodying traditional lifestyles relevant for the conservation and sustainable use of biological diversity" (UN Environment Programme, 1994, p. 9).

Different cultures within and between countries have differing spiritual and religious traditions and will place different values on land, biological diversity, and the integrity of living organisms. Cultural and religious traditions may reject altogether the genetic engineering of certain types of organisms. In a recent declaration, the Indigenous Peoples of the Western Hemisphere state,

---

2. I would like to thank Mark Winfield of the Canadian Institute for Environmental Law and Policy for pointing this out to me.

The principle of harmony requires that we do not violate the principles of Creation by manipulating and changing the natural order.... Genetic technologies which manipulate and change the fundamental core and identity of any life form are an absolute violation of these principles.... Therefore, we ... reject all programs involving genetic technology. (Indigenous Peoples of the Western Hemisphere, 1995, p. 63)

Importation of genetically engineered organisms may influence the value a particular culture places on aspects of its biological environment, altering its ability to conserve biological diversity. This could happen in two ways. If genetically engineered organisms alter the natural environment and totems on which particular peoples base their material and spiritual well-being, people could be profoundly depressed. Consider, for example, the U'wa people, who are currently threatening mass suicide because the Colombian government has just granted a permit to Occidental Petroleum for oil drilling on their ancestral lands. A group might also gradually lose or abandon cultural or spiritual values because of a degradation of the environment. Both of these sociocultural impacts could negatively influence the ability of a group to conserve biological diversity.

Impacts on Traditional Practices

Traditional communities depend greatly on the biological diversity that surrounds them. Environmental impacts on the biological diversity on which the community depends could make it difficult for the community to continue to support itself. For example, in Thailand, practitioners of traditional medicine are worried about the potential for cross-pollination by genetically engineered cotton of 16 different species in the cotton family (Malvaceae). According to the practitioners, they would be unable to continue to use those contaminated plants for medicinal purposes (Bhatiasevi, 1997). The inability to sustain use of the traditional medicines, and the impact that may have on the practitioners' ability to support themselves using those medicines, would have a further impact on their ability to conserve that valuable biological diversity.

In summary, there are valid reasons that indirect effects on the conservation and sustainable use of biodiversity, resulting from socioeconomic impacts, should be considered in biosafety assessment. SIA is a means to recognize and manage these impacts.

Introduction to SIA

Many countries take socioeconomic concerns into account in domestic planning decisions through their EIA process. It was in the United States that this means of assessing and incorporating consideration of social impacts first came into use, through implementation of the National Environmental Policy Act of 1970 (NEPA). Since that time, a great deal of rigorous social science research has been carried out to develop methodologies for such assessment, and a large scientific literature exists on the practice of SIA (see, for example, Finsterbusch, Ingersoll, & Llewellyn, 1990; Finsterbusch, Llewellyn, & Wolf, 1983; Freudenburg, 1986; Rickson, Hundloe, McDonald, & Burdge, 1990; Stoffle, 1990; Taylor, Bryan, & Goodrich, 1990). Data derived from SIA are in wide use in decision-making procedures throughout the world, including the World Bank's social assessment procedures and impact assessment procedures under the U.S. NEPA.

Definition of SIA

Burdge and Vanclay (1995, p. 32) define SIA as "the process of assessing or estimating, in advance, the social consequences that are likely to follow from specific policy actions or project development, particularly in the context of appropriate national, state, or provincial environmental policy legislation." Assessment consists of identifying the impacts and the social groups on which the impacts fall, evaluating them as to the probability of their occurrence and their magnitude, and investigating the equity aspects of their distribution because costs, risks, and benefits typically affect different segments of society (Lee & Bereano, 1981). Impact assessments measure both social impacts—"social and cultural consequences to populations that alter ways in which people: live, work, play, relate to one another, organize to meet their needs, cope as members of society" (p. 32)—and cultural impacts—"changes to norms, values, beliefs of individuals that guide and rationalize their cognition of themselves and their society" (Burdge & Vanclay, 1995, p. 32).

As noted above, an action may have impacts that are direct or indirect (sometimes the latter are called second or higher order impacts), intended or unintentional. Impacts often exist as chains of consequences in which one impact acts in turn to itself to cause higher order effects. For example, the use of certain insecticidal genes in genetically engineered plants could affect the lifespans of honeybees, which in turn could decrease the number of plants pollinated (Pham-Delègue, 1997).

Scope of Analysis

Current methodology of SIA is based on "identifying likely future impacts based on reconstructing social impacts of past events" (Burdge & Vanclay, 1995, p. 43). Reasoning by analogy is one of the most common analytic techniques.

> The basic SIA model is comparative and based on studying the course of events in communities where planned environmental change has occurred, and extrapolating from that analysis to predict what is likely to happen in another community where a similar developmental event or policy change is planned. (Burdge & Vanclay, 1995, p. 38)

(Although in carrying out such a procedure, one must bear in mind that analogies compare two situations that have differences as well as similarities; central to the validity of such an analysis is whether the differences are sufficiently small so that we may reason from the one situation we know to that which is unknown.)

Data and Variables Measured in SIA Analysis

Analysis of impact is based on a variety of social science data. "Such data range from the highly quantitative—such as demographic data—to more qualitative data on local traditions and beliefs" (Rickson & Rickson, 1990, p. 106). Sources of data for an ex post facto impact study on social and psychological impacts of the Exxon Valdez oil spill included

> (1) interviews with key community leaders, municipal department heads, and other citizens regarding impacts and responses; (2) interviews with psychological and social service providers regarding impacts; (3) compiled statistics regarding psychosocial impacts; and (4) a survey of about 596 households in 12 affected and 2 control communities. (Impact Assessment, Inc., 1990, p. 16)

In the United States, different agencies will analyze social impact based on a differing mix of social variables, depending on their statutory mandate. The categories of impact studied also will necessarily vary internationally. The following list is a summary of some of the major variables considered in impact assessment by the cited researchers and institutions:

- population change, community and institutional structures, political and social resources, individual and family changes, and community resources (Interorganizational Committee, 1995);
- population change; lifestyle; attitudes, beliefs, and values; and social organization (Taylor et al., 1990, as well as the U.S. Forest Service manual);
- demographic factors, socioeconomic determinants, social organization, sociopolitical context, needs and values (World Bank Environment Department, 1995); and
- unequal distribution of benefits and consequences of a particular action, changing power structures, family disruption, impacts on racial and cultural diversity, and disintegration of community cohesion (Burdge & Vanclay, 1995).

Characteristics of SIA Relevant to an MEA

A few characteristics of SIA need to be highlighted prior to our discussion of how it may be incorporated into a multilateral environmental agreement. First, it is important to note the wide array of techniques and variables used in impact assessment. Procedures between countries are likely to vary widely, as they do even between agencies within a single country. It is unlikely, and the Cartagena Protocol negotiations bear this out, that in negotiating legal text countries will agree to the proscription of actual procedures. Rather, in the protocol, the parameters to be taken into consideration during a risk assessment are relegated to an annex (Annex III), the text of which is not legally binding.

Furthermore, it is also important to note that both qualitative and quantitative data are used in impact analysis. As such, who carries out the assessment, and who is consulted during the assessment, will clearly have a bearing on the results of the assessment. In short, assessments will not be "objectively" duplicable. In fact, the subjective nature of impact assessments, as noted below, was seen as problematic by a number of countries during the Protocol negotiations. Any SIA is likely to be highly contested, in particular when the benefits and the costs of the impacts are not evenly distributed, and a finding goes against the interests of either the major beneficiaries or those bearing the largest burdens of impact. This, of course, does not mean that SIA should not be carried out, for they are important tools for predicting and possibly avoiding negative social impacts of technology. However, within the international legal arena, the subjectivity of the results will make them easy targets for challenge at the WTO. This point will be explored further below.

SIA and Genetic Engineering: Examples from Norway and New Zealand

What might national legislation look like that mandates consideration of the social impacts of LMOs in their approval process? Norway's genetic engineering law, the Gene Technology Act, states that its purpose is "to ensure that the production and use of genetically modified organisms takes place in an ethically and socially justifiable way" (Norway Ministry of Environment, 1993, p. 1). With respect to approval for environmental release of an LMO in Norway, the law states that "significant emphasis shall also be placed on whether the deliberate release represents a benefit to the community and a contribution to sustainable development" (Norway Ministry of Environment, 1993, p. 5).

New Zealand's Environmental Risk Management Authority has proposed procedures for the introduction of LMOs under the Hazardous Substances and New Organisms Act (New Zealand Environmental Risk Management Authority [ERMA], 1997, pp. 8-9). Under the act itself, *environment* is defined to include the following:

1. ecosystems and their constituent parts, including people and communities;
2. all natural and physical resources;
3. amenity values; and
4. the social, economic, aesthetic, and cultural conditions that affect the matters stated in paragraphs (a) to (c) of this definition or that are affected by those matters.

Included in the information that is to be supplied to the government for review and approval of a release of an LMO is information with particular regard for

- the maintenance and enhancement of the capacity of people and communities to provide for their own economic, social, and cultural well-being and for the reasonably foreseeable needs of future generations; and
- the relationships of Maori and their culture and traditions with their ancestral lands, sites, *waahi tapu*, valued flora and fauna, and other *taonga* (New Zealand ERMA, 1997).

Although Norway and New Zealand have not defined exact impact assessment procedures in their regulatory statutes, important socioeconomic and cultural variables have been identified that should be taken into consideration during impact assessment. Apparently, decisions on import and release of LMOs will be made based to some extent on the predicted socioeconomic and cultural impacts of those LMOs.

Proposals for Mechanisms to Include Socioeconomic Considerations in the Biosafety Protocol

SIA is an internationally accepted component of EIA, and has a set of coherent methodologies that could be referenced in international law. The key question for our analysis is the following: How might SIA be integrated into a protocol on biosafety?

As mentioned above, the central element of the biosafety protocol is a procedure called advance informed agreement (AIA). Under the AIA procedure, importing countries must explicitly agree to an importation of an LMO before export can proceed. The decisions taken under an AIA are based on information provided to, or generated by, the importing country, including the results of a risk assessment.

The initial African and Malaysian proposals for legal text provide clear examples of how social and economic impact assessments might figure in the language and procedures of the protocol. Their proposals had three primary mechanisms for incorporating socioeconomic considerations into a review of the risks posed by an LMO:

- mandatory inclusion of socioeconomic parameters, such as those data and variables noted in the earlier section on SIA, in the points to consider during the risk assessment;[3]

---

3. The original African position on the risk assessment article (Article 15) included the following clause:

> 1. Each Party shall ensure that, in accordance with the provisions of this Protocol, assessments prior to the use, transfer and release of living modified organisms or products thereof are undertaken as regards the risks or possible adverse impacts in their respective territories as well as in the territories of States of import, including the transboundary effects to human and animal health, the environment, biological diversity and *the socio-economic welfare of societies* [italics added]. (Federal Democratic Republic of Ethiopia, 1996, p. 7)

It also added the following parameters for risk assessment in what is now Annex III:

> 7. Socio-economic considerations:
> (a) Anticipated changes in the existing social and economic patterns resulting from the introduction of the living modified organism or product thereof;
> (b) Possible threats to biological diversity, traditional crops or other products and, in particular, farmers' varieties and sustainable agriculture;

- development of an early warning system for countries whose exports might be affected by development of genetically engineered substitutes, such as Malagasy vanilla;[4] and
- mandatory risk management of socioeconomic risks.[5]

> (c) Impacts likely to be posed by the possibility of substituting traditional crops, products and indigenous technologies through modern biotechnology outside of their agro-climatic zones;
> (d) Anticipated social and economic costs due to loss of genetic diversity, employment, market opportunities and, in general, means of livelihood of the communities likely to be affected by the introduction of the living modified organisms or products thereof;
> (e) Possible countries and/or communities to be affected in terms of disruptions to their social and economic welfare;
> (f) Possible effects which are contrary to the social, cultural, ethical and religious values of communities arising from the use or release of the living modified organism or the product thereof. (Federal Democratic Republic of Ethiopia, 1996, p. 17)

The Malaysian submission of legal text included the following text for a stand-alone article on socioeconomic considerations:

> 1. The Parties hereby agree that socio-economic imperatives must be taken into account at all levels during the transfer, handling or use of LMOs [living modified organisms]. To this end, the intending country Party shall ensure that the risk assessment prepared by it or person or entity under its jurisdiction under Article 6 [Risk Assessment, Article 15] shall incorporate specific assessments on the *socio-economic effects and impacts* of the transfer, handling or use of the LMO to or within the receiving country and its environment, in particular *to the conservation and sustainable use of biological diversity*, taking into account its human health, agriculture and welfare. (UN Environment Programme, 1997b, p. 3, italics added)

> 2. The risk assessment shall in particular include an assessment of whether introduction of LMOs in the environment of the receiving country may entail a *displacement of a particular agricultural and resource use system* or the *culture and livelihood of the local people*. (UN Environment Programme, 1997b, p. 3, italics added)

4. In addition to their proposals for the risk assessment article and annex, the African Group submission contained wording for a stand-alone article, which included the following clause describing an "early warning system" for commodities that would lose their market:

> 2. A Party that intends to produce, using a living modified organism, a hitherto imported commodity, shall notify the other Party or Parties whose export is to be affected long enough, and in no case less than seven years in advance so as to enable them to diversify their production and to implement measures concerning the biodiversity that would be reduced following the disruption of production of the commodity in question. The Party substituting its import in such an unnatural way shall, when the affected Party is a developing county, provide financial and technical assistance to the affected Party. (Federal Democratic Republic of Ethiopia, 1996, pp. 7-8)

5. From the Malaysian submission for a stand-alone article on socioeconomic considerations:

> 3. The intending Party shall ensure that the risk management strategies and measures proposed to be implemented by the receiving Party under Article 7 [Risk Management, Article 16] shall incorporate strategies and measures that will minimize, prevent or mitigate the potential socio-economic effects and impacts within the receiving country Party, in particular where the introduction of LMOs in the environment of the receiving country Party may entail a displacement of a particular agricultural or resource use system of the culture and livelihood of the local people. (UN Environment Programme, 1997b, p. 3)

These mechanisms were detailed in several places throughout the protocol: in the risk assessment article, in a stand-alone article on socioeconomic considerations, and in the annex detailing risk assessment parameters.

Results of the Cartagena Protocol Negotiations

The three elements listed above—an article on risk assessment, an annex on risk assessment parameters, and a stand-alone article on socioeconomic considerations—formed a solid framework for incorporating socioeconomic impact assessment into the language and procedures of the Protocol. However, a number of countries voiced strong opposition to including socioeconomic considerations under the procedures of the protocol at all. Arguments against including socioeconomic considerations in the risk assessment process, or as other legitimate criteria for decision making, included the nonquantifiable, nonscientific nature of the SIA, and as such, noncompatibility with provisions of the WTO agreements.

At the Cartagena negotiating session in January 1999, a delegate from Australia noted the subjectivity of socioeconomic considerations and argued against use of such nonobjective criteria in the risk assessment process. He suggested that these considerations are best dealt with domestically, taking into consideration a country's international obligations (anonymous delegate, official intervention, February 14, 1999). Japan used a more general argument, citing the extreme variability of relevant assessment parameters: "1. (Socio-Economic conditions vary too much from state to state to be measured by a standardized scale. Therefore, this item should not be dealt with in the Protocol.)" (UN Environment Programme, 1997b, p. 3). Both the United States and the European Union held that decisions should be "science-based."[6]

Early on in the negotiations, as names of articles were being decided on and working groups were established, a few important separations of topics occurred. The risk assessment article was assigned to Sub-Working Group 1 (SWG 1), the annex with risk assessment parameters was assigned to a contact group that reported to SWG 1, and the article on socioeconomic considerations was assigned to Sub-Working Group 2. This effectively precluded consideration of the environmental and social

---

6. Text for the risk assessment article submitted by the United States in 1997 required that "(d)ecisions shall be based on scientific principles . . . " (UN Environment Programme, 1997a, p. 41). The official position put forward by the European Commission at the Cartagena negotiating session was essentially the same: "Risk assessment should be science-based" (representative of the European Commission, personal communication, February 14, 1999).

impact assessment in a unified way, and it diluted the efforts that could be made by the African group and other members of what was to become the Like-Minded Group.[7] The group was minimally represented in many meetings, as most of the delegations were one-person delegations, and by separating the topics, it meant there were fewer delegates in the room at a time to argue for the Like-Minded Group position.

There was not just a physical separation of the discussion but also a philosophical one. The contact group discussing risk assessment parameters was also the group discussing definitions of terms such as *recombinant DNA*. Many of the diplomats in the room were also scientists. In a setting in which science is given priority, making the argument for including social science in risk assessment is difficult.

This emphasis on scientific assessment and quantifiability of risks by the majority of developed nations (Norway stood alone as a developed country supporting the position of the Like-Minded Group on socioeconomic considerations) was made stronger by a continued reference to the WTO and its requirements for "science-based" decision making under the Agreement on the Application of Sanitary and Phytosanitary Measures (the SPS Agreement).

The final Cartagena Protocol contains the following article as the only reference to socioeconomic considerations (reference was removed from both the risk assessment article—Article 15—and the annex on risk assessment):

Article 26 (Socioeconomic Considerations)
1. The Parties, in reaching a decision on import under this Protocol or under its domestic measures implementing the Protocol, may take into account, consistent with their international obligations, socioeconomic considerations arising from the impact of living modified organisms on the conservation and sustainable use of biological diversity, especially with regard to the value of biological diversity to indigenous and local communities.

2. The Parties are encouraged to cooperate on research and information exchange on any socioeconomic impacts of living modified organisms, especially on indigenous and local communities. (UN Environment Programme, 2000)

---

7. The Like-Minded Group, which coalesced during the Cartagena meeting, is formed by most members of the G77 and China, with the notable exceptions of Argentina, Chile, and Uruguay. These three South American nations joined with Australia, Canada, and the United States as the "Miami Group," of LMO-exporting (or soon-to-be exporting) nations. One other important extraregional grouping formed during the final meeting, the "Compromise Group," whose members include Japan, South Korea, Mexico, Norway, and Switzerland.

It should be noted that countries already have the ability to take domestic decisions regarding criteria for evaluation of imports. What the Like-Minded Group and Norway would have preferred in the Cartagena Protocol is an enabling provision that included SIA in internationally recognized criteria for decision making on LMO importation without the qualification regarding international obligations. Such a provision would have established a right under international law to ban an LMO based solely on socioeconomic considerations, if the downstream effects of socioeconomic impacts could be shown to be harmful to biological diversity. The Miami Group, composed of the United States, Canada, Australia, Argentina, Chile, and Uruguay,[8] argued such a right would be inconsistent with WTO obligations. What are those obligations, and why do they matter so much to the developed countries, the Miami Group in particular? Is a decision to restrict the importation of an LMO based on socioeconomic considerations a barrier to trade? What legal threats might there be against a country that decided to use information from an SIA in the risk assessment and decision-making process?

Is SIA Consistent With WTO Obligations?

The WTO agreements, including inter alia the General Agreement on Tariffs and Trade 1994 (the GATT 1994), the SPS Agreement, and the Agreement on Technical Barriers to Trade (the TBT Agreement), govern trade between member states. Three provisions of the GATT form its core obligations: Articles I, III, and XI. Articles I and III

> obligate parties to treat imports from any GATT party no less favorably than they treat any other imports . . . and no less favorably . . . then (*sic*) domestically produced "like products." Under Article XI, GATT parties also are obligated to convert all trade barriers to tariffs. (Nissen, 1997, p. 904)

This last provision prohibits trade measures such as quotas, embargoes, or bans.

Under the GATT, all barriers to trade are illegal unless they fit under a set of exceptions. The SPS Agreement and the TBT Agreement discuss particular types of exceptions allowed and the conditions under which

---

8. The Miami Group of LMO-exporting and potentially exporting countries was formed prior to the fourth negotiating session, at a meeting hosted by the United States in Miami.

those exceptions may be made. In the case of the SPS agreement, which describes allowable regulations to protect plant, animal, and human health, standards must be established based on "sound science." The agreement is very narrowly written and appears to apply only to protection from pests, diseases, disease-carrying organisms, or disease-causing organisms.[9] The TBT Agreement covers technical standards (voluntary) and regulations (mandatory) in relation to product characteristics or related processes and production methods.[10]

The Miami Group has asserted that any trade measures taken under the Biosafety Protocol would be governed by the SPS Agreement, and they argue that only those measures taken to protect animal, plant, and human health are WTO legal. This interpretation does not appear to be correct in light of the narrow definition of a sanitary or phytosanitary measure. Consider the introgression, or movement, of genes from genetically engineered varieties into populations of landraces by wind transfer of pollen. The impact of this occurrence on the conservation of genetic diversity could be very serious indeed but would not be covered under the narrow definition of "phytosanitary risks" of the SPS Agreement—genetically altered pollen is generally not considered a pest, disease, or disease-causing organism.

The TBT Agreement, which governs technical regulations in relation to product characteristics or related processes and production methods, does not appear to be relevant in this situation either. The TBT would perhaps cover the regulations that require a SIA to be carried out, that is, the establishment of potential parameters to be covered during a risk

---

9. Note the following definition of a sanitary or phytosanitary (SPS) measure under the SPS Agreement:

Sanitary or phytosanitary measure—Any measure applied:

(a) to protect animal or plant life or health within the territory of the Member *from risks arising from the entry, establishment or spread of pests, diseases, disease-carrying organisms or disease-causing organisms* [emphasis added];
(b) to protect human or animal life or health within the territory of the Member from risks arising from additives, contaminants, toxins or disease-causing organisms in foods, beverages or feedstuffs;
(c) to protect human life or health within the territory of the Member from risks arising from diseases carried by animals, plants or products thereof, or from the entry, establishment or spread of pests; or
(d) to prevent or limit other damage within the territory of the Member from the entry, establishment or spread of pests. (World Trade Organization [WTO], 1994, p. 77)

10. In the agreement, a technical regulation is defined as the following:

Document which lays down product characteristics or their related processes and production methods, including the applicable administrative provisions, with which compliance is mandatory. It may also include or deal exclusively with terminology, symbols, packaging, marking or labeling requirements as they apply to a product, process or production method. (WTO, 1994, p. 132)

assessment, but it would have nothing to say about any actual trade measures implemented. The agreement is concerned with import restrictions based on the characteristics of the product itself, whereas in the case of biosafety, regulators are concerned with the downstream effects of the importation of a particular product. Under the TBT, if international standards were developed, such as the designation of risk assessment parameters to be taken into consideration during the review for importation of an LMO, such "international standards" would be assumed to be WTO legal. The final text of the protocol did not establish such a standard regarding assessment of social impacts.[11] However, the TBT considers that one of the legitimate objectives of such standards is protection of the environment. Arguably, a basic international standard has already been established by the CBD itself, namely the conservation and sustainable use of biological diversity, and procedures developed under the protocol would be in accordance with the TBT Agreement.

Let us consider a specific example: Country A decides to ban or in some other way restrict trade in an LMO because of a determination of second-order negative impacts to biological diversity based on an SIA. The country's regulators came to the conclusion, through SIA, that the introduction of genetically engineered *Bt* corn (a corn engineered with a bacterial gene so that it becomes toxic to various Lepidopteran insects such as the European and Asian corn borers) into its agricultural system would cause a number of unwanted effects, including changes in the structure of agriculture. Country A determined that those changes in the land ownership and mix of crops grown would be significant for the conservation of biological diversity by smallholders.

If the country (a) banned the importation of *Bt* corn from all exporters, (b) did not allow its local biotechnology industry to develop *Bt* corn, and (c) the trade measure is not a disguised restriction on international trade, it would satisfy most of the major criteria of the WTO agreements. The country's moves, however, would not pass the test of Article XI, which forbids the use of bans or other types of quantitative restrictions. But if the government can demonstrate that such socioeconomic impacts have an impact on the conservation of biological diversity, it may be argued that the general exceptions article of the GATT 1994, Article XX, would allow trade-related measures, such as a ban, to be taken. The particular subclause of Article XX relevant in this case is Article XX (g).

---

11. The protocol would have established an international standard in this regard, if socioeconomic parameters had been included in the risk assessment annex.

Article XX (g)

The chapeau and relevant subclause of Article XX, both of which would have to be satisfied for such a ban to be legal, state that

> subject to the requirement that such measures are not applied in a manner which would constitute a means of *arbitrary or unjustifiable discrimination* between countries where the same conditions prevail, or *a disguised restriction on international trade*, nothing in this Agreement shall be construed to prevent the adoption or enforcement by any contracting party of measures . . . (g) relating to the conservation of exhaustible natural resources *if such measures are made effective in conjunction with restrictions on domestic production or consumption.* (WTO, 1994)

The conditions noted by the three italicized provisions would have to be met to justify a ban. Significantly, it appears that measures taken related to the conservation of biological diversity would clearly qualify under the exemption for measures relating to the conservation of exhaustible natural resources. If a country could demonstrate higher order links between socioeconomic impacts and impacts on the conservation of biodiversity, actions taken should be WTO legal.

The question then becomes, Was a specific enabling clause in the Biosafety Protocol necessary to legitimize trade measures taken based on the results of a socioeconomic impact assessment? The final version of the protocol merely states the status quo: that a country has the sovereign right to implement such measures, albeit under threat of a WTO challenge. An unqualified enabling provision would have given greater legitimacy to a country's actions and would bolster its defense in the face of a WTO complaint. As mentioned above, if the risk assessment standards are developed in the context of an international agreement, the TBT Agreement assumes that those standards are acceptable under the WTO. Given that risk assessment is a part of the current proposed protocol, that SIA is an accepted component of risk assessment around the world, and that social impacts can have a significant effect on a country's ability to conserve biological diversity, there seems no reason not to have included SIA parameters in the risk assessment annex and an enabling clause within the protocol saying that decisions based on SIA are legitimate. However, with strong opposition from the Miami Group and the European Union, this was not an outcome of the protocol negotiations.

Conclusions

Concurrent with the formation of the Miami Group came its demand that genetically engineered commodities—that is, LMOs used for food, feed, or processing rather than for direct planting into the environment—should not be subject to the AIA procedure.[12] One of the U.S. heads of delegation, Rafe Pomerance, was quoted as accusing the Like- Minded Group of being irresponsible, and in a raised voice during a late night closed-door session in Cartagena, informing negotiators that the protocol could have a negative impact on the United States's $40 billion agricultural export industry. The negotiator for the Like-Minded Group at that time, Tewolde Berhan Gebre Egziabher of Ethiopia, apparently calmly replied to Mr. Pomerance that the protocol was about the environment, not trade. Vandana Shiva of the Research Foundation for Science, Technology and Natural Resource Policy in India made an insightful intervention on this topic at one of the earlier negotiating sessions when she noted that the Miami Group's concern over subjecting commodities to the AIA procedure was a socioeconomic concern of the developed world and that their socioeconomic concerns always seemed to take precedence over those of the Third World.

Even with the qualified enabling clause contained in the protocol, it is likely that any country basing an LMO ban on the results of an SIA will face a challenge in the WTO. The United States (with the most advanced biotechnology industry and the world's largest LMO exporter) is unlikely to find acceptable a trade measure based on information derived from an SIA. As the United States will not likely be a party to the CBD, and hence the protocol as well, any time soon, it will not be bound to the dispute settlement provisions of the convention, and its only forum for lodging a complaint about a trade measure will be the WTO. It is difficult to predict the outcome of such a challenge, the merits of the case notwithstanding. However, the dispute resolution panels to this date have been quite successful at finding fault with every national environmental law that has been challenged to date, albeit often through legal technicalities rather than finding the environmental exceptions invalid.

If jurisprudence on Article XX(g) is an indication of how a dispute would be resolved, there is reason to think that the challenge of such a

---

12. The scientific rationale behind this is incredibly shaky. Corn imported into Mexico from the United States to be processed into tortillas will still germinate if it falls off the truck on the way to the processing plant, and will still have the ability to cause genetic pollution of the local landraces so important to world agriculture.

ban would be successful. Even though the text of XX(g) indicates that exceptions are allowed for measures "relating to the conservation of exhaustible natural resources," dispute panels have interpreted this to mean that the measures must be "primarily aimed at" conservation of the resource (Nissen, 1997). This is a high, and perhaps insurmountable, hurdle for a measure that aims to prevent second-order, rather than direct, impacts on the conservation of biological diversity.[13] Moreover, under GATT jurisprudence, the standard of justification for trade measures under Article XX(g) is a least restrictive means test, meaning the defending party must prove that there are no other potential measures that could be taken to prevent harm that are less trade restrictive than, say, the ban (Nissen, 1997).

There has yet to be a challenge of a trade-related environmental measure (TREM) taken pursuant to an MEA. The European Union and others have been putting forward proposals in the Committee for Trade and the Environment of the WTO for how to deal with potential conflicts between the WTO and MEAs. Among these proposals is the creation of what has been called an "environmental window," whereby TREMs taken pursuant to an MEA are automatically considered exempted under Article XX, provided that the MEA has met a certain set of procedural criteria.[14] Nissen (1997) suggests a new subclause (k) under Article XX: "(k) undertaken in pursuance of obligations under a multilateral environmental agreement listed in Annex 5, provided the measure is

---

13. The text of the risk assessment and risk management articles (UN Environment Programme, 2000, Articles 15 and 16, also provide some indication of the criteria that the dispute resolution panels will use (italics added):

Article 15 (Risk Assessment)
1. Risk assessments undertaken pursuant to this Protocol shall be carried out in a *scientifically* sound manner, in accordance with Annex III and taking into account recognized risk assessment techniques. Such risk assessments shall be based, at a minimum, on information provided in accordance with Article 8 and other available *scientific* evidence in order to identify and evaluate the possible adverse effects of living modified organisms on the conservation and sustainable use of biological diversity, taking also into account risks to human health.

Article 16 (Risk Management)
1. The Parties shall, taking into account Article 8 (g) of the Convention, establish and maintain appropriate mechanisms, measures and strategies to regulate, manage and control risks identified in the risk assessment provisions of this Protocol associated with the use, handling and transboundary movement of living modified organisms.
2. Measures based on risk assessment shall be imposed *to the extent necessary* to prevent adverse effects of the living modified organism on the conservation and sustainable use of biological diversity, taking also into account risks to human health, within the territory of the Party of import.

14. Potential criteria include "whether the MEA was open to participation by all parties concerned with the environmental objectives of the MEA, and reflected, through adequate participation, their interests, including significant trade and economic interests" (WTO, 1996, endnote 19).

proportional to the environmental harm. If the measure is not proportional, then the party may bring a dispute" (p. 926). She includes the concept of proportionality to avoid the present problem of the least restrictive means test.

Ironically for our story about SIA, it is the developing countries that have fought the move to establish an environmental window, citing the potential for the developed world to use TREMs as disguised protectionism. Also ironic is the nonpaper tabled by the United States in 1996, which noted that "WTO rules should not hamper the ability of MEAs to achieve their environmental objectives" and that "trade measures have been and will continue to be an important tool for achieving important environmental objectives" (WTO, 1996, paragraph 22).

It is interesting to note that the WTO itself claims that the exceptions clauses contained in Article XX of the GATT "subject to certain important conditions . . . allow a WTO member legitimately to place its . . . national environmental goals ahead of its general obligation not to raise trade restrictions or to apply discriminatory trade measures" (WTO, 1997). If countries include in their national environmental goals the conservation of various aspects of society and culture, trade-related measures based on results of SIA should be considered legitimate components of MEAs. Clearly, the proposals of the African Group and Malaysia to include socioeconomic considerations in the protocol would have been preferable to the present protocol text and arguably would have been consistent with international obligations as provided for by the WTO exceptions clauses. Given the likelihood of a WTO challenge, it is now up to countries to decide whether the exercise of their sovereign right to exclude LMOs based on predicted socioeconomic and downstream biodiversity impacts is worth the price they will pay.

Manuscript submitted December 6, 1999; revised manuscript accepted for publication April 18, 2000.

Acknowledgements

The author thanks two anonymous reviewers for the helpful comments provided.

References

Barrow, C. J. (1997). *Environmental and social impact assessment: An introduction*. London: Arnold.
Bhatiasevi, A. (1997, November 17). Cotton used in medicine poses threat: Genetically-altered cotton may not be safe. *Bangkok Post*.

Bowonder, B. (1979). Impact analysis of the green revolution in India. *Technological Forecasting and Social Change, 15,* 297-313.
Bray, F. (1994, July). Agriculture for developing nations. *Scientific American,* pp. 30-37.
Burdge, R. J., & Vanclay, F. (1995). Social impact assessment. In F. Vanclay & D. A. Bronstein (Eds.), *Environmental and social impact assessment* (pp. 31-65). New York: John Wiley.
Cleaver, H. M., Jr. (1972, June). Contradictions of the Green Revolution. *Monthly Review,* pp. 80-111.
Federal Democratic Republic of Ethiopia, Environmental Protection Authority. (1996). *Draft protocol to the Convention on Biological Diversity concerning safety in biotechnology.* Addis Ababa: Author.
Griffin, K. (1974). *The political economy of agrarian change.* Cambridge, MA: Harvard University Press.
Finsterbusch, K., Ingersoll, J., & Llewellyn, L. (Eds.). (1990). *Methods for social analysis in developing countries.* Boulder, CO: Westview.
Finsterbusch, K., Llewellyn, L. G., & Wolf, C. P. (Eds.). (1983). *Social impact assessment methods.* Beverly Hills, CA: Sage.
Freudenburg, W. R. (1986). Social impact assessment. *Annual Review of Sociology, 12,* 451-478.
Hewitt de Alcántara, C. (1976). *Modernizing Mexican agriculture: Socio-economic implications of technological change, 1940-1970.* Geneva: United Nations Research in Social Development.
Impact Assessment, Inc. (1990). *Social and psychological impacts of the Exxon Valdez oil spill* (Interim Report #3 of the Economic, Social, and Psychological Impact Assessment of the Exxon Valdez Oil Spill, prepared for Oiled Mayors Subcommittee, Alaska Conference of Mayors). La Jolla, CA: Author.
Indigenous Peoples of the Western Hemisphere. (1995). Declaration of indigenous peoples of the western hemisphere regarding the Human Genome Diversity Project. Reproduced in *Cultural Survival Quarterly, 20*(2), 63.
Interorganizational Committee on Guidelines and Principles for Social Impact Assessment. (1995). Guidelines and principles for social impact assessment. *Environmental Impact Assessment Review, 15*(1), 11-43.
Lee, A. M., & Bereano, P. L. (1981). Developing technology assessment methodology: Some insights and experiences. *Technological Forecasting and Social Change, 19*(1), 15-31.
New Zealand Environmental Risk Management Authority. (1997). *Considering applications: Proposed procedures and information requirements for the consideration of applications for the introduction of hazardous substances and new organisms under the HSNO Act 1996* (Consultation Doc. No. 2). Wellington: New Zealand Environmental Risk Management Agency.
Nissen, J. L. (1997). Achieving a balance between trade and the environment: The need to amend the WTO/GATT to include multilateral environmental agreements. *Law & Policy in International Business, 28*(3), 901-928.
Norway Ministry of Environment. (1993). *The Act relating to the production and use of genetically modified organisms.* Oslo: Author.
Pham-Delègue, M. (1997). Risk assessment of transgenic oilseed rape on the honeybee. *Safety of Our Foods and Life, 104,* 7-9.
Rickson, R. E., Hundloe, T., McDonald, G. T., & Burdge, R. J. (Eds.). (1990). Social impact of development: Putting theory and methods into practice. *Environmental Impact Assessment Review, 10*(1/2).
Rickson, R. E., & Rickson, S. T. (1990). Assessing rural development: The role of the social scientist. *Environmental Impact Assessment Review, 10*(1-2), 103-112.
Rural Advancement Foundation International. (1987, May). Cacao & biotechnology: A report on work in progress. *RAFI Communique,* pp. 1-9.
Rural Advancement Foundation International. (1989, July). Coffee and biotechnology. *RAFI Communique,* pp. 1-13.

Rural Advancement Foundation International. (1992, June). Genetic engineering of pyrethrins: Early warning for East African pyrethrum farmers. *RAFI Communique*, pp. 1-3.

Shiva, V. (1991). *The violence of the Green Revolution: Third world agriculture, ecology and politics*. London: Zed Books Ltd. and Third World Network.

Stoffle, R. W. (1990). Calculating the cultural significance of American Indian plants: Paiute and Shoshone ethnobotany at Yucca Mountain, Nevada. *American Anthropologist*, 92(2), 416-432.

Taylor, C. N., Bryan, C. H., & Goodrich, C.C. (1990). *Social assessment: Theory, process and techniques* (Studies in Resource Management No. 7). Canterbury, New Zealand: Lincoln University, Center for Resource Management.

UN Environment Programme. (1994). *Convention on Biological Diversity: Text and annexes* (UNEP/CBD/94/1). Montréal, Canada: Secretariat of the Convention on Biological Diversity.

UN Environment Programme. (1997a). *Compilation of government submissions of draft text on selected items* (UNEP/CBD/BSWG/3/3). Montréal, Canada: Secretariat of the Convention on Biological Diversity.

UN Environment Programme. (1997b). *Submissions on socio-economic considerations and liability & compensation* (UNEP/CBD/BSWG/3/3/Add.2). Montréal, Canada: Secretariat of the Convention on Biological Diversity.

UN Environment Programme. (2000). *Cartagena Protocol on Biosafety* [Online]. Available: http://www.biodiv.org/biosafe/Biosafe-Prot.html [retrieved 2000, March 26].

World Bank Environment Department. (1995, September). *Social assessment* (World Bank Environmental Department Dissemination Notes No. 36) [Brochure]. Washington, DC: World Bank.

World Trade Organization. (1994). *Uruguay round final act* [Online]. Available PDF: http//www.wto.org/wto.legal/finalact.htm [retrieved 2000, April 22].

World Trade Organization. (1996). *Report of the WTO Committee on Trade and Environment* [Online]. Available: http//iisd1.iisd.ca/trade/wto/ctereport.htm [retrieved 2000, April 22].

World Trade Organization. (1997). *WTO environment* [Online]. Available: http://www.wto.org [retrieved 2000, April 22].

Wright, A. (1990). *The death of Ramón González: The modern agricultural dilemma*. Austin, TX: University of Texas Press.

Doreen Stabinsky is an assistant professor of environmental studies at California State University at Sacramento. She was on leave during the academic year 1999-2000 for a Fulbright professorship at Central Luzon State University in Muñoz, Philippines. While in the Philippines, she also conducted research on NGO and peasant resistance to the patenting of life forms, in particular, patents on rice. Her Ph.D. is in genetics from the University of California at Davis, her BA in economics from Lehigh University. In addition to her Fulbright project, she conducts research on a number of other topics in the area of international biotechnology policy, including the negotiation of the Biosafety Protocol and the development of intellectual property rights policy in a number of international policy-making forums, including the Convention on Biological Diversity, the Food and Agriculture Organization, and the World Trade Organization. She is also a member of the board of directors of the Boston-based NGO, the Council for Responsible Genetics.

[32]

Environmental Impact Assessment Review

How is environmental conflict addressed by SIA?

C.J. Barrow *

Geography Department, School of the Environment and Society, Swansea University, Swansea SA2 8PP, UK

ARTICLE INFO

Available online 4 May 2010

Keywords:
Environmental conflicts
Natural resource conflicts
Peace and Conflict Impact Assessment
Environmental Conflict Management
Environmental Conflict Resolution
Conflict-aware SIA
Social Impact Assessment

ABSTRACT

The fields of Environmental Conflict Management (ECM), Environmental Conflict Resolution (ECR), and Peace and Conflict Impact Assessment (PCIA) have become well established; however, as yet there has not been much use of Social Impact Assessment (SIA) to manage environmental conflicts. ECM, ECR and PCIA are mainly undertaken when problems are advanced or, more likely, have run their course (post-conflict). This paper examines how conflict is addressed by SIA and whether there is potential to develop it for more proactive assessment of conflicts (pre-conflict or while things develop). SIA has the potential to identify and clarify the cause(s) of environmental and natural resources conflicts, and could possibly enable some avoidance or early mitigation. A promising approach may be for 'conflict-aware' SIA to watch for critical conflict stages or thresholds and to monitor stakeholders. Effective conflict-aware SIA might also significantly contribute to efforts to achieve sustainable development.

© 2010 Elsevier Inc. All rights reserved.

1. Introduction

This paper explores how Social Impact Assessment (SIA) might improve the management of environmental and natural resources conflicts. There are many post-conflict appraisals, but few attempts to provide advanced warning or make assessments before conflicts finish. Environmental Conflict Resolution (ECR), Environmental Conflict Management (ECM) and Peace and Conflict Impact Assessment (PCIA) are widely practiced but there has been little development of proactive conflict-aware SIA. This paper examines whether there are recognisable conflict stages and thresholds that could be used by conflict-aware SIA, and also tries to establish what might be promising approaches.

There is no universal definition of SIA; perhaps the best is that provided by Vanclay (2003:6): "…the process of analysing, monitoring and managing the social consequences of development." Alternatively, SIA could be described as a process that seeks to assess whether a proposed development will alter quality of life and sense of well-being, and how well individuals, groups and communities adapt to the changes (see also: Vanclay, 1999; 2002, 2004; Becker and Vanclay, 2003; Burdge, 2004). An SIA should consider what would happen if the proposed development did not take place, explore ways of avoiding or mitigating adverse (especially irreversible) impacts and flag likely or apparent beneficial impacts and opportunities. Increasingly the process also seeks to inform and involve stakeholders and make developers more reflective and accountable. There are three possible points for application of conflict-aware SIA: pre-conflict; in-conflict; and post-conflict. SIA must be applied early if it is to support proactive governance and management, so pre-conflict application is desirable but that is currently much less common than post-conflict usage. Whenever it is used SIA can aid in understanding the cause(s) of conflict, may help make developers more accountable, might help integrate diverse disciplines involved in planning, and thereby assist efforts to achieve sustainable development (Cox et al., 2000; Cavaye, 2003).

It is not uncommon for a project, programme or policy to 'succeed' in the sense that it meets its planned goals, yet be overshadowed by problems and conflict it provokes (Westman, 1985). Failed developments can also trigger conflict, change independent of any development that can cause or ease problems, and a development or an unrelated change may highlight or catalyse already developing conflict.

Before proceeding further it is useful to try to clarify the meanings of *development* and *conflict*. Definitions of *development* reflect the current values of those involved. So, what was once seen as development may no longer appear to be because opinions vary over time and between groups or among individuals. There can be no precise and universal definition. However, most accept it is a process of change, often multidimensional, and something many governments, bodies or individuals aspire to prompt and steer. Development may not progress toward 'better' conditions; there can be no change or deterioration. The focus of development can be economic, social, technological, cultural, etc. Progress may not be marked by more disposable income, but by greater security, improved sense of well-being, more fulfilled and healthy life, etc. Before the 1970s there was little concern for environmental quality or social welfare; that has changed and there has also been the establishment of the concept of sustainable development. The latter may be crudely defined as development,

---

* Tel.: +44 01792 205678x4362.
E-mail address: c.j.barrow@swansea.ac.uk.

0195-9255/$ – see front matter © 2010 Elsevier Inc. All rights reserved.
doi:10.1016/j.eiar.2010.04.001

which maintains achievements for those involved without reducing the options of others now and in the future. Development may be pursued at an individual, local, regional, national or international scale, through projects, programmes or policies, or simply the promulgation of a message. The process can be orchestrated from the bottom-up, or from the top-down; it can be short-term or longer-term in focus, planned and managed or more casual, even unconscious.

One definition of a *conflict* is that is a "...perceived divergence of interests, or belief that the various stakeholders' current aspirations cannot be achieved simultaneously" (Persson, 2006: 3). For a somewhat different definition, see: International Alert (2006). An environmental conflict can manifest as political, social, economic, ethnic, religious or territorial strife or discontent over resources, or national interests (Spillmann and Bächer, 2005). Conflict can be non-violent or violent but either can be damaging. Occasionally conflict prompts change and progress; often there are opportunities as well as problems. Cause(s) of conflict can often be identified, although there may be situations where perceptions are unclear or disagreement is based on long-forgotten events or unfounded prejudice. Sometimes a conflict is preceded by an obvious crisis, a realization that a threshold could be crossed leading to serious trouble. Crisis warning and crisis management may be able to contribute something to conflict prediction. For example, the crisis may be at a 'hot-spot' and occur well before a more general problem.

Divergence of interest may be expressed in ways short of public disagreement, let alone serious violence, but even restrained conflict can have serious consequences. Those in disagreement may fail to cooperate, might fail to share useful information, etc. Conflict can arise when stakeholders benefit, or are impartial outsiders can judge, to broadly the same degree. Often disagreement reflects divergent beliefs or habits. So, there may not always be a clear initial crisis.

2. Conflict and Social Impact Assessment

Projects, plans, programmes, policies, cultural development or socio-economic development in general and environmental changes run the risk of creating or exacerbating conflicts. During the process of preparing proposals SIA might be used to anticipate and thereby give a chance for reducing destructive conflicts. It may also be possible to run a SIA if precursors of conflict become apparent to monitoring bodies, NGOs, or whoever is vigilant. Vanclay (2004: 274) found that a number of conflict related SIAs had been conducted by 2003. However, most of those, and the majority of subsequent conflict related SIAs have been initiated post-conflict. So the potential of conflict-aware SIA has not really been adequately recognised or developed.

2.1. Social Impact Assessment

In some cases, developers do not adequately understand the potential and scope of SIA to improve proposals prior to decision-making, although this is changing (see Esteves and Vanclay, 2009). There may also be situations where things other than the proposed development are causing impacts, such as ongoing social or economic trends, environmental change, etc. SIA should be initiated before any developing conflict or proposal progresses too far to facilitate choice of best way forward and to give a chance of proactive management. In practice, SIA has mainly been applied to initiated projects, expected changes (social, economic, technical and environmental), already developing conflicts, ongoing programmes and policies, and post-development (or dispute) situations. Before those points, funding is unlikely to be forthcoming and the need little perceived. One of the basic demands for useful environmental SIA is to ensure it is applied as early as possible in order to try and: offer early-warning; establish causation; assess likely effects. Realistically, the best that can usually be expected is SIA application early in-conflict, which would at least offer the latter two benefits. It might be useful to explore ways to fund rapid response conflict-aware SIA and establish bodies to watch for situations which merit its application. If that sort of proactive approach found a situation deserving a full conflict-aware SIA, efforts should be made not to adopt too narrow a focus and to explore the full context of the dispute, proposal or development.

A *social impact* may be broadly defined as the consequences of any action that alters how people live, think, behave, and react to each other (Burdge, 2004). The impact lies somewhere on the scale from good via insignificant to bad. Social impacts include social, cultural, health, and psychological impacts. A social impact can be real or perceived and affect individuals, families, groups, societies, countries, and even the global community. Social impacts can result from environmental and/or socio-economic changes, including technical and cultural innovation Gleditsch, 1996. The negative manifestations include: increased insecurity, more vulnerability, frustration, hardship, and loss of livelihoods, alienation from land or social networks, and conflict. Positive manifestations include: improvements to confidence, social capital, and livelihoods, and better adaptability. It is important to stress that impacts may be beneficial and offer opportunities, not all are negative. It may take SIA to spot and flag such opportunities. Social impacts may occur without a planned development taking place, through ongoing change, such as: demographic shifts, altered tastes and fashions, unexpected disasters, and so forth. A given change can cause different impacts on various groups or among individuals within groups. For the same group or individual a similar change may cause different effects with passing time. Assessment may identify *outcomes* as well as impacts. For example, a development may cause learning or networking with little obvious effect (an outcome), which can mean similar events in the future, would be dealt with in a different way (Vanclay, 2002).

A development or environmental change can cause social impacts that contribute to conflict in a negative or positive manner (MacKay, 1981; Porter and Ganapin, 1988; Homer-Dixon, 1991; Baechler, 1998). Conflict can cause social impacts that affect the developer or the environment. The developer can cause environmental impacts, which contribute to conflict. Added to all that, there may be positive or negative feedbacks. As in EIA one can subdivide impacts into first-, second-, third-order, and so on. A first-order impact is a simple and relatively apparent relationship. Second-order impacts involve a two-step indirect causation, and so may be less obvious, and so on as the order-rises. Devising SIA methods for identifying first-order impacts is relatively easy; however, they are like weak dip-beam headlights, providing a broad close view, but failing to show things further away in the darkness. There is a risk if SIA assesses only first-order impacts those commissioning the assessment will get a false sense of security. Things are in reality even more difficult; indirect impacts may form often complex chains and webs of causation, whereby wholly unrelated impacts interact at some distant point in time and/or space in a significant manner (Slootweg et al., 2001; Taylor et al., 2004). Such chains of causation can be modelled, but it demands time, funds and expertise, and it is unlikely to be precise. Worse, human behaviour can be fickle and difficult to forecast (Barrow, 2000, 2002). There is also a need to exercise caution to avoid environmental determinism: environmental change or disaster do not invariably cause stress leading to conflict, there can be quite the opposite effect, or little change.

There is the potential for conflicts to arise between stakeholders involved in natural resources development or impacted by environmental change or disaster. A *stakeholder* may be defined as someone (it could also be an organism or local environment) that is affected or perceives they could be affected by something. The effect could be either positive or negative, and 'stakeholder' also includes those affected but unaware of it (including people in the future or off-site, possibly far away). In the early stages of an SIA stakeholders need to be identified and understood as accurately as possible. Complex multi-stakeholder situations with overlapping interests are common.

Sustainable development demands trade-offs and conflict resolution between present and future stakeholders. The latter are not able to voice their opinions so a proxy must represent them; SIA could be used to help identify such situations. Just as the 1969 US National Environmental Policy Act required EIAs to stress irreversible impacts it is desirable for SIAs to flag potential and actual sustainable development conflicts. SIA could be used more to supervise and help strengthen the social dimensions of sustainable development and to try to anticipate disruptive conflicts (Cramer et al., 2004).

SIA and social assessment are essentially the same. A technocratic-action orientation to SIA is typically adopted by government agencies. This approach is also commonly used by a range of public agencies seeking to meet legal requirements associated with EIA and natural resource planning and management, and by many private sector developers and consultants (Fig. 1). One can debate what is the best approach; each practitioner has their own ideology and set of experiences. Some favour a technocratic 'top-down' and others a more participatory 'bottom-up' strategy. There may also be conflicts between 'applied' or 'commissioned' research and 'academic' research. The former tends to have more practical objectives, while academic studies are shaped by a theoretical approach and may aim more for publishable results. For further details see Taylor et al. (2004: 27–29).

SIA, hazard assessment, technology assessment, and health impact assessment, often share weaknesses: a need for more standardised approaches; they usually present a 'snapshot' view; and often there are problems communicating between the different specialists and teams.

2.2. Conflict

A few people, even one, can cause serious conflict (e.g. Hitler, Stalin, and present day terrorist groups). Persson (2006) reported one USA animal liberation front (a handful of activists) caused US$18 million damage to property in 2002 alone. Conflict may arise over changes to the environment that is natural, caused by humans, or a combination of both. Social conflict may affect access to resources or the way the environment is used (Lockie et al., 2009; Thiranagama, 2009). Conflict can be generated by exploitation of resources and by people trying to adapt to environmental change, especially if they become eco-refugees. Sometimes conflicts appear at more than one level or locality or time and are in some way related (nested together). In spite of such diversity and complexity can causes, types of conflict and phase of evolution be identified fast and reliably enough to enable proactive conflict-aware SIA?

Studies of environmental and natural resources-related social conflicts have been undertaken by environmental conflict studies, PCIA, ECR, ECM, community psychology, economists, political economists, peace studies researchers, anthropologists, sociologists, economic geographers, etc. There have been attempts to model conflict development (Meissen and Cipriani, 1984; Fiaschi, 2008; http://www.uvm.edu/~shali/ecr.html accessed February, 2009). Overall, there is plenty of hindsight knowledge on conflict causation and progression.

This indicates conflicts tend to relate to one or more of the following:

- overuse of resources;
- access to resources;
- pollution;
- damage to environmental quality (e.g. pollution, overexploitation, overcrowding);
- differences in ethical and religious beliefs;
- simple scarcity;
- problems due to group identity;
- friction caused through deprivation of lower status groups.

The following are also possible causes of conflict:

- ☐ environmental changes (such as global warming);
- ☐ ethno-political differences;
- ☐ centre-periphery relationships;
- ☐ migration/displacement;
- ☐ demographic pressure;
- ☐ shared resources.

So, a body charged with conflict-aware SIA might watch for such situations.

The International Environmental Law Research Centre has published a typology of environmental conflicts, and explored environment-conflict linkages and causation (http://www.ielrc.org/activities/presentation_0410.htm accessed December 2007). Studies by the World Bank suggest that countries most likely to suffer conflict are those heavily dependent on natural resources, and it concluded conflict-aware impact

ACTION ORIENTATION

TECHNOCRATIC APPROACHES (product oriented) — Action based on centralised social planning and management (government agencies, consultants)

RESEARCH ORIENTATION

Academic research (uvniversities, private and public "think tanks")

ISSUES-ORIENTED APPROACH

PARTICIPATORY APPROACHES (process oriented) — Action based on social development at a community level (local community organisations, groups and community workers, organisers)

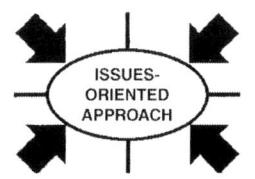

Advocacy research (foundation supported and independent research on behalf of special minority interests)

Fig. 1. Orientation to social assessment. Based on Taylor et al., 2004 Fig. 2.1 p.27.

assessment was desirable (Bannon and Collier, 2003: 259–263). Caution should be exercised because, while there is much written on environmental conflict causation, it is not adequately understood (Gleditsch and Diehl, 2001; Spillmann and Bächer, 2005).

PCIA is widely used but so far has not focused much on prediction and avoidance; efforts have been mainly directed to retro-assessing causation and on consensus building and reconciliation *after* a dispute has peaked or hostilities have ended (CIDA, 2004; CPR Network, 2005; Schmelzle, 2005; MacSweeney, 2008). PCIA has largely grown out of conflict mediation/resolution and conflict management since the 1970s. Often a neutral mutually accepted mediator is briefed to help to bring sides to agreement (rather like the *ombudsman* role in Sweden). There is no single overall PCIA approach; rather, most assessment is conducted on a case-by-case basis (Susskind and Thomas-Larmer, 2007).

PCIA, social psychologists and sociologists have recognised the following causes and phases:

☐ *Structural or root causes* – factors resulting from the structure and fabric of society and policies. These create the preconditions for conflict.
☐ *Proximate causes* – factors that are symptomatic of structural causes or precede/lead to escalation.
☐ *Triggers* – single events or series of events, or the anticipation of something, which sets-off conflict.

Thus, it is recognised that conflicts do evolve and may have recognisable thresholds and phases. Fig. 2 (redrawn with modifications from Kumar Rupesinghe, 1998) illustrates several phases of violent conflict. So, if there are thresholds and phases that can be recognised there are opportunities for proactive assessment. SIA will need to quickly identify conflict phases and the causes of stress; it may then be possible to assess how conflict is likely to unfold.

Caution should be exercised, because different types of conflict may overlap and not be clear-cut, also conflicts may vary in the way they evolve from theoretical patterns. Persson (2006) proposed a two-part subdivision of environmental conflicts. Firstly *value conflicts*, in which all parties feel they are right and are unlikely to negotiate. For example, a current value conflict between supporters of genetically modified organisms (GMOs) and their opponents. The outcome of a decision to either allow or prevent further introductions of GMOs into the environment and economy may have serious impacts. The opposing sides have very different perceptions and in some cases opponents to GMOs even turn to terrorism. Second, *conflicts of interest*, these Persson argued, were easier to mediate because trade-offs are possible without altering deeply held views. Manring et al. (1990: 255) also subdivided conflict into two. Firstly they recognised *crosscutting conflicts* – differences on a limited number of fronts, possibly with individuals in opposing groups sharing some similar interests. There is less likelihood of withdrawal into total opposition and more hope of successful negotiation than in a value conflict. Secondly, *overlapping conflicts* – stakeholders share little and tend to oppose their counterparts on virtually everything, consequently with little common ground, agreements are more difficult to achieve. (A reviewer of this paper noted that the Manring et al., taxonomy might link into the social capital literature which distinguishes 'bridging social capital' and 'bonding social capital').

Conflict may arise through one or a combination of:

• Emotional anger caused by jealousy, injured pride, insult, and so on.
• Imbalances in power relations.
• Inequitable distribution of resources.
• Fear, aggression, or indifference to others.
• Relocation as a consequence of natural disaster, social or economic forces.
• Habit: caused by not especially conscious thought, but by misunderstanding, prejudice or traditional views.
• Worldview; for example, religious beliefs, morals, or political outlook.
• Conscious reasoning: caused by rational thought (value beliefs).
• Opportunism: means to ends with the focus on a goal, which is often profit.

Policy and governance may trigger conflict; for example, a subsidy to selected groups may cause some users to over exploit and/or others to be jealous. Stakeholders may try to gain advantage through opportunism if they feel able to get away unobserved or if enforcement is inadequate.

In some situations conflict may upset the status quo and enable or encourage change (beneficial or damaging). The tension between conflicting parties might be used constructively: statesmen often practice 'divide and rule'; and NASA made use of Cold War rivalry to help spur development of its moon landing programme. SIA might help identify such opportunities. An example of a conflict situation leading to improvements in livelihoods and environmental management can be found in parts of the Sudan where males have migrated, leaving female heads of household. These female-headed households face a male-dominated society, yet in spite of conflict, have proved resilient and more innovative: improving family welfare, food security, and land use. Yet, in some other parts of Africa, male out-migration has resulted in family breakdown, loss of social capital, environmental degradation and deprivation. Subtle differences determine how societies change in vulnerability and resilience. Conflict-aware SIA might thus be usefully combined with assessment of the state of social capital (Buchan, 2003).

Conflict between individuals, between groups, between group(s) and 'outsiders' (central government, business, etc.), or between nations, may be a sign of effort to adapt to a challenge (environmental, social, economic, technical, political or combinations of these) (Warner, 2000). There are studies of how conflicts evolve which could be explored to help identify patterns and thresholds for SIA to work with (for example: Coy and Woehrle, 2000). Nevertheless, some conflicts arise where there are no challenges apparent. Developments can both counter or cause conflict. Sometimes a minority causes conflict, sometimes a majority group; it could be due to confident people or nervous people. Prediction of conflict evolution is unlikely to be precise and reliable; but even so, it would be valuable.

2.3. Established conflict impact assessment

PCIA is used by business, national governments, non-governmental organisations (NGOs) and aid agencies to develop appropriate strategies in country and, where refugees have settled; however, it is mainly reactive, not proactive (Austin et al., 2003; http://www.london.gov.uk/mayor/refugees/docs/destitution_by_design.pdf accessed November 2007; Broadwood and Sugden, 2008). Some sectors have generated considerable hindsight knowledge about

Phases of violent conflict

- Sustained violent conflict
- Outbreak of violence
- Unstable peace/latent conflict
- Stable peace
- Durable peace
- Stalemate/de-escalation/ceasefire
- Return to unstable peace/latent conflict
- Settlement/resolution

DURATION OF CONFLICT

Fig. 2. Phases of violent conflict.

social impacts, including conflict: large-scale mining, large dams (especially reservoir-related resettlement), irrigation projects, urban development, oil exploitation, logging, tourism development, road and rail building, creation of conservation areas, shopping mall provision, and (in Australia) casino development (Okoji, 2002; IPIECA, 2004). An increasing number of developers and governments have been adopting conflict management strategies (Ivanova et al., 2007). It should also be noted that the expanding fields of human vulnerability and adaptation studies overlap with conflict management. Human efforts to adapt to environmental or socio-economic change can sometimes cause marginalisation and the breakdown of established coping strategies. Some of the research on breakdown of established coping strategies might usefully feed into conflict-aware SIA. Studies in the USA and Europe of urban gentrification have included conflict-aware SIA. Businesses increasingly use PCIA to support their efforts to practice corporate social responsibility and to reduce costly and image-damaging disputes (Hoffman, 2007). The NGO International Alert has explored extractive industry-related conflict assessment in some depth, focusing on pre-existing social conflict (International Alert, 2006). Companies, NGOs, agencies and governments are keen to assess their operations in a proactive way to aid planning, reduce corruption, defuse opposition and inter-group conflict, anticipate human rights and resource access problems, and to improve benefit distribution. More proactive PCIA drawing on conflict-aware SIA would be welcomed (Daudelin, 1999; Berger, 2002; International Alert, 2006; Chandrasekara, undated; http://www.mazda.com/csr/environment accessed November 2007). ECR and ECM are also reactive, rather than proactive but do provide information on how conflicts evolve (Nath et al., 1998: 436–456; O'Leary and Bingham, 2003). The UNEP (2004: 38–47) has explored proactive conflict-aware SIA; but seems to have done little since then. Another exploration of proactive PCIA was provided by Carment and Schnabel (2004: 341–414). There is thus a knowledge base for conflict-aware SIA to draw upon.

2.4. Participation, empowerment and conflict avoidance

There is a widely held viewpoint that if stakeholders are encouraged and empowered to participate in planning and management the result is more likely to yield: sustainable results, cause less environmental damage, give better livelihoods, and avoid conflict (Rydin, 2003). Many fields adopt this view, including some SIAs, extractive reserves, participatory development, the sustainable livelihoods approach, and participatory conservation. But making it work can be a challenge: the established route for SIA is to involve representative stakeholders but often the marginalized or minorities are missed. The question should also be asked: how good is the judgement of those stakeholders consulted? SIA is often less about incorporating citizen views into planning and more concerned with legitimising what has been planned, i.e. orchestration of one-way communication to reduce conflict with the developer. There may be countries where participation is not a priority and situations where urgent problems or sensitive issues prompt more draconian ways. Participation or empowerment does not necessarily lead to conflict avoidance. Perhaps conflict-aware SIA should concentrate on assessing stakeholder potential to cause conflict and not get engrossed with ensuring participation or making development plans palatable.

Individuals and groups often differ in the things they value and in perception of opportunities and threats. Faced with the same development, confident people are likely to react differently from the fatalistic, weak and dispirited (but the result can be conflict in either case). A nation with a useful but unsustainable natural resource; for example, petroleum or groundwater has a choice: spend the benefits on short-term social welfare (and votes), or invest in long-term, hopefully sustainable, development (which may be unattractive to the electorate). Citizens and government can come into conflict over such decisions. Pursuit of sustainable development is not a costless strategy it can cause intergenerational conflict. SIA may therefore need to maintain some distance from those currently involved in development and identify ways to help represent the future in the present; not least because politicians and public servants are pressured to satisfy present demands.

3. SIA for environmental and resource development-related conflict management

ECM and political economy researchers have explored environmental conflicts in considerable depth (Modavi, 1991; Percival, 1992; Anon, 2000). But, the theory of environmental conflict is far from firmly established, particularly whether environmental changes commonly induce conflict, and if so how? Manring et al. (1990) explored the potential for linking SIA and ECM; they concluded that these two fields could work together, although they noted at that time that it had rarely happened. Their conclusion was that SIA could preemptively predict problems for ECM with (and presumably that would also be true of fields like PCIA). They were satisfied that SIA should be able to identify thresholds and help monitor and uncover causes of antagonism and posturing. Manring et al. (1990: 254) also felt that the social systems approach often adopted by SIA did little to support conflict management. Lockie (2007) argued for SIA to use deliberation theory and actor-networks to go beyond exploring social change to target consensus building among stakeholders; emphasise how values and perceptions change as development proceeds; help unravel what is crucial; and foster engagement between specialist and lay knowledge.

In some countries SIA is part of the regional or urban planning process and does explore conflict; issues focussed impact assessment also often deals with conflicts (Harrison and McDonald, 2003; Heikkinen and Sairinen, 2007; Jyväskylä, 2007; Wells et al., 2007). The spread of strategic environmental assessment (SEA) may offer opportunities for incorporating conflict-aware SIA in a way that enables it to seek out where it is needed early enough to support proactive governance and planning. Conflict management demands a proactive approach to give an opportunity to resolve differences and reach agreed solutions. It is also likely to require a neutral, respected SIA assessor and mediator with adequate 'teeth'.

Monitoring for situations where conflict-aware SIA should be applied might be made easier if it were applied using a manageable-sized bioregion. Bradshaw et al. (2001: 13) suggested a tiered methodology in their study of SIA applied to fisheries "stepping down through geographic scales and employing a range of methods, sources and techniques". New Zealand's Resource Management Act (1991) includes provision for environmental dispute resolution measures in the decision-making framework, but the focus of is not really on proactive assessment. Australia uses SIA for urban and regional planning with some consideration of conflicts, particularly as part of the quest for sustainable development and to help protect the rights of Aboriginal peoples (Rolf and Windle, 2003). In the UK several new town proposals have prompted SIA focused on conflict management; for example, existing communities around a possible development sited at Sherford (close to Plymouth) became aware and expressed concern, which triggered studies by the developers http://www.scotwilson.com/betasite/projects/property/education/sherford_ne (accessed November 2007). In cases like this conflict-aware SIA seems to be more a tool for 'value added', i.e. helping developers enhance achievements, rather than as a proactive means of shaping development. There is thus some risk that SIA may be used to support the interests of partisan sponsors and consequently inadequately explore the opportunity costs of developments and their alternatives (this was noted long ago by McDonald, 1990).

With any development a few dominant voices tend to be heeded (Boyle, 1998). These can be special interest groups, a business, government officials, or a powerful individual, and may lead to unsuitable decisions. There may also be problems when middle-class urban people make decisions affecting mainly rural folk and the poor because they are ill-informed or lack sympathy (Cernea, 1991; Chambers, 1997). SIA originated in western nations, so applying it in other countries, especially those socially, culturally and politically different, still poses challenges. Also, people may not be keen to participate (Tang Bo-sin et al., 2008), there may be limited funding for SIA, or a rush to develop or do something for strategic reasons.

Indigenous peoples have acquired rights and powers in many countries and may inhabit areas and rich natural resources. They can differ markedly from other groups in the ways they value natural features and resources so conflicts are often generated (O'Reilly and Eacott, 1999). SIA has been used in environmental and natural resources development conflicts between indigenous peoples and others in Australia, New Zealand, New Guinea, Canada, Finland, Alaska, Australia, the USA, South America, and several other countries, to clarify vulnerabilities and try to reduce impacts and conflicts. Mostly this has been done late: in-conflict or post-conflict, but there are signs of change (Rickson et al., 1989; O'Faircheallaigh, 1999; Lane et al., 2003; Roon, 2006).

3.1. Social Impact Assessment focused on social capital

Social capital may be defined as the networks of association and organisation at community level. It is the value gained from being part of a community, group, or institution achieved through informal and organised reciprocal networks of trust, obligation, and friendship, which together contribute to social organisation. It is the 'glue' that holds society together in a stable manner and it provides support to facilitate adaptation to adversity and innovation (Falk and Kirkpatrick, 2000). Social capital may support conflict resolution or help a stubborn group resist reconciliation. The networks can be horizontal: between family, friends, neighbourhood, community, culture, etc. And, they can be vertical: for example, access to resources through NGOs, government bodies, international agencies, political parties, etc. Social capital plays an important part in conflict and should be monitored. Williamson (2002) went further and suggested developers negotiate with community representatives and contract to develop social capital, and in return citizens would agree to support the development.

SIA could be a useful tool for warning of erosion of social capital, for identifying and recommending ways of building up social capital, and for identifying how to use it to support the quest for sustainable development. A number of local, regional and national investment programmes claim to have adopted proactive use of SIA, focusing on prediction of threats to or improvements in social capital (Sander, 1997; Anirudh and Shrader, 1999; Kingsley and Melkers, 1999; McGregor et al., 2000; Putnam, 2000; Chase, 2002; Randolph, 2004: 54–59). Business has also shown interest in assessing social capital, especially if community-based projects or programmes are involved (Grootaert and van Bastelaer, 2002). Subtle factors can affect social capital, including media, fashions, Internet access, and much more (Gaved and Andeson, 2006). So, making predictions about social capital is challenging, not least, because it has not been sufficiently established what strengthens and weakens it and it is difficult to measure.

3.2. Environmental and natural resource development-related impacts on stakeholders

Much of the SIA literature is focused on the impacts of development on local stakeholders. But it is not uncommon for development to impact on distant stakeholders (spatially and/or temporally). Some groups may be more prone to conflict: for example, people who are suspicious of outsiders; those habitually squabbling; those previously disrupted; those with a culture that hinders adaptation. Conflict generated when people are forced or encouraged to move impacts on the relocated and host population. The causes of relocation can include less than obvious gradual attitudinal changes. Poverty may play a role in conflict, poor people may find it difficult to maintain good environmental management and have little chance to adapt to or correct problems, withstand disasters, or innovate. If the causes, dynamics and impacts of poverty are established and monitored aid might be provided more effectively (http://www.worldbank.org/wbsite/external/topics/extpoverty/ex accessed November 2007). There are situations where local people damage the environment or natural resources through greed or traditions that hinder governance; it is also common for peoples in remote areas to be unfairly blamed without adequate efforts to assess root causes.

Conservation efforts can generate conflicts. Jackson et al. (2001) used SIA to explore conflicts between several stakeholders making multiple use of a wetland environment in Norfolk (UK). This greatly clarified causation but took place too late to enable proactive management and was a research study with no enforcement powers. In Australia saltwater crocodile conservation is blamed for more frequent human attacks so some stakeholders are unhappy (Axelrod, 1994). Similar conflicts occur in Florida (USA) over alligator conservation, in Scandinavia moose protection may mean more motor accidents, and lands around African game reserves suffer damage from elephants and people fear large land predators. Water is a crucial natural resource, which is widely seen to be coming under stress through rising population, poor management and global environmental change, together with growing demand. Because the resource is so vital, and sometimes has religious value, competition for it may lead to conflict. Rivers are frequently subject to different uses by a range of stakeholders and satisfactory sharing is not simply a matter of distributing a portion of available supplies, the usage must be integrated and seek to minimise conflict.

Social changes can gradually and often imperceptibly alter environmental and natural resources management. People can adopt seemingly minor innovations, such as nylon-line, cool boxes, outboard motors, skidoos, or mobile phones and the resulting impact on established resource use can be considerable. Allied with such changes there may be subtle breakdowns of traditional attitudes. For example, in Amazonia taboos against fishing in areas that acted as refuges prevented overexploitation, but social change has weakened these restrictions with serious impacts on sustainability and has caused friction between stakeholders. SIA might warn of such change before it progresses too far. The problems in doing this, apart from developing techniques, are: how to decide when conflict-aware SIA should be used and how to pay for doing it?

3.3. International environmental and natural resources development conflicts

World population is growing, an increasing proportion of people seek better standards of living, there is a likelihood of global environmental change, many natural resources are being degraded and legal safeguards evolve slowly. So, transnational and global conflict situations look likely to multiply. These conflicts are often about 'global commons' which are not under individual ownership or even national sovereignty and legislative controls tend to be weak. Overlapping territorial claims to areas rich in natural resources in the Arctic and Antarctica and their surrounding oceans have the potential to cause conflict as environmental change and technological development makes access easier. Now is the time, before ice melt, to start assessing how conflicts may evolve so that management can be planned and ways to co-operate can be encouraged before incidents develop. International commissions (like The International Whaling Commission) dealing with specific problems, resources or regions are possible platforms for such SIA to work from.

Fig. 3. Recent forest clearance in the Cameron Highlands in an area protected from farmers. It has been undertaken through a 'joint venture' between farmers and indigenous hunter-gatherers who are exempted from land use controls because they have traditional rights. Established enforcement either missed these clearances or they were seen as beneficial for the indigenous people.

4. SIA methods for proactive environmental and natural resources-related conflict assessment

It is possible to list useful inputs for proactive conflict-aware SIA:

- Look for early-warning signs of conflict.
- Establish deadlines for the SIA (the time available).
- List and study stakeholders.
- Identify relationships between stakeholders.
- Establish the history of any apparent conflict.
- Research the progress of similar conflicts (use of hindsight knowledge to help recognise thresholds and phases).
- Map areas of agreement and disagreement (in a stakeholder group there may be a range of views).
- Look for opportunities.

Desk research on environmental and natural resource development-related conflicts can help expose relevant legislation, collect case studies and information on how to mitigate and turn conflict situations into opportunities. These studies can be used to help to draw up checklists for conflict-aware SIA, but, alone are insufficient and should be supplemented with local field studies and perhaps modelling. A simple and quick Leopold-type matrix of tensions and conflicts against vulnerable environmental and social factors could be constructed to indicate direct (first-order) impacts. However, that is a crude tool and it would be desirable to conduct further assessment of indirect and cumulative impacts. Whatever methods are adopted, one question is: can pre-conflict SIA be effectively conducted without triggering or exacerbating existing conflicts?

Water resource development lessons suggest that conflict avoidance or reduction should be transparent, build long-term trust and dialogue among key parties, promote trust and dialogue among relevant stakeholders, and seek to support conflict resolution networks and water stakeholder or user groups. The aforementioned source notes the relative abundance of work on water disputes between states and fewer assessments of conflicts within states, yet the latter are more common. Conflict-aware SIA may be able to draw on water disputes experience to better develop approaches.

PCIA has used brainstorming workshops composed of selected experts and stakeholders (Besançon, 2005). Similar brainstorming might be suitable for conflict-aware SIA, at least as a starting point. This might also be a practical way to identify when and where SIA is needed. A more-ordered and controlled form of brainstorming is the Delphi technique, which is useful in complex situations where the data input is relatively patchy and the aim is relatively inaccurate longer range forecasting. Another possible tool is the self-assessment checklist issued to selected stakeholders. Focus groups, stakeholder analysis, and conflict mapping could be used to assess objectives, social dynamics and power relations. Manring et al. (1990: 259) explored what SIA approach and methods would best suit conflict management ends; they felt technical (impact assessment as technical analysis) and socio-political approaches were both useful. Lane et al. (2003: 91) came to a similar conclusion after researching development-Aboriginal people conflicts in northern Australia. They suggested that SIA should use technical methods along with more community-focused approaches to pick up subtle local issues. Conflict-aware SIA might also usefully borrow from adaptive environmental assessment and management (AEAM) (Gilmour and Walkerden, 1993).

SIA and sustainable development are often best pursued at a manageable project, community, sector, or regional level where there is some sense of 'context of place' (Hill et al., 2007: 197; Broadwood and Sugden, 2008). There are many ways to define a region: for example, through physical or cultural boundaries, sense of community, historical limits, areas of cultural cohesion/regional identity, catchments for service industries, transport networks, situations where a set of resources are used, etc. The important qualities for conflict management and sustainable development would be a unit that is not ephemeral and is clearly delineated. The domain of governance structures should match in spatial terms and function the natural resource system it is proposed to develop: for example: a river basin, or sub basin wholly within the jurisdiction of a governing authority. It is important that social and political systems are also aligned with biophysical systems to improve the chances of resolving natural resources-related conflicts. River basins or sub-basins are bioregions that have been widely used for integrated and holistic planning and management and have a clear region-wide theme: water development. Another potentially useful approach, developed in Brazil, is the extractive reserve. This is a smallish regional unit to cater for integrated management of complex and often conflicting human demands from a number of stakeholders on areas of forest or marine environments, defined for the purpose of promoting sustainable development. Even in small regions there will usually be a number of overlapping communities to assess, each with a number of stakeholders.

In the Cameron Highlands (Malaysia) about 2600 smallholders intensively farm an upland area of about 715 km^2. Wishing to avoid forest clearance and the pollution of streams through soil erosion and with agro-chemicals, the Malaysian Government has controlled land use by issuing a limited number of Temporary Occupation Licenses (TOLs) each year. This virtually stopped deforestation and led to a pool of landholdings and a 'survival of the fittest' situation that resulted in intensification and improvement of land husbandry with little abandonment and no clearance from the early 1980s. However, around 2004 a few entrepreneurs found loopholes in the legislation to restart forest clearance through 'joint ventures' with indigenous people or cleared plots in less regulated highlands some 30 km away (Fig. 3). The clearances cause conflicts between local stakeholders and cause serious environmental impacts (Barrow et al., 2008). Aerial remote sensing shows the deforestation extent but not its causation. Proactive SIA might have established causation and given a chance for avoidance of clearance before irreversible damage was done and conflict arose.

5. Conclusions

SIA combined with vigilance appears to have potential as a tool for understanding conflicts early enough to allow more proactive management. PCIA, ECR, and ECM mainly focus on conflicts that are well underway or, more often, on post-conflict situations. Conflict-aware SIA will need to apply available (and possibly develop new) rapid assessment tools. Research on conflicts indicates they often develop through phases and show thresholds, which could be useful for SIA. The complexity of conflict situations means that the SIA may not be precise so care must be taken to ensure that it does not give false messages. One challenge is to decide when and where conflict-aware SIA should be initiated; some sort of ongoing monitoring is desirable to flag cases for attention.

Acknowledgements

I am most grateful to Prof. Rauno Sairinen and other organisers of the *Conference on Environmental Conflict Mediation and Social Impact Assessment: approaches for enhanced environmental governance*, Helsinki University of Technology 14–15 February 2008. My thanks are also due to James Baines, Prof. Frank Vanclay and two anonymous referees for offering advice and comment on the draft of this paper.

References

Anirudh K, Shrader E. Social Capital Assessment Tool. Conference on Social Capital and Poverty Reduction 22–24 June. Washington DC: World Bank; 1999.
Anon. Bibliography. Washington DC: M.K. Udall Foundation; 2000.
Austin A, Fischer M, Wills O, editors. Peace and Conflict Impact Assessment. Berghof Handbook (Dialogue Series). Vienna: Berghof Research Centre for Constructive Conflict Management, (www.berghof-handbook.net); 2003.
Axelrod LJ. Balancing personal needs with environmental preservation: identifying the values that guide decisions in ecological dilemmas. J Soc Issues 1994;50(3): 83-1004.
Baechler G. Why environmental transformation causes violence. Environ Change Security Proj Rep 1998;4:24–44.
Bannon I, Collier P. Natural Resources and Violent Conflict: Options and Actions. Washington DC: World Bank Publications; 2003.
Barrow CJ. Social Impact Assessment: An Introduction. London: Arnold; 2000.
Barrow CJ. Evaluating the social impacts of environmental change and the environmental impacts of social change: an introductory review of social impact assessment. Int J Environ Stud 2002;59(2):185-96.
Barrow CJ, Chan NW, Bin Masron T. Evolving more sustainable agriculture in the Cameron Highlands Malaysia. Int J Agri Resources, Governance Ecology 2008;7(6): 450-68.
Becker HA, Vanclay F, editors. The International Handbook of Social Impact Assessment: Conceptual and Methodological Advances. Cheltenham: Edward Elgar; 2003.
Berger L. Private sector risk analysis and conflict impact assessment: measuring the reverse flow of risk; 2002. http://www.carleton.ca/ciifp (accessed November 2007).
Besançon C. Peace and Conflict Impact Assessment Briefing Workshop Report. Submitted to the International Gorilla Conservation Programme. Nairobi, Kenya. Published by IGCP Rutengen, Rwanda: Published by IGCP; 2005.
Boyle J. Cultural influences on implementing environmental impact assessment: insights from Thailand, Indonesia, and Malaysia. Environ Impact Asses Rev 1998;18 (1998):116-955.
Bradshaw M, Wood L, Williamson S. Applying qualitative and quantitative research: a social impact assessment of a fishery. Applied Geog 2001;21(1):69–85.
Broadwood J, Sugden N. Community Cohesion Impact Assessment and Community Conflict Prevention Tool. London: Communities and Local Government, Ottawa Queen's Printer; 2008. www.communities.gov.uk.
Buchan D. Buy-in and social capital: by-products of social impact assessment. Impact Assess Proj Apprais 2003;21(3):168–72.
Burdge RJ. The Concepts, Processes and Methods of Social Impact Assessment. Social Ecology Press, Middleton: Social Ecology Press; 2004.
Carment D, Schnabel A, editors. Conflict Prevention From Rhetoric to Reality: vol 2 opportunities and innovations. Lanham: Lexington Books; 2004.
Cavaye J. Integrating Economic and Social Issues in Regional Natural Resource Management Planning: a framework for regional bodies. Department of State Development, Queensland Government: Victoria (Australia); 2003. http://www.nrm.qld.gov.au/regional_planning/nap/priority_docs/pdf/regional_nrm_plan/se_regional_nrm_planning_1.pdf (accessed November 2007).
Cernea M. Putting People First: Sociological Variables in Rural Development. New York: Oxford University Press; 1991.
Chambers RJ. Whose Reality Counts? Putting the First Last. London: Intermediate Technology Publications; 1997.
Chandrasekara WS. Conflict Impact Assessment in Development Projects in Sri Lanka: a case study on Manwanella Communal Tension and Conflict Prevention in the Sataragamura Province. Colombo: Faculty of Arts, University of Colombo; undated.
Chase RS. Supporting communities in transition: the impact of the Armenian Social Investment Fund 2001. World Bank Econ Rep 2002;16:219–40.
CIDA. Peace and Conflict Impact Assessment. Ottawa: Canadian International Development Agency (CIDA); 2004.
Cox G, Dale A, Morrson T. Social assessment and resource management in Australia. In: Dale A, Lane M, editors. Social Assessment in Natural Resource Management Institutions. Collingswood: CSIRO Publishing; 2000. p. 74–82.
Coy PG, Woehrle LM. Social Conflicts and Collective Identities. Lanham: Rowman & Littlefield; 2000.
CPR Network. Peace and Conflict Impact Assessment (PCIA) Handbook. London: Conflict Prevention and Post-Conflict Reconstruction Network; 2005. www.cprnet.net
Cramer JC, Dietz T, Johnston RA. Social impact assessment of regional plans: a review of methods and issues and a recommended process. Policy Sci 2004;12(1):61–82.
Daudelin J. Conflict and development: exploring the links and assessing impacts. Rev N-S Inst Newsl 1999;3(3):1–6.
Esteves AM, Vanclay F. Social development needs analysis as a tool for SIA to guide corporate-community investment: applications in the minerals industry. Environ Impact Assess Rev 2009;29(2009):137-45.
Falk I, Kirkpatrick S. What is social capital? A study of interaction in a rural community. Sociologia Ruralis 2000;40(1):87–110.
Fiaschi D. Natural resources and social conflict: an explanation of sub-Saharan countries stagnation. In: Commendatori P, Salvadori P, Tamberi N, editors. Geography, Structural Change and Economic Development. Cheltenham: Edward Elgar; 2008. p. 66–85.
Gaved M, Anderson B. The impact of local ICT initiatives on social capital and quality of life. Chimera Working Paper 2006-06. Colchester: University of Essex; 2006.
Gilmour AJ, Walkerden G. A structured approach to conflict resolution in EIA: the use of adaptive environmental assessment and management (AEAM). IFIP Trans 1993; B-16:199–210.
Gleditsch NP, editor. Conflict and the Environment. NATO ASA Series 2 Dordrecht: Springer Kluwer Academic; 1996.

Gleditsch NP, Diehl PF, editors. Environmental Conflicts; An Anthology. Boulder: Westview Press; 2001.
Grootaert C, van Bastelaer T. The Role of Social Capital in Development: An Empirical Assessment. Cambridge: Cambridge University Press; 2002.
Harrison J, McDonald T. SIA in a regional development bank: the career of a concept. Impact Assess Proj Apprais 2003;21(3):155–60.
Heikkinen T, Sairinen R. Social Impact Assessment in Regional Land Use Planning – Best Practices from Finland. Stockholm: NORDREGIO, PO Box 1658; 2007.
Hill E, Lowe J. (2007) Regional impact assessment: An Australian Example. Impact Assess Proj Apprais 2007;25(3):189–97.
Hoffman M. Peace and Conflict Impact Assessment Methodology. Vienna: Berghof Research Centre for Constructive Conflict Management; 2001. http://www.berghof-handbook.net (accessed November 2007).
Homer-Dixon TF. On the Threshold: environmental changes as causes of acute conflict. Toronto: Trudeau Centre for Peace and Conflict Studies, University of Toronto; 1991. http://www.library.utoronto.ca/pcs/thresh/thresh1.html (accessed February 2009).
International Alert. Conflict-sensitive business practice: guidance for extractive industries. London: International Alert; 2006. http://www.international-alert.org (accessed November 2007).
IPIECA. A Guide to Social Impact Assessment in the Oil and Gas Industry. London: International Petroleum Industry Environmental Conservation Association; 2004.
Ivanova G, Rolfe J, Lockie S, Timmer V. Assessing social and economic impacts associated with changes in the coal mining industry in the Bowen Basin, Queensland, Australia. Manage Environ Qual 2007;19(2):211–28.
Jackson D, Georgiou S, Crookes S. Social Impact Assessment of the Hickling Broad Conflict. CSERGE Working Paper ECM01-02. Norwich: Centre for Social and Environmental Research on the Global Environment, University of East Anglia; 2001. http://www.cserge/pub/wp/ecm/ecm (accessed November 2007).
Jyväskylä ensuring social integrity through land use planning; 2007. http://www.info.stakes.fi/iva/EEN/examples/jyvasjyla.htm accessed November 2007).
Kingsley G, Melkers J. Value mapping social capital outcomes in state research and development programmes. Eval Model Assess 1999;28(3):165–75.
Kumar Rupesinghe. S.N.A. Civil Wars, Civil Peace: An Introduction to Conflict Research. London: Pluto Press; 1998.
Lane MB, Dale AP, Rickson RE. Sacred land, mineral wealth, and biodiversity at Coronation Hill, Northern Australia: indigenous knowledge and SIA. Impact Assess Proj Apprais 2003;21(2):89–98.
Lockie S. Deliberation and actor-networks: the "practical" implications of social theory for the assessment of large dams and other interventions. Soc Natur Resour 2007;20(9):785–99.
Lockie S, Momtaz S, Taylor B. Meaning and the construction of social impacts: water infrastructure development in Australia's Gladstone/Calliope region. Rural Soc J 2009;9(3):1–5.
MacKay A. Climate and popular unrest in late medieval Castille. In: Wigley TM, Ingram MJ, Farmer G, editors. Climate in History: Studies in Past Climates and their Impact on Man. Cambridge: Cambridge University Press; 1981.
MacSweeney N. Private Sector Development in Post-Conflict Countries: A Review of Current Literature and Practice. Cambridge: DCED; 2008.
Manring NJ, West PC, Bidol P. Social impact assessment and environmental conflict management: potential for integration and application. Environ Impact Assess Rev 1990;10(1990):253–65.
McDonald GT. Theory, methodology and policy: regional economic and social impact assessment. Environ Impact Assess Rev 1990;10(1990):25–36.
McGregor A, Mosley P, Johnson S, Simanowitz A. How can impact assessment take into account wider social and economic impacts? Impact Assessment Working Paper No. 3. Brighton: Institute of Development Studies, University of Sussex; 2000.
Meissen GJ, Cipriani JA. Community psychology and social impact assessment: an action model. American J Commmunity Psychol 1984;12(3):369–86.
Modavi N. The political economy of environmental conflicts: an analytical framework. Int J Conflict Manage 1991;12(1):27–44.
Nath B, Hens L, Compton P, Devuyst D, editors. Environmental Management in Practice: vol 1 instruments for the environmental manager. London: Routledge; 1998.
O'Faircheallaigh C. Making social impact assessment count: a negotiation-based approach for indigenous peoples. Soc Natur Resour 1999;12(1):63–80.
O'Leary R, Bingham LB, editors. The Practice and Performance of Environmental Conflict Resolution. Washington: Resources for the Future; 2003.

O'Reilly, K. Eacott, E. Aboriginal peoples and impact/benefit agreements. Report of a National Workshop, Yellowknife, Northwest Territories, Northern Minerals Programme, Working Paper No. 7. Ottawa: Canadian Arctic Resource Committee (CARC); 1999. www.carc.org/pubs/v25no4/2.htm.
Okoji MA. Social implications of the petroleum oil industry in the Niger Delta. Int J Environ Stud 2002;59(2):197–210.
Percival R. The ecology of environmental conflict: risk, uncertainty, and the transformation of environmental policy disputes. Stud Law Polit Soc 1992;12(2):209–46.
Persson J. Theoretical reflections on the connection between environmental assessment methods and conflict. Environ Impact Assess Rev 2006;26(2006):605–13.
Porter G, Ganapin jnrD. Resources, Population, and the Philippines' Future: a case study. WRI Paper No. 4. Washington: World Resources Institute; 1988.
Putnam R. Bowling Alone: the Collapse and Revival of American Community. New York: Simon & Schuster; 2000.
Randolph J. Environmental Land Use Planning and Management. New York: Island Press; 2004.
Rickson R, Hundloe T, Western J. Impact assessment in conflict situations: World Heritage listings of Queensland's northern tropical rainforests. Impact Assess Bull 1989;18:179–90.
Rolf J, Windle J. Valuing the protection of aboriginal cultural heritage sites. Econ Rec 2003;79:s85–95 June.
Roon T. Globalization of Sakhalin's oil industry: partnership or conflict? A reflection on the Etnolgicheskaia Eksspertiza. Siberica 2006;5(2):95–114.
Rydin Y. Conflict, Consensus, and Rationality in Environmental Planning: an institutional discourse approach. Oxford: Oxford University Press; 2003.
Sander T. Environmental impact statements and their lessons for social capital analysis. Saguaro III Background Readings: Environment & Social Capita. Kennedy School of Government. Cambridge (MA): Harvard University; 1997. http://www.ksg.harvard.edu/saguaro/mfg3.html (accessed November 2007).
Schmelzle B. New Trends in Peace and Conflict Impact Assessment (PCIA). Vienna: Berghof Research Centre for Constructive Conflict Management; 2005. http://www.berghof-handbook.net.
Slootweg R, Vanclay F, van Schooten M. Function evaluation as a framework for the integration of social and environmental impact assessment. Impact Assess Proj Apprais 2001;19(1):19–28.
Spillmann KR, Bächler G, editors Environment and Conflicts Project. ENCOP Occasional Papers. Center for Security Studies, ETH Zurich/Swiss Peace Foundation, Zurich; 2005. www.isn.ethz.ch.
Susskind L, Thomas-Larmer J. Constructing a conflict assessment; 2007. http://web.mit.edu/publicdisputes/practice/cbh_ch2.html (accessed December 2007).
Tang Bo-sin, Wong, Siu-wai, Chi-hong Lau M. Social impact assessment and public participation in China: a case study of land requisition in Guangzhou. Environ Impact Assess Rev 2008;28:57–72.
Taylor CN, Hobson B, Goodrich CG. Social Assessment: Theory, Process and Techniques. 3 rd edn. Middleton: Social Ecology Press; 2004.
Thiranagama S. The Social Impact of Conflict in Sri Lanka. London: Routledge, London; 2009.
UNEP. Understanding Environment, Conflict, and Cooperation. Nairobi: Division of Early Warning and Assessment, United Nations Environment Programme; 2004.
Vanclay F. Social impact assessment. In: Petts J, editor. Handbook of Environmental Impact Assessment, vol. 1. Oxford: Blackwell; 1999. p. 301–26.
Vanclay F. Conceptualising social impacts. Environ Impact Assess Rev 2002;22(2002):181–211.
Vanclay F. International principles for social impact assessment. Impact Assess Proj Apprais 2003;21(1):5–11.
Vanclay F. The triple bottom line and impact assessment: how do TBL, EIA, SIA, SEA and EMS relate to each other? J Environ Assess Policy Manage 2004;6(3):265–88.
Warner M. Conflict Management in Community-Based Natural Resource Projects: Experiences from Fiji and Papua New Guinea. London: Overseas Development Institute; 2000.
Wells V, Licata M, Kempton KA. A Social Impact Assessment on the Lower Hunter Regional Strategy: a guide for documenting a social impact assessment; 2007. (http://www.hiaconnect.edu.au/lower_hunter_regional_strategy.htm (accessed November 2007).
Westman WE. Ecology, Impact Assessment, and Environmental Planning. Chichester: Wiley; 1985.
Williamson A. Social Capital Impact Assessment. New York: Mimeo; 2002.

Part VIII
Case Studies of SIA around the World

Social Transformation in China and the Development of Social Assessment

Bettina Gransow

Since the late 1990s, China has been pursuing a policy of economic expansion with extensive investment in large-scale infrastructure projects. The social side effects of these projects—such as involuntary resettlement—are but the tip of the iceberg of so-called externalities of economic transformation. This paper introduces the background and methodology of social assessment in China and argues that the assessment of social risks in development projects and programmes, undertaken as an integral part of a larger complex of future-oriented sustainability strategies in China, can be analysed as particular 'governmental technologies' in the sense of the Foucauldian school.

Introduction

The transformation of China's former planned economy to a market economy which has been carried out in a politically authoritarian manner has led to (intended) economic growth on the one hand and to (unintended) forms of social disparities and social inequality on the other. A widening gap between urban and rural areas, unbalanced development between different regions, an increasing income gap between the rich and the poor, rural and urban poverty, unemployment and pressing employment issues, resource shortage and a worsening ecological environment, are all developments that are seen as possible challenges to social stability and harmonious growth in China.

After the 16th plenary session of the CPC, the Chinese government started to promote a new 'concept of scientific development' suggesting strategic adjustments with respect to the above mentioned problems. The new development perspective embraces a broader concept of development which includes environmental protection and promotes the slogan 'focus on people' (Hu, 2004). It comes close to the model of sustainable development, in which economic efficiency, social equity, and preservation of nature are considered to be equally significant interests.[1] Sustainability strategies are characterised by the following: they are oriented to future

---

Correspondence to: Professor Dr Bettina Gransow, East Asian Institute, Free University Berlin, Ehrenbergstr 26–28, 14195 Berlin, Germany. E-mail: bgransow@zedat.fu-berlin.de

ISSN 0390-6701 (print)/ISSN 1469-9273 (online) © 2007 University of Rome 'La Sapienza'
DOI: 10.1080/03906700701574321

development options; they view the role of nation states in relation to both supranational and local structures; they are action and agent-oriented to a greater degree; they include those affected in strategy formation and implementation processes. These characteristics have not least of all the consequence that instrumental expert rationality and purely academic analyses decline in significance if they are not combined with forms of social rationality based on the knowledge of local people. As such, sustainability strategies can be understood as ongoing political and social learning processes which are altering traditional political fields (see Beck, 1986, p. 298).

The development of social assessment in China can be seen as part of this broader strategical shift in Chinese development thinking at the beginning of the twenty-first century. This paper explores the development of social assessment in China and argues that the assessment of social risks in development projects and programmes, undertaken as an integral part of a larger complex of future-oriented sustainability strategies, can be analysed as particular 'governmental technologies' in the sense of the Foucauldian school.

Externalities of Economic Transformation: Social and Environmental Risks

China is a rapidly developing society, undergoing a three-fold transformation: from a planned to a market economy, from an agrarian to an industrial/service/information society, and from an isolated to a globalising society. However, this development is not only producing accelerated economic growth, but also accelerated processes that in turn generate new forms of poverty, deeper social polarisation, joblessness, damage to health and the environment, and other negative impacts. Embedded in such a dynamic social environment, the simultaneous occurrence of different types of environmental and social risks produces an extremely complex situation.

Given the fact that nearly half of the Chinese population is still engaged in farming, one could describe Chinese society as featuring agrarian, industrial and post-industrial development stages simultaneously. It is precisely the simultaneity of problems, which in the Western industrial nations occurred sequentially, that is creating highly charged and dynamic risks and uncertainties in Chinese society today. Concerning the environment in China, it has been noted that 'Chinese society ... has to deal all at once with problems that followed each other in the development of the industrial states: with the destruction of resources arising from pre-industrial over-utilisation—deforestation, soil erosion, desertification—and with the strain on the environment from harmful emissions generated by production and consumption' (Betke, 1998, p. 325). One could correspondingly say that China is having to overcome social risks associated with the transition from agrarian to industrial society, and at the same time those arising at the threshold to post-industrial society. Whereas the former are primarily a matter of combating *poverty*, the latter constitute risks that *new technologies* pose for society, requiring a new approach to uncertainty and incalculable results (cf. Evers & Nowotny, 1987).

Social Transformation in China and the Development of Social Assessment 541

Since the late 1990s, China has been pursuing a policy of economic expansion with extensive investment in the country's infrastructure, particularly in the transport, traffic, energy, telecommunications and water supply sectors.[2] New highways and expressways are under construction, and water and air transport networks are being more evenly distributed (Lu, 2000, p. 71ff). This development strategy attaches special significance to a series of large-scale projects, whose enormous magnitude and economic importance make them objects of national prestige on the one hand, but whose technical, environmental and social risks have exposed them to criticism on the other. The most well-known of these is the Three Gorges Dam on the Yangtze River.

As is clearly evident in the case of the Three Gorges project, risk situations exert a mutual effect on each other, and in the process create new side effects. The majority of those living on the banks of the Yangtze and scheduled for resettlement[3] were originally supposed to be moved up the mountainside in order to avoid the risks, problems and costs associated with long-distance resettlement. But environmental legislation stipulating that crops may only be planted on slopes of less than 25 degrees meant that other solutions had to be found, either in the form of non-agricultural employment or in long-distance resettlement. Both these solutions increase the levels of social risk and will in turn produce consequences of their own.

Additional large-scale projects include the railroad line from Golmud to Lhasa, which like the dam is part of the Western Region Development Strategy;[4] a water supply project to pump water from the south of the country to the north where it is in short supply; and a high-speed rail line from Beijing to Shanghai (and Hangzhou). There are also numerous smaller projects in which involuntary resettlement and farmland requisition also take place.[5]

The environmental and social side effects of these projects—those already manifest as well as those that must be feared in the future—are but the tip of the iceberg of so-called externalities of development, i.e., the external costs that have arisen and will continue to arise as a consequence of economic modernisation (cf. Zweig, 2000, p. 121). Destruction of the environment, damage to health, loss of jobs, involuntary resettlement with the potential for widespread impoverishment—all these external costs of Chinese economic development can well be characterised as self-generated social risks of development interventions.

Social Assessment in China: Background and Methodology

The origin of social assessment is closely linked to the institutionalisation of environmental assessment. This was especially evident in the USA, Canada and Australia in the 1980s and 1990s. In the USA, calls for social assessment were first made in connection with the National Environmental Policy Act (1969). Practice has shown that environmental impact can give rise to conditions or even conflicts that require more comprehensive and independent social assessment (Roue & Nakashima, 2002, p. 337).[6] As of the mid 1980s, multilateral development organisations started to require environmental and social assessments before financing development projects. At the beginning, however, these requirements tended to be given lip service only. At the start of the twenty-first century, social assessment has come to refer primarily to a management instrument for implementing sustainable development aims (Barrow, 2000, p. 2ff). This is also true for the development of social assessment in China.

The methodology of social assessment is introduced in a variety of handbooks and manuals. Some of these materials are mainly dealing with social impact assessment (e.g., Finsterbusch *et al.*, 1983; Finsterbusch, 1995; Becker, 1997; Roche, 1999; Barrow, 2000); others present social assessment in the context of social analysis (Social Development Department, 2002), community planning (Branch *et al.*, 1984), participation (Rietbergen-McCracken & Deepa Narayan, 1998) or poverty assessment (ADB, 2001). A more elaborated model of social assessment was introduced in the context of World Bank projects concerned with agricultural reform in central Asia and Turkey (Kudat *et al.*, 2000). It stresses the necessity to undertake social assessment throughout the whole project cycle and highlights four pillars of social assessment: the identification of social development issues, stakeholder identification and participation, institutional and organization issues and social impact monitoring and evaluation.

A two volume handbook on social assessment in investment projects (by Wang *et al.*, 1993 and Guojia, 1997, in Chinese) discusses the role of social assessment in development projects and gives valuable insights into sector specific questions and problems. It stresses social assessment in the preparation stage. As a means to more effectively plan and implement development programmes and projects, social assessment is gaining an ever greater degree of recognition in China. This applies to both joint international as well as internal Chinese operations. This is true not only for projects with explicit social aims (e.g., health and education), but also—and especially—for large-scale infrastructure projects such as the construction of railroads, roads, airports and dams. Beyond the previous rather technocratic understanding of social assessment, a more participatory understanding of the term has been crystallising to an ever greater degree.

The publication entitled 'Investment Projects' Feasibility Studies Guidelines' (Touzi, 2002),[7] confirmed and made an important contribution to establishing a policy and legislative framework for social assessment in China. Along with technical, economic, financial and environmental assessment, the guidelines list social assessment as an important component of investment project feasibility studies. This sent a signal indicating that social assessment, like environmental assessment before it, could well become established within a legislative and institutional framework, and consequently be addressed in practical terms as part of large-scale construction and technical co-operation projects.

The number of projects that have had positive experiences with social evaluation and participatory approaches is increasing. Some ministries, such as those in charge of water systems and railroads, have begun to apply sector-specific guidelines for social assessment. Of at least as much importance have been the practical experience and the hard lessons drawn from projects for which there have been no social assessment and in which the neglect of this dimension has led to health and environmental damage, impoverishment, social dissatisfaction, and gender-specific discrimination, which in turn impeded project implementation and generated additional costs. Protests on the part of the increasingly rights-conscious Chinese people are on the rise in rural as well as urban areas.

The NDRC guidelines request social assessment to be an integral part of project assessment. They describe the areas of application and the basic methodology. This is not merely a matter of establishing international standards within China, but also—as can be seen in many areas connected with China's joining the World Trade Organisation—of creating new legal regulations and institutional infrastructures that should function as indirect instruments of control compensating for an anticipated (further) decline in state control on economic operations. The guidelines consider social assessment necessary for investment projects that entail complex social factors, long-term social impact, notable social benefits, prominent social conflicts and/or major social risks. On the one hand, the guidelines refer primarily to projects involving large-scale resettlement or requisition of agricultural land such as transportation, key water conservation or mining and oil field projects; on the other hand, they also apply to poverty alleviation projects with rather explicit public benefits, such as development projects in agricultural areas or projects involving education and public health.

Social assessment requirements in feasibility studies consist of three parts. The first part defines the role and scope of social assessment, the second part introduces the major components of social assessment, and the third part gives an overview of procedures and techniques for social assessment. The Guidelines require that social assessment include a social impact analysis, an analysis of the mutual adaptability of the project and its regional social environment, and a social risk analysis.

The social impact analysis consists primarily of a study on how the project will affect local residents' income, a study of its impact on their standard of living and quality of life, an analysis of consequences for local employment, a section on the differing impact on various stakeholder groups, a study on how the project will affect the interests of disadvantaged groups in the area, an analysis of the impact on local culture, education and public health, a section on how local infrastructure and social service capacities will be affected, and an analysis of the impact on customs and religious beliefs of local ethnic minorities.

Analysis of the mutual suitability of a project and its regional social environment will generally consist of investigating and forecasting different interest groups' attitudes towards the project construction and operation and the degree to which these groups can be expected to become involved, with the aim of selecting a participatory method that can guarantee the success of the project. It will also assess and forecast the attitude of local organisations at various levels so as to determine in which regard and to what extent they are likely to support and co-operate with the project; and it will examine whether or not locally available technology and the local culture fit in with the project design in order to ensure sustainable development.

Social risk analysis is concerned with various social factors that might have a comprehensive and enduring impact on the project and thus represent a possible source of ethnic or religious conflict. It attempts to determine the social conditions and settings which could give rise to social risk and to design mitigating measures for these.

Social assessment guidelines are an important step on the way towards establishing a legislative and policy framework for social assessment in China. They can contribute to increasing the transparency of government procedures while helping to avoid or at least mitigate negative social impacts of project design. Nevertheless, the following measures seem necessary: *first*, to supplement those guidelines referring solely to the early stages of project planning with appropriate guidelines for the project implementation phase; *second*, to more clearly emphasise that alleviating poverty (or avoiding impoverishment arising from project interventions) is an integral part of the project aims; *third*, to accord more weight to gender-specific repercussions of projects and their consequences; and *fourth*, to create the necessary infrastructure for implementing the guidelines in the form of sector-specific guidelines, educational and research institutions, training courses, teaching materials and skilled personnel.

In 2004, the Chinese International Engineering Consulting Company published a social assessment manual describing in detail how to do social assessment in investment projects with a focus on participation of project affected men and women, especially poor and marginalized groups such as minority people and resettlers (Zhongguo, 2004). The manual considers social assessment as a strategic and action-oriented tool for project assessment. It puts forward the following as the main tasks for social assessment: identification and calculation of possible social impacts resulting from the project; identification of factors that could give rise to latent social risks; determination of specific social targets in relation to specific groups of project beneficiaries and project affected people, including gender and minority issues; identification of the contribution of the project to poverty alleviation; identification of opportunities to use participatory development strategies; suggestions for avoiding or reducing negative impacts.

The manual stresses the need for comprehensive, systematic social assessment throughout the project cycle, listing specific requirements for every project phase; it puts particular emphasis on the significance of social monitoring and evaluation in the implementation phase. It starts with a description of the current situation of social assessment in China, the development of research and practical application, its achievements, shortcomings and needs, such as social assessment regulations, institutions, procedures and trained personnel. The next chapter presents the methodological framework of social assessment and sets forth the objectives and the scope of social assessment, its characteristics in different project phases, and the main indicators and methods used. Building on this, the manual presents a participatory approach to social assessment and its methods and, from the perspective of stakeholder participation, discusses participatory methods, tools, and techniques. The following chapters deal with social assessment from the perspective of specific target groups, namely the poor, men and women, minority nationalities, and people affected by resettlement. Each chapter gives an account of the basic framework, including China's strategies and policies on gender equality, poverty reduction, minority issues and resettlement, and discusses the relevant analysis and planning methodologies as part of the project cycle. Finally, it discusses the characteristics of social assessment in different industry sectors. In addition, the appendix presents documents, case studies, research tools and an English–Chinese glossary of social assessment key terms.

In a certain sense, social assessment itself has gone through a learning process which is reflected in China and which shows that it should be performed throughout all phases of the project cycle, i.e., identification, preparation, and implementation. In the beginning, social assessment was performed as a *post evaluation* strategy. In such cases, however, it was not possible to intervene in the project proceedings and influence the design, but only to determine and evaluate the consequences ex post facto. Here it also became evident that the more time that had transpired since the project took place, the more difficult it was to determine which consequences could be ascribed to the project itself and which to other influences external to the project. The conclusion was drawn that in the interest of *early warning and preventive measures*, it was necessary to start social assessment at the earliest possible stage of the project cycle, in order to influence project design so as to avoid or reduce potential negative consequences. However, this approach was quickly recognised to be insufficient. For one thing, there was a danger that concrete recommendations existed only on paper and might not be implemented, perhaps because they were not feasible, or they could not be monitored, or because the necessary funds simply were not available. Because a project's social consequences, planned or otherwise, might not be evident until well into the implementation phase, unintended consequences are a quite normal occurrence during the implementation phase. Chain reactions can be set off and synergy effects activated, with the project area then displaying an increased speed and dynamic in social development that was difficult to foresee beforehand. The measures proposed in the preparation phase therefore need to be reworked in the *implementation* phase with the help of appropriate information and communication strategies and a corresponding monitoring process for these measures. Based on these experiences, the conviction has been strengthening that social assessment should be applied throughout all the main project phases.

Lessons from a Case Study: Social Assessment in a Chinese Railway Project

A full appreciation of the social dimensions and social dynamics of development interventions will require us to look beyond the so-called facts and figures and develop a deeper and more sensitive appreciation of the complexity of development processes, their structures and dynamics. This becomes clearer from an examination of case study material such as the following example of a Chinese railway project.[8]

Project Objectives and Project Area

The primary objective of the project was to promote economic growth by providing the necessary transport infrastructure in the project area. Poverty reduction was defined as a secondary project objective. It was to be achieved by creating new jobs for poor people, increasing incomes and providing access to basic education, health, communications, agricultural extension, and credit facilities. Thus, the living conditions should be improved and over 92,000 people or 40% of those living in the project area should be lifted out of poverty.

The project was located in a poor, mountainous region in the Southwest of China. It involved the construction and operation of a new 128.5-km railway line with 15 stations, 118 bridges and 72 tunnels. Construction began in the second half of 1998 and was finished by the end of 2002. The population in the project area is predominantly rural. It increased from 2 million in 1996 to 2.8 million in 2000. The rural per capita income in this region was ¥546 in 1996, only 10% of the national average. The project area has several coal mines and is rich in coal reserves. The exploitation of coal and other natural resources has been limited by insufficient transport infrastructure. The project was expected to allow the transport of coal to energy-deficient areas in neighbouring provinces. This, it was assumed, would facilitate the development of related industries, creating employment and income-generating opportunities that would help to reduce poverty.

Resettlement

The railway route was selected with the objective of technical suitability, while avoiding involuntary resettlement wherever feasible and minimizing such resettlement where population displacement was unavoidable. A resettlement plan was prepared ensuring that project-affected persons received assistance, so that they should be at least as well-off as they would have been in the absence of the project. If necessary, affected persons, particularly households headed by women, would be given additional assistance (as provided for under the Chinese land administration law) in order to restore income. The resettlement plan aimed at restoring the incomes of the resettled people with the minimum possible disruption to their economic and social environment. By the end of 2000, a total of 508 ha of land had been permanently acquired and an additional 150 ha of land were required for temporary use during construction; 882 households had been resettled.

The cost of land acquisition and resettlement were included in the project estimates. The compensation fees have all been paid in cash. No land redistribution or readjustment has been made. To restore and raise the income of the affected people the local governments have taken up the following measures: (1) increasing employment opportunities, (2) providing more loans and credits for poverty reduction programs, (3) helping to improve cultivation technologies, and (4) improving infrastructure.

The affected households have been resettled in different ways: one was scattered resettlement within original villages. This involved moving from the original houses to new house plots within the same village. If the new house was built on contracted land, the household got the old-house compensation fees, if not the village collective owned the compensation fees. Another way was the establishment of resettlement villages or resettlement towns. These were new villages and towns built for relocatees. For this kind of resettlement, infrastructure (such as water, power and roads) was provided and land-use programs worked out.

Land requisition for some of the affected households meant that they lost their land resources forever; though the households whose land was taken got some cash compensation preventing them from having any serious difficulties in the short term. In the long run, however, these families would tend to have problems with poverty unless they were able to find stable, non-rural employment or engage in private enterprise activity after land requisition. It is these poverty-stricken households, including elderly families and families with more women, who have fewer opportunities for non-rural employment and less capacity for opening up their own businesses. The loss of land had serious effects on poverty-stricken households, aged families, and single-mother families.

Obviously those whose land had been acquired and who moved were likely to suffer more long-term impacts than people who were simply resettled to another place nearby. Some relocated families only received small sums of compensation because their housing was in poor condition. They had to borrow money to build new houses, but were not able to pay the money back, particularly those whose land was acquired in its entirety or to a large extent, and who were unable to find other ways to make a viable livelihood. They were especially at risk of sliding into a cycle of poverty.

Poverty

Many people along the new railway depended on their land to make a living, with few opportunities for non-agricultural employment. Until the end of 2000, 55% of the workers hired under the project were local unskilled workers who had lived below the poverty line (according to the international poverty line of 1 US$ per day). They received monthly wages of ¥500. In the last quarter of 1998, there were 9,423 workers, this number decreased constantly to 4,212 by the last quarter of 2000 as the railway line approached completion.

The short-term effect of the new railway on local poverty was that it provided immediate and stable opportunities for employment for the poverty-stricken population during project construction as well as providing further employment opportunities through opening the way for railway-related service industries, construction materials industries and transportation. With increased opportunities in non-rural areas and increased income, many of those who were under the poverty line found themselves able to get out from under.

From 1998 to 2000, the poverty line in rural areas in China was set at 235–635 *yuan*. The standard for poverty alleviation set in the project area was 650 *yuan* net income per person, and 650 *jin* of grain per person. The annual income of the workers mentioned above, 4,350 *yuan*, was enough for any of these poor households to move to the other side of the poverty line. But two prerequisites were needed to reach the objective of true poverty alleviation. First, local skilled workers must be from the poorer families, and second, the poorer families must have stable opportunities for employment. Their annual working income must be sufficient for the per capita income of the household to exceed the poverty line.

According to the national poverty standards, 25% of the total population living in the railway area were living under the poverty line. Without special policies and measures, it would be impossible to draw most or all of the local unskilled labor force from this 25%, of families with the lowest incomes. However, the situation would be quite different if a higher poverty line was adopted.[9]

Gender Issues

It was estimated that 40–60% of household income in the project area was derived from activities performed by women. The socio-economic survey indicated that women headed 20% of households in the project area. They contribute significantly to agricultural production and raising livestock, fetching water and fuel, and played a major role in household management. Illiteracy among women was about 70%. Women also faced major health problems because of the absence of health services.

It was assumed that the railway would increase the flow of male labor to seek work elsewhere, and so accelerate the 'feminization of agriculture' in rural areas. This seems to be true for married women, whereas in most places with out-migration the unmarried young women between 16 and 24 are also leaving to look for work. In places where the husbands are already going out for work, married women are increasingly responsible for agriculture. Thus, they are more directly affected by the challenge of land acquisition.

In 1998, small credits were given to eight women-headed minority households who were affected by the project. In 1999, with the construction of the railway, as well as access and link roads, on monthly average, 1,103 unskilled women workers were employed (equivalent to 10% of the total number of unskilled workers). At the same time 1,826 women in the project area took up jobs in trades and services. More employment for women than expected was provided in trades and services relating to the migrant construction workers. There were also cases where local women married migrant construction workers or went away with them.

Project-induced resettlements presented a particular problem for women-headed households. Under normal to favorable conditions, adequate compensation payments would enable the construction of an equally valuable or better house. But women-headed households are frequently among the poorest households. Usually, the compensation for poor housing was not high and they were not able to draw upon savings necessary for building a new house. In addition, women-headed households often lacked the labor which could assist with building a house. It was much more difficult for women-headed households to activate the neighborhood social networks that could support them with construction, since, as a result of patrilocal traditions, they generally did not come from the same village in which they lived. For the same reason, it was difficult for women-headed households to provide reciprocal services for a project such as building a house, as was customary among men long established in the area. In general, women-headed households did not have the necessary materials or social capital at their disposal that would be necessary to take advantage of the resettlement situation.

Minority Issues

Access to technology and knowledge during the construction of the railway line not only provided people living along the new railway line with better job opportunities and rising incomes, but also provided them with access to new skills by way of interaction with the construction company and migrant workers. Minority households living in remote areas are often not used to taking their pigs and chickens to the local markets. The arrival of the railway construction teams led to increasing prices and attracted them to trade in markets and to produce more than before. As some villagers were afraid to look for jobs outside their home town, they were encouraged by the development taking place on their doorstep. Ethnic minorities were among those who were benefiting from the railway construction. Minority women started to learn Chinese because of their increased market activities and communication with the migrant construction workers.

However, not all experiences were positive. In a minority village, where different nationalities (Yi, Miao, Han, Bai and Mongol people) live together, many families spent all their compensation money on building new houses. Those who were better off could engage in small business, but others could not find work after the railway line was completed. An ethnic Miao with five brothers who got married and had children, received no additional land via land adjustment. The brothers had divided the family property and lived separately, therefore the compensation money for each of them was less than it would have been without division. They were not able to engage in any business other than agriculture, and all of them had difficulties in adapting to the new situation.

Intended and Unintended Social Impacts

The most obvious and biggest benefits that the new railway has brought to the communities on the railway line is in the small roads that have improved local transportation. The project built altogether 298 km of small roads and connected 265 km of main and trunk roads with 33 km of connecting roads. The next major effect was in the improvement of drinking water in many villages. Since the construction project needed to draw water to construction sites, villages nearby the sites could use their facilities to draw water for themselves. Water diversion in the towns on the railway line was 17% higher than in other areas of this county. The third effect, railway construction gave some villages access to electricity and thus improved conditions in rural households. Possible negative effects of the new railway which were not expected or were not given sufficient consideration during the preparatory phase of the project were mainly the following: broken roads, issues involving land utilized beyond the red line and drinking water problems.

Original roads being broken or cut off during the construction of the railway and highways was a common occurrence. If this problem was not handled properly, the effects on the lives and work of the inhabitants of these rural areas could be profound. These effects are usually magnified when those affected are fragile and poverty-bound groups such as the elderly, the disabled, and children. There were quite a few roads that were cut off and not properly restored. This has resulted in serious negative effects on the life and livelihood of nearby residents. In one village, for example, there used to be a small road connecting the village with the town. The nearest household was one kilometer away from the town headquarter, so this road made travel to and from the market and the school very convenient for children and other villagers. After the railway construction, the original road was cut off and the railway company built another road to the town headquarters which was less convenient. The new road was not only longer (4 km to the town headquarters), but also very steep. Children in the local area had to walk 4 km up and down hills to go to school every day; this has become the most intense issue voiced by the affected villagers. It has become significantly more difficult for the elderly and the disabled to get to the market at all. Since the road is steep and trucks with heavy loads cannot climb the hills, fruit sales in 2001 were greatly affected and incomes dropped.

The lands outside the red line which were covered during construction without compensation being paid, have been another source of contention during the construction of the railway. Because the project area was mostly mountainous and slopes are steep, it is hard to guarantee that sand and stones will stay inside the red line during construction. Particularly in the rainy season, landslides are common in these areas, and the construction has therefore inadvertently caused some lands outside the red lines, including even small roads, to be covered up.

The problem of potable water resulting from original water sources being cut off by railway construction has also been discussed. Sources are cut off or have dried up as a result of construction, and new water has not been found in sufficient quantities or in time to replace the old. This problem has not been mentioned as frequently as the others, but villagers in parts of the mountainous areas especially have raised the issue.

Short- and Long-term Effects

The short-term effect that the railway project had on poverty alleviation was in the creation of thousands of employment opportunities. Judged by international standards of poverty, these opportunities have been taken up mainly by poverty-stricken people. Those families who benefited from railway construction could overcome their poverty status with the help of wage income from their work on the railway.

There was much more short-term employment gain than long-term employment opportunities. Short-term employment was in road construction and the provision of services for migrant workers on the construction site rather than in railway construction itself. As construction worker teams are usually supplied by contractors from all over the country and the maintenance of the railway is carried out by skilled workers of the railway itself, there were not many employment opportunities for the unskilled local labor force in the construction of the railway itself. The idea of long-term employment in the production and transport of coal could not be realized as it ran counter to the national policy of closing down small coal mines due to a high rate of accidents. The local government had to face the challenge of transforming the short-term economic and social benefits into a long-term strategy of regional economic and social sustainability. Ideas of how to promote tourism in the region were discussed as one possibility to use the now more and more empty rooms local people had rented to construction workers.

As direct opportunities for employment decreased drastically after the construction of the railway was completed, and the migrant construction workers had left, the wage income of local rural families began to decrease. Whether the increase of wage income for local people during the railway construction can continue after completion will mainly depend on regional economic development and the employment opportunities created for poor and resettled people.

Social Impacts in Different Local Settings

Impacts varied according to the different local settings. In towns and cities more employment opportunities were available and the compensation rates were higher than in the villages along the railway. Some places were very capable of boosting regional development. Other local governments were not sufficiently farsighted to use the construction of the railway to develop their local economy. Different social and economic conditions showed different effects of the railway project.

There was much more mobility, social dynamics and exchange involved in the process of implementation of the project than was anticipated. Migrant workers as well as business people from outside were coming into the region, the possibilities for young people to go out for work were widening, some girls were marrying migrant workers, the opportunities and frequency of communication with people from outside were increasing and new ideas were flooding into the area.

In many cases households affected by land acquisition and resettled households in railway projects used their compensation money to rebuild their houses on a larger scale than before. They then normally lacked money to invest in small businesses which was more characteristic of business people from outside. But with the end of the construction process the commercial environment began to change, businesses declined and investors from outside began to withdraw. In summary, there were good opportunities during the construction phase to make a living by renting rooms to migrant construction workers, open small restaurants or karaoke bars. People compensated for their land or houses become landlords or landladies and rented rooms to people from outside the community—this is a pattern nowadays frequently to be observed in China.

This example shows clearly that the same project may have very different impacts on different social groups of project affected people, on different commmunities and in different local settings as well as in the context of short-term or long-term perspectives. In addition, projects and project management has to be seen as embedded in specific power relations and specific ways in which these power relations are exercised.

Assessing Social Risks. A Governmental Technology

Drawing on the orientation of the 'governmentality literature' and Michel Foucault's work, this paper treats social assessment as a form of calculative rationality. Foucault discusses the 'governmentality of the state' as a process of mutual constitution of the exercise of sovereignty over subjects and forms of knowledge (Foucault, 1991). His notion of government and the 'governmentality studies' which came into existence in the early 1990s 'displaces a concern for 'the state' onto the plurality of governing bodies and the practices, techniques and rationalities through which governing is accomplished and authority exercised' (Dean, 1998, p. 26). Social assessment can therefore be seen as a particular governmental technology which—instead of neglecting social risks—aims at making them a predictable, identifiable, quantifiable and calculable reality. It may in fact represent at least two different types of governmental technology: from above (technologies of the state) and from below (technologies of citizenship) (Dean, 1998, p. 35; Lemke, 2000, pp. 33, 36). These different approaches are manifested in the institutional framework of project organisation.

To start with, social risks are risks from the perspective of a project's decision-makers. They are concerned with possible obstacles to the project or delays that may cause budget constraints. From the perspective of those negatively affected, on the other hand, social risks are experienced as external dangers. The perception of social risks by different project stakeholders may differ widely. They may or may not participate in decision-making processes. Depending on specific impacts (or specific ways in which these impacts are perceived), project affected people will perceive social risks differently.

Social Transformation in China and the Development of Social Assessment 553

Let us take the example of roads bisected by a new railway and thus rendered impassable. In the absence of tunnels or bridges, peasants can be hindered in accessing their fields, or national minority peoples may now have difficulties reaching specific cultural sites. Children might have to take a much longer route to school, which can induce anxiety in them or their mothers. The elderly or people carrying loads on their backs may find it harder to get to the markets. Women fetching water might be affected, and so on. Different perceptions here depend on a gender-specific division of labour and different modes of using inner and outer spaces. Thus, risk does not have but a single objective and scientific definition, but rather a variety of definitions stressing the objective or subjective aspects of a project intervention to different degrees. Experts and project owners will probably utilise a different rationality than that of the project affected people.

Impoverishment as a consequence of project-induced farmland requisition and involuntary resettlement is one of the most deep-reaching social risks of project interventions. When local residents have to be resettled for an infrastructure project, those that can afford it endeavour to take the opportunity and combine their savings with the compensation money, which can be relatively low as well as delayed in payment, in order to build a larger and better house. Sometimes the opportunity is taken to split the household and to build two houses, one with the compensation money and the other with construction materials taken from the old house. If the new houses are located on what will become a shopping street or across from where a station will be built, additional economic benefits can be expected. Those people, however, who had only small dwellings and therefore received only a slight amount of compensation and who also did not have any significant savings were not in a position to use resettlement measures to their benefit. They will probably have to borrow money for house construction and possibly run into debt.

If affected households use their savings to build new and better houses, this also can represent a social risk because the reserves intended for social security are now no longer available in the event of illness or other unforeseen events. Thus, their standard of living may rise while their quality of life (in terms of social security) declines. Their lives are now less secure (cf. Li, 2000, p. 246ff). Nevertheless, these are examples of risks that the household undertakes of its own accord—in contrast to the resettlement situation as such, in which those affected have not made the decision themselves but rather had the new social dangers imposed upon them. This illustrates Niklas Luhmann's argument that social risks and social dangers cannot be clearly isolated from one another (Luhmann, 1991, p. 117)

When farmland is taken over for construction projects, those whose technical and social skills mean that they are not primarily dependent on the land or who have already made the transition from agricultural to non-agricultural employment will more easily be able to master the loss of land than those whose subsistence depends on farming, e.g., for reasons of age or lack of education. These are precisely the people who can end up in extremely perilous situations if they are not in a position to establish new livelihoods. Women in agrarian areas are often particularly affected by the requisition of farmland because many farming families display a gender-specific division of labour, with the husbands tending to pursue non-agricultural activities and their wives working the fields.

From the perspective of 'governmentality literature', it is argued that the analysis of risk must rid itself of the opposition between the calculable and the incalculable and instead must understand those practices, techniques and rationalities that seek to make the incalculable calculable, and the different ways they do so. As Mitchell Dean puts it, 'What is important about risk is not risk itself, but the forms of knowledge that make it thinkable from statistics, sociology, and epidemiology to management and accounting, the techniques that discover it from the calculus of probabilities to the interview, the social technologies that seek to govern it from risk screening, case-management and social insurance to situational crime prevention, and the political rationalities and programmes that deploy it, from those that dreamt of a welfare state to those that imagine an advanced liberal society of prudential individuals and communities' (Dean, 1998, p. 25).

If risk is seen as a form of calculative rationality for governing the conduct of individuals and populations, then social assessment can be defined as a specific mode of calculating social risks. Social assessment in China focuses on the impact and risks associated with development projects and programmes, with special attention devoted to the consequences of land acquisition and resettlement. Which kind of knowledge is needed in social assessment? The ways in which social risks are defined constitute the ways in which government is exercised, at least to a certain extent. This becomes clearer from looking at China's experience with infrastructure projects.

The very process of generating (new) knowledge about social impact and risks, i.e., the question of whose knowledge and needs are included or excluded in this process, is not only decisive for defining and assessing social risks, but also represents certain specific governmental technologies.[10] A preliminary typology of governmental technologies of social assessment in China comprises paternalistic, neo-liberal and participatory approaches.

Paternalistic approaches: local cadres responsible for resettlement activities are frequently of the opinion that they know best how to define risks and counter-measures for the local population. The male-dominated social hierarchies in which resettlement activities are embedded may lead to the neglect of local knowledge crucial for formulating an inclusive framework for assessing and managing social risks. A typical example can be taken from a transportation project where resettled households—already relocated several times—were compensated with comparably large new houses, whereby, however, the area of the house plot was reduced. Since the women were not questioned during the design stage of the project, it was only discovered during the project implementation that women from the resettled households were discontent because they no longer had sufficient land space for raising chickens and pigs—and this had been their primary source of income.

Neo-liberal approaches: compensation paid to the rural collective or the individual household constitutes specific patterns of responsibility transferred from the state to the collective or individual. Here the changing understanding of risk is a function of the transformation in modalities of governing. This approach comes closest to the concerns of governmentality studies (Lemke, 2000, p. 37).

Participatory approaches: participatory approaches may pursue and serve very different objectives in project management. On the one hand, they may be seen as an instrument for realising project objectives more smoothly by informing the public and the affected people. On the other hand, they may be viewed as an obstacle to implementing project objectives. Participation may be seen as an instrument for achieving transparency and public participation which will foster acceptance of the project, or as a Trojan horse that might introduce unwanted aspects of grass-roots democracy. In any case, by combining expert knowledge with the local knowledge of project affected people, as well as combining scientific knowledge with social rationality, social assessment can help identify and define social risks, avoid or reduce undesirable side effects, and anchor alternative development options in the design of projects and programmes.

Discussion

Social assessment is still in its infancy and much time is needed before the necessary legal and institutional conditions, bases for research, and human resources can be put into place. Comprehensive application of social assessment, however, can make development interventions more goal-oriented and better adapted to their respective social environments, and it can contribute to steering the benefits and resources of projects and programmes in such a manner that poor, vulnerable and marginalised groups can be specifically supported. Increased calculability and greater targeting accuracy are paradoxically achieved by combining quantitative with qualitative and participatory methods, which, from the standpoint of traditional social research, are pejoratively labelled 'fuzzy', or worse yet, 'unscientific'. PRA methods,[11] as frequently applied in project assessments, are considered 'quick and dirty' (Chambers, 1995, p. 518ff). But they provide social assessment practitioners with valuable insights, just as the blurred quality of a photo can offer evidence of authenticity (Ullrich, 2002, p. 90ff). Assessment of social risks needs to address both objective and subjective factors. As such it does not come without bias (see Douglas & Wildavsky, 1982, p. 67f.).

Experience with social assessment in national and international projects in China has thus far shown that the outlines of a new type of connection between academic and social rationality are beginning to appear, combining objective and subjective forms of action-oriented knowledge. Social analysis here anticipates options for addressing contingent developments. Social assessment must remain open for unforeseen events and prepared to address them in an innovative and improvisational manner. On account of its anticipatory components, its orientation toward changes in its field of research, and the participatory integration of specific target groups, social assessment cannot simply be equated with applied social research. Participatory

556   B. Gransow

social assessment (even if performed in an overall administrative environment that is predominately paternalistic) engenders new forms of collaboration, new forms of dialogue between experts, practitioners, policy-makers and local people. Social assessment as part of sustainability strategies weighs risks and dangers in order to anticipate or seek to avoid developments that have not yet transpired; and only thus can it gain significance as an action-oriented instrument of contingent development, and enable adequate measures to be implemented within the given spatial, temporal and financial limitations.

Notes

[1]   This model was agreed upon at the 1992 World Environmental and Development Summit in Rio de Janeiro. It was also incorporated into the Millennium Development Goals passed by the UN General Assembly in September of 2000. (http://www.developmentgoals.org/ 5 April 2003). The WTO preamble also lists sustainable development as one of its fundamental aims (Damian & Graz, 2001, pp. 597, 600).
[2]   This paragraph draws on Gransow 2003, p. 30, 36.
[3]   Official estimates for the Three Gorges project alone call for involuntary resettlement of at least 1.13 million people (Three Gorges Project: 25). Unofficial estimates suggest 2.5 million people to be resettled (Wang, 1997, p. 351).
[4]   The Western region development strategy started at the end of the 1990s and aims at accelerating the development of the Western and central provinces of China with priority given to minority and boarder areas, including the objective of further poverty reduction and integration of minority needs in the design and implementation of this strategy.
[5]   Since the People's Republic of China was founded, around 45 million people have been resettled to make room for construction projects. These also include 12 million farmers moved for dams. Since the 1990s the percentage of urban projects is on the rise (Asian Development Bank, 1999, p. 1, table 1.1.).
[6]   The energy crisis of the 1970s, for example, prompted the US government to exploit coal, oil and uranium reserves on Native American reservations, which in turn led to protests.
[7]   The Guidelines were approved by the National Development and Reform Commission (NDRC—former State Development and Planning Commission) in 2001 and released in the spring of 2002.
[8]   The following section is drawing on Gransow (2002).
[9]   The poverty line in China is two-thirds of the international standard set by the World Bank, that is, one dollar per day per person (calculated according to average purchasing power). According to this standard, China's poverty line should be around 1,000 *yuan*.
[10] This paragraph draws on Gransow 2003, p. 39.
[11] PRA stands for participatory rural assessment, participatory rapid appraisal, or variations thereon.

References

Asian Development Bank (1999) RETA 5781: *China Resettlement Policies and Practises. Review and Recommendations*, prepared by National Research Center for Resettlement (NRCR) at Hohai University, Nanjing.
Asian Development Bank (2001) *Handbook for Poverty and Social Analysis*. A Working Document (Manila).
Barrow, C. J. (2000) *Social Impact Assessment. An Introduction*, Oxford University Press, London.

Social Transformation in China and the Development of Social Assessment 557

Beck, U. (1986) *Risikogesellschaft. Auf dem Weg in eine andere Moderne*, edition suhrkamp, Frankfurt am Main.

Becker, H. (1997) *Social Impact Assessment: Method and Experience in Europe, North America and the Developing World*, UCL Press, London.

Betke, D. (1998) 'Umweltkrise und Umweltpolitik', in *Laenderbericht China*, eds C. Herrmann-Pillath & M. Lackner, Bundeszentrale für Politische Bildung, Bonn, pp. 325–357.

Branch, K., Hooper, D. A., Thompson, J. & Creighton, J. (1984) *Guide to Social Assessment. A Framework for Assessing Social Change*, Westview Press, Boulder, CO.

Chambers, R. (1995) 'Shortcut and participatory methods for gaining social information for projects', in *Putting People First. Sociological Variables in Rural Development*, ed. M. Cernea 2nd edn, The World Bank, Washington, DC, pp. 515–537.

Damian, M. & Graz, J. C. (2001) 'The World Trade Organization, the environment, and the ecological critique', *International Social Science Journal*, vol. 53, no. 170 (December), pp. 597–610.

Dean, M. (1998) 'Risk, calculable and incalculable', *Soziale Welt*, vol. 49, pp. 25–42.

Douglas, M. & Wildavsky, A. (1982) *Risk and Culture. An Essay on the Selection of Technical and Ecological Dangers*, University of California Press, Berkeley, CA.

Evers, A. & Nowotny, H. (1987) *Ueber den Umgang mit Unsicherheit. Die Entdeckung der Gestaltbarkeit von Gesellschaft*, Suhrkamp, Frankfurt am Main.

Finsterbusch, K. (1995) 'In praise of SIA: a personal review of the field of social impact assessment: evaluation, role, history, practice, methods, issues and future', *Impact Assessment*, vol. 13, no. 3, pp. 229–252.

Finsterbusch, K., Llewellyn, L. G. & Wolf, C. P (eds)(1983) *Social Impact Assessment Methods*, Sage, Los Angeles, CA.

Foucault, M. (1991) 'Governmentality', in *The Foucault Effect. Studies in Governmentality with two lectures by and an interview with Michel Foucault*, (eds) G. Burchell, C. Gordon, & P. Miller, Harvester Wheatsheaf, Hemel Hemstead, pp. 87–104.

Gransow, B. (2002) 'Yimin anzhi de shehui pingjia' (Social Assessment of Resettlement in Development Projects), in *Yimin yu shehui fazhan. Guoji yantaohui lunwenji* (Proceedings of International Symposium on Resettlement and Social Development), eds C. L. Tang & G. Q. Shi, Hehai University Press, Nanjing, pp. 647–654.

Gransow, B. (2003) 'Social assessment in China—Action learning for the risk society?', *Berliner China-Hefte*, no. 25 (October), pp. 30–43.

Guojia jiwei touzi yanjiusuo, jianshebu biaozhun ding'e yanjiusuo (Investment Institute of State Development and Planning Commission and Institute of Standards and Norms of the Ministry of Construction) (1997), ed. *Touzi xiangmu shehui pingjia zhinan (Guidelines on social assessment in investment projects)* Beijing, Economic Management Press.

Hu, A. G. (2004) *Zhongguo: Xin fazhanguan (China: New Development Strategy)*, Zhejiang People's Press, Hangzhou.

Kudat, A., Peabody, S. & Keyder, C. (2000) *Social Assessment and Agricultural Reform in Central Asia and Turkey*, World Bank, Washington, DC.

Lemke, T. (2000) 'Neoliberalismus, Staat und Selbsttechnologien. Ein kritischer Überblick über die governmentality studies', *Politische Vierteljahresschrift 1*, vol. 41, pp. 31–47.

Li, H. M. (2000) *Population Displacement and Resettlement in the Three Gorges Reservoir Area of the Yangtze River Central China*, Ph.D. Thesis University of Leeds.

Lu, J. R. (2000) 'China's Experience in Utilizing ODA and APEC Development Cooperation', in *Social Sciences: Chinese Academy of Social Sciences Forum*, ed. Foreign Affairs Bureau CASS, Beijing, pp. 55–83.

Luhmann, N. (1991) *Soziologie des Risikos*, de Gruyter, Berlin and New York.

Rietbergen-McCracken, J. & Deepa Narayan (1998) *Participation and Social Assessment. Tools and Techniques*, The World Bank, Washington, DC.

558 B. Gransow

Roche, C. (1999) *Impact Assessment for Development Agencies. Learning to Value Change*, Oxfam, Oxford.
Roue, M. & Nakashima, D. (2002) 'Knowledge and foresight: the predictive capacity of traditional knowledge applied to environmental assessment', in *International Social Science Journal* (Blackwell Publishing/UNESCO) No. 173 (Indigenous knowledge), (September) pp. 337–347.
Social Development Department, The World Bank (2002) *Social Analysis Sourcebook: Incorporating Social Dimensions into Bank-supported Projects* (Working draft, August 7).
Three Gorges Project, by China Yangtze Three Gorges Project Development Corporation (CTGPC), (undated—2002) 36 pp.
Touzi xiangmu kexingxing yanjiu zhinan bianxiezu (Guideline for Investment Project Feasibility Study. Compiled by the Compiling Group) (2002) *Touzi xiangmu kexingxing yanjiu zhinan Beijing (Guideline for Investment Project Feasibility Study)*, China Electric Power Press (Two volumes: Chinese and English).
Ullrich, W. (2002) *Die Geschichte der Unschärfe*, Wagenbach, Berlin.
Wang, W. L. (1997) 'Das Drei-Schluchten-Staudamprojekt am Jangtsekiang', in *Wasser in Asien. Elementare Konflikte*, ed. T. Hoffmann, Osnabrück, secolo, pp. 343–355.
Wang W. Y., Yu, S. F. & Zhang, H. Y. (1993) *Touzi xiangmu shehui pingjia fangfa (The method on social assessment for development project)*, Beijing.
Zhongguo guoji gongcheng zixun gongsi (China International Engineering Consulting Corporation) (2004) (ed.) *Zhongguo touzi xiangmu shehui pingjia zhinan* (Guidelines on social assessment in investment projects), Beijing, Zhongguo jihua chubanshe (China Planning Press).
Zweig, D. (2000) 'The "externalities of development": can new political institutions manage rural conflict?', in *Chinese Society. Change, Conflict and Resistance*, eds E. Perry & M. Selden, Routledge, London and New York, pp. 120–142.

Evaluating the use of Social Impact Assessment in the context of agricultural development projects in Iran

Mostafa Ahmadvand [a,*], Ezatollah Karami [b,1], Gholam Hossein Zamani [b,2], Frank Vanclay [c,3]

[a] Faculty of Agriculture, Yasuj University, Yasuj, Iran
[b] Department of Agricultural Extension and Education, College of Agriculture, Shiraz University, Shiraz, Iran
[c] Tasmanian Institute of Agricultural Research, University of Tasmania, Hobart, Australia

ARTICLE INFO

Article history:
Received 22 February 2009
Accepted 20 March 2009
Available online 8 April 2009

Keywords:
Social Impact Assessment
SIA
Environmental Impact Assessment
EIA
Agricultural development projects
Evaluation
Policy context
Iran

ABSTRACT

The utilisation of Social Impact Assessment (SIA) in Iran is analysed in terms of its policy context and its application in practice. Five case studies where SIA was employed in conjunction with Environmental Impact Assessments (EIA) for agricultural development projects are evaluated. In addition, the performance of the policy context is assessed. This research revealed that there are legal and institutional constraints to the effective functioning of SIA in Iran, and that there are deficiencies in the operating guidelines. There were serious problems associated with the way SIA was undertaken in all five case studies. Recommendations to improve the policy framework for the conduct of SIA are made. The recommendations advocate for a higher profile of SIA within legislation, for social issues to have greater emphasis in official guidelines for the conduct of EIA and SIA, and for a range of measures to increase the professionalism of SIA practice.

© 2009 Elsevier Inc. All rights reserved.

1. Introduction

Over the past few decades, many agricultural development projects (ADPs) have been initiated in Iran to alleviate poverty, unemployment, and an insufficient food supply. Although these projects were assumed to be beneficial for rural people, they often had unintended negative impacts on the environment and local communities. The projects were largely unregulated and the impacts often unmitigated. As a result, Iran has suffered from social and environmental degradation in many agricultural areas. Recently, however, ADPs in Iran and elsewhere have been criticized for their detrimental social and environmental impacts at the local level and to the world ecology at large (see Rezaei-Moghaddam et al., 2005; Ahmadvand and Karami, 2009).

Social Impact Assessment (SIA) is a useful mechanism for ensuring that ADPs can be implemented while maintaining the dynamics of social and human ecosystems (Slootweg et al., 2001). The International Principles for SIA (Vanclay, 2003, p.6) define SIA as including "the processes of analysing, monitoring and managing the intended and unintended social consequences, both positive and negative, of planned interventions (policies, programs, plans, projects) and any social change processes invoked by those interventions. Its primary purpose is to bring about a more sustainable and equitable biophysical and human environment". There is no doubt that in some ADPs (e.g. large dams, water management projects), the assessment of social impacts is as important as, if not more important than the assessment of the biophysical and economic aspects of these projects. SIA is important because it helps planners, project proponents, the impacted population and decision-makers to understand and be able to anticipate the possible social consequences on human communities of the proposed project (Pisani and Sandham, 2006). Vanclay (1999, 2000, 2004) considers that SIA makes projects more inclusive by involving key stakeholders; it makes them more socially-sound by minimizing or mitigating adverse social impacts, maximizing social benefits, and ensuring that projects are designed to be compatible with the local population. He also suggests that SIA is part of a democratic process in which equity, transparency and ownership are ensured through public participation. Therefore, SIA is necessary for building local capacity, and enhancing the performance of ADPs as a tool in sustainable development.

Although there has been an increase in awareness of SIA in Iran, its potential role in contributing to the identification and management of the social issues in ADPs is underestimated. This may be because of inadequate SIA processes and structures, insufficient regulation, or the lack of a framework for implementing SIA in Iran. Therefore, the purpose of this paper is to assess the role of SIA in Iran's agricultural

---

* Corresponding author. Tel./fax: +98 741 2224840.
E-mail addresses: ahmadvand_2000@yahoo.com (M. Ahmadvand), ekarami@shirazu.ac.ir (E. Karami), zamani@shirazu.ac.ir (G.H. Zamani), Frank.Vanclay@utas.edu.au (F. Vanclay).
[1] Tel.: +98 711 2286179; fax: +98 711 2286072.
[2] Tel.: +98 711 2286140; fax: +98 711 2286072.
[3] Tel.: +61 362262618; fax: +61 362267450.

development projects. The performance of the Iranian SIA system is reviewed and evaluated, and the role of SIA in Iran's agricultural development project cycle is examined. Recommendations to improve the effectiveness of the SIA process are provided. While the focus of the evaluation is the Iranian context, it is likely that the recommendations will have wider relevance.

2. Methodology

This investigation is two parts, an analysis of the SIA and EIA system or policy context in Iran, and a detailed evaluation of SIA as undertaken in actual practice, based on the assessment of five SIA reports of ADPs. The analysis of the policy context involved document research augmented with discussions with key informants. All major organizations involved in commissioning SIAs, especially for ADPs, were identified, including: Iran's Department of Environment (DoE) (*Sazeman-e-Mohit-e-Zist*), the Ministry of Agriculture (*Jihad-e-Keshavarzi*), the Management and Planning Organisation (MPO) (*Sazeman-e-Modiriat va Barnamerizi*), the Ministry of Energy (*Niroo*), and international organizations working in Iran such as the United Nations Development Program (UNDP) and the World Bank. The extent of consideration given to social impacts in the Iranian development process was examined through a review of legal, regulatory and guidance documents, related reports and the research literature. The analytical criteria developed by Ahmad and Wood (2002) were used to assess the performance of the Iranian SIA system (see Tables 1–4 later in the paper).

To assess the use of SIA in practice, we examined in detail five SIA reports for ADPs. These were selected from the SIA studies of ADPs undertaken between 2001 and 2006 in the Fars Province in the southwest of Iran. Since the majority of ADPs for which SIAs were required relate to the water and soil management sector, all five cases have this context. Because the power of purposeful sampling rests in being able to select information rich cases for in-depth study, the cases were chosen deliberately rather than randomly. Assessment of the quality of the SIAs was undertaken using an evaluation framework originally developed by Glasson et al. (1999) and further developed by Androulidakis and Karakassis (2006). For our purposes, it was revised for use with SIA (rather than EIA) reports.

3. Results part A: assessment of the performance of the Iranian SIA System

3.1. Provision for SIA in legislation

During the 1970s, many developing countries in Asia emerged at the forefront of EIA and SIA practice in the world (Gilpin, 1995). Today, EIA and SIA are firmly established in the planning processes of many

Table 1
Assessment of the adequacy of SIA Legislation in Iran.

Evaluation criteria	Assessment of the Iranian SIA system
1.1 Legal provision for SIA	Clause 82 of the Second State Economic, Social and Cultural Development Plan of 1994, as amended by Clause 105 of the Third Development Plan, Decree 138 of the Environmental Protection High Council, 1994, mandates the use of EIA. Arguably, assessment of social issues is implied within the provisions for EIA
1.2 Provision for appeal by the developer or the public against decisions	There is no provision for appeal; the decision of the Department of Environment is final
1.3 Legal or procedural specification of time limits	Time limits at various stages of the process, including for making a final decision on a development proposal following an EIA, are specified in law and are reasonable
1.4 Formal provision for Strategic Environmental Assessment (SEA)	SEA is not mentioned in the EIA/SIA legislation and procedures

Table 2
Assessment of the adequacy of the Administrative Arrangements for the conduct of SIAs in Iran.

Evaluation criteria	Assessment of the Iranian SIA system
2.1 Existence of a Competent Authority for EIA/SIA and procedures for the determination of social acceptability	The Competent Authority is defined in Note 2 of Decree 138 as being the Department of Environment. In practice there is a specialist EIA Bureau within the DoE. However, there is no specific procedure for determining social acceptability
2.2 Existence of a Review Body for EIA/SIA	The EIA Bureau within the DoE determines the appropriateness of EIA/SIA. It consults with other authorities with environmental and social responsibilities as appropriate
2.3 Specification of the responsibilities of sectoral authorities in the SIA process	Relevant sectoral authorities are represented in the EIA Bureau. Their roles and responsibilities are reasonably clear, although perhaps not specified in any formal sense
2.4 Level of coordination with other planning and management agencies	The Environment Bureau within the central Management and Planning Organisation has designated responsibility for coordination of environment-related issues. However, perhaps there is no coordination agency for social issues

Asian countries (Momtaz, 2002). Iran is one of the few developing countries that have the principle of environmental protection built into its constitutional law. Article 50 of the Constitution of the Islamic Republic of Iran 1979 states that (Islamic Republic of Iran, 1979):

The preservation of the environment, in which the present as well as the future generations have a right to flourishing social existence, is regarded as a public duty in the Islamic Republic. Economic and other activities that inevitably involve pollution of the environment or cause irreparable damage to it are therefore forbidden.

Iran has a history of environmental awareness, even prior to the 1979 revolution. For example, it was one of the 114 governments represented at the historic 1972 United Nations Stockholm Conference, which addressed problems of the human environment. As an outcome of this conference, Iran passed its first environmental legislation, the Environment Conservation and Restoration Act (ECRA), in 1974 (DoE, 2003). The aim of ECRA was not only to prevent and eliminate environmental degradation, but also to ensure management of natural and historic assets and the land in such a way as to utilize their richness and preserve it for future generations (DoE, 2004). Although the Iranian Government has made significant efforts to protect the environment, the conditions on approvals by the DoE were often not carried out due to weaknesses in implementation and compliance mechanisms, and a lack of an appropriate management and monitoring system (DoE, 1999).

The approach to environmental management has since been transformed. In the Second State Economic, Social and Cultural Development Plan of 1994, EIA became a legal requirement for a wide range of activities that may have a detrimental effect on the environment (METAP, 2002). According to Clause 82 of the enabling legislation, all major development plans (whether for production or service activities) must implement EIA activities and prepare an EIA report in conjunction with any feasibility study and before site selection. This regulation emphasizes the importance of the EIA instrument as a mechanism for developing a cooperative approach to the management of the environment. Therefore, since the 1990s a comprehensive legal framework for environmental governance and management has been established in Iran.

While there is no specific mention of SIA in any of the legal documents, in principle, SIA is a subset of EIA in Iran (El-Fadl and El-Fadel, 2004). Iranian policies, legislation and regulation have proceeded from the premise that 'the environment' ought to be

Table 3
Assessment of the adequacy of SIA Practice in Iran.

Evaluation criteria	Assessment of the Iranian SIA system
3.1 Specified screening categories (to establish when EIA/SIA is required)	Screening criteria exist with 17 project types designated as requiring EIA
3.2 Systematic screening approach	A systematic approach to screening exists and is in operation
3.3 Systematic scoping approach	The Department of Environment is responsible for defining the scope. Article 10 of the EIA Guidelines includes general statements about content. The DoE may identify significant issues to be addressed further in a final report, after submission of a preliminary report
3.4 Requirement to consider alternatives	There is no specified requirement to consider alternatives
3.5 Specified content of SIA report (to ensure quality and consistency)	The guidelines on preparing a preliminary EIA/SIA report provide a list of suggested chapter headings
3.6 Systematic process for review of SIA report	There is no fully-developed systematic process of review. However, the EPHC has a checklist of topics and a number of matrices of evaluation to determine whether proponent EIA/SIA reports are adequate
3.7 Public participation in SIA process	No requirements. Very rarely undertaken
3.8 Systematic decision-making approach	EIA/SIA report approved by the DoE with recommendations passed to the implementing authority
3.9 Requirement for social and environmental management plans	None
3.10 Requirement for mitigation of impacts	General requirements in EIA Regulation
3.11 Requirement for impact monitoring	DoE is responsible for follow-up monitoring
3.12 Experience of Strategic Environmental Assessment (SEA)	There is only limited experience of SEA in Iran; however UNEP is working with the DoE to increase skills in this area

defined very broadly, to include not only the biophysical, but also the economic and social components, in line with a triple bottom line approach to sustainable development (Vanclay, 2004). This breadth in definition stems from the official approach in Iran that environmental issues cannot be separated from the fundamental need for socio-economic development. Therefore, SIA is not regarded as a separate process in Iran, but is incorporated in all the important documents pertaining to the EIA system.

3.2. Adequacy of administrative arrangements relating to SIA

The administrative arrangements and roles of different agencies in the EIA/SIA process are defined in the various Iranian regulations and procedures. In order to conform to legal requirements, serious efforts have been made over the years to assess the environmental and social impacts of development projects. A Department of Environment (DoE) was established in Iran as early as 1971 (World Bank, 2003). Today, the DoE remains as the main actor for EIA and SIA, with responsibilities for protecting the environment, ensuring legitimate and sustainable utilization of natural resources to guarantee sustainable development, controlling pollution, preventing the destruction of the environment, and preserving Iran's biodiversity. The DoE established a specialist sub-agency, the Development Impact Assessment Bureau, under the Division of Human Environment in 1975, which was renamed the Bureau of Environmental Impact Assessment (*Daftar-e-Arzyabi Asarat-e-Mohiti*) in 1997. The EIA Bureau is responsible for supervising the screening process, managing the review of EIA/SIA reports, deciding on the acceptability of EIA/SIA reports, and issuing EIA Guidelines.

The EIA Bureau has approximately 15 staff members in its headquarters in the national capital, Tehran, about half of whom are professionally qualified. In addition, the DoE has offices in each of the 30 provinces, usually with one professional staff member but up to three in major cities. These professional staffs have the ability to contribute to EIAs at the screening stage (METAP, 2002).

In addition to the EIA Bureau, an Environment Bureau (*Daftar-e-Mohiti*) has been established within the Management and Planning Organization to ensure the effective coordination of EIA activities across ministries and departments at the national level for all new development projects. In order to prepare approvals, the Environmental Protection High Council (EPHC) (*Shuray-e-Âli-e-Hefazat Mohit-e-Zist*) was established within the DoE in 1994. The EPHC is an apex organization at the national level with the Republic President of Iran in the chair, which is responsible for the formulation and coordination of national environmental policies and programs. The EPHC was also given the responsibility of regulating the environment and ensuring the implementation of government policies on the environment (DoE, 1999). The EPHC has members from several ministries, including the Ministry of Agriculture, the Ministry of Energy, the Ministry of Health and Medical Education, the Ministry of Housing and Urban Development, the Ministry of Industries and Mines, the Ministry of Interior, the Department of Environment, and the Management and Planning Organisation.

The permit system is a three stage process (DOE, 1999): (1) at the project planning phase (preliminary permit); (2) prior to project implementation (construction permit); and (3) before the beginning of project operation (operation permit).

3.3. Performance of SIA in practice

Table 3 provides a summary of the performance of the Iranian EIA/SIA system in practice, evaluated against a comprehensive set of criteria that correspond to each stage of the EIA/SIA process, namely screening, scoping, consideration of alternatives, effective reporting, public participation, a decision-making process, establishment of social and environmental management plans, an impact mitigation strategy, and a monitoring process.

The Iranian EIA/SIA system uses an approach to screening that involves the use of both lists and thresholds. A relatively comprehensive set of project specifications is used to determine whether an EIA/SIA is required, and if so, whether a full EIA or only a preliminary or partial assessment is warranted. There are now 17 project types that are designated by the EPHC as being always subject to full EIA, including the proposal for any power plant, refinery, dam, bridge, airport, freeway, railroad, industrial city, irrigation project or forestry project (DoE, 1999). The EPHC may also require an EIA for any other large project.

Once the project proponent receives all the approvals, the proponent submits an application to the DoE for environmental clearance (METAP, 2002). Applications for development approval are submitted to the local DoE offices, which screen them to decide whether an EIA is required. If the project falls within any of the 17

Table 4
Assessment of the adequacy of foundational measures in the Iranian SIA system.

Evaluation criteria	Assessment of the Iranian SIA system
4.1 Existence of general and/or specific guidelines including any sectoral authority procedures	EIA Guidelines were prepared by the EPHC in 1997. These establish how EIA/SIA should be undertaken
4.2 SIA system implementation monitoring	There is no formal process to review the EIA/SIA system in Iran, although changes are made over time to improve its operation
4.3 Expertise in conducting SIA (national universities, institutes, consultancies with SIA technical expertise)	There is growing expertise in EIA, but expertise in SIA remains minimal
4.4 Training and capacity-building	Extensive introductory courses funded by UNDP exist, and there are a number of University units, especially at Masters level. Most concentrate on EIA, but some reference is made to SIA

categories subject to EIA, or is above any threshold specified by the EPHC, the developer is required to submit a preliminary EIA report as defined by the DoE Guidelines. The proponent is required to consult the DoE prior to preparation of the EIA and SIA reports. The EIA and SIA reports should be prepared according to the Guidelines, as well as the reports on project feasibility and site selection. The EIA/SIA must address both construction and operation phases.

According to the Guidelines (DoE, 1999), in the scoping stage four categories of impacts should be studied: impacts on physical, natural, and socio-cultural environments, and on development plans. Physical environment means land, water, air, and soil. Natural environment includes plant and animal species, habitats, landscapes, and bird migration routes. The impacts on development plans refers to the impact of proposed activities on other agricultural, industrial or service developments taking place in the region. Impacts on the socio-cultural environment includes people's health, employment, housing, education, religious and cultural beliefs, and cultural heritage. Special emphasis on social issues is also given in the section of the Guidelines outlining where in the EIA process public participation is regarded as being important.

The completed preliminary report is submitted to the local DoE office and passed to the national office in Tehran for review. In the review stage, the preliminary EIA report may be accepted without further assessment, or the DoE may, within one month, require further consideration of significant issues in a final EIA report. The final EIA report is required to include a baseline analysis, impact prediction, and impact mitigation measures. A comparison of project-induced environmental change with the expected environmental changes without the proposed project is assessed through a baseline analysis. It is mandatory that socio-economic and ecological impacts are included in this analysis.

After all relevant environmental information has been compiled; the potential consequences of the project are predicted. The prediction analysis should forecast the nature and significance of the expected impacts, or explain why no significant impacts are anticipated. Also, any mitigation measures that are proposed to avoid or reduce environmental and social impacts are outlined.

After submission of the final EIA report, the DoE has three months in which to submit its comments. The review and decision-making step starts when the proponent files an application accompanied by the EIA report and other documents. Based on this information and the review, the DoE either approves or rejects environment clearance for the project. The report may be accepted, rejected, or approved with recommended conditions.

Article 6 of the EIA Guidelines requires that EIA reports be prepared by individuals or organizations whose qualifications are approved by the relevant authorities. The Guidelines requires that the DoE publish a list of approved practitioners, but it is not clear that there is a focus on EIA expertise, and there is no requirement for expertise in SIA. As there is no legal requirement to involve the public in the EIA process, and EIA is generally regarded as a technical exercise solely involving government agencies and professional experts, social research expertise tends to be undervalued.

The DoE also has a post-project monitoring process. This aims to ensure that any conditions imposed on environment clearance approvals were implemented by the project proponent in accordance with what was specified.

3.4. Performance of the Iranian EIA/SIA System in relation to foundational activities

Drawing on Fuller (1999), Ahmad and Wood (2002) consider 'foundation measures' or activities to be those underlying features of the EIA system at a society level that promote good practice and underpin the successful application of EIA practice. The criteria relate to the existence of EIA/SIA guidelines, having a process of monitoring of the system in practice and being able to make improvements, the existence of expertise in conducting SIAs, and having training and capacity-building programs.

The use of SIA guidelines is widely advocated and many examples exist (e.g. Interorganizational Committee, 1994, 2003; Vanclay, 2003, 2006). As mentioned previously, in Iran SIA is incorporated into EIA. Therefore, there are no specific guidelines for SIA, however, several sector-specific guidelines have been developed and EIA Guidelines were issued by the EPHC in 1997 with assistance from the UNDP and other donors (METAP, 2002). These include, for example, guidelines for agro-industries, airports, dams, industrial estates, highways, irrigation and drainage projects, petrochemical plants, petroleum refineries, thermal power plants, railroads, reforestation projects, large industrial slaughter houses, and steel manufacturing industries.

The existence of guidelines does not necessarily mean that they are implemented in practice (Fuller, 1999). It has been found that the practical effectiveness of guidelines depends not only on the quality of their content, but on other measures that accompany their implementation. Such measures include monitoring the quality of EIA practice and providing agency and staff training in their use (Brew and Lee, 1996).

In Iran, there is no formal system monitoring in the legislation or Guidelines. However, some limited informal system monitoring by the environmental agencies has taken place to improve the EIA system by incorporating feedback from experience.

SIA can be undertaken by persons trained in variety of social sciences (Barrow, 2000), but in practice the majority of EIA and SIA consultants in Iran have a natural science rather than a social science background (METAP, 2002). Therefore, assessment of social aspects of EIA in Iran is often done by non-specialists. The training of EIA project managers, technical specialists and others involved in the EIA process is critical to the effectiveness of EIA and to increasing the standard of practice even in a mature EIA system (Fuller, 1999; Wood, 1999). The DoE places no constraints on the selection of practitioners, but requires the EIA report to give details of the experts who prepared it. There is no barrier to the EIA study being conducted by the developer, and both public and private sector developers and design engineering consultancies have used their own environmental staff to prepare EIA reports (Yousefi et al., 2002). Iran possesses some EIA expertise in universities, research and training institutes and consultancies, but many of them lack training in SIA. Iran has received some international funding for training. For example, many international agencies, such as the UNDP and World Bank, have funded various EIA training and capacity-building programs. Among these was the Mediterranean Environmental Technical Assistance Program (METAP), which was funded by the European Commission, the European Investment Bank, UNDP and the World Bank and, amongst other things, focussed on institutional strengthening of the EIA system.

4. Results part B: assessment of the performance of the application of SIA in agricultural development projects in Iran

While it has been established in the preceding section that there is a reasonable EIA/SIA system in Iran, an important issue is whether or not the actual SIA reports that are completed are adequate, and whether there are shortcomings in the way they are done. In order to address this issue, five SIA reports of ADPs in Iran were evaluated using the quality-related indicators used by Androulidakis and Karakassis (2006), which were originally developed by Glasson et al. (1999). The five ADPs were purposely selected to be indicative of SIA reports being undertaken. The aggregate evaluation results for the five cases are presented in Table 5. For each case and for each criterion, a three point rating scale of good, medium and poor was used. Scoring was based on a coding protocol adapted from Androulidakis and Karakassis (2006). As Table 5 reveals, the rating

Table 5
Assessment of the adequacy of five social impact studies for agricultural development projects in Iran.

Attribute	Project 1	Project 2	Project 3	Project 4	Project 5
Description of the environment					
Description of natural environment	Medium	Medium	Medium	Medium	Medium
Description of social environment	Medium	Medium	Medium	Medium	Medium
Reference to existing similar projects in the area	Poor	Poor	Poor	Poor	Poor
Description of the project					
Description of proposed project and construction phase	Poor	Poor	Poor	Poor	Poor
Description of operation of the project	Poor	Poor	Poor	Poor	Poor
Analysis of the entire life-cycle of the project	Poor	Poor	Poor	Poor	Poor
Justification of project's usefulness	Poor	Poor	Poor	Poor	Poor
Impact identification and prediction methods					
Adequacy of impact identification method	Medium	Medium	Poor	Poor	Poor
Estimation of positive and negative social impacts	Present	Present	Absent	Present	Present
Estimation of indirect and secondary social impacts	Absent	Absent	Absent	Absent	Absent
Use of suitable prediction models	Poor	Poor	Poor	Poor	Poor
Clarity and precision of the prediction	Poor	Poor	Poor	Poor	Poor
Mitigation and Monitoring					
Discussion of proposed mitigation	Absent	Present	Absent	Absent	Absent
Appropriateness of mitigation	Poor	Medium	Poor	Poor	Poor
Monitoring arrangements	Poor	Poor	Poor	Poor	Poor
Alternatives					
Reference to alternatives	Poor	Medium	Poor	Poor	Poor
Reference to procedures for selection among alternatives	Poor	Poor	Poor	Poor	Poor
Comparison to a "no-action option"	Present	Present	Absent	Present	Present
Public participation					
Contribution of public to the development of SIA	Poor	Poor	Medium	Poor	Poor

Explanatory notes to accompany table:
1. For most rows, the possible scores include: poor, medium, good. The score of 'good' was not allocated for any project for any attribute.
2. The attributes used here were derived from Androulidakis and Karakassis (2006) who drew on Glasson et al. (1999).
3. The Coding Protocol (rules for determining the appropriate score) used for this assessment were substantially similar to those in Appendix 1 in Androulidakis and Karakassis (2006).

of 'good' was never used, with the SIA reports being scored as 'poor' or 'medium' on all criteria. The five cases are considered in some detail below, and a comprehensive analysis of the EIA/SIA system in Iran follows.

4.1. Case Project 1: Gareh–Bygone plain floodwater spreading project

The Floodwater Spreading Project on the Gareh–Bygone Plain is located in the semi-arid Sheebkuh region of Fars Province. It was initiated by the Research Institute of Forests and Rangelands (*Moasese Tahqiqat-e-Jangalha va Marate*), utilizing the flow of the Bisheh-zard and Tchah-Qootch ephemeral rivers. It is one of the oldest floodwater spreading projects in Fars Province. The area utilised for floodwater spreading is about 2533 ha (1530 ha rangelands and drylands, and 503 ha of forests) out of the total of 6000 ha that comprises the plain. The aim of the project was to meet the needs of rural communities for water, food, and fodder (see Ahmadvand and Karami, 2009 for more details).

The review of the SIA report revealed that there were two parts to the SIA process: preparation of the SIA report (from scoping to documentation); and review and decision-making. Consistent with requirements, the report addressed the four dimensions of impacts on physical, natural and socio-cultural environments, and on development plans. However, the majority of the discussion of the socio-cultural environment addressed demographic issues using data acquired from the Statistics Centre of Iran (*Markaz-e-Âmar*). There was very little discussion of social dynamics in the absence of the proposed project. Another deficiency was a complete lack of discussion of issues during the operation stage of the project, nor was there an adequate justification of the project's usefulness. Only positive changes arising from the project were identified. In this way, the contractors tried to enhance the desirability of the proposed project. In the section regarding the identification and prediction of impacts, the contractors referred to potential effects and changes using descriptive text instead of models. Therefore, in spite of the possibility of a large socio-economic benefit deriving from the significant increase in irrigated farming lands, groundwater, and fodder, a large part of the report was allocated to the description of current state without any analysis being presented. This implies that the scoping stage of this report was poor.

In addition, the SIA did not adequately consider any cumulative impacts. The impact prediction step in this report was also very weak. The prediction technique that was used focused on primary impacts, rather than secondary and tertiary impacts. Accordingly, impact mitigation and monitoring were also ignored. No alternatives were considered. Finally, the contribution of the public to the SIA was ignored.

4.2. Case Project 2: Bid-zard mud dam project

Bid-zard (29°20′N, 51°50′E) is a village located 38 km southeast of Kazeroun City in Fars Province and has a history of drought, groundwater degradation and water shortages. The Bid-zard Mud Dam Project was initiated by the provincial Agricultural Organization (*Sazeman Jihad-e-Keshavarzi*) in 2003 utilizing the flow of the Bid-zard ephemeral river (see Fars Agricultural Organization, 2003 for more details).

The review of the SIA report of this project revealed that the process that was used followed the EPHC and DoE Guidelines. A mud dam is one of the 17 types of projects that are required to have EIA/SIA. However, the report was prepared by a team, which did not contain any social scientists. In the report, seven dimensions of the environment (rather than the usual four) were considered. The dimensions were climatology and hydrology; earthquake risk;

geology; geotechnical and geology engineering; agriculture, economy and society; water resource planning; and dam and related equipment. The agriculture and socio-economic dimension (i.e. the SIA component) included six sections. The report started by describing the site and project aim, which was stated as being to save floodwater in order to reduce water shortages in rural areas. The description of the environment was made on the basis of secondary data about topology, land use, climate, and socio-economic aspects. The baseline conditions – specifically groundwater condition, topsoil, geology and hydrology – were established by taking samples from the project site and obtaining tests from certified environmental testing laboratories.

Discussion of the separate impacts of the operation and construction phases of this project was inadequately done. Other significant elements, such as a lifecycle analysis and justification for the project, were also omitted. A large part of the report was allocated to a description of the characteristics of the project site without any analysis or interpretation. Further, for the majority of the report, the contractors discussed the problems that might emerge if the proposed project was not implemented, rather than assess the consequences of the project.

In the section regarding the identification and prediction of impacts, a range of issues relating to rural population, immigration, job opportunities, education, level of income, and production activities were considered, but without a sound basis for many of the predictions. The prediction technique employed in the report focused on primary impacts, rather than secondary and tertiary impacts.

While a number of alternatives were considered, there were problems with the way this was done. For example, three scenarios were defined for agricultural production in the project site. The first scenario represented 80% irrigated wheat and 20% irrigated barely to be cultivated in a wet year. In the second scenario, irrigated wheat and barley are cultivated, but they are irrigated only up to flowering stage. In the third scenario, a range of vegetables, e.g. tomatoes, potatoes, and cucumber, were cultivated in addition to irrigated wheat and barley. In spite of the scenario definition, the impacts of the project under these different scenarios on the rural community were not considered, nor was there any consideration of mitigation of negative consequences. Finally, there was no reference to public participation.

4.3. Case Project 3: Bane-kalaghi aquifer and flood control project

Bane-kalaghi (28°44'N, 55°02'E) is a plain with area of 4.07 km^2 located 116 km southeast of Neiriz City in Fars Province. The region has experienced a water crisis and drought since 1999. The Fars Agricultural Organization (Jihad-e-Keshavarzi) established an Aquifer and Flood Control project in 2005. The aim of the project was to control floods and recharge the groundwater of the plain (see Fars Agricultural Organization, 2004 for more details).

The baseline data mentioned in the description of the environment in the EIA/SIA report used both primary and secondary data. The data included physiographic information, and a discussion of geology and hydrology, meteorology, and socio-economic aspects. In terms of the socio-economic dimension, demographic characteristics, job opportunities, education, communication services, income, and agricultural production were studied. While the report was assessed as having sufficient baseline data, the analysis and interpretation of the data was weak.

There was a lack of discussion of the impacts of the operation stage, and the scoping stage was not well described. Analysis of alternatives was also weak with little assessment of the impacts of the project on the rural community, other than faith that a reduction in water shortages will benefit the region. There was little impact prediction and a lack of any attempt at impact mitigation. Socio-economic, cultural, and ecological assessments were given little emphasis.

However, in this EIA/SIA process there was some emphasis on public participation. The concerns, perceptions and judgments of the rural community were solicited and integrated into the EIA/SIA. A group discussion was held with the local leaders and members of the village council to identify the problems and constraints of the project. The discussion yielded a list of problems and constraints which informants believed would happen because of the project which was included in the report.

4.4. Case Project 4: Istahban groundwater recharge and flood control project

Iej (29°28'N, 45°30'E) is a district located 30 km southeast of Istahban City in Fars Province. The district is a floodway, and during major floods the entire district becomes inundated. The floods affect inhabitants considerably, with complete control of the floodwaters and/or prevention of damage not being feasible. Conversely, at various times, the plain also experiences water scarcity. Thus, a Groundwater Recharge and Flood Control Project was proposed by the Fars Agricultural Organization (see Fars Agricultural Organization, 2002 for more details).

In the EIA/SIA report that was undertaken, consistent with requirements, four dimensions of the environment including geography and topography, social situation, economic condition, and agricultural condition were considered. In the EIA/SIA report, the description of the environment was lacking in detail, and the baseline data was inadequate. The description of the environment was made on the basis of secondary data about topology, climatology, position and socio-economic aspects. Some illustrations regarding the agriculture and land use system in the area were presented. The description of the socioeconomic environment was addressed and included comments about population, socio-economic, and agricultural characteristics. The data was very general, without any analysis, basically just describing the present situation of the project site. The scoping stage had been neglected completely, and there was very little impact prediction or attempt at mitigation. There was no discussion of public participation.

4.5. Case Project 5: Sepidan irrigation networks and drainage project

Hossein-abad (29°28'N, 45°30'E) is a small plain in the Beyza district located 30 km east of Sepidan City in Fars Province. The level of groundwater is very high in the district, and farmlands are at risk of salinity. An Irrigation Network and Drainage Project was proposed by the Fars Agricultural Organization (Jihad-e-Keshavarzi) to improve soil quality and drainage management in the plain (see Fars Agricultural Organization, 2001 for more details).

The review of this EIA/SIA revealed serious shortcomings. First, the quality of the SIA report was very poor. The report started with describing the current state of the environment where the project was to be developed. Special attention was given to the natural environment, with an examination of climatic, geological, tectonic and ground characteristics. The geographical map of the project area was also presented. However, the fauna and flora of the project area were not examined and no attention was paid to endangered species or habitats. Second, the baseline data and the description of the environment were inadequate. The report tended to be a collection and compilation of data, with limited analysis or interpretation. Further, the report inadequately attempted a justification of the proposed project by using various economic data relating to the project area to suggest that the project was a positive move towards economic development. The scoping stage was neglected. The report failed to consider what would eventuate if the proposed project was not implemented. Third, a complete life cycle analysis of the proposed project was not included in the report, although it contained an outline of the various stages of the project life cycle and their respective duration. Fourth, under a section regarding the identification of predicted impacts, the report referred to the potential effects and changes by using simple descriptive text rather than analytical models. Therefore, the report failed to adequately describe and predict the environmental and social impacts of the project. The majority of the report focused on the direct effects of the project on the environment.

There was no consideration of alternatives. The proposed project was assumed to be the only possibility for the study contractor. There was also little assessment of the impacts of the project on the rural community. There was no discussion of public participation.

5. Discussion: enduring problems of SIA practice

To further evaluate SIA practice in Iran, this section considers the enduring problems of SIA practice that have been identified in the international literature, and the issues that arose from the review of the five case studies. The framework for SIA provided by the current Iranian legislation is assessed against these persistent issues to reflect on the degree to which they are likely to occur in practice in Iran.

5.1. Problems relating to the understanding of what is a social impact

The major shortcoming identified in the review of SIAs of ADPs in Iran was the lack of clarity in the legal definition about what should comprise a social assessment. In terms of environmental legislation and regulations, in Iran SIA is a subset of EIA. This has led to the misconception that consideration of social effects is only necessary if these result from environmental impacts. Furthermore, due to difficulties in quantifying many social impacts, they are often subsumed within economic impacts. As a result, this has led to very superficial treatment of the social aspects of development projects.

Another important issue is the selection of appropriate variables for inclusion in the SIA. In the EIA Guidelines, social impacts only include people's health, employment, housing, education, people's religious and cultural beliefs, and cultural heritage. In the international literature, a much wider range of variables has been suggested as being appropriate to consider in SIAs (see Branch et al., 1984; Burdge, 2004; Gramling and Freudenburg, 1992; Juslen, 1995; Taylor et al., 2004; Vanclay, 2002). Because of differences in the local context across projects, it is not possible to nominate a definitive list of variables that should be included across all time and place. Ideally, the scoping process should determine the important issues to include. However, a greater range of headings of types of social impacts should be included in the Guidelines to provide assistance to SIA practitioners and to the agencies commissioning reports.

5.2. Problems relating to the statutory framework

Despite fairly strong legal requirements to undertake an EIA study and obtain approval of the EIA report, the legal enforcement of any approval conditions or commitments made in any development application is weak (METAP, 2002). While the EIA Guidelines of the DoE give some indication of suggested coverage, there is no legal definition of environmental or Social Impact Assessment, nor of the required content of an EIA report. The EIA Guidelines have no legal standing, and DoE's requirements are largely restricted to the provision of information about the project and the host environment and community. This limits the Competent Authority's ability to require a detailed assessment of potential impacts.

The first major problem confronting EIA and SIA practitioners relates to screening that is, determining whether the size and type of a particular ADP means that it must be subject to an EIA/SIA process. According to the EPHC, only dams with a height of more than 15 m, and irrigation and drainage projects involving an area of more than 2500 ha are subject to EIA. While some ADPs that fall below these limits may be relatively harmless, some may have environmental and/or social impacts that would be significant. A smaller dam could still impact severely on cultural heritage or an archaeological site, for example.

While a comprehensive legal framework for environmental governance and management has been established in Iran by the EPHC, there is no mention of SIA in any of the legal documents and it is not treated as a priority issue. Because there is no mention of the requirement for social assessment, there is a danger of ignoring social factors where there are no apparent consequences on the natural environment.

5.3. Problems relating to the SIA process

The SIA process is typically similar to basic EIA procedures, comprising the phases of screening, scoping, baseline analysis, projection and estimation of effects, monitoring, mitigation and management, and evaluation (for further discussion of the SIA process, see Barrow, 2000; Becker, 1997; Burdge, 2004; Taylor et al., 2004; Vanclay, 1999).

The case study evaluations revealed that screening and scoping processes of the EIA/SIA for ADPs in Iran were not well defined. Screening occurs by reference to the Iranian EIA Guidelines which includes a list of 17 project types when EIA/SIA is mandated. In practice, this means that EIA/SIA is only undertaken for a small number of projects in the agricultural sector – as stated above, for dams with a height of over 15 m and irrigation and drainage projects involving an area of 2500 ha or more. Requirements (and guidelines) for scoping are inadequate, and scoping is basically left up to project proponents who, by and large, are not interested in considering a broader range of impacts than those they are currently required to assess. Nor do they consider secondary or higher-order impacts. In all five EIA/SIA reports analyzed, there was no evidence of project proponents attempting to consider the social impacts of their project beyond the most obvious. Furthermore, the evaluation findings revealed that the SIA reports were very poor in their prediction methodologies.

Another important shortcoming was insufficient baseline data. Despite the need for good quality data, there is no central databank in Iran. As a result, the data gathered by the different ADP proponents was not adequate. In all five cases, the baseline data presented was very general and superficial. A further issue is that there tends to be no monitoring of project impacts to identify and rectify impacts that were not identified by the EIA/SIA.

5.4. Problems relating to the lack of skilled EIA and SIA professionals

Project proponents tend to hire professional consultants to compile the EIA/SIA for their projects, although some are done in-house. While the SIA components of the report should be undertaken by persons trained in the social sciences, the majority of EIA consultants in Iran have a natural science rather than a social science background (METAP, 2002). The review of SIA reports on ADPs indicates that they were not done by social scientists. This will continue to be a problem while appropriate training programs to produce competent SIA practitioners do not exist, there is no professional accreditation and/or registration process for SIA competency, and while there is a shortage of social scientists interested in this type of work. There is also a lack of skilled EIA and SIA professionals within the DoE to make meaningful judgments on EIA/SIA reports prior to the issuance of any environmental clearance certificate (METAP, 2002). The DoE itself has identified the main problem with the review system of EIA reports as being the insufficient training and experience of the staff of the EIA Bureau

(DoE, 1999). EIA Bureau staffs themselves expresses frustration at their inability to evaluate EIA reports in greater depth (DoE, 2003).

5.5. Poor quality EIA/SIA reports

While there are guidelines for preparing EIA/SIA reports, and the quality of some of the reports was better than others, our research revealed that most reports tend to be a compilation of very general and superficial data, with a complete lack of interpretation and analysis.

5.6. The role of public participation

The participation of local people is central to SIA, and the combination of a participative approach with expert judgment is often regarded as strength of SIA (Burdge, 2003; Pisani and Sandham, 2006). Much has been written about the value of public participation for all stakeholders, particularly in bringing public values and social objectives to the decision-making process and in promoting accountability, efficiency, equity and empowerment (Stolp et al., 2002). The purpose of an SIA should be to enable proponents and decision-makers to make socially responsible decisions, and this requires involving people affected by those decisions (Taylor et al., 2004; Barrow, 2000; Burdge, 2003; Pisani and Sandham, 2006).

In developing countries, community participation is not typically enshrined in legislation or in EIA requirements, and is often neglected or started at a late stage of project development (Vanclay, 2000). This is also the case in Iran. Our research revealed that public participation was a disappointing feature of SIAs in Iran and there was little experience of public participation in the SIAs of ADPs. It was conducted in only one of the five cases (Project 3). However, the need for public participation is not specified in legal documents, nor in the EIA regulation and Guidelines. This can be attributed to lack of a culture of participation, poverty, and a low level of literacy. The role of public participation in the EIA/SIA process in Iran needs strengthening.

6. Conclusion and recommendations: improving the practice of SIA

Our research evaluated the application of Social Impact Assessment in agricultural development projects in Iran at both policy and practical dimensions. At the policy level, the review of the legislative and theoretical bases of SIA and EIA confirmed that SIA is meant to be an integral component of EIA in Iran, but is yet to be as firmly established in environmental planning as EIA. There are very evident conceptual and practical shortcomings in the current EIA/SIA system that affects the standing of SIA. A high standard of SIA practice will only be achieved when practitioners are professionally trained, accredited and monitored by a professional body. Then, professional ethics can be improved and international standards applied.

Although the term 'SIA' is not widely used in agricultural development projects, consideration of the negative effects of the proposed projects on people, their homes and their livelihoods is meant to be a major component of the EIAs that are conducted. Therefore, an appropriate amendment to the legislation on EIA would be to make specific mention of SIA, and to increase awareness of the importance of social issues. The legislation should also be changed so that SIAs are mandatory for projects that have significant social impacts, even if there are no impacts on the biophysical components of the environment. At the practical level, the review of EIA/SIA reports of ADPs in Iran revealed that the quality of the SIAs conducted was very weak, especially in terms of considering the social environment, in impact prediction and in the recommendation of mitigation measures.

To improve the policy and practical framework within which SIA is practiced, we make the following recommendations. While these recommendations specifically address the deficiencies revealed by our analysis of the use of SIA in ADPs in Iran, we trust that they may be more generally applicable.

1. 'Social Impact Assessment', and an outline of social issues to be considered in an SIA and EIA, should be more explicit in legislation.
2. SIA should be required whenever a project potentially creates social impacts, even when there may not be impacts on the biophysical environment.
3. In the current EIA Guidelines and regulations, the only agricultural development projects that require an EIA are dams over 15 m in height and large irrigation and drainage projects. Because many other types of ADPs have the potential to create significant impacts on the social and natural environment, we suggest that the screening list be modified to include a wider range of potential ADPs and/or that the screening process be changed so that projects that are not automatically required to undertake EIAs by the list are not automatically exempted, as seems to be the case at present.
4. We recommend the introduction of an accreditation system for the registration of SIA practitioners, and the mandatory use of practitioners from this list for every SIA or component of an EIA that addresses social issues.
5. Despite the importance of an effective scoping process to identify the locally significant impacts, this step is often neglected or does not receive due attention. Therefore, in order to improve the quality of SIAs, we recommend that the EIA Guidelines give more detail about how scoping should be undertaken, and that more attention is given to this step in the approvals process.
6. While strengthening the legislation for SIA is a priority need, parallel efforts to strengthen the country's administrative and institutional capacity for high quality SIA is also needed.
7. The lack of reliable and accurate baseline data is a problem for EIA and SIA. Therefore, it is suggested that a common database be created where all relevant agencies pool their data which would then be available to project proponents on request.
8. Our research revealed there was excessive attention given to construction impacts, and inadequate attention given to the longer-term operational impacts. It is suggested that SIA and EIA reports should clearly suggest mitigation, monitoring and institutional measures to eliminate, compensate, or reduce impacts to acceptable levels during operation as well as construction phases.
9. It is essential to involve local communities in SIA and EIA processes. Therefore, it is suggested that mechanisms be developed and resources provided to further enable the participation of community people in the SIA and EIA process, including in the monitoring of project implementation.
10. Specialized SIA training programs should be developed and offered. To ensure consistency and quality, they should be subject to accreditation by the Department of Environment. The likely content of such courses could follow the suggestions of Burdge (1998).

Acknowledgements

This paper is part of Ph.D. thesis submitted by senior author to the Shiraz University. The authors are grateful for the support of the managers of the Fars Agricultural Organization (Jihad-e-Keshavarzi) as well as the soil and water management staff who assisted in the data collection for this study. This research was funded by Fars Province Research, Statistics, and Information Technology Council.

References

Ahmad B, Wood C. A comparative evaluation of the EIA systems in Egypt, Turkey and Tunisia. Environ Impact Assess Rev 2002;22(3):213–34.

Ahmadvand M, Karami E. A social impact assessment of the floodwater spreading project on the Gareh-Bygone plain in Iran: a causal comparative approach. Environ Impact Assess Rev 2009;29(2):126–36.

Androulidakis I, Karakassis I. Evaluation of the EIA system performance in Greece using quality indicators. Environ Impact Assess Rev 2006;26(3):242–56.

Barrow CJ. Social Impact Assessment: An Introduction. London: Arnold; 2000.

Becker HA. Social Impact Assessment: Method and Experience in Europe, North America, and the Developing World. London: UCL Press; 1997.

Branch K, Hooper DA, Thompson J, Creighton JC. Guide to Social Assessment. Boulder: CO: Westview Press; 1984.

Brew D, Lee N. Reviewing the quality of donor agency environmental assessment guidelines. Proj Appraisal 1996;11(2):79–84.

Burdge RJ. A Conceptual Approach to Social Impact Assessment. Second ed. Middleton: Social Ecology Press; 1998.

Burdge RJ. The practice of social impact assessment: background. Impact Assess Proj Appraris 2003;21(2):84–8.

Burdge RJ. A Community Guide to Social Impact Assessment. Third ed. Middleton: Social Ecology Press; 2004.

DoE. Evaluation of impact assessment project: capacity building and institutional strengthening in Iran. Iran: The Department of Environment; 1999 (in Farsi).

DoE. The Environmental norms and standards: the human context. Department of Environment, Iran; 2003 (in Farsi).

DoE. The collection of regulations and rules of environmental protection in Iran. Iran: The Department of Environment; 2004 (in Farsi).

El-Fadl K, El-Fadel M. Comparative assessment of EIA systems in MENA countries: challenges and prospects. Environ Impact Assess Rev 2004;24(6):553–93.

Fars Agricultural Organization. Feasibility and justification studies of irrigation networks and drainage project, Sepidan. Fars Agricultural Organization Press; 2001 (in Farsi).

Fars Agricultural Organization. Feasibility and justification studies of groundwater recharge and flood control project, Istahban. Fars Agricultural Organization Press; 2002 (in Farsi).

Fars Agricultural Organization. Feasibility and justification studies of Bid-zard mud dam. Fars Agricultural Organization Press; 2003 (in Farsi).

Fars Agricultural Organization. Feasibility and justification studies of aquifer and flood control project, Neiriz. Fars Agricultural Organization Press; 2004 (in Farsi).

Fuller K. Quality and quality control in environmental impact assessment. In: Petts J, editor. Handbook of Environmental Impact Assessment, vol. 2. Oxford: Blackwell; 1999. p. 35–70.

Gilpin A. Environmental Impact Assessment: Cutting Edge for the Twenty-first Century. Cambridge: Cambridge University Press; 1995.

Glasson J, Therivel R, Chadwick A. Introduction to Environmental Impact Assessment. London: UCL Press; 1999.

Gramling R, Freudenburg WR. Opportunity-threat, development, and adoption: toward a comprehensive framework for social impact assessment. Rural Sociol 1992;57(2):216–34.

Interorganizational Committee on Guidelines and Principles for Social Impact Assessment. Guidelines and principles for social impact assessment. Impact Assess 1994;12(2):107–52.

Interorganizational Committee on Principles and Guidelines for Social Impact Assessment. Principles and guidelines for social impact assessment in the USA. Impact Assess Proj Appraris 2003;21(3):231–50.

Islamic Republic of Iran. The Constitutional Law of the Islamic Republic of Iran. Government Printer; 1979 (in Farsi).

Juslen J. Social impact assessment: a look at Finish experiences. Proj Appraisal 1995;10(3):163–70.

METAP. Evaluation and future development of the EIA system in the Islamic Republic of Iran. Mediterranean Environmental Technical Assistance Programme; 2002.

Momtaz S. Environmental impact assessment in Bangladesh: a critical review. Environ Impact Assess Rev 2002;22(2):163–79.

Pisani JAD, Sandham LA. Assessing the performance of SIA in the EIA context: a case study of South Africa. Environ Impact Assess Rev 2006;26(8):707–24.

Rezaei-Moghaddam K, Karami E, Gibson J. Conceptualizing sustainable agriculture: Iran as an illustrative case. J Sustain Agric System 2005;27(3):25–56.

Slootweg R, Vanclay F, van Schooten M. Function evaluation as a framework for the integration of social and environmental impact assessment. Imp Assess Proj Appraris 2001;19(1):19–28.

Stolp A, Groen W, van Vliet J, Vanclay F. Citizen values assessment: incorporating citizens' value judgements in environmental impact assessment. Imp Assess Proj Appraris 2002;20(1):11–23.

Taylor CN, Bryan CH, Goodrich CG. Social Assessment: Theory, Process and Techniques. Third ed. Lincoln: Taylor Baines and Associates; 2004.

Vanclay F. Social impact assessment. In: Petts J, editor. Handbook of Environmental Impact Assessment (Volume 1). Oxford: Blackwell Science; 1999. p. 301–26.

Vanclay F. Social impact assessment. In: Lee N, George C, editors. Environmental Assessment in Developing and Transitional Countries: Principles, Methods, and Practice. Chichester: John Wiley and Sons; 2000. p. 125–35.

Vanclay F. Conceptualizing social impacts. Environ Impact Assess Rev 2002;22:183–211.

Vanclay F. International principles for social impact assessment. Impact Assess Proj Appraris 2003;21(1):5–11.

Vanclay F. The triple bottom line and impact assessment: How do TBL, EIA, SIA, SEA and EMS relate to each other? J Environ Assess Policy Manag 2004;6(3):265–88.

Vanclay F. Principles for Social Impact Assessment: a critical comparison between the International and US documents. Environ Impact Assess Rev 2006;26(1):3–14.

Wood C. Comparative evaluation of environmental impact assessment systems. In: Petts J, editor. Handbook of Environmental Impact Assessment, vol. 2. Oxford: Blackwell; 1999. p. 10–34.

World Bank. Islamic Republic of Iran Environmental Support Program. Report Number PID11476 [online]; 2003. Available: http://www.wds.worldbank.org/servlet/WDSContentServer/WDSP/IB/2002/09/27/000094946_0209260416106/Render/PDF/multi0-page.pdf (May 22, 2003).

Yousefi H, Jabbaran B, Sohrab T, Azari F. Environmental impact assessment of Meshkinshahr geothermal power plant. Iran Energy Efficiency Organization, Report SABA/9/2002; 2002. p. 584. (in Farsi).

Mostafa Ahmadvand is a former Ph.D. student at Shiraz University, and currently an assistant professor of agricultural development and extension at the Faculty of Agriculture, Yasuj University, Iran. His interests and experience have been concentrated on Social Impact Assessment, conflict resolution, and sustainable development, especially in agricultural development projects in Iran.

Ezatollah Karami is professor of agricultural development and extension at the College of Agriculture, Shiraz University, Iran. He has published widely on issues of agricultural extension and sustainable agriculture. He has received an international award for his research on agriculture and environment.

Gholam Hossein Zamani is professor at the College of Agriculture, Shiraz University, Iran. He has published extensively in the area of agricultural education and rural development. He has served as Dean of the College of Agriculture, as well as Vice-Chancellor and Chancellor of Shiraz University. He received his Ph.D. from the University of Nebraska, USA.

Frank Vanclay is professor of rural sociology with the Tasmanian Institute of Agricultural Research at the University of Tasmania in Australia. He is a specialist in Social Impact Assessment and in social research in agriculture.

[35]

Assessing the performance of SIA in the EIA context: A case study of South Africa

Jacobus A. du Pisani [a,*], Luke A. Sandham [b]

[a] *School of Social and Government Studies, North-West University, Potchefstroom, P.O. Box 19772, 2522 Noordbrug, South Africa*
[b] *School of Environmental Sciences and Development, North-West University, Potchefstroom, South Africa*

Received 14 July 2006; accepted 17 July 2006
Available online 22 August 2006

Abstract

This article, a theoretical perspective based on a literature study, is a critical evaluation of SIA as part of the EIA process in South Africa against the background of international guidelines and best practices. It includes sections on the historical background of the development of SIA in South Africa, the legal status and requirements of SIA in the country, and a critical evaluation of SIA regulation in South Africa. The conclusion reached in the article is that the persistent problems of SIA practice, experienced in other parts of the world, are also evident in South Africa. Apart from institutional, financial and professional constraints, there are also serious problems associated with approach and methods. This conclusion confirms the findings of empirical studies that SIA in South Africa is neglected, that the practice of SIA in South Africa is not yet on a sound footing, and that it does not receive the professional attention it deserves in a country beset by enormous social challenges. To conclude the article recommendations are made to improve the level of SIA practice in South Africa, and the possible significance of this national case study for international practice is indicated.
© 2006 Elsevier Inc. All rights reserved.

Keywords: Social Impact Assessment (SIA); Environmental Impact Assessment (EIA); South Africa; National legislation; Integrated impact assessment

1. Introduction

In the development context "social" must be one of the hardest words to define, because it has such a broad range of meanings that it is often used in a rather fuzzy way. Development is by its

* Corresponding author. Tel.: +27 18 2991594; fax: +27 18 2991776.
 E-mail address: gskjadp@puk.ac.za (J.A. du Pisani).

nature social, because its means are social processes and institutions, its ends embody social values, and its costs and benefits are distributed across communities, social groups, and organisations (Francis and Jacobs, 1999). And yet, despite the pervasiveness of the social dimension of development, the integration of this crucial dimension into development practice, and subfields such as environmental impact assessment, has not been easy.

Social impacts are those impacts, stemming from a specific action, which alter "the day-to-day way in which people live, work, play, relate to one another, organize to meet their needs and generally cope as members of society" (Interorganizational Committee on Guidelines and Principles for Social Impact Assessment, 2003. For other definitions, see Barrow, 2000; Burdge, 2004).

Social Impact Assessment (SIA) refers to the efforts to assess, in advance, the social consequences, whether intended or unintended, positive or negative, that are likely to follow from specific actions, projects, policies and programmes (Becker, 1997; Interorganizational Committee on Guidelines and Principles for Social Impact Assessment, 2003; Vanclay, 2003. See also Burdge, 2004; Gilpin, 1996; IAIA, 2003; Taylor et al., 2004). Its purpose is to answer the following question: "Will there be a measurable difference in the quality of life in the community as a result of the proposed action?" (Barrow, 2000). SIA is used to assess how the costs and benefits of impacts are distributed among different stakeholders and over time. It is particularly relevant for understanding the quality of impact on different groups (World Bank, 2003). SIA has a hybrid nature, because it is linked to both scientific research and political policy and decision-making processes (Freudenburg, 1986).

There is no doubt that the assessment of social impacts is as important, in some cases even more important, than the assessment of biophysical and economic impacts of development projects. "Putting people first" is the first principle of the Rio Declaration, is at the heart of Agenda 21, and is regarded, in the broader social science community, as a non-negotiable imperative of development programmes (Cernea, 1991). SIA has considerable potential to give social criteria their rightful place alongside economic and environmental criteria in decision making (Taylor et al., 2004). One of its most important contributions is to move the focus of the policy debate away from the notion of a technical problem to be solved to a social issue to be managed (Baines et al., 2003). The value of SIA in social development, policy-making and planning, public involvement, conflict management, and sustainable development has been described (Barrow, 2000) and its significance in developing countries (Baines and Taylor, 2002; Becker, 1997; Burdge, 1990; Burdge, 1998; Henry, 1990; Momtaz, 2005) and in Africa in particular (Weaver et al., 2003) emphasised.

SIA is important, because it helps planners, project proponents, the impacted population and decision-makers to understand and be able to anticipate the possible social consequences on human populations and communities of proposed project development or policy changes. SIA should provide a realistic appraisal of possible social ramifications and suggestions for project alternatives and possible mitigation measures (Burdge, 2004) and must generate results that are meaningful, credible, and operationally relevant (Francis and Jacobs, 1999). It must, in other words, be practical and useful for all involved (Rivers and Buchan, 1995). SIA makes projects more inclusive by involving key stakeholders, it makes projects more socially sound by minimising or mitigating adverse social impacts, maximising social benefits, and ensuring that projects are designed to "fit" the populations to be reached, and it is part of a democratic process in which equity, transparency and ownership are ensured through public participation (Francis and Jacobs, 1999; Vanclay, 1999).

Since the 1970s there have been remarkable advances in the theory and practice of SIA. Despite these advances SIA has evolved in the shadow of Environmental Impact Assessment

(EIA). Dani (2003: abstract) attributes this to the fact that many practitioners regard EIA as the "mother of all impact assessments", and SIA as no more than a subset of EIA. Compared with the assessment of biophysical impacts, SIA is a bit of an "orphan" that has not been fully adopted by the assessment process for environmental and natural resource decision-making (Burdge, 2002, 2003a). This type of approach has led to the misconception that consideration of social effects is only necessary if these result from environmental impacts. In countries such as Canada, Australia, New Zealand, and the United States there is now a clearer distinction between EIA and SIA, because they often employ practitioners from different disciplines using different techniques. However, even in these countries the biophysical footprint is usually the overriding factor in impact assessment.

There has been a fierce debate among SIA theorists on whether SIA should be practised separate from or integrated with other impact assessments (Barrow, 2000). This is linked to the discussion among SIA practitioners as to whether the approach should be "technocratic" or "participative". According to Dani (2003: abstract) "SIA has been hamstrung by its attempt to emulate or ride on the coat-tails of environment... For SIA to realize its full potential it needs to go beyond the environmental paradigm". Vanclay (1999) and Burdge (2003b) view closer integration with, rather than separation from, EIA as the better way to strengthen the impact of SIA on decision-making, because it will have the benefit of increased awareness of social impacts among EIA practitioners, planners, proponents and the community.

Is SIA in South Africa also an infant that has not been successfully weaned from EIA? Or is there enough scope in the South African EIA context for SIA to come into its own in impact assessment practice? In this article the legal position of SIA in South Africa will be determined by analysing the relevant legislation and regulations. It will then be possible, by comparing the legal/ statutory requirements in South Africa to international theoretical perspectives on SIA, to come to a conclusion whether, theoretically, SIA receives sufficient attention in South Africa.

2. Historical background of the development of EIA and SIA in South Africa

In terms of the Environment Conservation Act (ECA), Act no. 73 of 1989 (Republic of South Africa, 1989), the National Environmental Management Act (NEMA), Act no. 107 of 1998 (Republic of South Africa, 1998b), and sectoral legislation such as the National Water Act, Act no. 36 of 1998 and the Mineral and Petroleum Resources Development Act (MPRDA), Act no. 28 of 2002 (Republic of South Africa, 2002c), EIA has become a legal requirement for a wide range of activities that may have a detrimental effect on the environment in South Africa (see Glazewski, 2000). Before the legislation, regulations and procedures pertaining to EIA and SIA in South Africa are discussed in more detail, it is necessary to sketch the historical background in which impact assessment evolved.

In the "old" (i.e. pre-1994) South Africa, environmental affairs were not really a top priority. Hamann et al. (2000), Sowman et al. (1995) and DEAT (2005) have documented the constraints to the development of proper environmental evaluation procedures in South Africa during the apartheid period and the reasons for the deep distrust among blacks to environmental conservation. Developments that had major negative impacts on the receiving environment and local communities went largely unregulated and unmitigated. In effect it meant that the poor and disenfranchised bore the heaviest burden of environmental pollution and degradation. Despite these constraints, significant progress was made towards the end of the old dispensation in the direction of developing an improved system of environmental governance. EIA was practiced on a non-mandatory basis as an input to decision-making from the mid-1970s. In the early 1980s a white paper and a draft bill culminated in the first Environment Conservation Act (Act no. 100 of 1982). A statutory Council for the Environment, with a Committee for EIA, was established. By the late 1980s increasing pressure from environmental groups prompted "progressive" initiatives to address concerns around the inadequate state of environmental management. A system of Integrated Environmental Management (IEM) was officially endorsed as the appropriate form of environmental assessment for South Africa (Glazewski, 2000; Sowman et al., 1995). ECA (the new Environment Conservation Act, Act no. 73 of 1989) was adopted, which gave the Minister of Environmental Affairs the power to identify activities which may have a detrimental effect on the environment and for which an environmental impact report would be required (Section 21) and to make regulations regarding environmental impact reports (Section 26) (Republic of South Africa, 1989). The promulgation of ECA coincided with the publication of an IEM procedural document, of which a revision, with a series of guideline documents and checklists, was finally published in 1992.

Since 1994 the approach to environmental management has been transformed in a positive way. In terms of the new South African Constitution, environmental issues are regarded as an integral element to be addressed in the democratic transition. An environmental right is enshrined in the Bill of Rights (chapter 2, Section 24), guaranteeing that everyone has the right to an environment "that is not harmful to their health or well-being", and to "have the environment protected, for the benefit of present and future generations, through reasonable legislative and other measures that prevent pollution and ecological degradation; promote conservation; and secure ecologically sustainable development and use of natural resources while promoting justifiable economic and social development" (Republic of South Africa, 1996).

It is claimed in publications by the current Department of Environmental Affairs and Tourism (DEAT) that after 1994 there was "a paradigm shift from narrow conservation to sustainable development" (DEAT, 1997) and that "major strides have been made in addressing environmental issues as part of an overall thrust towards the achievement of social justice, democracy and sustainable development" (DEAT, 2005). Although DEAT's self-evaluation may be exaggerated, the different approach of the new democratically elected government compared to that of the old government, with a particular socio-economic focus on improving the conditions in previously disadvantaged communities, has been reflected in environmental policy. In 1995 a Consultative National Environmental Policy Process (CONNEPP) was launched to democratise environmental governance in South Africa. Different stakeholders participated in drafting a framework for sustainable environmental management. In 1997 a blueprint for environmental governance was adopted by Parliament in the form of the White Paper on Environmental Management, setting out the vision, principles, strategic goals, objectives and regulatory approaches for environmental management in the country. Government appointed the national Department of Environmental Affairs and Tourism as lead agent responsible and accountable for all environmental issues, including the development and implementation of an integrated and holistic environmental management system (DEAT, 1997, DEAT, 2005). It is clear from the White Paper that the approach to environmental management has a sharp focus on social upliftment, which is in line with the shift in the main global development thrust during the 1990s to poverty alleviation. In South Africa DEAT recognises that "poverty alleviation and biodiversity conservation are themes of the Government agenda that should be seen as integrated solutions, rather than working against each other" (DEAT, 2005).

EIA practice in South Africa was formalised in 1997 when the first set of EIA regulations was published in the *Government Gazette*. Activities, which in terms of section 21 of ECA are subject to EIA procedures, were listed and amended in a series of government notices (Republic of South

Africa, 1997a,c, 1998a, 2002a). The categories of such activities include land use and transformation, water use and disposal, resource removal and renewal, agricultural, mining and industrial processes, transportation, energy generation and distribution, sewage disposal, chemical treatment and recreation (Republic of South Africa, 1989. See also DEAT, 1998). Regulations describing the procedure to be followed to apply for permission to conduct such activities in terms of Sections 26 and 28 of ECA were also published and amended on several occasions (Republic of South Africa, 1997b, 1998c, 2002b). In April 1998 the Department of Environmental Affairs and Tourism (DEAT) published a guideline document to assist stakeholders in the implementation of the EIA regulations (DEAT, 1998). For DEAT it is a major strategic objective that the potential negative environmental impacts of all significant new developments are avoided, mitigated, managed and/or controlled (DEAT, 2005).

Towards the end of the 1990s the first comprehensive environmental management legislation of the new democratically elected South African government evolved in the form of the National Environmental Management Act (NEMA), 1998, Act no. 107 of 1998. NEMA was promulgated on 27 November 1998 (Government Gazette 19519) and commenced on 29 January 1999 (Proclamation R8, Government Gazette 19703). This legislation reflected the spirit of the "new" South Africa, especially in terms of clearly formulating the social responsibilities of the government towards local communities. NEMA notes: "The environment is held in public trust for the people. The beneficial use of environmental resources must serve the public interest and the environment must be protected as the people's common heritage" (Republic of South Africa, 1998b). The central pillars of NEMA, according to DEAT (2005) are quality in environmental decision-making, cooperative governance in the environmental sector, facilitating the role of civil society in environmental governance and implementing the constitutional imperative to respect, protect, promote and fulfil the environmental right in the Bill of Rights. Chapter 5 of NEMA makes detailed provision for EIA (Republic of South Africa, 1998b). The competent authorities for administration of EIA are the nine provincial departments of environmental affairs, and for certain projects the national Department of Environmental Affairs and Tourism. New "quicker, simpler and better" EIA regulations under the relevant sections of NEMA, aimed at improving the efficiency and effectiveness of EIAs in South Africa, were promulgated in April 2006 for implementation in July 2006 (Republic of South Africa, 2006a,b. See also DEAT, 2006).

In terms of the Mineral and Petroleum Resources Development Act, Act no. 28 of 2002 (Republic of South Africa, 2002c, Sections 37, 38 and 39. See also Republic of South Africa, 2004) mining and related activities are also subject to the environmental principles and the IEM objectives of NEMA. Every person who has applied for a mining right must conduct an EIA, and for different types of mining activities either an environmental management programme or an environmental management plan (EMP) must be submitted. In the case of mining activities, the Department of Minerals and Energy is the competent authority.

A comprehensive legal framework for environmental governance and management has thus been established in South Africa.

3. Legal status and requirements of SIA in South Africa

Where does SIA fit into the broader EIA picture in South Africa? Theoretically, in terms of environmental legislation and regulations, SIA in South Africa is fully incorporated into EIA. Since the 1980s the South African government has in its policies, legislation and regulations proceeded from the assumption that "the environment", in line with the triple bottom line approach to sustainable development and the spirit of Agenda 21, ought to be defined very broadly, to include not only the biophysical environment, but also the economic and social components. This breadth of definition stems from the official approach that in South Africa environmental issues cannot be separated from the fundamental need for socio-economic development.

In Section 1(x) of ECA (Republic of South Africa, 1989), "environment" is defined as "the aggregate of surrounding objects, conditions and influences that influence the life and habits of man or any other organism or collection of organisms". This broad and inclusive definition of "environment" was continued in the post-apartheid era from 1994. In the White Paper on Environmental Management Policy, the word "environment" refers to "the conditions and influences under which any individual or thing exists, lives or develops", and it is emphasised that "people are part of the environment and are at the centre of concerns for its sustainability" (DEAT, 1997). When NEMA was drafted, in order to make the implementation of legislation more practicable, humans were given a prominent role in terms of their interrelationship with the environment, but without making them an explicit part of the definition of "environment" in Section 1(1)(xi) (Republic of South Africa, 1998b).

Because of this anthropocentric approach, SIA is not regarded as a separate process in South Africa, but incorporated, albeit mostly on a rather limited scale, into EIA. Social impacts have been included in all the important documents pertaining to the EIA system. It was clearly stated in Section 26 (a) (iv) and (v) of ECA that environmental impact reports would not be limited to biophysical impacts, but would also include impacts in the social and economic spheres. However, neither in ECA, nor in the EIA regulations and guidelines, nor in the White Paper on Environmental Management Policy, were "social impacts" clearly specified or a checklist supplied of possible social impacts that should receive attention in EIA procedures (see e.g. DEAT, 1998; DEAT, 1997).

NEMA seems to have a somewhat stronger social focus than the older legislation. In NEMA the social component of environmental management is given equal status with the economic and environmental components, and it is emphasised that people and their needs must be the first priority of environmental management. It is stated clearly in article 2 (4) (j) that the social impacts of activities must also be considered, assessed and evaluated. According to articles 23 (2) (b) and 24 (1) (a–c) impact assessment should focus on three aspects: (1) the environment, (2) socio-economic conditions and (3) cultural heritage. Potential impacts in these three spheres must be assessed in terms of article 24 (3) (a–b) in accordance with prescribed procedures set out in regulations and meeting the minimum requirements specified in article 24 (7). (Republic of South Africa, 1998b). In terms of the Mineral and Petroleum Resources Development Act, Act no. 28 of 2002 (Republic of South Africa, 2002c, Sections 37, 38 and 39) EIAs for mining activities should, apart from physical impacts, also assess socio-economic and heritage impacts.

It seems that the new EIA regulations, circulated by DEAT for comment on 25 June 2004 in terms of Section 24 (5) of NEMA, with revisions in January 2005 and finalised in 2006, reflect somewhat greater sensitivity to the importance of social impacts. Both site assessments in initial assessment reports and site and area assessments in environmental impact assessment reports should include an assessment of social impacts. Provision is also made for specialist reports, which could of course also deal with social impacts (DEAT, 2004).

4. Critical evaluation of SIA regulation in South Africa

It was indicated above that in South Africa SIA is incorporated into EIA. Carley and Bustelo (1984) warn that the inclusion of SIA as an integral part of EIA may lead to very superficial treatment of the socio-economic aspects of a project. The question is whether this has, indeed, been the case in South Africa.

In order to evaluate SIA regulation in South Africa theoretically, the persistent problems in SIA practice identified in the literature are used in this section as basis of discussion. The theoretical framework for SIA provided by the current South African legislation is measured against these persistent problems to reflect on the degree to which the problems are likely to occur in South African SIA practice. Where applicable, available empirical data on SIA practice in South Africa will be used.

4.1. Whose domain?

Clarifying the domain of SIA is a key issue for capacity building in SIA and to counter the poor representation of social scientists in planning, policy and research positions in natural resource management (Baines and Taylor, 2002). SIAs can be undertaken by persons trained in a variety of social sciences (Barrow, 2000), but in practice the majority of EIA consultants in South Africa have a natural science rather than a social science background (Sandham et al., 2005). Because social science staffing in natural resource management agencies remains below adequate levels to provide the necessary expertise for conducting SIAs, assessment of social aspects is often done by non-specialists. Furthermore, people involved in impact assessment may become members of regional branches of the International Association of Impact Assessment (IAIA), but there is still no formal system of registration of impact assessment practitioners in the country. As long as appropriate training programmes for SIA practitioners do not exist, qualified and experienced SIA practitioners are not required by law to register with a professional body, and more social scientists are not involved in EIAs, there will be no final answer to the problem around who is best qualified to take the lead in SIA. Professional accreditation and monitoring of practitioners would improve the practice of SIA, by establishing international standards and improving professional ethics (Barrow, 2000).

4.2. Integration v. segmentation

Segmentation of different types of impact assessment and lack of integration of results remain a problem. Disciplinary, institutional, organisational, capacity and conceptual considerations may stand in the way of closer integration (Rattle and Kwiatkowski, 2003). Suggestions have been made how SIA might be better integrated with other impact assessments (Barrow, 2000; Slootweg et al., 2003). Because SIA covers such a broad scope of social factors, it may become segmented in the EIA process, especially when social scientists from different disciplines are involved. Complex societal problems, often ill-defined and multifaceted, pose a special challenge to SIA practitioners. HIV/AIDS in South Africa is identified by DeTombe (2003) as a good example of such a problem. In South Africa, the application of a different set of EIA processes and requirements to mining activities may on the one hand complicate integration. On the other hand, SIA is incorporated into EIA and it seldom happens that several social scientists are involved in a single EIA, therefore integration may not be such a serious problem, except in very large-scale projects.

4.3. Focus

Determining the size and focus of an SIA is the first major problem confronting SIA practitioners (Becker, 1997). It is required of SIA as part of EIA to be done sufficiently quickly to meet the deadlines of the decision-makers and to be presented in a way that is useful to officials. A too encyclopaedic approach to SIA will take too much time and will produce unwieldy results (Taylor et al., 2004), but if the focus is too narrow and limited to a few standard variables the quality of the SIA will be prejudiced. Balance in this regard can be attained by proper use of scoping. To be useful to decision-makers, results will be limited to significant impacts and the focus will be issues oriented and not general (Taylor et al., 2004). In SIA practice in South Africa the focus tends to be too narrow rather than too broad. This is the result of the tendency among practitioners to meet only the minimum requirements of the law and of the preference among developers and authorities to appoint consultants who undertake EIAs in the shortest time and at the lowest cost (Rossouw et al., 2003). No specific guidelines in this regard have been developed by South African EIA authorities, and this aspect needs to be addressed in the guidelines that will follow the new EIA regulations.

4.4. Problems of concept

Conceptualisation has been problematic in SIA. Clear conceptual frameworks are necessary for SIA, because nobody can be expected to take responsibility for social impacts which are not properly conceptualised (Gramling and Freudenburg, 1992).

One area, identified by Taylor et al. (2004), where conceptual frameworks can be improved, is the analysis of community structure and change. SIA practitioners should have clear notions, grounded in social theory, of community formation and change. Theories of community and consultative techniques have evolved in the literature (see e.g. Armour et al., 1977; Burdge, 1998, 2004; DeLuca, 1977; Taylor et al., 2004). Proper knowledge of these theoretical aspects once again implies, in the South African context, that there should be accredited SIA training programmes to build the necessary capacity.

Another important area is the selection of relevant variables for SIA. If the promise of SIA, that it can provide better information for decision-making, is to be fulfilled, information should deal with the full range of significant social impacts and not just those that are conceptually or politically convenient (Gramling and Freudenburg, 1992). Therefore, the practitioner should have a clear concept of the "social universe", before the relevant significant impacts for a particular SIA can be identified from a list of social impact variables. With the expansion of the SIA literature, several lists, categories and frameworks of social impact monitoring variables have become available (see e.g. Barrow, 2000; Burdge, 1998; Fischer, 1999; Gilpin, 1996; Olsen and Merwin, 1977; Taylor et al., 2004; Vanclay, 1999; Vanclay, 2002; Van Schooten et al., 2003). In South Africa these should be integrated and compiled into guidelines suitable to local conditions, to provide markers for SIA practitioners.

4.5. Does the issue "count"?

Determining the significance of impacts and the weighting of impacts in relation to one another are crucial components of meaningful impact assessment. Sciences that use numerical analysis, such as economics, are more readily used by decision-makers than those that do not, because they present quantifiable measurements. Because the social sciences are regarded as being less accurate and their results as being more difficult to interpret, social impacts are often ignored by decision-makers (Barrow, 2000; Smith, 1993). However, much of the data of social analysis (jobs, income, population, etc.) can be quantified in one way or another and sophisticated computer models have been developed to project trends and create scenarios (see e.g. Aidala, 1977; Barrow, 2000; Becker, 1997; Miller, 1977; Vlachos, 1977). In order to address the difficulty of producing results that are useful to decision-makers SIA theorists have over many years debated the question how and to what extent quantitative techniques could be incorporated into SIA (see e.g. Barrow, 2000; Carley and Bustelo, 1984; Conopask and Reynolds, 1977; Dani, 2003; Sassone, 1977). Although it is recommended that information is summarised in numerical tables as much as possible in an SIA, the danger is that numbers may hide value judgements made in their compilation.

Some very significant social impacts, such as the social and psychological cost of changing lifestyles, cannot be easily quantified and they have to be analysed with qualitative data. For qualitative assessment survey data may be more useful than secondary data, but the SIA practitioner does not always have the luxury of enough time and money to collect primary data. In such a case the best option would be to review the available secondary data first and then fill the gaps by collecting new data (Taylor et al., 2004; See also Barrow, 2000). Whatever method is used, these crucial social variables are much more difficult to assess than others and this may also cause problems with the weighting of findings (Smith, 1993). SIA outcomes with regard to impacts that cannot be quantified may tend to be critical and discursive, rather than predictive and explanatory (Burdge, 1998). SIA recommendations may, therefore, seem less clear, concise and straightforward than other EIA recommendations (Barrow, 2000). However, Burdge (2003a) argues that an indicator, either quantitative or qualitative, can be found for every social impact. Cross-checking procedures (cross validation or triangulation) should be used to establish the validity of data (see Taylor et al., 2004).

From the above it is clear that due to the complexity of social systems the whole issue of determining the significance of social impacts calls for a reasonably expert knowledge of social research methods. Empirical studies of South African EIA practice (Kruger and Chapman, 2005; Sandham et al., 2002, 2005) have revealed that the SIA component of an EIA is often performed by non-specialists. Once again the need for sufficient training of SIA practitioners in South Africa is evident.

4.6. Problems of process

Different orientations towards the SIA process have been identified (Taylor et al., 2004), but regardless of whether a "technocratic" (product oriented) or "participatory" (process oriented) approach is followed, the SIA process usually includes basic EIA procedures, comprising phases of scoping, profiling, formulation of alternatives, projection and estimation of effects, monitoring, mitigation and management, and evaluation (For the key steps in the SIA process, see Becker, 1997; Burdge, 1998; Interorganizational Committee on Guidelines and Principles for Social Impact Assessment, 2003; Vanclay, 1999). In the South African EIA guidelines the process is clearly explained and this may be regarded as, theoretically, one of the strengths of our EIA system. The challenge lies in the ability of SIA practitioners to tap the available literature, methods and techniques and adapt them to particular social settings. Once more the need for SIAs in South Africa to be performed by well-trained SIA specialists is evident.

SIA should not be a once-off activity, producing a "snapshot" view of the social context. It should not be merely an approval mechanism to determine whether a project should proceed and what conditions should be set, but should also be used to ensure effective monitoring, mitigation of problems and management (Barrow, 2000; Burdge, 1998). Therefore social analysis should extend throughout and beyond the project or policy cycle (Francis and Jacobs, 1999). In terms of the World Bank's new PSIA (poverty and social impact analysis) approach, social assessment should be strengthened by including ex-ante analysis of the likely impacts of specific interventions, analysis during implementation, and ex-post analysis of completed interventions (World Bank, 2003; 1. See also Barrow, 2000; Burdge, 2003b; Égré and Senécal, 2003). The primary goal of SIA is "to anticipate a course of events following an environmental change and to manage them accordingly" (Taylor et al., 2004). Therefore SIA must adopt a strategy that can both anticipate and react to change.

In the South African context this approach would mean that SIA should not only be part of EIA, but also of the longer-term IEM, EMP and SEA processes. However, this is not the case in current EIA, mainly because of a lack of capacity in both the implementing authorities and in interested NGOs and CBOs (Rossouw et al., 2003). The South African EIA process does contain the generic phases of EIA, but in practice most EIAs in South Africa do not go beyond a scoping report followed by a record of decision (ROD). Apart from a description of the project and its potential impacts, the scoping report must also include information on alternatives considered and a description of the public participation process. Only in cases where information contained in the scoping report is considered to be insufficient, may the relevant authority request that information in the scoping report be supplemented by a full environmental impact assessment, to be submitted as an Environmental Impact Report (EIR) (DEAT, 1998). In order to short circuit a potentially drawn-out administrative procedure, many scoping reports take on the form of a "beefed-up" scoping or a "mini-EIA", which would usually also include public consultation, mitigation and environmental management steps (Sandham et al., 2005). Empirical studies have suggested that because of unsatisfactory follow-up procedures the "beefed-up" scoping tends to restrict EIA to exactly the type of "snapshot" view that ought to be avoided in SIA. Post-implementation monitoring and auditing are not enforced by law (Rossouw et al., 2003).

4.7. Flexibility v. standardisation

The balance between flexibility and standardisation has been a constant discussion point in SIA discourse. One problem is that when a standardised format of investigation and reporting is used, it may create a bureaucratic uniformity, where the formal requirements become more important than central issues. This is a very real danger in South African EIA practice. SIA often deals with the non-standard and unexpected, and inflexible procedures may prove to be dysfunctional (Barrow, 2000). SIA practitioners can overcome this problem by focusing on projecting social effects and staying issues oriented. It would be useful in the South African EIA system if methodological guidelines for the conduct of social assessments, such as those used by the US Forest Service (USDA Forest Service Collaborative Forest Restoration Program, 2005), could be formulated for South African conditions and appended to the EIA guidelines or better still, to give them mandatory power, incorporated into the EIA regulations. Such guidelines should elaborate on the tasks of the SIA practitioner in each phase of the EIA, but should be flexible.

Taylor et al. (2004) provide guidelines for the format of the SIA process, which are aimed at achieving a balance between standardisation and flexibility. The legitimacy of the contribution of SIA specialists will depend on their effectiveness in contributing to decisions. If such experts were used, instead of simply making do with the available EIA practitioners insufficiently trained for SIA, the contribution of SIA to the overall EIA process will be greatly enhanced. Unfortunately, this is not yet the case in South African EIA practice.

4.8. Decision criteria

Standards used to decide whether an environmental impact is positive or negative are called decision criteria. They are supposed to reflect basic values of what should be happening in a society, but decision-makers often shun making judgements in this regard and prefer to "let the facts speak for themselves". Therefore "social wellbeing" may become a rather fuzzy concept, depending on what different stakeholders assume it to be. It is often believed that social good will result from some very loosely defined "development" path. Citizen values assessment is regarded as a useful tool to avoid fuzziness (Stolp, 2003; See also Barrow, 2000). Taylor et al. (2004) argue that "much human reasoning is an exercise in creative rationalization to defend and promote things in which people have a vested interest". Therefore a crucial issue is who should determine the decision criteria. The danger is that, when those far away from the assessment process set the criteria, physical or technical considerations may take precedence over social considerations. There must be a policy framework, derived from wide public involvement, in place to guide sound thinking in this regard. Hidden agendas will then be avoided more easily. Setting appropriate decision criteria at an early stage will facilitate more careful accounting of costs and benefits of a project. Full disclosure of who gains and who loses and to what extent, is necessary (Burdge, 1998; Taylor et al., 2004).

Moral issues come into play here. SIA is regarded as a moral obligation of decision-makers to identify the future consequences of current or proposed actions, and to take knowledge about these consequences into consideration whenever they act (Becker, 1997). According to Finsterbusch (1995, cited in Becker, 1997) SIA shows a positive value in all seven ethical bases for evaluating public policies. The IAIA (2006) has formulated a code of ethics for EIA (also cited in Becker, 1997) and Lawrence (2003) provides a checklist of ethical aspects in the EIA process. SIA practice should be guided by ethical rules. In the final analysis the "effectiveness of SIA rests on the integrity of the SIA practitioners" (Burdge and Vanclay, 1996).

Because standard criteria of good EIA practice are not applied in South Africa, the EIA process depends to a large extent on consultants' interpretation of the EIA guidelines (Rossouw et al., 2003). One should think that the emphasis on public participation in the South African EIA processes ought to provide the necessary checks and balances, but unfortunately the more deprived communities, who are keen for more job opportunities, are not always in a position to successfully resist development projects which may eventually have more negative than positive social impacts. The government has a special responsibility towards them. Policy frameworks should remain sensitive to basic inequalities in South African society and oriented towards genuine empowerment. To protect the vulnerable an ethical code for EIA practice should be implemented.

4.9. The role of public participation

Public participation is central to SIA and the combination of technocratic and participative approaches is often regarded as SIA's strength (Burdge, 2003b). The purpose of an SIA should be to enable proponents and decision-makers to make socially responsible decisions, which would entail involving the people affected by these decisions (Taylor et al., 2004; See also Becker, 1997; Barrow, 2000; Burdge, 1998; Burdge, 2003b). The concerns, perceptions and judgements of interested and affected parties (IAPs) should be solicited and integrated into SIA processes. Ideally public participation should be included in good faith and at an early stage as an integral part of the assessment process. Effective public participation is regarded as a key to more valid social assessment, without which it would be meaningless (Harris et al., 2003; Wood, 1995). Much has been written about the value of public participation for all stakeholders, particularly in bringing public values and social objectives to the decision-making process and promoting accountability, efficiency, equity and empowerment. It makes a positive contribution towards realising both process and outcome objectives (Cernea, 1991; Glasson et al., 1999; Petts, 1999; Roberts, 2003). According to Buchan (2003) the effort of conducting a proper public participation exercise will be rewarded, because enhancing the capacity of communities to fully participate in decision-making will generate buy-in and social capital which, in the long run, will reduce costs.

Many obstacles, which may block effective public participation, have been identified (Bissett, 2000; Glasson et al., 1999; Hartley and Wood, 2005; Lawrence, 2003; Petts, 1999). Public involvement may in some cases be a genuine participatory exercise and in other cases just public manipulation, which may result in the hidden costs of projects being passed on to the affected communities (Taylor et al., 2004; See also Burdge, 1998; Burdge and Robertson, 1998; Hornback, 1977; PI Student Project, 1998; Roberts, 2003).

Different options have been mooted to facilitate more effective public participation. Webler et al. (1995) developed the idea of "cooperative discourse", involving a citizen panel type model augmented with stakeholder group participation. Petts (1999) refers to the example of successful community advisory committees in the USA. Lawrence (2003) recommends the establishment of public task forces, with EIA practitioners as facilitators. Harris et al. (2003) recommend the establishment of an interactive community forum to involve and empower local residents. All of these options thus imply the establishment of a specific public participation forum.

In developing countries, where the empowerment of the poor and weak should be a priority, SIA has the function to serve as a framework for facilitating public participation and promoting community empowerment (Gagnon et al., 1993; Ross, 1990; World Bank, 1995). However, in countries where there is not a culture of public participation, promoting meaningful participation may be difficult (Vanclay, 2000). This is also the case in South Africa, especially in disadvantaged communities. "Civil society" is a problematic concept in Africa, including South Africa where many members of the public are not properly educated about their rights in terms of the Constitution and NEMA (Hamann et al., 2000). On the other extreme NGOs or CBOs may use public participation to pursue other agendas and hijack the EIA processes.

Public participation is mandatory and receives much attention in South African EIA practice. Theoretically the South African EIA regulations provide an adequate framework for synchronising expert and public inputs in the SIA process. One could argue that both the public consultation and reporting procedures of the typical EIA process in South Africa leave room for attention to cultural and socio-economic impacts. One of the key principles underpinning the South African environmental management procedures is that the "social costs" of development proposals must be outweighed by the "social benefits" (Sowman et al., 1995). In practice the short-circuited EIA procedure makes it very difficult to realise this objective. Social impacts are not treated as a priority issue in the EIA legislation and regulations and it is left to a large extent to the discretion of the EIA practitioners and officials whether and to what extent SIA will be included in any EIA.

Empirical data suggest that in South Africa SIA is often neglected or treated as a less important aspect of an EIA (Kruger and Chapman, 2005; Sandham et al., 2002; Sandham et al., 2005). Public participation, in particular, is a disappointing feature of SIAs in South Africa. The response to invitations to take part in public participation activities is usually meager and very few objections to proposed projects are raised. Interested and affected parties (IAP) meetings take place in a low percentage of EIAs and are usually attended by very few stakeholders apart from the applicants and consultants. Disadvantaged communities tend to be underrepresented at IAP meetings (Hamann et al., 2000), which renders them voiceless in affairs which may be of crucial importance to them. Very few inputs on social impacts are made at public participation meetings, revealing the almost complete lack of public interest in the EIA process. The low interest levels in public participation can be attributed to poverty, low levels of education, and the fact that the environmental agenda is seen in some circles as an obstruction to wealth creation and poverty eradication (Kruger and Chapman, 2005; Sandham et al., 2002). Rossouw et al. (2003) point out that environmental consultants regard developers, by whom they are paid, as their sole clients. Therefore they seldom take the values and concerns of the affected communities into account. Appropriate engagement with poor, disadvantaged and rural communities is particularly inadequate.

The current public participation process in South Africa can therefore be seen as having serious shortcomings. It should be redesigned to make it more effective and truly participative. All relevant IAPs should be identified and adequate and appropriate representation should be introduced at an early stage in the project cycle. Attention should be paid to better means of communication and proper consultation with the IAPs in arranging public participation activities. Techniques should be employed to prepare the community for participation and to empower them to negotiate. More time for public inputs, particularly with regard to social impacts, should be allowed (Hamann et al., 2000; Kruger and Chapman, 2005; Preston et al., 1992). However, the most important single change that needs to be made is to institute an effective negotiating structure.

4.10. An "asocietal mentality"

This concept is attributed to Vanclay and Burdge. Burdge (1998) refers to a prevailing "asocietal mentality", an attitude that humans do not count, in the ranks of the management of regulatory agencies and corporations, politicians, public officials, engineers, economists and some planners. People with such a mindset are not sensitive to social processes. They have little understanding of the complexity and heterogeneity of society, and how the impacts of development benefit and disadvantage different sections of society in different ways. The implications of an "asocietal mentality" for SIA are that the need for SIA is overlooked, that the need for specialised expertise is not recognised, that there are very low expectations from SIA to produce only very superficial social baseline information, and a belief that only a very superficial public involvement process is all that is needed in terms of SIA. There may also be resistance to SIA among administrators and economists, who question its cost-effectiveness or who may be afraid that it will lead to delays or even the abandonment of development projects (Barrow, 2000).

Francis and Jacobs (1999) indicate four conditions necessary for countering an asocietal mentality: enhanced awareness, well-defined procedures and guidelines, proper social assessment methods, and the allocation of sufficient resources. EIA authorities and practitioners in South Africa should engage in a joint effort to meet these conditions in impact assessment practice.

5. Improvement of SIA in South Africa: recommendations and international significance

From the above it is clear that SIA, internationally and in South Africa, has been plagued by a number of problems, mainly related to approach and methods. In the SIA literature there is a clear understanding of the shortcomings that affect the standing of SIA, and recommendations for improvement in a number of areas have been made (Baines and Taylor, 2002; Barrow, 2000; Burdge, 1998; Peterson and Gemmell, 1977). However, as long as social impacts are assessed by consultants who have not been properly trained in social science methods, calls for improved professional standards for SIA will remain unanswered. Higher standards of SIA practice in South Africa can only be achieved when practitioners are professionally trained, accredited and monitored by a professional body. Then professional ethics can be improved and international standards applied (Barrow, 2000).

To improve the theoretical and legal framework within which SIA is practiced in South Africa, the following interventions are recommended:

- Introduce a system of mandatory registration of SIA practitioners.
- Specialised SIA training programmes should be developed and accredited by the South African Qualifications Authority (SAQA). Burdge (1998) makes recommendations on what should be taught in a university SIA course.
- Wherever significant social impacts are identified in an EIA, these should be assessed by an SIA specialist. This is in line with the principle emphasised in the guidelines of the US Interorganizational Committee on Guidelines and Principles for Social Impact Assessment (2003) that in SIA trained social scientists employing proper social science methods will produce the best results.
- A policy framework for SIAs, including a code of ethics for SIA, should be developed by the authorities responsible for EIAs in consultation with the impact assessment profession.
- In the guidelines that will follow the new EIA regulations, specific attention should also be paid to methodological guidelines for the conduct of SIAs. Such guidelines should elaborate on the tasks of the SIA practitioner in each phase of the EIA, but should be flexible. Aspects on which guidance for SIA practitioners is needed, include the features of an issues-oriented approach to SIA, how to identify the significant social impacts of a particular project from a list of social impact variables making up the "social universe", how to combine quantitative and qualitative assessment methods, how to use cross-checking procedures to establish the validity of data, and how to combine expert data and public participation to reach socially responsible decisions.
- The public participation process in South African EIAs should be redesigned to make it more effective and truly participative. An effective statutory negotiating structure should be instituted for this purpose. Vanclay (1999) notes: "Relying on volunteer interest by community members in participation processes is a sure way to achieve a non-representative or biased response." Therefore, statutory bodies on the pattern of the community forums employed in other countries should be introduced if public participation is to fulfill its purpose in South Africa. It is possible to utilise existing structures (e.g. those related to Integrated Development Plans or IDPs) to facilitate public participation. Local councillors, working in consultation with their ward committees, could be drafted into the EIA process with relative ease.

Social impacts will have to be taken much more seriously in South Africa, because they are crucial in empowering disadvantaged communities and in strengthening democratic processes. Some years ago Hamann et al. (2000) emphasised the need for proper balance between participatory processes and the decision-making responsibility of the elected representatives of the people in the context of the South African EIA system. In terms of SIA practice, despite DEAT's claims that environmental management is "part of an overall thrust towards social justice, democracy and sustainable development" (DEAT, 2005), this balance has not yet been achieved.

What is the significance of this national case study of South Africa for international SIA practice? Firstly, the lessons learnt are probably more applicable in developing than in developed countries. Many developing countries face the same basic challenge in terms of EIA and SIA, it is that the capacity is lacking to meet the high standards set in EIA legislation when it comes to the implementation phase. The assistance of stakeholders such as the World Bank should continue beyond the theoretical development of SIA to its practical implementation. Secondly, despite the shortcomings in SIA practice identified in this article, theoretically at least South Africa is a perfect exponent of the shift, identified by Vanclay (2006), from a more technocratic to a more participatory approach to SIA, "beyond the prevention of negative impacts, to include issues of building social capital, capacity building, good governance, community engagement and social inclusion". The above recommendations are meant to serve as markers on the way towards translating these desirable values into professional practice.

References

Aidala JV. Computer-assisted social profiling: some uses of computerized data banks in Social Impact Assessment. In: Finsterbusch K, Wolf CP, editors. Methodology of social impact assessment. Stroudsburg: Hutchinson Ross; 1977. p. 167–71.

Armour A, Bowron B, Miller E, Miloff M. A framework for community impact assessment. In: Finsterbusch K, Wolf CP, editors. Methodology of social impact assessment. Stroudsburg: Hutchinson Ross; 1977. p. 24–34.

Baines J, Taylor N. Institutionalising SIA in rapidly developing economies — the Malaysian case. Paper presented at the 22nd annual conference of the international association for impact assessment. The Netherlands: The Hague; 2002. p. 15–21 [June].

Baines J, Morgan B, Buckenham B. From technology-focused rules to socially responsible implementation: an SIA of proposed home heating rules in Christchurch, New Zealand. Impact Assess Proj Apprais 2003;21(3):187–94.

Barrow CJ. Social impact assessment: an introduction. London: Arnold, 2000.

Becker HA. Social impact assessment: method and experience in Europe, North America and the developing world. London: UCL Press, 1997.

Bissett R. Methods of consultation and public participation. In: Lee N, George C, editors. Environmental assessment in developing and transitional countries: principles, methods, and practice. Chichester: John Wiley and Sons; 2000. p. 149–60.

Buchan D. Buy-in and social capital: by-products of social impact assessment. Impact Assess Proj Apprais 2003;21(3):168–72.

Burdge RJ. A conceptual approach to social impact assessment. Second ed. Middleton: Social Ecology Press, 1998.

Burdge RJ. The benefits of Social Impact Assessment in Third World development. Environ Impact Assess Rev 1990;10:123–34.

Burdge RJ. Why is social impact assessment the orphan of the assessment process? Impact Assess Proj Apprais 2002;20(1):3–9.

Burdge RJ. The practice of social impact assessment — background. Impact Assess Proj Apprais 2003a;21(2):84–8.

Burdge RJ. Benefiting from the practice of social impact assessment. Impact Assess Proj Apprais 2003b;21(3):225–9.

Burdge, RJ. A Community Guide to Social Impact Assessment, Third ed. Social Ecology Press, Middleton; 2004 (1999, 1995). (First ed. 1995, second ed. 1999).

Burdge RJ, Robertson RA. Social Impact Assessment and the public involvement process. In: Burdge RJ, editor. A conceptual approach to social impact assessment. Second ed. Middleton: Social Ecology Press; 1998. p. 183–92.

Burdge RJ, Vanclay F. Social Impact Assessment: a contribution to the state of the art series. Impact Assess 1996;14(1):59–86.

Carley MJ, Bustelo ES. Social impact assessment and monitoring. A guide to the literature. Boulder: Westview Press, 1984.

Cernea MM. Putting people first: sociological variables in rural development, second revised and expanded ed. New York: Oxford University Press, 1991.

Conopask JV, Reynolds RR. Using cost-benefit analysis in Social Impact Assessment: hazards and promise. In: Finsterbusch K, Wolf CP, editors. Methodology of social impact assessment. Stroudsburg: Hutchinson Ross; 1977. p. 83–90.

Dani AA. From mitigating impacts to improving outcomes. Paper presented at the conference on new directions in impact assessment for development: methods and practice, Manchester, 24-25 November; 2003.

DEAT (Department of Environmental Affairs and Tourism), 1997. White Paper on Environmental Management Policy. http://www.environment.gov.za/ (accessed 3 October 2005).

DEAT, 1998. Guideline document, EIA Regulations, Implementation of sections 21, 22 and 26 of the Environment Conservation Act, Pretoria, [April].

DEAT, 2004. Proposed regulations under section 24(5) of the National Environmental Management Act, 1998 (Act no. 107 of 1998) as amended, Pretoria, 25 June.

DEAT, 2005. 10 year review, 1994–2004, Pretoria. http://www.environment.gov.za/ (accessed 3 October 2005).

DEAT, 2006. Environmental protection: quicker, simpler, better new EIA regulations for South Africa (media release), Pretoria, 19 April. http://www.environment.gov.za/ (accessed 13 July 2006).

DeLuca DR. Community structure, resources, and the capacity to respond to environmental problems: new concepts for Social Impact Assessments. In: Finsterbusch K, Wolf CP, editors. Methodology of social impact assessment. Stroudsburg: Hutchinson Ross; 1977. p. 224–34.

DeTombe D. Handling complex societal problems. In: Becker HA, Vanclay F, editors. The international handbook of social impact assessment: conceptual and methodological advances. Cheltenham: Edward Elgar; 2003. p. 278–95.

Égré D, Senécal P. Social impact assessments of large dams throughout the world: lessons learned over two decades. Impact Assess Proj Apprais 2003;21(3):215–24 [September].

Fischer TB. Comparative analysis of environmental and socio-economic impacts in SEA for transport-related policies, plans, and programs. Environ Impact Assess Rev 1999;19:275–303.

Francis P, Jacobs S. Institutionalizing social analysis at the World Bank. Environ Impact Assess Rev 1999;19:341–57.

Freudenburg WR. Social Impact Assessment. Annu Surv Sociol 1986;12:451–78.

Gagnon C, Hirsch P, Howitt R. Can SIA Empower Communities? Environ Impact Assess Rev 1993;13:229–53.

Gilpin A. Environmental Impact Assessment (EIA): cutting edge for the twenty-first century, 1995 edition, 1996 printing. Cambridge: Cambridge University Press, 1996.

Glasson J, Therivel R, Chadwick A. Introduction to environmental impact assessment: principles and procedures, process, practice, and prospects. Second ed. London: UCL Press, 1999.

Glazewski J. Environmental law in South Africa. Durban: Butterworths, 2000.

R.Gramling R, W.R.Freudenburg WR. Opportuniy-threat, development, and adaptation: toward a comprehensive framework for Social Impact Assessment. Rural Sociol 1992;57(2):216–34.

Hamann R, Booth L, O'Riordan T. South African environmental policy on the move. S Afr Geogr J 2000;82(2):11–22.

Harris CC, Nielsen EA, McLaughlin WJ, Becker DR. Community-based social impact assessment: the case of salmon-recovery on the lower Snake River. Impact Assess Proj Apprais 2003;21(2):109–18 [June].

Hartley N, Wood C. Public participation in environmental impact assessment—implementing the Aarhus Convention. Environ Impact Assess Rev 2005;25:319–40.

Henry R. Implementing Social Impact Assessment in developing countries: a comparative approach to the structural problems. Environ Impact Assess Rev 1990;10:91-101.

Hornback KE. Overcoming obstacles to agency and public involvement: a program and its methods. In: Finsterbusch K, Wolf CP, editors. Methodology of social impact assessment. Stroudsburg: Hutchinson Ross; 1977. p. 355–63.

International Association for Impact Assessment (IAIA). Code of ethics for IAIA Members; 2006. http://www.iaia.org/Non_Members/apply_renew_form/code_of_ethics.htm (accessed 13 July 2006).

Interorganizational Committee on Guidelines and Principles for Social Impact Assessment. Principles and guidelines for Social Impact Assessment in the USA. Impact Assess Proj Apprais 2003;21(3):231–50 [September].

Kruger E, Chapman OA. Quality aspects of Environmental Impact Assessment reports in the Free State Province, South Africa. S Afr Geogr J 2005;87(1):52–7.

Lawrence DP. Environmental impact assessment: practical solutions to recurrent problems. Hoboken, N.J.: Wiley-Interscience, 2003.

Miller DC. Methods for estimating societal futures. In: Finsterbusch K, Wolf CP, editors. Methodology of social impact assessment. Stroudsburg: Hutchinson Ross; 1977. p. 202–10.

Momtaz S. Institutionalizing social impact assessment in Bangladesh resource management: limitations and opportunities. Environ Impact Assess Rev 2005;25:33–45.

Olsen ME, Merwin DJ. Toward a methodology for conducting Social Impact Assessments using quality of social life indicators. In: Finsterbusch K, Wolf CP, editors. Methodology of social impact assessment. Stroudsburg: Hutchinson Ross; 1977. p. 43–73.

Peterson GL, Gemmell RS. Social Impact Assessment: comments on the state of the art. In: Finsterbusch K, Wolf CP, editors. Methodology of social impact assessment. Stroudsburg: Hutchinson Ross; 1977. p. 374–87.

Petts J. Public participation and Environmental Impact Assessment. In: Petts J, editor. Handbook of environmental impact assessment. Environmental impact assessment: process, methods and potential. Oxford: Blackwell Science; 1999. p. 145–77.

PI Student Project. Making a mountain out of a mole hill: using public involvement in recreation planning. In: Burdge RJ, editor. A conceptual approach to social impact assessment. Second ed. Middleton: Social Ecology Press; 1998. p. 219–30.

Preston GR, Robins N, Fuggle RF. Integrated environmental management. In: Fuggle RF, Rabie MA, editors. Environmental management in South Africa. Cape Town: Juta; 1992. p. 748–61.

Rattle R, Kwiatkowski RE. Integrating health and social impact assessment. In: Becker HA, Vanclay F, editors. The international handbook of social impact assessment: conceptual and methodological advances. Cheltenham: Edward Elgar; 2003. p. 92-107.

Republic of South Africa. Government gazette, vol. 288, 11927; 1989. Cape Town, 9 June. State President's Office no. 1188: Environment Conservation Act, 1989, Act no. 73 of 1989.

Republic of South Africa. The Constitution of the Republic of South Africa, 1996, Act no. 108 of 1996. Pretoria: Government Printer, 1996.

Republic of South Africa. Government gazette, vol. 387, 18261; 1997a. Government Notice R. 1182, Pretoria, 5 September.

Republic of South Africa. Government gazette, vol. 387, 18261; 1997b. Government Notice R. 1183, Pretoria, 5 September.

Republic of South Africa. Government gazette, vol. 388, 18362; 1997c. Government Notice R. 1355, Pretoria, 17 October.

Republic of South Africa. Government gazette, vol. 393, 18783; 1998a. Government Notice R. 448, Pretoria, 27 March.

Republic of South Africa. Government gazette, vol. 401, 19519; 1998b. Cape Town, 27 November 1998. National Environmental Management Act, Act no. 107 of 1998.

Republic of South Africa. Government gazette, vol. 402, 19599; 1998c. Government Notice R. 1645, Pretoria, 11 December.

Republic of South Africa. Government gazette, vol. 443, 23401; 2002a. Government Notice R. 670, Pretoria, 10 May.

Republic of South Africa. Government gazette, vol. 443, 23401; 2002b. Government Notice R. 672, Pretoria, 10 May.

Republic of South Africa. Government gazette, vol. 448, 23922; 2002c. Cape Town, 10 October. The Presidency, no. 1273: Mineral and Petroleum Resources Development Act, 2002, Act no. 28 of 2002.

Republic of South Africa. Government gazette, vol, 466, 26275; 2004. Regulation Gazette, No. 7949, Pretoria, 23 April 2004. Department of Minerals and Energy, Government Notice R. 527: Mineral and Petroleum Resources Development Act (28/2002): Mineral and Petroleum Resources Development Regulations, Schedule, chapter 2, Part III Environmental regulations for mineral development, petroleum exploration and production.

Republic of South Africa. Government gazette, vol. 28753; 2006a. Pretoria, 21 April 2006. Department of Environmental Affairs and Tourism, Government Notice R. 385: Regulations in terms of chapter 5 of the National Environmental Management Act, 1998.

Republic of South Africa. Government gazette, vol. 28753; 2006b. Pretoria, 21 April 2006. Department of Environmental Affairs and Tourism, Government Notice R. 386: List of activities and competent authorities identified in terms of Sections 24 and 24d of the National Environmental Management Act, 1998.

Rivers MJ, Buchan D. Social assessment and consultation: New Zealand cases. Proj Appraisal 1995;10(3):181–8 [September].

Roberts R. Involving the public. In: Becker HA, Vanclay F, editors. The international handbook of social impact assessment: conceptual and methodological advances. Cheltenham: Edward Elgar; 2003. p. 258–77.

Ross H. Community Social Impact Assessment: a framework for indigenous peoples. Environ Impact Assess Rev 1990;10:229–53.

Rossouw N, Davies S, Fortuin H, Rapholo B, De Wit M, South Africa. In: Tarr P, (comp.). Environmental Impact Assessment in Southern Africa. Southern African Institute for Environmental Assessment: Windhoek; 2003. p. 201-25.

Sandham LA, Siphugu MV, Tshivhandekano TR. Aspects of Environmental Impact Assessment (EIA) practice in the Limpopo Province — South Africa. Afr J Environ Assess Manag 2005;10:50–65 [March].

Sandham L, Van der Walt A, Retief F. Aspects of EIA in the North West Province. Powerpoint presentation of paper presented at the International Conference of the Geographical Union: Durban; 2002.

Sassone PG. Social Impact Assessment and cost-benefit analysis. In: Finsterbusch K, Wolf CP, editors. Methodology of social impact assessment. Stroudsburg: Hutchinson Ross; 1977. p. 74–82.

Smith LG. Impact assessment and sustainable resource management. Burnt Mill: Longman; 1993.

Slootweg R, Vanclay F, Van Schooten M. Integrating environmental and social impact assessment. In: Becker HA, Vanclay F, editors. The international handbook of social impact assessment: conceptual and methodological advances. Cheltenham: Edward Elgar; 2003. p. 56–73.

Sowman M, Fuggle R, Preston G. A review of the evolution of environmental evaluation procedures in South Africa. Environ Impact Assess Rev 1995;15:45–67.

Stolp A. Citizen values assessment. In: Becker HA, Vanclay F, editors. The international handbook of social impact assessment: conceptual and methodological advances. Cheltenham: Edward Elgar; 2003. p. 231–57.
Taylor CN, Bryan CH, Goodrich CG. Social assessment: theory, process and techniques. Third ed. Lincoln: Taylor Baines Associates, 2004.
USDA Forest Service Collaborative Forest Restoration Program. Handbook 5: monitoring social and economic effects of forest restoration. Flagstaff: Ecological Restoration Institute, Northern Arizona University, 2005.
F.Vanclay F. Social Impact Assessment. In: Petts J, editor. Handbook of environmental impact assessment. Environmental impact assessment: process, methods and potential. Oxford: Blackwell Science; 1999. p. 301–26.
Vanclay F. Social Impact Assessment. In: Lee N, George C, editors. Environmental assessment in developing and transitional countries: principles, methods, and practice. Chichester: John Wiley and Sons; 2000. p. 125–35.
Vanclay F. Conceptualising social impacts. Environ Impact Assess Rev 2002;22:183–211.
Vanclay F. International principles for Social Impact Assessment. Impact Assess Proj Apprais 2003;21(1):5-11.
Vanclay F. Principles for social impact assessment: a critical comparison between the international and US documents. Environ Impact Assess Rev 2006;26:3-14.
Van Schooten M, Vanclay F, Slootweg R. Conceptualizing social change processes and social impacts. In: Becker HA, Vanclay F, editors. The international handbook of social impact assessment: conceptual and methodological advances. Cheltenham: Edward Elgar; 2003. p. 74–91.
Vlachos E. The use of scenarios for Social Impact Assessment. In: Finsterbusch K, Wolf CP, editors. Methodology of social impact assessment. Stroudsburg: Hutchinson Ross; 1977. p. 211–23.
Weaver A, Chonguica E, Rukato H, Tarr P. NEPAD and environmental assessment. Afr J Environ Assess Manag 2003;7:1-13 [November].
Webler T, Kastenholz H, Renn O. Public participation in impact assessment: a social learning perspective. Environ Impact Assess Rev 1995;15:443–63.
Wood C. Environmental Impact Assessment: A Comparative Review. Harlow: Longman Group, 1995.
World Bank. Social assessment, environment department dissemination notes, vol. 36. Washington DC: World Bank, 1995.
World Bank. World bank poverty reduction group and social development department, a user's guide to poverty and social impact analysis. Washington D.C.: International Bank for Reconstruction and Development, 2003.

Jacobus A du Pisani is currently a Professor of History in the School of Social and Government Studies at the Potchefstroom campus of the North-West University in South Africa. In a research career of almost thirty years he has published on contemporary South African political history, masculinities studies and environmental history. He is now engaged in graduate studies in environmental science and this article is part of a master's dissertation focusing on SIA practice in the North West Province of South Africa.

Luke Sandham is a senior lecturer in Geography and Environmental Management. He has published in the field of remote sensing, and his current research interest is the effectiveness of Environmental Assessment in Southern Africa. In this context he has supervised several masters dissertations.

[36]

Journal of Environmental Management 90 (2009) S249–S257

Journal of Environmental Management

Social impacts of large dam projects: A comparison of international case studies and implications for best practice

Bryan Tilt [a,*], Yvonne Braun [b,1], Daming He [c,2]

[a] Oregon State University, Department of Anthropology, 238 Waldo Hall, Corvallis, OR 97331-6403, USA
[b] University of Oregon, Department of Sociology, 1291 University of Oregon, Eugene, OR 97403-1291, USA
[c] Asian International Rivers Center, Yunnan University, Wenjin Building, 6th Floor, No. 2 Green Lake North Road, Kunming, Yunnan 650091, People's Republic of China

ARTICLE INFO

Article history:
Received 15 September 2007
Received in revised form 1 April 2008
Accepted 30 July 2008
Available online 12 November 2008

Keywords:
Social impact assessment
Large dams
Displacement
Resettlement
Lesotho
China

ABSTRACT

This paper applies the tool of social impact assessment (SIA) to understand the effects of large dam projects on human communities. We draw upon data from two recent SIA projects: the Lesotho Highlands Water Project in Southern Africa, and the Manwan Dam, located on the upper Mekong River in southwestern China. These two cases allow us to examine the social impacts of large dam projects through time and across various geographical scales. We focus on a range of social impacts common to many large-scale dam projects, including: the migration and resettlement of people near the dam sites; changes in the rural economy and employment structure; effects on infrastructure and housing; impacts on non-material or cultural aspects of life; and impacts on community health and gender relations. By identifying potential impacts in advance of a large dam project, agencies and policymakers can make better decisions about which interventions should be undertaken, and how. We conclude our analysis with an overview of lessons learned from the case studies and suggestions for best practice in assessing the social impacts of large dams. Conducting proper social impact assessments can help to promote development strategies that address the most important concerns for local populations, enhancing the long-term sustainability of dam projects.

© 2008 Elsevier Ltd. All rights reserved.

1. Introduction

Over the past several decades, there have been heated debates over the pros and cons of building large dams.[3] Beyond the physical and ecological impacts associated with hydropower projects, such debates also focus on the geographical distribution of electrical power and water resources, the administrative decision-making process, the inclusion of relevant stakeholders, the relocation and resettlement of displaced inhabitants, and the disruption of social, cultural, and economic life in communities affected by dam construction. Growing global concern about the social costs of large dam projects, and about how to solicit meaningful participation from those most affected, resulted in the formation of the World Commission on Dams in 1998 and the publication of the first systematic assessment of large dams around the world in 2000 (World Commission on Dams, 2000a).

Since that time, social impact assessment (SIA) has been conducted on large dam projects in a variety of settings, including southern Africa (Thabane, 2000), China (Jackson and Sleigh, 2000; Jing, 2000), Guatemala (Aguiree, 2005), and India (Phadke, 2005). These research efforts have begun to shed light on the widespread, prominent and long-lasting effects of hydropower development. However, there is as yet little consensus about how best to use social impact assessment as a research tool for understanding the impacts of dams on human communities, and what variables to consider in the SIA process.

Our objective in this paper is to introduce the tool of social impact assessment and reflect on its usefulness for understanding the social impacts of large dam projects. To illustrate our points, we present the results of two recent SIA projects: the Lesotho Highlands Water Project in Southern Africa, and the Manwan Dam, located on the upper Mekong River in Yunnan Province, China. Large dam projects often attract controversy, and the two projects reviewed here rank among the most contentious in recent history. These two disparate cases allow us to examine the social impacts of large dam projects through time and across various geographical

---

* Corresponding author. Tel.: +1 541 737 3896.
E-mail addresses: bryan.tilt@oregonstate.edu (B. Tilt), ybraun@uoregon.edu (Y. Braun), hedaming@public.km.yn.cn (D. He).
[1] Tel.: +1 541 346 5752.
[2] Tel.: +86 871 503 4577.
[3] There are various interpretations of what exactly constitutes a "large dam." For the purposes of this paper, we follow the definition offered by the International Commission on Large Dams (ICOLD): those more than 15 m in height or having a storage capacity of more than 3 million cubic meters (ICOLD, 1998; see also Scudder, 2005: 2–3).

0301-4797/$ – see front matter © 2008 Elsevier Ltd. All rights reserved.
doi:10.1016/j.jenvman.2008.07.030

scales. We conclude our analysis with an overview of lessons learned from the case studies and suggestions for best practice in assessing the social impacts of large dams.

2. Assessing the social impacts of large dams

Vanclay (2002b: 388) defines SIA in the following manner:

Social impact assessment is the process of analyzing (predicting, evaluating and reflecting) and managing the intended and unintended consequences on the human environment of planned interventions (policies, programs, plans, projects) and any social change processes invoked by these interventions so as to bring about a more sustainable and equitable biophysical and human environment.

The goals of SIA are quite straightforward. By identifying potential impacts in advance of a large project, agencies and individuals can make better decisions about which interventions should be undertaken, and how. Furthermore, mitigation and compensation measures can be undertaken to minimize the undesirable impacts of development interventions. This is in line with Principle 1 of the Rio Declaration (1992), which affirmed that "human beings are at the center of concerns for sustainable development."

In the United States, social impact assessment often takes place under a federal mandate. Since the passage of the National Environmental Policy Act (NEPA) in 1970, environmental impact assessment has become an integral part of the environmental decision-making process in the United States. Under NEPA, federal agencies must conduct thorough environmental impact statements (EISs) prior to undertaking any actions with the potential to significantly affect the quality of the human environment. Environmental Impact Statements typically include a social science component that assists agencies in understanding the social consequences of policies, programs and projects. In 1994, the Interorganizational Committee on Guidelines and Principles for Social Impact Assessment produced basic guidelines for conducting SIA in federal projects, updated in 2003 (ICGP, 1994, 2003).

Because social, cultural and political conditions differ in disparate locations, conducting social impact assessment in international contexts can be particularly challenging. Responding to the need for internationally relevant guidelines for SIA, the International Association for Impact Assessment (IAIA) developed a set of principles that are broadly applicable to large development projects. These principles include, among other things, a dedication to the precautionary principle, intragenerational and intergenerational equity, the preservation of social and cultural diversity, and the internalization of costs associated with a planned intervention (Vanclay, 2003).

These principles can be used to predict and assess the impacts of large-scale dam projects. As might be expected, many of the most challenging socioeconomic impacts of dam construction relate to the migration and resettlement of people near the dam site or in the catchment area (Bartolome et al., 2000; Cernea, 2003; Egre and Senecal, 2003; Scudder, 1997, 2005). This primary impact results in a wide array of subsequent social impacts, including changes in household size and structure (Lerer and Scudder, 1999); changes in employment and income-generating opportunities; alteration of access and use of land and water resources; changes in social networks and community integrity (Fuggle and Smith, 2000); changes in the nature and magnitude of various health risks (Lerer and Scudder, 1999; McMillan, 1995); and often a disruption of the psycho-social wellbeing of displaced individuals (Scudder, 2005; World Commission on Dams, 2000b). Managing and mitigating the socioeconomic impacts of dam construction is an important task since, as the WCD noted in its seminal report, these effects are "spatially significant, locally disruptive, lasting, and often irreversible" (World Commission on Dams, 2000b: 102).

3. The Lesotho Highlands Water Project

3.1. Background and methods

The Lesotho Highlands Water Project (LHWP) was designed as a water delivery scheme between the governments of South Africa and Lesotho and is one of the five largest dam-development projects currently under construction in the world. Based on a treaty signed in 1986, the $8 billion project is funded in part by the World Bank, the African Development Bank, the European Community, and several European funding agencies, and implemented by the parastatal Lesotho Highlands Development Authority (LHDA) in Lesotho. The water delivery scheme will include five dams linked to cross-national tunnels constructed in four phases over a period of 30 years (1987–2017). Three dams (Katse, 'Muela, and Mohale) have been completed and two others (Mashai and Tsoelike) are still in the planning phases (see Fig. 1).

The first objective of the LHWP is to sell, transfer and deliver water from Lesotho's Senqu River and its tributaries to the Gauteng (including Johannesburg) industrial region of South Africa. In return, South Africa was estimated to pay approximately $55 million in royalties to Lesotho each year; however, recent reports show that Lesotho has received closer to $18 million in average annual revenues (Hassan, 2002; United Nations, 2003) because water levels were below initial projections. The second objective is to create a hydroelectric power station allowing Lesotho to generate electricity domestically.[4] An important documented obligation of the project is to not worsen the current standards of living of the project affected peoples (Lesotho Highlands Development Authority, 1986).

The prospect of large dams as a development strategy for Lesotho was first voiced in the 1950s, but only in the late 1970s and early 1980s was it seen as viable. For South Africa, the challenge was to identify an extensive water source for the prospering commercial and industrial sectors of the Gauteng region (including Johannesburg). In contrast, Lesotho was seen as having almost no other development options, for several reasons. Its predominantly rural population is engaged in primarily subsistence-oriented agriculture; its suffered from not having a viable market as exported crops could not compete with those of South Africa; and male labor migration rates to the mines of South Africa peaked during the late 1970s (Epprecht, 2000; Gordon, 1981). Ironically, the convergence at that time of the needs of the apartheid South African state and the military government of Lesotho, and the historical dominance of South Africa's relationship with Lesotho, seems to have set the stage for Lesotho's participation in the LHWP (Bardrill and Cobbe, 1985; Nkomo, 1990; Tsikoane, 1991).

As a "least developed country" (Ferguson, 2004; United Nations, 2003), Lesotho has a long history of externally funded development projects, but none quite as extensive as the LHWP.[5] The highlands

---

[4] The small number of households with electricity prior to the LHWP imported electricity from South Africa. Preliminary figures suggest that even after the operation of the 'Muela hydropower station, the cost of setting up electricity is prohibitively high for new consumers. The small proportion of households with electricity prior to the LHWP continues to import it.

[5] In fact, it is quite surprising for a small country with such minimal economic resources, and questionable institutional capacity for project of this extent, to have been eligible for receiving World Bank funding. At the time of the LHWP agreements, South Africa was under apartheid rule with full sanctions against aid of this type. Lesotho was made the proxy receiver of the loans despite their ineligibility (for a more detailed discussion see Tsikoane, 1991).

Fig. 1. Map of the Lesotho Highlands Water Project. Source: Trans-Caledon Tunnel Authority (TCTA, 2005).

areas chosen for construction of the completed dams (Katse, 'Muela, Mohale) contain some of the most remote and poorest communities within Lesotho, with some of the highest rates of unemployment and destitution. At the beginning of the LHWP, 60 percent of households in both areas of Katse and 'Muela fell below the average income for each area and were considered "very poor" (Sechaba Consultants, 1994; Tshabalala and Turner, 1989).

Construction of the dam-related infrastructure began in 1987, creating an extensive geographical area impacted by the LHWP before any dams were built. In 1993, dam construction at Katse began, eventually creating a reservoir to serve as the largest holding tank for the water being sold to South Africa (through 'Muela). The 185 m double curvature arch dam completed impoundment in 1998, creating a 1950 million m³ reservoir. The catchment area for 'Muela, the second dam of Phase 1A, underwent impoundment in 1999. Eighty-two kilometers of transfer and delivery tunnels from Katse and tunnels to the Ash River in South Africa connect at the tailpond site in 'Muela, thus impacting an extensive geographical area. Mohale Dam, a concrete-faced rockfill dam standing 145 m high, was still under construction during the social impact study (2000–2001), but the first of two phases of resettlement was in process and many Mohale communities had been impacted by the project for years prior. The Mohale dam was completed in November 2002 and in 2006 reached its full capacity as a 947 million m³ reservoir (Lesotho Highlands Development Authority, 2006).

Data for the social impact assessment of the LHWP is drawn from two periods of research. In 1997, one of the authors (Braun) spent two months working with an indigenous non-governmental organization, the Highlands Church Action Group (HCAG), at all three dam sites. Thirteen semi-structured, open-ended interviews were conducted (in English) with development officials. In addition, 25 semi-structured, open-ended interviews (in the Sesotho language, with English translation) were conducted with people directly impacted and living in the three dam project areas. During the second phase of research in 2000 and 2001, six teams of research assistants carried out two waves of surveys and interviews with a sample of 263 households in the three LHWP areas, revisiting approximately 15 percent of the original households in the second wave. Villages were stratified by dam site, categories of impact, and other socioeconomic characteristics for a total sample including 10 villages in the Katse area, fourteen villages in the 'Muela area, and 17 villages in the Mohale area. Households within these villages were then sampled randomly.

3.2. Social impacts of the LHWP

Most participants in the LHWP study had ambivalent feelings about the project as a whole. While there were benefits that most people embraced, such as new roads, many residents impacted directly by the LHWP reported intense disappointment, distrust, and specific grievances with the substance and execution of the policies of the project and its impacts on their lives. Below are some of the main categories of social impacts, by no means an exhaustive list, presented in three categories: effects on the rural economy; effects on culture, health and gender; and effects on infrastructure, transportation and housing.

3.2.1. Effects on the rural economy

Rural residents experienced changes in their relation to their environment and its resource base. These changes occurred either directly (through loss of access to land or other resources) or indirectly (through policies that had the effect of changing the nature of relations to resources or division of labor). The current geopolitical structure of wealth and power disadvantages the rural poor of the highlands in Lesotho. As the Lesotho government increasingly prioritizes the commercial uses of resources and the re-organization of rural resources towards the benefit of the state and urban areas, rural households undergo serious disruption to their livelihoods, absorbing the economic, ecological, and social costs of their resources being re-structured. Study participants reported losing sources of potable water and natural springs; decreased access to wild vegetables and herbs that are important food and medicinal resources; losing access to forests and wooded areas that were submerged in the reservoirs; losing some of the best arable land in the river basin areas; as well as stones and mud for building purposes (Braun, 2006). In losing these resources without compensation, the impacted population effectively subsidizes this international development project as they attempt to replace their lost resources using strategies of increased labor allocation, increased purchasing or a greater reliance on cash, or are left to go without these resources.

Development authorities are typically required to have compensation policies to mitigate some of the material losses that households absorb, as well as rural development programs that address some of the socioeconomic changes that result. Most development programs are typically justified as poverty-reduction measures and, in the case of dam infrastructure projects, as mitigative measures for those impacted. While the World Bank has declared that any subsidized economic project must also be a development project (Cernea, 1988), the programs that comprise the "development" portion of the LHWP generally are secondary measures that aim to serve the dual purpose of fulfilling the World Bank standards and the LHWP's treaty obligations to ensure that the standards of living of the affected peoples are not lowered.[6]

However, contextualizing the LHWP as part of this larger pattern of dam projects, the rural poor are in fact burdened with a disproportionate share of the losses from these schemes, and arguably receive an inadequate share of the benefits (Panel of Environmental Experts, 1997, 1995, 1994, 1993). This has clearly been in the case in

---

[6] See the LHDA Order of 1986, Article XII for the original conditions.

Lesotho; in fact, the experiences of suffering and difficulty faced by many of the people impacted and resettled stand in stark contrast to the development promises that came with the LHWP (Thamae and Pottinger, 2006). The struggle between the governments of South Africa and Lesotho to minimize their respective costs or to pass on costs to the other, including the costs of rural development and compensation programs, underlies the decision-making processes regarding planning and implementation (Panel of Environmental Experts, 1989).

The Rural Development Plan (RDP) of the LHWP was designed to provide skills training and alternative income-generating activities in recognition that those seriously impacted would be hard pressed to have a means to maintain their standard of living (Panel of Environmental Experts, 1995, 1991). However, the implementation and the planning were seriously underdeveloped and under-prioritized (Panel of Environmental Experts, 1995: 16). The costs of the RDP were in the "grey area" that neither Lesotho nor South Africa's development authority saw as its responsibility. While the loss of land and compensation policy began as early as 1988, the RDP was not in effect until 1993 and it is still not considered highly structured or effective.

Impacts on the employment structure of the area were also significant. Migrants from South Africa and other parts of Lesotho often settled on the outskirts of Khokhoba, a large village in close proximity to the employee housing at Katse Dam, while looking for work. Very few Basotho people, local or migrant, found formal work with the LHWP. In particular, the development authority hired men for almost all positions so most work available to women was informal, unregulated, and poorly paid. Some women from other villages came to the highlands area in the hope of getting jobs as domestic servants in the skilled employee village, thus creating more competition for the local women trying to obtain the few jobs available (Detter and Gunnewig, 1994). Jobs included cleaning, cooking, or sweeping at "whites' houses." These labor hierarchies created by the project contributed to a racialized and gendered landscape of increasing inequality.

3.2.2. Effects on infrastructure, transportation and housing

At Katse dam, an earthquake occurred in September 1996 as the reservoir was filling after impoundment. In the middle of the night, tremors shook the village of Mapeleng the hardest, scaring people out of their homes as they ran in fear for safety. Some homes suffered moderate damage while others experienced their belongings falling off the walls unexpectedly. Reservoir-induced seismicity is a less common, less discussed outcome of certain types of large dam projects. Lacking adequate preparation, education on the potential for earthquakes, or an early warning system, this seismic activity was a shocking and devastating event for those directly impacted. In addition to triaging the emergency conditions, this earthquake required the relocation of most of the village of Mapeleng and additional compensation for people impacted.

Approximately 20,500 residents in over 120 villages in the Maluti Mountains project areas were affected by the construction phase of the LHWP in a variety of ways (Tshabalala and Turner, 1989): by the construction of the dams themselves; by the construction of the infrastructure for the dam and tunnel system through Lesotho to South Africa; by the construction of roads through mountains; and by the construction of employee "camps" due to the long duration of LHWP (Braun, 2006; Detter and Gunnewig, 1994). When households were resettled, they were moved into new homes that approximated the same size of their previous homes and had some limited choices about style. Many resettled people expressed ambivalence about their new houses; most appreciated the beauty of the cement structures but complained of the difficulties of heating and cooking. Households who lost land during the resettlement process were given monetary compensation rather than replacement land, but most had a small garden space. In addition, resettled households received a financial "disturbance" allocation over a period of four years to help them get settled.

Households that would be submerged by the Katse reservoir were resettled within the same river basin area with no other options. While this avoided significantly altering social ties in affected villages, it proved problematic as those resettled often lost their agricultural lands and had few economic alternatives to farming. The resettlement program at Mohale was significantly different from the one at Katse in that it allowed resettled people to choose among several destinations. In particular, resettled people could choose to move uphill and stay in the larger Mohale area, to relocate to villages near Mohale (the lowlands), or to move to peri-urban areas near the capital, Maseru. Many households were moved in "clusters" into host villages which had agreed to absorb some of the resettled population. Host-settler conflicts occur in some villages, particularly over the allocation of burial space (Braun, 2005a).

Compensation to affected households was an important part of the LHWP. In large dam projects, affected people often subsidize the project with their agricultural and grazing lands, gardens, trees, river valleys and water sources, homes, burial grounds. Compensation packages that serve as mitigation for these losses depend on the sets of values determined by the development authorities, and on the successful implementation of those policies. For example, the compensation plans for Katse and 'Muela, the first two dam areas of the LHWP, were designed and implemented under the same project phase (1A). After significant local and international pressure, the compensation plans for these areas were retroactively changed. In the new plan, compensation for losses included lump sum cash payments for small plots of land and annual deliveries of maize and beans for larger agricultural plots, with some households receiving annuities in perpetuity. Private fruit and wood trees were to be replaced with saplings, but there are conflicting reports about whether this happened systematically, or at all. Compensation was not provided for communally owned or managed resources, except for small amounts of fodder for animal owners for five years.

At the third dam area, Mohale, the compensation plan was part of the second phase (1B) of the LHWP and was designed more comprehensively. This package includes annuities in perpetuity for agricultural land and assets of certain sizes. Households in the vicinity of the dam that lost arable land, but were not resettled, are being considered under a compensation policy that gives special consideration to those who have lost 50 percent or more of their landholdings. According to the LHDA, losses range from 309 m^2 to almost 5 ha per household (LHDA, 2006).

In addition to the direct losses that people experience in large dam projects, there is the social experience of having the physical presence of a large dam being built in close proximity. As the LHDA built roads and infrastructure in preparation for the construction of the dam, a main road was paved through the middle of the village of Makhoabeng on its way to Khokhoba village, arguably the most adversely affected village in the Katse area, which became centrally located just above the main traffic intersection. The LHDA then appropriated all of Khokhoba's pasture lands and built a hotel, shopping center, development authority offices, and a gated, suburban-style employee residential village just downslope from Khokhoba. The creation of a "gated foreign suburban community" next to the most severely affected village in the Katse basin, and actually built on their grazing land, stood in contradiction to the stated expectations that local businesses and local people would benefit from the presence of the large foreign workforce.

3.2.3. Effects on culture, health and gender

In many cases, the losses and impacts of large-scale dam development disproportionately burden the rural poor, and create especially intense pressures on women (Braun, 2005a). While the LHWP was justified as a national development strategy for poverty reduction, the implementation of the project has the potential to create contradictory circumstances for many Basotho women. Women are generally more vulnerable to the negative consequences of the LHWP. In particular, women reported increased workloads, the burden of having to make more household purchases, decreased nutritional status in some cases, less access to gatherable resources, and less access to the compensation benefits from the development authority (Braun, 2005b, 2006).

In contrast to other programs, the Rural Development component provided different training for men and women. Welding and masonry were training programs designated for men, while dairy and poultry programs were designed for women. The programs designed for men are generally outside the home, while for women they are tasks that can be done at or close to home. While this may be helpful for women with young children, it also serves to reinforce the identification of women's labor within the home.

Men's skills as designated by the RDP led to wage labor and did not require large investments for technical inputs. In contrast, women's labor under the plan centered around selling a marketable product and required a large investment for either dairy cows or poultry. Women do not generally have access to large amounts of money or cattle, which hold special importance as a source of financial security for rural households (Ferguson, 2004). Dairy cows are very rare in Lesotho and beginning a dairy business entails a very large capital expenditure. The poultry training program was more feasible in rural Lesotho; however, practical obstacles still existed for many women in trying to use the training they received.

More broadly, the position of rural Basotho households in the larger economy limits their ability to access large amounts of capital to fund these start up projects. The project authorities realized to a certain extent that these rural development programs would require a financial investment of households that would be beyond their capacity, and special credit availability was planned to be given to those directly impacted by the LHWP. However, by law in Lesotho women do not have access to credit and "special availability" was useless to women unless they received their husband's signature. Through the RDP, the development authorities in Lesotho reinforced women's customary secondary status by allowing women to access credit programs only through husbands or fathers, reinforcing and exacerbating existing gender inequalities. While the credit program was not implemented fully in most cases, this points to a more general problem of social programs being neglected, delayed, or underprioritized relative to the engineering and construction components of large dam projects.

The dam projects had other unforeseen effects on gender relations. As the first, largest, and most remote dam, the degree of infrastructure needed to support the building of the Katse dam demanded a large workforce of engineers, planners, and variously skilled laborers to be in the area for almost a decade. While foreigners—mostly white men—from more industrialized countries received the longer term, more secure, and higher paid professional, skilled, and semi-skilled positions with the project, most Basotho men only had access to insecure, casual, and low paid "piece" jobs demanding heavy physical labor. Women had almost no formal work opportunities. Many people directly impacted by the LHWP discussed with great concern the rise in sex work during the construction of the Katse dam, noting the impacts that these economic strategies had for women and girls, including health risks such as STDs, HIV/AIDS, and exposure to violence and stigma, as well as the impacts for marital relations and the broader community.

4. The Manwan Dam, upper Mekong River, China

4.1. Background and methods

China has a history of dam building that stretches more than 2000 years into the past. The Dujiangyan, for example, was constructed on the Chengdu Plain of southwest China 2200 years ago and is still used effectively today for flood control and irrigation. Dams remain an integral part of the national infrastructure; approximately 86,000 dams were built in China during the period from 1949 to 1990. The past several decades of rapid economic growth fuel China's ever-increasing demand for electrical power. Although basic environmental impact assessments have been conducted prior to major hydropower development in China since the 1980s, these were quite simple, often resulting in unforeseen social and environmental problems.

The exploitation of the upper Mekong River Basin (called the Lancang River in Chinese) for electric power potential commenced more than 60 years ago. The Tianshengqiao Hydropower Station, with an installed capacity of 400 kW, was completed in 1946. It is situated on the Xier River, a tributary of the Lancang River. Since the 1980s, Lancang hydropower development has taken place on the middle and downstream sections of the mainstem with a cascade development of eight dams planned (see Fig. 2). The Manwan hydropower station, with an installed capacity of 1500 MW, was completed in 1996. Dachaoshan hydropower station, with an installed capacity of 1350 MW, was completed in 2003. Both are currently in operation. The Xiaowan hydropower station, with an installed capacity of 4200 MW, is under construction and will be completed in 2012. Jinghong hydropower station, with an installed capacity of 1500 MW, began construction in 2006 (He and Chen, 2002).

This section of the paper addresses the impacts of the Manwan Dam, located in the middle reach of the Lancang River, and the first dam of the Lancang mainstream cascade development. The Manwan hydropower station was initially a joint project of the Yunnan

Fig. 2. The distribution of hydropower projects along the mainstem of the Lancang River.

provincial government and the Ministry of Water Resources and Electric Power, but has since become a stock company called Hydrolancang, a subsidiary of China Huaneng Group, which holds a state-granted monopoly on hydropower development in the region (Magee, 2006). Data for this section of the paper is drawn from a social and environmental impact study which was sponsored by Oxfam Hong Kong during the summer of 2000 and incorporated into a document entitled "Reasonable and Equitable Utilization of Water Resources and Water Environment Conservation in International Rivers in Southwest China," a key component of China's 9th National Five Year Plan for Science and Technology.[7]

The dam measures 132 m high with a crest length of 418 m and a backwater of 70 km. At the normal water level of 994 m, its reservoir covers an area of 23.6 km^2. After its completion, 6225 mu (411 ha) of farmland and 8508 mu (562 ha) of woodlands were inundated, resulting in significant impacts for 114 villages in 8 townships and 4 counties (Jingdong, Yun, Fengqing and Nanjian)[8] Prior to construction, the number of displaced farmers was estimated to be 3052, but the actual figure was 7260. Worldwide, dam resettlement programs often underestimate the number of potentially displaced people, which can be especially problematic when budgeting is based on the initial lower estimate. Resettlement of the local population can be classified into five types: (1) rural resettlement outside the reservoir region; (2) rural resettlement within the reservoir region; (3) resettlement into nearby cities and towns; (4) in situ resettlement with reallocation of resources; and (5) in situ resettlement without resource reallocation.

Several research methods were employed to assess the social impacts associated with the Manwan Dam. Our inquiry began with a survey of the relevant social science literature on dam impacts. Data were then gathered through participative processes that included case studies, focus groups, and home visits with affected individuals. Visits and interviews were conducted at the county, township, and village levels, as well as with farmers and power plant staff.

4.2. Social impacts of the Manwan Dam

4.2.1. Effects on the rural economy

The economy of the rural areas adjacent to the Manwan Dam experienced significant impacts, including a decline in productivity in agriculture and animal husbandry, shortages of water for irrigation, increasing costs for electricity, and depletion of forest resources.

The agricultural sector of the affected counties was severely impacted by the Manwan Dam project. In 1991, per-capita farmland ranged from 1.02 mu to 1.96 mu (0.067–0.129 ha), with an average holding of 1.79 mu (0.118 ha) per capita. Following the completion of the Manwan Dam in 1996, this figure dropped to 1.21 mu (0.08 ha). The quality of available agricultural lands also changed significantly. In rural China, paddy fields with intensive irrigation systems are the most highly valued land type and are used for growing the staple grain crop. Prior to the Manwan Dam project, the ratio of paddy fields to non-irrigated fields in the reservoir area was 6:4; this dropped to 4:6 after the inundation of the valley, resulting in decreased rice yields and a shift to other dryland crops such as maize and sugar cane. Many villagers have resorted to trading maize for rice to meet household consumption needs. Moreover, newly created paddy fields lack adequate irrigation and soil fertility, producing yields at approximately one-third previous levels.

While fruit trees provided a major source of cash income prior to inundation, 71.6% of orchard lands were lost after reservoir impoundment. Livestock production and breeding were also a mainstay of the local economy and centered on cattle, sheep and mules. Hundreds of mu of forage lands were inundated when the reservoir filled up, resulting in a drastic scale-back of animal husbandry. In Nanjian County alone, 4.8 km^2 of forage lands were submerged, placing the future viability of the livestock industry in question.

Ironically, while the impoundment of a massive reservoir at Manwan has meant a reliable irrigation source for downstream communities, it has resulted in water shortages for adjacent communities. In Hongyan Village, one of our study sites, the county government spent over RMB 3 million to provide at least 1 mu of irrigated paddy fields to each resettled household.[9] But the infrastructure required to deliver such a service proved too difficult to manage with local resources. The water originated in Yongde County and ran for 21 km, passing through three villages. A channel was dug through Mangguai Shan Mountain and a pump was installed to deliver water to the village. However, a year later, massive erosion and landslides rendered the project inoperable.

Meeting household heating and cooking needs has become an unforeseen problem in resettled villages. In Hongyan Village, located in Yun County, 800 mu (52.8 ha) of firewood slopes were allotted to the village when it was relocated in 1993. At present, only one-third remains due to intensive harvesting. As a result, villagers frequently walk 3–4 km in search of firewood, a task that generally falls to women. The county governments, in conjunction with the power company, have stepped up efforts to provide alternative energy sources to villagers, including biogas facilities which use human and animal waste from households. Such facilities require an investment of RMB 4500–5000 per household, only part of which is provided by government and private investment.

Ironically, chronic electricity shortages plague the area adjacent to the Manwan Dam, which is geared primarily towards sending electricity eastward to the booming cities of Guangdong province under a national plan called "Send Western Electricity East" (Magee, 2006). Although every resettled village has been connected to the power grid, power supplied by the Manwan facility can be purchased for RMB 0.9–1.5 per unit, which is several times more expensive than the electricity previously supplied by a micropower station on a small tributary, which was inundated by the reservoir.

These changes have brought a measurable downturn in economic productivity in the study area. According to surveys conducted by the Statistics Bureau of Yunnan Province on the rural economy of the province, per-capita income of Manwan resettlers in 1991 (before the valley was flooded) was 6.7% higher than the provincial average. By 1997, (after the valley was flooded), findings from our general survey on the livelihood of resettlers indicated that per-capita income in the reservoir region was only 46.7% of the provincial average. The available evidence suggests that the Manwan case is typical in this regard. A recent survey of 50 large dams around the world found that resettlers seldom see their living conditions improved, and in fact often slip further into poverty (Cernea, 2003; Scudder, 2005: 56–86).

4.2.2. Effects on transportation and housing

In general, the Manwan Dam has brought improved transportation infrastructure to the region, but there have been some

---

[7] This study draws upon data published in the "Master Report of the Study on Wanwan Dam Related to the Social, Economic and Environmental Impacts on the Lancang River," which was jointly completed by Daming He, Xiaogang Yu, Lihui Chen, Jiaji Guo, Shu Gan, and Qin Li, and translated by Oxfam Hong Kong from Chinese into English in 2002.

[8] The mu is a standard unit for measuring land area in China. One mu is equal to 0.066 ha or 0.165 acres.

[9] The renminbi (RMB, or "people's currency") was valued at 1 RMB = 8.3 USD in the late 1990s.

unanticipated effects on local communities. Prior to construction of the dam, State Route 214 passed through the area, running parallel to the Lancang River. After reservoir impoundment, the road was diverted away, and some village roads were submerged. Tractor roads, ferry piers and temporary bridges were built in all four affected counties as mitigation measures, but permanent bridges and tunnels were not provided. This has resulted in disruption of transportation, particularly during the summer monsoon season when landslides are frequent. Citing a lack of funds, county authorities have not yet built any roads in several resettled villages, including Jianbian and Abadi, located in Jingdong County. Insufficient transportation infrastructure makes it difficult for farmers to distribute their crops to markets.

Lack of roads and poor road conditions are perennial problems. In villages most affected by resettlement, like Jianbian and Abadi, not an inch of road had been built because of the funding shortages. Similar impacts exist in communities outside the reservoir region. In Bixi Township of Nanjian County, for example, more than 10,000 villagers typically participated in weekly produce markets. But dam construction turned their main thoroughfare into a dead-end road; participation in weekly markets has been cut by 90%, resulting in a drastic drop in local cash income from the sale of agricultural produce and livestock.

One of the key policies regarding dam-induced resettlement in China is the "developmental resettlement policy," which mandates that government agencies work to minimize social and economic impacts on communities affected by resettlement (Bartolome et al., 2000: 41). Compensation for lost housing is a key piece of this policy. In principle, resettlers in the Manwan reservoir area were to receive monetary compensation based on the size, quality and value of their houses. But the practicalities of rebuilding resettler housing proved difficult to manage. During the late 1980s and early 1990s, China was undergoing a massive transition from a centrally planned economy to a market economy. Government economic planners gradually allowed prices to fluctuate for a variety of commodities, including important construction materials such as steel and cement, which meant that these goods became considerably more expensive during the 1990s. Some villagers had difficulty using their compensation funds to build houses of comparable quality to the ones they had lost. The villages of Goujie and Wangjiang were particularly hard-hit; in these two villages, poor-quality construction and recurring landslides resulted in 17 houses being declared too dangerous for habitation.

4.2.3. Effects on culture, health and gender

With the help of resettlement aid, improvements were made in transport, medical services, education and market conditions of most of the affected villages. However, variation in the ability to utilize transport and market facilities brought about the widening of disparities in internal development among different sectors of new settlers. In addition, conflict over land and other resources between resettlers and neighboring villages is a growing problem. In villages that have been resettled far outside the reservoir region, traditional social capital and interpersonal relationships have dwindled. Northwest Yunnan, which is home to at least nine of China's 55 officially recognized "minority nationalities," is a region of remarkable cultural diversity. Many of the impacted villages in the Manwan case are home to minority populations, including the Yi and Dai minority nationalities. Displacement thus raises critical issues about the loss of traditional cultural and ecological knowledge.

Findings of a 1994 World Bank survey indicate that effects of resettlement on individuals varied by gender. One key problem relates to customs and traditions regarding the ownership or property. When money was provided as compensation to resettled villagers, for example, it was typically given to the man as household head; family property thus became liquidated and concentrated in the hands of elder males in the household, marginalizing the role of women.

Changes in the rural economy have also resulted in different work roles for men and women. Because of the downturn in agricultural productivity, many men have sought wage-earning jobs outside the community in construction, tourism and related industries, sending remittances back to their households. Meanwhile, agricultural production is becoming the purview of women, who even perform tasks such as plowing, which were traditionally seen as men's work. Gender ratios in secondary schools are likely to become more male-biased as household incomes drop and families must make a decision about which children to send to school. Because male children have a filial obligation to care for their family in Chinese society, many households may choose to educate their sons while keeping their daughters at home.

5. Discussion and conclusions: putting SIA to work in large dam projects

Despite the challenges outlined above, we believe that collaboration between natural and physical scientists, engineers, and social scientists can result in social impact assessment that accurately predicts and examines the effects of large dam projects. Based on our experiences with the above case studies, we present here an adaptation of best practices in SIA for assessing dam impacts, grounded in existing literature (Sadler et al., 2000; Scudder, 1997, 2005; Vanclay, 2002b, 2003; World Commission on Dams, 2000b). Table 1 provides a guide to SIA practitioners tasked with understanding dam impacts, including a description of steps to be followed and a brief discussion of the importance of each step. These steps may help to ensure that large dam projects meet the strategic priorities outlined by the World Commission on Dams (WCD, 2000a,b).

Conducting successful SIA of dam projects requires a dual emphasis on getting the impacts right and getting the process right. Both are crucial to the task of assessing dam impacts.

5.1. Getting the impacts right

One of the key challenges of assessing the social impacts of dam projects is establishing a standard set of variables to measure. As Vanclay (2002a: 200) has noted, "The variables that are important must be locally defined, and there may be local considerations that a generic listing does not adequately represent." The process of SIA itself provides a partial solution to this problem, however, since the step-by-step process described above involves an in situ evaluation of stakeholder identification and scoping of activities likely to result in impacts. While the important variables may differ considerably from project to project, a comprehensive SIA process should allow practitioners to identify and measure locally salient variables.

Certain socioeconomic variables, such as income or cost of housing, are easier to identify and measure than others. As a result, mitigation policies often suffer from a lack of emphasis on sociocultural impacts as well as the propensity to underestimate the economic and social value of prior livelihood strategies. Many assets, particularly those that are communally owned and managed or are non-material, are not likely to be prioritized in remuneration plans and may not be compensated for at all. "Irreplaceable" losses, such as those of social connections to lands held by families for generations, are challenging to evaluate in a cost-benefit driven analysis and, consequently, are often externalized by development authorities (World Commission on Dams, 2000b). As the Manwan Dam case study illustrates, displacement of indigenous people raises difficult questions about how to assess non-material losses such as traditional ecological knowledge.

Table 1
Steps in conducting social impact assessment of large dam projects.

Step	Description	Importance/significance
Step 1	Identify interested and affected individuals and communities (stakeholders).	Failure to include all stakeholders can result in improper assessment of impacts. For dam projects, stakeholders may include relocated people, upstream and downstream residents, communities affected by roads and transmission lines, and conservation groups concerned about environmental impacts.
Step 2	Facilitate the participation of stakeholders in the decision-making process.	Ensures that all affected individuals are included from the beginning. This increases the likelihood of local support for the intervention, minimizes impacts, and begins the process of considering measures to mitigate or compensate. All stakeholders should be able to contribute to the selection of variables to be considered in the SIA.
Step 3	Collect baseline data (social profiling).	May include published scientific literature, secondary data from census or other agencies, or the collection of primary data from survey research, interviews, etc. Both qualitative and quantitative research methods may be used. Ensures that demographic, economic, health, social and cultural information is understood about the present state of the community before the intervention, thus providing a baseline for comparison after project completion.
Step 4	Identify and describe the activities that are likely to cause impacts (scoping).	Should be described in enough detail to help identify what data is needed to predict impacts. For example, practitioners should assess the footprint of the reservoir, timeline for construction, number of people to be displaced, and other key variables.
Step 5	Predict likely impacts and determine how stakeholders may respond.	Compares the present baseline conditions with likely conditions following the intervention. Direct impacts (such as relocation) and secondary impacts (such as change in employment status, etc.) must be considered in sufficient detail to allow monitors to judge when post-resettlement living standard goals have been met.
Step 6	Identify possible intervention alternatives (including a non-intervention alternative).	Provides an array of alternatives for the location and design of dam projects. Each alternative should be assessed separately. This provides decision-makers with a range of options, in order to select an alternative that is both technically and financially feasible and minimizes environmental and social impacts.
Step 7	Recommend mitigation or compensation measures.	Mitigation or compensation measures may be built into the selected intervention alternative. Practitioners should also identify the agency or organization responsible for mitigation or compensation.
Step 8	Develop monitoring and management programs.	Assures that impacts are managed through the four phases in the life cycle of a dam, including planning, construction, operation, and decommissioning. Allow practitioners to compare actual impacts with projected impacts.

The distribution of impacts within communities can be highly variable. The Lesotho Highlands Water Project illustrates that many of the burdens associated with resettlement, including increased labor allocation and nutritional deficiencies, are borne by women and children and disproportionately affect poor families. Attempts to mitigate these burdens prove difficult, due to a cultural tendency to deny financial credit to women without permission from their husbands, thus reinforcing existing gender inequalities.

One of the most problematic aspects of conducting SIA of large dam projects is ensuring that the analysis takes place at the proper temporal and spatial scale. Multilateral development agencies, national governments, and private developers alike tend to primarily monitor the initial years of resettlement, for example, which has the effect of missing the long-term effects of these social adjustment processes. Evaluations during the initial years of resettlement may give a false reading of success. In the case of dam projects, practitioners should instead think about the "life cycle" of the project and anticipate impacts at each of four stages (Sadler et al., 2000), including conceptualization and planning, construction, operation, and decommissioning (Interorganizational Committee on Guidelines and Principles for Social Impact Assessment, 1994).

Analyzing the correct spatial scale can be equally troublesome. At what geographic location or level of analysis are the effects of dam projects best examined or understood? While people living near a dam site or reservoir may experience drastic negative impacts, the net effect downstream may in fact be positive due to increased reliability of irrigation water supply. Furthermore, if we consider impacts from a regional or national scale, large dam projects may appear to offer a net benefit due to increased hydropower. The Lesotho Highlands Water Project, for example, is embraced by the government as an important national development strategy, while many of its costs, including resettlement and lost economic opportunities, are borne by residents in the reservoir area. Similarly, in the case of China, the Manwan Dam and similar facilities in this underdeveloped region provide a growing share of electricity to fuel rapid industrial development in coastal areas with access to global capital some 2000 km away (Magee, 2006). In the case of large dam construction on trans-boundary rivers, the situation becomes even more complex due to limited data availability and geopolitical considerations. In the China case study, for example, downstream nations such as Laos, Myanmar, Thailand, Cambodia and Vietnam all experience biophysical, ecological and socioeconomic impacts from China's decision to seriously alter the hydrograph of the upper Mekong River.

5.2. Getting the process right

Beyond simply measuring the appropriate variables, meaningful social impact assessment must be grounded in current best practices that seek to empower stakeholders. Participatory social impact assessment is crucial, both as a pragmatic way of soliciting buy-in from stakeholders and as a moral and normative necessity in the field of international development, which increasingly espouses a community-driven development model. Stakeholders may have radically divergent ideas about whether and how a given project should proceed, and it is the task of social impact assessment to assure that these various voices are heard. The landmark report published by the World Commission on Dams in 2000 emphasizes the application of a "rights and risks" approach to evaluating large dam projects. This approach includes, among other things:

> Self-determination and the right to consultation in matters that affect people's lives, the right to democratic representation of people's views on such matters, the right to an adequate standard of living, freedom from arbitrary deprivation of property. (World Commission on Dams, 2000a: 200).

Best practices in SIA of large dam projects are ultimately grounded in the fundamental human rights frameworks agreed upon by the international community, including the United Nations Declaration of Human Rights (1947), the Declaration on the Right to Development (1986) and the Rio Declaration on Environment and Development Principles (1992). Attending to these ideals in SIA, through the encouragement of stakeholder participation in the decision-making process, increases the likelihood that dam projects are economically viable, socially equitable, and environmentally sustainable (World Bank, 2003; World Commission on Dams, 2000a: 202).

This presents us with a special challenge in undertaking SIA in international contexts, where cultural and political conditions may be markedly different from the Western, rights-based paradigm. China's Manwan Dam is a case in point. There, proper scoping and stakeholder involvement were limited by an authoritarian government with limited respect for individual rights and a severely restricted legal and institutional framework for including stakeholders in the decision-making process.[10] Furthermore, the effectiveness of SIA related to large dam projects often hinges on many outside factors, including cultural and political constraints on local populations to voice their concerns, the willingness of governmental, multilateral and private development agencies to support the measures proposed in the SIA, and the institutional capacity of these agencies to implement these measures (Egre and Senecal, 2003: 224).

It is important to remember that SIA serves only as a starting point which must be followed up with equitable mitigation and compensation measures appropriate to the project at hand. As development institutions continue to promote the use of hydropower projects, altering the social as well as ecological landscapes of many communities, it is crucial that we develop a systematic understanding of the impacts of dams. Such an undertaking can help to promote development strategies that address the most important concerns for local populations, enhancing the long-term sustainability of development interventions.

References

Aguiree, I., 2005. Social Investigation of the Communities Affected by the Chixoy Dam. Rights Action, Washington, DC.
Bardrill, J.D., Cobbe, J.H., 1985. Lesotho: Dilemmas of Dependence in Southern Africa. Westview Press, Boulder.
Bartolome, L.J., et al., 2000. Displacement, Resettlement, Rehabilitation, Reparation, and Development. World Commission on Dams, Cape Town.
Braun, Y.A., 2005a. Resettlement and risk: women's community work in Lesotho. Advances in Gender Research 9, 29–60.
Braun, Y.A., 2005b. Selling the river: gendered experiences of resource extraction and development in Lesotho. Research in Rural Sociology and Development 10, 373–396.
Braun, Y.A., 2006. Large dams as development: restructuring access to natural resources in Lesotho. In: Kick, E., Jorgenson, A. (Eds.), Globalization and the Environment. Brill Academic Press, Leiden, the Netherlands.
Cernea, M.M., 1988. Involuntary Resettlement in Development Projects: Policy Guidelines in World Bank-Financed Projects. World Bank Technical Paper 180. World Bank, Washington, DC.
Cernea, M.M., 2003. For a new economics of resettlement: a sociological critique of the compensation principle. International Social Science Journal 55 (175), 37–45.
Detter, A., Gunnewig, E., 1994. Transformations caused by Lesotho Highlands water project phase 1-A with a focus on the Ha Lejone and Ha Mensel in Katse local catchment, Maseru.
Egre, D., Senecal, P., 2003. Social impact assessments of large dams throughout the world: lessons learned over two decades. Impact Assessment and Project Appraisal 21 (3), 215–224.
Epprecht, M., 2000. This Matter of Women is Getting Very Bad: Gender, Development and Politics in Colonial Lesotho. University of Natal Press, Pietermaritzburg.
Ferguson, J., 2004. The Anti-Politics Machine: Development, Depoliticization, and Bureaucratic Power in Lesotho. University of Minnesota Press, Minneapolis.
Fuggle, R., Smith, W., 2000. Large Dams in Water and Energy Resource Development in the People's Republic of China. World Commission on Dams Country Review Paper. World Commission on Dams, Cape Town.
Gordon, E., 1981. An analysis of the impact of labour migration on the lives of women in Lesotho. In: Nelson, N. (Ed.), African Women in the Development Process Cass, London.

---

[10] There are some encouraging signs that China's central government is increasing its commitment to thorough environmental and social review of development projects. In 2003 the State Council passed a new Environmental Impact Assessment Law, which requires all significant development projects to undergo more rigorous regulatory oversight from the State Environmental Protection Agency (SEPA) as well as public hearings involving potentially effected stakeholders. Invoking the new law, Premier Wen Jiabao called a temporary halt to several hydropower projects on the Nu River, which is located adjacent to the Upper Mekong in Yunnan Province. More thorough environmental reviews are underway.

Hassan, F.M.A., 2002. Lesotho—Development in a Challenging Environment: a Joint World Bank–African Development Bank Evaluation. African Development Bank and World Bank, Washington, DC.
He, D., Chen, L., 2002. The impact of hydropower cascade development in the Lancang–Mekong Basin, Yunnan. Mekong Update and Dialogue 5 (3), 2–4.
International Commission on Large Dams, 1998. Register of Large Dams. ICOLD, Paris.
Interorganizational Committee on Guidelines and Principles for Social Impact Assessment, 1994. Guidelines and principles for social impact assessment. Impact Assessment 12 (2), 107–152.
Interorganizational Committee on Guidelines and Principles for Social Impact Assessment, 2003. Principles and guidelines for social impact assessment in the USA. Impact Assessment and Project Appraisal 21 (3), 231–250.
Jackson, S., Sleigh, A., 2000. Resettlement for China's three Gorges Dam: socio-economic impact and institutional tensions. Communist and Post-Communist Studies 33 (2), 223–241.
Jing, J., 2000. Displacement, Resettlement, Rehabilitation, Reparation and Development: China Report. In: World Commission on Dams Thematic Review 1.3. World Commission on Dams, Cape Town.
Lerer, L.B., Scudder, T., 1999. Health impacts of large dams. Environmental Impact Assessment Review 19 (2), 113–123.
Lesotho Highlands Development Authority, 1986. LHDA Order of 1986. Lesotho Government Gazette Extraordinary, Maseru.
Lesotho Highlands Development Authority, 2006. Mohale Dam Fills Up. Lesotho Highlands Development Authority, Maseru.
Magee, D., 2006. Powershed politics: hydropower and interprovincial relations under great western development. The China Quarterly 185, 23–41.
McMillan, D.E., 1995. Sahel Visions: Planned Settlement and River Blindness Control in Burkina Faso. University of Arizona Press, Tucson.
Nkomo, S., 1990. Confrontation and the challenge for independent development: the case of Lesotho. In: Mazur, R.E. (Ed.), Breaking the Links: Development Theory and Practice in Southern Africa. Africa World Press, Trenton.
Panel of Environmental Experts, 1989. Report to the LHDA and the World Bank. World Bank, Washington, DC.
Panel of Environmental Experts, 1991. Report to the LHDA and the World Bank. World Bank, Washington, DC.
Panel of Environmental Experts, 1993. Report to the LHDA and the World Bank. World Bank, Washington, DC.
Panel of Environmental Experts, 1994. Report to the LHDA and the World Bank. World Bank, Washington, DC.
Panel of Environmental Experts, 1995. Report to the LHDA and the World Bank. World Bank, Washington, DC.
Panel of Environmental Experts, 1997. Report to the LHDA and the World Bank. World Bank, Washington, DC.
Phadke, R., 2005. People's science in action: the politics of protest and knowledge brokering in India. Society and Natural Resources 18 (4), 363–378.
Sadler, B., et al., 2000. Environmental and Social Impact Assessment for Large Dams. In: World Commission on Dams Thematic Review v. 2. World Commission on Dams, Cape Town.
Scudder, T., 1997. Social impacts of large dams. In: Dorcey, T. (Ed.), Large Dams: Learning from the Past. IUCN, Gland, Switzerland.
Scudder, T., 2005. The Future of Large Dams: Dealing with Social, Environmental, Institutional and Political Costs. Earthscan, London.
Sechaba Consultants, 1994. Poverty in Lesotho: a Mapping Exercise. Government of Lesotho Working Document, Maseru.
Trans-Caledon Tunnel Authority, 2005. Map of the Water Flow of the Lesotho Highlands Water Project. TCTA, Maseru.
Thabane, M., 2000. Shifts from old to new social and ecological environments in the Lesotho Highlands water scheme: relocating residents of the Mohale Dam area. Journal of Southern African Studies 26 (4), 633–654.
Thamae, M.L., Pottinger, L., 2006. On the Wrong Side of Development: Lessons Learned From the Lesotho Highlands Water Projects. Transformation Resource Center, Maseru.
Tshabalala, M., Turner, S.D., 1989. Socioeconomic Census of the Lesotho Highlands Water Project Phase 1-A Areas, V. 1. Main Report. Lesotho Highlands Development Authority, Maseru.
Tsikoane, T., 1991. Towards a redefined role of the Lesotho Highlands water project in the post-apartheid South Africa. In: Santho, S., Sejanamane, M. (Eds.), South Africa After Apartheid: Prospects for the Inner Periphery in the 1990s. Sapes Truest, Harare.
United Nations, 2003. Investment Policy Review: Lesotho. United Nations Conference on Trade and Development. United Nations, New York.
Vanclay, F., 2002a. Conceptualizing social impacts. Environmental Impact Assessment Review 22 (3), 183–211.
Vanclay, F., 2002b. Social impact assessment. Encyclopedia of Global Environmental Change 4, 387–393.
Vanclay, F., 2003. International principles for social impact assessment. Impact Assessment and Project Appraisal 21 (1), 5–11.
World Bank, 2003. Stakeholder Involvement in Options Assessment: Promoting Dialogue in Meeting Water and Energy Needs—a Sourcebook. World Bank, Washington, DC.
World Commission on Dams, 2000a. Dams and Development: a New Framework for Decision-making. Earthscan, London.
World Commission on Dams, 2000b. Social Impact Assessment: WCD Thematic Review V. 2. Environmental and Social Assessment for Large Dams. World Commission on Dams, Cape Town.

Part IX
Historically Significant Documents

[37]

Cultural, Social, and Psychological Considerations in the Planning of Public Works

MAGOROH MARUYAMA

Introduction

As a result of the National Environmental Policy Act of 1969, agencies engaged in contruction of public works are required to incorporate cultural, social, and psychological considerations as well as economic and environmental considerations in their planning of public works.

This is a beginning of a new era characterized by an emergence of a social philosophy counteracting the hitherto dominant technocentricism in Western Civilization. Public agencies have begun an unprecedented task to implement this new social philosophy.

However, their efforts are handicapped by the fact that they are trying to attain the goals of a new social philosophy with an old conceptual and logical framework.

The purpose of this paper is to explore and discuss cultural, social, and psychological considerations in the planning of public works. However, before going into this main topic it is necessary to point out briefly the inadequacies of the traditional conceptual and logical structure, which is still widely used in the analysis of cultural, social and psychological considerations.

Inadequacies of the Traditional Conceptual and Logical Structure in the Analysis of Cultural, Social, and Psychological Considerations.

1. INADEQUACIES OF THE CONCEPT "IMPACT."

A current term used for the analysis of cultural, social and psychological considerations is "impact analysis." This way of thinking is based on the paradigm of unidirectional causality, which has been until recently considered as the "scientific" way of thinking.

However, recent advances in science have produced a newer paradigm of multilateral mutual causality [1–13]. This paradigm is applicable to many physical, biological, and social processes, and is indispensable in their analysis.

Since three decades this new paradigm has undergone increasing mathematical sophistication and has established itself on scientific rigor.

Mathematically, the mutual causal paradigm is completely different in nature from the unidirectional causal paradigm. Mutual causal analysis cannot be substituted by a succession of unidirectional causal analysis performed in alternating directions. It is easy to show mathematically that such substitution produces incorrect results.

In terms of public work planning, the notion of "impact analysis" is based on a wrong paradigm because social processes are basically mutual causal processes. "Impact

---

MAGOROH MARUMAYA is Professor of Systems Science, Portland State University, Portland, Oregon 97207

© American Elsevier Publishing Company, Inc., 1973

analysis'' cannot even be used with the excuse that it forms a part of the total mutual causal analysis and is to be supplemented later with the analysis in the other causal direction. Mutual causal analysis is not a sum of two unidirectional causal analyses in two different directions. As mentioned, such substitution produces mathematically incorrect results.

The notion of "impact analysis" must be replaced with the notion of causal *loop* analysis. For example, the construction of a highway or a dam may become a part of a self-perpetuating or self-amplifying loop: the construction of a highway through a corn field may cause residential areas or factories to grow along the highway, and such developments make the highway more necessary than before. Or the construction of a recreational lake may draw a large population to move to the lake area; soon the lake becomes overcrowded and more lakes must be constructed. These are examples of two-element loops (construction and population). There are also many-element loops, in which the causal effect comes back to the same element via a chain of several elements.

It must be recognized that it is wrong to consider a construction project as the cause and the society as the effect. The construction project is also an effect of the society in the first place, even before the project is started. *Therefore the community people's opinions and feelings must be inputted in the planning from the very beginning of the planning process.*

2. INADEQUACIES OF THE LOGIC OF "LIST OF CATEGORIES."

In almost all cases, the person who wants to perform an "impact analysis" begins with a list of categories. A typical list being used now consists of three large categories of "economic," "environmental," and "social," which are further divided into smaller categories or items. Such a list is an illusion resulting from the classificational Greek logic.

The classificational logic is based on the following assumptions which were derived from the physics of the Greek period. None of these assumptions hold today. Even if they did, none of them corresponds to actual social processes.

The Assumptions of the Classificational Logic

(1) The universe consists of material substances (and in some cases also of power substances).

(2) These substances persist in time.

(3) They obey the law of identity and the law of mutual exclusiveness, except that the power substance may penetrate into things.

(4) The substances are classifiable into mutually exclusive categories. The classification is unambiguous. The categories persist in time and in space. (The categories are believed to be uniformly and universally valid.)

(5) Categories may be divided into subcategories, and categories may be combined into supercategories. Thus, categories form a hierarchy.

(6) The categories can be constructed a priori, i.e., they can preexist before the things that are to be put into them. They have their reality independent from things, and higher than things. (Some later philosophers such as the nominalists in the medieval age challenged this last assumption. But it has remained nevertheless as a "mainstream" assumption in Western Civilization.)

We must realize that these are merely assumptions which do not correspond to reality. Nevertheless, many persons attempting an "impact analysis" proceed from a list of such categories as if these assumptions corresponded to reality.

We need to revise the structure of the list, applying the following new assumptions, which more closely correspond to our social reality:

New assumptions

(1) The universe consists of processes, many of which are interactive. Our interest is in the patterns of network, not isolated things.

(2) Culture, society, beliefs, philosophies, opinions, feelings, goals, purposes, etc. are mutually generative in interaction. They evolve and change in time, and they vary from place to place, from group to group, or from individual to individual.

(3) Mutual exclusiveness and isolatability are not a main relevance. Relatedness and overlapping are of our primary relevance.

(4) Classifications do not exist in things themselves. It is people who classify things *for convenience* and for specific purposes. Hence, categories may vary from person to person, from situation to situation, and from specific purpose to another specific purpose. Categories may overlap, and the same thing may be classfiable into several categories at the same time.

(5) For convenience, people may subdivide categories into subcategories, or combine categories into supercategories. Subcategories and supercategories may vary from person to person, from situation to situation, and from purpose to purpose. They may overlap Furthermore, what is a subcategory for a person in a given situation for a specific purpose may be a supercategory for a different purpose or in a different situation even for the same person, not to mention for different persons. Therefore, there is no unchanging hierarchy among subcategories and supercategories.

(6) Since categories may vary from person to person, from situation to situation, from purpose to purpose, from culture to culture, etc., the use of a prestructured list of categories distorts the varying reality. Ideally a list should be generated by each community for each specific purpose. Use of any prestructured list should be limited to suggestive purposes only.

The Range of Cultural, Social, and Psychological Considerations.

In most of the writings on "impact analysis" and "quality of life" that I have come across recently, there is one or more of the three tendencies which distort or limit what is to be examined under cultural, social and psychological considerations.

TENDENCY 1: ECONOMICOCENTRICISM

This is very common in the writings by agencies in which economists are given the responsibility of dealing with cultural, social, and psychological considerations. This is a tendency to equate human well-being with income level, low unemployment rate, and other economic considerations alone. This tendency also equates human needs with population density, population size, birth rate, and other demographic considerations alone. This type of thinking is based on the quantitative supply-and-demand model, with practically no cultural, social, or psychological considerations, and with practically no awareness of cultural and individual diversities in our society.

TENDENCY 2: MONETARY VALUE ASSIGNMENT.

Writers with this tendency may recognize the existence of noneconomic considerations in human well-being such as recreation or esthetic appreciation, but attempt to convert all these considerations into monetary values. For example, if a concert ticket costs $6, the value of the concert to the spectator is converted into the monetary value of $6. Some go so far as estimating the "value" of a fee-less recreation area at some arbitrary figure such as fifty cents per visitor per day.

TENDENCY 3: VALUE HIERARCHY MODEL.

The writers with this tendency recognize that there are individual and cultural differences in preferences, but assume ethnocentrically that the so-called values can be either scaled or rank-ordered in all cultures, i.e., they assume that all cultures have either a quantitative epistemology or a hierarchical epistemology. They do not realize that there are cultures with nonquantitative and nonhierarchical epistemologies. Furthermore, they assume that in all cultures people can give a definite response to an abstraction (such as "loyalty," "honesty," "freedom") as if such abstractions had reality independent from the context. They do not realize that in many cultures contextual and relational logics are practiced instead of the Western atomistic and classificational logic. A typical example of this tendency toward value hierarchy models is the widespread use of Maslow's hierarchy of values. This example is particularly illuminating because not only its structure is hierarchical but also its contents reflect an atomistic, unidirectional logic. The top item in Maslow's hierarchy of values is "self-actualization." The concept of "self" as an independent substance distinguishable from other "individuals" is a result of the atomistic and classificational logic. The concept of "actualization" is based on the unidirectional causal model. The result of "self-actualization" might as well turn out to be interaction with other people. But the conceptual detour needed to arrive at such reestablished interrelationship is quite characteristic of the classificational Greek logic. In many cultures the human being is inseparable from his natural environment and from his fellow human beings. The purpose of life for him is to enjoy beauty and harmony with nature and with fellow human beings. He is *not* identical with his fellow human beings. His skills and abilities place him in a *special* place in the harmony of the universe. His uniqueness is defined in terms of his place in the harmony. In cultures in which there is no separation between humans and their natural environment, a man may sit in a beautiful scenery, feel as a part of it, and be completely fulfilled. He does not have to first become "self," then actualize itself, and work his way back to interrelations.

As we have discussed regarding the classificational logic, the range of cultural, social, and psychological considerations cannot be and should not be rigidly defined. Yet, in order to remedy the three tendencies and other distorting tendencies, it is helpful to indicate a number of examples of cultural, social, and psychological considerations.

As discussed before, the three general categories of cultural, social, and psychological overlap to a great extent. Furthermore, what is considered as predominantly in one category in one situation or in one culture may be in another category in another situation or in another culture.

For example, in many cultures food exchange or food distribution is a social activity in addition to being a biological and economic activity. In the American middle-class culture, going to church is at the same time a social and psychological activity. In the Navajo culture, going to a "sing" is at the same time religious, esthetic, scientific, social, and psychological activity.

Furthermore, what goes into one category in a culture may go into the opposite category in another culture. For example, in some cultures a rat is considered as food. In many other cultures rats eat crops, and are considered as destroyers of food.

CULTURAL, SOCIAL, AND PSYCHOLOGICAL CONSIDERATIONS

With these cautions in mind, let us make a general outline of what are to be included in cultural, social, and psychological considerations.

CULTURAL.

Cultural pertains to philosophies and patterns of life shared by a number of interacting individuals. The group of interacting individuals who share the same philosophy and the same pattern of life may be an ethnic group, a professional group, a religious group, etc. There may be overlappings between groups in terms of some aspects of philosophies or of patterns of life. There may be individuals who are able to shift between different philosophies or different patterns of life. There may be individuals who belong to one culture according to one criterion, and to another culture according to another criterion. In all cases, cultural considerations are considerations of these different philosophies and patterns of life. Examples of philosophies and patterns of life are:

Example A:
Life is cut-throat competition. The stronger takes advantage of the weaker. Success depends on effort. If someone is unsuccessful, it is his fault because he is not making the necessary effort. Stab others in their backs or you will get stabbed. People who are equal to you are your competitors. People who are different are your enemies. Life is a zero-sum game. What someone gains is what someone else loses. Life is a constant exploitation.

Example B:
Life is a harmony of mutual relations. Life is a non-zero-sum game. People can help one another and gain from one another without anybody necessarily losing. Diversity enriches society. Different people can contribute different talents to one another. Some people are under disadvantaged conditions and they should be helped.

Example C:
As much as possible, life should be like a clockwork. It should run smoothly without disturbance. If everybody does his work, everything should go according to the book.

Example D:
Everybody should earn his living. He can work as much as he wants or as little as he wants. But he must budget his own life and be self-sufficient. He must save for his rainy days.

Example E:
I share with others what I earn, and others share with me what they earn. There is no need to save because others will help me on my rainy days. Therefore, I give away all my surplus. Saving is stinginess. You should not help people who are stingy.

The last example illustrates that the "value analysis" is meaningless if it is done out of cultural context. The person in the culture in Example E can afford to be generous because of the economic system of mutual resource distribution. At the same time, he cannot afford to be stingy. He can afford not to save, and he cannot afford to save. On the other hand, a person in the culture in Example D must have savings. He cannot afford not to save, and he can afford to save. If a value analysis is improperly conducted, it may be concluded that the culture in Example D is future-oriented, while the culture in Example E is more present-oriented. Such an analysis misses the more basic difference between the two cultures. The basic difference is that the culture in Example D is individualistic, while the culture in Example E is mutualistic. One is not necessarily more future-oriented than the other.

It is therefore important to note the following in the analysis of cultural considerations: (1) to analyze the total cultural context; (2) because preset methods of analysis may produce irrelevant conclusions and miss the relevant points, it is recommended that the cultural considerations be inputted from the community rather than measured by a preset test method constructed by outsiders.

Relation of Public Works to the Philosophies and the Life Patterns of the Community

Let us take the five examples of philosophies and patterns of life given above and illustrate some possible kinds of relationship between public works on the one hand and the philosophies and the life patterns of people on the other hand.

Example A: Competitive Philosophy. The arguents for or against the project may be influenced by such a cut-throat competitive philosophy, and the project in turn may create, accentuate or abate such a philosophy. If such a philosophy preexists in the community or in the planners, such a philosophy is likely to become the basis of arguments for or against the project. The project in turn can create competition which did not exist before, or increase the existing competitiveness, or in some cases decrease the existing competitiveness.

Example B: Philosophy of Harmony and Mutuality. This philosophy can influence the planning and can in turn be influenced by the project. If such a philosophy preexists, the arguments for or against the project can be made on the basis of the consideration as to whether the project can increase or disturb the harmony in the universe and in the community. The project, in turn, can reinforce or undermine the philosophy based on the harmony of mutual relations.

Example C: Bureaucratic Philosophy. If this type of philosophy preexists, the argument for or against the project can be made on the basis of the consideration as to whether the project itself is compatible with the "book," and whether the project will or will not disturb the clockwork system. The project, in turn, can create, enhance or undermine such a philosophy: the project may create a clockwork type of life in the community; enhance the existing clockwork type of life; or introduce nonclockwork type of elements in the life of the community.

Example D: Philosophy of Individual Self-Sufficiency. This type of philosophy can very well influence the decision regarding the plans. For example, the planner with this type of philosophy may argue that the community must be economically self-sufficient, and therefore it needs the proposed project. Or he may reject the project on the ground that the project would destroy the self-sufficiency of the community. If the community people hold this type of philosophy, they can use similar arguments for or against the project. The project, once carried out, may also create, enhance or decrease this type of philosophy. For example, if the community had a system of communal distribution of food, the project may introduce the money economy into the community as well as the salary system, which will destroy the traditional communal food distribution system and convert the community people into individual salary-budget-saving system.

Example E: Philosophy of Communal Resources. This type of philosophy may generate

CULTURAL, SOCIAL, AND PSYCHOLOGICAL CONSIDERATIONS

arguments for or against the project. For example, in a community in which the individual does not have to worry about his gain or loss as long as the gain of the community as a whole increases because of the community food distribution system, the fact that the project may decrease some individuals' crops is not a deterrent against the project as long as the total crops of the community increase. This eliminates one of the usual problems associated with the individual property. On the other hand, such a philosophy may generate arguments against the project if the project would benefit a small group but create disadvantages to the community as a whole. Thus, the commonly practiced strategy of using a small interest group as leverage to win the arguments for the project does not work. The project, once achieved, may enhance or undermine such a philosophy in turn.

SOCIAL:

Social pertains to interaction patterns of people in the community. They include the following considerations. The items listed are not mutually exclusive, nor exhaustive.

(1) *Family structure* : nuclear, extended, commune, transitory, etc.

(2) *Proxemics:* individual rooms or communal rooms, closed doors or open walls, spending much time with other people on the streets or in courtyards, etc.

(3) *Transient population, home-base population and sedentary population.*

(4) *Social activities:* churches, public religious feasts, market places used for social intercourse, bars, clubs, participant activities, spectator activities, types of housing (individual houses, highrises, etc.).

(5) *Social distance:* generation gap, ethnic distance, vertical and horizontal stratification, prejudices, alienation.

(6) *Forms of social organization:* hierarchical, nonhierarchical, homogenistic, heterogenistic, majority rule, consensual, diversity-symbiotizing, etc.

(7) *Communication:* telephone, newspapers, television, radio.

(8) *Public services:* hospitals, schools, libraries, parks, playgrounds, fire station, police.

(9) *Transportation:* roads, railways, buses, boats, snowways (snow-covered land facilitates transportation by sled, ski, etc.), iceways (ice-covered ocean and rivers facilitate transportation by car, sled, etc.), airports (including lake, river, frozen lake, snowland).

These social considerations influence the arguments for and against the proposed project, as well as are influenced by the project if the project is materialized.

PSYCHOLOGICAL

(1) *Direct feelings toward the project:*
(a) Feeling of being exploited.
(b) Feeling of not being respected or taken into consideration.
(c) Feeling of having participated in the planning.
(d) Feeling of being benefited.
(e) Feeling of being shortchanged.
(f) Feeling of being proud of the project.
(g) Feeling of being ashamed of the project.
(h) Feeling of indifference.

(i) Feeling that the project is irrelevant and is a waste of money.
(j) Indignation or anger toward the project.
(k) Enthusiasm or exhilaration.

(2) *Indirect psychological considerations:*
(a) Change in social interaction patterns, and consequent psychological reorientation.

(b) Change in social status or social position due to the project, and consequent psychological reorientation.

(c) Change from communal economy to individual economy, and consequent psychological reorientation.

(d) Change in working pattern and in attitude toward work (time-card mentality, etc.), and consequent psychological reorientation.

(e) Change in philosophy and life pattern, and consequent psychological reorientation.

The direct feelings toward the project generate arguments for or against the project. The materialized project, in turn, generates, increases or decreases some direct feelings toward the project. The indirect psychological considerations are secondary effects resulting from cultural and social considerations. However, once these secondary effects are generated, they in turn create, increase or decrease the direct feelings toward the project. The direct feelings, in turn, generate arguments for and against the project.

Multiple Entry Checklist

As cautioned, the "cultural," the "social," and the "psychological" are not mutually exclusive categories, nor are the items mentioned in each type of considerations to be considered as mutually exclusive nor preexisting before the actual situation is specified.

The method of establishing a list of preexisting categories and items should be discarded. Instead, the method of multiple entry checklist is suggested. In this method, there is no preestablished list of preexisting categories and items. For a given situation in a specific community, the specific considerations influencing the decision as well as those considerations which will be influenced by the project if it is materialized are first listed without the concern as to whether they are cultural, social, or psychological (or even economic or environmental). Some of these considerations may turn out to be any combination of cultural, social, and psychological (and even economic and environmental). If this is the case, make multiple entries in the check columns of cultural, social, and psychological.

Mutual Causal Relations Between the Cultural Considerations, Social Considerations, and Psychological Considerations as well as between Items within the Same Type of Considerations

We have seen that some indirect psychological considerations are influenced by cultural or social considerations. But direct feelings can also be influenced by cultural and social considerations. For example, the consideration that the project would disrupt the pattern of life in the community will undoubtedly result in a direct negative feeling toward the project. Furthermore, psychological considerations can also influence cultural and social considerations. For example, a strong feeling shared by community members against the project may unite the community which has not been cohesive. Cultural considerations and social considerations can also affect one another. For example, a rise of a competitive philosophy (cultural consideration) may divide the community (social consideration), and conversely a community physically divided by the project (social consideration) may develop a competitive philosophy (cultural consideration). There are also mutual interactions between the items within the same type of considerations. For example, establishment of schools may increase or decrease the social distance between the rich and the poor, and the change in social distance may create new kinds of schools.

Summary and Conclusion

The current efforts at incorporating the cultural, social, and psychological considerations in the planning of public works are handicapped by the fact that these efforts are directed at attaining the goals of a new social philosophy with the old conceptual and logical framework. In this paper the inadequacies of the paradigm of the "impact" model and the inadequacies of the classificational logic have been discussed. As an alternative paradigm, the mutual causal model has been proposed to replace the "impact" model. The mutual causal relations between the project planning on the one hand and the cultural, social and psychological considerations on the other hand have been discussed. Furthermore, mutual causal relations between cultural considerations, social considerations and psychological considerations as well as mutual causal relations between items under the same type of considerations have been pointed out. The range of the "cultural," the "social," and the "psychological" as related the project planning has been indicated with the caution that the lists and the examples are not to be interpreted in the classificational logic of exclusive and exhaustive categories. The method of multiple entry checklist beginning with the actual concrete situation in the specific community has been suggested to replace the use of preestablished list of categories.

References

1. W. Buckley, *Modern Systems Research for the Behavioral Scientist*, Aldine, Chicago (1968).
2. T. Gustafson and L. Wolpert, Cellular basis of morphogenesis in sea urchin development *Intern. Rev. Cy.* **15,** 139–214 (1963).
3. M. Maruyama, Morphogenesis and morphostasis, *Methodos* **12,** 251–296 (1961).
4. M. Maruyama, The second cybernetics: deviation-amplifying mutual causal processes, *American Scientist* **51,** 164–179; 250–256 (1963).
5. J. Milsum, *Positive Feedback*, Pergamon, Oxford (1968).
6. G. Myrdal, *American Dilemma*, Harper & Row, New York (1943).
7. G. Myrdal, *Economic Theory and Underdevelopped Regions*, Duckworth, London (1957).
8. H. Spemann, *Embryonic Development and Induction*, (1938).
9. S. Ulam, On some mathematical problems connected with growth of patterns. *Proceedings of the Symposium on Applied Mathematics* **14,** 215–224 (1962).
10. H. Von Foerster, *Transactions of Josiah Macy Jr. Foundation Conferences on Cybernetics*, Josiah Macy Jr. Foundation, New York (1949-53).
11. C. H. Waddington, *Towards a Theoretical Biology*, Aldine, Chicago (1969–71).
12. N. Wiener, *Cybernetics*, Herman et Cie, Paris (1948).
13. S. Wright, Evolution in Mendelian population, *Genetics* **16,** 97–159 (1931).

Received January 12, 1973

[38]

SOCIAL IMPACT ASSESSMENT: THE STATE OF THE ART
C. P. Wolf
Sociological Consultant
Institute for Water Resources
U. S. Army Corps of Engineers
Fort Belvoir, Virginia

Overview
This is a state of the art report on "social impact assessment." The argument of this report, and the organization of this volume, will be structured as a problem solving sequence according to the following analytic outline:

FIG. 1. SOCIAL IMPACT ASSESSMENT: ANALYTIC OUTLINE

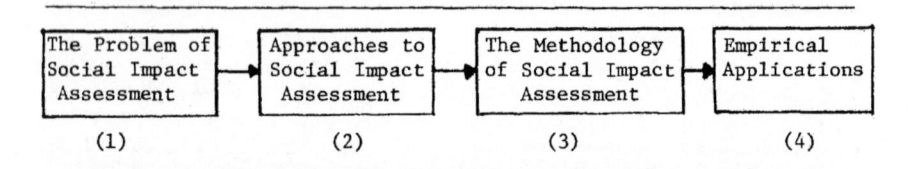

The Problem of Social Impact Assessment	Approaches to Social Impact Assessment	The Methodology of Social Impact Assessment	Empirical Applications
(1)	(2)	(3)	(4)

1. In the first section we will examine the nature of the analytic problem: the engagement of social science interests; the range of social impacts; and the position of social impact assessment in the overall planning process.

2. From this emerges a major orientation thesis, the "interactive approach" to social impact assessment. Section Two then arrays a wider variety of substantive and methodological approaches to the analytic problem and identifies their practitioners.

3. In Section Three, we undertake a brief "resource inventory" of social science methodologies and techniques that can be associated with varying approaches to the analytic problem. In the present state of the art these are not yet systematically related; however, a means for achieving this is proposed, keyed to one operational methodology for social impact assessment.

4. The fourth section refers to a few empirical applications of these approaches and methods that can be cited in the context of social impact assessment and provides a "check list" to guide field planners and reviewers.

The concluding discussion, on the future of social impact assessment, must be frankly programmatic and speculative. The current state of the art can best be summarized in one word: "explosive." We can anticipate orders-of-magnitude improvement on all present aspects and activities of

2 social impact assessment

social impact assessment to occur in the near term. While contributions
will continue to accrue from the advancement of social science generally,
social impact assessment may itself provide a distinctive focus and impetus
for their crystallization. Such at least is our hope.

1. THE PROBLEM OF SOCIAL IMPACT ASSESSMENT

Social Science and Social Impact Assessment
It is at least arguable that "social impact assessment" is what social
science is all about, and always has been. As social scientists, we
are concerned with analyzing the conditions, causes and consequences
of social phenomena and social life. The "social effects," "impacts"
or, more faintly, "implications of . . ." becomes merely an exercise
in filling in the blanks. It would appear then that "social impact
assessment" is only a novel expression for what is actually a traditional concern.

Even granting this argument, it does not follow that "social impact
assessment" (hereafter SIA) fairly describes what social scientists do,
their aspirations or achievements. Concentrated work in this interest
is only now beginning. The distinctive phrasing is useful in calling
attention to new contexts and concerns, to special approaches and settings.
In its broadest definition, SIA is practically coextensive with integrated
social science knowledge; doubtless that is part of its intellectual
appeal. While it is true that SIA does address this fundamental problem
of knowledge, it is not knowledge "for its own sake" alone. Its applications, as "use knowledge," are intensely practical. Correspondingly,
its practitioners must attain a level of professional competence and
assume a degree of professional responsibility to which few have been
accustomed.

What Is SIA?
There are many levels for answering to the question, "What is SIA?"
Operationally, it can be designated as formal compliance with legis-
lative acts such as Section 122 of PL 91-611, the River and Harbor and
Flood Control Act of 1970. Perhaps the most direct way of defining
SIA is by analogy with the environmental impact assessment required by
Section 102 of PL 91-190, the National Environmental Policy Act of 1969
(NEPA). Following the NEPA precedent, "social impacts" are then understood as an extension or broadening of environmental impacts, and indeed,
procedures for SIA do generally resemble those prescribed for environmental impact assessment. But at the most general level, the problem
of SIA is a problem of estimating and appraising the condition of a
society organized and changed by large-scale applications of high
technology.

If the broad definition of SIA can be given "simply" as the relatedness
of social things, it can be narrowed to particular situational and
institutional contexts and specified in particular aspects and concerns.
Situationally, it can be located in those circumstances and cases where
human, usually governmental, intervention is intended or believed
to affect the social condition. SIA is thus a procedure for anticipating,

social impact assessment 3

in Merton's (1936) phrase, "the unanticipated consequences of purposive social action," and thereby to forestall or offset adverse effects to which it may give rise. SIA is in this sense a hedge against uncertainty in the planning process.*

Institutionally, familiar contexts of concern for SIA have involved such areas of public works and private enterprise as dams and reservoirs (Wilkening and others, 1973), nuclear reactors (Peelle, 1974), power transmission lines (Young, 1973), highways (Perfater and Howell, 1973), large installations (Breese and others, 1965), weather modification (Haas, 1973), industrial location (Ireland, n.d.), planned community development (Bird, 1973), urban renewal (Williams, Jr., 1970) and resource exploitation (Krebs, 1973). Less common are studies of "natural" conditions where to "do nothing" is to hazard human community and hamper social progress.

Technology as Environment?
The relationship between environment and technology, or nature and culture, has become inverted in the evolution of society. Originally, social life was environmentally conditioned if not outright determined. A great reversal occurred with the advent of cultural controls over environmental conditions, primarily through the agency of technology. By means of such cultural interventions, passive at first and later actively asserted, the technosphere has come to dominate the biosphere. This "environmental revolution" (Nicholson, 1970) may yet encounter its counterrevolution, wherein these roles are reversed--that is the message of various catastrophisms and doomsday scenarios (e.g. Taylor, 1971). But in the historical present, it is the human impact on environment that predominates.

Now a curious transposition takes place. Technology, socially directed or influenced from its inception, merges with the environment. It is not only a matter of environment as the recipient of technological damage and the carrier of its malignancies. Technology is rather assimilated to environment in respect to its pervasiveness, its externality or human estrangement and the precariousness of cultural controls exercised over it. In this emergent condition of "technology as environment" (Ogburn, 1956), it appears that technology is acting on--"impacting"--us rather than we directing its course. The problem of SIA is not so much what we are doing to the environment; it is what we are doing to ourselves through the _medium_ of environment by technological misapplications.

The Technologic Bias
In the past, social scientists' own definition of the analytic situation has tended to reflect and reinforce this technologic bias. The main pattern for SIA was set in Ogburn's (1922) classic formulation of the "cultural lag hypothesis," wherein changes in material culture are said to induce alterations in the non-material, "adaptive culture." A classic study of this relationship--apart from Ogburn's own pioneering work (e.g. 1946)--was W. F. Cottrell's "Death by Dieselization" (1951):

---

*Conversely, by introducing relatively uncontrolled variables, SIA may work to _increase_ uncertainty in planning. The same is true of public involvement.

4 social impact assessment

> . . . here is the average American community with normal social life, subscribing to normal American codes. Nothing its members had been taught would indicate that the whole pattern of this normal existence depended completely upon a few elements of technology [e.g. high tensile steel for locomotive boilers] which were themselves in flux. For them the continued use of the steam engine was as "natural" a phenomenon as any other element in their physical environment. Yet suddenly their life pattern was destroyed by the announcement that the railroad was moving its division point, and with it destroying the economic basis of Caliente's existence. (p. 359)

As Cottrell observes (p. 360), "The story is an old one and often repeated in the economic history of America. It represents the 'loss' side of a profit and loss system of adjusting to technological change. Perhaps for sociological purposes we need an answer to the question, 'just who pays?'" Who paid most in Caliente were those who, by traditional American standards, were most moral—most conforming to settled community and family life (p. 361) and accepting of "our traditional system of assessing the costs of technological change . . . on the theory that the costs of such change are more than offset by the benefits to 'society as a whole'" (p. 363).

Social Technology
The strained assumption of a "market" model of society working distributive justice has in recent years been replaced by an assertion of public responsibility in adjusting to technological change (Turvey, 1966; Levitan and Sheppard, 1963). The "socialization" of technological change now enters on both sides of the equation, however—cause and effect. "Social technology" goes beyond recognition of the social effects of technological change to the application of systematic social knowledge in policy formulation and plan implementation. It has become active and often decisive in shaping the contours of society, and itself represents a source of major social impact. Nowhere has policy impact been more potent than on the Federal level, as a current Rand Corporation study of urban problems confirms (The Washington Post, 27 October 1973, p. F30).

What SIA Is
Above all, what SIA symbolizes is the assumption of social responsibility on the part of public authorities and its imposition on private interests. What is being requested—indeed, demanded—is nothing less than the use of social forecasts as a planning base. Insofar as participatory planning is involved, this becomes an exercise in what Toffler (1973) calls "anticipatory democracy." Clearly this implies a significantly higher standard of governmental performance than that previously attained or seriously contemplated. The evaluation of program effectiveness has become almost routine, as exampled in the areas of health (Witkin, 1971), housing (Aaron, 1972) and employment (Brecher, 1973). What SIA proposes is to place the expectation of desired outcomes, of legislative enactments and program operation, on a reliable and rational basis—to replace judgment with analysis.

social impact assessment 5

Scientific methodology is characterized by four analytic phases: description, explanation, prediction and control. SIA, as a mode of applied social science, also proceeds through these phases. But as an action-oriented concern, SIA differs from "pure" science largely because of its special relationship to <u>prediction</u> and <u>control</u>. SIA is operationally lodged in these latter phases by virtue of its "social engineering" and social (policy) planning emphases. <u>Prediction</u> is entailed in making "with" and "without" project projections of the impact area, and <u>control</u> is implied in the SIA requirement to mitigate adverse effects of project construction (Office of the Chief of Engineers, 1972: A-2-5).

What is the substance behind this impressive symbolism? "Is social science ready?" (Spengler, 1970). Can the scientific quality of social knowledge bear the analytic weight being pressed upon it? Does this ambitious program incline towards utopian planning on the one hand (Boguslaw, 1965) and totalitarian planning on the other (Popper, 1957)? Boguslaw's "new utopians," it will be recalled, were not social scientists but systems analysts; still the apprehension remains. Since the days of Joseph Wood Krutch's humanistic critiques, there has been an equal and opposite fear—not that social scientists will fail, but that they will succeed only too well. The Federal prison experiments on behavior modification, with all their "Clockwork Orange" overtones, betrayed (and belied) this great fear. There is a respectable body of opinion that holds social science will never be predictive in the same sense as physical science. A scientific attitude compels the reply, "That is an empirical question." And, on the faith of a rationalist, it is knowledge most worth the having.

Resistances to SIA
The "need to know" in SIA has been invoked primarily in regard to the "social effects" of technological change. As Eigerman (1973: 1) says, "Technology can visit upon its implementers wholly unforeseen and undesirable consequences. . . . It follows that prudent men will scrutinize the intensive application of any new technology and try to anticipate the changes in physical, social and economic environments that it may induce. Impact assessment is precisely this forecasting and analysis exercise." Moreover, Coates (1971: 228) observes, "The intended effect of a technology is rarely, if ever, the only impact it has on human life. Unintended, unknown, and delayed consequences may prove even more important in the long run than the direct and intended effects." Yet according to Bauer (1967: 5), there exists "a systematic bias against concern over second-order consequences of technical innovations." While in principle we can agree that "technical changes have proved historically to be particularly explosive sources of second-order social, economic, and political changes that were never envisioned," in practice they are viewed in sharply restricted context:

> An action is often labeled "technical" to offer reassurance as to its limited implications. The very phrase "purely technical" is used to convey the notion that an action does <u>not</u> have widespread

6 social impact assessment

> ramifications. Because a technical development is both seen and
> judged as an answer to a rather specific problem, there is . . .
> a strong bias against being concerned over, trying to anticipate,
> or even thinking about its possible wider consequences. (Bauer,
> 1967: 4)

"Social" Engineering
The very characterization of social impacts as "secondary" underscores
their relative neglect. Coupled with this is the often impressionistic
nature of SIA, contrasting with the more certain and precise knowledge
of technical effects. Fundamentally though, what engineering is about
is people and their values; it stands in the relation of providing material
means to the satisfaction of human needs. From this sociological commonplace it follows that civil works projects, say, are supposed to have
social impacts. Such impacts are not merely incidental; rather they are
the essence of engineering practice.

It is true that "social impacts" have acquired something of a negative
connotation, as things to be avoided or alleviated so far as possible.
Partly this stems from the lack of positive content to "social well-
being" as a planning objective, in water resources and other fields of
natural resource development and management (infra). Without upholding
a position of technological neutrality--an utterly pernicious doctrine,
in my view--it can be allowed that social impacts may be beneficial as
well as detrimental, and often both at the same time. Who decides, on
what rational basis and legal authority, and which the values and interests
served, are questions for major consideration (e.g. Ingram, 1972).

Distributive Effects
Further it follows that the effects of engineering works will be distributive in nature, the incidence of social benefits and detriments falling
unevenly and unequally over various sectors and segments of the population,
and that this will be more so the more highly differentiated the society
becomes.* Conversely, there are differing claims and demands for public
goods and services to be honored or refused. One value ascendant since
"Great Society" days is that of social equity; projects are meant to have
redistributive effects on the availability and accessibility of social
opportunities--in employment, recreation, cultural participation and the
like. This brings civil engineering perilously close to social policy,
the legitimacy and efficacy of which are widely open to question and
challenge (Rein, 1972; Alexander, 1972).

---

*There are various implicit models of these distributive effects,
notoriously the "pork barrel" model (Carter, 1973); Bonnen (1970)
contends the absence of knowledge of distributional impacts is a serious
obstacle to effective policy analysis and decision.

social impact assessment 7

"Structural" and "Nonstructural Effects"

The social character and functions of engineering work enter also in the common distinction between "structural" (physical) and "nonstructural" measures, a distinction reimpressed on planners by the declining political acceptability of physical solutions to social problems. It is scarcely too much to say that no large-scale engineering project, whatever its merits, can proceed uncontested by "intervenors." Paradoxically, the concerted opposition of aroused citizens and organized interests has surfaced at a time when societal needs—for energy, housing, transportation, water supply and waste disposal—have reached massive proportions. It is scarcely credible that these needs can be met without extensive physical planning and plan implementation. "Nonstructural" measures, such as the voluntary reduction of energy demand, are designed to complement structural ones, not wholly displace them. At the same time, nonstructural measures admit a range of "social" factors to the planning process that were previously excluded or underrepresented.

"Project Effects" and "Planning Effects"

Another set of needed distinctions is that between "project effects," referring to structural (and nonstructural) measures in the construction and operation stages of project life history, and "planning effects," the impacts of planning studies themselves. In many instances, the latter may be the weightier. For example, plans for a series of lakes along the Meramec River in Missouri have drastically affected land use, although a shovel of dirt has yet to be turned. Speculators have replaced farmers; a completely different "public" with different values, interests and outlooks has emerged. The plans have already had more impact than the structures (if built) will ever have.* Similarly, Filstead (personal communication) quotes a Chicago District planner's comment that before the Corps of Engineers came into a downstate Illinois town, "there wasn't any such thing as community cohesion." Nor are planning effects negligible increasingly large amounts of project costs are being alloted to planning as against construction. Robert Summitt of the Southwestern Division speculates that the day may come when a project cannot be justified because it costs more to plan than it does to build. Moreover, the "output" of the current "urban studies" (a euphemism for "wastewater management," I am told) are not structures but reports. Evidently, planning philosophy has evolved a considerable distance beyond simple project justification. That engineering practice has kept pace is less apparent.

---

*Frank Sharp attributes this example to E. Jackson Baur (personal communication).

8 social impact assessment

The Impact Assessment System
Earlier generations of public planners regarded their designs more as
blueprints than experiments. Wholey (1973: 39) states the contrary view,
"that every policy decision represents not an ultimate solution but a
hypothesis; that success lies in testing and applying the results of
tests of policy hypotheses."[*] This is so because:

> Experience with social planning teaches that two factors must
> be kept in mind when developing and carrying out Federal pro-
> grams: any course of action has many possible outcomes and any
> act has inherent error associated with it. We cannot predict
> with certainty which results will follow from the particular
> policies, nor should we be confident that policy implementation
> will conform to plan. Both factors imply that early determina-
> tion of effects is necessary in order to meet, and possibly re-
> direct, program goals. The limited resources available to meet
> grave social needs and the significant but largely unpredictable
> impact of federal domestic policies require timely feedback about
> both positive and negative effects from on-going programs to assure
> productive program planning and management. (Wholey and others,
> 1973: 21)

It is often asserted that impact assessment is an integral part of the
planning process and must proceed in series--or even, in parallel--with
other, related parts. What Raymond C. Hubley, Jr., Executive Director of
the Izaak Walton League of America, says of environmental impact assessment applies to SIA as well:

> All too often, agencies write impact statements merely to
> validate decisions long since made. The intent of NEPA is not to
> fill the archives with futile environmental statements, but to
> shape project planning. Environmental considerations should be
> taken into account from the inception of a project. If environ-
> mental studies were undertaken at the same time that initial
> engineering and economic studies were begun, the environmental
> information could be integrated into the decision making process.
> Environmental considerations would be built into the final pro-
> ject design and construction could begin without fear of legal
> delays. (The Washington Post, 15 March 1974)

---

[*]Attributed to Joseph H. Lewis of the Urban Institute. Wholey adds
a cautionary note, "This is the reverse of conventional management
practice and the conventional reward system."

social impact assessment 9

The "Adequacy" of Social Impact Statements
Again in parallel with EISs, we may repeat Lynch's (1972: 741) admonition:

> In order to judge the adequacy of the final statement, the court should ask "adequate" for what? The purpose of NEPA's reporting process is to advise the decisionmakers in the executive branch and in Congress of the relative merits and drawbacks of any ongoing or proposed major federal action. If an impact statement does that with reasonable clarity, it has accomplished its purpose; if not, it should be reworked and expanded. But agonizing over minutiae or pondering unmeasurable, speculative effects of that action have no real relationship to the essential purpose of NEPA; that is not what a "detailed statement" should have to consider. If there can be any one test of the sufficiency of a NEPA statement, it should be whether the statement fairly alerts the responsible decisionmakers to the significant factors involved in the project or program, and does so with enough clarity to allow the decisionmakers to weigh these factors in arriving at a decision.

The criterion of relevance, then, is what information is needed to enable decision makers to appreciate the major dimensions and implications of a situation and to weigh their effect on one or another planning alternative. The amount of irrelevant material a typical EIS contains implies that instead of entering the decision making/planning process, such reports are aimed at averting legal interference by project opponents. Overkill in EIS preparation is more nearly calculated to insure that objections are quashed than that all significant impacts are considered in reaching planning decisions.

Comprehensive Planning
Despite an occasional success (e.g. McCoy, 1973), what SIA has meant thus far in practice is no more, and frequently much less, than pro forma compliance with statutory requirements. Following the NEPA precedent, it is perceived from an agency bias as hindering accomplishment of planning objectives rather than as a valued aid to planning. Gradually its position may improve, to approximate the "open system planning process" Ortolano (1973) envisions and which is gaining wide acceptance as Corps planning doctrine (Office of the Chief of Engineers, 1974). Schematically, this consists of four planning tasks (problem identification, formulation of alternatives, impact assessment and evaluation) iterated with increasing detail over three planning stages. SIA is integral to this process and its involvement in it is continuous. One measure of effective integration would be the use of SIA data in formulation of alternative plans.

"Institutional" Impacts
SIA is not only a body of organized (or organizing) knowledge; it must make contact with a social environment and participate in an ongoing social organization. Effectively combining the ideas and supporting organization

10 social impact assessment

becomes then a central focus in pursuing the analytic problem.* Such a planning process as Ortolano describes intersects and interacts with a multiplicity of social systems, among them: the Congressional system, in respect to study authorization; the Federal system, in respect to prevailing definitions of the "Federal interest" such as cost-sharing provisions; the Corps' internal system of planning, contracting and reviewing; the community system, in regard to public involvement programs; other Federal agencies, in respect to multipurpose planning; and governmental bodies on state and local levels in coordinating plan development. All of these entangling relations, and others that may be invented (e.g. regional authorities for basin-wide planning and management) can be summed in the category, "institutional impacts." As with the other major category, technological impacts, the causal flow is two-directional (cf. Schmid, n.d.).

2. APPROACHES TO SOCIAL IMPACT ASSESSMENT

With this preliminary statement of the analytic problem, we can proceed to a review of approaches by which it might be effectively engaged. The leading contender is what Baur (1973: 3) terms the "interactive approach." He gives this rationale: "Instead of assuming that the social effect is the result of a specific cause or a chain of causes that are traced to a technological innovation, I propose that we think of an effect as the outcome in the form of altered human conduct of the interaction between the agents of change and the people who have an interest in the proposed public works project." On this approach we understand that social factors are as much the cause of SIA as they are the effects.

The Interactive Approach to SIA

Consider a simple S→R model where the stimulus is provided by some engineering project in planning, construction or operation, and the response is the social impact of that phase of project life. Undoubtedly, that is the simplistic view of the matter held by some. Complications arise when it is seen that in no case can the impact be considered a "point event"; rather the effects linger and intermingle with others appearing later. When these "interaction effects" are recognized, together with exogenous factors, the analytic problem appears anything but simple. The figure below suggests a number of the complexities:

---

*Similarly, for evaluative research Wholey (1973: **39**) says, "Evaluators have always recognized the need to understand the programs being evaluated but rarely, if ever, have they perceived the need to understand the decision-making process and the constraints on the options open to the policymakers or program managers for whom the study is being designed."

social impact assessment 11

FIG. 2. INTERACTION EFFECTS IN SIA

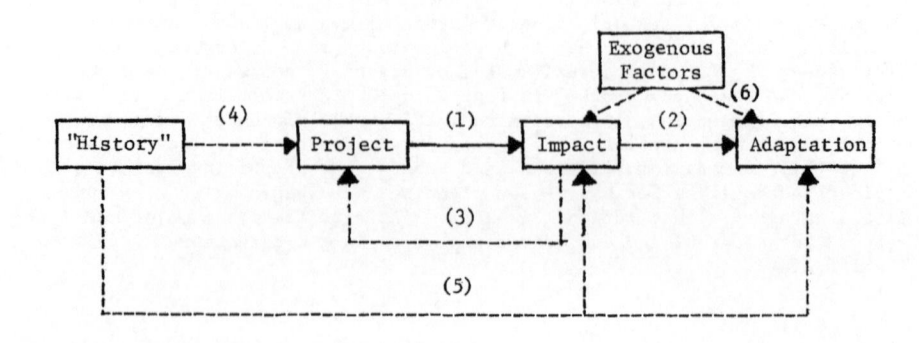

```
                                    Exogenous
                                    Factors
                   (4)         (1)        ↘  (2)  ↘(6)
    ┌─────────┐        ┌─────────┐    ┌────────┐      ┌────────────┐
    │"History"│------→ │ Project │ →  │ Impact │------→│ Adaptation │
    └─────────┘        └─────────┘    └────────┘      └────────────┘
         ¦                  ↑ (3)         ↑                ↑
         ¦                  ¦             ¦                ¦
         ¦                  ¦   (5)       ¦                ¦
         └──────────────────┴─────────────┴────────────────┘
```

The direct impact (1) is a deformation in the state variables describing initial conditions, but if analysis were to end there it would severely distort the reality situation of SIA. The continuing effects of readjustment and adaptive change represent a sort of "feed-forward" (2). We can further hypothesize a *differential* social responsiveness on the part of impacted units.* Conversely, in the planning phase the direct impact may result in a kind of "reaction formation" which impinges on project planning itself (3), in the form of public opposition and plan modification. Moreover, the project itself may be regarded as the social effect of a social cause--its "history" as a prospective solution to preexisting concerns, problems and issues residing in the affected area (4), and this history conditions public receptiveness at the points of impact and subsequent adaptation (5).** Finally, the intrusion of exogenous variables (6), whether random or systematic, compounds the problem of attributing measured effects to planned interventions.

---

*Economic studies of port development on the Arkansas River waterway (Belzung and Sonstegaard, 1973) suggest the hypothesis of differential social responsiveness to development opportunity (I owe this observation to Lloyd G. Antle of the Institute for Water Resources; see also Cox (1969)). If so, this has implications for differential impact prediction and directs attention to finer-grained analysis of community structural variables such as institutional capacity and learning.

**Antle insists that every current project Corps planners entertain is steeped in such a "history," although problem perceptions and project justifications may shift over time with institutional and opinion changes (e.g. in the definition of "Federal interest" and evaluative criteria).

12 social impact assessment

Given this situation of analytic complexity, Baur (1973: 2) concludes, it is "misleading to think of engineering projects as simply causing certain discrete social effects; rather, the effects are the resultants of a complex process of interchange between many persons, groups, organizations, and publics."

> Instead of a simple cause-effect model it is more in accord with the facts to use an interactive model based on an holistic approach to the situation. Some may prefer to call it a system model; but it is a very open, dynamic system. The approach is holistic in the sense that it tries to take account of multiple factors within and from outside the affected locality. Furthermore the agency or corporation that is planning the project should be viewed as part of the total social situation. It is a subsystem of national or regional scope which impinges on other subsystems within the area affected by the proposed project. Their interaction gives rise to new subsystems in the form of social movements and the groups instigated by the agency's public participation program.

What the interactive approach undertakes, then, is to "deresidualize" social impacts and to promote them to a position of causal importance. Supposing this approach to be the preferred metamethodological framework, it remains to be seen what are the variables interacting and which the systems of analysis by which they can be determined. The former indicates substantive approaches; the latter, methodological approaches. Naturally the two themselves interact.

Substantive Approaches
What selections and sets of variables can be drawn from the universe of impact parameters? Answering this question leads back into the cataloguing of social impact categories, and indeed, to the very conception of "the social" itself. This last point has proved especially troublesome (e.g. Enk and others, 1974: 37). General definitions have tended to be residual--"non-market," "non-biological," whatever is left after more definable entities and quantities have been deducted. In the effort to derive more specific content, Harris (1974: 37) isolated five principal vectors of the social domain relating to water resources planning by use of a multi-dimensional scaling technique: (1) fair allocation and conservation of water, (2) natural beauty of bodies of water, (3) public access to bodies of water, (4) quality of drinking water, and (5) public involvement in water-resources management. Perhaps this is getting too special; for present purposes it may suffice to simply distinguish between economic, social and environmental as major impact categories.*

---

*A case can be made out that "economic" and "environmental" are merely subsets of the "social" category. Regarding the economic, are we to believe it is non-social, or that economic phenomena exhaust the full range

Within the social category proper there are various aspects that receive varying emphasis: cultural impacts, which have been given operational definition in archeological sites and ethnic groups; value impacts; esthetic impacts (possibly a joint effect of "cultural" and "value" impacts); demographic impacts; institutional impacts, including specific functional areas such as recreation and family structure. The list could be extended and refined, and in keeping with the interactive approach we could introduce corresponding categories of social cause as well. For now this is enough to suggest some distinct objects of SIA.

Methodological Approaches

Exploring different content categories entails differing methodological approaches--for instance, the application of standard ethnographic techniques in assessing cultural impacts. Here our concern is with alternative research strategies, of which the "deductive" and "inductive" approaches are emblematic. On a deductive approach we would ideally begin with a concept, convert it to a variable, hypothesize a relationship between variables to achieve a theoretical formulation, then develop indicators (referents) and measurement techniques to determine the direction and test the strength of association, finally arriving at a parameter estimation. This ultrarational procedure is seldom followed, although experimental and quasi-experimental designs have been urged in evaluative research (Caporaso and Roos, Jr., 1973). To all appearances SIA is still in the "natural history" stage of science-building, at a point far removed from the mature stage of deductively formulated theory.

This being the case, inductive approaches--such as case studies of the community research variety--may be felt more fitting. Lest SIA remain in perpetual infancy, however, they should be fielded with a view towards building a _cumulative_ knowledge base. Perhaps the optimal strategy of inquiry is a "mixed" one, combining both inductive and deductive approaches. The method of "analytic induction," for example, is said to lend itself to "a simultaneous examination of the _particulars_ of a given event and those things which are _general_ and theoretical" (Manning, 1971: 39). Quite apart from forging theoretical linkages, however, inductive approaches have an undeniable immediacy and utility. Despite acute "causal ignorance" (Francis, 1973), Bauer (1967: 43) notes the legitimizing function of the social indicators approach:

> At the very least, a system of _social_ accounting, whether applied to a nation or any other organization, has the initial virtue of _legitimizing_ variables that are not included in the current systems of economic accounting. This fact, in itself, might bring about

of social phenomena? Regarding the environmental, from an anthropocentric viewpoint, it can be argued that _effective_ environment--"those parts of the total environment that are evidently of direct importance to the organism" (Allee and others, 1949: 1)--are fully encompassed in the realm of social concerns. My only point in sketching this _social_ reductionist argument is to suggest the desirability of preserving meaningful distinctions.

14 social impact assessment

rather rapid policy changes. There is a strong tendency for the managers of any system to improve the performance of the system on those variables that are regularly measured. Even a crude, approximate measure would reinforce the manager's judgment on the importance of what are now known as "qualitative" variables.

Levels of Impact Assessment: Policy, Program and Project Impacts
Along with systems of analysis, a levels of analysis problem intrudes in regard to methodological approaches. While SIA has been largely confined to specific, site-centered projects, as was environmental impact assessment in its earlier stages, this piecemeal approach is now suspect. A case-by-case treatment may well result in the whole being less than the sum of its parts. Rather, a systemic approach is indicated, in whose context specific projects can be assessed incrementally (even as they are now justified). Wholey and others (1973: 25) have stressed the necessity for program as well as project assessment,* and a few are now in progress on the side of environmental impacts (Baldwin, 1974: 3).

Just as projects are program elements, so programs emanate from policy-level deliberations. A good deal of policy analysis has been reported, but mainly on the topic of decision making. It remains, as Mowitz observes, "Policy analysis has seldom followed through to examine the impacts of policy decision once made. The most significant piece of information for the good of society is lacking, that is, did the policy decision trigger a chain of events for dealing effectively with the substantive problems at which the program was aimed" (quoted in Cook and Scioli, Jr., 1972: 329). These authors proceed to outline a research strategy for policy impact assessment in which program objectives and activities are cross-classified against primary-secondary and intended-unintended impact categories. Ideally then, SIA should make contact with public planning across levels of policy formulation, program development and project implementation.

Evaluation Research
Perhaps the most strategic approach to SIA might be expected to model itself on the growing research tradition of program evaluation. As defined by Wholey and others (1973: 23),

> Evaluation (1) assesses the **effectiveness** of an on-going program in achieving its objectives, (2) relies on the principles of research design to distinguish a program's effects from those of other forces working in a situation, and (3) aims at program improvement through a modification of current operations.

---

*The authors distinguish between "evaluative research" and "program" and "policy analysis," the latter two focusing on hypothetical alternative program solutions to problems of concern while the former deals exclusively with existing programs' effectiveness (pp. 23-24).

The "effectiveness" criterion stands in marked contrast to the cult of efficiency that placed administrative excellence over achieving desired results. In public assistance programs, for instance, "audit" and "compliance" took precedence, with scant attention paid to the impact of the system on direct "beneficiaries" or society at large. "Once it was enough to know that so many federal dollars bought so many miles of highway; now there is concern with 'secondary' impacts, such as the effects on community residents and the ecology," and generally, with "the actual effects that domestic federal policies and expenditures have on individuals, groups, neighborhoods and communities" (Wholey and others, 1973: 21).

There can be no quarrel with the effectiveness criterion, or with research designs that admit "sensitivity" or "discriminant analysis" (e.g. Decoursey, 1973), or with the "feedback link" in evaluative research that Wholey (1973: 31) says provides "the accountability and the information about program effectiveness that is normally provided by market action in the private sector." One major deviation incurred by SIA's role in planning methodology is that of employing ex ante instead of ex post designs, although that can be easily adjusted and SIA by no means precludes the latter. Rather, the principal difficulty revolves about the "criterion problem."

The Criterion Problem: Social Well-Being as a Planning Objective
The first condition of evaluative research is that program objectives be clearly stated; failing that, there is nothing to evaluate. The chief obstacle to SIA's adopting the evaluative research model is the unwillingness or inability to elevate social performance to the rank of a planning objective. Rather, social impact assessors are asked to treat their subject symptomatically, as unwanted and undesirable by-products or side effects of the serious (i.e. "structural") planning business. This structural pose misses the point of people; it is unsatisfactory and, I feel, ultimately untenable. A case in point is the inherently unstable situation existing in the water resources field, "two objectives, four accounts" (cf. Fairchild, 1973).

Senate Document 97 (U. S. Senate, 1962: 2) announces, "Well-being of all the people shall be the overriding determinant in considering the best use of water and related land resources." Its successor, the Water Resources Council's "Principles and Standards" (1973), reaffirms the overriding consideration for "quality of life" and purports to express "societal preference" in its planning guidance. The extent of its success in this endeavor appears quite limited.* "Social well-being" dwindles to

---

*Irving Fox, cited in National Academy of Public Administration and U. S. General Accounting Office (1973: 15-16). EPA's experience with the "Quality of Life" concept (Office of Research and Monitoring, 1973) is not at all dissimilar.

16 social impact assessment

the depressed status of an "account" consisting of real income distribution, health and safety, and a leftover from obsolete legislation on emergency preparedness.

"Straw Man"
It may be that "national economic development" (BCR) and "environmental quality" (a newcomer) are the only planning objectives on which social consensus can be reached. It may be too that regional development is best served from the pork barrel. Nevertheless, a more socially optimal solution has been advanced in the "Straw Man" modeling approach relating

> . . . water resource use to "social goals" . . . consisting of a hierarchical array of elements beginning at the top with nine general word-described goals, tentatively postulated as a comprehensive set describing general welfare, and successively delineated by expanding strata of sub-goal descriptors eventually to water related policy action variables through social indicators. (quoted in McDonald, 1971: 1).

The Straw Man modelers argued that "social well-being is the overriding objective of all water resources development activities such that any parameterized goal (such as national economic development) is not in itself the ultimate goal for planning, but serves as an achievement indicator of a project's impact on one sector of the national general welfare map" (McDonald, 1971: 1; see also Biswas and Durie, 1971). While experience thus far has failed to establish the conceptual meaning and operational measurement of "social well-being" (Special Task Force, 1970), this quest will doubtless command priority attention in future research.

Impact Assessors
Having quickly scanned a few plausible approaches to SIA, we should take notice of their practitioners. The present cohort of impact assessors strikes a fair balance of interests between governmental agencies, consultants and firms, institutes and academics. While there is not yet an effective division of labor between them, there does appear an increasing density of activity that holds promise for fruitful collaboration. The role of public participation in SIA is more problematic (infra).

The Federal Interest in SIA
On the Federal agency level, the tenured member is the Federal Highway Administration—actually the old Bureau of Public Roads. Its "Social Impact" program was advertised as "top priority research" as early as 1966 (Bureau of Public Roads, 1966; Kanwit, 1967). It is not at all reassuring that this effort faltered badly after its auspicious beginning. Lately it has been revived, however, under contract with the National Bureau of Standards (Llewellyn, 1973). FHWA's process guidelines for social, economic, and environmental effects of highway projects are set forth in "Policy and Procedure Memorandum 90.4" (1973).

social impact assessment 17

It might naturally be supposed that the lead agency in SIA would be the Environmental Protection Agency itself. In fact, after early sponsorship of Abt Associates' impact matrix methodology (1971), EPA's own initiative has been surprisingly limited. Though sophisticated in other respects, the large-scale modeling effort of House and his associates (1971) has yet to incorporate social impact categories. Systematic guideline formulation and enforcement will ultimately require model building on the grand scale but, divorced from theoretical grounding and empirical reality testing, present attempts seem premature (cf. Lee, Jr., 1973).

One occasion on which EPA has directly addressed SIA came at a recent conference on "The Assessment of the Social Impacts of Oil Spills." Conferees were asked, "Should the government, presumably under EPA auspices, undertake a program to research the assessment of social impacts (human community) from oil spills, which could then be used in the development of regulations and enforcement practices?" (Enk and others, 1974: 35). Their rhetorical question is still awaiting an official answer. At that same conference, Snyder (1974: 7) remarked, "Although I am not saying that EPA will automatically switch over from its biological emphasis to a social emphasis in its assessment process, I am saying that we do want to arrive at a better understanding of what can be done and how strong the demand is for us doing it." What Snyder actually discovered (personal communication) was a low signal-to-noise ratio among social impact assessors and a slack demand for their services. Far from advancing a social emphasis, EPA now threatens to recede past the biological and into straight environmental engineering. (In fairness, it should be added that SIA has lately infested the Office of Pesticides.)

If the Federal mandate for SIA is clear, organizational commitment on the part of Federal agencies remains uncertain. Budgetary allocations have been paltry, although Krebs (personal communication) recounts the arresting case of a Corps of Engineers dam project in eastern Ohio in which the SIA budget soared from one to 30% after community opposition. More than "public relations" will be required to appease the "locals." The agency picture is beginning to brighten, with stirrings in the Corps, the Bureau of Land Management and elsewhere. The newly-formed Office of Technology Assessment has an affinity with SIA, if not yet an active interest, and AEC, NASA and HUD may prove tractable. Efforts are now underway to constitute an "Ad Hoc Interagency Working Group on Social Impact Assessment" to review existing guidelines, procedures, methodologies, and to suggest improvements.

Special Interests in SIA
Special interests--corporate, professional and academic--are likely to be asserted somewhat proportional to the Federal interest: more exactly, to the level of Federal funding. The phenomenon of "instant expertise" which accompanied passage of NEPA is likely to be repeated, on a much diminished scale, in respect to SIA. Sensing a fundable project, one

18 social impact assessment

consulting firm grandly offered to prepare "a clearly written technical assistance bulletin of 20 to 40 pages in length, which would set forth the meaning of social impact assessment, the legal requirements under various applicable laws and administrative regulations, and ways in which social impacts, unrelated to economics, might be evaluated and mitigated." Moreover, their offer extended to "holding training sessions for project engineers and others in order to heighten their awareness of the social implications of projects in which they are involved." Evidently, this firm had at the time no more awareness of the dimensions of the problem than their intended clients, and probably a good deal less. With added experience, the corporate picture will doubtless improve.

Of course, the professional interest in SIA is not only to uphold "standards" of competence and conduct.* Also it is to constantly reimpress vexed adminstrators and planners with the complexity of the problem and the intricacy of the analysis, thus insuring a continuous flow of contract funds to themselves and their colleagues. The academic interest partakes not only of the genuine intellectual challenge inherent in SIA but also of the desire to "place" their clients--graduate students--in non-academic employment, thus relieving the problem of professional overpopulation (cf. Motz, 1974: 2). In asserting their right of interest, however, social scientists will have to match scientific pretentions with a convincing show of professional accomplishment. The record so far leaves small room for complacency.

For the short term, SIA appears fated to remain the intellectual property of non-experts. The "economist with a minor in sociology" will satisfy job descriptions, and retrained (or untrained) engineers will be pressed into "do-it-yourself" SIA. Gardner's (1973) social impact study of Willow Creek compares favorably with some in-house assessments, and no doubt proved a valuable learning experience for his Social Research Methods class of upper-division sociology majors at Walla Walla College, but if environmental impact assessment is any indication, the time will shortly arrive when as much professional expertise is demanded and received in SIA as in any other technical phase of project planning. Counsels of perfection are definitely misplaced, but nothing less than the highest level of professional competence will suffice to meet the analytic situation.

The Public Interest in SIA
Let us first establish that the "Federal interest" is neither definitive nor exhaustive of "the public interest." It _may_ be indicative, but even that is not a foregone conclusion. Irving Fox (National Academy of Public Admininstration and U. S. General Accounting Office, 1973: 15-16) questions

---

*The American Sociological Association has created an Ad Hoc Committee on Environmental Sociology "to establish guidelines for sociological contributions to environmental impact statements" (ASA Footnotes, 1, 9 (December 1973), p. 9).

social impact assessment 19

the embodiment of societal preference in public policy decisions as to (1) <u>whose</u> preferences are reflected in decisions about standards, (2) how well these preferences reflect the wishes of a cross-section of the general public affected, and (3) what institutional arrangements will facilitate consideration of the plan rankings and trade-offs by legitimate decision makers. The more fundamental point however is that our society is greater than the state and Federal decision rules provide only a minimalist definition of public interest. This condition implies needed scope for direct public involvement beyond the sometimes arbitrary and artificial boundaries of representative government. What provision SIA makes for this kind of public participation will be examined in the next section.

3. THE METHODOLOGY OF SOCIAL IMPACT ASSESSMENT

Ideally our aim in this section would be to associate various methodologies and techniques with the approaches introduced above, both from the side of causative factors and from that of social impact categories. Our acquaintance has been too casual and cursory to permit this in any codified fashion, however.* Instead, we will fasten on one coherent set of SIA procedures--those set forth in Section 122 Guidelines (Office of the Chief of Engineers, 1972)--and attempt to trace through them the methodological requirements implied. First a more general methodological discussion is in order.

<u>A Budget of Methodological Problems</u>
What are we solving for by application of selected methodologies? A characteristic list is presented in Ireland (n.d.: 21) with reference to industrial location:

1. How can the social structure of the receiving area be described and identified for the purposes of evaluation?
2. How can one identify and describe the changes in the economic, particularly the industrial, structure of the area?
3. How much of this change can be attributed to the action of regional policies of industrial location?
4. What is the relationship between changes in the industrial structure and changes in the micro socio-economic structure?
5. How can we evaluate the impact of changes in the industrial structure, in terms of the goals of members of the local community? in terms of the goals of the policy makers and planners? in terms of those members of the wider society who have social, economic or political interest in the receiving areas, or in the policy? in terms of an attempted sociological evaluation?

---

*Such a systematic codification is now in progress, following this basic format: approach, methodology, technique(s), data source(s), use, display, reference(s). In this process several other inventories are being generated, including criteria, descriptors, indicators, propositions and findings.

20 social impact assessment

Generalizing on Ireland, the questions are: (1) what is changing? (2) how can such change be detected and measured? (3) what is causing it? (4) what are the differentials in rates of change operating, e.g. as between sector proportions? and (5) what is the bearing of public policy and social choice on these changes?

Methodological Requirements for SIA

Eigerman (1973: 3) likewise considers that "To produce good information for the planner, an impact assessment methodology should handle at minimum:

1. Categories of impact stimuli (what in the plan may do the changing),
2. A baseline from which deviations can be measured,
3. Quantitative and qualitative impact measures (how much and what kind of change),
4. Temporal dimensions (frequency and duration of change),
5. And spatial dimensions (where the change takes place)."

The first of these are "causative factors" of a structural or nonstructural character, or the two in combination. The baseline, or initial conditions, is composed into a "profile" of the impact area, the salient features of which are the impact categories themselves. Then the problem for SIA methodology is to determine the relationships, their direction and magnitude, between categories of cause and effect. The general nature of the relationships can be described in terms of paired opposites such as: direct-indirect, intended-unintended, immediate-delayed, reversible-irreversible, random-systematic, concentrated-dispersed, homogenous-differential, and so on. Clearly SIA is speaking the language of causal analysis, but it is a situation of complex causality, with many-many relations and interactions between and within the respective category sets.

The general methodological requirement for SIA is essentially the same as for any controlled scientific experiment. Unfortunately, social impact assessors are seldom in a position to exert the requisite experimental controls. Moreover, they cannot establish truly experimental conditions because the analytic problem is predictive in nature. At best, they can perform what Weber called "mental experiments" and hope that the outcome will be isomorphic to the unfolding reality situation within some tolerable margin of error. The problem of social prediction is further complicated by the condition Duhl (1967) depicts of planning "when you don't know the names of the variables." Worse still, prediction must be contingent on public authorities and private interests orienting their future actions in accord with present expectations. That is the level of planning complexity SIA methodologies must engage. What are the intellectual resources that can be mobilized to this end?

social impact assessment 21

The Repertory of SIA Methodologies
"Assessing social impacts is an area of great interest and concern," Enk (1974: iii) believes, "but not one of established methodologies and expertise." Many of the methodological requirements of SIA do not radically depart from conventional social research, but Enk's assessment is accurate with respect to the more novel ones, e.g. social forecasting (cf. Duncan, 1969). All of the following social science methodologies enter SIA at one or another stage; what is crucial and problematic is their proper combination:

Demographic analysis	Evaluative research
Community studies	Institutional analysis
Causal modeling	Value analysis
Social indicators	Multivariate analysis
Ethnomethodology	Social network analysis
Archival research	Social forecasting
Survey research	Matrix methodologies

These can be further specified in particular techniques: cohort analysis, the "reputational" method, path analysis, index construction, etc. Because of its position in comprehensive planning, specialized methodologies from that domain are also implied: policy analysis, social accounting, simulation and gaming among many others. Now the question is how these assorted methodologies can be coordinated to yield the desired result, a social impact assessment.

Impact Assessment Steps
The series of impact assessment steps postulated in Section 122 Guidelines (Office of the Chief of Engineers, 1972), "tells the story" of SIA as operational procedure:*

FIG. 3. IMPACT ASSESSMENT STEPS (SECTION 122 GUIDELINES)

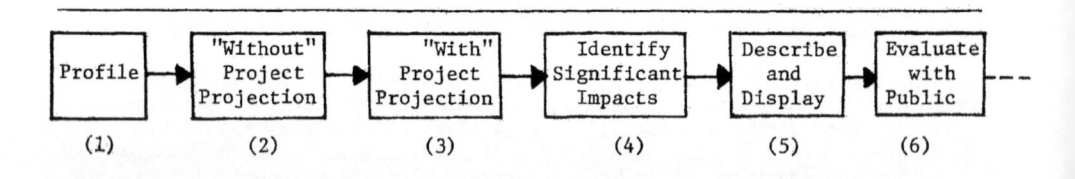

Profile (1) → "Without" Project Projection (2) → "With" Project Projection (3) → Identify Significant Impacts (4) → Describe and Display (5) → Evaluate with Public (6) → ─ ─

---

*Although technically the steps apply to economic and environmental impact assessment as well, our reading of Section 122 Guidelines is from the standpoint of SIA alone. The former two are well established elsewhere in Corps planning, and while their joint participation in an overall "impact assessment" process would be highly desirable, at present a serious disrelationship exists among the three (infra).

22 social impact assessment

The series continues with "mitigate adverse effects" (7) and then goes into a public hearing and official reporting sequence, ending with EIS preparation (11). The six initial steps are of primary concern here. They form a continuous, "value-added" process, each step of which is analyzable in terms of the input received, the analysis performed, and the output produced. In principle, the cumulative effect should be the systematic and comprehensive identification, measurement and evaluation of all significant impacts and their interrelations. In practice, this logic has yet to be carried through to a successful conclusion, though fragments of it have been assembled.

(1) <u>Profiling</u>: The purpose of profiling is to develop a set of social baseline data--in effect, a "before" measure of the impact situation, in anticipation of project-induced changes. Examples of this kind of analysis are Smith (1970) and Wilkening and others (1973).* Two methodological problems intrude at this point: (1) defining the impact area boundaries and (2) determining the data points that will dimensionalize and describe the referent system. The extent of impact predicted--and by implication the extent of system impacted--bears on the first question. Roughly speaking, the magnitude of impact can be assumed as proportional to the magnitude of the project, with intensity falling off as a gradient of undetermined steepness from the epicenter of impact.

Two basic attitudes can be taken towards bounding the impact area. One is "project-related" and presupposes an existing project proposal; the other and more difficult is "area-related" and focuses more on accurate problem identification than on specific project justification. Generally, Section 122 Guidelines is predicated on the former and "urban studies guidance" (Planning Division, 1973) on the latter. "Project-related" area bounding has the advantage of determinancy in what the presumed causative factors, and hence the predictable impacts, are to be--a harbor dredging operation, a floodway clearance, an upstream reservoir or whatever, while "area-related" is less well specified but more open to consideration of a wider range of social conditions and planning possibilities. On the

---

*The most ambitious undertaking of this type to date was the Office of Economic Opportunity's "Community Profile Series" (1968), establishing poverty indicators nationwide on the county level. This massive effort was to have been updated periodically to compile time series data, but the initial work has not been repeated and now OEO is itself practically defunct. Cook and Scioli, Jr.'s (1972: 337) comment on information requirements for SIA is pertinent here: "Impact analysis . . . cannot be constrained by present data sources but must instead stress the development of data sources that are relevant to the systematic evaluation of social programs. To do otherwise would result in the substitution of data availability for evaluation criteria as the primary analytical framework within which impact analysis is conducted." With all due regard for the cost of original data acquisition, it is no more reasonable to expect social impact assessors to conduct their business in an empirical vaccuum than to ask field geologists to abandon test borings.

social impact assessment 23

former, one might ask, "What are the impacts?"; on the latter, "What is the system?" While the water resources planner's typical unit of analysis is a hydrologic system, the social impact assessor's is likely to be a social system, in which the extent of functional dependence and degree of functional integration are crucial to stamping unit character. The "community bias" is especially pronounced in social analysis, though hard to localize in large-scale project planning (e.g. the Great Lakes water level).*

In either case, the profile features should cover the social impact categories prescribed in Section 122 and other relevant factors. The traits listed below in Table 1 derive from this source; social area indicators can also be developed for factors such as cultural intensity, extent and type of social uses, and "social orientation." "Proxy measures" are census titles whose data are pertinent to the traits listed; they are readily available at suitable levels of disaggregation on 1st and 4th count census tapes and the Bureau of Labor's detailed manpower indicators tapes.

TABLE 1. COMMUNITY PROFILE - CENSUS DATA & SOURCES**

Trait	Proxy Measures	Source	Detailed Source
Population Density	Population per sq. mi.[a]	US Population Census	Vol. 1. Characteristics of the Population, Pt. A, No. of Inhabitants
Population Mobility; Displacement	Total population A. Moved into unit 1965-1970 B. No. school years completed C. Residence in same house 5 years ago (total)	US Housing Census Pop Census " "	See Detailed Manpower Indicators, Table 12B 4th Count, Tabs 5301 thru 5308 Detailed Manpower Indicators, Table 12B

---

*Kent Rice (personal communication) offers the concept of "regional community" to comprehend such expansive planning areas. Scattered empirical findings likewise support the far-ranging effects of site-specific projects, e.g. watershed development. By use of cluster analysis, Wiebe (1972: 1197) demonstrated for the Tennessee River Valley that the incidence of benefits in employment, income and education "were not necessarily confined to isolated areas near projects but were rather of a regional dimension. . . ."

**Prepared by Frank Sharp, Office of the Chief of Engineers.

24 social impact assessment

Housing	A. Value count	Housing Census		Tabs 35AF01 thru 35AF08
	B. Rent count	"	"	Tabs 36AF01 thru 36AF10
	C. % in 1 unit structure	"	"	Tabs 27F01 thru 27F03
	D. % in structures built 1960 or later; or 1950 or earlier	"	"	Vol. 1, Housing characteristics for states, cities, or counties
Crowding	E. 1.01 or more persons per room	"	"	1st Count, Tabs 30F02 & 30F03
Transportation	A. With 1 or more autos	"	"	4th Count, Tabs 36.01 thru 36.09
	B. Used public transportation to work	"	"	
	C. Worked outside county of residence	Pop Census		4th Count, Tabs 35.25 and 35.26
Desirable Community Growth	A. Vacancy rate (Homeowner)	Housing Census		1st Count, Tabs 26AF07 thru 26AF09
	B. Median income (Family)	Pop Census		See (A) Community Cohesion
Health				
Community Cohesion	A. Families below 125% of low income level	"	"	4th Count, Tabs 75.01 thru 75.15
	B. No. of 1 person households	Housing Census		Vol. 1, Housing Characteristics for states, cities and counties
	C. % Homeowners	Pop Census		1st Count, Owner occupied Total occupied
	D. Employed by type of Industry 1. Manufacturing, wholesale & retail			Using Tabs 26AF01 and 26AF04
	2. Services 3. Educational 4. Construction 5. Government			4th Count, Tabs 62.01 thru 62.82

[a]Constraint: usually only available down to a city or county level.

These profile measures are only illustrative of a much wider array; owing to the "interchangeability of indices," selection among them might well be a matter of convenience or least-cost. The stricture on secondary data analysis noted above remains valid, although as Hyman (1972) has indicated, much productive work is possible along those lines. Noteworthy also is that all data series tabled above are retrievable through a comprehensive planning information system, SIRAP (System of Information Retrieval and Analysis for Planners) now coming on line. Social impact assessors should not bemuse themselves with visions of "instant analysis" at the touch of a button, however. Data interpretation is as much a part of SIA as data gathering and processing, and Kemper's (1974) inconvenient

social impact assessment 25

question, "What does it mean sociologically to be of a given age, sex, social class, educational level, race, religion, region, ethnicity, occupation, etc.?" is not easily answered. Conceptual analysis and elaboration of catagories such as "community cohesion" is a pressing need; the tacit assumption is one of a consensus model, whereas community conflict is often the situation of fact. Conceptual innovations on the order of Litwak's (1961) will likely be required.

(2-3) Projecting: The system profiled is a dynamic one; time series data must be generated for purposes of trend extrapolation, to forecast deviations from base conditions established in the profiling step. There are two states of the system projected over project life, which may be upwards of 100 years: "without" project and "with." As Eigerman (1973: 4) observes, "everything changes whether a given plan is implemented or not. Therefore, plan-induced change is not the difference between what is forecast 'with' a plan and some steady-state 'today.' It is the difference between two forecasts; what is anticipated 'with' the plan and what is anticipated 'without' it."* The second anticipation, "without project," entails making a general social forecast; "project-related" definitions of area and derivations of impact are insufficient.

The notion of "with" and "without" projections is employed in the California Tomorrow Plan (Heller, 1972), starting from a baseline of present-day conditions ("California Zero") and describing two future trajectories, one a negative extrapolation from the present ("California One") and the other "a proposal for the alternative ways of solving problems" ("California Two"). The former and "most probable future" is the "without" condition--without the California Tomorrow Plan--and the latter is the "with." Comparative advantage of the Two over the One is demonstrated by costing the two future Californias for open space, transportation and health care. A final section proposes institutional means for phasing in California Two.

While methodologically embryonic, the basic logic of the California Tomorrow Plan is identical with the "projecting" assessment steps prescribed in Section 122. A more advanced linear program model for multiobjective planning and evaluation, MOPE, uses OBERS projections in establishing comparison levels of resource availability and demand for "with" and "without plan" conditions (McKusick and others, 1973); deployment of this model to California data is proposed. Difficulties with forecasting techniques have been slightly relieved by advances in futures research and technology assessment (e.g. McHale, 1973; Stover, 1973; Jones, 1972; Kane, 1972; Helmer, 1972), although the fundamental problem of "predicting discontinuities in social change" (Moore, 1964) persists. Incremental gains rather than methodological breakthroughs are projecting's most probable future.

---

*Similarly, "Without-the-plan analysis is easily confused with existing conditions, ignoring ongoing programs and new developments which could be expected to come about even if no plan to meet future needs were developed. Without-the-plan analysis should be just as conscientious and objective a projection of the anticipated future without-the-plan as is made in support of it" (Water Resources Council Information Memorandum, 25 April 1974, p. 2).

26 social impact assessment

(4) <u>Identifying significant impacts</u>: This is not the simple operation of subtracting (2) from (3) to get (4). The criteria of significance are already preconceived in the categories of effect that enter the profiling step (1), and are predetermined in those of cause that initiated the study. Moreover, the net balance of effects can only be measured in (4), not weighed in comparative judgment until evaluative factors come into focus (5). What is sought in this step is an objective appraisal of impact magnitudes, without fear or favor. Yet even that dispassionate analysis is beset with difficulty.

Considering its myriad spin-offs and externalities, Bauer (1967: 14) believes it probable that "certain effects of the space program can never be distinguished from the effects of other developments in society. In many respects the program for space exploration is part and parcel of widespread developments in technology." It is precisely here of course where "discriminant" or "sensitivity" analysis is needed to partial out effects of planning projections (2-3). In the absence of experimental controls to neutralize what Campbell terms "internal threats to validity" and eliminate "plausible rival hypotheses" to the predicted change (Cook and Scioli, Jr., 1972: 332), such an analysis is impossible to perform.

> The essence of the experimental approach lies in two central concepts: control and the detection of interaction effects. Experimental control refers to the researcher's ability to regulate the values assumed by the experimental variables, both independent and control. In his attempt to determine the main effects of the independent variables, the researcher must include in his analysis those variables which may bear a functional relation to the independent-dependent relationship, that is, control variables. This inclusion allows the experimenter to determine whether or not the independent-dependent relationship is a direct relationship or is only operative at specific levels of the control variables. . . .
> (Cook and Scioli, Jr., 1972: 334)

The kind of experimental controls a social impact assessor can exercise over independent and dependent variables is given in the available mix and choice of planning alternatives. But assignment of hypothetical values, uncorrected in the predictive case by application of empirical controls, stretches the deductive chain to tenuous lengths after a few interactions. Although second-order consequences are generally acknowledged, little analysis has been directed to tracing indirect effects. Coates (1971: 228-29) has assessed the effects of automobiles, refrigeration and television through <u>sixth</u>-order consequences (all of them found conducive to breakdown in community and family life, perversely enough), and cross-impact computer programs such as Trend Impact Analysis (Becker and Gerjuoy, 1973) provide at least the technical capacity for analyzing complex interactions. Similarly with respect to "internalizing externalities," through more comprehensive systems mappings or other means, the methodological problems engendered by acceptance of an interactive approach appear overwhelming in the present state of the art. The social scientists' response to analytic complexity has been to intensely cultivate multivariate approaches. Cook and Scioli, Jr.'s (1972: 334-37) own "factorial design" leaves the problems for SIA still unresolved. Since the interactive approach seems compelling, for reasons discussed above, overcoming them may require ingenuity of a high order.

(5) <u>Displaying and describing impacts</u>: After this rather pessimistic account, it may appear that information displays based on such inoperable or invalid methodologies will be artifactual at best and mischievous at worst. Without denying the useful work of Miller and Byers (1973) and others, it seems fair to say that a clear and present danger exists of "premature quantification," foregoing the hard analysis prescribed above. The conjunction of terms, "describe <u>and</u> display," does signify a willingness to entertain "qualitative" variables, values and analyses, but the empiricist trend, propelled by the social indicators "movement" and allied forces, seems irresistable. Whether the outcome will be numerical analysis or numerology is in greater doubt.

(6) <u>Evaluating with the public</u>: Display features are encouraged as providing a basis for public participation in impact evaluation. A sharp distinction is made in Corps doctrine between "assessment" and "evaluation." To this point in the SIA process, technical neutrality has been the norm. "Going public" means now the attaching of values and assigning of weights as to the desirability or undesirability of the impacts assessed. Strict adherence to the fact-value dichotomy, and the segmentation of expert-public roles and relations attending it, is relaxed however in the initial problem identification phase, and the criterion of significance applied in (4) must be colored to an extent by subjective impressions of public preference. Moreover, the dichotomy may be false if it is assumed that "objective" assessments are value-free or that value positions lack factuality.

Two essential conditions must be met to elicit participation for purposes of impact evaluation: (1) the identification of publics (plural), and (2) some preliminary structuring of the situation to which their response is invited. The concept of "the public" is so elusive that, long ago (1925), Walter Lippmann declared it a "phantom." Emphasis falls on public<u>s</u> in recognition of the multiplicity of interests and associations to be included under that rubric. No one grouping is definitive of "the public," nor is any excluded. Most helpful for impact evaluation purposes would be a typology of impactee groups such as Mack (1974) and Peelle (1974) present. The following memorable exchange in a field interview situation points to the need for structuring:

28 social impact assessment

    Sociologist: How has the port affected life?

    Crane Operator: . . .

The quality of the questioning can be judged in the quality of the response. Public reaction is too easily dismissed as apathetic or ignorant; where an expectation of public input is encouraged, at least some attention should be paid to grounds on which the public is approachable and responsive. Use of simulation games such as IMPASSE (Impact Assessment) (Duke and others, 1973) and visual stimuli such as LAND (Landscape Analysis and Natural Design) (Everett, 1973) are richly deserving of much fuller employment. The discounting of public input occurs also in contention with expert judgments. The unpalatable alternative is to restore planner biases as to "what the people want." Manifestly, a method of articulating expert judgment and public opinion must be devised. Crawford's (1972) technique of expert responses to a Delphi instrument validated by a random sample's value analysis is instructive to this point.

There are two unavoidable problems of survey methodology we must confront, however. Supposing we succeed at obtaining verbal responses from a representative public, what is their relation to actual behavior? As matters presently stand, "the assumption that feelings are directly translated into actions has not been demonstrated" (Wicker, 1969; 75; see also Bruvold, 1973; Liska, 1974). But even if we grant some tenable relation between attitudes and actions, we are also aware of shifts in the schedules of public preference expressed over time. The advent of environmental concern as a public issue in the 1960s is one imposing instance. Moreover, we may further suppose that attitude change is itself a function of public involvement. If effective, public participation is a learning process throughout which attitude formation, crystallization and change occur. Anticipating shifts in public preference then becomes part of the predictive problem. Whatever the difficulties, we must agree with Baur's (1973: 2) assessment, "an understanding of social effects cannot be made without regard to the kind and extent of public involvement in the planning and management of the project."

4. EMPIRICAL APPLICATIONS OF SOCIAL IMPACT ASSESSMENT

Having completed our review of the procedures for SIA recommended in Section 122 Guidelines, we would normally expect to test their viability and validity against practical experience. We have found the assessment steps do form a logical progression, but that methodologically they falter. Issues raised in the operational context of Section 122 perhaps explain why no authentic case of SIA has yet been carried out or reported according to regulation. The closest approximation is a hypothetical case study of the Little Hunting Creek (VA) recreational navigation project (Office of the Chief of Engineers, 1973: Appendix A), intended "to demonstrate in theory how effect assessment can be conducted using an actual project

social impact assessment 29

in order to inject some realism into the task."* The authors generously included a sampling of its critical reception, e.g.:

> The process and analysis presented in the Little Hunting Creek example seem extremely cumbersome, abstract, and even vague.
>
> The Little Hunting Creek effect assessment is far too detailed than is necessary on a realistic basis.
>
> There are data lacking on the number of houses bordering Little Hunting Creek, and such things as how many owners have boats and docks.
>
> In the initial profile section of the Little Hunting Creek project example, the description is saturated with subjective judgments and non-quantified measurements.
>
> Information is lacking on the several creeks a few miles downstream from Little Hunting Creek that are not considered for improvement. Couldn't they be considered as alternatives?
>
> It appears that too many assumptions were made in the project setting that were not considered or studied properly before stating them as effects for assessment.
>
> Care should be taken about such statements as "the people of Gum Springs will desire any program that will improve their economic lot." Would the people desire a program that would break up families. . . ?

One commentator doubted the study's applicability to large-scale project planning, and another ventured, "What is needed in effect assessment is to identify how the area under analysis functions."

We have chosen Section 122 Guidelines for close scrutiny because it is a _strong_ case of attempted SIA, not because of the deficiencies revealed. No Federal, regional, state or local agency has done more than the Corps to honor a commitment to SIA; none has gone farther in its effort to provide specific procedural guidance. Yet having come this far we are entitled to ask what is wrong with SIA as conceived and executed by the Corps, and what about it can be put right. The underlying problem, of course, is the state of the art itself. Professional social scientists have not troubled themselves to think well or deeply about the problem. SIA Corps-style can perhaps be faulted both from the side of unrealizeable guidance and from that of methodological underdevelopment. Lack of rigorous field testing prior to instituting Section 122 Guidelines has

---

*"In March 1973, the Corps stopped work on the plan at the request of Fairfax County on the basis of apparent lack of local support."

30 social impact assessment

compounded these difficulties.* The attitude seems to be: "If it's a requirement, we can do it," following which untested procedures are issued as a normative forecast of subsequent field practice. Since this Policy of "forcing" appears overdemanding in the present state of the art, unless supported by a high density of activity and heavy commitment of resources, we might propose a more modest "incremental" strategy of inquiry.

Limiting Case Analysis: Mannford and Bank Stabilization
In closely adjoining areas, we are presented with two limiting cases of social impact ranging from total to negligible. These extremes define a continuum for registering the severity of social impact. At one stands the relocated town of Mannford, Oklahoma, which experienced direct, primary and immediate local impacts from construction of the Keystone Reservoir (Morgan, 1970). This was an instance of near-total physical impact, yet removal and recreation of Mannford served to maintain its social system virtually intact while three other nearby communities were undergoing physical dispersal and social disintegration.** The net balance of social

---

*A two-day "conference concerning the implementation of Section 122 Guidelines" was convened by the Office of the Chief of Engineers in April 1973, at which "pilot project" reports were presented by a number of districts and divisions. A token level of effort is reflected in these studies. One, a channel dredging project in Portland District, provoked environmentalist opposition:

> Environmentalists have stated that the EIS does not adequately reflect the multi-step effect assessment required by the Guidelines for Assessment of Economic, Social and Environmental Effects of Civil Works Projects. Therefore, they claim that, since the "Guidelines" have not been followed, the Corps is in violation of Federal Law (Sec. 122, PL 91-611), and that all work on processing the report and EIS should be halted until the full 11-step effect assessment process has been completed. It should be noted that the environmentalists did not object . . . on the basis of damage to the environment, but only on the basis that the Corps had not addressed in detail each and every word in the published "Guidelines" for accomplishing Sec. 122.

North Pacific Division offers the "pertinent comment,"

> Problems such as described above are the direct result of the Corps' published "Guidelines." In our opinion, the guidelines greatly exceed the intent of Congress set forth in Sec. 122 of PL 91-611. As an example, Sec. 122 makes no mention of NEPA. But, the "Guidelines" state that Sec. 122 supplements and extends the requirements of NEPA. Such declarations have no basis in fact, and have provided environmental extremists with still another "legal" means for obstructing our efforts on much needed and locally desired water resource projects.

**One has since adopted Mannford's "new town" model. The coupling of new town development with large-scale public works projects is a social innovation of considerable potential for deployment in urban settings as well.

social impact assessment 31

effects--reported by Mannford residents as a general improvement in community facilities, amenities and well-being and a general loosening of social ties--contrasts markedly to the magnitude of physical impacts accompanying project construction.

At the other extreme, that of "no impact," is the Corps' bank stabilization project extending from Keystone Dam to Webbers Falls Lock and Dam some hundred miles downstream on the Arkansas River. Although this stretch passes close by Tulsa, the areas of riverside abutment are largely unpopulated at present. While future settlement patterns may infringe on the protected area, "It is likely that the project itself will not generate growth" (Sparks, 1973: 13). The conclusion is that "the nature of the project and the general area under study are such that social impacts resulting from project construction, under alternative designs, are likely to be insignificant and indeterminate."

It must be noted however that the balanced growth concept of land use planning embodied in the Tulsa Metropolitan Area Planning Commission's "Vision 2000" aims at redirecting the population growth pattern towards the project area (Logue, 1974). While this is a "normative forecast" and its realization depends heavily on instituting and enforcing appropriate and effective land use controls, there is no indication given by Sparks that this expression of local interests has been weighted in the assessment. Moreover, the Corps' own "urban studies guidance" explicitly states that trend extrapolation which deviates from public preferences and planning objectives is unacceptable. In long-term effect, the "protected area" may expose a significantly increased number of people to flood risk both by increasing the attractiveness of residential occupancy and by changing the physical properties of the channel itself, through bank stabilization.

Preliminary study of these "limiting" cases underscores the analytic complexity inherent in SIA. By working in from extreme to more equivocal cases a higher resolving power may be obtained. Cumulative case analysis, such as "analytic induction" (Manning, 1971), may prove a superior choice of tactics for managing complexity under existing operational constraints. In building case history materials into systematic frameworks of analysis, "check lists" such as the following may prove of assistance.

TABLE 2. REVIEW CHECK LIST - SOCIAL EFFECTS[*]

A. Section 122 Guidelines (ER 1105-2-105)
Based on Information Supplement #1, Sep 73

Relationship to Planning Process	Selection of Significant Effects
Effect Assessment Steps	Descriptions and Display
With Projection	Systems Considerations
Without Projection	

---

[*]Prepared by Frank Sharp, Office of the Chief of Engineers, U. S. Army Corps of Engineers.

32 social impact assessment

Types of Effects

1. Population Density
   Density patterns

2. Population Mobility
   1. Growth and migration trends
   2. Age composition
   3. Ethnicity
   4. Relationship to regional distribution patterns

3. Housing
   1. Total units, single-multi occupancy
   2. Owner-renter
   3. Vacancy rates
   4. Median rent, or value
   5. Housing condition and age
   6. Construction trends, relocation programs
   7. Crowding--persons per room

4. Displacement of People*
   1. Educational attainment
   2. Political jurisdiction
   3. Municipal finance
   4. Public assistance recipients
   5. Employment characteristics
   6. Income characteristics

5. Transportation
   1. Highway access
   2. Commuter patterns
   3. Rail, airport and pipeline facilities

6. Desirable Community Growth*
   Reviewed by BOB Circular A:95 designated state agency

7. Institutional Dynamics

8. Health

9. Community Cohesion*
   1. Religious activities and civic groups
   2. Population stability
   3. Media--press, TV, etc.
   4. Community social service programs

10. Noise*

11. Leisure Cultural and Recreational Activities
    1. Parks
    2. Recreation facilities - outdoor, indoor

12. Aesthetic Effects

13. Other

Process
1. Was "affected area" adequately delineated?
2. Were systematic interdisciplinary approaches used?
3. Was there public participation and discussion concerning significant effects?
4. Was there coordination with local and regional planning agencies?
5. Was there adequate discussion of significant objections, problems, and alternatives?

Type of Methodology
1. Economic, environmental or sociological, psychological, intuitive
2. Quantitative vs. qualitative methods
3. Matrix
4. Reliability and validity testing
5. Survey techniques - mail, phone, etc.
6. a. Workshops and public meetings for input data and response feedback
   b. Use of brochures, media, etc.

---

*Mentioned specifically in Section 122.

(continued overleaf)

social impact assessment 33

7. **Statistical** analysis and proper research methodology
8. **Weighting** devices - ranking devices
9. **Models**
   1. Cause and effect
   2. Urban
   3. Growth
   4. Simulation
10. **Profiles** (community)
11. **Demographic** approach
12. Check list (simple or sophisticated)
13. SWAG Method
14. Political - Institutional
15. Chamber of Commerce Approach
16. In-House
    1. by Economics Section
    2. by Environmental Section
17. Contract
    1. University
    2. Consultant

B. Water Resources Council Principles and Standards (10 Sep 73)

1. **Measurement Standards**

2. **With and without analysis**

3. **Limitations**

4. **Classes of social well being effects**
   (a) Effects on real income
      1. Description of who benefits
      2. Description of who is affected detrimentally
   (b) Effects on security
      1. Life
      2. Health and safety and emergency preparedness
   (c) Opportunities: educational, cultural, recreational

5. THE FUTURE OF SOCIAL IMPACT ASSESSMENT

Our summary impression of SIA is a mixed one. While the imperative for SIA is manifest in statutory requirement and societal interest, its legal and administrative history has been ambiguous and ambivalent. The opportunity and occasion for social science knowledge making effective contact with pragmatic situations of genuine concern abound, yet proponents of SIA and the condition of organized knowledge in their field are in serious disarray. In the face of this, we might well heed Spengler's (1970: 70) cautious advice: "what is needed is that practitioners of each social science greatly improve its analytical apparatus, limit research commitments to what that apparatus is capable of doing, and so intensify internal discipline as to minimize the influence of ideology and the persistence of fallacy." Yet for reasons stated above (pp. 5-6), SIA is a radical act. Its adherents must be prepared to assume as much risk of ignorance and error as those who willingly proceed in its absence. In the midst of this confusion, we can however discern some central tendencies and impending trends.

34 social impact assessment

The Legal Challenge
Ours is a legalistic society; the legal system is our chief means of
conflict resolution, of relief and redress, as well as a prime mover
of social change. It would be surprising indeed if requirements and
provisions for SIA were not subjected to the same legal challenge as
environmental impact assessment. Often the two are inseparable, as one
informant, a penologist, disclosed in this communication:

> Ever since the 1969 environmental protection legislation, we have
> become increasingly involved in formulating statements regarding
> social, cultural, and physical impact of proposed correctional
> institutions. Our most recent work pertains to the proposed
> correctional institution at Lorton, Virginia. While construction
> of this facility would have been a grave error from a correctional
> point of view, it has been largely our environmental impact study
> which has brought the project to a halt.

In this instance, penology and not ecology is the point at issue. Is
this barely hidden agenda to be lightly regarded as a perversion of
Congressional intent? Or does it rather place a proper emphasis
on social impacts and their involvement in physical alterations? The
courts will decide, on the grounds of historical and cultural heritage
as well as environmental protection. Yet as Greenberg and Hordon (1974:
174) contend, the legal route is a hazardous one. Moreover, although
legal sanction is sometimes thought to constitute the sole means of
enforcing official conformity, they conclude, "judging by the several
score of impact statements we have reviewed, the courts have had a
minimal, if any, effect on the preparation of the vast majority of
environmental impact statements." It may be that SIA will be dragged
through the courts and the "impact fees" requiring developers to pay,
beyond normal property taxes, the cost of capital improvements that the
presence of a project would ordinarily place on the community (Nordheimer, 1974) will be ruled constitutional. However necessary legal
compulsion may appear, it is not likely to prove sufficient. Certainly
it will not substitute for the regular performance of professionally
competent assessments on the part of responsible administrators and their
staffs.

Acquiring Competence in SIA
For their part, responsible social scientists will strive to place their
best knowledge and judgment at the disposal of social impact assessors.
Their reward system will need realignment, extending professional recognition to colleagues who dedicate professional lives to this calling, or
who volunteer their expertise in advisory roles. Academics will have to
come out of their cloisters to engage real world problems on its terms,
not their own. They must grant the social truth of others' experience,
even as they demand respect for their own learning. In consultant roles,
they will regard the problem of SIA more as intellectual challenge than
income supplement. Administrators will relinquish the illusion that we
can spend our way into sagacity. They will renounce the "NIH" ("Not Invented Here") syndrome and other parochialisms. All of us know more than
any of us.

The Interrelation of Economic, Social and Environmental Impacts

SIA intersects with physical planning in environmental systems. In keeping with the multidisciplinary character of the analytic problem, the interrelations and interactions of major impact categories--ESE (economic, social, environmental)--is of utmost concern. Their present disrelation inhibits the development of compatible methodologies for discriminating, measuring and weighting joint effects. The most promising line for this development appears to be some modified version of input-output (I-O) analysis, already successfully employed in bridging between economic and environmental aspects (cf. Laurent and Hite, 1972; Lee and Fenwich, 1973; Victor, 1972; Wilen, 1973); its extension to social impacts would seem a natural one (e.g. Maki, 1973), as does the application of EES matrix methodologies for purposes of ESE assessment (Baker, Dee and Finley, 1974). Without such compatible systems of weights and measures, the idea of balances and tradeoffs in multi-criteria planning must remain vacuous.

Conclusion

Practice makes better. Though still primitive, the state of the art of SIA is rapidly improving. A year ago there was no such field, and scarcely more than a glimmer of interest. Today there are no fewer than six monographs and compendia in active preparation; the figure may be higher. The real cutting edge of SIA however is the actual practice of growing numbers of social impact assessors, in all quarters and sectors of an increasingly knowledgeable society. The contributors to this volume, whose statements speak for themselves, are but representative of this gathering trend. It is too early to speak of a SIA "movement," but the directions are set and movement is perceptible across a broad front of interest and activity. There will be obstacles in our path; nobody said it was easy. Overcoming them will be the work of perhaps generations to come, but a beginning has been achieved. What matters now is what follows afterward.

Acknowledgements

Mark Shields read and criticized this paper. My sincerest thanks to him and to contributors to this volume, my colleagues at the Institute for Water Resources and at large, especially Frank Sharp of the Office of the Chief of Engineers.

36 social impact assessment

References

Aaron, H. J. (1972) Shelter and Subsidies: Who Benefits from Federal Housing Policies? Washington, D.C.: Brookings Institution.

Abt Associates (1971) Identification and Assessment of Social Impacts. Cambridge, Mass.: Abt Associates, Inc.

Alexander, T. (1972) "The Social Engineers Retreat under Fire," Fortune, 86, 4 (October), 132-36, 140, 142, 146, 148.

Allee, W. C. and others (1949) Principles of Animal Ecology. Philadelphia: Saunders.

Baker, J. K., N. Dee and J. R. Finley (1974) "Measuring Impacts of Water Resource Developments on the Human Environment," Water Resources Bulletin, 10, 1 (February), 10-21.

Baldwin, M. F. (1974) "Report on Project Progress and Future Plans." Washington, D.C.: Environmental Impact Assessment Project, Institute of Ecology. 10 p. mimeo.

Bauer, R. A. (1967) "Detection and Anticipation of Impact: The Nature of the Task," pp. 1-67 in Bauer (ed.), Social Indicators. Cambridge, Mass.: M.I.T. Press.

Baur, E. J. (1973) "Assessing the Social Effects of Public Works Projects." Research Paper No. 3. Fort Belvoir, Va.: Board of Engineers for Rivers and Harbors, U. S. Army Corps of Engineers, July. 35 p. mimeo.

Becker, H. S. and H. Gerjuoy (1973) "Management of Risk Using Trend Impact Analysis: An Application of Computer Techniques for Corporate Planning and Decisionmaking." Glastonbury, Conn.: The Futures Group.

Belzung, L. D. and M. H. Sonstegaard (1973) Regional Response through Port Development: An Economic Case Study on the McClelland-Kerr Arkansas River Project. Fayetteville: Bureau of Business and Economic Research, University of Arkansas, January. 152 p. (I owe this reference to Lloyd G. Antle.)

Bird, H. P. (1972) "Environmental and Economic Impact of Rapid Growth on a Rural Area: Palm Coast," Environmental Affairs, 2, 1 (Spring), 154-71.

Biswas, A. K. and R. W. Durie (1971) "Sociological Aspects of Water Development," Water Resources Bulletin, 7, 6 (December), 1137-43.

Boguslaw, R. (1965) The New Utopians: A Study of System Design and Social Change. Englewood Cliffs, N.J.: Prentice-Hall.

Bonnen, J. T. (1970) "The Absence of Knowledge of Distributional Impacts: An Obstacle to Effective Policy Analysis and Decisions," pp. 246-70 in R. H. Haveman and J. Margolis (eds.), Public Expenditure and Policy Analysis. Chicago: Markham.

Brecher, C. (1973) The Impact of Federal Antipoverty Policies. New York: Praeger.

Breese, Gerald and others (1965) The Impact of Large Installations on Nearby Areas. Beverly Hills, Calif.: Sage.

Bruvold, W. H. (1973) "Belief and Behavior as Determinants of Environmental Attitudes," Environment and Behavior, 5, 2 (June), 202-18.

Caporaso, J. A. and L. L. Roos, Jr. (eds.) (1973) Quasi-Experimental Approaches: Testing Theory and Evaluating Policy. Evanston, Ill.: Northwestern University Press.

Carter, L. J. (1973) "Water Projects: How to Erase the 'Pork Barrel' Image?" Science, 182, 4109 (19 October), 266, 268-9, 316.

Coates, J. F. (1971) "Technology Assessment: The Benefits . . . the Costs . . . the Consequences," The Futurist, 5, 6 (December), 225-31.

Cook, T. J. and F. P. Scioli, Jr. (1972) "A Research Strategy for Analyzing the Impacts of Public Policy," Administrative Science Quarterly, 17, 3 (September), 328-39.

Cottrell, W. F. (1951) "Death by Dieselization: A Case Study in the Reaction to Technological Change," American Sociological Review, 16, 3 (June), 358-65.

Cox, P. T. (1969) "Success of Watershed Development in Local Communities," Natural Resources Journal, 9, 1 (January), 23-34.

Crawford, A. B. (1972) "A Method of Multiple Criteria Evaluation." Center Paper 72-2. Alexandria, Va.: Center for Advanced Planning, Institute for Water Resources, U. S. Army Corps of Engineers, June.

Decoursey, D. G. (1973) "Application of Discriminant Analysis in Design Review," Water Resources Research, 9, 1 (February), 93-102.

Duhl, L. J. (1967) "Planning and Predicting: Or What to Do When You Don't Know the Names of Variables," Daedalus, 96, 3 (Summer), 779-88.

Duke, R. D. and others (1973) "Regional Planning for Monterey Bay: A Trilogy of Issue-Oriented Games for Citizen Use." Ann Arbor: Environmental Simulation Laboratory, University of Michigan, December. (I owe this reference to Cathy Greenblat.)

38 social impact assessment

Duncan, O. D. (1969) "Social Forecasting: The State of the Art," The Public Interest, 17 (Fall), 88-118.

Eigerman, M. (1973) "Social and Economic Impacts of Waste Water Management in the Merrimack Basin." Paper presented at the National Meeting of the American Society of Civil Engineers, 30 January. 6 p.

Enk, G. A. (1974) "Preface," p. iii in Enk and others (1974).

Enk, G. A. and others (1974) Assessing the Social Impacts of Oil Spills: Proceedings of an Invitational Symposium Co-Sponsored by The Institute on Man and Science and the U. S. Environmental Protection Agency, 25-28 September 1973. Rensselaerville, N.Y.: Institute on Man and Science, February.

Everett, M. (1973) "LAND/Landscape Analysis and Natural Design," Bulletin of Rhode Island School of Design, Alumni Edition, 60, 3 (December), 7-12.

Fairchild, W. D. (1973) "2 Objectives, 4 Accounts," Water Spectrum, 5, 4, 22-27.

Federal Highway Administration (1973) "Process Guidelines (Social, Economic, and Environmental Effects of Highway Projects), Policy and Procedure Memorandum 90.4." Washington, D.C.: U. S. Department of Transportation, 1 June.

Francis, W. J. (1973) "A Report on Measurement and the Quality of Life." Washington, D.C.: U. S. Department of Health, Education, and Welfare, January.

Gardner, R. W. (1973) "Social Impact Study of the Proposed Willow Creek Flood Control Project." Walla Walla, Wash.: U. S. Army Engineer District, Walla Walla, June. 34 p. mimeo.

Greenberg, M. R. and R. M. Hordon (1974) "Environmental Impact Statements: Some Annoying Questions," Journal of the American Institute of Planners, 40, 3 (May), 164-75.

Haas, J. E. (1973) "Social Aspects of Weather Modification," Bulletin of the American Meterological Society, 54, 7 (July), 647-57.

Harris, D. H. (1974) The Social Dimensions of Water-Resources Planning. Technical Report 160. Santa Barbara, Calif.: Anacapa Sciences, March.

Heller, A. (ed.) (1972) The California Tomorrow Plan. Los Altos, Calif.: William Kaufman.

Helmer, O. (1972) "Cross-Impact Gaming," Futures, 4, 2 (June), 149-67.

House, Peter and others (1971) The River Basin Model: An Overview. Washington, D.C.: Envirometrics, Inc., December.

Hyman, H. H. (1972) Secondary Analysis of Sample Surveys: Principles, Procedures, and Potentialities. New York: John Wiley

Ingram, H. (1972) "The Changing Decision Rules in the Politics of Water," Water Resources Bulletin, 8, 6 (December), 1177-88.

Ireland, J. V. (n.d.) "Research Group in Planning Impact Evaluation Studies." London: Department of Social and Environmental Planning, Polytechnic of Central London. 27 p. mimeo.

Jones, M. V. (1972) "Generating Social Impact Scenarios, a Key Step in Making Technology Assessment Studies." Monograph No. 11. Washington, D.C.: Program of Policy Studies in Science and Technology, George Washington University, 20 January.

Kane, J. (1972) "A Primer for a New Cross-Impact Language--KSIM," Technological Forecasting and Social Change, 4, 2, 129-42.

Kanwit, E. L. (1967) "Some Aspects of the Social Impact of Urban Transportation." Paper presented at the Sesquicentennial Forum on Transportation Engineering, New York City, 29 August. 52 p. mimeo. (I owe this reference to Richard P. Wakefield.)

Kemper, T. D. (1974) "What Does It Mean Sociologically to Be of a Given Age, Sex, Social Class, Educational Level, Race, Religion, Region, Ethnicity, Occupation, Etc.?" Paper presented at the 44th Annual Meeting of the Eastern Sociological Society, Philadelphia, Pa., 6 April.

Krebs, G. E. (1973) "The Social Impact of Surface Mining," pp. 1076-87 in House Committee on Interior and Insular Affairs, U. S. House of Representatives, Washington, D.C., 16 April 1973. Regulation of Surface Mining, Part II. Washington, D.C.: U. S. Government Printing Office, Serial No. 93-11.

Levitan, S. A. and H. L. Sheppard (1963) "Technological Change and the Community," pp. 159-89 in G. G. Somers, E. L. Cushman and N. Weinberg (eds.), Adjusting to Technological Change. New York: Harper and Row.

Laurent, E. A. and J. C. Hite (1972) "Economic-Ecologic Linkages and Regional Growth: A Case Study," Land Economics, 48, 1 (February), 70-72.

Lee, D. B., Jr. (1973) "Requiem for Large-Scale Models," Journal of the American Institute of Planners, 39, 3 (May), 163-78.

Lee, T. R. and P. D. Fenwick (1973) "The Environmental Matrix: Input-Output Techniques Applied to Pollution Problems in Ontario," Water Resources Bulletin, 9, 1 (February), 25-33.

40 social impact assessment

Lippmann, W. (1925) The Phantom Public. New York: Harcourt, Brace.

Liska, A. E. (1974) "Emergent Issues in the Attitude-Behavior Consistency Controversy," American Sociological Review, 39, 2 (April), 261-72.

Litwak, E. (1961) "Models of Bureaucracy which Permit Conflict," American Journal of Sociology, 67, 2 (September), 177-84.

Llewellyn, L. G. (1973) "Social and Environmental Effects of Alternative Highway Locations." Paper presented at the First Federally Coordinated Program Research Review for Category 3: Environmental Considerations in Highway Design, Location, Construction, and Operation, Annapolis, Md., 9 August. 10 p. mimeo.

Logue, S. (1974) "Report Predicts Less Southeast Tulsa Growth," The Tulsa Tribune, 80, 73 (30 March), 1, 4. (I owe this reference to Lloyd G. Antle.)

Lynch, R. M. (1972) "Complying with NEPA: The Tortuous Path to an Adequate Environmental Impact Statement," Arizona Law Review, 14, 4, 717-45.

Mack, R. P. (1974) Criteria for Evaluation of Social Impacts of Flood Management Alternatives. Phase I Report submitted to the Connecticut River Basin Supplemental Flood Management Study. New York: Institute of Public Administration, 15 March. (I owe this reference to David A. Aggerholm.)

McCoy, C. G. (1973) "The Impact of an Impact Study upon Decision Making in Urban Government: Contributions of Sociology." Paper presented to the North American Action Group Conference on Sociology and Planning, New York City, 13 October. 15 p. mimeo.

McDonald, R. J. (1971) "Report on the Development of 'Straw Man.'" Internal working paper. Alexandria, Va.: Institute for Water Resources, U. S. Army Corps of Engineers, 15 November. 14 p. mimeo.

Maki, W. R. (1973) "Social/Environmental Systems for Regional Development Planning," Regional Science Perspectives, 3, 68-88.

Manning, P. K. (1971) "Analytic Induction." Paper presented at the 66th Annual Meeting of the American Sociological Association, Denver, Col., 1 September.

McHale, J. (1973) "The Changing Pattern of Futures Research in the USA," Futures, 5, 3 (June), 257-71.

McKusick, R. B. and others (1973) "The Development of a Plan of Study-- An Interagency Approach to Multiobjective Planning and Evaluation of Water and Land Resource Use," Water Resources Bulletin, 9, 3 (June), 467-84.

Merton, R. K. (1936) "The Unanticipated Consequences of Purposive Social Action," *American Sociological Review*, 1, 6 (December), 894-904.

Miller, W. L. and D. M. Byers (1973) "Development and Display of Multiple-Objective Project Impacts," *Water Resources Research*, 9, 1 (February), 11-20.

Moore, W. E. (1964) "Predicting Discontinuities in Social Change," *American Sociological Review*, 29, 3 (June), 331-38.

Morgan, W. C. (1970) *A Study of the Social and Economic Effects of Keystone Reservoir on the Community of Mannford, Oklahoma*. Unpublished masters thesis. Stillwater: Oklahoma State University, May. (I owe this reference to Robert Brown.)

Motz, A. B. (1974) "The Challenge of New Roles for Sociologists in Academic and Non-Academic Settings," *ASA Footnotes*, 2, 4 (April), 2-3.

National Academy of Public Administration and U. S. General Accounting Office (1973) "Evaluation of Federal Environmental Programs." Summary of a conference held at Silver Spring, Md., 24-26 May. 44 p. mimeo. (I owe this reference to Richard L. Chapman.)

Nicholson, M. (1970) *The Environmental Revolution: A Guide for the New Masters of the World*. New York: McGraw-Hill.

Nordheimer, J. (1974) "A Tiny Florida County Undertakes the Struggle against Too Much Growth," *The New York Times*, 17 February.

Office of Economic Opportunity (1968) *Poverty Indicators--Community Profile Series*. Springfield, Va.: National Technical Information Service.

Office of Research and Development (1966) "Social Impact: Environmental Quality, Community Effects, and Highway Transportation." Washington, D. C.: Bureau of Public Roads, U. S. Department of Commerce, 26 November. 14 p. mimeo. (I owe this reference to Richard P. Wakefield.)

Office of Research and Monitoring (ed.) (1973) *The Quality of Life Concept: A Potential New Tool for Decision-Makers*. Washington, D.C.: Environmental Studies Division, U. S. Environmental Protection Agency.

Office of the Chief of Engineers (1972) "Guidelines for Assessment of Economic, Social, and Environmental Effects of Civil Works Projects." ER 1105-2-105. Washington, D.C.: U. S. Army Corps of Engineers, 15 December.

Office of the Chief of Engineers (1973) "Information Supplement No. 1 to Section 122 Guidelines (ER 1105-2-105, 15 Dec. 1972)." Washington, D.C.: U. S. Army Corps of Engineers, September.

42 social impact assessment

Office of the Chief of Engineers (1974) "Planning Process: Implementation of Principles and Standards and Other Related Requirements." ER 1105-2-200. Washington, D.C.: U. S. Army Corps of Engineers, 5 May (draft).

Ogburn, W. F. (1922) Social Change. New York: B. W. Heubsch.

Ogburn, W. F. (1946) The Social Effects of Aviation. Boston: Houghton Mifflin.

Ogburn, W. F. (1956) "Technology as Environment," Sociology and Social Research, 41, 1 (September-October), 3-9.

Ortolano, L. (1973) "Impact Assessment in the Water Resources Planning Process." Unpublished manuscript. Stanford, Calif.: Department of Civil Engineering, Stanford University, June. 35 p. mimeo.

Peelle, E. (1974) "Social Impacts of a Remote Coastal Nuclear Power Plant: A Case Study of the Mendocino Proposal." Oak Ridge, Tenn.: Oak Ridge National Laboratory.

Perfater, M. A. and D. R. Howell (1973) "Evaluation of Social Impact: A Suggested Approach." VHRC 73-R10. Charlottesville: Virginia Highway Research Council, September. 15 p. mimeo.

Planning Division, Directorate of Civil Works (1973) "Urban Studies Program: Study Procedure." Washington, D.C.: Office of the Chief of Engineers, U. S. Army Corps of Engineers, 1 September.

Popper, K. R. (1957) The Poverty of Historicism. London: Routledge and Kegan Paul.

Rein, M. (1972) "Social Planning: The Search for Legitimacy," pp. 425-52 in M. Stewart (ed.), The City: Problems of Planning. Baltimore, Md.: Penguin.

Rosove, P. E. (1973) "A Trend Impact Matrix for Societal Impact Assessment." Los Angeles: Center for Futures Research, Graduate School of Business Administration, University of Southern California, April. 24 p. mimeo.

Schmid, A. A. (n.d.) "Impact of Alternative Federal Decision-Making Structures for Water Resources Development." Paper prepared for the National Water Commission.

Smith, C. R. (1970) Anticipations of Change: A Socio-Economic Description of a Kentucky County before Reservoir Construction. Research Report No. 28. Lexington: Water Resources Institute, University of Kentucky.

Snyder, H. (1974) "The Future Directions of Assessments of Impacts," pp. 7-8 in Enk and others (1974).

Sparks, C. (1973) "Assessment of Social Impacts Anticipated from the Proposed Project: Arkansas River--Keystone Lake to Webbers Falls Lock and Dam (Oklahoma)." Dallas, Tex.: Southwestern Division, U. S. Army Corps of Engineers, November. 15 p. mimeo. (I owe this reference to Frank Sharp.)

Special Task Force (1970) <u>A Summary Analysis of Nineteen Tests of Proposed Evaluation Procedures on Selected Water and Land Resource Projects</u>. Washington, D.C.: Water Resources Council, July.

Spengler, J. J. (1970) "Is Social Science Ready?" pp. 54-73 in L. A. Zurcher, Jr. and C. M. Bonjean (eds.), <u>Planned Social Intervention: An Interdisciplinary Anthology</u>. San Francisco: Chandler.

Stover, J. (1973) "Suggested Improvements to the Delphi/Cross-Impact Technique," <u>Futures</u>, 5, 3 (June), 308-13.

Taylor, G. R. (1971) <u>The Doomsday Book: Can the World Survive?</u> Greenwich, Conn.: Fawcett.

Toffler, A. (1973) "Anticipatory Democracy and the Prevention of Future Shock," pp. 74-78 in G. Chaplin and G. D. Paige (eds.), <u>Hawaii 2000: Continuing Experiment in Anticipatory Democracy</u>. Honolulu: University Press of Hawaii.

Turvey, R. (1966) "Side Effects of Resource Use," pp. 47-60 in H. Jarrett (ed.), <u>Environmental Quality in a Growing Economy</u>. Baltimore, Md.: Johns Hopkins Press.

U. S. Senate (1962) "Policies, Standards, and Procedures in the Formulation, Evaluation, and Review of Plans for Use and Development of Water and Related Land Resources." Document No. 97. Washington, D.C.: U. S. Government Printing Office.

Victor, P. A. (1972) <u>Pollution: Economy and Environment</u>. Toronto: University of Toronto Press.

Water Resources Council (1973) "Water and Related Land Resources: Establishment of Principles and Standards for Planning," <u>Federal Register</u>, 38, 174 (10 September), 24778-869.

Wholey, J. S. (1973) "Contributions of Social Intervention Research to Government Practices." Washington, D.C.: Urban Institute, September.

Wholey, J. S. and others (1973) "Federal Evaluation Policy: Analyzing the Effects of Public Programs." Washington, D.C.: Urban Institute.

Wicker, A. W. (1969) "Attitudes Versus Actions: The Relationship of Verbal and Overt Behavioral Responses to Attitude Objects," <u>Journal of Social Issues</u>, 25, 4 (Fall), 41-78.

44 social impact assessment

Wiebe, J. E. (1972) "Cluster Analysis and Water Project Evaluation," Water Resources Bulletin, 8, 6 (December), 1189-97.

Wilen, J. E. (1973) "A Model of Economic System-Ecosystem Interaction," Environment and Planning, 5, 3 (May-June).

Wilkening, E. A. and others (1973) Quality of Life in Kickapoo Valley Communities. Report 11. Madison: Institute for Environmental Studies, University of Wisconsin, September.

Williams, J. A., Jr. (1970) "The Effects of Urban Renewal upon a Black Community: Evaluation and Recommendations," pp. 377-86 in L. A. Zurcher, Jr. and C. M. Bonjean (eds.), Planned Social Intervention: An Interdisciplinary Anthology. San Francisco: Chandler.

Witkin, E. (1971) The Impact of Medicare. Springfield, Ill.: Charles C. Thomas.

Young, L. B. (1973) Power over People. New York: Oxford University Press.

[39]

SOCIAL IMPACT STATEMENTS: A TENTATIVE METHODOLOGY[1]

Sue Johnson, Program Assistant,[2]
Center for Developmental Change
University of Kentucky (Lexington)

Rabel J. Burdge[2]
Associate Professor of Sociology
University of Kentucky (Lexington)

Abstract
The general methodology presented here involves using post-construction analysis of a project similar in as many respects as possible to one being proposed to make social impact predictions (comparative diachronic analysis). Consideration is given to the kinds of similarities needed to "match" projects; e.g. geographical location, size and scope of project and the social and economic characteristics of the affected community. Further attention focuses on the degree of validity associated with primary and secondary data to make the necessary predictions for social impact statements. The examples here deal with reservoir construction projects; however, the general methodology with important adaptations can be used for other large-scale projects such as highway construction, urban renewal, waste disposal, and watershed management, among others. Social impact is here divided into two categories: the impact on persons who must be relocated and the project impact on the community and adjacent counties.

Situation
One of the more ambitious and laudable goals of an environmental impact statement is discovery and the concomitant possibility of preventing irreversible effects of physical development before they are facts to be bemoaned.

While planners and legislators often think of dirty air or a spoiled stream as impact, they often forget that irreparable damage can occur among the human population and in human communities. Part of this forgetfulness is due to beliefs in human capacity for adaptation (and for outwitting dismal predictions of social scientists). Undoubtedly, part of it is due to a less-than-spectacular track record among social scientists in their more publicized predictions. However, we must point out that a lack of concern for prediction and long-range planning on the part of scientists and technicians has led us to our present environmental fix. In an atmosphere of uncertainty about saying anything about the future, not to mention "predicting" it, yet one tempered by a need for action, we propose to outline in this paper a tentative predictive methodology for use in the social component of environmental impact statements.

Irreversible effects on an individual can be horrifying, as when an old person dies while being relocated for a new highway, or alarming, as when a poor person is forced further into debt to buy a "low income house" because rental property is scarce due to an urban renewal project. Other irreversible effects include the unseen erosion of self-confidence and psychological well-being of an aged widow deprived of her only home, that was in the family for generations, and who finds herself severed from

70 social impact assessment

personal relationships that have endured for decades, because her land is "needed" for reservoirs.

On the community level, we might find small villages serviced by county roads suddenly innundated with tourists who tear up the roads and wreak havoc with a pastoral routine. The traditionally-rural community may suddenly find its farmland more desirable for the construction of second homes for distant urbanites than for agricultural use. Some effects of resource development are temporary, such as the usual decline in tax base while a reservoir is in the construction phase, or the influx of workers during the construction phase. Others are irreversible, such as the loss of agricultural land, the disruption of a traditional rural community or the destruction of unique fauna and flora. The attempt here is not to distinguish reversible or temporary effects from irreversible ones; rather it is hoped that the suggested methodology will make it possible for planners to gauge the kinds of effects that are likely when natural resource developments are proposed.

While there are economic considerations in a social impact study, they are given only passing attention here. Examples of economic variables in the reservoir construction situation include number of recreational visitor days, changes in the tax base, agricultural crops, markets and subsidies, and changing demands on local services all of which affect the local budget (Goldman, Richardson, and McEvoy, 1973: 173). Nor are institutions and their behavior the focus of this paper. Attention is focused rather on those elusive, essentially qualitative considerations of impact, which may or may not have economic dimensions, but which tend to be ignored in current economically-slanted impact studies. Social interaction patterns, number of old people in an affected community, psychological well-being, and socio-economic status of potential migrants, and community residents, and their changing quality of life are examples of dimensions to be treated here. Attention is also focused on the varying degrees of validity and utility associated with data collected for a social impact study. It should be noted that the "ambitiousness" of this proposed methodology is possible because only recently have there been enough operating projects to make such suggestions even possible to implement.

Comparative Diachronic Studies
The major purpose of this paper is to propose comparative diachronic analysis as the proper methodology for assessing the social impact of a physical or resource development.

In its simplest form, diachronic analysis means investigation of a phenomenon at two different points in time such as before the construction of a reservoir and after construction. What we propose to add here is a comparative dimension: the post-construction analysis of a similar project or projects forms an empirical basis for making predictions in the pre-construction phase about the post-construction situation. In the remainder of this paper, the social impact segment of the study will be called "social impact situation" and the comparative segment of the study, "the

social impact assessment 71

comparison study." Figure 1 graphically presents the comparative dischronic model to be used in researching the social impact situation.

FIGURE 1. TIME DIMENSIONS OF A COMPARATIVE DIACHRONIC STUDY TO PREDICT SOCIAL IMPACT OF A PROPOSED RESOURCE DEVELOPMENT.

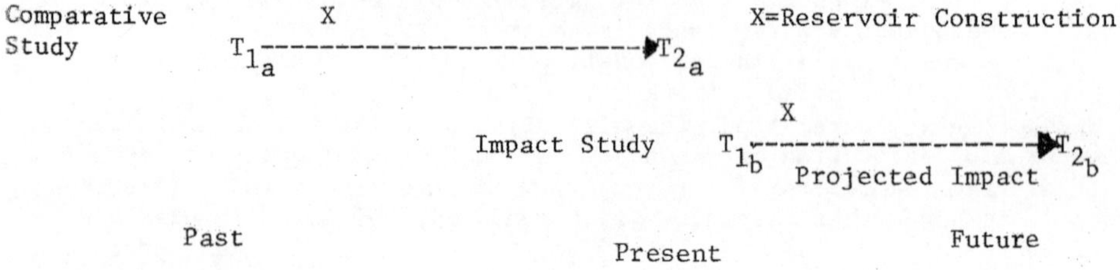

Comparative Study   X   X=Reservoir Construction
                  T_{1_a}----------------------▶T_{2_a}

                                                X
                           Impact Study T_{1_b}------------------▶T_{2_b}
                                                  Projected Impact

            Past   Present   Future

What we will describe here is the optimum case for making an empirical study, knowing full well that real life situations are often subject to temporal and monetary constraints, and as such, may fall short of the ideal. However, some idea of the kinds of data available and their relative virtues and costs should have practical utility.

The Time Dimension Factors Influencing Social Impact
The nature and scope of a project helps define the potential impact of a project, particularly if there are populations that must be relocated. These individuals and their families form a very special kind of subclass of social impact. Relocatees are among the first to be affected, and are often affected in major ways. Because of their special relationship to a development, they deserve study in and of themselves. The major social impact on relocatees begins long before actual reservoir construction starts. It begins with the "news" that a reservoir will be built and often extends past settlement in a new home. Therefore, the time dimension for studying those to be relocated may be long, depending on real estate transactions. Some projects remain in the pre-construction phase for decades. In the case of rural reservoir construction, the people who must move tend to relocate near their previous homes, which has an effect on the community (Johnson and Burdge, 1974a).

At the community level, the designation of time dimensions for studying the comparison community before and after construction of a resource development project and for predicting social impact is somewhat arbitrary. For example, in reservoir construction, lakes often take years to form and take on their full range of activities. However, given the kind of data available for measuring social impact, we recommend a five-year period as minimal and ten years or more as desirable for studying the comparison county and for making predictions about the impact county. Much of the data recommended for use is gathered at five- or ten-year intervals, and this forms part of the rationale for choice of time period. Remembering that even well-collected social science data lose their predictive utility with time, consideration is also given to periodic

72 social impact assessment

monitoring of other sources of data that appear more often because we feel future environmental impact statements are likely to require periodic updating to reflect the passage of time.

The Purpose of the Project
The reservoir itself will also have a discernable effect on the surrounding community, depending, among other things, on its intended use. A reservoir designed primarily for flood control and recreation, with industrial development and water storage and quality as secondary benefits, will have a different impact than a reservoir designed primarily to provide water for irrigation. The cost-benefit analysis of the proposed project should list the order of intended benefits and from that, a framework for assessing the potential impact of each component benefit can be made. Completed projects selected for comparative purposes should have basically the same hierarchy of benefits - e.g. recreation, flood control, industrial development, water quality, or whatever.

Before we proceed further, we must note that industrial development is evidently a very problematic aspect of the projection of future benefits from reservoir construction. As Hargrove has noted in his study of twenty reservoirs, "if the area is otherwise desirable for industrial location and the reservoir project provides key factors which were previously missing, the area will experience rapid development. However, if the area is deficient in location factors that are not provided by reservoir development, the project will not stimulate the local economy" (Hargrove, 1971: 4). Hargrove's generalization is somewhat limited, however, because recreational benefits were largely ignored. In keeping with the non-economic bias in this paper, industrial development and recreational benefits will be mentioned as only two of the many variables that may be analyzed in a social impact study.

Other Matching Criteria
The implicit recommendation above i
the community or the counties involveu ue the phenomena under study for a social impact statement. In keeping with this, general criteria for matching as shown in Figure 2 can be discussed. Later in this paper,

---

FIGURE 2. KEY DIMENSIONS FOR MATCHING PRESENT AND PROPOSED DEVELOPMENT PROJECTS

    ---County as unit of analysis (rural areas)
    ---Similar project size and purpose
    ---Similar geographical and cultural region
    ---Similar data time frames
    ---Use of comparable data sources

---

special comparisons will need to be made depending on whether one is studying the community as a whole, or people being relocated. Generally speaking, with regard to rural development projects, the geographic and political unit that most nearly reflects both community definition and identification is that of the county. It is also the easiest source of data to work with (Korsching, 1974). Therefore, except for relocation-type developments in large urban areas, we recommend the county as the unit of comparison.

Secondly, we recommend that the cost-benefit breakdown should be used as one matching criterion: projects should be selected as discussed above for comparative purposes. This will be simpler in the case of single purpose projects such as national recreational areas.

In matching for locational similarities, comparative projects should be selected from within the state of proposed construction, although nearby states will do if there is geographical similarity. For instance, reservoirs constructed in Kentucky are often located in the Appalachian area with its mountainous terrain and distinct Appalachian subculture. Comparisons of Eastern Kentucky reservoirs with reservoirs in neighboring states within the Appalachian region might be more appropriate than with reservoirs in Western Kentucky. Naturally, the more reservoirs or development projects available for comparison, the more reliable will be the results.

U.S. Censuses of Population, Agriculture, Business and Industry all form a useful body of data for matching population characteristics. In the initial selection of comparable counties, gross discrepancies in important demographic and social statistics should be avoided. Data collected in the matching process will also be used for predicting the social impact of a proposed reservoir, so care in collection and interpretation is essential.

Assuming that the prediction period for the social impact study is ten years into the future, data need to be collected for the comparison county for the ten-year Census period that overlaps the development. Often, the time match is less than ideal. For example, a reservoir that filled in 1959 would show a more complete impact in the 1970 census than in the 1960 census. Here a 1950, 1960 and 1970 census comparison to the community of impact would have to be made. In this case, one should also check back twenty years in the county of proposed impact to ensure a high degree of similarity. For purposes of matching development areas we recommend the following types of information: the age/sex structure of the population, the size of community (counties), the labor force patterns and the percentage urban and rural. Gross discrepancies in any of these basic dimensions between comparison and impact counties are likely to have a distorting effect on any predictions.

The U.S. Census of Agriculture, conducted at five-year intervals, includes key information on average farm size, average value of land and buildings, and the economic class of farms. If industrial development is already present or forms a large proportion of the benefits to be expected, the Census of Business and Industry, also conducted at five-year intervals, can be used to match basic retail, wholesale and service patterns of the

74 social impact assessment

areas under consideration. If needed, there is also a Census of Manufactures. Data on the above listed variables are then collected for the impact community and the comparison community(s) for the most recent Census, and for the previous ten years on the comparison community. Since Agricultural and Business Censuses are published every five years, the years most closely approximating the state of the comparison community before reservoir construction are utilized. If a twenty-year time frame is the case as in the example above, then these data would take on a more important role.

A most important step in our procedure is to establish a reasonable similarity for the pre-contruction periods in the comparison community and the impact community. Absolute magnitudes of difference naturally will change with time, and since one comparison may be ten years in the past, compared with the present, or recent past, no absolute standards for matching can be given at this time. Therefore, it is patterns in the variables used for matching that are to be studied. Ideally, we would also want a population that is similar in age structure, ten years ago, to the present comparison community, but this may be hard to achieve since rural areas have been losing population as well as steadily aging for some decades. However, if an age differential is present in one of several potential comparative communities, the age structure should assume high importance in the selection of a matching county since it is linked to the overall productiveness of a community. Other patterns that should be similar include industrial patterns and the economic class of farms.

If several reservoirs are operating near the proposed construction site, or in nearby states with geographical similarities, this stage of data-gathering can be used to winnow from the universe of possible comparative reservoirs those communities which most closely approximate the community of potential impact. Gathering secondary data on the variables listed above is not as time-consuming as it appears for these basic comparisons, and if carefully done, the closer the match on basic community characteristics, the greater the accuracy of impact predictions.

The Impact of Relocation on Family and Individuals
Relocation is a phenomenon, the effects of which are felt in the premigration period, during relocation, right after relocation, and in some cases for decades into the future (Johnson and Burdge, 1974a). What is important is being able to specify who is likely to be affected in what way by being relocated. This can only be known with some degree of precision by studying a population which has been relocated in the past. In the matching process described above, one thing that will be known is when the reservoirs were constructed and a recently-built reservoir will serve the best for making predictions about relocation. Field work, to include personal interviews, is a necessary component of this part of an impact study unless data about forced migrant populations are already available.

By way of illustration one of the authors is working with a project employing a similar methodology. Residents in three Eastern Kentucky counties are to be relocated due to the construction of two reservoirs. The authors had previously interviewed a post-relocation population of rural Kentuckians in a nearby reservoir area very similar to the one of proposed impact (Burdge and Johnson, 1973). The respondents were asked to reconstruct their relocation experience and to make comparisons between their pre- and post-migration situations.

In addition to the usual background information, we collected data on changes in social interaction patterns with friends and family and changes in organizational involvement. The respondents were asked questions about what kinds of assistance the Army Corps of Engineers gave them prior to and during the move. We also asked for the history and description of their previous and present residence, what had been important considerations in having to move, and what kinds of living conditions had been sought upon learning they had to move. They were asked about their satisfaction or dissatisfaction with their relocation and what economic areas of their life had been most affected by the move. Finally, attitudes toward reservoir construction in general and the reservoir that affected them directly, as well as attitudes toward the federal government, were measured.

A detailed analysis of survey data such as this is an invaluable tool for making social impact predictions. The proposed population to be relocated has been surveyed with regard to basic background data, attitudes toward present residence and toward moving, present social interaction patterns, and information on their current economic state. Respondents are then matched with those already relocated on basic demographic characteristics to predict how the post-relocation population will fare upon relocation.

The basic patterns of social impact will emerge from this kind of comparison. The predictions for those about to be relocated are that older, particularly retired, people and persons who were extremely attached to their place of residence or with little money will find relocation very painful and problematic. Many farmers will find they cannot afford land comparable to what has been taken and will settle for less acreage of lower quality if they resettle in the community. For many relocatees, the disruption of social interaction patterns with friends and family will be the heaviest blow and will contribute to poor adjustment to relocation. Those who will tend to fare well are those who are non-farmers, who are younger, and who have a decent job and education. Generally, the quality of housing for most migrants will improve (Burdge and Johnson, 1973).

Predictions like this can make it possible to identify "high-risk" populations, that is, those likely to suffer unduly from relocation, and make it possible for the relocation agency to take specific problems into account prior to making a development decision. At the present time, data needed for this part of a social impact study can only be collected somewhat expensively through survey research. However, as a body of data grows about relocation, the collection of additional data for every project will no longer be necessary. This assumes that some person or agency

76 social impact assessment

will take the leadership in organizing the proposed data bank or that we improve the communication network between scientists and agency officials.

Community Impact
This paper assumes that impact takes place at two levels when physical development occurs. As just described, individuals must move and the disruption of their lives is possibly the greatest tragedy. However, impact also occurs at the community or county level. Here the social changes may be less dramatic and less detectable on a daily basis, but their impact on the lives of people in the community is no less dramatic.

In Figure 3, we briefly outline seven categories of proposed information which should be obtained to present an accurate picture of the data which could be utilized in an environmental impact statement. These categories represent sources of information which have different levels of validity. We suggest that as one goes from census data, Category I, to survey data, Category VII, the data are more valid, because they are more and more reflective of the local community which is being impacted. Our use of the word validity here is not to be confused with the accepted context of validity and reliability in the social science measurement field.

For example, census data are widely heralded as being collected in a scientific manner and to be extremely reliable. However, data are summarized on such an aggregate level that it is often difficult to know which changes are due to resource development and which to other causes. In cases of highly aggregated data, we recommend choosing a "control" county, matched in the same fashion as the comparison county, but lacking a similar resource development project. Rates of change and absolute change in comparison, control, and impact counties can be compared to isolate changes due to resource development. County records on deed transfers are likely to be accurate because this is a major source of county taxes. Personal interviews are, of course, extremely valid data for our purposes here, because we are allowed to ask questions about how the project affects people.

The order presented in Figure 3 provides an approximate indication of the cost required to get the social impact information. As one moves from secondary information to primary data the cost will rise. Copying and correlating information from census data is much cheaper than searching out archive information or interviewing persons that are about to move. As one moves down from Categories I to VI, the data are collectable at more frequent time intervals for monitoring short-term impact.
As in all research situations, some trade-offs between price and validity must take place. However, we would argue that nothing less than all the suggested data sources is acceptable if a true picture of the social impact is to be gotten.

The remainder of the paper will be concerned with outlining in a very brief manner the kinds of information that will go in each one of the categories as shown in Table 1 and very briefly, without theoretical

social impact assessment 77

FIGURE 3: SCHEMATIC OUTLINE OF THE RELATIONSHIP OF KEY INFORMATION SOURCES TO OBSERVED AND PREDICTED IMPACT

10 Years Minimum Time Dimension (Hypothetical Dates)

Comparative Study:

$$T_{1_a} \longrightarrow T_{2_a}$$

(1960)   (1970)

I.   Census Data   I.   Census Data
II.   State Records   II.   State Records
III. Private Records and Reports   III. Private Records and Reports
IV. County Records   IV. County Records
V.   Selected Agency Information   V.   Selected Agency Information
VI. Archive Information   VI. Archive Information
                                                  VII. Survey Data

Impact Study:

$$T_{1_b} \longrightarrow T_{2_b}$$

(1970)   (1980)

I.   Census Data   I.   Census Data
II.   State Records   II.   State Records
III. Private Records and Reports   III. Private Records and Reports
IV. County Records   IV. County Records
V.   Selected Agency Information   V.   Selected Agency Information
VI. Archive Information   VI. Archive Information
VII. Survey Data   VII. Survey Data

Control Study: (when necessary)

$$T_{1_c} \longrightarrow T_{2_c}$$

(1970)   (1980)

I.   Census Data   I.   Census Data
II.   State Records   II.   State Records
III. County Records   III. County Records

---

rationale, what we feel are key variables which would reflect social impact on the quality of life of the residents if it occurs.

78 social impact assessment

TABLE 1: SUGGESTED OUTLINE OF INFORMATION SOURCES FOR SOCIAL IMPACT STATEMENTS AS OUTLINED IN FIGURE 3

I. Census Data
   a. Population
   b. Housing
   c. Agriculture
   d. Business, retail, services, and manufacturing
   e. Special reports

II. State Records
   a. Vital statistics
   b. Health
   c. Public assistance
   d. Tax assessment records
   e. Transportation

III. Private Records and Reports
   a. Family income
   b. Per capita income
   c. Personal disposable income

IV. County Records
   a. Transportation
   b. Natural resources
   c. Land transfer records

V. Selected Agency Information

VI. Archive Information
   a. Newspapers
   b. Transcripts of public hearings
   c. Agency records

VII. Survey Data
   a. Interviews with community leaders
   b. Interviews with a countywide sample of individuals
   c. Interviews with impacted persons and families

I. Census Information

The U.S. Bureau of Census routinely collects and reports information under several major headings. For an impact study the following are important: The Censuses of Population, Housing, Agriculture, Business and Industry, and Manufacturers. In most cases these data are available on a county basis, with much of the information available and relatively comparable in each Census since 1930. Data on agriculture, business, and manufacturers are collected every five years while information on population and housing is collected at ten-year intervals.

social impact assessment 79

The population census includes information on the age, sex, educational, occupational, racial, ethnic and residential composition of the population by city, county, and state aggregates. In addition, data are available on migration, size of family, ages of family members, previous residence and a family income figure. Most of these data would be useful in various impact statements. Hypotheses concerning impact are to be derived from the longitudinal analysis of the comparison county. Those given here are illustrative.

Social impact due to resource development might be found in the following variables: the age and sex structure of the population and the occupational structure of the county. Most other census variables would in some way be related to these. Age and sex structure, particularly if there is an improvement in the quality of life of rural residents, might show a trend toward increasing "younging" of the population if outmigration is slowed. The occupational opportunities in the community might show the addition of new occupations and increased services (increasing occupational diversity) due to resource development. Obviously, a control county is needed here to ensure that any attributions of increased well-being due to development have some empirical basis.

The decennial housing census reports data on the condition of housing, number of persons per room, and the average value of houses--all indirect data on the quality of life of residents. If resource development brings an increase in general prosperity, this should show up in these data.

The Agriculture Census, taken every five years, includes important data on farm size in acres, value of buildings, crops and livestock, plus social and demographic information on the farmer and the farm family. Data are summarized by economic class of farm, which is an important indicator of the commercial level of agriculture in a particular county. If a reservoir floods valuable bottomland, then changes in agricultural land use should be discernable in commodity composition, gross farm sales and the economic class of farms. A decline in commercial farming along with subdivision of farms is a likely impact.

The Census of Business and Industry and the Census of Manufactures are useful for such information as the kind or nature of businesses and the growth and decline of various industries. These censuses include items on retail and wholesale trade, employment figures, payrolls, taxes, general reserves and expenditures. Because it is taken every five years and supplemented by much private data, it represents an important barometer for economic and social change. Expectations about likely changes in business and industry patterns are similar to those listed under the population census--increased diversity and perhaps the presence of new businesses--but the data are given in greater detail on a more current basis and are much more useful. Control counties are needed here for a check on the rise in inflation and general economic growth.

Special reports of the Bureau of the Census which are of interest here include the County and City Data Book, published annually, which includes

80 social impact assessment

information from the various censuses, and is thus subject to their limitations. This is the best single substitute source if regular census publications are not available. Also, there are special reports on public employment, published annually, which can be used to monitor changes in public services back through 1952, and on county business patterns, which gives highly detailed data on major industry groups, number of employees by employment unit class and number of reporting units, employees and taxable payrolls. One of the latter report's virtues is that it tends to have comparable data for the past two business censuses given with the current census.

II. State Records

All states by law are required to keep current and vital statistics, which means information on births, marriages and deaths. Generally speaking, these data are accurate for persons born since 1910. The marriage rate is an index of potential household formation, an important component in economic growth. The age-specific fertility rate is a factor in population growth which may or may not have a beneficial effect. In poor areas, with high fertility, if the general quality of life improves, one would look for a decline in fertility and an increase in middle-class patterns of childbearing.

The infant and maternal mortality rate is an index of general health care and the death rate by age an index of the general health of the population. Information on all forms of public assistance is available through state records. The tax assessment records are an index of the aggregate wealth of the community under study. The federal government publishes a bibliography of state reports on state and local government finances. Transportation data, e.g. the condition of state and county roads, are valuable as are traffic counts. Often, if a community has a recreation-oriented resource development, roads and traffic patterns show noticeable impact (Drucker, 1973). Most state data are available on an annual basis.

III. Private Records and Reports

Unfortunately the census is not allowed to collect information which has been defined by the courts as being sensitive. Therefore, except for data on family income, little financial information is available from census data. Private record sources publish information on per capita income, disposable per capita income and measures of money flow on a county basis. (Sales Management is such a publication.) For impact statement purposes, a data source is needed which does not depend on the decennial census and which reflects the actual spending patterns of residents.

IV. County Records

The basic unit of analysis for our proposed impact statement is the county. The records here are important because they are close to the source of impact. Deed transfer records give the value of property, the kind of property, and prior ownership information and from these data, the rate of property transfer over time and the degree of subdivision can be shown. Important here is baseline data from before the project was even proposed so that relative changes due to resource development can be measured. Annual or semi-annual monitoring of these records gives a continuous survey of one form of impact—land use practices. Comparable data from the comparison county will suggest what the trend in land use practices will be.

V. Selected Agency Information

Both agencies of the state and federal government are increasingly collecting data on a local basis about a wide range of activities. These reports may be based on personal interviews as in the monthly survey of the labor force by the Department of Labor, or compiled from secondary sources such as health agency reports.

The question here is which are the relevant state and federal agencies associated with a particular resource development. In the case of reservoir construction in the Western U.S., it might be the Bureau of Land Management and the National Park Service. There are also state agency counterparts active in most projects.

These sources often have concrete data on several kinds of impact. The only difficulty with special agency reports is that they are of a recent vintage and may not have applicability to the long time frame necessary to develop an adequate impact statement.

VI. Archive Information

Here we mean mostly newspaper accounts. These data need to be collected by persons trained in content analysis and library research. The idea here is to assemble opinions, attitudes and descriptions of situations in the community which have developed as a result of the project. Because each source of information is biased in that it represents agency, official, or editorial opinion, it must be evaluated from that standpoint. Other sources, like the transcripts of hearings about projects, are located with the agency responsible for the hearings.

Archive information is very important in developing social impact statements for it deals with the actual event under study. It also represents an important transition between the aggregate data discussed above and data on individuals.

VII. Survey Data

Personal interviews from prepared pretested schedules and collected by trained social scientists represent the most reliable form of information about the social impact of a reservoir or other environmental development project. These data fit particularly our definition of validity because through interviews one is able to deal directly with the effects of a project on the community and the individuals that are relocated. Personal interviews have the disadvantage of being quite expensive, but this expense may be controlled through the use of careful sampling.

Under the category of survey data, we list interviews with community leaders of civic, business and important voluntary and religious organizations. Information on the attitudes of these persons toward the proposed

82 social impact assessment

project is important, because they control the opinions of many other persons. Also, the identification of community leaders allows us to establish the nature of power relationships in the community.

Interviews with a stratified random sample of persons in the county in which a reservoir has been constructed allows us to know what the degree and kind of personal impact has been. It may be that little interest is shown outside the immediate project area; on the other hand, the interest and the potential impact may be felt throughout the county. Planners often overestimate and underestimate many important parameters of the project impact. These survey data in a comparative diachronic study would be a useful basis for predicting impact at the individual level.

A listing of sources of data and possible key variables makes trade-offs due to limitations of time and money possible. For instance, in the project on which one of the authors is working, a twenty percent sub-sample of people to be relocated was studied intensively. Generalizations were made to the entire migrant population about which only basic background data were available, much of it gathered from informants. Another kind of trade-off would be to use Categories I, II, and III, all easily available data sources for studying community impact (using comparison and control counties) and then survey the population to be relocated, using past studies as a guide to what is likely to happen. However, when one does not collect data at the local level, Categories IV-VII, one is missing an entire level of social impact and one of greatest interest to those who live in the affected communities.

Finally, we strongly suggest that detailed personal interviews be conducted with the individuals who must be relocated due to project development. These are the people who suffer the most and their story can only be told by communicating their situation to an unbiased interviewer. Ideally, information on this phase of the study would include data on their present, past, and anticipated future situation. Information collected in such a systematic fashion will insure a proper comparative analysis.

Conclusion and Summary
The purposes of this paper have been threefold. First, we have suggested comparative diachronic analysis as a method for predicting the impact of a proposed natural resource project. Secondly, we have proposed some of the elements that we think must be included in a social impact statement, and finally we have suggested data sources and what we think are key variables contained therein. Our proposal is preliminary and exploratory and the substance of this outline is being developed in future publications (Burdge and Johnson, 1974; Johnson and Burdge, 1974b).

There are four major problems to overcome before this system is operational. First a statistical procedure must be appended to examine the changes that take place in the description variables between the various time frames. We must be able to establish whether or not the change has meaning and if it does what are the consequences for the individuals and the communities. Secondly, we have to relate the contents of this paper to the guidelines established by the Environmental Protection Agency. We have made the case that these should be some of the components of an Environmental Impact Statement. Thirdly, we must establish the actual measures that will fit under each of these broad categories. Finally, we have to translate our model into comprehensible terms that can be understood, not only by other scientists, but by the people who must use the information as well as those likely to be impacted.

As a final word, we wish to say that in order to accomplish this task in a valid manner, many data and indicators from primary and secondary data will have to be created. The collection of primary data and interpretation of the meaning of social impact on individuals from these data can form the vital underpinnings of a social impact assessment methodology that relies primarily on secondary data sources, yet doesn't stray too far from "people-concerns".

Footnotes

[1] Paper presented at the Workshop on "Social Impact Assessment" for the Fifth Annual Conferences of the Environmental Design Research Association, School of Architecture, University of Wisconsin, Milwaukee, May 30-June 1, 1974. For further information see Rabel J. Burdge and Sue Johnson, "Socio-Cultural Aspects of Resource Development with Special Emphasis on Impact Analysis," in James McEvoy, ed., Handbook of Legal, Social and Economic Assessment, Prentice-Hall, Englewood Cliffs, N.J., in preparation; Sue Johnson and Rabel J. Burdge, "A Methodology for Using Diachronic Studies to Predict the Social Impact of Resource Development," paper to be presented at the Annual Meetings of the Rural Sociological Society, McGill University, Montreal, Quebec, Canada, August 23-25, 1974, or contact the authors. For an anthropological example of this form of analysis, see Philip Drucker, Jerry Eugene Clark, and Lesker Dianne Smith, Sociocultural Impact of Reservoirs on Local Government Institutions, Lexington, Kentucky Water Resources Research Institute, 1973, Research Report No. 65. The authors are indebted to Dr. Drucker for introducing us to this form of analysis.

[2] Sue Johnson is Program Assistant at the Center for Developmental Change, University of Kentucky, Lexington, 40506. Her Ph.D. is in Sociology from the University of Texas at Austin with major training in demography and social psychology. Rabel J. Burdge is Associate Professor of Sociology, University of Kentucky, Lexington, 40506. His Ph.D. is in Rural Sociology from the Pennsylvania State University (University Park) with emphases on methodology, statistics and land economics. Both do extensive research on the social aspects of environmental change, natural resources and land development.

References

Burdge, R. J. and K. S. Johnson (1973) Social Costs and Benefits of Water Resource Development. Lexington, Kentucky: Kentucky Water Resources Research Institute, Research Report No. 64.

84 social impact assessment

Burdge, R. J. and S. Johnson (1974) "Socio-Cultural Aspects of Resource Development With Special Emphasis on Impact Analysis". James McEvoy, ed., Handbook of Legal, Social, and Economic Assessment. Englewood Cliffs, N.J.: Prentice-Hall, in preparation.

Drucker, P. and J. E. Clark, L. D. Smith (1973) Sociocultural Impact of Reservoirs on Local Government Institutions. Lexington, Kentucky: Kentucky Water Resources Research Institute, Research Report No. 65.

Goldman, C. R., McEvoy, J., and Richerson, P. J. (1973) Environmental Quality and Water Development. San Francisco: W. H. Freeman and Company.

Hargrove, M. B. (1971) Economic Development of Areas Contiguous to Multipurpose Reservoirs: The Kentucky-Tennessee Experience. Lexington, Kentucky: Kentucky Water Resources Institute, Research Report No. 21.

Johnson, S. and R. J. Burdge (1974a) "Analysis of Community and Individual Reactions to Forced Migration Due to Reservoir Construction". D. R. Field, J. Barron and B. Long, eds., Water and the Community. Ann Arbor: Ann Arbor Science Publishers, Inc., in press.

Johnson, S. and R. J. Burdge, (1974b) "A Methodology for Using Diachronic Studies to Predict the Social Impact of Resource Development". Paper to be presented at the Annual Meetings of the Rural Sociological Society, McGill University, Montreal Quebec, Canada, August 23-25.

Korsching, P. F. An Ecological Approach to Urban Dominance. Lexington, Kentucky, Ph.D. Dissertation in Progress, Sociology Department.

[40]
THE ROLE OF SOCIAL IMPACT ASSESSMENT IN HIGHWAY PLANNING

LYNN LLEWELLYN *received his Ph.D. in social psychology from George Washington University and is currently with the Division of Program Plans, U.S. Fish and Wildlife Service.*

ELAINE BUNTEN *holds a master's degree in clinical psychology from the University of West Virginia and is now with the Office of Programs of the National Bureau of Standards.*

CLARE GOODMAN *earned a B.S. in psychology from Bethany College and is currently employed by the Center for Consumer Product Technology, National Bureau of Standards.*

GAIL HARE *received a B.A. in psychology from the University of Maryland and is now with the Center for Consumer Product Technology, National Bureau of Standards.*

RICHARD MACH *earned a Ph.D. in social psychology from the University of Colorado and is now a member of the technical staff of Galler Associates in Arlington, Virginia.*

RALPH SWISHER *holds a Ph.D. in public and international affairs from the University of Pittsburgh and is now with the Office of Planning and Management of the Law Enforcement Assistance Administration.*

In 1973, at the request of the Federal Highway Administration (FHWA), the National Bureau of Standards (NBS) began a 26-month study of the social and environmental effects of alternative highway locations. The objective of this study is to

---

AUTHORS' NOTE: *This study was performed while the authors were colleagues in the Behavioral Science Group of the Technical Analysis Division, National Bureau of Standards. TAD died of unnatural causes on June 30, 1975. The views expressed in this paper are the authors' and do not necessarily reflect those of the Federal Highway Administration or the National Bureau of Standards.*

assist in the development of techniques which might be used to estimate the probable impact of new and improved highways on the values, attitudes, activity patterns, and quality of life of the communities through which they pass. Current plans call for compiling the techniques in a sourcebook on social impact assessment specifically for the use of state highway planners.

Following the completion last year of a comprehensive, critical review of the research literature on highway impacts (Llewellyn, 1974), it seemed clear that if the project were to accomplish its stated objectives we would need to know considerably more about the audience for which it was intended. To be more specific, there appeared to be little data available on the needs and capabilities of state highway department personnel responsible for social impact assessment under existing federal regulations.

METHOD

SAMPLE

In an effort to obtain the types of information which would enhance the acceptability of the sourcebook, NBS undertook a series of interviews with officials representing nine state highway departments, one from each of the Federal Highway Administration regions. The interviews were designed to (a) ascertain the range of social impacts currently being considered in highway planning; (b) identify the problems normally encountered in the assessment of social effects—particularly, areas of uncertainty or gaps in information as perceived by highway planners; and (c) seek advice on the content, format, and style of the sourcebook, which was scheduled for completion in May 1975.

At this point it seems appropriate to emphasize that a sample containing only nine states is not representative of highway planning in general; indeed, there is probably as much diversity within each FHWA region as there is between them. However, by including one state from each region in the sample, considerable variation was achieved in terms of geography, population density, degree of urbanization, economics, and transportation goals. Another point worth mentioning is that we sought to avoid any misconceptions about the purpose of the interviews in our preliminary contacts with each highway department; hence, we constantly stressed the fact that we were not part of any evaluation effort nor would any report to the sponsor mention individual states by name.

INTERVIEW PROCEDURE

The highway department interviews were conducted by senior staff members of the Technical Analysis Division between July and October 1974. A majority of the interviews were held in small groups to allow a free exchange of ideas and to minimize disruption of ongoing department activities. The composition of the discussion groups varied somewhat from state to state; generally, however, those in attendance included department officials concerned with social impact assessment, environmental quality, community factors and public involvement, location, and right of way. Additional information was supplied by district FHWA Planning and Research Engineers (or their designated representatives) who arranged the meetings with state personnel and frequently participated in the interview sessions. Moreover, in at least one instance state highway department planners were joined by both district and regional FHWA officials.

RESULTS

IMPLICATIONS OF THE ACTION PLAN

Background

State highway departments have long been concerned with the social consequences of new and improved highways, but not always in a formal, systematic fashion. The National Environmental Policy Act (NEPA) of 1969, and subsequent guidelines for the preparation of environmental impact statements issued by the Council on Environmental Quality, prompted renewed attention to the probable social (as well as environmental) effects of public works projects. More recently, FHWA Policy and Procedure Memorandum (PPM) 90-4 enjoined the development and implementation of approved state action plans which indicate the procedures to be followed in the evolution of highway projects. Of particular significance is the requirement for a detailed description of the process for identifying potentially adverse and beneficial social, economic, and environmental effects of highway projects. Some additional features of state action plans are (a) step-by-step procedures for consideration of alternative courses of action (including the no-build option); (b) means for involving other agencies and eliciting public participation in the planning process; and (c) the mechanics for organizing and staffing interdisciplinary project teams. The deadline for implementation of state action plans was November 1, 1974.

Development of the Action Plan

A majority of the officials interviewed during the site visits were favorably disposed toward the action plan concept. From a positive standpoint, PPM 90-4 clarified areas of major concern and, in some cases, assisted in the identification of concepts which previously were not considered in the highway planning process. In addition, several states mentioned improvements in departmental organization and communication. One state, for example, established a series of "check point" meetings of division chiefs which proved to be an effective management tool for improving intradepartmental communication; by the same token, the action plan opened channels of communication between sister agencies—in some instances, for the first time in recent memory. There were also indications that the process of alerting concerned citizens about public hearings had improved, primarily as the result of PPM 90-4.

As a rule, those states which had obtained assistance from other departments, outside consultants, and citizen groups at various stages in the development of the plan were generally optimistic about the benefits which might accrue following implementation. Some officials, though, were more cautious about their predictions and candidly admitted writing the action plan in very general terms ("flexible language"). Several factors seemed to dictate a carefully worded response to PPM 90-4:

- The action plan was viewed as a threat ("We are scared to death of it.");
- Explicit language might be held against them at some later date;
- It seemed important to document procedures already being followed at the state level;
- Officials were unhappy with what they considered to be unwarranted federal intervention;
- The technical skills which would have permitted a lengthier, more detailed response were not available.

Action Plan Implementation

One of the most frequently mentioned objections to the action plan was the money required for successful implementation. Several states complained that tight money was jeopardizing their ability to add more social scientists to fill out interdisciplinary teams, a problem addressed in greater detail in a subsequent section. In addition to personnel costs, time can also be thought of in monetary terms. One state, in particular, was concerned about the amount of time spent on paper work which inevitably led to project delays. Officials, however, were quick to point out that they frequently have gone beyond the requirements of PPM 90-4, and criticized the action plan for being overly involved and not allowing them enough flexibility to respond to highway projects on their individual merits. Other states were more inclined to take a "wait and see" attitude with respect to potential implementation problems.

STAFFING FOR SOCIAL IMPACT ASSESSMENT

Background

Although some highway departments have maintained social scientists on their payrolls for a number of years, primarily to offer advice about the displacement of families and to assist in the development of environmental impact statements, prior to PPM 90-4 many states were slow to hire sociologists and urban specialists. Their absence can be attributed to factors such as budgetary constraints, a preference for outside consultants or, in some instances, the attitude that the unique features of highway construction in the state made social scientists superfluous. Since so little information was available from federal government sources on the types of individuals who might be expected to use the proposed social assessment sourcebook, our questions concentrated on the following areas: (a) in-house staff capabilities, (b) experience with outside consultants, (c) assistance obtained from other agencies in social impact assessment, and (d) special problem areas.

In-House Staff

Generally speaking, the highway department's desire to maintain a strong social science capability or to augment existing personnel appeared to coincide with the attitudes toward environmentalism held by the state's elected leaders and a majority of the public. In states with strict environmental laws and a high degree of citizen activism in-house staffing was usually adequate, and sometimes outstanding. Three such state highway departments had at least one full-time Ph.D. sociologist or social psychologist. In addition, economists, geographers, urbanologists, land use planners, landscape architects, and, in one case, an archaeologist and a historian were in evidence.

Unfortunately, most highway departments appeared to lack sufficient manpower with social science backgrounds. Few staff members had advanced degrees, and often, those with undergraduate degrees in sociology and related disciplines had not been out of school long enough to acquire much training or experience. It should be noted, however, that at least one department did not perceive this as a disadvantage; in fact, department representatives went so far as to say that they had no desire to staff any social scientists. They chose, instead, to leave social assessment in the hands of outside consultants, an option that has not worked well in a number of areas.

Use of Outside Consultants

With one exception all the state highway departments we contacted had called on consultants from private corporations or academia to assist in some aspect of environmental impact analysis. When asked to evaluate overall consultant performance, most officials agreed that they were far from satisfied with the work that had been done. Private consultants, in particular, were not well liked—several interviewees described their efforts as a "rip-off." The basis for this antagonism could be traced to several factors: (a) consultants generally learned how highway departments operated, not at their own expense, but at considerable cost to the state; (b) consultants frequently ignored or were not responsive to department problems, preferring to act on their own preconceived notions as to what the job required; and (c) when a project was completed the consultant left, which meant that the department could no longer draw on his skills and knowledge.

Some states have concluded that the way to use consultants effectively is to maintain close supervision and control of their activities, and to hire them only for big projects when the work load is too heavy for indigenous personnel to handle. Another plan was to hire several subject matter specialists (e.g., air pollution experts) for specific jobs; each would submit separate reports which would then be compiled as an environmental impact statement by in-house staff. As indicated in the preceding section, however, some localities consider consultants more cost effective than hiring in-house specialists, especially if few federally-funded highway projects are anticipated.

Coordination with Other Agencies

There was every indication that most state highway departments are making effective use of sources outside their own agencies for planning purposes and in the preparation of impact statements. Some of the groups frequently consulted included fish and game departments, state and regional planning commissions, historical societies, health and welfare departments, economic development agencies, and police and fire departments. At the federal level, the Bureau of the Census and the U.S. Geological Survey are often contacted.

One of the few discordant notes was sounded by a state official who felt that agencies such as the Departments of Commerce, Housing and Urban Development, and Health, Education, and Welfare were quick to criticize draft environmental impact statements, but seldom offered constructive comments. In his opinion, comments which would allow the highway department to make appropriate changes (i.e., positive suggestions) would facilitate the impact statement process.

Areas of Concern Related to Staffing

Clearly, one of the most pressing problems faced by state highway departments was the inability to hire and to maintain an adequate social science complement. Highway departments which were dependent on the automotive industry or gasoline taxes for revenue were threatened by personnel cutbacks. Insufficient funds also prevented the hiring of additional social scientists in other localities despite an ever-increasing work load. One state, for example, was compelled to perform 175 impact assessments last year with a staff of 8 people, 2 of whom were sociologists. Another state maintained a total of 4 people trained in sociology. Two were concerned with social problems in the state's most populous city, where considerable opposition to highway construction had surfaced within old, established neighborhoods. Of the remaining 2, 1 had responsibility for other urban communities across the state, the second, for all rural settings.

In a similar vein, low salaries coupled with the difficulties inherent in a rigid civil service system kept one jurisdiction from hiring high quality specialists. The state's salary scale could not compete with that of private enterprise, and when good people were hired they usually left after a short period of time for better paying jobs. Moreover, the range of skills needed for impact assessment was difficult to obtain because job descriptions did not match the classification scheme maintained by the state employment agency.

Several states mentioned that some of their engineers were enrolled in cooperative programs with local colleges and universities to make them more sensitive to social factors in highway planning and to compensate for the scarcity of bona fide social scientists. However, despite the good intensions of such programs, the long-range consequences are difficult to predict. In all likelihood little class time will be devoted to sociopsychological theory; and without this fundamental background there is a strong possibility that social science principles and measurement techniques may be employed inappropriately.

SOCIAL EFFECTS IN HIGHWAY PLANNING

Social Accounting: The State of the Art

Considering the wide variation in academic training and professional experience among highway department social scientists, it is not surprising that the amount of coverage given to social effects in the planning process differs extensively. At the time these interviews were conducted no common set of social assessment guidelines existed, nor had any attempt been made to define social impact operationally. Considerable confusion appeared to exist among highway officials as to the exact meaning of "social" in the context of PPM 90-4. Some interviewees equated social with environmental effects; others felt that anything social could ultimately be reduced to economic costs and benefits. For example, displacement and relocation effects were the most frequently mentioned social costs—in some instances, the only ones—considered by highway planners. However, economic rather than social ramifications of displacement were generally emphasized. Specifically, problems related to the dislocation of businesses, just compensation, comparable replacement housing, and effect on employment were often discussed; yet little was said about the dismantling of community facilities which serve as the focal point of social interaction, the severance of family ties, or the grief reaction (particularly among elderly, long-term residents) associated with forced relocation (Fried, 1963).

In an attempt to elicit additional information on social impacts, officials were asked if they could recall any beneficial or adverse consequences of highways which seemed particularly noteworthy. Consistent with our earlier observations, the positive impacts most often described were largely economic in nature: tax revenues increased, living standards improved, and housing was upgraded. Interviewees from two departments were impressed by the positive changes in the physical appearance of certain localities. For instance, highways occasionally slow the pace of urban decay by creating physical boundaries or by encouraging the demarcation of idle land for specific functions such as recreation. It was also suggested that highways provide greater accessibility and encourage pedestrian safety—two benefits which are often not recognized.

Interestingly enough, spokesmen for three departments considered land-related impacts to be among the most lamentable consequences of highways: (a) changes which occur when the land is initially acquired; (b) the problems created by developers who attempt to obtain advanced information on highway location, cause land values to skyrocket, and make outrageous demands for compensation for recently purchased parcels of land; and (c) the drastic changes in land use patterns which sometimes occur, especially in rural areas following the completion of a new road system.

At this point it might be instructive to describe briefly the social factors currently considered in the planning process of two states, both of which put great emphasis on environmental concerns. The first state stresses three levels of social analysis which are outlined below.

Regional and community effects. Included in this category is the identification of basic social conditions within the community (e.g., the direction in which citizens would like to see the community developed; perceived transportation needs such as road systems, mass transit, and park-and-ride lots; estimates of the relative importance of various transportation requirements; and possible solutions to problem areas recommended by the public).

Right-of-way effects. Of concern here are problems related to displacement of homes, farms, small businesses; attitudes toward relocation; financial and sociopsychological adjustment to new housing.

Proximity effects. This stage treats the problems of the individuals who are by-passed or left behind (within approximately 500 feet of a highway), neighborhood cohesiveness and stability, and the creation of barriers.

Although there is a great deal of similarity in the way both states approach the identification of social effects, the second highway department appears to place greater emphasis on measuring "changes in community lifestyle." More specifically, data are collected on community values, expectations, vulnerabilities; strength of identification with the community, the extent to which elected officials are meeting the needs of constituents, how people live, and what sorts of changes they envisage. In developing a community profile, additional information is obtained on:

- population characteristics (e.g., size, age distribution, income, education, and ethnic composition);
- community characteristics (e.g., land use and housing)
- community facilities (e.g., educational, religious, health care, recreational, civic, commercial, and cultural);

- community organization (e.g., citizen groups, cooperative projects, communication networks, and interest groups); and, in common with other highway departments;

- displacement of residents and businesses (e.g., number and characteristics of people affected, characteristics of firms affected, and status of replacement housing and business facilities).

Unfortunately, the extensive social analyses summarized above appear to be the exception rather than the rule in the highway planning process.

Social Assessment Techniques

Despite a growing awareness of the tools of social science, only a modest number of techniques were employed with any regularity to forecast the consequences of highways; and seldom were they used in concert with other data sources. The decision as to which techniques to use was dictated, at times, by the size and location of the highway project, at other times, on the basis of past experience ("whatever seems to work"). Among the more sophisticated procedures which had been tried in various settings were computer mapping, aerial photography, color transparencies, weighting schemes, and delphi. If one disregards, for the time being, "guesstimates" and "good common sense," the data most often used were derived from census tapes and surveys, although even these sources were not without limitations.

Census. A majority of the departments in the sample were employing census data to aid in the regional analysis of transportation needs and the identification of transportation corridors during the "systems planning stage." One planning group was able to incorporate specific data elements (e.g., the percentage of people on public assistance and the percentage of households with head-of-household present) in a neighborhood stability index. For the most part, however, planners felt that census data were too gross and became obsolete too quickly to do them any good. As one authority noted: "The social facts that mean anything are simply not there."

Surveys. Questionnaires and household interviews constitute the main weapon in the social assessment arsenal. In a few states they are used almost exclusively, a practice that has limited their effectiveness in communities which have been "canvassed to death" and where there is a risk of stirring up old antagonisms. Nevertheless, with thoughtful planning, design, and administration, surveys have provided valuable information to planners at times when it was most needed. Survey instruments have been used by various departments to determine (a) community solidarity, (b) transportation priorities, (c) the potential adverse effects of highways on individual property owners, and (d) tradeoffs between noise abatement features and highway landscaping.

Some states appeared to be more successful than others in the use of surveys. A procedure which worked particularly well in one jurisdiction emphasized the use of questionnaires designed by an urban sociologist and administered by local college students. Two key ingredients were the stress placed on personal contact and the focus of the questionnaire on issues of specific interest to the community. Excellent return rates were obtained using a "drop-off" procedure; in fact, some of the highest returns came from population groups which were not expected to complete long, involved questionnaires. The fact that the highway department "cared enough to ask their opinion" was especially important to respondents.

Surveys have not worked well for highway departments which lack the expertise to design proper data collection instruments and sufficient manpower to administer them. Some practitioners also contend that attitude questionnaires are snapshots in time, reflecting existing conditions; hence, their value for long-range planning is limited. Clearly, such constraints apply to other techniques as well, a situation that has helped to create an information void in certain areas critical to social impact assessment.

Perceived Gaps in Social Information

Knowing that highway department personnel were frequently uncomfortable when called on to examine social effects, we found it appropriate to identify those areas of impact assessment which planners found most troublesome or where they felt critical information was lacking. In response to this query, four of nine departments reported that the concept of neighborhood gave them the most difficulty. The basic question they wanted answered was the following: when is a locality really a neighborhood in the sense that true social bonds exist between residents, and when is it merely a loose-knit collection of people? A number of officials expressed dissatisfaction with the measurement techniques they had used in the past—one state reported counting the number of people who stood up in a public hearing and referred to a given area as a neighborhood. It was generally agreed that the concept of neighborhood has at least two dimensions: (a) geographic reference points that mean something to residents and (b) a "community" of interests. Unfortunately, these dimensions do not always coincide.

Closely tied to the difficulty in delineating neighborhoods was the expressed need to know more about social interaction, community cohesion, and community disruption. As indicated earlier, much of the confusion surrounding these concepts has resulted from a lack of social assessment guidelines which, in turn, has led to widespread differences in interpretation from the standpoint of policy formulation. Community disruption, for example, was viewed by one state as consisting of three components: potential reduction in property values, visual disharmony, and increased traffic volume. These factors seemed to apply specifically to a large municipality containing old, established neighborhoods resentful of outside intrusion.

Anecdotal data obtained in the interviews suggest that, historically, the burden of disruption often was borne by less affluent communities. In one instance a highway was routed through a low income housing project despite conspicuous evidence of social interaction ("backyard conversations") among residents; whereas, in another area of the state, higher priced homes were spared even though no appreciable interaction was found. Interviews in another locality indicated that freeway locations and designs have not always been compatible with interaction patterns in the surrounding community. On more than one occasion predominantly lower class, black neighborhoods were severed by on-grade freeways despite prior recommendations that, in each case, an elevated design would be considerably less disruptive. Subsequently, as the result of massive protests that the neighborhood had been divided and schools isolated, overpasses were provided to restore access to disconnected portions of the community.

It should be understood that the examples cited above do not take into consideration countless other factors which had to be considered in the location and design decisions for those particular highways. They do, however, reflect increasing awareness of past mistakes and a genuine desire on the part of planners to reduce social costs. This growing sensitivity is also apparent in the desire to know more about what happens to the people who are not displaced—those who are left behind and now must cope with the sight and sound of a new highway. Several departments though that more information was needed on how specific individuals are affected (the cost to the person as opposed to institutions); on how long impacts are felt in an area; and on how damage can be ameliorated. As one highway department sociologist observed: "people's lives are often changed just as much by not moving as they are by relocating."

Interviewees in two states thought that highway planners often went about their jobs without knowing enough about the history of the communities they were dealing with, i.e., their age or "life cycle," changes in priorities and leadership, and most importantly, their past relationship with the highway department. Some communities have had painful experiences with highways which jeopardized subsequent projects. To quote another official: "The real question is how long are people's memories?"

Additional gaps in information mentioned in one or more states are as follows:

- What are "social impacts" and how do you weight them?
- What sort of communities do residents want?
- What are the immediate, short-term effects of a highway project?
- How does the construction phase of a highway project affect quality of life?
- What are the transportation needs of the disadvantaged in small urban communities?

Three Problems In Search of Solutions

Exogenous factors. One of the problems that plague planners is that, despite careful preparation and lengthy deliberation before decisions are made, there is no way of controlling exogenous factors which often contribute heavily to the overall impact of highway projects. The current plight of the housing market is one such example. In rural areas adequate replacement housing for low income families is virtually impossible to locate; and the same situation exists in most urban communities. Some states have touted mobile homes as a solution, but recent consumer-oriented investigations indicate that unwary buyers may encounter severe difficulties in locating and maintaining these units. One official explained how de facto segregation prevented black professionals from obtaining housing in the state's largest city. The situation has become so acute that attempts to involve the public in early highway planning efforts have sometimes failed, primarily because citizen groups refuse to participate until the housing problem is solved.

Tradeoffs: who benefits and who loses? Another difficult question for many highway departments is how to arrive at equitable tradeoffs between the satisfaction of transportation needs and the reduction of adverse social, environmental, and economic impacts. The problem has also been stated in a somewhat more simplistic fashion by highway advocates: how do you balance community desires against a facility which will be in the best interests of the majority population? Sometimes, as in the case of one interview site, a basic conflict exists between suburban commuters and inner-city neighborhoods; at other times the issue has transcended state boundaries and has become a matter of national priorities. Seldom have solutions been acceptable to all sides, and it has frequently been up to the courts to decide when costs outweigh benefits.

Rural highway impacts: a moral dilemma. State officials frequently point out that residents of rural areas are much more favorably disposed toward highway construction than their urban counterparts. Indeed, the question outside major population centers is not *if* a highway should be built; rather, *how soon* can you get started? Nonetheless, a sociologist who was interviewed about his experiences in rural communities was upset by the inability of many individuals to understand the profound changes, particularly in land use patterns, that might occur as the result of a new highway. Poor groups tended to see themselves as ineffective and were often fatalistic about the taking of their homes ("There is nothing I can do about the project."). As might be expected, there was little citizen participation in planning efforts: decisions were generally left to elected officials who, while more cognizant of harmful side effects, strongly supported highway construction on the basis of expected economic growth and development. The sociologist's dilemma was whether to try harder to inform the public and to invite citizen participation, even at the risk of delaying the project, or to let things go on in the time-honored tradition, thereby assuring that the highway would be expedited.

INTERACTION WITH THE PUBLIC

Background

It would be safe to say that highway departments no longer enjoy the same relationship with the public that existed a decade ago. Class action suits have delayed and sometimes halted highway projects in many areas of the country—a symptom of the growing estrangement between all levels of government and the people they are supposed to serve. In an effort to forestall further litigation, recent transportation planning guidelines have stressed implementation of programs designed to keep the public better informed and to promote citizen participation in the decision-making process.

The formal mechanism for citizen involvement is the public hearing. Highway departments generally hold two: a corridor hearing, which is scheduled prior to route location approval, but before the state is committed to a specific option, and a design hearing, which occurs after a route location has been approved, but prior to a final decision on highway design configurations. PPM 90-4 also encourages departments to find other ways of eliciting citizen participation. Although approaches vary from state to state, some of the program combinations which have been implemented include informal (pre-hearing) meetings, citizen advisory groups, and aggressive outreach. When well orchestrated, these techniques have proved to be far more efficacious than formal hearings in establishing a meaningful dialogue with the public.

The Public Hearing Process

In theory, route location and highway design hearings are supposed to provide citizens with a public forum for participation in decision-making and for expressing opinions on the potential consequences of project alternatives. In practice, however, few decisions are made and only a narrow band of the public opinion spectrum is heard from in open debate. According to highway department spokesmen, a majority of the people who attend public hearings (some estimates run as high as 80%) are "anti-highway." Furthermore, the same protesters tend to appear at all location and design hearings even though they often are not directly affected by the proposed project. Most interviewees depicted formal hearings as a useless, if not distasteful, experience and as a poor source of valid information.

Highway officials were openly critical of pro-highway factions for their failure to participate in the public hearing process. Indeed, one of their biggest concerns was to find some method of motivating the silent (or "lazy") majority to stand up and be counted. Solid evidence that such a group exists was difficult to produce, although in a few instances interviewees were able to cite the results of referendums or opinion polls which indicated that more people favored construction of a specific highway project than opposed it. Highway department spokesmen thought that the formal atmosphere of hearings and the fact that they often occur so late in the location process give people the impression that decisions have already been made. Whether or not a more representative showing of affected groups would eventuate, if hearings were less formal and held at a more opportune time, is open to conjecture.

Other Methods of Citizen Involvement

Informal meetings. In some localities highway departments have deemphasized public hearings in favor of informal meetings with concerned citizens. Meetings of this type can be held at any time although, generally, they are scheduled prior to, and following, formal public hearings. Highway officials have found them to be an effective procedure for exchanging information with the public, squelching rumors, reducing the probability that issues will become polarized, and obtaining comment on needed studies and the development of alternatives. One of the few drawbacks of pre-hearing meetings is that they are sometimes held too early: the public is psychologically unprepared to discuss the ramifications of a highway which may not be completed for many years.

Citizen advisory groups. The use of citizen advisory groups is a practice common to many highway departments; however, relatively few agencies in our sample had enlisted the aid of ordinary citizens rather than relying solely on the perceptions of elected officials and prestige figures in the community. One of the states which had moved in this direction established twelve citizen advisory groups—each varied in terms of racial and ethnic composition—for one highway segment alone. Two other states have attempted to identify informal leaders in the community to serve on advisory groups and to assist throughout the planning process. As defined by highway department spokesmen, informal leaders are people who others turn to for advice and help with their problems, and who frequently serve as intermediaries between local residents and outside groups.

Aggressive outreach. A third tactic that is sometimes employed puts great emphasis on the use of multiple communication channels to elicit citizen cooperation. The public is informed of department plans through radio, television, newspapers, posters, and occasionally through word of mouth. Some areas also stress the use of direct correspondence to homeowners. Experience has shown that early notification letters containing the names of department personnel to be contacted about specific issues often reduce anxiety. Another procedure is to open local information centers, particularly in outlying communities; the public is invited to drop in during convenient hours to view plans and to discuss alternatives with well-informed personnel. Mobile vans, equipped with aerial maps and tape and slide shows, are dispatched to remote areas in an effort to reach residents who otherwise might not see the department presentation.

In summary, the techniques described above accentuate candor, personal contact, and a willingness to communicate openly with the public—a refreshing departure from the stance taken by some highway departments just a few short years ago. It should be noted however that these programs are still in a formative stage and there is, as yet, no valid measure of their effectiveness. Problems remain unsolved in areas where there is a dearth of trained personnel to implement citizen participation programs or where officials still cling to a hard-line, union-management approach to bargaining. Some of these issues are discussed briefly in the final section.

CONCLUSION

There is compelling evidence that state action plans will have a significant impact on highway construction in the years to come. Indeed, it is gratifying even now—particularly for members of the scientific community concerned about the consequences of public works projects (Wolf, 1974)—to see social effects placed on an equal footing with environmental and economic effects. Unfortunately, implementation of the action plan has also created some new problems. Chief among these is the complaint that the ability to identify and minimize dysfunctional impacts has not kept pace with the law. To be more specific, federal regulations have outstripped the state's capacity to predict accurately the social repercussions of new and improved highways. Most highway departments do not maintain a large staff of well-trained social scientists, nor can they commit the resources necessary to comply fully with the requirements for social assessment set forth in PPM 90-4.

In a similar vein, confusion within some highway departments over the term "social" has precipitated a cautious approach in the preparation of environmental impact statements. Officials sometimes refuse to consider concepts which they think might be unfamiliar to federal reviewers. They feel that omitting a discussion of "marginal" social effects is preferable to risking rejection of an impact statement on the grounds that the state has not provided sufficient supporting evidence or has drawn the wrong conclusions. Spokesmen for the highway department argue, with some justification, that education about social impacts must begin at the top, i.e., with those federal agencies which pass judgment on the adequacy of environmental impact statements. At present, there are no concrete guidelines indicating the scope or the amount of coverage that must be given to the social effects of an individual highway project.

Despite implementation of some innovative citizen participation programs, an adversary relationship still prevails between the highway department and the public in many jurisdictions.

Opposition groups frequently accuse highway departments of devious tactics, closed-mindedness, and lack of concern for the rights of the individual; highway spokesmen criticize opponents for blocking progress, capriciousness, and total disregard for the transportation needs of the majority population. Regardless of which side is at fault, the social scientist employed by the highway department may find himself in a precarious position. While loyal to his employer, he is also likely to be in sympathy with the affected community, and, as a result, his perceptions may be discounted by both audiences. Contributing to this problem is the fact that engineers in the highway department sometimes find it difficult to accept the uncertainty and complexity associated with social science research. In the words of one highway planner: "Engineers like to draw straight lines. Once they get down on paper they have a way of becoming sacred." In the long run the task of the social scientist may be twofold: (1) to convince department engineers of the importance of social costs and benefits in the decision-making process; and (2) to convince the public that he is sincerely concerned about the highway's potential effect on the quality of life of the community.

REFERENCES

FRIED, M. (1963) "Grieving for a lost home," pp. 151-171 in L. Duhl (ed.) The Urban Condition. New York: Basic Books.

LLEWELLYN, L. G. (1974) "The social impact of urban highways," pp. 89-108 in C. P. Wolf (ed.) Social Impact Assessment. Milwaukee: Environmental Design Research Association.

WOLF, C. P. (1974) "Social impact assessment: the state of the art," pp. 1-44 in C. P. Wolf (ed.) Social Impact Assessment, Milwaukee: Environmental Design Research Association.

[41]
SOCIAL IMPACT STUDIES
An Expository Analysis

MARK A. SHIELDS *is a doctoral candidate in sociology at Brown University. His major interests are social planning and environmental sociology and his dissertation will explore the theoretical bases of social impact assessment.*

"Social impact" means different things to different people. Although one could recite a few definitions of the term, the best way to appreciate its diversity of meanings is to understand the concrete impacts identified in the empirical literature. That is the aim of this paper. Throughout, we implicitly think of social impacts as responses of social systems to the physical restructuring of their environments. By implication, then, social impacts involve adaptations on the part of social systems to "external" agents of change. This intentionally broad notion permits a large variety of specific types of impact. In this paper we discuss impacts in terms of six general categories: displacements and relocations, demographic, institutional, and economic impacts, and impacts on community cohesion and life styles. While the sources cited by no means exhaust the list of impact studies, they do represent a good sampling of recent work in the field.

AUTHOR'S NOTE: *This article is adapted from a report submitted to the U.S. Army Engineer Institute for Water Resources in October 1974, entitled "Social Impact Assessment: An Analytic Bibliography." My warmest thanks go to C. P. Wolf for his critical help in preparing that report.*

DEMOGRAPHIC IMPACTS

The general relationship between population and water resource development has been argued by Hollis and McEvoy (1973: 25): "From a demographic point of view, the crux of the water problem in the United States lies in the discrepancy between the natural distribution of the water supply and the distribution of the consumers." The history of water resource development in the United States has typically centered therefore on the problem of anticipating demographic shifts affecting water supply and demand. Smith and Hogg (1971b) identify three major phases in this relationship. The first, from the mid-nineteenth century to just before World War II, was a period during which water resource development was aimed toward stimulating population movement to the American frontier. The second phase, from the end of the war to roughly 1970 (symbolically marked by "Earth Day"), was characterized by the goal of keeping water development in pace with population growth. And the third, now emergent, is geared toward the use of water development as a strategic planning mechanism for regulating population growth and distribution. The latest phase is recognition of the fact that water development is an integral part of the total planning environment and can be used to guide other social changes.

Despite this growing attention to the interdependent impacts in population and water development, planning may achieve the paradoxical result of catalytically producing that which it is designed to avoid. Smith and Hogg (1971b) and Hollis and McEvoy (1973) argue that there is a tendency for admittedly tentative population projections to become compelling prophecy. Citing the prominent case of Los Angeles, the latter (1973: 25) comment:

> Projects are usually planned to meet the needs of the area in the "foreseeable future," that is, to support the population "projected" to be in the receiving area in about 30 years time. Yet the very act of constructing such projects usually ensures that the projected population becomes a reality, so projects become both self-fulfilling and self-perpetuating.

This is not to suggest that planning is a hopelessly impossible if not downright dangerous enterprise; rather, it cautions us to the independent causal impacts planning itself may have on the objects of its concern and impresses on us a present limitation of our ability to forecast. This warning is pertinent to all prediction in social impact assessment, not just to population prediction. Our forecasts should be better than "best guesses," but they are always constrained by the assumptions we make in extrapolating from current trends, some of which are likely to be significantly altered.

INSTITUTIONAL IMPACTS

There is a direct relationship between the planning and the construction of civil works projects and changes in the volume and distribution of populations. It is a relationship which cuts across project types and areas. The initial impact is felt via the influx of construction workers and others connected with a project (Peelle, 1974; Gold, 1974; Hogg and Smith, 1970; Wilkening et al., 1973). This influx, in turn, places extreme demands on local services and institutions. The typical pattern involves the receiving area in a series of impact crises. Invasion by outsiders stimulates demand for expanded services; the structure is then adapted to meet the demand; and a temporary "boom" is created during which local revenues show marked gains. After construction and well into the operations phase of the project, when demand has returned to a lower level, the area is faced with an underutilized but costly service and institutional structure which local residents must support through higher taxes. Not all project areas experience this extreme "boom-bust" pattern, but it is pervasive enough to raise doubts about the local community benefits of these programs.

While some communities view projects favorably, as a means to encourage population growth (Hogg and Smith, 1970), others fear the encouragement to growth signaled by projects (Gold, 1974) and still others are ambivalent (Wilkening et al.,

1973). What does seem clear, however, is that most communities are willing to look on population growth positively if it is accompanied by economic development. In short, there is a desire for *balanced* population and economic growth, an objective by which most projects are justified. But as the pattern described above would lead us to believe, this objective is frequently stymied. From a policy standpoint, this strongly argues for some action on the part of planning agencies to ameliorate these common negative impacts. Policy criteria should include some legal specification of the binding obligations of developers to ensure a just distribution of impact costs for some time following project construction. This speaks to the need for elevating "social well-being" to the status of a planning *objective,* alongside regional and national economic development, since by so doing local impacts of the sort described here could be given more central consideration.

DISPLACEMENT AND RELOCATION

The problem of displacement and relocation has probably received more attention than any other category of social impact. This is not surprising in view of the fact that, besides those impacts which may be broadly termed economic, displacements and relocations are among the most pervasive—and the most negative. Almost without exception, displacement and relocation connected with the construction of large public works projects are involuntary and preclude return to the former residence. They have the characteristics described by Ludtke and Burdge (1970) of "free compelled" migration: no choice about whether or not to move, but "free" choice of a new location. Free compelled migration has been studied in connection with the construction of large military installations (Breese et al., 1965), reservoirs (Burdge and Ludtke, 1973; Burdge and Johnson, 1973; Ludtke and Burdge, 1970), dams (Mack, 1974) and highways (Perfater, 1972; Llewellyn, 1974). Other studies have analyzed the impact of migrations which are different from the free compelled type, including urban renewal (Williams, 1969) and voluntary moves from one neighborhood to another (Booth and Camp, 1974).

Most studies of forced migration have found often severe psychological stresses and social strains associated with moving. In two papers reporting their findings on persons displaced by reservoirs in Kentucky and Ohio, Ludtke and Burdge (1970; Burdge and Ludtke, 1973) found that apprehension over moving is inversely related to people's willingness to separate themselves from current friends and homes. In addition, strong identification with place (i.e., attachment to a specific home or location) was associated with high levels of apprehension over moving. On the other hand, people with more favorable attitudes toward projects were less apprehensive and consequently more willing to engage in moves that required greater separation from friends and residences. A partial explanation for these differences may be that those whose vested interests are served by projects are more willing to engage in moves requiring major separation from current membership networks. Those whose vested interests are served by projects also tend to be those of relatively higher socioeconomic status, while those who tend to be hurt most by relocation are the poor and the elderly with relatively little formal education (Burdge and Johnson, 1973). Moreover, large numbers of these latter groups are also farmers and have a stronger attachment to their place of residence.

These difficulties are exacerbated by the financial costs of moving. In their study of persons displaced by a Corps of Engineers reservoir project, Burdge and Johnson (1973: 12) found that many felt mistreated by the corps: "They were not helped enough, or were not paid enough for the difficulty and inconvenience of finding a new home. About half the respondents experienced some difficulty in dealing with the Corps, and the major issue was financial cost." For these people the psychic loss of a highly valued attachment to place, coupled with inadequate financial compensation, can have catastrophic results.

In a study of displaced persons in selected Ohio and West Virginia communities, Napier (1972) reported considerable negative feelings expressed toward the planning agency. Mack (1974) also notes the distrust of the Corps created by the North Springfield, Vermont dam project and even suggests that it was extended to a general loss of confidence in government. While it is virtually inevitable that those adversely affected by civil works projects will feel maltreated by the responsible planning agency, it does appear that agencies like the Corps have not been highly sensitive to the serious problems their projects create. Burdge and Johnson (1973: 32) state the issue pointedly:

> The Corps' image is badly in need of refurbishing.... Current attitudes of Corps members toward condemned property and those who must move are alienating and may affect readjustment to relocation and reinforce or create negative attitudes toward the federal government as a whole. More humane treatment of forced migrants by the Corps might deter the vocalization of such sentiments as, in the words of one of our respondents, "The Corp's meaner than a barrel of fishhooks."

Clearly, then, an effective program of public involvement at all stages of planning is needed in responding to these disaffections.

Displacement due to highway construction produces impacts similar to those of reservoir projects. Llewellyn's (1974) analysis of the literature on the social impacts of urban highways concluded that loss of neighborliness, feelings of confusion and despondency, uncertainty about the actual time of moving, and high costs of relocating are among the most salient impacts. The bulk of the literature he reviewed argued that reimbursements for the costs of relocation could not adequately compensate for the tremendous psychic costs of moving. Llewellyn also found that highway impacts tend to be most severe in low income areas, or those communities heavily populated by minority groups or elderly, long-term residents. "All too often," he concluded, (1974: 98) "highway route selection has followed the path of least political resistance—precisely the localities just described." A different study, though emphasizing that most of the persons sampled in connection with a highway impact survey in Virginia were relatively satisfied with the treatment they received and the financial compensation for moving, nevertheless notes that "the social, economic and psychological impacts of relocation were relatively more severe upon the poor, the elderly, and the poorly educated" (Perfater, 1972: xi).

Breese and others (1965: 592) emphasize the economic costs of relocation:

> Generally, especially if the displaced people and uses do not have ready access to adequate capital and cannot act quickly before inflation appears or outside competition moves in, they are likely to be in a disadvantaged position as a result of site acquisition procedures and timing.

Mack (1974) describes similar negative impacts on people directly affected by dam construction in North Springfield, Vermont. In addition to the psychic costs mentioned above, they suffered reduction of income from capital invested in property, in time lost through relocating, and in litigation costs of obtaining fair settlement terms. In contrast, business interests tended to benefit from dam construction because of potential expansion in protected areas, and real estate dealers gained through the increased value of floodplain property.

Another type of forced relocation, urban renewal, displays many of these same characteristic impacts. In some ways, one might expect urban renewal relocation to be less disturbing than the relocations previously discussed because of the requirement to provide replacement housing. In his study of the impact of urban renewal on blacks in Austin, Texas, Williams (1969), however, found mostly negative and, at best, neutral impacts. Among them were the failure to obtain a "decent" home; heavy financial costs in changing residence; little, if any, improvement in the overall physical environment; no decrease in segregation and a significant degree of perceived "loss of community."

In generalizing about the literature on the human impact of displacement and relocation, one can reasonably conclude that relocatees are overwhelmingly placed in the role of benefactors and only rarely in the role of beneficiaries (Smith and Hogg, 1971a). What this says to those involved in planning and carrying out changes that entail these kinds of impacts has been aptly stated by Booth and Camp (1974: 127):

> Family stress is a factor that should be considered in weighing the costs of residential relocation programs which move families. ... Is the increased anxiety and tension the families will experience equal to the gains which might be realized from moving them? If prolonged stress contributes to mental illness, alcoholism or physical illness ... the cost to the community may exceed that of relocation alone.

ECONOMIC IMPACTS: INCOME, EMPLOYMENT, AND TAXES

Civil works projects are commonly justified on the basis of their expected contribution to economic development. But a critical question here is: *whose* economic development? If it is the affected community's development that is in question, then a large number of projects must assuredly be adjudged failures. What often happens is that the goals of national and/or regional economic development undermine or obscure the goals of citizens in the most directly affected communities. Severe community disruptions have been caused by the relative neglect of these goals. As Breese et al. (1965) have argued, financial adjustment is the single most crucial point of stress in a community's adaptation to new projects. If two of the central functions of water resource development are the "gaining of subsistence" and the "establishment of a meaningful community" (Smith and Hogg, 1971b), it is clear that failure to achieve the first makes realization of the second exceedingly difficult.

Impacts on regional economic development have been treated by Kraenzel (1957), who compared contrasting developmental patterns in the Tennessee and Missouri River valleys. Whereas the Tennessee River Valley, under TVA guidance, has had highly favorable development, the Missouri River Valley has not been nearly as fortunate. Kraenzel discusses a number of reasons for these differences. The Tennessee River Valley is a relatively small basin and the benefits have more easily and equitably reached more of the inhabitants. It also contains many indigenous metropolitan centers, is easily accessible to the urbanized, commercial-industrial complex of the East, and has favorable environmental conditions. The Missouri River Valley, on the other hand, is considerably larger and has a much greater diversity of resources and social structures. It also contains fewer metropolitan centers and those tend to be located on the periphery, largely serving interests outside the basin. Moreover, environmental conditions are generally less favorable than in the Tennessee River Valley. Kraenzel argues that the cluster of "plus" factors for the Tennessee River Valley are those which also receive support through the national ethos, a condition which does not hold for the Missouri River Valley. His point is that Tennessee River Valley development has succeeded because it is in special ways more "useful" to larger national interests than the Missouri River Valley.

On the more localized community level, a number of studies have analyzed the differential economic impacts of various types of projects on people and their communities. Mack (1974: 190) found that the North Springfield, Vermont dam brought substantial economic benefits to business interests in the community: "Economic impacts, largely positive, fell on the half dozen large ... manufacturers with plants along the river, and on present and future property owners farther north where some large commercial enterprises settled after the dam was built." In contrast, most residents—including those with property to be bought and cleared—tended to suffer major economic difficulties, particularly costs of displacement and relocation. Though partially counterbalanced by increased employment opportunities from construction, these were short-term gains and the total impact was negative for most townspeople.

Gold (1974) discovered a similar pattern in his study of the impact of strip mining on two communities in southeastern Montana. The total economic impact there presents a mixed picture. While the communities do seem to be experiencing at least a temporary "boom" from mining development, a sizeable number of ranchers in the area view it as a long-term threat because of land acquisitions by the mining company:

> Those who want to expand their ranches anticipate trouble in acquiring more land because the coal companies can always offer more money for acreage which becomes available. At the same time it is also doubtful that anyone interested in buying land for farming or ranching purposes would do so in this area, knowing of the press for coal development and the ramifications such industry brings [1974: 130].

In addition, ranchers worry about the demand for water supplies created by the mining developments and potential pollution hazards. All of these factors make them reluctant to expand or improve their holdings because of the uncertain return on investment.

By contrast, merchants and businessmen in the area are among the major beneficiaries of mining development, much to the resentment of the ranchers on whom the businessmen were formerly dependent for their livelihood. Accusations are made that the merchants are out to make a "quick buck." These suspicions, growing out of the differential interests served by coal mining, have produced a climate of distrust for those who previously contributed to each other's well-being and mutual regard. Gold also notes the rise in tax base accompanying the influx of mining development interests. There is some suspicion among area residents, however, that the extra tax dollars thus generated in the long run will not be pumped into the area, but into more populous regions of the state. There is, then, genuine fear of rising taxes to pay for the expanded service needs induced by development.

Impacts on taxes have been highlighted in other studies as well. Peelle (1974: 116), speaking of the impact of nuclear power plants, found that "if the huge increase in assessed valuation of the completed plant is felt primarily by a small governmental unit such as a town, tax rates will inevitably be affected and land prices may boom as the area becomes more attractive to new residents." Hogg and Smith (1970) found that most of the added tax burden due to dam construction in Sweet Home, Oregon was borne by local property owners on behalf of the short-term resident construction population. Income taxes paid by construction personnel went to the state government, not to support the expanded local service structure which they and their families used during the construction period. Overall, Hogg and Smith concluded that the people of Sweet Home, despite their hope and belief that the dams would spur economic development, were not substantially aided by the projects. The only minor positive impact—one which promises to continue—was a growth in sales of recreational supplies and other tourist-related business. Nevertheless, this will not be a sufficient base for sustained economic growth.

One case in which increased recreational development *did* serve to promote real economic growth has been discussed by Milliken and Mew (1969). They studied the impact of the Shadow Mountain/Granby and Horsetooth Reservoirs in Colorado and found large economic benefits, including increases in land and property values, tax revenues, retail business sales, and employment. Most residents in these areas are engaged in recreation-related business and since the effect of the reservoirs has been to increase recreational opportunities, nearly all of them received an economic boost. In like manner, Wilkening et al. (1973) found that a majority of respondents in the Kickapoo River Valley of Wisconsin expect construction of the LaFarge Dam to have positive economic impacts by improving recreational opportunities and thereby attracting more tourists. Finally, another study (Fullerton, 1972: 125) estimates recreation benefits on the order of $3 million per year from construction of the Cross Florida Barge Canal.

Thus it appears that a major potential economic benefit of a variety of water development projects is the additional revenue yielded by increased recreational opportunities. This is likely to continue. As Hollis and McEvoy (1973: 30) point out:

> Recreational demand has not gone unnoticed by water resources development planners and any increased recreational opportunities offered by a proposal are used as strong arguments for the project, not only from the point of view of amenities provided (or supposedly provided) but also because of the added income such facilities generate.

But as the studies by Mack, Peelle, Gold, and others cogently argue, there are likely to be pervasive economic costs as well. The problem for planners then becomes how to reduce such impacts, and this in turn implies some standard of equity. At the very least, equity means just compensation for costs incurred. But as we have seen, even when "just compensation" is defined in strictly economic terms, actual and perceived inequities persist. The problem is that in impact situations where significant costs are incurred by the people affected, mere economic accounting of damages is insufficient because of the second-order social impacts precipitated. Hence there is a need for an effective—i.e., practical and just—means of evaluating social and economic costs within the same framework. We shall later discuss one promising method for doing this in the section on "differential impacts."

COMMUNITY COHESION

Community cohesion is a problem of social integration. It refers to the bases and mechanisms by which individuals and groups within a defined ecological area maintain their functional and affective ties to one another. If we speak of a community as a social system, maintenance of its special unit character may be analyzed in terms of the ways in which it is integrated. A community has both ecological and conceptual boundaries within which membership and nonmembership are defined. Viewed in this way, the introduction of some external agent such as a construction project creates a need for adjustment by which system integration can be maintained. By this conception, social impacts on community cohesion are among the most crucial for in large measure they affect the entire range of structures and processes bearing on a community's identity and integrity.

Any of the types of impact thus far discussed may have some causal importance for community cohesion. In his study of the impact of coal mining developments on two Montana communities, Gold (1974) found many disruptions resulting from the superimposition of a new industrial technology on a relatively stable rural environment. These included shifts in friendship networks and new strains among old friends, intensification of class alignments and class awareness, a decline in "neighborliness," and the dissolution of old coalitions and the formation of new ones. These all contributed to what he (1974: 135) calls a pervasive sense of "loss of community":

> The old-time residents of Colstrip are finding that the community is no longer theirs; it already belongs to others. Locals here and at Forsyth are feeling socially uprooted, that is, feeling a loss of sense of community as the impact of newcomers becomes more apparent, as old-timers are elbowed out of established positions, and as traditional networks of relationships undergo continual strain and rupture. As locals contemplate future changes of greater magnitude and at a faster rate, they become very anxious about being able to manage their lives satisfactorily in the future. Factionalism related to the coal issue has added to the sense of being a stranger in one's own town.

Gold describes a not-atypical case here: the sudden impact of rapid development which most townspeople associate with the bad effects of an urban-industrial society—lack of privacy, fear for self, congestion, and the feeling that life is busier and more complicated than before.

The same kind of reaction has been described by Hogg and Smith (1970) in their study of the impact of dams on the communities of Sweet Home and Foster, in the Santiam River Basin. There too outsiders are seen as invading, taking over, and shaping anew the communities' character. Residents of Sweet Home, they note, have started to think differently about their community. At first, during the planning phase when the dams were being discussed, most looked on the projects as something which would bring greater prosperity and well-being. But few of the expected benefits were realized and the town now finds itself under the guidance of urban-suburban migrants associated with development. They have introduced formalistic, legalistic values and procedures which have tended to undercut the more traditional, informal, and personal orientations of most community residents. Overall, the dams have brought about social processes which have intensified disintegrative tendencies and increased the predominant "nonarticulation" of the system. Hogg and Smith argue that the structural configurations characterizing the rapid changes in these communities are similar to those of social and cultural disintegration.

Mack's (1974) report on North Springfield, Vermont portrays a similar picture—a town whose identity and development as a community have been adversely affected by the dam project. People there complain of the difficulties of forming new community and personal relationships because of the disruptions created by dam construction and its aftermath.

There is evidence which, on first glance, might suggest a different opinion. Gold (1974: 136), for example, speaks of the "excitement involved in opposing coal development" which has brought a few formerly opposed groups together for that shared purpose. And Wolf (1974: 7) relates the comment of a Chicago District planner "that before the Corps of Engineers came into a downstate Illinois town, 'there wasn't any such thing as community cohesion.'" But it would be silly to interpret instances like these as positive impacts on community cohesion. More properly, they should be viewed as alarmed efforts on the part of basically powerless groups to organize in the most effective way they can to counteract an external force that threatens to disrupt and trouble their lives profoundly.

LIFE STYLES

Much of what we have treated under the topic of "community cohesion" is related to the matter of life styles. The notion of life styles as used here has both a perceptual and a behavioral dimension: it refers jointly to symbols of what people value and how they behave on a day-to-day basis as well as to others' beliefs about these values and behaviors. The two are not necessarily synchronous, but W. I. Thomas's theorem that "if men define their situations as real, they are real in their consequences" fully applies here. Breese et al. (1965: 590) make the general point about life style impacts: "The preexisting public image of forthcoming installations [or projects] var[ies] greatly.... The public image is related not only to the kind of [project] but to the corresponding differences in the types of personnel attracted." The evidence from the studies examined points toward the conclusion that, at least in the case of relatively insulated and small rural communities, there is real trepidation about the "strange" life styles of those who migrate to the project area for employment. Gold (1974) and Mack (1974) both discuss the belief on the part of townspeople they interviewed that projects in their communities had brought in people whose life styles and values were threatening, and Wilkening et al. (1973) mentioned the concern expressed by Kickapoo Valley residents that a proposed dam would attract people with different social outlooks and life styles—as well as "undesirables."

Such references to undesirables are not mere parochial expressions reflecting an intolerance for the unconventional; in fact, they appear to have a real basis in experience. This is at least what Hogg and Smith's (1970) observations would lead us to conclude. They found that the people of Sweet Home and Foster not only had a hard time adjusting to the more formal operational modes of the newcomers, but also that the communities recorded a definite rise in crime during the construction phase and a return to preconstruction levels after completion of the dams. The findings of James and Brogan

(1974) are pertinent to this point. They studied a sample of Atlanta city blocks to determine the impact of land use on the well-being of neighborhood residents. The dominant pattern they discovered was that land uses which cause large numbers of nonresidents to frequent residential neighborhoods are regularly associated with problems for the neighborhood people—including narcotics, alcoholism, burglary, and juvenile delinquency. They conclude with a policy recommendation:

> If the implication that physical features that attract large numbers of outsiders contribute to certain community well-being problems while those that isolate the community reduce these problems is indeed true, the relationship needs to be factored into urban land use management decision making.

If this is so it carries serious implications for the negative impacts of outsiders in rural project areas like those discussed above, where disruptive effects may strike even harder than in more differentiated metropolitan areas.

CONCLUSION

DIFFERENTIAL IMPACTS

I am tempted to sum up this sketch of the literature in two words: *differential impacts.* The point is that the impacts of high technology projects affect different people in different ways at different times. Some people lose a great deal, others gain, and others most probably fall somewhere in between, gaining in some ways, but losing in others. And there are certainly some—indeed, many—who are virtually unaffected by project impacts. So it is quite clear that differential impacts are what social impact assessment is all about. The problem is: how do we measure, weigh, and compare the importance of impacts with such diverse complexity—how do we, in Mack's (1974: 182) words, go about 'summing non-commensurables?" Benefit-cost ratios—the conventional technique—are inadequate, for they assume that what is being analyzed is measurable in purely monetary terms. For many of the impacts we have discussed no such assumption can be made. It may be that some of them are immeasurable in any precise way ("non-quantifiables" in Peelle's words); or, perhaps more plausibly, we have not yet found the requisite measurement techniques; but with hard work we shall eventually succeed. The development of more valid and reliable social indicators is conceivably a basis for this sort of optimism. Yet even if we found good measures, there would still be the problem of converting them into a common currency for calculating tradeoffs.

One promising attempt to deal with this problem has been proposed by Mack (1974). Her "e-model" is an exploratory theoretical and methodological framework within which a diverse array of social, economic, and environmental impacts can be described and measured. The e-model is grounded in marginal utility theory and a theory of human needs postulating nine utility categories (or "want-satisfactions"). Assuming that individuals attempt to maximize utility, she argues that one way by which to assess the costs people incur from a project is to ask what proportion of the utility they could obtain with their last one percent of income would they be willing to give up in order to avoid an undesirable impact. This is measured in "utility index points," with one point representing the utility that a person or household expects to derive from spending the last percent of income. For a given type of impact, many utility categories may potentially be affected. The method of computation is to identify the impact and the relevant impacted group, the category(ies) of utility(ies) affected, and the imputed magnitude of the impact on the "average person" and on the group over a specified time period.

The approach makes some assumptions which might be disputed and raises other questions of substance (Shields, 1974), but it is nonetheless the most useful attempt to date to address the enormous problems of assessing differential impacts within a single analytic framework. From a practical standpoint, the approach is compatible with traditional benefit-cost techniques, but improves on these by the way in which it treats noneconomic impacts. It also places no constraints on the types of data gathering which might be used. Mack's approach is a lead well worth following, and future work in impact assessment should develop and refine the method by applying it to a variety of impact types and settings.

I have described one exemplary approach to the problem of assessing differential impacts. There are others (e.g., Bishop, 1972; Fitzsimmons and Salama, 1973). Whatever the preferred approach, social impact assessors must find an effective way to validate their observations in a manner which decision makers at all levels can appreciate. Otherwise we are in danger of frustrating our hopes and falling short of our goals. We may have confidence in the soundness of our judgments, but this faith will not be enough to convince skeptical administrators and planners. It is one thing to lament the precarious position of impact assessment in the overall planning process (Wilkinson and Cole, 1967), but it is another thing to "do something" about it. The way we do something is to improve on our knowledge and its potential application. For social impact assessment is nothing if not knowledge in use—applied social science in the broadest sense. If one extends this idea to the largest societal dimensions, the need for social impact assessment far transcends the task of single-agency planning. In principle, there is no reason why the analytic and methodological procedures of project-specific impact assessments cannot extend to the domain of overall societal assessment. It is not fantasy to think that within the foreseeable future, alongside the economic and foreign policy reports of the president, there will be an equivalent social report on the state of the society. The main obstacle at present is not so much the reluctance of political authorities to grant us equal opportunity, but the insufficiency of our efforts as social scientists to make our services one among the categories of "critical needs."

REFERENCES

BISHOP, A. B. (1972) "An approach to evaluating environmental, social and economic factors in water resources planning." Water Resources Bull. 8, 4 (August): 724-734.

BOOTH, A. and H. CAMP (1974) "Housing relocation and family social integration patterns." J. of the Amer. Institute of Planners 40, 2 (March): 124-128.

BREESE, G., R. J. KLINGENMEIER, Jr., H. P. CAHILL, Jr., J. E. WHELEN, and A. E. CHURCH, Jr. (1965) The Impact of Large Installations on Nearby Areas. Beverly Hills: Sage.

BURDGE, R. J. and K. S. JOHNSON (1973) Social Costs and Benefits of Water Resource Construction. Research Report 64. Lexington: University of Kentucky Water Resources Institute.

BURDGE, R. J. and R. L. LUDTKE (1973) "Social separation among displaced rural families: the case of flood control reservoirs," pp. 85-108 in W. R. Burch, Jr., N. H. Cheek, Jr., and L. Taylor (eds.) Social Behavior, Natural Resources and the Environment. New York: Harper & Row.

FITZSIMMONS, S. J. and O. A. SALAMA (1973) Man and Water—A Social Report. Cambridge, Mass.: Abt Associates, Inc.

FULLERTON, A. (1973) "Environmental, economic and social aspects of the Cross Florida Barge Canal," pp. 121-125 in L. B. Dworsky, D. J. Allee, and S. C. Csallany (eds.) Social and Economic Aspects of Water Resources Development. Urbana, Ill.: American Water Resources Association.

GOLD, R. L. (1974) "Social impacts of strip mining and other industrializations of coal resources," pp. 123-146 in C. P. Wolf (ed.) Social Impact Assessment. Milwaukee: Environmental Design Research Association.

HOGG, T. C. and C. L. SMITH (1970) Socio-Cultural Impacts of Water Resources Development in the Santiam River Basin. Corvallis: Oregon State University Water Resources Research Institute (October).

HOLLIS, J. and J. McEVOY III (1973) "Demographic effects of water development," pp. 216-232 in C. R. Goldman, J. McEvoy, and P. J. Richerson (eds.) Environmental Quality and Water Development. San Francisco: W. H. Freeman.

JAMES, L. D. and D. R. BROGAN (1974) "The impact of open urban land on community well-being," pp. 150-167 in C. P. Wolf (ed.) Social Impact Assessment. Milwaukee: Environmental Design Research Association.

KRAENZEL, C. F. (1957) "The social consequences of river basin development." Law and Contemporary Social Problems 22 (Spring): 221-236.

LLEWELLYN, L. G. (1974) "The social impact of urban highways," pp. 89-108 in C. P. Wolf (ed.) Social Impact Assessment. Milwaukee: Environmental Design Research Association.

LUDTKE, R. L. and R. J. BURDGE (1970) Evaluation of the Social Impact of Reservoir Construction on the Residential Plans of Displaced Persons in Kentucky and Ohio. Research Report 26. Lexington: University of Kentucky Water Resources Institute.

MACK, R. P. (1974) "Criteria for evaluation of social impacts of flood management alternatives," pp. 175-195 in C. P. Wolf (ed.) Social Impact Assessment. Milwaukee: Environmental Design Research Association.

MILLIKEN, J. G. and H. E. MEW, Jr. (1969) Economic and Social Impact of Recreation at Reclamation Reservoirs: An Exploratory Study of Selected Colorado Reservoir Areas. Denver: Denver Research Institute, University of Denver (March).

NAPIER, T. L. (1972) "Social-psychological response to forced relocation due to watershed development." Water Resources Bull. 8, 2 (August): 784-795.

PEELLE, E. (1974) "Social effects of nuclear power plants," pp. 113-120 in C. P. Wolf (ed.) Social Impact Assessment. Milwaukee: Environmental Design Research Association.

PERFATER, M. A. (1972) The Social and Economic Effects of Relocation Due to Highway Takings. Charlottesville: Virginia Highway Research Council (October).

SHIELDS, M. A. (1974) "Comment on 'Criteria for evaluation of social impacts of flood management alternatives,'" pp. 197-198 in C. P. Wolf (ed.) Social Impact Assessment. Milwaukee: Environmental Design Research Association.

SMITH, C. L. and T. C. HOGG (1971a) "Benefits and beneficiaries: contrasting economic and cultural distinctions." Water Resources Research 7, 2 (April): 254-262.

——— (1971b) "Cultural aspects of water resources development past, present, and future." Water Resources Bull. 7, 4 (August): 652-660.

WILKENING, E. A., P. WOPAT, J. G. LINN, C. GEISLER, and D. McGRANAHAN (1973) Quality of Life in Kickapoo Valley Communities. Report 11. Madison: University of Wisconsin Institute for Environmental Studies (September).

WILKINSON, K. P. and L. W. COLE (1967) Sociological Factors in Watershed Development. State College: Mississippi State University Water Resources Research Institute (July).

WILLIAMS, J. A., Jr. (1969) "The effects of urban renewal upon a black community: evaluation and recommendations." Social Sci. Q. 50, 3 (December): 703-712.

WOLF, C. P. (1974) "Social impact assessment: the state of the art," pp. 1-44 in C. P. Wolf (ed.) Social Impact Assessment. Milwaukee: Environmental Design Research Association.

Social Impact Assessment of Regional Plans: a review of methods and issues and a recommended process*

JAMES C. CRAMER, THOMAS DIETZ
Department of Sociology, University of California, Davis

ROBERT A. JOHNSTON
Division of Environmental Studies, University of California, Davis

ABSTRACT

Social impact assessment (SIA) is defined and related to other policy analysis techniques. Conceptual problems in conducting SIA are reviewed. Various SIA methods are identified and evaluated for their probable effectiveness in assessing regional plans. Regional planning conditions are identified and constraints to, and demands on, SIA are examined. A strategy for SIA is proposed which uses public inputs during cyclical planning iterations for efficiently identifying and assessing the most important social impacts.

Introduction

The purposes of this paper are to provide an introduction to social impact assessment (SIA) as a form of policy analysis and to propose a process for the social impact assessment of regional plans. The discussion will focus on the practical problems involved in assessing the social impacts of various types of plans — air and water quality, transportation, housing, land use — in a regional planning agency with limited time, money, and personnel. Sections I–IV of the paper provide an overview of SIA, with some discussion of the role SIA can play in the overall planning process. In Sections V and VI, methodological problems in social impact assessment are examined and we review methods that have been proposed. Organizational constraints found in regional planning agencies are discussed in Section VII and a strategy for conducting SIA of regional plans is recommended which efficiently copes with the problems of organization and methodological constraints.

---

* This article is primarily based on earlier work funded by the Kellogg Grant to the University of California at Davis (Kellogg-SRAPC Project). An earlier version of this paper was published by the Sacramento Regional Area Planning Commission (Sacramento, CA) in 1977.

As regional plans change from advisory documents to ones which legally control many local government actions, the assessment of these plans becomes more important to the quality of life in the United States. Regional (and state) planning bodies have recently begun producing plans for transportation, air quality, and water quality that will become guides for increasing state and federal authority over local government planning. The social assessment of these complex and large-scale plans presents formidable challenges.

I. Rationale for SIA

The logical arguments for SIA are straightforward. The rationale for committing public resources to various projects and plans is that such investments enhance people's well-being. Allocating resources effectively requires knowledge of how each investment might contribute to well-being. Benefit cost and related kinds of policy analysis were introduced as attempts to estimate the *economic* impacts of projects, first at the national level and more recently at the regional and local levels (Haveman and Margolis, 1977; Zeckhauser and Schaefer, 1968). With a rise in concern for the protection of environmental quality, political pressure led to a variety of statutes, court decisions, and administrative actions which require explicit consideration of the *environmental* consequences of governmental activities. The same political pressures deterred efforts to translate environmental impacts into economic terms (i.e. into strictly monetary values), and instead stipulated the development of environmental impact assessment (EIA), a mode of policy analysis quite different from economic approaches such as benefit–cost. Very broadly, the basic difference is between providing information on different means for attaining an agreed-upon goal, and providing information on competing goals and values. Despite this difference (and others), EIA and economic analyses share a common fault: the narrow focus on environmental impacts (or economic impacts) precludes consideration of other important dimensions of consequences, such as community solidarity, crime, mobility, or access to social services. Efforts to expand the scope of EIA to include *all* significant consequences of proposed projects (while maintaining its distinctive orientation toward competing goals and values) have resulted in social impact assessment. The movement toward SIA represents an attempt to reveal the existence of adverse impacts before they occur so that planners, the general public, and groups specially affected can conduct an informed debate over which impacts can be avoided, which are socially necessary, and which are socially intolerable (Daffron, 1975; Friesema and Culhane, 1976; Francis, 1974; Johnston, 1977).

At a more practical level, the impetus for social impact analysis comes from various legislative and administrative mandates. Key among these are the National Environmental Policy Act (NEPA) and the twenty-five roughly equivalent state statutes or administrative regulations. NEPA and the state equivalents call for assessment of the environmental impacts of governmental actions before these actions occur. The language of these laws and the administrative guidelines developed for implementing them call, in most cases, for an analysis of the social, as well as the biological and physical, effects of proposed actions. A variety of court decisions have noted the importance of social impacts. As a result, a number of agencies have incorporated requirements for SIA into their own guidelines and procedures and have imposed requirements for such analyses on their grantees and contractors. Legislatures at the national and state level have also included language calling for social impact assessment in several special purpose environmental laws (Coop, 1977).

NEPA requires an interdisciplinary approach to plan evaluation. The 1978 (and previous) Council on Environmental Quality regulations implementing NEPA urge the consideration of impacts on population growth, community facilities, land use, urban congestion, threats to health, transportation, noise, neighborhood character, low income populations, and recreation. Intangible (nonquantifiable) impacts must be considered. Section 1508.14 *requires* that social impacts be evaluated when they are "interrelated" with natural or physical impacts. Federal water agencies must evaluate project effects on social well-being under the Water Resources Council's Principles and Standards of 1973. Effects must be shown by geographic regions, income classes, and interest groups. Effects that should be considered include: population distribution, economic stability, income distribution, health, safety, and education. Furthermore, the Flood Control Act of 1970 requires these agencies to consider aesthetics, community cohesion, and displacement of people. Federal land management agencies, such as the Bureau of Land Management, consider a variety of social effects in their plan evaluation procedures. Federal and state transportation planning statutes and regulations require that a large number of social impacts be examined in plans.

It is evident even from this brief review that the requirements for SIA vary enormously, especially considering how different government agencies have interpreted and implemented the general laws and responded to various types of political pressures. In addition, not all types of "governmental action" are included within the legal mandates. Initially the requirements for environmental and social impact assessment were directed at administrative actions (e.g. issuance of permits) concerning specific projects such as construction of dams, river channels, and highway segments. Subsequently the mandates have been broadened to include urban and regional plans, even if the plans consist of general policies rather than lists of projects. Legislative and judicial decisions still are exempt from SIA, although a variety of policy analyses commissioned by Congress have examined social impacts systematically. An example with particular relevance for SIA of regional plans was the study by the U.S. Commission on Population Growth and the American Future (1972).

It should be noted that SIA can be conducted outside traditional institutional frameworks. Many of the practical and technical problems apply whether the impact analysis is being conducted by a planning agency in order to fulfill a legal requirement or by a community group trying to crystallize its position regarding a proposed governmental action. The discussion which follows focuses on the problems faced by planning agencies, but the methods discussed in Section VI could also be used by neighborhood organizations or other groups. The general development of applied social science at the "grass roots" level has been given little attention and is an area in which much fruitful work could be done (Ehrlich, n.d.).

II. The Definition of Social Impact Assessment

There are as many definitions of social impact assessment as there are individuals and organizations attempting to use the concept. At an intuitive level it is clear that various public and private projects, programs, and policies influence social life; if they did not, there would be little reason for committing resources to such actions. The difficulty in developing a working definition comes in delineating a manageable realm of inquiry. Definitions in the literature are oriented toward the practical problems of carrying out impact assessments. Some focus on differentiating social from other kinds of impacts (e.g. Mack, 1974: "Impacts on people other than those that operate primarily via the dollars in their wallet."). Others focus on the process of assessing social impacts (e.g. Army Corps of Engineers Section 122 Guidelines). Perhaps the best working definition is that developed by Duncan and Jones (1976): "A social impact assessment . . . is the identification, analysis and evaluation of a social impact resulting from a particular event" where a social impact is defined as a "significant improvement or deterioration in people's well-being or a significant change in an aspect of community concern." We shall often substitute "prediction" for "analysis" because it more accurately describes that part of the process: predicting the degree of impacts that will follow the event being assessed. We also will interpret the proposed "action programs" contained in regional plans as "events," although Duncan and Jones intended only specific projects.

This definition has several useful features. First, it focuses attention on individuals rather than institutions. Second, it includes matters of community concern, whether or not an outside expert considers them significant. Third, it focuses attention on significant impacts, rather than on all project effects. Finally, it breaks the process of impact assessment into identification, prediction, and evaluation, three distinct steps each with its own conceptual, methodological, and practical problems. (These points are elaborated in Duncan and Jones, 1976, Appendix A). Deficiencies in the definition are discussed in Section V.

III. Links to Other Fields

Social impact assessment resembles all other forms of policy analysis in that ideally it should identify, predict, and evaluate all costs and benefits caused directly or indirectly by a certain (proposed) event. In practice, however, SIA differs considerably from conventional forms of policy analysis such as benefit–cost or systems analysis. In part this is because SIA must be sufficiently flexible to be useful for analyzing diffuse plans as well as specific programs and projects. More importantly, several differences arise from the conclusion that not all impacts can be measured along the same dimension. One of the most frequently criticized aspects of benefit–cost analysis is the need to translate all relevant benefits and costs into dollar values (Nelson, 1977; Rivlin, 1971). This translation often is difficult even with projects having clear economic goals, and it has proved nearly impossible in social programs such as education. It is quite controversial whether the difficulties indicate inherent defects in the method or merely faulty applications of an inherently sound principle (compare the chapters by Williams and Rowan in Haveman and Margolis, 1977). Our position is that prices represent weighted averages of consumer preferences, and in the political arena the absence of agreed-upon weights precludes any assignment of (shadow) prices. (In some instances market prices themselves are recognized as products of political values – e.g. subsidies and other market distortions, the "arbitrary" distribution of income – and are rejected in favor of other, equally arbitrary, shadow prices.) Translating impacts into dollar values has been abandoned in environmental impact assessment, and this conclusion has been carried forward in SIA. As a result, impacts cannot be compared directly or summarized by a single ratio or index number; they can merely be listed – e.g. increase in community cohesion, reduced crime rate, lower unemployment, etc. – and (perhaps) their magnitudes estimated. When impacts are disaggregated in this fashion and measured in "natural" or "intuitive" units, it is clear that different people will attach different importance to them and there may even be disputes about whether an impact is "good" or "bad." Hence the legally mandated purpose of SIA is to provide information to the public. Clearly this is a political function, quite unlike the presumed technical function of benefit–cost analysis. Disaggregation in SIA (and EIA) extends beyond impacts to populations. Subgroups experiencing severe impacts must be identified regardless of the aggregate impact on "society." The strong emphasis on distributional impacts accentuates the political function of SIA and further distinguishes if from benefit-cost analysis. SIA was not developed strictly as a response to weaknesses in benefit-cost analysis, however; its heritage is actually quite diverse and eclectic.

At the conceptual and theoretical level, SIA is influenced by the sociological literature on social problems. By definition, social impacts aggravate or diminish social problems. Identifying impacts and defining social problems are conceptually similar tasks and research on the latter has demonstrated the significance of the frequent gap between objective social and physical conditions and people's subjective perceptions of well-being. Social problems research also is useful for its attention to group conflict and to distributional problems of social welfare and happiness.

Methodologically, social impact assessment is linked to three distinct traditions: social indicators, technology assessment, and futures research. The social indicators movement has its roots in the Twenties and is currently experiencing a florescence.

(See the special issue of the *American Journal of Sociology*, Vol. 82, No. 3, November, 1976 on "Social Change and Social Indicators" and the journal *Social Indicators Research* for examples of current work in this area.) Although the major goal of social indicators research is measurement, most practitioners seem to agree that a crucial test of any indicator is its ability to detect social change. Such measures are often justified because of their utility in evaluating various projects and programs (Duncan, 1969b; Campbell, 1976). Useful lists of many kinds of social impact categories can be found in the social indicators literature, along with proposed measurement definitions. There is also a vast literature on technology assessment, much of it on anticipating the social effects of the adoption of various technologies (Organization for Economic Cooperation and Development, 1975; Teich, 1977). Ogburn's study of the social effects of civilian aviation (1946) is a classic in the field. Technology assessment methodologies are informative but not directly transferable to SIA because of the latter's different legal mandate and, at least until recently, different purpose – i.e. policy analysis, as opposed to business forecasting or academic research.

Finally, there is the general forecasting and futures research tradition, which dates from the earliest social scientists, social philosophers, and science fiction writers and is active today in a variety of disciplines (Cornish, 1977). Futurists commonly focus on trend analysis and often ignore underlying causal processes, while social impact assessment requires an analysis which attempts to distinguish causes from effects. As a result the applicability of some forecasting techniques developed by futures researchers is limited. Nevertheless, most of the methods that have been proposed for SIA have their origins in futures research.

The importance to the planner of these parallel traditions lies in the prospect of utilizing the results of research from these fields in SIA. Most previous research on SIA has been conducted in the context of plan evaluation and environmental impact assessment. These approaches are useful, in that they ground SIA in practical concerns. But, while they have led to useful models for the process of SIA, they have not produced much methodological work. Closer attention to the work of social indicators researchers, forecasters, and technology assessors, combined with a general perspective derived from planning and EIA should lead to assessments of the social consequences of environmental change which are both practical and methodologically sound.

IV. Examples

At this point it would be useful to discuss a few examples of SIA. There are a large number of studies which have examined the social effects of various plans, projects, and programs *post hoc*. The information contained in these may be very valuable in preparing SIAs on proposed public projects. However, the methodological problems involved in determining what *has* happened are much different from those involved in determining what *will* or *might* happen, so *post hoc* studies will not be discussed here except as a guide to preparing SIAs (see Section VI).

The Yerba Buena Center redevelopment project EIS (San Francisco, City and County, 1973) discusses impacts on land use, population density, displacement of persons, urban design (aesthetics), traffic congestion, noise, community interests, employment, earthquake risks, housing quality and cost, utilities, fire safety, and historical sites. The methods used are generally not described but include economic base analysis, demographic projection, scenario writing, and analysis of newspaper files. Impacts were disaggregated by income classes and by geographic areas. Psychological effects of relocation were discussed briefly, as were other indirect social impacts. Many mitigation actions and alternative plans were examined in this lengthy report. Controversial issues are briefly described. Little subjective data was utilized.

Lichfield (1969) performed an evaluation of a town expansion plan for Peterborough, England. Several sketch plans were judgmentally evaluated for effects on current and new occupiers (industrial, commercial, residential), users of facilities, traffic, pedestrians, workers, recreators, displaced landowners and occupiers, and taxpayers. Analyses are reported for the various objectives of each affected group in detail. This study is useful chiefly for its handling of large amounts of data in a set of evaluation accounts and for its linking of impacts to physical plan alternatives. The sketch plans (maps) assessed by Lichfield's team are representative of the kinds of general policies or programs produced by regional planners and to which our discussion of SIA is directed.

The Final EIS on the California Coastal Management Program (U.S. Department of Commerce, 1977) examines potential effects on property rights, property values, employment stability, recreation/tourism, population, land use, public housing, public accomodations, aesthetics, historic objects, community character, and public involvement. This study projects impacts forward in time from both economic theory and from limited *post hoc* data from the program's first three years of operation. This report is valuable as an attempt to assess effects of a complex set of policies affecting a large and diverse social system (the California coastal zone), a system that interacts strongly with other geographic areas and is affected greatly by a myriad of other agencies, policies, and plans. The study deduces social impacts from economic effects in a thorough fashion.

An impressive study of an even more complex set of policies and conditions is the Mackenzie Valley Pipeline Inquiry, described by Gamble (1978). The inquiry commission was given a broad mandate by the Canadian government to study virtually all of the issues raised by the proposal to build a pipeline from the Arctic oil fields through Canada to the southern population centers. The inquiry was notable in many respects: (1) presentation of technical reports in an adversarial setting, with cross-examination by both experts and the public; (2) equal attention to technical experts and public opinion; (3) equal attention to economic, legal, environmental, social, and cultural issues; (4) careful consideration of inequities in the distribution of impacts between ethnic groups and geographically across Canada; and (5) consideration of impacts of additional development likely to be induced by the pipeline (rather than a narrow focus on the single proposal in isolation).

Analysis of growth impacts is central to SIA, since population and economic growth entail so many changes in society. A number of studies have assessed the effects of growth at the local and regional levels. The Boulder Area Growth Study Commission (1973, Vols. 8 and 9) explores the social impacts which would follow from four alternative growth patterns in the Boulder Valley of Colorado. The impact assessments used scenarios (Vol. 8) and interview data from self-selected respondents (Vol. 9). A variety of impacts were considered, with changes in population composition (income distribution, age, ethnic class, and cultural mix), changes in style of life, and equity effects identified as the most important impacts of alternative growth patterns. Appelbaum et al. (1976) have conducted extensive analyses of the possible impacts of growth in Santa Barbara, California. Using statistical techniques, results from previous studies, survey research and scenarios, they identified unemployment, municipal costs, taxes, and utility costs as key growth impacts.

V. Conceptual Problems in Defining Impacts

The first step in the SIA process is the identification of impacts, but impacts cannot be identified unless we know what to look for. Earlier we defined a social impact as "a significant improvement or deterioration in people's well-being or a significant change in an aspect of community concern." This definition was sufficient for providing a general idea of what is meant by "social impact," but it turns out to be unacceptably ambiguous in practical applications of deciding whether a projected situation is or is not an impact. We shall discuss four sources of ambiguity, in this order: (1) the two criteria may be inconsistent; (2) the inclusiveness of "people" and "community" is indeterminant; (3) the "significance" of an impact may be obscured by externalities; and (4) the same impact may be both an improvement in some respects and a deterioration in other respects.

"Well-being" and "Community Concern"

Our definition suggests two criteria of impacting, a change in people's well-being *or* in community concern. The first criterion refers to an objective physical or social reality while the second refers to public perceptions (what people think reality is). Several difficulties are apparent here: how do we observe the objective reality, how do we observe the subjective perceptions, and are the two realities likely to give the same evidence regarding impacts?

Numerous social scientists are working on measures of objective well-being, or quality of life (Sheldon and Moore, 1968; Campbell and Converse, 1972; De Neufville, 1975) and a few satisfactory solutions are beginning to emerge under the general title "social indicators." Several of these efforts are proceeding within the perspective of causal models and prediction (Land and Spilerman, 1975) and may be useful in SIA. A major difficulty with all objective measures of well-being is deciding what conditions actually contribute to quality of life and are desirable. For example, some models consider maximum quantity of employment as desirable while others are directed more at maximum quantity and quality of leisure. Another example is "community cohesion": which contributes more to well-being, ethnic enclaves or integration? The issue here is "What makes people happy?" The subjectivist solution is to ask people. Public opinion polling is, of course, a well-developed field, but systematic monitoring and prediction of "happiness" or concern (that is, creation of subjective social indicators useful in prediction) has barely begun (Campbell et al., 1976), and we can expect a great deal more experimentation and research in the near future. Specific techniques for measuring both objective and subjective well-being will be discussed below.

A more serious problem than measurement is the relationship between objective reality and subjective perceptions. We alluded to some of the issues above. A large amount of research on social problems has been devoted to this topic and the general conclusion is that objective conditions and subjective perceptions of well-being are only quite loosely associated (Mauss, 1975; Berger and Luckman, 1966). There are two general reasons for this. First, people often do not perceive reality accurately. Selective perception is a well-known psychological phenomenon, but there are other issues as well. Perceptions depend upon the availability of information, and this may be limited and uneven. Information can be controlled in both extent and accuracy. Examples abound of self-serving manipulations of information that have "created" social problems – e.g. fabricated crime waves (Mauss, 1975, pp. 88–100; Merton, 1976, p. 15), prohibitionist propaganda financed by bootleggers (McNall, 1975, p. 8), and the Bureau of Narcotics' campaign against marijuana (McNall, 1975, p. 213). In addition, some types of reality may be more visible than others, for temporal, physical, or cultural reasons. A single airplane crash is far more sensational than a number of auto accidents, leading many people to worry more about airplane than auto safety despite the lower risks of air travel (Merton, 1976, p. 16). Carcinogenic food additives and white-collar crime are problems even if people generally are unaware of them.

The second reason for the frequent disparity between objective reality and subjective perceptions is that even if people perceive a situation identically, their evaluation of whether it is problematic (and why) will vary depending on cultural values and beliefs as well as situational and personal factors. We assume this largely explains why for many years witches have not been problematic in Salem, Massachusetts, although they have continued to be problematic elsewhere. It also partly accounts for differences in definitions of what constitutes good health, poverty, alcoholism, or neighborhood attractiveness (to name a few examples), where such definitions are critical for evaluations. It should be noted, in this regard, that many technical experts and occupational groups who deal with social problems – for example police, doctors, teachers, psychologists, policy analysts – seem to learn somewhat distinctive values during their professional training, and they constitute subcultures as well as vested-interest groups (McCarthy and Zald, 1973; Mauss, 1975).

For the reasons mentioned above, and others we have chosen to neglect, there is considerable dispute about what is or will be a social problem – e.g. contrast Merton (1976, pp. 13–23) with Mauss (1975, "Prologue"). Resources for dealing with problems are scarce, so decisions about what are the important problems must be made. Many types of experts (e.g. planners, engineers, economists) have been trained to study the objectively real aspects of problems. Within the confines of scientific knowledge – which very often are severely limited – these experts have easier access to accurate information than the general public. But information must be evaluated before it is useful (in SIA as well as in the study of social problems), and here the general public is often more "expert" than the professionals. Hence, it is not clear what are the proper roles of technical experts and citizens. If people are more concerned about airplane than auto safety, where should the experts direct their attention (assuming scarce resources)? Nagel refers to this as the problem of "paternalism" (Nagel, 1972). It is our impression that many experts overlook the limitations to their expertise or are aware of the problem of paternalism in only a narrow and distant way (this may be one of the issues in the current wave of antigovernment feeling and tax revolt). But our point is not simply to demean experts. Experts may not realize what circumstances will be viewed as impacts or what impacts will be of greatest concern to people, nor are experts always nonpartisan, and the public may be short-sighted, misinformed, or ignorant about important impacts.

Previously we indicated that impacts are assessed in a three-step process of identification, prediction, and evaluation. The objective/subjective dilemma arises in somewhat different form at each step, because information is limited and/or value judgments are necessary. Clearly, potential impacts should be identified by both technical experts and representatives of the general public, as the two groups may have different ideas about what contributes to quality of life. Regardless of source of identification, some potential impacts can be predicted rigorously by technical experts using quantitative research methods, but other potential impacts must be predicted qualitatively by referring to selected case studies (i.e. experience elsewhere) and by asking experts and citizens if they think the impacts might occur. The mode of analysis depends on the resources available for research and on the state of scientific knowledge, both of which are often severely limited. Finally, after prediction has sorted out the most pertinent impacts, the importance of these impacts can be evaluated either by technical methods (analogous to benefit–cost analysis) or subjectively by crude ratings. Due to the frequent inability to quantify the relevant factors along a single dimension, the latter form of evaluation nearly always is used (Wolf, 1974; Duncan and Jones, 1976; Fitzsimmons et al., 1975). For example, specific impacts can be rated on a five-point scale from "very good" through "no impact" to "very bad." Again, both experts and citizens should participate at this step, as ratings require both technical and value judgments. To reiterate, identification, prediction, and evaluation of impacts all require objective and subjective methods of analysis.

"People" and "Community"

The second ambiguity in the definition of impacts has to do with boundaries. What people, and how large a community, will be impacted by a proposed plan or project? In theory, a web of causation extends from the physical site of the "event" to the rest of the planet. A global perspective may indeed be necessary for some proposals (e.g. commitment to breeder reactors, or deforestation in the Amazon Basin), but for most practical purposes more limited boundaries must be sought. One must be careful, however, not to define such narrow geographic boundaries that people "on the outside" will experience significant impacts, especially since these people probably are distant from the project site and hence most likely to be ignorant of potential impacts. This problem, familiar in all policy analyses as a type of externality, has no general solution. Usually boundaries are determined by law or political jurisdiction and one can merely exhort analysts to use good judgment and to be fair or at least sensitive to *long-term* expendiency.

"Significant Change"

The third ambiguity surrounding impacts also has to do with boundaries, but these are not geographic. The problem is best seen in terms of project or plan boundaries, or "compounding" in the terminology of environmental impact assessment. A specific event may not be significant in itself, but it may be part of a trend and thus contribute to an overall impact that is highly significant. If each proposed event is assessed separately and independently, none can be faulted as the cause of negative impacts. If the events are proposed at widely different times, the problem is even more difficult. For example, in the Mackenzie Valley Pipeline Inquiry discussed above, the only project actually proposed was a gas pipeline, and in all likelihood this project would pose few serious threats of adverse impacts. Almost certainly, however, the constructed pipeline would soon lead to proposals for roads, oil pipelines and refineries, and other forms of economic development. The most serious impacts were expected to be caused by these extensions of the initial proposal (Gamble, 1978). In this case, the scope of the SIA included the entire development trend, not simply the specific project that was tangibly proposed. Advocates of the gas pipeline bitterly contested this scope, arguing they were held "guilty by association."

From the perspective of doing SIAs, events usually must be taken as given (although a few court decisions have required redefinition of projects to take account of compounding). If a single project or plan must be assessed by itself, then the problem of compounding is redefined as a problem of "external impacts." This type of external impact is generated by a plan or project but is only manifested by another plan or project. Externalities generally occur where impacts are cumulative and where there are threshold effects or ceiling constraints (i.e. nonlinear impacts). A hypothetical example of a threshold effect is residential density and health: up to a certain point increasing density may have no impact on health, but beyond this point epidemics become problematic and increasing density seriously impacts health. There may also be threshold effects of automobile congestion on emission-caused disease and on deaths from collisions. A not-so-hypothetical example of a ceiling constraint is air pollution and unemployment. The auto industry has lobbied for relaxation of auto emission standards on the grounds of preventing unemployment in that industry. But local areas face legal limits on air pollution and if autos generate more pollution, there is less margin for local industrial pollution and hence unemployment occurs in other industries. These examples illustrate the nature of one type of externality. Externalities often are not physical impacts on people, but rather impacts on the range of future choices (i.e. impacts on future plans or projects). In assessing significant changes in well-being, these less-obvious and less-tangible impacts must not be overlooked.

"Aggregation Problem"

The final ambiguity in the definition of social impacts is perhaps the most obvious. Rarely will there be a single, unqualified experience of an impact throughout a community, so perhaps it is misleading even to speak of "an" impact. Probably in most cases impacts will be felt in different ways and different degrees by different people and these variations (at least the "significant" ones) should be noted in the assessment. Indeed it is very important (and prudent), as a routine part of the assessment process, to actively search for the most extreme distribution, where an impact causes the quality of life to improve for some people and to decline for others. The distribution of an impact should be fully reported in the SIA, not "averaged out" as an overall (aggregated) net impact (Johnston, 1977, 1975). For example, using the five-point scale of impact evaluation described above, indicating the number of people at each point would be preferable to a single summary score.

VI. Techniques for Assessing Social Impacts

Methods of identifying and measuring social impacts must satisfy the two requirements of validity and simplicity. The first requirement is somewhat ambiguous. To the extent that assessment is a process of objective forecasting, it is wasted effort and may be harmful unless it results in reasonably accurate and reliable forecasts of the consequences of proposed projects or plans. Unfortunately little is known about the validity of forecasting techniques for several reasons: social forecasting has a short history, few evaluations of past forecasts have been attempted because of methodological difficulties, and the criteria by which past forecasts should be judged are not at all clear (Duncan 1969a; Keyfitz, 1972). To the extent that assessments are based on subjective perceptions, the concern is more with identification of critical issues than with absolutely accurate forecasts (Duncan, 1969a) and validity is a question of identifying all truly critical issues, although accuracy cannot be completely disregarded. Furthermore, accuracy of prediction is a more appropriate criterion for assessments of specific projects than of general plans because the implementation of plans is almost always ambiguous and actual impacts depend on these subsequent events. Assessment programs should be designed so as to facilitate *post hoc* evaluation, so that in the future we will know more about validity. In the meantime, comparisons of the soundness of various methods must rest on judgments regarding the assumptions underlying the methods.

The second requirement of SIA techniques, simplicity, is imposed by the inevitable scarcity of such resources as time, money, personnel, and information. These constraints are nearly always serious and they may force the analyst to choose techniques which sacrifice methodological soundness for ease of use. Fortunately a variety of techniques are available, permitting some degree of flexibility in selecting a validity-simplicity tradeoff suited to the particular circumstances. Readers unfamiliair with these techniques may find detailed discussions and examples elsewhere (Finsterbusch and Wolf, 1977; McEvoy and Dietz, 1977; Runyan, 1977; Wolf, 1974).

The most obvious question of validity is, who does the assessment? We indicated earlier that both experts and the public should be involved in SIA. Since our particular concern here is assessing regional plans, we mean by "expert" the planning staff. Two definitions of "the public" have been used in the past. the more common one is to select for participating in SIA an elite sample consisting of a variety of non-staff technical experts and informed community leaders. The second approach is to use a representative sample of the general public. Each approach has advantages and disadvantages, and perhaps the best solution is to attempt to combine them in some way. The possibilities for doing this vary with the circumstances and the techniques of assessment being used.

Regardless of definition of "the public," there are several ways of obtaining their contribution to SIA. The most austere way is to do a survey of public opinion about probable impacts. This approach permits no interaction among the public participants, either at initial contact or in the form of feedback, and very limited interaction between them and the planning staff. The major drawbacks to surveys, in addition to the above, are the difficulty of posing intelligible questions on technical and complex issues, problems of obtaining cooperation (i.e. low response rates in many types of surveys), and the large burden on staff time or the expense of hiring consultants. The Delphi technique makes use of reinterviews to provide feedback among the participants and greater involvement of the staff; usually Delphi is used with elite samples.

The assumptions underlying Delphi have been cogently criticized (Hill and Fowles, 1975; Sackman, 1974), and it is not clear that it is an improvement over a single-round survey. Most of the advantages are due to using an elite sample, not to the technique itself, and it is more costly than simple surveys.

A different approach to public participation is to assemble the participants together for a conference. Conferences may be relatively unstructured "brainstorming" sessions, but more commonly they are highly structured in order to control group dynamics (Delbecq and Van de Ven, 1971; Greenblat and Duke, 1975; Runyan, 1977). The goal of structuring interaction is to increase motivation and creativity in the group setting yet protect individual opinions and judgments from group intimidation. Structured conferences permit interaction among participants and between participants and staff – allowing, for example, more complex questions than are possible in surveys – and consume less staff time than do surveys. Conferences consume much more of the participants' time than do surveys (and impose travel costs), however, so they pose greater problems of obtaining public cooperation.

All these forms of public participation require staff involvement, so the distinction between expert and public contributions to SIA is in practice a bit blurred. The staff impinge upon the public contribution in three ways: (1) selecting the public participants; (2) teaching the participants how to do SIA (e.g. sensitizing them to problems of externalities and distributional inequities); and (3) presenting information about the specific plan or project and asking questions about impacts, both of which may direct public attention toward certain impacts and away from others. Inevitably there is a risk that staff will use these opportunities to manipulate (deliberately or not) the public in order to obtain results desired by staff. This risk is greater with surveys (including Delphi) than in conferences, where participants are freer to initiate ideas and to determine which discussions deserve most attention. In a sense, the risk of manipulation may be lower with elite public samples, where participants are more technically sophisticated (and more accustomed to participating in such ventures) and need less "guidance." On the other hand, they may share the staff's values so that overt manipulation is not necessary – manipulation has occurred already with the choice of an elite sample.

We know of no SIA technique that guarantees the absence of manipulation; ultimately we must trust staff "professionalism." In addition, standardization of the process may reduce the risk. For example, checklists (or inventories, matrices, etc.) frequently are used in SIA. A checklist is simply a long list of impact categories. The list should include virtually every possible impact, but these should be grouped in categories so that the list is not too long and cumbersome. Using a checklist to guide conference discussion or to construct a survey questionnaire serves to insure that certain impacts are not deliberately overlooked. Good SIA checklists are readily available (Duncan and Jones, 1976; Finsterbusch and Wolf, 1977, pp. 43–73; Fitzsimmons et al., 1975; Wolf, 1974).

The public contributions to SIA are most important for identifying possible impact areas. In addition, with sufficient resources it may be possible to include technical analyses by experts (i.e. the planning staff) in an SIA. Several analytical techniques are commonly used. The simplest procedure is comparison of the proposed plan with one or more case studies. The staff may simply refer to their training and experience, or they may actively search for relevant case studies. Two drawbacks to using case studies are that they may be invalid (the reported causal relationships are spurious) or inappropriate (the causal relationships do not hold in different circumstances).

Statistical analysis of a large number of case studies may reduce the problem of appropriateness by parameterizing "local circumstances" and, in sophisticated models, may also increase validity. The case studies may be constructed from census and other official data as well as from one-site observations; they may include data on specific projects and plans, or more likely only data on primary and secondary impacts. Usually the analyses are cross-sectional, or synchronic – for example, Hoch's study (1976) of city size and level of crime. Because SIAs necessarily are dynamic, time series (diachronic) analyses of sequences of events are much more relevant (Burdge and Johnson, 1977) – for example, an analysis of population growth and changes in crime rates in a sample of urban areas observed at different historical periods. (The example would be stronger if it referred to specific projects or plans rather than to the relationship between a primary and a secondary impact.) We are investigating diachronic statistical models for SIA, but at present they seem to hold little promise. Data sets are difficult to assemble, statistical problems are formidable, few planners are competent in this area, and perhaps most important, the technical dazzle of numbers and models may obscure the underlying weaknesses of data quality and theoretical and statistical assumptions.

Other types of analysis commonly performed by expert staff include simulation and preparation of profiles and scenarios. Simulations of traffic flows and air pollution have been useful in planning, but simulations of social systems are likely to have quite limited value in SIA for the near future. Current understanding of social behavior is not sufficiently specific to lead to SIA-type predictions (Conn, 1976; Lee, 1973), due partly to the paucity of relevant diachronic statistical analyses. Also, existing simulation models have been found to be too inaccurate to be useful in SIA and they have been expensive to develop and maintain (Association of Bay Area Governments, 1977). Statistical profiles of areas or populations, based mainly on analysis of census data, are nearly essential for SIA, but profiles alone do not indicate impacts; too often, profiles are used in place of assessments. Scenarios are imaginative, qualitative profiles of future situations and are the oldest form of assessment (science fiction). They have no validity as an analytical tool, but they are useful – and sometimes quite powerful – in presenting the results of an SIA.

It should be clear from this very brief review that, although both experts and the public should contribute to SIA, the ways that they can actually do this usefully are limited. The main validity issue in expert assessments is accuracy; the state of research and data, and indeed the complexity of social life, do not give much comfort here. The main validity issue in public assessments is completeness (i.e. identifying all important impacts); prospects here are less discomforting, yet the problem of bias due to staff involvement is not negligible. Further discussion of these problems must take account of how regional planning agencies operate.

VII. SIA within Agency Constraints

Overview

As mentioned above, the current interest in social impact assessment is largely the result of legal requirements to include social factors in environmental impact assessments. As a result, a substantial portion of research on SIA has focused on incorporating such assessments into the overall planning and impact assessment process. A regional planning agency must prepare social impact assessments required by NEPA, various state impact assessment laws, and related administrative regulations on a variety of plans (air quality, water quality, housing, energy, transportation, land use, etc.). The plans themselves are prepared under severe constraints. The time and technical resources (including staff available) are limited. This sharply curtails the number of alternatives which can be examined and insures that the implications of any one alternative cannot be considered in as much depth as the planners might like. These constraints also imply that planners must be sensitive to the political implications of a given plan alternative. Resource constraints allow little opportunity for substantially modifying a nearly complete plan which contains elements highly objectionable to an organized power group. As a result, planners must attempt to anticipate objections which may be raised when the plan is submitted to the agency's governing body and receives general public scrutiny. A problem with this informal process is that it often forces planners to consider only the concerns of vocal interest groups who have made their influence manifest in the past. Groups which are not organized to protect their interests can easily be ignored in the abbreviated planning process.

Plan evaluation is difficult even in the absence of resource and political constraints. The current state of knowledge in the social and environmental sciences is such that few reliable forecasts of impacts can be generated even under ideal circumstances. The attempts that have been made to use large-scale models to evaluate plan alternatives have been disappointing (Johnston, 1977). The results produced may be technically impressive, but they often lack validity and are often politically irrelevant. More traditional research modes can elucidate specific impacts, but it is often difficult to integrate these individual analyses into an overall assessment.

These constraints suggest that SIA can best serve planners by becoming part of an iterative process. This approach takes into account our limited ability to produce objectively "correct" predictions or satisfactory plans based on these impact predictions in our first attempt. Instead, the process begins with an approximation. The approximation (rough draft or sketch plan) is evaluated and then the plan is revised in light of this first evaluation. The process continues and hopefully converges to a "good" plan. Cyclical planning for transportation systems has been recommended by Gruen Associates (1973) and by Boyce et al. (1970). A similar iterative process has been prescribed for water resources planning (Burke et al., 1973). A recent theoretical basis for iterative planning is found in Etzioni (1967).

Specific Constraints in Regional Planning Agencies

Most regional planning agencies are Councils of Government (COGs) with areawide planning organization, A-95 clearinghouse, indirect source pollutant ("208") water quality planning, and Air Quality Maintenance Agency (AQMA) authorizations. Regional plans being undertaken by these agencies include: land use, transportation/energy, housing, water quality/solid waste, and air quality. The first three types of plans have been broadened in most regional planning agencies to include significant new policy concerns such as energy efficiency and fair-share housing provision. The last two types of plans are new and involve untested policy issues and the development of analytical expertise in new areas of engineering and modeling. All of these plans pose substantial data management problems, staff coordination complexities, potential conflicts between plans, citizen education and participation challenges, and innovative political interchanges between staff and governing body and between governing body and local (member) jurisdictions.

In addition to the new subject matter included in the plans being done during the 1977–1980 period by regional agencies, the legal status of these plans has changed. Instead of the plans being advisory, they now have controlling legal status in the cases of water quality and air quality and considerable legal weight in the cases of transportation and perhaps housing. As a consequence of the much greater importance of these plans to the member jurisdictions, the plans will have to be carefully evaluated for impacts on local governments and be designed to be politically feasible to them. Of special concern to member governments, for example, is the 208 water quality plan which will entail serious local financial costs for nonpoint pollution control, with no federal funding presently available. Both the water quality and air quality plans have severe potential impacts on local government land-use planning discretion, in that these plans are to be enforced by state water and air boards and potentially by the EPA, after adoption by the regional planning agencies.

Experiences to date with 208 water quality plans and air quality maintenance plans indicate that modeling problems are severe, staff management is arduous, and political feasibility concerns are paramount. Funding is inadequate to comply with the congressional mandates and EPA and state guidelines for these plans. Furthermore, the available time periods are discouragingly short, considering the long plan review and approval pathways (three to nine months) and the considerable citizen education and participation requirements.

78

In spite of the rational view of planning that land-use and housing planners generally subscribe to, the systems analysis mentality that grips air quality, water quality, energy, and transportation planners, and the synthesis of these philosophies in the federal and state air quality, water quality, and transportation planning process guidelines and one-shot funding strategies, one must stand back and realize that our current knowledge is inadequate to accurately predict much of relevance. Furthermore, the politics of these plans are changing rapidly, within and among levels and branches of government. These planning processes will be going on indefinitely as political adjustments are made and as technical knowledge increases. Many variables can be known better, such as water runoff or atmospheric mixing; many variables, such as energy prices or consumer behavior, will never be susceptible to accurate prediction. A cursory examination of the many specific action (implementation) programs being considered in the regional planning processes of the San Diego Comprehensive Planning Organization and the Association of Bay Area Governments indicates that the problems of estimating the effects of water quality and air quality policies are well beyond current or future (budgetarily plausible) analysis capabilities (Association of Bay Area Governments, 1976a, 1976b; San Diego Air Quality Planning Team, 1976; San Diego County, 1974). To make matters worse, federal and state standards for air quality, water quality, energy, and housing opportunity are all rapidly changing and their deadlines are also subject to change.

From a theoretical standpoint, regional agencies are not faced with planning under certainty, or planning under risk, or even planning under uncertainty, but planning under "meta-uncertainty." In all probability, we do not know even the identity of some important future environmental (exogenous) variables (such as energy costs, or birth rates, or ?), much less the odds of their occurrence in various states. The only planning strategy appropriate under conditions of pure meta-uncertainty is trial-and-error, where plan effects are estimated from actual experience (Richerson and Johnston, 1975). Since some impacts can probably be estimated against certain assumed future states, however, and most of the important environmental variables are most likely known, we can proceed with a cautious short-term predictive plan evaluation, realizing that our models are subject to large errors in estimating impacts.

Cyclical Planning and SIA

Since we do not know the nature of many future environmental variables and we cannot objectively predict the political concerns that will result from these plan proposals, we should engage in cyclical planning, in order to identify policy issues and get a feel for their importance. Only when we have some idea of the relative importance of the evaluation variables should we expend significant resources in analyzing and evaluating impacts. In these early exploratory years (1977–1980), plan evaluation emphasis should be on the identification of impacts, their intelligent qualitative description and ordinal ranking. In other words, one should not spend time and money on exact but wrong-headed models (Alonso, 1968; Webber, 1968, 1969; Boyce et al., 1970; Holling and Goldberg, 1971; Lee, 1973; Conn, 1976). The evaluation variables that will probably be important, such as local government costs, health effects, effects on federal and state air quality and water quality standards, trip congestion/convenience, low- and moderate-cost housing availability, etc., can be studied now, however. Expending effort on large-scale models will probably be less effective than using sensible estimates of direction-of-change and crude ordinal scaling of impacts. There are too many unknown variables and poorly understood processes at work to place logical reliance on the present generation of models.

Given the untrodden nature of the political and technical paths being followed, investment in detailed research on an *a priori* set of indicators is probably inefficient. Only those evaluation criteria actually required by law or obviously of concern to organized interest groups or to member jurisdictions should even be identified in the early assessments of these plans. Furthermore, only crude analyses of the states of these evaluation variables should be performed until the plans have gone through at least one set of hearings. If at all possible, sketch plans should be "floated" early, either formally or informally to identify policy issues of community concern. Meanwhile, regional agencies should continue the development of their basic expertise in data management, learning from the experiences of large COGs, where, for example, large-scale models are expensive and generally uninformative, in terms of both technical and political concerns.

The cyclical, issue-oriented planning process recommended here – consisting of sketch plans, public and expert identification of impacts, revised plans, and more detailed public and expert SIA (Hudson et al., 1974; Sacramento Regional Area Planning Commission, 1978, 1977) – can be cost-effective and democratic by placing maximum reliance on decision-makers and citizens to reveal their concerns, which are then further studied. All data are heavily *interpreted,* in order to be meaningful to individuals, groups, and jurisdictions. Data portrayal is important: summary accounts need to be used to show trade-offs among alternatives, for example (Johnston, 1977, 1975). Indirect impacts can be identified only by careful thinking through of events by experts and laypersons.

This iterative process has a number of advantages. It encourages planners to brainstorm and to explore a wide range of alternatives in sketch plans. Some of these alternatives may not be viable in themselves, but they can lead to a broader range of options for final plans. The quick feedback from various sources also helps to identify "blind alleys" and potential problems and conflict points. The latter can be flagged for further research and analysis, which insures that scarce staff resources are allocated to problems which will be important in developing and adopting the final plan. The use of information from a variety of publics also promotes public participation.

In the evaluation study of alternative sites for the Third London Airport, perhaps the most expensive civilian public works expenditures analysis ever done, only two of the dozens of evaluation variables studied in great detail appear to have been of major political importance in the final decision: costs for surface transport to get from London to the airport (more for faraway sites) and number of families displaced (more for close-in sites). Millions of dollars were wasted overstudying other variables (Lichfield, 1971). It is nearly impossible to guess in advance what information will be important in the political process. Only by cycling plans can we learn what data, broken out by which groups over what time periods, will need to be estimated accurately. To summarize: plan evaluation, to be politically relevant, should seek to be roughly right rather than precisely wrong.

References

Alonso, W. (1968). "Predicting best with imperfect data," *Journal of the American Institute of Planners* 34: 248–255.
Appelbaum, R. P., Bigelow, J., Karmer, H., Molotch, H. and Relis, P. (1976). *The Effects of Urban Growth*. New York: Praeger.
Association of Bay Area Governments (1976a). "Surface runoff control measures." Draft memorandum dated 6/15/76. Berkeley, CA.
Association of Bay Area Governments (1976b). "Preliminary air quality maintenance candidate control measures." Draft memorandum dated 7/14/76. Berkeley, CA.
Association of Bay Area Governments (1977). "AQMP/Issue Paper 2." Berkeley, CA.
Burdge, R. and Johnson, S. (1977). "Socio-cultural Aspects of the Effects of Resource Development," in McEvoy, J., III and Dietz, T., eds. *Handbook for Environmental Planning*, pp. 241–276. New York: Wiley Interscience.
Berger, P. L. and Luckmann, T. (1966). *The Social Construction of Reality*. Garden City, N.Y.: Doubleday.
Boulder Area Growth Study Commission (1973). *Exploring Options for the Future*, Vols. 8 and 9. Boulder, Colo.: Boulder Area Growth Study Commission.
Boyce, D. E., Day, D., and McDonald, C. (1970). *Metropolitan Plan Making*. Monograph Series, No. 4. Philadelphia, Pa.: Regional Science Institute.
Burke, R., Heaney, J. P., and Pyatt, E. E. (1973). "Water resources and social choices," *Water Resources Bulletin* 9: 432–444.
Campbell, A. and Converse, P. E., eds. (1972). *The Human Meaning of Social Change*. New York: Russell Sage Foundation.
Campbell, A. Converse, P. E., and Rodgers, W. L. (1976). *The Quality of American Life*. New York: Russell Sage Foundation.
Campbell, D. T. (1976). "Focal local indicators for social program evaluation," *Social Indicators Research* 3: 237–256.
Conn, W. D. (1976). "The difficulty of forecasting ambient air quality," *Journal of the American Institute of Planners* 41: 334–346.
Coop, C. A. (1977). "Legal Requirements for Social Impact Analysis," in McEvoy, J., III and Dietz, T. eds., *A Handbook for Environmental Planning*. New York: Wiley Interscience.
Cornish, E. (1977). *The Study of the Future*. Washington, D.C.: World Future Society.
Daffron, C. (1975). "Using NEPA to exclude the poor," *Environmental Affairs* 4: 81–122.
Delbecq, A. and Van de Ven, A. (1971). "A group process model for problem identification and program planning," *Journal of Applied Behavioral Science* 7 (4): 466–492.
De Neufville, J. (1975). *Social Indicators and Public Policy*. New York: Elsevier.
Duncan, O. (1969a). "Social forecasting: The state of the art," *The Public Interest* 17: 88–118.
Duncan, O. (1969b). *Toward Social Reporting*. New York: Russell Sage Foundation.

Duncan and Jones (1976). *Methodology and Guidelines for Assessing Social Impacts of Development.* Berkeley, CA: Duncan and Jones, Inc.
Ehrlich, H. J., (n.d.). *Some Criteria for Radical Social Research.* Report No. 19, Research Group One, 2743 Maryland Ave., Baltimore, Maryland 21218.
Etzioni, A. (1967). "Mixed-scanning: A third approach to decision making," *Public Administration Review* 27: 385–392.
Finsterbusch, K. and Wolf, C. P. (1977). *Methodology of Social Impact Assessment.* Stroudsburg, Pa.: Dowden, Hutchinson and Ross.
Fitzsimmons, S. J., Stuart, L. I., and Wolff, P. C. (1975). *Social Assessment Manual.* Cambridge, Mass.: ABT Associates.
Francis, M. (1974). "The National Environmental Policy Act and the Urban Environment," in Wolf, C. P., ed., *Social Impact Assessment,* pp. 49–58. Milwaukee, Wis.: Environmental Design Research Association.
Friesema, H. P. and Culhane, P. J. (1976). "Social impacts, politics and the environmental impact process," *Natural Resources Journal* 16: 339–362.
Gamble, D. J. (1978). "The Berger inquiry: An impact assessment process," *Science* 199: 946–952.
Greenblat, C. S. and Duke, R. D., eds. (1975). *Gaming-Simulation: Rationale, Design and Applications,* New York: Halstead Press.
Gruen Associates (1973). *Transportation Evaluation Process.* Los Angeles, Calif: Southern California Association of Governments.
Hannan, M. T., (1971). *Aggregation and Disaggregation in Sociology.* Lexington, Mass: Heath.
Haveman, R. and Margolis, J. (1977). *Public Expenditures and Policy Analysis.* Chicago: Markham.
Hill, K. and Fowles, J. (1975). "The methodological worth of the Delphi forecasting technique," *Technological Forecasting and Social Change* 7: 179–192.
Hoch, I. (1976). "City size effects, trends and policies," *Science* 193: 856–863.
Holling, C. S. and Goldberg, M. A. (1971). "Ecology and planning," *Journal of the American Institute of Planners* 37: 221–230.
Hudson, B. M., Wachs, M., and Schofer, J. L. (1974). "Local impact evaluation in the design of large-scale urban systems," *Journal of the American Institute of Planners* 40 (4): 255.
Johnston, R. A., (1975). "Assessing Social and Economic Impacts," in Heffernan, P. and Corwin, R., eds., *Environmental Impact Assessment,* pp. 113–157. San Francisco: Freeman, Cooper and Co.
Johnston, R. A. (1977). "The Organization of Social Impact Information for Use by Decisionmakers and Citizens," in McEvoy, J. III and Dietz, T., eds., *Handbook for Environmental Planning.* New York: Wiley Interscience.
Keyfitz, N. (1972). "On future population," *Journal of the American Statistical Association* 67: 347–363.
Land, K. C. and Spilerman, S., eds. (1975). *Social Indicator Models.* New York: Russell Sage Foundation.
Lee, D. B. (1973). "Requiem for large-scale models," *Journal of the American Institute of Planners* 39: 163–178.
Lichfield, N. (1969). "Cost-benefit analysis in urban expansion: A case study – Peterborough," *Regional Studies* 3: 123–155.
Lichfield, N. (1971). "Cost-benefit analysis in planning: A critique of the Roskill Commission," *Regional Studies* 5: 157–183.
Mack, R. P. (1974). "Criteria for Evaluation of Social Impacts of Flood Management," in Wolf, C. P., ed., *Social Impact Assessment,* pp. 175–195. Milwaukee, Wis.: Environmental Design Research Association.
Mauss, A. L. (1975). *Social Problems and Social Movements.* Philadelphia Pa.: Lippincott.
McCarthy, J. D. and Zald, M. (1973). *The Trend of Social Movements in America: Professionalization and Resource Mobilization.* Morristown, N.J.: General Learning Press.
McEvoy, J., III and Dietz, T. (1977). *Handbook for Environmental Planning.* New York: Wiley Interscience.
McNall, S. G. (1975). *Social Problems Today.* Boston, Mass: Little, Brown.
Merton, R. K. (1976). "The Sociology of Social Problems," in Merton, R. and Nisbet, R., eds., *Contemporary Social Problems,* fourth edition, pp. 3–43. New York: Harcourt, Brace Jovanovitch.

Nagel, T. (1972). "Reason and national goals," *Science* 177: 766–770.
Nelson, R. R. (1977). *The Moon and the Ghetto*. New York: Norton.
Ogburn, W. F. (1946). *The Social Effects of Aviation*. Boston, Mass.: Houghton Mifflin.
Organization for Economic Cooperation and Development (1975). *Methodological Guidelines for Social Assessment of Technology*. Paris: Organization for Economic Cooperation and Development.
Revelle, R. (1971). *Rapid Population Growth*. Baltimore: The Johns Hopkins Press.
Richerson, P. J. and Johnston, R. A. (1975). "Environmental values and water quality planning," *Journal of the Hydraulics Division, American Society of Civil Engineers* 101 (HY2): 259–276. Proc. Paper 11135, February, pp. 259–276.
Rivlin, A. M. (1971). *Systematic Thinking for Social Action*. Washington D.C.: Brookings Institution.
Runyan, D. (1977). "Tools for community-managed impact assessment," *Journal of the American Institute of Planners* 43: 125–135.
Sackman, H. (1974). *Delphi Critique*. Lexington, Mass.: Lexington Books.
Sacramento Regional Area Planning Commission (1977). "Social and Economic Assessment of Regional Plans." Sacramento, CA.
Sacramento Regional Area Planning Commission (1978). "Social and Economic Impact Assessment of Regional Land Use Plan." Sacramento, CA.
San Diego Air Quality Planning Team (1976). "Regional Air Quality Strategies for the San Diego Air Basin." San Diego, CA: San Diego County.
San Diego County (1974). "Regional Organizational Structure for Air Resources Management." San Diego, CA.
San Francisco City and County (1973). "Yerba Buena Center Public Facilities and Private Development: Environmental Impact Report, Draft." San Francisco.
Schnaiberg, A. and Meidinger, E. (1978). "Social Reality Versus Analytic Mythology: Social Impact Assessment of Natural Resource Utilization." Paper presented at the American Sociological Association Annual Meeting, San Francisco.
Sheldon, E. B. and Moore, E. W., eds. (1968). *Indicators of Social Change*. New York: Russell Sage Foundation.
Teich, A. H., ed. (1977). *Technology and Man's Future*, second edition. New York: St. Martin's Press.
U.S. Army Corps of Engineers, Engineering Regulation ER 1105-2-507 ("Section 122 Guidelines").
U.S. Commission on Population Growth and the American Future (1972). *Population and the American Future*. New York: Signet.
U.S. Council on Environmental Quality (1973). "Guidelines to the National Environmental Quality Act," *Federal Register* 38 (147) (Wed., August 1).
U.S. Department of Commerce (1977). "State of California Coastal Management Program and Final Environmental Impact Statement." Washington, D.C.
U.S. Water Resource Council (1973). "Principles and standards for planning water and related land resources," *Federal Register* 38 (174): 24778 ff. (September 10).
Vlachos, E. (1977). "The Use of Scenarios for Social Impact Assessment," in Finsterbusch, K. and Wolf, C. P., eds., *Methodology of Social Impact Assessment*, pp. 211–223. Stroudsburg, Pa.: Dowden, Hutchinson and Ross.
Webber, M. M. (1968, 1969). "Planning in an environment of change," *Town Planning Review* 39 (3): 179–195 and (4): 277–295.
Wolf, C. P. (1974). "Social impact assessment: The state of the art," in Wolf, C. P., ed., *Social Impact Assessment*, pp. 1–44. Milwaukee, Wis.: Environmental Planning Research Association.
Zeckhauser, R. and Schaefer, E. (1968). "Public Policy and Normative Economic Theory," in Bauer, R. and Gergen, K., eds., *The Study of Policy Formation*. New York: The Free Press.

[43]

Getting Social Impact Assessment into the Policy Arena

C.P. Wolf

C.P. Wolf is Research Professor of Social Sciences at the Polytechnic Institute of New York. An active participant in the development of social impact assessment, he publishes a newsletter on that subject. For further information, write him at Box 587, Canal Street Station, New York, New York 10013.

"Social impact assessment" (SIA) is a newly emerging field of interdisciplinary knowledge and application. Its aim is to predict and evaluate the social effects of a policy, program, or project while still in the planning stage — before those effects have occurred. Unlike the more familiar "evaluation research," which gauges the effectiveness of programs already in operation, the task for SIA is *anticipatory* research. It seeks to place the expectation and attainment of desired outcomes — of policy formation, program development, and project implementation — on a more rational and reliable basis.

While the impetus for SIA came largely through passage of the National Environmental Policy Act of 1969 (NEPA), it is gaining prominence in such diverse fields as technology assessment and cultural resources management. Among the topical areas of SIA interest are:

community development	energy development
industrial development	highways and mass transportation
coastal zone management	buildings and housing
water resources	health and human services
weather and climate modification	education and manpower
parks, forests, and wildlands	hazardous and toxic substances

LEVELS OF ASSESSMENT

We can speak of three levels of assessment on which SIA must operate: policy, program, and project. On the policy level, social goals are established and priorities are set for their attainment; the values of environmental preservation and enhancement declared in NEPA are an example. On the program level, plans of action are devised for meeting more specific objectives, such as the Section 208 Program for clean water under P.L. 92-500, the Federal Water Pollution Control Act Amendments of 1972. The project level consists of concrete actions for carrying out these plans and reaching the stated objectives, such as construction of areawide wastewater treatment facilities. Logically, then, the three are interconnected levels of a comprehensive planning system, with program authorizations deriving from policy decisions and project actions supporting program objectives.

It follows that SIA should commence with policies and advance as the policies are translated into programs and embodied in projects. What has happened is just the reverse, however, and this was precisely the experience of environmental impact assessment under NEPA — first projects, next programs, and only then (if at all) the policies themselves: While the practice of SIA has become fairly standard at the project level, and is gradually improving at the program level, little has been attempted or achieved on the level of policy impact analysis. Once begun, we might reasonably expect that SIA would proceed in parallel on all three levels, with due attention to what decisions and actions on any one might imply for both the others. In actual practice, however, assessments conducted on the project level bear slight or no relation to those later conducted on higher levels. This kind of "disjointed incrementalism" is a faithful reflection of the way public business is done in our pluralistic society.

The Project Level

Although project-related SIA is now widely practiced, this is not to say it is consistently done well; as Friesema and Culhane (1976) have described, there are serious institutional methodological obstacles to preparing even minimally adequate social impact statements. On the institutional side, for instance, the full internalization of social costs and benefits would drastically alter the "economic feasibility" of many proposed projects. Analytically, the problem of reckoning those costs and benefits demands the full exercise of integrated social science knowledge crossing many conceptual boundaries. The articulation of institutional and analytic systems, whether they mesh or clash, is itself highly problematic.

Preoccupation with project-level assessments has diverted and distorted the systematic and cumulative development of SIA as a field. Short-term, site-specific assessments consume the bulk of available funding, to the detriment of the more orderly development of generic methodologies.

> As a consequence of this administrative decision making environment, where decision-makers need information about a particular project in a particular place and they need that information immediately, it is no small wonder that there is no universally accepted approach (paradigm) or methodology for conducting SIA.* (Carnes 1977, p. 3)

Because of the responsibilities and pressures under which sponsoring agencies must operate, their insistence on applications and solutions is justified. This kind of "off the shelf" capability must rest on a solid knowledge base, however. Assembling and consolidating that base is the role of research, which is marginal to most agency missions and jurisdictions. Assessment and research then appear as disparate types of professional activity, though progress in SIA depends on linking them firmly together.

The Program Level
While less accustomed in SIA practice, assessments at the program level are becoming more prevalent. Good recent examples are found in the Forest Service's draft of *Social Impact Assessment for Forest Planning and Deicisonmaking* (Bowen et al. 1979), the Bureau of Reclamation's "Revised Rules and Regulations on Excess Lands" and the Bureau of Land Management's request for proposals on "Social Effects of the Federal Coal Management Program in the West." In addition, President Carter's urban message of 27 March 1978 mandates that every new federal program undergo an "urban impact analysis" before it is implemented to determine if it would have a negative impact on cities. So far economic impacts — of revenue sharing, infrastructure investment, job training and the like (Glickman 1979) — have occupied the center of attention, but programs such as self-help neighborhood development capture more fully the social dimensions of urban impact. There is also a voluminous literature of evaluation research on program effectiveness that can be reprocessed for purposes of impact prediction and program design.

The Policy Level
The demand for policy impact analysis has arisen for several reasons: (1) issues of a policy nature are often encountered on the project level, yet they cannot be appropriately or effectively addressed or expressed on that level; (2) rightly or wrongly, it is perceived that environmental impact statements have little or no influence on decision making, and the locus of decision must be approached more directly; (3) there is need for greater compatibility in actions taken by governmental organ-

---

* Table 1 does reflect fairly the broad outlines of the "main pattern" of SIA, however.

izations at different levels of the federal system and for better coordination of governmental operations on the same level; and (4) greater attention to policy questions is required to forestall the side effects and spillovers of environmental modifications and other social interventions. For all these reasons, raising the level of assessment to the policy level is imperative.

Agency interests are nominally confined to executing rather than formulating policy, and few would like to see an agency such as the Corps of Engineers exceed its authority. Nevertheless, managers wield substantial discretionary authority in interpreting and administering policy directives, although their accountability in this regard is not readily apparent. What is evident is that policy questions often arise in conjunction with project actions. For example, Locks and Dam 26 was first presented as a local replacement project well within the Corps' existing authorization (Wade 1977). The Association of Western Railroads objected that this half-billion dollar project was subsidizing unfair competition from barge operators at the taxpayers' expense, and by court order the assessment was expanded to a system-wide consideration of navigation on the Upper Mississippi. Fundamentally, however, it is a question of national transportation (and energy) policy. The general imposition of "user charges" has already been one policy impact of what began as a "local" dispute.

The case of nuclear development is similarly instructive. At local levels, the licensing process has focused on alternative site selection, not whether construction should proceed at all. Public hearings have been limited to "disputed matters of material fact" — technical questions of reactor safety and local environmental and health effects — without regard for broader policy issues presumably "settled" at the federal level, or review of alternative energy systems. Such restrictive terms of reference may be the only ones available *given* existing institutional arrangements, but such arrangements themselves are variable and mutable.

The moral of these cases is that the project level of assessment may preclude considering policy issues of overriding soical importance. In the past, such concerns were relegated to the "normal politics" of elected officials and representative assemblies. Current provisions for public involvement clearly transcend these traditional structures and functions of democratic governance. Whoever "the public" may now be, it is no longer the electorate. This momentous change has come about in no small part because it has been unclear whom the representatives were representing. It remains to be seen how local publics can meaningfully engage national policy issues. Getting a hearing for local concerns is one constructive role SIA can play, if only it can get itself admitted into the policy arena. First of all, that means getting our own act together.

THE SIA "PROBLEMATIQUE"

The problem of SIA can be modestly stated as follows: "How to make public (and private) decisions that will look good in fifty years, after the evaluative criteria by which they are judged have changed." The problem can be further analyzed into these aspects:

1. *The criterion problem.* What does a "good decision look like? How can acceptable planning decisions be reached among multiple objectives for multiple publics employing multiple criteria of evaluation? What are "significant" social impacts? What is an "adequate" social impact statement? What are we "solving for" in SIA?

2. *The analytic problem.* What are the methodological requirements for SIA? How can they be established and satisfied? How can we reconcile questions of objectivity and subjectivity, uniqueness and comparability, within a unified analytic framework? How can we analyze the multiple and reciprocal relations between causes and effects typical of impact situations?

The first is a problem of values — of value conflict and consensus, and of value change and its prediction. The second is a problem of knowledge and the methods by which it can be obtained and verified. In both there is a problem of institutional analysis and institution building, and of organizational and professional commitment.

The Criterion Problem

The underlying (value) assumption of SIA is that "quality of life" or "social well-being" should be elevated to a status at least coequal with other planning objectives which now dominate federal policies and programs, in particular, "national economic efficiency" as conventionally estimated by benefit-cost analysis. This social goal orientation should be the basis and essence of all federal actions, yet in much policy guidance it is deficient or absent. For instance, the purpose of NEPA is to "encourage productive and enjoyable harmony between man and his environment and stimulate the health and welfare of man. . . ." Nonetheless, regulations approved by the Council on Environmental Quality (CEQ) reduce social welfare concerns to an inferior rank. Although NEPA recognizes "the profound impact of man's activities on the interrelations of all components of the natural environments," CEQ relegates the quality of human environments to a category of "secondary impacts." Granted that NEPA was not intended as omnibus social welfare legislation, the artificial separation of natural and human environments must ultimately prove counterproductive.

Even where acknowledged in official policy pronouncements, the relation between instrumental means and socially valued ends is far from certain. While Senate Document 97 (U.S. Senate 1962) proclaims that "Well-being of all the people shall be the overriding determinant in considering the best use of water and related land resources," the result of water project developments such as Tellicoe Dam resembles more the pork barrel than the public interest (Matthiessen 1980). In short, there is a separation of goals and actions that not only impedes progress toward meeting national needs but actively undermines public trust. It is to this condition that SIA is ultimately addressed.

It is a central tenet of SIA that attention be paid to social purposes as well as social consequences. What accounts then for the failure to institute normative planning as the basis for public policy making? Many explanations can be offered — the difficulty in forming societal consensus and forging national commitment, the dissociation of personal and social values, and so on. While SIA cannot remedy these constitutional disorders, it should contribute to the conceptual understanding and operational measurement of "quality of life" and "social well-being." Yet experience to date is not reassuring. EPA's venture into the "quality of life" concept as a tool for environmental management (U.S. Environmental Protection Agency 1973) and the Water Resources Council's efforts to habilitate the "social well-being" account (Andrews et al. 1973) proved unavailing in the past. Some recent work (Solomon et al. 1977) appears more promising, however.

The Analytic Problem

The analytic problem of SIA is to devise operational methodologies and deploy them in operational contexts. As matters now stand, even if responsible agencies and officials know they should take account of social impacts, they are far from confident about how this might be done and what to do with the results. As one HUD official observed,

> Guidance is needed regarding considerations of social impacts of various nature. These have caused difficulties to reviewers, even those with a social science background. The effects of a project on the social community do not lend themselves readily to clear analysis, and recognized criteria are lacking to objectively evaluate their significance and to weigh beneficial and detrimental consequences over [the] short and long term.

This is no isolated example; a comprehensive and continuing review of agency requirements on all governmental levels is a priority utilization research need. If SIA is to become "use knowledge" for societal problem solving, its potential uses and users must be clearly identified. Effective assertion of the federal interest in SIA must necessarily proceed on an agency-by-agency basis, however. For example, Llewellyn (1976) has urged a concern for social well-being by the U.S. Fish and Wildlife Service on grounds of the changing constituency of the Service, the secondary effects of highways on fragile ecosystems, and the viability of the endangered species program. In any case, agency acceptance will depend on SIA's perceived utility in satisfying mission requirements as they exist and evolve. Such acceptance will be facilitated by state-of-the-art improvements in the methodology of SIA.

SIA is a multi-method approach, and part of the analytic problem is to evaluate the wide variety of methodologies and techniques that practitioners employ (Finsterbusch and Wolf 1977; McEvoy and Dietz 1977). As Carnes notes:

> The methodology of SIA is quite varied, and has included ethnographic research (Gold), survey research (Finsterbusch), secondary data analysis (Dunning), content analysis (Motz), and community studies (Carnes), among others. While each and every one of these methodological approaches can contribute to the analysis of outcomes of social change, we desperately need to analyze exactly what each of these approaches can contribute at what cost, with what validity, and with respect to what kind of results. (1977, p. 7)

The critical factor for methodological development, however, is to fit this array into a continuous and self-consistent series of assessment steps.

The main pattern of analysis in SIA is shown in Table 1; this pattern can be explicated at great length and elaborated in minute detail. In problem identification, for example, determining what "the problem" is incurs complications of who the definers are and what definitions they employ. In one instance of local flooding around Athens, Ohio, the problem might be stated as "keeping the water away from the people," in which case the reasonable alternatives would be different configurations of flood control structures. Conversely, however, the problem might be stated as "keeping the people away from the water," in which case the reasonable alternatives would be different measures for floodplain management. Similar questions can be posed for the remaining assessment steps in the series.

Further elaborations involve associating general methodologies with each analytic operation — e.g., demographic (cohort) analysis with needs assessment; specific techniques with each methodological approach — e.g., cluster analysis with impact area delineation; and data sources and sets with each technique — e.g., census tract data with indicator measurement. This pattern of analysis exhibits an exponential rate of expansion and has not yet been rigorously unfolded to a high level of detail. As it stands, the series possesses undoubted heuristic value, for example, in mapping convergence or divergence with other methodological approaches and assimilating their findings. For specific application to actual impact situations, it requires extensive adaptation and calibration.

Special problems requiring intensive methodological development arise at many — in fact, most — points in the series. For example, regarding the specification of broad societal trends to local impact predictions, Christopher Freeman of the Science Policy Research Unit, University of Sussex, underscores "the need to relate 'macro' forecasts to the underlying 'micro' processes. . . ." In the case of energy impacts of residential development, for instance, population projections would need to be analyzed in terms of number, size, and composition of households; their likely preferences for various housing types; and

Table 1

SOCIAL IMPACT ASSESSMENT:
THE MAIN PATTERN

QUESTIONS	ASSESSMENT STEPS	ANALYTIC OPERATIONS
0. What are the "terms of reference"?	SCOPING (preassessment)	Set level(s) of assessment (policy/program/project) Determine impact area boundaries Establish time horizons
1. What is the problem? What is causing it?	PROBLEM IDENTIFICATION	Formulate policy goals, planning objectives Identify publics and concerns Perform needs assessment Determine evaluative criteria
2. What are the alternatives?	FORMULATION OF ALTERNATIVES	Define set of "reasonable" alternatives (corresponding to identified concerns) Determine change agents and instruments Characterize and describe technical systems Analyze for social (institutional/behavioral) components and correlatives Analyze economic and environmental impacts for secondary social impacts
3. What is the system? Who is being affected and how?	PROFILING	Dimension impact categories Select impact categories Assign impact indicators Perform indicator measurements Compile social profile
4. What is it causing?	PROJECTION	Explicate "state of society" assumptions Perform trend impact analysis Construct dynamic system models Estimate impact indicator values for alternative plans ("with and without" implementation)
5. What difference does it make?	ASSESSMENT	Perform sensitivity analysis for alternative outcomes of alternative plans Perform cross-impact analysis Describe and display "significant" impacts
6. How do you like it?	EVALUATION	Reidentify publics and concerns Reformulate evaluative criteria Rank and weight preferences for aternatives Perform tradeoff analysis Identify preferred alternative
7. What can you do about it if you don't like it?	MITIGATION	Review unavoidable adverse impacts Identify possible mitigation measures Perform sensitivity analysis of possible measures
8. How good are your guesses?	MONITORING	Measure actual vs. predicted impacts Feed back measurements to policy makers and publics Adjust planning objectives, operating procedures, design specifications

Now associate and integrate *general methodologies,*
specific techniques, and *relevant data.*

the relative energy efficiencies of these different structures and settlement patterns.

One particularly obdurate problem that deserves special mention is that of data availability and quality. A preliminary reconnaissance of social impact data requirements and existing resources (Tunstall 1978) has disclosed major gaps in the information available for environmental policy planning in many areas of governmental operation. This survey was limited to national policy data; equivalent needs and lacks are encountered at regional, state, and local levels. Detailed, site-specific data are required for every planning project. Often the data collection is so laborious that data analysis is slighted, and whether the data gathered are the *right* ones for analytic purposes is seldom questioned or tested. Ideally, data requirements would be generated by analytic requirements, themselves structured according to the nature of the problem or situation being investigated. In practice, the ideal is usually abandoned in favor of convenience, with indeterminate results.

SUMMARY

From this discussion, it can safely be inferred that the problem of SIA remains "ill-defined" in respect to the desired outcomes and steps necessary for achieving them. Yet policy questions are also of this order, and methodologies suited to policy analysis must share in its ambiguity. It would be misleading and mischevious to believe that greater analytic precision alone will improve the quality of policy decisions. The resolving power required must begin with determining "the direction of the sign" — whether predicted impacts are positive or negative. For example, it is not obvious whether the number of lawyers or hospital beds per thousand population is a good or bad thing. "Getting the numbers right" in most policy decisions is a matter of orders of magnitude, not parts per million. In the case of anticipatory research, moreover, the facts in question are "future facts" which have no empirical existence. The first approximation to an answer, then, is to get the question right.

For all its problems, there is growing acceptance that SIA ought and can be done and done well. Doing it consistently and competently will require further theoretical, methodological, institutional and professional development across a wide range of interests and activities. A substantial body of experience and expertise has accumulated within an active community of seasoned and skilled practitioners. If the problems are imposing, so also are the possibilities.

REFERENCES

Andrews, W.H. et al., eds. 1973. *The Social Well-Being and Quality of Life Dimensions in Water Resources Planning and Development.* Institute for Social Science Research on Natural Resources, Utah State University, Logan, Utah.

Bowen, P. et al., 1979. *Social Impact Assessment for Forest Planning and Decisionmaking.* Technical review draft. Northern Region, Forest Service, U.S. Department of Agriculture, Missoula, Montana.

Carnes, S. 1977. *Electric Centralization Research Project: Theoretical Background and a Preliminary Research Plan.* Discussion draft. Center for Urban Affairs, Northwestern University, Evanston, Illinois.

Finsterbusch, K., and Wolf, C.F., eds. 1977. *Methodology of Social Impact Assessment.* Stroudsburg, Penn.: Dowden, Hutchinson and Ross.

Friesema, H.P., and Culhane, P.J. 1976. Social Impacts, Politics and the Environmental Impact Statement Process. *Natural Resourcs Journal* 16:339-56.

Glickman, N.J. ed. 1979. *The Urban Impacts of Federal Policies.* Baltimore, Md.: Johns Hopkins University Press.

Llewellyn, L.G. 1976. Toward a Social Science Role in the Fish and Wildlife Service. Unpublished manuscript. Division of Program Plans, U.S. Fish and Wildlife Service, Washington, D.C.

Matthiessen, P. 1980. How to Kill a Valley. *The New York Review of Books* 27:31-36.

McEvoy, J., and Dietz, T., eds. 1977. *Handbook for Environmental Planning: The Social Consequences of Environmental Change.* New York: John Wiley.

Solomon, R.C. et al. 1977. *Water Resources Assessment Methodology (WRAM) — Impact Assessment and Alternative Evaluation.* Technical Report Y-77-1 (interim report). Environmental Effects Laboratory, U.S. Army Engineer Waterways Experiment Station, Vicksburg, Mississippi.

Tunstall, D.B. 1978. Investigating and Identifying Social Data Needs for Environmental Analysis: A Draft Report to the Socioeconomic Working Group (unpublished manuscript).

U.S. Environmental Protection Agency 1973. *The Quality of Life Concept — A Potential New Tool for Decision-Makers.* Washington, D.C.: U.S. Government Printing Office.

U.S. Senate 1962. Policies, Standards, and Procedures in the Formulation, Evaluation, and Review of Plans for Use and Development of Water and Related Land Resources. Document No. 97. Washington, D.C.: U.S. Government Printing Office.

Wade, R. 1977. Social Impact Assessment for the Locks and Dam No. 26 Study. In Institute for Water Resources, ed., *Social Scientists Conference: III. Water Transportation Planning,* pp. 106-16. U.S. Army Engineer Institute for Water Resources, Fort Belvoir, Virginia.

[44]
STATE OF THE ART IN SOCIAL IMPACT ASSESSMENT

KURT FINSTERBUSCH is an Associate Professor of Sociology at the University of Maryland. He received his Ph.D. from Columbia University and was Executive Associate of the American Sociological Association. He is author of Understanding Social Impact and is co-editor of Social Impact Assessment Methods and Methodology of Social Impact Methods. His current interest is in the field of impact assessment of development projects in Third World countries.

ABSTRACT: This article reviews the state of the art in social impact assessment (SIA). SIA is distinguished from problem analysis, policy development research, and evaluation research. Five sub-fields in SIA are identified. The general methodology for SIA is outlined, and a sophisticated methodology for assessing the social impacts of constructing major facilities is explained in detail. Several innovative research techniques or methodologies have been adapted to SIA requirements and are reviewed. New directions in SIA are identified including cumulative impact analysis, accounting of positive social impacts, monetizing stress factors, and new public involvement techniques.

AUTHOR'S NOTE: *This is a revision of an article presented at the annual meetings of the International Sociological Association, Session on Social Policy Research and Social Policy Analysis, Mexico City, August 16-24, 1982.*

The practice of social impact assessment (SIA) has improved dramatically since it began as a distinct field of applied social science around 1970. At first, there was considerable uncertainty about what SIAs should study and how to go about it. During the 1970s, the general methodology of SIA was developed along with specific methodologies designed for specific types of SIAs. In this review, the general SIA methodology and an SIA methodology designed for the construction of facilities is reported. These methodologies require the use of the standard social science research procedures of surveys of respondents, informant interviews, field observations, use of records and documents, and study of published accounts and statistics. They also use a number of special or innovative research procedures of which nine were selected for brief explication.

Past accomplishments and areas of needed and likely development are identified. Accordingly, seven new directions for SIA methodology are suggested.

DEFINING AND DISTINGUISHING SIA

Social impact assessment is a current buzz word, and is used to describe almost any type of research that looks at social factors. In this state of the art review, however, it is used as a technical term for the estimation of all significant impacts of potential policies, programs, or projects on individuals, groups, organizations, neighborhoods, communities, institutions, and other social units. To define it more precisely, it is distinguished from other types of policy research below.

There are five basic types of policy research, though actual studies may contain elements of several types. Each type answers a different question. The five types and their related questions are:

(1) Problem identification: "What is the problem?"
(2) Policy development: "What should be done?"

(3) Impact assessment: "Which alternative is best?"
(4) Program evaluation: "Is the program worthwhile?"
(5) Program improvement: "How can it be improved?"

The first two basic policy types occur after there is a governmental concern about a problem that needs to be addressed and before the policy or program is devised. The first, *problem identification,* attempts to identify the parameters of the problem. How many people are in need? Where are current facilities or programs inadequate and additional ones needed? How much harm is caused by various unregulated actions of people and organizations?

An understanding of the extent of a problem and its many dimensions is the first step in a policy analysis. A solid grasp of the problem's dimensions often suggests by itself the policy or program that is needed, such as when badly congested or delayed traffic suggests the need for a highway. Often, however, additional research is needed to develop appropriate policies and programs. *Policy development* research normally produces information in three areas: characteristics of the target population, policy analysis in terms of requirements and expected effects, and the expected actions of affected parties. For example, if problem identification research has scoped out the dimensions of child abuse in a county, policy development research would specify the characteristics of abusing parents and abused children, identify potential policies or programs for dealing with the problem, and suggest how abusing parents might respond to various government actions toward them. Policy development research also would have to find out why parents abuse their children in order to know how to handle abusing parents, and would have to find out more about the abused children to reach them with help.

Impact assessment fits into policy research after the policy or program has been devised and before it is implemented. Impact assessment seeks to compare the impacts of alternative policies or programs in order to choose the "best" policy for implementation. The impacts are normally divided into the economic, environmental, and social. The economic impacts include the cost of implementing the action and the economic costs and benefits to the society in terms of jobs, sales, taxes, expenditures, and revenues. Social impacts involve impacts on individuals, groups, organizations, communities, regions, institutions, and other social units. They include impacts on specific governments and other political consequences, though these impacts are sometimes separated out into a separate political impact analysis.

Program evaluation analyzes already existing policies, programs, and projects in order to determine whether they should be continued or stopped, expanded or contracted, slowed down or accelerated. *Program improvement* is the final basic type of policy research and normally is conducted as part of a program evaluation study. Program improvement research gathers information that identifies program defects to be corrected and evaluates ways to improve the program.

The five basic types of policy research require different research strategies. Problem identification must define and measure the problem. Policy development must analyze the causes of the problem and identify the variables that can be manipulated or controlled. Impact assessment must estimate all potentially significant impacts of a potential project. It does not measure what has happened but it must try to predict what will happen. Program evaluation must determine evaluation criteria and then measure the policy or program effects in terms of these criteria. After it measures changes that have taken place, it must determine whether the changes are due to the program or to other factors. Finally, program improvement must predict the effects of program modifications. It is similar to impact assessment in predicting rather than measuring impacts, but it deals with much smaller changes, and it focuses on the evaluation criteria rather than on the total array of significant impacts.

SIA SUBFIELDS

SIA is a mode of analysis that could be used for any potential government or nongovernment action, but, in fact, has been essentially limited to five sets of actions that define the major subfields in SIA:

(1) new technologies
(2) constructed facilities
(3) environment use plans
(4) environmental designs
(5) development projects in the third world

The assessment of *new technology* is probably the most difficult SIA subfield, because the action that has its impacts assessed is unique, for example, the application of technologies for predicting earthquakes, determining the sex of one's offspring, retarding the aging process, controlling weather, offshore mining, harnessing solar energy, or telecommunicating. Assessors must predict potential impacts with little or no comparable historical experience on which to base predictions. As a result, subjective judgments and methods for making them as rigorous as possible such as the delphi technique (discussed later) are important for these studies.

The largest and most developed SIA subfield is SIAs for *constructed facilities* such as highways, dams, power plants, waste disposal or treatment plants, airports, pipelines, and transmission lines. Unlike technology assessments, SIAs for constructed facilities can predict on the basis of past case studies. This feature has allowed for a considerable amount of accumulated knowledge on the social impacts of constructed facilities that I have tried to summarize elsewhere (Finsterbusch, 1980). Methodologies for SIAs of constructed facilities are also well developed and fairly standardized. A summary is presented in a later section.

Environment use plans include many government activities for which environmental impact assessments are mandated but that either do not involve construction or treat it as only a secondary consideration. These include many policies and programs of agencies that manage public lands or provide wildlife services such as Fish and Wildlife Service, Bureau of Land Management, Forest Service, and the Park Service. The SIAs for such actions have less standardized information to build on than SIAs for constructed facilities, but excellent progress has been made in SIA methodology in this area. A particularly strong feature of many SIAs of this type is the heavy use of public participation and the development of effective techniques for generating and using public participation (see later section).

Research on *environmental design* is the offspring of the marriage of architecture and psychology and is professionally represented by the Environmental Design Research Association. It focuses on the relationship between constructed environments and human behavior. It usually involves the construction of facilities, but it is distinguished from the constructed facilities subfield for two reasons: (1) They involve two fairly separate networks of social scientists and look at very different problems. Constructed facilities are usually large buildings that displace significant numbers of people and activities and/or require a large labor force that significantly increases the population of nearby communities. (2) Environmental design research is more concerned with the impacts of constructed environments on the people who use and occupy them, and it is interested in the effects of different designs on behavior and satisfaction.

Development projects in the third world is a subfield of SIA that takes into account third world conditions, the politics of joint sponsorship by the development agency and the recipient country, and the economic and social criteria of the development agency. This subfield is distinguished from constructed facilities only by the foreign settings for its projects and some unique traditions about conducting SIAs.

GENERAL METHODOLOGY FOR SIA

In the early 1970s, considerable effort was devoted to the development of general methodologies. This phase of the development of the field of SIA has been completed for several years and several reviews of general methodologies are available including Finsterbusch, 1975; Finsterbusch and Motz, 1980; Fitzimmons et al., 1977; Leistritz and Murdock, 1981; and the three general SIA methodologies found in Finsterbusch and Wolf, 1981; i.e., by Armour et al., 1981; by Watkins, 1981; and by Olsen et al., 1981. Each version uses somewhat different terms and seems to give somewhat different directives, but essentially they are variations on the same themes.

In the interest of standardization, Wolf's (1983) outline of a general SIA methodology is adopted for presentation here. His methodology is based on the ten steps presented in Table 1. Often, the government agencies that sponsor SIAs limit them to steps 4, 5, and 6, but SIAs should ideally include steps 1, 2, 3, 7, and 8. When SIA researchers are left out of steps 1-3, projects are likely to produce more adverse effects. SIA researchers can help scope and define the assessment issues and help formulate alternatives in a manner that makes them more socially acceptable. SIA researchers should also have an active role in evaluation and mitigation in order to minimize the negative effects and to maximize the benefits of the project or policy.

Three important stages of the SIA are profiling, projecting, and assessing. SIAs start with descriptions of the current situation and then attempt to project the future situation in order to estimate the impact. Monitoring and management are not usually suggested as part of SIA, but

TABLE 1
Social Impact Assessment: General Methodology

Assessment Steps	Analytic Operations
Scoping How big a problem is it? How much is enough?	Set level(s) of assessment (policy/program/project). Determine impact area boundaries. Establish time horizons. Develop study design.
Problem Identification What is the problem? What is causing it?	Formulate policy goals, planning objectives. Identify publics and concerns. Perform needs assessment. Determine evaluative criteria.
Formulation of Alternatives What are the alternatives?	Define set of "reasonable" alternatives (corresponding to identified concerns). Determine change agents, instruments. Characterize and describe technical systems; analyze for social (institutional/behavioral) components and correlates. Analyze economic and environmental impacts for secondary social impacts.
Profiling Who is being affected?	Dimensionalize impact categories. Select impact categories. Assign impact indicators. Perform indicator measurements. Compile social profile.
Projection What is it causing?	Explicate "state of society" assumptions. Perform trend impact analysis. Construct dynamic system models. Estimate impact indicator values for alternative plans ("with and without" implementation).
Assessment What difference does it make?	Perform sensitivity analysis for alternative outcomes of alternative plans. Perform cross-impact analysis. Describe and display "significant" impacts.
Evaluation How do you like it?	Reidentify publics and concerns. Reformulate evaluative criteria. Rank and weight preferences for alternatives. Perform trade-off analysis. Identify preferred alternative.
Mitigation What can you do about it? if you do not like it?	Review unavoidable adverse impacts. Identify possible mitigation measures. Perform sensitivity analysis of possible measures.

(continued)

TABLE 1 Continued

Assessment Steps	Analytic Operations
Monitoring How good are your guesses?	Measure actual versus predicted impacts. Provide feedback of measurements to policy-makers and publics.
Management Who is in charge here?	Devise management plan. Adjust planning objectives, operating procedures, design specifications.
(Bottom Line) Who benefits and who loses?	(All of the above.)

Now, associate and integrate general methodologies, specific techniques, and relevant data.

SOURCE: Wolf (1983)

Wolf says that SIA should incorporate these steps and monitoring is discussed in a later section.

AN SIA METHODOLOGY FOR FACILITY CONSTRUCTION

The SIA literature on facility construction has reached a consensus on the basic elements of methodology. These elements will be outlined below and the reader is referred to Leistritz and Murdock (1981), Olsen et al. (1981), Flynn and Flynn (1982), and Flynn et al. (1983) for three different and effective elaborations on this basic model.

The SIA for facility construction needs to examine or predict the following socioeconomic conditions or changes:

(1) dimensions of the project
(2) existing social and economic conditions
(3) economic changes
(4) demographic changes
(5) supply/demand changes in housing, private goods and services, and public goods and services

(6) changes in community structure (government, intergroup relations, organizations)
(7) changes in quality of life or social well-being

The connections between these factors are as follows: the project directly and indirectly changes the other factors within limits determined by the social and economic conditions. Subsequently, the major causal flow is down the list. The project creates jobs and income that cause demographic changes. Together, these cause changes in the supply and demand for goods and services. Thereupon all of these changes cause changes in community structure and subsequently cause changes in quality of life and social-well being. In effect, the SIA compares the community without the project on these dimensions to the anticipated community with the project.

Figures 1 and 2 present the flow diagrams for Olsen et al. (1981) and Flynn et al. (1983) methodologies. They embody the above list of elements and add some additional elements. Olsen et al. add a management component that emphasizes amelioration of negative social impacts. Flynn and her colleagues emphasize the principal functional groups in the community, their interaction patterns, the distribution of positive and negative effects on the different groups, and the response of the groups to the project and its impacts. The special emphases of both Olsen et al. and Flynn et al. are important for effective SIAs for facility construction and should be consulted in the originals because they cannot be covered adequately here. We will briefly elaborate, however, on Flynn and her colleagues' plan for assessing social structure effects because this is the most original contribution of their methodology.

This distinctive feature of the social effects methodology of Flynn and her colleagues is its focus on functional groups, that is, groupings that are discernible to area residents and have identifiable roles in the political and

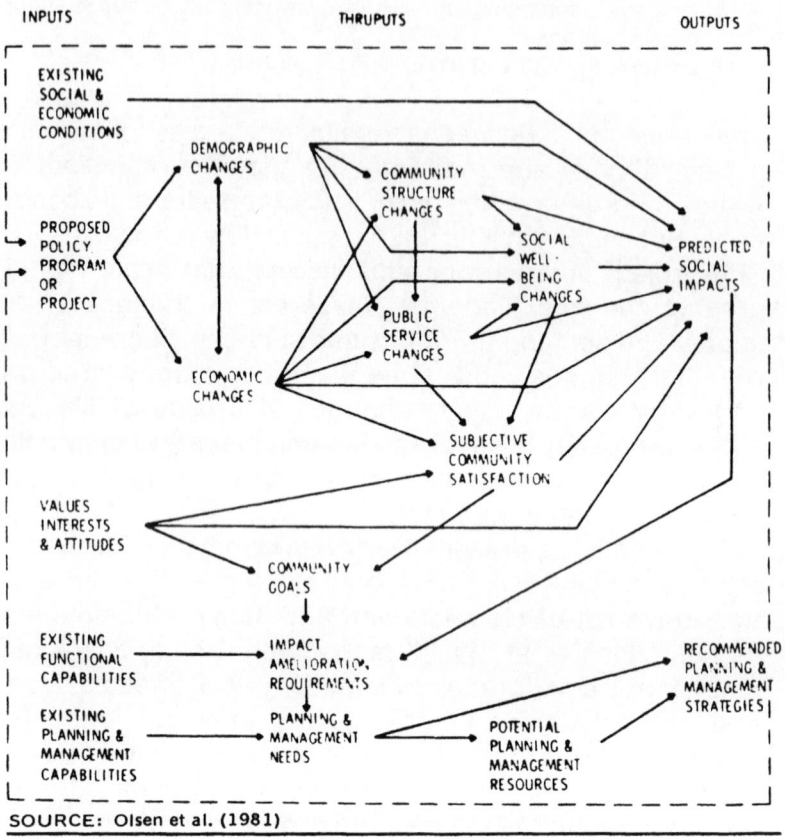

Figure 1: General Social Impact Assessment and Management Model

SOURCE: Olsen et al. (1981)

social structure of the community. Through interviews they develop a profile of each group in terms of seven attributes:

(1) size of the group
(2) livelihood of group members
(3) demographic characteristics
(4) geographic location (residential and occupational)
(5) property ownership characteristics
(6) dominant attitudes and values toward growth, environment, community participation, and planning.
(7) patterns of interaction among group members (cohesion)

SOURCE: Flynn et al. (1983)

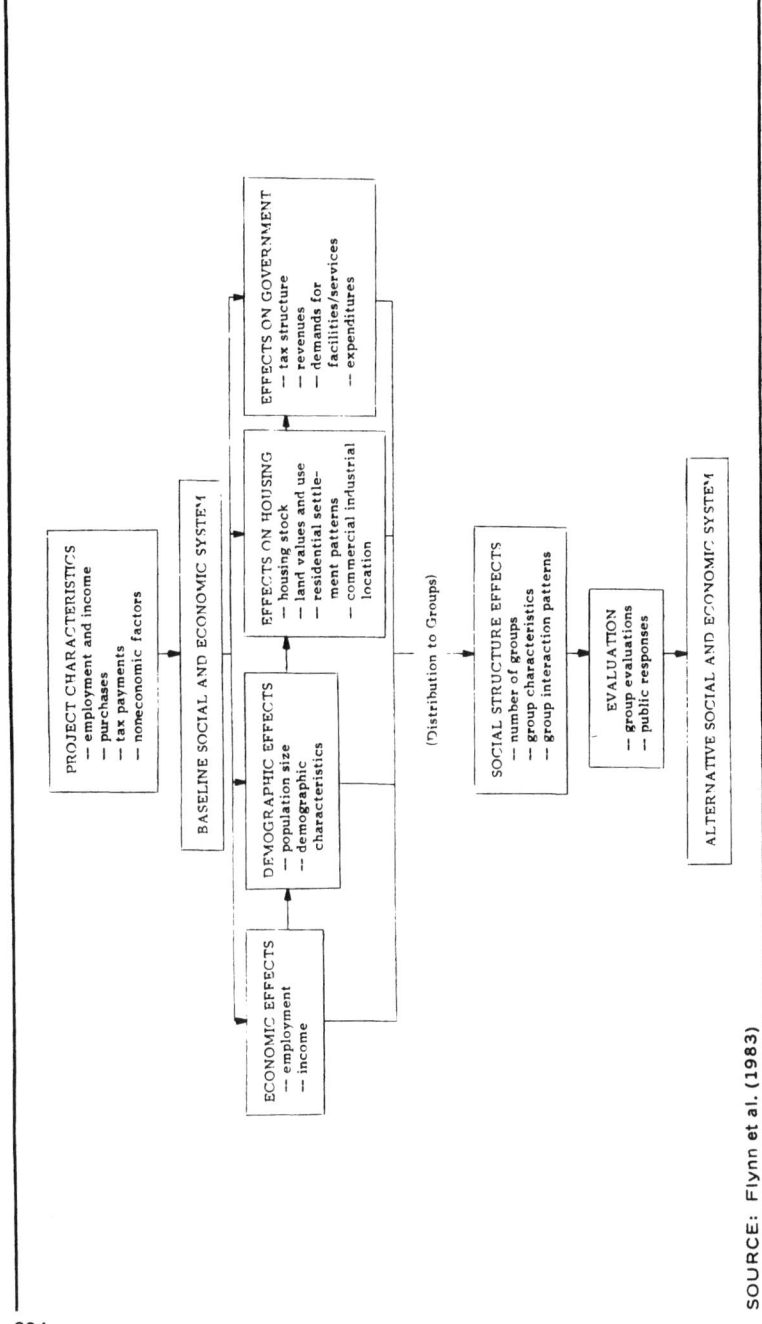

Figure 2: Group Ecology Model for the Assessment of Social and Economic Change

where possible averages and standard deviations on these attributes are calculated for each group. Then the patterns of interactions between each pair of groups are assessed in the areas of economic, political, and social relations in terms of dimensions such as cooperation/competition/conflict, superordination/subordination, or positive/negative attitudes. Next, these patterns of interaction are projected into the future both with and without the project using standard projection techniques such as we review in the next section. These projections need to take into account changing demographic characteristics of local groups and economic changes in the study area on the one hand, and relevant national trends on the other. Finally, the distribution among groups of the economic, demographic, housing, government, and fiscal effects of the project are estimated.

SPECIAL RESEARCH TECHNIQUES

SIA uses the full array of standard research techniques, but also has developed some special techniques for dealing with its own peculiar research needs. In this section, a number of these special research techniques are introduced, and their role in the general SIA methodology is identified.

Profiling is the SIA step that describes the social units affected by the policy, program, or project. I call the basic research procedure for profiling "data hunting." The social scientist acts like a newsperson and ferets out available statistical and descriptive information on these social units. In more substantial SIAs, surveys and systematic field observations are also used.

An innovation profiling technique is *regional statistical modeling* (it is also a projecting technique). The most handy explication of socio-economic statistical models that have been developed for use in SIA is found in Murdock and Leistritz (1983), Leistritz and Murdock (1981), and

Leistritz et al., (1979). These models are designed to profile and project the economic, demographic, public service, and fiscal impacts of large construction or development projects on the surrounding region. They use site specific primary statistical data and state, county, and subcounty secondary statistical data in dynamic systems models. The models predict supply and demand for public services and government expenditures on the basis of the project's economic and demographic impacts.

To date, these models have not been tested adequately. Partial tests of the types of projections used in these models, however, do suggest their forecasting accuracy needs to be improved before they can be widely used in SIAs (Gilmore et al., 1981; Murdock et al., 1982). The major source of error found in these tests was a significant underestimation of the peak construction labor force and these estimates were obtained from the construction companies themselves.

Projection is the SIA step that predicts the impacts of potential policies, programs, and projects. The basic research procedure for projecting is to find out what has happened in similar cases and to estimate whether the same thing will happen again. The researcher must consider whether there are unique aspects of the potential action or situation that would cause a deviation from the general pattern of previous cases. The basis for this type of prediction should be systematic summarization and case studies for common types of government actions such as highways or power plants. Finsterbusch (1980) presents this type of summary for a number of social impact assessment areas.

Two innovative projecting techniques are scenarios and delphi projections. A *scenario* provides "narrative descriptions of potential courses of development. It attempts to sketch a logical sequence of events in order to show how, under present conditions and assumptions, a future state or set of alternative states might evolve" (Vlachos, 1981: 162).

It is not a prediction of what will occur but of what might occur. By describing an array of possible future consequences of an action, a set of scenarios can apprise decision makers and potentially affected parties of the possible costs and benefits of the action. They can also suggest steps for preventing certain potential consequences.

Anyone with an uninhibited imagination can create scenarios, but there are guidelines and techniques that can aid the process (Abt et al., 1973; deLeon, 1975; Gerardin, 1973). Perhaps the most important rule is to identify the key assumptions used in the scenarios so that the reader can better judge their plausibility. They should be reasonable and reflect probabilities suggested by past experiences with similar actions. They should be reasonably complete in that the levels of all major relevant variables should be identified. Finally, scenarios should be critiqued by other experts and their credibility discussed. The delphi procedure discussed below can be employed usefully in the critiquing of the scenarios.

Delphi projection is a technique for maximizing the reliability of the subjective judgments of a group of experts (see Delbecq, 1975). When social impacts are estimated for standard actions such as highway or dam construction, there is little need for subjective judgments by experts. The more distinct the situation or action, however, the greater the importance of subjective judgments. These judgments can be obtained from the experts either individually or in groups and both methods have drawbacks. Experts' judgments gathered individually do not have the benefit of criticism and debate. Experts' judgments gathered in a group are adversely affected by normal group dynamics. One or two opinion leaders come to dominate the group and many of the opinions of others are not expressed.

The delphi technique is designed to solve the problem of both individual and group judgments. It involves several rounds of individually conducted interviews with the experts. After each round, the experts critique each others' ideas and means and standard deviations for quantified judgments are computed for the group. These are fed back to each expert so he or she is informed of the degree of unpopularity or deviance of his or her views. He or she can then revise or defend them in the next round and the process is repeated until the group opinion stabilizes. The delphi projection reports the mean opinion and the degree of consensus (standard deviation) on it. Minority opinions that hold out to the last round are also reported. (Also see Delbecq, 1975, for a description of the nominal group technique for generating group judgments.)

Assessment of impacts is an SIA step that estimates the difference that the action makes. It compares the projected state of affairs with and without the action. Again, a wide range of commonly used techniques in the social sciences are appropriate to this process, but we single out three uncommon techniques as especially appropriate for SIAs: mini surveys, visual impact techniques, and the cross impact matrix.

Mini surveys are especially appropriate for SIAs because research funds are often insufficient for full scale surveys. A mini survey is a normal random sample survey with an abnormally small sample size, that is, 20 to 100 respondents. Mini surveys can be conducted in one or two days at a low cost and they provide rich informational returns per dollar spent. In fact, the cost of each additional respondent is practically constant and the benefit in statistical accuracy declines in ratio to $\sqrt{n-1}$. In other words, one must roughly quadruple the sample size in order to double the accuracy of the results (halve the confidence interval). Sophisticated multivariate analyses of a complex system of variables should be based on several hundred respondents at least, but SIAs report mainly univariate distributions that require far fewer respondents. Finsterbusch (1977) describes elsewhere several ways that mini surveys can be used in SIAs and argues that surveys of small samples are useful for many research needs (Finsterbusch, 1976a, 1976b).

The application of *visual techniques* to SIA has been described by Palmer (1981). He delineates two basic approaches to the assessment of visual impacts; professional appraisals and landscape perception. Professional appraisals are standardized criteria to assess visual quality in terms of visibility, landscape features, land use patterns, and aesthetic composition. "The scenic value of these criteria are primarily based on traditional values within the landscape architecture profession. However, they are supported to some extent by recent landscape perception research" (Palmer, 1981: 285).

Landscape perception approaches for assessing visual quality selects a medium to present or simulate the environment in testing the response of a sample of the viewing public to various environmental designs. The presentation media might be sketches, models, computer graphics, photographs, or photographic composites. The evaluators then rate the presentations using rating scales or objective check lists.

Another procedure is to give the evaluators cameras and have them take pictures of what they like as they pass through an area. A final method is cognitive mapping in which respondents draw an area in terms of features that are important to them.

The *cross impact matrix* is a simple assessment aid that forces the analyst to consider higher order impacts of the proposed action. Each significant impact is placed in both a column and a row of matrix and each cell is subjectively scored for the degree of impact that the column change (impact) might have on the row change. Obviously all of the impacts will not occur independently of each other and the cross impact matrix forces an accounting of interdependent effects. Once they are subjectively identified, important higher order or cross impacts should be assessed more rigorously.

Evaluation is the SIA step that judges the value of both positive and negative impacts. It is a subjective act based on the values of the evaluator. Evaluation techniques aid this process and thereby improve the judgments. Many SIAs stop with assessment and make no attempt to evaluate. Evaluation is left up to the decision maker. When the decision involves many types of impacts and no one alternative emerges as the obvious best choice, the decision maker could benefit from evaluation aids such as the three discussed below.

Subjective weighting is the simplest procedure. It can be applied directly to the alternatives or applied to the impact dimensions. In the former, each judge rates each alternative on a scale (1 to 10 or 1 to 100) or simply ranks them. The judges' scores are added up and the highest score wins as in gymnastic events. Judgmental psychology research has shown, however, that judges can only keep a few criteria in mind at once and will reduce the decision to manageable proportions by practically excluding some criteria and overemphasizing others (see Mumpower and Anderson, 1983). For complex judgments, it may be advisable to have the judges rate the impact criteria. The set of average ratings are then used as weights to be multiplied by the impact scores (standardized) in computing a total rating for each alternative (for a variety of weighting techniques, see Finsterbusch, 1981; Nijkamp and Sprank, 1981; Hwang and Masud, 1979; MacCrimmon, 1973).

Interpretive structural modeling is one of several computer methods for assisting group decision making for complex problems. The group generates the elements (impacts, objectives, criteria) being evaluated and judges how pairs relate to each other or compare to each other. The computer orders the questions, ensuring that all elements are fitted into the hierarchical structure of objectives or criteria. The computer then computes and graphically displays the structure among the elements that evolves from the group process. This graph can serve as a focus for communication and debate. In the process, both the group and the individuals separately sharpen their understanding of their goal structure or evaluation framework (for material on interpretative structural modeling, see Kawamura and Malone, 1981; Malone, 1975).

Risk analysis is mainly concerned with evaluating low probability but high consequence impacts. It is essential to evaluations for siting hazardous facilities such as nuclear power plants and other projects involving high risks. It is a specialty with a recent history but already it has produced a substantial literature (see for example Schwing and Albers, 1980 and *Risk Analysis: An International Journal*). Nevertheless, much of the vitality of this specialty is because of the difficulty of developing satisfactory procedures.

Perhaps the major concept in this specialty is "acceptable risk" and no single all-purpose number can be proposed to express it. The entire subject depends on beliefs and values on which there is no consensus. Competing approaches emphasize different features of acceptable-risk problems and tend to favor different interests. As a result, approaches and definitions of the problem are subject to heated political debates. The researchers can clarify the debate by separating issues of fact from issues of value, but even this task is usually only partially successful.

NEW DIRECTIONS IN SIA METHODOLOGY

Considerable progress has been achieved in SIA method and knowledge. The basic general methodology has been worked out and methodologies for specific types of actions have been refined to sophisticated levels. The knowledge base has been growing fairly rapidly (for a summary see Finsterbusch, 1980) but still has a long way to go. At this point the major need in SIA is to improve the knowledge base even further. For this purpose, the expansion of two types of studies is recommended: before/after impact studies and the specification and testing of commonly accepted impact hypotheses. Other new directions that are emerging and should be encouraged are: (1) better identification of positive social impacts, (2) advances in the quantification of nonmarket impacts, (3) advances in public participation processes, (4) extending the impact assessment time frame further in the future, and (5) using SIA in the monitoring function. These new departures will be briefly discussed below.

Knowledge of the past is the basis for predicting the future, so estimating potential future impacts in SIAs requires systematic knowledge of past cases. *Before/after* studies are needed to provide this knowledge. Few such studies are funded even though the entire SIA community knows how important they are. Ideally, the before/after study would compare the changes in the treated community and a control community. The most common study attempting to document impacts of actions, however, is the retroactive post construction study in which the impacted community is examined after the project is constructed and compared to data on the community before construction. Findings from retroactive studies should be treated cautiously, however, until they are retested with before/after data.

Currently, a major need in SIA is the testing of assumptions and accepted generalizations. Cumulated experience leads social impact assessors to expect certain impacts to occur when certain kinds of projects are implemented, but these expectations should be tested for each new case. For example, it has been commonly assumed that constructing major facilities in rural regions lowers unemployment, increases profits for local merchants, creates excessive demands on schools and public services, and causes community disintegration and individual psychological problems. All of these impacts have occurred in certain cases, but they have also failed to occur in other cases. Therefore, the frequency and intensity of these impacts must be tested, and the factors determining their occurrence need to be identified. In the study of negative social impacts of facility construction, the conventional wisdom has been challenged by Wilkinson et al. (1982) and Reynolds et al. (1982), and the testing of assumptions has begun (e.g., Freudenburg et al., 1982; Wilkinson et al., 1982).

The assessment of social impacts has improved greatly over the past decade but two additional improvements are badly needed: registration of positive social impacts and advances in the quantification of subjective impacts. SIA has emphasized negative social impacts of projects. The typical project has been justified by its economic benefits and challenged for its negative social effects. The efforts to find positive social impacts have not been nearly as vigorous. It would be nice to see more projects justified by their social impacts even when they cannot be justified by normal cost-benefit accounting. SIA researchers have been slow to advance positive social impact analysis but some jurisdictions are now requiring them. In 1975, Illinois mandated that economic impact studies of environmental control measures must also assess their benefits including social benefits (See Forrester et. al., 1981). The Corps of Engineers has begun to take positive social impacts seriously into account in its project assessments (Delli Priscoli, 1981).

The second improvement needed in the assessment of social impacts is more quantification. It is easy to criticize efforts to quantify the nonquantifiable and Finsterbusch (1981) has contributed to the chorus of criticism. Nevertheless, impacts that are not quantified, and quantified impacts that are not translated into monetary terms, are slighted by decision makers. To make impacts count in assessments, they must be quantified and priced.

A commendable effort to quantify subjective impacts is found in the Institute for Water Resources's (1980) study of the human costs of flooding in the Tug Fork Valley. A sample of 278 flood survivors were surveyed to identify factors potentially contributing to psychological impacts (flood trauma) of the flood. In the areas of general health, physical injuries, psychological effects, and serious inconveniences (e.g., forced evacuation), 22 factors were rated as likely (1) or not likely (0) "to contribute to the overall trauma of the flood experience" (1980: 69). The summed scores for households were arrayed into three levels that closely corresponded to the American Medical Association's three-level scale of psychological impairment as follows:

```
Level I   =  1 -  9 points   (84 households)
Level II  = 10 - 12 points   (114 households)
Level III = 13 - 20 points   (80 households)
```

The household trauma levels were assigned to individuals and matched to Veterans' Administration disability compensation payments for comparable median percentages of impairment. Assuming payments would average 2 years, the mean cost per household computes to around $18,000. Because 5,300 residences were actually damaged in the flood, the total psychological trauma damage is estimated at around $95,000,000, which exceeded residential property losses by about 50%.

IWR also computed the costs of psychological trauma in two other ways. First, the payment schedule for psychological impairment used in court settlements of Buffalo Creek flood victims was applied to corresponding trauma experiences in Tug Fork, and the costs sum to $93,205,656. Second, the Social Readjustment Rating Scale (SRRS) of Holmes and Rahe (1967) was used to compute an average Tug Fork flood victim score based on the survey information. Then the 1975 workman's compensation award for the death of a spouse was used as a money value for the "death of a spouse" position on the SRRS, and all other scale positions were priced in ratio to this value. By this method, the average Tug Fork flood victim incurred psychological trauma valued at $9,164. When the SRRS is monetized using workers' compensation for the average personal injury, however, the average level of psychological trauma is valued at $1,348. Both of these average trauma values are used to compute a total cost for flood trauma following two sets of assumptions (see original for details) and the results are $18 million to $125 million using assumption A and $24 to $164 million using assumption B. The midpoint between $18 million and $164 million is $91 million.

An examination of the Tug Fork study demonstrates that choosing different assumptions and procedures can produce very different results. This study ended up with fairly similar results by three different methods, but the consensus masks considerable variability in the results of various options. Nevertheless, this study advances the state of the art in quantifying and pricing subjective impacts and indicates the direction in which SIAs will move.

The next way SIAs need to be improved is by improving the participation of the public in the SIA process and by extending the process to include longer time periods. Public participation in SIA has been an area of considerable improvement over the past decade but the advances need to be more widely diffused to SIA researchers and further advances need to be made. Too often, agencies continue to limit participation to hearings and letters. There are many other public involvement techniques and most increase the value to decision makers of the public input. Large public meetings could break away from the formality and noninteractive character of formal hearings. Alternative formats are: a) briefing/questions and answers; b) town meeting (all speakers generally address the audience); c) panel of presenters of viewpoints and questions; d) sequence of a presentation, small group discussions, and summary reports; and e) workshops. For further information, see Creighton (1980), Burdge (1983), Forest Service (1977), and Ueland and Junker (1974).

Nonmeeting techniques should be explored as supplemental to public meetings. The most important is the use of surveys and questionnaires as sources of public input. They probably provide the most accurate guide to public opinion of all available techniques. The proportion having various views can be quantified with known degrees of accuracy whereas hearings only obtain inputs from the outspoken. Another technique is to interview spokespersons for various interested parties and viewpoints, but one must be cautious in using the results because group leaders see things differently than the rank and file. Creighton (1980) describes 16 other "public involvement techniques" ranging from maintaining field offices to computer-based methods.

The SIA process needs to be improved in still another way, that is, by lengthening the time horizon for the impacts predicted. The methodology for examining long-term impacts is *cumulative impact analysis*. At this time, this methodology is in the initial stages of development so we identify it as a new direction, but have little progress to report (see Vlachos, 1982, for a report on his Cumulative Impact Analysis Project). We can specify, however, some of the requirements for a methodology for analyzing cumulative impacts.

First, the longer the time frame, the greater the importance of changes in the state of society for projecting the extent, severity, and distribution of impacts. Few SIAs to date have used any forecast of changes in the state of society. They have short time frames and can assume that current societal conditions or trends continue more or less as they are. SIAs with long-term time frames must consider changes in life-styles, economic growth patterns, and political conditions. Cumulative impact analysis, therefore, will forge a marriage between SIA and futures forecasting.

Second, the longer time frame necessitates a more holistic approach. For short time periods, many individual series can be projected with reasonable probabilities without taking into account interactions with other series. The errors in the projections caused by these interactions are small at first but grow with time. Cross impact matrices, as described earlier, are a judgmental method for taking into account the interactions of components of dynamic systems. Dynamic systems modeling as popularized by Forrester (1968) and illustrated in the Club of Rome Limits to Growth Model (Meadows et al., 1972) is the procedure to be used when the critical variables can be quantified.

Finally, cumulative impact analysis must give larger scope than do short-term SIA's to values and to shaping the future in desirable conditions. The future should not be simply projected as though it is uncontrollable and inevitable. Society should act to try to bring about preferred futures. This requires determining, first of all, the preferred futures through a values analysis; then a policy analysis is required to determime what can be manipulated to bring about the preferred futures. Shaping the future, however, must be a continual process involving continual analysis (monitoring) and policy adjustments. We never would have landed on the moon if we tried to develop the ability to aim perfectly from the launching pad. We achieved this spectacular feat through reasonably good original aim and many adjustments. In societal futures, the adjustments are more important than the original aim.

The ultimate direction for SIA is the expansion of its role. The major function of SIA is to provide information on impacts to assist in the decision to act or not act and in the choice of the course of action from a set of alternatives. A secondary function that has become increasingly important since the mid-1970s is the planning of policies to mitigate negative social impacts. Another secondary function that more recently has become important in some agencies is the monitoring and guiding of projects as they are implemented. The leading agencies for incorporating monitoring functions in SIAs are the development assistance agencies such as Agency for International Development, World Bank, and Inter-American Development Bank. These agencies were not leaders in the SIA field in the 1970s but may become leaders in the mid-1980s, especially in the development of the monitoring role for SIA.

FINAL THOUGHT

Lipset (1979) presents a discouraging documentation of the inability of the social sciences to predict accurately. Most of the major developments since World War II were not foreseen. He concludes "It seems clear that social scientists... can explain only a small part of the variance, of the causal factors, involved in dealing with the major societal or worldwide issues that concern him" (1979: 21). Lipset's thesis is that our knowledge and methods are not up to the task of predicting. Because SIAs are predictions, his view is disturbing. We would point out, however, that it is easier to predict the effects of a highway or dam than the course of history so SIAs should predict better than the scientists whom Lipset reviewed. Nevertheless, reliable SIAs are difficult to produce. SIA work has improved considerably in its short history and gained some badly needed respectability. Now it needs to be fashioned into a truly valuable decision-making tool.

REFERENCES

ABT, C. C. et al. (1973) "A scenario generating methodology," pp. 191-214 in J. R. Bright and M.E.G. Schoenman (eds.) A Guide to Practical Technological Forecasting. Englewood Cliffs, NJ: Prentice-Hall.

ARMOUR, A., B. BOWRON, E. MILLER, and M. MILOFF (1981) "A framework for community impact assessment," pp. 24-34 in K. Finsterbusch and C. P. Wolf (eds.) Methodology of Social Impact Assessment. Stroudsburg, PA: Hutchinson Ross.

BURDGE, R. J. (1983) "Community needs assessment and techniques," pp. 191-213 in K. Finsterbusch et al. (eds.) Social Impact Assessment Methods. Beverly Hills, CA: Sage.

CREIGHTON, J. L. (1980) Public Involvement Manual: Involving the Public in Water and Power Resources Decisions. Washington, DC: U.S. Department of Interior, Government Printing Office.

DELBECQ, A. L., A. H. VAN DE VEN, and D. H. GUSTAFSON (1975) Group Techniques for Program Planning: A Guide to Nominal Group and Delphi Processes. Glenview, IL: Scott Foresman.

DeLEON, P. (1975) "Scenario designs: An overview." Simulations and Games 6: 39-60.

DELLI PRISCOLI, J. (1981) "People and water: Social impact assessment research." Water Spectrum (Summer): 8-17.

FINSTERBUSCH, K. (1981) "A survey of methods for evaluating social impacts," pp. 343-360 in K. Finsterbusch and C. P. Wolf (eds.) Methodology of Social Impact Assessment. Stroudsburg, PA: Hutchinson Ross.
——— (1980) Understanding Social Impacts. Beverly Hills, CA: Sage.
——— (1977) "The use of mini surveys in social impact assessments," pp. 291-296 in K. Finsterbusch and C. P. Wolf (eds.) Methodology of Social Impact Assessment. Stroudsburg, PA: Hutchinson Ross.
——— (1976a) "The mini survey: An underemployed research tool." Social Science Research 5 (March): 81-93.
——— (1976b) "Demonstrating the value of mini surveys in social research." Soc. Methods and Research 5 (August): 117-136.
——— (1975) "A policy analysis methodology for social impacts." J. of the International Society for Technology Assessment 1 (March): 5-15.
——— and A. B. MOTZ (1980) Social Research for Policy Decisions. Belmont, CA: Wadsworth.
FINSTERBUSCH, K. and C. P. WOLF [eds.] (1981) Methodology of Social Impact Assessment. Stroudsburg, PA: Hutchinson Ross.
FITZSIMMONS, S. J., L. I. STUART, and C. P. WOLF (1977) Social Assessment Manual: A Guide to the Preparation of the Social Well-Being Account. Washington, DC: Bureau of Reclamations.
FLYNN, C. B. and J. H. FLYNN (1982) "The group ecology method: A new conceptual design for social impact assessment." Impact Assessment Bull. 1, 4: 11-19.
FLYNN, C. B., J. H. FLYNN, J. A. CHALMERS, D. PIJAWKA, and K. BRANCH (1983) "An integrated methodology for large-scale development projects," pp. 55-72 in K. Finsterbush et al. (eds.) Social Impact Assessment Methods. Beverly Hills, CA: Sage.
Forest Service (1977) Inform and Involve Handbook. Washington, DC: U.S. Department of Agriculture.
FORESTER, B., H. A. ROBERTS, and H. SIEVERING (1981) "Social impact assessment in economics impact studies," pp. 79-90 in K. Finsterbusch and C. P. Wolf (eds.) Methodology of Social Impact Assessment. Stroudsburg, PA: Hutchinson Ross.
FORRESTER, J. W. (1968) Principles of Systems. Cambridge, MA: Wright-Allen.
FREUDENBERG, W. R., L. M. BACIGALUPI, and C. TANDOLL-YOUNG (1982) "Mental health consequences of rapid community growth: A report from the longitudinal study of boomtown mental heatlh impacts." J. of Health and Human Resources Administration 4 (Winter): 334-352.
GERARDIN, L. (1973) "Study of alternative futures: A scenario writing method," pp. 276-288 in J. R. Bright and M.E.F. Schoenman (eds.) A Guide to Practical Technological Forecasting. Englewood Cliffs, NJ: Prentice-Hall.
GILMORE, J. S., D. HAMMOND, K. D. MOORE, J. F. JOHNSON, and D. C. CODDINGTON (1981) Socioeconomic Impacts of Power Plants. Denver, CO: Denver Research Institute.
HOLMES, T. H. and R. H. RAHE (1967) "The social readjustment rating scale." J. of Psychosomatic Research 11: 213-218.
HWANG, C. and A.S.M. MASUD (1979) Multiple Objective Decision Making: Methods and Applications: A State-of-the-Art Survey. New York: Springer Verlag.

Institute for Water Resources, U.S. Army Corps of Engineers (1980) Human Costs Assessment: The Impacts of Flooding and Nonstructural Solutions. Report by D. Atlee et al., Fort Belvoir, Virginia, April.

KAWAMURA, K. and D. W. MALONE (1981) "Probing complexity in social systems through interpretive structural modeling," pp. 335-342 in K. Finsterbusch and C. P. Wolf (eds.) Methodology of Social Impact Assessment. Stroudsburg, PA: Hutchinson Ross.

LEISTRITZ, F. L. and S. H. MURDOCK (1981) The Socioeconomic Impact of Resource Development: Methods for Assessment. Boulder, CO: Westview.

LEISTRITZ, F. L., S. H. MURDOCK, N. E. TOMAN, and T. A. HORTSGAARD (1979) "A model for projecting localized economic, demographic, and fiscal impacts of large-scale projects." Western J. of Agricultural Economics 4, 2: 1-16.

LIPSET, S. M. (1979) "Predicting the future of post-industrial society: Can we do it?" pp. 1-35 in S. M. Lipset (ed.) The Third Century: America as a Post-Industrial Society. Stanford, CA: Hoover Institution Press.

MacCRIMMON, K. R. (1973) "An overview of multiple objective decision-making," pp. 18-44 in J. L. Cochrane and M. Zeleny (eds.) Multiple Criteria Decision Making. Columbia: Univ. of South Carolina Press.

MALONE, D. W. (1975) "An introduction to the application of interpretive structural modeling." Proceedings of the IEEE 63 (March): 397-404.

MEADOWS, D. H., D. L. MEADOWS, J. RANDERS, and W. W. BEHRENS, III (1972) The Limits to Growth: A Report for the Club of Rome's Project on the Predicament of Mankind. New York: Universe Books.

MURDOCK, S. H. and F. L. LEISTRITZ (1983) "Computerized socioeconomic assessment models," pp. 171-190 in K. Finsterbusch et al. (eds.) Social Impact Assessment Methods. Beverly Hills, CA: Sage.

MURDOCK, S. H. et al. (1982) "An assessment of the accuracy and utility of socioeconomic impact assessments." Presented at the Symposium on Paradoxes of Resource Development in the Arid West, American Association for the Advancement of Science Annual Meeting, Washington D.C., January 5.

MUMPOWER, J. and B. F. ANDERSON (1983) "Causes and correctives for errors of judgment," pp. 241-262 in K. Finsterbusch et al. (eds.) Social Impact Assessment: Methods. Beverly Hills, CA: Sage.

NIJKAMP, P. and J. SPRANK 9 [eds.] (1981) Multiple Criteria Analysis: Operational Methods. Aldershot, England: Gower.

OLSEN, M. E., B. D. MELBER, and D. S. MERWIN (1981) "A methodology for conducting social impact assessment using quality of social life indicators," pp. 43-78 in K. Finsterbusch and C. P. Wolf (eds.) Methodology of Social Impact Assessment. Stroudsburg, PA: Hutchinson Ross.

PALMER, J. F. (1981) "Approaches for assessing visual quality and visual impacts," pp. 284-301 in K. Finsterbusch and C. P. Wolf (eds.) Methodology of Social Impact Assesment. Stroudsburg, PA: Hutchinson Ross.

REYNOLDS, R. R., JR., K. P. WILKINSON, J. G. THOMPSON, and L. M. OSTRESH (1982) "Problems in the social impact assessment literature base for Western energy development communities," Impact Assessment Bull. 1 (Summer): 44-59.

SCHWING, R. C. and W. A. ALBERS, JR. [eds.] (1980) Societal Risk Assessment: How Safe is Safe Enough? New York: Plenum.

Ueland and Junker Architects and Planners and Portfolio Associates (1974) A Manual for Achieving Effective Community Participation in Transportation Planning. Philadelphia: Pennsylvania Department of Transportation.

VLACHOS, E. (1981) "The use of scenarios for social impact assessment," pp. 162-174 in K. Finsterbusch and C. P. Wolf (eds.) Methodology of Social Impact Assessment. Stroudsburg, PA: Hutchinson Ross.

WATKINS, G. (1981) "Development of a social impact assessment methodology (SIAM)," pp. 35-42 in K. Finsterbusch and C. P. Wolf (eds.) Methodology of Social Impact Assessment. Stroudsburg, PA: Hutchinson Ross.

WATTS, W. and F. A. FREE (1978) State of the Nation III. Lexington, MA: Lexington Books.

――――(1974) State of the Nation 1974. Washington, DC: Potomac Associates.

――――(1973) State of the Nation 1972. Washington, DC: Potomac Associates.

WELLMAN, B. (1979) "The community question: The intimate networks of East Yonkers," Amer. J. of Sociology 84, 5: 1201-1229.

――――(1972) "Who needs neighborhoods," pp. 94-100 in A. Powell (ed.) Attacking Modern Myths. Toronto: McClelland and Stewart.

WILKINSON, K. P., J. G. THOMPSON, R. R. REYNOLDS, JR., and L. M. OSTRESH (1982) "Local social disruption and Western energy development: A critical review." Pacific Soc. Rev. 25 (July): 275-296.

WOLF, C. P. (1983) "Social Impact Assessment: A Methodological Overview," pp. 25-33 in K. Finsterbusch et al. (eds.) Social Impact Assessment Methods. Beverly Hills, CA: Sage.

SOCIAL IMPACT ASSESSMENT

*William R. Freudenburg**

Department of Rural Sociology, Washington State University, Pullman, Washington 99164

Abstract

This article reviews the large and growing literature on social or socioeconomic impact assessment (SIA). Sociologists and other social scientists have been examining various "impacts" or consequences for decades, but the field of SIA emerged during the 1970s as a response to new environmental legislation. Both in its origins and its contributions, SIA is thus a hybrid, a field of social science and a component of the policy-making process. SIAs are generally anticipatory—efforts to project likely impacts before they occur—but empirical SIA work has looked at a broad range of social consequences. The largest subset of empirical SIA work has focused on relatively specific construction projects, particularly large-scale energy development projects in rural areas. Important advances have taken place in documenting economic/demographic and also social and cultural impacts. Further developments in findings, theory, and techniques will be necessary to meet the challenges of the future. The field is showing increasing consensus on a number of earlier controversies, e.g. on the need for SIAs to cross the usual disciplinary boundaries and to develop original data where "available" data are not sufficient. The main issue on which consensus has not yet emerged involves the question of how best to incorporate scientific input in what will remain largely political decisions. The field's efforts to deal with this fundamental and perhaps enduring question, however, may provide useful guidance for other efforts to include scientific input in political decision-making—efforts that may take on growing importance as society begins to deal with the increasingly complex risks posed by technological developments.

*Current address: Department of Rural Sociology, University of Wisconsin, Madison, Wisconsin 53706.

452 FREUDENBURG

INTRODUCTION

> Technology is neither good nor bad.
> Nor is it neutral.
>
> Kranzberg's Law.

Social impact assessment (SIA) is a hybrid, an offspring both of science and of the political process. Its lineage is ancient, but its emergence is recent, a response to society's increased concern with environmental degradation and the social implications of technology. For the most part, the hybrid has only begun to bear fruit within the last decade.

Reflecting SIA's hybrid heritage, this review will discuss both the policy and the scientific aspects of SIA. Of necessity, the review will be limited to what might be called mainstream SIA literature, which tends to form a subarea of "environmental sociology" (Dunlap & Catton 1979). SIA also draws heavily from other traditions in sociology, such as human ecology, social change, social problems, social indicators, and evaluation research, but these and other bodies of work are outside the scope of the present review.

Under some of the broadest definitions, SIA can be seen as including all of the social sciences and a good deal more besides. In general, however, *social impact assessment* refers to *assessing* (as in measuring or summarizing) a broad range of *impacts* (or effects, or consequences) that are likely to be experienced by an equally broad range of *social groups* as a result of some course of action. Although SIA is among the policy sciences and has a certain similarity to evaluation research (Carley & Bustelo 1984, Wolf 1977), it is also distinctive in at least three main respects. First, SIA tends to focus on the consequences of technological developments—usually developments that lead to alterations in the biophysical environment—while evaluation research tends to focus on programs or policies, especially social policies. Second, while evaluation research commonly focuses on stated or intended goals of public policy initiatives, SIA generally focuses on unintended consequences of developments that are often initiated by private, profit-oriented firms (cf Merton 1936). Third, under most definitions, SIA is a planning tool, prospective rather than retrospective—an attempt to foresee and hence avoid or minimize unwanted impacts—while evaluation research tends to take place after a policy has been set into motion.

As is noted below, however, there are many variations around these central tendencies. Despite the future-oriented focus of SIA as a whole, for example, some of the most important contributions to the field have been empirical analyses of impacts actually experienced after development has proceeded. Most practitioners in the United States appear to see SIA's major role as one of providing information and analysis to be taken into account in political decision-making. Yet SIA practitioners also often work to involve the public in the decision-making process (Daneke et al 1983), and the practitioners range from academic scientists who strive for dispassionate analysis to political activists whose analyses are impassioned indeed.

These and other forms of diversity make it difficult to provide a simple review of the entire field, but the task is aided by a number of excellent summaries that have become available recently. Accordingly, this review provides an overview at a somewhat broader level of abstraction, referring to more specific works as appropriate. It is divided into three main sections. The first deals with the historical development of the field as we know it today. The second notes some of the main empirical findings about social impacts and controversies about social impact assessment that have become the focus for SIA scholarship over the past decade and a half. The third and final section turns to some of the implications that grow out of the accumulated literature, including implications for the broader role to be played by science in the policy-making process.

HISTORICAL DEVELOPMENT

The Policy Context

The phrase "social impacts" means something like "social consequences," and the scientific genealogy of SIA can be traced back to the earliest days of sociology—to the concerns of Toennies and Durkheim, for example, with the social consequences of the Industrial Revolution. But the field as we know it today can be traced to legislation that took effect in 1970.

The first presidential act of the 1970s was the signing of a law passed just a few days earlier: the National Environmental Policy Act of 1969, or NEPA. This short and apparently simple act, five pages long in its entirety, has had enormous repercussions. Under NEPA, before a federal agency is allowed to take actions "significantly affecting the quality of the human environment," it must first prepare a balanced, interdisciplinary, and publicly available assessment of the action's likely impacts or consequences—an assessment now known as an environmental impact statement, or EIS. It is in the EIS context that much if not most SIA work is done, at least in the United States.

Section 102 of NEPA requires Federal agencies to make "integrated use of the natural *and social* sciences" in "decisionmaking which may have an impact on man's environment" (emphasis added). Like many provisions of the Act, however, those dealing with the social sciences were not immediately grasped. "Integrated use" is sometimes difficult to find even today, but it was virtually impossible to find in some of the earliest EISs. In one notable example, the *total* assessment of the social impacts to be created by relocating a community consisted of the following sentence: "Acquisition of approximately 130 acres

454   FREUDENBURG

used by [the community of] North Bonneville will affect the human population that resides there and also some mouse, rat, and domestic animal habitat that is normally associated with intense human use areas" (US Army Corps of Engineers 1971:3.1). The agency's concern for the community was later increased, but only after almost a decade-long battle had been fought in agency corridors, the media, and even the halls of Congress.

One major reason for the early lack of integrated use may have been the low proportion of NEPA lawsuits that had social impacts as a major focus. Before NEPA had been in effect for its first full decade, over 12,000 EISs had been prepared, and over 1,200 EIS-related lawsuits had been filed, but virtually none of the early suits focused on the social impact portions of the EISs (Freudenburg & Keating 1982). The few early suits dealing with social impacts, moreover, could scarcely have been less propitious for establishing legal precedents. Most of the cases were efforts to require the preparation of EISs on "socioeconomic" grounds alone, in cases where Federal decisions had negligible impacts on biophysical environments. Two important early examples were the closing of a military base and the development of a job training center on a site where a campus had previously stood. In both cases there were actually to be fewer people on the sites—generating fewer impacts in the form of air pollution, dust, noise, etc—than would have been the case previously. Not surprisingly, the courts ruled that no EISs were required in these and similar cases.

The US Council on Environmental Quality, the agency charged with overseeing implementation of NEPA, issued regulations for implementing the procedural provisions of the Act in 1973 and then again in 1978. The official 1978 regulations have clarified the situation: "Social and economic effects by themselves do *not* require preparation of an EIS," but if an EIS must be prepared because of physical environmental impacts, and if the social and bioenvironmental impacts are "interrelated," then the EIS is required to discuss "*all* of these impacts on the human environment" (US Council on Environmental Quality 1978:29; emphasis added).

Even after these clarifications were issued, the flow of SIA-related litigation could scarcely be said to have created a heavy burden for courts: It appears that the first case making clear use of social science expertise was not decided until 1983, and the first case presenting the type of issue envisioned in the Council on Environmental Quality's regulations was not decided until May of 1985. The 1983 decision involved an effort to require the Nuclear Regulatory Commission to prepare an EIS before permitting the undamaged nuclear reactor at Three Mile Island to resume operation (the reactor happened to be shut down for refueling when its twin unit malfunctioned). The case argued that restarting the undamaged unit would damage the psychological health of citizens living nearby, that psychological health is a form of "health" protected by NEPA, and thus that an environmental impact statement was required even though no other environmental impacts were alleged. A high court in the District of Columbia agreed with the citizens' contention, but the US Supreme Court—in *Metropolitan Edison Co. v. People Against Nuclear Energy,* 460 U.S. 766, 103 S. Ct. 1556 (1983)—did not. While noting that psychological health could be a form of health as defined under NEPA, the Justices ruled that they had not been shown "a sufficiently close causal connection" between the physical act of restarting the reactor and the hypothesized increase in mental health problems. A group of respected mental health researchers had reached essentially the same conclusion about one year earlier (Walker et al 1982; for fuller discussions of the case and its implications, see Jordan 1984, Meidinger & Freudenburg 1983).

It was not until May of 1985, more than 15 years after the Act was passed, that the first decision was rendered on the type of case envisioned in the Council or Environmental Quality regulations (and presumably in NEPA itself). The case—*Northern Cheyenne Tribe v. Hodel,* No. CV 82-116-BLG (D. Mont. May 28, 1985)—involved the largest federal coal lease sale that had ever been held. While the Department of the Interior had prepared an EIS on the affected area (the Northern Powder River Basin of Wyoming and Montana), the EIS included virtually no discussion of the sale's likely social, cultural, or economic impacts on the Northern Cheyenne Tribe, and thus the Northern Cheyennes sued to have the EIS overturned. They succeeded. In a strongly worded decision, Judge James F. Batten overturned the EIS, voided the sale of over 350 million tons of Federal coal (with a market value of well over $4 billion), and chided the Department of Interior for failing to turn its "ostensible concern" with socioeconomic impacts into "any meaningful analysis of the extent of such impacts on certain groups of residents within the affected area, particularly the Northern Cheyenne Tribe" (pp. 14–15; see also the discussion in Freudenburg & Keating 1985).

The Social Science Context

The early years under NEPA, from roughly 1970–1975, were a time of humble beginnings for the field, with most SIA work being a relatively straightforward continuation of research that had been underway before the Act was passed. Some of the earliest signs of the emergence of a self-conscious field of SIA came when the Council of the American Sociological Association (ASA) authorized the formation in 1973 of a committee "to develop guidelines for sociological contributions to environmental impact statements" (Dunlap & Catton 1979:246). Given the newness and relative lack of development of the field at the time, the Committee ultimately disbanded without making formal recommendations on EIS criteria (Wolf 1975), but its efforts prepared the groundwork for establishing the Environmental Sociology Section of the ASA.

In addition, the field of SIA could also be said to have emerged from the efforts of the Committee—especially its chair, C. P. Wolf, described by some as the founder of the field but by himself as its "finder" (Wolf 1977). Wolf was also the convener of the Ad Hoc Interagency Working Group on SIA that began to meet in Washington, DC in June of 1974. In early 1974, he organized a session on social impact assessment at the annual meeting of the Environmental Design Research Association and later turned the session into the field's first published volume (Wolf 1974). June 1975 saw publication of the first special journal issue on SIA (*Environment and Behavior*, Vol. 7, No. 3), again with Wolf as its editor. In January 1976, he turned over his earlier *Environmental Sociology* newsletter to the ASA and established a second newsletter, *Social Impact Assessment*. This he still edits for a subscription list that has grown to more than 1000; it remains the field's most important channel of communication. At about the same time, he was also working with Kurt Finsterbusch on *Methodology of Social Impact Assessment* (Finsterbusch & Wolf 1977), which led to a second edition and then a sequel (Finsterbusch et al 1983). The original was identified in a later survey of practitioners (Davidson 1983) as the most influential volume in SIA. (Both the original volume and its successors are useful sources on SIA methodologies, which receive little attention in this review.) When the ASA's Section on Environmental Sociology established its award for Distinguished Contributions to Environmental Sociology, the Section's Council unanimously chose Wolf as the first recipient.

If the first few years after NEPA were a period of humble beginnings, the following years (from roughly 1975–1980) might be identified as a second era—a time of not-so-humble claims and aspirations. Agencies were accustomed to measuring "adequacy" in terms of following official procedures, rather than in scientific terms, and they desired procedural guidance for dealing with SIAs. One of the results was a multiplying of how-to manuals and a dramatic growth in the enthusiasm of their claims. Unlike the Ad Hoc ASA committee, writers of these manuals indicated little difficulty in deciding what to include in SIAs. One claimed, for example, "All of the information necessary to conduct a social assessment, analyze data, present findings, and make recommendations is contained within this book" (Fitzsimmons et al 1977:3). While the manual making this claim received mixed reviews (Flynn 1976, Shields 1976), it was still one of the more widely respected of the early guides—along with the more sociological guide produced for the US Forest Service by Richard Gale (1975)—and it was the first to be commercially published. Even so, such a claim would have required more than a little bravery, particularly at such an early state of the development of the field. It also may have proved to be less than entirely convincing—a conclusion suggested by the proliferation of other publications on "How To Do Social Impact Assessment," numbering roughly two dozen at last count. (Other agencies, such as the Corps of Engineers, also considered producing their own manuals

SOCIAL IMPACT ASSESSMENT   457

but decided instead to draw on empirical case studies—R. Love, personal communication.) More recent volumes often reflect more modest goals, such as producing "a reference manual that can be consulted either for general advice or for more specific direction on particular problems" (Branch et al 1984:3), although, the advertising for a manual being published as this article went to press claimed without qualification, "with this book you can conduct socio-economic impact assessments."

The enthusiasm of the claims was not simply a response to agency needs, however. Some of the field's most important early progress did in fact occur in adapting established social science methods (such as surveys, demographic projections, and field research techniques) to the new demands of SIA (see e.g. the collections in Finsterbusch & Wolf 1977, Wolf 1974). In addition, the field's growth during the late 1970s was exceptional. In Canada, for example, a 1975 study found only two dozen SIAs, and even that only "by stretching the definition of social impact research" (Boothroyd 1978:131). At the time of a nation-wide conference three years later, participants were able to identify over 3000 SIAs (D'Amore 1981). Also, SIA practitioners may have been influenced by the broader culture of the industrial developments they assessed, and during the late 1970s, this culture was dominated by "big thinking" and massive projects—to say nothing of consulting opportunities—particularly in the field of energy development.

Conversely, during the third post-NEPA era of SIA, extending roughly from 1981 to the present, the field began not only to think more seriously about the "bust" side of development but to experience those very problems itself. In the United States, a new President took office, one who placed relatively low priorities both on social science and on environmental protection and who tended to view impact assessment as a form of "paralysis by analysis." In addition, the combination of a recession and the increasing effectiveness of energy conservation led to the cancellation of one large-scale energy project after another. As the projects were cancelled, so were formerly lucrative consulting contracts for SIA firms, many of which were forced to scale back, close branch offices, refocus their efforts in other areas of work, or even go out of business entirely.

Yet an examination of SIA literature reveals that the early 1980s were a time not of disastrous decline, but of exceptional productivity—a time of retrenchment, to be sure, but also one of reflection and reconsideration, resulting in what may be a higher level of quality than was found in previous periods of SIA work. While there can be little doubt that many factors were at work, three seem to have been particularly important. First, researchers who had previously been in high demand for project-specific assessments, one contract after another, began to find time to do the more detailed analyses that many had wanted to do all along. Second, a pair of important conferences were held in summer and fall of 1982—the Alaska Symposium on the Social, Economic and Cultural Impacts of Natural Resource Development (many of the formal papers from which were published in Yarie 1983) and the International Conference on SIA, held in Vancouver, British Columbia, Canada, two months later. These conferences gave researchers the opportunity to consider the contrasts, complementarities, and contributions to be gained from those whose contexts and philosophies differed from their own. This cross-national cross-fertilization seems to have been particularly important for US practitioners, who had previously paid too little attention to developments in other countries. Third, a lag of several years is common before work in any field begins to climb the learning curve and to appear in scientific journals; SIA was not immune from this general tendency.

It is mainly in the past few years that the accumulating evidence has begun to permit more confident statements about the actual impacts of projects. The first "SIA textbook" to focus not on how to do SIAs but on what was known about social impacts was published in 1980 (Finsterbusch 1980), and the first books to summarize literature on the impacts of a given type of development (rapid community growth) appeared at roughly the same time (Murdock & Leistritz 1979, Weber & Howell 1982). A special issue of *The Social Science Journal* (Vol. 16, No. 2) was devoted to "the social impacts of energy development in the West" in 1979, and a July 1982 special issue of *Pacific Sociological Review* (Vol. 25, No. 3) was devoted to sociological research on boomtowns in particular. The Westview Press series on social impact assessment, which included only four titles before 1981, roughly quadrupled its number of titles by the end of 1985. And finally, as this list reflects, the proportion of SIA discussions appearing only in the "underground" literature or technical reports has declined since 1980, and publications have begun to appear increasingly in refereed journals and other mainstream publications.

MAJOR FINDINGS AND FEUDS

Empirical Findings

Empirical work in SIA has been extraordinarily varied, studying "social impacts" associated with sources as disparate as highways and high technology (Llewellyn et al 1982, Berardi & Geisler 1984). Some work has gone beyond technology to urge an emphasis on local regional-/ or national-level programs and policies (see e.g. Cramer et al 1980, Dietz 1984, Freeman et al 1982); some has even gone beyond strictly human actions to look at the social impacts of natural events such as disasters (Dillman et al 1983, Erikson 1976).

An important area of early research focused on forests and recreation; indeed, this work provided an impetus for the development of the entire field of environmental or natural resource sociology (Dunlap & Catton 1979). Particularly significant studies included those dealing with the impacts of increased population densities on the experiences of outdoor recreationists (Lucas 1964, Wagar 1964), the impact of the outdoor setting per se on the activities of recreationists (Burch 1965), and the impacts of forestry management practices on recreationists and other social groups (Hendee et al 1978). Related work, using a somewhat different definition of SIA, has looked at "social impacts" on quasi-natural systems such as National Parks of the human populations living nearby (e.g. Baxter et al 1984).

Entire reviews could be devoted to forest recreation or many of the other topics noted above. In addition, a number of authors have stressed SIA's potential to contribute to broader policy considerations (e.g. Finsterbusch 1984, 1985; Carley & Bustelo 1984; Wolf 1977). To date, however, the largest and most important area of empirical work in SIA has dealt with relatively specific construction projects.

In the earliest days after NEPA, the most important types of projects may have been water resource developments such as dams and urban undertakings such as highways. Work on water resources led to what appear to have been the first set of actual agency guidelines, namely those issued by the US Water Resources Council. In addition, some of the empirical studies from this era remain among the best yet done on the social impacts of reservoir construction and relocation. For example, Burdge & Johnson (1973) used a longitudinal design, included interviews with people who had actually been relocated by reservoir development, and focused on social and psychological impacts as well as easier-to-quantify economic impacts. They found, among other things, that younger, more affluent, and better-educated migrants fared better in the relocation process than those who were older, poorer, and less educated. The primary beneficiaries of development were found to live in different locations than the victims; in addition, those who refused to accept initial offers for their land were found to receive higher prices, and those who were relocated were found to express dissatisfaction with their interpersonal as well as economic dealings with the agency building the dam (Burdge & Johnson 1973; see also Andrews 1981, or the compilation by Field et al 1974; see also the later summary provided by Finsterbusch 1980).

Similarly, some of the most important work on urban highway construction dates from the first few years after the passage of NEPA, and some of the significant work on urban renewal dates from the period before NEPA was enacted (e.g. Fried 1963, Gans 1962). By the mid-1970s, studies showed that (at least after the Uniform Relocation Assistance and Real Property Acquisition Policies Act of 1970) relocatees generally received sufficient payments to allow them to move into comparable or superior housing. One notable study found that about 80% of the relocatees moved into equal or better housing and neighborhoods, that 50% of the previous renters became homeowners, and that a portion of the cost of the improved housing was borne by the government, although a portion was also borne by the relocatees themselves (Buffington et al 1974). Only 6% of the relocatees in this study thought that they had downgraded the quality of their housing. Another study found that "sixty percent of the respondents were more pleased with their new homes than the old, while the reverse was true for 27 percent" (Burkhardt et al 1976: 34). The bad news is that relocation was found to lead to declines in neighboring and neighborly assistance, use of neighborhood facilities, and participation in neighborhood organizations (Burkhardt et al 1976: 46–50). In addition, as was the case with rural relocation for reservoir construction, the stresses of relocation appear to have been greater for long-term residents and the elderly (Buffington et al 1974; Fried 1963). Fried (1963) also noted problems related to spatial identity—i.e. for those persons having especially strong ties to their neighborhoods (see also Fellman & Brandt 1970). For more detailed reviews, the most extensive treatment available is the seven-volume compilation by Llewellyn et al (1982); see also Finsterbusch (1980).

But projects such as new highway construction and urban renewal became increasingly rare after the early 1970s, just as the larger field of SIA was beginning to crystallize. This fact may reflect both the increased national concern with protecting natural and human environments that led to NEPA and the effectiveness of NEPA itself in giving expression to such concerns. In addition, the "energy crisis" that followed the oil embargo of 1973–1974 led to a decline in gasoline consumption and hence in the revenues for new highway construction. That same energy crisis, however, led to a remarkable growth in opportunities for rural SIA work in studying the impacts of large-scale energy development, particularly in the Rocky Mountain region of the United States and Canada.

As did other areas of SIA, this one draws on work that was underway before NEPA (see especially the summary by Summers et al 1976), but this area saw explosive growth during the late 1970s. Until the middle years of that decade, studies of rural industrialization had tended to view even large-scale developments in rural areas as generally beneficial, providing "an important tool for solving the twin problems of rural poverty and urban crisis" (Summers et al 1976: 1). Even after NEPA, environmental impact statements tended to note in detail the likely economic benefits of growth and the need for expanding municipal services but to say virtually nothing about the broader range of potential sociocultural impacts. In the later 1970s, however, reports from so-called "energy boomtowns" frequently (but by no means always) began to note a pattern of problems similar to the "social pathologies" that Durkheim, for example, might have predicted—suicide attempts, increased crime, and drug abuse problems, and so forth—and the field became the focus for considerably increased controversy and contention.

To oversimplify only slightly the picture that has since emerged, the major conclusion appears to be that the impacts have neither been as positive as claimed by project proponents nor as negative as claimed by opponents. Most rural communities in the United States continue to favor industrial developments (Murdock & Leistritz 1979, Stout-Wiegand & Trent 1983), with the clear exception of nuclear facility development (Freudenburg & Baxter 1984), although the support appears to be more a reflection of general cultural favorability toward development than the expectation that a respondent will benefit personally from growth (Gartrell et al 1980; Gates 1982).

Where local benefits have been expected from large-scale projects, the focus has been primarily economic, specifically including jobs for local unemployed or young persons, whether in the large-scale developments themselves or in the so-called secondary, ancillary, service, or spin-off employment—i.e. in local restaurants, clothing stores, filling stations, and other services set up or expanded to serve the workers brought in by development. Virtually all service employment benefits appear to have been overestimated. First, as Murdock & Leistritz (1979) note, early impact projections commonly incorporated "multipliers" of approximately 1.6 and 2.5, respectively, during the construction and operational phases of major facilities; these imply the creation of 0.6 and 1.5 secondary jobs, respectively, for each job on the development project itself. Empirical evaluations have produced far lower numbers. Summers et al (1976:55) found "the most significant aspect" of findings on the operation of facilities to be the "very low multipliers—half of them are below 1.2." In other words, only 2 additional jobs were created for every 15 that had been anticipated. An analysis of 12 major power plant construction sites (Gilmore et al 1982) calculated actual construction-phase employment multipliers to be 1.2 to 1.3 for sparsely populated areas and only 1.3 to 1.4 even for areas with moderate population densities. In another retrospective analysis of 12 nuclear power plants, Pijawka & Chalmers (1983) estimated actual local employment multipliers to have averaged 1.16 during construction and 1.23 during operation of the facilities. The major monitoring effort on the Huntly Power Project in New Zealand (Fookes 1981) also developed an estimate of 1.125 for the local construction employment multiplier.

An analysis of the accuracy of 1980 population projections from 225 EISs found that "many statements simply ignore the socioeconomic dimensions entirely, others fail to provide necessary baseline or impact projections and still others do not provide data for jurisdictions that are useful for local and state-level decisionmaking." Even for EISs providing projections on identifiable jurisdictions, the analysis found their projections to be "of questionable value" (Murdock et al 1984:292). The mean error in cities' projected populations was over 50% and was apparently "not merely a result of the rapid growth or small population sizes of the projected areas" (Murdock et al 1984:291). Much of the inaccuracy, however, was due not to social scientists

462   FREUDENBURG

but to engineers who significantly underestimated the construction workforces needed (see also Braid 1981, Dietz 1984, Finsterbusch 1985, Gilmore et al 1982).

Most of the in-migrating workers tend to come from within the state or at least from within a thousand miles or so of a project (Mountain West Research 1975, Murdock & Leistritz 1979, Wieland et al 1979), and sizable minorities or even majorities of the workers tend to report having lived "in the area" at least briefly prior to taking employment at the facilities (Mountain West Research 1975, Chalmers 1977). The proportion of "local hires" tends to be higher where the host area populations are larger and/or the projects are smaller (Dunning 1981, DeVeney 1977, Malhotra & Manninen 1980). Even so, local employment often falls below initial expectations, for three reasons. First, local workers tend to be concentrated in the less-skilled job categories (Summers et al 1976, Mountain West Research 1975), although even these jobs often provide higher wages than are otherwise available in many rural areas (Murdock & Leistritz 1979). Second, the projects do not generally appear to lead to a decrease in the local unemployment rate, apparently in part because "new jobs often do not go to the local unemployed, underemployed, minorities and marginally employable persons likely to be near or below the poverty level" (Summers et al 1976:3). Third and finally, while such projects generally do halt or even reverse patterns of population decline, they apparently do not increase the propensity of local youth to stay in their home communities (Summers et al 1976, Seyfrit 1986).

Just as the anticipated benefits of development may not prove to be as substantial as sometimes hoped, however, there is also increasing evidence that *negative* impacts of growth may not be as severe as sometimes feared. Outside of the area of housing, the "soaring costs of living" often mentioned in the early SIA literature (and sometimes asserted even in more recent documents) have proved difficult to find in practice (Thompson et al 1979). Aggregate-level statistics do often reflect significant increases in per capita indicators of disruption, particularly in the areas of crime, substance abuse, and the need for human services more generally (Thompson et al 1979, Bacigalupi & Freudenburg 1983, Baring-Gould & Bennett 1976, Colorado Division of Criminal Justice 1981, Freudenburg 1982, Lantz & McKeown 1979, Lovejoy 1977, Milkman et al 1980, Montana Energy Advisory Council 1975, Suzman et al 1980). The interpretation of many of these statistics, however, remains highly controversial (see Weber & Howell 1982, Murdock et al 1985, or the July 1982 issue of *Pacific Sociological Review,* Vol. 25, No. 3; for aggregate-level statistics on crime rates in particular, compare Colorado Division of Criminal Justice 1981 to Wilkinson et al 1984). Despite these community-level statistics, surveys in affected communities have repeatedly failed to find evidence of psychological pathologies in the general population (England & Albrecht 1984,

Freudenburg 1981, Gartrell 1980, Krannich & Greider 1984, Suzman et al 1980). Similarly, empirical evidence has provided little support for the assumption that energy boomtowns are particularly stressful for the elderly (Gilmore et al 1982, Freudenburg 1982) or for women (Freudenburg 1981; but see Moen et al 1981, Stout-Wiegand & Trent 1983). On the other hand, more careful empirical analysis (Freudenburg 1984) has shown evidence of significant disruption in a group often identified in early SIA work as being likely to benefit from growth, namely the young people of rapidly growing communities (see also Seyfrit 1986; for further reviews, see Cortese & Jones 1977, Finsterbusch 1980, Freudenburg 1982, Murdock & Leistritz 1979; for a comprehensive set of reviews, see Weber & Howell 1982; and for a "critical review," see Wilkinson et al 1982).

Controversial Conceptions

As noted at the outset, SIA is not merely an area of empirical social science; it also draws from and contributes to the policy-making process. Particularly given the increasing availability of empirical summaries of SIA work (see the specific items cited above; see also Finsterbusch 1985), it would be inappropriate for this review to focus exclusively on the empirical work. Instead, something like equal space needs to be devoted to the large and increasingly important body of scholarship dealing with what might be called the metatheoretical issues of SIA—efforts to conceptualize and clarify the field. As in the case of the empirical literature, the metatheoretical literature can only be summarized here in greatly simplified form (for further discussions, see e.g. Boothroyd 1978, 1982; Bowles 1981b; Carley & Bustelo 1984; Cramer et al 1980; Dietz 1984; Finsterbusch 1984, 1985; Freudenburg & Keating 1985; Gale 1984; Jobes 1985; Murdock et al 1985; Tester & Mykes 1981; Wolf 1974, 1977).

The task is aided by the fact that many of the issues that would have been considered controversial and deserving of mention in the late 1970s appear today to be the focus of much higher levels of consensus—or more accurately, of pluralism. For example, many authors speak not of social but of "socioeconomic" impact assessment. The two terms have become essentially interchangeable in common usage, but in earlier years, the "*social* social impacts" were so often ignored that many "socioeconomic" assessments were strictly economic, rarely going beyond roads, sewer and water systems, and the other facilities and services making up what might be called "the edifice complex." Today, both "social" and "socioeconomic" impact assessment essentially refer not just to sociology, economics, or any other single discipline, but to interdisciplinary social science efforts. The general consensus appears to be that noneconomic or sociocultural variables need to be examined as well as economic or demographic ones (Albrecht 1982; Branch et al 1984; Carley &

Bustelo 1984; Finsterbusch 1980, 1985; Freudenburg & Keating 1982; Murdock et al 1979, 1985; National Academy of Sciences 1984).

Similarly, arguments might once have centered on several other issues that no longer appear to warrant extensive discussion—e.g. the role to be played by quantitative vs qualitative data, the importance of attitudes vs those impacts not mediated by attitudes, the need for original vs publicly "available" data, or the appropriateness of combining all impacts in terms of a single metric (whether dollars or some other system such as a listing of pluses and minuses). In general, just as the leading practitioners in the field appear to have moved away from analyses based narrowly on a specialist's own disciplinary background, most appear to be in agreement today on the inappropriateness of limiting the SIA to whatever data may happen to be available (see e.g. Finsterbusch 1980, Freudenburg 1982, Little 1977, Schnaiberg 1980). They recognize that SIAs should not be limited to variables that are easily quantified and/or politically salient (Carley & Bustelo 1984, Dietz 1984, Freudenburg & Keating 1982, Holden 1980, Murdock et al 1985, Wolf 1977). Agreement is also growing that, while decisionmakers should be provided with a concise summary of likely impacts, the attempt to "add" or otherwise combine incommensurables goes against the intent of NEPA, which is to provide relevant information for a decisionmaker's judgment, not to hide the analyst's own judgments behind a single, overall figure. Science provides no basis for combining impacts that may be as dissimilar as apples, oranges, and orangutans; efforts to add incommensurables may merely hide the value decisions that are inherent in the analyst's efforts. A decision as simple as dividing a category into two subcategories, for example, can effectively "double the weighting of the original category" (Boothroyd 1978:130; see also Flynn 1976, Holden 1980, Shields 1976).

Perhaps the main issue on which increasing consensus is *not* evident is the manner in which scientific and political considerations can best coexist. In some views, SIA is essentially synonymous with applied social science, while in others, SIA becomes almost synonymous with the political process (Carley & Bustelo 1984:10, discussing Torgerson 1981). Divergent opinions on this issue were brought out particularly clearly by the First International Conference on SIA. In his comments on the Conference, for example, Boothroyd (1982) noted the divergence between the "technical" and "political" approaches to SIA, while Carley & Bustelo (1984:7) later differentiated between "research" and "participatory" approaches. Numerous practitioners have since commented informally if a bit inaccurately about the "U.S." and "Canadian" approaches, respectively.

There have been important examples of empirical work in Canada (for a summary, see Bowles 1981b), as there have been in a number of other nations that have received little attention in this review, particularly including New

Zealand (Taylor et al 1982), Australia (Armstrong 1982), and a broad range of third-world countries that are the focus of social impact research in the context of international development (Finsterbusch 1985, Bailey 1985). The key difference is that in the United States, most "action" efforts have taken place inside the normal channels of agency decision-making; social scientists have served as important "internal proponents" for community interests and also have produced extensive bodies of work on efforts to "mitigate" or lessen the negative impacts (see e.g. Metz 1980, Davenport & Davenport 1979; Halstead et al 1984). "Action" orientations in other countries have often been more politicized—in the sense of working directly with affected communities, helping to organize opposition to projects, etc—and some of the most articulate spokespersons for this approach have been Canadians (see e.g. Carley & Bustelo 1984 or the collection in Tester & Mykes 1981).

The institutional settings for SIA differ greatly between the United States and Canada. While Canada has important environmental laws and regulations, along with agency traditions that some practitioners view as being more neutral toward development than those in the United States, Canadians do not have a statutory basis for SIA comparable to the National Environmental Policy Act. Instead, it is only a minor exaggeration to note that, if SIA in the United States can be traced to NEPA, SIA in Canada can be traced to the Berger Commission (Berger 1977). Justice Thomas R. Berger of the British Columbia Supreme Court was appointed by the Canadian Government to examine the social, economic, and environmental impacts of "the greatest project, in terms of capital expenditure, ever undertaken by private enterprise anywhere" (Berger 1983:22)—a proposed pipeline along the Mackenzie Valley that would have brought natural gas from the Arctic to midcontinent. The pipeline would have crossed a region as large as western Europe but inhabited by only 30,000 people, half of them natives. Berger held hearings skillfully and empathetically, complete with native translations, in a series of northern communities; his inquiry helped to educate his countrymen about their neighbors to the north as well as to investigate the implications of the pipeline itself. His final recommendation—to delay pipeline permits for 10 years to allow settlement of native claims—did not carry the force of law, but it had a greater impact on policy outcomes than have most social impact recommendations in the United States.

Particularly since the time of the International Conference, US practitioners have devoted increasing thought to the political dimensions of SIA. Before that time, the general if unspoken consensus appears to have been that, if SIA could be said to have possessed a "bias," whether in its practice or practitioners, that bias would have been a "conservative" one, in the sense of working against disruptions or other changes in preexisting communities. It is clear that developers have tended to see SIA practitioners in this light—if only because SIAs, like EISs in general, have rarely been used to build a stronger case for development but have sometimes identified reasons why developments should not proceed (but see Allee et al 1980, Finsterbusch 1985). Indeed, social scientists in agencies have sometimes served as internal advocates for community interests that were otherwise being ignored by development-oriented agencies. As a number of writers have recently pointed out, however, there actually may be a pro- as much as an anti-development bias in SIA, although the pro-development bias may operate at a deeper and more subtle level.

Two key factors that tend to make assessments more supportive of development are the selective availability of data (Schnaiberg 1980) and the analysts' tendency to focus on certain questions while ignoring others (Susskind 1983). In addition, analysts work within a system that contains its own biases—although those biases may not be consciously recognized—a possibility perhaps indicated by the common terminology. EISs will often weigh local "preferences" against a national "need" for energy, for example, rather than balancing a national "preference" for cheap energy against the "need" to preserve the vitality of local communities. Assessments on particularly controversial facilities (e.g. for nuclear waste) claim to assess both "real" and (locally) "perceived" impacts, rather than assessing both the impacts that are "acknowledged" by (project-hired) experts and those that are not. From another perspective, some of the "non-acknowledged" nuclear waste impacts result from the credibility problems of the nuclear industry and the Department of Energy, which are unable to "sell" their claims about the safety of planned facilities because communities contrast early industry claims about clean and cheap nuclear power against more recent news reports about cost overruns, management difficulties, leaks of radioactive waste, and efforts to cover up damaging evidence. Similarly, the mitigations proposed in most EISs have to do with changes that are suggested for local communities, rather than for the proposed developments. EISs and SIA practitioners will often conclude that the decent and humane thing to do is to "help communities cope" with developments that are "destined to go ahead" as planned, rather than helping *developers* learn how to do a better job of adapting to the ways in which local communities do business (Bowles 1981a). In short, while it would be inappropriate in the extreme to drop efforts to improve the empirical quality of SIA work, it also needs to be recognized that the work is affected in both subtle and significant ways by the context within which it takes place (for further discussion, see Jobes 1985, Freudenburg & Keating 1985).

IMPLICATIONS

The Policy Context

As the foregoing discussion should suggest, NEPA and SIA are worthy of increased sociological interest for more reasons than merely the new setting for applied sociology they helped create. In the empirical realm, SIA has led to important new opportunities for testing and extending the hypotheses drawn from the broader body of sociology. Perhaps in part because SIA requires a focus on change over time, it holds promise for its practitioners to rethink and to contribute to basic research in a variety of areas, such as human ecology and community change, that will help to make those fields more dynamic. In the policy context, NEPA has helped to institutionalize what is in many ways a new approach to the use of scientific information in political decision-making. This section will turn to the latter of these contributions first.

As Frank (1932) pointed out in a classic law article, societies have long shown distrust for the "human" element in decision-making. Under what might be called the first models for dealing with this problem, the early modes of trial—ordeals, judicial duels, "floating" tests for witches, etc.—were "considered to involve no human element. The judgment [was] the judgment of the supernatural, or 'the judgment of God' " (Frank 1932:582). The nineteenth-century equivalent of the earlier distrust for human judgment, according to Frank, was reliance on a body of impersonal legal rules. Under this second model of decision-making, "rationality" was thought to emerge through a dependence on rules that were derived from self-evident principles, thus reducing the human element in decision-making to a minimum (for a fuller discussion of this second approach, also known as "formal jurisprudence," see Monahan & Walker 1985:1–31). In the twentieth-century, largely in response to a school known as "sociological jurisprudence" (e.g. Pound 1912), the emphasis on such abstract "universal principles" declined, and a third model emerged, placing increased emphasis on empirical evidence. One could even argue that with society's increasing replacement of the sacred by the secular, this model attempted to replace the presumably fair or even sacred decisions of the supernatural with those of the scientist, where in the extreme case the scientist would replace the judge or the elected official as the actual decisionmaker. Perhaps the illustration with which social scientists would be most familiar is the cost-benefit analysis: Rather than having public works projects built primarily on the basis of pork-barrel politics, the argument goes, a dispassionate and scientific analysis should be used, and the project should only be built if the benefits outweigh the costs.

Yet it may not be that simple. One of the major points of Frank's article was that "the human element in the administration of justice by judges is irrepressible. . . .[T]he more you try to conceal the fact that judges are swayed by human prejudices, passions and weaknesses, the more likely you are to augment those prejudices, passions and weaknesses. . . . For judges behave substantially like the human beings who are not judges" (Frank 1932:580–81). Similarly, "scientific" decision-making has come under fire more recently, as in the case of the cost-benefit analysis, for being anything but value-free. It appears that scientists also tend to behave much like the other human beings who are neither scientists nor judges. Fallibilities include a susceptibility to political pressure and a sensitivity to the conclusions desired by clients; purportedly scientific assessments have sometimes succeeded not so much in eliminating human fallibilities and political pressures as in hiding them behind a statistical smokescreen (Schnaiberg 1980, Hoos 1979).

The approach taken by NEPA is a fourth and very different one; indeed, one way of viewing the extent of the difference is to see how often the law is misunderstood. Despite many references to a "balancing" of costs and benefits, both in legal decisions and in the technical literature, NEPA is a radical departure from the more familiar cost-benefit assessments of old. While the law does ask at least implicitly for an identification of the full range of significant costs and benefits that are likely to result from a given action, the key provision is the way in which the identified information is incorporated into decisionmaking. In a nutshell, the EIS must contain a full and fair discussion of likely impacts or effects (along with possible measures to lessen or "mitigate" negative impacts). The EIS is then distributed to interested parties, first in draft and then in final form, before it is used by policymakers (along with political considerations) as a basis for making an actual decision. Notably, NEPA does *not* require a policymaker to come up with a "right" or "best" decision, and it does not require projects to be stopped if they would be likely to create negative impacts. It merely requires that these impacts be publicly disclosed, and that the impacts and their potential mitigation be "considered" by policymakers, before certain federal actions may be taken (US Council on Environmental Quality 1978; see also Caldwell 1982, Freudenburg & Keating 1985).

This approach has aroused more than a little controversy. Perhaps the most common criticism is that the law has been wasteful of time and other human resources, encouraging greater emphasis on "paperwork" (the EISs) than on actual decisions and policy outcomes. Indeed, only a tiny handful of NEPA-related lawsuits have succeeded by attacking agency *decisions;* more successful by far have been the lawsuits focusing on the adequacy of EISs.

On a pragmatic basis, however, NEPA decisions are by no means the only area in which courts have been reluctant to intervene in the operations of government agencies. On the contrary, this is a well-established precedent in what lawyers call "administrative law" (for discussions, see Monahan & Walker 1985, Rodgers 1981), and it is also governed by other legal rules such as the Administrative Procedures Act. In addition, NEPA has by no means proved to be a "toothless" law. "What NEPA did was to change the rules of the game; the new rules have changed the pattern of access to decisionmaking, and they have shown definite signs of changing actual outcomes, as well" (Freudenburg & Keating 1982:77; for a fuller discussion, see Caldwell 1982). One indication of the change in access comes from a study that found "consumptive users" such as logging companies to account for nearly 80% of the personal business contacts of Forest Service personnel, but for only 17% of the public comments on Forest Service EISs studied. The EIS process caused agency decisions to be "altered to some degree in approximately half of the decisions" in which the authors of that study were involved (Friesema & Culhane 1976: 349–50, 354). In another study, an early evaluation of the Michigan Environmental Protection Act, Sax & DiMento found evidence of the effectiveness of actual litigation on a NEPA-type statute. Environmentalists won over 50% of the lawsuits they initiated; most of the cases were settled out of court for an average cost of less than $2,000 for the environmentalists, and even the cases that went to court had an average expense of only $10,000 (Sax & DiMento 1974: 7–8).

In a broader sense, moreover, it is the law's very focus on the adequacy of EISs that can strengthen the role of truly scientific analysis in decision-making. Unlike the case with the more traditional cost-benefit analysis, where it is to a proponent's advantage to have the analysis "slanted" in favor of a proposed development, the focus on adequacy and accuracy in EISs can place a premium on fair and full disclosure of impacts. In addition, as Dietz (1984) notes, the more effectively the EIS identifies the likely impacts and implications of the decision, the more clearly it can be seen that a given decision indicates that a policymaker sees one set of values or considerations as more important than another. Rather than using a thin veneer of scientific respectability to hide political considerations, in this view, the proper application of the NEPA model acknowledges that both facts and values are likely to play significant roles in political outcomes, and it helps to clarify the relationship between the two. In short, while the NEPA model is still an unusual and novel one, it may deserve greater attention in the future from those who are concerned with the role of science in societal decision-making.

The Research Context

In the case of empirical studies of social impacts, perhaps the most visible need is for a continued increase in the links between SIA and the broader body of social scientific research. The recent increase in empirical testing of what Wilkinson et al (1982) call the "boomtown disruption hypothesis" is a particularly noteworthy example of this tendency. The potential for advancement of empirical work will be further enhanced if several other recent trends are continued. The first is an increasing consensus that SIAs need to include a specific focus on *sociological variables,* instead of allowing the analysis to be guided by data availability, political pressures, or whatever "laundry lists" of potential impacts happen to be available (Little 1977, Cramer et al 1980, Murdock et al 1985, Finsterbusch 1985, Jobes 1985). This change is particularly heartening in contrast to an earlier tendency, still not entirely extinct, for EISs to deal in great detail with services and facilities but to become suddenly

470   FREUDENBURG

vague when dealing with human behavior. In early assessments, the matters of traditional sociological concern were sometimes dealt with, if at all, as being related to few if any considerations beyond the provision of municipal services. One scarcely needs to be a sociologist to know that people rarely attempt or commit suicide because of inadequate sewage treatment facilities, yet recognition of that fact by EISs has at times been painfully slow in coming.

A second development, related to the first, is increasing agreement on a key dependent variable, namely *quality of life* (Wolf 1974, Boothroyd 1978, Freudenburg & Keating 1982, Freeman et al 1982, Carley 1983, Dietz 1984, Branch et al 1984, Olsen et al 1985). The field of SIA is likely to remain a diverse one both empirically and theoretically, but a careful reading of the SIA literature suggests that it may now be possible to be more specific in deciding just which "social impacts" are deserving of study: Those that are identified by a relevant body of social science research as having specifiable implications for a social group's quality of life. Indeed, Burdge (1983: 193) defines SIA in terms of this variable: "The purpose of social impact studies is to answer the following question: Will there be a measurable difference in the quality of life in the community as a result of what the proposed project is doing or might do in the future?" Quality of life is not as tangible as trailers and toilets, nor is it as easy to quantify as are dollars, but the concept has been the focus of a good deal of work, allowing SIA specialists to draw on established bodies of social science research. Most specialists agree that the concept can be measured reasonably effectively through a combination of so-called "subjective" and "objective" indicators (for discussions, see Carley 1983, Land 1983, Schuessler & Fisher 1985).

The third development is an increasing emphasis on *disaggregation* and *distributional impacts* (Elkind-Savatsky 1986, Flynn et al 1983, Gale 1984). In the literature on rapid community growth, one major reason behind the early overestimation of both anticipated benefits and drawbacks may have been the tendency for policymakers to search for an "overall" answer—"Well, so is the new mine going to be good or bad for the community?" Similarly, researchers often searched for "social pathologies" or "benefits of development" in relatively undifferentiated terms. One of the reasons for the improved progress of the field in recent years, on the other hand, may be researchers' increasing tendency to focus on specific population groups, notably women (Moen et al 1981, Freudenburg 1981), youths (Freudenburg 1984), "newcomers" (Massey & Lewis 1979), and native or other population groups that differ markedly from Anglo or "mainstream" cultures (Bowles 1981a, Geisler et al 1982, O'Sullivan 1981). In addition, researchers are beginning to focus more on the tendency of projects to redistribute resources, ranging from the broad level of national or even international changes (Lovejoy & Krannich 1982, Newton 1979) down to a microlevel focus on developments' implications for redistributing wealth and/or negative impacts in given localities. There is more than a little irony to the fact that the literature speaks so often of "socioeconomic" impacts and yet has tended until recently to avoid discussing the implications of projects for socioeconomic *status* and other distributional considerations (cf Schnaiberg 1980). As Freudenburg & Keating note (1985:15), "Even presumably 'public' projects will tend to have *distributive* impacts . . . [that] will rarely work to the disadvantage of the 'advantaged.' . . . Highways are generally built through poor neighborhoods, not rich ones."

The fourth and final development is an emphasis on *theories of the middle range*—of a level of abstraction high enough to allow conclusions from one setting to be usefully applied in another, but not of such high levels as to attempt to explain everything while in fact explaining very little. As Merton noted (1967:56), there is enduring truth in Plato's observation that "Particulars are infinite, and the higher generalities give no sufficient direction." An illustration of middle-range concepts can be drawn from the present author's own work on energy boomtowns. It may be that findings in this area are best understood not in terms of relatively global assertions about "damaged" or "improved" social functioning, but in terms of a narrower focus on a community's "density of acquaintanceship"—essentially the proportion of the community residents who are acquainted with one another. Rapid population growth and turnover in a boomtown can create a lowered density of acquaintanceship, but these changes do not lead to dramatic increases in the number of people who are truly isolated or "atomized." The decreased density of acquaintanceship may be responsible for disrupting informal mechanisms of watchfulness, socialization, and deviance control—and hence for frequent increases in boomtowns' crime rates—but the continued vitality of friendships and support networks may provide a kind of "social buffering" that greatly lessens any psychosocial disruptions that might otherwise be created (Freudenburg 1986).

The Challenges Ahead

A number of major issues are likely to prove important in the years ahead. Three that are currently discernible appear to be particularly deserving of mention.

"NON-PROJECT" IMPACTS   The first issue is one that is already being noted by a number of SIA practitioners (Finsterbusch 1984, 1985; Carley & Bustelo 1984; Dietz 1984; Wolf 1977). While the field is devoting increasing attention to the empirical impacts of specific, large-scale facilities in relatively isolated areas, there is a need to explore SIA's potential to contribute in "non-project" contexts—dealing with "impacts" that range from long-term but localized problems, such as the presence of toxic wastes or the erosion of a community's economic base, to short-term but broadly distributed impacts, such as those that result from changes in state or national policies or programs. These new contexts, moreover, may require the development of new approaches as well as creative adaptations of established SIA techniques, perhaps leading to a bridging of some of the gaps between SIA and evaluation research.

ASSESSING JUDGMENTAL BIASES   Second, SIA provides unique opportunities to contribute information on the decision-making process itself. In an increasing number of technological decisions, "expert" judgments have come to take on considerable significance. Particularly given the long-term social impacts that can result from what might appear at the time to be narrowly "technical" decisions, previous debates over expert "vs" citizen perceptions can take on new meaning. Unfortunately, "experts" are not infallible. Mumpower & Anderson (1983) and Hogarth & Makridakis (1981), among others, have provided excellent overviews of the types of judgmental errors that are as likely to be present in the predictions of purported "experts" as of the general public. By virtue of at least occasional membership in interdisciplinary teams preparing EISs and a familiarity with social science literature that many of their "more technical" colleagues lack, SIA practitioners may be in a unique position to see that such error-prone "expert judgments" are interpreted with caution rather than deference, both in the EISs and in decision-making more generally. Indeed, this contribution may prove to be particularly important for emerging field of risk assessment.

PLANNING FOR "SURPRISES"   Third, SIA practitioners may also need to devote more attention to the fallibility of their own projections. This point goes beyond Merton's (1936) conception of "unintended consequences." In addition to the potential for developments to create unintended impacts, external sources of "surprises" seem to be an inescapable fact of life in industrialized societies. SIA practitioners may need to explore approaches that differ in at least one significant way from the typical scientific tendency to make ceteris paribus or "surprise-free" projections. "All other things being equal," the analyst will say, "X is likely to lead to Y." In many ways, this approach is eminently reasonable, since the logic is explicitly stated, and the analyst does not expect variations in those "other things" (i.e. factors not included in the analysis). If other changes were expected, they could be explicitly taken into account. In other ways, however, recent experience seems to indicate that this approach is profoundly unreasonable. In practice, "other things" have shown very little inclination to remain "equal." The world-wide decline in petroleum prices in the 1980s was as unexpected as the sudden increases in petroleum prices during the 1970s, but in both decades, people who had based plans on apparently reasonable extrapolations from previous trends found their lives to be badly disrupted as a consequence. Particularly given today's changeability both in society and technology, perhaps what is needed from SIA is not only a set of "surprise-free" or ceteris paribus projections but also a more systematic examination of the implications of other things *not* being equal (cf Henshel 1983).

The most appropriate strategies for dealing with uncertainty per se can be quite different from those that are appropriate for dealing with whatever outcome is judged "most likely." An illustration can be provided by electric power planning. In earlier years, even when point estimates were bracketed by ranges of alternative projections, utilities tended to base their planning on whatever level of demand was projected to be "most likely" by forecasters. This approach worked quite reasonably as long as demand continued to rise at historically high rates—roughly doubling every ten years—but the approach put a premium on facilities with high generating capacities, especially nuclear power plants, and it turns out in retrospect to have had little flexibility. If the projections had been reasonably close to the mark, the utilities could have responded in a relatively straightforward way, slowing down planned construction or adding new or larger facilities to their schedules. Yet the very reliance on building nuclear power plants caused the planning situation to change. All nuclear reactors finished in recent years have cost far more than original estimates, and the increased electricity prices have contributed to a national trend toward energy conservation—leaving utilities with expensive problems of excess capacity despite the cancellation of almost half of all the commercial nuclear reactors ever ordered in the US (Rosa & Freudenburg 1984). In response to earlier problems, the Pacific Northwest (where the problem first became too obvious to ignore) recently adopted a policy of "planning for uncertainty." Rather than depending on the generating resources that appear most economical to meet a *given level of projected demand,* this approach emphasizes resources that can respond most quickly to *changes* in projected demand, thus placing greater emphasis on flexible, small-scale generators that can be put into operation quickly, and on manipulating the level of demand through conservation. It may be that future SIAs will need to explore similar approaches, emphasizing not relatively specific projections of impacts but the steps that appear best-suited for maintaining the flexibility to respond to a range of potential outcomes (for further discussion of the trade-offs between flexibility and apparent "efficiency," see Ayres 1980).

CONCLUSION

In short, much remains to be done. The mating of science and politics in SIA has often been uneasy, and further conflicts are likely in the future. While there are reasons for concern as well as for continued effort, however, fairness requires that the accomplishments as well as the problems of the field be noted. Like most teenagers, SIA has endured growing pains, identity crises, and overblown expectations. Further challenges lie ahead, as well, and the coming decade is likely to be a key time in the field's development. But in realistic terms, SIA has shown considerable growth and maturation in its decade and a half of existence. With the proper combination of support and guidance, this field has the potential to grow into the type of maturity that will contribute significantly to the legacy it has received both from its scientific and its political predecessors.

ACKNOWLEDGMENTS

Colleagues too numerous to mention have contributed the papers, ideas, and brainstorming time that helped make this paper possible. I thank all of them collectively here, and I hope they will all forgive me for not thanking them individually. The University of Denver Department of Sociology provided both a congenial setting and intellectual stimulation for developing this paper during the 1984–1985 academic year. Both the initial development and the final revisions of the paper were supported at Washington State University. During the process of writing the paper, reviews and particularly helpful suggestions were provided by Peter Boothroyd, Riley Dunlap, Kurt Finsterbusch, Cynthia Flynn-Brown, James Flynn, John Gartrell, Thomas Heberlein, Robert Jones, Ruth Love, Robert Mitchell, Steve Murdock, Thomas Rudel, Carole Seyfrit, and C. P. Wolf. Other helpful suggestions were provided by *Annual Review* referees. These valued colleagues are responsible, individually and collectively, for many of the strengths of this review, but they bear no responsibility for its shortcomings. This is Scientific Paper No. 7264, Research Project 0478, Agricultural Research Center, Washington State University.

Literature Cited

Albrecht, S. L. 1982. Commentary. *Pac. Sociol. Rev.* 25:297–306

Allee, D. J., Osgood, B. T., Antle, L. G., Simpkins, C. E., Motz, A. B., Van Der Slice, A. 1980. *Human costs of flooding and implementability of non-structural damage reduction in the Tug Fork Valley of West Virginia and Kentucky: IWR Research Report.* Fort Belvoir, Va: US Army Engineer Inst. for Water Resourc.

Andrews, W. H. 1981. *Evaluating Social Effects in Water Resources Planning: First Set.* Washington, DC: US Water Resourc. Counc.

Armstrong, A. F. 1982. *First Directory of Australian Social Impact Assessment.* Parkville, Victoria, Australia: Univ. Melbourne

Ayers, R. U. 1980. Growth, risk and technological choice. *Technol. Soc.* 2:413–31

Bacigalupi, L. M., Freudenburg, W. R. 1983. Increased mental health caseloads in an energy boomtown. *Admin. Ment. Health* 10:306–22

Bailey, C. 1985. The blue revolution: The impact of technological innovation on third-world fisheries. *The Rural Sociol.* 5:259–66

Baring-Gould, M., Bennett, M. 1976. *Social impact of the trans-Alaska pipeline construction in Valdez, Alaska, 1974–1975.* Testimony prepared for the Mackenzie Valley Pipeline Inquiry

Baxter, J., Cortese, C. F., Key, W. H. 1984. *The Social Impacts of Energy Development on National Parks: Final Report.* Washington, DC: Natl. Parks Serv., US Dept. Interior

Berardi, G. M., Geisler, C. C. 1984. *The Social Consequences and Challenges of New Agricultural Technologies.* Boulder, Colo.: Westview

Berger, T. R. 1977. *Northern Frontier, Northern Homeland: The Report of the Mackenzie Valley Pipeline Inquiry.* 2 Vols. Ottawa: Supplies & Services Canada

Berger, T. R. 1983. Energy resources develop-

ment and human values. *Canadian J. Comm. Ment. Health* (Special suppl.) 1:21–31
Boothroyd, P. 1978. Issues in social impact assessment. *Plan Canada* 18:118–133
Boothroyd, P. 1982. *Overview of the issues raised at the international conference on social impact assessment.* Presented at Int. Conf. Soc. Impact Assessment, Vancouver, British Columbia, Canada
Bowles, R. T. 1981a. Preserving the contributions of traditional local economies. *Hum. Serv. Rural Environ.* 6:16–21
Bowles, R. T. 1981b. *Social Impact Assessment in Small Communities: An Integrative Review of Selected Literature.* Toronto: Butterworth
Bowles, R. T. 1982. *A quick and dirty profile of the social impact assessment community.* Presented at Int. Conf. Soc. Impact Assessment, Vancouver, British Columbia, Canada
Braid, R. Jr. 1981. Better work force projections needed for nuclear plant construction. *Power Engineer.* (April):91–95
Branch, K., Hooper, D. A., Thompson, J., Creighton, J. 1984. *Guide to Social Assessment: A Framework for Assessing Social Change.* Boulder, Colo: Westview
Buffington, J. L. Meuth, H. G., Schafer, D. L., Pledger, R., Bollion, C. 1974. *Attitudes, Opinions, and Experiences of Residents Displaced by Highways Under the 1970 Relocation Assistance Program.* College Park, Tex: Texas A&M Univ.
Burkhardt, J. E. Boyd, N. K., Martin, T. K. 1976. *Residential Dislocation: Consequences and Compensation, Final Report.* Washington, DC: NCHR Program
Burch, W. R. 1965. The play world of camping: Research into the social meaning of outdoor recreation. *Am. J. Sociol.* 70:604–12
Burdge, R. J. 1983. Community needs assessments and techniques. See Finsterbusch et al 1983, pp. 191–213
Burdge, R. J., Johnson, K. S. 1973. *Social Costs and Benefits of Water Resource Construction.* Lexington, Ky: Univ. Kentucky Water Resources Res. Inst. Rep. No. 64
Caldwell, L. K. 1982. *Science and the National Environmental Policy Act: Redirecting Policy through Procedural Reform.* University, Ala: Univ. Ala. Press
Carley, M. J. 1983. Social indicators research. See Finsterbusch et al 1983, pp. 151–67
Carley, M. J., Bustelo, E. S. 1984. *Social Impact Assessment and Monitoring: A Guide to the Literature.* Boulder, Colo: Westview
Chalmers, J. A. 1977. *Construction Worker Survey.* Denver, Colo: US Bur. Reclamation
Colorado Division of Criminal Justice. 1981. *Colorado's Energy Boom: Impact on Crime and Criminal Justice.* Denver, Colo: Colo. Div. Criminal Justice, Dep. Local Affairs
Cortese, C. F., Jones, B. 1977. The sociological analysis of boom towns. *Western Sociol. Rev.* 8:76–90
Cramer, J. C., Dietz, T., Johnston, R. A. 1980. Social impact assessment of regional plans: A review of methods and issues and a recommended process. *Policy Sci.* 12:61–82
D'Amore, L. J. 1981. An overview of SIA. See Tester & Mykes 1981, pp. 366–73
Daneke, G. A., Garcia, M. W., Priscoli, J. D. 1983. *Public Involvement and Social Impact Assessment.* Boulder, Colo: Westview
Davenport, J. A., Davenport, J. Jr. 1979. *Boom Towns and Human Services.* Laramie, Wyo: Univ. Wyoming Press
Davidson, G. K. 1983. *Social Impact Assessment: A Survey of Its Practitoners.* Alexandria, Va: Santa Fe Corp.
DeVeney, G. R. 1977. *Construction Employee Monitoring.* Knoxville, Tenn: Tenn. Valley Authority
Dietz, T. 1984. Social impact assessment as a tool for rangelands management. In *Developing Strategies for Range Lands Management,* ed. Natl. Acad. Sci. Boulder, Colo: Westview
Dillman, D. A., Schwalbe, M. L., Short, J. F. Jr. 1983. Communication behavior and social impacts following the May 18, 1980, eruption of Mt. St. Helen's. In *Mt. St. Helens, One Year Later,* ed. S. A. C. Keller, pp. 191–98. Cheney, Wash: Eastern Wash. Univ. Press
Dunlap, R. E., Catton, W. R. Jr. 1979. Environmental Sociology. *Ann. Rev. Sociol.* 5:243–73
Dunning, C. M. 1981. *Report of Survey of Corps of Engineers Construction Workforce.* Fort Belvoir, Va: US Army Corps of Engineers Inst. Water Resources Res. Rep. 81-R0
Elkind-Savatsky, P. D. 1986. *Differential Social Impacts of Rural Resource Development.* Boulder, Colo: Westview
England, J. L., Albrecht, S. L. 1984. Boomtowns and social disruption. *Rural Sociol.* 49:230–46
Erikson, K. T. 1976. *Everything In Its Path: Destruction of Community in the Buffalo Creek Flood.* New York, NY: Simon & Schuster
Fellman, G., Brandt, B. 1970. A neighborhood a highway would destroy. *Environ. Behav.* 2:281–301
Field, D. R., Barron, J. C., Long, B. F., eds. 1974. *Water and Community Development: Social and Economic Perspectives.* Ann Arbor, Ann Arbor Sci.
Finsterbusch, K. 1980. *Understanding Social Impacts: Assessing the Effects of Public Projects.* Beverly Hills, Calif: Sage
Finsterbusch, K. 1984. Social impact assessment as a policy science methodology. *Impact Assess. Bull.* 3:37–43
Finsterbusch, K. 1985. State of the art in social

impact assessment. *Environ. Behav.* 17: 193–221

Finsterbusch, K., Llewellyn, L. G., Wolf, C. P. 1983. *Social Impact Assessment Methods.* Beverly Hills, Calif: Sage

Finsterbush, K., Wolf, C. P. 1977. *Methodology of Social Impact Assessment.* Stroudsburg, Penn: Dowden, Hutchinson & Ross. (1st ed.)

Fitzsimmons, S. J., Stuart, L. I., Wolff, P. C. 1977. *Social Assessment Manual: A Guide to the Preparation of the Social Well-Being Account for Planning Water Resource Projects.* Boulder, Colo: Westview

Flynn, C. B. 1976. Science and speculation in social impact assessment. *Soc. Impact Assess.* No. 11/12:5–14

Flynn, C. B., Flynn, J. H., Chalmers, J. A., Pijawaka, D., Branch, K. 1983. An integrated methodology for large-scale development projects. See Finsterbusch et al 1983, pp. 55–72

Fookes, T. W. 1981. *Monitoring Social and Economic Impact: Huntly Case Study, Final Report Series.* Hamilton, New Zealand: Univ. Waikato

Frank, J. 1932. Mr. Justice Holmes and non-euclidean legal thinking. *Cornell Law Q.* 17:568–603

Freeman, D. M., Frey, R. S., Quint, J. M. 1982. Assessing resource management policies: A social well-being framework with a national level application. *Environ. Impact Assess. Rev.* 3:59–73

Freudenburg, W. R. 1981. Women and men in an energy boomtown: Adjustment, alienation and adaptation. *Rural Sociol.* 46:220–44

Freudenburg, W. R. 1982. Coping with rapid growth in rural communities. See Weber & Howell 1982, pp. 137–69

Freudenburg, W. R. 1984. Boomtown's youth: The differential impacts of rapid community growth on adolescents and adults. *Am. Sociol. Rev.* 49:697–705

Freudenburg, W. R. 1986. The density of acquaintanceship: An overlooked variable in community research? *Am. J. Sociol.* 92. In press

Freudenburg, W. R., Baxter, R. K. 1984. Host community attitudes toward nuclear power plants: A reassessment. *Soc. Sci. Q.* 65:1129–36

Freudenburg, W. R., Keating, K. M. 1982. Increasing the impact of sociology on social impact assessments: Toward ending the inattention. *Am. Sociol.* 17:71–80

Freudenburg, W. R., Keating, K. M. 1985. Applying sociology to policy: Social science and the environmental impact statement. *Rural Sociol.* 50:578–605

Fried, M. 1963. Grieving for a lost home. In *The Urban Condition: People and Policy in the Metropolis,* ed. L. J. Duhl, pp. 151–70. New York: Basic

Friesema, H. P., Culhane, P. J. 1976. Social impacts, politics, and the environmental impact statement process. *Natl. Resource J.* 16:339–356

Gale, R. P. 1975. *The U.S. Forest Service and Social Impact Assessment.* Eugene, Oreg: US Forest Serv. Staff Paper

Gale, R. P. 1984. The evolution of social impact assessment: Post-functionalist view. *Impact Assess. Bull.* 3:27–35

Gans, H. J. 1962. *The Urban Villagers: Group and Class in the Life of Italian-Americans.* New York: Free Press

Gartrell, J. W., Krahn, H. N., Sunahara, D. F. 1980. *Cold Lake Baseline Study: Phase II.* Peace River, Alberta, Canada: Alberta Small Bus. Tourism, Northern Dev. Branch

Gates, D. P. 1982. *Social Profile: Rifle.* Craig, Colo: US Bur. Land Mgmt.

Geisler, C. C., Green, R., Usner, D., West, P. C. 1982. *Indian SIA: The Social Impact Assessment of Rapid Resource Development on Native Peoples.* Monograph No. 3. Ann Arbor, Mich: Univ. Mich. Natl. Resources Sociol. Res. Lab.

Gilmore, J. S., Hammond, D. M., Moore, K. D., Johnson, J., Coddington, D. C. 1982. *Socio-Economic Impacts of Power Plants.* Palo Alto, Calif: Electric Power Res. Inst.

Halstead, J. M., Chase, R. A., Murdock, S. H., Leistritz, F. L. 1984. *Socioeconomic Impact Management: Design and Implementation.* Boulder, Colo: Westview

Hammond, K. R., Mumpower, J., Dennis, R. L., Fitch, S., Crumpacker, D. W. 1983. Fundamental obstacles to the use of scientific information in public policy making. See Rossini & Porter 1983, pp. 168–83

Hendee, J. C., Stankey, G. H., Lucas, R. C. 1978. *Wilderness Management.* Washington, DC: US Forest Serv. Misc. Pub. No. 1365

Henshel, R. L. 1982. Sociology and social forecasting. *Ann. Rev. Sociol.* 8:57–79

Hogarth, R. M., Makridakis, S. 1981. Forecasting and planning: An evaluation. *Mgmt. Sci.* 27:115–89

Holden, A. G. 1980. *Estimation of social effects: Social science in the planning process.* Portland, Ore: US Forest Ser. Work. Pap.

Hoos, I. R. 1979. Societal aspects of technology assessment. *Technol. Forecasting Soc. Change* 13:191–202

Jobes, P. C. 1985. Social control of dirty work: Conflict avoidance in social-impact assessment. *The Rural Sociol.* 5:104–111

Jordan, W. S. III. 1984. Psychological harm after PANE: NEPA's requirements to consider psychological damage. *Harv. Environ. Law Rev.* 8:55–87

Krannich, R. S., Greider, T. 1984. Personal well-being in rapid growth and stable communities: Multiple indicators and contrasting results. *Rural Sociol.* 49:541–52

Land, K. C. 1983. Social indicators. *Ann. Rev. Sociol.* 9:1–26

Lantz, A. E., McKeown, R. L. 1979. Social/psychological problems of women and their families associated with rapid growth. In *Energy Resource Development: Implications for Women and Minorities in the Intermountain West*, ed. US Commiss. Civil Rights. Washington, DC: USGPO

Little, R. L. 1977. Some social consequences of boom towns. *N. Dak. Law Rev.* 53:401–25

Llewellyn, L. G., Goodman, C., Hare, G. 1982. *Social Impact Assessment: A Source Book for Highway Planners.* FHWA/RD-81/023-029 Washington, DC: US Dep. Transport.

Lovejoy, S. L. 1977. *Local Perceptions of Energy Development: The Case of the Kaiparowitz Plateau.* Los Angeles: Lake Powell Res. Proj. Bull. 62

Lovejoy, S. B., Krannich, R. S. 1982. Rural industrial development and domestic dependency relations: Toward an integrated perspective. *Rural Sociol.* 47:475–95

Lucas, R. C. 1964. *Recreational Use of the Quetico-Superior Area.* St. Paul, Minn: US Forest Serv. Res. Pap. LS-8

Malhotra, S., Manninen, D. 1980. *Migration and Residential Location of Workers at Nuclear Power Plant Construction Sites*, 2 Vols. Seattle, Wash: Battelle Hum. Affairs Res. Centers

Massey, G., Lewis, D. 1979. Energy development and mobile home living: The myth of suburbia revisited. *Soc. Sci. J.* 16:81–91

Meidinger, E. E., Freudenburg, W. R. 1983. The legal status of social impact assessments: Recent developments. *Environ. Sociol.* No. 34:30–33

Merton, R. K. 1936. The Unanticipated Consequences of Purposive Social Action. *Am. Sociol. Rev.* 1:894–904

Merton, R. K. 1967. *On Theoretical Sociology: Five Essays, Old and New.* New York: Free Press

Metz, W. C. 1980. The mitigation of socioeconomic impacts by electric utilities. *Public Util. Fortnightly* 106 (Sept. 11):34–42

Milkman, R. H., Hunt, L. G., Pease, W., Perez, U. M., Crowley, L. J., Boyd, B. 1980. *Drug and Alcohol Abuse in Booming and Depressed Communities.* Washington, DC: Nat. Inst. Drug Abuse, US Dep. Health, Educ. Welfare

Moen, E., Boulding, E., Lillydahl, J., Palm, R. 1981. *Women and the Social Costs of Economic Development: Two Colorado Case Studies.* Boulder, Colo: Westview

Monahan, J., Walker, L. 1985. *Social Science in Law: Cases and Materials.* Mineola, NY: Found. Press

Montana Energy Advisory Council. 1975. *Coal Development Information Packet: Supplement I.* Helena, Mont: Off. Lt. Gov.

Mountain West Research, Inc. 1975. *Construction Worker Profile.* Washington, DC: Old West Reg. Comm.

Mumpower, J., Anderson, B. F. 1983. Causes and correctives for errors of judgment. See Finsterbusch et al 1983. pp. 241–62

Murdock, S. H., Leistritz, F. L. 1979. *Energy Development in the Western United States: Impact on Rural Areas.* New York: Praeger

Murdock, S. H., Leistritz, F. L., Hamm, R. R. 1985. The state of socio-economic impact analysis: Limitations and opportunities for alternative futures. Presented at Ann. Meet. So. Assoc. Agric. Sci., Biloxi, Miss.

Murdock, S. H., Leistritz, F. L., Hamm, R. R., Hwang, S. S. 1984. An assessment of the accuracy and utility of socio-economic impact assessments. In *Paradoxes of Western Energy Development*, ed. C. M. McKell, D. G. Brown, E. C. Cruze, W. R. Freudenburg, R. L. Perrine, F. Roach: pp. 265–96. Boulder, Colo: Westview

National Academy of Sciences, National Research Council. 1984. *Social and Economic Aspects of Radioactive Waste Disposal: Considerations for Institutional Management.* Washington, DC: Natl. Acad. Press

Newton, P. W. 1979. In the North, overseas priorities inhibit local identity, with ultimate economic and social costs. *Royal Australian Plan. Inst. J.* 17:189–92

Olsen, M. E., Canan, P., Hennessy, M. 1985. A value-based community assessment process: Integrating quality of life and social impact studies. *Sociol. Methods Res.* 13:325–61

O'Sullivan, M. J. 1981. *The psychological impact of the threat of relocation on the Fort McDowell Indian community.* Ph.D. thesis. St. Louis Univ., Mo.

Pijawka, D., Chalmers, J. A. 1983. Impacts of nuclear generating plants on local areas. *Econ. Geog.* 59:66–80

Pound, R. 1912. The scope and purpose of sociological jurisprudence. *Harv. Law Rev.* 25:489–516

Rodgers, W. H. Jr. 1981. Judicial review of risk assessments: The role of decision theory in unscrambling the Benzene decision. *Environ. Law.* 11:301–20

Rosa, E. A., Freudenburg, W. R. 1984. Nuclear power at the crossroads. In *Public Reactions to Nuclear Power: Are there Critical Masses?* ed. W. R. Freudenburg, E. A. Rosa. pp. 3–34. Boulder, Colo: Westview

Rossini, F. A., Porter, A. L. 1983. *Integrated*

Impact Assessment. Boulder, Colo: Westview
Sax, J. L., DiMento, J. F. 1974. Environmental citizen suits: Three years' experience under the Michigan Environmental Protection Act. *Ecol. Law Q.* 4:1–62
Schnaiberg, A. 1980. *The Environment: From Surplus to Scarcity.* New York: Oxford Univ. Press
Seyfrit, C. L. 1986. Migration intentions of rural youth: Testing an assumed benefit of rapid growth. *Rural Sociol.* 51:199–211
Shields, M. 1976. Review of *Social Assessment Manual. Soc. Impact Assess.* No. 6:16–19
Stout-Wiegand, N., Trent, R. B. 1983. Sex differences in attitudes toward new energy resource developments. *Rural Sociol.* 48:637–46
Summers, G. F., Evans, S. D., Clemente, F., Beck, E. M., Minkoff, J. 1976. *Industrial Invasion of Non-Metropolitan America: A Quarter Century of Experience.* New York: Praeger
Susskind, L. E. 1983. The uses of negotiation and mediation in environmental impact assessment. See Rossini & Porter 1983, pp. 154–167
Suzman, R. M., Voorhees-Rosen, D. J., Rosen, D. H. 1980. *The impact of the North Sea oil development on mental and physical health: a longitudinal study of the consequences of an economic boom and rapid social change.* Presented to Ann. Meet. Am. Sociol. Assoc., New York
Taylor, C. N., Bettesworth, C. M., Kerslake, J. G. 1982. *Social Implications of Rapid Industrialisation: A Bibliography of New Zealand Experiences.* Canterbury (New Zealand): Ctr. Resource Mgmt. Lincoln Coll.
Tester, F. J., Mykes, W. 1981. *Social Impact Assessment: Theory, Method and Practice.* Calgary, Alberta, Canada: Detselig
Thompson, J. G., Blevins, A. L. Jr., Watts, G. L. 1979. *Socio-Economic Longitunal Monitoring Project: Final Report: Vol. 1. Summary.* Washington, DC: Old West Reg. Comm.
Torgerson, D. 1981. SIA as a social phenomenon: The problems of contextuality. See Tester & Mykes 1981, pp. 68–92
US Army Corps of Engineers. 1971. *Final Environmental Statement: Second Powerhouse, Bonneville Lock and Dam, Columbia River, Oregon and Washington.* Portland, Ore: US Army Engineer Dist.
US Council on Environmental Quality. 1978. *Regulations for Implementing the Procedural Provisions of the National Environmental Policy Act* (40 CFR 1500-1508). Washington, DC: US Council Environ. Qual.
Wagar, J. A. 1964. *The Carrying Capacity of Recreational Lands: A Review.* Washington, DC: Soc. Am. Foresters, Occas. Pap. No. 7
Walker, P., Fraize, W. E., Gordon, J. J., Johnson, R. C. 1982. *Workshop on Psychological Stress Associated with the Proposed Restart of Three Mile Island Unit One.* McLean, Va: Mitre Corp.
Weber, B. A., Howell, R. E. 1982. *Coping with Rapid Growth in Rural Communities.* Boulder, Colo: Westview
Wieland, J. S., Leistritz, F. L., Murdock, S. H. 1979. Characteristics and residential patterns of energy-related work forces in the Northern Great Plains. *Western J. Agric. Econ.* 4:57–68
Wilkinson, K. P., Reynolds, R. R. Jr., Thompson, J. G., Ostresh, L. M. 1984. Violent crime in the Western energy-development region. *Sociol. Perspec.* 27:241–56
Wilkinson, K. P., Thompson, J. G., Reynolds, R. R. Jr., Ostresh, L. M. 1982. Local disruption and western energy development: A critical review. *Pac. Sociol. Rev.* 25:275–96
Wolf, C. P. 1974. *Social Impact Assessment.* Stoudsburg, Penn: Dowden, Hutchinson & Ross
Wolf, C. P. 1975. Report of the committee on environmental sociology. *ASA Footnotes* 3 (Aug):15–16
Wolf, C. P. 1977. Social impact assessment: The state of the art updated. *Soc. Impact Assess.* No. 20(Aug):3–22
Yarie, S. 1983. *Alaska Symposium on the Social, Economic, and Cultural Impacts of Natural Resource Development.* Fairbanks: Univ. Alaska Press

[46]

A BRIEF HISTORY AND MAJOR TRENDS IN THE FIELD OF IMPACT ASSESSMENT

Rabel J. Burdge [*]

The purpose of this paper is to report on the history and major trends in the field of environmental and social impact assessment from the perspective of a long-time participant and most recently, President of the International Association for Impact Assessment (IAIA).

The roots of IAIA as an organization began when the National Environmental Policy Act of 1969 (NEPA) was signed by the U.S. President Richard Nixon on January 1, 1970. Under that law, proponents of development projects that involved U.S. federal land, federal tax dollars or federal jurisdictions were required to file an environmental impact statement detailing the impacts of the proposed project, as well as project alternatives, on the physical, cultural and human environments. The NEPA legislation also required mitigation measures for each impact and a monitoring program to ensure that mitigation measures were actually working (NEPA, 1970). I am sure that very few members of Congress, the industrial development community, the environmentalists, or indeed Nixon himself, foresaw how the new law would change the way the world community looked at environment issues and development projects. Henry "Scoop" Jackson, the late Senator from the State of Washington, was responsible for including the "triggering mechanism" in the NEPA legislation, which required an EIA if Federal land, laws or monies were involved. The inclusion of the triggering mechanism was a unique legislative requirement and ensured that EIS statements would be written. The Figure provides a chronology of some key events in the history of impact assessment, particularly in North America. In February, 1970, the Bureau of Land Management in the U.S. Department of the Interior submitted a eight-page EIS statement to accompany the application for

---

[*] Professor of Environmental Studies and Rural Sociology & 1990-91 President of the International Association for Impact Assessment, Institute for Environmental Studies, University of Illinois at Urbana-Champaign, Urbana, Il 61801 –USA

the Trans-Alaska pipeline permit. Two days later the Wilderness Society, the Friends of the Earth and the Environmental Defense Fund filed suit contending that the EIS statement was inadequate because it did not consider possible damage to the permafrost caused by pumping hot oil through a pipe laying on the ground. In addition, no provision was made for a possible disruption of the annual migration of several caribou herds due to the pipeline and the road that was to be built beside it. Although not specifically mentioned in the litigation, some wondered where all those construction workers and their families would be housed (Dixon, 1978: 3).

Three years later the permit to build the pipeline was issued. In the meantime, the EIS statement had grown in height from eight pages to eight feet. More importantly, most of the potential environmental problems had been addressed to the satisfaction of the courts, the plaintiffs and the Alyeska Pipeline Company (a collection of U.S. and Canadian oil companies that owned leases on Prudhoe Bay). Anticipatory planning had worked and all sides agreed that the NEPA process had allowed project proponents to deal with issues that might otherwise have been overlooked. Until the Exxon Valdez set sail on Prince William Sound in 1989, no unforseen environmental damage could be traced to pipeline activity. After the decision to build the pipeline was made, one of the Inuit Chiefs made the following comment "...now that we have dealt with the problem of the permafrost and the caribou and what we will do with hot oil, what about changes in the customs and ways of my people..." (Dixon, 1978: 4).

Unfortunately, as the Inuit chief pointed out, the social impacts on both the indigenous and white Alaskan populations were never addressed. Would the traditional cultures and way of life be changed by so massive of a construction project? What about the influx of construction workers that spoke a different dialect (of English) and brought a distinctive life style with them? Obviously, with a total population of 300,000 (in 1973) the State of Alaska could provide only a fraction of the estimated 42,000 persons that would work on the pipeline during the periods of peak construction. Because of these and other related events the impacts of development on the human populations began to be discussed alongside bio-physical and economic alterations (Dixon, 1978: 8).

One of the key events in establishing the importance of impact assessment in project appraisal was the inquiry by Justice Berger regarding the proposed Mackenzie Valley gas pipeline. Between 1974 and 1978 Justice T.R. Berger, of the British Columbia Supreme Court, conducted an extensive inquiry into the proposed pipeline from Mackenzie Bay in the Beaufort Sea along the Richardson Mountains with eventual connections to pipelines in British Columbia and Alberta (Gamble, 1978 and Berger, 1983). Although the pipeline was proposed by Canadian oil companies, the money to build it came from the U.S., because the gas and oil would end up in the Chicago market. The assessment was important because social impacts on the native populations were considered in depth. Furthermore, native populations were provided money to present their views, and the hearings were conducted in the native village in the local dialect.

The founding of the International Association for Impact Assessment in 1981 provided an international forum for persons interested in research and the practice of EIA, SIA and technology assessment. A year later, IAIA first published a journal titled *Impact Assessment Bulletin*, which provides an outlet for both scholarly and practical research. In 1979, the *Environmental Impact Assessment Review* was first published. It too, provides a forum for academics and practitioners to review the state of the art of impact assessment and related fields. By 1983, most U.S. federal agencies had formalized environmental and social impact assessment procedures in agency regulations. The social impact variables listed for assessment were often included under the label of "socio-economic" impacts.

The European Economic Community began to recommend environmental impact statements for their members in 1985. By 1989, the recommendation became a requirement. The event is significant, not only because of the diversity of language and culture involved, but because it was now apparent that the British Towne Planning tradition could not adequately deal with environmental problems.

An equally important event happened in 1986 when the World Bank made a public commitment to include environmental impact assessment in their project appraisal process. The event was important for two reasons; first, the requirement represented a split with the Reagan Administration policy of minimizing environmental assessment and secondly, it was a recognition that many bank funded projects were failing due to environmental problems and a lack of fit with the social and cultural milieu of the project communities. Taking their cue from the World Bank, regional donor and lending organizations began to incorporate environmental and social impact assessment into their project appraisal procedures.

The decision of the World Bank was further reinforced by publication in 1987 of *Our Common Future* by the United Nations Committee on Environment and Development. Commonly known as the Brundtland Commission Report, the recommendations on sustainability received wide acceptance outside the United States and further accelerated the interest in environmental and social impact assessment. The need for impact assessment was enhanced by a continued string of environmental disasters due primarily to the lack of prior planning. Decision makers within many governments and donor agencies were turning away from narrow economic criteria in project evaluation and instead opting for an emphasis on long-run ecosystem sustainability.

OBSERVATIONS ON TRENDS IN EIA AND SIA

The second portion of this paper presents my observations on how social and environmental impact assessment have altered project planning and appraisal and development in general. The key to the NEPA legislation was anticipatory change. If nothing else, the process changed our way of thinking about project planning. The major benefit was that many bad projects were never proposed or at least were stalled, because the consequences of the development (other than economic), never previously regarded, were now considered in the planning stage.

Important Consequences of EIA-SIA Legislation

The 70s in North America was the decade in which the largest number of EIA statements were completed. By the end of that time, agreement had been reached on the components of the statements, and we began to observe the long-run importance of the NEPA process.

1. The process changed policy makers' thinking about the benefits of pre-planning (although only a little bit in most cases). This change was particularly true for engineers and others from technical backgrounds.

2. As environmental planning before the event became more accepted, officials in more development-oriented agencies and ministries saw the process as stopping or slowing economic development. However, the string of environmental disasters resulting from decisions made on narrow technical and economic data reinforced the need for environmental assessment during the planning process.

Figure 1: Key Events in The History of NEPA (National Environmental Policy Act)

1970	Passage of NEPA (last day of 1969)
1970	1st Earth Day, April 22nd
1970	Suit filed against Alyeska Pipeline Company and Department of the Interior over the EIS prepared for the permit allowing construction of the Trans-Alaska Pipeline
1971-1976	Expansion of NEPA-style legislation into 23 U.S. states
1970-1973	Initial attempts to prepare Environmental Impact Statements by the U.S. Army Corps of Engineers
1970-1976	Courts clarify the requirements of EIA and SIA
1973	Council on Environmental Quality (CEQ) issues guidelines for the preparation of environmental impact statements
1973	Environmental Assessment and Review Process (EARP) established in Canada (amended in 1977)
1974	Beginning of Berger Inquiry regarding the proposed Mackenzie Valley Pipeline from the Beaufort Sea to connections in British Columbia and Alberta
1974	EDRA-1 Environmental Design Research Association meet in Milwaukee, Wisconsin-first professional meeting on EIA
1978	Final CEQ Guidelines issued for preparation of environmental impact statements

Figure 1 continued

1980 *Environmental Impact Assessment Review* – first issue

1981 International Association for Impact Assessment founded in Toronto at the 1981 meeting of the American Association for the Advancement of Science (AAAS)

1981 Reagan Administration reduces funding for the Council on Environmental Quality which overseas the NEPA process

1982 First International Social Impact Assessment Conference in Vancouver, B.C.

1983 Most U.S. federal agencies develop regulations for environmental and social impact analysis

1986 World Bank requires social and environmental impact assessment for all development projects

1987 *Our Common Future* (the Brundtland commission report published)

1989 European Economic Community requires environmental impact assessment for member countries

1991 International Association for Impact Assessment holds tenth annual meeting (IAIA '91)

3. The NEPA process initiated a more general movement to examine other development and policy settings on an ex-ante basis. Knowledge gained in a variety of development settings made it possible to understand and predict future development events by looking at past events. It was found that planning based on social science research could actually be forward looking.

4. Research on the types and frequency of exposure risks made health effects an important part of the assessment process. The continued interest by the World Health Organization in environmental assessment is an indication of this trend.

Tentative Agreement on Content of the Bio-Physical Impact Statement

1. By the early 80s, most researchers and practitioners agreed upon the ecological, biological and physical components of an EIA. Federally subsidized water-related research in the 60s provided a good theoretical and empirical basis for organizing impact statements because impoundments and diversion projects were large scale and included basic alteration effects. In the late 70s and the 80s that research effort spread to health and human impacts.

2. Research funds for ex-post facto studies in the field of bio-physical impact assessment were reduced in the late 70s and 80s in the U.S. The result was a slowing of the accumulation of data that could have been added to the storehouse of knowledge about future impacts.

3. However, just as funding looked bleak, the emergence of bio-sustainability as a research focus in the late 80s provided an opportunity to extend impact assessment research to biological and conservation issues.

Lack of Integration of EIA-SIA into the Planning Process

The failure to include environmental assessment in the planning process is a classic case of "who's to blame." The *Impact Assessment Bulletin* recently devoted two issues (Vol. 8 [1-2], 1990) to analyzing the problem and suggesting some remedies.

1. The first problem, which is only now being overcome, is that EIS and SIA statements were seldom prepared by planners or those trained

in the planning process. Because EIAs were generally completed by the project proponent, engineering and architectural consulting firms were the first to take a stab at the content of the statements.

2. The engineers were not the only profession unprepared; the planners themselves often ignored environmental concerns and information in the planning process. Trained in land use allocation and aesthetics, planners were also ignorant as to how they might incorporate environmental and social concerns into the planning process.

3. The traditional British Towne Planning system is very useful in land use allocation and preservation decisions and in allowing public comment during the decision period. However, the British approach does not specifically include an environmental component. The integration of EIA-SIA into the planning process has been slowed because many countries that used the British system assumed that environmental concerns would be accounted for through that process. The recent decision by the European Community to require EIA is an indication of dissatisfaction with the traditional planning process.

4. However, if the goal of integrating EIA-SIA into the planning process is achieved, another potential problem surfaces. Do practitioners of EIA-SIA have to be certified by university planning departments or organizations of professional planners to practice their trade? Graduation from departments and schools of planning leads to certification and membership in the planning profession. Persons who do EIA-SIA and are not graduates of planning departments may be left on the outside if they do not have some type of formal certification.

Rediscovery of the EIA-SIA Process

The time worn phrase "reinventing the wheel," probably applies more to impact assessment than any other type of planning activity. At the annual meeting of IAIA we have every range of experience represented, from new persons in agencies assigned to do impact assessment to persons who have devoted their life to practicing and promoting impact assessment. However, there are some other good reasons for the perpetuation of the "rediscovery of the wheel" phenomena.

1. The first problem is the continued shifting of ministries and agencies in both federal and provincial governments charged with reviewing

and the implementation of impact assessment. For example, under the parliamentary form of government, ministerial portfolios often change with each new government, thereby creating much confusion as to which ministry is responsible for environmental assessment.

2. Also, there appears to be a constant shift in personnel actually responsible for administration and supervision of the EIA-SIA process. Rather than seeking trained practitioners or people with experience, assessment responsibilities are given to the lowest paid and the most recent additions to the agency. In the U.S., the SIA positions are often seen as an opportunity to fill affirmative action quotas.

3. However, and perhaps more damaging, is that the content of the impact statements, to including the findings and the procedures, never becomes part of the extant body of literature. Persons in consulting firms and government agencies who prepare EIA and SIA statements do not receive credit for writing their findings and experiences for research publications. While EIA-SIA documents are not intended to be research, they do represent any important source of knowledge about the types of impacts that occur in different project settings. An *EIS Digest* first appeared in the early 70s, however, it ceased publication when the numbers of EIAs in the USA began to decline.

4. Another "rediscovery of the wheel" problem is that we do not have a series of agreed upon concepts or list of variables around which to accumulate research knowledge. The problem is particularly acute for the field of social impact assessment and when EIA and SIA statements are used as the basis for environmental policy analysis. Certainly a goal for academics and practitioners of social impact assessment is to reach some tentative agreement on procedure and content.

5. If planning departments begin to offer courses in EIA and SIA, hopefully the practitioners will have some input to the content. Some courses teach compliance with the letter of regulation, while others teach the spirit of the NEPA process and that environmental concerns should always be considered in the planning process.

"Project" or "Policy" Level?

Problems in establishing the boundaries of an impact assessment have made it difficult to generalize the findings and communicate the results to policy makers. The geo-political boundaries of the assessment delineate the range of data collection and areas to which impact events may be projected. In general, it can be said that the bio-physical and social impacts are most observable and can be measured at the project or community level. The economic benefits of a project generally occur and can only be measured at the regional or national level. It is very difficult to talk about bio-physical and social impacts at a regional level because research knowledge has accumulated in these areas at the project level.

It is also quite difficult to specify social impacts at the community or local level resulting from a decision made or an event occurring in a different part of the world. For example, what would be the likely social impacts of bringing 36-channel satellite television to the indigenous populations of Alaska and the Yukon and Northwest territories? If a worldwide embargo continues on elephant tusks, how would that policy influence game management practices in the southern countries of Africa?

Future Role of IAIA in Integrated Environmental Management

Based on my observations during the year as president and from presentations at the IAIA annual meeting, the collective fields of impact assessment must put more emphasis on monitoring, post-impact evaluation of impacts and mitigation procedures, and cumulative effects. Another frequently asked question is how to weigh the significance of different environmental, social, and economic effects in the decision process. IAIA, as an organization of practitioners and professionals, can assist in addressing these issues.

1. First we must continue the networking function by expanding the newsletter to include items of immediate interest to the profession; continue to provide opportunities to purchase journals, bulletins and books which report the latest research in the field; officially sponsor and promote new titles for the Westview EIA-SIA series thereby ensuring the financial viability of the series; in cooperation with affiliated organizations, such as the Centre for Environmental Management and Planning at Aberdeen and the Environmental Evaluation Unit of the University of Capetown, offer training programs during the annual meeting; and finally detailing interest areas in the semi-annual membership directory.

2. Encourage the formation of, provide support for and eventually affiliate with regional and national organizations in impact assessment. Examples of such organizations include the Environmental Institute of Australia, the Institute for Social Impact Assessment in Canada and the Association for Social Assessment in New Zealand. Similar groups are forming in South Africa, Quebec, and The Philippines. The European chapter of IAIA now holds at least two seminars each year.

3. Encourage the formation of topical and content interest groups within IAIA. These interest groups would then be allocated program space at the annual meeting.

4. Develop, maintain and publish a worldwide directory of federal, provincial, state and municipal ministries and agencies responsible for or who conduct all types of impact assessment.

5. Both Canada and New Zealand are attempting to pass and implement legislation which would include the basic components of environmental and social impact assessment within the larger context of integrated environmental and project management. These proposals see impact assessment as but one component of an overall goal to achieve sustainability by including environmental concerns along with economic analysis in the decision process. Much of the impetus for integrated environmental management came from the recommendations first detailed in *Our Common Future*. Certainly, the International Association for Impact Assessment has an opportunity to participate in the implementation of impact assessment into the larger context of environmental policy and planning.

References

[] Berger, T.R. 1983. "Resources Development, and Human Values," *Impact Assessment Bulletin* Vol. 2 (2): 129-147.

[] Council on Environmental Quality (CEQ) 1978, National Environmental Policy Act – Regulation, Federal Register, Vol. 43 (230): 55979-5600.7 Washington, D.C.: U.S. Government Printing Office.

[] Dixon, M. 1978. *What Happened to Fairbanks: The Effects of the Trans-Alaska Oil Pipeline on the Community of Fairbanks, Alaska*, Boulder, CO: Westview Press.

[] Gamble, D.J. 1978. "The Berger Inquiry: An Impact Assessment Process." *Science*. Vol. 199: 3 March, 946-952.

[] NEPA, The National Environmental Policy Act of 1969, Public Law 91-190: 852-859. 42 U.S.C.

[] United Nations Environmental Programme. 1987. *Our Common Future*. Toronto and London: Oxford Press.◻

Opportunity-Threat, Development, and Adaptation: Toward a Comprehensive Framework for Social Impact Assessment[1]

Robert Gramling and William R. Freudenburg*
University of Southwestern Louisiana, Lafayette, Louisiana 70504
*University of Wisconsin, Madison, Wisconsin 53706

ABSTRACT Partly because of the field's efforts to deal first with the kinds of impacts that have been the most obvious and pressing, the traditional focus of social impact assessment has been on the impacts taking place during the most intensive phases of developmental activity. Recently it has become increasingly clear that a number of predictable, significant impacts take place both before and after the periods of most intense activity; these impacts are missed by social impact assessment approaches that are excessively narrow in focus. This paper offers a conceptual framework that is relatively simple but that deals with impacts both across time and across potentially affected systems of the human environment, doing so in such a way as to improve the promise of social impact assessment to become more nearly comprehensive.

Introduction

The impacts of technological and environmental change on human social systems, long of interest to rural sociologists, began to receive more focused attention following the passage of the National Environmental Policy Act (NEPA) in 1969, which led to the development of social impact assessment (SIA) in the 1970s (Field and Burch 1991). NEPA requires agencies to assess the impacts of a project before implementation, and the primary focus of social impact assessment to date has been on predicting impacts that will occur in response to a project, activity, or other proposed action (see Freudenburg 1986a for an analysis of historical trends in SIA). SIA has been increasingly recognized as a valuable tool to assess the impacts taking place across a broader range of time frames, including those taking place before (National Research Council 1989) or after (Seyfrit 1988) the periods of most intense activity. SIA techniques have been utilized in these broader time frames for analysis (Gramling and Freudenburg 1990), mitigation (Impact Assessment Inc. 1990), and litigation (Gill and Picou 1991).

As part of this trend, Freudenburg and Gramling (1992) have offered a longitudinal framework for conceptualizing the temporal

---

[1] An earlier version of this paper was presented at the annual meeting of the International Association of Impact Assessment in Urbana, Illinois, in 1991. This research was funded in part by a grant from the U.S. Department of Interior, Minerals Management Service. All analyses and conclusions are those of the authors and should not be taken to represent the views of the Minerals Management Service or any other component of the U.S. government.

scope of social impacts. They note that impacts to the human environment can begin as soon as new information becomes available, with various social actors competing to define, as well as to respond to, the opportunities and threats presented by a proposed activity. Impacts can also continue after the development or activity has ended, as when mining activity ceases and a formerly booming community goes bust (Gulliford 1989), or when local businesses manage to survive the construction phase of a highway or dam but later, having lost a significant fraction of their clientele because of residential relocation, are forced to close (Llewellyn 1981). What is still needed, however, is an analytical framework for dealing with the impacts that can take place across different temporal stages and across different systems of the human environment. It is toward meeting this need that the present paper is devoted. We provide a description of one framework that offers a way of conceptualizing the broad and complex range of challenges to which SIA has been applied.

This typology arises from our experiences with a variety of impact assessment situations, but it was greatly assisted by our involvement with the long-term, massive exploitation of oil and gas resources beneath the continental shelf in many parts of the world (Gramling and Brabant 1986; Gramling and Freudenburg 1990; Freudenburg and Gramling 1992). Because this developmental scenario spans temporal, geographic, and human systems, we draw heavily on offshore oil development for examples.

We examine impacts that take place within six different systems of the human environment and across three periods of time—the impacts that occur during planning phases; those that occur as a project, activity, or development is being implemented; and those that take place as a result of adaptation over the longer term. Obviously, projects, activities, and events will vary in the extent to which they produce impacts in the various cells of the typology; indeed, in many cases there will be numerous empty cells. Even in such cases, it is useful to recognize that certain categories of impacts are not a matter of substantial concern, particularly if it is possible to identify explicitly the reasoning behind the lack of concern. A summary and overview of the framework is provided in Table 1.

Opportunity-threat impacts

In the biological or physical sciences, it may be true that impacts do not take place until concrete alterations of physical or biological conditions have occurred. With the human environment, however, measurable impacts begin as soon as there are changes in *social* conditions—often from the time when information about a project first becomes available. As Freudenburg and Gramling (1992:941) note, "Speculators buy property, politicians maneuver for position, interest

Table 1. Temporal phases and affected systems

System affected	Temporal phase		
	Opportunity-threat	Development/event	Adaptation/post-development
Physical	Anticipatory construction or lack of maintenance, decay of existing structures and facilities	Potentially massive alteration of the physical environment, construction of new and upgrading of existing facilities	Creation of development-specific facilities, deterioration of alternative productive facilities, destruction of environment
Cultural	Initial contact, new ideas, potential for loss of cultural continuity	Suspension of activities that assure cultural continuity (e.g., subsistence harvest)	Gradual erosion of culture; loss of unique knowledge, skills, and/or perspectives
Social	Organizational changes; investment of time, money, or energy for support or resistance; differential construction of risk	Population increases, influx of outsiders; decline in density of acquaintanceship; social change	Gradual loss of social human capital (e.g., organizational networks and skills, replacements having limited optional application)
Political/legal	Litigation to force or block proposed development, heightened political claims-making	Intrusion of development activity into community politics, litigation and conflict over activity impacts	Zoning and regulatory changes in search of new development, new laws/ruling in response to impacts
Economic	Decline or increase in property values, speculation, investment	Traditional boom/bust effects, inflation, entrance of outsiders into local labor market	Loss of economic flexibility, specialization of businesses
Psychological	Anxiety, stress, anger; gains or loses in perceived efficacy	Stress associated with rapid growth, psycho-social pathology, loss of efficacy	Acquisition of coping strategies that are potentially maladaptive under future scenarios

groups form or redirect their energies, stresses mount, and a variety of other social and economic impacts take place, particularly in the case of facilities that are large, controversial, risky, or otherwise out of the range of ordinary experiences for the local community. These changes have sometimes been called 'pre-development' or 'anticipatory' impacts, but they are far more real and measurable than such terminology might imply."

Even before any physical disturbances take place, a community can experience what we call opportunity-threat impacts. These impacts result, to a large extent, from the efforts of interested parties to identify, define, and to respond to the ongoing and the anticipated implications of development, whether as opportunities (to those who see the changes as positive) and/or as threats (to those who feel otherwise). Impacts occur not just when social groups are faced with threats over which they have little effective control, but also when there are conflicts over the extent to which a proposed development represents threats and/or opportunities.

The emergent definitions of opportunities and threats are shaped by a community's prior experience and present interests. The process of developing definitions, however, far from being automatic, is inherently social, often contentious, and capable of leading to impacts in and of itself. Facilities that are seen as involving unacceptable risks generate intense concerns. Recent proposals for outer continental shelf (OCS) oil development along the coasts of Florida and northern California, for example, have been so contentious that they eventually required Presidential intervention (National Research Council 1989; Bush 1990). In contrast, similar proposals for areas off the coasts of Texas and Louisiana have inspired consistent support, in spite of the fact that offshore oil development in the northern Gulf of Mexico has reached a much higher level of intensity than has even been suggested for regions such as Florida and California (there are currently over 3,800 offshore production platforms in federal waters, and all but approximately two dozen of them are in the Gulf of Mexico).

While there can be significant overlap, opportunity-threat impacts can be seen as having implications for six systems of the human environment. Each is explained briefly in the following paragraphs.

Biophysical and health systems. Impacts occur as individuals and groups engage in alterations of the physical environment, based on anticipated future development. These include the development of coastlines or harbors, renovation of transportation routes and facilities, or upgrading of community infrastructure and/or health or social services. Initial decay of existing facilities, often due to lack of maintenance, may also occur during this phase.

Less commonly recognized is that proposed developments can also be interpreted as opportunities for direct improvements to the environment or public health. Particularly during the early-to-mid 1970s, when ever-increasing energy prices led a number of rural communities to anticipate episodes of very rapid growth, the expected prosperity helped a number of these communities, including some in coastal Louisiana, to attract industry donations, government grants, local financing, and other resources for building improved medical and sanitation facilities. The expected increases in client populations also helped some communities to attract increased numbers of doctors, dealing in part with one of the chronic problems of such rural communities.

Cultural systems. Developments and other external activities most obviously affect indigenous or native cultures, whose very survival may be threatened by increased contact with mainstream industrialized cultures and increased integration into the cash economy during the planning stage of development. During this phase leaders of native cultures can find themselves effectively powerless to oppose unwanted development. The accompanying loss of status to elders and increased levels of anomie can worsen the erosion of traditional cultures. To a lesser extent, these same impacts occur in so-called mainstream rural communities. In addition, both in traditional cultures and in mainstream-culture communities, the battles that ensue over proposals for new developments can threaten citizens' views of how the world ought to work, particularly with respect to expected and actual actions of governmental and other authorities (Finsterbusch 1988; Edelstein 1988; Clarke 1988).

Social systems. Impacts to social systems occur as interest groups form or redirect their energies, promoting or opposing the proposed activity and engaging in attempts to define the activity as involving opportunities or threats. Interaction patterns change, old friendships are lost, and new ones are made. Potential threats include the risk of the disruptions that have characterized large-scale industrial developments in rural areas, such as increased crime (Freudenburg 1986a; Krannich et al. 1984), drug and alcohol abuse (Lantz and McKeown 1979; Milkman et al. 1980), mental health problems (Freudenburg et al. 1982; Bacigalupi and Freudenburg 1983), or even deterioration of the sense of community. Often community residents are aware of instances where these impacts have occurred in other communities. As a result, potential for such impacts becomes part of the definition process (Wilson 1982). Threats may also be seen for characteristics of the social system frequently ignored by researchers but highly prized by rural residents, such as a slow-paced, peaceful, and friendly community (Dillman and Tremblay 1977) or one where everybody knows everybody else (Freudenburg 1986b). An example of such concerns is provided by OCS proposals for the northern California coast. Although jobs in the Mendocino/Fort Bragg region are scarce, the interpretation among local residents is that this means people have to really want to live there. The slow-paced life style was considered so valuable that even real estate agents said they would not want to endanger it with offshore development.

Political/legal systems. Some of the most contentious of all opportunity-threat impacts come through the altercations that surround litigation and/or political activities in favor of or opposed to a project or activity. The battles over OCS development off California and Florida, which have been going on for decades, provide an excellent example (National Research Council 1989). Not only have numerous lawsuits resulted from this proposed activity, but political interventions have taken place at the highest level. Congressional moratoria have repeatedly been used to stop lease sales off California, and currently a Presidential moratorium is in effect barring leasing off much of the east and west coasts until the year 2000 (Bush 1990).

The litigious nature of the debate over the perceived opportunities and threats associated with OCS development has greatly increased the tendencies toward intractable positions in coastal communities and federal agencies. Legal processes start from the assumption that the relevant parties are adversaries and often exacerbate the degree to which the process becomes adversarial. Once the conflict enters the arena of litigation, lawyers for all parties insist the parties must not do precisely what virtually all risk communication literature insists that people *must* do, which is to talk to people on the other side (e.g., Hance et al. 1988). The net result is a spiral of stereotypes. Once the information loop is severed by the litigation process, individuals on both sides begin to talk not *to* the other side but *about* the other side. Experience shows that, lacking any real information, the participants will make something up, so that rumors and speculation become for both sides the primary sources of information about one's adversaries (Freudenburg and Pastor in press; Coleman 1957).

Economic systems. With economic institutions, threats often receive less early attention than do opportunities. Opportunities include potential increases in business revenue and in real estate values, but primary attention is often devoted to the possibilities for new jobs—even though findings suggest that such jobs often prove to be less numerous (Molotch 1976; Summers et al. 1976) and/or less attractive to local young persons (Seyfrit 1986) than is commonly assumed. Still, jobs have often been created locally. In southern Louisiana, offshore oil development has largely been defined as an opportunity, providing tens of thousands of coastal jobs. In part, this is because of the relatively good fit between the OCS jobs and the local human environment. When offshore oil development began in the Gulf of Mexico in the 1930s, it proceeded as a natural extension of land-based activities. It also occurred in a region with an extractive orientation toward the environment, and few other economically attractive options, as well as taking place during an exuberant era, "... when humans seemed exempt from ecological constraints" (Catton and Dunlap 1980: 15).

The same activities, however, can also lead to economic threats. In California and Florida today the same activity would constitute a potential economic threat to those who are more dependent on the preservation (i.e., for tourism, recreation) than on the extractive exploitation of the environment. Those who are living on low or fixed incomes can be threatened by rising costs, or by the higher taxes that, contrary to expectations, often accompany industrial development and growth (Real Estate Research Corporation 1974). Finally, facilities that are generally seen as undesirable have the ability to stigmatize a region (Slovic 1987; Kunreuther et al. 1988) and may be opposed even by promoters of industrial growth, given the potentially problematic implications for the area's ability to attract more desirable kinds of economic development in the future.

Psychological systems. Finally, both the proposals and the battles over their meanings can create threats and/or opportunities for psychological systems. Not just the perceived threats of a development, but also the contentiousness surrounding the definition process, can lead to anxiety and stress. In addition, the decisions that are made, and the ways in which they are made, can alter residents' abilities to maintain the view of themselves as efficacious persons. On the other hand, citizens who respond to threats can find that not only their friends and neighbors but they themselves may possess greater effectiveness than they had previously realized. One Mendocino resident, active in the fight against offshore oil, went from being the owner and manager of a bed and breakfast to being an acknowledged regional leader.

These examples do not deal with expected impacts, but with actual impacts—significant, empirically verifiable changes that would not have taken place but for the announcement of a proposed development; the actions that were taken to encourage, discourage, or otherwise influence the outcome of the proposed development; and the social definitions of the development that emerge as a result of such negotiation processes (Freudenburg and Gramling 1992). In these negotiations, moreover, project proponents and relevant government agencies are far from being impartial observers; in fact they are key participants. Their behavior as well as the behavior of community residents can have considerable influence on the type and extent of opportunity-threat impacts associated with proposed activities.

Development-stage impacts

The overwhelming majority of the social impact literature to date has involved examination of impacts associated with the actual onset of development and/or operation of a project or activity (for detailed overviews of this literature, see Finsterbusch and Freudenburg in press; Freudenburg 1986a; Leistritz and Ekstrom 1986; Murdock and Leistritz 1979). Social actors will continue to respond to opportunities, threats, and the opportunity-threat debates, even when the most intensive phases of development or construction are taking place. In the case of particularly controversial activities, it is even possible for the opportunity-threat impacts to remain more significant than the impacts that result directly from the physical and demographic changes created by a project or activity. The same six systems of the human environment that are vulnerable to opportunity-threat impacts are relevant for the consideration of development-stage impacts.

Biophysical and health systems. The more dramatic of impacts to biophysical and health systems during development, such as those taking place at Love Canal and Chernobyl, have not only received attention in the popular literature but are increasingly becoming objects of scientific study (e.g., Couch and Kroll-Smith 1985; Erikson 1976; Freudenburg and Jones 1991; Levine 1982). More mundane, but also far more common, are the types of impacts associated with stresses on community services brought on by development-related growth. The litany of impacts can range from inadequate sewage treatment facilities to overburdened hospitals to contamination of ground water from hastily constructed landfills.

Development can also lead to improvements in biophysical/health systems, as when increased prosperity leads to the construction of new hospitals or water systems or to a cleaning up of previously problematic waste-disposal facilities. In coastal Louisiana, the most intensive phase of offshore development (1974–1981) led to concerted efforts to obtain federal assistance to upgrade inadequate water and sanitation facilities and in one case to build a new hospital. Because these types of impacts are at least partially embedded in tangible physical systems, often involve unknown or unaccepted risks (Slovic 1987), and are amenable to the types of solutions conceptually available to local politicians, they frequently become among the most contentious of all impacts related to development.

Cultural systems. Cultural systems also are affected by the onset of developmental activities. The most obvious examples occur when two distinct cultures are involved. The most blatant impacts occur when cultures are deliberately manipulated or destroyed for developmental or political goals, such as those created for native cultures through the "settling" of the American west and the "development" of many other areas of the globe. Although initially appearing benign, other impacts have far-reaching implications, as in the case of contacts that introduce alien cultural traits (Sharp 1952). Isolated native cultures are particularly vulnerable to developmental contact and subsequent impacts. The increasing integration of North Slope Alaskan Native

Americans into the monied economy with the construction of the Trans-Alaskan Pipeline is a well-documented example (Worl and Smythe 1986).

Impacts also occur with non-indigenous cultures, as in the dilution of Cajun culture from inmigration associated with the offshore oil boom in coastal Louisiana (Gramling et al. 1987) and the alteration of community values in the aftermath of the "money spill," Exxon's $2 billion clean-up attempt to Prince William Sound (Impact Assessment Inc. 1990). These impacts occur as new behavioral options are required for altered situations. On the other hand, if conditions are appropriate, development can also help to preserve traditional cultures; the offshore oil industry in Louisiana may have led to significant inmigration, but it also helped to stem outmigration of relatively traditional Cajuns. Because of concentrated work scheduling (e.g., a schedule where a worker spends 14 consecutive days on an offshore oil rig, but is then able to return to home for the next 14 days) it was possible for workers to continue living in their home towns, often hundreds of miles from the offshore work locations, and even to continue to engage in traditional activities such as hunting and fishing while enjoying highly paid employment.

Social systems. In addition to the alteration of fundamental cultural values and assumptions, there are a variety of ways in which external activities and developments can affect social systems. Under certain circumstances, development can create positive impacts for social systems, sometimes by allowing people to stay in place, continuing to participate in established social networks and to fulfill extended-family obligations, as in the case of Louisiana offshore workers. At other times, development can lead to changes in social patterns, but can do so in ways that many observers would find positive, as in allowing the development of a healthier range of social options in a previously isolated and closed community. Under other circumstances, however, the impacts can be negative, and even the introduction of new options can have unforeseen implications for social well-being. Impacts on social systems have been documented in the literature, but the potential here is practically infinite. At the most fundamental level, these activities alter the way in which people interact with one another or even the extent (Freudenburg 1986b) to which they interact with one another. The impacts may involve alteration of authority relationships, as when younger Native American men were put in positions of authority over their elders during the Exxon Valdez oil spill clean-up attempt (Impact Assessment Inc. 1990); of social practices, such as decreased community involvement (Freudenburg 1986b); of interaction patterns, including fears of criminal victimization (Krannich et al. 1984); and of all the long-noted changes that occur as communities move from more traditional to more rational/legal forms of interaction (Weber 1947 [1922]).

Political / Legal systems. Litigation to regulate, stop, or gain compensation for the damages associated with a development has become increasingly common in recent years. The maze of litigation surrounding the Exxon Valdez oil spill is almost impossible to comprehend, much less sort out, and the drain on the resources of individuals, agencies, corporations, communities, and even state and federal governments in such situations is enormous.

Over longer periods, rapid development of the sort created by offshore development led to wholesale changes in the political structure of many rural communities, as the stresses of development quickly exceed the capacity of traditional political leaders (Gilmore 1976), a form of impact that can be seen as positive by some and as negative by others. In addition, signal events (Slovic 1987) may lead to political action resulting ultimately in changes in the entire legal structure. The Santa Barbara oil spill has been at least partially credited with Earth Day and the enactment of NEPA, and the Exxon Valdez spill is directly linked to the passage of the Federal Oil Pollution Act of 1990.

Economic systems. The economic impacts of external events have long been noted. In the case of developmental activities, particularly those sought by local community leaders, alteration of the economic system is a basic goal of the entire process. In these cases, injection of more jobs and capital into the community, at least from the local perspective, is both a highly desirable impact and the manifest function of the development. The distribution of economic benefits may be another matter, however; while unequal distributions of benefits can often be anticipated by actors guiding and constituting the local growth machine (Molotch 1976), the often unanticipated economic function of such development is not only to distribute negative impacts of development unequally but to impose the greatest burdens on the members of a community who are least able to afford them.

The disproportionate percentage of new jobs captured by those who move to the community (Cortese and Jones 1977; Moen et al. 1981), the inflation caused by the scarcity of goods and housing (Gilmore 1976), the impact of this on those with fixed or declining incomes (Cortese and Jones 1977), and the influx of outsiders into the labor market, with subsequent increases in unemployment levels (Molotch 1976), tend not to be anticipated. This is particularly true in cases where the economic benefits of development prove to be smaller in magnitude or shorter in duration than originally promised (Gulliford 1989). Indeed, with more massive developmental scenarios, even the best intentions and planning may be of little effect in preventing adverse economic impacts (Gramling and Freudenburg 1990). In situations where the external activity is thrust on the community, the economic disruption may even be worse. The massive injection of capital into local communities associated with the attempted clean-up of the Exxon Valdez spill, and the random, or even manipulative, way in which it was distributed, had significant impacts on the local economy (Impact Assessment Inc. 1990).

Psychological systems. Finally, there is considerable evidence that the disruptions caused by many external activities bring on psychological impacts. These impacts are evidenced by increased loads on community mental health facilities (Freudenburg et al. 1982; Bacigalupi and Freudenburg 1983) and even by widespread and systematic psychological testing for depression and post-traumatic stress disorder (Impact Assessment Inc. 1990). Mental health impacts appear to be far more common in the case of technological disasters than of natural ones (Kroll-Smith and Couch 1990; Freudenburg and Jones 1991).

Alternatively, financial rewards may lead to the easing of psychological pressure created by indebtedness or by long periods of high unemployment rates. Offshore oil development has generally been welcomed in Newfoundland, for example, where unemployment levels of about 20 percent have been common for decades. Options for distributing employment benefits more widely throughout the province have been explored as official policy (House et al. 1986).

Longer-term impacts: adaptation and overadaptation

Seyfrit (1988) indicated the need to move beyond the past focus on predicting future impacts toward post-impact assessment. Although the call for extending the analysis of impacts longitudinally is on target, the terminology of post-impact assessment tends to obscure the fact that impacts continue long after the activity in question has ceased. Impacts continue primarily because the systems in question have adapted to the activity (Freudenburg and Gramling 1992).

The usual assumption is that adaptation is a positive characteristic; indeed, the favorable implications of adaptation are sufficiently obvious that they do not need to be explained here. The focus, instead, will be on the generally unforeseen problems that can result from becoming too precisely adapted to a given set of circumstances, particularly if, as is so often the case in isolated rural communities that come to be dependent on natural resource development, the dependence proves to be prone to great instabilities (Gramling and Freudenburg 1990).

Virtually by definition, we would argue, human environments do adapt to impacts; they cannot fail to do so. The problem is not that the various systems so far identified—environmental, cultural, social, political, economic, or psychological—fail to adapt either to externally generated perturbations or to internally negotiated threats and opportunities. Instead, the relevant question has to do not with the possibility of adaptation, but with the consequences. In most instances, the consequences are neither a return to normal nor a true case of underdevelopment (Bunker 1984). Instead, adaptation may lead to situations where over-specialization results in a loss of flexibility or to situations where altered behaviors are adaptive in some situations but not in others. The net result can more properly be called overadaptation (Freudenburg and Gramling 1992). The same systems that are vulnerable to opportunity-threat and development-stage impacts are relevant for considering the potential for overadaptation.

Biophysical and health systems. Overadaptation occurs in the physical environment primarily with the construction of facilities and infrastructure and through the exhaustion or damaging of important environmental resources. If a developmental activity continues for a significant period, then the likely outcome is the construction of additional facilities to accommodate growth. Often, however, facilities are specific to a particular activity. Specific utilization of the environment for a development activity—e.g., dumping industrial wastes in a local river—may damage elements of the environment to the extent that alternative uses are lost. Furthermore, the process of construction may deplete locally available resources (Bunker 1984). When the activity ceases, as it surely must in the case of extractive enterprises, the community is often left with facilities that are of limited value to other economic endeavors. Also, the consumption of resources may have reduced local capacity to construct new facilities for other potential economic alternatives.

Offshore oil development in Louisiana provides an excellent example. As development expanded during the 1970s and early 1980s, local communities moved to increase their share of the offshore support activity. Several coastal communities produced marine versions of the industrial park. This often involved digging or enlarging canals through the coastal marsh, creating stable staging areas for heavy equipment in the low terrain, and establishing road and utility access. In several instances, this construction was funded by public bonds. With the crash of the world oil markets in 1985–1986, these facilities became liabilities for the communities in question, failing to bring in anticipated income while continuing to require payment on bonded indebtedness.

In addition to the creation of facilities that lose relevance with the decline of the dominant economic activity, overadaptation involves the loss or deterioration of pre-existing facilities that might otherwise have provided an alternative to the developmental activity in question. The physical capital of buildings and equipment can decay from lack of maintenance during the period of rapid growth. This impairs a community's ability to return to previous activities and thus increases dependency on the new development.

Cultural systems. Because cultural systems generally take millennia to develop and hone tools for survival, overadaptation in cultural systems usually involves the decay of techniques and knowledge as well as the creation of development-specific ones. While it may take many generations to create techniques that are embedded in cultures, the techniques can be lost in a single generation through the simple failure to be transmitted.

On the North Slope, the increasing native reliance on the snowmobile provides a case in point. It is doubtful that many in the younger generation have the skills to return to earlier animal-powered forms of transportation should the need arise. Both knowledge associated with the training and maintenance of dogs and construction of sleds from local materials may be lost in the not-too-distant future. Indeed, even the requisite knowledge to obtain some of the materials (e.g., the bones of large marine mammals) may also perish (as may the mammals themselves). These assembledges of knowledge and behaviors have been in existence for tens of thousands of years. North Slope oil, in comparison, is a distinctly finite commodity.

Social systems. Social systems are affected not only by the decay of existing skills and the acquisition of development-specific ones, but also by the opportunity costs associated with the failure to acquire more generic ones. Although the problem is often overlooked, the potential for depletion or loss may be at least equally important for resources associated with human and social capital—e.g., skills, knowledge, experience, teamwork, and networks of supply and distribution—as for the physical capital of buildings and equipment. Offshore oil development in coastal Louisiana resulted in just such alterations of the region's human capital. One particular example has to do with the inversion of the status hierarchy with respect to education; while many local leaders worked hard to increase the seriousness with which the region's young people approached the educational system, the reality, at least during the boom, was that young males, in particular, could drop out of high school, learn a specialized skill, and start making more money than did the teachers. During the bust, unfortunately, both the individual-level and the community-level consequences of the resultant loss of human capital have become far more readily apparent.

In addition, overadaptation may be characteristic of subsystems embedded within communities. Forsyth and Gramling (1987) examined strategies families used to adapt to the periodic absence of one family member (usually the male) in situations such as those associated with employment in the offshore oil sector (see also Forsyth and Gauthier 1991). Their basic argument was that the resulting interaction within families, while different from interactions in families experiencing more traditional forms of work scheduling, was not evidence of pathology but of adaptation. Unfortunately, these altered forms of interaction are likely to become maladaptive if the situation changes and work offshore is no longer available.

Economic systems. It is perhaps with economic systems that the capacity for overadaptation becomes most clear. Here again, the pattern involves both the loss of capacity and the acquisition of development-specific skills. A straightforward measure of economic overadaptation involves the degree to which a region's economic fortunes have become tied to a single industry. This is particularly problematic for rural communities that become heavily dependent on (or closely adapted to) large-scale extractive industries (Gramling and Freudenburg 1990). The critical concern with extractive economies is that the very employment opportunities seen as advantages by many proponents of development will, instead, lead their communities to develop an excessive dependency on a single, volatile sector of the economy and hence to become susceptible to the vagaries of the world commodity markets.

To note only the most obvious example, Morgan City, Louisiana, was the self-proclaimed shrimp capital of the world when offshore oil development was first beginning in the 1950s. After some 30 years of oil development, when a dramatic drop in oil prices (and employment) led many residents to think of returning to shrimping to maintain their livelihood, the area no longer had a resident shrimp fleet or shrimp-processing facility (Gramling and Brabant 1986). In rare cases, this danger has been recognized by local communities, and steps have been taken to protect against loss (Wybrow 1986). As resource extraction activities continue to grow in capital-intensity, often being developed in regions that are increasingly remote, the likelihood for success of such protective measures declines (Gramling and Freudenburg 1990).

Psychological systems. Overadaptation at the psychological level occurs as individuals habitually utilize coping strategies. Coping strategies emerge as individuals learn or invent ways to mitigate the psychological impacts of unacceptable situations in their physical and social environment. Although coping strategies are numerous, dictates of the situation may limit available strategies. Bettelheim (1943), for example, noted how extremely restrictive situations (e.g., concentration camps) may allow only a few coping strategies to emerge. Likewise, the things that individuals find unacceptable are numerous, but are also frequently agreed-upon. Most people object to living in the flight path of a major airport or being exposed to a toxic waste site, but if forced to live under these situations, they will develop a coping strategy. The available strategies, however, may alleviate certain types of psychological pressures in some situations while failing in others. The passive approach associated with the "periodic guest" adaptation to frequent absence of the father/husband from the nuclear family, where the father's behavior at home takes on many of the elements of the role of guest due to work scheduling associated with offshore oil production (Forsyth and Gramling 1987), may work well as long as the periodic absences continue. If the employment opportunities associated with this type of scheduling decline and he returns to normal work patterning, the male's minimal involvement with the day-to-day activities of the family may well be maladaptive. Similarly, Llewellyn (1981) notes how the learned ability of lower-class children living next to urban freeways to disregard traffic noise may impair their ability to pay attention in school.

Discussion

Clearly, there will be variation in the degree to which the three temporal stages of development are distinct. In general, or at least in cases where information and rumors about a project begin to circulate before physical disturbances take place, opportunity-threat impacts would be expected to materialize first. Similarly, the so-called post-development stage is likely to be characterized primarily by the accumulated consequences of earlier adaptations, although adaptations can begin to accumulate even before a project or action directly disrupts the physical environment, as when landlords learn that their properties have been identified as being in the impoundment area for a new dam or the route for a new highway and stop all maintenance and repair activities (Llewellyn 1981).

The six systems of the human environment were chosen not because they are completely distinct; they clearly are not. They were chosen because traditional disciplinary boundaries have tended to create relatively distinct lines of research surrounding these systems, which accordingly lead to a convenient way of organizing findings.

This conceptual framework is being offered not as a simple checklist but as a tool to aid conceptualization of social impacts. We make no claim that this is the only possible approach for dealing with the fuller range of social impacts; indeed, if dissatisfaction with this framework inspires any of our colleagues to improve on what we offer here, then this paper will have filled its purpose.

What we do claim is that a form of improved conceptualization is very much required, both for policy and for scientific reasons. Although few of the traditionally rural forms of economic activity have experienced growth during recent decades, one important if not always helpful growth industry has been an increasing tendency for rural areas to be asked to accept the types of facilities that are seen as too risky or in some cases simply as too contentious for areas that are more heavily populated. In all too many cases to date, even in the midst of supposed efforts to assess the local impacts of such facilities, agencies and project proponents have hidden behind the ambiguity and inadequacy of past terminology. Rather than working actively to deal with the full range of likely impacts, such actors have often followed bureaucratically simpler courses of action, insisting that they see no need to deal with impacts that are "merely perceptual," those that could be described as "anticipatory" rather than "real," or those that purportedly are so far in the future as to be "beyond our control."

In empirical fact, of course, these impacts have often proved to be every bit as real, as quantifiable, and as significant as the development-phase impacts that have been officially acknowledged. Given that impacts do not cease to exist if they are simply ignored, failure to deal with the broader range of impacts has meant that we have effectively transferred the risks, shifting the burdens away from the principal beneficiaries of development, and imposing them instead on the often-rural communities and residents nearby. Too frequently in the past, the full range of social impacts have been not so much beyond our *control* as beyond our *concepts*. In the case of many projects, it has been only a short step to treating these real and predictable impacts as having been beyond our responsibilities as well.

One promise of social impact assessment is that it can provide better information for decision-making. If the promise of the field is to be fulfilled, however, that information needs to deal with the full range of social impacts that are significant in their human consequences—not just those that are conceptually or politically convenient.

References

Bacigalupi, Linda M., and William R. Freudenburg
    1983 "Increased mental health caseloads in an energy boomtown." Administration in Mental Health 10:306–22.
Bettelheim, Bruno
    1943 "Individual and mass behavior in extreme situations." Journal of Abnormal and Social Psychology 38:417–52.
Bunker, Stephen G.
    1984 "Modes of extraction, unequal exchange, and the progressive underdevelopment of an extreme periphery: the Brazilian Amazon, 1600–1980." American Journal of Sociology 89:1017–64.
Bush, George
    1990 Presidential Decisions Concerning Oil and Gas Development on the Outer Continental Shelf. Washington DC: Fact Sheet, June 26, 1990, Office of the Press Secretary, White House.
Catton, William R., Jr., and Riley E. Dunlap
    1980 "A new ecological paradigm for post-exuberant sociology." American Behavioral Scientist 24:15–47.
Clarke, Lee
    1988 "Politics and bias in risk assessment." Social Science Journal 25:155–65.
Coleman, James S.
    1957 Community Conflict. Glencoe, IL: Free Press.
Cortese, Charles F., and Bernie Jones
    1977 "The sociological analysis of boomtowns." Western Sociological Review 8: 76–90.
Couch, Stephen R., and J. Stephen Kroll-Smith
    1985 "Chronic technical disaster: toward a social scientific perspective." Social Science Quarterly 66:564–75.

Dillman, Don A., and Kenneth R. Tremblay, Jr.
  1977 "The quality of life in rural America." Annals of the American Academy of Political and Social Science 429:115–29.
Edelstein, Michael R.
  1988 Contaminated Communities: The Social and Psychological Impacts of Residential Toxic Exposure. Boulder, CO: Westview Press.
Erikson, Kai T.
  1976 Everything in Its Path: The Destruction of Community in the Buffalo Creek Flood. New York: Simon and Schuster.
Field, Donald R., and William R. Burch, Jr.
  1991 Rural Sociology and the Environment. Middleton, WI: Social Ecology Press.
Finsterbusch, Kurt
  1988 "Citizens' encounters with unresponsive authorities in obtaining protection from hazardous wastes." Presented at the Society for the Study of Social Problems meeting, Atlanta, August.
Finsterbusch, Kurt F., and William R. Freudenburg
  In Press "Social impact assessment and technology assessment." In R. Dunlap and W. Michelson (eds.), Handbook of Environmental Sociology. Westport, CT: Greenwood Press.
Forsyth, Craig, and Deann Gauthier
  1991 "Families of offshore oil workers: adaptations to cyclical father absence/presence." Sociological Spectrum 11:177–202.
Forsyth, Craig, and Robert Gramling
  1987 "Feast or famine: alternative management techniques among periodic father absence single career families." International Journal of Sociology of the Family 17:183–95.
Freudenburg, William R.
  1986a "Social impact assessment." Annual Review of Sociology 12:451–78.
  1986b "The density of acquaintanceship: an overlooked variable in community research." American Journal of Sociology 92:27–63.
Freudenburg, William R., Linda M. Bacigalupi, and Cheryl Landoll-Young
  1982 "Mental health consequences of rapid community growth: a report from the longitudinal study of boomtown mental impacts." Journal of Health and Human Resources Administration 4:334–52.
Freudenburg, William R., and Robert Gramling
  1992 "Community impacts of technological change: toward a longitudinal perspective." Social Forces 50:937–55.
Freudenburg, William R., and Timothy R. Jones.
  1991. "Attitudes and stress in the presence of technological risk: a test of the Supreme Court hypothesis." Social Forces 69:1143–68.
Freudenburg, William R., and Susan K. Pastor
  In Press "Public responses to technological risks: toward a sociological perspective." Sociological Quarterly.
Gill, Duane A., and J. Steven Picou
  1991 "The social psychological impacts of a technological accident: collective stress and perceived health risks." Journal of Hazardous Materials 27:77–89.
Gilmore, John S.
  1976 "Boomtowns may hinder energy resource development." Science 191:535–40.
Gramling, Robert, and Sarah Brabant
  1986 "Boom towns and offshore energy impact assessment: the development of a comprehensive model." Sociological Perspectives 29:177–201.
Gramling, Robert, Craig Forsyth, and Linda Mooney
  1987 "The Protestant ethic and the spirit of Cajunism." Journal of Ethnic Studies 15:33–47.
Gramling, Robert, and William R. Freudenburg
  1990 "A closer look at 'local control': communities, commodities, and the collapse of the coast." Rural Sociology 55:541–58.

Gulliford, Andrew
  1989 Boomtown Blues: Colorado Oil Shale 1885–1985. Niwot, CO: University of Colorado Press.
Hance, Billie Jo, Caron Chess, and Peter M. Sandman
  1988 Improving Dialogue with Communities: A Risk Communication Manual for Government. New Brunswick, NJ: Rutgers University Environmental Communication Research Program.
House, J. D., Harold Lundirgan, Stephen Delaney, Linda Inkpen, and Andrew Wells
  1986 Building on Our Strengths: Report of the Royal Commission on Employment and Unemployment. St. John's, Newfoundland: Office of the Queen's Printer.
Impact Assessment Inc.
  1990 Economic, Social, and Psychological Impact Assessment of the Exxon Valdez Oil Spill. La Jolla, CA: Impact Assessment Inc.
Krannich, Richard S., Thomas Greider, and Ronald L. Little
  1984 "Rapid growth and fear of crime: a four-community comparison." Rural Sociology 50:193–209.
Kroll-Smith, J. Stephen, and Stephen R. Couch
  1990 The Real Disaster is Above Ground: A Mine Fire and Social Conflict. Lexington: University Press of Kentucky.
Kunreuther, Howard, William H. Desvousges, and Paul Slovic
  1988 "Nevada's predicament: public perceptions of risk from the proposed nuclear repository." Environment 30:16–20, 30–33.
Lantz, Alma E., and Robert L. McKeown
  1979 "Social/psychological problems of women and their families associated with rapid growth." Pp. 42–54 in U.S. Commission on Civil Rights (eds.), Energy Resources Development: Implications for Women and Minorities in the Intermountain West. Washington, DC: U.S. Government Printing Office.
Leistritz, Larry, and Brenda Ekstrom
  1986 Social Impact Assessment and Management: An Annotated Bibliography. New York: Garland.
Levine, Adeline G.
  1982 Love Canal: Science, Politics, and People. Lexington, MA: Lexington.
Llewellyn, Lynn G.
  1981 "The social costs of urban transportation." Pp. 169–201 in I. Altman, J. Wohlwill, and P. Everette (eds.), Transportation and Behavior. New York: Plenum.
Milkman, Raymond H., L. G. Hunt, William Pease, Una Perez, L. J. Crowley, and Brian Boyd
  1980 Drug and Alcohol Abuse in Booming and Depressed Communities. Washington, DC: National Institute on Drug Abuse, U.S. Department of Health, Education and Welfare.
Moen, Elizabeth, E. Boulding, E. Lillydahl, and R. Palm
  1981 Women and the Social Costs of Economic Development: Two Colorado Case Studies. Boulder, CO: Westview Press.
Molotch, Harvey
  1976 "The city as a growth machine: toward a political economy of place." American Journal of Sociology 82:309–32.
Murdock, Steve H., and F. Larry Leistritz
  1979 Energy Development in the Western United States: Impact on Rural Areas. New York: Praeger.
National Research Council
  1989 The Adequacy of Environmental Information for Outer Continental Shelf Oil and Gas Decisions: Florida and California. DC: National Academy Press, National Academy of Sciences.
Real Estate Research Corporation
  1974 The Costs of Sprawl: Detailed Cost Analysis. Washington, DC: U.S. Council on Environmental Quality.

Seyfrit, Carole L.
  1986 "Migration intentions of rural youth: testing an assumed benefit of rapid growth." Rural Sociology 51:199–211.
  1988 "A need for post-impact and policy studies: the case of the 'Shetland experience'." Sociological Inquiry 58:206–15.
Sharp, Lauriston
  1952 "Steel axes for stone age Australians." Human Organization 11:17–22.
Slovic, Paul
  1987 "Perception of risk." Science 236:280–85.
Summers, Gene F., Sharon D. Evans, Frank Clemente, Elwood M. Beck, and Jon Minkoff
  1976 Industrial Invasion of Nonmetropolitan America: A Quarter Century of Experience. New York: Praeger.
Weber, Max
  1947 The Theory of Social and Economic Organization. New York: Free Press.
  [1922]
Wilson, Edward
  1982 "MAGCRD: a classic model for state/federal communication and cooperation." Pp. 72–90 in J. Goldstein (ed.), The Politics of Offshore Oil. New York: Praeger.
Worl, Rosita, and Charles Smythe
  1986 Barrow: A Decade of Modernization. Technical Report 124 (MMS 86-0088) Prepared for the Minerals Management Service, Alaska OCS Region, Socioeconomic Studies program. Anchorage, AL: Minerals Management Service.
Wybrow, Peter
  1986 "Comparative responses and experiences to migration due to oil development in Scotland." Pp. 53–73 in ISER Conference Papers No. 1. St. John's, Newfoundland: Institute of Social and Economic Research, Memorial University of Newfoundland.

SOCIAL IMPACT ASSESSMENT

CAN SIA EMPOWER COMMUNITIES?

Christiane Gagnon
Université du Québec à Chicoutimi

Philip Hirsch
University of Sydney

Richard Howitt
Macquarie University

Public participation in social impact assessment (SIA) has been identified as a source of improved decision-making about resource development in several countries, with an implicit assumption that this sort of participation provides an avenue for empowerment of affected communities in these decision-making processes. This paper provides a critical discussion of the effectiveness of SIA as a means of local empowerment through case studies of resource projects in Australia, Canada, and Southeast Asia.

Public participation in social impact assessment (SIA) has been identified as a source of improved decision-making about resource development in several countries, with an implicit assumption that this sort of participation provides an avenue for empowerment of local communities in these decision-making processes (Burdge and Robertson 1990; Garcia 1983; Priscoli 1983; but also see Canan 1989; Gale 1983; and Gariepy 1991). This paper provides a critical discussion of the efficiency of SIA as a means of local empowerment, drawing on the authors' multinational experience of resource projects in Canada, Southeast Asia, and Australia.

Address correspondence to: Christiane Gagnon, Département des sciences humaines de l'Université du Québec à Chicoutimi and Groupe de recherche et d'intervention régionales, 555 boul. de l'université, Chicoutimi, Québec, G7H 2B1, Canada.

Craig (1990) has provided a useful distinction between "political" and "technical" approaches to SIA, arguing that with a political approach to SIA "a closer connection can be made between SIA and the policy and planning process" (1990, p. 45). It is clear, however, that the technical approach which Craig distinguishes from an overtly political approach, also has significant political content and consequences, promoting a corporate and state power rather than fostering community development or empowerment (Howitt 1989, pp. 159–160).

Building on the benchmark work of the East Kimberley Impact Assessment Project (Western Australia), Ross (1990) supports a perspective related to Craig's "political" approach, which she labels community SIA. This requires, Ross suggests, a cumulative view rather than a project-based approach and involves a high level of community control. In many ways, the East Kimberley Project tried to apply Berger's approach to formal SIA (Berger 1977), into a less formal setting. While this approach clearly shifts the balance of power toward the impacted communities, its wider application is influenced by political processes that demand formal procedures and positive community responses to project-based development without support for community-controlled research into cumulative impacts of regional changes.

In the context of resource-based projects, social, ecological, economic, and cultural changes experienced at the local level may involve impacts on regional and local development. It is now recognized that these impacts are still underevaluated and not sufficiently taken into account in many decision-making processes. For many communities, existing exogenous models of control and management of local resources, and their relations with indigenous approaches, have not only economic and political importance, but also play a major role in cultural identity and consequently in local development (Bassand 1990). Changing patterns of resource ownership, use, control, and management, therefore, have far-reaching consequences in these settings. This is apparent in the context of Aboriginal people affected by the Comalco bauxite mine in Northern Australia, or the peasant communities impacted by dam developments in Southeast Asia, and the remote urban and rural communities of Canada and Australia all of whom are claiming greater autonomy in decision-making and more local control and management of resources.

To date, most of the compelling work on local empowerment in SIA has been linked to indigenous peoples' organizations (Geisler et al. 1982; Gondolf and Wells 1986; Howitt 1992a; Mulvihill and Keith 1989; Nottingham 1990; Ross 1990b; 1992). Yet there are also examples of regional and urban planners and other groups who are interested in local empowerment through bottom-up responses to the impacts of changing control and management of local resources (e.g., Newcastle Ecology Centre 1980; Sthör and Taylor 1981). There has also been incorporation of some of the participatory approach of local empowerment into the discourse of institutions such as the World Bank, normally associated with top-down approaches to development (e.g., Hirsch 1991; IWGIA 1991).

This paper pursues three interrelated objectives in contributing to debate on the issues of local empowerment and SIA:

1. Reflection on recent experience of social impact assessment (SIA) of resource projects affecting people and environments in three contrasting localities in Canada, Australia, and Southeast Asia;
2. Construction of a framework that incorporates formal and informal, technocratic and participatory approaches to SIA, and allows for consideration of the interactions between them as a means of achieving improved local outcomes in resource management and decisions; and
3. Demonstration that SIA can empower communities affected by resource-based projects.

In pursuing these objectives, we acknowledge that considerable ambiguity and confusion exist in key terms and concepts. For example, terms such as locality, SIA, and empowerment, along with categories such as state, capital, and community are all subject to debates relevant to these objectives.[1] This paper, however, aims not so much to clear up these ambiguities and confusions, but rather to show how a critical questioning of categories, readily incorporated into analysis as conceptual givens, may contribute to improved practice of SIA.

Central to the opportunities for local empowerment involved has been the existence of tensions and contradictions within the ranks of entities commonly assumed to be defined as homogeneous—the "state," "capital," and "locality." In the Quebec case, municipal and regional governments, often uncritically supportive of any economic proposals, provided only conditional and divided support for Hydro-Quebec's proposal. In the Thai case, the previously unimportant and divergent provincial interests emerged as an influential coalition to challenge the hegemony of national government institutions. In the Australian case, staff within the mining company itself supported involvement of local indigenous people in a genuinely participatory review of the proposal. The importance of these changes and tensions open up opportunities for using SIA to pursue increased local empowerment and development.

Case Studies

Three very different social, cultural and physical settings in Quebec, Western Thailand, and North Queensland have been chosen for the case studies presented. Each deals with proposals to develop large-scale projects to exploit natural resources in previously remote localities. In each case, a formal impact assessment was required as part of the project review and decision process. In each case study, a dispute between the social actors and the proponents highlighted the inadequacy of initial approaches to impact assessment for addressing social and environmental concerns with the proposals. In each case,

---

[1] For relevant examples of these debates, see Smith 1989; Kemp 1987; Jonas 1988; Howitt 1992b inter alia.

the outcome remains undecided to some extent, but the political campaigns involved at several scales have had significance well beyond the individual projects, such as the question of energy demand and export (Quebec), regional geopolitics (Thailand), or mining operations and indigenous rights (Australia).

Canada: Quebec's Disputed Ashuapmushuan River

The Ashuapmushuan is one of Quebec's wild rivers. It is 193 km in length, flowing into a vast hydrographical basin, covering an area of 15,000 km^2 (Figure 1). This area is under the jurisdiction of two Regional County Municipalities (MRCs) in the region of Saguenay- Lac-Saint-Jean: the MRC Domaine-du-Roy and the MRC Maria- Chapdelaine. The combined population of these two MRCs exceeds 60,000 inhabitants. In 1989, Hydro-Quebec revised an earlier proposal to construct four dams in this area, announcing its intention to construct two dams (778 MW), and create two reservoirs of 610 km^2 (Figure 1). The Ashuapmushuan project was based upon projections made by Hydro-Quebec, which foresaw an increase on the provincial demand for electricity by 2.7% in the next 20 years (Hydro-Quebec 1989, p. 5).

This hydroelectric project is part of the new Quebec provincial government policy that aims to increase Hydro-Quebec's output to 30,000 MW, with a manageable further potential[2] of 18,000 MW, in order to make Hydro-Quebec a "driving force of the economic development" (Quebec 1988, p. 48). This policy relies on the expansion of the industrial sector within Quebec, particularly relocation of aluminum plants and export of electric power. Export contracts have already been signed with the United States. The objective is to export around 10% of the hydroelectric production by the year 2005.[3] However, the cancellation in March 1992 of a 1000 MW contract by the New York Power Authority (NYPA) prompted deferral of the work schedule for the proposed Grande-Baleine and Ashuapmushuan dams (*Le Quotidien*, 28/03/92 and 01/04/92).

Historically, the region of Saguenay–Lac-Saint-Jean was the first in Canada to experience intensive exploitation of hydroelectric power for industrial purposes, when Alcan Aluminum Company developed more than 2000 MW, largely on the Saguenay and the Peribonca Rivers. In 1982, Hydro-Quebec abandoned its original project on the Ashuapmushuan because it faced the recession, a surplus of electricity, a decline in demand, severe environmental impacts (Hydro-Quebec 1989, p. 3) and regional opposition. Seven years later, Hydro-Quebec has revised and revived its project, which has started a lively debate. Three types of protagonist defended different points of view of the revised proposal. The

---

[2] Putting aside the Ashuapmushuan River, Hydro-Quebec is studying the feasibility of a number of other sites as well as the megaproject of Grande-Baleine (James Bay).
[3] In 1992, the exportation will reach close to 7% (Entrevue Hydro-Quebec: 03/27/92).

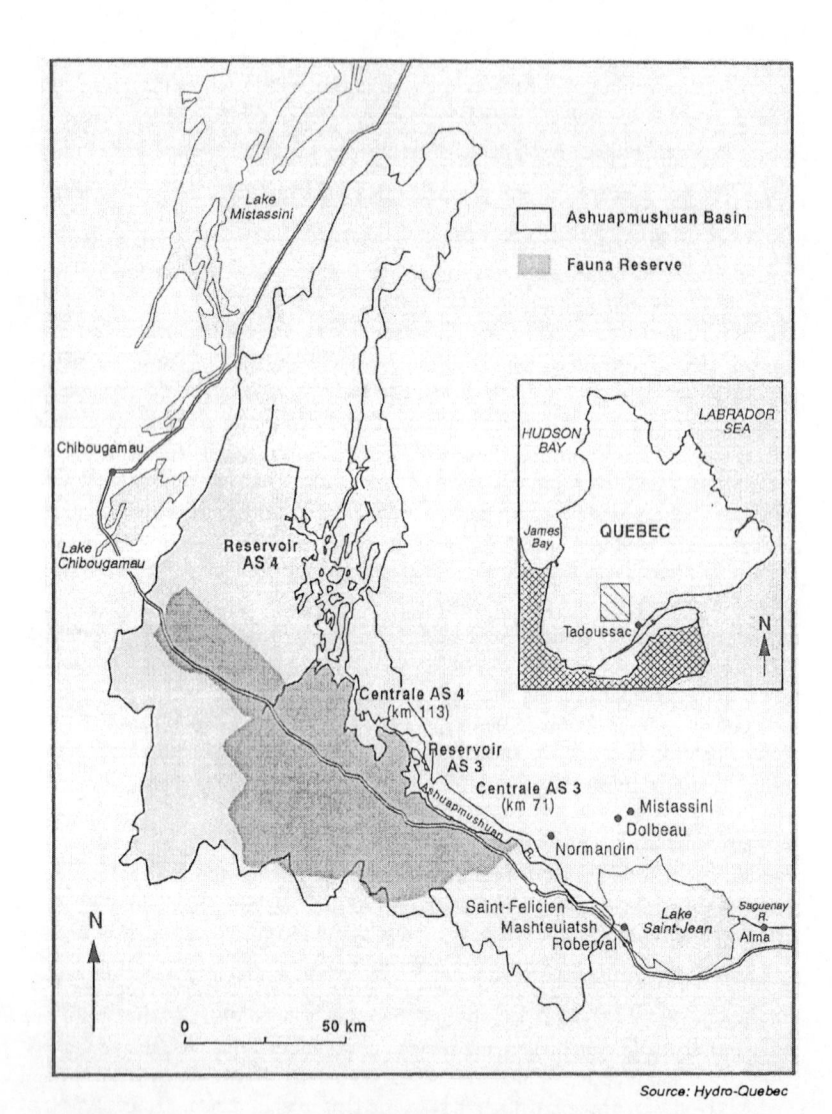

FIGURE 1. Location of the Ashuapmushuan Fauna Reserve within the Ashuapmushuan Basin, Quebec.

proponent, Hydro-Quebec, emphasized the social acceptability of the project. An unconditional opponent of the proposal was The Coalition for the Protection of Ashuapmushuan (RPA), which advocated complete conservation of the river. The two counties and additional municipalities emerged as conditional protagonists, seeking maximization of the economic benefits for the local communities.

Within the context of recent consultation led by Hydro-Quebec, about 100 individuals and organizations responded, mostly with conditional or restrictive submissions.[4] On the side of the opposition, the RPA, made up of 12,000 members, obtained the support of some 40 organizations including unions, municipalities, and regional and provincial groups. The Council of the Montagnais of Mashteuiatsh (Figure 1) disapproved of the proposal (*Le Quotidien*, 01/22/91). As for the regional population, two opinion polls, carried out at the expense of the RPA, concluded that two out of three people opposed the dam. Will the opposition be judged sufficient for the project to be abandoned, an outcome acknowledged as possible by Hydro-Quebec?[5] In fact, negotiations were taking place between Hydro-Quebec and the MRCs to obtain guarantees on local economic results and complementary studies.

The preliminary impact study, carried out by Hydro-Quebec and its consultants, gave major emphasis to the physical environment (Hydro-Quebec 1991). In one bulletin, all the impacts were identified as effects on the environment, such as the situation of the natives of Mashteuiatsh. They would be deprived of some 600 km^2 of land for traditional activities such as hunting and fishing, due to the inundation of the territory. This territory, which signifies for the Montagnais, "where we watch for moose," is composed of a multitude of archeological sites because it covers a part of the historic fur trail route from James Bay to Tadoussac (Figure 1) (Hydro-Quebec 1991b, p. 18). As for the forest, the flood would represent a virtual loss of 84,000 m^3 per year of logging (Hydro-Quebec 1991b, p. 18). The construction of the dam would significantly affect reproduction of the fresh water salmon and sport fishing.[6] Some occupations connected with tourism and leisure activities will be permanently altered.

In a region where a lot of jobs depend on the forest industry or more and more on tourism, and where the natives claim territory, a cumulative SIA study (Ross 1990a) should be essential as well as an environmental impact study (EIA). In the pre-project study (stage 1), however, the social impact is a sectoral description of "the human environment" alone, collecting known data (see Hydro-Quebec 1991a, pp. 107–138). There are no alternative scenarios concerning regional development relating to tourism or forestry industries. The study reveals a captive approach which ensures that negative local impacts are not emphasized.

Therefore, while technical and political issues related to the impact studies do exist, the major issue involves the communities' autonomy in orienting their mode of development or setting the conditions for development according to their needs, strategies, and priorities. The report from the Joint Committee, formed by

---

[4] Interview Hydro-Quebec: 03/27/92. On Hydro-Quebec's public consultations see also Gariepy 1991.
[5] Declaration made at the time of the official announcement of the studies of the pre-project in 1989.
[6] The Joint Committee report of the two municipalities of Domaine-du-Roy and Maria-Chapdelaine estimated this loss between one and two million dollars.

the two counties, gives evidence of this issue. They require that, before coming to a decision on the social acceptability, Hydro-Quebec provides:

- some complementary environmental studies;
- an agreement which ensures that some of the money ($344 million) will be spent locally;
- the creation of a regional fund, supplied by the revenues and royalties on public and private exploitation (Hydro-Quebec and Alcan) of the hydraulic forces (Comité conjoint des MRC du Domaine-Du-Roy et de Maria-Chapdelaine 1991, p. 12).

In a region historically oriented to resource development, and characterized by unemployment, economic and demographical slowdowns, and increased gaps between the regions of Quebec, the MRC's response is a significant step toward achieving increased control of exogenous projects and on their impacts.

Responses and solutions were identified by the individuals and social groups to stop the project: to develop leisure, forestry, fauna, and cultural aspects (RPA, no date, p. 11); to promote programs of energy conservation; to use of the hydraulic potential still available on the Peribonca, etc. Broadly, what is strongly questioned by many elements of the Quebec population is the necessity, viability, and effectiveness[7] of this type of project. The creation of an independent commission on energy is demanded.

There is a deep unrest in Quebec about formal impact assessment procedures, especially for resources projects. The public consultation process and the "technical" approach to making the assessment have failed to meet the expectations of the affected communities. In the case of the Ashuapmushuan River, the opponents believe that if the project reaches the step of the public hearings, it will already have been lost. They doubt the credibility, the balance of power of the Public Hearings Environmental Board of Quebec,[8] and the impartiality of the results of the impact study carried out by the proponent. Then, it happens that the negotiations between the official (elected) protagonists are made before the formal process of assessment. In the present case, the MRC is negotiating with Hydro-Quebec at the pre-project stage. This type of mediation process raises other questions such as the place of public hearings. Whatever happens, the debate on the Ashuapmushuan River involves a strong public demand for community viability, much greater political rationality and accountability in the decision-making process. The present and future needs as well as the apprehensions of the local and regional communities have to be considered by the proponent and politicians.

---

[7] Belanger and Bernard (1991) estimated that the cheap price for hydroelectric power of the aluminum industry would represent a loss of $300 million per year for the Quebec, relative to export of the same amount of power.
[8] The cases of the hearings on the banks of Lac Saint-Jean and Soligaz are referred to here.

Southeast Asia: the Case of Thailand's Nam Choan Dam and its Aftermath[9]

On April 5, 1988, the Thai Council of Economic Ministers accepted a high-level committee's recommendation to shelve plans to construct the Nam Choan Dam in Kanchanaburi Province near the western border with Burma (Figure 2). This decision was both a culmination of rapidly escalating and broadening concern over the environmental and social impacts of large resource projects in Thailand, and a precursor to intensified public debate and conflict over a host of other resource-related social and environmental issues. In this way, Nam Choan was something of a watershed in popular participation in impact assessment, albeit a participation that continues to lie well outside formal EIA or SIA procedures.

The Nam Choan Dam was initially proposed in 1972 by the Electricity Generating Authority of Thailand (EGAT), the state enterprise responsible for electricity generation nationwide. A 187-m high dam was to provide 580 MW hydroelectric generating potential to feed into the national grid. The World Bank was actively involved as a potential source of loan funding for the project. The dam would be the third major dam on the two branches of the Khwae River, upstream of the Srinakharin Dam on the Khwae Yai (Figure 2), and the largest hydro-project to date in Thailand.

There were several major concerns regarding Nam Choan, primary among which was its impact on the Thung Yai Naresuan Wildlife Reserve. The reservoir would only flood about 4% of the reserve's area, but this would include most of the rare lowland riverine forest habitat and, even more significantly, greatly increase accessibility for loggers and follow-on settlers. Moreover, migration routes for the larger mammals would be disrupted. Six Karen communities would be flooded, all of which had been in the area for many generations. None of these concerns were addressed in any detail in the EGAT-commissioned environmental impact assessment in 1980 (Stewart–Cox 1987).[10]

Potential downstream impacts were uncertain. One of the major concerns that emerged during the controversy engendered by the proposal was the threat of dam failure due to earthquakes, with one of Thailand's leading geologists expressing doubts over the wisdom of building a large dam in such a seismically unstable area (Prinya 1987). The dam would have had few irrigation or flood control benefits other than supplementing the storage capacity of the Srinakharin Dam, so the debate became focused around the issue of sacrifices being asked of rural people and environments to cater to urban and industrial development interests.

In 1982, a number of Thai student environmental groups, concerned academics, and other government officials organized a campaign of opposition to

---

[9] For more detailed discussion of Nam Choan and its implications, refer to Nart 1984; Stewart–Cox 1987; Prinya 1987; Hirsch 1987; Dhira and Widhanya 1989; Hirsch and Lohmann 1989; Hirsch forthcoming.
[10] Under existing legislation, the National Environment Board required EGAT to carry out an EIA for the project.

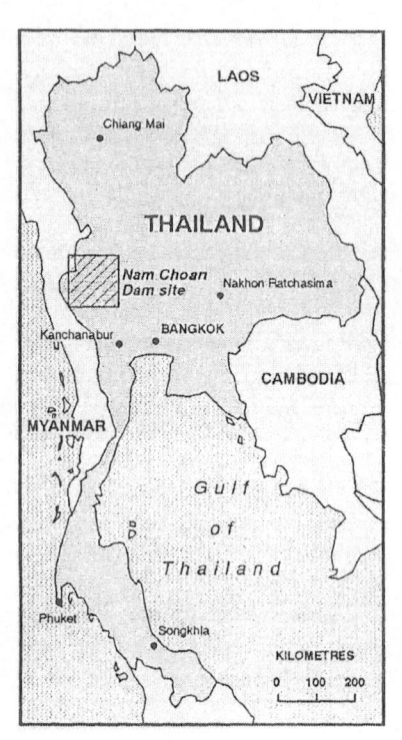

FIGURE 2. Nam Choan Dam site in Thailand.

the dam and in April 1983 succeeded in having it shelved. At this stage there was little question of local involvement in protest action or petitioning, partly due to the still politically sensitive nature of the area in question, which until very recently had been one of the most secure base areas of the outlawed Communist Party of Thailand. However, concerned officials of the Royal Forestry Department, including the management of the Thung Yai Naresuan Wildlife Reserve, were actively opposed to the dam, to the extent that a decree was issued forbidding government officials, including academics, to comment publicly on the project.

In 1986, Nam Choan was quietly revived. This time, however, the considerable liberalization that was occurring in Thai society, growing concern about deforestation, increased sophistication among urban-based environmental groups, but above all growing confidence among the rural population of the legitimacy of voicing protest within the system, led to a different order of campaign against the dam, one that ultimately involved groups from the Karen who would have been flooded out of their homes and land, through Kanchanaburi residents worried about the earthquake risk and further depredations on the province's forests, student environmental groups, to international environmental groups concerned about an area being considered for nomination as a World Heritage site.

Although all of these groups and the coalition of diverse interests contributed to the opposition to the dam, perhaps most novel and significant in the Nam Choan case was response at the provincial level. Past campaigns and controversies over resource projects had usually only emerged at the national level and among student environmental groups, with local opposition rarely being voiced and never being influential. The emergence of a coalition of teachers, lawyers, women's groups, civic and business groups and others in the province of Kanchanaburi was a crucial link between local people's aspirations and Bangkok-based groups. In particular, the leadership of the Kanchanaburi Nam Choan Opposition Centre by the president of the elected Provincial Assembly, and the acceptance of position of secretary by the manager to the Thung Yai reserve (i.e., a civil servant), gave legitimacy to local concerns and allowed the coalition the chance to confront head-on the EGAT insinuation that opposition groups were "communist-inspired," a charge that had in the past contributed to silencing local voices.

In September 1987, amidst public controversy a committee headed by General Thienchai Sirisamphan was appointed to carry out studies by five sub-committees and make a recommendation.[11] Initially the committee appeared to be stacked with pro-dam officials, but by March 1988 public opposition, supported by the media, was such as to leave little option other than to recommend cancellation.

Following the cancellation of the Nam Choan Dam resulting from political pressure from grassroots to international levels, a number of other environmentally sensitive resource projects came onto the national agenda. The three principal recurring areas of controversy have been dams, logging, and reforestation with eucalyptus. Following Nam Choan, the Kaeng Krung, Kaeng Sua Ten, and Pak Mul Dams in the South, North, and Northeast respectively have all met with local and wider opposition. Pak Mul made international headlines in 1991 when for the first time, executive directors of the Bank (being asked to provide partial loan funding for the dam), in Bangkok for their annual meeting, were forced to confront farmers due to lose their land. Logging became a national issue following floods in southern Thailand in late 1988 attributed in part to illegal logging, which led to a national ban on logging in January 1989. Reforestation with eucalyptus has become a major issue in the Northeast as farmers are moved off forest reserve land to make way for plantations (Hirsch and Lohmann 1989).

---

[11] None of these included impact on communities to be flooded. The five areas were: forest and wildlife; seismic potential; economics, energy and finance; archaeological values; water quality and public health (Dhira ad Widhanya 1989).

All these responses to what are at first sight primarily environmental issues have in common local concern at encroachment on rural communities' resource base. It is primarily this material concern that has led to heightened community involvement in resource and environmental debates over Thailand's development path. To date, there are still few channels for integrating these concerns into environmental or social impact assessment procedures, and as a result resource development and associated social and environmental impact remains highly polarized.

The most recent development in this area has been the increasing tendency for Thailand to turn to the natural resources of neighboring countries, particularly for timber and new sources of hydropower in Burma, Cambodia, and Laos. This is facilitated by changing regional geopolitics and is partly due to the greatly diminished natural resource base of Thailand as a result of past exploitation, but it is also due to the much more limited opportunities for community response in neighboring countries. The legacy of Nam Choan, therefore, is highly complex, having provided the precedent to give confidence for increased community involvement in response to actual or impending impacts of resource projects, but also to some extent encouraging a shift to areas where such response is not so easily articulated and organized into simultaneous campaigns at a number of scales.

Australia: Proposed Alumina Refinery at Weipa, Queensland

Weipa, on the west coast of Queensland's Cape York Peninsula (Figure 3), is the location of one of the world's largest bauxite mines, operated since 1963 by Comalco, an Australian company with links to the Rio Tinto Zinc Corporation group in the UK.[12] Weipa bauxite is integrated into international markets through direct exports and exports of alumina from the Queensland Alumina Ltd refinery in Gladstone, on Queensland's east coast, a joint venture in which Comalco holds a 30.3% interest.

In the 1980s a degree of doubt over the Weipa operation had arisen following dramatic restructuring in the international aluminum industry, including the closure of all alumina refining capacity and most smelting capacity in Japan, previously a major destination for Weipa bauxite exports. In 1990 Comalco announced a proposal to construct a large new refinery at Weipa aimed at reducing transport costs and increasing viability of processing lower ore grades.

During 1990 Alcan joined Comalco in a joint project (Weipa Alumina Plant Project—WAPP) to determine the feasibility of the Weipa proposal. Alcan has held undeveloped bauxite leases adjacent to the Comalco leases since 1965, and their participation in the project increases the likelihood of development of these lease areas by integrating them with the Comalco leases.

---

[12] For overviews the RTZ Group generally see e.g., Howitt and Douglas 1983, ch. 2, and Moody 1991. For more historical background on Weipa see Howitt, 1992c and the references therein.

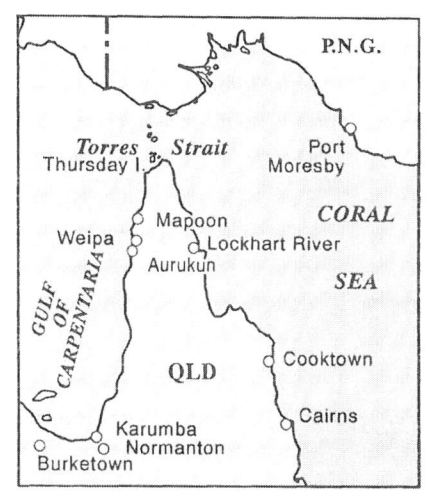

FIGURE 3. Site of proposed alumina refinery at Weipa, Queensland.

An initial advice statement to the Queensland Government in October 1990 reported preliminary investigation of five Weipa area sites. The Whiting site, three kilometers south of the Aboriginal settlement of Napranum, was identified at this stage as the "technically preferred site," although a refinery on the site and its associated infrastructure would have left Napranum completely surrounded by industrial development (Figure 4). Social and environmental implications of the Whiting site for the nearby Napranum community were glossed over in the initial advice statement with an inconclusive undertaking to future action:

> The effects on the existing community and social structure including the aboriginal [sic][13] population in particular Napranum, will be addressed (Hollingsworth Dames and Moore, 1990, p. 29).

After further investigation and discussions with local community groups, all five initial sites were rejected during 1991. This review identified several additional local sites, including some suggested by local people, as worthy of further investigation. By mid-1991 WAPP confirmed two local sites, East Andoom and Humbug (Figure 4), as possible development sites. These would be compared in detailed studies with an alternative site at Bowen on the east coast.

At an early stage of discussions about the proposed refinery, Napranum Council, the local Aboriginal and Islander community government organization, indicated

---

[13] Australian conventions require the word "Aboriginal" to be capitalized. Failure to do so, as in this statement, indicates a lack of sensitivity to Aboriginal cultural and political issues.

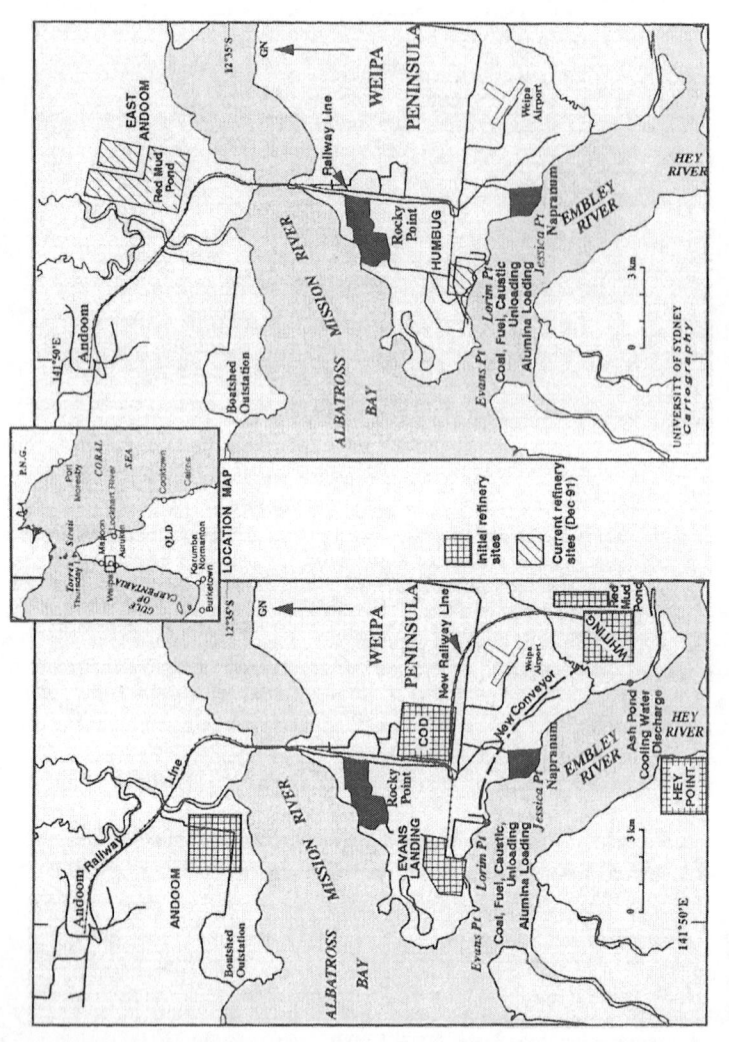

FIGURE 4. East Andoon and Humbug—additional possible development sites.

that it would expect to control any impact assessment studies involving the people of Napranum. One of the authors was involved in an independent study of impact issues related to the existing mine at the time this proposal was raised (Howitt 1992b). When asked by WAPP personnel, he counseled that conventional technical approaches to SIA at Napranum would create rather than resolve conflicts between the refinery project and Napranum. He further suggested that a Napranum social impact study should be "participatory, interventionist and responsive to local dynamics rather than adopting the conventions which have marginalised Aboriginal peoples in others EISs" (Howitt 1991, p. 3).

Soon after, Napranum Council and Tharpuntoo commissioned a critique of the proposal as part of the Queensland Government's public process of developing impact assessment guidelines for this proposal. This made clear the Aboriginal community's desire and determination to control any impact research affecting them. The guidelines, however, did not go nearly far enough to meet the Council's expectations. Although the Environmental Impact Study was to be required to:

... specifically address the impact on, and concerns of, Aboriginal communities ... [and that] In these matters there should be close liaison with traditional Aboriginals of the region (Australia and Queensland 1991, pp. 4–5).

the Council felt that Aboriginal people and their organizations should, as a matter of principle, not be seen as optional consultants to be liaised with at the discretion of the developers' impact assessment consultant. Rather, they asserted, they should be empowered to act to address negative impact directly and to engage in the assessment and amelioration of impacts directly. From the Council's point of view it would be completely unacceptable to have an impact study that accurately monitored the speed and direction in which the community was "going down the drain" as a result of negative impacts of development.

For the Napranum community, the refinery proposal raised a number of serious impact issues. First was a series of concerns about being besieged by an influx of construction workers. The proposal to accommodate workers at the Whiting site, where the Napranum Tavern would be the closest bar, was seen as particularly threatening because previously experience in other parts of Australia has confirmed alcohol-related violence and disturbance as a major source of impacts. Second was a complex set of issues concerning existing unresolved impacts from the development of the mine, the mining town, and recent proposals to "normalize" the mining town[14] and recognize Aboriginal land rights.[15] Third,

---

[14] Under normalization proposals, Comalco would take a less dominant role in administration of local government functions in the mining town areas. Prospects for sale of mining lease land to private interests, development of an elected local government structure parallel to the Napranum Community Government Council, and other aspects of the process all raised concerns among local Aboriginal people.

[15] Under the terms of the Aboriginal Land Act 1991, Queensland Aboriginal people have been able to lodge claims for limited amounts of Crown land. Alienation of the former Aboriginal Reserve lands currently covered by the mining and special purpose leases at Weipa was seen as threat to people's ability to pursue longstanding grievances over the unilateral revocation of the Aboriginal Reserve in the early 1950s when bauxite was discovered.

there were serious concerns about the interaction of biophysical environmental impacts and social, cultural, and economic effects on Napranum. The Whiting site area is used for subsistence fishing and other activities, and fears of continued access to these resources existed. There is also an aquacultural industry under investigation by Comalco and local Aboriginal groups, and damage to sensitive estuarine ecosystems was seen as a threat to this. Fourth, all parties had concerns about the effects the proposal might have on generally improving relations between the Comalco mining operation and the Aboriginal population. Finally, the involvement of Alcan, which has held undeveloped mining leases in areas of continuing interest to Aboriginal traditional owners at Weipa[16] for many years, raised serious questions about the expansion of mining operations into new areas.

While the Government's guidelines for the project assessment fell below the standards desired by Napranum Council, WAPP made it clear throughout its discussions with the Council that they not only accepted a high level of community participation in the impact research, but they would also welcome and support this. From Napranum's point of view, this provided a window of opportunity to pursue a community development agenda throughout the impact assessment process.[17] After several months of formal and informal discussions and negotiations Napranum Council and WAPP reached in-principle agreement about the processes to be used for a Napranum social impact study as part of the formal environment assessment of the refinery proposal:

- the Council itself would be employed as the consultant for the study;
- the Council would have complete freedom to select its own expert consultants in specialist areas;
- the full text of the Council's Napranum social impact study would be published as part of the final EIS; and
- an advisory a committee consisting of WAPP, Napranum Council and its subconsultants, WAPP's principal consultant, and open to others as required, would be established and funded to meet as a forum for free and open exchange and discussion of research in all areas of the EIS.

In September 1991 WAPP announced that it would undertake a detailed review of economics issues associated with the refinery proposal, including a detailed

---

[16] Under the Queensland Aboriginal Land Act 1991, some limited opportunities for Aboriginal people's traditional claims to land ownership prior to non-Aboriginal invasion and occupation emerged. The land held by Alcan, however, would not be available for claim under this legislation.

[17] It is worth noting here that Napranum is not the only Aboriginal community affected by the refinery proposal, although it clearly faces the most direct and dramatic impacts. Aurukun, 60 kilometers south, and Mapoon, 40 kilometers north, will also face significant effects from the proposal. In the wider Cape York Peninsula region, communities at Lockhart River, Iron Range, Coen, and other locations will face impacts from increased local tourism, increased pressure on resources, and other regional impacts. Howitt's involvement with Napranum Council in negotiations with WAPP has restricted his treatment of the broader issues. Although the Council raised the need to ensure high levels of regional Aboriginal involvement in studying the project during the negotiations, they were principally concerned to protect their own local interests rather than pursuing a wider regional agenda.

comparison with costs at the Bowen site. The Weipa site office was closed and the arrangements for impact assessment research placed on hold for at least twelve months. From the Council's point of view, this removes an unwelcome and unneeded source of social pressure on the community, although prospects for using the Napranum social impact study to formally review unresolved grievances from previous development was something to which many looked forward. It remains a possibility that the project will be revived at Weipa, in which case the Napranum social impact study will again become a focus of community strategies in securing improved Aboriginal participation in local development decisions.

Discussion

Despite the particularities in these three examples, each exemplifies important issues to guide SIA approaches and practice toward community empowerment outcomes. We identify three types of issues: divided power, win–win scenario, and territorially based action.

Divided Power

In each case study, nominally unified and powerful actors, generally oriented to specific self-interest concerns within the statutory impact assessment and decision-making, e.g., corporate proponents, state, central, and local institutions, exhibit a range of internal tensions and divisions that created opportunities for locally empowering interventions.

The centralized power of institutions, such as resource transnationals like Comalco, state authorities like Hydro-Quebec and EGAT, international organizations such as the World Bank, and government structures, is fragmenting under various pressures. Recognition of this situation can be an important first step in establishing empowerment strategies relevant to formal SIA processes. Areas of common ground or strategic weakness or grounds for cross-factional and inter-regional alliances may emerge for investigations in this area.[18] In many cases, simply recognizing that decisions of powerful statutory authorities and transnational corporations are not independent of human intervention is itself empowering—specific decisions (or even policies) are no longer felt to be irreversible, and possibilities for alteration or even cancellation of undesirable development proposals can be discussed as realistic options rather than pipedreams. Recognition of divided power is a source of empowerment in terms of viable and acceptable responses to affected groups.

---

[18] Michalenko (1981) provides a useful overview of the need to assess the corporations producing social assessment as part of the broader SIA process.

Win–Win Approaches to Conflict

The dangers of conventional win–lose approaches to resource decisions are dramatically illustrated in the circumstances surrounding the closure of the Bougainville Copper Mine in Papua New Guinea in 1989. This example highlights the extent to which development of projects on terms that excessively favor a powerful company creates timebombs of social tension that can ultimately destroy most of the apparent benefits generated.[19] If a project proponent can be persuaded to realize that social dissatisfaction can affect long-term viability and security of investments, before decisions are made instead of retrospectively, it is possible for many proposals to be transformed into more locally acceptable forms, from which a wider range of impacted groups derive some direct and meaningful benefits (e.g., acceptable compensation, training, and employment guarantees, associated educational, infrastructural, and other investments valued by the affected groups, even decentralized infrastructure such as power lines from hydro-electric schemes so that affected groups gain the benefits of electrification).

Even where regional or local priorities require abandonment or marked changes to a project, the process of negotiating with the affected social actors affords the proponent an alternative. In the Quebec case, negotiations between Hydro-Quebec and the two MRCs addressed possibilities for a sustainable regional economic development that could lead to a win–win scenario, following agreement to the conditions from all the major intervenors. Local communities did shape alternatives to the proposed Ashuapmushuan project, as well as a change in external circumstances (export markets), a program of energy savings, and more effective use of sites and facilities.

The Weipa case provides a good example of both the positive outcomes and considerable difficulties involved in pursuing a win–win approach. The weakness, from the perspective of the affected communities, is their lack of secure standing in most formal SIA procedures. The agreement secured from WAPP concerning the proposed study for the refinery remains only an in-principle agreement, not a statutory requirement. A change of management, a change of external economic imperatives, or a change of political circumstances could easily see a return of pressures for the companies involved to pursue more conventional win–lose results, in which local Aboriginal people again become marginalized losers in another round of win–lose development decisions in the Cape York region.

In the case of Southeast Asia, failure to involve local people in the Pak Mul and other projects has resulted in severe difficulties for the project proponents and funding bodies. Applying the participatory lessons of the Nam Choan case suggests that potential exists for win–win scenarios to be constructed in these cases, although in the case of another Nam Choan the "win" for EGAT may be

---

[19] The timebomb analogy comes from Filer (1990). See also Connell (1991) for background in Bougainville.

reduced loss of time, money, or faith rather than ultimate success in going ahead with the dam. Certainly, the prospects for local community participation in constructing win–win outcomes through preparatory studies funded under the new World Bank guidelines (IWGIA 1991) are substantially greater than existed prior to the Nam Choan controversy.

Territorially Based Action

Central to community empowerment is the formation and transformation of political alliances around proposed development projects. In many cases common ground between sometimes antagonistic groups (landlords and tenants; farmers and mineworkers; indigenous peoples and urban middle classes; peasants and environmentalists) establishes the base for territorial action and campaigns. In the context of the opportunities presented to communities in formal SIA processes, these pragmatic alliances present a substantial challenge to political approaches which assume that such coalitions should be entrenched in institutionalized politics. For example, popular front politics often assume that such solidarity is the first step in the creation of a broader national revolutionary politics or foundations for challenges to established political structures. The practicalities of pragmatic community politics generally ensure that the alliances are campaign-specific, temporary, and flexible. As a result a territorially based action may also be tenuous, and vulnerable to all sorts of pressures, from within and without. Nevertheless, they have proved empowering to a significant degree in the cases examined here.

In the case of Hydro-Quebec's proposed Ashuapmushuan project, local and regional governments did a kind of partnership with social forces, and a new alliance was recently done by social groups about a dam project on Peribonca River (harnessed river). Members of the Industrial Commission called the state authority to account. The articulation between the actors in an alternative regional development strategy, including local conservation and tourism projects, wider energy conservation programs and better utilization of existing dam sites, provided a strong challenge to Hydro-Quebec, and enhanced the local and regional value of the proposal.[20] While an SIA that adopts a participatory–emancipatory orientation to disputes does not avoid conflict, it facilitates win–win outcomes through territorially based interventions.

In other cases, links between local affected groups and wider social actors active in multi-scale forums, present opportunities to insert local concerns that would otherwise be characterized as merely parochial, into formulation of decisions and approval procedures. The Nam Choan Dam provides an excellent example of this process at work, as the championing of the local and provincial

---

[20] For a useful parallel to Hydro-Quebec see Crabb (1986) and Thompson (1986) on the role of Tasmani's Hydro-Electric Commission in the case of the Franklin Dam in World Heritage areas of Tasmania.

opposition to the dam by national environmental groups within Thailand, and later international green groups, not only transformed the national approach to this proposal and others, but together with similar movements elsewhere has influenced the wider procedures adopted by the World Bank.

In the Weipa case, it was a coalition between local Aboriginal groups and the regional Aboriginal legal service, and a second tenuous alliance between the Aboriginal groups and a faction within the corporate proponent that accepted the validity of Aboriginal concerns, which provided the opportunity for the Aboriginal group to negotiate a way of controlling the SIA research, if not the actual development proposal itself.

A Framework for Community Empowerment through SIA

These points suggest that community empowerment in SIA does not involve any singular, simple form of "preferred research" procedure. Rather a community empowerment approach to SIA involves multi-directional efforts by affected grassroots groups to secure influence over and standing (even if tenuous, circumstantial, or informal) in formal SIA procedures by:

- appropriating the formal SIA procedures to community priorities;
- extending the formal procedures into less formal settings, where avenues for community influence are greater;
- exercising increased levels of community control over technical inputs into SIA inquiries;
- negotiating popular participation in territorially based campaigns for more acceptable local outcomes to project proposals and the mobilization of popular support.

This matrix of processes is illustrated in Figure 5. In this diagram, the horizontal axis represents the degree of formality of the procedures. That statutory requirements may impose specific formal procedures for an SIA is recognized without excluding the possibility that affected communities or groups can independently pursue SIA-style research or a range of other actions aimed at influencing development outcomes. That is, although a formal SIA study may provide some opportunities for community empowerment, it is not suggested that in any particular situation, this would be the only, or even the preferred, option for pursuing community goals. The vertical axis represents the orientation of the SIA process from technocratic at one pole to participatory at the other. There is scope both for communities to establish greater control over technical input and the resources that go with them, and for the more conventional "managers" of SIA to benefit from greater community involvement.

Each of these processes can be illustrated from the case studies presented here. The appropriation of formal SIA procedures by community groups is clearly demonstrated in the Weipa case, where the proponent accepted an arrangement in which a community organization would control the relevant sections of the

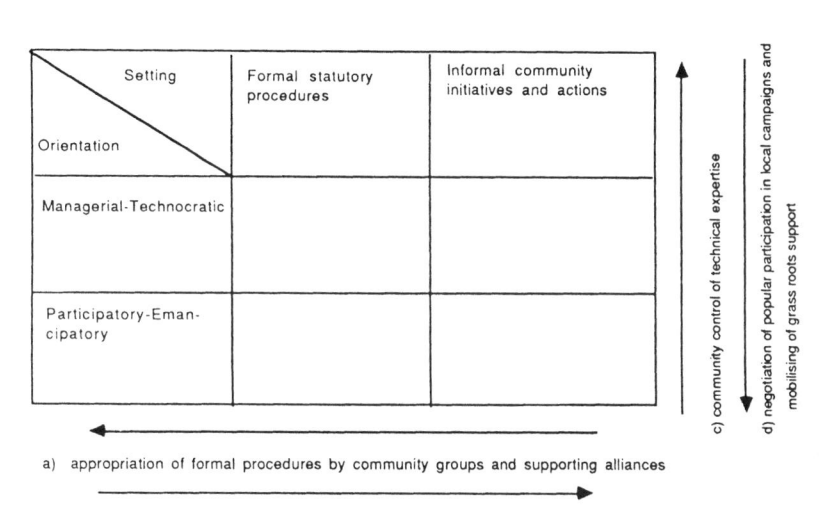

Setting / Orientation	Formal statutory procedures	Informal community initiatives and actions
Managerial-Technocratic		
Participatory-Emancipatory		

c) community control of technical expertise
d) negotiation of popular participation in local campaigns and mobilising of grass roots support

a) appropriation of formal procedures by community groups and supporting alliances

b) extension of community groups' influence over statutory procedures in wider political setting

FIGURE 5. Processes in a community empowerment framework for SIA.

formal social impact study. While committing the Napranum Council to the formal research process, the agreement involved adequate protection of those issues emphasized by the Council (full disclosure; access to full range of EIS data; selection of technical experts; one line funding of the Council for the study).

The process of extending the formal procedures into less formal settings, where greater levels of community influence can be developed, is illustrated in the Nam Choan case, where a committee, initially established to justify approving the dam, was confronted with community-based opposition that left it with little option other than to recommend cancellation of the proposal. In this case, the attempt to circumvent community opposition by institutional means was itself circumvented by community-based political efforts that pushed the committee's inquiry into the arenas of greatest community concern and influence.

The Nam Choan case also illustrates the importance of opportunistic coalitions and territorially based action in securing a more participatory approach to impact assessment and development decisions. In this case, extension of these alliances into international arenas has had consequences far beyond the original project, and is, for example, now influencing the development of hydro-electric projects in Indochina.

The important roles played by a regional municipal committee and community-based environmental interests in the Ashuapmushuan case in Quebec highlights the importance of locality-related common interests as a basis for campaign alliances. In this case, the alliance produced negotiation and mediation processes aimed at securing improved environmental and economic outcomes—

to transform a locally unacceptable proposal into a more widely acceptable one. The relevance of these proposals to local aspirations was central to the development of a politically effective alliance.

Establishing mechanisms for increased community control of technical inputs for formal (and informal) SIA is fundamental to the empowerment process outlined here. Without this, one is really only talking about advocacy, not empowerment.[21] In the Weipa case, control over selection of technical experts was supplemented by direct community presence on the advisory committee. The extent to which these mechanisms would actually deliver community control of the process remains untested following postponement of the study. Ross (1989, p. 12) acknowledges this issue of community control of technical expertise as a difficult area in the East Kimberley study, and there are no unproblematic examples of this process to guide individual practice.

The point is, however, to identify this as a basic issue in the empowerment process. Control of technical inputs into SIA (e.g., who directs the research, what data is used, which scenarios will be considered), and control of the resources needed to assemble, analyze, interpret and debate these inputs, is often the crux of community disempowerment in formal SIA research.[22] As a result, community critiques of technical documents are left to depend on volunteer "experts," independent funding sources, or emotional arguments against technically sophisticated research. Placing technical research at the disposal of community interests rather than solely in the control of project proponents substantially alters the conventional balance of power in impact studies. This was the logic behind Berger's funding of community groups to prepare and present submission to his environmental inquiry in northern Canada (Berger 1977, pp. 241–246). This important innovation, however, remains far from standard practice in the field of impact assessment.

Community strategies targeting basic processes (appropriating, extending, exercising, negotiating, and mobilizing local support) as a means of challenging the conventional power relationships in formal SIA will, as the case studies presented demonstrate, vary considerably in different community settings. The purpose of the framework outlined here is not to prescribe a universally applicable method of "empowerment SIA," but to identify general issues and processes that need to be addressed in developing strategies in particular circumstances. Supplemented with a range of other strategies and interventions—to adapt formal impact assessment procedures into the realm of community research and action—will move formal procedures away from the status of post-facto justifications of predetermined development decisions. This involves recognition of the role of community empowerment in planning and decision-

---

[21] For a useful discussion of the politics of voluntary technical experts in environmental conflicts, see Frankena (1988).

[22] This is probably the reason why the Cree, the native community affected by the Grand-Baleine dams project, claimed and received $5 million to undertake their own SIA studies concerning that project.

making that influences not just quality-of-life, but in many cases, community survival and the viability of future livelihoods in these regions.

The author Christiane Gagnon thanks the Social Sciences and Humanities Research Council of Canada (SSHRCC) and La Fondation de l'Université du Québec à Chicoutimi for their postdoctoral research sponsorship.

References

Australia: Environmental Assessment Branch, Department of the Arts, Sport, the Environment, Tourism and Territories, and Queensland: Department the Premier Economic and Trade Development, 1991, Guidelines for an Environmental Impact Statement: proposed bauxite refinery, Weipa, Queensland, Canberra and Brisbane.

Bassand, M. 1990. *Culture et Régions d'Europe*. Lausanne: Presses Polytechniques et Universitaires Romandes.

Bélanger, G., and Bernad, J.T. 1991. Aluminium ou exportation: de l'usage de l'électricité québécoise. *Analyse de Politiques* XVII(2):197–204.

Berger, T. 1977. *Northern Frontier, Northern Homeland: The Report of the Mackenzie Valley Pipeline Inquiry*, Toronto: Lorimer & Co. (2 volumes).

Burdge, R.J., and Robertson, R.A., 1990. Social impact assessment and the public involvement process. *Environmental Impact Assessment Review*, 10:81–90.

Canan, P., 1989, Citizen participation: protecting the democratic approach to environmental disputes. *Environmental Impact Assessment Review*, 9:333–335.

Comité conjoint des MRC Du Domaine-Du-Roy et De Maria-Chapdelaine. 1991. *Projet d'aménagement hydroélectrique de l'Ashuapmushuan*.

Connell, J. 1991. Compensation and conflict: the Bougainville Copper Mine, Papua New Guinea. In *Mining and Indigenous Peoples in Australasia*, J. Connell and R. Howitt (eds). Sydney: Sydney University Press.

Crabb, P. 1986. Hydroelectric Power in Newfoundland, Tasmania and the South Island of New Zealand. In *The Social and Environmental Effects of Large Dams, Volume 2: Case Studies*, E. Goldsmith and N. Hildyard (eds). Camelford, Cornwall: Wadebridge Ecological Centre.

Craig, D. 1990. Social impact assessment: Politically oriented approaches and applications. *Environmental Impact Assessment Review* 10:37–54.

Dhira, Phantumvanit, and Widhanya, Nandhabiwat. 1989. The Nam Choan controversy: An EIA in practice. *Environmental Impact Assessment Review* 9:135–147.

Filer, C. 1990. The Bougainville Rebellion, the mining industry and the process of social disintegration in Papua New Guinea. In *The Bougainville Crisis*, R. May and M. Spriggs (eds). Bathurst, NSW: Crawford House.

Frankena, F. 1988. The emergent social role and political impact of the voluntary technical expert. *Environmental Impact Assessment Review* 8:73–82.

Gagnon, C. 1992. Industrial Reorganisation and Modernisation Strategies in the Aluminium Industry: Sociospatial: Impacts on Quebec's Local Communities. ERRRU Working Paper No. 11. Sydney: University of Sydney.

Gale, R.P., 1983, The conciousness-raising potential of social impact assessment. In *Public Involvement and Social Impact Assessment*, G.A. Daneke, M.W. Garcia and J.D. Priscolli (eds). Boulder: Westview Press.

Garcia, M.W., 1983 Public involvement and social impact assessment: a case history of the Coronado National Forest. In *Public Involvement and Social Impact Assessment*, G.A. Deneke, M.W. Garcia and J.D. Priscolli (eds). Boulder: Westview Press.

Gariepy, M. 1991. Toward a dual-influence system: assessing the effects of public participation in environmental impact assessment for Hydro-Quebec projects. *Environmental Impact Assessment Review* 11:353–375.

Geisler, C.G., Green, R., Usner, D., and West, P. (eds). 1982. *Indian SIA: The Social Impact Assessment of Rapid Resource Development on Native Peoples*. Michigan: Natural Resources Research Lab, University of Michigan.

Gondolf, E.W., and Wells, S.R. 1986. Empowered native community: Modified SIA. *Environmental Impact Assessment Review* 6:373–383.

Hirsch, P. 1987. Nam Choan: Benefits for whom? *The Ecologist* 17(6):220–222.

Hirsch, P. 1991. Environmental and Social Implications of the Nam Theun Dam, *ERRRU Working Paper No.5*, Sydney: University of Sydney.

Hirsch, P. Political economy of environment in Thailand. *Journal of Contemporary Asia Publishers* (forthcoming).

Hirsch, P., and Lohmann, L. 1989. The Contemporary Politics of Environment in Thailand. *Asian Survey* 29(4):439–451.

Hollingsworth, D., and Moore. 1990. *Initial Advice Statement: Project to Refine Weipa Bauxite into Alumina*. Brisbane: Hollingsworth Dames & Moore.

Howitt, R. 1989. Social impact assessment and resource development: Issues from the Australian experience. *Australian Geographer* 20(2):153–166.

Howitt, R. 1991. *Social impact assessment and community empowerment at Weipa*, unpublished paper. Sydney: University of Sydney.

Howitt, R. 1992a. *Industrialisation, impact assessment and community empowerment*. Paper presented to the New Zealand Geographical Society and Institute of Australian Geographers Conference. Auckland: University of Auckland.

Howitt, R. 1992b. The political relevance of locality studies: A remote Antipoden viewpoint. *Area* 24(1):73–81.

Howitt, R. 1992c. Weipa: Industrialisation and indigenous rights in a remote Australian mining region. *Geography* 77.3:223–235.

Howitt, R. and Douglas, J., 1983, *Aborigines and Mining Companies in North Australia*, Sydney, Alternative Publishing Co-operative.

Hydro-Quebec. 1989. *Aménagement hydroélectrique de l'Ashuapmushuan: Renseignements généraux*.

Hydro-Quebec. 1991a. *L'aménagement hydroélectrique de l'Ashuapmushuan:* (Bulletin no. 4).

Hydro-Quebec. 1991b. *Aménagement hydroélectrique de l'Ashuapmushuan: Synthèse des études sectorielles. Avant-projet, Phase 1.*

IWGIA. 1991. The World Bank Operational Manual. *International Working Group on Indigenous Affairs Newsletter*, December 1991:19–22.

Jacobs, J. 1985. *Cities and the Wealth of Nations: Principles of Economic Life.* New York: Vintage Books.

Jonas, A. 1988. A new regional geography of localities? *Area* 20(1):101–110.

Kemp, J. 1987. *Seductive Mirage: The Search for the Village Community in Southeast Asia.* Amsterdam: Centre for Asian Studies.

Michalenko, G. 1981. The social assessment of corporations. In *SIA: Theory, Method and Practice*, Detselig, Tester, and Mykes (eds).

Moody, R. 1991. *Plunder!*, London: PARTiZANS/CAFCA.

Mulvihill, P.R., and Keith, R.F. 1989. Institutional requirements for adaptive EIA: The Kativik environmental quality commission. *Environmental Impact Assessment Review* 9:399–412.

Nart T. 1984. Public perception of rain forest and its perception in Thailand. *Environment, Development, and Natural Resource Crisis in Asia and the Pacific.* Penang: Proceedings of symposium organized by Sahabat Alam Malaysia.

Newcastle Ecology Centre. 1980. *Who Asked Us? Coal, Power, Aluminium—the Hunter Region's Only Future?* Newcastle: Newcastle Ecology Centre.

Nottingham. I. 1990. Social impact reporting: A Maori perspective—the Taharoa case. *Environmental Impact Assessment Review* 10:175–284.

Prinya, Nutalai. 1987. Earthquakes and the Nam Choan Dam. *The Ecologist* 17(6):223–225.

Priscoli, J.D., 1983, Public involvement and social impact assessment: a union seeking a marriage. In *Public Involvement and Social Impact Assessment*, G.A. Daneke, M.W. Garcia and J.D. Priscolli (eds). Boulder: Westview Press.

Québec. 1977. *Livre blanc sur la politique énergetique québécoise.* Québec: Éditeur officiel.

Québec. 1988. *L'énergie force motrice du développement économique. Politique énergétique pour les années 1990.* Québec: Direction des communications du ministère de l'Énergie et des ressources.

Regroupement pour la protection de l'Ashuapmushuan (RPA). (S.D.). *Le projet de barrages sur l'Ashuapmushuan. Au moins quinze bonnes raisons de s'y opposer.*

Ross, H. 1989. Community social impact assessment: A cumulative study in the Turkey Creek area, Western Australia. *East Kimberley Working Paper No 27*, Canberra: Centre for Resource and Environmental Studies, Australian National University.

Ross, H. 1990a. Community social impact assessment: A framework for indigenous peoples. *Environmental Impact Assessment Review* 10:185–193.

Ross, H. 1990b. Progress and prospects in Aboriginal SIA. *Australian Aboriginal Studies* 1990(1):11–17.

Ross, H. 1992. Opportunities for Aboriginal participation in Australian social impact assessment. *Impact Assessment Bulletin* 10(1):47–75.

Smith, B. 1989. The concept of "community" in Aboriginal policy and service delivery. *NADU Occasional Paper No 1*, Darwin: Department of Social Security.

Stewart–Cox, B. 1987. Thailand's Nam Choan Dam: Disaster in the making. *The Ecologist* 17(6):212–219.

Sthör, W.B., and Taylor, F. 1981. *Development from Above or Below?* Chichester: John Wiley and Sons.

TDRI [Thailand Development Research Institute]. 1987. *Thailand Natural Resources Profile: Is the Resource Base for Thailand's Development Sustainable?* Bangkok: TDRI.

Thompson, P. 1986. Saving Tasmania's Franklin and Gordon wild rivers. In *The Social and Environmental Effects of Large Dams, Volume 2: Case Studies*, E. Goldsmith and N. Hildyard (eds). Camelford, Cornwall: Wadebridge Ecological Centre.

[49]

IN PRAISE OF SIA —
A PERSONAL REVIEW OF THE FIELD OF SOCIAL IMPACT ASSESSMENT: FEASIBILITY, JUSTIFICATION, HISTORY, METHODS, ISSUES[1]

Kurt Finsterbusch[2]

This paper presents an overview of the field of social impact assessment (SIA) in the United States. I argue in the following sections that SIA is manageable and justifiable, is seldom conducted unless legally required, has declined as an activity since the late 1970s, has a widely accepted methodology, and can be conducted at reasonable costs. This assessment of SIA begins with the recognition of the difficulties inherent in the task of predicting all the significant future impacts of events or activities on people and social collectives, but suggests that the task is usually quite feasible for recurring government actions. Next, the ethical foundations for SIA are spelled out. It is justified by all ethically based policy value systems if its costs are within reason.

---

[1] A version of this paper was presented at the colloquium, *SIA: A step toward sustainable development?*, at the University of Québec at Chicoutimi, June 1994, and at the annual meeting of IAIA, Québec City, June 1994.

[2] Prof. Kurt Finsterbusch is in the Department of Sociology, University of Maryland, College Park MD 20742 USA.

A review of its history emphasizes the legal mandate for SIA in the United States in the National Environmental Policy Act of 1969, the production of thousands of SIAs in the 1970s for Environmental Impact Statements, and the dramatic decline from the late 1970s in federally sponsored construction activities that require an SIA. The next section spells out the standard methodology for SIAs. The final section discusses some key issues that affect the quality of SIAs. Our thesis is that SIAs can be cost effective in improving the knowledge needed for good policy decisions and improve the decision-making process.

On the other hand, it does have limits. It cannot eliminate uncertainty but it can help minimize it. It cannot study all social impacts, but when scoped to manageable limits it is an effective policy analysis tool.

FEASIBILITY

Given the complex nature of social phenomena, a complete and accurate social impact assessment (SIA) is nearly an impossible task except for highly standardized events. SIA commits the researcher to the challenging task of estimating all the significant future impacts of proposed projects and programs on people and social collectives and this can be an extremely difficult and endless job. SIA is difficult because it is mostly prediction. Often the proposed actions will change the course of the history of the nearby communities and the direction of that course might be contingent on numerous unique factors such as a weak or strong leader.

We can illustrate the difficulty of impact predictions by looking at some retrospective impact assessments where a later situation is attributed to earlier causes, but the later situation could not have been predicted when those causes first occurred. For example, White (1962) attributes the emergence of feudalism to the invention of the stirrup and Weber (1958) attributes "the disenchantment of the world" to industrialization. In the same work Weber attributed the rise of capitalism in the West to the impacts of Calvinistic protestantism. Most of us sociologists, if we had done an SIA at the time, would have missed these impacts.

On recent events social scientists have not predicted any better. We did not predict the transformations in Eastern Europe and the Soviet Union, the resurgence of racial and ethnic identification in modern industrial societies, the women's movement, or the extreme instability of the American family. (See Lipset (1979) for a review of the failure of each of the social sciences to predict many of the major trends since World War II.) We might also ask who predicted the consequences of the automobile or of television? Even today social scientists are not accepted as reliable futurists. For example, do any sociologists credibly predict the future impacts that computers and new communication technologies will have on society?

The fact of the matter is that the nature of social phenomena prevents precise behavioral predictions for two major reasons: *social units are not fixed structures* and *social phenomena involve adaptive interactions*. Social units are not like a billiard ball that has a fixed structure and perfectly translates inputs into outputs. Once we know the angle and force of the ball that hits 'our' ball, we can determine the direction and speed of its movement. But the most common units in sociology are individuals and social systems. These units have reasonably meaningful boundaries and regularities and hence are amenable to probabilistic but not deterministic theories. Since they lack fixed structure, they exhibit *equifinality*, i.e., different inputs result in the same outcomes as when either a threat or love obtains the same complying response, and *multifinality*, i.e., the same inputs result in different outcomes as when a scolding can produce contrition or defiant anger. Other social units are less bounded social collectives that are even less amenable to predictable regularities.

The second reason why most social phenomena are not predictable is that they involve adaptive interactions where individuals and organizations act in reaction to changing contingencies and thereby change the contingencies for other individuals and organizations and so on. Two major figures in the environmental movement can be used to illustrate the importance of this feature of social phenomena. The first is Paul Ehrlich who has been one of the major crusaders for environmental protection and the ecological perspective against the economic growth perspective. Many of his predictions, however, have failed badly, because he ignored human adaptation. He extrapolated linear or exponential trends without considering the effects of social systems adapting to changing conditions.

The second is Jay Forrester who was the intellectual guru of the *Limits to Growth* team (Meadows et al. 1972) that shook up the rosy assumptions of the dominant economic growth paradigm of the day. Forrester had some understanding of the complex nature of social systems and proposed dynamic systems models to anticipate their functioning. He posed the problem this way:

> It is my basic theme that the human mind is not adapted to interpreting how social systems behave. Our social systems belong to the class called multiple-loop nonlinear feedback systems. In the long history of human evolution it has not been necessary for man to understand these systems until very recent historical times. Evolutionary processes have not given us the mental skill needed to interpret properly the dynamic behavior of the systems of which we have now become a part (Forrester 1973: 5).

Forrester's dynamic systems models involving many dozens of simultaneous multivariate equations was able to capture some of the complexities of social systems but not their adaptive interactions and restructuring. He and the Limits to Growth team could not include policy adaptations in their world dynamic models. They had to insert policy adaptations on an ad hoc basis and then run the model to see how they affected other dimensions. As those dimensions changed, however, their models could not anticipate further policy adaptations to the changing conditions.

In fact, no one to date has done so except in fairly simple conflict and escalation games. I argue that it cannot be done in real-life situations, because each action in an interaction sequence has, at best, only a modest predictability unless many parameters such as the relative power of participating groups remain essentially unchanged. As a result, the probability of predicting a number of sequential interactive actions rapidly approaches zero. Predictive SIA, like weather predictions beyond two weeks, is a nearly impossible task unless the social phenomena involve highly constrained interactions.

Nevertheless, I seek not to bury SIA, but to praise it. The above remarks are somewhat misleading. They point out that SIAs are limited in what they can predict with confidence because of the difficulties of predicting single events and relatively unrestrained interaction chains. Most SIAs, however, are not so difficult. What most SIAs do is to predict either the types of impacts that might occur, or nearly inevitable direct impacts, or likely patterns of responses. These are far easier to predict than single events, so the bulk of most SIA work is quite manageable.

For example, a highway will definitely force the relocation of residents and businesses in the route alignment and subject nearby residents to noise levels that can be estimated on the basis of estimated traffic levels, distance, and land contours. The traffic estimates may be too low and the noise impacts may be somewhat higher than predicted, but the fact of noise impacts is certain if the highway is used. The assessor can predict, on the basis of past findings, that people generally do not like to be relocated. This will not be true for every single person (the difficulty of predicting the single event), but it will be true as a pattern or tendency. In sum, the feasibility of SIA depends on the type of information that is required and most SIAs provide credible and valuable information for decision makers based on relatively predictable patterns.

THE MORAL BASIS FOR SIA

Feasibility does not establish legitimacy. Value systems do. There are seven major ethical bases for evaluating public policies and SIA has positive value in all seven ethical paradigms. The first is *utilitarianism* which judges the policy that produces the greatest good for the greatest number as the best. This translates into the largest excess of benefits over costs. Since a SIA is needed to determine the full set of benefits and costs, it contributes to the information basis for good policy choices according to the utilitarian paradigm.

The second is the *libertarian* view that elevates individuals and their rights (mainly their freedoms) above all other values. According to Nozick (1974), this translates into limiting the state almost entirely to defense and law enforcement. Nozick views most other state actions as unacceptable because they would step on individual rights, especially property rights. In its pure form this is a rather radical view that is impractical and unpopular. It also has little use for SIA. If most potential government actions are dismissed out of hand, then SIAs and other policy analyses are not needed. In its less extreme form, however, libertarianism would find SIA useful. When government actions are taken, SIA could estimate how the actions will affect individuals and their rights and help minimize and compensate for the negative impacts. In this way SIA would serve a major concern of libertarianism.

The third ethical basis for evaluating public policies is Rawls' (1971) theory of *justice* which requires that policies treat all members of the contractual society equally. When policies must involve inequality, as they must in the real world, they are 'just' if they benefit everyone and if all members have an equal chance to get the better positions. If, in fact, some must bear more costs than benefits, the policy may still be just if the more advantaged groups rather than the less advantaged groups are the ones to bear these costs. The justice paradigm justifies SIAs because they provide the information whereby one can monitor the justice criteria. It usually is the major research tool that reveals who gets the negative and positive impacts and estimates how well the less and more advantaged groups fare from the policy. It thereby facilitates a more equal distribution of costs and benefits and facilitates the implementation of the criteria of justice.

The fourth ethical basis for evaluating policies is the marxian *condemnation of exploitation*. Marx argued that social institutions are created by the powerful and are structured to serve the interests of the powerful, so they consistently produce biased results. Marxism calls for the eradication of all exploitation and bias. This requires radical reform and sometimes even a revolution. SIA is not an instrument for the revolution of social institutions to equalize power and results. However, by bringing to light information on the distribution of costs and benefits of government actions, it tends to reduce the generation of inequality by government actions, because governments produce the most inequality when they act in relative secrecy. In other words, SIA increases the accountability of government actions and creates some interference in the reproduction of unequal distributions of power and benefits.

The fifth ethical basis for evaluating policies is *functionalism* in which policies are judged good if they improve the functioning of the target system and the larger system of which it is a part. The units of analysis are not individuals but the collectives that express the communal life of individuals—such as the society, state, or community and the subsystems within them that are the setting for the policy. SIA enhances system functioning by providing information for better decisions and project designs. The information it provides on dysfunctional side effects of planned government actions can be used to engineer a better fit between the project and local conditions and communities. By improving performance and expanding the opportunities for public inputs SIA increases the legitimacy of the system.

Sometimes the implementing agency may view SIA more as a hindrance than a help, but this view is short sighted. The requirement of aa SIA may make the agency less able to just do what it wants and force it to be more responsive to the public. Nevertheless, in the long run better service will be provided and public trust will be built up, which helps state agencies to function more effectively. In fact, many of the recent difficulties of infrastructure agencies are due to the low level of public trust in them, the results of ramrodding methods and underhanded procedures that were often used when undertaking projects and programs in the past. SIA encourages and enables agencies to pursue win-win policies to create infrastructure projects such as highways that benefit large numbers of users while minimizing, compensating, and protecting the displaced and noise-impacted. The current practice of negotiated compromises are an improvement over the more brutal zero sum policies of several decades ago.

The sixth ethical basis for evaluating policies is a truly *democratic decision-making process*. The previous five criteria emphasize good outcomes and this criterion emphasizes a good process (which may or may not produce the best outcome). Habermas (1970, 1971, 1977) argues that truly democratic decision making requires that knowledge be relatively equally shared among the parties affected by policy decisions. An SIA that clearly reveals who is adversely or beneficially affected would serve this need. Habermas points out, however, that not only must the substance of the SIA cover the impacts on all groups but also the form of the SIA must be accessible to all groups (i.e., be written in lay terms). Habermas sees technical language as a way of keeping the policy process relatively inaccessible to the public and, in effect, of subtly disenfranchising the less-educated groups. An unbiased SIA written without technical jargon, however, greatly facilitates the democratic process, because it provides information to citizens on which they can act in the political arena.

It should also be pointed out that SIAs generally activate and facilitate public participation in the decision-making process. At the very least, an SIA provides an opportunity for people to voice their concerns in a mode that is less combative and more reliable than the public hearing process, which has numerous deficiencies as a communication between agencies and the public (Hornback 1981). Done well, the SIA enhances the democratic process.

The final ethical basis for evaluating policies is *ethical pluralism*. This view remains unpersuaded by the proponents of the other views which emphasize one criterion over the others. Instead pluralism assumes that the weights for the various relevant criteria vary from case to case, so they must be traded off against each other anew in each situation. The pluralist paradigm probably requires an SIA more than the other ethical paradigms, because the philosophy of pluralism is to examine all significant impacts and it must consider all relevant values to achieve this.

There are two major methods for trading off values one against another: (1) a fair political process or (2) a technically rational procedure. An SIA that fully identifies the distribution of all significant impacts (both benefits and costs) on various groups is essential to both a fair political process (stakeholders need the SIA to act politically on their interests) and a rational technical process of assigning weights for impacts. In sum, SIA is required in all ethically grounded decision-making processes and, therefore, should be widely used in all public decisions regarding projects and programs.

An exception

There is one ethical basis for claiming that certain SIAs should not be conducted—when the costs exceed the benefits of the SIA. This can occur when research costs are high and findings are highly uncertain. Because agencies usually budget SIAs on the low side, this is not a common condition. Furthermore, throughout the past two decades the SIA community has developed the methodological and empirical bases for SIAs to increase their reliability, precision, and certainty while reducing their costs. (Some methods for cost cutting and precision-enhancing research will be discussed below). Another situation that might result in higher costs than benefits is when the SIA research process itself produces significant unintended negative consequences. This is a legitimate criticism that can only be silenced by social impact assessors acting to minimize the chances of such negative impacts.

A BRIEF HISTORY OF SIA IN THE UNITED STATES

For practical purposes the history of SIA began with the passage of the National Environmental Policy Act (NEPA) in 1969. Before NEPA, very little published research in the social sciences attempted to estimate future impacts. Speculative remarks on the future often graced concluding chapters of books or sections of papers, but research that systematically attempted to describe the likely results of potential events was very rare. After NEPA, however, SIA became a cottage industry in the United States and by the end of the 1970s, about 1,000 professional social scientists had become part of an SIA network.

NEPA requires "major federal actions significantly affecting the quality of the human environment" to have an environmental impact statement (EIS) that estimates the action's impacts. Sections 101 and 102 suggest that social impacts should be included in the impacts estimated, and section 1508 of the official *Regulations for Implementing NEPA* (US-CEQ 1978) calls for the study of direct and indirect social and cultural impacts. The subsequent judicial history has created considerable ambiguity as to exactly what the law requires concerning the study of social and cultural impacts (see Llewellyn and Freudenburg 1990), but it is clear that social impacts are to be assessed when they result from changes in the physical environment.

During the 1970s, a tremendous number of environmental impact assessments were produced—10,475 up to May 1980 (Culhane, Friesema, and Beecher 1987: 50,51); many of them included SIAs. Since 1980 the production of EISs has declined greatly; 352 final EISs were filed with EPA in 1980 and only 189 in 1993 (information obtained from EPA). EISs for construction projects (roads, dams, power plants, airports, tunnels, bridges, power lines, etc.) have declined the most. In the beginning, the agency that was involved in the most SIAs was the Federal Highway Administration (FHA), although most of the actual SIA work was done by the state highway departments and their contractors. FHA produced 31.3 percent of all SIAs filed up to May 1980—a total of 3277. By the end of the 1970s, however, the federal highway system was largely completed and federal support for state highway programs was cut back in the 1980s. As a result, the number of FHA SIAs conducted under NEPA requirements have declined substantially. In fact only 24 final EISs were filed by FHA with EPA in 1993 compared to 56 in 1980.

Using project titles and maps, I estimate that the 24 road projects assessed in the final EISs filed in 1993 will not exceed 200 miles of constructed roads. None of them should have many person years to assess their social impacts, and the ones that I have looked at showed no evidence of extensive social impact assessment activity (mainly because they were very straightforward and unproblematic).

The Corps of Engineers was the second most active agency in the field of SIA in the 1970s. It produced 2,031 EISs (19.4 percent of the total) and was involved in a number of dam projects that involved relatively complicated SIAs. Since 1980, however, dam construction has declined greatly because higher and more realistic discount rates became required. As a result many proposed new dams had cost–benefit ratios that did not qualify them for funding. The slump in the dam business is evidenced by the fact that the Corps of Engineers filed only one final EIS for a dam project in 1992 and none in 1993, and the 1992 dam project was a relatively small flood control and recreation project in Los Angeles County, California.

Although the dam business has dried up, so to speak, the actions of Corps of Engineers significantly affect the environment. It filed 16 final EISs in 1993 (the third highest behind the Forestry Service and the Federal Highway Administration). Most of them, however, are for navigation, flood control, and beach erosion control projects, or for various non-construction projects that have few social impacts.

Another very important type of government action that requires an EIS with an SIA component has been energy developments in rural areas that create boomtowns. These were not numerous but they became a major focus of SIA research and account for many of the best academic publications involving SIAs (see, for example, Finsterbusch 1980; Freudenburg 1984, 1986a, 1986b; Freudenburg and Jones 1992; Seyfrit 1986; Weber and Howell 1982). Since 1980, however, energy developments have slackened considerably and some boomtowns have become busttowns. The craft industry of boomtown SIAs has crashed.

One major construction activity requiring EISs with associated SIAs that has not slackened since 1980 is the siting of hazardous and nonhazardous waste landfills or facilities. In fact, this activity has become a growing national concern and a major contributor to the virulent national NIMBY (not-in-my-backyard) syndrome. Even here, however, a bust has occurred in the most toxic sector of these government actions—the siting of a national nuclear waste repository. The Nuclear Waste Policy Act was passed in 1982, and in 1983 nine sites in six states were selected for characterization. By 1985 only three sites remained for consideration, and political factors seemed to play a larger role in the elimination of sites than environmental factors. In 1987 Congress legislated that the repository would be located at the Yuca Mountain site in Nevada which was on federal land and therefore the least susceptible of the sites to public protests.

Since millions of dollars were budgeted by federal and state governments for the impact assessments of each of the nine sites, and later for the three that survived the first cut, a large amount of SIA work was contracted for and underway, but most of it was canceled in mid-process. The SIA cottage industry has also crashed.

In sum, the field of SIA in the United States has declined dramatically since 1980 both in personpower and in research funds, because construction of highways, dams, and energy facilities has declined dramatically and the nuclear hazardous waste candidate sites have shrunk from nine to one. At the same time the practice of SIA has greatly increased in Canada and Western Europe and is developing in other parts of the world.

Another noteworthy development is the expansion of EISs for land and resource use management plans. Such plans for the Forest Service have became the leading government actions requiring an EIS, increasing from 16 final EISs in 1980 to 54 in 1993. Another agency that is active in land and resource use plans is the Bureau of Land Management which filed 15 final EISs in 1993 (fourth behind Forestry Service, Federal Highway, and Corps of Engineers mentioned above).

Another important area for the practice of SIA is Third World development projects. The practice of SIA in the Agency for International Development (AID) regarding development projects has a separate history from domestic SIAs. NEPA regulations do not apply to these projects. Nevertheless, social impacts have normally been considered in the project design and selection processes since AID issued guidelines for "Social Soundness Analysis" in 1975. In most cases, however, the SIAs were more social feasibility studies than impact assessments; they did not try to identify all the significant potential social impacts of the project. The purpose of these SIAs was to discover whether there were cultural or institutional factors that would hinder the success or feasibility of the project.

The guidelines governing the Social Soundness Analysis were much vaguer than the SIA guidelines adopted by agencies working under NEPA requirements. The social soundness guidelines set few research requirements; experienced anthropologists or other social scientists would be hired and they would figure out for themselves what needed to be studied in order to assess how the project fit with the affected communities and cultures. In fact, there is considerable wisdom in this approach if it is carried out as designed. It is better to chose a very good researcher and offer little guidance than to choose mediocre researchers and give them a lot of guidance. Nevertheless, in a review of project design documents which I did with Van Wicklin (Finsterbusch and Van Wicklin 1988), we found generally weak social soundness analyses; and negative sociocultural factors often contribute substantially to poor project performance (see also Morgan 1985).

The World Bank and the Inter-American Development Bank incorporate less SIA in their project planning than AID. Because they are banks, it is understandable that economic factors are emphasized in project design. Both banks, however, have been criticized for the negative environmental and social impacts of some of their projects, so they have become more sensitive to these issues. For example, the World Bank has just completed a major report on involuntary relocation from infrastructure projects and is strengthening its requirements for relocation programs. Over the years, in fact, the World Bank has substantially increased the number of sociologists and anthropologists on staff who contribute to World Bank policies and project designs. The Inter-American Development Bank is also trying to take social factors more into account in planning its projects, but has not yet made a major commitment in this direction.

Development agencies have also been criticized for doing the wrong things and for doing things the wrong way, and a stronger role for SIA should raise their scores on both these criteria. Nelson (1985) accuses development agencies of helping the rich more than the poor, and the Paddocks (1973) and Kottak (1985) accuse them of starting event chains that have unanticipated and unaddressed serious negative social impacts. Since SIAs address these problems, they deserve to be more fully utilized in development agencies.

The criticism of development agencies' procedures focuses on their top-down approach which usually fails to attain significant client participation in design, redesign, implementation, operation, and maintenance of projects (see Derman and Whiteford 1985; Finsterbusch and Van Wicklin 1987, 1989; Gran 1983; Korten 1980; Morgan 1985; Paddock and Paddock 1973). SIAs can help address this problem because they are often used to make the project process more participatory.

Perhaps the strongest evidence for the need for SIAs in the development project process is Kottak's (1985: 328) study of 68 projects, which concludes:

> Many of the experiences documented here illustrate the tendency to address technical and financial factors and to neglect social issues. Perhaps the most significant finding of the present study is that attention to social issues, which presumably enhances sociocultural fit and results in a better social strategy for economic development, pays off in concrete economic terms: the average economic rates of return for projects that were socioculturally compatible and were based on an adequate understanding and analysis of social conditions were more than twice as high as those for socially incompatible and poorly analyzed projects .

METHODOLOGY OF SIA

During the 1970s the methodology for SIA was developed. A consensus had emerged on the basic methodology by 1980, and this methodology has recently been incorporated into an official set of *Guidelines and Principles for Social Impact Assessment* (ICGP 1994). These guidelines were produced by a committee made up of representatives from the professional associations that are most directly concerned with SIA. Since the *Guidelines* are readily available, I will not present them in detail, but I will use them to present the methodology for SIA.

There are 10 generic steps in the ideal SIA process. It begins with **a public involvement program** that dialogues with affected parties for their input throughout the impact assessment process. This is both a scientific and political requirement in the SIA methodology. These guidelines present the view of most social scientists that the assessment of social impacts is not complete nor fully valid unless the inputs of affected parties are obtained. Social scientists, even using sophisticated measurements of peoples' conditions and expected impacts, cannot speak for them with complete confidence. The public involvement step is also a political statement that affected parties should participate in the decision-making process.

Steps 2 and 3 obtain information on the **alternatives being considered** and on the **existing relevant conditions**. This is basic information for both the

Impact Assessment

SIA and for any policy decisions that claim to be rational. Step 4, **'scoping'**, is probably the key step in designing the SIA. It involves two steps: (1) the development of a relatively exhaustive list of potential impacts of the action, and (2) the selection from that list of the potential impacts to be studied in the SIA (some procedures for making this selection are reviewed by Canter and Canty (1993) and some criteria are provided in the *Guidelines* (ICGP 1994)). It is vitally important that the public participate in this scoping process or at least that public concerns are well represented. Otherwise public trust will be broken and public protest is likely.

The main research step is step 5, **projection of estimated effects**. There are three main information sources for impact estimation (in addition to the information collected to this point): (1) the literature, (2) experts, and (3) field research, including informant interviews. On the basis of the literature, the social impact assessor tries to establish what happened in similar past cases as a guide to what will happen in the study case. Then experts can advise how they think the study case will deviate from or conform to the normal patterns in past cases. The focus of the field study can then be to test the hypotheses of the experts and the applicability to the study case of the general patterns of impacts found in past cases.

The sixth step is the difficult task of **predicting how the affected parties will respond**. It must be admitted that most SIAs do not do this step or do very little of it. It is essential, however, to estimate higher-order impacts and the political consequences of the action—information in which decision makers should be interested. Step 6 entails asking affected parties their attitudes toward both the action and its direct impacts and their probable responses to the impacts. Respondents' statements about their responses might poorly predict their later actions, but the statements can at least alert the agency of potential problems that might be resolved by appropriate agency actions.

Step 7 is the **estimation of indirect and cumulative impacts**. This is an obvious next step, but is often neglected or shortchanged. Again the patterns found in past cases can guide this step. The eighth step is to **recommend changes in the action or alternatives** that would avoid the predicted negative impacts and enhance the positive impacts. These changes, however, should be put through the SIA process before implementing. Step 9 is to **mitigate the negative impacts** by avoiding, minimizing, rectifying, reducing, or providing compensation.

Finally, step 10 involves **a monitoring program** to be sure that negative impacts are dealt with as they happen. Again, most SIAs lack this step, but it should be remembered that the purpose of assessing impacts is to manage them. It should also be remembered that assessing social impacts is often a very difficult task, and not all problems can be dealt with ahead of time. An adequate SIA must be supplemented by a program that monitors the impacts and adjusts the action to unanticipated new conditions.

SELECTED METHODOLOGICAL ISSUES IN SIA

Increasing the Cost Effectiveness of SIA

The first and most important issue for the practice of SIA is its cost effectiveness. SIA is now an established field of sociological practice. The activity level has declined significantly since the big construction days of the 1970s, but the field has matured and earned sufficient legitimacy to become a standard intellectual tool for decision making. Its acceptance, however, is still incomplete. SIA is opposed by some economists and engineers who are not convinced that its benefits will be greater than its costs. Many of these professionals want to proceed with various projects as rapidly as possible, and they fear that an SIA will slow down the process. They also fear that the SIA process may give opposition groups additional opportunities to mobilize against the project. The first issue for consideration, therefore, is the value of SIA relative to the costs.

We have argued throughout that SIA is valuable, but this conclusion presumes that costs are reasonable. The methods used in most SIAs, therefore, should be relatively inexpensive but provide the key information for effective policy decisions and the management of negative impacts. The SIA should use the full range of social science research techniques as appropriate, but keep an eye on costs. In this section I will suggest methods that should make SIAs more cost-effective by improving the collection of information obtained from the literature, from experts, and from field research.

Information from the literature

The more we know from the past, the better able we are to estimate future impacts. At the moment the major problem is not the availability of information from the past but our understanding of that information. Knowledge is the systematic loss of information. Infinite factual details confuse more than they inform. The masses of details must be systematically reduced to summary statements that are true to the details and informative for the information users. For example, large research projects often are reported in a few dozen or a few hundred pages that serve most audiences far better than the thousands of pages of raw data. Another example of useful condensation is when large literatures are summarized in article-length literature reviews for the convenience of laypersons, students, and even professionals.

For SIAs, past case studies and the relevant literatures should be summarized in what I call a *standard information module* (SIM). (See Finsterbusch and Hamilton (1978) for a fuller description of the SIM method.) In brief, the SIM method for impact assessments examines past research with a sharp focus on dominant impact patterns for the type of event or action under review. For maximum effectiveness of the SIA, these events should happen repeatedly, e.g., the building of highways or the boomtown phenomenon. If so, then the new case will usually approximate the patterns identified in the previous cases. It is also important that the SIM identify significant minority patterns and the contextual factors that determine when the minority or majority pattern holds. The SIM should also determine the factors that are responsible for various impacts.

As SIMs are created and revised, they can be used in future SIAs to reduce costs and improve predictions. A good example of a well-developed SIM is the *Report of the National Advisory Commission on Civil Disorders* (1968), which studied the civil disorders in the 1960s (up to 1968) and developed a profile of the typical riot that helped authorities to know how to deal with subsequent riots. Social impact assessors in the context of an actual SIA probably will not have the time and resources to do thorough SIMs, but they could profitably follow these principles.

Another method that massages the general knowledge out of previous cases is the *systematic case review* (SCR). (See Finsterbusch and Van Wicklin (1987) for a fuller description of the SCR method.) This method gathers a large set of case studies, creates an information questionnaire that contains a question with a subjective scale from high to low for each variable of interest, has two coders read the case material and fill out a questionnaire for each case, and then statistically analyzes the results. This procedure is **not** recommended for the typical social impact assessor who is in the midst of an underbudgeted SIA, because it is too time consuming. Rather, scholars should conduct SCRs on more general research grants and create SCRs to build up the general information base for SIAs and for wider scholarly knowledge. Once SCRs are available in an SIA area the cost-effectiveness of SIAs in that area is greatly increased.

The experts

Experts also bring past findings to the SIA in that each expert is an idiosyncratic compilation and synthesis of past experience. Experts also contribute disciplinary perspectives and frameworks through which to understand and interpret past experience and the study case. The following comments suggest some ways to maximize the contributions of experts.

First, in order to enrich the analysis, several outside experts should be used from different disciplines and perspectives. Second, these experts should be used to supply information and expert advice, help with the research design, estimate what will happen, review and critique the work of the SIA team, and help interpret the findings. I especially recommend using a panel of outside experts to review and critique the work of the SIA team at several points in the process unless the SIA is very routine. Third, there are several methods for effectively obtaining inputs from experts, including the delphi and nominal group techniques that should be applied when appropriate (see Finsterbusch and Hamilton 1978; Delbecq et al. 1975).

Field research

The SIA should use the full range of social science research techniques. SIA field research mainly uses informant interviews and when funds are available also uses surveys. Two variations on informant interviews that can be very cost-effective in the SIA context are *focus groups* and *workshops*.

Focus groups are a way of interviewing several people together as a group and thus benefiting from the way opinions develop through discussion. Several groups should be interviewed to increase reliability. This method is used extensively in marketing research because it reveals the reasons behind people's choices, e.g., why they like a TV program. The focus group technique may not give carefully controlled scientific precision, but it does provide very valuable information for decision makers with acceptable reliability (see Kruger 1994; Merton, et al. 1990; Morgan 1993; Morgan and Spanish 1984). Focus groups are used extensively in Third World settings where private interviews can create suspicions, fear, and difficulties (see Kumar 1987). The technique merits greater use in SIAs; focus groups can identify people's concerns, needs, reasons, attitudes, wants, values, and expectations and have the advantage over individual interviews of having the group respond not only to the interviewer's questions but also to each other's ideas. The group can be a natural group or made up of randomly selected participants. The facilitator sets the topic and lets the group carry the conversation, stepping in only to stimulate the dialogue when needed through follow-up questions or to set the next topic. The focus group process continues until a list of issues has been adequately addressed.

Workshops are another method for working with groups and learning how the group mind develops in dialogue with the action agency and other affected parties.

Surveys can also be useful to SIAs, but they are often not used because they require too much time and money for some projects. *Mini surveys* (small samples of 20 to 100 respondents) are the answer in such situations because the time and money requirements are greatly reduced. They do not give pinpoint accuracy nor can they sustain a robust multivariate analysis, but they give adequate frequency distributions or, for very small mini surveys, they offer a telltale 'straw in the wind' that can be very useful for testing or spot-checking the hypotheses of the experts and the patterns in the SIM (Finsterbusch 1976a; 1976b; 1990). And finally, *mediation* is an important tool of SIA, because an SIA not only studies conflicts of interest but also participates in minimizing those conflicts (Amy 1983a, 1983b, 1987; Carpenter and Kennedy 1988; Curtis 1983; Lake 1980; Mernitz 1980; Ozawa 1991; Talbot 1983; Watson and Danielson 1982).

Some Impediments to Effective SIAs

Another issue is the intrusion of politics into the practice of SIA. We do know how to do good SIAs, and they can easily be cost-effective. But that does not necessarily mean that good and cost-effective SIAs will be done. Political agendas can prevent this. Politics is the main reason why SIAs are often not conducted when they are needed, why SIAs are sometimes not done well, and why they are sometimes purposely biased. (For a recent example of an SIA dominated by politics, see the exposé of the Canadian feasibility study of the Three Gorges Dam in China by Philip Fearnside (1994).) It is the obligation of the SIA community to use political and bureaucratic influence to attain the adoption of professional standards so that fraudulent SIAs are more difficult to get away with. It should be noticed that the public is usually allied with SIA advocates in this political battle.

A further impediment to effective SIAs is the impact of bureaucratization, including standardization and routinization, on SIAs. Bureaucratization is supposed to standardize by taking the formula that works best and to routinize the process by developing workable procedures for implementing it and institutionalizing the procedures as practices, guidelines, or regulations. These bureaucratic processes are efficient **if** the activity being analyzed is a relatively standard event (not unique but repetitive). But relatively inflexible procedures can become dysfunctional for all nonstandard cases.

Unfortunately, sometimes the bureaucratic way of operating is to promulgate rigid requirements that may not be the best formula but in fact might hinder effectiveness, as when an agency requires that a lengthy list of specified impacts be assessed in a routinized way. This tends to produce a large quantity of information, much of which might be of marginal value. The agency can claim that the appropriate impacts have been addressed, but this is no guarantee that a deep understanding of the issues has been gained that can guide decision makers to successful actions while avoiding pitfalls. Therefore, the community of social impact assessors must actively participate in the drafting and review of such guidelines and keep the SIA process flexible and professional.

It must be remembered that regulations are both good and bad. Without bureaucratic regulations requiring SIAs, few would be conducted. On the other hand, bureaucratic regulations tend to define the minimum acceptable SIA and some agencies shoot for the minimum. Another problem is the waste of time and money on relatively useless but required information. In my judgment, having SIAs reviewed by a board of competent professionals is preferable to rigid requirements.

The Scope of SIAs

A very important issue is what is included in the SIA, especially what the law requires. A minimum SIA includes the identification and investigation of probable impacts. A full description of the action alternatives and the baseline conditions is necessary to successfully investigate impacts, as are the estimation of the probable responses by the impacted parties and cumulative impacts. Therefore, steps two through seven in the *Guidelines* are necessary for a minimal but adequate SIA. The professional SIA community, however, in the *Guidelines* recommends that public involvement (step one), recommendations of revisions in the alternatives (eight), monitoring (nine), and mitigation (ten) also be included in SIAs. Defined narrowly, SIAs end with the estimation of expected impacts, but the resulting information base provides a strong basis for monitoring and managing the impacts, and therefore, should extend into these activities.

Another recommendation made in the *Guidelines* is that SIAs extend to the very end of the project or program. All projects and programs involve four phases: (1) design, (2) construction or program start-up, (3) maintenance and operation, and (4) ending, decommissioning, or replacement. The SIA should assess and plan the management of the impacts for all four phases of the action. Typically the first and fourth phases are ignored.

Another scope issue for SIAs is the inclusion of stakeholder analysis in it. Stakeholder analysis is the identification of all stakeholders (groups affected by the action) and the assessment of all significant impacts upon them. A normal SIA does this to some extent already, but a formal stakeholder analysis does it more rigorously and helps agencies in designing their actions and their strategies toward stakeholders. Babiuch and Farhar (1994) at the National Renewable Energy Laboratory have already developed a stakeholder analysis for their agency and it will probably diffuse to other agencies.

In summary, I have not sought to bury SIA but to praise it, justify it, describe its development, explain its methodology, and advise on how to improve it. I argue for expanding the role of social impact assessment in policy research, but I am not recommending a big job-expansion welfare program for social impact assessors. Rather, the SIA community should be working on reducing the costs while increasing the quality and usefulness of SIAs.

REFERENCES AND SOURCES OF INFORMATION

Amy, Douglas James. 1983a. "Environmental Mediation: An Alternative approach to Policy Stalemates." *Policy Sciences* 15: 343–365.

Amy, Douglas James. 1983b. "The Politics of Environmental Mediation." *Ecology Law Quarterly* 11: 1–19.

Amy, Douglas James. 1987. *The Politics of Environmental Mediation.* New York: Columbia University Press.

Babiuch, William and Barbara C. Farhar. 1994. *Stakeholder Analysis Methodologies: Resource Book.* Golden, CO: National Renewable Energy Laboratory.

Canter, L.W. and G.A. Canty. 1993. "Impact Significance Determination—Basic Considerations and a Sequenced Approach." *Environmental Impact Assessment Review* 13: 275-297.

Carpenter, L. Susan and W.J.D. Kennedy. 1988. *Managing Public Disputes: A Practical Guide to Handling Disputes and Reaching Agreement.* San Francisco: Jossey-Bass.

Culhane, Paul J., H. Paul Friesema, and Janice A. Beecher. 1987. *Forecasts and Environmental Decisionmaking: The Content and Predictive Accuracy of Environmental Impact Statements.* Boulder, CO: Westview Press.

Curtis, Fred A. 1983. "Integrating Environmental Mediation into EIA." *Impact Assessment Bulletin* 2(3): 17-25.

Delbecq, Andre L., Andrew H. Van De Van, and David H. Gustafson. 1975. *Group Techniques for Program Planning: A Guide to Nominal Group and Delphi Processes.* Glenview, IL: Scott Foresman.

Derman, William and Scott Whiteford, eds. 1985. *Social Impact Analysis and Development Planning in the Third World.* Boulder, CO: Westview Press.

Fearnside, Philip M. 1994. "The Canadian Feasibility Study of the Three Gorges Dam Proposed for China's Yangzi River: A Grave Embarrassment to the Impact Assessment Profession." *Impact Assessment* 12(1): 21-57.

Finsterbusch, Kurt. 1976a. "The Mini Survey: An Underemployed Research Tool." *Social Science Research* 5(1): 81-93.

Finsterbusch, Kurt. 1976b. "Demonstrating the Value of Mini Surveys in Social Research." *Sociological Methods and Research* 5(1): 117-136.

Finsterbusch, Kurt. 1980. *Understanding Social Impacts: Assessing the Effects of Public Projects.* Beverly Hills: Sage.

Finsterbusch, Kurt. 1990. "A Bayesian Perspective on Social Impact Assessment Data Collection." In *Methods for Social Analysis for Third World Countries,* edited by Kurt Finsterbusch, Jasper Ingersoll, and Lynn Llewellyn. Boulder, CO: Westview Press.

Finsterbusch, Kurt and Mary R. Hamilton. 1978. "The Rationalization of Social Science Research in Policy Studies." *International Journal of Comparative Sociology* 19(1-2): 88-106.

Finsterbusch, Kurt and Warren Van Wicklin, III. 1987. "The Contributions of Beneficiary Participation to Development Project Effectiveness." *Public Administration and Development* 7(1): 1-23.

Finsterbusch, Kurt and Warren Van Wicklin, III. 1988. "Unanticipated Consequences of A.I.D. Projects: Lessons from Impact Assessment for Project Planning." *Policy Studies Review* 8(1): 126-136.

Finsterbusch, Kurt and Warren Van Wicklin, III. 1989. "Beneficiary Participation in Development Projects: Empirical Tests of Popular Theories." *Economic Development and Cultural Change* 37(3): 573-593.

Forrester, Jay. 1973. "Counterintuitive Behavior of Social Systems." In *Toward Global Equilibrium: Collected Papers*, edited by Dennis L. Meadows and Donella H. Meadows. Cambridge, MA: Wright-Allen.

Freudenburg, William R. 1984. "Boomtown's Youth: The Differential Impacts of Rapid Community Growth on Adolescents and Adults." *American Sociological Review.* 49: 697–705.

Freudenburg, William R. 1986a. "The Density of Acquaintanceship: An overlooked variable in community research?" *American Journal of Sociology* 92(1):27–63.

Freudenburg, William R. 1986b. "Assessing the Social Impacts of Rural Resource Developments: An overview." In *Differential Social Impacts of Rural Resource Development*, edited by Pamela D. Elkind-Savatsky. Boulder, CO: Westview Press.

Freudenburg, W.R. and R.E. Jones. 1992. "Criminal Behavior and Rapid Community Growth: Examining the evidence." *Rural Sociology* 56(4): 619–645.

Gran, Guy. 1983. *Development by People*. New York: Praeger.

Habermas, Jurgen. 1970. *Toward a Rational Society*. Boston: Beacon.

Habermas, Jurgen. 1971. *Knowledge and Human Interests*. Boston: Beacon.

Habermas, Jurgen. 1977. *Communication and the Evolution of Society*. Boston: Beacon.

Hornback, Kenneth E. 1981. "Overcoming Obstacles to Agency and Public Involvement: A Program and Its Methods." In *Methodology of Social Impact Assessment*, 2nd ed., edited by Kurt Finsterbusch and C.P. Wolf. Stroudsburg PA: Hutchinson Ross.

Interorganizational Committee on Guidelines and Principles (ICGP). 1994. "Guidelines and Principles for Social Impact Assessment." *Impact Assessment* 12(2): 107–152. Also in *Environmental Impact Assessment Review* 15: 11–43.

Korten, David C. 1980. "Community Organization and Rural Development: A Learning Process Approach." *Public Administration Review* 40(5): 480–510.

Kottak, Conrad Phillip. 1985. "When People Don't Come First: Some Sociological Lessons from Completed Projects." In *Putting People First: Sociological Variables in Rural Development*, edited by Michael M. Cernea. New York: Oxford.

Kruger, Richard A. 1994. *Focus Groups: A Practical Guide for Applied Research*, 2nd ed. Thousand Oaks, CA: Sage.

Kumar, Krishna. 1987. *Conducting Group Interviews in Developing Counties*. Washington, DC: U.S. Agency for International Development, Program Design and Evaluation Methodology Report No. 8.

Lake, Laura M., ed. 1980. *Environmental Mediation: The Search for Consensus.* Boulder, CO: Westview Press.

Lipset, Seymour Martin. 1979. "Predicting the Future of Post-Industrial Society: Can We Do It?" In *The Third Century: America as a Post-Industrial Society,* edited by Seymour Martin Lipset. Stanford, CA: Hoover Institution Press.

Llewellyn, Lynn G. and William R. Freudenburg. 1990. "Legal Requirements for Social Impact Assessments: Assessing the Social Science Fallout from Three Mile Island." *Society and Natural Resources* 2(3): 193–208.

Meadows, Donella, et al. 1972. *Limits to Growth.* New York: Universe Books.

Mernitz, S. 1980. *Mediation of Environmental Disputes: A Sourcebook.* New York: Praeger.

Merton, Robert K., Marjorie Fiske, and Patricia L. Kendall. 1990. *The Focused Interview,* 2nd ed. Glencoe, IL: The Free Press (first published in 1956).

Morgan, David L., ed. 1993. *Successful Focus Groups.* Newbury Park, CA: Sage.

Morgan David L. and Margaret T. Spanish. 1984. "Focus Groups: A New Tool for Qualitative Research." *Qualitative Sociology* 7(3): 253–270.

Morgan, E. Phillip. 1985. "Social Analysis and the Dynamics of Advocacy in Development Assistance." In *Social Impact Analysis and Development Planning in the Third World,* edited by William Derman and Scott Whiteford. Boulder, CO: Westview Press.

National Advisory Commission on Civil Disorders. 1968. *Report of the National Advisory Commission.* . . . New York: Bantam Books.

Nelson, Paul. 1985. "Development Aid: An Agenda for Change." Background Paper No. 86, *Bread for the World.* Washington, DC (November).

Nozick, Robert. 1974. *Anarchy, State and Utopia.* New York: Basic Books.

Ozawa, Connie P. 1991. *Recasting Science.* Boulder, CO: Westview Press.

Paddock, William and Elizabeth Paddock. 1973. *We Don't Know How: An independent audit of what they call success in foreign assistance.* Ames: Iowa State University Press.

Rawls, John. 1971. *A Theory of Justice.* Cambridge, MA: Harvard University Press.

Seyfrit, Carole L. 1986. "Migration Intentions of Rural Youth: Testing an Assumed Benefit of Rapid Growth." *Rural Sociology* 51(2): 199–211.

Talbot, A.R. 1983. *Settling Things: Six Case Studies in Environmental Mediation.* Washington, DC: The Conservation Foundation.

U.S. Council on Environmental Quality (US–CEQ). 1978. Regulations for Implementing the Procedural Provisions of the National Environmental Policy Act. Washington, DC: U.S. Council on Environmental Quality, 40 CFR Parts 1500–1508.

Watson, J.L. and L.J. Danielson. 1982. "Environmental Mediation." *Natural Resources Lawyer* 15: 687–723.

Weber, Max. 1958. *The Protestant Ethic and the Spirit of Capitalism*, translated by Talcott Parsons. New York: Scribner's Sons.

White, Lynn, Jr. 1962. *Medieval Technology and Social Change*. New York: Free Press.

Weber, Bruce A. and Robert E. Howell. 1982. *Coping with Rapid Growth in Rural Communities*. Boulder, CO: Westview Press.

[50]

SOCIAL IMPACT ASSESSMENT:
A CONTRIBUTION TO THE STATE OF THE ART SERIES[1]

Rabel J. Burdge and Frank Vanclay[2]

Social impact assessment can be defined as the process of assessing or estimating, in advance, the social consequences that are likely to follow from specific policy actions or project development, particularly in the context of appropriate national, state, or provincial environmental policy legislation. Social impacts include all social and cultural consequences to human populations of any public or private actions that alter the ways in which people live, work, play, relate to one another, organize to meet their needs, and generally cope as members of society. Cultural impacts involve changes to the norms, values, and beliefs of individuals that guide and rationalize their cognition of themselves and their society.[3]

While SIA is normally undertaken within the relevant national environmental policy framework, it is not restricted to this, and SIA as a process and methodology has the potential to contribute greatly to the planning process. As an example, New Zealand health professionals have recently been planning the introduction of new health care systems in the indigenous Maori communities and were looking at SIA to assist in the process of evaluation of alternatives, and to help in their understanding and management of the process of social change (Association for Social Assessment 1994).

---

[1] A longer version of this article has appeared in *Environmental and Social Impact Assessment* published by John Wiley and Sons (UK) in 1995.

[2] Rabel Burdge is professor of rural sociology in the Institute of Environmental Studies, University of Illinois–Urbana/Champaign, USA. Frank Vanclay is a key researcher with the Centre for Rural Social Research and teaches sociology at Charles Sturt University, Wagga Wagga, Australia.

[3] Largely based on the definition provided by the Interorganizational Committee (1994).

These professionals realized that social change would occur as the result of the introduction of new health care delivery programs. They realized that they needed a way to involve and integrate Maoris in planning for the proposed programs. Although none of these health care professionals had formal training either in managing social change or in undertaking SIA, they at least recognized the need to understand in advance what changes would likely occur depending upon the type of health care system that was implemented—precisely the type of information provided by a well-done SIA. This New Zealand example highlights opportunities for SIA. From the standpoint of a practitioner implementing social policy decisions, SIA research provides a direction for understanding the process, and guidance in the management of social change in advance of the implementation of the proposed changes. It thus facilitates a decision-making process to choose between alternative possibilities.

In general, the SIA process provides direction in (1) understanding, managing, and controlling change; (2) predicting probable impacts from change strategies or development projects that are to be implemented; (3) identifying, developing, and implementing mitigation strategies in order to minimize potential social impacts (that is, identified social impacts that would occur if no mitigation strategies were to be implemented); (4) developing and implementing monitoring programs to identify unanticipated social impacts that may develop as a result of the social change; (5) developing and implementing mitigation mechanisms to deal with unexpected impacts as they develop; and finally (6) evaluating social impacts caused by earlier developments, projects, technological change, specific technology, and government policy.

Benefits Gained from Conducting Social Impact Assessment

Often, the greatest social impact of many projects or policies, particularly those planned for community benefit (as in the New Zealand health care delivery program), is the stress that results from the uncertainty associated with it—for example, living near a major development and being uncertain about the impacts that the project may have. Sometimes just experiencing a situation of rapid change is the cause of stress. By maximizing community involvement in the SIA process—not just by consultation, but by directly involving locals in planning teams—uncertainty is reduced, the legitimacy of the SIA and the development project is enhanced, the accuracy of the SIA is increased, and the capacity for the SIA to mitigate impacts is maximized. Previous research has shown that local people from the affected communities have made substantial contributions to SIAs even though they may not be experienced in administrative procedures.

While the requirement to undertake SIAs may seem to be an unnecessary luxury that adds to the costs of projects, there are substantial benefits to be gained from undertaking them—for governments, communities, and developers. SIAs that involve the community minimize local resistance to projects, thereby reducing disruption; they increase project success; and they prevent major planning disasters and associated costs. In fact, SIAs may save money in the long run. It is particularly important that communities and governments insist on SIAs being undertaken because in the majority of cases, the costs of rectifying social and environmental impacts of development are borne by the public sector, not by the corporations that created them.

Even where there are mechanisms (for example, regulatory or legal action) for extracting compensation from companies for damage or impact they may create, the compensation is likely to only cover direct impacts and not the vast amounts of indirect impacts. In local community settings, the compensation itself may have a considerable social impact. It is possible that some groups would be less affected by the development than by the compensation. Nevertheless, there are examples where compensation and other payments (mining royalties, for example) to local peoples have been used in very positive ways for community development. The establishment of an Aboriginal-owned and -managed airline service, and an Aboriginal radio/television station in the Northern Territory of Australia, are examples.

In any case, the onus of proof to establish that a community, or certain groups within a community, did experience significant social impacts would rest with the community. For social impacts especially, it would be difficult to establish proof to the satisfaction of the courts. Furthermore, there are many impacts that cannot be mitigated or rectified so compensation is not necessarily a desirable strategy. Once local cultural life is affected, it is affected for good; therefore, it is important to prevent the majority of impacts before they actually happen. SIAs should be required of all public and private activities (projects, programs, policies) that are likely to affect social life.

Impact Assessment

The costs of undertaking an SIA should be included as part of the costs of the project and should not be borne by the government or by the local community. However, care must be taken that the standard of the SIA undertaken satisfies the government and the community. Some review process is required to ensure that all SIAs and EIAs are up to a required standard.

A BRIEF HISTORY

Social impact assessment was formalized with the introduction of the U.S. National Environmental Policy Act (NEPA) legislation of 1969. It became evident that altering the environment of the natural ecosystem also altered the culture and social organization of human populations. In 1973, after the decision had been made to build the Alaskan pipeline from Prudhoe Bay on the Arctic Sea to Valdez on Prince William Sound, an Inuit tribal chief commented, "Now that we have dealt with the problem of the permafrost and the caribou and what to do with hot oil, what about changes in the customs and ways of my people?" (cited by Dixon 1978:4; see also Berry 1975; McGrath 1977). Would the traditional culture and way of life be changed by such a massive construction project? Furthermore, because Alaska had a very small population, few of the estimated 42,000 persons needed to work on the pipeline during peak periods would come from the state. How would the influx of construction workers that spoke a different dialect (of English) and brought a distinctive lifestyle with them affect the local culture? Because of these impacts on human populations, the term 'social impact assessment' probably was first used in 1973 to refer to the changes in the indigenous Inuit culture due to the pipeline.[4]

The new field of SIA grew out of a need to apply the knowledge of sociology and other social sciences in an attempt to predict the social effects of environmental alterations by development projects that were subject to the NEPA legislation in the United States and the Canadian Environmental Assessment and Review Process (EARP) which was passed in 1973. Most of the early SIA procedures were developed by social scientists located within federal, state, and provincial agencies, or by consultants hired by the engineering and architectural firms that prepared the larger environmental impact statements (EIS). These early impact assessors used social science

---

[4] In Europe, a 1973 study into the social impacts of the then proposed Channel tunnel (which was not completed until 1994) represents one of the first European predictive SIA studies undertaken (Economic Consultants 1973).

labels in their EISs, but few of the concepts had a connection to prior literature on community and cultural change. U.S. assessors opted for models that required such data as the number and types of new workers as an input to predict quantitative social changes in the geo-political area of impact (Leistritz, Murdock 1981). The Canadian assessors focused more on a social action model, with emphasis on helping the impacted population adjust to the impending change (Bowles 1981, 1982).

The inquiry by Chief Justice Thomas Berger of the province of British Columbia (Canada) into the proposed Mackenzie Valley pipeline, from the Beaufort Sea in the Yukon Territory to Edmonton (Alberta), was the first case where social impacts were considered in project decision making (Berger 1977,1983; Gamble 1978; Gray, Gray 1977). The inquiry was important because social impacts on indigenous populations were considered in depth. Furthermore, native populations were provided with funding to present their views and hearings were conducted in native villages and in local dialects.

Of course, social impacts have been considered in different contexts throughout history. In anthropological analysis, retrospective analysis of social impacts has been a major feature of the discipline. Examples that form part of the literature of SIA include Cottrell (1951) and Sharp (1952). The social impacts of tourism has been a major field of study in SIA as the international tourism market has expanded, with early anthropological analyses dating back to Forster (1964). Eric Cohen (1971, 1972, 1979, 1984) has been a leading researcher in this area of study. The social impacts of mining has also been a major field of study for SIA, with social scientists being consulted to improve the design of mining towns in order to minimize social problems. An early Scottish example is Francis (1973); in Australia a number of studies were undertaken by the Pilbara Study Group, part of the Commonwealth Scientific and Industrial Research Organisation (CSIRO) (eg Pilbara Study Group 1974; Brealey 1974; Burvill 1975); while in Canada, the Institute of Social and Economic Research at the Memorial University of Newfoundland has undertaken and published numerous studies into the impacts of oil exploration and mining. Development studies is another area with an interest in social impacts. An early study into the social impacts of relocation due to the construction of a dam in Africa is Colson (1971). In addition to tourism, mining and dams, nuclear power and new road (highway) construction have also provided the impetus for much SIA research.

Impact Assessment

The first international conference on SIA was held in Vancouver, British Columbia in 1982 and gave academic and political credibility to the new field. Since then, the activities of this first conference have been combined into the International Association for Impact Assessment (IAIA) which held its first meeting in 1981 in Toronto, Canada.

By 1983, most US federal agencies had formalized environmental and social assessment procedures in agency regulations. The European Economic Community began to recommend EISs for their members in 1985, and by 1989 the recommendations became a requirement. In 1986, the World Bank decided to include both environmental and social assessment in their project evaluation procedures because liabilities were increasing for projects evaluated strictly on economic and financial criteria. Since then, SIA has become an important requirement (although to varying degrees) around the world as nations adopted and modified the original NEPA model.

In the United States, SIA reached its highest legitimacy when at the conclusion of the April 1993 'Forest Summit' in Portland, Oregon, President Bill Clinton mandated that a social assessment of each timber-dependent community in the Pacific Northwest would be a required component in deciding among alternative management futures for old growth forests. This directive was significant because it formally recognized SIA as a component of the policy-making process. Although the social assessment team of the federal eco-system management assessment team (FEMAT) did not conduct a formal SIA for each of 300 communities under study, they did use much of the literature on community change and cultural history (particularly for indigenous populations) as a basis for making assessments of community response to forest management alternatives (see Clark, Stankey 1994; Stone 1993).

SIA IN THE LARGER CONTEXT OF EIA

SIA has become a part of project planning and policy evaluation and part of environmental impact assessment (EIA) as a result of the recognition that social considerations must be included alongside and even in lieu of solely economic criteria in the evaluation and decision process. The definition of the environment in impact assessment has been expanded to include a 'social component'. SIA now increasingly carries equal weight with both economic and environmental impact assessment in decisions to change policy or approve ecosystem alteration (USCEQ 1986).

However, there are few documented cases where SIA has actually made a difference in the decision process. Two decades later, the Berger Inquiry continues to be cited as **the** case where the findings from a SIA provided the justification not to proceed with the proposed development.[5] In that case, the SIA provided justification to stop the project. Similarly, there a few cases which point to SIA as a way to enhance benefits or make a better policy decision. The spirit of the NEPA was that knowing about and understanding project effects in advance could make the proposal better through the implementation of mitigation and monitoring procedures. Although not benefiting from the same level of legal support as EIA, SIA has achieved wide acceptance as evidenced by the following:

- The document, *Guidelines and Principles for Social Impact Assessment*, is important, not only because social scientists could agree on the content, but also because it is written to fit within the NEPA process and regulations now used by U.S. Federal and State agencies. SIA is tied directly to EIA by including public involvement, identification of alternatives, baseline conditions, scoping, projection, evaluation of alternatives, mitigation and monitoring in the SIA process.
- In early 1993, the U.S. Council on Environmental Quality began to explore ways to formally incorporate SIA into their revised EIA regulations. While the 1978 Guidelines for NEPA (amended in 1986) have served as a model for project evaluation, they do not specifically require SIA. Rather, the courts have mandated that selected social components must be included and some federal agencies have included SIA in their regulations and handbooks. In addition, American Indian concerns and rights have been incorporated into the NEPA process particularly with regard to historic lands and spiritual places.
- The American Sociological Association held a professional workshop on SIA in August 1993 and has plans for another on integrative SIA.
- The number of universities listing courses in SIA is increasing, particularly in urban and regional planning departments as part of an environmental planning program. As well, universities are incorporating

---

[5] There have been other examples. For example, in Australia, a proposed mine at Coronation Hill in the Northern Territory, and a High Temperature Incinerator for Intractable Waste which was to have been built in Corowa in rural NSW, provide examples of situations where social impacts stopped the projects even though they were arguably acceptable on environmental grounds. However, these do not come close to the international fame of the Berger Inquiry.

SIA in curricula on community development, health and educational needs assessment and as a component in policy analysis.
- The U.S. Agency for International Development has continued to respond to the NEPA directives and has incorporated SIA-like procedures (which they term Social Soundness Analysis) into their project proposal and project identification documents.
- Recent rulings by U.S. courts have upheld the need for SIA in project evaluation procedures; a February 1994 U.S. Presidential Executive Order expanded SIA to include the issues of environmental racism and justice; and the FEMAT project, referred to earlier, highlighted the need for a 'social component' in all ecosystem management activity.

Despite these advances, the fact remains that in the two decades since SIA became a recognized sub-field of research and policy application, there are few examples where its use has made a difference in the project/policy decision process. On the other hand, EIA has been shown to be one of the most far ranging and significant methodologies to improve projects and policies. SIA is recognized as important, but has yet to be integrated sufficiently in the EIA process. Integration into the institutionalized policy and decision making process will depend upon a proven track record of making projects and policies better, as well as an understanding by policy makers as to what SIA actually is all about. However, the SIA process must always help communities understand the impacts of external change, and defend communities' interests.

PROBLEMS CONFRONTING SIA

Despite the advances of SIA, some conceptual, procedural and methodological difficulties remain. These can be grouped into four major categories:

1. Difficulties in applying the social sciences to SIA
   - Units of analysis, theoretical models, and the language of the various social science disciplines are sometimes contradictory or inconsistent, making interdisciplinary communication difficult.
   - Social science traditions, especially sociology, tend to be critical and discursive, rather than predictive and explanatory. Thus the core theoretical disciplines which comprise SIA fail to provide background in the processes of developing conceptual frameworks or valid measures for testing the interrelationships among variables.

2. Difficulties with the SIA process itself
   - Data are often poorly collected, and therefore projections are based on inadequate information which is often isolated, not systematically collected and therefore lacks validity checks. Estimates about the consequences to human communities of likely future events should be based on conceptual relationships developed from theory and previous research supported by data collected utilising the appropriate methods and subject to empirical verification.
   - The methodologies for assessing social impacts are numerous and complex, and exist as a process as much as a discrete entity. Consequently, they are difficult to document and to evaluate.

3. Problems with the procedures applying to SIA
   - SIAs are often done by consultants who do not know relevant social and economic theory, and who may not be trained in either SIA or social science methodology. There is no registration of suitably qualified and experienced SIA practitioners and some overly-zealous consultants have claimed expertise that they didn't have.
   - Regulatory agencies and corporations have not checked the credentials of consultants who undertake SIAs or insist that SIA consultants have appropriate social science training.
   - There is little evaluation or audit of SIA reports, and agencies and corporations receiving SIA statements seldom take the time to determine the validity and reliability of the contents of these reports.
   - Relevant literature on SIA is hard to find, and often not accessible. Many valuable resources are not published, but exist only as consultancy reports. Because of both litigation and commercial secrecy concerns, consultants, proponents and government agencies often prefer not to publish or make widely available many reports. Where reports are published, they often do not provide the detail necessary to fully evaluate the methodologies used and the validity of the claims.
   - SIA is seen as a single event, as a discrete statement of impacts, not as a process which develops its full potential in the mitigation of impacts, and as a process which governs the planning and development process. The regulatory frameworks under which EIA-SIA are undertaken (including NEPA and NEPA-like structures) impose this discrete event mentality.
   - Because of its project-based conceptualization, SIA, when undertaken according to the regulatory guidelines, although not to its full

potential, can not address cumulative impacts resulting from multiple projects.
- While mitigation is part of the project-based conceptualization, the potential for the development and implementation of effective and ongoing mitigation strategies is limited by the failure to see SIA as a process.
- Impact statements tend to be used to determine whether a project should go ahead or not; and if approval is given under what conditions, such as what mitigation strategies and/or what compensation should be paid. The failure to utilize SIA as a process with effective monitoring, mitigation and management, means a reliance on the use of SIA as an approval mechanism and to determine the level or form of compensation. Thus, approval may be denied to projects that potentially could be acceptable provided that certain mitigation strategies were in place. And other projects are approved, with compensation paid, even though the project and the compensation (or royalties) itself may create considerable social impact that appropriate mitigation and planning may have avoided (Connell and Howitt 1991; O'Hare 1977; Swartzman, Croke, and Swibel 1985).
- In some countries, there are statutory requirements to undertake SIAs, but even in these countries there is seldom a requirement for the results of SIAs to be seriously considered. SIAs often go unread, at least unheeded, and mitigation measures seldom taken seriously.
- As a component of the policy-making process, SIAs will come under increased scrutiny in the adversarial setting of the public hearing and judicial review process, therefore, the assessment must be based on rigor and at least a minimal level of quantification. If an assessment is questioned in a legal setting, it will be by another social scientist hired to critique the methods and conclusions. Because of the nature of public settings, data and ideas will be evaluated in the context of special interests. In the United States and Canada, the various reviews of SIAs are done in the setting of formal hearing. As such, the SIA practitioner needs some peer-supported guidelines and principles for justification of the general methodological approach and sociological content (that is, social variables) of the study. These are provided by, in the United States, at least, the *Guidelines and Principles for Social Impact Assessment*.

4. There is what can be described as a prevailing 'asocietal mentality'— an attitude that humans don't count—amongst the management of regulatory agencies and corporations (proponents undertaking the proposed development) which commission SIAs. This mentality also extends to politicians at all levels of government, public officials, physical scientists, engineers, and even economists and some planners. Persons with this mindset do not understand—and are often antithetical to—the social processes and social scientific theories and methodologies which are very different in form from those in the physical sciences in which these people are often trained. Because of the power of this mentality within the regulatory and administrative subcultures, even when sympathetic individuals join, they are often socialized into this mentality.

The implications of this asocietal mentality for SIA are—
- A failure to accept the need for SIA in the first place. This mentality naively assumes that development is good and that there are no social (and sometimes no environmental) consequences of development.
- There is no recognition of the need for special skills or expertise to assess social impacts. Since no credence is given to society as a special entity, it is assumed that anyone can determine the social consequences of development. The legitimacy and unique knowledge of the applied field called SIA is not yet fully recognized, understood and accepted.
- Since there was no understanding of the nature of potential impacts, or of the concerns that community members might have, there was no expectation that SIA statements should provide anything other than a statement about the change in the number of jobs, and the number of children going to school. SIA was little more than primitive demographic impact assessment and fiscal impact assessment. With this expectation, it was not in the interests of consultants to provide more, even if they were capable of doing so.
- Persons not familiar with SIA have difficulty in understanding the use and integration of public involvement in the SIA process. In some organizations and agencies, public involvement has been equated with SIA. The problem comes when administrators or decision-makers believe, that because they have done public involvement, they have done SIA. Public involvement is a component of the SIA process and may be used to collect data on key SIA variables. Public involvement is also part of the initial

scoping (and is required under the NEPA regulations) and must be incorporated throughout the entire process, but is not social impact assessment!
- Consultants who intended to undertake a thorough SIA were thwarted because of the lack of understanding about how long it would take and how much it would cost to do the job adequately. Reputable consultants were under-bid in the tender process by charlatan (at least with respect to SIA) consultants intending to do a superficial analysis.
- There is a lack of understanding, and often disagreement with the results of SIA studies. Because individuals possessing this asocietal mentality do not understand social processes, they often rejected the results of bone-fide consultants whose results often contradicted their notions of common sense.
- Another problem is articulating the complex stakeholder network (both corporate and community-based) in which SIA and EIA is conducted. Special interest groups will define problems and see results of studies from their point of view, and attempt to use SIAs to their particular advantage, possibly distorting the intent of the study or the specific result in the process. In a litigious and/or confrontationist situation, altruism and concern for such global (and even regional) goals as a quality environment and the future welfare of an impacted community are seldom part of the debate.
- Because in the physical sciences generally there tends to be clearly defined problems for which singular solutions can be identified with the appropriate analysis, there is a belief that social issues are similar, and an expectation that SIA statements will deliver clear statements of social impacts and that singular mitigation strategies can be identified.
- There is a complete lack of recognition of the complexity and heterogeneity of society, and how the impacts of developments benefit and disadvantage different components of society in different ways.

FUNDAMENTAL ISSUES IN SIA

In addition to the difficulties confronting SIA, there are a number of more complex, fundamental issues affecting SIA, which are problematic in most situations where SIA is to be applied. These issues are best expressed as questions to which definitive answers can not be easily given.

Who have legitimate interests in the community? How is the 'affected community' to be defined and identified?

It is fundamental to SIA that in all development projects, the distribution of costs and benefits is not equal across the community (Elkind-Savatsky 1986; Freudenburg 1984). One of the tasks of SIA is to identify the stakeholders, the winners, and the losers in any development. Usually, those examining social impacts are concerned about the social distribution of costs and benefits, usually in terms of social class and ethnic minority groups. A further concern of SIA is to predict how the nature of the community will change as a result of a specific project. However, 'community' is a reified concept in sociology. In a stable community (one in which the rate of change of members is low) faced with a single project development, it is relatively easy to identify bona fide members of the community. Most projects bring newcomers to a community, and development itself promotes additional growth in service industries (the regional multiplier). In a community experiencing rapid growth, newcomers to the community may be very different in values, attitudes, and behaviors to the existing community members. Their concerns vis-à-vis any development project may be very different from the established local community's. If a community is experiencing rapid growth, should newcomers be regarded as part of the community and their concerns be included in any impact assessment? Or are they part of the problem?

Rural rezoning and rural-urban fringe development provide many examples of situations where newcomers, predominantly middle-aged professionals, have very different concerns with respect to further development than the pre-existing (often farming) communities. Attractive locations, such as coastal zones, which are subject to tourist development and inundation of new settlers provide additional examples of such situations. The environmental assets of many coastal locations attract city leavers. In the case of Port Douglas in northern Queensland (Australia) and northern NSW (Australia), successive waves of newcomers have each arrived, each causing their own impact. At the time when each wave of new settlers arrives: these new arrivals typically either want no further development and no more settlers (thus pulling up the ladder); or want the opportunity to develop income producing activities that may have significant social (and environmental) impacts. Because of the rate of growth experienced by the community, and the successive waves of immigration to the region, at any point in time when an SIA is to be undertaken, how is the SIA consultant to establish what the views of the community are? Whose views are entitled to be considered? The problem may be further compounded by the seasonal nature of the residence of many new arrivals. In many cases, the original inhabitants are forced out of the community: by rate and rent increases; by local councils that become dominated by socially and politically astute new arrivals who set certain building standards that exclude, in the extreme case, the hermit-type existence of some original inhabitants; and simply by their own desire to escape from the development in order to find another place where they can regain some of their lost solitude (where doubtless the same process will occur again in a few years' time).

There are often conflicts, especially in locations of tourist potential or ecological value, between the local community (defined as residents living and working in the area for the majority of the year) and other sections of the community such as holiday makers and the broader community that experiences vicarious satisfaction from knowing about an area. Thus, when an ecologically significant old growth forest that was intended to be logged is protected from logging, the local community may experience social impacts in the form of job loss, forced migration from their home in search of work, or long-term unemployment, loss of identity and self worth, loss of their sense of their community, etc. But had the logging proceeded, the wider public may have experienced social impacts in the form of lost opportunities for holiday-making or ecotourism to that location, as well having experienced grief at the knowledge of further environmental destruction.

Although not usually considered in SIA, future communities of generations not yet born perhaps ought to be considered as part of the public whose interests ought to be protected. Future communities will suffer social and environmental impacts as the result of present human activities.

SIA cannot deal with these questions, nor should it. These questions are political. The role of SIA is to identify how different sections of the broader community are effected by development projects (and what can be done to minimize these impacts). SIA tends, and probably correctly so, to pay more attention to local concerns over the concerns of the broader distant public; but in so doing, SIA practitioners, and local communities must accept that broader concerns may outweigh purely local concerns in the ultimate decision about whether a project or policy ought to proceed.

What should be the role of community participation in the SIA?
This question raises many issues about the extent and validity of the knowledge and opinion of local communities, and about the right of local communities to determine their own destinies independent of outside interference. While one might take the view that community involvement is an intrinsic good or right and that community involvement will always lead to an increased knowledge of the project by the community and therefore reduce potential impact caused by uncertainty, there are two situations likely to be of concern in the SIA process: one where the public is opposed to the project, yet by independent assessment the project is likely to be beneficial; the other, where the public is in favor of the project, but independent assessment of the project suggests that the social (and/or environmental) problems are likely to outweigh the benefits.

The general community does not necessarily know what the likely effects of development will be. The public may be manipulated by advertising, and may be deceived by promises of economic prosperity. Public support for, or opposition to, a project may simply be a matter of timing, the role of the media and public relations exercises by the developer.

Strong public support for a project does not mean that there will not be any major social impacts, or that a project should necessarily proceed. Independent, non-partisan, expert assessment of likely impacts needs to be undertaken. On the other hand, where the public is opposed to the project, it is possible the public perception of risks associated with a project may be over-inflated, and actual impacts may be slight—except that fear and associated psychosocial stress are themselves major social impacts, although they can be mitigated by careful management, usually through a public involvement process. Research into residents' concerns about nuclear power stations (Travis, Etnier 1983; Brown 1989; Gwin 1990)—and probably other major and different projects, such as high-temperature toxic waste incinerators for intractable waste—indicates that the fear of danger associated with these plants far exceeds the actual probability of the risk involved. However, for everyday risks, such as those associated with the effects of smoking, excessive alcohol consumption, and probability of road accident, the risks are under-perceived. Perception of risk is an emotive issue and does not correlate with the actual risk (expressed as a probability of occurrence).

The other major concern affecting public participation is that the nature of the public participation methodologies used may mean that the view gained from the so-called participation is not representative of the community. Public meetings, sadly often the only format of public participation that is used, constitute neither participation nor representation. They are not participative because they usually consist of one way information transfer, and they are not representative because only certain groups come to such meetings, and only some individuals representing some of these groups say anything, and almost none of them have any attention paid to them. Other forms of participation do not necessarily guarantee representation either. Invariably, elite or power groups, the very same groups that tend to benefit most from developments, are also the most likely to gain representation through the various avenues that are used to involve the public and certain groups of people, especially social underclasses, tend to be excluded from public participation exercises.

Public participation, not matter how carefully undertaken with respect to community concerns, is not a substitute for a thorough SIA using appropriately qualified SIA professionals, although it remains an essential component of SIA.

What impacts are to be considered?

SIAs are usually undertaken at the behest of a community group, local or regional government, or the developer. Each one of these bodies has vested interests that they are keen to promote or protect. Consequently, the regulatory framework under which SIAs and EIAs are undertaken affects the integrity of the SIA or EIA (Buckley 1991). Where EIA-SIA consultants are engaged directly by developers, with no review procedure other than public comments, the consultants tend only to give a pro-development line, with any negative or critical comments couched in very masked terms. Consequently the impacts that are considered (both perceived as impacts and/or measured) are those that are politically or socially determined at the time the study is done. Many potential impacts are excluded from consideration because they may not be regarded as important at the time. Therefore, unless SIA is an ongoing process undertaken by truly independent and professional individuals, all SIA statements will be inadequate. There needs to be a procedure for ensuring that all potential impacts are considered. Adoption and promotion of the understanding contained in the *Guidelines and Principles* is step toward ensuring appropriate and professional SIA practice.

How should impacts be weighted?

Certain impacts, such as changes to the nature or character of a community may be perceived as negative by some members of the community, and as positive by other members. Thus impacts are not simply positive or negative in themselves (such as job growth is positive; job loss is negative), but are subject to the value judgements of individuals. For example, one of the consequences of the siting of a new prison in a rural community might be the movement of previously city-based families of prisoners (that is, wives and children) to that community. Some existing members of the community may view this as a negative experience and may be concerned about the loss of community integration, the changing nature of the community, and may have concerns about their personal safety and the security of their belongings. Other members of the community might believe that the community was too narrow minded to begin with, and therefore the intrusion of new and a largely different type of people might be good for the community because it will lead to a broadening of the mental horizons of the more conservative members of the community. Thus the same consequence of development is both a positive impact and a negative impact depending on the perspective of individuals.

This situation of whether consequences are positive or negative is even more problematic because individuals may change their mind over time. Thus a consequence may be a negative impact for a period, and a positive impact thereafter, or vice-versa. In this situation what should be the position of the SIA practitioner?

Other concerns about the weighting of impacts include difficulties for SIA about different strengths of feelings different individuals attribute to impacts. Some individuals may regard an impact as a mild unpleasantness or inconvenience, while for other individuals, the same impact may create a major change in life. Many individuals over time will adapt to a new environment, even if the (romanticized) past is reflected on as having been preferable. However, there are certain vulnerable groups, particularly the aged and the socially disadvantaged, who are unlikely to be able to adapt and who bear most of the social impacts. These groups need special attention by SIA practitioners.

SIA can not judge. It can merely report the how different segments of a community are likely to respond to development projects or policies, and advise on appropriate mitigation mechanisms.

Impact Assessment

Who judges?
A nation's regulatory framework usually specifies the role of the SIA or EIA in decision making and planning. Although EIAs and SIAs are compulsory in many countries, in most cases they are perfunctory; and regulatory bodies tend not to be bound by the outcomes. In any case, because of the issues outlined above—and cost–benefit analysis and other economic decision-making techniques notwithstanding—SIA cannot, except in very obvious cases, make definitive decisions about whether a given project ought to go ahead or not. SIA is not, of course, accorded regulatory power sufficient for this to happen even if it could decide. Decisions are about whether a project should proceed, or what compensation a developer should pay, are ultimately and inherently political. Even in the examples cited as being successes of SIA in stopping a project (the Berger inquiry, Coronation Hill, and the intractable waste incinerator), it could be argued that it was not the SIA study that stopped the project, but other political pressures, with the SIA providing the convenient excuse (Toyne 1994). Consequently, it could be argued that SIA is no better than the normal political process, complete with social and power inequalities that are vested in the political system. However, to the extent that SIA provides information for informed decision making, media commentary, and public discussion, SIAs can do no harm, and have the potential to contribute. It is unlikely, however, that SIAs can change the inherently political process of decision making and planning.

Even in a benevolent political system where SIA was genuinely desired as a decision-making tool, SIA could not deliver a decision-making mechanism. The inherent social inequalities of costs and benefits of projects, will mean that on simple cost benefit analysis, where benefits are greater than costs, projects will proceed even if the same social groups will always be adversely affected. Even if mitigatory action is taken to minimize these impacts or if affected groups are compensated, the compensation probably will not cover the full extent of costs actually experienced. It is also unlikely that any government would have sufficient courage or conviction to enforce full compensation, and no developer would engage in such practices voluntarily. Decisions about projects are ultimately and inevitably political.

WHAT SIA SHOULD DO TO ADDRESS THE PROBLEMS IT FACES

With acceptance comes expectations—a general cliche that is particularly appropriate for the field of SIA at the present time. With general agreement within the SIA field on procedures and content, as well as the general conceptual orientation of SIA becoming more widely accepted, attention must now shift to the development of conceptual and methodological issues which will strengthen the field. Two overriding issues are: (1) the application of SIA in the larger policy context, and (2) whether SIA can be successfully integrated into the planning and development process to improve projects and planning generally, rather than being seen solely as methodology to provide only a statement of potential impacts to determine whether a project ought, or ought not proceed.

Such a narrow view wastes so much of the potential of SIA because many possible impacts can be easily avoided by simple and cost effective mitigation strategies that can turn development projects with negative social impacts into projects with positive impacts, at least for many members of the community. Such an enlightened approach to SIA has been recognized in certain industries, particularly the mining industry, where through the use of SIA and community development consultants, practical social strategies and social design concepts can have a profound influence on community well-being which flows through to reduced costs and enhanced productivity for the company. Conversely, early mining developments which had no social planning often were social disasters with severe social problems which had, not only social impacts on the workforce and surrounding (often indigenous) populations, but also on productivity through lost work due to sick leave, alcoholism, strikes, and 'slow days'.

SIA needs to address the issue of scale, i.e. how the concepts and procedures of SIA can be applied to larger geographical regions than the immediate vicinity of a specific project, such as a large river basin, an ecosystem, or even regional and national political units. Some assessors are even calling for the analysis of global processes, such as the effects of world trade and GATT negotiations on agricultural and rural restructuring in peripheral and semi-peripheral nations (e.g., Lawrence and Vanclay 1994; Vanclay and Lawrence 1995). The social effects of some developments can be extremely dispersed from the original site of the development. This is perhaps best illustrated by the impacts of satellite television on locations which had no previous exposure to outside cultures (see O'Rourke 1980). Social and biophysical EIAs rely on localized, project level measures to predict impacts. As the scale is expanded, it becomes more difficult to establish significance because larger geo-political units tend to wash out project level impacts. Burdge's (1994b:2) axiom is pertinent:

The social benefits and consequences of project development, consolidation, and closure (abandonment) always occur, can be measured, and are usually borne at the community and local level—but the rationale for projects and the decisions are justified and sold on the basis of regional and national economic goals.

There are two general approaches to SIA, a generic one and the project level approach. The strengths of each need to be examined. The generic approach to SIA sensitises people to general social change. It assumes the presence of major impacts and a rather wide policy application. Project and policy impacts are seen as leading to radical shifts in the distribution of the population and in turn producing recognizable changes in how human groups relate to each other. Implicit in the generic approach to SIA is the notion of understanding social change through experience. Being sensitive to the existence of social impacts is seen as more important than actually being able to identify them. Often the objective of the generic type of SIA is to get the social science point of view across to the non-social scientist.

The project level approach to SIA assumes that social change is ubiquitous, but that a new project or policy change alters the normal flow of social change. Furthermore, this approach stresses that impact events will vary in specificity, intensity, duration, and a variety of other characteristics. It then becomes important to understand what will be the actual social impacts of a particular development rather than only being aware that social change will take place. The researcher or practitioner uses past social science research to better understand what is likely to happen to human populations given different development events.

SIA will be most successful when fully integrated with planning at the appropriate level of jurisdiction where project development or a proposed policy development will occur. When this integration is accomplished, both social and environmental factors become central to planning decisions, rather than being treated as external or peripheral to the planning process. Achieving such integration requires a sound understanding of the nature of planning on the one hand, and how advances in knowledge about impact assessment and its many methodologies can fit into modern planning models on the other. Additionally, functional integration of the key components of the planning process from project inception to post-development monitoring, is an important goal of modern comprehensive planning. This kind of integration is essential because, as a dynamic process, planning requires data collection across time and ongoing revision of plans to ensure that planning goals are being met (Armour 1990). Similarly, SIA requires successful integration of all phases from scoping to monitoring, mediation to mitigation, as well as continual and cumulative assessment of results.

The methodology for measuring, and the substance of, cumulative effects in SIA need to be researched. Certain cumulative effects are obvious—such as basic infrastructural needs generally provided by local government and utility companies. Infrastructure payments and other financial arrangements can generally satisfactorily compensate existing communities for these impacts. Other, still basic, questions are less obvious, for example, does increased population require an increased size of local government? At what stage should the assessment consider the community infrastructure needs? Finally, and most importantly, there are a whole range of questions relating to cumulative impacts that the SIA process raises that it cannot answer. Communities have a basic resilience and can accept a certain amount of change or impact. Impacts become important when the number or extent of changes exceeds a certain threshold. This threshold is likely to be unknown and unknowable for any community. Very large projects with major social impacts may exceed this threshold, but so may many different small projects. When the SIA procedure is undertaken on a project by project basis, it is very difficult to determine if this threshold will be exceeded, and of course, no specific project was individually responsible for exceeding that threshold. Overall advance planning is required to ensure that the threshold is not exceeded for any community, and to maximize the benefits and minimize the negative impacts for each project.

SIA achieves its greatest benefit to society through its ability to advise on mitigation of impacts. However, not only must mitigation procedures be developed and improved, but appropriate political procedures must be established to determine who is responsible for mitigation and monitoring at each step of a project, not only during construction and operation of projects, but also for the decades and centuries after the project has been abandoned or the policy implemented, especially in the case of projects with long term impacts (such as nuclear waste repositories where the wastes have radioactive half-lives of thousands of years!).

These issues imply both policy and administrative procedures as well as mechanisms to pin point responsibility. A well thought out public involvement program is a necessity for the mitigation and monitoring steps of the SIA process.

Impact Assessment

As pointed out earlier, early SIA assessors faced ideological resistance (the asocietal mentality) as well as political and legal obstacles, not only in including SIA within EISs, but also in deciding which variables to use in the analysis. Social variables were often considered suspect. To ensure the presence of a social component in an EIA statement, SIA was changed to socio-economic indicators, and as a result many US federal agencies adopted the term 'socio-economic' impacts. In practice, the social part of the hyphenation was not done and socio-economic became an economic impact assessment, with a concentration on demographic changes and regional multipliers. The linkage persists today and a goal for SIA must be to separate further the social from socio-economic impact assessment, and to enhance the legitimacy of purely social concerns.

The SIA research community needs to publish more widely, making available the really good case studies which point out where SIA actually made a difference in the decision process, not only cases in which the SIA stopped the development, but the cases for which SIA substantially improved it. Now that there are agreed upon methods, long range research on case studies using good SIA practice needs to be undertaken. Well-conceptualized, long-range research projects will provide the legitimacy for the verification of existing—and the identification of new—SIA variables.

SIA needs to be considered in the broader policy context. In the FEMAT project in the Pacific Northwest of the United States (see Clark, Stankey 1994), the researchers could not differentiate between impacts to an individual community and social impacts that occurred over the entire region as a result of proposed alternatives in levels of timber harvesting. The social assessment team was asked to do an SIA for a region without the benefit of data on any one of the impacted communities. Thus a regional data base to study social impacts which are ongoing and cumulative is needed. The FEMAT social scientists had no longitudinal data base (other than census information) as a starting point to measure social impacts. They needed an agreed upon list of SIA variables and the funds to maintain this information over time. As part of the data base problem, the FEMAT exercise highlighted the problems of integrating qualitative and quantitative data. Qualitative SIA indicators are just as valid and in many cases are more insightful and provide a more holistic perspective than quantitative indicators. However qualitative data are more difficult to store on a cumulative basis and are difficult to sell to non-social scientists. Furthermore, both types of social science indicators when used in SIA, are usually in some form of small area analysis, and consequently face the problem of 'statistical significance'. The FEMAT team of social assessors were repeatedly asked to defend the significance of the social impacts identified in the assessment process and probability levels seemed the only acceptable answer, even though these were impossible to provide (Clark, Stankey 1994).

All types of assessment face the problem of integration. How do EIA and SIA fit together in providing a comprehensive picture of likely project impacts? At present, most SIA statements are stapled to an EIA, and the total recommendations are the sum of the parts. No attempt is made to integrate and interpret the collective findings. This needs to be improved. Higher order impacts are possible. Thus environmental impacts can have social impacts, and social impacts can turn into environmental impacts. Mitigation strategies (both biophysical and social) can also have their own environmental and social impacts which may not be considered in impact statements because impact statements tend not to go past first order impacts.

The relationship between SIA and public involvement needs clarification, especially to managers of agencies and corporations who often confuse them. Public involvement is an important process which goes on throughout the EIA, SIA and planning process, but it does not tell us what social impacts will occur as a result of a policy or future project (Burdge, Robertson 1990).

The broadening of, and increased acceptance of, a cultural understanding of society and social processes may be the most important contribution of SIA to the assessment process. The science and research of EIA assume a logical-positivist model in the analysis and implementation of the planning process. The model is generally reductionist and therefore lacks a holistic approach. It also assumes that all interested and affected parties have the same perspective and goals. In order to be acceptable to the EIA masters, some SIA practitioners have adopted a similar perspective in their approach to social impacts. Such an approach is inadequate in dealing with many of the real social impacts that may arise, that are purely cultural, and that will be identified if such a perspective is adopted.

For example, to many individuals and groups, particularly but not exclusively indigenous peoples, there are many spiritual and religious issues that need to be considered in SIA (Greider, Garkovich 1994). Concepts such as attachment to the land and identification with place are very difficult to quantify and easily discounted in the formal decision process, yet are the most important factors in determining project success and probable acceptance by local populations (Burdge 1994b; Chase 1990).

One dimension of culture is spirituality, which is profoundly evident in the many indigenous cultures of the world—although anthropologists would argue it applies equally to all cultures, even if it may take on various forms which many people may not recognize as spiritual. The reference to and the use of the 'spiritual' in understanding human interaction with ecosystems is a jolting revelation for decision makers and runs counter to traditional western positivist thought. The alteration of scared ground is a good example. A new airport built in Denver, Colorado (USA) was completed and scheduled to be opened in 1993. However, an automated baggage system could never be perfected and a series of other mechanical failures delayed the opening indefinitely. When the airport was first proposed, the American Indian tribe who lived in the area said the site was on sacred ground and that the 'spirits' would never allow the project to be completed. The natives were right, at least up until the time this paper was published! The SIA for a mining project in Australia (Coronation Hill) revealed a similar story, where if the sacred ground was disturbed, the spirit of Bula would rise up and destroy the world (Lane et al. 1990). In this case, the SIA resulted in a Federal Government decision not to allow mining. Unfortunately, most EIA-SIA statements allude to the importance of culture, but never really admit that cultural history is a key component in the decision process. Again much more legitimacy must be placed on the social and cultural factors of society.

CONCLUSION

The progress of the field of SIA has been remarkable. There have been some major agreements: a shared definition and understanding of the SIA process; a basic framework; and an outline of what ought to go into an SIA. However, more longitudinal research case studies are needed, particularly to evaluate (audit) past studies and predictions. There is widespread consensus that human or social impacts should be considered as part of the environment. In particular, the SIA process has raised awareness of how projects and policies and political change alter the cultures of indigenous populations. Experience has provided a realistic appraisal of what is likely to happen in the future as a result of particular policies or actions. SIA is beginning to be fully integrated into the EIA process, and EIA (and SIA) into the planning process.

Despite the success of the last ten years, the big issue ahead is how project specific knowledge about social, economic and environmental impacts can be used for larger policy assessments. SIA has yet to bridge the schism between project level research findings and the larger scale assessments which are needed for regional and national policy decisions.

SIA should also be considered an integral part of the development process, not a step or hurdle to be overcome. Done poorly, SIA may be nothing more than a public relations exercise for illegitimate development by unscrupulous corporations. SIA is not designed to hamper development, but is designed to maximize the potential benefit for all parties associated with the development. For the community this means minimising social impacts on the community and maximising community benefits. For the developer it means minimising social impacts and therefore the costs of rectification of these impacts in the future. Effective SIA increases the legitimacy of the development, and may well facilitate the development process. SIA removes uncertainty from the process, for both the community and the developer. To a small extent, SIA reduces impacts on the workforce and has the potential to increase productivity and reduce disruption.

The effectiveness of SIA rests on the integrity of the SIA practitioner. Community participation is essential, as is community evaluation of any report or recommendations. However, public participation exercises are not of themselves social impact assessments. Governments should consider appropriate measures to ensure that SIA and EIA that is undertaken are to a satisfactory standard. Furthermore, it must be accepted that SIA can not be an ultimate guide in decision making. Decisions were always and will always, of necessity, be political. Nevertheless, SIA can be a useful tool in providing information that will assist in that process.

Predicting the future based on the past is tricky but is what impact assessment is all about. Charlie Wolf's analogy of the binoculars with a lens pointed to the front and another to the back, with a weather vane at the top to give an indication of which way the (political) wind is blowing, is exemplary. Perhaps the analogy should be expanded by attaching a wheel to remind SIA practitioners not to reinvent it! The challenge ahead is to make sure that the field of SIA can deliver what it promises, and at the same time present a realistic picture of what the field of SIA can provide in the planning/decision making process.

Impact Assessment

REFERENCES

Armour, A. 1990. "Integrating impact assessment into the planning process." *Impact Assessment Bulletin* 8(1/2): 3–14.

Association for Social Assessment (New Zealand). 1994. "Social assessment and Maori policy development." *Social Impact Assessment Newsletter* 35: 10–11.

Berger, T.R. 1977. *Northern Frontier, Northern Homeland: The report of the Mackenzie Valley pipeline inquiry* (2 vols). Ottawa: Ministry of Supply and Services Canada.

Berger, T.R. 1983. "Resources development and human values." *Impact Assessment Bulletin* 2(2): 129–147.

Berger, T.R. 1985. *Village Journey: The report of the Alaskan Native Review Commission*. New York: Hill and Wang.

Berry, M.C. 1975. *The Alaska Pipeline: The politics of oil and native land claims*. Bloomington: Indiana University Press.

Bowles, R.T. 1981. *Social Impact Assessment in Small Communities*. Toronto: Butterworths.

Bowles, R.T. (ed.) 1982. *Little Communities and Big Industries*. Toronto: Butterworths.

Brealey, T.B. 1974. "Mining towns are for people." *Search* 5(1/2): 54–59.

Brown, J. (ed.) 1989. *Environmental Threats: Perception, Analysis and Management*. London: Belhaven.

Buckley, R. 1991. "Should environmental impact assessment be carried out by independent consultants?" *Environment Institute of Australia Newsletter* 16: 12–13.

Burdge, R.J. 1994a. *A Conceptual Approach to Social Impact Assessment*, Middleton, WI: Social Ecology Press.

Burdge, R.J. 1994b. *A Community Guide to Social Impact Assessment*, Middleton, WI: Social Ecology Press.

Burdge, R.J. and R.A. Robertson. 1990. "Social impact assessment and the public involvement process." *Environmental Impact Assessment Review* 10(1/2): 81–90.

Burvill, P.W. 1975. "Mental health in isolated new mining towns in Australia." *Australian and New Zealand Journal of Psychiatry* 9(2): 77–83.

Chase, A. 1990. "Anthropology and impact assessment: development pressures and indigenous interests in Australia." *Environmental Impact Assessment Review* 10(1/2): 11–23.

Clark, R.N. and G.H. Stankey. 1994. "FEMAT's social assessment: Framework, key concepts and lessons learned." *Journal of Forestry* 92(4): 32–35.

Cohen, E. 1971. "Arab boys and tourist girls in a mixed Jewish-Arab community." *International Journal of Comparative Sociology* 12(4): 217–233.

Cohen, E. 1972. "Towards a sociology of international tourism." *Social Research* 39(1): 164–182.

Cohen, E. 1979. "Rethinking the sociology of tourism." *Annals of Tourism Research* 6(1): 18–35.

Cohen, E. 1984. "The sociology of tourism." *Annual Review of Sociology* 10: 373-392.

Colson, E. 1971. *The Social Consequences of Resettlement: The Impact of the Kariba Resettlement upon the Gwembe Tongo.* Manchester: Manchester Univ. Press.

Connell, J. and R. Howitt. (eds). 1991. *Mining and Indigenous People in Australasia.* Melbourne: Oxford University Press.

Cottrell, W.F. 1951. "Death by dieselization." *American Sociological Review* 16(3): 358-365.

Dixon, M. 1978. *What Happened to Fairbanks: The effects of the Trans-Alaska oil pipeline on the community of Fairbanks, Alaska.* Boulder: Westview Press.

Economic Consultants Ltd. 1973. *The Channel Tunnel: Its economic and social impacts on Kent.* Report presented to the Secretary of State for the Environment, London: Her Majesty's Stationery Office.

Elkind-Savatsky, P. (ed.) 1986. *Differential Social Impacts of Rural Resource Development.* Boulder: Westview Press.

Forster, J. 1964. "The sociological consequences of tourism." *International Journal of Comparative Sociology* 5(2): 217-227.

Francis, J. 1973. *Scotland in Turmoil: A social and environmental assessment of the impact of North Sea oil and gas.* Edinburgh: St Andrews Press.

Freudenburg, W.R. 1984. "Differential impacts of rapid community growth." *American Sociological Review* 49(5): 697-705.

Gamble, D.J. 1978. "The Berger inquiry: an impact assessment process." *Science* 199, 3 March, 946-952.

Gray, J.A. and P.J. Gray. 1977. "The Berger report: its impact on northern pipelines and decisionmaking in northern development." *Canadian Public Policy* 3(4): 509-514.

Greider, T. and L. Garkovich. 1994. "Landscapes: the social construction of nature and the environment." *Rural Sociology* 59(1): 1-24.

Gwin, L. 1990. *Speak No Evil: The promotional heritage of nuclear risk communication.* New York: Praeger.

Interorganizational Committee on Guidelines and Principles for Social Impact Assessment. 1994. "Guidelines and principles for social impact assessment." *Impact Assessment* 12(2): 107-152.

Lane, M. et al. (1990). *Social Impact of Development: An analysis of the social impacts of development on aboriginal communities of the region, Kakadu conservation zone inquiry.* Resource Assessment Commission Consultancy Series, Canberra: Australian Government Publishing Service.

Lawrence, G. and F. Vanclay. 1994. "Agricultural change in the semiperiphery." In *The Global Restructuring of Agro-Food Systems*, edited by P. McMichael, 76-103. Ithaca: Cornell University Press.

Leistritz, F.L. and S.H. Murdock. 1981. *The Socioeconomic Impact of Resource Development: Methods of Assessment.* Boulder: Westview Press.

McGrath, E. 1977. *Inside the Alaska Pipeline.* Milbrae: Celestial Arts.

O'Hare, M. 1977. "Not on my block you don't: facility siting and the strategic importance of compensation." *Public Policy* 25(4): 407–458.

O'Rourke, D. 1980. *Yap: How did you know we'd like TV* (video). Canberra: Ronin Films.

Pilbara Study Group. 1974. *The Pilbara Study*. Canberra: Australian Government Publishing Service.

Swartzman, D., K. Croke and S. Swibel. 1985. "Reducing aversion to living near hazardous waste facilities through compensation and risk reduction." *Journal of Environmental Management* 20(1): 43–50.

Sharp, L. 1952. "Steel axes for stone age Australians." In *Human Problems in Technological Change*, edited by E. Spicer, 69–90. New York: Russell Sage.

Stone, R. 1993. "Spotted owl plan kindles debate on salvage logging." *Science* 261.

Toyne, P. 1994. *The Reluctant Nation: Environment, Law and Politics in Australia*. Sydney: Australian Broadcasting Commission.

Travis, C.C. and E.L. Etnier (eds.) 1983. *Health Risks of Energy Technologies*. Boulder: Westview.

United States, Council on Environmental Quality (USCEQ). 1978. National Environmental Policy Act—Regulation, Federal Register, Vol. 43 (230): 55979–5600-7 Washington DC, Government Printing Office.

United States, Council on Environmental Quality (USCEQ). 1986. Regulations for Implementing the Procedural Provisions of the National Environmental Policy Act (40 CFR 1500-1508). Washington DC: Government Printing Office.

United States, The National Environmental Policy Act of 1969 (NEPA). 1969. 42 USC 4321 (1994).

Vanclay, F. 1989-95. *Social Impact Assessment Bibliography: A Database and Interrogation Program for DOS-Based Personal Computers*. Wagga Wagga: Centre for Rural Social Research, Charles Sturt University.

Vanclay, F. and G. Lawrence. 1995. *The Environmental Imperative*. Rockhampton: Central Queensland University Press.